Advance Praise for *Mergers, Acquisitions, and Other Restructuring Activities, Fifth Edition*

"This is a truly comprehensive text and does a wonderful job at supplying the underlying motives and theory as well as the critical 'in practice' elements that many books lack. It spans all types of M&A and restructuring transactions and covers all the relevant knowledge from the academic research to the practical legal, accounting, and regulatory details. The book is up-to-date and teaches the state of the art techniques used today. The book contains numerous cases and spreadsheet support that enable the reader to put into practice everything that is covered. The combination of great writing and active case learning make this book the best I have seen in the M&A and restructuring arena."

—**Matthew T. Billett**, Associate Professor of Finance, Henry B. Tippie Research Fellow, University of Iowa

*"I am happy to recommend the fifth edition of **Mergers, Acquisitions, and Other Restructuring Activities**. Having used prior editions of Don DePamphilis' text, I can affirm that the newest edition builds on a firm foundation of coverage, real-world examples, and readability. My students have consistently responded favorably to prior editions of the book. In the newest edition, I was delighted to discover that Don is expanding his coverage of family-owned businesses, already a strength in his earlier editions that were distinguished by their coverage of the valuation of privately held businesses. Additional attention is paid to restructuring, bankruptcy, and liquidation as well as risk management, which are clearly topics of interest to every business person in today's economic climate."*

—**Kent Hickman**, Professor of Finance, Gonzaga University, WA

"This new edition is one of the most comprehensive books on mergers and acquisitions. The text combines theories, valuation models, and real-life cases to give business students an overall insight into the M&A deal process. The up-to-date real-life examples and cases provide opportunities for readers to explore and to apply theories to a wide variety of scenarios such as cross-border transactions, highly levered deals, firms in financial distress, and family-own businesses. The chapter on restructuring under bankruptcy and liquidation both inside and outside the protection of bankruptcy court is timely and most useful in light of today's economic crisis. Overall, this is an excellent book on mergers, acquisitions, and corporate restructuring activities."

—**Tao-Hsien Dolly King**, Rush S. Dickson Professor of Finance, Associate Professor, Department of Finance, The Belk College of Business, University of North Carolina at Charlotte

*"**Mergers, Acquisitions, and Other Restructuring Activities** is an interesting and comprehensive look at the most important aspects of M&A and corporate restructuring — from strategic and regulatory considerations and M&A deal process, through several chapters on M&A valuation and deal structuring, to other types of restructuring activities. It not only provides a road map for the M&A and other corporate restructuring transactions, but also highlights the key things to watch for. The book is clearly written with extensive but easy-to-follow case examples and empirical findings and cases to illustrate the points in the text. It is a book by an expert, and for M&A instructors and students as well as practitioners."*

—**Qiao Lui**, Faculty of Business and Economics, The University of Hong Kong

and the chapter on private equity and hedge funds is interesting because M&A activities by these players are not well-documented in the literature. Overall, I believe that MBA students would find the book useful both as a textbook in class and as a reference book for later use."

—**Raghavendra Rau**, Purdue University, IN, and Barclays Global Investors

"This book is truly outstanding among the textbooks on takeovers, valuation and corporate restructuring for several reasons: the DePamphilis book not only gives a very up-to-date overview of the recent research findings on takeovers around the world, but also offers nearly 100 recent business cases. The book treats all the valuation techniques in depth and also offers much institutional detail on M&A and LBO transactions. Not just takeover successes are analyzed, but also how financially distressed companies should be restructured. In short, the ideal textbook for any M&A graduate course."

—**Luc Renneboog**, Professor of Corporate Finance, Tilburg University, The Netherlands

"The fifth Edition of the textbook **Mergers, Acquisitions, and Other Restructuring Activities** by Professor Donald DePamphilis is an excellent book. Among its many strengths, I could easily identify three features that stand out. First, it is up-to-date, covering the recent knowledge published in most of the academic journals. Second, it offers a comprehensive coverage of the subject matter, including chapters on the U.S. institutional, legal, and accounting environment; on technical aspects; valuation techniques; and strategic issues. Third, it is practical by including Excel Spread Sheet Models, and a large number of real cases. These three aspects along with the large number of end-of-chapter discussion and review questions, problems, and exercises make this book one of the best choices for the particular subject."

—**Nickolaos G. Travlos**, The Kitty Kyriacopoulos Chair in Finance, and Dean, ALBA Graduate Business School, Greece

"It is difficult to imagine that his fourth edition could be improved upon, but Dr. DePamphilis has done just that. His latest edition is clearer, better organized, and contains a wealth of vitally important new material for these challenging times. I especially recommend the new chapter on liquidation for members of boards of directors who face extreme circumstances. This is a remarkably useful book for readers at any level—students, instructors, company executives, as well as board members. Bravo Don!"

—**Wesley B. Truitt**, Adjunct Professor, School of Public Policy, Pepperdine University, CA

"The book is an excellent source for both academicians and practitioners. In addition to detailed cases, it provides tools contributing to value creation in M&A. A must book for an M&A course."

—**Vahap Uysal**, Assistant Professor of Finance, Price College of Business, University of Oklahoma

"An impressive detailed overview of all aspects of Mergers and Acquisitions. Numerous recent case studies and examples convince the reader that all the material is very relevant in today's business environment."

—**Theo Vermaelen**, Professor of Finance, Insead

Mergers, Acquisitions, and Other Restructuring Activities

An Integrated Approach to Process, Tools, Cases, and Solutions

Fifth Edition

Donald M. DePamphilis, Ph.D.
College of Business Administration
Loyola Marymount University
Los Angeles, California

AMSTERDAM • BOSTON • HEIDELBERG • LONDON
NEW YORK • OXFORD • PARIS • SAN DIEGO
SAN FRANCISCO • SINGAPORE • SYDNEY • TOKYO
Academic Press is an imprint of Elsevier

Academic Press is an imprint of Elsevier
30 Corporate Drive, Suite 400, Burlington, MA 01803, USA
525 B Street, Suite 1900, San Diego, California 92101-4495, USA
84 Theobald's Road, London WC1X 8RR, UK

Library of Congress Cataloging-in-Publication Data
DePamphilis, Donald M.
   Mergers, acquisitions, and other restructuring activities / Donald M. DePamphilis. – 5th ed.
      p. cm. – (Academic Press advanced finance series)
   Includes bibliographical references and index.
   ISBN 978-0-12-374878-2 (hardcover)
   1. Organizational change–United States–Management. 2. Consolidation and merger of corporations–
United States–Management. 3. Corporate reorganizations–United States–Management. I. Title.
   HD58.8.D467 2009
   658.1′6—dc22

2009005306

British Library Cataloguing-in-Publication Data
A catalogue record for this book is available from the British Library.

For information on all Academic Press publications
visit our website at www.elsevierdirect.com

Printed in the United States of America
   10   11   12   13   7   6   5   4   3   2

Dedication

I extend my heartfelt gratitude to my wife, Cheryl, and my daughter, Cara, without whose patience and understanding this book could not have been completed, and to my brother, Mel, without whose encouragement this book would never have been undertaken.

Contents

Part IV. Deal Structuring and Financing Strategies

11. Structuring the Deal: Payment and Legal Considerations

Part V. Alternative Business and Restructuring Strategies

14. Joint Ventures, Partnerships, Strategic Alliances, and Licensing

Contents of CD-ROM Accompanying Textbook

Acquirer Due Diligence Question List

Acquisition Process: The Gee Whiz Media Integrative Case Study

Example of Applying Experience Curves to M&A

Example of Supernormal Growth Model

Example of Market Attractiveness Matrix (New)

Examples of Merger and Acquisition Agreements of Purchase and Sale

Excel-Based Mergers and Acquisitions Valuation and Structuring Model

Excel-Based Leveraged Buyout Valuation and Structuring Model

Excel-Based Decision Tree M&A Valuation Model

Excel-Based Model to Estimate Firm Borrowing Capacity (New)

Excel-Based Offer Price Simulation Model (New)

Excel-Based Spreadsheet of How to Adjust Target Firm's Financial Statements (New)

Guidelines for Organizing ESOPs

Interactive Learning Library (Updated)

MCI/Verizon 2005 Merger Agreement

Primer on Cash Flow Forecasting (New)

Primer on Applying and Interpreting Financial Ratios

Student Chapter PowerPoint Presentations (updated)

Student Study Guide, Practice Questions and Answers (updated)

Business Case Studies

---

*A single asterisk indicates that the case study is new since the fourth edition of this book.
**A double asterisk indicates that the case study has been updated since the fourth edition.

Preface to the Fifth Edition

To the Reader

Mergers, acquisitions, business alliances, and corporate restructuring activities are increasingly commonplace in both developed and emerging countries. Given the frequency with which such activities occur, it is critical for business people and officials at all levels of government to have a basic understanding of why and how such activities take place. The objective of this book is to bring clarity to what can be an exciting, complex, and sometimes frustrating subject. This book is intended to help the reader think of the activities involved in mergers, acquisitions, business alliances, and corporate restructuring in an integrated way.

The fifth edition contains exciting new content, including one new and seven substantially revised, updated, or reorganized chapters. The new chapter (Chapter 16) is entirely devoted to restructuring under bankruptcy and liquidation. This chapter is particularly timely, following the global economic slowdown of recent years, as financially distressed companies seek the protection of bankruptcy courts or are liquidated over the next several years.

Chapter 1 has been reorganized to improve the ease of reading and to increase the focus on the empirical results of recent academic studies. The chapter provides recent evidence that the success of mergers and acquisitions is largely situational and suggests that the results of aggregate studies may be misleading. The number of real world examples has been greatly increased in the discussion of alternative valuation methods in Chapter 8. Chapter 9 includes a discussion and illustration of how M&A Excel-based simulation models can be useful tools in the negotiation process. Chapter 10 includes an expanded discussion of the operating and governance characteristics of family-owned businesses, a streamlined discussion of how to address the challenges associated with privately owned firms, and a practical way to estimate and apply liquidity discounts, control premiums, and minority discounts as part of the valuation process.

The section in Chapter 11 on managing risk and alternative methods for closing the gap on price between the buyer and seller has been expanded significantly. Chapter 12 has been updated to include a discussion of the implications of the recent changes to accounting rules applying to business combinations, as well as recent regulations increasing the flexibility of statutory mergers in qualifying for tax-free reorganizations. Chapter 13 has been expanded in its discussion of financing transactions, the role of private equity and hedge funds as LBO sponsors, how to structure and analyze highly leveraged transactions, and how to build LBO models. Through an Excel spreadsheet model, this chapter also deals with estimating a firm's borrowing capacity and adjusting the valuation process for the probability of financial distress.

Including the 40 new cases, about 95 percent of the 95 business case studies in the book involve transactions that have taken place since 2006. The case studies involve transactions in many industries. Ten of the case studies have been updated to reflect recent developments. Twenty-one of the case studies involve cross-border transactions, 6 cases deal with highly leveraged transactions, 6 involve private or family-owned businesses, 10 address various aspects of deal structuring, and 8 case studies deal with firms experiencing financial distress. All case studies include discussion questions, with answers for all end-of-chapter and many "in-chapter" case study questions available in the online instructors' manual. All chapters reflect the latest academic research.

The textbook contains more than 280 end-of-chapter discussion and review questions, problems, and exercises to allow readers to test their knowledge of the material. A number of the exercises enable students to find their own solutions based on different sets of assumptions, using Excel-based spreadsheet models available on the CD-ROM accompanying this textbook. Solutions to all questions, problems, and exercises are available on the expanded online instructors' manual available to instructors using this book. The online manual now contains more than 1,600 true/false, multiple choice, and short essay questions as well as numerical problems

In addition to Excel-based customizable M&A and LBO valuation and structuring software, PowerPoint presentations, and due diligence materials, the CD-ROM accompanying this book provides access to an interactive learning library. The learning library enables readers to test their knowledge by having their answers to specific questions scored immediately. The CD-ROM also contains a student study guide and models for estimating a firm's borrowing capacity, adjusting a firm's financial statements, and numerous illustrations of concepts discussed in the book.

This book is intended for students in mergers and acquisitions, corporate restructuring, business strategy, management, and entrepreneurship courses. This book works well at both the undergraduate and graduate levels. The text also should interest financial analysts, chief financial officers, operating managers, investment bankers, and portfolio managers. Others who may have an interest include bank lending officers, venture capitalists, government regulators, human resource managers, entrepreneurs, and board members. Hence, from the classroom to the boardroom, this text offers something for anyone with an interest in mergers and acquisitions, business alliances, and other forms of corporate restructuring.

To the Instructor

This text is an attempt to provide organization to a topic that is inherently complex due to the diversity of applicable subject matter and the breadth of disciplines that must be applied to complete most transactions. Consequently, the discussion of M&A is not easily divisible into highly focused chapters. Efforts to compartmentalize the topic often result in the reader not understanding how the various seemingly independent topics are integrated. Understanding M&A involves an understanding of a full range of topics, including management, finance, economics, business law, financial and tax accounting, organizational dynamics, and the role of leadership.

With this in mind, this book attempts to provide a new organizational paradigm for discussing the complex and dynamically changing world of M&A. The book is organized according to the context in which topics normally occur in the M&A process. As such, the book is divided into five parts: M&A environment, M&A process, M&A valuation and modeling, deal structuring and financing, and alternative business and restructuring strategies. Topics that are highly integrated are discussed within these five groupings. See Figure 1 for the organizational layout of the book.

This book equips the instructor with the information and tools needed to communicate effectively with students having differing levels of preparation. The generous use of examples and contemporary business cases makes the text suitable for distance learning and self-study programs, as well as large, lecture-focused courses. Prerequisites for this text include familiarity with basic accounting, finance, economics, and general management concepts.

Online Instructors' Manual

The manual contains PowerPoint presentations for each chapter (completely consistent with those found on the CD-ROM), suggested learning objectives, recommended ways for teaching the materials, detailed syllabi for both undergraduate- and graduate-level classes, examples of excellent papers submitted by the author's students, and an exhaustive test bank. The test bank contains more than 1,600 test questions and answers (including true/false, multiple choice, short essay questions, case studies, and computational problems) and solutions to end-of-chapter discussion questions and end-of-chapter business case studies in the book.

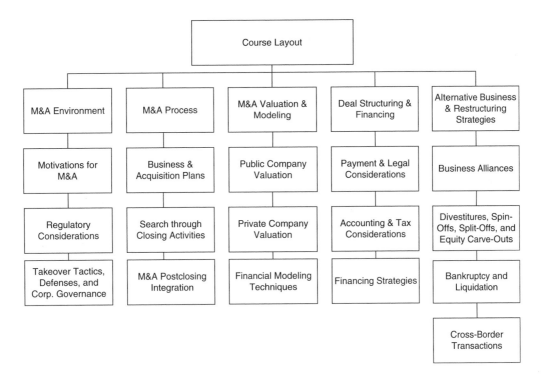

FIGURE 1 Course layout: Mergers, acquisitions, and other restructuring activities.

The online manual also contains, in a file folder named Preface to the Online Instructors' Manual and Table of Contents, suggestions as to how to teach the course to both undergraduate and graduate classes.

Please email the publisher at textbook@elsevier.com (within North America) and emea .textbook@elsevier.com (outside of North America) for access to the online manual. Please include your contact information (name, department, college, address, email, and phone number) along with your course information: course name and number, annual enrollment, ISBN, book title, and author. All requests are subject to approval by the company's representatives. For instructors who have already adopted this book, please go to textbooks.elsevier.com (Elsevier's instructors' website) and click on the button in the upper left hand corner entitled "instructors' manual." You will find detailed instructions on how to gain access to the online manual for this book.

Student Study Guide

The guide contained on the CD-ROM accompanying this book includes chapter summaries highlighting key learning objectives for each chapter, as well as true/false, multiple choice, and numerical questions and answers to enhance the student's learning experience.

Many Practical, Timely, and Diverse Examples and Current Business Cases

Each chapter begins with a vignette intended to illustrate a key point or points described in more detail as the chapter unfolds. Hundreds of examples, business cases, tables, graphs, and figures illustrate the application of key concepts. Many exhibits and diagrams summarize otherwise diffuse information and the results of numerous empirical studies substantiating key points made in each chapter. Each chapter concludes with a series of 15 discussion questions and two integrative end-of-chapter business cases intended to stimulate critical thinking and test the reader's understanding of the material. Some chapters include a series of practice problems and exercises to facilitate learning the chapter's content.

Comprehensive Yet Flexible Organization

Although the text is sequential, each chapter was developed as a self-contained unit to enable adaptation of the text to various teaching strategies and students with diverse backgrounds. The flexibility of the organization also makes the material suitable for courses of various lengths, from one quarter to two full semesters. The amount of time required depends on the students' level of sophistication and the desired focus of the instructor. Undergraduates have consistently demonstrated the ability to master eight or nine chapters of the book during a typical semester, whereas graduate-level students are able to cover effectively 12 to 14 chapters during the same period.

Acknowledgments

I would like to express my sincere appreciation for the many helpful suggestions received from a number of reviewers, including Kent Hickman, Gonzaga University; James Horan, LaSalle University; Tao-Hsien Dolly King, University of North Carolina at Charlotte; Hamilton Lin, Wall St. Training; and Matthew M. Wirgau, Walsh College; and the many resources of Academic Press/Butterworth–Heinemann/Elsevier. Finally, I would like to thank Alan Cherry, Ross Bengel, Patricia Douglas, Jeff Gale, Jim Healy, Charles Higgins, Michael Lovelady, John Mellen, Jon Saxon, David Offenberg, Chris Manning, and Maria Quijada for their many constructive comments and Karen Maloney, managing editor at Academic Press/Butterworth–Heinemann/Elsevier, for her ongoing support and guidance.

About the Author

Dr. DePamphilis has managed through closing more than 30 transactions including acquisitions, divestitures, joint ventures, minority investments, licensing, and supply agreements in a variety of different industries. These industries include the following: financial services, software, metals manufacturing, business consulting, health care, automotive, communications, textile, and real estate. He earned a Masters and Ph.D. in economics from Harvard University and B.A. in economics from the University of Pittsburgh. He is currently a Clinical Professor of Finance at Loyola Marymount University in Los Angeles, where he teaches undergraduate, MBA, and Executive MBA students mergers and acquisitions, corporate restructuring, deal making, finance, micro- and macroeconomics, and corporate governance. He has served as Chair of the Student Investment Fund in the Loyola Marymount University College of Business. Furthermore, Dr. DePamphilis also has been a lecturer on M&A and corporate restructuring, finance, and economics at the University of California, at Irvine, Chapman University, and Concordia University. As a visiting professor, he also has taught mergers and acquisitions at the Antai School of Management, Shanghai Jiao Tong University, in Shanghai, China.

Dr. DePamphilis has more than 25 years of experience in business in various industries and with varying degrees of responsibility. Previously, he served as Vice President of Electronic Commerce for Experian Corporation, Vice President of Business Development at TRW Information Systems and Services, Senior Vice President of Planning and Marketing at PUH Health Systems, Director of Corporate Business Planning at TRW, and Chief Economist for National

Steel Corporation. He also served as Director of Banking and Insurance Economics for Chase Econometric Associates and as an Economic Analyst for United California Bank. While at United California Bank, he developed a complex, interactive econometric forecasting model of the U.S. economy. Dr. DePamphilis has also spoken to numerous industry trade associations and customer groups at his former employers and Los Angeles community and business groups. He also is a graduate of the TRW and National Steel Corporation Executive Management programs.

Dr. DePamphilis has authored numerous articles, book chapters, and monographs on M&A, business planning and development, marketing, and economics in peer-reviewed academic journals as well as business and trade publications. Dr. DePamphilis serves as a consultant in product infringement and personal liability lawsuits, including but not limited to providing expert analysis and deposition in cases primarily related to mergers and acquisitions. Several other books by the author are forthcoming through Academic Press in 2010. These include *Merger and Acquisition Basics: All You Need to Know* and *Merger and Acquisition Negotiation and Deal Structuring: All You Need to Know.* Please forward any comments you may have about this book to the author at ddepamph@lmu.edu.

The Mergers and Acquisitions Environment

1

Introduction to Mergers and Acquisitions (M&As)

If you give a man a fish, you feed him for a day.
If you teach a man to fish, you feed him for a lifetime.

—Lao Tze

Inside M&A: Mars Buys Wrigley in One Sweet Deal

Under considerable profit pressure from escalating commodity prices and eroding market share, Wrigley Corporation, a U.S. based leader in gum and confectionery products, faced increasing competition from Cadbury Schweppes in the U.S. gum market. Wrigley had been losing market share to Cadbury since 2006. Mars Corporation, a privately owned candy company with annual global sales of $22 billion, sensed an opportunity to achieve sales, marketing, and distribution synergies by acquiring Wrigley Corporation.

On April 28, 2008, Mars announced that it had reached an agreement to merge with Wrigley Corporation for $23 billion in cash. Under the terms of the agreement, unanimously approved by the boards of the two firms, shareholders of Wrigley would receive $80 in cash for each share of common stock outstanding. The purchase price represented a 28 percent premium to Wrigley's closing share price of $62.45 on the announcement date. The merged firms in 2008 would have a 14.4 percent share of the global confectionary market, annual revenue of $27 billion, and 64,000 employees worldwide. The merger of the two family-controlled firms represents a strategic blow to competitor Cadbury Schweppes's efforts to continue as the market leader in the global confectionary market with its gum and chocolate business. Prior to the announcement, Cadbury had a 10 percent worldwide market share.

Wrigley would become a separate stand-alone subsidiary of Mars, with $5.4 billion in sales. The deal would help Wrigley augment its sales, marketing, and distribution capabilities. To provide more focus to Mars' brands in an effort to stimulate growth, Mars would transfer its global nonchocolate confectionery sugar brands to Wrigley. Bill Wrigley, Jr., who controls 37 percent of the firm's outstanding shares, would remain executive chairman of Wrigley. The Wrigley management team also would remain in place after closing. The combined companies would have substantial brand recognition and product diversity in six growth categories: chocolate, nonchocolate confectionary, gum, food, drinks, and pet-care products. The resulting confectionary powerhouse also would expect to achieve significant cost savings by combining manufacturing operations and have a substantial presence in emerging markets.

While mergers among competitors are not unusual, the deal's highly leveraged financial structure is atypical of transactions of this type. Almost 90 percent of the purchase price would be financed through borrowed funds, with the remainder financed largely by a third party equity investor. Mars's upfront costs would consist of paying for closing costs from its cash balances in excess of its operating needs. The debt financing for the transaction would consist of $11 billion and $5.5 billion provided by J.P. Morgan Chase and Goldman Sachs, respectively. An additional $4.4 billion in subordinated debt would come from Warren Buffet's investment company, Berkshire Hathaway, a nontraditional source of high-yield financing. Historically, such financing would have been provided by investment banks or hedge funds and subsequently repackaged into securities and sold to long-term investors, such as pension funds, insurance companies, and foreign investors. However, the meltdown in the global credit markets in 2008 forced investment banks and hedge funds to withdraw from the high-yield market in an effort to strengthen their balance sheets. Berkshire Hathaway completed the financing of the purchase price by providing $2.1 billion in equity financing for a 9.1 percent ownership stake in Wrigley.

Chapter Overview

The first decade of the new millennium heralded an era of global megamergers, followed by a period of extended turbulence in the global credit markets. As was true of the frenetic levels of mergers and acquisitions (M&As) in the 1980s and 1990s, the level of activity through mid-2007 was fueled by readily available credit, historically low interest rates, rising equity markets, technological change, global competition, and industry consolidation. In terms of dollar volume, M&A transactions reached a record level worldwide in 2007. The largely debt financed, speculative housing bubble in the United States and elsewhere burst during the second half of the year. Banks, concerned about the value of many of their own assets, became exceedingly selective in terms of the types of transactions they would finance, largely withdrawing from financing the highly leveraged transactions that had become commonplace in 2006. In view of the global nature of the credit markets, the quality of assets held by banks throughout Europe and Asia became suspect. As the availability of credit dried up, the malaise in the market for highly leveraged M&A transactions spread worldwide. The combination of record high oil prices and a reduced availability of credit caused most of the world's economies to slip into recession in 2008, substantially reducing global M&A activity. Despite a dramatic drop in energy prices and highly stimulative monetary and fiscal policies, the global recession continued in 2009, extending the slump in M&A activity.

In recent years, governments worldwide have intervened aggressively in global credit markets as well as manufacturing and other sectors of the economy in an effort to restore business and consumer confidence and offset deflationary pressures. While it is still too early to determine the impact of such actions on mergers and acquisitions, the implications may be significant. As will be noted in the coming chapters, M&As represent an important means of transferring resources to where they are most needed and removing underperforming managers. Government decisions to save some firms while allowing others to fail are likely to disrupt this process. Such decisions often are based on the notion that some firms are simply too big to fail because of their potential impact on the economy. The choices made by government could potentially produce perverse incentives for businesses to merge to minimize the risk of failing if they can achieve a size that is viewed as "too big too fail." Such actions disrupt the smooth functioning of markets, which reward good decisions while penalizing those having made poor decisions. There is very little historical evidence that governments can decide who is to fail and who is to survive better than markets.

The intent of this chapter is to provide the reader with an understanding of the underlying dynamics of M&As in the context of an increasingly interconnected world. The chapter begins with a discussion of M&A as a change agent in the context of corporate restructuring. Although other aspects of corporate restructuring are discussed elsewhere in this book, the focus in this chapter is on M&As, why they happen and why they tend to cluster in waves. The author also introduces the reader to various legal structures and strategies employed to restructure corporations. Moreover, the role of the various participants in the M&A process is explained. Using the results of the latest empirical studies, the chapter addresses the question of whether mergers pay off for target and acquiring company shareholders and bondholders, as well as for society. Finally, the most commonly cited reasons why some M&As fail to meet expectations are discussed. Major chapter segments include the following:

- Mergers and Acquisitions as Change Agents
- Common Motivations for Mergers and Acquisitions
- Merger and Acquisition Waves
- Alternative Forms of Corporate Restructuring
- Friendly versus Hostile Takeovers
- The Role of Holding Companies in Mergers and Acquisitions
- The Role of Employee Stock Ownership Plans in Mergers and Acquisitions
- Business Alliances as Alternatives to Mergers and Acquisitions
- Participants in the M&A Process
- Do Mergers and Acquisitions Pay Off for Shareholders?
- Do Mergers and Acquisitions Pay Off for Bondholders?
- Do Mergers and Acquisitions Pay Off for Society?
- Commonly Cited Reasons Some M&As Fail to Meet Expectations
- Long-Term Performance Similar for M&As, Business Alliances, and Solo Ventures
- Things to Remember

Words in italicized bold type are considered by the author to be important and are also found in the glossary at the end of this text for future reference. Throughout this book, a firm that attempts to acquire or merge with another company is called an *acquiring company*, *acquirer*, or *bidder*. The *target company*, or the target, is the firm that is being solicited by the acquiring company. *Takeovers* or *buyouts* are generic terms referring to a change in the controlling ownership interest of a corporation.

A review of this chapter (including practice questions and answers) is available in the file folder entitled Student Study Guide, contained on the CD-ROM accompanying this book. The CD-ROM also contains a Learning Interactions Library enabling students to test their knowledge of this chapter in a "real-time" environment.

Mergers and Acquisitions as Change Agents

Many have observed how businesses come and go. This continuous churn in businesses is perhaps best illustrated by the ever-changing composition of the 500 largest U.S. corporations. The so-called Fortune 500 illustrates remarkable change, in which only 70 of the original 500 firms on the list at its inception in 1955 can be found on the list today. About 2000 firms have appeared on the list at one time or another (aggdata.com, 2008). Most have been eliminated either through merger, acquisition, bankruptcy, downsizing, or some other form of corporate restructuring. Examples of such companies include such icons as Bethlehem Steel, Scott Paper, Zenith, Rubbermaid, and Warner Lambert.

In the popular media, actions taken to expand or contract a firm's basic operations or fundamentally change its asset or financial structure are referred to as ***corporate restructuring*** activities. Corporate restructuring is a catchall term that refers to a broad array of activities, ranging from reorganizing business units to takeovers and joint ventures to divestitures and spin-offs and equity carve-outs. Consequently, virtually all of the material covered in this book can be viewed as part of the corporate restructuring process. While the focus in this chapter is on corporate restructuring involving mergers and acquisitions, non-M&A corporate restructuring is discussed in more detail elsewhere in this book.

Common Motivations for Mergers and Acquisitions

The reasons M&As occur are numerous and the importance of factors giving rise to M&A activity varies over time. Table 1–1 lists some of the more prominent theories about why M&As happen. Each theory is discussed in greater detail in the remainder of this section.

Synergy

Synergy is the rather simplistic notion that the combination of two businesses creates greater shareholder value than if they are operated separately. The two basic types of synergy are operating and financial.

Table 1–1   Common Theories of What Causes Mergers and Acquisitions

Theory	Motivation

Operating synergy
   Economies of scale
   Economies of scope
	Improve operating efficiency through economies of scale or scope by acquiring a customer, supplier, or competitor

Financial synergy	Lower cost of capital

Diversification
   New products/current markets
   New products/new markets
   Current products/new markets
	Position the firm in higher-growth products or markets

Strategic realignment
   Technological change
   Regulatory and political change
	Acquire capabilities to adapt more rapidly to environmental changes than could be achieved if developed internally

Hubris (managerial pride)	Acquirers believe their valuation of target more accurate than the market's, causing them to overpay by overestimating synergy
Buying undervalued assets (q ratio)	Acquire assets more cheaply when the equity of existing companies is less than the cost of buying or building the assets
Mismanagement (agency problems)	Replace managers not acting in the best interests of the owners
Managerialism	Increase the size of a company to increase the power and pay of managers
Tax considerations	Obtain unused net operating losses and tax credits, asset write-ups, and substitute capital gains for ordinary income
Market power	Increase market share to improve ability to set prices above competitive levels
Misvaluation	Investor overvaluation of acquirer's stock encourages M&As

Operating Synergy (Economies of Scale and Scope)

Operating synergy consists of both economies of scale and economies of scope. Gains in efficiency can come from either factor and from improved managerial practices. Empirical studies suggest that such synergies are important determinants of shareholder wealth creation (Houston, James, and Ryngaert, 2001; DeLong, 2003).

Economies of scale refer to the spreading of fixed costs over increasing production levels. Scale is defined by such fixed costs as depreciation of equipment and amortization of capitalized software; normal maintenance spending; obligations, such as interest expense, lease payments, and union, customer, and vendor contracts; and taxes. Such costs are fixed in the sense that they cannot be altered in the short run. Consequently, for a given scale or amount of fixed expenses, the dollar value of fixed expenses per dollar of revenue decreases as output and sales increase. To illustrate the potential profit improvement impact of economies of scale, assume an auto plant can assemble 10 cars per hour or 240 cars per day and that fixed expenses per day are $1 million. Average fixed costs per car per day are $4,167 (i.e., $1 million/240). If improved assembly line speed increases car assembly rates to 20 cars per hour or 480 per day, the average fixed cost per car per day falls to $2,083 (i.e., $1 million/480). If variable costs per car do not increase and the selling price per car remains the same, the profit improvement per car due to the decline in average fixed costs per car per day is $2,084 (i.e., $4,167 – $2,083).

A firm with high fixed costs as a percent of total costs has greater earnings variability than one with a lower ratio of fixed to total costs. Assume two firms have annual revenues of $1 billion and operating profit of $50 million. However, fixed costs are 100 percent and 50 percent of total costs for the first and second firms, respectively. Assume revenues at both firms increase by $50 million. The first firm's income increases to $100 million, because all its costs are fixed. However, income at the second firm rises to only $75 million, as one half of the $50 million increase in revenue goes to pay for increased variable costs.

Economies of scope refers to using a specific set of skills or an asset currently employed in producing a specific product or service to produce related products or services. They are most often found when it is cheaper to combine two or more product lines in one firm than to produce them in separate firms. For example, Procter and Gamble, the consumer products giant, uses its highly regarded consumer marketing skills to sell a full range of personal care as well as pharmaceutical products. Honda utilizes its skills in enhancing internal combustion engines to develop motorcycles, lawn mowers, and snow blowers, as well as automobiles. Sequent Technology lets customers run applications on UNIX and NT operating systems on a single computer system. Citigroup uses the same computer center to process loan applications, deposits, trust services, and mutual fund accounts for its bank's customers. In each example, a specific set of skills or assets are used to generate more revenue by applying those skills or assets to producing or selling multiple products.

Financial Synergy (Lowering the Cost of Capital)

Financial synergy refers to the impact of mergers and acquisitions on the cost of capital (i.e., the minimum return required by investors and lenders) of the acquiring firm or the newly formed firm, resulting from the merger or acquisition. Theoretically, the cost of capital could be reduced if the merged firms have uncorrelated cash flows (i.e., so-called coinsurance), realize financial economies of scale from lower securities and transactions costs, or result in a better matching of investment opportunities with internally generated funds. Combining a firm with excess cash flows with one whose internally generated cash flow is insufficient to fund its investment opportunities may result in a lower cost of borrowing. A firm in a mature industry whose growth is slowing may produce cash flows well in excess of available investment opportunities. Another firm in a high-growth industry may have more investment opportunities than the cash to fund them. Reflecting their different growth rates and risk levels, the firm in the mature industry may have a lower cost of capital than the one in the high-growth industry. Combining the two firms might result in a lower cost of capital for the merged firms.

Diversification

Diversification refers to a strategy of buying firms outside of a company's current primary lines of business. There are two commonly used justifications for diversification. The first relates to the creation of financial synergy, resulting in a reduced cost of capital. The second common argument for diversification is for firms to shift from their core product lines or markets into product lines or markets that have higher growth prospects. Such diversification can be either related or unrelated to the firm's current products or markets.

The product–market matrix illustrated in Table 1–2 identifies a firm's primary diversification options. If a firm is facing slower growth in its current markets, it may be able to accelerate growth by selling its current products in new markets that are somewhat unfamiliar and, therefore, more risky. For example, pharmaceutical giant Johnson and Johnson's announced unsuccessful takeover attempt of Guidant Corporation in late 2004 reflected its attempt to give its medical devices business an entrée into the fast growing market for implantable devices, a market in which it does not currently participate. Similarly, a firm may attempt to achieve higher growth rates by developing or acquiring new products, with which it is relatively unfamiliar, and selling them into familiar and less risky current markets. Examples of this strategy include retailer JCPenney's acquisition of the Eckerd Drugstore chain or J&J's $16 billion acquisition of Pfizer's consumer health-care products line in 2006. In each instance, the firm is assuming additional risk. However, each of these related diversification strategies is generally less risky than an unrelated diversification strategy of developing new products for sale in new markets.

Empirical studies support the conclusion that investors do not benefit from unrelated diversification. The share prices of conglomerates often trade at a discount from shares of focused firms or from their value if they were broken up and sold in pieces by as much as 10 to 15 percent (Berger and Ofek, 1995; Lins and Servaes, 1999). This discount is called the *conglomerate*, or *diversification, discount*. Investors often perceive companies diversified in unrelated areas (i.e., those in different standard industrial classifications) as riskier, because they are difficult for management to understand and management often fails to fully fund the most attractive investment opportunities (Morck, Shleifer, and Vishny, 1990). Moreover, outside investors may have a difficult time understanding how to value the various parts of highly diversified businesses (Best and Hodges, 2004).

Table 1–2   Product–Market Matrix

Products \ Markets	Current	New
Current	Lower growth/lower risk	Higher growth/higher risk (related diversification)
New	Higher growth/higher risk (related diversification)	Highest growth/highest risk (unrelated diversification)

Some studies argue that the magnitude of the conglomerate discount is overstated. The discount is more related to the fact that diversifying firms are often poor performers before becoming conglomerates than to the simple act of diversification (Campa and Simi, 2002; Hyland, 2001). Still others conclude that the conglomerate discount is a result of how the sample studied is constructed (Villalonga, 2004; Graham, Lemmon, and Wolf, 2002).

Numerous studies suggest that the conglomerate discount is reduced when firms either divest or spin off businesses in an effort to achieve greater focus in the core business portfolio (Comment and Jarrell, 1993; Daley, Mehrotra, and Sivakumar, 1997; Lamont and Polk, 1997; Shin and Stulz, 1998; Scharfstein, 1998; Gertner, Powers, and Scharfstein, 2002; Dittmar and Shivdasani, 2003). Harding and Rovit (2004) and Megginson, Morgan, and Nail (2003) find evidence that the most successful mergers are those that focus on deals that promote the acquirer's core business. Singh and Montgomery (2008) find related acquisitions are more likely to experience higher financial returns than unrelated acquisitions. This should not be surprising, in that related firms are more likely to be able to realize cost savings due to overlapping functions and product lines than unrelated firms.

Although the empirical evidence suggests that corporate performance is likely to be greatest for firms that tend to pursue a more focused corporate strategy, there are always exceptions. Among the most famous are the legendary CEO of Berkshire Hathaway, Warren Buffet, and Jack Welch of General Electric (see Case Study 2–10, Chapter 2 of this book). Fauver, Houston, and Narrango (2003) argue that diversified firms in developing countries, where access to capital markets is limited, may sell at a premium to more focused firms. Under these circumstances, corporate diversification may enable more efficient investment, as diversified firms may use cash generated by mature subsidiaries to fund those with higher growth potential.

Strategic Realignment

The strategic realignment theory suggests that firms use M&As as ways of rapidly adjusting to changes in their external environments. Although change can come from many sources, only changes in the regulatory environment and technological innovation are considered. During the last 20 years, these two factors have been major forces in creating new opportunities for growth or threats to a firm's primary line of business, made obsolete by new technologies or changing regulations. This process of "creative destruction" is illustrated in Case Study 1–2.

Regulatory Change

M&A activity in recent years centered on industries subject to significant deregulation. These industries include financial services, health care, utilities, media, telecommunications, and defense. There is significant empirical evidence that takeover activity is higher in deregulated industries than in regulated ones (Jensen, 1993; Mitchell and Mulherin, 1996; Mulherin and Boone, 2000). The advent of deregulation broke down artificial barriers in these industries and stimulated competition. In some states, utilities now are required to sell power to competitors, which can resell the power in the utility's own marketplace. Some utilities are responding to this increased competition by attempting to achieve greater operating efficiency through mergers and acquisitions. In financial services, commercial banks have moved well beyond their historical role of accepting deposits and granting loans and into investment banking, insurance, and mutual funds. The Financial Services Modernization Act of 1999 repealed legislation dating back to the Great Depression that prevented banks, securities firms, and insurance companies from merging. The legislation accelerated the trend toward huge financial services companies typified by the 1998 Citicorp-Travelers merger. Some observers argue that allowing commercial banks to venture well beyond their traditional lines of business contributed to the breakdown in the global financial markets in 2008 and 2009.

Historically, local and long-distance phone companies were not allowed to compete against each other. Cable companies were essentially monopolies. Following the Telecommunications Reform Act of 1996, local and long-distance companies are actively encouraged to compete in each other's markets. Cable companies are offering both Internet access and local telephone service. During the first half of the 1990s, the U.S. Department of Defense actively encouraged consolidation of the nation's major defense contractors to improve their overall operating efficiency. In early 2002, a Federal Appeals Court rejected a Federal Communications Commission regulation that prohibited a company from owning a cable television system and a TV station in the same city. Moreover, it also overturned a rule that barred a company from owning TV stations that reach more than 35 percent of U.S. households. These rulings encourage combinations among the largest media companies or purchases of smaller broadcasters.

Technological Change

Technological advances create new products and industries. The development of the airplane created the passenger airline, avionics, and satellite industries. The emergence of satellite delivery of cable network to local systems ignited explosive growth in the cable industry. Today, with the expansion of broadband technology, we are witnessing the convergence of voice, data, and video technologies on the Internet. The emergence of digital camera technology has dramatically reduced the demand for analog cameras and film, causing such household names in photography as Kodak and Polaroid to shift their focus to the newer digital technology. The advent of satellite radio is increasing its share of the radio advertising market at the expense of traditional radio stations.

As the pace of technological change accelerates, M&A often is viewed as a way of rapidly exploiting new products and industries made possible by the emergence of new technologies. Large, more bureaucratic firms often are unable to exhibit the creativity and speed smaller, more nimble players display. With engineering talent often in short supply and product life cycles shortening, firms often do not have the luxury of time or the resources to innovate. Consequently, large companies often look to M&As as a fast and sometimes less expensive way to acquire new technologies and proprietary know-how to fill gaps in their current product offering or to enter entirely new businesses. Acquiring technologies also can be used as a defensive weapon to keep important new technologies out of the hands of competitors. In 2006, eBay acquired Skype Technologies, the Internet phone provider, for $2.6 billion in cash and stock. EBay hopes that the move will boost trading on its online auction site and prevent competitors from gaining access to the technology.

Hubris and the "Winners Curse"

As a result of hubris, managers sometimes believe that their own valuation of a target firm is superior to the market's valuation. Thus, the acquiring company tends to overpay for the target because of over-optimism in evaluating synergies. Competition among bidders also is likely to result in the winner overpaying because of hubris, even if significant synergies are present (Roll, 1986). Senior managers tend to be very competitive and sometimes self-important. The desire not to lose can result in a bidding war that can drive the purchase price of an acquisition well in excess of the actual economic value (i.e., cash generating capability) of that company.

Hubris, or excessive overconfidence, is a factor contributing to the so-called winner's curse. In an auction environment where there are many bidders, there is likely to be a wide range of bids for a target company. The winning bid is often substantially in excess of the expected value of the target company. This is attributable to the difficulty all participants have in estimating the actual value of the target and the competitive nature of the process. The winner is cursed in that he or she paid more than the company is worth and ultimately may feel remorse in having done so.

Buying Undervalued Assets (the *q* Ratio)

The *q ratio* is the ratio of the market value of the acquiring firm's stock to the replacement cost of its assets. Firms interested in expansion have a choice of investing in new plant and equipment or obtaining the assets by acquiring a company whose market value is less than the replacement cost of its assets (i.e., *q* ratio < 1). This theory was very useful in explaining M&A activity during the 1970s, when high inflation and interest rates depressed stock prices well below the book value of many firms. High inflation also caused the replacement cost of assets to be much higher than the book value of assets. More recently, gasoline refiner Valero Energy Corp. acquired Premcor Inc. in an $8 billion transaction that created the largest refiner in North America. The estimated cost of building a new refinery with capacity equivalent to Premcor would have cost 40 percent more than the acquisition price (Zellner, 2005). Similarly, the flurry of mergers among steel and copper companies in 2006 reflected the belief that the stock price of the target firms did not fully reflect the true market value of their assets.

Mismanagement (Agency Problems)

Agency problems arise when there is a difference between the interests of incumbent managers (i.e., those currently managing the firm) and the firm's shareholders. This happens when management owns a small fraction of the outstanding shares of the firm. These managers, who serve as agents of the shareholder, may be more inclined to focus on maintaining job security and a lavish lifestyle than on maximizing shareholder value. When the shares of a company are widely held, the cost of mismanagement is spread across a large number of shareholders. Each shareholder bears only a small portion of the cost. This allows for such mismanagement to be tolerated for long periods. According to this theory, mergers take place to correct situations where there is a separation between what the managers want and what the owners want. Low stock prices put pressure on managers to take actions to raise the share price or become the target of acquirers, who perceive the stock to be undervalued (Fama and Jensen, 1983). Mehran and Peristiani (2006) found that agency problems also are an important factor contributing to management-initiated buyouts, particularly when managers and shareholders disagree over how excess cash flow should be used.

Managerialism

The managerialism motive for acquisitions asserts that managers make acquisitions for selfish reasons. Masulis, Wang, and Xie (2007) hypothesize that managers sometimes are motivated to make acquisitions to build their spheres of influence and augment their compensation to the extent that such compensation depends on the size of the firms they manage. Gorton, Kahl, and Rosen (2007) argue that managers make "empire building" acquisitions as a means of defending their firms from being acquired. These conclusions ignore the pressure that managers of larger firms experience to sustain earnings growth in order to support their firms' share price. As the market value of a firm increases, senior managers are compelled to make ever larger investment bets to sustain the increases in shareholder value. Small acquisitions simply do not have sufficient impact on earnings growth to justify the effort required to complete them. Consequently, even though the resulting acquisitions may destroy value, the motive for making them may be more to support shareholder interests than to preserve management autonomy.

Tax Considerations

There are two important issues in discussing the role of taxes as a motive for M&As. First, tax benefits, such as loss carry forwards and investment tax credits, can be used to offset the combined firms' taxable income. Additional tax shelter is created if the acquisition is recorded under the purchase method of accounting, which requires the net book value of the acquired assets to be revalued to their current market value. The resulting depreciation of these generally higher asset values also reduces the amount of future taxable income generated by the combined companies. Second, the taxable nature of the transaction frequently plays a more important role in determining if the merger takes place than any tax benefits that accrue to the acquiring company. The tax-free status of the transaction may be viewed by the seller as a prerequisite for the deal to take place. A properly structured transaction can allow the target shareholders to defer any capital gain resulting from the transaction. If the transaction is not tax free, the seller normally wants a higher purchase price to compensate for the tax liability resulting from the transaction (Ayers, Lefanowicz, and Robinson, 2003). These issues are discussed in more detail in Chapter 12.

Market Power

The *market power* theory suggests that firms merge to improve their monopoly power to set product prices at levels not sustainable in a more competitive market. There is very little empirical support for this theory. Many recent studies conclude that increased merger activity is much more likely to contribute to improved operating efficiency of the combined firms than to increased market power (see the section of this chapter entitled "Do Mergers Pay Off for Society?").

Misvaluation

This explanation as to why takeovers happen has traditionally been overshadowed by the presumption that markets are efficient. Efficiency implies that a target's share price reflects accurately its true economic value (i.e., cash generation potential). While the empirical evidence that, over time, asset values reflect their true economic value is substantial, the evidence that assets may temporarily not reflect their underlying economic value is growing. The Internet bubble in the late 1990s is the most recent example of market inefficiencies. Just as these market inefficiencies affect investor decisions in buying individual stocks, they also affect the M&A market. Shleifer and Vishny (2003) suggest that irrational changes in investors' sentiment sometimes affect takeover decisions. While evident in earlier periods, empirical support for the misvaluation hypothesis was stronger in the 1990s than during earlier periods (Dong et al., 2006). The authors suggest that acquirers can periodically profit by buying undervalued targets for cash at a price below its actual value or by using equity (even if the target is overvalued) as long as the target is less overvalued than the bidding firm's stock. The tendency of overvalued acquirers to use stock as long as it is more overvalued than the target's stock (including premium) also is supported by Ang and Cheng (2006).

Overvalued shares enable the acquirer to purchase a target firm in a share for share exchange by issuing fewer shares. This reduces the probability of diluting the ownership position of current acquirer shareholders in the new company created by combining the acquirer and target firms. For example, assume the acquirer offers the target firm shareholders $10 for each share they own and that the acquirer's current share price is $10. As such, the acquirer would have to issue one new share for each target share outstanding. If the acquirer's share price is currently valued at $20, only 0.5 new shares would have to be issued and so forth. Consequently, the initial dilution of the current acquirer's shareholders ownership position in the new firm is less the higher is the acquirer's share price compared to the price offered for each share of target stock outstanding.

Merger and Acquisition Waves

Why M&A Waves Occur

M&A activity has tended to cluster in the United States in six multiyear waves since the late 1890s. There are two competing theories that attempt to explain this phenomenon. The first, sometimes referred to as the *neoclassical hypothesis*, argues that merger waves occur when firms in industries react to "shocks" in their operating environments (Martynova and Renneboog, 2008a; Brealey and Myers, 2003; Mitchell and Mulherin, 1996). Shocks could reflect such events as deregulation; the emergence of new technologies, distribution channels, or substitute products; or a sustained rise in commodity prices. The size and length of the M&A wave depends largely on the number of industries affected and the extent to which they are affected by such shocks. Some shocks, such as the emergence of the Internet, are pervasive in their impact, while others are more specific, such as deregulation of financial services and utilities or rapidly escalating commodity prices. In response to shocks, firms within the industry often acquire either all or parts of other firms.

The second theory, sometimes referred to as the *behavioral hypothesis*, is based on the misvaluation hypothesis discussed earlier and suggests that managers use overvalued stock to buy the assets of lower-valued firms. For M&As to cluster in waves, this theory requires that valuations of many firms measured by their price-to-earnings or market-to-book ratios compared to other firms must increase at the same time. Managers, whose stocks are believed to be overvalued, move concurrently to acquire companies whose stock prices are lesser valued (Rhodes-Kropf and Viswanathan, 2004; Shleifer and Vishny, 2003). The use of overvalued stock means the acquirer can issue fewer shares, resulting in less earnings dilution. Reflecting the influence of overvaluation, the method of payment according to this theory would normally be stock. Numerous studies confirm that long-term fluctuations in market valuations and the number of takeovers are positively correlated (Dong et al., 2006; Ang and Cheng, 2006; Andrade, Mitchell, and Stafford, 2001; Holmstrom and Kaplan, 2001; Daniel, Hirschleifer, and Subrahmanyam, 1998). However, whether high valuations contribute to greater takeover activity or increased M&A activity boosts market valuations is less clear.

In comparing these two theories, Harford (2005) finds greater support for the neoclassical or "shock" model, modified to include the effects of the availability of capital, in causing and sustaining merger waves. Harford underscores the critical role played by capital availability in determining merger waves. He points out that shocks alone, without sufficient liquidity to finance the transactions, do not initiate a wave of merger activity. Moreover, readily available, low-cost capital may cause a surge in M&A activity, even if industry shocks are absent. The low cost of capital was a particularly important factor in the most recent M&A boom.

Why It Is Important to Anticipate Merger Waves

Not surprisingly, there is evidence that the stock market rewards firms that see promising opportunities early and punishes those that imitate the moves of the early participants. Those pursuing these opportunities early on pay lower prices for target firms than those that are followers. In a review of 3,194 public companies that acquired other firms between 1984 and 2004, McNamara, Dykes, and Haleblian (2008) found that deals completed during the first 15 percent of a consolidation wave have share prices that out-perform significantly the overall stock market, as well as those deals that follow much later in the cycle, when the purchase price of target firms tends to escalate. Consequently, those that are late in pursuing acquisition targets are more likely to overpay for acquisitions. The study defines a *merger consolidation wave* as a cycle in which the peak year had a greater than 100 percent increase from the first year of the wave followed by a decline in acquisition activity of greater than 50 percent from the peak year. For some of the 12 industries studied, consolidation waves were as long as six years. Gell, Kengelbach, and Roos (2008) also found evidence that acquisitions early in the M&A cycle produce financial returns over 50 percent and, on average, create 14.5 percent more value for acquirer shareholders.

Trends in Recent M&A Activity

An explosion of highly leveraged buyouts and private equity investments (i.e., takeovers financed by limited partnerships) and the proliferation of complex securities collatera-lized by pools of debt and loan obligations of varying levels of risk characterized the U.S. financial markets from 2005 through 2007. Much of the financing of these transac-tions, as well as mortgage-backed security issues, has taken the form of syndicated debt (i.e., debt purchased by underwriters for resale to the investing public).

Because of the syndication process, such debt is dispersed among many investors. The issuers of the debt discharge much of the responsibility for the loans to others (except where investors have recourse to the originators if default occurs within a stipulated time). Under such circumstances, lenders have an incentive to increase the volume of lending to generate fee income by reducing their underwriting standards to accept riskier loans. Once sold to others, loan originators are likely to reduce monitoring of such loans. These practices, coupled with exceedingly low interest rates, made possible by a world awash in liquidity, contributed to excessive lending, and encouraged acquirers to overpay for target firms. Figure 1–1 illustrates how these factors spread risk throughout the global credit markets.

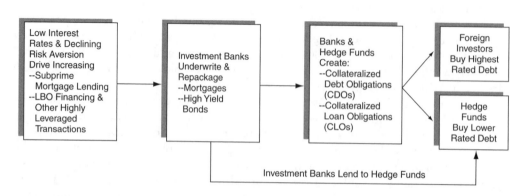

FIGURE 1–1 Debt-financed 2003–2007 M&A boom.

Since it is difficult to determine the ultimate holders of the debt once it is sold, declining home prices and a relatively few defaults in 2007 triggered concerns among lenders that the market value of their assets was actually well below the value listed on their balance sheets. Subsequent write-downs in the value of these assets reduced bank capital. Regulators require banks to maintain certain capital-to-asset ratios. To restore these ratios to a level comfortably above regulatory requirements, lenders restricted new lending. Bank lending continued to lag despite efforts by the Federal Reserve to increase sharply the amount of liquidity in the banking system by directly acquiring bank assets and expanding the types of financial services firms that could borrow from the central bank or by the U.S. Treasury's direct investment in selected commercial banks and other financial institutions. Thus, the repackaging and sale of debt in many different forms contributed to instability in the financial markets in 2008. The limitations of credit availability affected not only the ability of private equity and hedge funds to finance new or refinance existing transactions but also limited the ability of other businesses to fund their normal operations. Compounded by rapidly escalating oil prices in 2007 and during the first half of 2008, these conditions contributed to the global economic slowdown in 2008 and 2009 and the concomitant slump in M&A transactions, particularly those that were highly leveraged.

Table 1–3 provides the historical data underlying the trends in both global and U.S. merger and acquisition activity in recent years. M&A activity worldwide reached an historical peak in 2000 in terms of both the number and the dollar value of transactions, following surging economic growth and the Internet bubble of the late 1990s. During 2000, the dollar value of transactions in the United States accounted for almost one half of the global total. The ensuing recession in 2001, escalating concerns about terrorism, and the subsequent decline in the world's stock markets caused both the number and dollar value of global and U.S. transactions to decline through 2002. However, by that time, conditions were in place for a resurgence in M&A activity. Partially reflecting catch-up to the frenetic pace of U.S. M&A activity in the late 1990s, the dollar value and number of announced global M&A transactions outside of the United States reached new highs in 2007 (see Figures 1–2 and 1–3). However, global merger activity dropped

Table 1–3 Trends in Announced Mergers and Acquisitions (M&As)

Year	Global M&As Number	Global M&As $Value (billions)	U.S. M&As Number	U.S. M&As $Value (billions)	U.S. Share of Global M&As Number (%)	U.S. Share of Global M&As $Value (%)
1995	22,027	980	3,510	356	15.9	36.3
1996	23,166	1,146	5,848	495	25.2	43.2
1997	22.642	1,676	7,800	657	34.5	39.2
1998	27,256	2,581	7,809	1,192	28.7	46.2
1999	31,701	3,439	9,278	1,426	29.3	41.5
2000	37.204	3,497	9,566	1,706	25.7	48.8
2001	28,828	1,745	8,290	759	28.8	43.5
2002	26.270	1,207	7,303	441	27.7	36.5
2003	27,753	1,333	8,131	559	29.3	41.9
2004	31,467	1,949	9,783	812	31.1	41.7
2005	33,574	2,775	10,644	1,045	31.7	37.7
2006	38,602	3,794	10,977	1,563	28.4	41.2
2007	42,921	4,784	10,554	1,579	24.6	33.0
2008	27,478	2,898	6,237	947	22.7	32.7

Source: Thompson Reuters and Dealogic.

Note: All valuations include the value of debt assumed by the acquirer.

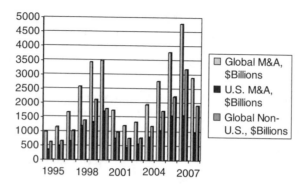

FIGURE 1–2 Dollar value of transactions: U.S. versus global M&A. All valuations include the value of debt assumed by the acquirer. *Source:* Thompson Reuters and Dealogic.

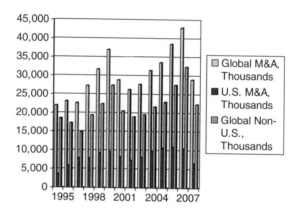

FIGURE 1–3 Number of transactions: U.S. versus global M&A. All valuations include the value of debt assumed by the acquirer. *Source:* Thompson Reuters and Dealogic.

precipitously in 2008, reflecting a lack of credit, plunging equity markets, and the world-wide financial crisis. According to Dealogic, 1,307 previously announced deals valued at $911 billion were canceled in 2008, underscoring the malaise affecting the global M&A market. Deals sponsored by private equity firms hit a five-year low worldwide, falling 71 percent in 2008 from the prior year to $188 billion. Both the number of and dollar value of U.S. mergers and acquisitions as a percent of global M&A activity continued to decline in 2008.

Similarities and Differences among Merger Waves

While patterns of takeover activity and their profitability vary significantly across M&A waves, all waves have common elements. Mergers tended to occur during periods of sustained high rates of economic growth, low or declining interest rates, and a rising stock market. Historically, each merger wave differed in terms of a specific development, such as the emergence of a new technology; industry focus such as rail, oil, or financial services; degree of regulation; and type of transaction, such as horizontal, vertical, conglomerate, strategic, or financial. The different types of transactions are discussed in more detail later in this chapter. See Table 1–4 for a comparison of the six historical merger waves.

Table 1–4 U.S. Historical Merger Waves

Time Period	Driving Force(s)	Type of M&A Activity	Key Impact	Key Transactions	Factors Contributing to End of Wave
1897–1904	Drive for efficiency Lax antitrust law enforcement Westward migration Technological change	Horizontal consolidation	Increasing concentration: Primary metals Transportation Mining	U.S. Steel Standard Oil Eastman Kodak American Tobacco General Electric	Fraudulent financing 1904 stock market crash
1916–1929	Entry into WWI Post-WW I boom	Largely horizontal consolidation	Increased industry concentration	Samuel Insull builds utility empire in 39 states called Middle West Utilities	1929 stock market crash Clayton Antitrust Act
1965–1969	Rising stock market Sustained economic boom	Growth of conglomerates	Financial engineering and conglomeration	LTV ITT Litton Industries Gulf and Western Northwest Industries	Escalating purchase prices Excessive leverage
1981–1989	Rising stock market Economic boom Underperformance of conglomerates Relative weakness of U.S. dollar Favorable regulatory environment Favorable foreign accounting practices	Retrenchment era Rise of hostile takeovers Corporate raiders Proliferation of financial buyers using highly leveraged transactions Increased takeover of U.S. firms by foreign buyers	Break-up of conglomerates Increased use of junk (unrated) bonds to finance transactions	RJR Nabisco MBO Beecham Group (U.K.) buys SmithKline Campeau of Canada buys Federated Stores	Widely publicized bankruptcies 1990 recession
2003–2007	Low interest rates Rising stock market Booming global economy Globalization High commodity prices	Age of cross-border transactions, horizontal megamergers, and growing influence of private equity investors	Increasing synchronicity among world's economies	Mittal acquires Arcelor P&G buys Gillette Verizon acquires MCI Blackstone buys Equity Office Properties	Loss of confidence in global capital markets Economic slowdown in industrial nations

Alternative Forms of Corporate Restructuring

In the academic literature, corporate restructuring activities often are broken into two specific categories: operational and financial restructuring. *Operational restructuring* usually refers to the outright or partial sale of companies or product lines or downsizing by closing unprofitable or nonstrategic facilities. *Financial restructuring* describes actions by the firm to change its total debt and equity structure. Examples of financial restructuring include share repurchases or adding debt to either lower the corporation's overall cost of capital or as part of an antitakeover defense (see Chapter 3).

Mergers and Consolidations

Mergers can be described from a legal perspective and an economic perspective. This distinction is relevant to discussions concerning deal structuring, regulatory issues, and strategic planning.

A Legal Perspective

This perspective refers to the legal structure used to consummate the transaction. Such structures may take on many forms depending on the nature of the transaction. A *merger* is a combination of two or more firms in which all but one *legally* cease to exist, and the combined organization continues under the original name of the surviving firm. In a typical merger, shareholders of the target firm exchange their shares for those of the acquiring firm, after a shareholder vote approving the merger. Minority shareholders, those not voting in favor of the merger, are required to accept the merger and exchange their shares for those of the acquirer. If the parent firm is the primary shareholder in the subsidiary, the merger does not require approval of the parent's shareholders in the majority of states. Such a merger is called a *short form merger.* The principal requirement is that the parent's ownership exceeds the minimum threshold set by the state. For example, Delaware allows a parent corporation to merge without a shareholder vote with a subsidiary if the parent owns at least 90 percent of the outstanding voting shares. A *statutory merger* is one in which the acquiring company assumes the assets and liabilities of the target in accordance with the statutes of the state in which the combined companies will be incorporated. A *subsidiary merger* involves the target becoming a subsidiary of the parent. To the public, the target firm may be operated under its brand name, but it will be owned and controlled by the acquirer.

Although the terms *mergers* and *consolidations* often are used interchangeably, a *statutory consolidation,* which involves two or more companies joining to form a new company, is technically not a merger. All legal entities that are consolidated are dissolved during the formation of the new company, which usually has a new name. In a merger, either the acquirer or the target survives. The 1999 combination of Daimler-Benz and Chrysler to form DaimlerChrysler is an example of a consolidation. The new corporate entity created as a result of consolidation or the surviving entity following a merger usually assumes ownership of the assets and liabilities of the merged or consolidated organizations. Stockholders in merged companies typically exchange their shares for shares in the new company.

A *merger of equals* is a merger framework usually applied whenever the merger participants are comparable in size, competitive position, profitability, and market capitalization. Under such circumstances, it is unclear if either party is ceding control to the other and which party is providing the greater synergy. Consequently, target firm shareholders rarely receive any significant premium for their shares. It is common for the new firm to be managed by the former CEOs of the merged firms, who will be coequal, and for the composition of the new firm's board to have equal representation from the boards of the merged firms. In such transactions, it is uncommon for the ownership split to be equally divided, with only 14 percent having a 50/50 split (Mallea, 2008). The 1998 formation of Citigroup from Citibank and Travelers is an example of a merger of equals. Research suggests that the CEOs of target firms often negotiate to retain a significant degree of control in the merged firm for both their board and management in exchange for a lower premium for their shareholders (Wulf, 2004).

An Economic Perspective

Business combinations also may be classified as horizontal, vertical, and conglomerate mergers. How a merger is classified depends on whether the merging firms are in the same or different industries and their positions in the corporate value chain (Porter, 1985). Defining business combinations in this manner is particularly important from the standpoint of antitrust analysis (see Chapter 2). Horizontal and conglomerate mergers are best understood in the context of whether the merging firms are in the same or different industries. A *horizontal merger* occurs between two firms within the same industry. Examples of horizontal acquisitions include Procter & Gamble and Gillette (2006) in household products, Oracle and PeopleSoft in business application software (2004), oil giants Exxon and Mobil (1999), SBC Communications and Ameritech (1998) in telecommunications, and NationsBank and BankAmerica (1998) in commercial banking. *Conglomerate mergers* are those in which the acquiring company purchases firms in largely unrelated industries. An example would be U.S. Steel's acquisition of Marathon Oil to form USX in the mid-1980s.

Vertical mergers are best understood operationally in the context of the corporate value chain (see Figure 1–4). Vertical mergers are those in which the two firms participate at different stages of the production or value chain. A simple value chain in the basic steel industry may distinguish between raw materials, such as coal or iron ore; steel making, such as "hot metal" and rolling operations; and metals distribution. Similarly, a value chain in the oil and gas industry would separate exploration activities from production, refining, and marketing. An Internet value chain might distinguish between infrastructure providers, such as Cisco; content providers, such as Dow Jones; and portals, such as Yahoo and Google. In the context of the value chain, a *vertical merger* is one in which companies that do not own operations in each major segment of the value chain choose to "backward integrate" by acquiring a supplier or to "forward integrate" by acquiring a distributor. An example of forward integration includes paper manufacturer Boise Cascade's acquisition of office products distributor, Office Max, for $1.1 billion in 2003. An example of backward integration in the technology and media industry is America Online's purchase of media and content provider Time Warner in 2000. In another example of backward integration, American steel company Nucor Corporation announced in 2008 the acquisition of the North American scrap metal operations of privately held Dutch conglomerate SHV Holdings NV. The acquisition further secures Nucor's supply of scrap metal used to fire its electric arc furnaces.

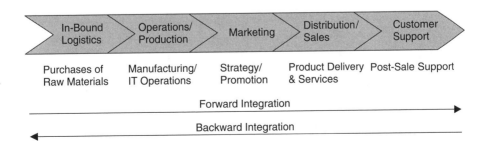

FIGURE 1–4 Corporate VALUE chain. *Note:* IT refers to information technology.

According to Gugler et al. (2003), horizontal, conglomerate, and vertical mergers accounted for 42 percent, 54 percent, and 4 percent of the 45,000 transactions analyzed between 1981 and 1998. While pure vertical mergers are rare, Fan and Goyal (2006) find that about one fifth of the mergers analyzed between 1962 and 1996 exhibited some degree of vertical relatedness.

Acquisitions, Divestitures, Spin-Offs, Carve-Outs, and Buyouts

Generally speaking, an *acquisition* occurs when one company takes a controlling ownership interest in another firm, a legal subsidiary of another firm, or selected assets of another firm, such as a manufacturing facility. An acquisition may involve the purchase of another firm's assets or stock, with the acquired firm continuing to exist as a legally owned subsidiary. In contrast, a *divestiture* is the sale of all or substantially all of a company or product line to another party for cash or securities. A *spin-off* is a transaction in which a parent creates a new legal subsidiary and distributes shares in the subsidiary to its current shareholders as a stock dividend. An *equity carve-out* is a transaction in which the parent firm issues a portion of its stock or that of a subsidiary to the public. See Chapter 15 for more about divestitures, spin-offs, and carve-outs.

A *leveraged buyout* (LBO) or *highly leveraged transaction* involves the purchase of a company financed primarily by debt. While LBOs commonly involve privately owned firms, the term often is applied to a firm that buys back its stock using primarily borrowed funds to convert from a publicly owned to a privately owned company (see Chapter 13). See Figure 1–5 for a summary of the various forms of corporate restructuring.

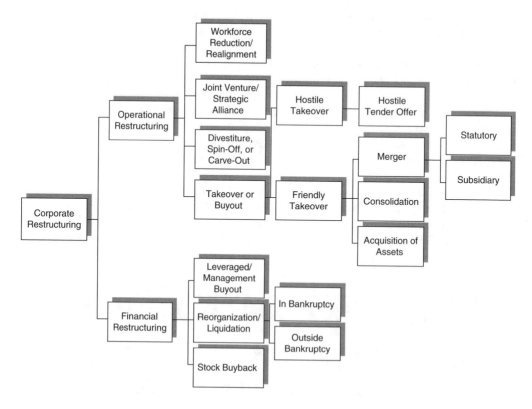

FIGURE 1–5 Corporate restructuring process.

Friendly versus Hostile Takeovers

In a *friendly takeover* of control, the target's board and management are receptive to the idea and recommend shareholder approval. To gain control, the acquiring company generally must offer a premium to the current stock price. The excess of the offer price over the target's premerger share price is called a *purchase*, or acquisition, *premium*. U.S. merger premiums averaged about 38 percent between 1973 and 1998 (Andrade et al., 2001). Rossi and Volpin (2004) document an average premium of 44 percent during the 1990s for U.S. mergers. The authors also found premiums in 49 countries ranging from 10 percent for Brazil and Switzerland to 120 percent for Israel and Indonesia. The wide range of estimates may reflect the value attached to the special privileges associated with control in various countries. For example, insiders in Russian oil companies have been able to capture a large fraction of profits by selling some of their oil to their own companies at below market prices.

The purchase premium reflects the perceived value of obtaining a controlling interest (i.e., the ability to direct the activities of the firm) in the target, the value of expected synergies (e.g., cost savings) resulting from combining the two firms, and any overpayment for the target firm. Overpayment is the amount an acquirer pays for a target firm in excess of the present value of future cash flows, including synergy. Analysts often attempt to identify the amount of premium paid for a controlling interest (i.e., *control premium*) and the amount of incremental value created the acquirer is willing to share with the target's shareholders (see Chapter 9). An example of a pure control premium is a conglomerate willing to pay a price significantly above the prevailing market price for a target firm to gain a controlling interest even though potential operating synergies are limited. In this instance, the acquirer often believes it will be able to recover the value of the control premium by making better management decisions for the target firm. It is important to emphasize that what often is called a *control premium* in the popular or trade press is actually a purchase or acquisition premium including both a premium for synergy and a premium for control.

The offer to buy shares in another firm, usually for cash, securities, or both, is called a *tender offer*. While tender offers are used in a number of circumstances, they most often result from friendly negotiations (i.e., negotiated tender offers) between the acquirer's and the target firm's boards. *Self-tender offers* are used when a firm seeks to repurchase its stock. Finally, those that are unwanted by the target's board are referred to as *hostile tender offers*.

An unfriendly or *hostile takeover* occurs when the initial approach was unsolicited, the target was not seeking a merger at that time, the approach was contested by the target's management, and control changed hands (i.e., usually requiring the purchase of more than half of the target's voting common stock). The acquirer may attempt to circumvent management by offering to buy shares directly from the target's shareholders (i.e., a hostile tender offer) and by buying shares in a public stock exchange (i.e., an open market purchase).

Friendly takeovers often are consummated at a lower purchase price than hostile transactions. A hostile takeover attempt may attract new bidders, who otherwise may not have been interested in the target. Such an outcome often is referred to as putting the target *in play*. In the ensuing auction, the final purchase price may be bid up to a point well above the initial offer price. Acquirers also prefer friendly takeovers, because the postmerger integration process usually is accomplished more expeditiously when both parties cooperate fully. For these reasons, most transactions tend to be friendly.

The Role of Holding Companies in Mergers and Acquisitions

A *holding company* is a legal entity having a controlling interest in one or more companies. The primary function of a holding company is to own stock in other corporations. In general, the parent firm has no wholly owned operating units. The segments owned by the holding company are separate legal entities, which in practice are controlled by the holding company. The key advantage of the holding company structure is the leverage achieved by gaining effective control of other companies' assets at a lower overall cost than if the firm were to acquire 100 percent of the target's outstanding shares. Effective control sometimes can be achieved by owning as little as 30 percent of the voting stock of another company when the firm's bylaws require approval of major decisions by a majority of votes cast rather than a majority of the voting shares outstanding. This is particularly true when the target company's ownership is highly fragmented, with few shareholders owning large blocks of stock. Effective control generally is achieved by acquiring less than 100 percent but usually more than 50 percent of another firm's equity. One firm is said to have *effective control* when control has been achieved by buying voting stock; it is not likely to be temporary, there are no legal restrictions on control (such as from a bankruptcy court), and there are no powerful minority shareholders.

The holding company structure can create significant management challenges. Because it can gain effective control with less than 100 percent ownership, the holding company is left with minority shareholders, who may not always agree with the strategic direction of the company. Consequently, implementing holding company strategies may become very contentious. Furthermore, in highly diversified holding companies, managers also may have difficulty making optimal investment decisions because of their limited understanding of the different competitive dynamics of each business. The holding company structure also can create significant tax problems for its shareholders. Subsidiaries of holding companies pay taxes on their operating profits. The holding company then pays taxes on dividends it receives from its subsidiaries. Finally, holding company shareholders pay taxes on dividends they receive from the holding company. This is equivalent to triple taxation of the subsidiary's operating earnings.

The Role of Employee Stock Ownership Plans in Mergers and Acquisitions

An *employee stock ownership plan* (ESOP) is a trust fund that invests in the securities of the firm sponsoring the plan. About 13,000 ESOPs exist nationwide, with most formed by privately owned firms. Such plans are defined contribution employee benefit pension plans that invest at least 50 percent of the plan's assets in the common shares of the firm sponsoring the ESOP. The plans may receive the employer's stock or cash, which is used to buy the sponsoring employer's stock. The sponsoring corporation can make tax-deductible contributions of cash, stock, or other assets into the trust. The plan's trustee holds title to the assets for the benefit of the employees (i.e., beneficiaries). The trustee is charged with investing the trust assets productively, and unless specifically limited, the trustee can sell, mortgage, or lease the assets.

Stock acquired by the ESOP is allocated to accounts for individual employees based on some formula and vested over time. Often participants become fully vested after six years. When employees leave the company they receive their vested shares, which the company or the ESOP buys back at an appraised fair market value. ESOP participants must be allowed to vote their allocated shares at least on major issues, such as selling the company. However, there is no requirement that they be allowed to vote on other issues such as choosing the board of directors. The assets are allocated to employees and not taxed until withdrawn by employees. Cash contributions made by the sponsoring firm to pay both interest and principal payments on bank loans to ESOPs are tax deductible by the firm. Dividends paid on stock contributed to ESOPs also are deductible if they are used to repay ESOP debt. The sponsoring firm could use tax credits equal to .5 percent of payroll, if contributions in that amount were made to the ESOP. Finally, lenders must pay taxes on only one half of the interest received on loans made to ESOP's owning more than 50 percent of the sponsoring firm's stock.

ESOPs as an Alternative to Divestiture

If a subsidiary cannot be sold at what the parent firm believes to be a reasonable price and liquidating the subsidiary would be disruptive to customers, the parent may sell directly to employees through a shell corporation. A *shell corporation* is one that is incorporated but has no significant assets. The shell sets up the ESOP, which borrows the money to buy the subsidiary. The parent guarantees the loan. The shell operates the subsidiary, whereas the ESOP holds the stock. As income is generated from the subsidiary, tax-deductible contributions are made by the shell to the ESOP to service the debt. As the loan is repaid, the shares are allocated to employees who eventually own the firm.

ESOPs and Management Buyouts

ESOPs may be used by employees in leveraged or management buyouts to purchase the shares of owners of privately held firms. This is particularly common when the owners have most of their net worth tied up in their firms. The mechanism is similar to owner-initiated sales to employees.

ESOPs as an Antitakeover Defense

A firm concerned about the potential for a hostile takeover creates an ESOP. The ESOP borrows with the aid of the sponsoring firm's guarantee and uses the loan proceeds to buy stock issued by the sponsoring firm. While the loan is outstanding, the ESOP's trustees retain voting rights on the stock. Once the loan is repaid, it generally is assumed that employees will tend to vote against bidders who they perceive as jeopardizing their jobs.

Business Alliances as Alternatives to Mergers and Acquisitions

In addition to mergers and acquisitions, businesses also may combine through joint ventures (JVs), strategic alliances, minority investments, franchises, and licenses. These alternative forms of combining businesses are addressed in more detail in Chapter 14. The term *business alliance* is used to refer to all forms of business combinations other than mergers and acquisitions.

Joint ventures are cooperative business relationships formed by two or more separate parties to achieve common strategic objectives. While the JV is often an independent legal entity in the form of a corporation or partnership formed for a specific time period and a specific purpose, they may take any organizational form deemed appropriate by the parties involved. JV corporations have their own management reporting to a board of directors consisting of representatives of those companies participating in the JV. The JV generally is established for a limited time. Each of the JV partners continues to exist as separate entities. In contrast, **strategic alliances** generally fall short of creating a separate legal entity. They can be an agreement to sell each firm's products to the other's customers or to codevelop a technology, product, or process. The terms of such an agreement may be legally binding or largely informal. **Minority investments** require little commitment of management time and may be highly liquid if the investment is in a publicly traded company. Investing companies may choose to assist small or startup companies in the development of products or technologies useful to the investing company. The investing company often receives representation on the board of the firm in which the investor has made the investment. Such investments may also be opportunistic in that passive investors take a long-term position in a firm believed to have significant appreciation potential. In 2008, Berkshire Hathaway, Warren Buffett's investment company, invested $5 billion in investment bank Goldman Sachs by acquiring convertible preferred stock paying a 10 percent dividend. Berkshire Hathaway also received warrants (i.e., rights) to purchase $5 billion of Goldman Sachs's common stock at $115 per share. This exercise price was less one half of the firm's year-earlier share price.

Licenses require no initial capital and represent a convenient way for a company to extend its brand to new products and new markets by licensing their brand name to others. Alternatively, a company may gain access to a proprietary technology through the licensing process. A **franchise** is a specialized form of a license agreement granting a privilege to a dealer by a manufacturer or a franchise service organization to sell the franchiser's products or services in a given area. Such arrangements can be exclusive or nonexclusive. Under a franchise agreement, the franchiser may offer the franchisee consultation, promotional assistance, financing, and other benefits in exchange for a share of the franchise's revenue. Franchises represent a low-cost way for the franchisor to expand, because the capital usually is provided by the franchisee. However, the success of franchising has been limited largely to such industries as fast food services and retailing, in which a successful business model can be more easily replicated.

The major attraction of these alternatives to outright acquisition is the opportunity for each partner to gain access to the other's skills, products, and markets at a lower overall cost in terms of management time and money. Major disadvantages include limited control, the need to share profits, and the potential loss of trade secrets and skills to competitors.

Participants in the Mergers and Acquisitions Process

Investment Bankers

Amid the turmoil of the 2008 credit crisis, the traditional model of the mega independent investment bank as a highly leveraged, largely unregulated, innovative securities underwriter and M&A advisor foundered. Lehman Brothers was liquidated and Bear Stearns and Merrill Lynch were acquired by commercial banks J.P. Morgan Chase and Bank of America, respectively. In an effort to attract retail deposits and borrow from the U.S. Federal Reserve System (the "Fed"), Goldman Sachs and Morgan Stanley converted to commercial bank holding companies subject to Fed regulation.

While the financial markets continue to require investment banking services, they will be provided increasingly through "universal banks" (e.g., Bank of America/Merrill Lynch and Citibank/Smith Barney), which provide the customary commercial banking as well as investment banking services. In addition to those already mentioned, traditional investment banking activities also include providing strategic and tactical advice and acquisition opportunities; screening potential buyers and sellers; making initial contact with a seller or buyer; and providing negotiation support, valuation, and deal structuring guidance. Along with these investment banking functions, the large firms usually maintain substantial broker-dealer operations serving wholesale and retail clients in brokerage and advisory capacities. While the era of the thriving independent investment banking behemoth may be over, the role of investment banking boutiques providing specialized expertise is likely to continue to thrive.

Fairness Opinion Letters and Advisory Fees

Investment bankers derive significant income from writing so-called fairness opinion letters. A *fairness opinion letter* is a written and signed third-party assertion certifying the appropriateness of the price of a proposed deal involving a tender offer, merger, asset sale, or leveraged buyout. It discusses the price and terms of the deal in the context of comparable transactions. A typical fairness opinion provides a range of "fair" prices, with the presumption that the actual deal price should fall within that range. Although such opinions are intended to inform investors, they often are developed as legal protection for members of the boards of directors against possible shareholder challenges of their decisions.

The size of an investment banking advisory fee is often contingent on the completion of the deal and may run about 1–2 percent of the value of the transaction. Such fees generally vary with the size of the transaction. The size of the fee paid may exceed 1–2 percent, if the advisors achieve certain incentive goals. Fairness opinion fees often amount to about one fourth of the total advisory fee paid on a transaction (Sweeney, 1999). Although the size of the fee may vary with the size of the transaction, the fairness opinion fee usually is paid whether or not the deal is consummated. Problems associated with fairness opinions include the potential conflicts of interest with investment banks that generate large fees. In many cases, the investment bank that brought the deal to a potential acquirer is the same one that writes the fairness opinion. Moreover, they are often out of date by the time shareholders vote on the deal, they do not address whether the firm could have gotten a better deal, and the overly broad range of value given in such letters reduces their relevance. Courts agree that, because the opinions are written for boards of directors, the investment bankers have no obligation to the shareholders (Henry, 2003).

Selecting Investment Banks

The size of the transaction often determines the size of the investment bank that can be used as an advisor. The largest investment banks are unlikely to consider any transaction valued at less than $100 million. Investment banking boutiques can be very helpful in providing specialized industry knowledge and contacts. Investment banks often provide large databases of recent transactions, which are critical in valuing potential target companies. For highly specialized transactions, the boutiques are apt to have more relevant data. Finally, the large investment banks are more likely to be able to assist in funding large transactions because of their current relationships with institutional lenders and broker distribution networks.

In large transactions, a group of investment banks, also referred to as a *syndicate*, agrees to purchase a new issue of securities (e.g., debt, preferred, or common stock) from the acquiring company for sale to the investing public. Within the syndicate, the banks underwriting or purchasing the issue are often different from the group selling the issue. The selling group often consists of those firms with the best broker distribution networks. After registering with the Securities and Exchange Commission (SEC), such securities may be offered to the investing public as an *initial public offering* (IPO), at a price agreed on by the issuer and the investment banking group. Alternatively, security issues may avoid the public markets and be privately placed with institutional investors, such as pension funds and insurance companies. Unlike public offerings, *private placements* do not have to be registered with the SEC if the securities are purchased for investment rather than for resale. Bao and Edmans (2008) find that, in selecting an investment bank as a transaction advisor, the average magnitude of the financial returns on the announcement dates for those deals for which they serve as an advisor is far more important than the investment bank's size or market share.

Lawyers

The legal framework surrounding a typical transaction has become so complex that no one individual can have sufficient expertise to address all the issues. On large, complicated transactions, legal teams can consist of more than a dozen attorneys, each of whom represents a specialized aspect of the law. Areas of expertise include the following: M&As, corporate, tax, employee benefits, real estate, antitrust, securities, environmental, and intellectual property. In a hostile transaction, the team may grow to include litigation experts. Leading law firms in terms of their share of the dollar value of transactions include Wachtell Lipton Rosen & Katz, Simpson Thatcher & Bartlett, Skadden Arps Slate Meagher & Flom, Sullivan & Cromwell, and Davis Polk & Wardwell.

Accountants

Services provided by accountants include advice on the optimal tax structure, financial structuring, and performing financial due diligence. A transaction can be structured in many ways, with each having different tax implications for the parties involved (see Chapter 12). In conducting due diligence, accountants also perform the role of auditors by reviewing the target's financial statements and operations through a series of onsite visits and interviews with senior and middle-level managers. The accounting industry is dominated by the group of firms called the *big four*: Ernst & Young, Pricewaterhouse-Cooper, KPMG, and Deloitte & Touche. Regional firms are those likely to have some national and possibly some international clients, but they are largely tied to specific regional accounts. Examples of large regional firms include Grant Thornton and BDO Seidman. Local accounting firms operate in a number of cities and tend to focus on small businesses and individuals.

Proxy Solicitors

Proxy battles are attempts to change management control of a company by gaining the right to cast votes on behalf of other shareholders. In contests for the control of the board of directors of a target company, it is often difficult to compile mailing lists of stockholders' addresses. Proxy solicitors often are hired to obtain such addresses by the acquiring firm or dissident shareholders. The target's management may also hire proxy solicitors to design strategies to educate shareholders and communicate why shareholders should follow the board's recommendations. Major proxy-solicitation companies include Georgeson & Company and D. F. King & Company.

Public Relations

Communicating a consistent position during a takeover attempt is vital, as inconsistent messages reduce the credibility of the parties involved. From the viewpoint of the acquiring company in a hostile takeover attempt, the message to the shareholders must be that their plans for the company will increase shareholder value more than the plans of the incumbent management. The target company's management frequently will hire private investigators, such as Kroll Associates, to develop detailed financial data on the company and do background checks on key personnel. The target firm may use such information to discredit publicly the management of the acquiring firm. Major public relations firms with significant experience in the M&A arena include Kekst & Company, Hill & Knowlton, and Robinson Lerer & Montgomery.

Institutional Investors

Institutional investors include public and private pension funds, insurance companies, investment companies, bank trust departments, and mutual funds. Although a single institution generally cannot influence a company's actions, a collection of institutions can. Federal regulations require institutional shareholders who are seeking actual proxies or hold a large percentage of a company's stock to file a proxy statement with the SEC (see Chapter 3). Shareholders may announce how they intend to vote on a matter and advertise their position to seek support. Institutional investors also influence M&A activity by providing an important source of financing. While commercial banks have always played an important role in providing both short- and long-term financing, often backed by the assets of the target firm, institutional investors have become increasingly important as sources of financing for corporate takeovers.

Hedge and Private Equity Funds

Private equity funds and *hedge funds* are usually limited partnerships (for U.S. investors) or offshore investment corporations (for non-U.S. or tax exempt investors) in which the general partner has made a substantial personal investment. This structure permits the general partner to achieve extensive control over the funds it manages subject to relatively few legal restrictions. Other characteristics of partnerships that make them attractive include favorable tax benefits, a finite life, and limitations on risk for individual investors to the amount of their investment. Once a partnership has reached its target size, the partnership closes to further investment from new investors or even existing investors. Reflecting the importance of being nimble, smaller funds tend to perform better on average than larger funds (Boyson, 2008).

Companies in which the private equity or hedge fund has made investments are called *portfolio companies*. Institutional investors such as pension funds, endowments, insurance companies, and private banks, as well as high net worth individuals, commonly invest in these types of funds. According to the Thomson Reuters Lipper/TASS Asset Flow report, about 9,000 hedge funds worldwide had $1.9 trillion under management at the end of 2007. This compares to about 3,000 private equity funds with about $500 billion under management. A survey by Hedge Fund Research indicates that hedge fund assets under management fell to about $1 trillion by the end of 2008 reflecting a combination of losses on invested assets and redemptions. Investors pulled a record $155 billion out of hedge funds in 2008. The number of hedge funds and private equity firms is likely to shrink dramatically by the end of 2009 due to the credit meltdown and global economic slowdown in 2008 and 2009.

Hedge funds can be distinguished from private equity funds in terms of their investment strategies, lock-up periods (i.e., the length of time investors are required to commit funds), and the liquidity of their portfolios. Hedge fund investment strategies include trading a variety of financial instruments, such as debt, equity, options, futures, and foreign currencies, as well as higher-risk strategies, such as corporate restructurings (e.g., LBOs) and credit derivatives (e.g., credit default swaps). Hedge fund investors usually receive more frequent access to their money than those who invest in private equity funds. The need to maintain liquidity to satisfy investor withdrawals causes hedge funds to focus on investments that can be converted to cash relatively easily, such as comparatively small investments in companies. Hedge funds often sell their investments after 6 to 18 months in order to keep sufficient liquidity to satisfy investor withdrawals, with lock-up periods for partners ranging from one to three years.

In contrast, private equity fund managers often make highly illiquid investments in non-publicly listed securities of private companies. Investments often are made during the first two or three years of the fund, which then maintains these investments for five to seven years, during which there are few new investments. Private equity funds partnerships usually last about 10 years, followed by a distribution of cash or shares in companies within the portfolio. Such funds invest in IPOs, LBOs, and corporate restructurings. Private equity funds attempt to control risk by getting more actively involved in managing the firm in which they have invested.

In the past, one could generalize by saying that hedge funds are traders, while private equity funds are more likely to be long-term investors. However, in recent years, this distinction has blurred, as hedge funds have taken more active roles in acquiring entire companies. For example, Highfields Capital Management, a hedge fund, which owned 7 percent of Circuit City, made a bid to buy the entire company in 2005. That same year, hedge fund manager Edward Lampert, after buying a large stake in Kmart, engineered an $11 billion takeover of Sears. The Blackstone Group (a private equity firm) and Lio Capital (a hedge fund) banded together to purchase the European beverage division of Cadbury Schweppes in early 2006. Blackstone also acted like a hedge fund that year with its purchase of a 4.5 percent stake in Deutsche Telekom. According to Dealogic, hedge funds accounted for at least 50 leveraged buyouts in 2006. The blurring of the differences between hedge and private equity funds reflects increased competition among the growing number of funds and the huge infusion of capital between 2005 and mid-2007, making it more difficult for fund managers to generate superior returns.

Unlike mutual funds, hedge funds generally do not have to register with the Securities and Exchange Commission. Consequently, a hedge fund is allowed to use aggressive strategies that are unavailable to mutual funds. Hedge funds are exempt from many of the rules and regulations governing mutual funds. However, hedge funds and their advisors are likely to come under increasing regulatory scrutiny in the coming years, due to their highly aggressive lending and investment practices. In early 2009, U.S. Treasury Secretary, Timothy Geithner, argued for legislation that would require managers of large pools of capital such as hedge funds and private equity firms to register and to supply more information about themselves as part of the process.

Like mutual funds, hedge and private equity funds receive a management fee from participating investors. Such fees usually average about 2 percent of the assets under management. In addition, hedge funds managers also receive "carried interest" of 20 percent of any profits realized from the sale of portfolio companies before any monies are distributed to investors. Furthermore, hedge funds and private equity investors usually receive fees from their portfolio companies for completing transactions, arranging financing, performing due diligence, and monitoring business performance while the company is in the fund's portfolio. Kaplan and Schoar (2005) found little evidence that private equity funds, on average, outperform the overall stock market, once their fees are taken into account. In contrast, hedge funds have tended to outperform the overall market by 1–2 percentage points over long periods of time, even after fees are considered, although the difference varies with the time period selected (The Deal, 2006). Moreover, hedge fund returns appear to be less risky than the overall market, as measured by the standard deviation of their returns. However, these data may be problematic, since hedge fund financial returns are self-reported and not subject to public audit. Furthermore, such returns could be upward biased due to the failure to report poorly performing funds. For a sample of 238 LBO funds from 1992 to 2006, Metrick and Yasuda (2007) found that the average private equity fund collected about $10.35 in management fees for every $100 under management, as compared to $5.41 for every $100 under management that came from carried interest. Consequently, about two thirds of fund income comes from fees. For more detail on private equity and hedge fund investment strategies, see Chapter 13. For an exhaustive discussion of hedge fund investing, see Stefanini (2006).

M&A Arbitrageurs

When a bid is made for a target company, the target company's stock price often trades at a small discount to the actual bid. This reflects the risk that the offer may not be accepted. *Merger arbitrage* refers to an investment strategy that attempts to profit from this spread. *Arbitrageurs* ("arbs") buy the stock and make a profit on the difference between the bid price and the current stock price if the deal is consummated. Hedge fund managers often play the role of arbs.

Arbs may accumulate a substantial percentage of the stock held outside of institutions to be in a position to influence the outcome of the takeover attempt. For example, if other offers for the target firm appear, arbs promote their positions directly to managers and institutional investors with phone calls and through leaks to the financial press. Their intention is to sell their shares to the highest bidder. Acquirers involved in a hostile take-over attempt often encourage hedge funds to buy as much target stock as possible with the objective of gaining control of the target by buying the stock from the hedge funds. In 2006, hedge funds, acting as arbitrageurs, were the deciding factor in the battle over Swedish insurance company Skandia AB. Skandia opposed a takeover bid by Old Mutual PLC, but Old Mutual eventually gained control of Skandia because enough hedge funds purchased Skandia shares and sold their stock to Old Mutual.

Arbs monitor rumors and stock price movements to determine if investors are accumulating a particular stock. Their objective is to identify the target before the potential acquirer is required by law to announce its intentions. Reflecting arb activity and possibly insider trading, empirical studies show that the price of a target company's stock often starts to rise in advance of the announcement of a takeover attempt (Ascioglu, McInish, and Wood, 2002). Also, if one firm in an industry is acquired, it is commonplace for the share prices of other firms in the same industry to also increase, because they are viewed as potential takeover targets.

Arbs also provide market liquidity (i.e., the ease with which a security can be bought or sold without affecting its current market price) during transactions. In a cash-financed merger, the merger arbitrageur seeking to buy the target firm's shares provides liquidity to the target's shareholders that want to sell on the announcement day or shortly thereafter. While arbitrageurs may provide some liquidity in the target firm's stock, they may reduce liquidity for the acquirer's stock in a stock-for-stock merger, because they immediately "short" the acquirer shares (i.e., sell borrowed shares—paying interest to the share owner based on the value of the shares when borrowed—hoping to buy them back at a lower price). The downward pressure on the acquirer's share price at the time the transaction is announced from widespread arb short selling makes it difficult for others to sell without incurring a loss from the premerger announcement price. Merger arbitrage short selling may account for about one half of the downward pressure on acquirer share prices around the announcement of a stock-financed merger (Mitchell, Pulvino, and Stafford, 2004). Merger arbitrage also has the potential to be highly profitable. A number of studies find that such arbitrage generates financial returns ranging from 4.5 percent to more than 100 percent in excess of what would be considered normal in a highly competitive market (Dukes, Frohlich, and Ma, 1992; Jindra and Walkling, 1999; Karolyi and Shannon, 1998; Mitchell and Pulvino, 2001).

Do Mergers and Acquisitions Pay Off for Shareholders?

The answer seems to depend on for whom and over what period of time. On average, total shareholder gains around the announcement date of an acquisition are significantly positive; however, most of the gain accrues to target firm shareholders. Moreover, over the three to five years following the takeover, many acquirer firms either underperform their industry peers or destroy shareholder value. However, it is less clear if the reason for this subpar performance and value destruction is due to the acquisition or other factors. Recent empirical evidence suggests that the success rate among acquisitions may be considerably higher than widely believed when M&As are analyzed in terms of the characteristics of the deal.

Zola and Meier (2008), in an analysis of 88 empirical studies between 1970 and 2006, identify 12 approaches to measuring the impact of takeovers on shareholder value. Of these studies, 41 percent use the event study method to analyze premerger returns and 28 percent utilize long-term accounting measures to analyze postmerger returns. Other assessment methodologies utilize proxies for financial returns, such as postmerger productivity and operating efficiency improvements, revenue enhancement, and customer retention and satisfaction. The most common approach, the analysis of premerger returns, involves the examination of abnormal stock returns to the shareholders of both bidders and targets around the announcement of an offer and includes both successful (i.e., completed transactions) and unsuccessful takeovers. Such analyses are referred to as *event studies*, with the event being the takeover announcement. The second approach, postmerger returns using accounting measures, gauges the impact on shareholder value after the merger has been completed. What follows is a discussion of the results of the two most common types of analyses of pre- and postmerger returns.

Premerger Returns to Shareholders

Positive abnormal returns represent gains for shareholders, which could be explained by such factors as improved efficiency, pricing power, or tax benefits. They are abnormal in the sense that they exceed what an investor would normally expect to earn for accepting a certain level of risk. For example, if an investor can reasonably expect to earn a 10 percent return on a stock but actually earns 25 percent due to a takeover, the abnormal or excess return to the shareholder would be 15 percent. Abnormal returns are calculated by subtracting the actual return on the announcement date from a benchmark indicating investors' required financial returns, which often are approximated by the capital asset pricing model (see Chapter 7) or the return on the S&P 500 stock index. Abnormal returns are forward looking in that share prices usually represent the present value of expected future cash flows. Therefore, the large positive M&A announcement date returns could reflect anticipated future synergies resulting from the combination of the target and acquiring firms.

Abnormal or excess returns to target shareholders are not necessarily the same as the purchase price premium they receive for their shares. While the purchase price premium is calculated with respect to the premerger share price, abnormal or excess returns reflect the difference between the premium shareholders receive for their stock and what is considered a normal return for the risk they are assuming. The abnormal/excess return would be the same as the purchase price premium only if the premerger share price reflected accurately the normal rate of return for the level of risk assumed by investors in the target stock.

Table 1–5 summarizes the key results of 65 studies of friendly and hostile takeovers of nonfinancial firms in the United States, United Kingdom, and continental Europe. These studies include horizontal, vertical, and conglomerate mergers, as well as hostile

Table 1–5   Empirical Evidence on Abnormal Returns to Bidders and Targets around Announcement Dates

Total Gains from Takeovers[1]	Target Shareholders	Bidder Shareholders

1. Takeovers increase, on average, the combined market value of the merged firms, with target shareholders earning large positive returns and bidding firm shareholders on average showing little or no abnormal return.
2. Largest gains are realized at the beginning of a takeover wave
3. Takeovers with the largest losses come during the second half of a takeover wave
	1. For the two-week period around the announcement date, returns range from 14% to 44%.
	2. Average returns vary by time period:
	    1960s: 18–19%
	    1980s: 32–35%
	    1990s: 32–45%
	3. Average returns vary by type of bid:
	    Hostile bids: 32%
	    Friendly bids: 22%
	4. Returns higher for all-cash bids than all-equity offers
	5. Target share prices often react as much as six weeks prior to an announcement, reflecting speculation or insider trading.
		1. For the two-week period around the announcement date, average returns are close to zero when the target is a public firm; some studies show small positive gains and others small losses.
		2. Returns can be 1.5–2.6% when the target is a private firm (or a subsidiary of a public firm) due to improved performance from increased monitoring by the acquiring firm, frequent absence of multiple bidders, and liquidity discount resulting from difficulty in valuing such firms
		3. In U.S., all-equity financed takeovers of public firms frequently exhibit negative abnormal returns and underperform all-cash bids
		4. In Europe, all-equity financed M&As are frequently associated with positive returns (often exceeding all-cash bids), reflecting the greater concentration of ownership and the tendency of holders of large blocks of stock to more closely monitor management.

Source: Adapted from Martynova and Renneboog (2008a).

Note: Results based on 65 studies of successful nonfinancial (friendly and hostile) M&As in the United States, United Kingdom, and continental Europe. Studies include horizontal, vertical, and conglomerate mergers as well as tender offers. The studies also include related and unrelated takeovers; all-stock, all-cash, and mixed forms of payment involving both public and private firms.

[1]Includes the sum of the returns to target and acquirer shareholders.

Table 1–6   Acquirer Returns Differ by Characteristics of the Acquirer, Target, and Deal

Characteristic	Empirical Support
Type of Target	
Acquirer returns often positive when targets are privately owned (or subsidiaries of public companies) and slightly negative when targets are publicly traded (i.e., so-called listing effect) regardless of country	Faccio, McConnell, and Stolin (2006) Draper and Paudyal (2006) Moeller, Schlingemann, and Stulz (2005) Fuller, Netter, and Stegemoller (2002)
Form of Payment	
Acquirer returns on equity financed acquisitions of public firms often *less than* cash financed deals in U.S.	Schleifer and Vishny (2003) Megginson et al. (2003) Heron and Lie (2002) Linn and Switzer (2001)
Acquirer returns on equity financed acquisitions of public or private firms frequently *more than* all-cash financed deals in European Union countries	Martynova and Renneboog (2008a)
Acquirer returns on equity financed acquisitions of private firms often exceed significantly cash deals, particularly when the target is difficult to value	Chang (1998) Officer, Poulsen, and Stegemoller (2009)
Acquirer/Target Size	
Smaller acquirers may realize higher returns than larger acquirers	Moeller, Schlingemann, and Stulz (2004, 2005) Gorton, Kahl, and Rosen (2009)[1]
Relatively small deals may generate higher acquirer returns than larger ones	Hackbarth and Morellec (2008) Frick and Torres (2002)
Acquirer returns may be higher when the size of the acquisition is large relative to buyer and small relative to seller	Gell et al. (2008)

[1]Size is measured not in absolute but relative terms compared to other firms within an industry.

tender offers. The studies also include related and unrelated takeovers: all-stock, all-cash, and mixed forms of payment involving both public and private firms. For more detail about each study, see Martynova and Reneeboog (2008a). Financial returns in these studies usually are computed over a period starting immediately before and ending shortly after the announcement date of the transaction. Moreover, these studies usually assume that share prices fully adjust to reflect anticipated synergies; therefore, they are believed to reflect both the short- and long-term effects of the acquisition. See Table 1–6 for greater detail on how the specific characteristics of the acquirer and the target and the deal affect acquirer returns.

Target Shareholders Realize High Returns in Both Successful and Unsuccessful Bids

While averaging 30 percent between 1962 and 2001, Bhagat, Dong, Hirshleifer, and Noah (2005) document that abnormal returns for tender offers have risen steadily over time. These substantial returns reflect the frequent bidder strategy of offering a substantial premium to preempt other potential bidders and the potential for revising the initial offer because of competing bids. Other contributing factors include the increasing sophistication of takeover defenses and federal and state laws requiring bidders to notify target shareholders of their intentions before completing the transaction (see Chapters 2 and 3 for more details). Moreover, the abnormal gains tend to be higher for shareholders of target firms, whose financial performance is expected to deteriorate over the long term (Ghosh and Lee, 2000). This may suggest that the bidding firms see the highest potential for gain among those target firms whose management is viewed as incompetent. Returns from hostile tender offers typically exceed those from friendly mergers, which are characterized by less contentious negotiated settlements between the boards and management of the bidder and the target firm. Moreover, friendly takeovers often do not receive competing bids.

Unsuccessful takeovers (i.e., those whose bids are not accepted and are eventually withdrawn) also may result in significant returns for target company shareholders around the announcement date, but much of the gain dissipates if another bidder does not appear. Studies show that the immediate gain in target share prices following a merger announcement disappears within one year if the takeover attempt fails (Akhigbe, Borde, and Whyte, 2000; Asquith, 1983; Bradley, Desai, and Kim, 1988; Sullivan, Jensen, and Hudson, 1994). Consequently, target firm shareholders, in an unsuccessful bid, must sell their shares shortly after the announcement of a failed takeover attempt to realize abnormal returns.

Acquirer Returns to Shareholders May Not Be as Disappointing as They Often Appear

In the aggregate, for successful takeovers, acquirer returns are modest to slightly negative for both tender offers and mergers. Bidder returns generally have declined slightly over time, as the premiums paid for targets have increased. Even if the excess returns are zero or slightly negative, these returns are consistent with returns in competitive markets in which financial returns are proportional to risk assumed by the average competitor in the industry. For unsuccessful takeovers, bidder shareholders have experienced negative returns in the 5–8 percent range (Bradley, Desai, and Kim, 1988). Such returns may reflect investors' reassessment of the acquirer's business plan more than it does about the acquisition (Grinblatt and Titman, 2002).

Bidders with low leverage show a tendency to pay high purchase premiums (Hackbarth and Morellec, 2008; Uysal, 2006). This tendency may result in such bidders overpaying for target firms, which increases the difficulty in earning the acquirer's cost of capital on net acquired assets once they are restated to reflect their fair market value.

Focusing on aggregate returns to acquirers can by highly misleading. First, the results can be distorted by a relatively few large transactions. Acquirer abnormal returns around transaction dates were, in the aggregate, positive during the 1990s (around 1.5 percent), particularly during the 1990–1997 period (Moeller et al., 2005). However, losses incurred by a relatively few megatransactions between 1998 and 2001 offset the gains during the earlier period.

Second, event studies treat acquisitions as a single event, however, Barkema and Schijven (2008) find that gains from a specific acquisition often depend on subsequent acquisitions undertaken to implement a firm's business strategy. For example, in an effort to become the nation's largest consumer lender, Bank of America spent more than $100 billion to acquire credit card company MBNA in 2005, mortgage lender Countrywide in 2007, and the investment firm/broker Merrill Lynch in 2008. Because of potential synergies among the acquired firms (e.g., cost savings and cross-selling opportunities), the success or failure of these acquisitions should be evaluated in the context of the entire strategy and not as stand-alone transactions.

Third, Harrison, Oler, and Allen (2005) provide evidence that the initial stock market reaction to the announcement of an acquisition often is biased. Event studies assume that markets are efficient and share prices reflect all the information available about the transaction. In practice, much of the data provided by the seller to the buyer is confidential and therefore unavailable to the public. Furthermore, the investing public often is unaware of the target's specific business plan at the time of the announcement, making a comparison of whether to hold or sell the target's stock difficult. Zola and Meier (2008) also provide evidence that announcement period returns are not good predictors of the ultimate success or failure of an acquisition.

Fourth, whether abnormal returns to acquirers are positive or negative varies with the characteristics of the acquirer, target, and the deal. The situations in which these characteristics result in positive abnormal returns are discussed in detail later in this chapter.

Postmerger Returns to Shareholders

The second approach to assessing the performance of M&As has been to examine accounting measures, such as cash flow and operating profit, during the three- to five-year period following completed transactions. The objective is to determine how performance changed following closing. Unfortunately, these studies provide conflicting evidence about the long-term impact of M&A activity. Some studies find that M&As create shareholder value; however, others have found that as many as 50–80 percent underperformed their industry peers or failed to earn their cost of capital. If this were true, it would imply that CEOs and boards do not learn from the past (perhaps due to hubris), since the number and size of transactions continues to increase over time. However, the author believes that failure to account for issues unrelated to the transaction often leads to an understatement of potential returns to acquirers and that CEOs and boards in the aggregate do learn from past performance.

In a review of 26 studies of postmerger performance during the three to five years after the merger, Martynova and Renneboog (2008a) found that 14 of the 26 studies showed a decline in operating returns, 7 provided positive (but statistically insignificant) changes in profitability, and 5 showed a positive and statistically significant increase in profitability. The diversity of conclusions about postmerger returns may be the result of sample and time period selections, methodology employed in the studies, or factors unrelated to the merger, such as a slowing economy (Barber and Lyon, 1997; Fama, 1998; Lyon, Barber, and Tsai, 1999). Presumably, the longer the postmerger time period analyzed, the greater is the likelihood that other factors, wholly unrelated to the merger, will affect financial returns. Moreover, these longer-term studies are not able to compare how well the acquirer would have done without the acquisition.

Acquirer Returns Vary with the Characteristics of the Acquirer, the Target, and the Deal

Research in recent years has shown that abnormal returns to acquirer shareholders may vary according to type of acquirer (i.e., publicly traded or private), form of payment (i.e., cash or stock), and size of acquirer and target. See Table 1–6 for a summary of these findings. What follows is a discussion of findings indicating how these factors can affect acquirer returns.

Impact of Type of Target on Acquirer Returns

U.S. acquirers of private firms or subsidiaries of publicly traded firms often realize positive excess returns of 1.5–2.6 percent (Moeller et al., 2005; Fuller et al., 2002; Ang and Kohers, 2001; Chang, 1998). Draper and Paudyal (2006) found similar results in an exhaustive study of U.K. acquirers making bids for private firms or subsidiaries of public firms. In a 17-nation study between 1996 and 2001, Faccio et al. (2006) show that acquirers of privately owned or unlisted companies earn abnormal returns of 1.48 percent, while acquirers of listed firms earn a statistically insignificant negative 0.38 percent. Moreover, this study finds that the so-called listing effect persists over time and across countries.

Why acquirer returns tend to be positive when targets are private or subsidiaries of public firms and zero or slightly negative when targets are publicly traded is not well documented. However, there are four plausible explanations. First, private businesses often are difficult to value due to a lack of publicly available information, potentially questionable operating and accounting practices, substantial intangible assets, and unknown off-balance-sheet liabilities. As such, buyers frequently offer a lower price to compensate for this perceived risk. Subsidiaries of larger firms often represent an even greater valuation challenge. A portion of their revenue may be under- or overstated, in that products are sold to other units controlled by the parent at prices that do not reflect actual market prices. Similarly, the cost of sales may be misstated due to purchases of products or services (e.g., accounting or legal) from other parent-controlled units at non-market prices. Second, sellers of private firms frequently are inclined to accept lower prices to "cash out" to realize their immediate goals of retiring or pursing other interests (Poulsen and Stegemoller, 2007; Officer, 2007; Faccio and Masulis, 2005). Third, sellers may also be willing to accept a lower price because of their own naivety, the lack of good financial advice, and a preference for a particular buyer willing to manage the business in accordance with the seller's wishes over the highest bidder (Capron and Shen, 2007). Fourth, public firms are more likely to receive multiple bids than private firms due to the 1968 Williams Act, which mandates public disclosure and waiting periods in acquisitions of private firms. The resulting auction environment for publicly traded firms often raises the purchase price and the potential for overpaying for the target firm.

As a result of these factors, private firms or subsidiaries of public firms are more likely to be acquired at a discount from their actual economic value (i.e., cash generation potential) than public firms. As a consequence of this discount, bidder shareholders are able to realize a larger share of the anticipated synergies resulting from combining the acquirer and target firms, which is reflected in the significant positive abnormal announcement date returns.

Impact of Form of Payment on Acquirer Returns

Situations in which one party has access to information not available to others are referred to as *information asymmetries*. An example of such a situation would be one in which managers tend to issue stock when they believe it is overvalued (Myers and Majluf, 1984). However, over time, investors learn to treat such decisions as signals that the stock is overvalued and sell their shares when the new equity issue is announced, causing the firm's share price to decline.

Applying the same concept of information asymmetries to mergers and acquisitions, numerous studies have found that bidding firms using cash to purchase the target firm exhibit better long-term performance than do those using stock. These studies argue that stock-financed mergers underperform because investors treat stock financing as a signal that shares are overvalued (Schleifer and Vishny, 2003; Megginson et al., 2003; Heron and Lie, 2002; Linn and Switzer, 2001; Walker, 2000). The use of stock to acquire a firm often results in announcement period gains to bidder shareholders dissipating within three to five years, even if the acquisition is successful (Deogun and Lipin, 2000; Black, Carnes, and Jandik, 2000; Agrawal and Jaffe, 1999; Rau and Vermaelen, 1998;

Loughran and Vijh, 1997; and Sirower, 1997). These findings imply that shareholders selling around the announcement dates may realize the largest gains from either tender offers or mergers. Those who hold onto the acquirer's stock received as payment for their shares may see their gains diminish over time.

Jensen (2005) argues that equity overvaluation occurs when a firm's management believes it cannot make investments that will sustain the current share price except by chance. Therefore, management pursues larger, more risky investments, such as unrelated acquisitions, in a vain attempt to support the overvalued share price. These actions destroy shareholder value as the firm is unable to earn its cost of capital. Consequently, the longer-term performance of the combined firms suffers as the stock price declines to its industry average performance.

Consistent with previous findings, Moeller, Schlingemann, and Stulz (2007) find that abnormal returns to acquirers are negatively related to equity offers but not to cash bids. However, they conclude that there is no difference in abnormal returns for cash offers for public firms, equity offers for public firms, and equity offers for private firms when such firms exhibit similar business specific risk (e.g., institutional ownership, growth rates, leverage, or product offerings).

Savor and Lu (2009) find that successful acquirers using stock as the form of payment outperform unsuccessful attempts by a wide margin. Over the first year, abnormal returns for acquirers using stock is a negative 7 percent, reaching a negative cumulative 13 percent at the end of three years. However, acquirers using stock who fail in their takeover attempts do even worse, experiencing negative returns of 21 percent and 32 percent after one year and three years, respectively, following their aborted takeover attempts. The authors attribute the relatively better performance of successful stock-financed acquirers to their ability to use their overvalued stock to buy the target firm's assets relatively inexpensively.

In contrast to findings of studies of U.S. firms that bidder returns on cash deals exceed those of equity-financed deals, Martynova and Renneboog (2008a) conclude that studies of European firms indicate that postmerger returns to bidders using stock often are higher than those using cash. These results reflect the greater concentration of ownership in European firms than in the United States and the tendency of large shareholders to monitor more closely management actions.

Acquirers using stock to buy privately owned firms often display positive abnormal returns (Chang, 1998). Chang attributes this positive abnormal return to the creation of large stockholders, who more closely monitor performance than might be the case when ownership is diffuse, as is often true for listed firms. Officer et al. (2009) argue that the use of acquirer stock affects bidder returns when the target is difficult to value (e.g., target characterized by large intangible assets). The authors contend that the use of acquirer stock helps acquirers share the risk of overpayment with target shareholders. However, this is likely to be true only if target shareholders retain their acquirer stock following closing. Consequently, the use of acquirer stock is likely to be most effective when some portion of the purchase price is deferred until after closing (e.g., through an escrow account). By accepting stock, target shareholders willing to retain their equity interest in the combined firms are more likely to be forthcoming during due diligence about the true value of the target's operations.

Impact of Acquirer and Target Size on Acquirer Returns

Moeller et al. (2004) conclude that the absolute size of the acquirer and financial returns realized in M&As are inversely related. Relatively smaller acquirers often realize larger abnormal returns than larger acquirers. The authors attribute these findings to management overconfidence and the empire-building tendencies of large firms. Another explanation is that smaller firms tend to be more focused and may be more likely to make acquisitions related to products or markets they more readily understand. For the 20-year period ending in 2001, Moeller et al. (2005) found that large firms destroyed shareholder wealth while small firms created wealth. Small firms are defined as the smallest 25 percent of firms listed on the New York Stock Exchange each year during that 20-year period. Regardless of how they were financed (i.e., stock or cash) or whether they were public or private targets, acquisitions made by smaller firms had announcement returns 1.55 percent higher than a comparable acquisition made by a larger firm. Gorton et al. (2009) also demonstrate that smaller acquirers realize larger abnormal returns than larger buyers. In this study, size is defined relative to other firms within an industry. According to their theory, larger acquirers tend to overpay for "defensive" acquisitions in an effort to grow the size of their firms to avoid being taken over. Smaller firms are believed to make profitable "positioning" acquisitions to make their firms attractive acquisition targets.

Average target size appears to play an important role in determining financial returns to acquirer shareholders. For the 10-year period ending in 2000, high-tech companies averaging 39 percent annual total return to shareholders acquired targets with an average size of less than $400 million, about 1 percent of the market value of the acquiring firms (Frick and Torres, 2002). High-tech firms often acquire small but related target firms to fill gaps in their product offerings as part of their overall business strategy. Hackbarth and Morellec (2008) found that larger deals tend to be more risky for acquirers. Larger deals as a percentage of the acquiring firms' equity experience consistently lower postmerger performance, possibly reflecting the challenges of integrating large target firms and realizing projected synergies on a timely basis.

Under certain circumstances, larger deals may offer significant positive abnormal rates of returns. Gell et al. (2008) found that acquirer's returns from buying product lines and subsidiaries of other companies tend to be higher when the size of the asset is large relative to the buyer and small relative to the seller. Specifically, in deals where the divested unit represents more than 50 percent of the value of the buyer but less than 10 percent of the value of the seller, acquirer returns are three times those of deals in which the divested unit represents about the same share of value to the buyer and seller. This implies that parent firms interested in funding new opportunities are more likely to divest relatively small businesses not germane to their core business strategy at relatively low prices to raise capital quickly. Buyers are able to acquire sizeable businesses at favorable prices, increasing the potential to earn their cost of capital.

Acquirer Experience May Not Improve Long-Term Performance of Combined Companies

Abnormal returns to serial acquirers (i.e., firms making frequent acquisitions) have tended to decline from one transaction to the next (Fuller et al., 2002; Billett and Qian, 2006; Conn et al., 2005; Croci, 2005; Ismail, 2005). The explanation for this trend given in most studies is that the CEO of the serial acquirer becomes overconfident with each successive acquisition and tends to overestimate the value of synergies and the ease with which they can be realized. Consequently, overconfident or excessively optimistic CEOs tend to overpay for their acquisitions. These findings differ from those of Harding and Rovit (2004) and Hayward (2002), who show that acquirers learn from their mistakes, suggesting that serial acquirers are more likely to earn returns in excess of their cost of capital. Finally, experience is a necessary but not sufficient condition for successful acquisitions. Barkema and Schijven (2008), in an extensive survey of the literature on how firms learn from past acquisitions, conclude that experience contributes to improved financial returns if it is applied to targets in the same or similar industries or in the same or similar geographic regions.

Do Mergers and Acquisitions Pay Off for Bondholders?

Mergers and acquisitions have relatively little impact on abnormal returns to either acquirer or target bondholders, except in special situations (Renneboog and Szilagyi, 2007). The limited impact of M&As on bondholder wealth is in part due to the relationship between leverage and management discipline. Increasing leverage imposes discipline on management to improve operating performance, while decreasing leverage has the opposite effect. Moreover, decreasing leverage encourages controlling shareholders to increase future borrowing to enhance financial returns to equity. Therefore, even if the transaction results in a less leveraged business, the impact on abnormal returns to bondholders may be negligible. This results from the tendency of controlling shareholders to borrow at low levels of indebtedness to enhance financial returns being partially offset by reduced pressure on management to improve operating performance.

The empirical evidence is ambiguous. Billet, King, and Mauer (2004), for a sample of 831 U.S. transactions between 1979 and 1998, find slightly negative abnormal returns to acquirer bondholders regardless of the acquirer's bond rating. However, they find that target firm holders of below investment grade bonds (i.e., BBB–) earn average excess returns of 4.3 percent or higher around the merger announcement date, when the target firm's credit rating is less than the acquirer's and when the merger is expected to decrease the target's risk or leverage. In a sample of 253 U.S. transactions from 1963 to 1996, Maquierira, Megginson, and Nail (1998) find positive excess returns to acquirer bondholders of 1.9 percent and .5 percent for target bondholders but only for nonconglomerate transactions. Renneboog and Szilagyi (2006), using a sample of 225 European transactions between 1995 and 2004, find small positive returns to acquirer bondholders of 0.56 percent around the announcement date of the transaction.

Do Mergers and Acquisitions Pay Off for Society?

Although postmerger performance study results are ambiguous, event studies show generally consistent results. Such studies suggest that M&A activity tends to improve aggregate shareholder value (i.e., the sum of the shareholder value of both the target and acquiring firms). If financial markets are efficient, the large increase in the combined shareholder values of the two firms reflect future efficiencies resulting from the merger. However, the target firm's shareholders often capture most of this increase. Also, there is no evidence that M&As result in increasing industry concentration. Mergers and acquisitions have continued to increase in number and average size during the last 30 years. Despite this trend, M&As have not increased industry concentration in terms of the share of output or value produced by the largest firms in the industry since 1970 (Carlton and Perloff, 1999). Finally, recent research suggests that gains in aggregate shareholder value are due more to the improved operating efficiency of the combined firms than to increased pricing power (Shahrur, 2005; Fee and Thomas, 2004; Ghosh, 2004; Song and Walking, 2000; Akhigbe et al., 2000; Benerjee and Eckard, 1998). In an exhaustive study of 10,079 transactions between 1974 and 1992, Maksimovic and Phillips (2001) conclude that corporate transactions result in an overall improvement in efficiency by transferring assets from those who are not using them effectively to those who can.

Commonly Cited Reasons Why Some Mergers and Acquisitions Fail to Meet Expectations

In a survey of acquiring firm managers, Brouthers (2000) found that whether M&As are viewed as having failed depends on whether *failure* is defined in terms of easily measurable outcomes. If *failure* is defined as the eventual sale or liquidation of the business, the failure rate tends to be low. If *failure* is defined as the inability to meet or exceed financial objectives, the rate of failure is higher. If *failure* is defined as not achieving largely strategic objectives, managers often are very satisfied with their acquisitions.

The notion that most M&As fail in some substantive manner is not supported by the data. As noted previously, event studies identified a number of situations in which acquirers earn positive abnormal returns. These situations include acquisition of private firms and subsidiaries of public firms (often accounting for more than one half the total number of annual transactions), relatively small acquirers, when targets are small relative to acquirers, acquisitions of target firms early in a consolidation cycle, and when acquirers use cash rather than stock as a form of payment. Moreover, such firms often continue to outperform their peers in the years immediately following closing. Even though the average abnormal return for all bidders tends to be about zero, the average firm still earns at or close to its cost of capital.

Of those M&As that fail to meet expectations, it is unlikely that there is a single factor that caused their underperformance. Table 1–7 identifies three commonly cited reasons, ranked by the number of studies in which they are mentioned. These include overestimation of synergy or overpaying, the slow pace of postmerger integration, and a flawed strategy. Conversely, acquiring firms that tend not to overpay, focus on rapid integration of the target firm, and have a well-thought-out strategy tend to meet or exceed expectations.

Overpayment increases the hurdles an acquirer must overcome to earn its cost of capital, since there is little margin for error in achieving anticipated synergies on a timely basis. In an exhaustive study of 22 papers examining long-run postmerger returns, Agrawal, Jaffe, and Mandelker (1999) reviewed a number of arguments purporting to explain postmerger performance. They found the argument that acquirers tend to overpay for so-called high-growth glamour companies based on their past performance to be most convincing. Consequently, the postmerger share price for such firms should underperform broader industry averages as future growth slows to more normal levels. As noted in Chapter 6, integration frequently turns out to be more challenging than anticipated. Consequently, paying less than "fair market value" may enable acquirers to still earn their cost of capital despite not realizing planned synergies. However, no matter what is paid for the target firm, success is elusive if the strategy justifying the acquisition is flawed.

Long-Term Performance Similar for Mergers and Acquisitions, Business Alliances, and Solo Ventures

Even if a substantial percentage of M&As underperformed their peers or failed to earn appropriate financial returns, it is important to note that there is little compelling evidence that growth strategies undertaken as an alternative to M&As fare any better. Such alternatives include solo ventures, in which firms reinvest excess cash flows, and business alliances, including joint ventures, licensing, franchising, and minority investments. Failure rates among alternative strategies tend to be remarkably similar to those documented for M&As. The estimated failure rate for new product introductions is well

Table 1–7   Commonly Cited Reasons for M&A Failure

Overestimating synergy/overpaying[1]	Cao (2008)
	Harper and Schneider (2004)
	Christofferson, McNish, and Sias (2004)
	Boston Consulting Group (2003)
	Henry (2002)
	Bekier, Bogardus, and Oldham (2001)
	Chapman et al. (1998)
	Agrawal, Jaffe, and Mandelker (1999)
	Rau and Vermaelen (1998)
	Sirower (1997)
	Mercer Management Consulting (1998)
	Hillyer and Smolowitz (1996)
	McKinsey & Company (1990)
	Bradley, Desai, and Kim (1988)
Slow pace of integration	Adolph (2006)
	Carey and Ogden (2004)
	Coopers & Lybrand (1996)
	Anslinger and Copeland (1996)
	Mitchell (1998)
	Business Week (1995)
	McKinsey & Company (1990)
Poor strategy	Mercer Management Consulting (1998)
	Bogler (1996)
	McKinsey & Company (1990)
	Salter and Weinhold (1979)

Note: Factors are ranked by the number of times they have been mentioned in studies.

[1]Some studies conclude that postmerger underperformance is a result of overpayment. However, it is difficult to determine if overpayment is a cause of merger failure or a result of other factors, such as overestimating synergy, the slow pace of integration, a poor strategy, or simply the bidder overextrapolating past performance.

over 70 percent (ACNielsen, 2002), while failure rates for alliances of all types exceeds 60 percent (Ellis, 1996; Klein, 2004). See Chapters 4 and 14 for a more detailed discussion of these issues.

Things to Remember

Businesses are in a state of constant churn, with only the most innovative and nimble surviving. Those falling to the competition often have been eliminated either through merger, acquisition, bankruptcy, downsizing, or some other form of corporate restructuring. In this way, M&As represent an important change agent.

There are many theories of why M&As take place. Operating and financial synergies are commonly used rationales for takeovers. Diversification is a strategy of buying firms outside of the company's primary line of business; however, recent studies suggest that corporate strategies emphasizing focus deliver more benefit to shareholders. Strategic realignment suggests that firms use takeovers as a means of rapidly adjusting to changes in their external environment, such as deregulation and technological innovation. Hubris is an explanation for takeovers that attributes a tendency to overpay to excessive optimism about the value of a deal's potential synergy or excessive confidence in management's ability to manage the acquisition. The undervaluation of assets theory (q ratio) states that takeovers occur when the target's market value is less than its replacement value. The mismanagement (agency) theory states that mergers occur when there are different manager and shareholder expectations. Low share prices of such firms pressure managers to take action to either raise the share price or become the target of an acquirer.

Tax considerations are generally not the driving factor behind acquisitions, except when sellers demand a tax-free transaction. While lacking in empirical support, the market power hypothesis suggests that firms merge to gain greater control over pricing. According to the managerialism theory, managers acquire companies to increase the acquirer's size and their own remuneration. Finally, the misevaluation theory suggests that firms are periodically improperly valued, making it possible for an acquirer to buy another firm at a discount from its true economic value.

Although M&As clearly pay off for target company shareholders around announcement dates, shareholder wealth creation in the three to five years following closing is problematic. However, the results of postmerger performance studies are subject to substantial uncertainty, in that the longer the postacquisition time period, the greater is the likelihood that other factors will affect performance. Studies show that abnormal returns to bidder firms are influenced by the type of acquirer, form of payment, and the size of the acquirer and target. Acquirers of private (unlisted) firms or subsidiaries of public firms frequently show larger returns than M&As involving publicly listed firms. U.S. acquirers using cash rather than equity often show larger returns compared to those using equity, although these results are reversed for European acquirers. Also, abnormal returns tend to be larger when acquirers are relatively small and the target is relatively large compared to the acquirer but represents a small portion of the selling firm. Finally, acquirer returns tend to be larger when the transaction occurs early in a merger wave.

The most consistent finding among studies explaining merger waves is that they are triggered by industry shocks, assuming there is sufficient credit market liquidity to finance the upsurge in transactions. The most common reasons for a merger to fail to satisfy expectations are the overestimation of synergies and subsequent overpayment, the slow pace of postmerger integration, and the lack of a coherent business strategy. Empirical studies also suggest that M&As tend to pay off for society due to the improved operating efficiency of the combined firms. The success rate for M&As is very similar to alternative growth strategies that may be undertaken. Such strategies may include reinvesting excess cash flow in the firm (i.e., solo ventures) or business alliances.

Chapter Discussion Questions

1–1. Discuss why mergers and acquisitions occur.

1–2. What are the advantages and disadvantages of holding companies in making M&As?

1–3. How might a leveraged ESOP be used as an alternative to a divestiture, to take a company private, or as a defense against an unwanted takeover?

1–4. What is the role of the investment banker in the M&A process?

1–5. Describe how arbitrage typically takes place in a takeover of a publicly traded company.

1–6. Why is potential synergy often overestimated by acquirers in evaluating a target company?

1–7. What are the major differences between the merger waves of the 1980s and 1990s?

1–8. In your judgment, what are the motivations for two M&As currently in the news?

1–9. What are the arguments for and against corporate diversification through acquisition? Which do you support and why?

1–10. What are the primary differences between operating and financial synergy? Give examples to illustrate your statements.

1–11. At a time when natural gas and oil prices were at record levels, oil and natural gas producer, Andarko Petroleum, announced on June 23, 2006, the acquisition of two competitors, Kerr-McGee Corp. and Western Gas Resources, for $16.4 billion and $4.7 billion in cash, respectively. These purchase prices represent a substantial 40 percent premium for Kerr-McGee and a 49 percent premium for Western Gas. The acquired assets strongly complement Andarko's existing operations, providing the scale and focus necessary to cut overlapping expenses and concentrate resources in adjacent properties. What do you believe were the primary forces driving Andarko's acquisition? How will greater scale and focus help Andarko cut costs? Be specific. What are the key assumptions implicit in your answer to the first question?

1–12. On September 30, 2000, Mattel, a major toy manufacturer, virtually gave away The Learning Company, a maker of software for toys, to rid itself of a disastrous acquisition of a software publishing firm that actually had cost the firm hundreds of millions of dollars. Mattel, which had paid $3.5 billion for the firm in 1999, sold the unit to an affiliate of Gores Technology Group for rights to a share of future profits. Was this related or unrelated diversification for Mattel? Explain your answer. How might your answer to the first question have influenced the outcome?

1–13. In 2000, AOL acquired Time Warner in a deal valued at $160 billion. Time Warner is the world's largest media and entertainment company, whose major business segments include cable networks, magazine publishing, book publishing, direct marketing, recorded music and music publishing, and film and TV production and broadcasting. AOL viewed itself as the world leader in providing interactive services, Web brands, Internet technologies, and electronic commerce services. Would you classify this business combination as a vertical, horizontal, or conglomerate transaction? Explain your answer.

1–14. On July 15, 2002, Pfizer, a leading pharmaceutical company, acquired drug maker Pharmacia for $60 billion. The purchase price represented a 34 percent premium to Pharmacia's preannouncement price. Pfizer is betting that size is what matters in the new millennium. As the market leader, Pfizer was finding it increasingly difficult to sustain the double-digit earnings growth demanded by investors. Such growth meant the firm needed to grow revenue by $3–5 billion annually while maintaining or improving profit margins. This became more difficult, due to the skyrocketing costs of developing and commercializing new drugs. Expiring patents on a number of so-called blockbuster drugs intensified pressure to bring new drugs to market. In your judgment, what were the primary motivations for Pfizer wanting to acquire Pharmacia? Categorize these in terms of the primary motivations for mergers and acquisitions discussed in this chapter.

1–15. Dow Chemical, a leading chemical manufacturer, announced that it had reached an agreement to acquire, in late 2008, Rohm and Haas Company for $15.3 billion. While Dow has competed profitably in the plastics business for years, this business has proven to have thin margins and to be highly cyclical. By acquiring Rohm and Haas, Dow would be able to offer less-cyclical and higher-margin products such as paints, coatings, and electronic materials. Would you consider this related or unrelated diversification? Explain your answer. Would you consider this a cost effective way for the Dow shareholders to achieve better diversification of their investment portfolios?

Answers to these Chapter Discussion Questions are available in the Online Instructor's Manual for instructors using this book.

Chapter Business Cases

Case Study 1–1. Procter & Gamble Acquires Competitor

Procter & Gamble Company (P&G) announced, on January 28, 2005, an agreement to buy Gillette Company (Gillette) in a share-for-share exchange valued at $55.6 billion. This represented an 18 percent premium over Gillette's preannouncement share price. P&G also announced a stock buyback of $18 to $22 billion, funded largely by issuing new debt. The combined companies would retain the P&G name and have annual 2005 revenue of more than $60 billion. Half of the new firm's product portfolio would consist of personal care, health-care, and beauty products, with the remainder consisting of razors and blades and batteries. The deal would be expected to dilute P&G's 2006 earnings by about 15 cents per share. To gain regulatory approval, the two firms would have to divest overlapping operations, such as deodorants and oral care.

P&G is often viewed as a premier marketing and product innovator. Consequently, some of P&G's R&D and marketing skills in developing and promoting women's personal care products could be used to enhance and promote Gillette's women's razors. Gillette is best known for its ability to sell an inexpensive product (e.g., razors) and hook customers to a lifetime of refills (e.g., razor blades). Although Gillette is the number 1 and number 2 supplier in the lucrative toothbrush and men's deodorant markets, respectively, it has been much less successful in improving the profitability of its Duracell battery brand. Despite its number 1 market share position, it has been beset by intense price competition from Energizer and Rayovac Corp., which generally sell for less than Duracell batteries.

Suppliers such as P&G and Gillette have been under considerable pressure from the continuing consolidation in the retail industry due to the ongoing growth of Walmart and industry mergers, such as Sears and Kmart. About 17 percent of P&G's $51 billion in 2005 revenues and 13 percent of Gillette's $9 billion annual revenue came from sales to Walmart. Moreover, the sales of both Gillette and P&G to Walmart have grown much faster than sales to other retailers. The new company would have more negotiating leverage with retailers for shelf space and in determining selling prices, as well as with its own suppliers, such as advertisers and media companies. The broad geographic presence of P&G would facilitate the marketing of such products as razors and batteries in huge developing markets, such as China and India. Cumulative cost cutting was expected to reach $16 billion, including layoffs of about 4 percent of the new company's workforce of 140,000. Such cost reductions would be likely to be realized by integrating Gillette's deodorant products into P&G's structure as quickly as possible. Other Gillette product lines, such as the razor and battery businesses, would be expected to remain intact.

P&G's corporate culture is often described as conservative, with a "promote-from-within" philosophy. While Gillette's CEO would become vice chairman of the new company, it is unclear what would happen to other Gillette senior managers in view of the perception that P&G is laden with highly talented top management. Obtaining regulatory approval requires divesting certain Gillette businesses that, in combination with P&G's current businesses, could have given the new firm dominant market positions in certain markets.

Discussion Questions

1. Is this deal a merger or a consolidation from a legal standpoint? Explain your answer.
2. Is this a horizontal or vertical merger? What is the significance of this distinction from a regulatory perspective? Explain your answer.
3. What are the motives for the deal? Discuss the logic underlying each motive you identify.
4. Immediately following the announcement, P&G's share price dropped by 2 percent and Gillette's share price rose by 13 percent. Explain why this may have happened.
5. P&G announced that it would be buying back $18–22 billion of its stock over the 18 months following the closing of the transaction. Much of the cash required to repurchase these shares requires significant new borrowing by the new companies. Explain what P&G is trying to achieve in buying back its own stock. Explain how the incremental borrowing may help or hurt P&G in the long run.
6. Explain how actions required by antitrust regulators may hurt P&G's ability to realize anticipated synergy. Be specific.
7. Identify some of the obstacles that P&G and Gillette are likely to face in integrating the two businesses. Be specific. How would you overcome these obstacles?

Answers to these questions are found in the Online Instructor's Manual available to instructors using this book.

Case Study 1–2. The Free Market Process of Creative Destruction: Consolidation in the Telecommunications Industry

Background: The Role of Technological Change and Deregulation

Economic historian Joseph Schumpeter described the free-market process by which new technologies and deregulation create new industries, often at the expense of existing ones, as "creative destruction." In the short run, the process of "creative destruction" can have a highly disruptive impact on current employees, whose skills are made obsolete; investors and business owners, whose businesses are no longer competitive; and communities, which are ravaged by increasing unemployment and diminished tax revenues. However, in the long run, the process tends to raise living standards by boosting worker productivity and increasing real income and leisure time, stimulating innovation, and expanding the range of products and services offered, often at a lower price, to consumers. Much of the change spurred by the process of "creative destruction" takes the form of mergers and acquisitions.

Consolidation in the Telecommunications Industry

The blur of consolidation in the U.S. telecommunications industry in recent years is a dramatic illustration of how free market forces can radically restructure the competitive landscape, spurring improved efficiency and innovation. Verizon's and SBC's acquisition of MCI and AT&T, respectively, in 2005, and SBC's merger with BellSouth, in 2006, pushed these two firms to the top of the U.S. telecommunications industry. In 2006, SBC was renamed AT&T to take advantage of the globally recognized brand name. In all, Verizon and SBC spent about $170 billion in acquisitions during this two-year period.

By buying BellSouth, AT&T won full control of the two firms' wireless joint venture, Cingular (later renamed AT&T Wireless), which is the biggest mobile operator in the

United States. Following this acquisition, one third of the firm's combined revenues came from cellular service, up from 28 percent prior to the acquisition. Unlike Europe, where markets are saturated, there still is room for growth, with only 70 percent of the U.S. population having cell phones. This exposure to cell phones helps offset the decline in the number of fixed lines, as some subscribers go to wireless only or utilize Internet telephony.

Both Verizon and SBC bought their long-distance rivals to obtain access to corporate customers to whom they can sell packages of services. SBC and Verizon had the ability to buy AT&T and MCI's networks and business customers at a price that was less than the cost of obtaining these customers and replicating their networks. The combination of these companies created opportunities for cost savings by eliminating overlapping functions. A 2004 ruling by the FCC to roll back the requirement that local phone companies offer their networks at regulated rates to long-distance carriers made it prohibitively expensive for MCI and AT&T to offer price-competitive local phone service. This factor increased the inevitability of their eventual sale.

The Emergence of Nontraditional Telecom Competitors

Many cable companies have been racing to add phone service to the TV and Internet packages they already offer. Phone companies are responding with offers of combined cell phone, Internet, and landline phone service. The pace at which TV services are being offered will accelerate once the new fiber-optic networks are completed. Besides cable and telephone companies, consumers also have the option of such new technologies as Vonage, which has signed up more than 600,000 customers for its Internet calling services. Local phone companies are also expected to face increasing competition from wireless calling. In December 2004, Sprint and Nextel Communications merged to form a wireless giant in a $35 billion transaction intending to compete directly with traditional phone lines.

Changes in technology mean that there will likely be many more companies competing against the phone companies than just cable companies. The integration of voice and data on digital networks and the arrival of Internet calling have attracted many new competitors for phone companies. These include Microsoft, Sony, Time Warner's AOL subsidiary, and Google.

Implications of Telecom Industry Consolidation for Businesses and Consumers

Some analysts say that fewer providers will leave business customers with less leverage in their negotiations with the telecommunications companies. Others believe that pricing for consumers is going to continue to be very competitive. In the business market, cable is not an effective alternative to phone service, since the nation's cable infrastructure was built to offer television service to homes. Consequently, existing cable networks do not reach all commercial areas. Cable companies are often unwilling to invest the capital required, because it is unclear if they will be able to acquire the customer density to achieve the financial returns they require. In the consumer market, telecom companies are rushing to sell consumers bundles of services, including local and long-distance service, cellular service, and Internet access for one monthly fee. These competitive forces are likely to prevent higher prices for local phone service, which is already eroding at a rapid rate due to emerging technologies, like Internet calling.

Concluding Comments

The free market forces of "creative destruction" resulted in a dramatic transformation of the competitive landscape in the U.S. telecommunications industry. Historically, the U.S. telecom industry was clearly defined, with the former monopolist AT&T providing the bulk of local and long-distance services in the United States. However, "Ma Bell" was required by the government to spin off its local telephone operating companies in the mid-1980s in an attempt to stimulate competition for both local and long-distance services. The telecommunications industry changed from a single provider of both local and long-distance services to many aggressive competitors.

In the wake of far reaching deregulation in the 1990s, various competitors began to combine, increasing industry concentration. However, incursions by the cable industry into the traditional market for telephone services and the proliferation of new technologies, such as WiFi and Internet telephony, changed the competitive landscape once again. Today, software, entertainment, media, and consumer electronics firms now compete with the more traditional phone companies. When adjusted for inflation, prices paid by consumers and businesses are a fraction of what they were a generation ago. While the effects of these changes may influence the business and consumer telecom markets differently, the unmistakable imprint of the free market's "creative destruction" process is highly visible.

Discussion Questions

1. How have technological and regulatory change affected competition in the telecommunications industry?
2. How have technological and regulatory change affected the rate of innovation and customer choice in the telecom industry?
3. The process of "creative destruction" stimulated substantial consolidation in the U.S. telecom industry. Is bigger always better? Why or why not? (Hint: Consider the impact on a firm's operating efficiency, speed of decision making, creativity, ability to affect product and service pricing, etc.)
4. To determine the extent to which industry consolidation is likely to lead to higher, lower, or unchanged product selling prices, it is necessary to consider current competitors, potential competitors, the availability of substitutes, and customer pricing sensitivity. Explain why.
5. What factors motivated Verizon and SBC to acquire MCI and AT&T, respectively? Discuss these in terms of the motives for mergers and acquisitions described in Chapter 1 of the textbook.

Answers to these questions are found in the Online Instructor's Manual available to instructors using this book.

2
Regulatory Considerations

Character is doing the right thing when no one is looking.

—J. C. Watts

Inside M&A: Justice Department Approves Maytag/Whirlpool Combination Despite Resulting Increase in Concentration

When announced in late 2005, many analysts believed that the $1.7 billion transaction would face heated regulatory opposition. The proposed bid was approved despite the combined firms' dominant market share of the U.S. major appliance market. The combined companies would control an estimated 72 percent of the washer market, 81 percent of the gas dryer market, 74 percent of electric dryers, and 31 percent of refrigerators. Analysts believed that the combined firms would be required to divest certain Maytag product lines to receive approval. Recognizing the potential difficulty in getting regulatory approval, the Whirlpool/Maytag contract allowed Whirlpool (the acquirer) to withdraw from the contract by paying a "reverse breakup" fee of $120 million to Maytag (the target). Breakup fees are normally paid by targets to acquirers if they choose to withdraw from the contract.

U.S. regulators tended to view the market as global in nature. When the appliance market is defined in a global sense, the combined firms' share drops to about one fourth of the previously mentioned levels. The number and diversity of foreign manufacturers offered a wide array of alternatives for consumers. Moreover, there are few barriers to entry for these manufacturers wishing to do business in the United States. Many of Whirlpool's independent retail outlets wrote letters supporting the proposal to acquire Maytag as a means of sustaining financially weakened companies. Regulators also viewed the preservation of jobs as an important consideration in its favorable ruling.

Chapter Overview

Regulations that affect merger and acquisition (M&A) activity exist at all levels of government. Regulatory considerations can be classified as either general or industry specific. General considerations are those affecting all firms, whereas industry-specific considerations influence only certain types of transactions in particular industries. General considerations include federal security, antitrust, environmental, racketeering, and employee benefits laws. Public utilities, insurance, banking, broadcasting, telecommunications, defense contracting, and transportation are examples of industries subject to substantial regulation. M&A activities in these industries often require government approvals to transfer government-granted licenses, permits, and franchises. State antitakeover statutes place limitations on how and when a hostile takeover may be implemented. Moreover, approval may have to be received to make deals in certain industries at both the state and federal levels. Cross-border transactions may be even more complicated, because it may be necessary to get approval from regulatory authorities in all countries in which the acquirer and target companies do business.

While regulating the financial markets is essential to limiting excesses, it is unrealistic to expect government controls to eliminate future speculative bubbles. Following the credit market meltdown of 2008, governments rushed to impose new regulations. However, as history has shown, regulations tend to lag behind changes in dynamic markets (Foster and Kaplan, 2001). Managers and investors move quickly to adapt to the new rules by avoiding activities that fall within the scope of such regulations. The explosion of credit default swaps (thinly disguised insurance products) in recent years is an example of how financial markets adapt to regulations.

This chapter focuses on the key elements of selected federal and state regulations and their implications for M&As. Considerable time is devoted to discussing the pre-notification and disclosure requirements of current legislation and how decisions are made within the key securities law and antitrust enforcement agencies. This chapter provides only an overview of the labyrinth of environmental, labor, benefit, and foreign (for cross-border transactions) laws affecting M&As. See Table 2–1 for a summary of applicable legislation. Major chapter segments include the following:

- Federal Securities Laws
- Antitrust Laws
- State Regulations Affecting Mergers and Acquisitions
- National Security-Related Restrictions on Direct Foreign Investment in the United States
- U.S. Foreign Corrupt Practices Act
- Regulated Industries
- Environmental Laws
- Labor and Benefit Laws
- Cross-Border Transactions
- Things to Remember

A review of this chapter is available (including practice questions) in the file folder entitled Student Study Guide contained on the CD-ROM accompanying this book. The CD-ROM also contains a Learning Interactions Library, enabling students to test their knowledge of this chapter in a "real-time" environment.

Note that the discussion of regulations affecting M&As is current as of the publication of this book. However, the meltdown of the global financial markets in late 2008 and early 2009 has raised questions about the efficacy of certain regulatory agencies, particularly the U.S. Securities and Exchange Commission. Therefore, the reader should be aware that major changes in existing regulations and enforcement agencies may occur during the next several years that are not discussed in this book.

Federal Securities Laws

Whenever either the acquiring or the target company is publicly traded, the firms are subject to the substantial reporting requirements of the current federal securities laws. Passed in the early 1930s, these laws were a direct result of the loss of confidence in the

Table 2–1   Laws Affecting M&A

Law	Intent
Federal securities laws	
Securities Act (1933)	Prevents the public offering of securities without a registration statement; specifies minimum data requirements and noncompliance penalties
Securities Exchange Act (1934)	Established the Securities and Exchange Commission (SEC) to regulate securities trading. Empowers the SEC to revoke registration of a security if the issuer is in violation of any provision of the 1934 act
Section 13	Specifies content and frequency of, as well as events triggering, SEC filings
Section 14	Specifies disclosure requirements for proxy solicitation
Section 16(a)	Specifies what insider trading is and who is an insider
Section 16(b)	Specifies investor rights with respect to insider trading
Williams Act (1968)	Regulates tender offers
Section 13D	Specifies disclosure requirements
Sarbanes–Oxley Act (2002)	Initiates extensive reform of regulations governing financial disclosure, governance, auditing standards, analyst reports, and insider trading
Federal antitrust laws	
Sherman Act (1890)	Made "restraint of trade" illegal. Establishes criminal penalties for behaviors that unreasonably limit competition
Section 1	Makes mergers creating monopolies or "unreasonable" market control illegal
Section 2	Applies to firms already dominant in their served markets to prevent them from "unfairly" restraining trade
Clayton Act (1914)	Outlawed certain practices not prohibited by the Sherman Act, such as price discrimination, exclusive contracts, and tie-in contracts, and created civil penalties for illegally restraining trade. Also established law governing mergers
Celler–Kefauver Act of 1950	Amended the Clayton Act to cover asset as well as stock purchases
Federal Trade Commission Act (1914)	Established a federal antitrust enforcement agency; made it illegal to engage in deceptive business practices.
Hart–Scott–Rodino Antitrust Improvement Act (1976)	Requires waiting period before a transaction can be completed and sets regulatory data submission requirements
Title I	Specifies what must be filed
Title II	Specifies who must file and when
Title III	Enables state attorneys general to file triple damage suits on behalf of injured parties
Other legislation affecting M&As	
State antitakeover laws	Specify conditions under which a change in corporate ownership can take place; may differ by state
State antitrust laws	Similar to federal antitrust laws; states may sue to block mergers, even if the mergers are not challenged by federal regulators
Exon–Florio Amendment to the Defense Protection Act of 1950	Establishes authority of the Committee on Foreign Investment in the United States (CFIUS) to review the impact of foreign direct investment (including M&As) on national security.
Industry specific regulations	Banking, communications, railroads, defense, insurance, and public utilities
Environmental laws (federal and state)	Specify disclosure requirements
Labor and benefit laws (federal and state)	Specify disclosure requirements
Applicable foreign laws	Cross-border transactions subject to jurisdictions of countries in which the bidder and target firms have operations

securities markets following the crash of the stock market in 1929. See the Securities and Exchange Commission website (www.sec.gov); Coffee, Seligman, and Sale (2008); and Gilson and Black (1995) for a comprehensive discussion of federal securities laws.

Securities Act of 1933

Originally administered by the FTC, the Securities Act of 1933 requires that all securities offered to the public must be registered with the government. Registration requires, but does not guarantee, that the facts represented in the registration statement and prospectus are accurate. Also, the law makes providing inaccurate or misleading statements in the sale of securities to the public punishable with a fine, imprisonment, or both. The registration process requires a description of the company's properties and business, a description of the securities, information about management, and financial statements certified by public accountants. Section 8 of the law permits the registration statement to automatically become effective 20 days after it is filed with the SEC. However, the SEC may delay or stop the process by requesting additional information.

Securities Exchange Act of 1934

The Securities Exchange Act of 1934 extends disclosure requirements stipulated under the Securities Act of 1933 covering new issues to include securities already trading on the national exchanges. In 1964, coverage was expanded to include securities traded on the Over-the-Counter (OTC) Market. Moreover, the act prohibits brokerage firms working with a company and others related to the securities transaction from engaging in fraudulent and unfair behavior, such as insider trading. The act also covers proxy solicitations (i.e., mailings to shareholders requesting their vote on a particular issue) by a company or shareholders. For a more detailed discussion of proxy statements, see Chapter 3.

Registration Requirements

Companies required to register are those with assets of more than $10 million and more than 500 shareholders. Even if both parties are privately owned, an M&A transaction is subject to federal securities laws if a portion of the purchase price is going to be financed by an initial public offering of stock or a public offering of debt by the acquiring firm.

Section 13. Periodic Reports

Form 10K or the annual report summarizes and documents the firm's financial activities during the preceding year. The four key financial statements that must be included are the income statement, balance sheet, statement of retained earnings, and the statement of cash flows. The statements must be well documented with information on accounting policies and procedures, calculations, and transactions underlying the financial statements. Form 10K also includes a relatively detailed description of the business, the markets served, major events and their impact on the business, key competitors, and competitive market conditions. Form 10Q is a highly succinct quarterly update of such information.

If an acquisition or divestiture is deemed significant, Form 8K must be submitted to the SEC within 15 days of the event. Form 8K describes the assets acquired or disposed, the type and amount of consideration (i.e., payment) given or received, and the identity of the person (or persons) for whom the assets were acquired. In an acquisition, Form 8K also must identify who is providing the funds used to finance the purchase and the financial statements of the acquired business. Acquisitions and divestitures are deemed significant if the equity interest in the acquired assets or the amount paid or received exceeds 10 percent of the total book value of the assets of the registrant and its subsidiaries.

Section 14. Proxy Solicitations

Where proxy contests for control of corporate management are involved, the act requires the names and interests of all participants in the proxy contest. Proxy materials must be filed in advance of their distribution to ensure that they are in compliance with disclosure requirements. If the transaction involves the shareholder approval of either the acquirer or target firm, any materials distributed to shareholders must conform to the SEC's rules for proxy materials.

Insider Trading Regulations

Insider trading involves individuals buying or selling securities based on knowledge not available to the general public. Historically, insider trading has been covered under the Securities and Exchange Act of 1934. Section 16(a) of the act defines insiders as corporate officers, directors, and any person owning 10 percent or more of any class of securities of a company. The Sarbanes–Oxley Act (SOA) of 2002 amended Section 16(a) of the 1934 act by requiring that insiders disclose any changes in ownership within two business days of the transaction, compared to the previous requirement that it be done on a monthly basis. Furthermore, the SOA requires that changes in ownership be filed electronically, rather than on paper. The SEC is required to post the filing on the Internet within one business day after the filing is received.

The SEC is responsible for investigating insider trading. Regulation 10b-5 issued by the SEC under powers granted by the 1934 Securities and Exchange Act prohibits the commission of fraud in relation to securities transactions. In addition, Regulation 14e-3 prohibits trading securities in connection with a tender offer based on information not available to the general public. According to the Insider Trading Sanctions Act of 1984, those convicted of engaging in insider trading are required to give back their illegal profits. They also are required to pay a penalty three times the magnitude of such profits. A 1988 U.S. Supreme Court ruling gives investors the right to claim damages from a firm that falsely denied it was involved in negotiations that subsequently resulted in a merger.

Williams Act: Regulation of Tender Offers

Passed in 1968, the Williams Act consists of a series of amendments to the Securities Act of 1934. The Williams Act was intended to protect target firm shareholders from lightning-fast takeovers in which they would not have enough information or time to assess adequately the value of an acquirer's offer. This protection was achieved by requiring more disclosure by the bidding company, establishing a minimum period during which a tender offer must remain open, and authorizing targets to sue bidding firms. The disclosure requirements of the Williams Act apply to anyone, including the target, asking shareholders to accept or reject a takeover bid. The major sections of the Williams Act as they affect M&As are in Sections 13(D) and 14(D). Note that the procedures outlined in the Williams Act for prenotification must be followed diligently. The Williams Act requirements apply to all types of tender offers including those negotiated with the target firm (i.e., negotiated or friendly tender offers), those undertaken by a firm to repurchase its own stock (i.e., self-tender offers), and those that are unwanted by the target firm (i.e., hostile tender offers).

Sections 13(D) and 13(G) Provide for Ownership Disclosure Requirements

Section 13(D) of the Williams Act is intended to regulate "substantial share" or large acquisitions and serves to provide an early warning for a target company's shareholders and management of a pending bid. Any person or firm acquiring 5 percent or more of the stock of a public corporation must file a Schedule 13D with the SEC within 10 days of reaching that percentage ownership threshold. The disclosure is necessary even if the accumulation of the stock is not followed by a tender offer.

Under Section 13(G), any stock accumulated by related parties, such as affiliates, brokers, or investment bankers working on behalf of the person or firm are counted toward the 5 percent threshold. This prevents an acquirer from avoiding filing by accumulating more than 5 percent of the target's stock through a series of related parties. Institutional investors, such as registered brokers and dealers, banks, and insurance companies, can file a Schedule 13G, a shortened version of the Schedule 13D, if the securities were acquired in the normal course of business.

The information required by the Schedule 13D includes the identities of the acquirer, his or her occupation and associations, sources of financing, and the purpose of the acquisition. If the purpose of the acquisition of the stock is to take control of the target firm, the acquirer must reveal its business plan for the target firm. The plans could include the breakup of the firm, the suspension of dividends, a recapitalization of the firm, or the intention to merge it with another firm. Otherwise, the purchaser of the stock could indicate that the accumulation was for investment purposes only. Whenever a material change in the information on the Schedule 13D occurs, a new filing must be made with the SEC and the public securities exchanges. The Williams Act is vague when it comes to defining what constitutes a material change. It is generally acceptable to file within 10 days of the material change.

Section 14(D) Created Rules for the Tender Offer Process

Although Section 14(D) of the Williams Act relates to public tender offers only, it applies to acquisitions of any size. The 5 percent notification threshold also applies.

- **Obligations of the acquirer.** An acquiring firm must disclose its intentions, business plans, and any agreements between the acquirer and the target firm in a Schedule 14D-1. The schedule is called a *tender offer statement.* The commencement date of the tender offer is defined as the date on which the tender offer is published, advertised, or submitted to the target. Schedule 14D-1 must contain the identity of the target company and the type of securities involved; the identity of the person, partnership, syndicate, or corporation that is filing; and any past contracts between the bidder and the target company. The schedule also must include the source of the funds used to finance the tender offer, its purpose, and any other information material to the transaction.
- **Obligations of the target firm.** The management of the target company cannot advise its shareholders how to respond to a tender offer until it has filed a Schedule 14D-9 with the SEC within 10 days after the tender offer's commencement date. This schedule is called a *tender offer solicitation/recommendation statement.* Target management is limited to telling its shareholders to defer responding to the tender offer until it has completed its consideration of the offer. The target also must send copies of the Schedule 14D-9 to each of the public exchanges on which its stock is traded.
- **Shareholder rights: 14(D) (4)–(7).** The tender offer must be left open for a minimum of 20 trading days. The acquiring firm must accept all shares that are tendered

during this period. The firm making the tender offer may get an extension of the 20-day period if it believes that there is a better chance of getting the shares it needs. The firm must purchase the shares tendered at the offer price, at least on a pro rata basis, unless the firm does not receive the total number of shares it requested under the tender offer. The tender offer also may be contingent on attaining the approval of such regulatory agencies as the Department of Justice (DoJ) and the Federal Trade Commission (FTC). Shareholders have the right to withdraw shares that they may have tendered previously. They may withdraw their shares at any time during which the tender offer remains open. The law also requires that, when a new bid for the target is made from another party, the target firm's shareholders must have an additional 10 days to consider the bid.

- **Best price rule: 14(D)-10.** The "best price" rule requires that all shareholders be paid the same price in a tender offer. As a result of SEC rule changes on October 18, 2006, the best price rule was clarified to underscore that compensation for services that might be paid to a shareholder should not be included as part of the price paid for their shares. The rule changes also protect special compensation arrangements that are approved by independent members of a firm's board and specifically exclude compensation in the form of severance and other employee benefits. The rule changes make it clear that the best price rule only applies to the consideration (i.e., cash, securities, or both) offered and paid for securities tendered by shareholders.

The best price rule need not apply in tender offers in which a controlling shareholder, a management group, or a third party makes a tender offer for all the outstanding publicly held shares of a firm with the goal of obtaining at least a certain threshold percentage of the total outstanding shares. Once this threshold has been reached, the acquirer can implement a short form merger and buy out the remaining shareholders (see Chapter 1). This threshold may be as high as 90 percent in states such as Delaware. Under such circumstances, the courts have ruled that the controlling shareholder is not legally compelled to purchase the remaining shares at any particular price, unless there is evidence that material information concerning its tender offer has been withheld or misrepresented (Siliconix Inc. Shareholders Litigation, 2001).

Acquirers routinely initiate two-tiered tender offers, in which target shareholders receive a higher price if they tender their shares in the first tier (round) than those submitting their shares in the second tier. The best price rule in these situations simply means that all shareholders tendering their shares in first tier must be paid the price offered for those shares in the first tier and those tendering shares in the second tier are paid the price offered for second tier shares. See Chapter 3 for more about two-tiered tender offers.

Sarbanes–Oxley Act of 2002

The Sarbanes-Oxley Act was signed in the wake of the egregious scandals at such corporate giants as Enron, MCI WorldCom, ImClone, Qwest, Adelphia, and Tyco. The act has implications ranging from financial disclosure to auditing practices to corporate governance. Section 302 of the act requires quarterly certification of financial statements and disclosure controls and procedures for CEOs and CFOs. This section became effective in September 2002.

Section 404 requires most public companies to certify annually that their internal control system is designed and operating successfully and became effective November 15, 2004. The legislation, in concert with new listing requirements at public stock exchanges, requires a greater number of directors on the board who do not work for the company (i.e., so-called independent directors). In addition, the act requires board audit committees to have at least one financial expert while the full committee must review financial statements every quarter after the CEO and chief financial officer certify them. Independent directors are encouraged to meet separately from management on a regular basis. Table 2–2 outlines the key elements of the act.

Coates (2007) argues that the SOA offers the potential for a reduction in investor risk of losses due to fraud and theft. The act also provides for an increase in reliable financial reporting, transparency or visibility into a firm's financial statements, as well as for greater accountability. If true, firms should realize a lower cost of capital and the economy would benefit from a more efficient allocation of capital. However, the egregious practices of some financial services firms (e.g., AIG, Bear Stearns, and Lehman Brothers) in recent years cast doubt on how effective the SOA has been in achieving its transparency and accountability objectives.

The costs associated with implementing SOA have been substantial. As noted in a number of studies cited in Chapter 13, there is growing evidence that the monitoring costs imposed by Sarbanes–Oxley have been a factor in many small firms going private

Table 2–2 Sarbanes–Oxley Bill (7/31/02)

Key Elements of Legislation	Key Actions
Creates Public Company Accounting Oversight Board (PCAOB)	Private, nonprofit corporate entity separate from SEC, but subject to SEC oversight; five members appointed by SEC for a five-year term Duties include — Register public accounting firms — Establish audit report standards — Inspect registered public accounting firms — Suspend registrations or impose fines on public accounting firms for violations — Promote a professional standard of conduct
Promotes auditor independence	Prohibits a registered public accounting firm from providing certain nonaudit services (e.g., information technology) to clients contemporaneously with the audit
Promotes corporate responsibility reform	Directs stock markets to require that audit committees of listed firms: — Be responsible for appointment, compensation, and oversight of auditors — Be composed of independent members of the board of directors — Have the authority to engage independent counsel to carry out duties Requires CEOs and CFOs to certify that financial statements do not violate antifraud and disclosure standards
Provides for financial disclosure reform	Requires detailed disclosure of all material off-balance sheet transactions Pro-forma financial statements must be consistent with generally accepted accounting practices (GAAP) Generally prohibits personal loans to executives Reduces period for principal stockholders, officers, and directors to disclose stock sales to two business days after the transaction is executed.
Expands corporate and criminal fraud accountability	Increases criminal penalties to include a prison sentence of up to 20 years for destroying records with intent to impede a criminal investigation

since the introduction of the legislation. However, a recent study illustrates the positive impact this legislation can have for the shareholders of firms that were required to overhaul their existing governance systems because of Sarbanes–Oxley. Chaochharia and Grinstein (2007) conclude that large firms that are the least compliant with the rules around the announcement dates of certain rule implementations are more likely to display significantly positive abnormal financial returns. In contrast, small firms that are less compliant earn negative abnormal returns.

In an effort to reduce some of the negative effects of Sarbanes–Oxley, the U.S. Securities and Exchange Commission allowed foreign firms to avoid having to comply with the reporting requirements of the act. Effective June 15, 2007, foreign firms whose shares traded on U.S. exchanges constituted less than 5 percent of the global trading volume of such shares during the previous 12 months are not subject to the Sarbanes–Oxley Act. This action was taken to enhance the attractiveness of U.S. exchanges as a place for foreign firms to list their stock. This regulatory change affects about 360 of the 1,200 foreign firms listed on U.S. stock exchanges (Grant, 2007).

Sarbanes–Oxley versus European Union's 8th Directive

While both focus on the relationship between the auditing firm and top company management, transparency, and accountability, the European Union's (EU's) 8th Directive is widely viewed as less onerous than the U.S.'s Sarbanes–Oxley legislation. In contrast to rapid action taken in the United States following the wave of corporate scandals in 2001 and 2002, the EU took longer to overhaul European company law, having started the process in the mid-1990s. While U.S. law mandates only independent (i.e., nonexecutive) directors can serve on audit committees, the 8th Directive allows the audit committee to consist of both independent and inside directors, as long as the committee contains at least one independent member with substantial accounting and auditing experience. Furthermore, the 8th Directive contains far fewer reporting requirements, but it does require auditing firms to report on key issues arising from the audit, such as weak internal controls for financial reporting. Unlike Sarbanes–Oxley, the 8th Directive requires firms rotate auditing companies as well as senior audit partners.

Sarbanes–Oxley versus Public Stock Exchange Regulations

New York Stock Exchange listing requirements far exceed the auditor independence requirements of the Sarbanes–Oxley Act. Companies must have board audit committees consisting of at least three independent directors and a written charter describing its responsibilities in detail. Moreover, the majority of all board members must be independent and nonmanagement directors must meet periodically without management. Board compensation and nominating committees must consist entirely of independent directors. Shareholders must be able to vote on all stock option plans. Listed firms must also adopt a set of governance guidelines and a code of business ethics.

Impact of Sarbanes–Oxley on Mergers and Acquisitions

While the act does not specifically address M&As, its implications are likely to be far reaching. Acquirers will do more intensive due diligence on target firms viewed as having weak internal controls. Due diligence will become more complex and take longer to complete. This will be especially true when the target firm is highly significant to the buyer. The timing of Sections 302 and 404 certification reporting requirements could increasingly cause delays in deal closings. Failure to properly coordinate a firm's responses to Section 302 and 404 could undermine management's credibility and lead to SEC investigations.

The Effectiveness of Public versus Private Enforcement of Securities Laws

The SEC and Justice Department enforce U.S. securities laws by filing lawsuits and imposing financial and criminal penalties. Additional resources come in the form of "whistle-blowers" that make public allegations of fraud and private law firms that file lawsuits against firms in instances of alleged shareholder abuse. Critics of private lawsuits often argue that the system for private enforcement of securities laws is poorly designed. Private law firms have a financial incentive to file lawsuits that are cheaper for a firm to settle out of court than go to trial. A firm may choose to settle even if the basis of the lawsuit is questionable. In these instances, the firm incurs significant expenses related to the settlement, which erode earnings that rightly belong to the firm's shareholders. Moreover, in the case of lawsuits filed on behalf of a class of shareholders, the shareholders usually receive a relatively small percentage of the recovered damages, with the majority of the dollars going to the law firm. Jackson and Roe (2008) argue that, if properly resourced in terms of staffing levels and budgets, public enforcement agencies can be at least as effective in protecting shareholder rights as private enforcement mechanisms, such as disclosure and privately filed lawsuits.

Antitrust Laws

Federal antitrust laws exist to prevent individual corporations from assuming too much market power such that they can limit their output and raise prices without concern for any significant competitor reaction. The DoJ and the FTC have the primary responsibility for enforcing federal antitrust laws. The FTC was established in the Federal Trade Commission Act of 1914 with the specific purpose of enforcing antitrust laws such as the Sherman, Clayton, and Federal Trade Commission Acts. For excellent discussions of antitrust law, see the DoJ (www.usdoj.gov) and FTC (www.ftc.gov) websites, and the American Bar Association (2006).

Generally speaking, national laws do not affect firms outside their domestic political boundaries. There are two important exceptions. These include antitrust laws and laws applying to the bribery of foreign government officials (Truitt, 2006). Outside the United States, antitrust regulation laws are described as competitiveness laws, intended to minimize or eliminate anticompetitive behavior. As illustrated in Case Study 2–7, the European Union antitrust regulators were able to thwart the attempted takeover of Honeywell by General Electric, two U.S. corporations with operations in the European Union. Remarkably, this occurred following the approval of the proposed takeover by U.S. antitrust authorities. The other exception, the Foreign Corrupt Practices Act, is discussed later in this chapter.

Sherman Act

Passed in 1890, the Sherman Act makes illegal all contracts, combinations, and conspiracies that "unreasonably" restrain trade (U.S. Department of Justice, 1999). Examples include agreements to fix prices, rig bids, allocate customers among competitors, or monopolize any part of interstate commerce. Section I of the Sherman Act prohibits new business combinations that result in monopolies or in a significant concentration of pricing power in a single firm. Section II applies to firms that already are dominant in their targeted markets.

The Sherman Act remains the most important source of antitrust law today. The act specifies broad conditions and remedies for such firms that are deemed to be in violation of current antitrust laws. The act applies to all transactions and businesses involved in interstate commerce or, if the activities are local, all transactions and business "affecting" interstate commerce. The latter phrase has been interpreted to allow broad application of the Sherman Act. Most states have comparable statutes prohibiting monopolistic conduct, price-fixing agreements, and other acts in restraint of trade having strictly local impact.

Clayton Act

Passed in 1914 to strengthen the Sherman Act, the Clayton Act was created to outlaw certain practices not prohibited by the Sherman Act and help government stop a monopoly before it developed. Section 5 of the act made price discrimination between customers illegal, unless it could be justified by cost savings associated with bulk purchases. Tying of contracts—in which a firm refused to sell certain important products to a customer unless the customer agreed to buy other products from the firm—also was prohibited. Section 7 prohibits mergers and acquisitions that may substantially lessen competition or tend to create a monopoly. Under Section 7 of the act, it is illegal for one company to purchase the stock of another company if their combination results in reduced competition within the industry. Interlocking directorates also were made illegal when the directors were on the boards of competing firms.

Unlike the Sherman Act, which contains criminal penalties, the Clayton Act is a civil statute. The Clayton Act allows private parties injured by the antitrust violation to sue in federal court for three times their actual damages. State attorneys general also may bring civil suits. If the plaintiff wins, costs must be borne by the party violating prevailing antitrust law, in addition to the criminal penalties imposed under the Sherman Act.

Acquirers soon learned how to circumvent the original statutes of the Clayton Act of 1914, which applied to the purchase of stock. They simply would acquire the assets, rather than the stock, of a target firm. In the Celler–Kefauver Act of 1950, the Clayton Act was amended to give the FTC the power to prohibit asset as well as stock purchases. The FTC also may block mergers if it believes that the combination will result in increased market concentration (i.e., fewer firms having increased market shares) as measured by the sales of the largest firms.

Federal Trade Commission Act of 1914

This act created the FTC, consisting of five full-time commissioners appointed by the president for a seven-year term. The commissioners are supported by a staff of economists, lawyers, and accountants to assist in the enforcement of antitrust laws.

Hart–Scott–Rodino (HSR) Antitrust Improvements Act of 1976

Acquisitions involving companies of a certain size cannot be completed until certain information is supplied to the federal government and a specified waiting period has elapsed. The premerger notification allows the FTC and the DoJ sufficient time to challenge acquisitions believed to be anticompetitive before they are completed. Once the merger has taken place, it is often exceedingly difficult to break it up. See Table 2–3 for a summary of prenotification filing requirements.

Title I: What Must Be Filed?

Title I of the act gives the DoJ the power to request internal corporate records if it suspects potential antitrust violations. In some cases, the requests for information result in truckloads of information being delivered to the regulatory authorities because of the

Table 2–3   Summary of Regulatory Prenotification Filing Requirements

	Williams Act	Hart–Scott–Rodino Act
Required filing	1. Schedule 13D within 10 days of acquiring 5% stock ownership in another firm 2. Ownership includes stock held by affiliates or agents of bidder 3. Schedule 14D-1 for tender offers 4. Disclosure required even if 5% accumulation not followed by a tender offer	HSR filing is necessary when[1] 1. Size of transaction test: The buyer purchases assets or securities >$65.2 million or 2. Size of person test:[2] Buyer or seller has annual sales or assets ≥$126.2 million and other party has sales or assets ≥$12.6 million Thresholds in 1 and 2 are adjusted annually by the increase in gross domestic product.
File with whom	Schedule 13D 1. 6 copies to SEC 2. 1 copy via registered mail to target's executive office 3. 1 copy via registered mail to each public exchange on which target stock traded Schedule 14D-1 1. 10 copies to SEC 2. 1 copy hand delivered to target's executive offices 3. 1 copy hand delivered to other bidders 4. 1 copy mailed to each public exchange on which target stock traded (each exchange also must be phoned)	1. Pre-Merger Notification Office of the Federal Trade Commission 2. Director of Operations of the DoJ Antitrust Division
Time period	1. Tender offers must stay open a minimum of 20 business days 2. Begins on date of publication, advertisement, or submission of materials to target 3. Unless the tender offer has closed, shareholders may withdraw tendered shares up to 60 days after the initial offer	1. Review/waiting period: 30 days 2. Target must file within 15 days of bidder's filing 3. Period begins for all cash offer when bidder files; for cash/stock bids, period begins when both bidder and target have filed 4. Regulators can request 20-day extension

[1]Note that these are the thresholds as of January 13, 2009.

[2]The size of person test measures the size of the "ultimate parent entity" of the buyer and seller. The "ultimate parent entity" is the entity that controls the buyer and seller and is not itself controlled by anyone else. Transactions valued at more than $260.7 million are not subject to the size of person test and are therefore reportable.

extensive nature of the prenotification form. The information requirements include background information on the "ultimate parent entity" of the acquiring and target parents, a description of the transaction, and all background studies relating to the transaction. The "ultimate parent entity" is the corporation at the top of the chain of ownership if the actual buyer is a subsidiary. In addition, the reporting firm must supply detailed product line breakdowns, a listing of competitors, and an analysis of sales trends.

Title II: Who Must File and When?

Title II addresses the conditions under which filings must take place. Effective January 13, 2009, to comply with the "size-of-transaction" test, transactions in which the buyer purchases voting securities or assets valued in excess of $65.2 million must be reported under the HSR Act. However, according to the "size-of-person" test, transactions valued at less than $65.2 million may still require filing if the acquirer or the target firm has annual net sales or total assets of at least $126.2 million and the other party has annual net sales or total assets of at least $12.6 million. These thresholds are adjusted upward by the annual rate of increase in gross domestic product.

Bidding firms must execute an HSR filing at the same time as they make an offer to a target firm. The target firm also is required to file within 15 days following the bidder's filing. Filings consist of information on the operations of the two companies and their financial statements. The required forms also request any information on internal documents, such as the estimated market share of the combined companies, before extending the offer. Consequently, any such analyses should be undertaken with the understanding that the information ultimately will be shared with the antitrust regulatory authorities. The waiting period begins when both the acquirer and target have filed. Either the FTC or the DoJ may request a 20-day extension of the waiting period for transactions involving securities and 10 days for cash tender offers. If the acquiring firm believes that there is little likelihood of anticompetitive effects, it can request early termination. However, the decision is entirely at the discretion of the regulatory agencies.

In 2007, there were 2,201 HSR filings with the FTC (about one fifth of total transactions) compared to 1,768 in 2006 (Barnett, 2008). Of these, about 4 percent typically are challenged and about 2 percent require second requests for information (Lindell, 2006). This represents a continuation of a longer-term trend. About 97 percent of the 37,701 M&A deals filed with the FTC between 1991 and 2004 were approved without further scrutiny (*Business Week*, 2008).

If the regulatory authorities suspect anticompetitive effects, they will file a lawsuit to obtain a court injunction to prevent completion of the proposed transaction. Although it is rare for either the bidder or the target to contest the lawsuit, because of the expense involved, and even rarer for the government to lose, it does happen. Regulators filed a suit on February 27, 2004, to block Oracle's $26 per share hostile bid for PeopleSoft on antitrust grounds. On September 9, 2004, a U.S. District Court judge denied a request by U.S. antitrust authorities that he issue an injunction against the deal, arguing that the government failed to prove that large businesses can turn to only three suppliers (i.e., Oracle, PeopleSoft, and SAP) for business applications software. Government antitrust authorities indicated that, given the strong findings on behalf of the plaintiff by the judge, they would not attempt to appeal the ruling.

If fully litigated, a government lawsuit can result in substantial legal expenses as well as a significant cost in management time. The acquiring firm may be required to operate the target firm as a wholly independent subsidiary until the litigation has been resolved. Even if the FTC's lawsuit is ultimately overturned, the perceived benefits of the merger often have disappeared by the time the lawsuit has been decided. Potential customers and suppliers are less likely to sign lengthy contracts with the target firm during the period of trial. Moreover, new investment in the target is likely to be limited, and employees and communities where the target's operations are located would be subject to substantial uncertainty. For these reasons, both regulators and acquirers often seek to avoid litigation.

How Does HSR Affect State Antitrust Regulators?

Title III expands the powers of state attorneys general to initiate triple damage suits on behalf of individuals in their states injured by violations of the antitrust laws. This additional authority gives states the incentive to file such suits to increase state revenues.

Procedural Rules

When the DoJ files an antitrust suit, it is adjudicated in the federal court system. When the FTC initiates the action, it is heard before an administrative law judge at the FTC. The results of the hearing are subject to review by the commissioners of the FTC. Criminal actions are reserved for the DoJ, which may seek fines or imprisonment for violators. Individuals and companies also may file antitrust lawsuits. The FTC reviews complaints that have been recommended by its staff and approved by the commission. Each complaint is reviewed by one of the FTC's hearing examiners. The commission as a whole then votes whether to accept or reject the hearing examiner's findings. The decision of the commission then can be appealed in the federal circuit courts. In 1999, the FTC implemented new "fast-track" guidelines that commit the FTC to making a final decision on a complaint within 13 months.

As an alternative to litigation, a company may seek to negotiate a voluntary settlement of its differences with the FTC. Such settlements usually are negotiated during the review process and are called *consent decrees*. The FTC then files a complaint in the federal court along with the proposed consent decree. The federal court judge routinely approves the consent decree.

The Consent Decree

A typical **consent decree** requires the merging parties to divest overlapping businesses or restrict anticompetitive practices. If a potential acquisition is likely to be challenged by the regulatory authorities, an acquirer may seek to negotiate a consent decree in advance of consummating the deal. In the absence of a consent decree, a buyer often requires that an agreement of purchase and sale includes a provision that allows the acquirer to back out of the transaction if it is challenged by the FTC or the DoJ on antitrust grounds. In a report evaluating the results of 35 divestiture orders entered between 1990 and 1994, the FTC concluded that the use of consent decrees to limit market power resulting from a business combination has proven to be successful by creating viable competitors (Federal Trade Commission, 1999). The study found that the divestiture is likely to be more successful if it is made to a firm in a related business rather than a new entrant into the business. (See Case Study 2–1.)

Case Study 2–1 Justice Department Requires Verizon Wireless to Sell Assets Before Approving Alltel Merger

In late 2008, Verizon Wireless, a joint venture between Verizon Communications and Vodafone Group, agreed to sell certain assets to obtain Justice Department approval of their $28 billion deal with Alltel Corporation. The merger created the nation's largest wireless carrier. Under the terms of the deal, Verizon Wireless planned to buy Alltel for $5.9 billion and assume $22.2 billion in debt. The combined firms would have about 78 million subscribers nationwide.

The consent decree was required following a lawsuit initiated by the Justice Department and seven states to block the merger. Fearing the merger would limit competition, drive up consumer prices, and potentially reduce the quality of service, the settlement would require Verizon Wireless to divest assets in 100 markets in

22 states. The proposed merger had raised concerns about the impact on competition in the mainly rural, inland markets that Alltel serves. Consumer advocates had argued that Verizon would not have the same incentive as Alltel to strike roaming agreements with other regional and small wireless carriers that rely on the firm to provide service in areas where they lack operations. By requiring the sale of assets, the Justice Department hoped to ensure continued competition in the affected markets.

Discussion Questions

1. Do you believe consent decrees involving the acquiring firm to dispose of certain target company assets is an abuse of government power? Why or why not?
2. What alternative actions could the government take to limit market power resulting from a business combination?

Antitrust Merger Guidelines for Horizontal Mergers

Understanding an industry begins with understanding its market structure. *Market structure* may be defined in terms of the number of firms in an industry; their concentration, cost, demand, and technological conditions; and ease of entry and exit. The size of individual competitors does not tell one much about the competitive dynamics of an industry. Some industries give rise to larger firms than other industries because of the importance of economies of scale or huge capital and research and development requirements. For example, although Boeing and Airbus dominate the commercial airframe industry, industry rivalry is intense.

Beginning in 1968, the DoJ issued guidelines indicating the types of M&As the government would oppose. Intended to clarify the provisions of the Sherman and Clayton Acts, the largely quantitative guidelines were presented in terms of specific market share percentages and concentration ratios. Concentration ratios were defined in terms of the market shares of the industry's top four or eight firms. Because of their rigidity, the guidelines have been revised to reflect the role of both quantitative and qualitative data. Qualitative data include factors such as the enhanced efficiency that might result from a combination of firms, the financial viability of potential merger candidates, and the ability of U.S. firms to compete globally.

In 1992, both the FTC and the DoJ announced a new set of guidelines indicating that they would challenge mergers creating or enhancing market power, even if there are measurable efficiency benefits. *Market power* is defined as a situation in which the combined firms will be able to profitably maintain prices above competitive levels for a significant period. M&As that do not increase market power are acceptable. The 1992 guidelines were revised in 1997 to reflect the regulatory authorities' willingness to recognize that improvements in efficiency over the long term could more than offset the effects of increases in market power. Consequently, a combination of firms that enhances market power would be acceptable to the regulatory authorities if it could be shown that the increase in efficiency resulting from the combination more than offsets the increase in market power. Numerous recent empirical studies support this conclusion (see Chapter 1).

In the 1980s and 1990s, a merger in an industry with five major competitors would face scrutiny from either the Federal Trade Commission or the Department of Justice and might face significant regulatory opposition. Today, mergers reducing the number of competitors from three to two are the only ones regulators are likely to block due to the supposition that the efficiencies the merger partners might realize would be offset by the potential harm to consumers of reduced competition. Indeed, even under this scenario, unusually high market concentration may be overlooked if the market is broadly defined to include foreign competitors. For example, Whirlpool Corporation's acquisition of Maytag Corporation resulted in a combined postmerger market share of about 70 percent of the U.S. home appliance market. (See the section entitled "Inside M&A" at the beginning of this chapter.)

In general, horizontal mergers, those between current or potential competitors, are most likely to be challenged by regulators. Vertical mergers, those involving customer-supplier relationships, are considered much less likely to result in anticompetitive effects, unless they deprive other market participants of access to an important resource. The antitrust regulators seldom contest conglomerate mergers involving the combination of dissimilar products into a single firm.

The 1992 guidelines describe the process the antitrust authorities go through to make their decisions. This process falls into five discrete steps.

Step 1. Market Definition, Measurement, and Concentration

A substantial number of factors are examined to determine if a proposed transaction will result in a violation of law. However, calculating the respective market shares of the combining companies and the degree of industry concentration in terms of the number of competitors is the starting point for any investigation.

- **Defining the market.** Regulators define a market as a product or group of products offered in a specific geographic area. Market participants are those currently producing and selling these products in this geographic area as well as potential entrants. Regulators calculate market shares for all firms or plants identified as market participants based on total sales or capacity currently devoted to the relevant markets. In certain cases, the regulatory agencies have chosen to segment a market more narrowly by size or type of competitor.

- **Determining market concentration.** The number of firms in the market and their respective market shares determine market concentration (i.e., the extent to which a single or a few firms control a disproportionate share of the total market). Concentration ratios are an incomplete measure of industry concentration. Such ratios measure how much of the total output of an industry is produced by the n largest firms in the industry. The shortcomings of this approach include the frequent inability to define accurately what constitutes an industry, the failure to reflect ease of entry or exit, foreign competition, regional competition, and the distribution of firm size.

In an effort to account for the distribution of firm size in an industry, the FTC measures concentration using the **Herfindahl–Hirschman Index** (HHI), which is calculated by summing the squares of the market shares for each firm competing in the market. For example, a market consisting of five firms with market shares of 30, 25, 20, 15, and 10 percent, respectively, would have an HHI of 2,250 ($30^2 + 25^2 + 20^2 + 15^2 + 10^2$). Note that an industry consisting of five competitors with market shares of 70, 10, 5, 5, and 5 percent, respectively, will have a much higher HHI score of 5,075, because the process of squaring the market shares gives the greatest weight to the firm with the largest market shares.

FIGURE 2–1 Federal Trade Commission actions at various market share concentration levels. HHI, Herfindahl–Hirschman index (From FTC Merger Guidelines, www.ftc.gov).

- **Likely FTC actions based on the Herfindahl–Hirschman index.** The HHI ranges from 10,000 for an almost pure monopoly to approximately 0 in the case of a highly competitive market. The index gives proportionately more weight to the market shares of larger firms to reflect their relatively greater pricing power. The FTC developed a scoring system, described in Figure 2–1, which is used as one factor in determining whether the FTC will challenge a proposed merger or acquisition.

Step 2. Potential Adverse Competitive Effects of Mergers

Market concentration and market share data are based on historical data. Consequently, changing market conditions may distort the significance of market share. Suppose a new technology that is important to the long-term competitive viability of the firms within a market has been licensed to other firms within the market but not to the firm with the largest market share. Regulators may conclude that market share information overstates the potential for an increase in the market power of the firm with the largest market share. Therefore, before deciding to challenge a proposed transaction, regulators will consider factors other than simply market share and concentration to determine if a proposed merger will have "adverse competitive effects." These other factors include evidence of coordinated interaction, differentiated products, and similarity of substitute products.

- **Coordinated interaction.** Regulators consider the extent to which a small group of firms may exercise market power collectively by cooperating in restricting output or setting prices. Collusion may take the form of firms agreeing to follow simple guidelines, such as maintaining common prices, fixed price differentials, stable market shares, or customer or territorial restrictions.
- **Differentiated products.** In some markets, the products are differentiated in the eyes of the consumer. Consequently, products sold by different firms in the market are not good substitutes for one another. A merger between firms in a market for differentiated products may diminish competition by enabling the merged firms to profit by raising the price of one or both products above premerger levels.
- **Similarity of substitutes.** Market concentration may be increased if two firms whose products are viewed by customers as equally desirable merge. In this instance, market share may understate the anticompetitive impact of the merger if the products of the merging firms are more similar in their various attributes to one another than to other products in the relevant market. In contrast, market share may overstate the perceived undesirable competitive effects when the relevant products are less similar in their attributes to one another than to other products in the relevant market.

Step 3. Entry Analysis

The ease of entry into the market by new competitors is considered a very important factor in determining if a proposed business combination is anticompetitive. Ease of entry is defined as entry that would be timely, likely to occur, and sufficient to counter the competitive effects of a combination of firms that temporarily increases market concentration. Barriers to entry—such as proprietary technology or knowledge, patents, government regulations, exclusive ownership of natural resources, or huge investment requirements—can limit the number of new competitors and the pace at which they enter a market. In such instances, a regulatory agency may rule that a proposed transaction will reduce competitiveness. Ease of entry appears to have been a factor in the DoJ's assessment of Maytag's proposal to acquire Whirlpool (see "Inside M&A" at the beginning of this chapter).

Step 4. Efficiencies

Increases in efficiency that result from a merger or acquisition can enhance the combined firms' ability to compete and result in lower prices, improved quality, better service, or new products. However, efficiencies are difficult to measure and verify, because they will be realized only after the merger has taken place. Efficiencies are most likely to make a difference in the FTC's decision to challenge when the likely effects of market concentration are not considered significant. An example of verifiable efficiency improvements would be a reduction in the average fixed cost of production due to economies of scale.

Step 5. Alternative to Imminent Failure

Regulators also take into account the likelihood that a firm would fail and exit a market if it is not allowed to merge with another firm. The regulators must weigh the potential cost of the failing firm, such as a loss of jobs, against any potential increase in market power that might result from the merger of the two firms. The failing firm must be able to demonstrate that it is unable to meet its financial obligations, that it would be unable to successfully reorganize under the protection of the U.S. bankruptcy court, and that it has been unsuccessful in its good-faith efforts to find other potential merger partners. In 2008, U.S. antitrust regulators approved the merger of XM Radio and Serius Radio, the U.S. satellite radio industry's only competitors, virtually creating a monopoly in that industry. The authorities recognized that neither firm would be financially viable if compelled to remain independent. The firms also argued successfully that other forms of media, such as conventional radio, represented viable competition since they were free and XM and Serius offer paid subscription services.

Antitrust Guidelines for Vertical Mergers

The guidelines described for horizontal mergers also apply to vertical mergers between customers and suppliers. Vertical mergers may become a concern if an acquisition by a supplier of a customer prevents the supplier's competitors from having access to the customer. Regulators are not likely to challenge this type of merger unless the relevant market has few customers and, as such, is highly concentrated (i.e., an HHI score in excess of 1800). Alternatively, the acquisition by a customer of a supplier could become a concern if it prevents the customer's competitors from having access to the supplier. The concern is greatest if the supplier's products or services are critical to the competitor's operations (see Case Study 2–2).

Case Study 2–2 JDS Uniphase Acquires SDL—What a Difference Seven Months Makes!

What started out as the biggest technology merger in history, at that time, saw its value plummet in line with the declining stock market, a weakening economy, and concerns about the cash flow impact of actions the acquirer would have to take to gain regulatory approval. The challenge facing JDS Uniphase (JDSU) was to get Department of Justice approval of a merger that could result in a supplier (i.e., JDS Uniphase/SDL) that could exercise pricing power over products ranging from components to packaged products purchased by equipment manufacturers. The regulatory review lengthened the period between the signing of the merger agreement and the closing to seven months.

JDSU manufactures and distributes fiber-optic components and modules to telecommunication and cable systems providers worldwide. The company is the dominant supplier in its market for fiber-optic components. JDSU's strategy is to package entire systems into a single integrated unit, thereby reducing the number of vendors that fiber network firms must deal with when purchasing systems that produce the light transmitted over fiber. SDL's products, including pump lasers, support the transmission of data, voice, video, and Internet information over fiber-optic networks by expanding its fiber-optic communications networks much more quickly and efficiently than conventional technologies. Consequently, SDL fit the JDSU strategy perfectly.

Regulators expressed concern that the combined entities could control the market for a specific type of laser used in a wide range of optical equipment. SDL is one of the largest suppliers of this type of laser, and JDS is one of the largest suppliers of the chips used to build them. Other manufacturers of pump lasers, such as Nortel Networks, Lucent Technologies, and Corning, complained to regulators that they would have to buy some of the chips necessary to manufacture pump lasers from a supplier (i.e., JDSU), which in combination with SDL also would be a competitor.

On February 6, 2001, JDSU agreed as part of a consent decree to sell a Swiss subsidiary, which manufactures pump laser chips, to Nortel Networks Corporation, a JDSU customer, to satisfy DoJ concerns about the proposed merger. The divestiture of this operation set up an alternative supplier of such chips. The deal finally closed on February 12, 2001. JDSU shares had fallen from their 12-month high of $153.42 to $53.19. The deal that originally had been valued at $41 billion when first announced, more than seven months earlier, had fallen to $13.5 billion on the day of closing, a staggering loss of more than two thirds of its value.

Discussion Questions

1. The JDS Uniphase/SDL merger proposal was somewhat unusual in that it represented a vertical rather than horizontal merger. Why does the FTC tend to focus primarily on horizontal rather than vertical mergers?
2. How can an extended regulatory approval process change the value of a proposed acquisition to the acquiring company? Explain your answer.
3. Do you think that JDS Uniphase's competitors had legitimate concerns, or were they simply trying to use the antitrust regulatory process to prevent the firm from gaining a competitive advantage? Explain your answer.

Antitrust Guidelines for Collaborative Efforts

On April 7, 2000, the FTC and DoJ jointly issued new guidelines, entitled "Antitrust Guidelines for Collaborations among Competitors," intended to explain how the agencies analyze antitrust issues with respect to collaborative efforts. *Collaborative effort* is the term used by the regulatory agencies to describe a range of horizontal agreements among competitors, such as joint ventures, strategic alliances, and other competitor agreements. Note that competitors include both actual and potential ones. Collaborative efforts that might be examined include production, marketing or distribution, and R&D activities.

The analytical framework for determining if the proposed collaborative effort is pro- or anticompetitive is similar to that described earlier in this chapter for horizontal mergers. The agencies evaluate the impact on market share and the potential increase in market power. The agencies may be willing to overlook any temporary increase in market power if the participants can demonstrate that future increases in efficiency and innovation will result in lower overall selling prices or increased product quality in the long term. In general, the agencies are less likely to find a collaborative effort to be anticompetitive under the following conditions: (1) the participants have continued to compete through separate, independent operations or through participation in other collaborative efforts; (2) the financial interest in the effort by each participant is relatively small; (3) each participant's ability to control the effort is limited; (4) effective safeguards prevent information sharing; and (5) the duration of the collaborative effort is short.

The regulatory agencies have established two "safety zones" that provide collaborating firms a degree of certainty that the agencies will not challenge them. First, the market shares of the collaborative effort and the participants collectively accounts for no more than 20 percent of the served market. Second, for R&D activities, there must be at least three or more independently controlled research efforts, in addition to those of the collaborative effort. These independent efforts must possess the required specialized assets and the incentive to engage in R&D that is a close substitute for the R&D activity of the collaborative effort. Market share considerations resulted in the Justice Department threatening to file suit if Google and Yahoo proceeded to implement an advertising alliance in late 2008 (see Case Study 2–3).

Case Study 2–3 Google Thwarted in Proposed Advertising Deal with Chief Rival, Yahoo

A proposal that gave Yahoo an alternative to selling itself to Microsoft was killed in the face of opposition by U.S. government antitrust regulators. The deal called for Google to place ads alongside some of Yahoo's search results. Google and Yahoo would share in the revenues generated by this arrangement. The deal was supposed to bring Yahoo $250 million to $450 million in incremental cash flow in the first full year of the agreement. The deal was especially important to Yahoo, due to the continued erosion in the firm's profitability and share of the online search market.

The Justice Department argued that the alliance would have limited competition for online advertising, resulting in higher fees charged online advertisers. The regulatory agency further alleged that the arrangement would make Yahoo more reliant on Google's already superior search capability and reduce Yahoo's efforts to invest in its own online search business. The regulators feared this would limit innovation in the online search industry.

On November 6, 2008, Google and Yahoo announced that they would cease any further efforts to implement an advertising alliance. Google expressed concern that continuing the effort would result in a protracted legal battle and risked damaging lucrative relationships with their advertising partners. The Justice Department's threat to block the proposal may be a sign that Google can expect increased scrutiny in the future. High-tech markets often lend themselves to becoming "natural monopolies" in markets in which special factors foster market dominance by a single firm. Examples include Intel's domination of the microchip business, as economies of scale create huge barriers to entry for new competitors; Microsoft's preeminent market share in PC operating systems and related application software, due to its large installed customer base; and Google's dominance of Internet search, resulting from its demonstrably superior online search capability.

Discussion Questions

1. In what way might the Justice Department's actions result in increased concentration in the online search business in the future?
2. What are the arguments for and against regulators permitting "natural monopolies"?

The Limitations of Antitrust Laws

Antitrust laws have faced serious challenges in recent years in terms of accurately defining market share, accommodating rapidly changing technologies, and promoting competition without discouraging innovation. Efforts to measure market share or concentration inevitably must take into account the explosion of international trade during the last 20 years. Actions by a single domestic firm to restrict its output to raise its selling price may be thwarted by a surge in imports of similar products. Moreover, the pace of technological change is creating many new substitute products and services, which may make a firm's dominant position in a rapidly changing market indefensible almost overnight. The rapid growth of electronic commerce, as a marketplace without geographic boundaries, has tended to reduce the usefulness of conventional measures of market share and market concentration. What constitutes a market on the Internet often is difficult to define.

State Regulations Affecting Mergers and Acquisitions

Numerous regulations affecting takeovers exist at the state level. The regulations often differ from one state to another, making compliance with all applicable regulations a challenge. State regulations often are a result of special interests that appeal to state legislators to establish a particular type of antitakeover statute to make it more difficult to complete unfriendly takeover attempts. Such appeals usually are made in the context of an attempt to save jobs in the state.

State Antitakeover Laws

States regulate corporate charters. *Corporate charters* define the powers of the firm and the rights and responsibilities of its shareholders, boards of directors, and managers. However, states are not allowed to pass any laws that impose restrictions on interstate commerce or conflict in any way with federal laws regulating interstate commerce. State laws affecting M&As tend to apply only to corporations incorporated in the state or that conduct a substantial amount of their business within the state. These laws typically contain *fair price provisions*, requiring that all target shareholders of a successful tender offer receive the same price as those tendering their shares. In a specific attempt to prevent highly leveraged transactions, such as leveraged buyouts, some state laws include *business combination provisions,* which may specifically rule out the sale of the target's assets for a specific period. By precluding such actions, these provisions limit LBOs from using the proceeds of asset sales to reduce indebtedness.

Other common characteristics of state antitakeover laws include cash-out and control share provisions. *Cash-out provisions* require a bidder whose purchases of stock exceed a stipulated amount to buy the remainder of the target stock on the same terms granted those shareholders whose stock was purchased at an earlier date. By forcing the acquiring firm to purchase 100 percent of the stock, potential bidders lacking substantial financial resources effectively are eliminated from bidding on the target. *Share control provisions* require that a bidder obtain prior approval from stockholders holding large blocks of target stock once the bidder's purchases of stock exceed some threshold level. The latter provision can be particularly troublesome to an acquiring company when the holders of the large blocks of stock tend to support target management.

Such state measures may be set aside if sufficient target firm votes can be obtained at a special meeting of shareholders called for that purpose. Ohio's share control law forced Northrop Grumman to increase its offer price from its original bid of $47 in March 2002 to $53 in mid-April 2002 to encourage those holding large blocks of TRW shares to tender their shares. Such shareholders had balked at the lower price, expressing support for a counterproposal made by TRW to spin off its automotive business and divest certain other assets. TRW had valued its proposal at more than $60 per share. The Ohio law, among the toughest in the nation, prevented Northrop from acquiring more than 20 percent of TRW's stock without getting the support of other large shareholders.

State Antitrust Laws

As part of the Hart–Scott–Rodino Act of 1976, the states were granted increased antitrust power. The state laws are often similar to federal laws. Under federal law, states have the right to sue to block mergers they believe are anticompetitive, even if the DoJ or FTC does not challenge them.

State Securities Laws

State blue sky laws are designed to protect individuals from investing in fraudulent security offerings. State restrictions can be more onerous than federal ones. An issuer seeking exemption from federal registration will not be exempt from all relevant registration requirements until a state-by-state exemption has been received from all states in which the issuer and offerees reside.

National Security–Related Restrictions on Direct Foreign Investment in the United States

While in existence for more than 50 years, the Committee on Foreign Investment in the United States made the headlines in early 2006 when Dubai Ports Worldwide proposed to acquire control of certain U.S. port terminal operations. The subsequent political firestorm catapulted what had previously been a relatively obscure committee into the public limelight. CFIUS operates under the authority granted by Congress in the Exon-Florio amendment (Section 721 of the Defense Production Act of 1950). CFIUS includes representatives from an amalgam of government departments and agencies with diverse expertise to ensure that all national security issues are identified and considered in the review of foreign acquisitions of U.S. businesses.

Concerns expressed by CFIUS about a proposed technology deal prevented U.S. networking company 3Com from being taken private by private equity firm Bain Capital in early 2008. Under the terms of the transaction, a Chinese networking equipment company, Huaewi Technologies, would have obtained a 16.6 percent stake and board representation in 3Com. CFIUS became alarmed because of 3Com's involvement in networking security software, a field in which it is a supplier to the U.S. military.

The president can, under the authority granted under Section 721 (also known as the Exon-Florio provision), block the acquisition of a U.S. corporation under certain conditions. These conditions include the existence of credible evidence that the foreign entity exercising control might take action that threatens national security and that existing laws do not adequately protect national security if the transaction is permitted. To assist in making this determination, Section 721 provides for the president to receive written notice of an acquisition, merger, or takeover of a U.S. corporation by a foreign entity. Once CFIUS has received a complete notification, it begins a thorough investigation. Section 721 provides for a 30-day review process, which can be extended an additional 45 days. After the review is completed, the findings are submitted to the president, whose decision must, by law, be announced within 15 days. The total process is not to exceed 90 days.

Section 721 requires that the impact of the proposed transaction on the following factors be considered during the review process:

1. Domestic production needed for projected national defense requirements.
2. The capability and capacity of domestic industries to meet national defense requirements.
3. The control of domestic industries and commercial activity by foreign citizens as it affects the capability and capacity to meet the requirements of national security.
4. The effects of the transaction on the sales of military equipment and technology to a country that supports terrorism or the proliferation of missile technology or chemical or biological weapon technology.
5. The potential effects of the transaction on U.S. technological leadership areas affecting U.S. national security.

Following the public furor over the proposed Dubai Ports World deal, CFIUS was amended to cover investments involving critical infrastructure. The intention is to cover cross-border transactions involving energy, technology, shipping, and transportation. Some argue that it may also apply to large U.S. financial institutions, in that they represent an important component of the U.S. monetary system.

Foreign Corrupt Practices Act

Originally passed in 1976 and later amended in 1988, the Foreign Corrupt Practices Act prohibits individuals, firms, and foreign subsidiaries of U.S. firms from paying anything of value to foreign government officials in exchange for obtaining new business or retaining existing contracts. This type of law is unique to the United States. Even though many nations have laws prohibiting bribery of public officials, enforcement often tends to be lax. The act permits so-called facilitation payments to foreign government officials if relatively small amounts of money are required to expedite goods through foreign custom inspections, gain approval for exports, obtain speedy passport approval, and related considerations. Such payments are considered legal according to U.S. law and the laws of countries in which such payments are considered routine (Truitt, 2006).

In 2004, while performing due diligence on Titan Corporation, Lockheed Corporation uncovered a series of bribes that Titan had paid to certain West African government officials to win a telecommunications contract. After Lockheed reported the infraction, Titan was required to pay $28.5 million to resolve the case. In 1996, Lockheed was required to pay $24.8 million for similar violations of the act.

Regulated Industries

In addition to the DoJ and the FTC, a variety of other agencies monitor activities in certain industries, such as commercial banking, railroads, defense, and cable TV. In each industry, the agency is typically responsible for both the approval of M&As and subsequent oversight. Mergers in these industries often take much longer to complete because of the additional filing requirements.

Banking

According to the Bank Merger Act of 1966, any bank merger not challenged by the attorney general within 30 days of its approval by the pertinent regulatory agency cannot be challenged under the Clayton Antitrust Act. Moreover, the Bank Merger Act stated that anticompetitive effects could be offset by a finding that the deal meets the "convenience and needs" of the communities served by the bank. Currently, three agencies review banking mergers. Which agency has authority depends on the parties involved in the transaction. The comptroller of the currency has responsibility for transactions in which the acquirer is a national bank. The Federal Deposit Insurance Corporation oversees mergers where the acquiring or the bank resulting from combining the acquirer and target will be a federally insured, state-chartered bank that operates outside the Federal Reserve System. The third agency is the Board of Governors of the Federal Reserve System (Fed). It has the authority to regulate mergers in which the acquirer or the resulting bank will be a state bank that is also a member of the Federal Reserve System. Although all three agencies conduct their own review, they consider reviews undertaken by the DoJ in their decision-making process.

The upheaval in the capital markets in 2008 saw the Federal Reserve move well beyond its traditional regulatory role when it engineered a merger between commercial bank J. P. Morgan Chase and failing investment bank, Bear Stearns. The financial collapse of Bear Stearns was triggered by a panic among its creditors and customers concerned about the quality of the firm's assets and commitments. The illiquidity of the financial markets in March 2008 was so poor that creditors lost confidence that they could recover their loans by selling the underlying collateral. Consequently, they refused to renew their loans and demanded repayment. Unable to meet these cash demands, Bear Stearns's options were to seek bankruptcy protection or merge with a viable firm. The Fed was concerned that liquidation in bankruptcy would be at "fire sale" prices, which would have created additional stress when the capital markets were already in disarray. The failure of Bear Stearns to pay its obligations could have made its creditors illiquid and forced them to renege on their obligations, thereby creating a chain reaction throughout the financial markets. Case Study 2–4 illustrates the Fed's role in facilitating this transaction.

Case Study 2–4 The Bear Stearns Saga—When Failure Is Not an Option

Prodded by the Fed and the U.S. Treasury Department, J.P. Morgan Chase (JPM), the nation's third largest bank, announced, on March 17, 2008, that it had reached an agreement to buy 100 percent of Bear Stearns's outstanding equity for $2 per share. As one of the nation's larger investment banks, Bear Stearns had a reputation for being aggressive in the financial derivatives markets. Hammered out in two days, the agreement called for the Fed to guarantee up to $30 billion of Bear Stearns's "less liquid" assets. In an effort to avoid what was characterized as a "systemic meltdown," regulatory approval was obtained at a breakneck pace. The Office of the Comptroller of Currency and the Federal Reserve approvals were in place at the time of the announcement. The SEC elected not to review the deal. Federal and state antitrust regulatory approvals were obtained in record time.

   With investors fleeing mortgage-backed securities, the Fed was hoping to prevent any further deterioration in the value of such investments. The concern was that a bankruptcy at Bear Stearns could trigger a run on the assets of other financial services firms. The fear was that the financial crisis that beset Bear Stearns could spread to other companies and ultimately test the Fed's resources after it had said publicly that it would lend up to $200 billion to banks in exchange for their holdings of mortgages.

   Interestingly, Bear Stearns was not that big among investment banks when measured by asset size. However, it was theoretically liable for as much as $10 trillion due to its holdings of such financial derivatives as credit default swaps, in which it agreed to pay lenders in the event of a borrower defaulting. If credit defaults became widespread, Bear Stearns would not have been able to honor its contractual commitments, and the ability of other investment banks in similar positions would have been questioned and the panic could have spread. . .

   With Bear Stearns's shareholders threatening not to approve what they viewed as a "fire sale," JPM provided an alternative bid, within several days of the initial bid, in which it offered $2.4 billion for about 40 percent of the stock, or about $10 per share. In exchange for the higher offer, Bear Stearns agreed to sell 95 million newly issued shares to JPM, giving JPM a 39.5 percent stake and an almost certain majority in any shareholder vote, effectively discouraging any alternative bids. Under the new offer, JPM assumed responsibility for the first $1 billion in asset losses, before the Fed's guarantee of up to $30 billion takes effect.

   For JPM, the deal provides a major entry to the so-called prime brokerage market, which provides financing to hedge funds. The deal also gives the firm a much larger presence in the mortgage securities business. However, the risks are significant. Combining the firms' investment banking businesses could result in a serious loss of talent. The prime brokerage business requires a sizeable investment to upgrade technology. There also are potentially severe cultural issues and management overlap. In addition, JPM is acquiring assets whose future market value is in doubt; however, the Fed's guarantee promises to offset a major portion of future asset-related losses.

Continued

Case Study 2–4 The Bear Stearns Saga—When Failure Is Not an Option — Cont'd

Discussion Questions

1. Why do you believe government regulators encouraged a private firm (J.P. Morgan Chase) to acquire Bear Stearns rather than have the government take control? Do you believe this was the appropriate course of action? Explain your answer.

2. By facilitating the merger, the Fed sent a message to Wall Street that certain financial institutions are "too big to fail." What effect do you think the merger will have on the future investment activities of investment banks? Be specific.

3. Do you believe JPM's management and board were acting in the best interests of their shareholders? Explain your answer.

Communications

The federal agency charged with oversight deferred to the DoJ and the FTC for antitrust enforcement. The Federal Communications Commission (FCC) is an independent U.S. government agency directly responsible to Congress. Established by the 1934 Communications Act, the FCC is charged with regulating interstate and international communication by radio, television, wire, satellite, and cable. The FCC is responsible for the enforcement of such legislation as the Telecommunications Act of 1996. This act is intended to promote competition and reduce regulation while promoting lower prices and higher-quality services (see the Federal Communications Commission website at www.fcc.gov).

In Case Study 2–5, the FCC blocked the proposed combination of EchoStar and Hughes's DirecTV satellite TV operations in late 2002, because it believed the merger would inhibit competition in the market for cable services.

Case Study 2–5 FCC Blocks EchoStar, Hughes Merger

On October 10, 2002, the FCC voted 4–0 to block a proposed $18.8 billion merger of the two largest satellite TV companies in the United States. The commission stated that the merger would create a virtual monopoly that would be particularly harmful to millions of Americans without access to cable television. Living largely in rural areas, such Americans would have no viable alternative to subscribing to a satellite TV hook-up. This was the first time the commission had blocked a major media merger since 1967. The companies were also facing opposition from the Justice Department and 23 states, which were seeking to block the merger.

EchoStar manages the DISH Network, while Hughes operates DirecTV. Together they serve about 18 million subscribers and, if allowed, would have been the largest pay-television service. The two companies argued that the merger was needed to offset competition from cable TV. In presenting the proposal to the commission, the companies offered to maintain uniform pricing nationwide to ease fears they would gouge consumers where no alternative is available.

While expressing disappointment, the two firms pledged to work with the FCC to achieve approval. On November 30, 2002, EchoStar and Hughes offered to sell more assets to help create a viable satellite-television rival to overcome the regulators' opposition. The companies proposed selling 62 frequencies to Cablevision Systems Corporation. Continued opposition from the FCC, Justice Department, and numerous states caused Hughes and EchoStar to terminate the merger on December 14, 2002.

Discussion Questions

1. Why do you believe the regulators continued to oppose the merger after EchoStar and Hughes agreed to help establish a competitor?
2. What alternatives could the regulators have proposed that might have made the merger acceptable?

Railroads

The Surface Transportation Board (STB), the successor to the Interstate Commerce Commission (ICC), governs mergers of railroads. Under the ICC Termination Act of 1995, the STB employs five criteria to determine if a merger should be approved. These criteria include the impact of the proposed transaction on the adequacy of public transportation, the impact on the areas currently served by the carriers involved in the proposed transaction, and the burden of the total fixed charges resulting from completing the transaction. In addition, the interest of railroad employees is considered, as well as whether the transaction would have an adverse impact on competition among rail carriers in regions affected by the merger.

Defense

During the 1990s, the defense industry in the United States underwent substantial consolidation. The consolidation swept the defense industry is consistent with the Department of Defense's (DoD) philosophy that it is preferable to have three or four highly viable defense contractors that could more effectively compete than a dozen weaker contractors. Examples of transactions include the merger of Lockheed and Martin Marietta, Boeing's acquisition of Rockwell's defense and aerospace business, Raytheon's acquisition of the assets of defense-related product lines of Hughes Electronics, Boeing's acquisition of Hughes space and communication business, and Northrop Grumman's takeover of TRW's defense business. However, regulators did prevent the proposed acquisition by Lockheed Martin of Northrop Grumman. Although defense industry mergers are technically subject to current antitrust regulations, the DoJ and FTC have assumed a secondary role to the DoD. As noted previously, efforts by a foreign entity to acquire national security–related assets must be reviewed by the Council on Foreign Investment in the United States.

Other Regulated Industries

The insurance industry is regulated largely at the state level. Acquiring an insurance company normally requires the approval of state government and is subject to substantial financial disclosure by the acquiring company. The acquisition of more than 10 percent of a U.S. airline's shares outstanding is subject to approval of the Federal Aviation Administration. Effective March 8, 2008, the 27-nation European Union and the United States agreed to reduce substantially restrictions on cross-border flights under the Open Skies Act. While the act permits foreign investors to acquire more than 50 percent of the total shares of a U.S. airline, they cannot purchase more than 25 percent of the voting shares. In contrast, U.S. investors are permitted to own as much as 49 percent of the voting shares of EU-nation airlines. The accord allows the European Union to suspend air traffic rights of U.S. airlines if the United States fails to open its domestic market further by the end of 2010.

Public utilities are highly regulated at the state level. Like insurance companies, their acquisition requires state government approval. In 2006, the federal government eliminated the 1935 Public Utility Holding Company Act, which limited consolidation among electric utilities unless they are in geographically contiguous areas. Proponents of the repeal argue that mergers would produce economies of scale, improve financial strength, and increase investment in the nation's aging electricity transmission grid. With more than 3,000 utilities nationwide, the relaxation of regulation has the potential to stimulate future industry consolidation. However, state regulators will continue to have the final say in such matters. Case Study 2–6 illustrates the challenges of satisfying a multiplicity of regulatory bodies.

Case Study 2–6 Exelon Abandons the Acquisition of PSEG Due to State Regulatory Hurdles

On September 14, 2006, Exelon, owner of utilities in Chicago and Philadelphia, announced that it was discontinuing its effort to acquire New Jersey's Public Service Enterprise Group (PSEG) due to an impasse with New Jersey state regulators. If completed, the transaction would have created the nation's largest utility. Exelon had reached an agreement to buy PSEG in December 2004. Exelon's management argued that they could manage PSEG's facilities, especially its nuclear power plants, more efficiently because of their more extensive experience. Exelon's management also argued that improved efficiency would increase the supply of electricity available in New Jersey's competitive wholesale electricity market and ultimately lower prices. The combined companies would have created an energy giant serving 7.1 million electricity customers and 2.2 million natural gas customers in three states.

Exelon offered $600 million in cash, with additional future rate concessions, if New Jersey would agree to approve the acquisition. Both Exelon and PSEG had agreed previously to sell six power plants in New Jersey and Pennsylvania and place 2,600 megawatts of nuclear power capacity under contract for as long as 15 years to win approval from the U.S. Department of Justice and the Federal Energy Regulatory Commission. However, New Jersey regulators felt that, even with these concessions, the combined companies would exert too much pricing power.

The demise of this transaction marked the fourth such utility takeover blocked by state regulatory officials in recent years. In 2003, Exelon was also forced to drop its offer for Dynergy Inc.'s Illinois Power Co after the Illinois legislature rejected the proposal. Kohlberg Kravis Roberts & Co., J.P. Morgan Chase, and Wachovia Corp abandoned an $800 million bid in 2004 for Tucson's UniSource Energy Corp. after the Arizona Corporation Commission required buyers to put in more equity to reduce the amount of debt the utility would have had to carry. Oregon's public utility commission prevented the $1.4 billion sale of Portland General Electric Company in mid-2005, deciding the proposed takeover by Texas Pacific Group would hurt customers.

Discussion Questions

1. Why do you believe that federal regulators accepted the proposed transaction while it was rejected at the state level?
2. Many other nonutility transactions have been approved both at the federal and the state on the basis of the anticipated improved efficiency of the combined firms. Why does the efficiency argument seem to be less convincing to regulators when it is applied to proposed utility mergers?

Environmental Laws

Environmental laws create numerous reporting requirements for both acquirers and target firms. Failure to comply adequately with these laws can result in enormous potential liabilities to all parties involved in a transaction. These laws require full disclosure of the existence of hazardous materials and the extent to which they are being released into the environment, as well as any new occurrences. Such laws include the Clean Water Act (1974), the Toxic Substances Control Act of 1978, the Resource Conservation and Recovery Act (1976), and the Comprehensive Environmental Response, Compensation, and Liability Act (Superfund) of 1980. Additional reporting requirements were imposed in 1986 with the passage of the Emergency Planning and Community Right to Know Act (EPCRA). In addition to EPCRA, several states also passed "right-to-know" laws, such as California's Proposition 65. The importance of state reporting laws has diminished because EPCRA is implemented by the states.

Labor and Benefit Laws

A diligent buyer also must ensure that the target is in compliance with the labyrinth of labor and benefit laws. These laws govern such areas as employment discrimination, immigration law, sexual harassment, age discrimination, drug testing, and wage and hour laws. Labor and benefit laws include the Family Medical Leave Act, the Americans with Disabilities Act, and the Worker Adjustment and Retraining Notification Act (WARN). WARN governs notification before plant closings and requirements to retrain workers.

Benefit Plan Liabilities

Employee benefit plans frequently represent one of the biggest areas of liability to a buyer. The greatest potential liabilities often are found in defined pension benefit plans, postretirement medical plans, life insurance benefits, and deferred compensation plans. Such liabilities arise when the reserve shown on the seller's balance sheet does not accurately indicate the true extent of the future liability. The potential liability from improperly structured benefit plans grows with each new round of legislation starting with the passage of the Employee Retirement Income and Security Act of 1974. Laws affecting employee retirement and pensions were strengthened by additional legislation including the following: the Multi-Employer Pension Plan Amendments Act of 1980, the Retirement Equity Act of 1984, the Single Employer Pension Plan Amendments Act of 1986, the Tax Reform Act of 1986, and the Omnibus Budget Reconciliation Acts of 1987, 1989, 1990, and 1993. Buyers and sellers also must be aware of the Unemployment Compensation Act of 1992, the Retirement Protection Act of 1994, and Statements 87, 88, and 106 of the Financial Accounting Standards Board (Sherman, 2006).

The Pension Protection Act of 2006 places a potentially increasing burden on acquirers of targets with underfunded pension plans. The new legislation requires employers with defined benefit plans to make sufficient contributions to meet a 100 percent funding target and erase funding shortfalls over seven years. Furthermore, the legislation requires employers with so-called at-risk plans to accelerate contributions. "At-risk" plans are those whose pension fund assets cover less than 70 percent of future pension obligations.

Cross-Border Transactions

Transactions involving firms in different countries are complicated by having to deal with multiple regulatory jurisdictions in specific countries or regions. Antitrust regulators historically tended to follow different standards, impose different fee structures from one country to another, and require differing amounts of information for review by the country's regulatory agency. The number of antitrust regulatory authorities globally has grown to 100 from 6 in the early 1990s (*New York Times*, 2001). More antitrust agencies mean more international scrutiny for mergers.

Reflecting the effects of this mishmash of regulations and fee structures, Coca-Cola's 1999 acquisition of Cadbury Schweppes involved obtaining antitrust approval in 40 jurisdictions globally. Fees paid to regulators ranged from $77 in Austria to $2.5 million in Argentina. In contrast, the fee in the United States is limited to $280,000 for transactions whose value exceeds $500 million. Following the failed merger attempt of Alcan Aluminum, Pechiney, and Alusuisse, Jacques Bougie, CEO of Alcan Aluminum, complained that his company had to file for antitrust approval in 16 countries and in eight languages. In addition, his firm had to submit more than 400 boxes of documents and send more than 1 million pages of email due to the different reporting requirements of various countries (Garten, 2000).

The collapse of the General Electric and Honeywell transaction in 2001 underscores how much philosophical differences in the application of antitrust regulations can jeopardize major deals (see Case Study 2–8 at the end of the chapter). Mario Monti, then head of the EU Competition Office, had taken a highly aggressive posture in this transaction. The GE–Honeywell deal was under attack almost from the day it was announced in October 2000. Rival aerospace companies, including United Technologies, Rockwell, Lufthansa, Thales, and Rolls Royce, considered it inimical to their ability to compete. Philosophically, U.S. antitrust regulators focus on the impact of a proposed deal on customers; in contrast, EU antitrust regulators were more concerned about maintaining a level playing field for rivals in the industry. Reflecting this disparate thinking, U.S. antitrust regulators approved the transaction rapidly, concluding that it would have a salutary impact on customers. EU regulators refused to approve the transaction without GE making major concessions, which it was unwilling to do.

While the collapse of the GE–Honeywell transaction reflects the risks of not properly coordinating antitrust regulatory transactions, the 2007 combination of information companies Thomson and Reuters highlights what happens when regulatory authorities are willing to work together. The transaction required approval from antitrust regulators in the U.S., European, and Canadian agencies. Designing a deal acceptable to each country's regulator required extensive cooperation and coordination.

Acutely aware of the problem, the International Competition Network (ICN), representing 103 enforcement agencies in 91 countries, and the 30-country Organization for Economic Cooperation and Development continue their efforts to achieve consistency among the world's antitrust regulatory agencies. Based on the ICN's "Recommended Practices for Merger Notification and Review Procedures," almost one half of the ICN's membership has made changes in their systems to achieve greater conformity with the practices promoted by the ICN (Barnett, 2008). Consequently, many antitrust regulators have moved away from the mechanical application of rigid criteria to a more comprehensive evaluation of competitive conditions in a properly defined market. China was the most recent large country to pass antitrust legislation, which took effect in August 2008.

Things to Remember

The Securities Acts of 1933 and 1934 established the SEC and require that all securities offered to the public must be registered with the government. The registration process requires a description of the company's properties and business, a description of the securities, information about management, and financial statements certified by public accountants. Passed in 1968, the Williams Act consists of a series of amendments to the 1934 Securities Exchange Act intended to provide target firm shareholders with sufficient information and time to adequately assess the value of an acquirer's offer. Any person or firm acquiring 5 percent or more of the stock of a public corporation must file a Schedule 13D disclosing its intentions and business plans with the SEC within 10 days of reaching that percentage ownership threshold.

Federal antitrust laws exist to prevent individual corporations from assuming too much market power. Passed in 1890, the Sherman Act makes illegal such practices as agreements to fix prices and allocate customers among competitors, as well as attempts to monopolize any part of interstate commerce. In an attempt to strengthen the Sherman Act, the Clayton Act was passed in 1914 to make illegal the purchase of stock of another company if their combination results in reduced competition within the industry. Current antitrust law requires prenotification of mergers or acquisitions involving companies of a certain size to allow the FTC and the DoJ sufficient time to challenge business combinations believed to be anticompetitive before they are completed.

Numerous state regulations affect M&As, such as state antitakeover and antitrust laws. A number of industries also are subject to regulatory approval at the federal and state levels. Considerable effort must be made to ensure that a transaction is in full compliance with applicable environmental and employee benefit laws. Failure to do so can result in litigation and fines that could erode the profitability of the combined firms or even result in bankruptcy. Finally, gaining regulatory approval in cross-border transactions can be nightmarish because of the potential for the inconsistent application of antitrust laws, as well as differing reporting requirements, fee structures, and legal jurisdictions.

Chapter Discussion Questions

2–1. What were the motivations for the Federal Securities Acts of 1933 and 1934?

2–2. What was the rationale for the Williams Act?

2–3. What factors do U.S. antitrust regulators consider before challenging a transaction?

2–4. What are the obligations of the acquirer and target firms according to the Williams Act?

2–5. Discuss the pros and cons of federal antitrust laws.

2–6. Why is premerger notification (HSR filing) required by U.S. antitrust regulatory authorities?

2–7. When is a person or firm required to submit a Schedule 13D to the SEC? What is the purpose of such a filing?

2–8. What is the rationale behind state antitakeover legislation?

2–9. Give examples of the types of actions that may be required by the parties to a proposed merger subject to a FTC consent decree.

2–10. How might the growth of the Internet affect the application of current antitrust laws?

2–11. Having received approval from the Justice Department and the Federal Trade Commission, Ameritech and SBC Communications received permission from the Federal Communications Commission to combine to form the nation's largest local telephone company. The FCC gave its approval of the $74 billion transaction, subject to conditions requiring that the companies open their markets to rivals and enter new markets to compete with established local phone companies, in an effort to reduce the cost of local phone calls and give smaller communities access to appropriate phone service. SBC had considerable difficulty in complying with its agreement with the FCC. Between December 2000 and July 2001, SBC paid the U.S. government $38.5 million for failing to provide rivals with adequate access to its network. The government noted that SBC failed repeatedly to make available its network in a timely manner, meet installation deadlines, and notify competitors when their orders were filled. Comment on the fairness and effectiveness of using the imposition of heavy fines to promote government imposed outcomes, rather than free market outcomes.

2–12. In an effort to gain approval of their proposed merger from the FTC, top executives from Exxon Corporation and Mobil Corporation argued that they needed to merge because of the increasingly competitive world oil market. Falling oil prices during much of the late 1990s put a squeeze on oil industry profits. Moreover, giant state-owned oil companies pose a competitive threat because of their access to huge amounts of capital. To offset these factors, Exxon and Mobil argued that they had to combine to achieve substantial cost savings. Why were the Exxon and Mobil executives emphasizing efficiencies as a justification for this merger?

2–13. Assume that you are an antitrust regulator. How important is properly defining the market segment in which the acquirer and target companies compete in determining the potential increase in market power if the two firms are permitted to combine? Explain your answer.

2–14. Comment on whether antitrust policy can be used as an effective means of encouraging innovation. Explain your answer.

2–15. The Sarbanes–Oxley Act has been very controversial. Discuss the arguments for and against the act. Which side do you find more convincing and why?

Answers to these Chapter Discussion Questions are available in the Online Instructor's Guide for instructors using this book.

Chapter Business Cases

Case Study 2–7. Global Financial Exchanges Pose Regulatory Challenges

Background

In mid-2006, the NYSE Group, the operator of the New York Stock Exchange, and Euronext NV, the European exchange operator, announced plans to merge. This merger created the first transatlantic stock and derivatives market. The transaction is valued at $20 billion. Organizationally, NYSE–Euronext would be operated as a holding company and be the world's largest publicly traded exchange company. The combined firms would trade stocks and derivatives through the New York Stock Exchange, on the electronic Euronext Liffe exchange in London, and on the stock exchanges in Paris, Lisbon, Brussels, and Amsterdam.

In recent years, most of the world's major exchanges have gone public and pursued acquisitions. Before this latest deal, the NYSE merged with electronic trading firm Archipelago Holdings, while NASDAQ Stock Market Inc. acquired the electronic trading unit of rival Instinet. This consolidation of exchanges within countries and between countries is being driven by declining trading fees, improving trading information technology, and relaxed cross-border restrictions on capital flows and in part increased regulation in the United States. U.S. regulation, driven by Sarbanes–Oxley, contributed to the transfer of new listings (IPOs) overseas. The best strategy U.S. exchanges have for recapturing lost business is to follow these new listings overseas.

Larger companies that operate across multiple continents also promise to attract more investors to trading in specific stocks and derivatives contracts, which could lead to cheaper, faster, and easier trading. As exchange operators become larger, they can more easily cut operating and processing costs by eliminating redundant or overlapping staff and facilities and, in theory, pass the savings along to investors. Moreover, by attracting more buyers and sellers, the gap between prices at which investors are willing to buy and sell any given stock (i.e., the bid and ask prices) should narrow. The presence of more traders means more people are bidding to buy and sell any given stock. This results in prices that more accurately reflect the true underlying value of the security because of more competition. Furthermore, the cross-border mergers also should make it easier and cheaper for individual investors to buy and sell foreign shares. Currently, the cost and complexity of buying an overseas stock typically limits most U.S. investors to buying mutual funds that invest in foreign stocks. Finally, corporations now can sell their shares on several continents through a single exchange.

Regulatory Challenges

Before these benefits are realized, numerous regulatory hurdles have to be overcome. Even if exchanges merge, they must still abide by local government rules when trading in the shares of a particular company, depending on where the company is listed. Generally, companies are not eager to list on multiple exchanges worldwide because that subjects them to many countries' securities regulations and a bookkeeping nightmare.

At the local level, little would change in how markets are regulated under the new holding company. European companies would list their shares on exchanges owned by the combined companies. These exchanges would still be overseen by individual national regulators, which cooperate but are still technically separate. In the United States, the SEC would still oversee the NYSE but not have a direct say over Europe, except in that it would oversee the parent company, since it would be headquartered in New York.

Whether this will work in practice is another question. EU member states continue to set their own rules for clearing and settlement of trades. If the NYSE and Euronext truly want a more unified and seamless trading system, the process could spark a regulatory war over which rules prevail. Consequently, it may be years before much of the anticipated synergies are realized.

Discussion Questions

1. What key challenges face regulators resulting from the merger of financial exchanges in different countries? How do you see these challenges being resolved?
2. In what way are these regulatory issues similar or different from those confronting the SEC and state regulators and the European Union and individual country regulators?
3. Who should or could regulate global financial markets? Explain your answer.
4. In your opinion, would the merging of financial exchanges increase or decrease international financial stability?

Solutions to these case study questions are found in the Online Instructor's Manual available to instructors using this book.

Case Study 2–8. GE's Aborted Attempt to Merge with Honeywell

Many observers anticipated significant regulatory review because of the size of the transaction and the increase in concentration it would create in the markets served by the two firms. Nonetheless, most believed that, after making some concessions to regulatory authorities, the transaction would be approved, due to its widely perceived benefits. Although the pundits were indeed correct in noting that it would receive close scrutiny, they were completely caught off guard by divergent approaches taken by the U.S. and EU antitrust authorities. U.S regulators ruled that the merger should be approved because of its potential benefits to customers. In marked contrast, EU regulators ruled against the transaction based on its perceived negative impact on competitors.

Background

Honeywell's avionics and engines unit would add significant strength to GE's jet-engine business. The deal would add about 10 cents to GE's 2001 earnings and could eventually result in $1.5 billion in annual cost savings. The purchase also would enable GE to continue its shift away from manufacturing and into services, which already constituted 70 percent of its revenues in 2000 (*Business Week*, 2000b). The best fit is clearly in the combination of the two firms' aerospace businesses. Revenues from these two businesses alone would total $22 billion, combining Honeywell's strength in jet engines and cockpit avionics with GE's substantial business in larger jet engines. As the largest supplier in the aerospace industry, GE could offer airplane manufacturers "one-stop shopping" for everything from engines to complex software systems by cross-selling each other's products to their biggest customers.

Honeywell had been on the block for a number of months before the deal was consummated with GE. Its merger with Allied Signal had not been going well and contributed to deteriorating earnings and a much lower stock price. Honeywell's shares had declined in price by more than 40 percent since its acquisition of Allied Signal. While the euphoria surrounding the deal in late 2000 lingered into the early months of 2001, rumblings from the European regulators began to create an uneasy feeling among GE's and Honeywell's management.

Regulatory Hurdles Slow the Process

Mario Monti, the European competition commissioner at that time, expressed concern about possible "conglomerate effects" or the total influence a combined GE and Honeywell would wield in the aircraft industry. He was referring to GE's perceived ability to expand its influence in the aerospace industry through service initiatives. GE's service offerings help differentiate it from others at a time when the prices of many industrial parts are under pressure from increased competition, including low-cost manufacturers overseas. In a world in which manufactured products are becoming increasingly commoditylike, the true winners are those able to differentiate their product offering. GE and Honeywell's European competitors complained to the EU regulatory commission that GE's extensive service offering would give it entrée into many more points of contact among airplane manufacturers, from communications systems to the expanded line of spare parts GE would be able to supply. This so-called range effect or portfolio power is a relatively new legal doctrine that has not been tested in transactions the size of this one (Murray, 2001).

U.S. Regulators Approve the Deal

On May 3, 2001, the U.S. Department of Justice approved the buyout after the companies agreed to sell Honeywell's helicopter engine unit and take other steps to protect competition. The U.S. regulatory authorities believed that the combined companies could sell more products to more customers and therefore could realize improved efficiencies, although it would not hold a dominant market share in any particular market. Thus, customers would benefit from GE's greater range of products and possibly lower prices, but they still could shop elsewhere if they chose. The U.S. regulators expressed little concern that bundling of products and services could hurt customers, since buyers can choose from among a relative handful of viable suppliers.

Understanding the EU Position

To understand the European position, it is necessary to comprehend the nature of competition in the European Union. France, Germany, and Spain spent billions subsidizing their aerospace industry over the years. The GE–Honeywell deal has been attacked by their European rivals from Rolls-Royce and Lufthansa to French avionics manufacturer Thales. Although the European Union imported much of its antitrust law from the United States, the antitrust law doctrine evolved in fundamentally different ways. In Europe, the main goal of antitrust law is to guarantee that all companies be able to compete on an equal playing field. The implication is that the European Union is just as concerned about how a transaction affects rivals as it is consumers. Complaints from competitors are taken more seriously in Europe, whereas in the United States it is the impact on consumers that constitutes the litmus test. Europeans accepted the legal concept of "portfolio power," which argues that a firm may achieve an unfair advantage over its competitors by bundling goods and services. Also, in Europe, the European Commission's Merger Task Force can prevent a merger without taking a company to court. By removing this judicial remedy, the European Union makes it possible for the regulators, who are political appointees, to be biased.

GE Walks away from the Deal

The EU authorities continued to balk at approving the transaction without major concessions from the participants, concessions that GE believed would render the deal unattractive. On June 15, 2001, GE submitted its final offer to the EU regulators in a last-ditch attempt to breathe life into the moribund deal. GE knew that, if it walked away, it could continue as it had before the deal was struck, secure in the knowledge that its current portfolio of businesses offered substantial revenue growth or profit potential. Honeywell clearly would fuel such growth, but it made sense to GE's management and shareholders only if it would be allowed to realize potential synergies between the GE and Honeywell businesses.

GE said it was willing to divest Honeywell units with annual revenue of $2.2 billion, including regional jet engines, air-turbine starters, and other aerospace products. Anything more would jeopardize the rationale for the deal. Specifically, GE was unwilling to agree not to bundle (i.e., sell a package of components and services at a single price) its products and services when selling to customers. Another stumbling block was the GE Capital Aviation Services unit, the airplane-financing arm of GE Capital. The EU Competition Commission argued that that this unit would use its influence as one of the world's largest purchasers of airplanes to pressure airplane manufacturers into using GE products. The commission seemed to ignore that GE had only an 8 percent share of the global airplane leasing market and would therefore seemingly lack the market power the commission believed it could exert.

On July 4, 2001, the European Union vetoed the GE purchase of Honeywell, marking it the first time a proposed merger between two U.S. companies has been blocked solely by European regulators. Having received U.S. regulatory approval, GE could ignore the EU decision and proceed with the merger as long as it would be willing to forego sales in Europe. GE decided not to appeal the decision to the EU Court of First Instance (the second highest court in the European Union), knowing that it could take years to resolve the decision, and withdrew its offer to merge with Honeywell.

The GE–Honeywell Legacy

On December 15, 2005, a European court upheld the European regulator's decision to block the transaction, although the ruling partly vindicated GE's position. The European Court of First Instance said regulators were in error in assuming without sufficient evidence that a combined GE–Honeywell could crush competition in several markets. However, the court demonstrated that regulators would have to provide data to support either their approval or rejection of mergers by ruling on July 18, 2006, that regulators erred in approving the combination of Sony BMG in 2004. In this instance, regulators failed to provide sufficient data to document their decision. These decisions affirm that the European Union needs strong economic justification to overrule cross-border deals. GE and Honeywell, in filing the suit, said that their appeal had been made to clarify European rules with an eye toward future deals, as they had no desire to resurrect the deal.

Discussion Questions

1. What are the important philosophical differences between U.S. and EU antitrust regulators? Explain the logic underlying these differences. To what extent are these differences influenced by political rather than economic considerations? Explain your answer.

2. This is the first time that a foreign regulatory body prevented a deal involving only U.S. firms from occurring. What are the long-term implications, if any, of this precedent?

3. What were the major stumbling blocks between GE and the EU regulators? Why do you think these were stumbling blocks? Do you think the EU regulators were justified in their position?

4. Do you think that competitors are using antitrust to their advantage? Explain your answer.

5. Do you think the EU regulators would have taken a different position if the deal had involved a less visible firm than General Electric? Explain your answer.

Solutions to these case study questions are found in the Online Instructor's Manual available to instructors using this book.

3

The Corporate Takeover Market

Common Takeover Tactics, Antitakeover Defenses, and Corporate Governance

Treat a person as he is, and he will remain as he is. Treat him as he could be, and he will become what he should be.

—Jimmy Johnson

Inside M&A: InBev Buys an American Icon for $52 Billion

For many Americans, Budweiser is synonymous with American beer and American beer is synonymous with Anheuser-Busch (AB). Ownership of the American icon changed hands on July 14, 2008, when beer giant Anheuser Busch agreed to be acquired by Belgian brewer InBev for $52 billion in an all-cash deal. The combined firms would have annual revenue of about $36 billion and control about 25 percent of the global beer market and 40 percent of the U.S. market. The purchase is the most recent in a wave of consolidation in the global beer industry. The consolidation reflected an attempt to offset rising commodity costs by achieving greater scale and purchasing power. While likely to generate cost savings of about $1.5 billion annually by 2011, InBev stated publicly that the transaction is more about the two firms being complementary rather than overlapping.

The announcement marked a reversal from AB's position the previous week when it said publicly that the InBev offer undervalued the firm and subsequently sued InBev for "misleading statements" it had allegedly made about the strength of its financing. To court public support, AB publicized its history as a major benefactor in its hometown area (St. Louis, Missouri). The firm also argued that its own long-term business plan would create more shareholder value than the proposed deal. AB also investigated the possibility of acquiring the half of Grupo Modelo, the Mexican brewer of Corona beer, which it did not already own to make the transaction too expensive for InBev.

While it publicly professed to want a friendly transaction, InBev wasted no time in turning up the heat. The firm launched a campaign to remove Anheuser's board and replace it with its own slate of candidates, including a Busch family member. However, AB was under substantial pressure from major investors, including Warren Buffet, to agree to the deal since the firm's stock had been lackluster during the preceding several years. In an effort to gain additional shareholder support, InBev raised its initial $65 bid to $70. To eliminate concerns over its ability to finance the deal, InBev agreed to fully document its credit sources rather than rely on the more traditional but less certain credit commitment letters. In an effort to placate AB's board, management, and the myriad politicians who railed against the proposed transaction, InBev agreed to name the new firm Anheuser-Busch InBev and keep Budweiser as the new firm's flagship brand and St. Louis as its North American headquarters. In addition, AB would be given two seats on the board, including August A. Busch IV, AB's CEO and patriarch of the firm's founding family. InBev also announced that AB's 12 U.S. breweries would remain open.

Chapter Overview

The corporate takeover has been dramatized in Hollywood as motivated by excessive greed, reviled in the press as a job destroyer, hailed as a means of dislodging incompetent management, and often heralded by shareholders as a source of windfall gains. The reality is that corporate takeovers may be a little of all of these things. The purpose of this chapter is to discuss the effectiveness of commonly used tactics to acquire a company and evaluate the effectiveness of various takeover defenses. The market in which such takeover tactics and defenses are employed is called the *corporate takeover market*, which serves two important functions in a free market economy. First, it facilitates the allocation of resources to sectors in which they can be used most efficiently. Second, it serves as a mechanism for disciplining underperforming corporate managers. By replacing such managers through hostile takeover attempts or proxy fights, the corporate takeover market can help to promote good corporate governance practices.

There is no universally accepted definition of corporate governance. Traditionally, the goal of corporate governance has been viewed as the protection of shareholder rights. More recently, the goal has expanded to include more corporate stakeholders, including customers, employees, the government, lenders, communities, regulators, and suppliers. For our purposes, corporate governance is defined as factors internal and external to the firm, which interact to protect the rights of corporate stakeholders. In the final analysis, corporate governance is about leadership and accountability. For leaders to be held accountable requires full disclosure of accurate and complete information regarding a firm's performance.

Figure 3–1 illustrates the factors affecting corporate governance, including the corporate takeover market. Following a discussion of these factors, the corporate takeover market is discussed in more detail in terms of commonly used takeover tactics and defenses. Finally, case studies at the end of the chapter provide an excellent illustration of how takeover tactics are used in a hostile takeover to penetrate a firm's defenses. Major chapter segments include the following:

- Factors Affecting Corporate Governance
- Alternative Takeover Tactics in the Corporate Takeover Market
- Developing a Bidding or Takeover Strategy Decision Tree
- Alternative Takeover Defenses in the Corporate Takeover Market
- Things to Remember

A chapter review (including practice questions) is available in the file folder entitled Student Study Guide contained on the CD-ROM accompanying this book. The CD-ROM also contains a Learning Interactions Library, enabling students to test their knowledge of this chapter in a "real-time" environment.

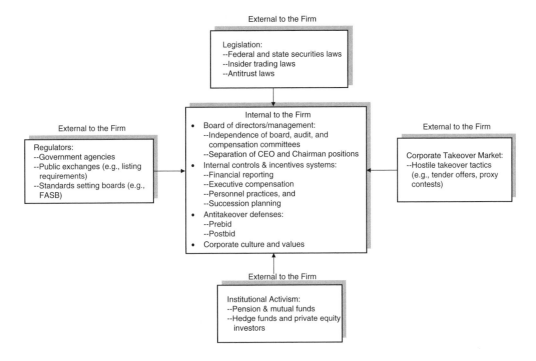

FIGURE 3–1 Factors affecting corporate governance.

Factors Affecting Corporate Governance

Alternative Models of Corporate Governance

The ultimate goal of a successful corporate governance system should be to hold those in power accountable for their actions. Where capital markets are liquid, investors discipline bad managers by selling their shares. This situation is referred to as the *market model of corporate governance*. Where capital markets are illiquid, bad managers are disciplined by those owning large blocks of stock in the firm or those whose degree of control is disproportionate to their ownership position. The latter situation (called the *control model*) may develop through the concentration of shares having multiple voting rights in the hands of a few investors. See Table 3–1 for the characteristics of these two common models of corporate governance.

This chapter focuses on governance under the market model, while the control model is discussed in more detail in Chapter 10, which deals with analyzing privately and family-owned firms.

Table 3–1   Alternative Models of Corporate Governance

Market Model Is Applicable When	Control Model Is Applicable When
Capital markets are highly liquid	Capital markets are illiquid
Equity ownership is widely dispersed	Ownership is heavily concentrated
Board members are largely independent	Board members largely are "insiders"
Ownership and control are separate	Ownership and control overlap
Financial disclosure is high	Financial disclosure is limited
Shareholders focus more on short-term gains	Shareholder focus more on long-term gains

The market model relies on two basic principles. First, the incentives of managers should be aligned with the goals of the shareholders and other primary stakeholders. Second, the firm's financial condition should be sufficiently transparent to enable shareholders and other stakeholders to evaluate the performance of managers based on public information. Accountability is achieved through market forces, regulation, or some combination of the two. What follows is a discussion of those factors internal and external to the firm that affect corporate governance.

Factors Internal to the Firm

Corporate governance is affected by the integrity and professionalism of the firm's board of directors, as well as the effectiveness of the firm's internal controls and incentive systems, takeover defenses, and corporate culture and values.

Board of Directors and Management

Boards serve as advisors to the CEO and review the quality of recommendations received by the CEO from corporate management. Boards also hire, fire, and set compensation for a company's chief executive, who runs the daily operations of the firm. Moreover, boards are expected to oversee management, corporate strategy, and the company's financial reports to shareholders. The board's role also is to resolve instances where decisions made by managers (as agents of the shareholder) are not in the best interests of the shareholder (i.e., the agency problem). Board members, who are also employees or family members, may be subject to conflicts of interest, which may cause them to act in ways not necessarily in the stakeholders' interest. Some observers often argue that boards should be dominated by independent directors and that the CEO and chairman of the board should be separate positions. Byrd and Hickman (1992) provide evidence that monitoring of management by independent board members can contribute to better acquisition decisions.

Operationally, the board's role in ensuring good corporate governance practices is performed by board committees. The committee structure is designed to take advantage of the particular background and experience of certain members. Committees common to public companies include audit, compensation, governance, nominating, and so-called special committees. Audit committees usually consist of three independent directors charged with providing oversight in areas related to internal controls, risk management, financial reporting, and audit activities. Compensation committees also consist of three independent directors, who design, review, and implement directors' and executives' compensation plans. Also consisting of three independent members, the nominating committee's purpose is to monitor issues pertaining to the recommendation, nomination, and election activities of directors. Consisting of both independent and executive (i.e., those who may also be company employees) directors, the role of the governance committee is to advise, review, and approve management strategic plans, decisions, and actions in effectively managing the firm. Special committees may be formed to assist the board in executing oversight on financing, budgeting, investment, mergers, and acquisitions. Special committees may include both independent and executive board members.

Hermalin (2006); Huson, Parrino, and Starks (2001); and Dahya and McConnell (2001) documented the following trends with respect to board composition and compensation. First, the proportion of independent directors has steadily increased in the United States and other countries. The average percentage of outside directors increased from 35 percent in 1989 to 61 percent in 1999. Second, the use of incentive compensation for outside directors increased significantly. Of firms reporting to a Conference Board

Survey, 84 percent used stock-based compensation for outside directors in 1997 versus 6 percent in 1989. Unfortunately, empirical studies have not consistently demonstrated that such proposals improve shareholder wealth (*Economic Report to the President*, 2003, p. 90).

In the United States, the standard of review for a director's conduct in an acquisition begins with the ***business judgment rule***. Directors are expected to conduct themselves in a manner that could reasonably be seen as being in the best interests of the shareholders. This "rule" is a presumption with which the courts will not interfere, or second guess, business decisions made by directors. However, when a party to the transaction is seen as having a conflict of interest, the business judgment rule does not apply. In such circumstances, the director's actions are subject to the so-called fairness test, consisting of fair dealing (i.e., a fair process) and a fair price. An example of a fair process would be when a seller does not favor one bidder over another. An example of a fair price would be when the seller accepts the highest price offered for the business. However, the determination of what constitutes the highest price may be ambiguous when the purchase price consists of stock (whose value will fluctuate) rather than cash.

So-called bright-line standards have been enacted by the Securities and Exchange Commission and the New York Stock Exchange (NYSE), requiring that a majority of directors and board members sitting on key board committees, such as compensation and audit, be independent. According to the NYSE, directors having received more than $100,000 over the prior three years from a company cannot be considered independent. For the SEC, the amount is $60,000. The NYSE also requires that firms explain even nonfinancial relationships to shareholders so that they may determine if such relationships should be viewed as material and, if so, whether they should disqualify the director from being considered independent.

In a survey of 586 corporate directors from 378 private and 161 public companies, McKinsey & Company noted that boards that are highly influential in creating shareholder value are distinguished less by whether they are privately or publicly held and more by their strategic focus and relationship with management. Specifically, the most influential boards focus on long-term strategy. Highly influential boards also have substantial expertise in how the firm operates, access to many levels of management, and engage management in substantive debates about long-term strategy (McKinsey & Co., 2008).

Coles, Daniel, and Naveen (2008) and Boone, Casaeres Field, and Karpoff (2007) show that complex firms have a greater need for advisors, larger boards, and more outside directors. Recognizing that excessive monitoring of management can restrict the firm's tactical flexibility, Linck, Netter, and Yang (2008) find that public firms structure their boards in ways consistent with the costs and benefits of the monitoring and advisory roles of the board. Adams and Ferreira (2007) argue that management-friendly (i.e., less independent) boards often can more effectively advise and monitor the CEO, thereby creating shareholder value, than more independent boards, which often are less knowledgeable about the firm's operations.

Internal Controls and Incentive Systems

Tax rules and accounting standards in the United States send mixed signals. On the one hand, the U.S. tax code requires compensation above $1 million to be "performance based" to be tax deductible. This encourages firms to pay executives with stock options rather than cash. In contrast, firms are now required to charge the cost of options against current earnings, as opposed to their ability to defer such costs in the past. This has a dampening effect on the widespread use of options. Moreover, the current practice of fixed strike or exercise prices (i.e., prices at which option holders can buy company stock) for options led to enormous profits simply because the overall stock market rose even though the firm's performance lagged the overall market.

By eliminating such tax rules, boards would be encouraged to design compensation plans that reward exceptional performance rather than the exploitation of tax rules. Furthermore, linking option strike prices to the performance of the company's stock price relative to the stock market would ensure that increases in the stock market do not benefit managers whose companies are underperforming. Indexing option strike prices would also reduce the incentive to reset the strike price of existing options when a stock price declines and renders current options worthless.

Another way to align corporate managers' interests with those of other stakeholders is for managers to own a significant portion of the firm's outstanding stock or for the manager's ownership of the firm's stock to constitute a substantial share of his or her personal wealth. The proportion of shares owned by managers of public firms grew since 1935, from an average of 12.9 percent to an average of 21.1 percent in 1998 (*Economic Report to the President*, 2003, p. 86). There appears to have been little change in this ownership percentage in recent years. An alternative to concentrating ownership in management is for one or more shareholders who are not managers to accumulate a significant block of voting shares. Corporations having outside shareholders with large blocks of stock may be easier to acquire, thereby increasing management's risk of being ousted due to poor performance. While concentrating stock ownership may contribute to minimizing agency problems, there is evidence that management may become more entrenched as the level of stock ownership in the hands of executives reaches 30–50 percent. Moreover, the quality of earnings may also deteriorate as decisions are made to boost short-term results to maximize profit earned on exercising stock options (Pergola, 2005).

There is some evidence that the composition of a manager's compensation may affect what he or she is willing to pay for an acquisition. The share prices of acquirers whose managers' total compensation includes a large amount of equity tend to exhibit positive responses to the announcement of an acquisition. In contrast, the share price of those firms whose managers' compensation is largely cash based display negative responses (Dutta, Iskandar-Dutta, and Raman, 2001).

Antitakeover Defenses

Takeover defenses may be employed by a firm's management and board to gain leverage in negotiating with a potential suitor. Alternatively, such practices may be used to solidify current management's position within the firm. The range of such defenses available to a target's management is discussed in some detail later in this chapter.

Corporate Culture and Values

Regulations, monitoring systems, and incentive plans are only part of the answer to improved corporate governance. While internal systems and controls are important, good governance is also a result of instilling the employee culture with appropriate core values and behaviors. Setting the right tone and direction comes from the board of directors and senior management and their willingness to behave in a manner consistent with what they demand from other employees. One can only speculate as to the degree to which the scandal that rocked Hewlett Packard in late 2006 undermined the firm's internal culture. The scandal made it clear that some members of top management sanctioned internal spying on the firm's board members and illegally gaining access to their private information. Such missteps understandably drastically reduce employee confidence in senior management's pronouncements about desired corporate values and behaviors. See Chapter 6 for a more detailed discussion of corporate culture.

Factors External to the Firm

Federal and state legislation, the court system, regulators, institutional activists, and the corporate takeover market all play an important role in maintaining good corporate governance practices.

Legislation and the Legal System

As noted in Chapter 2, the basis of modern securities legislation can be found with the Securities Acts of 1933 and 1934, which created the SEC and delegated to it the task of writing and enforcing securities regulations. The U.S. Congress has also transferred some of the enforcement task to public stock exchanges, such as the New York Stock Exchange. Such exchanges operate under SEC oversight as self-regulatory organizations. Furthermore, the SEC has delegated certain responsibilities for setting and maintaining accounting standards to the Financial Accounting Standards Board. Under the Sarbanes–Oxley Act, the SEC oversees the new Public Company Accounting Oversight Board, whose primary task is to develop, maintain, and enforce the standards that guide auditors in monitoring and certifying corporate financial reports. State legislation also has a significant impact on governance practices by requiring corporate charters to define the responsibilities of boards and managers with respect to shareholders.

Regulators

Regulators, such as the FTC, SEC, and DoJ, can discipline firms with inappropriate governance practices through formal and informal investigations, lawsuits, and settlements. Data suggest that the announcement of a regulatory investigation punishes firms, with firms subject to investigations suffering an average decline in share prices of 6 percent around the announcement date (Hirschey, 2003). In mid-2003, the SEC approved new listing standards for the NYSE that would require many lucrative, stock-based pay plans to be subject to a vote by shareholders. This means that investors in more than 6,200 companies listed on the NYSE, NASDAQ, and other major markets can exercise significant control over CEO pay packages. Effective January 1, 2007, the SEC implemented additional disclosure requirements about CEO pay and perks. The new rules require companies to disclose perks whose value exceeds $10,000. In contrast, the old rules required disclosure of perks valued at more than $50,000 (White and Lublin, 2007).

Institutional Activists

Even if shareholders vote overwhelmingly in favor of specific resolutions to amend a firm's charter, boards need not implement these resolutions, as most are simply advisory only. Managers often need to be able to manage the business without significant outside interference from single-agenda dissident shareholders. It is analogous to the distinction between pure democracy in which everyone has a vote in changing a law and a representative democracy in which only elected representatives vote on new legislation. Reflecting this distinction, shareholder proposals tend to be nonbinding, because in many states, including Delaware, it is the firm's board representing the shareholders and not the shareholders that must initiate charter amendments.

Mutual Funds and Pension Funds   Activist efforts in prior years by institutional investors, particularly mutual funds and pension funds, often failed to achieve significant benefits for shareholders (Karpoff, 2001; Romano, 2001; Black, 1998; Gillan and Starks, 2007). During the 1970s and 1980s, institutional ownership of public firms increased substantially, with the percent of equity held by institutions at 49.1 percent in 2001 versus 31 percent in 1970 (*Federal Reserve Bulletin*, 2003, p. 33). In the 1980s, pension funds, mutual funds, and insurance firms were often passive investors, showing little interest in matters of corporate governance. While pension funds became more aggressive in the 1990s, the Investment Company Act of 1940 restricts the ability of institutions to discipline corporate management. For example, to achieve diversification, mutual funds are limited in the amount they can invest in any one firm's outstanding stock. State regulations often restrict the share of a life insurance or property casualty company's assets that can be invested in stock to as little as 2 percent. Nevertheless, institutional investors that have huge portfolios can be very effective in demanding governance changes.

Despite these limitations, there is evidence that institutions are taking increasingly aggressive stands against management. TIAA-CREF, the New York-based investment company that manages pension plans for teachers, colleges, universities, and research institutions, believes it has a responsibility to push for better corporate governance as well as stock performance. The Louisiana Teachers Retirement System brought legal pressure to bear on Siebel Systems Inc., resulting in a settlement in mid-2003 in which the software company agreed to make changes in its board and disclose how it sets executive compensation, which has been criticized as excessive. In a case brought against some officers and directors of Sprint Corp. in 2003 by labor unions and pension funds, Sprint settled by agreeing to governance changes that require at least two thirds of its board members to be independent.

Following the SEC requirement in late 2004 to make their proxy votes public, mutual funds are increasingly challenging management on such hot-button issues as antitakeover defenses, lavish severance benefits for CEOs, and employee stock option accounting. A study of the 24 largest mutual funds in the United States indicated that the American Funds, T. Rowe Price, and Vanguard voted against management and for key shareholder proposals, in 2004, 70, 61, and 51 percent of the time, respectively, sharply higher than in 2003. However, industry leader Fidelity voted against management only 33 percent of the time. Voting against management could become more problematic as some mutual funds manage both retirement plans and increasingly a host of outsourcing services from payroll to health benefits for their business clients (Farzad, 2006; Davis and Kim, 2007).

Kini, Kracaw, and Mian (2004) document a decline in the number of executives serving as both chairman of the board and chief executive officer from about 91 percent during the 1980s to 58 percent during the 1990s. This general decline may be attributable to increased pressure from shareholder activists (Brickley, Coles, and Jarrell, 1997; Goyal and Park, 2002). In some instances, CEOs are willing to negotiate with activists rather than face a showdown in an annual shareholders meeting. Activists are finding that they may avoid the expense of a full blown proxy fight by simply threatening to withhold their votes in support of a CEO or management proposal. Institutional investors may choose to express their dissatisfaction by abstaining rather than casting a "no" vote, although in some instances, they may have the choice only of abstaining or voting affirmatively. By abstaining, institutional investors can indicate their dissatisfaction with a CEO or a firm's policy without jeopardizing future underwriting or M&A business for the institution. In early 2004, in an unprecedented expression of no confidence, 43 percent of the votes cast were in opposition to the continuation of Disney chairman of the board and chief executive officer Michael Eisner as chairman of the board. While he had still received a majority of the votes, the Disney board voted to strip Eisner of his role as chairman of the board. In late 2004, Michael Eisner announced that he would retire at the end of his current contract in 2006.

Activist strategies in which votes are withheld are likely to have a greater impact on removing board members in the future, as more firms adopt majority voting policies, which require directors to be reelected by a majority of the votes cast. Under the traditional voting system, votes withheld were not counted and such activity was largely a symbolic gesture. With 53 percent of all S&P 500 firms having adopted majority voting as of early 2007, directors are less likely to get majority approval (Whitehouse, 2007). For example, traditionally, if 40 percent of votes were withheld, a director receiving 60 percent of the votes counted would win, even though she had received only 36 percent (i.e., .6 × (1 − 0.4)) of total possible votes (including those withheld). Under the majority voting system in which withheld votes are counted, the same director would not win, having received (i.e., 36 percent) less than a majority of total possible votes.

The importance of institutional ownership in maintaining good governance practices is evident in the highly concentrated ownership of firms in Europe. Ownership in U.S. companies tends to be dispersed, which makes close monitoring of board and management practices difficult. European companies are characterized by concentrated ownership. While this ownership structure facilitates closer operational monitoring and removal of key managers, it also enables the controlling shareholder to extract certain benefits at the expense of other shareholders (Coffee, 2005). Controlling shareholders may have their company purchase products and services at above-market prices directly from another firm they own. European firms Parmalat and Hollinger are examples of firms whose principal shareholders exploited their firms.

Hedge Funds and Private Equity Firms   In recent years, hedge funds and private equity investors have assumed increasing roles as activist investors, with much greater success than other institutional investors have in previous years. In 2006, a shareholder revolt led by New York-based Knight Vinke Asset Management prompted the $9.6 billion sale of the underperforming Dutch conglomerate VNU to a group of private equity investors. In 2007, U.S. hedge fund Trian prompted soft drink and candy giant Cadbury Schweppes to split the firm in two after taking a 3 percent ownership position and threatening a proxy contest.

Using a sample of 236 activist hedge funds and 1,059 instances of activism from 2001 to 2006, Brav et al. (2006) document that activist hedge funds are successful (or partially so) about two thirds of the time in their efforts to change a firm's strategic, operational, or financial strategies. While seldom seeking control (with ownership stakes averaging about 9 percent) and most often nonconfrontational, the authors document an approximate 7 percent abnormal return around the date of the announcement that the hedge fund is initiating some form of action. Hedge fund activists tend to rely on cooperation from management or other shareholders to promote their agendas. The authors argue that activist hedge funds occupy a middle ground between internal monitoring by large shareholders and external monitoring by corporate raiders. Clifford (2007) and Klein and Zur (2009) also found that hedge fund activism can generate significant abnormal financial returns to shareholders.

The relative success of hedge funds as activists is attributable to their use of managers highly motivated by the prospect of financial gain, who manage large pools of relatively unregulated capital. Because they are not currently subject to the regulation governing mutual funds and pension funds, they can hold highly concentrated positions in small numbers of firms. Moreover, hedge funds are not limited by the same conflicts of interests that afflict mutual funds and pension funds, because they have few financial ties to the management of the firms whose shares they own.

Hedge funds as activist investors tend to have the greatest impact on financial returns to shareholders when they prod management to put a company up for sale. However, their impact rapidly dissipates when the company is unsuccessful. Greenwood and Schor (2007) found that, under such circumstances, there is little change in the firm's share price or financial performance during the next 18 months, even if the firm follows the activist's recommendations and buys back shares or adds new directors. However, firms once targeted by activists are more likely to be acquired.

Corporate Takeover Market

Changes in corporate control can occur because of a hostile (i.e., bids contested by the target's board and management) or friendly takeover of a target firm or because of a proxy contest initiated by dissident shareholders. When mechanisms internal to the firm governing management control are relatively weak, there is significant empirical evidence that the corporate takeover market acts as a "court of last resort" to discipline inappropriate management behavior (Kini, Kracaw, and Mian, 2004). In contrast, when a firm's internal governance mechanisms are strong, the role of the takeover threat as a disciplinary factor is lessened. Moreover, the disciplining effect of a takeover threat on a firm's management can be reinforced when it is paired with a large shareholding by an institutional investor (Cremers and Nair, 2005). Offenberg (2008), in a sample of nearly 8,000 acquisitions between 1980 and 1999, found evidence that the corporate takeover market and boards of directors discipline managers of larger firms better than managers of smaller firms.

Several theories have evolved as to why managers may resist a takeover attempt. The **management entrenchment theory** suggests that managers use a variety of takeover defenses to ensure their longevity with the firm. Hostile takeovers or the threat of such takeovers have historically played a useful role in maintaining good corporate governance by removing bad managers and installing better ones (Morck, Shleifer, and Vishny, 1988). Indeed, there is evidence of frequent management turnover even if a takeover attempt is defeated, as takeover targets are often poor financial performers *(Economic Report to the President,* 2003, p. 81). An alternative viewpoint is the **shareholders' interest theory**, which suggests that management resistance to proposed takeovers is a good bargaining strategy to increase the purchase price to the benefit of the target firm's shareholders (Franks and Mayer, 1996; Schwert, 2000).

Proxy contests are attempts by a dissident group of shareholders to gain representation on a firm's board of directors or to change management proposals. Proxy contests addressing issues other than board representation do not bind a firm's board of directors. However, there is evidence that boards are becoming more responsive. While nonbinding, boards implemented 41 percent of shareholder proposals for majority voting in 2004 versus only 22 percent in 1997, possibly reflecting fallout from the Enron-type scandals in 2001 and 2002. A board was more likely to adopt a shareholder proposal if a competitor had adopted a similar plan (Ertimur, Ferri, and Stubben, 2008). Even unsuccessful proxy contests often lead to a change in management, a restructuring of the firm, or investor expectations that the firm ultimately will be acquired.

As of the printing of this book, the U.S. Securities and Exchange Commission is considering rule changes that would give shareholders of firms whose market value exceeds $700 million greater say in nominating company directors. Under the proposed rules, investors owning at least one percent of a firm's equity would be allowed to nominate up to one-fourth of the firm's board in corporate proxy statements which are then distributed to the firm's shareholders by the company. Under current rules, investors wanting to submit their own candidates have to mail their nominees to shareholders at their own expense. The SEC also is considering limiting the ability of boards to ignore shareholder proposals.

Many firms stripped away their takeover defenses to satisfy shareholder demands for better governance practices. For example, in 2006, Thomson Financial data indicates that only 118 companies adopted poison pills (i.e., plans giving shareholders the right to buy stock below the current market price) compared to an average of 234 annually throughout the 1990s. To explain these developments in more detail, the remainder of this chapter describes the common takeover tactics and antitakeover defenses that characterize the corporate takeover market.

Alternative Takeover Tactics in the Corporate Takeover Market

As noted in Chapter 1, takeovers may be classified as friendly or hostile. Friendly takeovers may be viewed as ones in which a negotiated settlement is possible without the acquirer resorting to such aggressive tactics as the bear hug, proxy contest, or tender offer. A *bear hug* involves the mailing of a letter containing an acquisition proposal to the board of directors of a target company without prior warning and demanding a rapid decision. A *proxy contest* is an attempt by dissident shareholders to obtain representation on the board of directors or to change a firm's bylaws by obtaining the right to vote on behalf of other shareholders. A *hostile tender offer* is a takeover tactic in which the acquirer bypasses the target's board and management and goes directly to the target's shareholders with an offer to purchase their shares. Unlike a merger in which the minority must agree to the terms of the agreement negotiated by the board, once the majority of the firms' shareholders (i.e., 50.1 percent or more) approve the proposal, the tender offer specifically allows for minority shareholders. In a traditional merger, minority shareholders are said to be frozen out of their positions. This majority approval requirement is intended to prevent minority shareholders from stopping a merger until they are paid a premium over the purchase price agreed to by the majority.

Following the tender offer, the target firm becomes a partially owned subsidiary of the acquiring company. In some instances, the terms of the transaction may be *crammed down* or imposed on the minority. This is achieved by the parent firm merging the partially owned subsidiary that resulted from the failure of the tender offer to get substantially all of the target firm's shares into a new, wholly owned subsidiary. Alternatively, the acquirer may decide not to acquire 100 percent of the target's stock. In this case, the minority is subject to a *freeze-out* or squeeze-out, in which the remaining shareholders are dependent on the decisions made by the majority shareholders. See Chapter 11 for a more detailed discussion of these terms.

The Friendly Approach

Friendly takeovers involve the initiation by the potential acquirer of an informal dialogue with the target's top management. In a friendly takeover, the acquirer and target reach agreement on key issues early in the process. These key issues usually include the combined businesses' long-term strategy, how the combined businesses will be operated in the short term, and who will be in key management positions. A *standstill agreement* often is negotiated, in which the acquirer agrees not to make any further investments in the target's stock for a stipulated period. This compels the acquirer to pursue the acquisition only on friendly terms, at least for the time period covered by the agreement. It also permits negotiations to proceed without the threat of more aggressive tactics, such as a tender offer or a proxy contest.

According to Thompson Reuters, the vast majority of transactions were classified as friendly during the 1990s. However, this was not always the case. The 1970s and early

1980s were characterized by blitzkrieg-style takeovers. Hostile takeovers of U.S. firms peaked at about 14 percent in the 1980s, before dropping to a low of about 4 percent in the 1990s. The decline in hostile takeovers can be partly attributable to the soaring stock market in the 1990s, as target shareholders were more willing to accept a takeover bid when their shares are overvalued. In addition, the federal prenotification regulations slowed the process dramatically (see Chapter 2). A number of states and public stock exchanges also require shareholder approval for certain types of offers. Moreover, most large companies have antitakeover defenses in place, such as poison pills. Hostile takeover battles are now more likely to last for months. Hostile or unsolicited deals reached their highest level in more than ten years in 2008, despite the inhospitable credit environment, as firms with cash on their balance sheets moved to exploit the decline in target company share prices.

In contrast to the United States and the United Kingdom, the frequency of hostile takeovers in continental Europe increased during the 1990s. In the 1980s, heavy ownership concentration made the success of hostile takeovers problematic. In the 1990s, ownership gradually became more dispersed and deregulation made unwanted takeovers easier.

Although hostile takeovers today are certainly more challenging than in the past, they have certain advantages over the friendly approach. In taking the friendly approach, the acquirer surrenders the element of surprise. Even a warning of a few days gives the target's management time to take defensive action to impede the actions of the suitor. Negotiation also raises the likelihood of a leak and a spike in the price of the target's stock as arbitrageurs ("arbs") seek to profit from the spread between the offer price and the target's current stock price. The speculative increase in the target's share price can add dramatically to the cost of the transaction, because the initial offer by the bidder generally includes a premium over the target's current share price. Because a premium usually is expressed as a percentage of the target's share price, a speculative increase in the target firm's current share price adds to the overall purchase price paid by the acquiring firm. For these reasons, a bidder may opt for a more aggressive approach.

The Aggressive Approach

Successful hostile takeovers depend on the premium offered to target shareholders, the board's composition, and the composition, sentiment, and investment horizon of the target's current shareholders. Other factors include the provisions of the target's bylaws and the potential for the target to implement additional takeover defenses.

The target's board finds it more difficult to reject offers exhibiting substantial premiums to the target's current stock price. Concern about their fiduciary responsibility and stockholder lawsuits puts pressure on the target's board to accept the offer. Despite the pressure of an attractive premium, the composition of the target's board also greatly influences what the board does and the timing of its decisions. A board dominated by independent directors, nonemployees, or family members is more likely to resist offers in an effort to induce the bidder to raise the offer price or to gain time to solicit competing bids than to protect itself and current management. Shivdasani (1993) concluded that the shareholder gain from the inception of the offer to its resolution is 62.3 percent for targets with an independent board, as compared with 40.9 percent for targets without an independent board.

Furthermore, the final outcome of a hostile takeover is also heavily dependent on the composition of the target's stock ownership, how stockholders feel about management's performance, and how long they intend to hold the stock. Gaspara and Massa (2005) found that firms held predominately by short-term investors (i.e., less than four months) show a greater likelihood of receiving a bid and exhibit a lower average premium of as much as 3 percent when acquired. The authors speculate that firms held by short-term investors have a weaker bargaining position with the bidder. To assess these factors, an acquirer compiles, to the extent possible, lists of stock ownership by category including management, officers, employees, and institutions such as pension and mutual funds. Such information can be used to estimate the target's *float*, the number of shares outstanding, not held by block shareholders, and available for trading by the public. The larger the share of stock held by corporate officers, family members, and employees, the smaller is the float, as these types of shareholders are less likely to sell their shares. The float is likely to be largest for those companies in which shareholders are disappointed with the financial performance of the firm.

Finally, an astute bidder always analyzes the target firm's bylaws (often easily accessible through a firm's website) for provisions potentially adding to the cost of a takeover. Such provisions could include a staggered board, the inability to remove directors without cause, or supermajority voting requirements for approval of mergers. These and other measures are discussed in more detail later in this chapter.

The Bear Hug: Limiting the Target's Options

If the friendly approach is considered inappropriate or is unsuccessful, the acquiring company may attempt to limit the options of the target's senior management by making a formal acquisition proposal, usually involving a public announcement, to the board of directors of the target. The intent is to move the board to a negotiated settlement. The board may be motivated to do so because of its fiduciary responsibility to the target's shareholders. Directors who vote against the proposal may be subject to lawsuits from target stockholders. This is especially true if the offer is at a substantial premium to the target's current stock price. Once the bid is made public, the company is effectively "put into play" (i.e., likely to attract additional bidders). Institutional investors and arbitrageurs add to the pressure by lobbying the board to accept the offer. Arbs are likely to acquire the target's stock and sell the bidder's stock short (see Chapter 1). The accumulation of stock by arbs makes purchases of blocks of stock by the bidder easier.

Proxy Contests in Support of a Takeover

The primary forms of proxy contests are those for seats on the board of directors, those concerning management proposals (e.g., an acquisition), and those seeking to force management to take some particular action (e.g., dividend payments and share repurchases). The most common reasons for dissidents to initiate a proxy fight are to remove management due to poor corporate performance, a desire to promote a specific type of restructuring of the firm (e.g., sell or spin off a business), the outright sale of the business, and to force a distribution of excess cash to shareholders (Faleye, 2004). Proxy fights enable dissident shareholders to replace specific board members or management with those more willing to support their positions. By replacing board members, proxy contests can be an effective means of gaining control without owning 50.1 percent of the voting stock, or they can be used to eliminate takeover defenses, such as poison pills, as a precursor to a tender offer. In 2001, Weyerhauser Co. placed three directors on rival Willamette Industries nine-member board. The prospect of losing an additional three seats the following year ultimately brought Willamette to the bargaining table and ended Weyerhauser's 13-month attempt to takeover Willamette. In mid-2005, billionaire Carl Icahn and his two dissident nominees won seats on the board of Blockbuster, ousting chairman John Antioco.

The cost of initiating a proxy contest to replace a board explains why so few board elections are contested. Between 1996 and 2004, an average of 12 firms annually faced contested board elections (*Economist*, 2006a). For the official slates of directors nominated by the board, campaigns can be paid out of corporate funds. For the shareholder promoting his or her own slate of candidates, substantial fees must be paid to hire proxy solicitors, investment bankers, and attorneys. Other expenses include those related to printing and mailing the proxy statement, as well as advertising. Litigation expenses also may be substantial. The cost of litigation easily can become the largest single expense item in highly contentious proxy contests. Nonetheless, a successful proxy fight represents a far less expensive means of gaining control over a target than a tender offer, which may require purchasing at a substantial premium a controlling interest in the target.

Implementing a Proxy Contest

When the bidder is also a shareholder in the target firm, the proxy process may begin with the bidder attempting to call a special stockholders' meeting. Alternatively, the bidder may put a proposal to replace the board or management at a regularly scheduled stockholders' meeting. Before the meeting, the bidder may undertake an aggressive public relations campaign, consisting of direct solicitations sent to shareholders and full-page advertisements in the press, in an attempt to convince shareholders to support the bidder's proposals. The target undertakes a similar campaign, but it has a distinct advantage in being able to deal directly with its own shareholders. The bidder may have to sue the target corporation to get a list of its shareholders' names and addresses. Often such shares are held in the name of banks or brokerage houses under a "street name," and these depositories generally have no authority to vote such shares.

Once the proxies are received by shareholders, they may then sign and send their proxies directly to a designated collection point, such as a brokerage house or bank. Shareholders may change their votes until the votes are counted. The votes are counted, often under the strict supervision of voting inspectors to ensure accuracy. Both the target firm and the bidder generally have their own proxy solicitors present during the tabulation process.

Legal Filings in Undertaking Proxy Contests

Securities Exchange Commission regulations cover the solicitation of the target's shareholders for their proxy, or right to vote their shares, on an issue that is being contested. All materials distributed to shareholders must be submitted to the SEC for review at least 10 days before they are distributed. Proxy solicitations are regulated by Section 14(A) of the Securities Exchange Act of 1934. The party attempting to solicit proxies from the target's shareholders must file a *proxy statement* and Schedule 14A with the SEC and mail it to the target's shareholders. Proxy statements include the date of the future shareholders' meeting at which approval of the transaction is to be solicited, details of the merger agreement, company backgrounds, reasons for the proposed merger, and opinions of legal and financial advisors. Proxy statements may be obtained from the companies involved, as well as on the Internet at the SEC site (www.sec.gov) and represent excellent sources of information about a proposed transaction.

The Impact of Proxy Contests on Shareholder Value

Despite a low success rate, there is some empirical evidence that proxy fights result in abnormal returns to shareholders of the target company regardless of the outcome. The gain in share prices occurs despite only one fifth to one third of all proxy fights actually resulting in a change in board control. In studies covering proxy battles during the 1980s through the mid-1990s, abnormal returns ranged from 6 to 19 percent, even if the dissident shareholders were unsuccessful in the proxy contest (DeAngelo and DeAngelo, 1989; Dodd and Warner, 1983; Mulherin and Poulsen, 1998; Faleye, 2004). Reasons for gains of this magnitude may include the eventual change in management at firms embroiled in proxy fights, the tendency for new management to restructure the firm, investor expectations of a future change in control due to M&A activity, and possible special cash payouts for firms with excess cash holdings.

Pre-Tender Offer Tactics: Purchasing Target Stock in the Open Market

Potential bidders often purchase stock in a target before a formal bid, to accumulate stock at a price lower than the eventual offer price. Such purchases are normally kept secret to avoid driving up the price and increasing the average price paid for such shares. The primary advantage accruing to the bidder of accumulating target stock before an offer is the potential leverage achieved with the voting rights associated with the stock it has purchased. This voting power is important in a proxy contest to remove takeover defenses, to win shareholder approval under state antitakeover statutes, or for the election of members of the target's board. In addition, the target stock accumulated before the acquisition can be later sold, possibly at a gain, by the bidder in the event the bidder is unsuccessful in acquiring the target firm.

Once the bidder has established a toehold ownership position in the voting stock of the target through open-market purchases, the bidder may attempt to call a special stockholders' meeting. The purpose of such a meeting may be to call for a replacement of the board of directors or the removal of takeover defenses. The conditions under which such a meeting can be called are determined by the firm's articles of incorporation, governed by the laws of the state in which the firm is incorporated. A copy of a firm's articles of incorporation can usually be obtained for a nominal fee from the Office of the Secretary of State of the state in which the firm is incorporated.

Using a Hostile Tender Offer to Circumvent the Target's Board

The hostile tender offer is a deliberate effort to go around the target's board and management. The early successes of the hostile tender offer generated new, more effective defenses (discussed later in this chapter). Takeover tactics had to adapt to the proliferation of more formidable defenses. For example, during the 1990s, hostile tender offers were used in combination with proxy contests to coerce the target's board into rescinding takeover defenses.

While target boards often discourage unwanted bids initially, they are more likely to relent when a hostile tender offer is initiated. In a study of 1,018 tender offers between 1962 and 2001, target boards resisted tender offers about one fifth of the time (Bhagat et al., 2005). While they have become more common in recent years, hostile takeovers are also rare outside the United States. Rossi and Volpin (2004) found, in a study of 49 countries, that only about 1 percent of 45,686 M&A transactions considered between 1990 and 2002 were opposed by target firm boards.

Implementing a Tender Offer

Tender offers can be for cash, stock, debt, or some combination. Unlike mergers, tender offers frequently use cash as the form of payment. Securities transactions involve a longer period for the takeover to be completed, because new security issues must be registered with and approved by the SEC, as well as with states having security registration requirements. During the approval period, target firms are able to prepare defenses and solicit other bids, resulting in a potentially higher purchase price for the target. If the tender offer involves a share-for-share exchange, it is referred to as an ***exchange offer.*** Whether cash or securities, the offer is made directly to target shareholders. The offer is extended for a specific period and may be unrestricted (any-or-all offer) or restricted to a certain percentage or number of the target's share.

Tender offers restricted to purchasing less than 100 percent of the target's outstanding shares may be oversubscribed. Because the Williams Act of 1968 requires that all shareholders tendering shares must be treated equally, the bidder may either purchase all the target stock that is tendered or only a portion of the tendered stock. For example, if the bidder has extended a tender offer for 70 percent of the target's outstanding shares and 90 percent of the target's stock actually is offered, the bidder may choose to prorate the purchase of stock by buying only 63 percent (i.e., 0.7×0.9) of the tendered stock from each shareholder.

If the bidder chooses to revise the tender offer, the waiting period automatically is extended. If another bid is made to the target shareholders, the waiting period also must be extended by another 10 days to give them adequate time to consider the new bid. Once initiated, tender offers for publicly traded firms are usually successful, although the success rate is lower if it is contested. Between 1980 and 2000, the success rate of total attempted tender offers was more than 80 percent, with the success rate for uncontested offers more than 90 percent and for contested (i.e., by the target's board) offers slightly more than 50 percent (*Mergerstat Review*, 2001).

Multitiered Offers

The form of the bid for the target firm can be presented to target shareholders as either a one-tier or a two-tiered offer. In a **one-tiered offer**, the acquirer announces the same offer to all target shareholders. This strategy provides the acquirer with the potential for quickly purchasing control of the target, thereby discouraging other potential bidders from attempting to disrupt the transaction. A **two-tiered offer** occurs when the acquirer offers to buy a certain number of shares at one price and more shares at a lower price at a later date. The form of payment in the second tier may also be less attractive, consisting of securities rather than cash. The intent of the two-tiered approach is to give target shareholders an incentive to tender their shares early in the process to receive the higher price. Once the bidding firm accumulates enough shares to gain control of the target (usually 50.1 percent), the bidder may initiate a so-called **back end merger** by calling a special shareholders meeting seeking approval for a merger in which minority shareholders are required to accede to the majority vote. Alternatively, the bidder may operate the target firm as a partially owned subsidiary, later merging it into a newly created wholly owned subsidiary.

While the courts have determined that two-tier tender offers are not illegal, many state statutes have been amended requiring equal treatment for all tendering shareholders. Many states also give target shareholders **appraisal rights**, so that those not tendering shares in the first or second tier may seek to have the state court determine a "fair value" for the shares. The appraised value for the shares may be more or less than the offer made by the bidding firm. The minority shares may be subject to a "minority discount," since they are worth less to the bidder than those acquired in the process of gaining control. State statutes may also contain fair price provisions, in which all target shareholders, including those in the second tier, receive the same price and redemption rights, enabling target shareholders in the second tier to redeem their shares at a price similar to that paid in the first tier.

If the objective of the acquirer is to gain a controlling interest in the target firm, it may initiate a **creeping takeover** strategy, in which it purchases target voting stock in relatively small increments until it has gained effective control of the firm. This may occur at less than 50.1 percent if the target firm's ownership is widely dispersed. If about 60 percent of a firm's eligible shareholders vote in elections for directors, a minority owning as little as 35 percent can vote in its own slate of directors. Acquirers generally pay more for the initial voting shares than for shares acquired at a later time. The amount in excess of the target's current share price paid to target shareholders tendering their shares first often is referred to as a *control premium*.

The disadvantages to owning less than 100 percent of the target's voting stock include the potential for dissident minority shareholders to disrupt efforts to implement important management decisions, the cost incurred in providing financial statements to both majority and minority shareholders, and current accounting and tax rules. Owning less than 50.1 percent means that the target cannot be consolidated for purposes of financial reporting but rather must be accounted for using the equity method. Since the equity method includes the investor's share of the target's income, it will not change consolidated income; however, the target's assets, liabilities, revenues, and expenses are not shown on the investor's financial statements. Consequently, potential increases in borrowing capacity from showing a larger asset or sales base would not be realized. Furthermore, target losses cannot be used to offset bidder gains, since consolidation, for tax purposes, requires owning 80.1 percent of the target. How control premiums and minority discounts are determined is discussed in detail in Chapter 10.

Legal Filings in Undertaking Tender Offers

Federal securities laws impose a number of reporting, disclosure, and antifraud requirements on acquirers initiating tender offers. Once the tender offer has been made, the acquirer cannot purchase any target shares other than the number specified in the tender offer. As noted in Chapter 2, Section 14(D) of the Williams Act covers tender offers. It requires that any individual or entity making a tender offer resulting in owning more than 5 percent of any class of equity must file a Schedule 14D-1 and all solicitation material with the SEC. For additional details, see Chapter 2.

Other Potential Takeover Strategies

With the average length of time between signing the initial agreement and completion or termination of the agreement about six months, both the buyer and seller have an incentive to hold up the deal to renegotiate the terms of the agreement based on new information. A number of strategies have been designed to minimize the so-called hold-up problem.

To heighten the chance of a successful takeover, the bidder includes a variety of provisions in a letter of intent designed to discourage the target firm from backing out of any preliminary agreements. The **letter of intent** (**LOI**) is a preliminary agreement between two companies intending to merge that stipulates major areas of agreement between the parties, as well as their rights and limitations. The LOI may contain a number of features protecting the buyer. The **no-shop agreement** is among the most common. This agreement prohibits the takeover target from seeking other bids or making public information not currently readily available. Related agreements commit the target firm's management to use its best efforts to secure shareholder approval of the bidder's offer.

Contracts often grant the target the right to forego the merger and pursue an alternative strategy instead and the acquirer to withdraw from the agreement. However, the right to break the agreement is usually not free. **Breakup**, or termination, **fees** are sums paid to the initial bidder or target if the transaction is not completed. This fee reflects legal and advisory expenses, executive management time, and the costs associated with opportunities that may have been lost to the bidder involved in trying to close this deal. Hotchkiss, Qian, and Song (2005) found, for a sample of 1,100 stock mergers between 1994 and 1999, that, in 55 percent of all deals, a target termination or breakup fee is included in the initial agreement, while in 21 percent of the deals both target and acquirer termination fees are included. Termination fees are used more frequently on the target side than on the acquirer because targets have greater incentives to break contracts and seek other bidders. Such fees tend to average about 3 percent of the purchase price.

Officer (2003) found that the use of such fees increases the probability of a deal being completed. When breakup fees are paid by the bidder to the target firm, they are called *reverse breakup fees.*

Another form of protection for the bidder is the *stock lockup,* an option granted to the bidder to buy the target firm's stock at the bidder's initial offer, which is triggered whenever a competing bid is accepted by the target firm. Because the target may choose to sell to a higher bidder, the stock lockup arrangement usually ensures that the initial bidder will make a profit on its purchase of the target's stock. The initial bidder also may require that the seller agree to a *crown jewels lockup,* in which the initial bidder has an option to buy important strategic assets of the seller, if the seller chooses to sell to another party. There is evidence that target firms use lockup options to enhance their bargaining power in dealing with a bidding firm (Burch, 2001).

Developing a Bidding or Takeover Strategy Decision Tree

The tactics that may be used in developing a bidding strategy should be viewed as a series of decision points, with objectives and options usually well defined and understood before a takeover attempt is initiated. Prebid planning should involve a review of the target's current defenses, an assessment of the defenses that could be put in place by the target after an offer is made, and the size of the float associated with the target's stock. Poor planning can result in poor bidding, which can be costly to CEOs. Lehn and Zhao (2006) found that, between 1990 and 1998, for a sample of 714 acquisitions, 47 percent of acquiring firm CEOs were replaced within five years. Moreover, top executives are more likely to be replaced at firms that had made poor acquisitions some time during the prior five years.

Common bidding strategy objectives include winning control of the target, minimizing the control premium, minimizing transaction costs, and facilitating postacquisition integration. If minimizing the purchase and transaction costs while maximizing cooperation between the two parties is considered critical, the bidder may choose the "friendly" approach.

The friendly approach has the advantage of generally being less costly than more aggressive tactics and minimizes the loss of key personnel, customers, and suppliers during the fight for control of the target. Friendly takeovers avoid an auction environment, which may raise the target's purchase price. Moreover, as noted in Chapter 6, friendly acquisitions facilitate premerger integration planning and increase the likelihood that the combined businesses will be quickly integrated following closing. The primary risk of this approach is the loss of surprise. If the target is unwilling to reach a negotiated settlement, the acquirer is faced with the choice of abandoning the effort or resorting to more aggressive tactics. Such tactics are likely to be less effective, because of the extra time afforded the target's management to put additional takeover defenses in place. In reality, the risk of loss of surprise may not be very great because of the prenotification requirements of the Williams and the Hart–Scott–Rodino Acts.

Reading Figure 3–2 from left to right, the bidder initiates contact casually through an intermediary (i.e., a casual pass) or a more formal inquiry. The bidder's options under the friendly approach are to either walk away or adopt more aggressive tactics, if the target's management and board spurn the bidder's initial offer. If the choice is to become more aggressive, the bidder may undertake a simple bear hug to nudge the target toward a negotiated settlement due to pressure from large institutional shareholders and arbs.

If the bear hug fails to convince the target's management to negotiate, the bidder may choose to buy stock on the open market. This tactic is most effective when ownership in the target is concentrated among relatively few shareholders. The bidder may

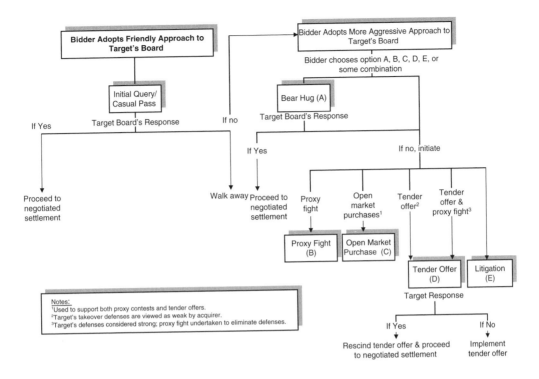

FIGURE 3–2 Alternative takeover tactics.

accumulate a sufficient number of voting rights to call a special stockholders' meeting, if a proxy fight is deemed necessary to change board members or to dismember the target's defenses. If the target's defenses are viewed as relatively weak, the bidder may forego a proxy contest and initiate a tender offer for the target's stock. In contrast, if the target's defenses appear formidable, the bidder may implement a proxy contest and a tender offer concurrently. However, implementing both simultaneously is a very expensive strategy. Tender offers are costly, because they are offers to buy up to 100 percent of the target's outstanding stock at a significant premium. While a proxy fight is cheaper, they are still costly, involving professional fees paid to such advisors as proxy solicitors, investment bankers, and attorneys. Printing, mailing, and advertising costs can also be substantial. Finally, both proxy fights and tender offers involve significant legal fees due to the likelihood of extensive litigation. Litigation is a common tactic used to put pressure on the target board to relent to the bidder's proposal or to remove defenses. Litigation is most effective if the firm's defenses appear to be especially onerous. The board may be accused of not giving the bidder's offer sufficient review or it may be told that the target's defenses are intended only to entrench senior management. As such, the acquirer will allege that the board is violating its fiduciary responsibility to the target shareholders. Table 3–2 relates takeover tactics to specific bidder objectives and strategies.

Alternative Takeover Defenses in the Corporate Takeover Market

Alternative takeover defenses can be grouped into two categories: those put in place before receiving a bid and those implemented after receipt of a bid. Prebid defenses are used to prevent a sudden, unexpected hostile bid from gaining control of the company

Table 3–2 Advantages and Disadvantages of Alternative Takeover Tactics

Tactics	Advantages	Disadvantages
Casual pass (i.e., informal inquiry)	May learn target is receptive to offer	Gives advance warning
Bear hug (i.e., letter to target board forcefully proposing takeover)	Raises pressure on target to negotiate a deal	Gives advance warning
Open market purchases (i.e., acquirer buys target shares on public markets)	May lower cost of transaction Creates profit if target agrees to buy back bidder's toehold position (i.e., greenmail) May discourage other bidders	Can result in a less than controlling interest Limits on amount can purchase without disclosure Some shareholders could hold out for higher price Could suffer losses if takeover attempt fails
Proxy contest (i.e., effort to obtain target shareholder support to change target board)	Less expensive than tender offer May obviate need for tender offer	Relatively low probability of success if target stock widely held Adds to transactions costs
Tender offer (i.e., direct offer to target shareholders to buy shares)	Pressures target shareholders to sell stock Bidder not bound to purchase tendered shares unless desired number of shares tendered	Tends to be most expensive tactic Disruptive to postclosing integration due to potential loss of key target management, customers, and suppliers.
Litigation (i.e., lawsuits accusing target board of improper conduct)	Puts pressure on target board	Expense

Note: Common bidder strategy objectives:

Gain control of target firm

Minimize the size of the control premium

Minimize transactions costs

Facilitate postacquisition integration

before management has time to assess the options properly. If the prebid defenses are sufficient to delay a change in control, the target firm has time to erect additional defenses after an unsolicited bid is received. Table 3–3 identifies the most commonly used defenses. Public companies, on average, make use of about three of the various pre- and postbid defenses listed in this table (Field and Karpoff, 2000). These defenses are discussed in more detail later in this chapter.

The Role of Planning

The best defense against unwanted suitors may be advance planning and a strong financial performance. Large public companies routinely review their takeover defenses. Many companies have "stock watch" programs in place that are intended to identify stock accumulations or stock price movements that reflect an impending takeover attempt. Such a program tracks trading patterns in a company's stock. Companies require their stock transfer agent to provide up-to-date, accurate stock transfer sheets and report any unusual movements in stock transfer activity. Stock watch programs routinely review SEC records for any Schedule 13D filings.

The rapidity of events once a takeover is underway may make an effective defense impossible unless certain defenses are already in place. A prebid strategy involves building defenses that are adequate to the task of slowing down a bidder to give the target

Table 3–3   Alternative Prebid and Postbid Takeover Defenses

Prebid Defenses	Postbid Defenses
Poison pills[1]: 　Flip-over rights plans 　Flip-in rights plans	Greenmail (bidder's investment purchased at a premium to what stockholders paid as inducement to refrain from any further activity)
Shark repellants (implemented by changing bylaws or charter): 　Strengthening the board's defenses 　Staggered or classified board elections 　Cumulative voting rights 　"For-cause" provisions 　Limiting shareholder actions 　Calling special meetings 　Consent solicitations 　Advance notice provisions 　Supermajority rules	Standstill agreements (often used in conjunction with an agreement to buy bidder's investment)
Other shark repellents: 　Antigreenmail provisions (discourages target's use of greenmail as a takeover tactic) 　Fair price provisions 　Super voting stock 　Reincorporation	
Golden parachutes	Pac-Man defense White knights Employee stock ownership plans Leveraged recapitalization Share repurchase or buyback plans Corporate restructuring Litigation

[1]While many types of poison pills are used, only the most common forms are discussed in this text. Note also that the distinction between pre- and postbid defenses is becoming murky, as increasingly poison pill plans are put in place immediately following the announcement of a bid. Pills can be adopted without a shareholder vote, because they are issued as a dividend and the board has the exclusive authority to issue dividends.

company's management and board time to assess the situation and decide on an appropriate response to an offer. A company's strategy should never be to try to build insurmountable defenses. Courts will disallow defenses that appear to be designed only to entrench the firm's management.

Once a bid has been received, most companies choose never to comment on merger discussions until an agreement has been signed. When such an event must be disclosed depends on how far along discussions are with the bidder. The U.S. Supreme Court has said that a company has an obligation to make accurate, nonmisleading statements once it has commented on a situation (Wasserstein, 1998, p. 689). The Supreme Court also has said that a company's statement of "no comment" will be taken as silence and therefore will not be considered misleading.

Prebid Defenses

Prebid defenses generally fall into three categories: poison pills, shark repellants, and golden parachutes. The sophistication of such measures has increased dramatically since 1980, in lockstep with the effectiveness of takeover tactics. The objective of these defensive measures is to slow the pace of the takeover attempt and make it more costly for the bidder.

Poison Pills

In the popular press, the *poison pill* is a generic name that refers to a range of protections against unsolicited tender offers. In practice, they represent a very specific type of anti-takeover defense. Often referred to as shareholder rights plans, **poison pills** represent a new class of securities issued by a company to its shareholders. Because pills are issued as a dividend and the board has the exclusive authority to issue dividends, a pill can often be adopted without a shareholder vote. Therefore, poison pills can be adopted not only before but also after the onset of a hostile bid. Consequently, even a company that does not have a poison pill in place can be regarded as having a "shadow poison pill," which could be used in the event of a hostile bid (Coates, 2000). In 2007, almost one fourth of first-time pill adoptions were implemented when the firm was "in play." This compares to about 3 percent of all first-time pill adoptions in 2002 (sharkrepellent.com).

Poison pill securities have no value unless an investor acquires a specific percentage (often as low as 10 percent) of the target firm's voting stock. If this threshold percentage is exceeded and the pill is a so-called **flip-in pill**, the poison pill securities are activated and typically allow existing target shareholders to purchase additional shares of the target's firm's common stock at a discount from the current market price. Alternatively, if the pill is a **flip-over pill**, existing shareholders may purchase additional shares of the acquirer or surviving firm's common shares (i.e., the shares of the combined companies), also at a discount.

Triggering the flip-in pill has the effect of increasing the cost of the transaction for the acquirer by increasing the number of target shares that need to be purchased for cash in a cash-for-share exchange or the number of new shares that must issued by the acquirer in a share-for-share exchange. In a cash-for-share exchange, the change in the acquirer's cash outlay depends on the number of target shareholders exercising their right to buy additional target shares. For example, if the number of target shares outstanding doubles and the price per share offered by the acquirer remains unchanged, the amount of cash required to buy all or a specific portion of the target's shares would double. In share-for-share exchange, the increased number of acquirer shares issued imposes a cost on acquirer shareholders by diluting their ownership position. News Corp's November 8, 2004, announcement that it would give its shareholders the right to buy one News Corp share at half price for each share they own, if any party buys a 15 percent stake in the firm, is a recent example of a flip-in poison pill. The flip-in rights plan would exclude the purchaser of the 15 percent stake.

Table 3–4 illustrates the dilution of the acquirer's shareholders ownership position resulting from a poison pill in a share-for-share exchange offer. Assume the acquirer has 1 million shares currently outstanding and agrees to acquire the 1 million shares of target stock outstanding by exchanging one share of acquirer stock for each share of target stock. To complete the transaction, the acquirer must issue 1 million shares of new stock, with the target's stock being canceled. The total number of shares outstanding for the new company would be 2 million shares (i.e., 1 million of existing acquirer stock plus 1 million in newly issued shares). Target company and acquirer shareholders would each own one half of the new company. However, if target company shareholders are able to buy at a nominal price 1 million new shares of target stock because of a flip-in pill, the number of shares that now must be acquired would total 2 million. The total number of shares of the new company would be 3 million, of which target company shareholders would own two thirds and acquirer shareholders one third. Note that a flip-in or flip-over pill has the same dilutive effect on acquirer shareholders. With the flip-in pill, target shareholders purchased 1 million new shares of target stock, while for a flip-over pill, they bought 1 million new shares of the acquirer or surviving firm's shares. In either case, the acquirer had to issue 1 million new shares.

Table 3–4   Acquirer Shareholder Dilution Due to Poison Pill

	New Company Shares Outstanding[1]		Ownership Distribution in New Company (%)	
	Without Pill	**With Pill**	**Without Pill**	**With Pill**
Flip-in Pill Defenses[2]				
Target firm shareholders				
Shares currently outstanding	1,000,000	2,000,000	50	67[3]
Total shares outstanding	1,000,000	2,000,000		
Acquiring firm shareholders				
Shares currently outstanding	1,000,000	1,000,000		
New shares issued	1,000,000	2,000,000	50	33
Total shares outstanding	2,000,000	3,000,000		
Flip-over Pill Defense[4]				
Target firm shareholders				
Shares currently outstanding	1,000,000	1,000,000	50	67
Total shares outstanding	1,000,000	1,000,000		
Acquiring firm shareholders				
Shares currently outstanding	1,000,000	1,000,000	50	33
New shares issued	1,000,000	2,000,000		
Total shares outstanding	2,000,000	3,000,000		

[1]Acquirer agrees to exchange one share of acquirer stock for each share of target stock. The target shares outstanding are canceled.

[2]Poison pill provisions enable each target shareholder to buy one share of target stock for each share they own at a nominal price.

[3]2,000,000/3,000,000

[4]One million new shares must be issued to target shareholders exercising their right to buy shares in the surviving or new company at a nominal price.

Proponents of the pill defense argue that it prevents a raider from acquiring a substantial portion of the firm's stock without board permission. Since the board generally has the power to rescind the pill, bidders are compelled to negotiate with the target's board, potentially resulting in a higher offer price. Pill defenses may be most effective when used with staggered board defenses in which a raider would be unable to remove the pill without winning two successive elections. With such a combination of defenses, the likelihood of remaining independent rose from 34 percent to 61 percent, and the probability that the first bidder would be successful dropped from 34 to 14 percent (Bebchuk, Coates, and Subramanian, 2002). Detractors argue that pill defenses simply serve to entrench management and encourage disaffected shareholders to litigate. In recent years, boards have been under pressure to require a shareholder approval of all rights plans and to rescind existing pill defenses.

Most pills are put in place with an *escape clause*, enabling the board of the issuing company to redeem the pill through a nominal payment to the shareholders. This is necessary to avoid dilution of the bidder's ownership position in the event the acquiring company is considered friendly. However, the existence of this redemption feature has made pill defenses vulnerable. For example, a tender offer may be made conditional on the board's redemption of the pill. The target's board is under substantial pressure from institutions and arbs to redeem the pill if the bidder offers a significant premium over the current price of the target's stock. Alternatively, such takeover defenses could be dismantled through a proxy fight. One strategy that has sometimes been used to mitigate this redemption feature is the *dead hand* poison pill. This security is issued with special characteristics, which prevent the board of directors from taking action to redeem or rescind the pill unless the directors were the same directors who adopted the pill. However, dead hand poison pills are routinely struck down by the courts as excessively protecting a firm's board and management.

Shark Repellants

Shark repellants are specific types of takeover defenses that can be adopted by amending either a corporate charter or its bylaws. The charter gives the corporation its legal existence. The **corporate charter** consists of the **articles of incorporation,** a document filed with a state government by the founders of a corporation, and a **certificate of incorporation,** a document received from the state once the articles have been approved. The charter contains the corporation's name, purpose, amount of authorized shares, and number and identity of directors. The corporation's powers thus derive from the laws of the state and the provisions of the charter. Rules governing the internal management of the corporation are described in the **corporation's bylaws,** which are determined by the corporation's founders.

Shark repellants are put in place largely to reinforce the ability of a firm's board of directors to retain control. Although shark repellants predate poison pills, their success in slowing down and making takeovers more expensive has been mixed. These developments have given rise to more creative defenses, such as the poison pill. Today, shark repellants are intended largely as supplements to the poison pill defenses. Their role is primarily to make gaining control of the board through a proxy fight at an annual or special meeting more difficult. In practice, most shark repellants require amendments to the firm's charter, which necessitate a shareholder vote. Despite many variations of shark repellants, the most typical include staggered board elections, restrictions on shareholder actions, antigreenmail provisions, super voting, and debt-based defenses. Table 3–5 summarizes the primary advantages and disadvantages of each type of shark repellant defense, divided into three categories: those that strengthen the board's defenses, those limiting shareholder actions, and all others. Note that golden parachutes are generally

Table 3–5   Advantages and Disadvantages of Prebid Takeover Defenses—Poison Pills, Shark Repellents, and Golden Parachutes

Type of Defense	Advantages for Target Firm	Disadvantages for Target Firm
Poison Pills: Raising the Cost of Acquisition		
Flip-over pills (rights to buy stock in the acquirer, activated with 100% change in ownership)	Dilutes ownership position of current acquirer shareholders Rights redeemable by buying them back from shareholders at nominal price	Ineffective in preventing acquisition of <100% of target (bidders could buy controlling interest only and buy remainder after rights expire) Subject to hostile tender contingent on target board's redemption of pill Makes issuer less attractive to white knights
Flip-in pills (rights to buy stock in the target, activated when acquirer purchases <100% change in ownership)	Dilutes target stock regardless of amount purchased by potential acquirer Discriminatory, as not given to investor who activated the rights Rights redeemable at any point prior to triggering event	Not permissible in some states due discriminatory nature No poison pill provides any protection against proxy contests

Table 3–5 — Cont'd

Type of Defense	Advantages for Target Firm	Disadvantages for Target Firm
Shark Repellents: Strengthening the Board's Defenses		
Staggered or classified boards	Delays assumption of control by a majority shareholder	May be circumvented by increasing size of board, unless prevented by charter or bylaws
Cumulative voting	Delays assumption of control by a majority shareholder	Gives dissident shareholder a board seat and access to confidential information
Limitations on removal of directors	"For-cause" provisions narrow range of reasons for removal	Can be circumvented unless supported by a supermajority requirement for repeal
Shark Repellents: Limiting Shareholder Actions		
Limitations on calling special meetings	Limits ability to use special meetings to add board seats or remove or elect new members	States may require a special meeting if a certain percentage of shareholders request a meeting.
Limiting consent solicitations	Limits ability of dissident shareholders to expedite a proxy contest process	May be subject to court challenge
Advance notice provisions	Gives board time to select its own slate of candidates and decide on an appropriate response	May be subject to court challenge
Supermajority provisions	May be applied selectively to events such as hostile takeovers	Can be circumvented unless a supermajority of shareholders are required to change the provision
Other Shark Repellents		
Antigreenmail provision	Eliminates profit opportunity for raiders	Eliminates greenmail as a takeover defense
Fair-price provisions	Increases the cost of a two-tiered tender offer	Raises the cost to a white knight, unless waived by typically 95% of shareholders
Super voting stock	Concentrates control by giving "friendly" shareholders more voting power than others.	Difficult to implement because requires shareholder approval and useful only when voting power can be given to pro-management shareholders.
Reincorporation	Takes advantage of most favorable state antitakeover statutes	Requires shareholder approval; time consuming to implement unless subsidiary established before takeover solicitation
Golden parachutes[1]	Emboldens target management to negotiate for a higher premium and raises the cost of a takeover to the hostile bidder	Negative public perception; makes termination of top management expensive; cost not tax deductible.

[1]Generally not considered a shark repellent but included in this table, as they are usually put in place before a bid is made for the firm.

not considered shark repellents, as they are designed more to raise the cost of the buyout to the bidder and to retain management rather than to gain time for the target board. They are discussed here as they are generally put in place prior to a takeover bid.

Strengthening the Board's Defenses   A *staggered*, or *classified*, *board election* involves dividing the firm's directors into a number of classes, only one of which is up for reelection each year. For example, for a board consisting of 12 members, the directors may be divided into four classes, with each director elected for a four-year period. In the first year, the three directors, designated as class 1 directors, are up for election; in the second year, class 2 directors are up for election; and so on. Consequently, an insurgent stockholder, who may hold the majority of the stock, still would have to wait for three elections to gain control of the board. Moreover, the size of the board is limited by the firm's bylaws to preclude the insurgent stockholder from adding board seats to take control of the board. The target may have to accede to the majority stockholder's demands because of litigation initiated by dissident shareholder groups. The likelihood of litigation is highest and pressure on the board is greatest whenever the offer price for the target is substantially above the target firm's current share price. Bebchuk, Coates, and Subramanian (2002, 2003) find that staggered boards can be effective in helping a target to ward off a hostile takeover attempt.

Some firms have common stock carrying **cumulative voting rights** to maximize minority representation. Cumulative voting in the election of directors means each shareholder is entitled to as many votes as shall equal the number of shares the shareholder owns multiplied by the number of directors to be elected. Furthermore, the shareholder may cast all these votes for a single candidate or for any two or more of them. Using the preceding example of a 12-member board, a shareholder who has 100 shares of stock has 300 votes for the three open seats for class 1 directors. The shareholder may cumulate her votes and cast them for a specific candidate. A dissident stockholder may choose this approach to obtain a single seat on the board to gain access to useful information that is not otherwise readily available. However, cumulative voting rights also may backfire against the dissident shareholder. Cumulative voting may be used to counter the ability of insurgents to gain control of the board by cumulating the votes of opposing shareholders and casting them for candidates who would vigorously represent the board's positions. **For-cause provisions** specify the conditions for removing a member of the board of directors. This narrows the range of reasons for removal and limits the flexibility of dissident shareholders in contesting board seats.

Limiting Shareholder Actions   Other means of reinforcing the board's ability to retain control include limiting the ability of shareholders to gain control of the firm by bypassing the board altogether. These include limiting their ability to call special meetings and engage in consent solicitations and limiting the use of supermajority rules.

Many states require a firm to call a special shareholders' meeting if it is requested by a certain percentage of its shareholders. Special meetings may be used as a forum for insurgent shareholders to take control by replacing current directors with those likely to be more cooperative or increasing the number of board seats. To limit this type of action, firms frequently rely on the conditions under which directors can be removed (i.e., the "for-cause" provision discussed earlier) and a limitation on the number of board seats is defined in the firm's bylaws or charter. Furthermore, special meetings may be used by shareholders to engage in a nonbinding vote to remove certain types of defenses, such as a poison pill. The board then must decide to ignore the will of the shareholders or to remove the defenses.

In some states, shareholders may take action to add to the number of seats on the board, remove specific board members, or elect new members without a special shareholders' meeting. These states allow dissident shareholders to obtain shareholder support for their proposals by simply obtaining the written consent of shareholders under what is known as **consent solicitation**. Although the consent solicitation must abide by the disclosure requirements applicable to proxy contests, dissident stockholders may use this process to expedite their efforts to seize control of the board or remove defenses without waiting for a shareholders meeting to gain approval of their proposals, as is required in a proxy contest. This process circumvents the delays inherent in setting up a meeting to conduct a stockholder vote. An important difference between a consent solicitation and a proxy contest is that the winning vote in a consent solicitation is determined as a percentage of the number of shares outstanding. In a proxy fight, the winner is determined as a percentage of the number of votes actually cast (unless majority voting rules are in place that require the counting of votes withheld). Therefore, it may be easier for a dissident shareholder to win by initiating a proxy contest rather than a consent solicitation, because many shareholders simply do not vote. Companies have attempted to limit shareholders' ability to use this procedure by amending charters or bylaws. Bylaw amendments may not require shareholder approval. However, the courts frequently have frowned on actions restricting shareholder rights without shareholder approval.

Advance notice provisions in corporate bylaws require the announcement of shareholder proposals and board nominations well in advance of an actual vote. Some bylaws require advance notice of as long as two months, buying time for the target's management. *Supermajority rules* require a higher level of approval for amending the charter or for certain types of transactions, such as a merger or acquisition. Such rules are triggered if an "interested party" acquires a specific percentage of the ownership shares (e.g., 5–10 percent). Supermajority rules may require that as much as 80 percent of the shareholders must approve a proposed merger or a simple majority of all shareholders except the "interested party." Supermajority rules often include escape clauses, which allow the board to waive the requirement. For example, supermajority rules may not apply to mergers approved by the board.

Other Shark Repellents   The final category of prebid defenses includes antigreenmail and fair price provisions, as well as super voting stock and reincorporation.

During the 1980s, many raiders profited by taking an equity position in a target firm, threatening takeover, and subsequently selling their ownership position back to the target firm at a premium over what they paid for the target's shares. Many corporations adopted charter amendments called *antigreenmail provisions* restricting the firm's ability to repurchase shares at a premium. By removing the incentive for greenmail, companies believed they were making themselves less attractive as potential takeover targets. As such, antigreenmail provisions may be viewed as an antitakeover tactic.

Fair price provisions require that any acquirer pay minority shareholders at least a fair market price for their stock. The fair market price may be expressed as some historical multiple of the company's earnings or as a specific price equal to the maximum price paid when the buyer acquired shares in the company. Fair price provisions are most effective when the target firm is subject to a two-tiered tender offer. The fair price provision forces the bidder to pay target shareholders who tender their stock in the second tier the same terms offered to those tendering their stock in the first tier. Most such provisions do not apply if the proposed takeover is approved by the target firm's board of directors or if the bidder obtains a specified supermajority level of approval from the target's shareholders.

A firm may create more than one class of stock for many reasons, including separating the performance of individual operating subsidiaries, compensating subsidiary operating management, maintaining control with the founders, and preventing hostile takeovers. As a takeover defense, a firm may undertake a *dual class recapitalization*, in which the objective is to concentrate stock with the greatest voting rights in the hands of those most likely to support management. One class of stock may have 10 to 100 times the voting rights of another class of stock. Such stock is called *super voting stock*. Super voting stock is issued to all shareholders along with the right to exchange it for ordinary stock. Most shareholders are likely to exchange it for ordinary stock, because the stock with the multiple voting rights usually has a limited resale market and pays a lower dividend than other types of voting stock issued by the corporation. Management usually retains the special stock. This effectively increases the voting control of the corporation in the hands of management. For example, Ford's dual class or super voting shares enable the Ford family to control 40 percent of the voting power while owning only 4 percent of the total equity of the company.

Under the voting rights policies of the SEC and the major public exchanges, U.S. firms are allowed to list dual class shares. However, once such shares are listed, firms cannot reduce the voting rights of existing shares or issue a new class of superior voting shares. Several hundred U.S. companies issue dual class shares, including the New York Times, Dow Jones, the Washington Post, Coors, Tyson Foods, Adelphia, Comcast, Viacom, and Google. While relatively limited among U.S. firms, dual class firms are very common in other countries. Recent research suggests that firms with dual class shares often underperform the overall stock market. This may result from efforts to entrench controlling shareholders by erecting excessive takeover defenses and policies that are not in the best interests of noncontrolling shareholders, such as excessive compensation for key managers and board members and making value-destroying acquisitions. Moreover, such firms often have excessive leverage, due to an unwillingness to raise additional funds by selling shares that could dilute the controlling shareholders (Masulis, Wang, and Xie, 2009; Gompers, Ishii, and Metrick, 2008; and Harvey et al., 2004).

Reincorporation involves a potential target firm changing its state of incorporation to one in which the laws are more favorable for implementing takeover defenses. Several factors need to be considered in selecting a state for possible reincorporation. These include how the state's courts have ruled in lawsuits alleging breach of corporate director fiduciary responsibility in takeover situations and the state's laws pertaining to poison pills, staggered boards, and hostile tender offers. Reincorporation involves the creation of a subsidiary in the new state into which the parent is merged at a later date. Reincorporation requires shareholder approval.

Golden Parachutes

Golden parachutes are employee severance arrangements that are triggered whenever a change in control takes place. Such a plan usually covers only a few dozen employees and obligates the company to make a lump-sum payment to employees covered under the plan whose jobs are terminated following a change in control. A change in control usually is defined to occur whenever an investor accumulates more than a fixed percentage of the corporation's voting stock. Such severance packages may serve the interests of shareholders by making senior management more willing to accept an acquisition. The 1986 Tax Act imposed stiff penalties on these types of plans if they create what is deemed an excessive payment. Excessive payments are those exceeding three times the employee's average pay over the previous five years and are not tax deductible by the paying corporation. The employee receiving the parachute payment also must pay a 20 percent surcharge in addition to the normal tax due on the parachute payment.

Postbid Defenses

Once an unwanted suitor has approached a firm, a variety of additional defenses can be introduced. These include greenmail to dissuade the bidder from continuing the pursuit; defenses designed to make the target less attractive, such as restructuring and recapitalization strategies; and efforts to place an increasing share of the company's ownership in friendly hands by establishing ESOPs and seeking white knights. Table 3–6 summarizes the primary advantages and disadvantages of such postbid defenses.

Table 3–6 Advantages and Disadvantages of Postbid Takeover Defenses

Type of Defense	Advantages for Target Firm	Disadvantages for Target Firm
Greenmail	Encourages raider to go away (usually accompanied by a standstill agreement)	Reduces risk to raider of losing money on a takeover attempt; unfairly discriminates against nonparticipating shareholders; often generates litigation; and triggers unfavorable tax consequences and negative public image
Standstill agreement	Prevents raider from returning for a specific time period	Increases amount of greenmail paid to get raider to sign standstill; provides only temporary reprieve
White knights	May be a preferable to the hostile bidder	Involves loss of the target's independence
ESOPs	Alternative to white knight and highly effective if used in conjunction with certain states' antitakeover laws	Employee support not guaranteed. ESOP cannot overpay for stock because transaction could be disallowed by federal law.
Recapitalizations	Makes target less attractive to bidder and may increase target shareholder value if incumbent management is motivated to improve performance	Increased leverage reduces target's borrowing capacity.
Share buyback plans	Reduces number of target shares available for purchase by bidder, arbs, and others who may sell to bidder	Securities laws limit ability to self-tender without SEC filing once hostile tender is under way. A reduction in the shares outstanding may facilitate bidder's gaining control
Corporate restructuring	Going private may be attractive alternative to bidder's offer for target shareholders and incumbent management	Going private, sale of attractive assets, making defensive acquisitions, or liquidation may reduce target's shareholder value versus bidder's offer
Litigation	May buy time for target to build defenses and increases takeover cost to the bidder	May have negative impact on target shareholder returns

Greenmail

Greenmail is the practice of paying a potential acquirer to leave you alone. It consists of a payment to buy back shares at a premium price in exchange for the acquirer's agreement to not undertake a hostile takeover. In exchange for the payment, the potential acquirer is required to sign a *standstill agreement*, which typically specifies the amount of stock, if any, that the investor can own, the circumstances under which the raider can sell stock currently owned, and the term of the agreement. Despite their discriminatory nature, courts in certain states, such as Delaware, have found greenmail an appropriate response as long as it is made for valid business reasons. However, courts in other states, such as California, have favored shareholder lawsuits, contending that greenmail breaches fiduciary responsibility (Wasserstein, 1998, pp. 719–720).

White Knights

A target company seeking to avoid being taken over by a specific bidder may try to be acquired by another firm, a *white knight*, that is viewed as a more appropriate suitor. To complete such a transaction, the white knight must be willing to acquire the target on more favorable terms than those of other bidders. More favorable terms need not involve an offer price higher than the current bidder's proposal. The presumed white knight may be viewed as more favorable in terms of its willingness to allow the target firm's management to stay in place and continue to pursue their current strategy.

Fearing that a bidding war might ensue, the white knight often demands some protection in the form of a lockup. The lockup may involve giving the white knight options to buy stock in the target that has not yet been issued at a fixed price or to acquire at a fair price specific target assets. Such lockups usually have the effect of making the target less attractive to other bidders. In the event a bidding war ensues, the knight may exercise the stock options and sell the shares at a profit to the acquiring company. German drug and chemical firm Bayer AG's white knight bid for Schering AG in 2006 (which was recommended by the Schering board) was designed to trump a hostile offer from a German rival, Merck KGaS.

Employee Stock Ownership Plans

ESOPs are trusts that hold a firm's stock as an investment for their employees' retirement program. They can be established quickly, with the company either issuing shares directly to the ESOP or having an ESOP purchase shares on the open market. The stock held by ESOPs is likely to be voted in support of management in the event of a hostile takeover attempt.

Leveraged Recapitalization

Recapitalization may require shareholder approval, depending on the company's charter and the laws of the state in which it is incorporated. A company may recapitalize by assuming substantial amounts of new debt, which is used to either buy back stock or finance a dividend payment to shareholders. In doing so, the target becomes less attractive to a bidder, because the additional debt reduces its borrowing capacity, which may have been used by the bidder to help finance the takeover of the target. Moreover, the payment of a dividend or a stock buyback may persuade shareholders to support the target's management in a proxy contest or hostile tender offer. The target firm is left in a highly leveraged position. Whether the recapitalization actually weakens the target firm in the long term depends on its impact on the target firm's shareholder value. Shareholders benefit from the receipt of a dividend or capital gains resulting from a stock repurchase. Furthermore, the increased debt service requirements of the additional debt shelters a substantial amount of the firm's taxable income and may encourage management to be more conscientious about improving the firm's performance. Thus, the combination of these factors may result in current shareholders benefiting more from this takeover defense than from a hostile takeover of the firm. The primary differences between a leveraged recapitalization and a leveraged buyout are that the firm remains a public company and management does not take a significant equity stake in the firm.

Share Repurchase or Buyback Plans

Firms may repurchase shares in one of two ways: through a tender offer or by direct purchases of shares in public markets. Firms engage in such activities for a variety of reasons, including rewarding shareholders, signaling undervaluation, funding employee stock option plans, adjusting capital structure, and defending against unwanted takeovers. Firms frequently increase their share repurchase activities when confronted with an imminent takeover threat (Billet and Xue, 2007). When used as an antitakeover tactic, share repurchase or buyback plans are intended to reduce the number of shares that could be purchased by the potential acquirer or by those such as arbitrageurs who would sell to the highest bidder. This tactic reflects the belief that, when a firm initiates a tender offer (i.e., a self-tender) for a portion of its own shares, the shareholders who offer their shares for sale are those most susceptible to a tender offer by a hostile bidder. This leaves the target firm's shares concentrated in the hands of shareholders who are less likely to sell, thereby reducing so-called float. Therefore, for a hostile tender offer to succeed in purchasing the remaining shares, the premium offered would have to be higher. The resulting higher premium might discourage some prospective bidders. A share buyback may work well in combination with a self-tender by allowing the firm to buy shares (perhaps at a somewhat higher price) in addition to those tendered to the firm. The deterrent effect of buyback strategies has been supported in a number of studies. Potential acquirers are less likely to pursue firms with substantial excess cash, which could be used to adopt highly aggressive share repurchase programs (Harford, 1999; Pinkowitz, 2002; Faleye, 2004).

The repurchase tactic may in fact be subject to the "law of unintended consequences." By reducing the number of shares on the open market, it is easier for the buyer to gain control, because fewer shares have to be purchased to achieve 50.1 percent of the target's voting shares. Moreover, self-tenders actually may attract potential bidders, if they are seen as a harbinger of improving target company cash flows. Federal securities law prohibits purchase by an issuer of its own shares during a hostile tender offer for its shares. An exception is made if the firm files a statement with the SEC disclosing the identity of the purchaser, stock exchanges that will be used for the purchase, the intent of the purchase, and the intended disposition of the shares.

Corporate Restructuring

Restructuring may involve taking the company private, the sale of attractive assets, undertaking a major acquisition, or even liquidating the company. "Going private" typically involves the management team's purchase of the bulk of a firm's shares. This may create a win-win situation for shareholders, who receive a premium for their stock, and management, who retain control. To avoid lawsuits, the price paid for the stock must represent a substantial premium to the current market price. Alternatively, the target may make itself less attractive by divesting assets the bidder wants. The cash proceeds of the sale could fund other defenses, such as share buybacks or payment of a special stockholder dividend. A target company also may undertake a so-called *defensive acquisition* to draw down any excess cash balances and exhaust its current borrowing capacity. A firm may choose to liquidate the company, pay off outstanding obligations to creditors, and distribute the remaining proceeds to shareholders as a *liquidating dividend*. This makes sense only if the liquidating dividend exceeds what the shareholders would have received from the bidder (see Chapter 15).

Litigation

Takeover litigation often includes antitrust concerns, alleged violations of federal securities laws, inadequate disclosure by the bidder as required by the Williams Act, and alleged fraudulent behavior. Targets often try to get a court injunction temporarily stopping the takeover attempt until the court has decided that the target's allegations are groundless. By preventing the potential acquirer from buying more stock, the target firm buys time to erect additional takeover defenses. In mid-2008, Anheuser-Busch, in an effort to stop its suitor, InBev, from attempting to replace its board of directors, filed a lawsuit in federal court. The suit alleged that InBev had made numerous "false and misleading statements" in touting its financing as fully committed, because the commitments that it had received from lenders were full of conditions allowing them to walk away.

Impact on Shareholder and Bondholder Value of Takeover Defenses

As noted in Chapter 1 of this book, average abnormal returns to target shareholders about the time of a hostile tender offer announcement have increased dramatically since the 1960s to more than 30 percent, whereas abnormal returns to acquirer shareholders have deteriorated from marginally positive to slightly negative. Abnormal returns to target shareholders in friendly takeovers have remained at about 20 percent. The increase in target company shareholder returns in hostile bids may be attributable to potential improvements in efficiency, tax savings, or market power. However, if this were true, one would have expected abnormal returns for mergers to also show a correspondingly large increase over time. Consequently, other factors must be at work.

It is probably more than coincidental that the increase in abnormal returns began with the introduction of the 1967 Wallace Act prenotification period. This provided a respite for target firms to erect takeover defenses and search for other potential bidders. Takeover defenses, such as poison pills, although unlikely to prevent a takeover, could add significantly to the overall purchase price. The purchase price could be further boosted by any auction that might take place as the initial bidder lost precious time in trying to overcome myriad defenses the target may have in place. Thus, the increasing sophistication of takeover defenses since 1980 would seem to be a highly plausible factor explaining the sustained increase in abnormal returns to target shareholders following the announcement of a hostile tender offer.

Early Empirical Studies Show Mixed Results

Unfortunately, it is difficult to substantiate this intuitive argument empirically. Those studies showing a negative return to shareholders of firms with takeover defenses support the argument that incumbent management acts in its own self-interest, the management entrenchment hypothesis. Studies showing a positive shareholder return support the argument that incumbent management acts in the best interests of shareholders, the shareholder interests' hypothesis. For many takeover defenses, empirical results cannot be confirmed by multiple studies, the available evidence is largely contradictory, or the findings are statistically insignificant. The empirical evidence seems to suggest that takeover defenses in general have virtually no statistically significant impact on shareholder returns or, as in the case of poison pills, have a positive impact.

In a comprehensive review of previous studies, Comment and Schwert (1995) found that most takeover defensives, such as staggered boards, supermajority provisions, fair price provisions, reincorporation, and dual capitalization, resulted in a slightly negative decline in shareholder returns of about 0.5 percent. These studies included the following: Jarrell and Poulsen, 1987; Malatesta and Walkling, 1988; Ryngaert, 1988; Karpoff and Malatesta, 1989; Romano, 1993. Other studies found no statistically significant negative results (DeAngelo and Rice, 1983; Linn and McConnell, 1983). Yet another study found that shareholder efforts to remove takeover defenses had no significant impact on shareholder returns, suggesting that such efforts were viewed by investors as largely inconsequential (Karpoff and Walkling, 1996). Field and Karpoff (2002) concluded, in a study of 1,019 initial public offerings between 1988 and 1992, that takeover defenses had no impact on the takeover premiums of those firms acquired after the IPO.

The Comment and Schwert (1995) study also found that poison pills would have a positive impact on shareholder returns if their addition by the target were viewed by investors as a signal that a takeover was imminent or that the firm's management would use such a defense to improve the purchase price during negotiation. The existence of poison pills often requires the bidder to raise its bid or change the composition of its bid to an all-cash offer to put the target's board under pressure to dismantle its pill defenses. Timing also is important. For example, whenever a merger announcement coincided with the announcement of a poison pill, abnormal returns to target shareholders increased by 3–4 percent. A number of studies suggest that investors react positively to the announcement of the adoption of takeover defenses if the firm's management interests are viewed as aligned with those of the shareholders and negatively if management is viewed as seeking to entrench itself (McWilliams, 1993; Bhaghat and Jefferis, 1994; Boyle, Carer, and Stover, 1998; Malekzadeh et al., 1998).

More Recent Empirical Studies

Despite the largely mixed results of earlier studies, more recent studies suggest that takeover defenses may destroy shareholder value. In an effort to assess which of 24 governance provisions tracked by the Investor Responsibility Research Center (IRRC) had the greatest impact on shareholder value, Bebchuk, Cohen, and Ferrell (2005) created a "management entrenchment index" that is negatively correlated with firm value between 1990 and 2003. The index consists of staggered boards, limits to shareholder bylaw amendments, supermajority requirements for mergers, supermajority requirements for charter amendments, poison pills, and golden parachutes. The study's major finding is that firms with a low entrenchment index (i.e., management's interests are more aligned with those of the shareholders) have larger abnormal returns than firms with a high entrenchment index. The authors found no correlation between firm value and the other 18 IRRC provisions during the sample period. The authors note that the mere existence of correlation does not necessarily mean that these takeover defenses cause a reduction in the value of the firm. The correlation could reflect the tendency of underperforming firms that are likely to be takeover targets to adopt takeover defenses. These results support the findings of an earlier study by Bebchuk, Cohen, and Ferrell (2004), which used a shorter time period.

Masulis et al. (2007) provide additional support for the destructive effect of takeover defenses on shareholder value. In a study of 3,333 completed acquisitions between 1990 and 2003, they conclude that managers at firms protected by takeover defenses are less subject to the disciplinary power of the market for corporate control. Moreover, such managers are more likely to engage in "empire building" acquisitions that destroy shareholder value. Guo, Hotchkiss, and Song (2008) found that firms that move immediately from staggered board elections to annual elections of directors experience a cumulative abnormal return of 1.82 percent, reflecting investor expectations that the firm is more likely to be subject to a takeover. The authors found that such firms often are subject to substantial pressure from activist shareholders and are more likely to have a greater proportion of independent directors than those that retain staggered boards.

Takeover Defenses May Benefit Initial Public Offerings

Event studies examine only how takeover defenses affect shareholder wealth after the corporation has been formed, shareholders have purchased its stock, and employees and managers have been hired. Takeover defenses may, in fact, create significant firm value at the point when the firm is formed. Consequently, to fully evaluate the impact of takeover defenses on firm value, the analyst must consider both the potentially beneficial effects before the event of a takeover attempt and the potentially destructive effect on firm value after the announcement.

Takeover defenses may add to firm value before a takeover attempt if they help the firm to attract, retain, and motivate effective managers and employees. Furthermore, such defenses give the new firm time to fully implement its business plan and invest in upgrading the skills of employees (Stout, 2002). Coates (2001) found that the percentage of IPO firms with staggered boards in their charters at the time of the initial public offering rose from 34 percent in the early 1990s to 82 percent in 1999. This finding suggests that investors may prefer the adoption of takeover defenses during the early stages of a firm's development.

Takeover Defenses May Benefit Bondholders

Companies with limited takeover defenses are often vulnerable to hostile takeovers, which may hurt bondholders (Cremers, Nair, and Wei, 2004). While the increased potential for takeover may benefit shareholder investors, existing bondholders stand to lose if the takeover results in a significant increase in leverage, which is typical of a leveraged buyout. Higher leverage can reduce the value of outstanding debt by increasing the potential for future bankruptcy. This impact on existing bondholders is explored in more detail in Chapter 16.

Trends in Takeover Defenses

During the five years ending in 2007, U.S. corporations have been largely dismantling their takeover defenses. While the trend began with large capitalization firms, it has spread to firms of all sizes in recent years. At the end of 2007, 1,400 U.S. firms had poison pills in place. This compares to 2,200 firms with poison pills at the end of 2002. The percentage of S&P 500 firms with poison pills in place fell below 30 percent, compared to 60 percent in 2002. While the pace at which large capitalization firms are removing defenses is slowing, it is accelerating for smaller firms (see Table 3–7). According to FactSet sharkrepellent.com, the decline in overall takeover defenses resulted primarily from the removal of poison pills and the switch to annually elected boards from a staggered board system. However, preliminary estimates for 2008 suggest a reversal of these trends. In response to depressed equity prices, hostile takeover activity surged upward, comprising as much as one fifth of 2008 announced U.S. deals. In an effort to ward off takeovers, 53 U.S. firms adopted their first pills, 20 percent more than in 2007. Of these 53 firms, one fourth were "in-play" adoptions undertaken in response to an unwanted takeover attempt according to FactSet Merger Metrics.

Things to Remember

The market in which takeover tactics and defenses are employed is called the *corporate takeover market*, which in a free market economy facilitates the allocation of resources and disciplines underperforming managers. By replacing such managers through hostile

Table 3–7 Trend in Takeover Defenses

Index	Market Capitalization	2005	2006	2007	% Change 2005–2006	% Change 2006–2007
S&P 500	Large cap	4.89	4.28	3.89	(12.47)	(9.11)
S&P 400	Mid cap	5.84	5.45	5.05	(6.68)	(7.34)
S&P 600	Small cap	5.46	5.19	4.81	(4.95)	(7.32)

Source: FactSet sharkrepellent.com Bullet Proof Rating (BPR). BPR is a relative measurement of a company's takeover defense protection. It is based on an index that considers charter and bylaw provisions and procedural items that contribute to defending against hostile takeovers and proxy battles. The scale ranges from 0 to 10, with 10 representing the highest relative protection.

takeover attempts or proxy fights, the corporate takeover market can help promote good corporate governance practices, which protect stakeholder interests. In addition to the corporate takeover market, other factors external to the firm, such as federal and state legislation, the court system, regulators, and institutional activism serve important roles in maintaining good corporate governance practices. Corporate governance is also affected by the integrity and professionalism of the firm's board of directors, as well as the effectiveness of the firm's internal controls and incentive systems, takeover defenses, and corporate culture.

Takeovers often are divided into friendly and hostile categories. A hostile takeover generally is considered an unsolicited offer made by a potential acquirer that is resisted by the target's management. If the friendly approach is considered inappropriate or is unsuccessful, the acquiring company may attempt to limit the options of the target's senior management by making a formal acquisition proposal, usually involving a public announcement, to the target's board of directors. This tactic, called a *bear hug*, is an attempt to pressure the target's board into making a rapid decision. Alternatively, the bidder may undertake a proxy contest. By replacing board members, proxy contests can be an effective means of gaining control without owning 50.1 percent of the voting stock, or they can be used to eliminate takeover defenses as a precursor to a tender offer. In a tender offer, the bidding company goes directly to the target shareholders with an offer to buy their stock.

Takeover defenses are designed to raise the overall cost of the takeover attempt and provide the target firm with more time to install additional takeover defenses. Prebid defenses usually require shareholder approval and fall into three categories: poison pills, shark repellants, and golden parachutes. Postbid defenses are those undertaken in response to a bid. For example, a target company seeking to avoid being taken over by a specific bidder may try to be acquired by another firm, a white knight, which is viewed as a more appropriate suitor.

Takeover defenses may benefit the shareholders of firms that are performing well and whose managers' interests are aligned with those of their shareholders. In contrast, shareholders of underperforming firms are often penalized by significant takeover defenses, as they may tend to entrench incompetent management. The results of earlier empirical studies are mixed, while more recent studies suggest that takeover defenses have a small negative impact on abnormal shareholder returns. However, takeover defenses put in place prior to an IPO can benefit shareholders. Finally, in some situations, bondholders may lose due to the absence of takeover defenses, which make the firm more vulnerable to hostile takeovers.

Chapter Discussion Questions

3–1. What are the management entrenchment and shareholder interests hypotheses? Which seems more realistic in your judgment? Explain your answer.

3–2. What are the advantages and disadvantages of the friendly versus hostile approaches to a corporate takeover? Be specific.

3–3. What are proxy contests and how are they used?

3–4. What is a tender offer? How does it differ from open market purchases of stock?

3–5. How are target shareholders affected by a hostile takeover attempt?

3–6. How are the bidder's shareholders affected by a hostile takeover attempt?

3–7. What are the primary advantages and disadvantages of commonly used takeover defenses?

3–8. Of the most commonly used takeover defenses, which seem to have the most favorable impact on target shareholders? Explain your answer.

3–9. How may golden parachutes for senior management help a target firm's shareholders? Are such severance packages justified in your judgment? Explain your answer.

3–10. How might recapitalization as a takeover defense help or hurt a target firm's shareholders?

3–11. Anheuser-Busch rejected InBev's all-cash offer price of $65 per share on June 30, 2008, saying it undervalued the company, despite the offer representing a 35 percent premium to AB's preannouncement share price. InBev refused to raise its offer while repeating its strong preference for a friendly takeover. Speculate as to why InBev refused to raise its initial offer price. Why do you believe that InBev continued to prefer a friendly takeover? What do you think InBev should have done to raise pressure on the AB board to accept the offer?

3–12. What do you believe are the primary factors a target firm's board should consider when evaluating a bid from a potential acquirer?

3–13. If you were the CEO of a target firm, what strategy would you recommend to convince institutional shareholders to support your position in a proxy battle with the bidding firm?

3–14. Anheuser-Busch reduced its antitakeover defenses in 2006, when it removed its staggered board structure. Two years earlier, it did not renew its poison pill provision. Speculate as to why the board acquiesced in these instances. Explain how these events affected the firm's vulnerability to a takeover.

3–15. In response to Microsoft's efforts to acquire the firm, the Yahoo board adopted a "change in-control" compensation plan in May 2008. The plan states that, if a Yahoo employee's job is terminated by Yahoo without cause (i.e., the employee is performing his or her duties appropriately) or if an employee leaves voluntarily due to a change in position or responsibilities within two years after Microsoft acquires a controlling interest in Yahoo, the employee will receive one year's salary. Also, the plan provides for accelerated vesting of all stock options. Yahoo notes that the adoption of the severance plan is an effort to ensure that employees are treated fairly if Microsoft wins control. Microsoft views the tactic as an effort to discourage a takeover. With whom do you agree and why?

Answers to these Chapter Discussion Questions are available in the Online Instructor's Manual for instructors using this book.

Chapter Business Cases

Case Study 3–1. Mittal Acquires Arcelor—A Battle of Global Titans in the European Market for Corporate Control

Ending five months of maneuvering, Arcelor agreed on June 26, 2006, to be acquired by larger rival Mittal Steel Co. for $33.8 billion in cash and stock. The takeover battle was one of the most acrimonious in recent European Union history. After decades in which hostile transactions were rare, the battle between the two steel titans illustrates Europe's move toward less-regulated markets. Hostile takeovers are now increasingly common in

Europe. The battle is widely viewed as a test case as to how far a firm can go in attempting to prevent an unwanted takeover.

Arcelor was created in 2001 by melding steel companies in Spain, France, and Luxembourg. Most of its 90 plants are in Europe. In contrast, most of Mittal's plants are outside of Europe in areas with lower labor costs. Lakshmi Mittal, Mittal's CEO and a member of an important industrial family in India, started the firm and built it into a powerhouse through two decades of acquisitions in emerging nations. The company is headquartered in the Netherlands for tax reasons. Prior to the Arcelor acquisition, Mr. Mittal owned 88 percent of the firm's stock.

Mittal acquired Arcelor to accelerate steel industry consolidation to reduce industry overcapacity. The combined firms' could have more leverage in setting prices and negotiating contracts with major customers such as auto and appliance manufacturers, suppliers such as iron ore and coal vendors, and eventually realize $1 billion annually in pretax cost savings.

The War of Words

After having been rebuffed by Guy Dolle, Arcelor's president, in an effort to consummate a friendly merger, Mittal launched a tender offer in January 2006 consisting of mostly stock and cash for all of Arcelor's outstanding equity. The offer constituted a 27 percent premium over Arcelor's share price at that time. The reaction from Arcelor's management, European unions, and government officials was swift and furious. Guy Dolle stated flatly that the offer was "inadequate and strategically unsound." European politicians supported Mr. Dolle. Luxembourg's prime minister Jean Claude Juncker said a hostile bid "calls for a hostile response." French finance minister Thierry Breton said that Mittal's logic ran contrary to what he called "the grammar of business." Trade unions expressed concern about potential job loss.

The Chess Match Begins

Dolle engaged in one of the most aggressive takeover defenses in recent corporate history. In early February, Arcelor doubled its dividend and announced plans to buy back about $8.75 billion in stock at a price well above the then current market price for Arcelor stock. These actions were taken to motivate Arcelor shareholders not to tender their shares to Mittal. Arcelor also backed a move to change the law so that Mittal would be required to pay in cash. However, the Luxembourg parliament rejected that effort.

To counter these moves, Mittal Steel said in mid-February that, if it received more than one half of the Arcelor shares submitted in the initial tender offer, it would hold a second tender offer for the remaining shares at a slightly lower price. Mittal pointed out that it could acquire the remaining shares through a merger or corporate reorganization. Such rhetoric was designed to encourage Arcelor shareholders to tender their shares during the first offer.

In late 2005, Arcelor outbid German steelmaker Metallgeschaft to buy Canadian steelmaker Dofasco for $5 billion. Mittal was proposing to sell Dofasco to raise money and avoid North American antitrust concerns. Following completion of the Dofasco deal in April 2006, Arcelor set up a special Dutch trust to prevent Mittal from getting access to the asset. The trust is run by a board of three Arcelor appointees. The trio has the power to determine if Dofasco can be sold during the next five years. Mittal immediately sued to test the legality of this tactic.

In a deal with Russian steel maker OAO Severstahl, Arcelor agreed to exchange its shares for Alexei Mordashov's 90 percent stake in Severstahl. The transaction would give Mr. Mordashov a 32 percent stake in Arcelor. Arcelor also scheduled an unusual vote that created very tough conditions for Arcelor shareholders to prevent the deal with Severstahl from being completed. Arcelor's board stated that the Severstahl deal could be blocked only if at least 50 percent of all Arcelor shareholders would vote against it. However, Arcelor knew that only about one third of shareholders actually attend meetings. This is a tactic permissible under Luxembourg law, where Arcelor is incorporated.

Arcelor Shareholders Revolt

Investors holding more than 30 percent of Arcelor shares signed a petition to force the company to make the deal with Severstahl subject to a traditional 50.1 percent or more of actual votes cast. After major shareholders pressured the Arcelor board to at least talk to Mr. Mittal, Arcelor demanded an intricate business plan from Mittal as a condition that had to be met. Despite Mittal's submission of such a plan, Arcelor still refused to talk. In late May, Mittal raised its bid by 34 percent and said that, if the bid succeeded, Mittal would eliminate his firm's two-tiered share structure, giving the Mittal family shares ten times the voting rights of other shareholders.

A week after receiving the shareholder petition, the Arcelor board rejected Mittal's sweetened bid and repeated its support of the Severstahl deal. Shareholder anger continued, as many investors said they would reject the share buyback. Some investors opposed the buyback, because it would increase Mr. Mordashov's ultimate stake in Arcelor to 38 percent by reducing the number of Arcelor shares outstanding. Under the laws of most European countries, any entity owning more than a third of a company is said to have effective control. Arcelor canceled a scheduled June 21st shareholder vote on the buyback. Despite Mr. Mordashov's efforts to enhance his bid, the Arcelor board asked both Mordashov and Mittal to submit their final bids by June 25.

Arcelor finally agreed to Mittal's final bid which had been increased by 14 percent. The new offer consisted of $15.70 in cash and 1.0833 Mittal shares for each Arcelor share. The new bid is valued at $50.54 per Arcelor share, up from Mittal's initial bid in January 2006 of $35.26. The final offer represented an unprecedented 93 percent premium over Arcelor's share price of $26.25 immediately before Mittal's initial bid. Lakshmi Mittal will control 43.5 percent of the combined firm's stock. Mr. Mordashov would receive a $175 million breakup fee due to Arcelor's failure to complete its agreement with him. Finally, Mittal agreed not to make any layoffs beyond what Arcelor already has planned.

Discussion Questions

1. Identify the takeover tactics employed by Mittal. Explain why each was used.
2. Identify the takeover defenses employed by Arcelor. Explain why each was used.
3. Using the information in this case study, discuss the arguments for and against encouraging hostile corporate takeovers. Be specific.
4. Was Arcelor's board and management acting to protect their own positions (i.e., the management entrenchment hypothesis) or the best interests of the shareholders (i.e., the shareholder interests hypothesis)? Explain your answer.

Solutions to these questions are found in the Online Instructor's Manual available to instructors using this book.

Case Study 3–2. Verizon Acquires MCI—The Anatomy of Alternative Bidding Strategies

While many parties were interested in acquiring MCI, the major players included Verizon and Qwest. U.S.-based Qwest is an integrated communications company that provides data, multimedia, and Internet-based communication services on a national and global basis. The acquisition would ease the firm's huge debt burden of $17.3 billion (more than twice its stock market value), because the debt would be supported by the combined company with a much larger revenue and asset base. The deal would also give the firm access to new business customers and opportunities to cut costs.

Verizon Communications, created through the merger of Bell Atlantic and GTE in 2000, is the largest telecommunications provider in the United States. The company provides local exchange, long distance, Internet, and other related services to residential, business, and government customers. In addition, the company provides wireless services to over 42 million customers in the United States, through its 55 percent-owned joint venture with Vodafone Group PLC.

Interest Grows in MCI

By mid-2004, MCI had received several expressions of interest from Verizon and Qwest regarding potential strategic relationships. By July, Qwest and MCI entered into a confidentiality agreement and proceeded to perform more detailed due diligence. Others also expressed interest in acquiring or converting MCI to a private company through a leveraged buyout. However, they were rebuffed by the MCI board. Ivan Seidenberg, Verizon's chairman and CEO, inquired about a potential takeover and was rebuffed by MCI's board, which was evaluating its strategic options. These included Qwest's proposal regarding a share-for-share merger, following a one-time cash dividend to MCI shareholders from MCI's cash in excess of its required operating balances (i.e., excess cash). In view of Verizon's interest, MCI's board of directors directed management to advise Richard Notebaert, the chairman and CEO of Qwest, that MCI was not prepared to move forward with a potential transaction.

The stage was set for what would become Qwest's laboriously long and ultimately unsuccessful pursuit of MCI, in which the firm would be rejected by MCI four times. The key events of this 11-week period are summarized in Table 3–8.

Verizon's Reasons for the Merger

Verizon stated that the merger would enable it to more efficiently provide a broader range of services, give the firm access to MCI's business customer base, accelerate new product development using MCI's fiber-optic network infrastructure, and create substantial cost savings.

MCI's Reasons for the Merger

After assessing its strategic alternatives, including the option to remain a stand-alone company, MCI's board of directors concluded that the merger with Verizon was in the best interests of the MCI stockholders. MCI's board of directors noted that Verizon's bid of $26 per share represented a 41.5 percent premium over the closing price of MCI's common stock on January 26, 2005. Furthermore, the offer included "price protection" in the form of a collar.

The merger agreement also provided for the MCI board to declare a special dividend of $5.60 once the firm's shareholders approved the deal. MCI's board of directors

Table 3–8 Transaction Timeline

Key Date	Bidder	Price per MCI Share	Comment
4/20/04			MCI emerged from bankruptcy after a multibillion accounting scandal nearly destroyed the company.
2/2/05	Qwest	$19.45	At $6.32 billion, the offer consisted of $17.85 per share in cash and provided for the payment of $0.40 per share in quarterly dividends for the four quarters anticipated between signing and closing.
2/7/05	Verizon	$20.00	At $6.5 billion, the proposal consisted of $5.99 per share payable in cash plus the conversion of each MCI share into 0.3802 shares of Verizon stock.
2/10/05	Qwest	$19.87	Valued at $6.46 billion, the all-cash offer included four quarterly dividends between signing and closing dates.
2/11/05	Qwest	$24.60	The revised offer was valued at $7.5 billion, consisting of $7.50 in cash and 3.735 shares of Qwest stock for each share of MCI stock. It continued to include the dividend payouts of its previous offers.
2/14/05	Verizon	$20.75	MCI agreed to a $6.75 billion deal in which Verizon would convert each MCI share into 0.4062 shares of Verizon stock and pay cash in the amount of $1.50 per MCI share. MCI stockholders would also receive a special cash dividend of $4.50 per share (first rejection of Qwest).
2/24/05	Qwest	$24.60	Valued at $8.1 billion, the revised proposal provided for $6.00 in cash in quarterly and special dividends, $3.10 in cash at closing, and 3.735 shares of Qwest common stock for each share of MCI common stock.
3/29/05	Verizon	$23.50	Verizon increased its bid to $8.45 billion, consisting of $8.75 per share in cash and the higher of 0.4032 shares of Verizon or $14.75 in stock (second rejection of Qwest).
3/31/05	Qwest	$27.50	Qwest raised bid to $8.9 billion, consisting of 3.733 shares of Qwest stock and $13.50 in cash.
4/6/05			MCI's board voted to reject Qwest's $8.9 billion offer (third rejection of Qwest).
4/8/05			Qwest said a survey of investors indicated that investors controlling more than 50% of MCI's stock favor the higher Qwest bid.
4/9/05			Verizon bought out MCI's largest shareholder, Mexican millionaire Carlos Slim Helu, for $1.1 billion. Mr. Slim had invested $700 million in MCI.
4/12/05			MCI announced that it will not amend its rights plan allowing shareholders to buy more shares if a single investor acquires 15% or more of MCI's stock.
4/21/05	Qwest	$30.00	Qwest raised its bid to $9.9 billion, saying this was its final offer, after having been rejected three times. Qwest added $2.50 in cash per share to the previous bid.
4/25/05			MCI declared the Qwest offer superior to the accepted merger with Verizon.
5/2/05	Verizon	$26.00	Verizon raised it bid to $8.45 billion or $26 per share, consisting of $5.60 per share in cash payable on approval by MCI shareholders plus the greater of 0.5743 Verizon shares for every MCI common share or the equivalent number of Verizon shares equal to $20.40, whichever is higher. This collar enabled MCI shareholders to benefit from a floor of $20.40 and would benefit from the upside potential of an increase in Verizon's share price. MCI's board voted to accept the Verizon offer (fourth and final rejection of Qwest).

also considered the additional value that its stockholders would realize, since the merger is expected to be a tax-free reorganization. Consequently, only the cash portion of the purchase price would be taxable, with the payment of taxes on any gains from the receipt of Verizon stock deferred until the MCI shareholders chose to sell their shares. MCI's board of directors also noted that a large number of MCI's most important business customers had indicated that they preferred a transaction between MCI and Verizon rather than a transaction between MCI and Qwest.

Analysis of Verizon's Bidding Strategies

While it is clearly impossible to know for sure, the sequence of events reveals a great deal about Verizon's possible bidding strategy. Any bidding strategy must begin with a series of management assumptions about how to approach the target firm. It was certainly in Verizon's interest to attempt a friendly rather than hostile takeover of MCI, due to the challenges of integrating these two complex businesses. Verizon also employed an increasingly popular technique, in which the merger agreement includes a special dividend payable by the target firm to its shareholders contingent upon their approval of the transaction. This special dividend is an inducement to gain shareholder approval.

Given the modest 3 percent premium over the first Qwest bid, Verizon's initial bidding strategy appears to have been based on the low end of the purchase price range it was willing to offer MCI. Verizon was initially prepared to share relatively little of the potential synergy with MCI shareholders, believing that a bidding war for MCI would be unlikely in view of the recent spate of mergers in the telecommunications industry and the weak financial position of other competitors. SBC and Nextel were busy integrating AT&T and Sprint, respectively. Moreover, Qwest appeared to be unable to finance a substantial all-cash offer due to its current excessive debt burden, and its stock appeared to have little appreciation potential because of ongoing operating losses. Perhaps stunned by the persistence with which Qwest pursued MCI, Verizon believed that its combination of cash and stock would ultimately be more attractive to MCI investors than Qwest's primarily all-cash offer, due to the partial tax-free nature of the bid.

Throughout the bidding process, many hedge funds criticized MCI's board publicly for accepting the initial Verizon bid. Since its emergence from Chapter 11, hedge funds had acquired significant positions in MCI's stock, with the expectation that MCI constituted an attractive merger candidate. In particular, Carlos Slim Helu, the Mexican telecommunications magnate and largest MCI shareholder, complained loudly and publicly about the failure of MCI's board to get full value for the firm's shares. Pressure from hedge funds and other dissident MCI shareholders may have triggered a shareholder lawsuit to void the February 14, 2005, signed merger agreement with Verizon.

In preparation for a possible proxy fight, Verizon entered into negotiations with Carlos Slim Helu to acquire his shares. Verizon acquired Mr. Slim's 13.7 percent stake in MCI in April 2005. Despite this purchase, Verizon's total stake in MCI remained below the 15 percent ownership level that would trigger the MCI rights plan.

About 70 percent (i.e., $1.4 billion) of the cash portion of Verizon's proposed purchase price consisted of a special MCI dividend payable by MCI when the firm's shareholders approved the merger agreement. Verizon's management argued that the deal would cost their shareholders only $7.05 billion (i.e., the $8.45 billion purchase price less the MCI special dividend). The promise of the special dividend served as an inducement for the MCI shareholders to approve the deal. The $1.4 billion special dividend reduced MCI's cash in excess of what was required to meet its normal operating cash requirements.

Analysis of Qwest's Bidding Strategy

Qwest consistently attempted to outmaneuver Verizon by establishing a significant premium between its bid and Verizon's, often as much as 25 percent. Qwest realized that its current level of indebtedness would preclude it from significantly increasing the cash portion of the bid. Consequently, it had to rely on the premium to attract enough investor interest, particularly among hedge funds, to pressure the MCI board to accept the higher bid. However, Qwest was unable to satisfy enough investors that its stock would not simply lose value once more shares were issued to consummate the stock and cash transaction.

Qwest could have initiated a tender or exchange offer directly to MCI shareholders proposing to purchase or exchange their shares without going through the merger process. The tender process requires lengthy regulatory approval. However, if Qwest initiated a tender offer, it could trigger MCI's poison pill. Alternatively, a proxy contest might have been preferable because Qwest already had a bid on the table and the contest would enable Qwest to lobby MCI shareholders to vote against the Verizon bid. This strategy would have avoided triggering the poison pill.

Ultimately, Qwest was forced to capitulate simply because it did not have the financial wherewithal to increase the $9.9 billion bid. It could not borrow any more because of its excessive leverage. Additional stock would have contributed to earnings dilution and caused the firm's share price to fall.

Governance Issues

It is unusual for a board to turn down a higher bid, especially when the competing bid was 17 percent higher. In accepting the Verizon bid, MCI stated that a number of its large business customers had expressed a preference for the company to be bought by Verizon rather than Qwest. MCI noted that these customer concerns posed a significant risk in being acquired by Qwest. The MCI board's acceptance of the lower Verizon bid could serve as a test case of how well MCI directors are conducting their fiduciary responsibilities. The central issue is how far boards can go in rejecting a higher offer in favor of one they believe offers more long-term stability for the firm's stakeholders.

The bidding war illustrates how forces outside of the company can force management and boards to modify their decisions. The bidding war featured an almost daily exchange between the bidders and the powerful role of hedge funds and arbitrageurs, who owned a majority of MCI shares and pushed the company to extract two higher bids from Verizon.

Ron Perlman, the 1980s takeover mogul, saw his higher all-cash bid rejected by the board of directors of Revlon Corporation, which accepted a lower offer from another bidder. In a subsequent lawsuit, a court overruled the decision by the Revlon board in favor of the Perlman bid. Consequently, from a governance perspective, legal precedent compels boards to accept higher bids from bona fide bidders where the value of the bid is unambiguous, as in the case of an all-cash offer. However, for transactions in which the purchase price is composed largely of acquirer stock, the value is less certain. Consequently, the target's board may rule that the lower bidder's shares have higher appreciation potential or at least are less likely to decline than those shares of other bidders. This is a particularly important consideration when the time between the signing of a merger agreement and the actual closing is expected to be lengthy.

MCI's president and CEO Michael Capellas and other executives could collect $107 million in severance, payouts of restricted stock, and monies to compensate them for taxes owed on the payouts. In particular, Capellas stood to receive $39.2 million if his job is terminated "without cause" or if he leaves the company for "good reason."

Discussion Questions

1. Discuss how changing industry conditions have encouraged consolidation within the telecommunications industry.
2. What alternative strategies could Verizon, Qwest, and MCI have pursued? Was the decision to acquire MCI the best alternative for Verizon? Explain your answer.
3. Who are the winners and losers in the Verizon-MCI merger? Be specific.
4. What takeover tactics were employed or threatened to be employed by Verizon? By Qwest? Be specific.
5. What specific takeover defenses did MCI employ?
6. How did the actions of certain shareholders affect the bidding process? Be specific.
7. In your opinion, did the MCI board act in the best interests of their shareholders? Of all their stakeholders? Be specific.
8. Do you believe that the potential severance payments that could be paid to Capellas were excessive? Explain your answer. What are the arguments for and against such severance plans for senior executives?
9. Should the antitrust regulators approve the Verizon-MCI merger? Explain your answer.
10. Verizon's management argued that the final purchase price from the perspective of Verizon shareholders was not $8.45 billion but rather $7.05. This was so, they argued, because MCI was paying the difference of $1.4 billion from their excess cash balances as a special dividend to MCI shareholders. Why is this misleading?

Solutions to these discussion questions are available in the Online Instructor's Manual for instructors using this book.

The Mergers and Acquisitions Process: Phases 1–10

4

Planning: Developing Business and Acquisition Plans

Phases 1 and 2 of the Acquisition Process

If you don't know where you are going, any road will get you there.
—Lewis Carroll, *Alice in Wonderland*

Inside M&A: Nokia Moves to Establish Industry Standards

The ultimate success or failure of any transaction to satisfy expectations often is heavily dependent on the answer to a simple question: Was the justification for buying the target firm based on a sound business strategy? No matter how bold, innovative, or precedent setting a bad strategy is, it is still a bad strategy. In a bold move, reminiscent of the roll-out of Linux, Nokia, a Finnish phone handset manufacturer, announced in mid-2008 that it had reached an agreement to acquire Symbian, its supplier of smart phone operating system software. Nokia also announced its intention to give away Symbian's software for free.

Symbian currently supplies 56 percent of the operating system software for smart phones. Nokia hopes to establish an industry standard based on the Symbian software, using it as a platform for providing online services to smart phone users. Such services could include online music and photo sharing. The market for such services is expected to increase from $46 billion in 2007 to $92 billion in 2012, with an increasing portion of these services delivered via smart phones. By supplying the Symbian code free, Nokia hopes that more independent software developers will make their service offering compatible with the Symbian system. Microsoft is likely to be hurt by these developments as it charges royalties to use its software.

Nokia's ability to grow its offering to the smart phone market is heavily dependent on its ability to grow its customer base using Nokia-supplied handsets capable of downloading online services. The firm hopes to move from more expensive niche products such as its N series handsets to less-expensive, mass market products. Currently, many handsets in wide use employ proprietary operating software, which makes it difficult to provide online services.

The opportunity has not been lost on Nokia's competitors. Google is backing an operating system called *Android* to create a Web-friendly software platform. The LiMO Foundation has garnered widespread support for using Linux software for mobile phones. The pervasive popularity of Apple's iPhone has captured the imagination of many independent software developers targeting the smart phone as a conduit for distributing online services to consumers.

In its *vision* for the future, Nokia seems to be positioning itself as the premier supplier of online services to the smart phone market. Its *business strategy* or model is to dominate the smart phone market with handsets reliant on the Symbian operating system. Nokia hopes to exploit economies of scale by spreading any fixed cost associated with online services over an expanding customer base. Such fixed expenses could include a requirement by content service providers that Nokia pay a minimum level of royalties in addition to royalties that vary with usage. Similarly, the development cost incurred by service providers can be defrayed by selling into a growing customer base. The *implementation strategy* is to acquire the leading supplier of handset operating systems and subsequently give away the Symbian software free. The success or failure of this vision, business strategy, and implementation strategy depends on whether Symbian can do a better job of recruiting other handset makers, service providers, and consumers than Nokia's competitors. Nokia may have been too optimistic as its success in establishing an industry operating system standard is dependent on its ability to enlist the support of other manufacturers of handsets, who may be understandably reluctant to do anything that would strengthen a competitor. Many smart phone manufacturers already are hedging their bets. For example, while Motorola and NTT DoCoMo serve on the Symbian board, they also are involved in various ways with LiMO and Android.

Chapter Overview

A poorly designed or inappropriate business strategy is among the most frequently cited reasons for the failure of mergers and acquisitions (M&As) to satisfy expectations. Surprisingly, many textbooks on the subject of M&As fail to address adequately the overarching role that planning should take in conceptualizing and implementing business combinations. The purpose of this chapter is to introduce a planning-based approach to mergers and acquisitions, which discusses M&A activity in the context of an integrated process consisting of 10 interrelated phases. This chapter focuses on the first two phases of the process—building the business and acquisition plans—and on tools commonly used to evaluate, display, and communicate information to key constituencies both inside (e.g., board of directors and management) and outside (e.g., lenders and stockholders) the corporation. Phases 3–10 are discussed in Chapter 5.

Many companies view M&A as a business growth strategy. In this book, mergers and acquisitions are not considered a business strategy but rather a means of implementing a business strategy. Palter and Srinivasan (2006) note that successful acquirers tend to view acquisitions as a tool to support strategy rather than as a business strategy itself. While firms may accelerate overall growth in the short run through acquisition, the higher growth rate often is not sustainable without a business plan. It also serves as a roadmap for identifying additional acquisitions to fuel future growth. Moreover, the business plan facilitates the integration of the acquired firms and the realization of synergy. Bank of America's acquisition of Merrill Lynch in late 2008 illustrates how its vision of becoming the number 1 financial services provider in its domestic market drove the firm's business strategy, focused in the United States, of broadening its product offering and expanding its geographic coverage. This strategy was implemented by opportunistically making acquisitions. The ultimate success of these acquisitions will not be known for some time. While Bank of America's vision and business strategy may have been reasonable, the firm's decision to acquire opportunistically Countrywide and Merrill Lynch without performing adequate due diligence may lead to the eventual failure of these acquisitions. See the case study at the beginning of Chapter 5.

The planning concepts described in this chapter are largely prescriptive in nature, in that they recommend certain strategies based on the results generated by applying specific tools (e.g., experience curves) and answering checklists of relevant questions. Although these tools introduce some degree of rigor to strategic planning, their application should not be viewed as a completion of the planning process. Business plans must be updated frequently to account for changes in the firm's operating environment and its competitive position within that environment. Indeed, business planning is not an event, it is an evolving process. Major chapter segments include the following:

- A Planning-Based Approach to Mergers and Acquisitions
- Phase 1. Building the Business Plan
- The Business Plan as a Communications Document
- Phase 2. Building the Merger–Acquisition Implementation Plan
- Things to Remember

A review of this chapter (including practice questions) is available in the file folder entitled Student Study Guide contained on the CD-ROM accompanying this book. The CD-ROM also contains a Learning Interactions Library, enabling students to test their knowledge of this chapter in a "real-time" environment. For a more detailed discussion of business planning, see Hunger and Wheeler (2007); Thompson (2007); and Deusen, Williamson, and Babson (2007).

A Planning-Based Approach to Mergers and Acquisitions

The acquisition process envisioned in this chapter can be separated into a planning stage and an implementation stage. The planning stage consists of the development of the business and the acquisition plans. The implementation stage includes the search, screening, contacting the target, negotiation, integration planning, closing, integration, and evaluation activities. To understand the role of planning in the M&A process, it is necessary to understand the purpose of the acquiring firm's mission and strategy.

Key Business Planning Concepts

A planning-based acquisition process consists of both a business plan and a merger–acquisition plan, which drive all subsequent phases of the acquisition process. The *business plan* articulates a mission or vision for the firm and a *business strategy* for realizing that mission for all of the firm's stakeholders. *Stakeholders* include such constituent groups as customers, shareholders, employees, suppliers, lenders, regulators, and communities. The business strategy is long-term oriented and usually cuts across organizational lines to affect many functional areas. It often is broadly defined and provides relatively little detail.

With respect to business strategy, it is often appropriate to distinguish between corporate level strategy, where decisions are made by the management of a diversified or multiproduct firm, and business-level strategy, where decisions are made by the management of the operating unit within the corporate organizational structure. *Corporate-level strategies* generally cross business unit organizational lines and entail such decisions as financing the growth of certain businesses, operating others to generate cash, divesting some units, or pursuing diversification. *Business-level strategies* pertain to a specific operating unit and may involve the business unit attempting to achieve a low-cost position in its served markets, differentiating its product offering, or narrowing its operational focus to a specific market niche.

The *implementation strategy* refers to the way in which the firm chooses to execute the business strategy. It is usually far more detailed than the business strategy.

The *merger–acquisition plan* is a specific type of implementation strategy and describes in detail the motivation for the acquisition and how and when it will be achieved. *Functional strategies* describe in detail how each major function (e.g., manufacturing, marketing, and human resources) within the firm will support the business strategy. *Contingency plans* specify actions taken as an alternative to the firm's current business strategy. The selection of which alternative action to pursue is often contingent on certain events occurring (e.g., failure to realize revenue targets or cost savings). Such events are called *trigger points*. At such points, a firm is faced with a number of alternatives, which are sometimes referred to as *real options*. These options include abandoning, delaying, or accelerating an investment strategy. Real options are not the same as strategic options, discussed later in this chapter, as they represent decisions that can be made *after* a business strategy has been implemented. See Chapter 8 for a more detailed discussion of how real options may be applied to M&As.

The Acquisition Process

It is sometimes convenient to think of an acquisition process as a series of largely independent events, culminating in the transfer of ownership from the seller to the buyer. In theory, thinking of the process as discrete events facilitates the communication and understanding of the numerous activities required to complete the transaction. Thinking of M&As in the context of a transaction-tested process, while not ensuring success, increases the likelihood of meeting or exceeding expectations.

Good Planning Expedites Sound Decision Making

Some individuals tend to shudder at the thought of following a structured process because of perceived delays in responding to both anticipated and unanticipated opportunities. Anticipated opportunities are those identified as a result of the business planning process. This process consists of understanding the firm's external operating environment, assessing internal resources, reviewing a range of reasonable options, and articulating a clear vision of the future of the business and a realistic strategy for achieving that vision (Hill and Jones, 2001). Unanticipated opportunities result from new information becoming available. Rather than delaying the pursuit of an opportunity, the presence of a well-designed business plan provides for a rapid yet substantive evaluation of the perceived opportunity based on work completed while having developed the business plan. Decisions made in the context of a business plan are made with the confidence that comes from already having asked and answered the difficult questions.

Mergers and Acquisitions Are a Process, Not an Event

Figure 4–1 illustrates the 10 phases of the acquisition process described in this chapter and Chapter 5. These phases fall into two distinct sets of activities: pre- and postpurchase decision activities. The crucial phase of the acquisition process is the negotiation phase. Negotiation consists of four largely concurrent and interrelated activities. The decision to purchase or walk away is determined as a result of continuous iteration through the four activities making up the negotiation phase. Assuming the transaction ultimately is completed, the price paid for the target is actually determined during the negotiation phase. The phases of the acquisition process are summarized as follows:

Phase 1. Develop a strategic plan for the entire business (Business Plan).

Phase 2. Develop the acquisition plan supporting the business plan (Acquisition Plan).

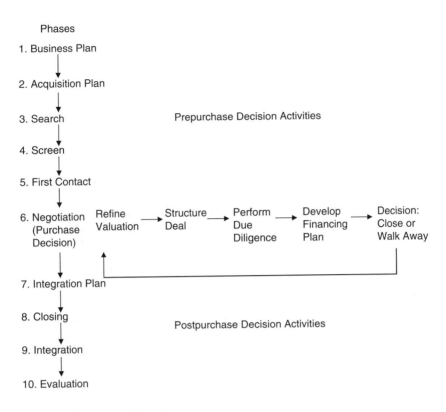

Phases

1. Business Plan

2. Acquisition Plan

3. Search   Prepurchase Decision Activities

4. Screen

5. First Contact

6. Negotiation   Refine ⟶ Structure ⟶ Perform ⟶ Develop ⟶ Decision:
   (Purchase   Valuation   Deal   Due   Financing   Close or
   Decision)   Diligence Plan   Walk Away

7. Integration Plan

8. Closing   Postpurchase Decision Activities

9. Integration

10. Evaluation

FIGURE 4–1 The acquisition process flow diagram.

Phase 3. Actively search for acquisition candidates (Search).

Phase 4. Screen and prioritize potential acquisition candidates (Screen).

Phase 5. Initiate contact with the target (First Contact).

Phase 6. Refine valuation, structure deal, perform due diligence, and develop financing plan (Negotiation).

Phase 7. Develop plan for integrating the acquired business (Integration Plan).

Phase 8. Obtain necessary approvals, resolve postclosing issues, and execute closing (Closing).

Phase 9. Implement postclosing integration (Integration).

Phase 10. Conduct postclosing evaluation of acquisition (Evaluation).

Phase 1. Building the Business Plan

Key Activities

A well-designed business plan is a result of the following activities:

1. External analysis involves determining where to compete (i.e., the industry or market in which the firm has chosen to compete) and how to compete (i.e., how the firm can most effectively compete in its chosen market or markets).

2. Internal analysis or self-assessment (i.e., conducting an internal analysis of the firm's strengths and weaknesses relative to its competition).

3. Defining a mission statement (i.e., summarizing where and how the firm has chosen to compete and the basic operating beliefs and values of management).
4. Setting objectives (i.e., developing quantitative measures of financial and nonfinancial performance).
5. Business strategy selection (i.e., selecting the strategy most likely to achieve the objectives in an acceptable time period, subject to constraints identified in the self-assessment).
6. Implementation strategy selection (i.e., selecting the best means of implementing the business strategy from a range of reasonable options).
7. Functional strategy development (i.e., defines the roles, responsibilities, and resource requirements of each major functional area within the firm needed to implement the firm's business strategy).
8. Establishing strategic controls (i.e., monitoring actual performance to plan, implementing incentive systems, and taking corrective actions as necessary).

The first two activities, the external and internal analyses, often are referred to in the planning literature as a **SWOT *analysis*** (i.e., the determination of a business's strengths, weaknesses, opportunities, and threats). In practice, the process of actually developing a business plan can be facilitated by addressing a number of detailed questions corresponding to each activity listed previously. Extensive checklists can be found in Porter (1985) and Stryker (1986). Answering these questions requires the accumulation of substantial amounts of economic, industry, and market information. See the chapter appendix for common sources of such data.

Following an exhaustive analysis of the external environment and an internal assessment of the firm, management has a clearer understanding of emerging opportunities and threats to the firm and of the firm's primary internal strengths and weaknesses. Table 4–1 illustrates how SWOT analysis could be used to identify opportunities and threats for Amazon.com. This hypothetical example suggests that Amazon.com sees its greatest opportunity as becoming an "online department store" and the growing Internet presence of sophisticated competitors as its greatest threat. The table then summarizes how Amazon.com sees its major strengths and weaknesses compared to the primary perceived opportunity and threat. This information enables management to set a direction

Table 4–1 Hypothetical Amazon.com SWOT Matrix

	Opportunity	**Threat**
	To be perceived by Internet users as the preferred online "department store" to exploit accelerating online retail sales	Wal-Mart, Best Buy, Costco, etc., are increasing their presence on the Internet
Strengths	• Brand recognition • Convenient online order entry system • Information technology infrastructure • Fulfillment infrastructure for selected products (e.g., books)	• Extensive experience in online marketing, advertising, and fulfillment (i.e., satisfying customer orders)
Weaknesses	• Inadequate warehousing and inventory management systems to support rapid sales growth • Limited experience in merchandising noncore retail products (e.g., pharmaceuticals, sports equipment) • Limited financial resources	• Substantially smaller retail sales volume limits ability to exploit purchase economies • Limited financial resources • Limited name recognition in selected markets (e.g., consumer electronics) • Retail management depth

for the firm in terms of where and how the firm intends to compete, which is communicated to the firm's stakeholders in the form of a mission–vision statement and a set of quantifiable financial and nonfinancial objectives.

Information gleaned from the external and internal analyses drives the development of business, implementation, and functional strategies. Each level of strategy involves an increased level of detail. The business strategy defines in general terms how the business intends to compete (i.e., through cost leadership, differentiation, or increased focus). The implementation strategy identifies how the business strategy will be realized (i.e., the firm acts on its own, partners with others, or acquires–merges with another firm). Finally, functional strategies define in considerable detail how each functional department (e.g., legal, finance, and human resources) in the firm will support the implementation strategy. Functional strategies often entail setting objectives and performance milestones for each employee supporting the implementation strategy. Strategic controls are put in place to heighten the prospect that vision, objectives, and strategies will be realized on schedule. Such controls involve establishing bonus plans and other incentive mechanisms to motivate all employees to achieve their individual objectives on or ahead of schedule. Systems are also put in place to track the firm's actual performance to the plan. Significant deviations from the implementation plan may require switching to contingency plans.

The eight key activities involved in developing an appropriate business plan are discussed in more detail during the remainder of this chapter. Of the various implementation strategy alternatives, the merger–acquisition implementation plan is discussed in considerable detail. Shared growth and shared control or partnering strategies are discussed in detail in Chapter 14. Implementing solo ventures are beyond the scope of this book.

External Analysis

External analysis involves the development of an in-depth understanding of the business's customers and their needs, the underlying market dynamics or factors determining profitability, and the emerging trends that affect customer needs and market dynamics. This analysis starts with answering two basic questions, which involve determining where and how the firm should compete. The primary output of the external analysis is the identification of important growth opportunities and competitive threats.

Determining Where to Compete

Deciding where a firm should compete starts with identifying the firm's current and potential customers and their primary needs. This is the single most important activity in building a business plan and is based on the process of market segmentation.

Market Segmentation

Market segmentation involves identifying customers with common characteristics and needs. Whether individual consumers or other firms, collections of customers form *markets.* A collection of markets is said to make up an *industry.* In manufacturing, examples include the automotive industry, which could be defined to consist of the new and used car markets as well as the aftermarket for replacement parts. Markets may be further subdivided by examining cars by makes and model years. The automotive market also could be defined regionally (e.g., North America) or by country. Each subdivision, whether by product or geographic area, defines a new market within the automotive industry.

The process for identifying a target market involves a three-step procedure. The first step entails establishing evaluation criteria used to distinguish the market to be targeted by the firm from other potential target markets. This requires the management of the firm conducting the market segmentation to determine the factors likely to affect a market's overall attractiveness. The evaluation criteria may include market size and growth rate, profitability, cyclicality, the price sensitivity of customers, amount of regulation, degree of unionization, and entry and exit barriers. The second step entails continuously subdividing industries and the markets within these industries and analyzing the overall attractiveness of these markets in terms of the evaluation criteria. For each market, the evaluation criteria are given a numerical weight, reflecting the firm's perception of the relative importance of each criterion applied to that market to determine overall attractiveness. Higher numbers imply greater perceived significance. Note that some criteria may be given a zero weight. The evaluation criteria then are ranked from 1 to 5, with 5 indicating that the firm finds a market to be highly favorable in terms of a specific evaluation criterion. In the third step, a weighted average score is calculated for each market and the markets are ranked according to their respective scores. For an example of how these selection criteria may be applied, see a Word document on the CD-ROM accompanying this text book entitled "Constructing Market Attractiveness Matrices."

Determining How to Compete

Determining how to compete involves a clear understanding of the factors critical for successfully competing in the targeted market. This outward-looking analysis applies to the primary factors governing the environment external to the firm. Understanding market dynamics and knowing in what areas the firm must excel when compared with the competition is crucial if the firm is to compete effectively in its chosen market.

Profiling the Targeted Markets

Market profiling entails collecting sufficient data to accurately assess and characterize a firm's competitive environment within its chosen markets. Using Michael Porter's (1985) Five Forces framework, the market or industry environment can be described in terms of such competitive dynamics as the firm's customers, suppliers, current competitors, potential competitors, and product or service substitutes. The three potential determinants of the intensity of competition in an industry include competition among existing firms, the threat of entry of new firms, and the threat of substitute products or services. While the degree of competition determines whether there is potential to earn abnormal profits (i.e., those in excess of what would be expected for the degree of assumed risk), the actual profits or cash flow are influenced by the relative bargaining power of the industry's customers and suppliers.

This framework may be modified to include other factors that determine actual industry profitability and cash flow, such as the severity of government regulation and the impact of global influences (e.g., fluctuations in exchange rates). While labor costs often represent a relatively small percentage of total expenses in many areas of manufacturing, they frequently constitute the largest portion of the nonmanufacturing sector. With the manufacturing sector in most industrialized nations continuing its long-term decline as a percentage of the total economy, the analyst should also include the factors affecting the bargaining power of labor (Figure 4–2).

The data required to analyze industry competitive dynamics include the following: (1) types of products and services, (2) market share in terms of dollars and units, (3) pricing metrics, (4) selling and distribution channels and associated costs, (5) type, location, and age of production facilities, (6) product quality metrics, (7) customer service metrics, (8) compensation by major labor category, (9) research and development (R&D)

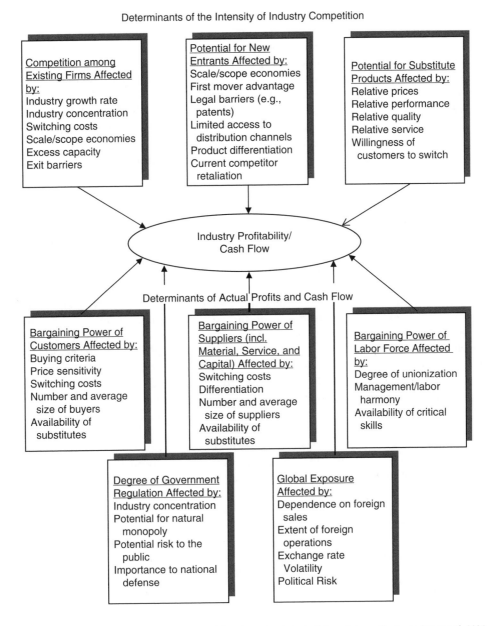

FIGURE 4–2 Defining market and industry competitive dynamics (adapted from Palepu, Healy, and Bernard, 2004, p. 2–2).

expenditures, (10) supplier performance metrics, and (11) financial performance in terms of growth and profitability. These data must be collected on all significant competitors in the firm's chosen markets.

Determinants of the Intensity of Industry Competition

How intense industry competition becomes is affected by competition among existing firms, the potential for new entrants, and the potential for substitute products and services.

The intensity of competition among current industry competitors is affected by industry growth rate, industry concentration, degree of differentiation and switching costs, scale and scope economies, excess capacity, and exit barriers. If an industry is growing rapidly, existing firms have less need to compete for market share. If an industry is highly concentrated, firms can more easily coordinate their pricing activities in contrast to a highly fragmented industry in which price competition is likely to be very intense. If the cost of switching from one supplier to another is minimal because of low perceived differentiation, customers are likely to switch based on relatively small differences in price. In industries in which production volume is important, companies may compete aggressively for market share to realize economies of scale. Moreover, firms in industries exhibiting substantial excess capacity often reduce prices to fill unused capacity. Finally, competition may be intensified in industries in which it is difficult for firms to exit due to high exit barriers such as large unfunded pension liabilities and single-purpose assets.

Current competitors within an industry characterized by low barriers to entry have limited pricing power. Attempts to raise prices resulting in abnormally large profits will attract new competitors, thereby adding to the industry's productive capacity. In contrast, high entry barriers may give existing competitors significant pricing power. Barriers to new entrants include situations in which the large-scale operations of existing competitors give them a potential cost advantage due to economies of scale. New entrants may enter only if they are willing to invest in substantial additional new capacity. "First mover advantage" (i.e., being an early competitor in an industry) may also create entry barriers as such firms achieve widespread brand recognition, establish industry standards, or develop exclusive relationships with key suppliers and distributors. Finally, legal constraints, such as copyrights and patents, may inhibit the entry of new firms. Examples of new entrants abound. Internet-based technologies loom as an enormous threat to cable. Phone giants AT&T and Verizon are using such technologies to offer consumers a variety of movies and TV shows that could be watched at any time. Furthermore, program owners such as ESPN are working with consumer electronics manufacturers to develop a set-top box that would provide access to college football games not available on cable or satellite. Users of Apple Computer's iPod can watch shows from Disney's ABC unit.

The relative price (i.e., the selling price of one product compared to a close substitute) or performance of competing products, perceived quality, and the willingness of the customer to switch products determine the threat of substitution. Potential substitutes include those that are substantially similar to existing products and those performing the same function. Examples include the shift of many products formerly ordered through traditional brick and mortar retail outlets to the Internet, such as books, compact discs, and airline tickets. Other examples include e-mail and faxes as substitutes for letters.

Determinants of Actual Profits and Cash Flow

The bargaining power of customers, suppliers, and the labor force are important factors affecting profits and cash flow. Other factors include the degree of government regulation and global exposure. The relative bargaining power of buyers depends on their primary buying criteria (i.e., price, quality or reliability, service, convenience, or some combination), price sensitivity or elasticity, switching costs, and their number and size compared to the number and size of suppliers. For example, if customers' primary criterion for making a purchase is product quality and reliability, they may be willing to pay a premium for a Toyota, due to its perceived higher relative quality. Customers are more likely to be highly price sensitive in industries characterized by largely undifferentiated products and low switching costs. Finally, buyers are likely to have considerable bargaining power when there are relatively few large buyers relative to the number of suppliers.

The relative leverage of suppliers reflects the ease with which customers can switch suppliers, perceived differentiation, their number, and how critical they are to the customer. Switching costs are highest when customers must pay penalties to exit long-term supply contracts or new suppliers would have to undergo an intensive learning process to meet the customers' requirements. Moreover, reliance on a single or a small number of suppliers shifts pricing power from the buyer to the seller. Examples include Intel's global dominance of the microchip market and Microsoft's worldwide supremacy in the market for personal computer operating systems.

Work stoppages create opportunities for competitors to gain market share. Customers are forced to satisfy their product and service needs elsewhere. Although the loss of customers may be temporary, it may become permanent if the customer finds that another firm's product or service is superior. Frequent work stoppages also may have long-term impacts on productivity and production costs as a result of a less-motivated labor force and increased labor turnover. High turnover can contribute to escalating operating expenses as firms incur substantial search and retraining expenses to fill positions.

Governments may choose to regulate industries that are heavily concentrated, are natural monopolies (e.g., electric utilities), or provide a potential risk to the public. Regulatory compliance adds significantly to an industry's operating costs. Regulations also create barriers to both entering and exiting an industry. The government may choose to regulate heavily concentrated industries to minimize anticompetitive practices or those such as utilities whose economics justifies relatively few competitors. Companies wishing to enter the pharmaceutical industry must have the capability to produce and test new drugs to the satisfaction of the Food and Drug Administration. Companies with large unfunded or underfunded pension liabilities may find exiting an industry impossible until they have met their pension obligations to the satisfaction of the U.S. Pension Benefit Guaranty Corporation.

Global exposure refers to the extent to which participation in an industry necessitates having a multinational presence. For example, the automotive industry is widely viewed as a global industry in which participation requires having assembly plants and distribution networks in major markets throughout the world. As the major auto assemblers move abroad, they also are requiring their parts suppliers to build nearby facilities to ensure "just-in-time" delivery of parts. Global exposure introduces the firm to significant currency risk as well as political risk that could result in the confiscation of the firm's properties (see Chapter 17).

Internal Analysis

The primary output of internal analysis is the determination of the firm's strengths and weaknesses. What are the firm's critical strengths and weaknesses compared to the competition? Can the firm's critical strengths be easily duplicated and surpassed by the competition? Can these critical strengths be used to gain advantage in the firm's chosen market? Can the firm's key weaknesses be exploited by competitors? These questions must be answered as objectively as possible for the information to be useful in formulating a viable strategy.

Success Factors

Competing successfully ultimately means satisfying the firm's targeted customers' needs better than competitors can. Conducting a self-assessment consists of identifying those strengths or competencies necessary to compete successfully in the firm's chosen or targeted market. These strengths often are referred to as *success factors*. Examples of success factors could include the following: high market share compared to the competition, product line breadth, cost-effective sales distribution channels, age and geographic location of production facilities, relative product quality, price competitiveness, R&D effectiveness, customer service effectiveness, corporate culture, and profitability.

Core Competencies

Gary Hamel and C. K. Prahalad (1994) argue that a firm's strategy should be based on core competencies, which represent bundles of skills that can be applied to extend a firm's product offering in new areas. For example, Honda Motor Corporation traditionally has had a reputation for being able to manufacture highly efficient internal combustion engines. In addition to cars, these skills have been applied to lawnmowers and snowblowers. Similarly, Hewlett-Packard was able to utilize its skills in producing highly precise measurement instruments to move successfully into calculators and later into PCs.

Defining the Mission Statement

At a minimum, a corporate mission statement seeks to describe the corporation's purpose for being and where the corporation hopes to go. The mission statement should not be so general as to provide little practical direction. A good mission statement should include references to such areas as the firm's targeted markets, product or service offering, distribution channels, and management beliefs with respect to the firm's primary stakeholders. Ultimately, the market targeted by the firm should reflect the fit between the corporation's primary strengths and competencies and its ability to satisfy customer needs better than the competition. The product and service offering should be relatively broadly defined to allow for the introduction of new products, which can be derived from the firm's core competencies. Distribution channels address how the firm chooses to distribute its products (e.g., through a direct sales force, agents, distributors, resellers, the Internet, or some combination). Customers are those targeted by the firm's products and services. Management beliefs establish the underpinnings of how the firm intends to behave with respect to its stakeholders.

Setting Strategic or Long-Term Business Objectives

Business objectives specify what is to be accomplished within a specific time period. A good objective is measurable and has a time frame in which it is to be realized. Typical corporate objectives include revenue growth rates, minimum acceptable financial returns, and market share. A good objective might state that the firm seeks to increase revenue from $1 billion currently to $5 billion by the year 20XX. A poorly written objective would be that the firm seeks to increase revenue substantially.

Common Business Objectives

- **Return.** The firm seeks to achieve a rate of return that will equal or exceed the return required by its shareholders (cost of equity), lenders (cost of debt), or the combination of the two (cost of capital) by 20XX.
- **Size.** The firm seeks to achieve the critical mass defined in terms of sales volume to realize economies of scale by 20XX.
- **Growth.** Accounting objectives: The firm seeks to grow earnings per share, revenue, or assets at a specific rate of growth per year. Valuation objectives: Such objectives may be expressed in terms of the firm's common stock price per share divided by earnings per share, book value, cash flow, or revenue.

- **Diversification.** The firm desires to sell current products in new markets, new products in current markets, or new products in new markets. For example, the firm intends to derive 25 percent of its revenue from new products by 20XX.
- **Flexibility.** The firm desires to possess production facilities and distribution capabilities that can be shifted rapidly to exploit new opportunities as they arise. For example, the major automotive companies have moved toward standardizing parts across car and truck platforms to reduce the time required to introduce new products and to facilitate the companies' ability to shift production from one region to another.
- **Technology.** The firm desires to possess capabilities in core or rapidly advancing technologies. Microchip and software manufacturers, as well as defense contractors, are good examples of industries in which staying abreast of new technologies is a prerequisite for survival.

Selecting the Appropriate Corporate-Level Strategy

Corporate-level strategies are adopted at the corporate or holding company level and may include all or some of the business units either wholly or partially owned by the corporation. A *growth strategy* entails a focus on accelerating the firm's consolidated revenue, profit, and cash-flow growth. This strategy may be implemented in many different ways. This will be described in more detail later in this chapter in the discussion of implementation strategies. A *diversification* strategy involves a decision at the corporate level to enter new businesses. These businesses may be either related or totally unrelated to the corporation's existing business portfolio. An *operational restructuring* strategy, sometimes referred to as a *turnaround or defensive strategy*, usually refers to the outright or partial sale of companies or product lines, downsizing by closing unprofitable or nonstrategic facilities, obtaining protection from creditors in bankruptcy court, or liquidation. A *financial restructuring* strategy describes actions by the firm to change its total debt and equity structure. The motivation for this strategy may entail better utilization of corporate excess cash balances through share-repurchase programs, reducing the firm's cost of capital by increasing leverage or management's control by acquiring a company's shares through a management buyout. The latter strategy is discussed in more detail in Chapter 13.

Selecting the Appropriate Business-Level Strategy

A firm should choose the business strategy from among the range of reasonable alternatives that enables it to achieve its stated objectives in an acceptable time period subject to resource constraints. Resource constraints include limitations on the availability of management talent and funds. Gaining access to highly competent management talent is frequently the more difficult of the two to overcome. Strategies can be reduced to one of four basic categories: (1) price or cost leadership, (2) product differentiation, (3) focus or niche strategies, and (4) hybrid strategies.

Price or Cost Leadership

The price or cost leadership strategy reflects the influence of a series of tools introduced and popularized by the Boston Consulting Group (BCG). These tools include the experience curve and the product life cycle (Boston Consulting Group, 1985). Cost leadership is designed to make a firm the cost leader in its market by constructing efficient production facilities, tightly controlling overhead expense, and eliminating marginally profitable customer accounts. The *experience curve* postulates that, as the cumulative historical volume of a firm's output increases, the cost per unit of output decreases geometrically as the firm becomes more efficient in producing that product. Therefore, the firm with the largest historical output also should be the lowest-cost producer. The implied strategy for this firm should be to enter markets as early as possible and reduce product prices aggressively to maximize market share. See the CD-ROM accompanying this book for an example of how to calculate an experience curve.

The applicability of the experience curve varies across industries. It seems to work best for largely commodity-type industries, in which scale economies can lead to substantial reductions in per-unit production costs. Examples include the manufacturing of PCs or cell-phone handsets. The strategy of continuously driving down production costs may make most sense for the existing industry market share leader. If the leader already has a cost advantage over its competitors because of its significantly larger market share compared with its competitors, it may be able to improve its cost advantage by more aggressively pursuing market share through price cutting. This strategy may be destructive if pursued concurrently by a number of firms with approximately the same market share in an industry whose customers do not see measurable differences in the products or services offered by the various competitors. Therefore, repetitive price cutting by firms within the industry is likely to drive down profitability for all firms in the industry. Case Study 4–1 illustrates how Anheuser-Busch attempted to reduce its per-unit production costs in the rapidly consolidating Chinese beer market.

Case Study 4–1 The Market Share Game: Anheuser-Busch Battles SABMiller to Acquire China's Harbin Brewery

China's beer industry is the world's fastest growing and second largest, after the United States. It is highly fragmented and offers many potential acquisition targets. At the end of 2000, there were about 470 independent brewers; however, industry consolidation reduced the number from almost 800 in 1992. The level of concentration is still relatively low, with the top 10 brewers producing about 30 percent of the country's total annual production. This compares to the United States, where Anheuser-Busch alone controls about one half of the American beer market.

Foreign brewers found it nearly impossible to achieve profitability in the highly price-competitive Chinese market and scaled back their operations in the late 1990s. However, China's brewing industry entered a new round of acquisitions ever since Anheuser-Busch, the world's largest brewery, announced in October 2002 plans to increase its share in Tsingtao Beer, China's largest brewery, from 4.5 percent to 27 percent by 2006. The difference, this time, from the merger boom in the early 1990s, is that foreign breweries are concentrating on building market share in local beer markets rather than trying to roll out their international brands.

On July 12, 2004, Anheuser-Busch acquired 99.7 percent of the issued shares of Harbin Brewery Group Ltd. for $720 million, by offering to pay a 30 percent premium over the next highest bid. The takeover of Harbin began with the May 2, 2004, announcement by Anheuser-Busch that it had completed its purchase of approximately 29 percent of Harbin for $139 million. This announcement triggered a hostile takeover bid for Harbin by its largest shareholder, SABMiller, the world's second largest brewer, which had a 29.6 percent stake in Harbin. The SABMiller bid was the first hostile takeover attempt of a publicly traded Chinese company by a foreign firm. With the Harbin takeover, Anheuser-Busch's market share would be more than twice that of any other competitor in northeastern China.

Conceding to Anheuser-Busch, SABMiller agreed to sell its share of Harbin to Anheuser-Busch. SABMiller indicated that it would receive $211 million from Anheuser Busch for its stake in Harbin, which it had acquired in July 2003 for $87 million. SABMiller said publicly that Anheuser-Busch placed a greater value on Harbin's growth potential than it did and that Harbin was not of great value to their growth strategy in China. Reflecting the extent to which existing Chinese brewery assets have increased in value in recent years compared to the cost of starting up a new brewery, SABMiller announced in late 2004 its intention to invest $82.2 million in 2005 to build a new brewery in affluent Guangdong in southeast China.

Discussion Questions

1. In your judgment, why was Anheuser-Busch willing to pay more than SABMiller for Harbin? Be specific.
2. In what way did SABMiller gain from its failure to acquire Harbin in the short run? How might it lose in the long run? Explain your answer.

BCG's second major contribution is the *product life cycle*, which characterizes a product's evolution in four stages: embryonic, growth, maturity, and decline. Strong sales growth and low barriers to entry characterize the first two stages. However, over time, entry becomes more costly, as early entrants into the market accumulate market share and experience lower per-unit production costs as a result of the effects of the experience curve. New entrants have substantially poorer cost positions as a result of their small market shares when compared with earlier entrants and cannot catch up to the market leaders as overall market growth slows. During the later phases, characterized by slow market growth, falling product prices force marginal firms and unprofitable firms out of the market or to consolidate with other firms.

Management can obtain insight into the firm's probable future cash requirements and in turn its value by determining its position in its industry's product life cycle. During the high-growth phase, firms in the industry normally have high investment requirements associated with capacity expansion and increasing working capital needs. Operating cash flow is normally negative. During the mature and declining growth phases, investment requirements are lower and cash flow becomes positive. Although the phase of the product life cycle provides insights into current and future cash requirements for both the acquiring and target companies, determining the approximate length of each phase can be challenging. The introduction of significant product innovation can reinvigorate industry growth and extend the length of the current growth phase. This is particularly true in such industries as microchip, PC, and cellular.

In addition to its applicability to valuing the firm, the product life cycle also can be useful in selecting the firm's business strategy. In the early stages of the product life cycle, the industry tends to be highly fragmented, with many participants having very small market shares. Often firms in the early stages adopt a niche strategy in which they focus their marketing efforts on a relatively small and homogeneous customer group. If economies of scale are possible, the industry will begin to consolidate as firms aggressively pursue cost leadership strategies.

In 2005, Mittal Steel announced a $4.5 billion deal to buy International Steel Group (ISG), a collection of five once-bankrupt steel companies consolidated by U.S. workout specialist, Wilbur Ross. With the transaction, Mittal became the largest steel producer in the world. In a creative application of a cost leadership strategy, Mittal operated its eight U.S. mills (ISG and three others it already owned)—clustered around the Great Lakes—to achieve "regional" economies of scale. By running the facilities as a single unit, the firm hopes to extract better terms from iron ore, coal, and electricity suppliers. Moreover, Mittal hopes to gain better pricing power with the individual plants no longer competing with each other.

Product Differentiation

Differentiation represents a range of strategies in which the product offered is perceived to be slightly different by customers from other product offerings in the marketplace. Differentiation can be accomplished through brand image, technology features, or through alternative distribution channels, such as the ability to download products via the Internet. Firms may compete by offering customers a range of features or functions. For example, many banks issue credit cards such as MasterCard or Visa. Each bank tries to differentiate its card by offering a higher credit line, a lower interest rate or annual fee, or by providing prizes. Software companies justify charging for upgrades based on additional features to word-processing or spreadsheet programs, which are not found on competing software packages. Other firms compete on the basis of consistent product quality or by providing excellent service. Some firms attempt to compete by offering their customers excellent convenience. Amazon.com falls in this category by offering consumers the opportunity to buy books and other products whenever and from wherever they choose. Apple Computer has used innovative technology to stay ahead of competitors selling MP3 players, most recently with the video capabilities of its newer iPods.

Focus or Niche Strategies

Firms adopting these types of strategies tend to concentrate their efforts by selling a few products or services to a single market and compete primarily on the basis of understanding their customers' needs better than the competition does. In this strategy, the firm seeks to carve a specific niche with respect to a certain group of customers, a narrow geographic area, or a particular use of a product. Examples include the major airlines, airplane manufacturers (e.g., Boeing), and major defense contractors (e.g., Lockheed-Martin).

Hybrid Strategies

Hybrid strategies involve some combination of the previously mentioned strategies (see Table 4–2). For example, Coca-Cola pursues both a differentiated and highly market-focused strategy. Coca-Cola derives the bulk of its revenues by focusing on the worldwide soft drink market. Its product is differentiated in that consumers perceive it to have a distinctly refreshing taste. Other companies that pursue focused yet differentiated strategies include fast-food industry giant McDonald's, which competes on the basis of providing fast food of a consistent quality in a clean, comfortable environment.

Table 4–2   Hybrid Strategies

	Cost Leadership	Product Differentiation
Niche focus approach	Cisco Systems WD-40	Coca-Cola McDonald's
Multimarket approach	Wal-Mart Oracle	America Online Microsoft

Selecting the Appropriate Implementation Strategy

Once a firm has determined the appropriate business strategy, attention must turn to deciding the best means of implementing the desired strategy. Implementation involves selecting the right option from the range of reasonable options. Generally, a firm has five choices: (1) solo venture, go it alone, or build (i.e., implement the strategy based solely on internal resources); (2) partner; (3) invest; (4) acquire; or (5) swap assets. Each option has significantly different implications. Table 4–3 provides a comparison of the different options in terms of their advantages and disadvantages. In theory, the decision to choose among alternative options should be made based on the discounting of the projected cash-flow stream to the firm resulting from each option. In practice, many other considerations are at work. For an illustration of this process, see DePamphilis (2001).

The Role of Intangible Factors

Although financial analyses are conducted to evaluate the various options, the option chosen ultimately may depend on such nonquantifiable factors as the senior manager's risk profile, patience, and ego. The degree of control offered by the various alternatives, displayed in Table 4–3, is often the central issue confronted by senior management in choosing among the various options. Although the solo venture and acquisition options offer the highest degree of control, they are often among the most expensive but for very

Table 4–3   Strategy Implementation: Solo Venture, Partner, Invest, Acquire, or Asset Swap

Basic Options	Advantages	Disadvantages
Solo venture or build (organic growth)	Control	Capital and expense requirements Speed

Partner (shared growth, shared control)
   Marketing–distribution alliance
   Joint venture
   License
   Franchise
	Limits capital and expense investment requirements
	May be precursor to acquisition
		Lack of or limited control
		Potential for diverging objectives
		Potential for creating a competitor

Invest (e.g., minority investments in other firms)	Limits initial capital and /expense requirements	High risk of failure Lack of control Time
Acquire or merge	Speed Control	Capital and expense requirements Potential earnings dilution
Swap assets	Limits use of cash No earnings dilution Limits tax liability if basis in assets swapped remains unchanged	Finding willing parties Reaching agreement on assets to be exchanged

different reasons. Typically, a build strategy takes considerably longer to realize key strategic objectives, and it may, depending on the magnitude and timing of cash flows generated from the investments, have a significantly lower current value than the alternatives. In contrast, gaining control through acquisition also can be very expensive because of the substantial premium the acquirer normally has to pay to gain a controlling interest in another company.

The joint venture may represent a practical alternative to either a build or acquire strategy by giving a firm access to such factors as skills, product distribution channels, proprietary processes, and patents at a lower initial expense than might be involved otherwise. The joint venture is frequently a precursor to acquisition, because it gives both parties time to determine if their respective corporate cultures and strategic objectives are compatible (see Chapter 14).

Asset swaps may represent an attractive alternative to the other options, but they are generally very difficult to establish in most industries, unless the assets involved are substantially similar in terms of physical characteristics and use. The best example of an industry in which this practice is relatively common is in commercial and industrial real estate. The cable industry is another example of how asset swaps can be used to achieve strategic objectives. In recent years, the cable industry has been swapping customers in different geographic areas to allow a single company to dominate a specific geographic area and realize the full benefits of economies of scale. In 2005, Citigroup exchanged its fund management business for Legg Mason's brokerage and capital markets businesses, with difference in the valuation of the businesses being paid in cash and stock. Similarly, Royal Dutch Shell and Russia's Gazprom reached a deal to swap major natural gas producing properties in late 2005. In 2007, British Petroleum swapped half of its stake in its Toledo, Ohio, oil refinery for half of Husky Energy's position in the Sunrise oil sands field in Alberta, Canada.

Accounting Considerations

Table 4–3 distinguishes between capital investment and expense investment. Although both types of investment have an immediate impact on actual cash flow, they have substantially different effects on accounting or reported profits. The impact of capital spending affects reported profits by adding to depreciation expense. This effect is spread over the accounting life of the investment. In contrast, *expense investment* refers to expenditures made on such things as application software development, database construction, research and development, training, and advertising to build brand recognition. Although it may be possible to capitalize and amortize some portion of these investments over several years, they usually are expensed in the year in which the monies are spent. Publicly traded firms may base strategic investment decisions on accounting considerations (e.g., the preservation of earnings per share) rather than on purely economic considerations. Consequently, a publicly traded company may be inclined to purchase a piece of depreciable equipment rather than develop a potentially superior piece of equipment internally through R&D expenditures, which may have to be expensed.

Analyzing Assumptions

With the assumptions displayed, the reasonableness of the various options can be compared more readily. The option with the highest net present value is not necessarily the preferred strategy, if the assumptions underlying the analysis strain credulity. Understanding the assumptions underlying the chosen strategy and those underlying alternative strategies force senior management to make choices based on a discussion of the reasonableness of the assumptions associated with each option. This is generally preferable to placing a disproportionately high level of confidence in the numerical output of computer models. Case Study 4–2 illustrates some of the complexities of selecting the appropriate implementation strategy.

Case Study 4–2 Disney Buys Pixar—A Deal Based Largely on Intangible Value

In the wake of a stagnating share price, Walt Disney Corporation (Disney) sought to revive its animation capabilities as investors flocked to more successful animation studios such as Pixar Animation Studios (Pixar) and DreamWorks Inc. Disney's efforts in animated films in recent years have been disappointing. In an industry in which creative talent rules, Disney had simply not been able to assemble the right combination of talent in an environment conducive to creating blockbuster animation films. Disney and Pixar had been in a joint venture involving three pictures since 1991, in which Disney shared the production costs and profits. Disney benefited from Pixar's success by cofinancing and distributing Pixar films. Talks to extend this arrangement disintegrated in 2004 due to the failure of Pixar CEO Steve Jobs and Disney CEO Michael Eisner to reach agreement on allowing Pixar to own films it produces in the future.

With the current distribution agreement set to expire in June 2006, Robert Iger, Eisner's replacement, moved to repair the relationship with Pixar. Consequently, a deal that was unthinkable a few years earlier became possible. Disney announced the acquisition of Pixar, one of the most successful moviemakers in Hollywood history, on January 25, 2006. The move reflected Disney's desire to infuse the firm's internal animation resources with those from a proven animation company. A key Disney strategy is to use popular Disney movie characters across different venues (i.e., theme parks, merchandise, and television). Disney exchanged its stock for Pixar shares in a deal valued at $7.4 billion for the Pixar stock or $6.4 billion including $1 billion of Pixar cash that Disney would receive.

Despite near-term dilution of Disney's earnings per share by as much as 10 percent, investors seem focused on the long-term impact to growth in Disney's shares. Disney's shares rose 1 percent on news of the announcement. Nevertheless, the risk associated with the transaction can be measured in terms of what Disney could have done with cash raised by issuing the same number of new shares to the public. At $6.4 billion, Disney could make 64 sequels at $100 million each. Moreover, Disney was probably paying top dollar for Pixar, as the filmmaker was coming off a string of six consecutive movie blockbusters. Finally, revenue from DVD sales might have been maturing.

The long-term success of the combination hinges on the ability of the two firms to meld their corporate cultures without losing Pixar's creative capabilities. Pixar president, Ed Catmull would become president of the combined Pixar–Disney animation business. John Lasseter, Pixar's creative director, would assume the role of chief creative officer of the combined firms, helping to design attractions for the theme parks and advising Disney's Imagineering division. In an effort to insulate the Pixar culture from the Disney culture, Pixar would remain based in Emeryville, California, far from Disney's Burbank, California, headquarters. As a condition of the closing, all key Pixar employees would have to sign long-term employment contracts.

Continued

Case Study 4–2 Disney Buys Pixar—A Deal Based Largely on Intangible Value — Cont'd

As part of the deal, Pixar chairman and chief executive Steve Jobs, holder of 50.6 percent of Pixar stock, would become Disney's largest individual shareholder, at about 6.5 percent of Disney stock, and a member of Disney's board of directors. Jobs's advice was hoped to rejuvenate the Disney board at a time when the entertainment industry was scrambling to reinvent itself in the digital age. Jobs, who is also the chairman and CEO of Apple Computer Inc. (Apple), is in a position to apply Apple's substantial technical skills to Disney's animation efforts.

It is unclear if Disney could not have achieved many of these benefits at a much lower cost by partnering with Pixar and offering Steve Jobs a seat on the Disney board. Ultimately, the opportunity to prevent Pixar's acquisition by a competitor may have been the primary reason why Disney moved so aggressively to acquire the animation powerhouse.

Discussion Questions

1. Discuss the advantages and disadvantages of an acquisition of Pixar versus a partnership. What would you have recommended and why? Be specific.
2. Pixar's key creative employees have long-term contracts and assumed key roles in the combined firms. Does such an arrangement heighten the prospects for Disney producing successful animated films? What challenges is Disney likely to face?

Functional Strategies

Functional strategies are focused on short-term results and generally are developed by functional areas; they also tend to be very detailed and highly structured. Such strategies result in a series of concrete actions for each function or business group, depending on the company's organization. It is common to see separate plans containing specific goals and actions for such functions as marketing, manufacturing, R&D, engineering, and financial and human resources. Functional strategies should include clearly defined objectives, actions, timetables for achieving those actions, resources required, and the individual responsible for ensuring that the actions are completed on time and within budget.

Specific functional strategies could read as follows:

- Set up a product distribution network in the northeastern United States capable of handling a minimum of 1 million units of product annually by 12/31/20XX. (Individual responsible, Oliver Tran; estimated budget, $5 million.)
- Develop and execute an advertising campaign to support the sales effort in the northeastern United States by 10/31/20XX. (Individual responsible, Maria Gomez; estimated budget, $.5 million.)
- Hire a logistics manager to administer the distribution network by 9/15/20XX. (Individual responsible, Patrick Petty; estimated budget, $150,000.)
- Acquire a manufacturing company with sufficient capacity to meet the projected demand for the next three years by 6/30/20XX at a purchase price not to exceed $250 million. (Individual responsible, Chang Lee.)

The relationship between the business mission, business strategy, implementation strategy, and functional strategies can be illustrated for an application software company targeting the credit card industry:

- **Mission.** To be recognized by its customers as the leader in providing accurate high-speed, high-volume transactional software for processing credit card remittances by 20XX.
- **Business strategy.** Upgrade the firm's current software by adding the necessary features and functions to differentiate the firm's product and service offering from its primary competitors and satisfy projected customer requirements through 20XX.
- **Implementation strategy.** Purchase a software company, at a price not to exceed $400 million, capable of developing "state-of-the-art" remittance processing software by 12/21/20XX. (Individual responsible, Donald Stuckee.) Note that this assumes that the firm has completed an analysis of available options including internal development, collaborating, licensing, and acquisition.
- **Functional strategies to support implementation strategy.**
  Research and development—Identify and develop new applications for remittance processing software.

  Marketing and sales—Assess impact of new product offering on revenue generated from current and new customers.

  Human resources—Determine appropriate staffing requirements to support the combined firms (i.e., the acquirer and target firms).

  Finance—Identify and quantify potential cost savings generated from improved productivity as a result of replacing existing software with the newly acquired software and the elimination of duplicate personnel in acquirer and target companies. Evaluate the impact of the acquisition on the combined companies' financial statements.

  Legal—Ensure that all target company customers have valid contracts and such contracts are transferable to the acquirer without penalty. Also, ensure that the acquirer will have exclusive and unlimited rights to use the remittance processing software.

  Tax—Assess the tax impact of the acquisition on the acquiring firm's cash flow.

Strategic Controls

Strategic controls consist of both incentive and monitoring systems. *Incentive systems* include bonus, profit sharing, or other performance-based payments made to motivate both acquirer and target company employees to work to implement the business strategy for the combined firms. Such a strategy normally would have been agreed to during negotiation. Incentives often include *retention bonuses* made to key employees of the target firm, if they remain with the combined companies for a specific period following completion of the transaction. *Monitoring systems* are implemented to track the actual performance of the combined firms against the business plan. Such systems can be accounting based (i.e., monitoring such financial measures as revenue, profits, and cash flow) or activity based. Activity-based systems monitor variables that drive financial performance. Such variables include customer retention, average revenue per customer, employee turnover, and revenue per employee.

The Business Plan as a Communication Document

The necessary output of the planning process is a document designed to communicate effectively with key decision makers and stakeholders. Although there are many ways to develop such documents, Exhibit 4–1 outlines the key features that should be addressed in a good business plan (i.e., one so well reasoned and compelling as to cause decision makers to accept its recommendations). A good business plan should be short, focused, and well documented. Supporting documentation should be referred to in the text but placed primarily in appendices to the business plan. The executive summary may be the most important and difficult piece of the business plan to write. It must communicate succinctly and compellingly what is being proposed, why it is being proposed, how it is to be achieved, and by when. It also must identify the major resource requirements and risks associated with the critical assumptions underlying the plan. The executive summary is often the first and only portion of the business plan read by the time-constrained chief executive officer (CEO), lender, or venture capitalist. As such, it may represent the first and last chance to catch the attention of the key decision maker (DePamphilis, 2010a).

Exhibit 4–1 Typical Business Unit–Level Business Plan Format

1. **Executive summary.** In one or two pages, describe what you are proposing to do, why, how it will be accomplished, by what date, critical assumptions, risks, and major resource requirements.
2. **Industry/market definition.** Define the industry or market in which the firm competes in terms of size, growth rate, product offering, and other pertinent characteristics.
3. **External analysis.** Describe industry or market competitive dynamics in terms of the factors affecting customers, competitors, potential entrants, product or service substitutes, and suppliers and how they interact to determine profitability and cash flow (e.g., Porter or modified Porter framework; Porter, 1985). Discuss major opportunities and threats that exist because of the industry's competitive dynamics. Information accumulated in this section should be used to develop the assumptions underlying revenue and cost projections in building financial statements.
4. **Internal analysis.** Describe the company's strengths and weaknesses and how they compare with the competition. Identify which of these strengths and weaknesses are important to the firm's targeted customers, and explain why. These data can be used to develop cost and revenue assumptions underlying the businesses projected financial statements.
5. **Business mission/vision statement.** Describe the purpose of the corporation, what it intends to achieve, and how it wishes to be perceived by its stakeholders. For example, an automotive parts manufacturer may envision itself as being perceived by the end of the decade as the leading supplier of high-quality components worldwide by its customers and as fair and honest by its employees, the communities in which it operates, and its suppliers.
6. **Quantified strategic objectives** (including completion dates). Indicate both financial (e.g., rates of return, sales, cash flow, share price) and nonfinancial goals (e.g., market share; being perceived by customers or investors as number 1 in the targeted market in terms of market share, product quality, price, innovation).

7. **Business strategy.** Identify how the mission and objectives will be achieved (e.g., become a cost leader, adopt a differentiation strategy, focus on a specific market segment, or some combination of these strategies). Show how the chosen business strategy satisfies a key customer need or builds on a major strength possessed by the firm. For example, a firm whose targeted customers are highly price sensitive may pursue a cost leadership strategy to enable it to lower selling prices and increase market share and profitability. Alternatively, a firm with a well-established brand name may choose to pursue a differentiation strategy by adding features to its product that are perceived by its customers as valuable.

8. **Implementation strategy.** From a range of reasonable options (i.e., solo venture or "go it alone" strategy; partner via a joint venture or less formal business alliance, license, or minority investment; or acquire–merge), indicate which option would enable the firm to best implement its chosen business strategy. Indicate why the chosen implementation strategy is superior to alternative options. For example, an acquisition strategy may be appropriate if the perceived "window of opportunity" is believed to be brief. Alternatively, a solo venture may be preferable if there are few attractive acquisition opportunities or the firm believes it has the necessary resources to develop the needed processes or technologies.

9. **Functional strategies.** Identify plans and resources required by major functional areas including manufacturing, engineering, sales and marketing, research and development, finance, legal, and human resources.

10. **Business plan financials and valuation.** Provide projected five-year income, balance sheet, and cash flow statements for the firm and estimate the firm's value based on the projected cash flows. State key forecast assumptions underlying the projected financials and valuation.

11. **Risk assessment.** Evaluate the potential impact on valuation by changing selected key assumptions one at a time. Briefly identify contingency plans (i.e., alternative ways of achieving the firm's mission or objectives) that would be undertaken if critical assumptions prove inaccurate. Identify specific events that would cause the firm to pursue a contingency plan. Such "trigger points" could include deviations in revenue growth of more than x percent or the failure to acquire or develop a needed technology within a specific period.

Phase 2. Building the Merger–Acquisition Implementation Plan

A merger–acquisition plan is required, if it is determined that an acquisition or merger is necessary to implement the business strategy. (The merger–acquisition implementation plan subsequently will be referred to as the *acquisition plan.*) The acquisition plan is a specific type of implementation strategy. The acquisition plan focuses on tactical or short-term rather than strategic or longer-term issues. It consists of management objectives, a resource assessment, a market analysis, senior management's preferences about how the acquisition process should be managed, a timetable for completing the acquisition, and the name of the individual responsible for making it all happen. The acquisition plan communicates to those charged with acquiring a company senior management's intentions. These are expressed in terms of management objectives and preferences. The objectives specify management's expectations for the acquisition and how it supports business plan objectives, and management preferences provide guidance on how the acquisition process should be managed. This guidance could include the specification of the criteria for selecting potential acquisition targets and willingness to engage in a hostile takeover. Moreover, preferences also could indicate management's choice of the form of payment (stock, cash, or debt), willingness to accept temporary earnings per share dilution, preference for a stock or asset purchase, and limitations on contacting competitors.

The "deal owner" should direct the development of the acquisition plan. Such individuals are frequently high-performing managers accountable for specific acquisitions. Senior management very early in the process should appoint these individuals. This position could be full or part time could go to someone in the firm's business development unit or an individual expected to manage the operation once acquired. In some instances, the deal owner may be someone on the firm's business development team who has had substantial deal-making experience. Often the deal owner should be the individual who will be responsible for eventual operation and integration of the target, with an experienced deal maker in a supporting role.

Management Objectives

The acquisition plan's stated objectives should be completely consistent with the firm's strategic objectives. Objectives include both financial and nonfinancial considerations.

Financial objectives in the acquisition plan could include a minimum rate of return or operating profit, revenue, and cash-flow targets to be achieved within a specified time period. Minimum or required rates of return targets may be substantially higher than those specified in the business plan, which relate to the required return to shareholders or to total capital. The required return for the acquisition may reflect a substantially higher level of risk as a result of the perceived variability of the amount and timing of the expected cash flows resulting from the acquisition.

Nonfinancial objectives address the motivations for making the acquisition that support the achievement of the financial returns stipulated in the business plan. In many instances, such objectives provide substantially more guidance for those responsible for managing the acquisition process than financial targets. Nonfinancial objectives in the acquisition plan could include the following:

1. Obtain rights to specific products, patents, copyrights, or brand names.
2. Provide growth opportunities in the same or related markets.
3. Develop new distribution channels in the same or related markets.
4. Obtain additional production capacity in strategically located facilities.
5. Add R&D capability.
6. Obtain access to proprietary technologies, processes, and skills.

Market Analysis

Assuming the proposed acquisition is in the firm's target market, there is no need to conduct a separate external or internal assessment, which was completed as part of the business plan. If the market to be entered is new to the firm, a complete market assessment is required. Market assessments were discussed earlier in this chapter under the modified Porter Five Forces framework (see Figure 4–2).

Resource Availability

Early in the acquisition process it is important to determine the maximum amount of the firm's available resources that senior management will commit to a merger or acquisition. This information is used when the firm develops target selection criteria before undertaking a search for target firms. Financial resources that are potentially available to the acquirer include those provided by internally generated cash flow in excess of normal operating requirements plus funds from the equity and debt markets. If the target firm is known, the potential financing pool includes funds provided by the internal cash flow of the combined companies in excess of normal operating requirements, as well as the capacity of the combined firms to issue equity or increase leverage.

Financial theory suggests that a firm always will be able to attract sufficient funding for an acquisition if the acquiring firm can demonstrate that it can earn its cost of capital. In practice, senior management's risk tolerance plays an important role in determining what the acquirer believes it can afford to spend on a merger or acquisition. Consequently, risk-adverse management may be inclined to commit only a small portion of the total financial resources potentially available to the firm.

Three basic types of risk confront senior management considering making an acquisition. These risks affect how they feel about the affordability of an acquisition opportunity. These include operating risk, financial risk, and overpayment risk. How managers perceive these risks will determine how much of their potential available resources they will be willing to commit to making an acquisition.

Operating risk addresses the ability of the buyer to manage the acquired company. It generally is perceived to be higher for M&As in markets unrelated to the acquirer's core business. The limited understanding of managers in the acquiring company of the competitive dynamics of the new market and the inner workings of the target firm may negatively affect the postmerger integration effort as well as the ongoing management of the combined companies.

Financial risk refers to the buyer's willingness and ability to leverage a transaction as well as the willingness of shareholders to accept dilution of near-term earnings per share (EPS). To retain a specific credit rating, the acquiring company must maintain certain levels of financial ratios, such as debt-to-total capital and interest coverage (i.e., earnings before interest and taxes divided by interest expense). A firm's incremental debt capacity can be approximated by comparing the relevant financial ratios to those of comparable firms in the same industry that are rated by the credit rating agencies. The difference represents the amount they theoretically could borrow without jeopardizing their current credit rating. For example, suppose the combined acquirer and target firms' interest coverage ratio is 3 and the combined firms' debt-to-total capital ratio is 0.25. Assume further that other firms within the same industry with comparable interest coverage ratios have debt-to-total capital ratios of 0.5. Consequently, the combined acquirer and target firms could increase borrowing without jeopardizing their combined credit rating until their debt-to-total capital ratio equals 0.5. Senior management could also gain insight into how much EPS dilution equity investors may be willing to tolerate through informal discussions with Wall Street analysts and an examination of comparable transactions financed by issuing stock. See Chapter 13 for a more detailed discussion of how to estimate the combined firms' incremental borrowing capacity.

Overpayment risk involves the dilution of EPS or a reduction in its growth rate resulting from paying significantly more than the economic value of the acquired company. The effects of overpayment on earnings dilution can last for years. To illustrate the effects of overpayment risk, assume the acquiring company's shareholders are satisfied with the company's projected annual average increase in EPS of 20 percent annually for the next five years. The company announces that it will be acquiring another company and that a series of "restructuring" expenses will slow EPS growth in the coming year to 10 percent. However, management argues that the savings resulting from combining the two companies will raise the combined companies' EPS growth rate to 30 percent in the second through fifth year of the forecast. The risk is that the savings cannot be realized in the time assumed by management and the slowdown in earnings extends well beyond the first year.

Management Preferences

Senior management's preferences for conducting the acquisition process are usually expressed in terms of boundaries or limits management chooses to impose on the process. To ensure that the process is managed in a manner consistent with management's risk tolerance and biases, management must provide guidance to those responsible for finding and valuing the target, as well as negotiating the transaction, in the following areas:

1. Determining the criteria used to evaluate prospective candidates (e.g., size, price range, current profitability, growth rate, geographic location, and cultural compatibility).
2. Specifying acceptable methods for finding candidates (e.g., soliciting board members; analyzing competitors; and contacting brokers, investment bankers, lenders, law firms, and the trade press).
3. Establishing roles and responsibilities of the acquisition team, including the use of outside consultants and determining the team's budget.
4. Identifying acceptable sources of financing (e.g., equity issues, bank loans, unsecured bonds, seller financing, or asset sales).
5. Preferences for an asset or stock purchase and form of payment (cash, stock, or debt).
6. Tolerance for goodwill.
7. Openness to partial rather than full ownership.
8. Willingness to launch an unfriendly takeover.
9. Setting affordability limits (such limits can be expressed as a maximum price to aftertax earnings, earnings before interest and taxes, or cash-flow multiple or a maximum dollar amount).
10. Desire for related or unrelated acquisitions.

Substantial upfront participation by management helps dramatically in the successful implementation of the acquisition process. Unfortunately, senior management frequently avoids providing significant input early in the process, despite recognizing the value of communication. Limited participation by management inevitably leads to miscommunication, confusion, and poor execution later in the process by those charged with making it happen.

Schedule

The final component of a properly constructed acquisition plan is a schedule that recognizes all the key events that must take place throughout the acquisition process. Each event should be characterized by beginning and ending milestones or dates as well as the name of the individual responsible for ensuring that each milestone is achieved. The timetable of events should be aggressive but realistic. The timetable should be sufficiently aggressive to motivate all participants in the process to work as expeditiously as possible to meet the management objectives established in the acquisition plan. However, overly optimistic timetables may be demotivating, because uncontrollable circumstances may delay reaching certain milestones.

Exhibit 4–2 outlines the contents of a typical acquisition plan as discussed in this chapter. The linkage between the acquisition plan and business plan is that the former describes how the firm will realize the business strategy, whose execution is believed to require an acquisition or merger. Note the same logic would apply if the implementation of the firm's business strategy required some other business combination, such as a joint venture or business alliance (see Chapter 14). Exhibit 4–3 provides a number of examples of how carefully crafted acquisition plan objectives can be linked directly to specific business plan objectives.

Exhibit 4–2 Acquisition Plan for the Acquiring Firm

1. **Plan objectives**. Identify the specific purpose of the acquisition. This should include what specific goals are to be achieved (e.g., cost reduction, access to new customers, distribution channels or proprietary technology, expanded production capacity) and how the achievement of these goals will better enable the acquiring firm to implement its business strategy.

2. **Timetable**. Establish a timetable for completing the acquisition, including integration, if the target firm is to be merged with the acquiring firm's operations.

3. **Resource and capability evaluation**. Evaluate the acquirer's financial and managerial capability to complete an acquisition. Identify affordability limits in terms of the maximum amount the acquirer should pay for an acquisition. Explain how this figure is determined.

4. **Management preferences**. Indicate the acquirer's preferences for a "friendly" acquisition; controlling interest; using stock, debt, cash, or some combination; and the like.

5. **Search plan**. Develop criteria for identifying target firms and explain plans for conducting the search, why the target ultimately selected was chosen, and how to make initial contact with the target firm. This activity is explained in more detail in Chapter 5.

6. **Negotiation strategy**. Identify key buyer and seller issues. Recommend a deal structure that addresses the primary needs of all parties involved. Comment on the characteristics of the deal structure. Such characteristics include the proposed acquisition vehicle (i.e., the legal structure used to acquire the target firm), the postclosing organization (i.e., the legal framework used to manage the combined businesses following closing), and form of payment (i.e., cash, stock, or some combination). Other characteristics include the form of acquisition (i.e., whether assets or stock are being acquired) and tax structure (i.e., whether it is a taxable or a nontaxable transaction). Indicate how you might "close the gap" between the seller's price expectations and the offer price. These considerations are discussed in more detail in Chapter 5.

7. **Determine initial offer price**. Provide projected five-year income, balance sheet, and cash-flow statements for the acquiring and target firms individually and for the consolidated acquirer and target firms with and without the effects of synergy. (Note that the projected forecast period can be longer than five years if deemed appropriate.) Develop a preliminary minimum and maximum

Continued

Exhibit 4–2 Acquisition Plan for the Acquiring Firm — Cont'd

purchase price range for the target. List key forecast assumptions. Identify an initial offer price, the composition (i.e., cash, stock, debt, or some combination) of the offer price, and why this price is appropriate in terms of meeting the primary needs of both target and acquirer shareholders. The appropriateness of the offer price should reflect your preliminary thinking about the deal structure. See Chapters 11 and 12 for a detailed discussion of the deal structuring process.

8. **Financing plan.** Determine if the proposed offer price can be financed without endangering the combined firm's credit worthiness or seriously eroding near-term profitability and cash flow. For publicly traded firms, pay particular attention to the near-term impact of the acquisition on the earnings per share of the combined firms. For a more detailed explanation of M&A financial modeling, see Chapter 9.

9. **Integration plan.** Identify integration challenges and possible solutions. (See Chapter 6 for a detailed discussion of how to develop integration strategies.) For financial buyers, identify an "exit strategy." Highly leveraged transactions are discussed in detail in Chapter 13.

Things to Remember

The success of an acquisition frequently depends on the focus, understanding, and discipline inherent in a thorough business plan. Four overarching questions must be addressed in developing a viable business plan:

1. Where should the firm compete?
2. How should the firm compete?
3. How can the firm satisfy customer needs better than the competition?
4. Why is the chosen strategy preferable to other reasonable options?

To answer these questions, the business planning process should consist of a thorough analysis of customers and their needs and an intensive analysis of the firm's strengths and weaknesses compared with the competition. In addition, the planning process should result in a clearly articulated mission and set of quantified objectives with associated time frames and individuals responsible for meeting these objectives by the targeted dates. Using this information, a strategy is selected from a range of reasonable options. An acquisition is only one of many options available for implementing a business strategy. The decision to pursue an acquisition often rests on the desire to achieve control and a perception that the acquisition will result in achieving the desired objectives more rapidly than other options. Firms all too often pay far too much for control. Alternative options may prove to be less risky. A firm may choose to implement what amounts to a phased acquisition by first entering into a joint venture with another company before acquiring it at a later date.

Once a firm has decided that an acquisition is critical to realizing the strategic direction defined in the business plan, a merger–acquisition plan should be developed. The acquisition plan provides the detail needed to implement effectively the firm's business strategy. The acquisition plan defines the specific objectives management hopes to

Exhibit 4–3 Examples of Linkages between Business and Acquisition Plan Objectives

Business Plan Objective

Financial: The firm will
Achieve rates of return that equal or exceed its cost of equity or capital by 20XX.
Maintain a debt/total capital ratio of x%.

Size: The firm will
Be the number 1 or 2 market share leader by 20XX.
Achieve revenue of $x million by 20XX.

Growth: The firm will achieve through 20XX annual averages
Revenue growth of y%.
Earnings per share growth of y%.
Operating cash-flow growth of z%.

Diversification: The firm will reduce earnings variability by x%.

Flexibility: The firm will achieve flexibility in manufacturing and design.

Technology: The firm will be recognized by its customers as the industry's technology leader.

Quality: The firm will be recognized by its customers as the industry's quality leader.

Service: The firm will be recognized by its customers as the industry's service leader.

Cost: The firm will be recognized by its customers as the industry's low-cost provider.

Innovation: The firm will be recognized by its customers as the industry's innovation leader.

Acquisition Plan Objective

Financial returns: The target firm should have
A minimum return on assets of x%.
A debt/total capital ratio $\leq y$%.
Unencumbered assets of $z million.
Cash flow in excess of operating requirements of $x million.

Size: The target firm should be at least $x million in revenue.

Growth: The target firm should
Have annual revenue, earnings, and operating cash-flow growth of at least x%, y%, and z%.
Provide new products and markets.
Possess excess annual production capacity of x million units.

Diversification: The target firm's earnings should be largely uncorrelated with the acquirer's earnings.

Flexibility: The target firm should use flexible manufacturing techniques.

Technology: The target firm should possess important patents, copyrights, and other forms of intellectual property.

Quality: The target firm's product defects must be $<x$ per million units manufactured.

Warranty record: The target firm's customer claims per million units sold should be no greater than x.

Labor costs: The target firm should be nonunion and not subject to significant government regulation.

R&D capabilities: The target firm should have introduced at least x new products in the previous 18 months.

achieve by completing an acquisition, addresses issues of resource availability, and identifies the specific boundaries management chooses to use to complete a transaction. The acquisition plan also establishes a schedule of milestones to keep the process on track and clearly defines the authority and responsibilities of the individual charged with managing the acquisition process.

Chapter Discussion Questions

4-1. Why is it important to think of an acquisition or merger in the context of a process rather than as a series of semi-related, discrete events?

4-2. How does planning facilitate the acquisition process?

4-3. What major activities should be undertaken in building a business plan?

4-4. What is market segmentation and why is it important?

4-5. What basic types of strategies do companies commonly pursue and how are they different?

4-6. What is the difference between a business plan and an acquisition plan?

4-7. What are the advantages and disadvantages of using an acquisition to implement a business strategy compared with a joint venture?

4-8. Why is it important to understand the assumptions underlying a business plan or an acquisition plan?

4-9. Why is it important to get senior management heavily involved early in the acquisition process?

4-10. In your judgment, which of the acquisition plan tactical limits discussed in this chapter are the most important and why?

4-11. After having acquired the OfficeMax superstore chain in 2003, Boise Cascade announced the sale of its core paper and timber products operations in late 2004 to reduce its dependence on this highly cyclical business. Reflecting its new emphasis on distribution, the company changed its name to OfficeMax, Inc. How would you describe the OfficeMax mission and business strategy implicit in these actions?

4-12. Dell Computer is one of the best-known global technology companies. In your opinion, who are Dell's primary customers? Current and potential competitors? Suppliers? How would you assess Dell's bargaining power with respect to its customers and suppliers? What are Dell's strengths and weaknesses versus its current competitors?

4-13. In your opinion, what market need(s) was Dell Computer able to satisfy better than its competition? Be specific.

4-14. Discuss the types of analyses inside GE that may have preceded GE's 2008 announcement that it would spin off its consumer and industrial business to its shareholders.

4-15. Ashland Chemical, the largest U.S. chemical distributor, acquired chemical manufacturer, Hercules Inc., for $3.3 billion in 2008. This move followed Dow Chemical Company's purchase of Rohm & Haas. The justification for both acquisitions was to diversify earnings and offset higher oil costs. How will these combinations offset escalating oil costs?

Answers to these Chapter Discussion Questions are available in the Online Instructor's Manual for instructors using this book.

Chapter Business Cases

Case Study 4–3. BofA Acquires Countrywide Financial Corporation

On January 12, 2008, Bank of America Corp (BofA) announced plans to buy mortgage lender Countrywide Financial Corp (Countrywide) for $4 billion, a 70 percent discount from BofA's book value. Countrywide originates, purchases, and securitizes residential and commercial loans; provides loan closing services, such as appraisals and flood determinations; and performs other residential real estate–related services. This marked another major (but risky) acquisition by Bank of America's chief executive Kenneth Lewis in recent years. BofA's long-term intent has been to become the nation's largest consumer bank, while achieving double-digit earnings growth. The acquisition would help the firm realize that vision and create the second largest U.S. bank. In 2003, BofA paid $48 billion for FleetBoston Financial, which gave it the most branches, customers, and checking deposits of any U.S. bank. In 2005, BofA became the largest credit card issuer when it bought MBNA for $35 billion.

The purchase of the troubled mortgage lender averted the threat of a collapse of a major financial institution because of the U.S. 2007–2008 subprime loan crisis. U.S. regulators were quick to approve the takeover because of the potentially negative implications for U.S. capital markets of a major bank failure. Countrywide had lost $1.2 billion in the third quarter of 2007. Countrywide's exposure to the subprime loan market (i.e., residential loans made to borrowers with poor or nonexistent credit histories) had driven its shares down by almost 80 percent from year-earlier levels. The bank was widely viewed as teetering on the brink of bankruptcy as it lost access to the short-term debt markets, its traditional source of borrowing.

Bank of America deployed 60 analysts to Countrywide's headquarters in Calabasas, California. After four weeks of analyzing Countrywide's legal and financial challenges and modeling how its loan portfolio was likely to perform, BofA offered an all-stock deal valued at $4 billion. The deal values Countrywide at $7.16 per share, a 7.6 discount to its closing price the day before the announcement. BofA issued 0.18 shares of its stock for each Countrywide share. The deal could be renegotiated if Countrywide experienced a material change that adversely affects the business. BofA made its initial investment in Countrywide in August 2007, purchasing preferred shares convertible to a 16 percent stake in the company. By the time of the announced acquisition, Countrywide had a $1.3 billon paper loss on the $2 billion it invested in Countrywide in 2007.

The acquisition provided an opportunity to buy a market leader at a distressed price. The risks relate to the amount of potential loan losses and the length of the U.S. housing slump. The purchase will make BofA the nation's largest mortgage lender and servicer, consistent with the firm's business strategy, which is to help consumers meet all their financial needs. BofA has been one of the relatively few major banks to be successful in increasing revenue and profit following acquisitions by "cross-selling" its products to the acquired bank's customers. Countrywide's extensive retail distribution network enhances BofA's network of more than 6,100 banking centers throughout the United States. BofA anticipates $670 million in aftertax cost savings in combining the two firms. Two thirds of the annual cost savings would be realized in 2010 and the remainder in 2011.

Discussion Questions

1. How did the acquisition of Countrywide fit BofA's business strategy? Be specific. What were the key assumptions implicit the BofA's business strategy? How did the existence of BofA's mission and business strategy help the firm move quickly in acquiring Countrywide?

2. How would you classify the BofA business strategy (cost leadership, differentiation, focus, or some combination)? Explain your answer.

3. Describe what the likely objectives of the BofA acquisition plan might have been. Be specific. What key assumptions are implicit in BofA's acquisition plan? What are some of the key risks associated with integrating Countrywide? In addition to the purchase price, how would you determine BofA's potential resource commitment in making this acquisition?

4. What capabilities did the acquisition of FleetBoston Financial and MBNA provide BofA? How did the acquisition of Countrywide complement previous acquisitions?

5. What alternatives to outright acquisition did BofA have? Why do you believe BofA chose to acquire Countrywide rather than to pursue an alternative strategy? Be specific.

Solutions to these case discussion questions are available in the Online Instructor's Manual for instructors using this book.

Case Study 4–4. Oracle Continues Its Efforts to Consolidate the Software Industry

Oracle CEO Larry Ellison continued his effort to implement his software industry strategy when he announced the acquisition of Siebel Systems Inc. for $5.85 billion in stock and cash on September 13, 2005. The global software industry includes hundreds of firms. During the first nine months of 2005, Oracle had closed seven acquisitions, including its recently completed $10.6 billion hostile takeover of PeopleSoft. In each case, Oracle realized substantial cost savings by terminating duplicate employees and related overhead expenses. The Siebel acquisition accelerates the drive by Oracle to overtake SAP as the world's largest maker of business applications software, which automates a wide range of administrative tasks. The consolidation strategy seeks to add the existing business of a competitor, while broadening the customer base for Oracle's existing product offering.

Siebel, founded by Ellison's one-time protégé turned bitter rival, Tom Siebel, gained prominence in Silicon Valley in the late 1990s as a leader in customer relationship management (CRM) software. CRM software helps firms track sales, customer service, and marketing functions. Siebel's dominance of this market has since eroded amidst complaints that the software was complicated and expensive to install. Moreover, Siebel ignored customer requests to deliver the software via the Internet. Also, aggressive rivals, like SAP and online upstart Salesforce.com have cut into Siebel's business in recent years with simpler offerings. Siebel's annual revenue had plunged from about $2.1 billion in 2001 to $1.3 billion in 2004.

In the past, Mr. Ellison attempted to hasten Siebel's demise, declaring in 2003 that Siebel would vanish and putting pressure on the smaller company by revealing he had held takeover talks with the firm's CEO, Thomas Siebel. Ellison's public announcement of these talks heightened the personal enmity between the two CEOs, making Siebel an unwilling seller.

Oracle's intensifying focus on business applications software largely reflects the slowing growth of its database product line, which accounts for more than three fourths of the company's sales.

Siebel's technology and deep customer relationships give Oracle a competitive software bundle that includes a database, middleware (i.e., software that helps a variety of applications work together as if they were a single system), and high-quality customer relationship management software. The acquisition also deprives Oracle competitors, such as IBM, of customers for their services business.

Customers, who once bought the so-called best-of-breed products, now seek a single supplier to provide programs that work well together. Oracle pledged to deliver an integrated suite of applications by 2007. What brought Oracle and Siebel together in the past was a shift in market dynamics. The customer and the partner community is communicating quite clearly that they are looking for an integrated set of products.

Germany's SAP, Oracle's major competitor in the business applications software market, played down the impact of the merger, saying they had no reason to react and described any deals SAP is likely to make as "targeted, fill-in acquisitions." For IBM, the Siebel deal raised concerns about the computer giant's partners falling under the control of a competitor. IBM and Oracle compete fiercely in the database software market. Siebel has worked closely with IBM, as did PeopleSoft and J.D. Edwards, which had been purchased by PeopleSoft shortly before its acquisition by Oracle. Retek, another major partner of IBM, had also been recently acquired by Oracle. IBM had declared its strategy to be a key partner to thousands of software vendors and that it would continue to provide customers with IBM hardware, middleware, and other applications.

Discussion Questions

1. How would you characterize the Oracle business strategy (i.e., cost leadership, differentiation, niche, or some combination of all three)? Explain your answer.
2. What other benefits for Oracle, and the remaining competitors such as SAP, do you see from further industry consolidation? Be specific.
3. Conduct an external and internal analysis of Oracle. Briefly describe those factors that influenced the development of Oracle's business strategy. Be specific.
4. In what way do you think the Oracle strategy was targeting key competitors? Be specific.

Solutions to these questions are found in the Online Instructor's Manual available for instructors using this book.

Appendix: Common Sources of Economic, Industry, and Market Data

Economic Information

Business Cycle Development (U.S. Department of Commerce)

Current Business Reports (U.S. Department of Commerce)

Economic Indicators (U.S. Joint Economic Indicators)

Economic Report of the President to the Congress (U.S. Government Printing Office)

Long-Term Economic Growth (U.S. Department of Commerce)

Regional statistics and forecasts from large commercial banks

Monthly Labor Review (U.S. Department of Labor)

Monthly Bulletin of Statistics (United Nations)

Overseas Business Reports (By country, published by U.S. Department of Commerce)

World Trade Annual (United Nations)

U.S. Industrial Outlook (U.S. Department of Commerce)

Survey of Current Business (U.S. Department of Commerce)

Statistical Yearbook (United Nations)

Statistical Abstract of the United States (U.S. Department of Commerce)

Industry Information

Forbes (Mid-January issues provides performance data on firms in various industries)

Business Week (provides weekly economic and business information, and quarterly profit and sales rankings of corporations)

Fortune (April issues include listings of financial information on corporations within selected industries)

Industry Survey (Published quarterly by Standard and Poor's Corporation)

Industry Week (March–April issue provides information on 14 industry groups)

Inc. (May and December issues give information on entrepreneurial firms)

Directories of National Trade Associations

Encyclopedia of Associations

Funk and Scott's *Index of Corporations and Industries*

Thomas' *Register of American Manufacturers*

Wall Street Journal Index

5

Implementation

Search through Closing—Phases 3–10

A man that is very good at making excuses is probably good at nothing else.
—Ben Franklin

Inside M&A: Bank of America Acquires Merrill Lynch

Against the backdrop of the Lehman Brothers' Chapter 11 bankruptcy filing, Bank of America (BofA) CEO Kenneth Lewis announced on September 15, 2008, that the bank had reached agreement to acquire megaretail broker and investment bank, Merrill Lynch. Hammered out in a few days, investors expressed concern that the BofA's swift action on the all-stock $50 billion transaction would saddle the firm with billions of dollars in problem assets by pushing BofA's share price down by 21 percent.

BofA saw the takeover of Merrill as an important step toward achieving its long-held vision of becoming the number 1 provider of financial services in its domestic market. The firm's business strategy was to focus its efforts on the U.S. market by expanding its product offering and geographic coverage. The firm implemented its business strategy by acquiring selected financial services companies to fill gaps in its product offering and geographic coverage. The existence of a clear and measurable vision for the future enabled BofA to make acquisitions as the opportunity arose. Since 2001, the firm completed a series of acquisitions valued at more than $150 billion. The firm acquired FleetBoston Financial, greatly expanding its network of branches on the East Coast and LaSalle Bank to improve its coverage in the Midwest. The acquisitions of credit card issuing powerhouse MBNA, U.S. Trust (a major private wealth manager), and Country-wide (the nation's largest residential mortgage loan company) were made to broaden the firm's financial services offering.

The acquisition of Merrill makes BofA the country's largest provider of wealth management services to go with its current status as the nation's largest branch banking network and the largest issuer of small business, home equity, credit card, and residential mortgage loans. The deal creates the largest domestic retail brokerage and puts the bank among the top five largest global investment banks. Merrill also owns 45 percent of the profitable asset manager BlackRock Inc., worth an estimated $10 billion. BofA expects to realize $7 billion in pretax cost saving by 2012. BofA's retail network should help sell Merrill and BlackRock's investment products to BofA customers.

The hurried takeover encouraged by the U.S. Treasury and Federal Reserve did not allow for proper due diligence. The extent of the troubled assets on Merrill's books was largely unknown. While the losses at Merrill proved to be stunning in the short run, $15 billion alone in the fourth quarter of 2008, the acquisition by Bank of America averted the possible demise of Merrill Lynch. By the end of the first quarter of 2009, the U.S. government had injected $45 billion in loans and capital into BofA in an effort to offset some of the asset writeoffs associated with the acquisition. While BofA's vision and strategy may still prove to be sound, the rushed execution of the acquisition could hobble the financial performance of BofA for years to come.

Chapter Overview

The firm's business plan sets the overall direction for the business. It defines where the firm has chosen to compete (i.e., target market) and how the firm has chosen to compete (i.e., through price-cost leadership, differentiation, or a focused strategy). A merger-acquisition implementation plan (subsequently referred to as the *acquisition plan*) is required if the firm decides that an acquisition is needed to execute the firm's business strategy. The acquisition plan communicates to those charged with acquiring a company the preferences of senior management about the key objectives to be achieved and how the process should be managed. It ensures that the acquisition team conducts itself in a manner consistent with management's risk tolerance.

The acquisition plan defines the criteria (such as size, profitability, industry, growth rate, and cultural compatibility) used to select potential acquisition candidates. It may specify the degree of relatedness to the acquiring firm's current businesses and define the types of firms that should not be considered (e.g., current competitors). The plan also stipulates the roles and responsibilities of team members, including outside consultants, and sets the team's budget. Moreover, the plan indicates management's preference for such things as the form of payment (stock, cash, or debt), acquiring stock or assets, and partial or full ownership. It may preclude any hostile takeover attempts or indicate a desire to limit goodwill. It also may specify management's desire to minimize the impact of the acquisition on the earnings per share of the combined companies immediately following closing. Finally, the acquisition plan may establish limits as determined by management on what the acquiring firm is willing to pay for any acquisition by setting a ceiling on the purchase price in terms of a maximum price-to-earnings multiple or multiple of some other measure of value.

This chapter starts with the presumption that a firm has developed a viable business plan that requires an acquisition to realize the firm's strategic direction. Whereas Chapter 4 addressed the creation of business and acquisition plans (Phases 1 and 2), this chapter focuses on Phases 3–10 of the acquisition process, including search, screening, first contact, negotiation, integration planning, closing, integration implementation, and evaluation. The negotiation phase is the most complex aspect of the acquisition process, involving refining the preliminary valuation, deal structuring, due diligence, and developing a financing plan. It is in the negotiation phase that all elements of the purchase price are determined. The major segments of this chapter include the following:

- The Search Process
- The Screening Process
- First Contact
- Negotiation

- Developing the Integration Plan
- Closing
- Postclosing Integration
- Conducting Postclosing Evaluation
- Things to Remember

A review of this chapter (including practice questions) is contained in the file folder entitled Student Study Guide on the CD-ROM accompanying this book. The CD-ROM also contains a comprehensive acquirer due diligence question list and redacted agreements of purchase and sale for stock and asset purchases. The CD-ROM also contains a Learning Interactions Library enabling students to test their knowledge of this chapter in a "real-time" environment.

Phase 3. The Search Process

Initiating the Search

Initiating the search for potential acquisition candidates involves a two-step procedure. The first step is to establish the primary screening or selection criteria. At this stage of the search process, it is best to use a relatively small number of criteria. The primary criteria should include the industry and size of the transaction. It also may be appropriate to add a geographic restriction. The size of the transaction is best defined in terms of the maximum purchase price a firm is willing to pay. This can be expressed as a maximum price-to-earnings, book, cash-flow, or revenue ratio or a maximum purchase price stated in terms of dollars.

For example, an acute-care private hospital holding company wants to buy a skilled nursing facility within a range of 50 miles of its largest acute-care hospital in Allegheny County, Pennsylvania. Management believes that it cannot afford to pay more than $45 million for the facility. Its primary selection criteria could include the following: an industry (skilled nursing), location (Allegheny County), and maximum price (five times cash flow not to exceed $45 million). Similarly, a Texas-based manufacturer of patio furniture with manufacturing operations in the southwestern United States is seeking to expand its sales in California by purchasing a patio furniture manufacturer in the far western United States for an amount not to exceed $100 million. Its primary selection criteria could include an industry (outdoor furniture), a location (California, Arizona, and Nevada), and a maximum purchase price (15 times aftertax earnings not to exceed $100 million).

The second step is to develop a search strategy. Such strategies normally entail using computerized databases and directory services such as Disclosure, Dun & Bradstreet, Standard & Poor's *Corporate Register,* or Thomas' *Register* and *Million Dollar Directories* to identify qualified candidates. Firms also may query their law, banking, and accounting firms to identify other candidates. Investment banks, brokers, and leveraged buyout firms are also fertile sources of candidates, although they are likely to require an advisory or finder's fee. The Internet makes research much easier than in the past. Today, analysts have much more information at their fingertips. Such services as Google Finance, Yahoo!, Finance, Hoover's, or EDGAR Online enable researchers to gather quickly data about competitors and customers. These sites provide easy access to a variety of public documents filed with the Securities and Exchange Commission. Exhibit 5–1 provides a listing of commonly used sources of information that can be highly useful in conducting a search for prospective acquisition candidates.

Exhibit 5–1 Information Sources on Individual Companies

SEC Filings (Public Companies Only)

10-K. Provides detailed information on a company's annual operations, business conditions, competitors, market conditions, legal proceedings, risk factors in holding the stock, and other related information.

10-Q. Updates investors about the company's operations each quarter.

S-1. Filed when a company wants to register new stock. Can contain information about the company's operating history and business risks.

S-2. Filed when a company is completing a material transaction, such as a merger or acquisition. Provides substantial detail underlying the terms and conditions of the transaction, the events surrounding the transaction, and justification for the merger or acquisition.

8-K. Filed when a company faces a "material event," such as a merger.

Schedule 14A. A proxy statement. Gives details about the annual meeting and biographies of company officials and directors including stock ownership and pay.

Websites

www.capitaliq.com
www.factset.com
www.sec.gov
www.edgar-online.com
www.freeedgar.com
www.quicken.com
www.hooversonline.com
www.aol.com
http://finance.yahoo.com
www.bizbuysell.com
www.dialog.com
www.lexisnexis.com
www.mergernetwork.com
www.mergers.net
www.washingtonresearchers.com
www.worldm-anetwork.com
www.onesource.com
http://edgarscan.pwcglobal.com/serviets.edgarscan

Organizations

Value Line Investment Survey: Information on public companies
Directory of Corporate Affiliations: Corporate affiliations
Lexis/Nexis: Database of general business and legal information
Thomas Register: Organizes firms by products and services
Frost & Sullivan: Industry research
Findex.com: Financial information

Competitive Intelligence Professionals: Information about industries
Dialog Corporation: Industry databases
Wards Business Directory of U.S. and public companies
Predicasts: Provides databases through libraries
Business Periodicals Index: Business and technical article index
Dun & Bradstreet Directories: Information about private and public companies
Experian: Information about private and public companies
Nelson's Directory of Investment Research: Wall Street Research Reports
Standard and Poor's Publications: Industry surveys and corporate records
Harris Infosource: Information about manufacturing companies
Hoover's Handbook of Private Companies: Information on large private firms
Washington Researchers: Information on public and private firms, markets, and industries
The *Wall Street Journal* Transcripts: Wall Street research reports
Directory of Corporate Affiliations (Published by Lexis-Nexis Group)

If confidentiality is not an issue, a firm may seek to advertise its interest in acquiring a particular type of firm in the *Wall Street Journal* or the trade press. Although this is likely to generate substantial interest, it is less likely to generate high-quality prospects. Considerable time is wasted sorting through responses from those interested in getting a free valuation of their own company to those responses from brokers claiming their clients fit the buyer's criteria as a ruse to convince the buyer that they need the broker's services.

Finding reliable information about privately owned firms is a major problem. Often by using sources such as Dun & Bradstreet or Experian, an analyst is able to accumulate fragmentary data. Nonetheless, it is possible to use publicly available information to obtain additional detail. For example, industry surveys provided by trade associations or the U.S. Census Bureau often provide such data as average sales per employee for specific industries. A private firm's sales can be estimated by multiplying an estimate of its workforce by the industry average ratio of sales per employee. An estimate of the private firm's workforce may be obtained by searching the firm's product literature, website, or trade show speeches or even by counting the number of cars in the firm's parking lot. For additional detail on how to develop information on private firms, see Chapter 10.

Brokers and Finders: Do You Really Need to Hire an Outside Investment Banker?

Increasingly, companies are moving investment banking "in house." Such companies are identifying potential targets on their own and doing their own valuation as well as due diligence. While large companies, such as General Electric, PepsiCo, and Johnson & Johnson, have long handled many deals themselves, even mid-size firms, such as funeral services chain Hillenbrand Industries Inc. and diet empire Weight Watchers International Inc., are doing their own work. The trend toward in-house banking reflects efforts to save on investment banking fees, which could easily be more than $5 million plus expenses on a $500 million transaction.

Employing Brokers and Finders in the Search Process

Brokers or so-called finders may be used to supplement the search process. A broker has a fiduciary responsibility to either the potential buyer or seller. The broker is not permitted to represent both parties. The broker is compensated by his or her client. In some states, the government licenses brokers. In contrast, a finder is someone who introduces both parties, without representing either one. The finder has no fiduciary responsibility to either party and is compensated by either party or both. Generally, finders are not regulated; consequently, they do not require a license. Determining whether an agent is a broker or a finder is challenging. Courts often identify a finder as a broker if the finder discusses price or any significant terms of the transaction. Brokers are regulated at the state or local level.

Fees Paid to Brokers and Finders

It is important to respond in writing if you receive a solicitation from a broker or finder, particularly if rejecting the offered services. If, at a later date, you acquire the firm they claim to have represented, the broker or finder may sue your firm for compensation. If you choose to use the broker or finder, make sure that the fees and terms are clearly stipulated in writing. Keep a written record of all telephone conversations and meetings with the finder or broker. These may be used in court if the broker or finder sues for fees that may be in dispute.

Actual fee formulas are most often based on the purchase price. The so-called **Lehman formula** was at one time a commonly used fee structure, in which broker or finder fees would be equal to 5 percent of the first million dollars of the purchase price, 4 percent of the second, 3 percent of the third, 2 percent of the fourth, and 1 percent of the remainder. Today, this formula often is ignored in favor of a negotiated fee structure. A common fee structure consists of a basic fee, a closing fee, and an "extraordinary" fee. A basic fee or retainer is paid regardless of whether the deal is consummated. The closing fee is an additional amount paid on closing. Finally, the "extraordinary" fee is paid under unusual circumstances, which may delay eventual closing, such as gaining antitrust approval or achieving a hostile takeover. Fees vary widely, but 1 percent of the total purchase price plus reimbursement of expenses is often considered reasonable. For small deals, investment bankers often insist on the Lehman formula.

Phase 4. The Screening Process

The screening process is a refinement of the search process. It starts with a pruning of the initial list of potential candidates created by applying such primary criteria as the type of industry and the maximum size of the transaction. Because relatively few primary criteria are used, the initial list of potential acquisition candidates may be lengthy. Additional or secondary selection criteria may be used to shorten the list.

Care should be taken to limit the number of secondary criteria used. An excessively long list of selection criteria severely limits the number of candidates that will pass the screening process. Whenever possible, the selection criteria should be quantified. In addition to the maximum purchase price, industry, or geographic location criteria used to develop the initial list, secondary selection criteria may include a specific market segment within the industry or a specific product line within a market segment. Other measures often include the firm's profitability, degree of leverage, and market share. Cultural compatibility also should be considered an important screening criterion.

Market Segment

The search process involved specification of the target industry. It is now necessary to identify the target segment in the industry. For example, a steel fabrication company may decide to diversify by acquiring a manufacturer of aluminum flat-rolled products. A primary search criterion would include only firms in the aluminum flat-rolled products industry. Subsequent searches may involve a further segmenting of the market to identify only those companies that manufacture aluminum tubular products.

Product Line

The product line criterion identifies a specific product line within the target market segment. The steel fabrication company in the previous example may decide to focus its search on companies manufacturing aluminum tubular products used in the manufacturing of lawn and patio furniture.

Profitability

The profitability criterion should be specified in terms of the percentage return on sales, assets, or total investment. This enables a more accurate comparison among candidates of different sizes. A firm with after-tax earnings of $5 million on sales of $100 million may be less attractive than a firm earning $3 million on sales of $50 million, because the latter firm may be more efficient.

Degree of Leverage

Debt-to-equity or debt-to-total capital ratios are used to measure the level of leverage or indebtedness. The acquiring company may not want to purchase a company whose heavy debt burden may cause the combined company's leverage ratios to jeopardize its credit rating. A firm's credit rating is an evaluation by such companies as Standard and Poor's or Moody's of the likelihood that a firm will repay its debt and interest on a timely basis.

Market Share

The acquiring firm may be interested only in firms that are number 1 or 2 in market share in the targeted industry or in firms whose market share is some multiple (e.g., 2 × the next largest competitor). Firms having substantially greater market share than their competitors often are able to achieve lower cost positions than their competitors because of economies of scale and experience curve effects.

Cultural Compatibility

While more difficult to quantify, insights can be gained by examining employee demographics such as the approximate average age and diversity of the workforce and the number of years a potential target has been in business. America Online's 2001 acquisition of Time Warner highlighted the difficulties in integrating a much more youthful and heterogeneous employee population with a much older, more homogeneous group. Also, as a much newer firm, AOL had a much less-structured management style than Time Warner's more staid environment. Public statements about the target's vision for the future and governance practices as well as reputation as a responsible corporate citizen within its industry provide other subjective measures of compatibility. Finally, an acquirer needs to determine if it can adapt to the challenges of dealing with foreign firms, such as different languages and customs.

Phase 5. First Contact

Alternative Approach Strategies

The approach suggested for initiating contact with a target company depends on the size of the company, if the target is publicly or privately held, and the acquirer's timeframe for completing a transaction. The last factor can be extremely important. If time permits, there is no substitute for developing a personal relationship with the sellers. Often, if a rapport is developed, companies can be acquired that are not perceived to be for sale. Such relationships can be formed only at the highest level within the target firm. In large and small privately owned firms, founders or their heirs often have a strong paternalistic view of their businesses. Such firms often have great flexibility in negotiating a deal that "feels right" rather than simply holding out for the highest possible price. Relationship building often is a critical factor in cross-border transactions (see Chapter 17). However, personal relationships can go only so far in negotiating with a public company, which has a fiduciary responsibility to get the best price.

If time is a critical factor, acquirers may not have the luxury of developing close personal relationships with the seller. Under these circumstances, a more expeditious approach might be taken. However, the approach taken may well differ depending on the size or public/private status of the potential target firm.

Small Companies

For small companies (<$25 million in sales) in which the buyer has no direct contacts, a vaguely worded letter expressing interest in a joint venture or marketing alliance and indicating that you will follow up with a telephone call often is all that is necessary. During the follow-up call, be prepared to discuss a range of options with the seller. Preparation before the first telephone contact is essential. If possible, script your comments. Get to the point quickly but indirectly. Identify yourself, your company, and its strengths. Demonstrate your understanding of the contact's business and how an informal partnership could make sense. Be able to quickly and succinctly explain the benefits of your proposal to the contact. If the opportunity arises, propose a range of options, including an acquisition. Listen carefully to the contact's reaction. Request a face-to-face meeting, if the contact is willing to entertain the notion of an acquisition. To assure confidentiality, choose a meeting place that provides sufficient privacy. Create a written agenda for the meeting after soliciting input from all participants. The meeting should start with a review of your company and your perspective on the outlook for the industry. Encourage the potential target firm to provide information on its own operations and its outlook for the industry. Look for areas of consensus.

Medium-Sized Companies

For medium-sized companies (between $25 and $100 million), make contact at the highest level possible in the potential target firm's organization through an intermediary. Intermediaries can be less intimidating than a direct approach. Intermediaries include members of the acquirer's board of directors or the firm's outside legal counsel, accounting firm, lender, broker-finder, or investment banker.

Large Companies

For large, publicly traded companies, contact also should be made through an intermediary at the highest level possible. Discretion is extremely important because of the target's concern about being "put into play." A company is said to be in play if circumstances suggest that it may be an attractive investment opportunity for other firms. Even rumors of an acquisition can have substantial, adverse consequences for the target. Current or potential customers may express concern about the uncertainty associated with a change of ownership. Such a change could imply variation in product or service quality, reliability, and the level of service provided under product warranty or maintenance contracts. Suppliers worry about possible disruptions in their production schedules as the transition to the new owner takes place. Employees worry about possible layoffs or changes in compensation. Competitors do what they can to fan these concerns to persuade current customers to switch and potential customers to defer buying decisions; key employees are encouraged to defect to the competition. Shareholders may experience a dizzying ride as arbitrageurs buying on the rumor bid up the price of the stock only to bail out if denial of the rumor appears credible.

Discussing Value

Neither the buyer nor seller has an incentive to be the first to provide an estimate of value. Getting a range may be the best you can do. This may be accomplished by discussing values for recent acquisitions of similar businesses. Listen carefully to the contact's reasons for wanting to sell, so that any proposal made can be structured to satisfy as many of the seller's primary needs as possible. With the seller's consent, establish a timeline consisting of next steps and stick to it.

Preliminary Legal Documents

A common first step in many transactions is to negotiate a confidentiality agreement, term sheet, and letter of intent (LOI). Usually, all parties to the deal desire to have a confidentiality agreement. This may not be true for a letter of intent. The LOI is useful in that it generally stipulates the initial areas of agreement, the rights of all parties to the transaction, and certain provisions protecting the interests of both the buyer and seller. However, the LOI could result in some legal risk to either the buyer or seller if the deal is not consummated. The LOI may create legal liabilities if one of the parties is later accused of not negotiating in "good faith." This often is the basis for many lawsuits filed when transactions are undertaken but not completed as a result of disagreements emerging during lengthy and often heated negotiations. For illustrations of legal documents associated with M&As, see Oesterlie (2006) and the CD-ROM accompanying this book.

Confidentiality Agreement

A confidentiality agreement (also called a *nondisclosure agreement*) is generally mutually binding, in that it covers all parties to the transaction. In negotiating the confidentiality agreement, the buyer requests as much audited historical data and supplemental information as the seller is willing to provide. The prudent seller requests similar information about the buyer to assess the buyer's financial credibility. It is important for the seller to determine the buyer's credibility early in the process so as not to waste time with a potential buyer incapable of raising the financing to complete the transaction. The agreement should cover only information that is not publicly available and should have a reasonable expiration date. Note that the confidentiality agreement can be negotiated independently or as part of the term sheet or letter of intent.

Term Sheet

A term sheet outlines the primary terms with the seller and is often used as the basis for a more detailed letter of intent. The involvement of lawyers and accountants is often unnecessary at this stage. It is the last stage in the negotiation before the parties to the potential transaction start incurring significant legal, accounting, and consulting expenses. A standard term sheet may be two to four pages in length. It stipulates the total consideration or purchase price (often as a range), what is being acquired (i.e., assets or stock), limitations on the use of proprietary data, a *no-shop agreement* preventing the seller from sharing the terms of the buyer's proposal with other potential buyers with the hope of instigating an auction environment, and a termination date. Many transactions skip the term sheet and go straight to the negotiating of a letter of intent.

Letter of Intent

The LOI often is useful in identifying, early in the process, areas of agreement and disagreement. However, it may delay the signing of a definitive agreement of purchase and sale. For public companies, it may necessitate a public announcement to be in compliance with securities laws if the agreement is likely to have a "material" impact on the buyer or seller. Depending on how it is written, it may or may not be legally binding. The LOI formally stipulates the reason for the agreement and major terms and conditions. It also indicates the responsibilities of both parties while the agreement is in force, a reasonable expiration date, and how all fees associated with the transaction will be paid. Major terms and conditions include a brief outline of the structure of the transaction, which may entail the payment of cash or stock for certain assets and the assumption of certain target company liabilities. The letter also may specify certain conditions, such as an agreement that selected personnel of the target will not compete with the combined companies for some time period if they should leave. Another condition may indicate that a certain portion of the purchase price will be allocated to the noncompete agreement. Such an allocation of the purchase price is in the interests of the buyer, because the amount of the allocation can be amortized over the life of the agreement. As such, it can be taken as a tax-deductible expense. However, it may constitute taxable income for the seller. The agreement also may place a portion of the purchase price in escrow.

The proposed purchase price may be expressed as a specific dollar figure, as a range, or as a multiple of some measure of value, such as operating earnings or cash flow. The LOI also specifies the types of data to be exchanged and the duration and extent of the initial due diligence. The LOI usually terminates if the buyer and the seller do not reach agreement by a certain date. Legal, consulting, and deed transfer fees (i.e., payments made to government entities when ownership changes hands) may be paid for by the buyer or seller or they may be shared. As discussed in Chapter 3, buyers are sometimes able to negotiate breakup fees and options to purchase target stock or selected assets if the deal is not completed.

A well-written LOI usually contains language limiting the extent to which the agreement binds the two parties. Price or other provisions are generally subject to *closing conditions.* Such conditions could include the buyer having full access to all of the seller's books and records; having completed due diligence; obtaining financing; and having received approval from boards of directors, stockholders, and regulatory bodies. Other standard conditions include the requirement for signed employment contracts for key target firm executives and the completion of all necessary M&A documents. Failure to satisfy any of these conditions invalidates the agreement. A well-written LOI also should describe the due diligence process in some detail. It should stipulate how the potential buyer should access the potential seller's premises, the frequency and duration of such access, and how intrusive such activities should be. The LOI also should indicate how the buyer should meet and discuss the deal with the seller's employees, customers, and suppliers. Sometimes, the provisions of a standard confidentiality agreement are negotiated as part of the LOI. The letter of intent becomes the governing document for the deal that the potential acquirer can show to prospective financing sources.

In recent years, letters of intent sometimes include *go-shop* provisions, which allow the seller to continue to solicit higher bids for several months. However, if the seller accepts another bid, the seller would have to pay the bidder with whom it has a signed agreement a breakup fee. In early 2007, auto parts manufacturer Lear Corp announced that it had signed a deal to be acquired by financier Carl Icahn's American Real Estate Partners. Under the terms of the deal, Lear had 45 days to find another suitor.

Phase 6. Negotiation

Unlike the previous phases, the negotiation phase is an interactive, iterative process. Many activities are conducted concurrently by various members of the acquisition team. The actual purchase price paid for the acquired business is determined during this phase and frequently will be considerably different from the initial valuation of the target company made before due diligence and based on limited publicly available information. For a more detailed discussion of the M&A negotiation and deal structuring process, see DePamphilis (2010b).

Developing a Negotiating Strategy

Negotiating is essentially a process in which two or more parties, representing different interests, attempt to achieve a consensus on a particular issue. A useful starting point in any negotiation is to determine the areas of disagreement as soon as possible. This may be achieved by having the parties review and agree on the facts pertaining to the deal. In general, parties will be able to reach agreement on most facts relatively easily. Once a list of areas of agreement has been compiled, it is easy to identify areas in dispute. Each party then determines if the list of disputed subjects contains any "deal breakers." *Deal breakers* are issues that a party to the negotiation cannot concede without making the deal unacceptable. Good negotiators make concessions on issues not considered deal breakers, but only if they receive something in return. The easiest areas of disagreement should be resolved first until only a few remain on the list. By this point, all parties to the negotiation have invested a great deal of money, time, and emotional commitment to the process. All parties generally are looking forward to a near-term resolution of the remaining issues. All positions should be explained logically. Unreasonable demands at this point in the negotiation are likely to evoke frustration by the other party and encourage that party to end discussions. If the parties can reach a point where one side is willing to state at least a price range, a final agreement is in sight. Avoid disclosing information when you are not compelled to do so.

Defining the Purchase Price

The three commonly used definitions of purchase price are the total consideration, the total purchase price or enterprise value, and the net purchase price. Each definition serves a different purpose.

Total Consideration

In the agreement of purchase and sale, the ***total consideration*** consists of cash (*C*), stock (*S*), new debt issues (*D*), or some combination of all three. It is a term commonly used in legal documents to reflect the different types of remuneration received by target company shareholders. Note that the remuneration can include both financial and nonfinancial assets, such as real estate. Nonfinancial compensation sometimes is referred to as *payment in kind.* The debt counted in the total consideration is what the target company shareholders receive as payment for their stock, along with any cash or acquiring company stock.

Each component of the total consideration may be viewed in present value terms; therefore, the total consideration is itself expressed in present value terms (PV_{TC}). The present value of cash is its face value. The stock component of the total consideration are the present value (PV_S) of future dividends or net cash flows or the acquiring firm's stock price per share times the number of shares to be exchanged for each outstanding share of the seller's stock. New debt issued by the acquiring company as part of the compensation paid to shareholders can be expressed as the present value (PV_{ND}) of the cumulative interest payments plus principal discounted at some appropriate market rate of interest (see Chapter 7).

Total Purchase Price (Enterprise Value)

The **total purchase price** (PV_{TPP}) or **enterprise value** of the target firm consists of the total consideration (PV_{TC}) plus the market value of the target firm's debt (PV_{AD}) assumed by the acquiring company. The enterprise value is sometimes expressed as the total purchase price plus net debt. **Net debt** includes the market value of debt assumed by the acquirer less cash and marketable securities on the books of the target firm. The enterprise value of the firm often is quoted in the media as the purchase price, because it is most visible to those not familiar with the details. It is important to analysts and shareholders alike, because it approximates the total investment made by the acquiring firm. It is an approximation because it does not necessarily measure liabilities the acquirer is assuming that are not visible on the target firm's balance sheet. Nor does it reflect the potential for recovering a portion of the total consideration paid to target company shareholders by selling undervalued or redundant assets.

Net Purchase Price

The **net purchase price** (PV_{NPP}) is the total purchase price plus other assumed liabilities (PV_{OAL}) less the proceeds from the sale of discretionary or redundant target assets (PV_{DA}) on or off the balance sheet. PV_{OAL} are those assumed liabilities not fully reflected on the target firm's balance sheet or in the estimation of the economic value of the target firm. Other assumed liabilities and discretionary assets are explained in more detail later.

The net purchase price is the most comprehensive measure of the actual price paid for the target firm. It includes all known cash obligations assumed by the acquirer as well as any portion of the purchase price that is recovered through the sale of assets. It may be larger or smaller than the total purchase price. The various definitions of price can be summarized as follows:

Total consideration $= PV_{TC} = C + PV_S + PV_{ND}$

Total purchase price or enterprise value $= PV_{TPP} = PV_{TC} + PV_{AD}$

Net purchase price $= PV_{NPP} = PV_{TPP} + PV_{OAL} - PV_{DA}$
$$= (C + PV_S + PV_{ND} + PV_{AD}) + PV_{OAL} - PV_{DA}$$

Although the total consideration is most important to the target company's shareholders as a measure of what they receive in exchange for their stock, the acquirer's shareholders should focus on the total purchase price/enterprise value as the actual amount paid for the target firm. However, the total purchase price tends to ignore other adjustments that should be made to determine actual or pending "out-of-pocket" cash spent by the acquirer. The net purchase price reflects adjustments to the total purchase price and is a much better indicator of whether the acquirer overpaid (i.e., paid more than its economic value including synergy) for the target firm. *Economic value* is the present value of a firm's projected cash flows. The application of the various definitions of the purchase price is addressed in more detail in Chapter 9.

Other Assumed Liabilities

The adjustment to the total purchase price referred to as *other assumed liabilities* consists of items not adequately accounted for on the target's balance sheet. If all the target firm's balance sheet reserves reflected accurately all known future obligations and there were no significant potential off-balance sheet liabilities, there would be no need to adjust the purchase price for assumed liabilities other than for short- and long-term debt assumed by the acquiring company. Earnings would accurately reflect the expected impact of known liabilities. Operating cash flows, which reflect both earnings and changes in balance sheet items, would also accurately reflect future liabilities. Therefore, valuations based on a multiple of earnings, book value, or discounted cash flow would accurately reflect the economic value of the business.

In practice, this is rarely the case. Reserves are often inadequate to satisfy pending claims. This is particularly true if the selling company attempts to improve current earnings performance by understating reserves. Common examples include underfunded or underreserved employee pension and health-care obligations and uncollectable receivables, as well as underaccrued vacation and holidays, bonuses, and deferred compensation, such as employee stock options. Other examples include product warranties, environmental liabilities, pending lawsuits, severance expenses, maintenance and service agreements, and any other obligations of the selling company accepted by the buyer at closing. To the extent that such factors represent a future use of cash, the present value of their future impact, to the extent possible, should be estimated.

Discretionary Assets

Discretionary assets are undervalued or redundant assets not required to operate the acquired business that can be used by the buyer to recover some portion of the purchase price. Such assets include land valued at its historical cost on the balance sheet or inventory and equipment whose resale value exceeds its fully depreciated value. Other examples include cash balances in excess of normal working capital needs and product lines or operating units considered nonstrategic by the buyer. The sale of discretionary assets is not considered in the calculation of the economic value of the target firm because economic value is determined by future operating cash flows before consideration is given to how the transaction will be financed.

Concurrent Activities

The negotiation phase consists of four concurrent activities: (1) refining valuation, (2) deal structuring, (3) due diligence, and (4) developing a financing plan. Refining the preliminary valuation based on new information uncovered during due diligence provides the starting point for negotiating the agreement of purchase and sale. Deal structuring involves meeting the needs of both parties by addressing issues of risk and reward by constructing an appropriate set of compensation, legal, tax, and accounting structures. Due diligence provides additional information enabling the buyer to better understand the nature of the liabilities the buyer is being asked to assume and confirm perceived sources of value. Finally, the financing plan provides a reality check on the buyer, because it defines the maximum amount the buyer can reasonably expect to finance and in turn pay for the target company.

Refining Valuation

The first activity within the negotiation phase of the acquisition process deals with updating the preliminary target company valuation based on new information. At this stage, the buyer requests and reviews at least three to five years of historical financial data. Although it is highly desirable to examine data that have been audited in accordance with Generally Accepted Accounting Principals (GAAP), such data may not be available for small, privately owned companies. In fact, small companies rarely hire outside accounting firms to conduct expensive audits unless they are required to do so as part of a loan agreement.

The three to five years of historical data should be *normalized*, or adjusted for nonrecurring gains, losses, or expenses. Nonrecurring gains or losses can result from the sale of land, equipment, product lines, patents, software, or copyrights. Nonrecurring expenses include severance, employee signing bonuses, and settlement of litigation. These adjustments are necessary to allow the buyer to smooth out irregularities in the historical information and better understand the underlying dynamics of the business. Once the data have been normalized, each major expense category should be expressed as a percentage of revenue. By observing year-to-year changes in these ratios, sustainable trends in the data are more discernable. The process of refining valuations using standard financial modeling techniques is described in more detail in Chapter 9.

Deal Structuring

In purely financial terms, deal structuring involves the allocation of cash-flow streams (with respect to amount and timing); the allocation of risk; and, therefore, the allocation of value between different parties to the transaction. In terms of the personalities of the parties involved, deal structuring is the process of identifying and satisfying as many of the highest priority objectives of the parties involved in the transaction subject to their tolerance for risk. In practice, deal structuring is about understanding the potential sources of disagreement from a simple argument over basic facts to substantially more complex issues, such as the form of payment, legal, accounting, and tax structures. It also requires understanding the potential conflicts of interest that can influence the outcome of the discussions. For example, when a portion of the purchase price depends on the long-term performance of the acquired business, the management of the business, often the former owner, may not behave in a manner that is in the best interests of the acquirer. The deal-structuring process also embodies feedback effects, in which one element of the process, such as the nature of payment, including amount, timing, and risk, may affect tax strategies.

Decisions made throughout the deal-structuring process influence various attributes of the deal. These attributes include, but are not limited to, how ownership is determined, how assets are transferred, how ownership is protected (i.e., governance), and how risk is apportioned among parties to the transaction. Other attributes include the type, number, and complexity of the documents required for closing; the types of approvals required; and the time needed to complete the transaction. These decisions also influence how the combined companies will be managed, the amount and timing of resources committed, and the magnitude and timing of current and future tax liabilities (McCarthy, 1998; Tillinghast, 1998).

Reflecting this complexity, the deal-structuring process should be viewed as consisting of a number of interdependent components. At a minimum, these include the acquisition vehicle, the postclosing organization, the legal form of the selling entity, the form of payment, the form of acquisition, and tax considerations. The process starts with the determination by each party of their initial negotiating positions, potential risks, options for managing risk, levels of tolerance for risk, and conditions under which either party will "walk away" from the negotiations. The term *acquisition vehicle* refers to the legal structure (e.g., corporation or partnership) used to acquire the target company. The *postclosing organization* is the organizational and legal framework (e.g., corporation or partnership) used to manage the combined businesses following the completion of the transaction. The *legal form of the selling entity* refers to whether the seller is a C or subchapter S corporation, a limited liability company, or a partnership. These considerations affect both the tax structure of the deal and the form of payment. The *form of payment* may consist of cash, common stock, debt, or some combination. Some portion of the payment may be deferred or dependent on the future performance of the acquired entity. The *form of acquisition* reflects both what is being acquired (e.g., stock or assets) and the form of payment. Consequently, the form of acquisition largely determines the tax structures. As a general rule, a transaction is taxable if remuneration paid to the target company's shareholders is primarily something other than the acquirer's stock, and it is nontaxable (i.e., tax deferred) if what they receive is largely acquirer stock. How and why these things happen are discussed in substantial detail in Chapters 11 and 12.

Conducting Due Diligence

Although some degree of protection is achieved through a well-written contract, legal documents should never be viewed as a substitute for conducting formal due diligence. Exhibit 5–2 lists convenient online sources of information helpful in conducting due diligence. A detailed preliminary acquirer due diligence question list is provided on the CD-ROM included with this book. For a detailed discussion of the due diligence process and best practices, see Selim (2003).

Exhibit 5–2 Convenient Information Sources for Conducting Due Diligence

Web Address	Content
Securities and Exchange Commission	Financial information/security law violations
www.sec.gov	Public filings for almost 10 years available through the Edgar database
http://www.sec.gov/litigation.shtml	Enforcement actions
U.S. Patent Office	Intellectual property rights information
www.uspto.gov	Search patent database
www.uspto.gov/patft/index.html	Database if you have patent number
Federal Communications Commission:	Regulates various commercial practices
www.fcc.gov	General information
www.fcc.gov/searchtools.html	Access to database of individuals sanctioned for illegal marketing practices

Continued

Exhibit 5–2 Convenient Information Sources for Conducting Due Diligence — Cont'd	
U.S. and states attorneys general offices	Information on criminal activities
www.naag.org/ag/full_ag_table.php	Listing of states attorneys general
National Association of Securities Dealers	Regulates securities industry
www.nasdr.com	Information on investment bankers Database
Better Business Bureau (BBB)	Compiles consumer complaints
http://search.bbb.org/search.html	Database
Paid services	Information on
U.S. Search (www.ussearch.com)	Criminal violations
KnowX (www.knowx.com)	Liens/bankruptcies
	Credit history
	Litigation

Buyer Due Diligence

Buyer due diligence is the process of validating assumptions underlying valuation. The primary objectives are to identify and confirm "sources of value" and mitigate real or potential liability by looking for fatal flaws that reduce value. Table 5–1 provides a way of categorizing sources of synergy and their impact on operating performance. Chapter 9 provides examples of how to quantify and include these sources of value in the valuation and financial modeling process.

Due diligence involves three primary reviews: (1) a strategic, operational, and marketing review conducted by senior operations and marketing management; (2) a financial review directed by financial and accounting personnel; and (3) a legal review conducted by the buyer's legal counsel. Rigorous due diligence requires the creation of comprehensive checklists. The strategic and operational review questions focus on the seller's management team, operations, and sales and marketing strategies. The financial review questions focus on the accuracy, timeliness, and completeness of the seller's financial statements. Finally, legal questions deal with corporate records, financial matters, management and employee issues, tangible and intangible assets of the seller, and material contracts and obligations of the seller, such as litigation and claims. The interview process provides invaluable sources of information. By asking the same questions of a number of key managers, the acquirer is able to validate the accuracy of their conclusions. See the appendix to this chapter for a further discussion of buyer due diligence question lists and the CD-ROM accompanying this book for an example of a detailed buyer due diligence question list.

Limiting Due Diligence

Due diligence is an expensive and exhausting process. The buyer frequently wants as much time as necessary to complete due diligence. In contrast, the seller often wants to limit the length and scope as much as possible. By its nature, due diligence is highly intrusive and places substantial demands on managers' time and attention. Due diligence rarely works

Table 5–1   Identifying Potential Sources of Value

Potential Source of Value	Examples	Potential Impact
Operating Synergy		
Eliminating functional overlap	Reducing duplicate overhead positions	Improved margins
Productivity improvement	Increasing output per employee	Same
Purchasing discounts	Volume discounts on material purchases	Same
Working capital management	Reduced days in receivables due to improved collection of accounts receivable	Improved return on total assets
	Fewer days in inventory due to improved inventory turns	Same
Facilities management		
Economies of scale	Increased production in underutilized facilities	Improved return on total assets
Economies of scope	Data centers, R&D functions, call centers, etc. support multiple product lines/ operations	Same
Organizational realignment	Reducing the number of layers of management	Improved communication Reduced bureaucratic inertia
Financial Synergy		
Increased borrowing capacity	Target has little debt and many unencumbered assets	Increased access to financing
Increased leverage	Access to lower cost source of funds	Lower cost of capital
Marketing/Product Synergy		
Access to new distribution channels	Increased sales opportunities	Increased revenue
Cross-selling opportunities	Selling acquirer products to target customers and vice versa	Same
Research and development	Cross-fertilization of ideas	More innovation
Product development	Increased advertising budget	Improved market share
Control		
Opportunity identification	Acquirer sees opportunities not seen by target's management	New growth opportunities
More proactive management style	More decisive decision making	Improved financial returns

to the advantage of the seller, because a long and detailed due diligence is likely to uncover items that the buyer will use as an excuse to lower the purchase price. Consequently, sellers may seek to terminate due diligence before the buyer feels it is appropriate.

In some instances, buyers and sellers may agree to an abbreviated due diligence period. The theory is that the buyer can be protected in a well-written agreement of purchase and sale. In the agreement, the seller is required to make certain representations and warrant that they are true. Such "reps and warranties" could include the seller's acknowledgment that it owns all assets listed in the agreement "free and clear" of any liens. If the representation is breached (i.e., found not to be true), the agreement generally includes a mechanism for compensating the buyer for any material loss. What constitutes material loss is defined in the contract. Relying on reps and warranties as a substitute for a thorough due diligence is rarely a good idea (see Case Study 5–1).

Case Study 5–1   When "Reps and Warranties" Do Not Provide Adequate Protection

A large financial services firm in the mid-1990s acquired a small database company that provided data supporting the lending process. The seller signed a contract with all the necessary reps and warranties that all its computer systems were fully operational and in compliance with prevailing laws. The buyer also withheld about 20 percent of the purchase price in the event that the operational effectiveness of the systems was not at the level specified in the contract. The combination of the assurances in the contract and the portion of the purchase price held in escrow made the buyer confident that it was fully protected.

It became apparent almost immediately after closing that the seller had misstated dramatically the viability of his business. The buyer had to eventually shut down the business and write off the full purchase price. The buyer also had to submit to binding arbitration to recover the portion of the purchase price that had been placed in escrow. The buyer had virtually no recourse to the seller which had few assets in its own name and may have moved the bulk of the cash received for its stock to banks beyond the jurisdiction of the U.S. legal system.

Discussion Questions

1. Comment on the statement that there is no substitute for thorough due diligence.
2. How might the acquirer have been better able to protect itself in this situation?

Using a **data room** is another method commonly used by sellers to limit due diligence. This amounts to the seller sequestering the acquirer's team in a single room to complete due diligence. Typically, the data room consists of a conference room filled with file cabinets and boxes of documents requested by the buyer's due diligence team. Formal presentations by the seller's key managers are given in the often cramped conditions of the data room. Not surprisingly, the data room is a poor substitute for a tour of the seller's facilities. Large investment banks frequently provide access to such data via the Internet.

Seller's Due Diligence

Although the bulk of due diligence is performed by the buyer on the seller, the prudent seller also should perform due diligence on the buyer and on themselves. In doing so, the seller can determine if the buyer has the financial wherewithal to finance the purchase price. In addition, a seller, as part of its own due diligence process, frequently requires all its managers to sign documents (i.e., affidavits) stating that to the "best of their knowledge" what is being represented in the contract that pertains to their area of responsibility is indeed true. By conducting an internal investigation of its own operations, the seller hopes to mitigate liability stemming from inaccuracies in the seller's representations and warranties made in the definitive agreement of purchase and sale.

Lender's Due Diligence

If the acquirer is borrowing to buy a target firm, the lender(s) will want to perform their own due diligence independent of the buyer's. It is easy to see how burdensome multiple lender due diligences, often performed concurrently, can be on the target firm's management and employees. The seller should not agree to such disruptive activities unless confident that the transaction will be consummated within a reasonable period.

Developing the Financing Plan: The Reality Check

The final activity of the negotiation phase is to develop balance sheet, income, and cash-flow statements for the combined firms. Unlike the financial projections of cash flow made to value the target, these statements should include the expected cost of financing the transaction. This activity is a key input into the determination of the purchase price, because it places a limitation on the amount of the purchase price the buyer can offer the seller.

According to capital budgeting theory, an investment should be funded as long as its net present value (NPV) is greater than or equal to 0. The same concept could be applied to an acquisition. The buyer should be able to finance a purchase price (P_{TPP}) up to the present value of the target company as an independent or stand-alone entity (PV_I) plus synergy (PV_{SYN}) created by combining the acquiring and target companies discounted at the appropriate cost of capital:

$$NPV = (PV_I + PV_{SYN}) - P_{TPP} \geq 0$$

The financing plan is appended to the acquirer's business and acquisition plans and used to obtain financing for the transaction. No matter what size the transaction, lenders and investors will want to see a coherent analysis explaining why the proposed transaction is a good investment opportunity for them. Regardless of the intended audience, the financing plan largely is used as a marketing or sales document to negotiate the best possible terms for financing the proposed transaction. See Chapters 9 and 13 for more detail on developing the financing plan.

Obtaining Bridge or Interim Financing

For an all-cash transaction, the buyer goes to the traditional sources of financing: banks, insurance companies, investment bankers and underwriters, venture capitalists and private equity funds, and the seller. Banks commonly are used to provide temporary, or *bridge*, financing to pay all or a portion of the purchase price and meet possible working capital requirements until permanent or long-term financing is found. Buyers usually seek more long-term sources of financing to replace bank debt because of the onerous covenants that restrict how the buyer may operate the combined firms. *Covenants* are promises made by the borrower that certain acts will be performed and others will be avoided. Covenants are designed to protect the lender's interests and may require the borrower to maintain a certain ratio of working capital to sales, debt-to-equity ratio, and credit rating. Covenants also may limit the amount of dividends the borrower can pay and future acquisitions or divestitures.

Case Study 5–2 describes how acquiring companies arrange interim financing to meet immediate cash requirements at closing. These cash requirements consist of the need to pay target company shareholders the cash portion of the total consideration as well as the payment of cash for fractional shares. For large transactions, banking syndicates include many banks to spread the risk of the transaction. These bank loans are usually short term in nature and either "rolled over" (i.e., continued) at the prevailing rate of interest or refinanced using long-term debt.

Case Study 5–2 Vodafone Finances the Acquisition of AirTouch

In April 1999, Vodafone Group PLC reached an agreement with 11 banks to underwrite and arrange the "facility" or line of credit for financing the merger with AirTouch Communications, Inc. Under the terms of the transaction, AirTouch common shareholders would receive five Vodafone AirTouch ADSs (equivalent to five Vodafone AirTouch ordinary shares) plus $9 in cash. The transaction closed in July 1999 and was valued at $55 billion. The banking syndicate consisted of Bank of America, Barclay's, Banque Nationale de Paris, Citibank, Deutsche Bank, Goldman Sachs, HSBC, ING Barings, National Australia Bank, NatWest, and WestLB. The total facility, or amount that could be borrowed, was set at between $10 and $13 billion. The actual amount required could not be determined until the closing, when a more precise estimate of cash requirements could be determined. The term of the major part of the facility was for 364 days, with the remaining balance multiyear. The initial borrowing rate was to be 60 basis points (six tenths of 1 percent) above the London Interbank Overnight Rate. This rate is similar to the U.S. federal funds rate. The actual spread would vary with the tranche (term) selected, utilization level (amount borrowed), and guarantee structure (the creditworthiness of those banks issuing letters of credit). Following completion of the merger, much of the facility was to be refinanced in the bond and commercial paper markets through the banks, which had arranged the facility.

Discussion Questions

1. Why is short-term bank financing often used to finance an acquisition?
2. Why did Vodafone seek to convert the short-term bank financing to longer-term debt?

Mezzanine and Permanent Financing

Mezzanine financing refers to capital that, in liquidation, has a repayment priority between senior debt and common stock. Although mezzanine financing may take the form of redeemable preferred stock, it generally is subordinated debt, with warrants convertible into common stock. It generally is unsecured, with a fixed coupon rate and a maturity of 5–10 years. Mezzanine investors usually look for firms with revenues in excess of $10 million. *Permanent financing* usually consists of long-term unsecured debt. Such debt is generally not rated by the major credit-rating agencies, such as Standard & Poor's and Moody's services, and may be referred to as junk bond financing. Such financing may be obtained by investment bankers or underwriters raising funds by a "private placement" of all or a portion of the bond issue with investors willing to hold the bonds for long periods. Private placements avoid going through the public securities markets. Investors in private transactions often include insurance companies and pension funds, which are interested in matching their investment income stream with their obligations to policyholders and pensioners. Such debt is usually subordinate to bank debt if the firm is forced into bankruptcy. In addition, junk bonds may be sold to mutual funds or directly to the public. If a significant percentage of the debt is to be sold to the public, raising permanent financing will require many months to satisfy SEC requirements for full disclosure of risks.

Venture Capital Firms

Venture capitalists (VCs) are also a significant source of funds for financing both startups and acquisitions. VC firms identify and screen opportunities, transact and close deals, monitor and add value, and raise additional capital. General partners receive a 2–3 percent fee and 15–25 percent of any capital gains from initial public offerings and mergers. The remaining 75–85 percent of capital gains plus a return of principal goes back to investors in the VC fund (Bygrave and Timmons, 1992). Only 2–4 percent of the firms contacting VC firms actually receive funding (Vachon, 1993). VCs sometimes are willing to lend when the more traditional sources, such as banks, insurance companies, and pension funds, are not. VCs usually demand a large equity position in the firm in exchange for paying the firm a relatively low price per share.

Angel Investors

Angel investors are wealthy individuals who often band together in "investment clubs" or groups in loose affiliations or networks. The objective of such groups or networks is to generate deal flow, pool money, and share expertise. Some angel groups imitate professional investment funds, some affiliate with universities, while others engage in for-profit philanthropy. Angel investors often expect annual average returns of about 27 percent (Wiltbank and Boeker, 2007). However, the variability of such returns can be substantial. In their study of 1,137 "exits" between 1990 and 2007 through mergers, acquisitions, initial public offerings, reorganizations, and liquidations, Wiltbank and Boeker (2007) found that 7 percent of their sample had returns 10 times their original investments. Thirty-nine percent earned less than one time their initial investment.

Seller Financing

Seller financing represents a very important source of financing for buyers and involves the seller deferring the receipt of a portion of the purchase price until some future date or making an investment in the buyer. The advantages to the buyer include a lower overall risk of the transaction because of the need to provide less capital at the time of closing and the shifting of operational risk to the seller if the buyer ultimately defaults on the loan to the seller.

In an effort to reduce the amount it would have to borrow to finance its purchase of chemical company Rohm & Haas, Dow Chemical renegotiated the terms of its original July 2008 agreement in March 2009 before it was willing to close the deal. While Rohm shareholders received $78 per share in cash (consistent with the original terms), the way it would be financed was considerably different. In the original transaction, Dow would have had to borrow most of the $15.3 billion purchase price. Under the new deal, Rohm's largest shareholders, Rohm's founding Haas family and the hedge fund Paulson & Company, agreed to buy up to $2.5 billion in preferred stock in Dow in what effectively represented seller financing. See Table 5–2 for a summary of alternative financing methods.

The "Road Show"

To arrange both bridge and permanent financing, the buyer develops elaborate presentations to take on a "road show" to convince potential lenders of the attractiveness of the lending opportunity. It is referred to as a *road show* for good reason—immaculately dressed borrowers passionately display confidence in their business plan through carefully rehearsed and choreographed multimedia presentations in stuffy conference rooms throughout the country. It represents an opportunity for potential lenders to see management and ask the "tough questions." If the "road show" is successful, at least several lenders compete for all or a portion of the bond issue, resulting in lower interest rates and less onerous loan covenants.

Table 5–2   Financing Mergers and Acquisitions

	Debt	Equity
Asset-based lending (collateralized by fixed assets, accounts receivable, and inventories)	Revolving credit lines Term loans Sale/lease-back	
Cash-flow-based lending (based on projected cash flow)		
Seller-financing	Deferred payments Earn-outs Installment sales	Common stock Preferred stock
Public offering and private placements	Senior Convertible Subordinated	Common stock Preferred stock
Alternative sources	Commercial banks Insurance companies Pension funds Investment/merchant banks Hedge funds and private equity partnerships	Hedge or buyout funds Private equity investors Venture capital Strategic investors Individual investors ("angels")

Selecting Alternative Financial Structures

Computer models that simulate the financial impact of various financial structures on the combined firms are excellent tools for determining the appropriate capital structure (see Chapter 9). Although leverage raises the potential rate of return to equity investors, it also adds to risk. Increasing credit obligations to lenders implies increasing fixed interest expense, which raises the point at which the firm's revenue covers its costs (i.e., its breakeven point). An unanticipated downturn in the economy or aggressive pricing actions by competitors can erode cash flow and the firm's ability to meet its interest expense. This ultimately could lead to bankruptcy. This risk can be measured by creating various scenarios, each representing a different capital structure and determining the impact of lower-than-expected sales growth.

Financing Contingencies

Most well-written agreements of purchase and sale contain a financing contingency. The buyer is not subject to the terms of the contract if the buyer cannot obtain adequate funding to complete the transaction. As previously discussed, breakup fees can be particularly useful to ensure that the buyer attempts to obtain financing as aggressively as possible. In some instances, the seller may require the buyer to put a nonrefundable deposit in escrow to be forfeited if the buyer is unable to obtain financing to complete the transaction.

Phase 7. Developing the Integration Plan

The euphoria that surrounds the successful completion of a transaction erodes quickly once the challenges of making the combined firms perform in line with the predictions laid out in the business and acquisition plans become apparent. Once the documents are signed, the buyer has lost most, if not all, leverage over the seller.

Earning Trust

Decisions made before closing affect postclosing integration activity. Benefits packages, employment contracts, and bonuses to retain key employees (i.e., retention bonuses) normally are negotiated before closing. Contractual covenants and conditions also affect integration. *Earn-outs*, payments to the seller based on the acquired business achieving certain profit or revenue targets, and ***deferred purchase price payments***, involving the placement of some portion of the purchase price in escrow until certain contractual conditions have been realized, can limit the buyer's ability to effectively integrate the target into the acquirer's operations. Successfully integrating firms requires getting employees in both firms to work toward achieving common objectives. This comes about through building credibility and trust, not through superficial slogans, pep talks, and empty promises. Trust comes from cooperation and experiencing success.

Earn-Outs

Earn-outs are generally very poor ways to create trust and often represent major impediments to the integration process. The two firms generally are kept physically separate. Accounting and management reporting systems are not merged immediately, data centers remain separate, and sales forces remain largely independent. The buyer's concern is that the effort to integrate the firms as soon as possible after closing will make tracking the financial progress of the acquired company toward meeting its earn-out goals difficult. Moreover, the merging of facilities and sales forces could create a highly contentious situation once the earn-out period has elapsed, if the acquired company did not meet the earn-out goals. Employees covered by the earn-out could plead in court that they were prevented from doing so by not being allowed by the buyer to implement the business plan on which the earn-out was based. See Chapter 11 for a discussion of how to calculate earn-out payments.

Choosing the Integration Manager and Other Critical Decisions

This person should have excellent interpersonal and project management skills. During the integration phase, interpersonal skills are frequently more important than professional and technical skills. The buyer must determine what is critical for continuation of the acquired company's success during the first 12–24 months following closing. Critical activities include the identification of key managers, vendors, and customers and what is needed to retain these valued assets. The preclosing integration planning activity also should include the determination of operating norms or standards required for continued operation of the businesses. These include executive compensation, labor contracts, billing procedures, product delivery times, and quality metrics. Finally, a communication plan must be designed for all stakeholders to be implemented immediately following closing (Porter and Wood, 1998). Preclosing planning and postclosing integration are discussed in considerable detail in Chapter 6.

Phase 8. Closing

The closing phase of the acquisition process consists of obtaining all necessary shareholder, regulatory, and third party consents (e.g., customer and vendor contracts), as well as completing the definitive agreement of purchase and sale. Like all other phases, this activity requires significant planning at the outset if it is to go smoothly. Unfortunately, this is frequently impractical, in view of all the activities under way during the acquisition process. All such activities tend to converge on the closing date.

Assigning Customer and Vendor Contracts

In a purchase of assets, many customer and vendor contracts cannot be assigned to the buyer without receiving written approval from the other parties. Although this may be a largely mechanical process, both vendors and customers may view this as an opportunity to attempt to negotiate more favorable terms. Licenses also must receive approval from the licensor, and they also can be a major impediment to a timely closing if not properly planned. For example, a major software vendor demanded a substantial increase in royalty payments before it would transfer the software license to the buyer. The vendor knew that the software was critical for the ongoing operation of the business's data center. The exorbitant increase in the fee had an adverse impact on the economics of the transaction from the buyer's viewpoint and almost caused the deal to collapse.

A number of transitional issues also must be addressed before closing. These include continued payroll processing support by the seller on behalf of the buyer until the buyer is able to assume this function and the return of checks received by the seller from customers continuing to send checks to the seller's bank accounts after closing. Similarly, the buyer wants to be reimbursed by the seller for payments made by the buyer to vendors for materials supplied or services provided before closing but not paid until after closing.

Gaining the Necessary Approvals

The buyer's legal counsel is responsible for ensuring that the transaction is in full compliance with securities, antitrust, and state corporation laws. Significant planning before closing is again crucial to minimizing roadblocks that a target company may place before the buyer. Great care must be exercised to ensure that all the filings required by law have been made with the Federal Trade Commission and the Department of Justice. Noncompliance can delay or prevent a merger or acquisition (see Chapter 2). Finally, many transactions require approval by the acquirer and target company shareholders.

Completing the Acquisition-Merger Agreement

The cornerstone of the closing documents is the acquisition-merger agreement, which indicates all the rights and obligations of the parties both before and after closing. This agreement also may be referred to as the *definitive agreement of purchase and sale*. The length of the definitive agreement depends on the complexity of the transaction. See Chapters 11 and 12 for additional detail on definitive agreements.

Deal Provisions

In an asset or stock purchase, this section of the agreement defines the consideration or form of payment and how it will be paid and the specific assets or shares to be acquired. In a merger, this section of the agreement defines the number of (or fraction of) acquirer shares to be exchanged for each target share.

Price

The purchase price or total consideration may be fixed at the time of closing, subject to future adjustment, or it may be contingent on future performance. The purchase price may be initially fixed based on the seller's representations of the firm's total assets, total book value, tangible book value, or some other measure of value. However, the price may be adjusted following a postclosing audit. In asset transactions, cash on the target's balance sheet frequently is excluded from the transaction; the price paid for noncurrent assets, such as plant and intangible assets, is fixed, but the price for current assets depends on their levels at closing. Chapter 11 discusses how the postclosing adjustment to current assets is calculated.

Allocation of Price

The buyer typically has an incentive to allocate as much of the purchase price as possible to depreciable assets, such as fixed assets, customer lists, and noncompete agreements, which enable the buyer to depreciate or amortize these upwardly revised assets and reduce future taxable income. However, such an allocation may constitute taxable income to the seller. Both parties should agree on how the purchase price should be allocated to the various assets acquired in an asset transaction before closing. This eliminates the chance that the parties involved will take different positions for tax purposes. Nonetheless, the IRS may still challenge the transaction.

Payment Mechanism

Payment may be made at closing by wire transfer or cashier's check. The buyer may defer the payment of a portion of the purchase price by issuing a promissory note to the seller. The buyer and seller also may agree to put the unpaid portion of the purchase price in escrow or through a holdback allowance, thereby facilitating the settlement of claims that might be made in the future. The escrow account involves the buyer putting a portion of the purchase price in an account held by a third party, while the holdback allowance generally does not.

Assumption of Liabilities

The seller retains those liabilities not assumed by the buyer. In instances such as environmental liabilities, unpaid taxes, and inadequately funded pension obligations, the courts may go after the buyer and seller. In contrast, the buyer assumes all known and unknown liabilities in a merger or purchase of shares.

Representations and Warranties

"Reps and warranties" are intended to provide for full disclosure of all information germane to the transaction. They typically cover the areas of greatest concern to both parties. Areas commonly covered include the following: corporate organization and good standing, capitalization, financial statements, absence of undisclosed liabilities, current litigation, contracts, title to assets, taxes and tax returns, no violation of laws or regulations, employee benefit plans, labor issues, and insurance coverage.

Covenants

Covenants are agreements by the parties about actions they agree to take or refrain from taking between signing the definitive agreement and the closing. An example is the requirement that the seller continues to conduct business in the usual and customary manner. The seller often is required to seek approval for all expenditures that may be considered out of the ordinary, such as one-time dividend payments or sizeable increases in management compensation.

Closing Conditions

The satisfaction of the conditions negotiated determines whether a party to the agreement has to go forward and consummate the deal. These conditions could include the continued accuracy of the seller's representations and warranties and extent to which the seller is living up to its obligations under the covenants. Other examples include obtaining all necessary legal opinions, the execution of other agreements such as promissory notes, and the absence of any "material adverse change" in the condition of the target company.

The effects of material adverse change clauses in agreements of purchase and sale became very visible during the disruption in the financial markets in 2008. Many firms that had signed M&A contracts looked for a way out. The challenge in negotiating most such clauses is defining what constitutes materiality. Is it a 20 percent reduction in earnings or sales? Because of the inherent ambiguity, the contract language is usually vague. It is this ambiguity that enabled so many acquirers to withdraw from contracts and lenders to withdraw financing.

Indemnification

The definitive agreement requires the seller to indemnify or absolve the buyer of liability in the event of misrepresentations or breaches of warranties or covenants. Similarly, the buyer usually agrees to indemnify the seller. In effect, indemnification is the reimbursement to the other party for a loss incurred following closing for which it was not responsible. Both parties generally want to limit the period during which the indemnity clauses remain in force. At least one full year of operation and a full audit is necessary to identify claims. Some claims (e.g., environmental) extend beyond the survival period of the indemnity clause. Usually, neither party can submit claims to the other until some minimum threshold, expressed in terms of the number or dollar size of claims, has been exceeded.

Merger Agreements

A merger is structurally simpler than an asset agreement, because it does not require the stipulation of assets being transferred to the buyer and liabilities assumed by the buyer. Although it may take less time to negotiate and draft than an asset agreement, it may take longer to complete. A merger with a public company generally requires approval of the target companies' shareholders and must comply with the full public disclosure and filing requirements of both federal and state securities laws (see Chapter 2).

Other Closing Documents

In addition to resolving the issues outlined previously, closing may be complicated by the number of and complexity of the documents required to complete the transaction. In addition to the agreement of purchase and sale, the more important documents often include the following (Sherman, 2006):

1. Patents, licenses, royalty agreements, trade names, and trademarks.
2. Labor and employment agreements.
3. Leases.
4. Mortgages, loan agreements, and lines of credit.
5. Stock and bond commitments and details.
6. Supplier and customer contracts.
7. Distributor and sales representative agreements.
8. Stock option and employee incentive programs.
9. Health and other benefit plans (must be in place at closing to eliminate lapsed coverage).

10. Complete description of all foreign patents, facilities, and investments.

11. Insurance policies, coverage, and claims pending.

12. Intermediary fee arrangements.

13. Litigation pending for and against each party.

14. Environmental compliance issues resolved or on track to be resolved.

15. Seller's corporate minutes of the board of directors and any other significant committee information.

16. Articles of incorporation, bylaws, stock certificates, and corporate seals.

See the folder entitled "Example M&A Legal Documents" found on the CD-ROM accompanying this book for examples of an agreement of purchase and sale and associated legal documents. These documents were reproduced with permission of Eric Steinmann, director of development, and Glenn Ishihara, president of NTCH Inc.

Is Closing Ever Simple?

The closing experience runs the gamut from mind-numbing routine to bombastic confrontation. How smoothly the process goes depends on its overall complexity and the level of trust among the parties involved. The size of the transaction is not a good indicator of complexity. Small transactions in terms of revenue or purchase price can be horrifically complicated where multiple parties are involved, significant off-balance sheet liabilities exist, or multiple levels of regulatory approval are required. Even when it appears that both parties have reached agreement on the major issues, what were previously minor issues seem to resurface on a more challenging scale. Sometimes this happens because the parties did not realize the significance of an item until the last minute. Other times, one party intentionally takes a hard line on an issue as the closing date approaches in the hope of gaining a negotiating advantage. In one instance, a buyer of a computer maintenance business sat in the seller's mahogany-filled boardroom just minutes before the closing documents were to be signed and began to enumerate concerns he had with the deal. Tempers began to flare. Only after the seller threatened to walk away from the transaction did the buyer relent and the transaction closed. This strategy is ill advised.

Although closing normally involves one central location, offsite locations may be needed if documents for transferring deeds and titles to assets must be signed and filed from remote locations. Remote signings may be completed by having power of attorney for the buyer and seller transferred to local attorneys at each remote site. It is also a good idea to have separate conference rooms for the buyer and seller to ensure privacy and another room in which the parties meet to execute the documents. Finally, lenders should be kept separate from each other to minimize any exchange of information during closing that might cause them to reopen discussions between the buyer and the lender about the terms and conditions of loans.

For small, uncomplicated transactions, the closing can consist of a simple faxing back and forth of documents between the buyer and seller to ensure that there is complete agreement on the closing documents. Signature pages then are signed by one party and sent via overnight mail to the other party for signature.

Phase 9. Implementing Postclosing Integration

The postclosing integration activity is widely viewed as among the most important phase of the acquisition process. Postclosing integration is discussed in considerable detail in Chapter 6. What follows is a discussion of those activities required immediately following closing. Such activities generally fall into five categories: (1) implementing an effective communication plan, (2) retaining key managers, (3) identifying immediate operating cash-flow requirements, (4) employing the best practices of both companies, and (5) addressing cultural issues.

Communication Plans

Implementing an effective communication plan immediately following closing is crucial for retaining employees of the acquired firm and maintaining or boosting morale and productivity. The plan should address employee, customer, and vendor concerns. The message always should be honest and consistent. Employees need to understand how their compensation, including benefits, might change under new ownership. Employees may find a loss of specific benefits palatable if they are perceived as offset by improvements in other benefits or working conditions. Customers want reassurance that there will be no deterioration in product or service quality or delivery time during the transition from old to new ownership. Vendors also are very interested in understanding how the change in ownership will affect their sales to the new firm. Whenever possible, communication is best done on a face-to-face basis. Senior officers of the acquiring company can be sent to address employee groups (on site, if possible). Senior officers also should contact key customers (preferably in person or at least by telephone) to provide the needed reassurances. Meeting reasonable requests for information from employees, customers, and vendors immediately following closing with complete candor will contribute greatly to the sense of trust among stakeholders that is necessary for the ultimate success of the acquisition.

Employee Retention

Retaining middle-level managers should be a top priority during this phase of the acquisition process. Frequently, senior managers of the target company that the buyer chooses to retain are asked to sign employment agreements as a condition of closing. Without these signed agreements, the buyer would not have completed the transaction. Although senior managers provide overall direction for the firm, middle-level managers execute the day-to-day operations of the firm. Plans should be in place to minimize the loss of such people. Bonuses, stock options, and enhanced sales commission schedules are commonly put in place to keep such managers.

Satisfying Cash-Flow Requirements

Invariably, operating cash-flow requirements are higher than expected. Conversations with middle-level managers following closing often reveal areas in which maintenance expenditures have been deferred. Receivables previously thought to be collectable may have to be written off. Production may be disrupted as employees of the acquired firm find it difficult to adapt to new practices introduced by the acquiring company's management or if inventory levels are inadequate to maintain desired customer delivery times. Finally, more customers than had been anticipated may be lost to competitors, which use the change in ownership as an opportunity to woo them away with various types of incentives.

Employing Best Practices

An important motivation for takeovers is to realize specific operating synergies, which result in improved operating efficiency, product quality, customer service, and on-time delivery. The parties in a transaction are likely to excel in different areas. An excellent way for the combined companies to take advantage of the strengths of both companies is to use the "best practices" of both. However, in some areas, neither company may be employing what its customers believe to be the best practices in the industry. In these circumstances, management should look beyond its own operations to accept the practices of other companies.

Cultural Issues

Corporate cultures reflect the set of beliefs and behaviors of the management and employees of a corporation. Some corporations are very paternalistic, and others are very "bottom-line" oriented. Some empower employees, whereas others believe in highly centralized control. Some promote problem solving within a team environment; others encourage individual performance. Inevitably, different corporate cultures impede post-acquisition integration efforts. The key to success is to be sensitive to these differences and take the time to explain to all employees of the new firm what is expected and why these behaviors are desired in the new company.

Phase 10. Conducting a Postclosing Evaluation

The primary reasons for conducting a postclosing evaluation of all acquisitions are to determine if the acquisition is meeting expectations, determine corrective actions if necessary, and identify what was done well and what should be done better in future acquisitions.

Do Not Change Performance Benchmarks

Once the acquisition appears to be operating normally, evaluate the actual performance to that projected in the acquisition plan. Success should be defined in terms of actual to planned performance. Too often, management simply ignores the performance targets in the acquisition plan and accepts less than plan performance to justify the acquisition. This may be appropriate if circumstances beyond the firm's control cause a change in the operating environment. Examples include a recession, which slows the growth in revenue, or changing regulations, which preclude the introduction of a new product.

Ask the Difficult Questions

The types of questions asked should vary, depending on the elapsed time since closing. After six months, what has the buyer learned about the business? Were the original valuation assumptions reasonable? If not, what did the buyer not understand about the target company and why? What did the buyer do well? What should have been done differently? What can be done to ensure that the same mistakes are not made in future acquisitions? After 12 months, is the business meeting expectations? If not, what can be done to put the business back on track? Is the cost of fixing the business offset by expected returns? Are the right people in place to manage the business for the long term? After 24 months, does the acquired business still appear attractive? If not, should it be divested? If yes, when and to whom?

Learn from Mistakes

It always pays to take the time to identify lessons learned from each transaction. This is often a neglected exercise and results in firms repeating the same mistakes. This occurs even in the most highly acquisitive firms, because those involved in the acquisition process may change from one acquisition to another. Lessons learned in an acquisition completed by the management of one of the firm's product lines may not be readily communicated to those about to undertake acquisitions in other parts of the company. Highly acquisitive companies can benefit greatly by dedicating certain legal, human resource, marketing, financial, and business development resources to support acquisitions made throughout the company.

Things to Remember

The acquisition process consists of 10 identifiable phases. During the first phase, the business plan defines the overall direction of the business. If an acquisition is believed necessary to implement the firm's business strategy, an acquisition plan, developed during the second phase, defines the key objectives, available resources, and management preferences for completing an acquisition. The next phase consists of the search for appropriate acquisition candidates. To initiate this phase, selection criteria need to be developed. At this stage, selection criteria should be relatively few in number and, whenever possible, quantified. The screening phase is a refinement of the search phase and entails applying more criteria to reduce the list of candidates that surfaced during the search process.

How the potential acquirer initiates first contact depends on the urgency of completing a transaction, the size of the target, and the availability of intermediaries with highly placed contacts within the target firm. If the target is interested in proceeding, a letter of intent formally defining the reasons for the agreement, responsibilities of the two parties while the agreement is in force, and the expiration date is negotiated. Confidentiality agreements covering both parties also should be negotiated. The negotiation phase consists of the following activities: refining valuation, structuring the deal, conducting due diligence, and developing a financing plan. The actual amount and composition of the purchase price is determined during this phase.

There is no substitute for performing a complete due diligence on the target company. Refining a valuation based on new information uncovered during due diligence affects the determination of the total consideration to be paid to the seller. The financing plan may be affected by the discovery during due diligence of assets that can be sold to pay off debt incurred to finance the transaction. Due diligence is not limited to the buyer. The seller should perform due diligence on the buyer to ensure that it will be able to finance the purchase price. Moreover, the seller also should perform due diligence on its own operations to ensure that its representations and warranties in the definitive agreement are accurate. Lenders also want to perform due diligence.

Integration planning is a highly important aspect of the acquisition process that must be done before closing. Without adequate planning, integration is unlikely to provide the synergies anticipated by, at the cost included in, and on the timetable provided in the acquisition plan. The closing phase goes well beyond organizing, finalizing, and signing all the necessary legal documents. It includes wading through the logistical quagmire of getting all the necessary third party consents and regulatory and shareholder approvals. The postclosing integration phase consists of communicating effectively with all stakeholders, retaining key employees, and identifying and resolving immediate cash-flow needs. The postclosing evaluation phase is the most commonly overlooked phase. Although many acquiring companies closely monitor the performance of the acquisition to plan, many stop short of formally questioning how effective they were in managing the acquisition process.

Chapter Discussion Questions

5–1. What resources are commonly used to conduct a search for potential acquisition targets?

5–2. Identify at least three criteria that might be used to select a manufacturing firm as a potential acquisition candidate. A financial services firm? A high-technology firm?

5–3. Identify alternative ways to make "first contact" with a potential acquisition target. Why is confidentiality important? Under what circumstances might a potential acquirer make its intentions public?

5–4. What are the advantages and disadvantages of a letter of intent?

5–5. How do the various activities undertaken concurrently as part of the negotiation phase affect the determination of the purchase price?

5–6. What are the differences between total consideration, total purchase price, enterprise value, and net purchase price? How are these different concepts used?

5–7. What is the purpose of the buyer and seller performing due diligence?

5–8. What is the purpose of a financing plan? In what sense is it a "reality check"?

5–9. Why is preclosing integration planning important?

5–10. What key activities make up a typical closing?

5–11. In a rush to complete its purchase of health software producer HBO, McKesson did not perform adequate due diligence but rather relied on representations and warranties in the agreement of sale and purchase. Within six months following closing, McKesson announced that it would have to reduce revenue by $327 million and net income by $191.5 million for the preceding three fiscal years to correct for accounting irregularities. The company's stock fell by 48 percent. If HBO's financial statements had been declared to be in accordance with GAAP, would McKesson have been justified in believing that HBO's revenue and profit figures were 100 percent accurate? Explain your answer.

5–12. Find a transaction currently in the news. Speculate as to what criteria the buyer may have employed to identify the target company as an attractive takeover candidate. Be specific.

5–13. In mid-2008, Fresenius, a German manufacturer of dialysis equipment, acquired APP Pharmaceuticals for $4.6 billion. The deal includes an earn-out, under which Fresenius would pay as much as $970 million if APP reaches certain future financial targets. What is the purpose of the earn-out? How does it affect the buyer and seller?

5–14. Material adverse change clauses (MACs) are a means for the parties to the contract to determine who will bear the risk of adverse events that occur between the signing of an agreement and the closing. MACs are frequently not stated in dollar terms. How might MACs affect the negotiating strategies of the parties to the agreement during the period between signing and closing?

5–15. Despite disturbing discoveries during due diligence, Mattel acquired The Learning Company (TLC), a leading developer of software for toys, in a stock-for-stock transaction valued at $3.5 billion on May 13, 1999. Mattel had determined that TLC's receivables were overstated, a $50 million licensing deal had been prematurely put on the balance sheet, and TLC's brands were becoming outdated. TLC also had substantially exaggerated the amount of money put into research and development for new software products. Nevertheless, driven by the appeal of rapidly becoming a big player in the children's software market, Mattel closed on the transaction, aware that TLC's cash flows were overstated. After restructuring charges associated with the acquisition, Mattel's consolidated 1999 net loss was $82.4 million on sales of $5.5 billion. Mattel's stock fell by more than 35 percent during 1999 to end the year at about $14 per share. What could Mattel have done to better protect its interests? Be specific.

Answers to these Chapter Discussion Questions are available in the Online Instructor's Manual for instructors using this book.

Chapter Business Cases

Case Study 5–3. The Anatomy of a Transaction: K2 Incorporated Acquires Fotoball USA

On January 26, 2004, K2 Inc. completed the purchase of Fotoball USA in an all-stock transaction. What follows is an attempt to reconstruct the preclosing events to illustrate how the acquisition process discussed in Chapters 4 and 5 may have been applied in this transaction. Note that this is a highly condensed version of an actual business and acquisition plan.

Industry-Market Definition

K2 is a sporting goods equipment manufacturer. K2's portfolio of brands includes Rawlings, Worth, Shakespeare, Pflueger, Stearns, K2, Ride, Olin, Morrow, Tubbs, and Atlas. The company's diversified mix of products is used primarily in team and individual sports activities, such as baseball, softball, fishing, water sports activities, alpine skiing, snowboarding, snowshoeing, in-line skating, and mountain biking.

External Analysis

The firm's current top competitors include Adidas-Salomon; Rollerblade, Inc.; and Skis Rossignol S.A. While other sporting goods suppliers, such as Amer Group PLC, Head N.V., Nike, Inc., Fila USA, and Reebok International Ltd, do not currently compete in K2's served markets, they could easily enter them, due to their substantial brand recognition and financial resources. Not only must K2 be concerned about existing and potential competitors, a variety of substitute popular sports, such as horseback riding, ice hockey, sky diving, surfing, and cross country skiing, could erode growth in their targeted markets.

The firm's primary customers are sporting goods retailers. Many of K2's smaller retailers and some larger retailers are not strongly capitalized. Adverse conditions in the sporting goods retail industry can adversely affect the ability of retailers to purchase K2 products. Secondary customers include individuals, both hobbyists and professionals. K2's success depends on its ability to keep abreast of changes in taste and style and its ability to provide high-quality products at competitive prices.

The majority of K2 products are manufactured in China, which helps to ensure cost competitiveness. However, disruptions in international trade or shipping could adversely affect the availability or cost of K2 products. K2's revenue from international operations was approximately 32 percent of total revenue for fiscal 2002, and approximately

26 percent of K2's sales are denominated in foreign currencies. K2's international operations are subject to a variety of risks, including recessions in foreign economies, currency conversion risks and fluctuations, limitations on repatriation of earnings, and reduced protection of intellectual property rights in some countries. Other factors include social, political, and economic instability; the adoption and expansion of government trade restrictions; unfavorable political developments affecting international trade; and unexpected changes in regulatory requirements.

K2 believes that the most successful sporting goods suppliers will be those with the greatest resources. In addition to financial capabilities, such resources include the ability to produce or source high-quality, low-cost products and deliver these products on a timely basis and the ability to access distribution channels with a broad array of products and brands. As the influence of large sporting goods retailers grows, management believes these retailers will prefer to rely on fewer and larger sporting goods suppliers to help them manage the supply of products and the allocation of shelf space.

Internal Analysis

K2 has a number of leading brands in major sporting goods markets. K2 is also involved in the sports apparel business and faces stiff competition in this industry from Nike and Reebok. Wal-Mart accounted for over 10 percent and 5 percent of K2's consolidated annual net sales and operating income, respectively, in 2003. No one customer of K2 accounted for 10 percent or more of its consolidated annual net sales or 5 percent of its operating income in 2002.

Despite its strong brand names, K2 is susceptible to imitation. The sporting goods markets and recreational products markets are generally highly competitive, with competition centered on product innovation, performance and styling, price, marketing, and delivery. Competition in these products consists of a relatively small number of large producers, some of whom have substantially greater financial resources than K2. K2's relationships with collegiate and professional leagues and teams cannot be easily usurped by smaller competitors that may want to enter into these markets. It takes time for the necessary trust to build up in these relationships. Larger competitors may have the capacity to take away some of these relationships, but K2 has so many that the loss of one or two would not seriously hinder its overall revenue growth.

Its relatively small size in comparison to major competitors is the firm's primary weakness. Historically, the firm has been able to achieve profitable growth by introducing new products into fast growing markets. The firm has historically applied its core competencies of producing fiberglass and assembling structures for manufacturing skis to new markets, such as snowboarding and in-line skating.

Mission Statement and Strategic Objectives

"K2 will accept nothing less than the best ... We will create ever better products that raise the bar of performance and celebrate the human spirit ... We will build value by growing and succeeding where others have failed." The firm's long-term objective is to achieve the number 1 market share position in its served markets. Toward that end, K2 seeks to meet or exceed its corporate cost of capital of 15 percent. In addition, K2 intends to achieve sustained double-digit revenue growth, gross profit margins above 35 percent, and net profit margins in excess of 5 percent within the next five years. The firm also seeks to reduce its debt-to-equity ratio to the industry average of 25 percent in the next five years.

Business Strategy

K2 intends to achieve its mission and objectives by becoming the low-cost supplier in each of its niche markets. The firm intends to achieve a low-cost position by using its existing administrative and logistical infrastructure to support entry into new niche segments within the sporting goods and recreational markets, new distribution channels, and new product launches through existing distribution channels. Furthermore, the firm intends to pursue continued aggressive cost cutting and to expand its global sourcing to include other low-cost countries in addition to mainland China.

Implementation Strategy

In view of its great success in acquiring and integrating a series of small acquisitions in recent years, K2 has decided to avoid product or market extension through partnering because of the potential for loss of control and for creating competitors once such agreements lapse. Consequently, K2 believes that it can accelerate its growth strategy by seeking strategic acquisitions of other sporting goods companies with well-established brands and with complementary distribution channels.

M&A-Related Functional Strategies

Functional strategies have been developed based on an acquisition-oriented implementation strategy. A potential target for acquisition is a company that holds many licenses with professional sports teams. Through their relationship with these sports teams, K2 can further promote its long line of sporting gear and equipment. All the different business functions within K2 have roles to play in supporting the implementation strategy.

Research and Development

K2's R&D activities are focused on developing only the highest-quality sports equipment and apparel. The NBA, NFL, and the Major League Baseball are all potential licensing partners. To support these critical activities, the research and development budget would be increased by 10 percent annually during the next five years. High-quality and innovative new products can be sold into the customer bases of firms acquired during this period.

Marketing and Sales

The licensing agreements in existence between the target firm and its partners can be enhanced to include the many products that K2 now offers. It must be determined whether one sales force can sell both the products sold by K2 currently and those obtained through an acquisition. If so, the two sales forces can be merged, resulting in significant cost savings.

The human resources department is charged with the responsibility to determine appropriate staffing requirements and how those can be best satisfied immediately following a merger. Potential job overlaps are expected to contribute to significant cost savings. The finance department is charged with quantifying the potential increase in revenue from cross-selling K2 and the target's products into each firm's existing customer bases and determining the feasibility of realizing anticipated cost synergies. Such information would be used to determine the initial offer price for the target firm. The legal department is responsible for determining the validity of customer and supplier contracts and, in conjunction with the finance department, their overall profitability.

Finally, the tax department is responsible for assessing the tax impact an acquisition would have on K2's after-tax cash flow and shareholders.

Strategic Controls

Incentives Systems   K2 has incentive systems in place to motivate employees to work toward implementing its business strategy. Employees are awarded yearly bonuses based on their performance throughout the year. At the end of the year, employees working in sales are given up to 5 percent of the sales revenues for which they were personally responsible. Management is given a bonus based on how well the manager's department has performed. Managers are given a bonus made up of 10 percent of the operating income achieved by their department. This way they are motivated not only to increase sales but to minimize costs.

Monitoring Systems   Monitoring systems are in place to monitor the actual performance of the firm against the business plan. Activity-based systems monitor variables that drive financial performance. Such variables include customer retention, revenue per customer, and revenue per dealer.

Business Plan Financials and Valuation

K2's net revenue was projected to grow from $790 million in 2004 to $988 million in 2008 on a stand-alone basis. After-tax income is expected to increase from $17.6 million to $41.2 million during the same period. Reflecting a sharp improvement in free cash flow from ($7.6) million in 2004 to $46 million in 2008, K2's current valuation based on discounted cash flow (with no new acquisitions) is $812 million or $23.79 per share.

Acquisition Plan

K2's overarching financial objective for any acquisition is to at least earn its cost of capital, and its primary nonfinancial objective is to acquire a firm with well-established brands and complementary distribution channels. More specifically, K2 is seeking a firm with a successful franchise in the marketing and manufacturing of souvenir and promotional products that could be easily integrated into K2's current operations.

Timetable

February 28, 2003	Acquisition plan completed.
March 30, 2003	Search for potential target companies completed.
May 30, 2003	Screening for potential target companies completed.
June 30, 2003	First contact completed.
October 30, 2003	Negotiations completed.
November 30, 2003	Integration plan developed.
December 30, 2003	Closing completed.
June 30, 2004	Integration completed.
September 30, 2004	Acquisition process evaluation completed.

Resource-Capability Evaluation

- **Operating risk.** After completion of a merger, K2 must successfully integrate the target's sourcing and manufacturing capabilities into K2's sourcing and manufacturing operations. The firm must sell K2's portfolio of products and brands through the target's distribution channels, increase the target's sales to team sports and sporting goods retailers, and develop a licensing and cobranding program. K2 would need to retain the management, key employees, customers, distributors, vendors, and other business partners of both companies. It is possible that these integration efforts would not be completed as planned, which could have an adverse impact on the operations of the combined company. K2 believes that, given its successful track record in acquiring and integrating businesses, its management team can deal with these challenges.

- **Financial risk.** Borrowing under K2's existing $205 million revolving credit facility and under its $20 million term loan, as well as potential future financings, may substantially increase K2's current leverage. Among other things, such increased indebtedness could adversely affect K2's ability to expand its business, market its products, make needed infrastructure investments, and the cost and availability of funds from commercial lenders.

- **Overpayment risk.** If new shares of K2 stock are issued to pay for the target firm, K2's earnings per share may be diluted if anticipated synergies are not realized in a timely fashion. Moreover, overpaying for any firm could result in K2 failing to earn its cost of capital.

Management Preferences

- The target should be smaller than $100 million in market capitalization and have positive cash flows. Also, it should be focused on the sports or outdoor activities market.
- The search should be conducted initially by analyzing current competitors.
- The company has an experienced acquisition team in place, which would be utilized to complete this acquisition.
- The form of payment would be new K2 nonvoting common stock.
- The form of acquisition would be a purchase of stock.
- K2 will not consider takeovers involving less than 100 percent of the target's stock.
- Only friendly takeovers will be considered.
- The target firm's current year P/E should not exceed 20.

Search Plan

After an exhaustive search, K2 identified Fotoball USA as its most attractive target due to its size, predictable cash flows, complementary product offering, and many licenses with most of the major sports leagues and college teams. Fotoball USA represented a premier platform for expansion of K2's marketing capabilities because of its expertise in the industry and place as an industry leader in many sports and entertainment souvenir and promotional product categories. The fit with the Rawlings division would make both companies stronger in the marketplace. Fotoball also had proven expertise in licensing programs, which would assist K2 in developing additional revenue sources for its portfolio of brands.

Negotiation Strategy

K2 has positioned itself as a holding company and does not take an active management role in the businesses it acquires. The firm generally allows acquired companies to function independently. In 2003, Fotoball lost $3.2 million so it was anticipated that the firm would be receptive to an acquisition proposal. A stock-for-stock exchange offer would be very attractive to the shareholders of Fotoball due to the combined firms' anticipated high-earnings growth rate. The transaction was expected to qualify as a "tax-free" reorganization for federal income tax purposes. Additionally, management and most employees would be retained.

Fotoball was a very young company and many of its investors were looking to make their profits through the growth of the stock. The stock-for-stock offer contains a significant premium, which would be well received, considering that the company had been in the red; and it would allow Fotoball shareholders to defer taxes until they decided to sell their stocks and be taxed at the capital gains rate. Earn-outs would be included in the deal to give management incentive to run the company effectively and meet deadlines in a timely order.

The acquisition vehicle used in the deal would be a C-type corporation. Postclosing, Fotoball would be run as a wholly owned subsidiary of K2. This form would work best, because K2 is in the process of acquiring many companies, and it cannot actively manage all of them. In addition, such an organizational structure would be most conducive to a possible earn-out and the preservation of the unique culture at Fotoball.

Determining the Initial Offer Price

Valuations for both K2 Inc. and Fotoball were done using discounted cash-free flow methods. The valuations reflect the following anticipated synergies due to economies of scale and scope: a reduction in selling expenses of approximately $1 million per year, a reduction in distribution expenses of approximately $500,000 per year, and an annual reduction in general and administrative expenses of approximately $470,000. The stand-alone value of K2 was $23.79 per share or $812 million. The stand-alone value of Fotoball was $3.97 per share or $14.3 million. Including the effects of anticipated synergy, the estimated combined market value of the two firms is $909 million. This represents an increase in the shareholder value of the combined firms of $82.7 million over the sum of the stand-alone values of the two firms.

Based on Fotoball's outstanding common stock of 3.6 million shares and the current stock price of $4.02 at that time, a minimum offer price was determined by multiplying the current stock price by the number of shares outstanding. The minimum offer price was $14.5 million. If K2 were to concede 100 percent of the value of synergy to Fotoball, the value of the firm would be $97.2 million. However, sharing more than 45 percent of synergy with Fotoball would cause a serious dilution of earnings. To determine the amount of synergy to share with Fotoball's shareholders, K2 looked at what portion of the combined firms' revenues would be contributed by each player and applied that proportion to the synergy. Since 96 percent of the projected combined firms' revenues in fiscal year 2004 were expected to come from K2, only 4 percent of the synergy value was added to the minimum offer price to come up with an initial offer price of $17.8 million or $4.94 per share. This represented a premium of 23 percent over the then current market value of Fotoball's stock.

Financing Plan

Due to the synergies involved in this transaction, as well as the relatively small size of the target (Fotoball) as compared to the acquirer (K2), it is unlikely that this merger would endanger K2's creditworthiness or near-term profitability. Although the contribution to earnings would be relatively small, the addition of Fotoball would help diversify and smooth K2's revenue stream, which has been subject to seasonality in the past.

Integration Plan

Organizationally, the integration of Fotoball into K2 would be achieved by operating Fotoball as a wholly owned subsidiary of K2, with current Fotoball management remaining in place. All key employees would receive retention bonuses as a condition of closing. Integration teams consisting of employees from both firms would move expeditiously according to a schedule put in place prior to closing to implement the best practices of both firms. Immediately following closing, senior K2 managers would communicate on site, if possible, with Fotoball customers, suppliers, and employees to allay their immediate concerns.

Source: This case study is adapted from a paper written by Curt Charles, Tuukka Luolamo, Jeffrey Rathel, Ryan Komagome, and Julius Kumar, Loyola Marymount University, April 28, 2004.

Discussion Questions

1. How did K2's acquisition plan objectives support the realization of its corporate mission and business plan objectives?
2. What alternatives to M&As could K2 have employed to pursue its growth strategy? Why were the alternatives rejected?
3. What was the role of "strategic controls" in implementing the K2 business plan?
4. How did the K2 negotiating strategy seek to meet the primary needs of the Fotoball shareholders and employees?

Solutions to these case study discussion questions are found in the Online Instructor's Manual available to instructors using this book.

Case Study 5–4. Cingular Acquires AT&T Wireless in a Record-Setting Cash Transaction

By entering the bidding at the last moment, Vodafone, an investor in Verizon Wireless, forced Cingular's parents, SBC Communications and BellSouth, to pay a 37 percent premium over their initial bid. By possibly paying too much, Cingular put itself at a major disadvantage in the U.S. cellular phone market. The merger did not close until October 26, 2004, due to the need to get regulatory and shareholder approvals. This gave Verizon, the industry leader in terms of operating margins, time to woo away customers from AT&T Wireless, which was already hemorrhaging a loss of subscribers because of poor customer service. By paying $11 billion more than its initial bid, Cingular would have to execute the integration, expected to take at least 18 months, flawlessly to make the merger pay for its shareholders.

With AT&T Wireless, Cingular would have a combined subscriber base of 46 million, as compared to Verizon Wireless's 37.5 million subscribers. Together, Cingular and Verizon control almost one half of the nation's 170 million wireless customers. The transaction gives SBC and BellSouth the opportunity to have a greater stake in the rapidly expanding wireless industry. Cingular was assuming it would be able to achieve substantial operating synergies and a reduction in capital outlays by melding AT&T Wireless's network into its own. Cingular expected to trim combined capital costs by $600 to $900 million in 2005 and $800 million to $1.2 billion annually thereafter. However, Cingular might feel pressure from Verizon Wireless, which was investing heavily in new mobile wireless services. If Cingular were forced to offer such services quickly, it might not be able to realize the reduction in projected capital outlays. Operational savings might be even more difficult to realize. Cingular expected to save $100 to $400 million in 2005, $500 to $800 million in 2006, and $1.2 billion in each successive year. However, in view of AT&T Wireless's continued loss of customers, Cingular might have to increase spending to improve customer service. To gain regulatory approval, Cingular agreed to sell assets in 13 markets in 11 states. The firm would have six months to sell the assets before a trustee appointed by the FCC would become responsible for disposing of the assets.

SBC and BellSouth, Cingular's parents, would have limited flexibility in financing new spending if it were required by Cingular. SBC and BellSouth each borrowed $10 billion to finance the transaction. With the added debt, S&P put SBC, BellSouth, and Cingular on credit watch, which often is a prelude in a downgrade of a firm's credit rating.

Discussion Questions

1. What was the total purchase price of the merger?
2. What are some of the reasons Cingular used cash rather than stock or some combination to acquire AT&T Wireless? Explain your answer.
3. How might the amount and composition of the purchase price affect Cingular's, SBC's, and BellSouth's cost of capital?
4. With substantially higher operating margins than Cingular, what strategies would you expect Verizon Wireless to pursue? Explain your answer.

Solutions to these case study discussion questions are found in the Online Instructor's Manual for instructors using this book.

Appendix: Legal Due Diligence Preliminary Information Request

The due diligence question list, found in the file folder entitled Acquirer Due Diligence Question List contained on the CD-ROM accompanying this book, applies mainly to transactions involving large public companies. For smaller, privately owned target firms, the list may be substantially more focused. Normally, the length and complexity of a "due diligence question list" submitted by the acquiring firm to the target firm's management is determined through negotiation. The management of the target firm normally would view a lengthy list as both intrusive and costly to complete. Consequently, the target firm's management often will try to narrow both the number and breadth of the questions included in the initial request for information. The request for such a list often is included as part of the letter of intent signed by the acquirer and target firms.

The acquirer typically attempts to protect itself, either through an exhaustive review of the target's records and facilities (i.e., due diligence), extensive representations and warranties (i.e., claims and promises made by the seller), or some combination of the two. If the target firm is successful in reducing the amount of information disclosed to the acquiring firm, it can expect to be required to make more representations and warranties as to the accuracy of its claims and promises in the agreement of purchase and sale. This no doubt adds to the time required to negotiate such a document. Notwithstanding the intrusiveness of the due diligence question list contained on the CD-ROM accompanying this book, the buyer is well advised to rely more on an on-site review of facilities and records and personnel interviews than on the seller's contract obligations. If the seller declares bankruptcy, cannot be found, or moves assets to offshore accounts, receiving remuneration for breach of contract may be impossible. Note that all references to the company in the due diligence question list refer to the target.

6

Integration Mergers, Acquisitions, and Business Alliances

What could be worse than being without sight?
Being born with sight and no vision.

—Helen Keller

Inside M&A: GE's Water Business Fails to Meet Expectations

When Jeffrey Immelt, GE's CEO, assumed his position in September 2001, he identified water as one of five industries that would fuel future growth for the firm. Since 2001, General Electric (GE) has invested more than $4 billion in acquiring four companies to grow its water treatment business. In an unusual strategy for GE, the firm's intention was to build a business from scratch through acquisition to enter the $400 billion global water treatment business. In doing so, GE would be competing against a number of global competitors. GE had historically entered many new markets by growing a small portion of a larger existing business unit through a series of relatively small but highly complementary acquisitions.

GE's experience in integrating these so-called bolt-on acquisitions emboldened the firm to pursue this more aggressive strategy. However, the challenge proved to be more daunting than originally assumed. The largest of the units, which sells chemicals, faced aggressive price competition in what has become a commodity business. Furthermore, expectations of huge contracts to build water treatment plants have not yet materialized.

Amid the unit's failure to spur revenue growth, GE has been struggling to meld thousands of employees from competing corporate cultures into its own highly disciplined culture with its focus on excellent financial performance. As the cornerstone to accelerating revenue growth, GE attempted to restructure radically the diverse sales forces of the four acquired companies. The new sales and marketing structure divides the combined sales forces into teams that are geographically focused. Within each region, one sales team is responsible for pursuing new business opportunities. More than 1,500 engineers have been retrained to sell the unit's entire portfolio from chemicals to equipment that removes salt and debris from water. Another group is focused on servicing customers in "vertical markets," or industries such as dairy products, electronics, and health care. However, the task of retraining even highly educated engineers to do substantially different things has required much more time and expense than anticipated. For example, in an effort to rapidly redirect the business, GE retrained a group of 2,000 engineers who had previously sold chemicals to sell sophisticated equipment. The latter sales effort required a much different set of skills than what the engineers had been originally trained to do.

Reflecting these problems, in mid-2006, Immelt reduced the water business unit's operating profit forecast for the year from $400 to $200 million. Immelt also replaced George Oliver, the executive he put in charge of the water business in 2002. "We probably moved quicker than we should have in some areas," Immelt conceded, adding that "training has taken longer than expected" (Kranhold, 2006).

Chapter Overview

Motives for purchasing a company vary widely. Acquirers tend to fall into two broad categories: strategic buyers and financial buyers. Financial buyers are typically those who buy a business for eventual resale. In general, they do not intend to integrate the acquired business into another entity. Moreover, instead of managing the business, they are inclined to monitor the effectiveness of current management, intervening only if there is a significant and sustained deviation between actual and projected performance. In contrast, strategic buyers are interested in making a profit by managing a business for an extended period. The strategic buyer may choose to manage the acquisition as a separate subsidiary in a holding company or merge it into another business. These choices influence greatly the extent of and speed with which integration takes place.

This chapter assumes that the goal of the acquirer is integration immediately after the transaction closes. The purpose of this chapter is to discuss a practical process for integrating businesses effectively. The chapter begins by stressing the importance of the integration phase of the acquisition process in contributing to the eventual success of the merger or acquisition. As noted in Chapter 1, ineffective integration is the second most commonly cited factor contributing to the failure of mergers and acquisitions to meet or exceed expectations. The factors critical to the success of any integration activity are addressed in this chapter. These include careful premerger planning, candid and continuous communication, the pace at which the businesses are combined, the appointment of an integration manager and team with clearly defined goals and lines of authority, and making the difficult decisions early in the process. This chapter views integration as a process consisting of six activities: planning, developing communication plans, creating a new organization, developing staffing plans, implementing functional integration, and integrating corporate cultures. The chapter concludes with a discussion of how to overcome some of the unique obstacles encountered in integrating business alliances. The major segments of this chapter include the following:

- The Role of Integration in Successful Mergers and Acquisitions
- Viewing Integration as a Process
- Integrating Business Alliances
- Things to Remember

A chapter review (consisting of practice questions and answers) is available in the file folder entitled Student Study Guide contained on the CD-ROM accompanying this book. The CD-ROM also contains a Learning Interactions Library, enabling students to test their knowledge of this chapter in a "real-time" environment.

The Role of Integration in Successful Mergers and Acquisitions

While overpayment and poor strategy are among the most common explanations for the failure of M&As, numerous studies support the conclusion that rapid integration efforts are more likely to result in mergers that achieve the acquirer's expectations (*Business Week,* 1995; Coopers and Lybrand, 1996; Marks, 1996; McKinsey Company, 1987). In a global study of 100 acquisitions, each of which is valued at more than $500 million, Andersen Consulting (1999) concluded that most postmerger activities are completed within six months to one year. Moreover, the study suggests that integration must be done quickly to generate the financial returns expected by shareholders and to minimize employee turnover and customer attrition.

Realizing Projected Financial Returns

For our purposes, the term *rapid* is defined relative to the pace of normal operations for a firm. The importance of rapid integration can be demonstrated using a simple numerical example. Suppose a firm has a current market value of $100 million and this value accurately reflects the firm's future cash flows discounted at its cost of capital. Assume an acquirer is willing to pay a $25 million premium for this firm, believing that it can recover the premium by realizing cost savings resulting from integrating the two firms. The amount of cash the acquirer has to generate to recover the premium increases the longer it takes to integrate the target company. If the cost of capital is 10 percent and integration is completed by the end of the first year, the acquirer has to earn $27.5 million by the end of the first year to recover the control premium plus its cost of capital (i.e., $25 + ($25 × 0.10)). If integration is not completed until the end of the second year, the acquirer has to earn an incremental cash flow of $30.25 million (i.e., $27.5 + ($27.5 × 0.10)).

The Impact of Employee Turnover

Although there is little evidence that firms necessarily experience an actual reduction in their total workforce following an acquisition, studies do show that turnover among management and key employees increases after a corporate takeover (Hayes, 1979; Shivdasani, 1993; Walsh, 1989; Walsh and Ellwood, 1991). Some loss of managers is intentional, as part of an effort to eliminate redundancies and overlapping positions, whereas others quit during the turmoil of integration. Flanagan and O'Shaughnessy (1998) found that layoffs were announced around the same time as mergers about 50 percent of the time. What is difficult to measure in any of these studies is whether the employees that leave represent a significant "brain drain," or loss of key managers. For many acquisitions, talent and management skills represent the primary value of the target company to the acquirer. This is especially true in high-technology and service companies, for which assets are largely the embodied knowledge of their employees (Lord and Ranft, 2000). Consequently, the loss of key employees rapidly degrades the value of the target company, making the recovery of any premium paid to target shareholders difficult for the buyer.

The cost also may be high when the integration results in the removal of a target firm's top managers because of the high failure rate of new managers. When a firm selects an insider (i.e., a person already in the employ of the merged firms) to replace a top manager (e.g., CEO), the failure rate of the successor (i.e., the successor is no longer with the firm 18 months later) is 34 percent. When the board selects an outside successor (i.e., a person selected who as not in the employ of the merged firms) to replace the departing senior manager, the 18-month failure rate is 55 percent. Therefore, more than half of the time, an outside successor will not succeed, with an insider succeeding about two thirds of the time (Dalton, 2006).

The cost of employee turnover does not stop with the loss of key employees. The loss of any significant number of employees can be very costly. Current employees already have been recruited and trained. Firms incur both recruitment and training costs again when equally qualified employees are hired to replace those lost. Moreover, the loss of employees is likely to reduce the morale and productivity of those who remain.

Acquisition-Related Customer Attrition

During normal operations, businesses can expect a certain level of churn in their customer list. Depending on the industry, normal churn as a result of competitive conditions can be anywhere from 20 to 40 percent. A newly merged company will experience a loss of another 5–10 percent of its existing customers as a direct result of the merger (Down, 1995). The loss of customers may reflect uncertainty about on-time delivery and product quality, as well as more aggressive pricing by competitors following the merger. Moreover, many companies lose revenue momentum as they concentrate on realizing expected cost synergies. The loss of customers may continue well after closing. A McKinsey study of 160 acquisitions by 157 publicly traded firms in 11 industries in 1995 and 1996 found that on average these firms grew 4 percentage points less than their peers during the three years following closing. Moreover, 42 percent of the sample actually lost ground. Only 12 percent of the sample showed revenue growth significantly ahead of their peers (Bekier, Bogardus, and Oldham, 2001).

Rapid Integration Does Not Mean Doing Everything at the Same Pace

Rapid integration may result in more immediate realization of synergies, but it also contributes to employee and customer attrition. Therefore, intelligent integration involves managing these trade-offs by quickly identifying and implementing those projects offering the most immediate payoff while deferring those whose disruption would result in the greatest loss in revenue. Acquirers often postpone integrating data processing and customer service call centers until much later in the integration process, if such activities are viewed as pivotal to maintaining on-time delivery and high-quality customer service. Moreover, sometimes significant differences in the corporate cultures of the acquirer and target firms require a more measured pace of integration. This was certainly the situation in GE's effort to integrate the four acquisitions constituting its water treatment business, illustrated in the opening case study to this chapter.

Viewing Integration as a Process

The activities involved in integrating an acquired business into the acquirer's operations do not fall neatly into a well-defined process. Some activities fall into a logical sequence, whereas others are continuous and, in some respects, unending. The major activities fall loosely into the following sequence: premerger planning, resolving communication issues, defining the new organization, developing staffing plans, integrating functions and departments, and building a new corporate culture. In practice, communicating with all major stakeholder groups and developing a new corporate culture are largely continuous activities, running through the integration period and beyond. Each of these six activities is discussed in the coming sections of this chapter in the sequence outlined in Figure 6–1.

Integration Planning	Developing Communication Plans	Creating a New Organization	Developing Staffing Plans	Functional Integration	Building a New Corporate Culture
Premerger planning: -Refine valuation -Resolve transition issues -Negotiate contract assurances	Stakeholders: -Employees -Customers -Suppliers -Investors -Lenders -Communities (including regulators)	Learn from the past	Determine personnel requirements for the new organization	Revalidate due diligence data	Identify cultural issues through corporate profiling
		Business needs drive organizational structure	Determine resource availability	Conduct performance benchmarking	Integrate through shared: -Goals -Standards -Services -Space
			Establish staffing plans and timetables	Integrate functions: -Operations -Information technology -Finance -Sales -Marketing -Purchasing -R&D -Human resources	
			Develop compensation strategy		
			Create needed information systems		

FIGURE 6–1 Viewing merger integration as a process.

Integration Planning

Carey and Ogden (2004) argue that integration planning should begin as soon as the merger is announced. However, assumptions made before the closing, based on information accumulated during due diligence, must be reexamined once the transaction is consummated to ensure their validity. For an excellent discussion of the challenges of integration, see Schweiger (2002) and Galpin and Herndon (2007).

Premerger Integration Planning: Begin Planning before Closing

The planning process enables the acquiring company to refine further its original estimate of the value of the target company and deal with transition issues in the context of the definitive agreement of purchase and sale. Furthermore, the buyer has an opportunity to insert into the agreement the appropriate representations (claims) and warranties (promises), as well as conditions of closing that facilitate the postmerger integration process.

Finally, the planning process creates a postmerger integration organization to expedite the integration process following closing. It is important to include representatives from the negotiating team on the postmerger integration organization. As negotiators hand off to those responsible for postmerger integration, there is often a lack of shared understanding as to why certain items were included and others excluded from the agreement and what certain contract terms mean. To minimize potential confusion arising when those responsible for negotiating the contract hand off to those responsible for integrating the target, it is critical to get the integration manager involved in the process as early as possible.

Uhlaner and West (2008) argue that integration managers should become involved as soon as the target has been identified or at least well before the evaluation and negotiation process begins. By doing so, it is more likely that the strategic rationale for the deal remains well understood by those involved in conducting due diligence and postmerger integration. The 2002 acquisition of Compaq Computer by Hewlett-Packard offers some interesting insights into the benefits of preclosing planning (see Case Study 6–1).

Case Study 6–1 HP Acquires Compaq—The Importance of Preplanning Integration

The proposed marriage between Hewlett-Packard (HP) and Compaq Computer got off to a rocky start when the sons of the founders came out against the transaction. The resulting long, drawn out proxy battle threatened to divert management's attention from planning for the postclosing integration effort. The complexity of the pending integration effort appeared daunting. The two companies would need to meld employees in 160 countries and assimilate a large array of products ranging from personal computers to consulting services. When the transaction closed on May 7, 2002, critics predicted that the combined businesses, like so many tech mergers over the years, would become stalled in a mess of technical and personal entanglements.

Instead, HP's then CEO Carly Fiorina methodically began to plan for integration prior to the deal closing. She formed an elite team that studied past tech mergers, mapped out the merger's most important tasks, and checked regularly whether key projects were on schedule. A month before the deal was even announced on September 4, 2001, Carly Fiorina and Compaq CEO Michael Capellas each tapped a top manager to tackle the integration effort. The integration managers immediately moved to form a 30-person integration team. The team learned, for example, that, during Compaq's merger with Digital, some server computers slated for elimination were never eliminated. In contrast, HP executives quickly decided what to jettison. Every week they pored over progress charts to review how each product exit was proceeding. By early 2003, HP had eliminated 33 product lines it had inherited from the two companies, thereby reducing the remaining number to 27. Another six were phased out in 2004.

After reviewing other recent transactions, the team recommended offering retention bonuses to employees the firms wanted to keep, as Citigroup had done when combining with Travelers. The team also recommended that moves be taken to create a unified culture to avoid the kind of divisions that plagued AOL Time Warner. HP executives learned to move quickly, making tough decisions early with respect to departments, products, and executives. By studying the 1984 merger between Chevron and Gulf Oil, where it had taken months to name new managers, integration was delayed and employee morale suffered. In contrast, after Chevron merged with Texaco in 2001, new managers were appointed in days, contributing to a smooth merger.

Disputes between HP and former Compaq staff sometimes emerged over issues such as the different approaches to compensating sales people. These issues were resolved by setting up a panel of up to six sales managers enlisted from both firms to referee the disagreements. HP also created a team to deal with combining the corporate cultures and hired consultants to document the differences. For example, HP staff typically used voicemail while Compaq employees used email. Compaq managers were viewed by HP managers as impulsive, while HP managers were viewed as bureaucrats. A series of workshops involving employees from both organizations were established to find ways to bridge actual or perceived differences. Teams of sales personnel from both firms were set up to standardize ways to market to common customers. Schedules were set up to ensure that agreed-upon tactics were actually implemented in a timely manner. The integration managers met with Ms. Fiorina weekly.

The results of this intense preplanning effort were evident by the end of the first year following closing. HP eliminated numerous duplicate product lines and closed dozens of facilities. The firm cut 12,000 jobs, 2,000 more than had been planned at that point in time, from its combined 150,000 employees. HP achieved $3 billion in savings from layoffs, office closures, and consolidating its supply chain. Its original target was for savings of $2.4 billion after the first 18 months.

Despite realizing greater than anticipated cost savings, operating margins by 2004 in the PC business fell far short of expectations. This shortfall was due largely to declining selling prices and a slower than assumed recovery in PC unit sales. The failure to achieve the level of profitability forecast at this time of the acquisition contributed to the termination of Ms. Fiorina in early 2005.

Discussion Questions

1. Explain how premerger planning aided in the integration of HP and Compaq.
2. What did HP learn by studying other mergers? Give examples.
3. Cite key cultural differences between the two organizations. How were they resolved?

Part of the integration planning process involves the preclosing due diligence activity. One responsibility of the due diligence team is to identify ways in which assets, processes, and other resources can be combined to realize cost savings, productivity improvements, or other perceived synergies. This information is also essential for refining the valuation process by enabling planners to better understand the necessary sequencing of events and the resulting pace at which the expected synergies may be realized. Consequently, understanding how and over what time period the integration will be implemented is important in determining the magnitude and timing of the cash flows of the combined companies used in making the final assessment of value.

Integration planning also involves addressing human resource, customer, and supplier issues that overlap the change of ownership. These issues should be resolved as part of the agreement of purchase and sale. For example, the agreement may stipulate how target company employees will be paid and how their benefit claims will be processed.

Payroll systems must be in place to ensure that employees of the acquired company continue to be paid without disruption. For a small number of employees, this may be accommodated easily by loading the acquirer's payroll computer system with the necessary salary and personal information before closing or by having a third-party payroll processor perform these services. For larger operations or where employees are dispersed geographically, the target's employees may continue to be paid for a specific time period using the target's existing payroll system.

Employee health care or disability claims tend to escalate just before a transaction closes. Studies by the American Management Association and CIGNA Corporation show that employees, whether they leave or stay with the new firm, file more disability claims for longer periods after downsizing (*Wall Street Journal*, 1996c). The sharp increase in such expenses can pose an unexpected financial burden for the acquirer if the responsibility for payment of such claims has not been addressed in the merger agreement. For example, the agreement may read that all claims incurred within a specific number of days before closing but not submitted by employees for processing until after closing would be reimbursed by the seller after the closing. Alternatively, such claims may be paid from an escrow account containing a portion of the purchase price set aside to cover these types of expenses.

Similar timing issues exist for target company customers and suppliers. For example, the merger agreement should specify how the seller should be reimbursed for products shipped or services provided by the seller before closing but not paid for by the customer until after closing. A prudent buyer typically would be the recipient of such payments because the seller's previous lockboxes (i.e., checking accounts) would have been closed and replaced by the buyer's. Likewise, the buyer would want to be reimbursed by the seller for monies owed to suppliers for products or services provided to the seller before closing but not billed until after closing. The merger agreement may indicate that both parties will keep track of customer and supplier invoices paid during the 60–90 days following closing and submit them for reimbursement to the other party at the end of that period.

A prudent buyer would want to include certain assurances in the agreement of purchase and sale to limit its postclosing risk. Most seller representations and warranties made to the buyer refer to the past and present condition of the seller's business. Such "reps and warranties" usually pertain to such items as the ownership of securities; real and intellectual property; current levels of receivables, inventory, and debt; and pending lawsuits, worker disability, customer warranty claims, and that the target's accounting practices are in accordance with generally accepted accounting principles. Although "reps and warranties" apply primarily to the past and current state of the seller's business, they have ramifications for the future. For example, if a seller claims that there are no lawsuits pending and a lawsuit is filed shortly after closing, the buyer may seek to recover damages from the seller.

The buyer also may insist that certain conditions be satisfied before closing can take place. Common conditions include employment contracts, agreements not to compete, financing, and regulatory and shareholder approval. The buyer usually insists that key target company employees sign contracts obligating them to remain with the newly formed company for a specific period. The former owners, managers, and other key employees also are asked to sign agreements precluding them from going into any business that would directly compete with the new company during the duration of the noncompete agreement. Finally, the buyer would want to make the final closing contingent on receiving approval from the appropriate regulatory agencies and shareholders of both companies before any money changes hands.

Postmerger Integration Organization: Put in Place before Closing

A postmerger integration organization with clearly defined goals and responsibilities should be in place before closing. For friendly mergers, the organization, including supporting work teams, should consist of individuals from both the acquiring and target companies who have a vested interest in the newly formed company. The extent to which such an organization can be assembled during a hostile takeover is problematic, given the lack of trust that may exist between the parties to the transaction. In such circumstances, the acquiring company is likely to find it difficult to gain access to the necessary information and get the involvement of the target company's management in the planning process before the transaction actually closes.

In those instances where the target firm is going to be integrated into one of the acquirer's business units, it is critical to place responsibility for integration in that business unit. Personnel from the business unit should be well represented on the due diligence team to ensure they understand how best to integrate the target to expeditiously realize synergies.

Postmerger Integration Organization: Composition and Responsibilities

The postmerger integration organization should consist of a management integration team (MIT) and a series of integration work teams. Each work team is focused on implementing a specific portion of the integration plan. The MIT consists of senior managers from the two merged organizations and is charged with implementing synergies identified during the preclosing due diligence. The use of senior managers from both firms not only enables the combined firms to capture the best talent from both organizations but also to give employees from both firms comfort in knowing that there are decision makers who understand their respective situations.

The composition of the work teams also should reflect employees from both the acquiring and target companies. Other team members might include outside advisors, such as investment bankers, accountants, attorneys, and consultants. The MIT's emphasis during the integration period should be on those activities creating the greatest value for shareholders. The MIT's primary responsibility is to focus on key concerns such as long-term revenue, cost, and cash-flow performance targets, as well as product and customer strategies. Exhibit 6-1 summarizes the key tasks that should be performed by the MIT to realize anticipated synergies.

Exhibit 6–1 Key Management Integration Team Responsibilities

1. Build a master schedule of what should be done by whom and by what date.
2. Determine the required economic performance for the combined entity.
3. Establish work teams to determine how each function and business unit will be combined (e.g., structure, job design, and staffing levels).
4. Focus the organization on meeting ongoing business commitments and operational performance targets during the integration process.
5. Create an early warning system consisting of performance indicators to ensure that both integration activities and business performance stay on plan.
6. Monitor and expedite key decisions.
7. Establish a rigorous communication campaign to support aggressively the integration plan. Address both internal (e.g., employees) and external (e.g., customers, suppliers, and regulatory authorities) constituencies.

In addition to driving the integration effort, the MIT ensures that the managers not involved in the endeavor remain focused on running the business. Dedicated integration work teams perform the detailed integration work. The MIT allocates dedicated resources to the integration effort and clarifies non-team-membership roles and enables day-to-day operations to continue at premerger levels. The MIT should be careful to give the work teams not only the responsibility to do certain tasks but also the authority to get the job done. The teams should be encouraged to inject ideas into the process to foster creativity by encouraging solutions rather than by dictating processes and procedures. To be effective, the work teams must have access to accurate, timely information and should receive candid, timely feedback. The teams also should be given adequate resources to execute their responsibilities and be kept informed of the broader perspective of the overall integration effort to avoid becoming too narrowly focused.

Institutionalizing the Integration Process

In recognition of the importance of integration, firms that frequently acquire companies in the same industry often have staffs fully dedicated to managing the integration process. The presumption is that integration is likely to proceed more smoothly and rapidly if those guiding the process have substantial experience in integrating certain types of businesses. It is ironic that some firms can have such discipline when it comes to postacquisition integration but display such poor judgment by consistently overpaying for acquisitions. By overpaying for the target, the acquirer implicitly assumes that all anticipated synergies used to justify the exorbitant purchase price can be realized in a reasonable time period following closing. Thus, overpayment leaves little room for errors during the integration process.

Developing Communication Plans: Talking to Key Stakeholders

Before publicly announcing an acquisition, the acquirer should have prepared a communication plan. The plan should be developed jointly by the MIT and the public relations (PR) department or outside PR consultant. It should contain key messages and specify target stakeholders and appropriate media for conveying the messages to each group. The major stakeholder groups should include employees, customers, suppliers, investors, lenders, communities, and regulators.

Employees: Address the "Me Issues" Immediately

As noted earlier, target company employees typically represent a substantial portion of the value of the acquired business. This is particularly true for technology and service-related businesses, having few tangible assets. Therefore, preserving the value of an acquisition requires that companies must be sensitive to when and how something is communicated to employees and the accuracy of its content. Communication, particularly during crisis periods, should be as frequent as possible. It is better to report that there is no change than to remain silent. Silence breeds uncertainty, which adds to the stress associated with the integration effort. Deteriorating job performance and absences from work are clear signs of workforce anxiety. However, anxiety is not limited to employees of the target firm but also those within the acquirer firm. The acquirer's employees understand that most mergers result in staff reductions at both the target and acquirer firms. Consequently, it is critical to direct communication to all employees at both firms.

The CEO should lead the effort to communicate to employees at all levels through employee meetings on site or via teleconferencing. Many companies find it useful to create a single source of information accessible to all employees. This may be an individual whose job it is to answer questions or a menu-driven automated phone system programmed to respond to commonly asked questions. The best forum for communication in a crisis is through regularly scheduled employee meetings. All external communication in the form of press releases should be coordinated with the PR department to ensure that the same information is released concurrently to all employees. This minimizes the likelihood that employees will learn about important developments second hand. Internal email systems, voicemail, or intranets may be used to facilitate employee communications. In addition, personal letters, question-and-answer sessions, newsletters, or videotapes are highly effective ways of delivering the desired messages.

Employees are interested in any information pertaining to the merger and how it will affect them. They want to know how changes affect the overall strategy, business operations, job security, working conditions, and total compensation. The human resources (HR) staff plays an important role in communicating to employees. HR representatives must learn what employees know and want to know, what the prevailing rumors are, and what employees find most disconcerting. This can be achieved through surveys, interviews, focus groups, or employee meetings.

Customers: Undercommit and Overdeliver

To minimize customer attrition, the newly merged firm must commit to customers that it will maintain or improve product quality, on-time delivery, and customer service. The commitments should be realistic in terms of what needs to be accomplished during the integration phase. Despite these efforts some attrition related to the acquisition is inevitable. The firm continuously must communicate to customers realistic benefits associated with the merger. From the customer's perspective, the merger can increase the range of products or services offered or provide lower selling prices as a result of economies of scale and new applications of technology. However, the firm's actions must support its talk.

When rival PeopleSoft agreed to be acquired in a $10.3 billion cash deal on December 14, 2004 after a protracted 18-month struggle for control, Larry Ellison, Oracle's CEO, immediately took steps to reduce customer attrition. The final purchase price of $26.30 per share represented a 75 percent premium over its original offer made on June 5, 2003, and Ellison believed he had to move quickly to earn back this huge premium (see Case Study 6–2).

Case Study 6–2 Promises to PeopleSoft's Customers Complicate Oracle's Integration Efforts

When Oracle first announced its bid for PeopleSoft in mid-2003, the firm indicated that it planned to stop selling PeopleSoft's existing software programs and halt any additions to its product lines. This would result in the termination of much of PeopleSoft's engineering, sales, and support staff. Oracle indicated that it was more interested in PeopleSoft's customer list than its technology. PeopleSoft earned sizeable profit margins on its software maintenance contracts, under which customers pay for product updates, fixing software errors, and other forms of product support. Maintenance fees represented an annuity stream that could improve profitability even when new product sales are listless. However, PeopleSoft's customers worried that they would have to go through the costly and time-consuming process of switching

Continued

Case Study 6–2 Promises to PeopleSoft's Customers Complicate Oracle's Integration Efforts — Cont'd

software. To win customer support for the merger and to avoid triggering $2 billion in guarantees PeopleSoft had offered its customers in the event Oracle failed to support its products, Oracle had to change dramatically its position over the next 18 months.

One day after reaching agreement with the PeopleSoft board, Oracle announced it would release a new version of PeopleSoft's products and would develop another version of J.D. Edwards's software, which PeopleSoft had acquired in 2003. Oracle committed itself to support the acquired products even longer than PeopleSoft's guarantees would have required. Consequently, Oracle had to maintain programs that run with database software sold by rivals such as IBM. Oracle also had to retain the bulk of PeopleSoft's engineering staff and sales and customer support teams.

Among the biggest beneficiaries of the protracted takeover battle was German software giant SAP. SAP was successful in winning customers uncomfortable about dealing with either Oracle or PeopleSoft. SAP claimed that its worldwide market share had grown from 51 percent in mid-2003 to 56 percent by late 2004. SAP took advantage of the highly public hostile takeover by using sales representatives, email, and an international print advertising campaign to target PeopleSoft customers. The firm touted its reputation for maintaining the highest quality of support and service for its products.

Discussion Questions

1. How might the commitments Oracle made to PeopleSoft's customers affect its ability to realize anticipated synergies? Be specific.
2. Explain why Oracles willingness to pay such a high premium for PeopleSoft and its willingness to change its position on supporting PeopleSoft products and retaining the firm's employees may have had a negative impact on Oracle shareholders. Be specific.

Suppliers: Develop Long-Term Vendor Relationships

Just as a current customer is often worth more than a new one, a current supplier with a proven track record also may be worth more than a new one. Although substantial cost savings are possible by "managing" suppliers, the new company should seek a long-term relationship rather than simply a way to reduce costs. Aggressive negotiation can get high-quality products and services at lower prices in the short run, but it may be transitory if the new company is a large customer of the supplier and if the supplier's margins are squeezed continuously. The supplier's product or service quality will suffer, and the supplier eventually may exit the business. Ways to effectively manage suppliers following an acquisition is discussed later in this chapter.

Investors: Maintain Shareholder Loyalty

The new firm must be able to present a compelling vision of the future to investors. In a share-for-share exchange, there are compelling reasons for appealing to current investors of both the acquirer and target companies. Target shareholders will become shareholders in the newly formed company. Loyal shareholders tend to provide a more stable ownership base, and they may contribute to lower share price volatility. All firms attract particular types of investors—some with a preference for high dividends and others for capital gains. The acquisition of Time Warner by America Online in January 2000 illustrated the potential clash between investor preferences. The combined market value of the two firms lost 11 percent in the four days following the announcement, as investors fretted over what had been created. The selling frenzy following the announcement may have involved different groups of investors who bought Time Warner for its stable growth and America Online for its meteoric growth rate of 70 percent per year. The new company may not have met the expectations of either group.

Communities: Build Strong, Credible Relationships

Companies should communicate plans to build or keep plants, stores, or office buildings in a community as soon as they can be confident that these actions will be implemented. These pronouncements translate readily into new jobs and increased taxes for the community. Good working relations with surrounding communities are simply good public relations.

Creating a New Organization

The combined firms' new leaders must appoint the best possible top management team for achieving the goals of the new company. In turn, the management team must be highly supportive of achieving these goals. Individual senior manager's roles must be clearly defined to achieve effective collaboration. While easy to articulate, the appointment of the new team at the top is highly challenging in the frenetic period immediately before or after closing. The process can become time consuming in that it can involve the appointment of anywhere from 10 to 40 executives, including key functional, group, and often divisional heads. Nonetheless, it must be done adroitly and expeditiously. McKinsey & Company, in a study of 161 mergers, found that the early appointment of the top management team was a strong predictor of the long-term success of the combined firms (Fubini, Price, and Zollo, 2006).

Business Needs Drive the Structure

Organization or structure traditionally is defined in terms of titles and reporting relationships. For the purpose of this chapter, we follow this definition. A properly structured organization should support, not retard, the acceptance of a culture in the new company that is desired by top management. An effective starting point in setting up a structure is to learn from the past and recognize that the needs of the business drive structure and not the other way around.

Learn from the Past

Building new reporting structures for combining companies requires knowledge of the target company's prior organization, some sense as to the effectiveness of this organization in the decision-making process, and the future business needs of the newly combined companies. Therefore, in creating the new organization, it is necessary to start with previous organization charts. They provide insights into how individuals from both the target and acquiring companies will interact within the new company, because they reveal the past experience and future expectations of individuals with regard to reporting relationships.

Structure Facilitates Decision Making, Provides Internal Controls, and Promotes Desired Behaviors

The next step is to move from the past into the future by creating a structure that focuses on meeting the business needs of the combined companies rather than attempting to please everyone. Often, acquiring companies simply impose their reporting structures on the target company, especially if the acquirer is much larger than the target. By ignoring the target's existing organizational structure, the acquiring company, in effect, ignores the expectations of the target's employees.

The three basic types of structures are functional, product or service, and divisional. The functional tends to be the most centralized, and the divisional tends to be the most decentralized.

In a *functional organization*, people are assigned to specific groups or departments such as accounting, engineering, marketing, sales, distribution, customer service, manufacturing, or maintenance. This type of structure tends to be highly centralized and is becoming less common. In a *product or service organization*, functional specialists are grouped by product line or service offering. Each product line or service offering has its own accounting, human resources, sales, marketing, customer service, and product development staffs. These types of organizations tend to be somewhat decentralized. *Divisional organizations* continue to be the dominant form of organizational structure, in which groups of products are combined into independent divisions or "strategic business units." Such organizations have their own management teams and tend to be highly decentralized.

The popularity of decentralized versus centralized management structures varies with the state of the economy. During recessions, when top management is under great pressure to cut costs, companies often tend to move toward centralized management structures, only to decentralize when the economy recovers. Highly decentralized authority can retard the pace of integration, because there is no single authority to resolve issues or determine policies. In contrast, a centralized structure may make postmerger integration much easier. Senior management can dictate policies governing all aspects of the combined companies, centralize all types of functions providing support to operating units, and resolve issues among the operating units.

Although centralized control does provide significant advantages during postmerger integration, it also can be highly detrimental if the policies imposed by the central headquarters are inappropriate for the operating units. Highly centralized management may destroy value by imposing too many rigid controls, focusing on the wrong issues, hiring or promoting the wrong managers, or focusing on the wrong performance measures. Moreover, centralized companies often have multiple layers of management and centralized functions providing services to the operating units. The parent companies pass the costs of centralized management and support services on to the operating units. Studies suggest that the costs of this type of structure often outweigh the benefits (Alexander, Campbell, and Gould, 1995; Campbell, Sadler, and Koch, 1997; Chakrabarti, 1990).

The right structure may be an evolving one. The substantial benefits of a well-managed, rapid integration of the two businesses suggest a centralized management structure initially with relatively few layers of management. In general, flatter organizations are becoming common among large companies. The distance between the CEO and division heads, measured in terms of intermediate positions, decreased by 25 percent between 1986 and 1999. Moreover, the span of a CEO's authority has widened, with about 50 percent more positions reporting directly to the CEO (Wulf and Rajan, 2003). This does not mean that all integration activities should be driven from the top without input from middle managers and supervisors of both companies. It does mean taking decisive and timely action based on the best information available.

Once the integration is viewed as relatively complete, the new company should move to a more decentralized structure in view of the well-documented costs of centralized corporate organizations. Case Study 6–3 shows how Lenovo reacted to organizational issues following its acquisition of IBM's personal computer operations in mid-2005.

Developing Staffing Plans

Staffing plans should be formulated as soon as possible in the integration process. In friendly acquisitions, the process should begin before closing. The early development of such plans provides an opportunity to include the key personnel from both firms in the integration effort. Other benefits from early planning include the increased likelihood of retaining those with key skills and talents, maintaining corporate continuity, and team building. Figure 6–2 describes the logical sequencing of staffing plans and the major issues addressed in each segment.

Case Study 6–3 Lenovo Adopts a Highly Decentralized Organization Following Its Acquisition of IBM's Personal Computer Business

China's largest computer manufacturer completed its acquisition of IBM's ThinkPad PC business in mid-2005, creating overnight the world's third largest personal computer manufacturer behind Hewlett-Packard and Dell. Lenovo tapped Bill Amelio, former head of Dell's Asian operations, to run the combined firms. The initial challenge in merging the two firms was where to locate the headquarters.

ThinkPad's operations were based in Raleigh, North Carolina, while Lenovo was headquartered in Beijing. Rather than identify a single corporate headquarters location, Amelio decided to go without a corporate headquarters. He works out of Singapore, Lenovo chairman Yang Yuanqing relocated to Raleigh, and top executives hold meetings in different locations each month. In mid-2007, Lenovo announced it would base its companywide marketing operations in Bangalore, India, reflecting the firm's desire to base teams where the talent is greatest. The decision reflected Amelio's belief that the team at this location was the strongest. Lenovo's software development team was transferred to Raleigh to capitalize on IBM's talent base at that location. English is the firm's official language.

These actions seemed to work. With profits soaring and Lenovo shares at an all-time high in late 2007, Lenovo decided to change the brand from ThinkPad to Lenovo two years earlier than required under the terms of the acquisition agreement with IBM.

Discussion Questions

1. What do you believe are some of the benefits and challenges of Lenovo's decision to disperse the management, design, and marketing functions? Be specific.
2. Why do you believe Lenovo selected an American to run the global operations and adopted English as the language in which business would be conducted inside the firm?

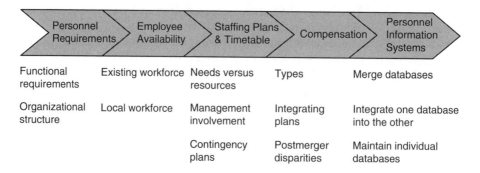

FIGURE 6–2 Staffing strategy sequencing.

Personnel Requirements

The appropriate organizational structure is one able to meet the current functional require-ments or needs of the business and flexible enough to be expanded to satisfy future busi-ness requirements. The process for creating such a structure should involve input from all levels of management, be consistent with the combined firm's business strategy, and reflect expected sales growth. Before establishing the organizational structure, the integra-tion team should agree on what specific functions are needed to run the combined busi-nesses. Once the necessary functions have been identified, the effort to project personnel requirements by function should start with each functional department describing the ideal structure to meet the roles and responsibilities assigned by senior management. By asking for their input, department personnel are involved in the process, can communicate useful insights, and can contribute to the creation of a consensus for changing the organization.

Employee Availability

Employee availability refers to the number of each type of employee required by the new organization that can be identified in the new company's existing workforce and the local communities in which the new company has operations. The skills of the existing work-force should be documented and compared with the current and future functional requirements of the new company. The local labor pool can be used to augment the exist-ing workforce. These workers represent potential new hires for the combined firms. Data should be collected on the educational levels, skills, and demographic composition of the local workforce, as well as prevailing wage rates by skill category.

Staffing Plans and Timetable

Following the determination of the organizational structure and the pool of current and potential employees available to staff the new organization, a detailed staffing plan can be developed.

By matching the number of workers and skills required to support current and future business requirements with the current workforce, gaps in the firm's workforce needing to be filled from recruiting outside the company can be readily identified. The effort to recruit externally should be tempered by its potentially adverse impact on cur-rent employee morale. Filing needed jobs should be given high priority and phased in over time in recognition of the time required to fill certain types of positions and the impact of major hiring programs on local wage rates in communities with a limited avail-ability of labor.

Once management positions have been filled, the managers should evaluate and select new employees to fill job openings in their departments and operations. Senior management should stress the importance of filling job openings, particularly when the skills required are crucial to completing the integration of the acquired business. During integration, managers are under the stress of having to conduct normal business operations as well as integrate portions of the acquired business. In view of the increased workload, it is common for managers to defer the time-consuming hiring process by assuming multiple responsibilities. This hurts the manager's morale and health and the completion of the integration process, because managers often are insufficiently trained to handle many of the responsibilities they have assumed. Key employees inevitably are lost to the new company. Other employees should be trained to fill positions considered critical to the long-term viability of the organization.

Compensation

Merging compensation plans can be one of the most challenging activities of the integration process. Such activities must be conducted in compliance with prevailing regulations and with a high degree of sensitivity. Total compensation consists of base pay, bonuses or incentive plans, benefits, and special contractual agreements. Bonuses may take the form of a lump sum of cash or stock paid to an employee for meeting or exceeding these targets. Special contractual agreements may consist of noncompete agreements, in which key employees, in exchange for an agreed on amount of compensation, sign agreements not to compete against the newly formed company if they should leave. Special agreements also may take the form of golden parachutes (i.e., lucrative severance packages) for senior management. Finally, retention bonuses often are given to employees if they agree to stay with the new company for a specific time period. Following its acquisition of Merrill Lynch in 2008, Bank of America offered Merrill's top financial advisers retention bonuses to minimize potential attrition. For a more detailed discussion of these issues, see Page (2006) and Ferenczy (2005).

Personnel Information Systems

The extent to which compensation plans are integrated depends on whether the two companies are going to be managed separately or integrated. Financial acquirers may be intent on reselling the acquired business in a few years; as such, they may choose to keep compensation plans separate. The strategic acquirer also may keep the plans separate especially if it is moving into an industry in which compensation differs from that prevailing in its current industry. In instances in which the parent chooses to combine plans, the design of the new plan generally is done in consultation with the acquired unit's management. The parent sets guidelines, such as how much stock senior executives should own (e.g., a percentage of base pay) and how managers receive the stock (e.g., whether they are awarded stock or have to buy it at a discount from its current market price). The parent also sets guidelines for base pay. For example, the parent may decide that base pay is to be at the market, below the market, or above the market, adjusted for regional differences in the cost of living. Moreover, the parent may also decide how bonuses are paid, with the operating unit determining who receives them. Finally, the parent determines the benefits policy and plans.

The acquiring company may choose to merge all personnel data into a new database, merge one corporate database into another, or maintain the personnel databases of each business. A single database enables authorized users to access employee data more readily, plan for future staffing requirements more efficiently, and conduct workforce analyses. Maintenance expense associated with a single database also may be lower. The decision to keep personnel databases separate may reflect plans to divest the unit at some time in the future.

Functional Integration

Previous activities within the integration process dealt primarily with planning for the actual integration of the acquired business into the acquirer's business. *Functional integration* refers to the actual execution of the plans. The first consideration of the MIT is to determine the extent to which the two companies' operations and support staffs are to be centralized or decentralized. The main areas of focus should be information technology (IT), manufacturing operations, sales, marketing, finance, purchasing, R&D, and the requirements to staff these functions. However, before any actual integration takes place, it is crucial to revalidate data collected during due diligence and benchmark all operations by comparing them to industry standards.

Due Diligence Data Revalidation: Verify Assumptions

Data collected during due diligence should be revalidated immediately after closing. The pressure exerted by both the buyer and the seller to complete the transaction often results in a haphazard preclosing due diligence review. For example, in an effort to compress the time devoted to due diligence, sellers often allow buyers' access to senior managers only. Middle-level managers, supervisory personnel, and equipment operators often are excluded from the interview process. For similar reasons, site visits by the buyer often are limited to those with the largest number of employees, thus ignoring the risks and opportunities that might exist at sites not visited. The buyer's legal and financial reviews normally are conducted only on the largest customer and supplier contracts, promissory notes, and operating and capital leases. Receivables are evaluated and physical inventory counted using sampling techniques. The effort to determine if intellectual property has been properly protected, with key trademarks or service marks properly registered and copyrights and patents filed, is often spotty.

Performance Benchmarking

Benchmarking important functions, such as the acquirer's and the target's manufacturing and IT operations and processes, is a useful starting point for determining how to integrate these activities. Standard benchmarks include the International Standards Organization's (ISO) 9000 Quality Systems-Model for Quality Assurance in Design, Development, Production, Installation, and Servicing. Other benchmarks that can be used include the U.S. Food and Drug Administration's Good Manufacturing Practices and the Department of Commerce's Malcolm Baldridge Award. Sanderson and Uzumeri (1997, p. 135) provide a comprehensive list of standards-setting organizations.

Integrating Manufacturing Operations

The data revalidation process for integrating and rationalizing facilities and operations requires in-depth discussions with key target company personnel and on-site visits to all facilities. The objective should be to reevaluate overall capacity, the potential for future cost reductions, the age and condition of facilities, adequacy of maintenance budgets, and compliance with environmental laws. Careful consideration should be given to manufacturing capabilities that duplicate those of the acquirer. The integration team also needs to determine if the duplicate facilities are potentially more efficient than those of the buyer. As part of the benchmarking process, the operations of both the acquirer and the target company should be compared with industry standards to properly evaluate their efficiency.

Process effectiveness is an accurate indicator of overall operational efficiency (Porter and Wood, 1998). The four processes that should be examined are planning, materials ordering, order entry, and quality control. For example, production planning is often very inaccurate, particularly when the operations are not easily changed and require long-term sales forecasts. The production planning and materials ordering functions need to coordinate activities, because the quantity and composition of the materials ordered depends on the accuracy of sales projections. Inaccurate projections result in shortages or costly excess inventory accumulation.

The order entry activity may offer significant opportunities for cost savings. Companies that produce in anticipation of sales often carry large finished goods inventories. For this reason, companies such as personal computer manufacturers build inventory according to orders received to minimize working capital requirements. A key indicator of the effectiveness of quality control is the percentage of products that go through the manufacturing process without being inspected. Companies whose "first-run yield" (i.e., the percentage of finished products that do not have to be reworked due to quality problems) is in the 70–80 percent range may have serious quality problems.

Plant consolidation starts with the adoption of a common set of systems and standards for all manufacturing activities. Such standards include cycle time between production runs, cost per unit of output, first-run yield, and scrap rates. Links between the facilities then are created by sharing information management and processing systems, inventory control, supplier relationships, and transportation links. Vertical integration can be achieved by focusing on different stages of production. Different facilities specialize in the production of selected components, which then are shipped to other facilities to assemble the finished product. Finally, a company may close certain facilities whenever there is excess capacity.

Integrating Information Technology

IT spending constitutes an ever-increasing share of most businesses' budgets. Studies have shown that about 80 percent of software projects fail to meet their performance expectations or deadlines (*Financial Times*, 1996). Almost one half are scrapped before they are completed, and about one half cost two or three times their original budgets and take three times as long as expected to complete (*Wall Street Journal*, 1996b). Studies conclude that managers tend to focus too much on technology and not enough on the people and processes that will use it. If the buyer intends to operate the target company independently, the information systems of the two companies may be kept separate as long as communications links between the two companies' systems can be established. However, if the buyer intends to integrate the target, the process can be daunting. Studies show that nearly 70 percent of buyers choose to combine their information systems immediately after closing. Almost 90 percent of acquirers eventually combine these operations (Cossey, 1991). Case Study 6–4 illustrates how Dutch fragrance maker Coty overcame successfully many of the challenges of integrating its supply chain with that of Unilever Cosmetics International.

Case Study 6–4 Integrating Supply Chains: Coty Cosmetics Integrates Unilever Cosmetics International

In mid-August, 2005, Coty, one of the world's largest cosmetic and fragrance manufacturers, acquired Unilever Cosmetics International (UCI), a subsidiary of the Unilever global conglomerate for $800 million. Coty viewed the transaction as one in which it could become a larger player in the prestigious fragrance market of expensive perfumes. Coty believed it could reap economies of scale from having just one sales force, marketing group, and the like, selling and managing the two sets of products. It hoped to retain the best people from both organizations. However, Coty's management understood that, if it were not done quickly enough, it might not realize the potential cost savings and would risk losing key personnel.

By mid-December, Coty's IT team had just completed moving UCI's employees from Unilever's infrastructure to Coty's. This involved such tedious work as switching employees from Microsoft's Outlook to Lotus Notes. Coty's information technology team was faced with the challenge of combining and standardizing the two firms' supply chains, including order entry, purchasing, processing, financial, warehouse, and shipping systems. At the end of 2006, Coty's management announced that it anticipated that the two firms would be fully integrated by June 30, 2006. From an IT perspective, the challenges were daunting. The new company's supply chain spanned 10 countries and employed four different enterprise resource planning (ERP) systems that had three warehouse systems running five major distribution facilities on two continents. ERP is an information system or process that integrates all production and related applications across an entire corporation.

On January 11–12, 2006, 25 process or function "owners," including the heads of finance, customer service, distribution, and IT, met to create the integration plan for the firm's disparate supply chains. In addition to the multiple distribution centers and ERP systems, operations in each country had unique processes that had to be included in the integration planning effort. For example, Italy was already using the SAP system on which Coty would eventually standardize. The largest customers there placed orders at the individual store level and expected products to be delivered to these stores. In contrast, the United Kingdom used a legacy (i.e., a highly customized, nonstandard) ERP system and Coty's largest customer in the United Kingdom, the Boots pharmacy chain, placed orders electronically and had them delivered to central warehouses. Smaller but important differences among the various operations included such things as label reformatting.

Coty's IT team, facing a very demanding schedule, knew it could not accomplish all that needed to be done in the time frame required. Therefore, it started with any system directly affecting the customer, such as sending an order to the warehouse, shipment notification, and billing. The decision to focus on "customer-facing" systems came at the expense of internal systems, such as daily management reports tracking sales and inventory levels. These systems were to be completed after the June 30, 2006, deadline imposed by senior management.

To minimize confusion, Coty created small project teams, consisting of project managers, IT directors, and external consultants. Smaller teams did not require costly overhead, like dedicated office space, and eliminated chains of command that might have prevented senior IT management from receiving timely, candid feedback on actual progress against the integration plan. The use of such teams is credited with allowing Coty's IT department to combine sales and marketing forces as planned at the beginning of the 2007 fiscal year in July 2006. While much of the "customer-facing" work was done, many tasks remained. The IT department now had to go back and work out the details it had neglected during the previous integration effort, such as those daily reports its senior managers wanted and the real-time monitoring of transactions. By setting priorities early in the process and employing small project-focused teams, Coty was able to integrate successfully the complex supply chains of the firms in a timely manner.

Discussion Questions

1. Do you agree with Coty management's decision to focus on integrating "customer-facing" systems first? Explain your answer.
2. How might this emphasis on integrating "customer-facing" systems have affected the new firm's ability to realize anticipated synergies? Be specific.
3. Discuss the advantages and disadvantages of using small project teams. Be specific.

Integrating Finance

Some target companies are operated as stand-alone operations, whereas others are completely merged with the acquirer's existing business. Many international acquisitions involve companies in areas geographically remote from the parent company and operate largely independently from the parent. Such situations require a great deal of effort to ensure that the buyer can monitor the financial results of the new business's operations from a distance, even if the parent has its representative permanently on site. The acquirer also should establish a budgeting process and signature approval levels to control spending. Signing authority levels refer to levels of expenditures that must be approved in writing by a designated manager. The magnitude of approval levels vary by the size of the firm. At a minimum, the budget should require projections of monthly cash inflows and outflows for the coming year.

Integrating Sales: It Is Often Hard to Teach an Old Dog New Tricks

The extent to which the sales forces of the two firms are combined depends on their relative size, the nature of their products and markets, and geographic location. Based on these considerations, the sales forces may be wholly integrated or operated separately. A relatively small sales force may be readily combined with the larger sales force if the products they sell and the markets they serve are sufficiently similar. In contrast, the sales forces may be kept separate if the products they sell require in-depth understanding of the customers' needs and a detailed knowledge of the product. For example, firms using the "consultative selling" approach employ highly trained specialists to advise current or potential customers on how the firm's product and service offering can be used to solve particular customer problems. Consequently, a firm may have a separate sales force for each product or service sold to specific markets. Sales forces in globally dispersed businesses often are kept separate to reflect the uniqueness of their markets. However, support activities such as sales training or technical support often are centralized and used to support sales forces in several different countries.

The benefits of integrating sales forces include significant cost savings by eliminating duplicate sales representatives and related support expenses, such as travel and entertainment expenses, training, and management. A single sales force also may minimize potential confusion by enabling customers to deal with a single sales representative in the purchase of multiple products and services. Moreover, an integrated sales force may facilitate product cross-selling (i.e., the sale of one firm's products to the other firm's customers).

Integrating Marketing: Avoid Brand Confusion

Enabling the customer to see a consistent image in advertising and promotional campaigns is often the greatest challenge facing the integration of the marketing function. For example, the acquired company may offer an explicit or implied warranty that the acquirer finds unacceptable. However, ensuring consistency should not result in confusing the customer by radically changing a product's image or how it is sold. The location and degree of integration of the marketing function depends on the global nature of the business, the diversity or uniqueness of product lines, and the pace of change in the marketplace. A business with operations worldwide often is inclined to decentralize marketing to the local countries to increase awareness of local laws and cultural patterns. Companies with a large number of product lines, which can be grouped into logical categories or require extensive product knowledge, may decide to disperse the marketing function to the various operating units. Finally, it is crucial that the marketing function be kept as close to the customer as possible when the market is changing rapidly. This expedites the inclusion of changing customer requirements into product development cycles and changes in the advertising and promotional campaigns needed to support the selling effort.

Integrating Purchasing

According to an analysis of 50 M&As, managing the merged firm's purchasing function efficiently can reduce the total cost of goods and services purchased by merged companies by 10–15 percent. Companies in this sample were able to recover at least half the premium paid for the target company by moving aggressively to manage their purchasing activities (Chapman et al., 1998). For these firms, purchased goods and services, including office furniture, raw materials, and outside contractors, constituted up to 75 percent of the firms' total spending. The opportunity to reap these substantial savings from suppliers comes immediately following closing of the transaction. A merger creates uncertainty among both companies' suppliers, particularly if they might have to compete against each other for business with the combined firms. Many offer cost savings and new partnership arrangements, given the merged organization's greater bargaining power to renegotiate contracts. The new company may choose to realize savings by reducing the number of suppliers. As part of the premerger due diligence, both the acquirer and the acquired company should identify their critical suppliers. The list should be kept relatively short. The focus should be on those accounting for the largest share of purchased materials expenses.

Integrating Research and Development

The role of R&D is an extremely important source of value in many M&As. Often the buyer's and seller's organizations are either working on duplicate projects or projects not germane to the buyer's long-term strategy. The integration team responsible for managing the integration of R&D activities needs to define future areas of R&D

collaboration and set priorities for future R&D research subject to senior management approval. Barriers to R&D integration abound. Some projects require more time to produce results than others. For example, some scientists and engineers may feel that their current projects require at least 10 years of continuing research, whereas others are looking for results in a much shorter time frame. Another obstacle is that some personnel stand to lose titles, prestige, and power if they collaborate. Finally, the acquirer's and the target's R&D financial return expectations may be different. The acquirer may wish to give R&D a higher or lower priority in the combined operation of the two companies. A starting point for integrating R&D is to have researchers from both companies share their work with each other and colocate. Work teams also can follow a balanced scorecard approach for obtaining funding for their projects. In this process, R&D projects are scored according to their impact on key stakeholders, such as shareholders and customers. Those projects receiving the highest scores are fully funded.

Integrating Human Resources

Traditionally, HR departments have been highly centralized and responsible for conducting opinion surveys, assessing managerial effectiveness, developing hiring and staffing plans, and providing training. HR departments are often instrumental in conducting strategic reviews of the strengths and weaknesses of potential target companies, integrating the acquirer's and target's management teams, recommending and implementing pay and benefit plans, and disseminating information about acquisitions. More recently, the trend has been to move the HR function to the operating unit. Highly centralized HR functions have been found to be very expensive and not responsive to the needs of the operating units. Hiring and training often can be more effectively done at the operating unit level. Most of the traditional HR activities are conducted at the operating units with the exception of the administration of benefit plans, management of HR information systems, and in some cases, organizational development (Porter and Wood, 1998).

Building a New Corporate Culture

Corporate culture refers to a common set of values, traditions, and beliefs that influence management and employee behavior within a firm. Large, diverse businesses have an overarching culture and a series of subcultures that reflect local conditions. When two companies with different cultures merge, the newly formed company often takes on a new culture, quite different from either the acquirer's or the target's culture. Cultural differences are not inherently bad or good. They can instill creativity in the new company or create a contentious environment.

Employee acceptance of a common culture can breed identification with and trust in the corporation. Trust in the corporation is initially undermined after a merger, in part by the ambiguity of the new organization's identity. However, once this ambiguity is lessened, as acceptance of a common culture grows, trust can be restored, especially among those who closely identified with their previous organization (Maguire and Phillips, 2008).

A firm's culture takes both tangible and intangible forms. Tangible symbols of culture include statements hung on walls containing the firm's mission and principles, as well as status associated with the executive office floor and designated parking spaces. Intangible forms of corporate culture include the behavioral norms communicated through implicit messages about how people are expected to act. Since they represent the extent to which employees and managers actually "walk the talk," these behavioral messages are often far more influential in forming and sustaining corporate culture than the tangible trappings of corporate culture. Kennedy and Moore (2003) argue that the most important source of communication of cultural biases in an organization is the individual behavior of others, especially those with the power to reward appropriate and punish inappropriate behavior. Since speed in integrating the acquirer and target firms is critical to realizing anticipated synergies, dealing with potentially contentious cultural issues early in the integration process is crucial. For an excellent discussion of how to analyze cultural issues during preintegration planning, see Carleton and Lineberry (2004).

Identifying Cultural Issues through Cultural Profiling

The first step in building corporate cultures is to develop a cultural profile of both the acquirer and the acquired companies. The information may be obtained from employee surveys and interviews and by observing management styles and practices in both companies. The information then is used to show how the two cultures are alike or different and what are the comparative strengths and weaknesses of each culture. Common differences may include having one culture value individualism and the other value teamwork. Cultural issues can be categorized in terms of company size, maturity, and industry, as well as geographic and international considerations. For our purposes, maturity is defined by the number of years in business.

The relative size and maturity of the acquirer and target firms can have major implications for cultural integration. Startup companies are usually highly unstructured and informal in terms of dress and decision making. Compensation may consist largely of stock options and other forms of deferred income. Benefits, beyond those required by state and federal law, and other "perks," such as company cars, are largely nonexistent. Company policies are frequently either nonexistent, not in writing, or drawn up as needed. Internal controls covering items such as employee expense accounts are often minimal. In contrast, larger, mature companies are frequently more highly structured with well-defined internal controls, compensation structures, benefits packages, and employment policies. Such firms have grown too large and complex to function in an orderly manner without some structure in the form of internal policies and controls. Employees usually have clearly defined job descriptions and career paths. Decision making can be either decentralized at the operating unit level or centralized within a corporate office. In either case, the process for decision making often is well defined. Decision making may be ponderous, requiring consensus within a large management bureaucracy. Cultural differences may be exacerbated in combining firms in different industries or even across segments within the same industry. For example, when Travelers merged with Citicorp, resentment arose as a result of the huge differences between investment banking salaries and those elsewhere in the combined companies.

Geographic and international considerations also represent important challenges in integrating corporate cultures. Language barriers and different customs, working conditions, work ethics, and legal structures create an entirely new set of challenges in integrating cross-border transactions. If cultures are extremely different, integration may be inappropriate. For this reason, acquiring and acquired companies in international transactions frequently maintain separate corporate headquarters, stock listings, and CEOs for an extended period (*Wall Street Journal*, 1996a). Moreover, in choosing how to manage an acquisition in a new country, a manager with an in-depth knowledge of the acquirer's priorities, decision-making processes, and operations is appropriate, especially when the acquirer expects to make very large new investments. However, when the acquirer already has existing operations within the country, a manager with substantial industry experience in the country is generally preferable because of that person's cultural sensitivity and knowledge of local laws and regulations.

Recent studies suggest that acquisitions involving firms from countries with very dissimilar cultures perform better in the long run than those between firms from countries with similar cultures (Chakrabarti, Jayaraman, and Mukherjee, 2005; Langford and Brown, 2004; and Morosini, Shane, and Singh, 1998). These studies distinguish between national culture and corporate culture. Diversity arising from very different national cultures may help the combined acquirer and target firms to compete more effectively in the global marketplace. However, differences in corporate cultures that impair cooperation offset such synergy. The salutary effects of diverse national cultures often tend to outweigh the undermining effects of diverse corporate cultures.

Following a review of the information obtained from the corporate profile, senior management must decide those characteristics of both cultures that should be emphasized in the new business's culture. As noted previously, when two separate corporate cultures combine, it is crucial to realize from the outset that the combined companies often create a new culture that, in some respects, may be distinctly different from the two previous cultures. Because a company's culture is something that evolves over a long time, it often is wishful thinking that changing the culture can be managed carefully or quickly. A more realistic expectation is that employees in the new company can be encouraged to take on a shared vision, set of core values, and behaviors deemed important by senior management. However, getting to the point at which employees wholly embrace management's desired culture may take years and be unachievable in practice. Case Study 6–5 illustrates how the Tribune Corporation's inattention to the profound cultural differences between itself and the Times Mirror Corporation may have contributed to the failure of this merger to meet expectations.

Case Study 6–5 Culture Clash Exacerbates Efforts of the Tribune Corporation to Integrate the Times Mirror Corporation

Chicago-based Tribune Corporation (Tribune), at that time, owned 11 newspapers, including such flagship publications as the *Chicago Tribune*, the *Los Angeles Times*, and *Newsday*, as well as 25 television stations. Attempting to offset the long-term decline in newspaper readership and advertising revenue, Tribune acquired the Times Mirror (owner of the *Los Angeles Times* newspaper) for $8 billion in 2000. The merger combined two firms that historically had been intensely competitive and had dramatically different corporate cultures. The Tribune was famous for its emphasis on local coverage, with even its international stories having a connection to Chicago. In contrast, the *L.A. Times* had always maintained a strong overseas and Washington, D.C. presence, with local coverage often ceded to local suburban newspapers. To some Tribune executives, the *LA Times* was arrogant and overstaffed. To *L.A. Times* executives, Tribune executives seemed too focused on the "bottom line" to be considered good newspaper people (Ellison, 2006).

The overarching strategy for the new company was to sell packages of newspaper and local TV advertising in the big urban markets. It soon became apparent that the strategy would be unsuccessful. Consequently, the Tribune's management turned to aggressive cost cutting to improve profitability. The Tribune wanted to encourage centralization and cooperation among its newspapers to cut overlapping coverage and redundant jobs.

Coverage of the same stories by different newspapers owned by the Tribune added substantially to costs. After months of planning, the Tribune moved five bureaus belonging to Times Mirror papers (including the *L.A. Times*) to the same

Continued

Case Study 6–5 Culture Clash Exacerbates Efforts of the Tribune Corporation to Integrate the Times Mirror Corporation — Cont'd

location as its four other bureaus in Washington, D.C. *L.A. Times'* staffers objected strenuously to the move saying that their stories needed to be tailored to individual markets and they did not want to share reporters with local newspapers. As a result of the consolidation, the Tribune's newspapers shared as much as 40 percent of the content from Washington, D.C., among the papers in 2006, compared to as little as 8 percent in 2000. Such changes allowed for significant staffing reductions.

In trying to achieve cost savings, the firm ran aground in a culture war. Historically, the Times Mirror, unlike the Tribune, had operated its newspapers more as a loose confederation of separate newspapers. Moreover, the Tribune wanted more local focus, while the *L.A. Times* wanted to retain its national and international presence. The controversy came to a head when the *L.A. Times'* editor was forced out in late 2006.

Many newspaper stocks, including the Tribune, had lost more than half of their value between 2004 and 2006. The long-term decline in readership within the Tribune appears to have been exacerbated by the internal culture clash. As a result, the Chandler Trusts, Tribune's largest shareholder, put pressure on the firm to boost shareholder value. In September, the Tribune announced that it wanted to sell the entire newspaper; however, by November, after receiving bids that were a fraction of what had been paid to acquire the newspaper, it was willing to sell parts of the firm. The Tribune was taken private by legendary investor Sam Zell in 2007. See Case Study 12–3 for more details.

Discussion Questions

1. Why do you believe the Tribune thought it could overcome the substantial cultural differences between itself and the Times Mirror Corporation? Be specific.
2. What would you have done differently following closing to overcome the cultural challenges faced by the Tribune? Be specific.

Integrating Corporate Cultures

Sharing common goals, standards, services, and space can be a highly effective and practical way to integrate disparate cultures (Lajoux, 1998, pp. 187–191; Malekzadeh and Nahavandi, 1990). Common goals serve to drive different units to cooperate. For example, at the functional level, setting exact timetables and processes for new product development can drive different operating units to collaborate as project teams to introduce the product by the target date. At the corporate level, incentive plans spanning many years can focus all operating units to pursue the same goals. Although it is helpful in the integration process to have shared or common goals, individuals still must have specific goals to minimize the tendency of some to underperform while benefiting from the collective performance of others. Shared standards or practices enable the adoption of the "best practices" found in one unit or function by another entity. Standards include operating procedures, technological specifications, ethical values, internal controls, employee performance measures, and comparable reward systems throughout the combined companies. Finally, some functional services can be centralized and shared by multiple departments or operating units. The centralized functions then provide services to the operating units. Commonly centralized services include accounting, legal, public relations, internal audit, and information technology. The most common way to share services is to use a common staff. Alternatively, a firm can create a support services unit and allow operating units to purchase services from it or buy similar services outside the company.

Isolating target company employees in a separate building or even a floor of the same building impairs the integration process. Mixing offices or even locating acquired company employees in space adjacent to the parent's offices is a highly desirable way to improve communication and idea sharing. Sharing laboratories, computer rooms, or libraries also can facilitate communication and cooperation.

Despite the various approaches taken to achieve cooperation in corporations with significantly disparate cultures, the challenges are enormous. In early 2006, Time Warner president Jeffrey Bewkes stopped requiring the company's corporate units to cooperate. This was a complete philosophical turnabout from what the firm espoused following its 2001 merger with AOL. At that time, executives promised to create a well-oiled, vertically integrated profit generator. Books and magazines and other forms of content would feed the television, movie, and Internet operations. Now managers are encouraged to cooperate only if they cannot make more money on the outside. Other media companies such as Viacom and Liberty Media have already broken themselves up because their efforts to achieve corporatewide synergies with disparate media businesses proved unsuccessful.

Integrating Business Alliances

Business alliances, particularly those created to consolidate resources such as manufacturing facilities or sales forces, also must pay close attention to integration activities. Unlike M&As, alliances usually involve shared control. Successful implementation requires maintaining a good working relationship between venture partners. When partners cannot maintain a good working relationship, the alliance is destined to fail. The breakdown in the working relationship is often a result of an inadequate integration (Lynch, 1993, pp. 189–205).

Integrating Mechanisms

Robert Porter Lynch suggests six integration mechanisms to apply to business alliances: (1) leadership, (2) teamwork and role clarification, (3) control by coordination, (4) policies and values, (5) consensus decision making, and (6) resource commitments.

Leadership

Although the terms *leadership* and *management* often are used interchangeably, there are critical differences. A leader sets direction and makes things happen, whereas a manager follows through and ensures that things continue to happen. Leadership involves vision, drive, enthusiasm, and strong selling skills; management involves communication, planning, delegating, coordinating, problem solving, making choices, and clarifying lines of responsibility. Successful alliances require the proper mix of both sets of skills. The leader must provide clear direction, values, and behaviors to create a culture that focuses on the alliance's strategic objectives as its top priority. Managers foster teamwork and promote long-term stability in the shared control environment of the business alliance.

Teamwork and Role Clarification

Teamwork is the underpinning that makes alliances work. Teamwork comes from trust, fairness, and discipline. Teams reach across functional lines and often consist of diverse experts or lower-level managers with critical problem-solving skills. The team provides functional managers with the broader, flexible staffing to augment their own specialized staff. Teams tend to create better coordination and communication at lower levels of the alliance, as well as between partners in the venture. Because teams represent individuals with varied backgrounds and possibly conflicting agendas, they may foster rather than resolve conflict. The alliance manager must be diligent in clarifying what behaviors will not be tolerated.

Coordination

In contrast to an acquisition, no one company is in charge. Alliances do not lend themselves to control through mandate; rather, in the alliance, control is best exerted through coordination. The best alliance managers are those who coordinate activities through effective communication. When problems arise, the manager's role is to manage the decision-making process, not necessarily to make the decision.

Policies and Values

Alliance employees need to understand how decisions are made, what has high priority, who will be held accountable, and how rewards will be determined. When people know where they stand and what to expect, they are better able to deal with ambiguity and uncertainty. This level of clarity can be communicated through a distinct set of policies and procedures that are well understood by joint venture or partnership employees.

Consensus Decision Making

Consensus decision making does not mean that decisions are based on unanimity. Rather, decisions are based on the premise that all participants have had an opportunity to express their opinions and they are willing to accept the final decision. Like any other business, operating decisions must be made within a reasonable time frame. The formal decision-making structure varies with the type of legal structure. Joint ventures often have a board of directors and a management committee, which meet quarterly and monthly, respectively. Projects normally are governed by steering committees. Many alliances are started to take advantage of complementary skills or resources available from alliance participants. The alliance can achieve its strategic objective only if all parties to the alliance live up to the resources they agreed to commit. The failure of one party to meet its commitments erodes trust and limits the alliance's ability to meet its objectives.

Things to Remember

Postclosing integration is a critical phase of the M&A process. Integration itself can be viewed in terms of a process consisting of six activities: integration planning, developing communication plans, creating a new organization, developing staffing plans, functional integration, and integrating corporate cultures. Both communication and cultural integration extend beyond what normally is considered the conclusion of the integration period. Combining companies must be done quickly (i.e., 6–12 months) to achieve proper staffing levels, eliminate redundant assets, and generate the financial returns expected by shareholders. Delay contributes to employee anxiety and accelerates the loss of key talent and managers; delay also contributes to the deterioration of employee morale among those that remain. The loss of key talent and managers often is viewed as the greatest risk associated with the integration phase. Nevertheless, although speed is important to realize cost savings and retain key employees, highly complex operations must be integrated in a more deliberate and systematic fashion to minimize long-term problems.

Successfully integrated M&As are those that demonstrate leadership by candidly and continuously communicating a clear vision, a set of values, and clear priorities to all employees. Successful integration efforts are those that are well planned, appoint an integration manager and a team with clearly defined lines of authority, and make the tough decisions early in the process. These decisions include organizational structure, reporting relationships, spans of control, people selection, roles and responsibilities, and workforce reduction. During integration, the focus should be on those issues having the greatest near-term impact.

Unlike M&As, the integration of business alliances tends to be phased. Resources are contributed at the outset to enable the formation of the alliance. Subsequent resource contributions are subject to a lengthy negotiation process in which the partners are trying to get the most favorable terms. Because alliances involve shared control, the integration process requires good working relationships with the other participants. Successful integration also requires leadership capable of defining a clear sense of direction and well-defined priorities and managers who accomplish their objectives as much by coordinating activities through effective communication as by unilateral decision making. Like M&As, cross-functional teams are used widely to achieve integration. Finally, the successful integration of business alliances, as well as M&As, demands that the necessary resources, in terms of the best people, the appropriate skills, and sufficient capital, be committed to the process.

Chapter Discussion Questions

6–1. Why is the integration phase of the acquisition process considered so important?

6–2. Why should acquired companies be integrated quickly?

6–3. Why might the time required to integrate acquisitions vary by industry?

6–4. What are the costs of employee turnover?

6–5. Why is candid and continuous communication so important during the integration phase?

6–6. What messages might be communicated to the various audiences or stakeholders of the new company?

6–7. Cite examples of difficult decisions that should be made early in the integration process.

6–8. Cite the contract-related "transition issues" that should be resolved before closing.

6–9. How does the process for integrating business alliances differ from that of integrating an acquisition?

6–10. How are the processes for integrating business alliances and M&As similar?

6–11. When Daimler Benz acquired Chrysler Corporation, it announced that it could take six to eight years to fully integrate the combined firm's global manufacturing operations and certain functions, such as purchasing. Why do you believe it might take that long?

6–12. In your judgment, are acquirers more likely to under- or overestimate anticipated cost savings? Explain your answer.

6–13. Cite examples of expenses you believe are commonly incurred in integrating target companies. Be specific.

6–14. A common justification for mergers of competitors are the potential cross-selling opportunities it would provide. Comment on the challenges that might be involved in making such a marketing strategy work.

6–15. Billed as a merger of equals, Citibank and Travelers resorted to a co-CEO arrangement when they merged in 1998. Why do you think they adopted this arrangement? What are the advantages and disadvantages of such an arrangement?

Answers to these Chapter Discussion Questions are available in the Online Instructor's Manual for instructors using this book.

Chapter Business Cases

Case Study 6–6. The Challenges of Integrating Steel Giants Arcelor and Mittal

The merger of Arcelor and Mittal into ArcelorMittal in June 2006 resulted in the creation of the world's largest steel company. With 2007 revenues of $105 billion and its steel production accounting for about 10 percent of global output, the behemoth has 320,000 employees in 60 countries, and it is a global leader in all its target markets. Arcelor was a product of three European steel companies (Arbed, Aceralia, and Usinor). Similarly, Mittal resulted from a series of international acquisitions. The two firms' downstream (raw material) and upstream (distribution) operations proved to be highly complementary, with Mittal owning much of its iron ore and coal reserves and Arcelor having extensive distribution and service center operations. Like most mergers, Arcelor-Mittal faced the challenge of integrating management teams; sales, marketing, and product functions; production facilities; and purchasing operations. Unlike many mergers involving direct competitors, a relatively small portion of cost savings would come from eliminating duplicate functions and operations.

This case study relies upon information provided in an interview with Jerome Ganboulan (formerly of Arcelor) and William A. Scotting (formerly of Mittal), the two executives charged with directing the postmerger integration effort.[1] The focus in the case study is on the formation of the integration team, the importance of communications, and the realization of anticipated synergies.

Top Management Sets Expectations

ArcelorMittal's top management set three driving objectives before undertaking the postmerger integration effort: (1) achieve rapid integration, (2) manage daily operations effectively, and (3) accelerate revenue and profit growth. The third objective was viewed as the primary motivation for the merger. The goal was to combine what were viewed as entities having highly complementary assets and skills. This goal was quite different from the way Mittal had grown historically, which was a result of acquisitions of turnaround targets focused on cost and productivity improvements.

---

[1]Adapted from Jan De Mdedt and Michel Van Hoey, "Integrating Steel Giants: An Interview with the Arcelor-Mittal Post-Merger Managers," *McKinsey Quarterly*, February 2008.

Developing the Integration Team

The formal phase of the integration effort was to be completed in six months. Consequently, it was crucial to agree on the role of the management integration team (MIT); key aspects of the integration process, such as how decisions would be made; and the roles and responsibilities of team members. Activities were undertaken in parallel rather than sequentially. Teams consisted of employees from the two firms. People leading task forces came from the business units. For example, commercial integration issues were resolved by the commercial business units.

The teams were then asked to propose a draft organization to the MIT, including the profiles of the people who were to become senior managers. Once the senior managers were selected, they were to build their own teams to identify the synergies and create action plans for realizing the synergies. Teams were formed before the organization was announced and implementation of certain actions began before detailed plans had been developed fully. Progress to plan was monitored on a weekly basis, enabling the MIT to identify obstacles facing the 25 decentralized task forces and, when necessary, resolve issues.

Developing Communication Plans

Considerable effort was spent in getting line managers involved in the planning process and selling the merger to their respective operating teams. Initial communication efforts included the launch of a top-management "road show." The new company also established a website and introduced Web TV. Senior executives reported two- to three-minute interviews on various topics, giving everyone with access to a personal computer the ability to watch the interviews onscreen.

Owing to the employee duress resulting from the merger, uncertainty was high, as employees with both firms wondered how the merger would affect them. To address employee concerns, managers were given a well-structured message about the significance of the merger and the direction of the new company. Furthermore, the new brand, ArcelorMittal, was launched in a meeting attended by 500 of the firm's top managers during the spring of 2007. This meeting marked the end of the formal integration process. Finally, all communication of information disseminated throughout the organization was focused rather than of a general nature.

External communication was conducted in several ways. Immediately following closing, senior managers traveled to all the major cities and sites of operations, talking to local management and employees in these sites. Typically, media interviews were also conducted around these visits, providing an opportunity to convey the ArcelorMittal message to the communities through the press. In March 2007, the new firm held a media day in Brussels, which involved presentations on the status of the merger. Journalists were invited to go to the different businesses and review the progress themselves.

Within the first three months following closing, customers were informed about the advantages of the merger for them, such as enhanced R&D capabilities and wider global coverage. The sales forces of the two organizations were charged with the task of creating a single "face" to the market.

Creating a New Organization

ArcelorMittal's management viewed the merger as an opportunity to conduct interviews and surveys with employees to gain an understanding of their views about the two companies. Employees were asked about the combined firm's strengths and weaknesses and how the new firm should present itself to its various stakeholder groups. This process resulted in a complete rebranding of the combined firms.

Achieving Operational and Functional Integration

ArcelorMittal management set a target for annual cost savings of $1.6 billion, based on experience with earlier acquisitions. The role of the task forces was first to validate this number from the bottom up then to tell the MIT how the synergies would be achieved. As the merger progressed, it was necessary to get the business units to assume ownership of the process to formulate the initiatives, timetables, and key performance indicators that could be used to track performance against objectives. In some cases, the synergy potential was larger than anticipated while smaller in other situations. The expectation was that the synergy could be realized by mid-2009. The integration objectives were included in the 2007 annual budget plan. As of the end of 2007, the combined firms were on track to realize their goal with annualized cost savings running $1.4 billion.

Concluding Formal Integration Activities

The integration was deemed complete when the new organization, the brand, the "one face to the customer" requirement, and the synergies were finalized. This occurred within eight months of the closing. However, integration would continue for some time to achieve cultural integration. Cultural differences within the two firms are significant. In effect, neither company was homogeneous from a cultural perspective. ArcelorMittal management viewed this diversity as an advantage, in that it provided an opportunity to learn new ideas.

Discussion Questions

1. Why is it important to establish both top-down (i.e., provided by top management) and bottom-up (provided by operating units) estimates of synergy?
2. How did ArcelorMittal attempt to bridge cultural differences during the integration? Be specific.
3. Why are communication plans so important? What methods did ArcelorMittal employ to achieve these objectives? Be specific.
4. Comment on ArcelorMittal management's belief that the cultural diversity within the combined firms was an advantage. Be specific.
5. The formal phase of the post-merger integration period was to be completed within six months. Why do you believe that ArcelorMittal's management was eager to integrate the two businesses rapidly? Be specific. What integration activities were to extend beyond the proposed six-month integration period?

Solutions to these questions are found in the Online Instructor's Manual for instructors using this book.

Case Study 6–7. Alcatel Merges with Lucent, Highlighting Cross-Cultural Issues

Alcatel SA and Lucent Technologies signed a merger pact on April 3, 2006, to form a Paris-based telecommunications equipment giant. The combined firms would be led by Lucent's chief executive officer Patricia Russo. Her charge would be to meld two cultures during a period of dynamic industry change. Lucent and Alcatel have been considered natural merger partners, because they have overlapping product lines and different strengths. More than two thirds of Alcatel 's business comes from Europe, Latin America, the Middle East, and Africa. The French firm is particularly strong in equipment that enables regular telephone lines to carry high-speed Internet and digital television traffic. Nearly two thirds of Lucent's business is in the United States. The new company was expected to eliminate 10 percent of its workforce of 88,000 and save $1.7 billion annually within three years by eliminating overlapping functions.

While billed as a merger of equals, Alcatel of France, the larger of the two, would take the lead in shaping the future of the new firm, whose shares would be listed in Paris, not in the United States. The board would have six members from the current Alcatel board and six from the current Lucent board, as well as two independent directors that must be European nationals. Alcatel CEO Serge Tehuruk would serve as the chairman of the board. Much of Ms. Russo's senior management team, including the chief operating officer, chief financial officer, the head of the key emerging markets unit, and the director of human resources would come from Alcatel. To allay U.S. national security concerns, the new company would form an independent U.S. subsidiary to administer American government contracts. This subsidiary would be managed separately by a board composed of three U.S. citizens acceptable to the U.S. government.

International combinations involving U.S. companies have had a spotty history in the telecommunications industry. For example, British Telecommunications PLC and AT&T Corp. saw their joint venture, Concert, formed in the late 1990s, collapse after only a few years. Even outside the telecom industry, trans-Atlantic mergers have been fraught with problems. For example, Daimler Benz's 1998 deal with Chrysler, which was also billed as a merger of equals, was heavily weighted toward the German company from the outset.

In integrating Lucent and Alcatel, Russo faces a number of practical obstacles, including who will work out of Alcatel's Paris headquarters. Russo, who became Lucent's chief executive in 2000 and does not speak French, would have to navigate the challenges of doing business in France. The French government has a big influence on French companies and remains a large shareholder in the telecom and defense sectors. Russo's first big fight might come over job cuts anticipated in the merger plan. French unions tend to be strong, and employees enjoy more legal protections than elsewhere. Hundreds of thousands took to the streets in mid-2006 to protest a new law that would make it easier for firms to hire and fire younger workers. Russo has had extensive experience with big layoffs. At Lucent, she helped orchestrate spin-offs, layoffs, and buyouts involving nearly four fifths of the firm's workforce.

Making choices about cuts in a combined company would likely be even more difficult, with Russo facing a level of resistance in France unheard of in the United States, where it is generally accepted that most workers are subject to layoffs and dismissals. Alcatel has been able to make many of its job cuts in recent years outside France, thereby avoiding the greater difficulty of shedding French workers. Lucent workers might fear that they would be dismissed first simply because it is easier than dismissing their French counterparts.

Since the 2006 merger, the company posted six quarterly losses and took more than $4.5 billion in write-offs, while its stock plummeted more than 60 percent. An economic slowdown and tight credit limited spending by phone companies. Moreover, the market has been getting more competitive, with China's Huawei aggressively pricing its products. However, other telecommunications equipment manufacturers facing the same conditions have not fared nearly as badly as Alcatel-Lucent. Melding two fundamentally different cultures (Alcatel's entrepreneurial and Lucent's centrally controlled cultures) has proven daunting. Customers uncertain about the new firm's products are migrating to competitors, forcing Alcatel-Lucent to slash prices even more. Despite the aggressive job cuts, a substantial portion of the projected $3.1 billion in savings from the layoffs were lost to discounts the company made to customers in an effort to rebuild market share.

Frustrated by the lack of progress in turning around the business, the Alcatel-Lucent board announced in July 2008 that Patricia Russo, the American chief executive, and Serge Tchuruk, the French chairman, would leave the company by the end of the year. The board also announced that, as part of the shake-up, the size of the board would be reduced, with Henry Schacht, a former chief executive at Lucent, stepping down. Perhaps hamstrung by its dual personality, the French-American company seemed poised to take on a new personality of its own by jettisoning previous leadership.

Discussion Questions

1. Explain the logic behind combining the two companies. Be specific.
2. What major challenges are the management of the combined companies likely to face? How would you recommend resolving these issues?
3. Most corporate mergers are beset by differences in corporate cultures. How do cross-border transactions compound these differences?
4. Why do you think mergers, both domestic and cross-border, are often communicated by the acquirer and target firms' management as mergers of equals?
5. In what way would you characterize this transaction as a merger of equals? In what ways should it not be considered a merger of equals?

Solutions to these questions are found in the Online Instructor's Manual for instructors using this book.

Merger and Acquisition Valuation and Modeling

7

A Primer on Merger and Acquisition Cash-Flow Valuation

The greater danger for most of us is not that our aim is too high and we might miss it, but that it is too low and we reach it.

—Michelangelo

Inside M&A: The Importance of Distinguishing between Operating and Nonoperating Assets

On February 14, 2005, Verizon Communications and MCI Inc. executives announced that they had agreed to a deal in which MCI shareholders would receive $6.7 billion for 100 percent of MCI stock. Verizon's management argued that the deal would cost their shareholders only $5.3 billion in Verizon stock, with MCI agreeing to pay its shareholders a special dividend of $1.4 billion contingent on their approval of the transaction. The $1.4 billion special dividend reduced MCI's cash in excess of what was required to meet its normal operating cash requirements.

To understand the actual purchase price, it is necessary to distinguish between operating and nonoperating assets. Without the special dividend, the $1.4 billion in cash would transfer automatically to Verizon as a result of the purchase of MCI's stock. Verizon would have to increase its purchase price by an equivalent amount to reflect the face value of this nonoperating cash asset. Consequently, the purchase price would be $6.7 billion. With the special dividend, the excess cash transferred to Verizon is reduced by $1.4 billion, and the purchase price is $5.3 billion. In fact, the alleged price reduction is no price reduction at all. It simply reflects Verizon's shareholders receiving $1.4 billion less in acquired assets. Moreover, since the $1.4 billion represents excess cash that would have been reinvested in MCI or paid out to shareholders anyway, the MCI shareholders are simply getting the cash earlier than they may have otherwise.

Chapter Overview

There are five basic methods of valuation: income or discounted cash flow (DCF), market based, asset oriented, replacement cost, and the contingent claims or real options approach. The purpose of this chapter is to provide an overview of the basics of valuing mergers and acquisitions using discounted cash-flow methods. The remaining valuation methods are discussed in Chapter 8.

The chapter begins with a brief review of rudimentary finance concepts, including measuring risk and return, the capital-asset pricing model, and the effects of leverage on risk and return. The cash-flow definitions, free cash flow to equity or to the firm, discussed in this chapter are used in valuation problems in subsequent chapters. The distinction between these cash-flow definitions is particularly relevant for the discussion of leveraged buyouts in Chapter 13. The chapter concludes with a discussion of the valuation of a firm's debt and other obligations and nonoperating assets, such as excess cash and marketable securities, investments in other firms, unutilized and pension fund assets, and intangible assets. For more exhaustive analyses of valuation, see Damodaran (2001); Copeland, Koller, and Murrin (2005); and Chambers and Lacey (2008). For those seeking a more rigorous quantitative approach to valuation, see Abrams (2001) and Levy (2004). The major segments of this chapter include the following:

- Required Returns
- Analyzing Risk
- Calculating Free Cash Flows
- Applying Income or Discounted Cash-Flow Methods
- Valuing Firms under Special Situations
- Valuing a Firm's Debt and Other Obligations
- Valuing Nonoperating Assets
- Adjusting the Target Firm's Equity Value for Nonoperating Assets, Debt, and Other Obligations
- Things to Remember

A review of this chapter (including additional practice problems with solutions) is available in the file folder entitled Student Study Guide contained on the CD-ROM accompanying this book. The CD-ROM also contains a Learning Interactions Library, enabling students to test their knowledge of this chapter in a "real-time" environment and a discussion of how to project cash flows in a file entitled "Primer on Cash Flow Forecasting."

Required Returns

Investors require a minimum rate of return on an investment to compensate them for the level of perceived risk associated with that investment. The required rate of return must be at least equal to what the investor can receive on alternative investments exhibiting a comparable level of perceived risk. For an excellent discussion of the basic concepts of finance, see Gitman (2008).

Cost of Equity and the Capital Asset Pricing Model

The cost of equity (k_e) is the rate of return required to induce investors to purchase a firm's equity. The cost of equity also can be viewed as an **opportunity cost** (i.e., a foregone opportunity), because it represents the rate of return investors could earn by investing in equities of comparable risk. The cost of equity can be estimated using the capital asset pricing model (CAPM), which measures the relationship between expected risk and expected return. It postulates that investors require higher rates of return for accepting higher levels of risk. Specifically, the CAPM states that the expected return on an asset or security is equal to a risk-free rate of return plus a risk premium.

A *risk-free rate of return* is one for which the expected return is certain. For a return to be considered risk free over some future time period, it must be free of default risk and there must be no uncertainty about the reinvestment rate (i.e., the rate of return that can be earned at the end of the investor's holding period). Despite widespread agreement on the use of U.S. Treasury securities as assets that are free of default risk, there is some controversy over whether a short- or long-term Treasury rate should be used in applying the CAPM. Whether you should use a short- or long-term rate depends on how long the investor intends to hold the investment. Consequently, the investor who anticipates holding an investment for 5 or 10 years needs to use either a 5- or 10-year Treasury bond rate. A three-month Treasury bill rate is not free of risk for a 5- or 10-year period, since interest and principal received at maturity must be reinvested at three-month intervals, resulting in considerable reinvestment risk. In this book, a 10-year Treasury bond rate is used to represent the risk-free rate of return. This would be most appropriate for a strategic acquirer interested in valuing a target firm with the intent of operating the firm over an extended time period.

Estimating Market Risk Premiums

The *market risk* or *equity premium* refers to the additional rate of return in excess of the risk-free rate that investors require to purchase a firm's equity. While the risk premium represents the perceived risk of the stock and should therefore be forward looking, obtaining precise estimates of future market returns often is exceedingly difficult. The objectivity of Wall Street analysts' projections is problematic, and efforts to develop sophisticated models show results that vary widely in their underlying assumptions. Consequently, analysts often look to historical data, despite results that vary based on the time periods selected and whether returns are calculated as arithmetic or geometric averages. CAPM relates the cost of equity to the risk-free rate of return and market risk premium as follows:

$$\text{CAPM} = k_e = R_f + \beta(R_m - R_f) \tag{7–1}$$

where

R_f = risk free rate of return.

β = beta (see the section of this chapter entitled "Analyzing Risk").

R_m = the expected rate of return on equities.

$R_m - R_f = 5.5\%$.

(i.e., the simple long-term average of the arithmetic and geometric average equity premium).

The author used the simple average of arithmetic and geometric means, since the choice of either methodology may result in different estimates of the historical equity premium. The 5.5 percent equity risk premium used in this book is consistent with long-term averages calculated elsewhere. Based on survey results of 510 finance and economics professors, Welch (2001) estimates an equity premium over a 30-year horizon of 5.5 percent. Using data provided by Dimson, March, and Staunton (2003), the equity risk premium relative to bonds during the period from 1900 and 2002 in the United States, calculated as a simple average of the geometric and arithmetic means, was 5.75 percent in the United States and 4.9 percent for a 16-country average. However, the standard error of estimate for the United States is 1.9 percent, with the range of standard errors extending from a low of 1.7 percent for Australia and Canada to a high of 3.5 percent for Germany. Therefore, for the United States, we can be only two thirds confident that the true mean lies within one standard error of the estimate (i.e., the true mean lies within 5.75 ± 1.9 percent or between 3.85 and 7.65 percent).

Despite its intuitive appeal, the CAPM has limitations. Betas tend to vary over time and are quite sensitive to the time period and methodology employed in their estimation. For a detailed discussion of these issues, see Fama and French (1992, 1993, 2006). Other studies show that the market risk premium is unstable, lower during periods of prosperity and higher during periods of economic slowdowns (Claus and Thomas, 2001; Easton et al., 2001).

Some analysts argue that the "risk premium" should be changed to reflect fluctuations in the stock market. However, history shows that such fluctuations are relatively short term in nature. Consequently, the risk premium should reflect more long-term considerations, such as the expected holding period of the investor or acquiring company. Therefore, for the strategic or long-term investor or acquirer, the risk premium should approximate the 5.5 premium long-term historical average. Escherich (1998), in a survey of 200 companies, found that most firms estimate the cost of equity using CAPM and use an equity risk premium of between 5 and 7 percent.

Since CAPM measures a stock's risk only relative to the overall market and ignores returns on assets other than stocks, some analysts have begun using *multifactor models*. Such models adjust the CAPM by adding other risk factors that determine asset returns, such as firm size, bond default premiums, the bond term structure (i.e., difference between short- and long-term interest rates on securities that differ only by maturity), and inflation.

Studies show that, of these factors, firm size appears to be among the most important (Bernard, Healy, and Palepu, 2004; Pastor and Stambaugh, 2001). The size factor serves as a proxy for factors such as smaller firms being subject to higher default risk and generally being less liquid than large capitalization firms (Berk, 1995). While the specific stock risk for an owner of a properly diversified portfolio can be eliminated, this is not true of the owner of a privately owned business. Table 7–1 provides estimates of the amount of the adjustment to the cost of equity to correct for firm size, as measured by market value, based on actual data since 1926. This is explored in more detail in Chapter 9, in the discussion of adjusting CAPM for firm-specific risk. The analyst should use this data as guidelines only. Specific firm business risk is largely unobservable. Consequently, in applying a firm size premium, analysts should use their judgment in selecting a proper size premium. This magnitude of the firm size premium should be tempered by such

Table 7–1   Estimates of the Size Premium

Market Value (000,000)	Percentage Points Added to CAPM Estimate
>$12,400	0.0
$5,250 to $12,400	0.3
$2,600 to $5,250	0.6
$1,650 to $2,600	0.8
$700 to $1,650	1.2
$450 to $700	1.3
$250 to $450	1.9
$100 to $250	2.4
$50 to $100	3.5
<$50 million	9.2

Source: Adapted from estimates provided by Ibbotson's *Stocks, Bills, Bonds, and Inflation Valuation Yearbook* (Chicago: Ibbotson Associates, 2005).

factors as a comparison of the firm's key financial ratios (e.g., liquidity and leverage) with comparable firms and after interviewing management. The selection of the proper magnitude is addressed in more detail in Chapter 10.

Equation (7–1) can be rewritten to reflect an adjustment for firm size as follows:

$$\text{CAPM} = k_e = R_f + \beta(R_m - R_f) + \text{FSP} \tag{7–2}$$

where FSP = firm size premium.

Assume a firm has a market value of less than \$50 million and a β of 1.75. Also, assume the risk-free rates of return and equity premium are 5.0 and 5.5 percent, respectively. The firm's cost of equity using the CAPM method adjusted for firm size can be estimated as follows:

$$k_e = 0.05 + 1.75(0.055) + 0.092 \text{ (see Table 7–1)} = .238 = 23.8\%$$

Pretax Cost of Debt

The cost of debt represents the cost to the firm of borrowed funds. It reflects the current level of interest rates and the level of default risk as perceived by investors. Interest paid on debt is tax deductible by the firm. In bankruptcy, bondholders are paid before shareholders as the firm's assets are liquidated. Default risk can be measured by the firm's credit rating. Default rates vary from an average of 0.52 percent of AAA-rated firms for the 15-year period ending in 2001 to 54.38 percent for those rated CCC by Standard and Poor's Corporation (Burrus and McNamee, 2002).

For nonrated firms, the analyst may estimate the pretax cost of debt for an individual firm by comparing debt-to-equity ratios, interest coverage ratios, and operating margins with those of similar rated firms. Alternatively, the analyst may use the firm's actual interest expense as a percent of total debt outstanding. Some analysts prefer to use the average yield to maturity of the firm's outstanding bonds. Much of this information can be found in local libraries in such publications as Moody's *Company Data*; Standard & Poor's *Descriptions, The Outlook,* and *Bond Guide*; and Value Line's *Investment Survey*.

Cost of Preferred Stock

Preferred stock exhibits some of the characteristics of long-term debt, in that its dividend is generally constant and preferred stockholders are paid before common shareholders in the event the firm is liquidated. Unlike interest payments on debt, preferred dividends are not tax deductible. Because preferred stock is riskier than debt but less risky than common stock in bankruptcy, the cost to the company to issue preferred stock should be less than the cost of equity but greater than the cost of debt. Viewing preferred dividends as paid in perpetuity, the cost of preferred stock (k_{pr}) can be calculated as dividends per share of preferred stock (d_{pr}) divided by the market value of the preferred stock (PR) (see the section of this chapter entitled "Zero-Growth Valuation Model"). Consequently, if a firm pays a \$2 dividend on its preferred stock whose current market value is \$50, the firm's cost of preferred stock is 4 percent (i.e., \$2/\$50). The cost of preferred stock can be generalized as follows:

$$k_{pr} = \frac{d_{pr}}{\text{PR}} \tag{7–3}$$

Cost of Capital

The weighted average cost of capital (WACC) is the broadest measure of the firm's cost of funds and represents the return that a firm must earn to induce investors to buy its common stock, preferred stock, and bonds. The WACC is calculated using a weighted average of the firm's cost of equity (k_e), cost of preferred stock (k_{pr}), and pretax cost of debt (i):

$$\text{WACC} = k_e \times \frac{E}{D + E + \text{PR}} + i \times (1 - t) \times \frac{D}{D + E + \text{PR}} + k_{pr} \times \frac{\text{PR}}{D + E + \text{PR}} \quad (7\text{--}4)$$

where

E = the market value of common equity.

D = the market value of debt.

PR = the market value of preferred stock.

t = the firm's marginal tax rate.

A portion of interest paid on borrowed funds is recoverable by the firm because of the tax deductibility of interest. For every dollar of taxable income, the tax owed is equal to $1 multiplied by t. Since each dollar of interest expense reduces taxable income by an equivalent amount, the actual cost of borrowing is reduced by $(1 - t)$. Therefore, the after-tax cost of borrowed funds to the firm is estimated by multiplying the pretax interest rate, i, by $(1 - t)$.

Note that the weights, $[E/(D + E + \text{PR})]$, $[D/(D + E + \text{PR})]$, and $[\text{PR}/(D + E + \text{PR})]$, associated with the cost of equity, preferred stock, and debt, respectively, reflect the firm's target capital structure or capitalization. These are targets, in that they represent the capital structure the firm hopes to achieve and sustain in the future. The actual market value of equity, preferred stock, and debt as a percentage of total capital (i.e., $D + E + \text{PF}$) may differ from the target. Market values rather than book values are used, because the WACC measures the cost of issuing debt, preferred stock, and equity securities. Such securities are issued at market and not book value. The use of the target capital structure avoids the circular reasoning associated with using the current market value of equity to construct the weighted average cost of capital, which is subsequently used to estimate the firm's current market value.

Non-interest-bearing liabilities, such as accounts payable, are excluded from the estimation of the cost of capital for the firm to simplify the calculation of WACC. Although such liabilities have an associated cost of capital, it is assumed to have been included in the price paid for the products and services whose purchase generated the accounts payable. Consequently, the cost of capital associated with these types of liabilities affects cash flow through its inclusion in operating expenses (e.g., the price paid for raw materials). Estimates of industry betas, cost of equity, and WACC are provided by firms such as Ibbotson Associates, Value Line, Standard and Poor's, and Bloomberg. Such estimates provide a "reality check," since they serve as a benchmark against which the analyst's estimate of a firm's WACC can be compared.

Analyzing Risk

Risk is the degree of uncertainty associated with the outcome of an investment. It takes into consideration the probability of a loss as well as a gain on an investment. Risk consists of a **diversifiable risk** (also called *nonsystematic risk*) component, such as strikes, defaulting on debt repayments, and lawsuits, and a **nondiversifiable risk** (also called *systematic risk*) component, such as inflation and war, that affects all firms. **Beta** (β) is a measure of nondiversifiable risk or the extent to which a firm's (or asset's) return changes because of a change in the market's return. An **equity beta** is a measure of the risk of a stock's financial returns, compared with the risk of the financial returns to the general stock market, which in turn is affected by the overall economy. When $\beta = 1$, the stock is as risky as the general market; when $\beta < 1$, the stock is less risky; whereas when $\beta > 1$, the stock is more risky than the overall stock market. Investors are compensated only for risk that cannot be eliminated through diversification (i.e., systematic or nondiversifiable risk).

The value of β may be estimated by applying linear regression analysis to explain the relationship between the dependent variable, stock returns (R_j), and the independent variable, market returns (R_m). The intercept or constant term (also referred to as the *alpha*) of the regression equation provides a measure of R_j's performance compared with the general market during the regression period. In Wall Street parlance, alpha is the premium (or discount) an investment earns above (below) some performance benchmark, such as the S&P 500 index.

The following equations express R_j as defined by the linear regression model and R_j as defined by the CAPM:

$$R_j = \alpha + \beta R_m \text{ (regression equation formulation)}$$
$$R_j = R_f + \beta(R_m - R_f)$$
$$= R_f + \beta R_m - \beta$$
$$= R_f(1 - \beta) + \beta R_m \text{ (CAPM formulation)}$$

If α is greater than $R_f(1 - \beta)$, this particular stock's rate of return, R_j, performed better than would have been expected using the CAPM during the same time period. The cumulative daily difference between α (i.e., actual returns) and $R_f(1 - \beta)$ (i.e., expected returns) is a measure of "abnormal" or "excess return" for a specified number of days around the announcement of a transaction. Abnormal returns often are calculated in empirical "event" studies to assess the impact of acquisitions on the shareholder value of both acquiring and target firms (Exhibit 7–1).

In practice, betas are frequently estimated using the most recent three to five years of data. Consequently, betas are sensitive to the time period selected. The relationship between the overall market and a specific firm's equity beta may change significantly if

---

Exhibit 7–1 Estimating β for Publicly Traded Companies

Calculate the return to the *j*th company's shareholders as capital gains (or losses) plus dividends paid during the period adjusted for stock splits that take place in the current period. This adjusted return should then be regressed against a similarly defined return for a broadly defined market index:

$$\frac{SP(P_{jt} - P_{jt-1}) + SP \text{ Dividends}}{P_{jt-1}} = \alpha + \beta \frac{(S\&P500_t - S\&P500_{t-1}) + \text{Dividends}}{S\&P500_{t-1}}$$

Notes:

1. SP is equal to 2 for a two-for-one stock split, 1.5 for a three-for-two split, 1.33 for a four-for-three split, and so forth. If we do not adjust for stock splits that may take place in the current period, the stock price drops, resulting in a negative return.

2. Betas for public companies can be obtained from estimation services such as Value Line, Standard & Poor's, Ibbotson, and Bloomberg. Betas for private companies can be obtained by substituting a beta for comparable publicly traded companies (see Chapter 10).

a large sector of stocks that make up the overall index increase or decrease substantially. While over longer periods of time the impact on beta is problematic, it may be quite substantial over relatively short time periods. For example, the telecommunications, media, and technology sectors of the S&P 500 rose dramatically in the late 1990s and fell precipitously after 2000. Other sectors were relatively unaffected by the wild fluctuations in the overall market, resulting in a reduction in their betas. To illustrate, the equity beta for electric utilities fell to 0.1 (reflecting its reduced correlation with the overall stock market) in 2001 from 0.6 in 1998, falsely suggesting that the sector's risk and, in turn, cost of equity had declined (Annema and Goedhart, 2006).

Effects of Leverage on Beta

In the absence of debt, the equity β measures the volatility of a firm's financial return to changes in the general equity market's overall financial return. Such a measure of volatility or risk is called an *unlevered* β, denoted β_u. The unlevered beta of a firm is determined by the type of industry in which the firm operates (e.g., cyclical or noncyclical) and its operating leverage. Operating leverage is measured by the ratio of a firm's fixed costs to total costs. Firms having high operating leverage have higher operating earnings (i.e., earnings before interest and taxes, or EBIT) volatility than a firm producing a comparable product with lower operating leverage. For example, a firm, whose fixed expenses constitute 60 percent of total costs, would experience a 60 percent improvement in operating profit for each dollar of incremental revenue in excess of their fixed costs. Operating leverage is difficult to estimate unless an analyst has access to such financial details as variable and fixed expenses, which are often aggregated on a firm's public financial statements.

The presence of debt magnifies financial returns to shareholders. A firm whose total capital consists of $1 million in equity generates a return to shareholders of 10 percent if its after-tax profits are $100,000. A firm whose total capital is $1 million, consisting of $500,000 in equity and $500,000 in debt, achieves a 20 percent return ($100,000/$500,000) to shareholders given the same level of after-tax profits. If the firm experienced an after-tax loss of $100,000, the firm's financial return would be a negative 10 percent; if the firm had borrowed $500,000, the return would have been a negative 20 percent. Consequently, the presence of financial leverage (i.e., debt) increases the variability of the firm's financial performance.

The impact of financial leverage on the firm suggests that an increase in financial leverage would increase a firm's equity beta, assuming nothing else changes to offset the effects of the financial leverage. The obligation of the firm to pay interest and principal on the debt increases the variance of the firm's net income and financial returns. In general, financial leverage would boost financial returns during periods of economic prosperity and depress returns during economic slowdowns.

Risk to shareholders may also be viewed as the likelihood that they are going to receive a sufficiently large enough share of the firm's future cash flow to meet or exceed their minimum required returns. Increasing leverage raises the level of risk or uncertainty and increases the value of a firm's equity β, because interest payments represent fixed expenses that must be paid before any payments can be made to shareholders. However, this is offset somewhat by the tax deductibility of interest, which reduces shareholder risk by increasing after-tax cash flow available for shareholders. The reduction in the firm's tax liability due to the tax deductibility of interest is often referred as a ***tax shield***. A beta reflecting the effects of both the increased volatility of earnings and the tax shield or shelter effects of leverage is called a *leveraged* or *levered* β, denoted β_l. If a firm's stockholders bear all the risk from operating and financial leverage and interest paid on debt is tax deductible, these relationships can be expressed as follows for a firm whose debt-to-equity ratio is denoted by D/E:

$$\beta_l = \beta_u[1 + (1 - t)(D/E)] \tag{7–5}$$

and

$$\beta_u = \frac{\beta_l}{1 + (1 - t)(D/E)} \tag{7–6}$$

In summary, β_u is determined by the characteristics of the industry in which the firm competes and its degree of operating leverage. The value of β_l is determined by the same factors and the degree of the firm's financial leverage. Using equations (7–5) and (7–6), a firm's capital structure can be analyzed by estimating its cost of equity at different levels of leverage as follows:

1. Determine a firm's current equity β^* and $(D/E)^*$.
2. Estimate the unlevered beta:

$$\beta_u = \beta^*/[1 + (1 - t)(D/E)^*]$$

3. Estimate the firm's levered beta:

$$\beta_l = \beta_u[1 + (1 - t)(D/E)^{**}]$$

4. Estimate the firm's cost of equity for the new levered beta

where β^* and $(D/E)^*$ represent the firm's current equity beta and the market value of the firm's debt-to-equity ratio before additional borrowing takes place. The term $(D/E)^{**}$ is the firm's debt-to-equity ratio after additional borrowing occurs, and t is the firm's marginal tax rate.

In an acquisition, an acquirer may anticipate increasing significantly the target firm's current debt level following closing. The target's unlevered beta should be adjusted to estimate its degree of risk with no debt. As such, the unlevered beta approximates the target's operating risk before any debt financing. A levered beta is then estimated, reflecting the postacquisition borrowing. See Exhibit 7–2.

Exhibit 7–2 Calculating a Levered β

Assume a target's current or preacquisition debt-to-equity ratio is 25 percent, current levered beta is 1.05, and marginal tax rate is 0.4. After the acquisition, the debt-to-equity ratio is expected to rise to 75 percent. What is the target's postacquisition levered beta?

Answer: Using equations (7–5) and (7–6),

$$\beta_u = \frac{\beta_l^*}{1 + (1 - t)(D/E)^*} = \frac{1.05}{1 + (1 - 0.4)(0.25)} = 0.91$$

$$\beta_l = \beta_u[1 + (1 - t)(D/E)^{**}] = 0.91[1 + (1 - 0.4)(0.75)] = 1.32$$

where $(D/E)^*$ and $(D/E)^{**}$ are the target's pre- and postacquisition debt-to-equity ratios and β_l^* is the target's preacquisition equity beta.

Continued

> ## Exhibit 7–2 Calculating a Levered β — Cont'd
>
> Notes:
>
> 1. Corporate income at the time of publication of this book is generally taxed by the U.S. government at rates that begin at 15 percent and go up to 35 percent on taxable income of $10 million or more. A typical state tax rate is 5 percent. Since larger firms generally pay approximately 40 percent of their pretax income in taxes, this is the marginal rate used in examples in this textbook.
> 2. Simply adjusting the target firm's current levered beta for the incremental borrowing implicitly assumes that the impact on beta would be linear or additive, which may not be the case, particularly if the target is already highly levered. Consequently, it is appropriate to calculate the unlevered beta before estimating the new levered beta.

The definition of a levered beta in equation (7–5) is based on the assumption that all market risk is borne by equity investors (i.e., the firm's debt beta, β_{debt}, is 0). In reality, some portion of a firm's risk is borne by bondholders, particularly for more highly leveraged firms, where economic volatility can affect investor perceptions of the probability of default. An alternative formulation of equation (7–5) may be used to estimate the levered beta by apportioning some of the firm's market risk to lenders. Rewriting equation (7–5) by multiplying through by β_u then assuming some portion of the firm's risk is borne by the firm's bondholders (i.e., $\beta_{debt} > 0$) provides the following:

$$\beta_r = \beta_u + (\beta_u - \beta_{debt})(1 - t)(D/E) \qquad (7\text{–}7)$$

and

$$\beta_r = \beta_u[1 + (1 - t)(D/E)] - \beta_{debt}(1 - t)(D/E) \qquad (7\text{–}8)$$

Debt betas are based on the credit rating of the bond and are estimated by regressing each rating category of debt (e.g., AA, A, etc.) against returns on a market index composed of debt issues. Debt betas for investment grade issues are relatively small at 0.17, but they can be significantly higher for non-investment-grade debt issues (Brealey and Myers, 2003). The levered betas estimated using equation (7–7) or (7–8) is lower than those estimated using equation (7–5).

Calculating Free Cash Flows (D/E)

Free cash flow to the firm is more frequently used for valuation than free cash flow to equity investors or equity cash flow for several reasons. First, it is simpler to apply, because it does not require estimation of principal repayments and preferred dividends. FCFF is most helpful when a firm's level of future borrowing is expected to change substantially during the forecast period, thereby making the estimation of debt repayment schedules difficult. However, the estimation starting with EBIT does require assumptions about the acquiring firm's target debt-to-equity ratio to calculate the firm's weighted average cost of capital. Second, it can be applied to the valuation of the total firm or individual operations. Free cash flow to equity investors is best suited for special situations such as for valuing financial institutions and leveraged buyouts.

Free Cash Flow to the Firm (Enterprise Cash Flow)

Free cash flow to the firm represents cash available to satisfy all investors holding claims against the firm's resources. These claim holders include common stockholders, lenders, and preferred stockholders. This definition assumes implicitly that a firm can always get financing if it can generate sufficient future cash flows to meet or exceed minimum returns required by investors and lenders. Consequently, enterprise cash flow is calculated before the sources of financing are determined and, as such, is not affected by the firm's financial structure. However, the financial structure may affect the firm's cost of capital and, therefore, its value due to the potential for bankruptcy (see Chapter 16 for a more detailed discussion of financial distress).

FCFF can be calculated by adjusting operating earnings before interest and taxes (EBIT) as follows:

$$\text{FCFF} = \text{EBIT}(1 - \text{Tax rate}) + \text{Depreciation and amortization} \\ - \text{Gross capital expenditures} - \Delta \text{Net working capital} \quad (7\text{–}9)$$

Under this definition, only cash flow from operating and investment activities, but not financing activities, is included. The tax rate refers to the firm's marginal tax rate. Net working capital is defined as current operating assets less cash balances in excess of the amount required to meet normal operating requirements less current operating liabilities.

Selecting the Right Tax Rate

The calculation of after-tax operating income requires multiplying EBIT by either a firm's marginal tax rate (i.e., the rate paid on each additional dollar of earnings) or effective tax rate (i.e., taxes due divided by taxable income). The effective tax rate is calculated from actual taxes paid, based on accounting statements prepared for tax reporting purposes. The marginal tax rate in the United States is usually 40 percent, 35 percent for federal taxes for firms earning more than $10 million and 5 percent for most state and local taxes, and it is typically used to calculate after-tax income on the firm's accounting statements prepared for financial reporting purposes (e.g., to the public). The effective rate is usually less than the marginal tax rate and varies among firms due to the use of tax credits to reduce actual taxes paid or accelerated depreciation to defer the payment of taxes. While favorable tax rules may temporarily reduce the effective tax rate, it is unlikely to be permanently reduced. Once tax credits have been used and the ability to further defer taxes exhausted, the effective rate can exceed the marginal rate at some point in the future. For example, if future capital expenditures are expected to diminish, projected depreciation also declines and the difference between taxable income reported on financial statements and that recorded for tax purposes shrinks, requiring firms to eventually pay deferred taxes. How deferred taxes can be treated for valuation purposes is discussed later in this chapter.

Because favorable tax treatment cannot be extended indefinitely, the marginal tax rate should be used if taxable income is going to be multiplied by the same tax rate during each future period. However, an effective tax rate lower than the marginal rate may be used in the early years of cash flow projections and eventually increased to the firm's marginal tax rate, if the analyst has reason to believe that the current favorable tax treatment is likely to continue into the foreseeable future. However, whatever the analyst chooses to do with respect to the selection of a tax rate, it is critical to use the marginal rate in calculating after-tax operating income in perpetuity. Otherwise, the implicit assumption is that taxes can be deferred indefinitely.

For many firms, future operating lease commitments are substantial. As noted later in this chapter, future lease commitments should be discounted to the present at the firm's pretax cost of debt (i), since leasing equipment represents an alternative to borrowing to buying a piece of equipment, and its present value should be included in the firm's total debt outstanding. Once operating leases are converted to debt, operating lease expense (OLE_{EXP}) must be added to EBIT, because it is a financial expense and EBIT represents operating income before such expenses. Lease payments include both an interest expense component to reflect the cost of borrowing and a depreciation component to reflect the anticipated decline in the value of the leased asset. An estimate of depreciation expense associated with the leased asset (DEP_{OL}) then must be deducted from EBIT, as is depreciation expense associated with other fixed assets owned by the firm, to calculate an "adjusted" EBIT ($EBIT_{ADJ}$). The $EBIT_{ADJ}$ then is used to calculate free cash flow to the firm. EBIT may be adjusted as follows:

$$EBIT_{ADJ} = EBIT + OLE_{EXP} - DEP_{OL} \qquad (7\text{--}10)$$

Alternatively, adjusted EBIT may be calculated by adding back an estimate of the interest rate, i, on the debt value of the operating lease (PV_{OL}). By adding back an estimate of the interest expense associated with the present value of the leased asset, we are viewing the leased asset from the liability side of the firm's balance sheet in terms of how it is being financed. Depreciation expense associated with the leased assets need not be deducted from EBIT if they are assumed to represent the principal portion of the debt being repaid, because free cash flow to the firm is calculated before how the expenditure will be financed is considered. Consequently, adjusted EBIT ($EBIT_{ADJ}$) also may be shown as follows:

$$EBIT_{ADJ} = EBIT + PV_{OL} \times i \qquad (7\text{--}11)$$

Free Cash Flow to Equity Investors (Equity Cash Flow)

Free cash flow to equity investors is the cash flow remaining for returning cash through dividends or share repurchases to current common equity investors or for reinvesting in the firm after the firm satisfies all obligations (Damodaran, 2002). These obligations include debt payments, capital expenditures, changes in net working capital, and preferred dividend payments. Income and cash-flow statements differ in terms of how they treat depreciation. The income statement amortizes the cost of equipment over its depreciable accounting life and deducts depreciation expense from revenue. Depreciation is an expense item that does not actually involve an outlay of cash by the firm. Although depreciation reduces income, it does not reduce cash flow. In calculating FCFE, depreciation is added back to net income. FCFE can be defined as follows:

$$
\begin{aligned}
FCFE = \ & \text{Net income} + \text{Depreciation and amortization} \\
& - \text{Gross capital expenditures} - \Delta\,\text{Net working capital} \\
& + \text{New debt and equity issues} - \text{Principal repayments} \\
& - \text{Preferred dividends}
\end{aligned}
\qquad (7\text{--}12)
$$

Other expense items that do not involve an actual expenditure of cash that should be added back to net income in the calculation of free cash flow include the amortization expense associated with such items as capitalized software and changes in deferred taxes. Deferred taxes may arise if a company uses accelerated depreciation for tax purposes but straight-line depreciation for reporting its financial statements to investors.

Exhibit 7–3 summarizes the key elements of enterprise, equation (7–9), and equity cash flow, equation (7–12). The example delineates the difference between equity and

Exhibit 7–3 Defining Valuation Cash Flows: Equity and Enterprise Cash Flows

Free Cash Flow to Equity: (Equity Cash Flow: FCFE)

FCFE = {Net income + Depreciation and amortization – Δ Working capital}[1] – Gross capital expenditures[2] + {New preferred equity issues – Preferred dividends + New debt issues – Principal repayments}[3]

→ Cash flow (after taxes, debt repayments and new debt issues, preferred dividends, preferred equity issues, and all reinvestment requirements) available for paying dividends on or repurchasing common equity.

Free Cash Flow to the Firm: (Enterprise Cash Flow: FCFF)

FCFF = {Earnings before interest and taxes (1 – Tax RATE) + Depreciation and amortization – Δ Working capital}[1] – Gross capital expenditures[2]

→ Cash flow (after taxes and reinvestment requirements) available to repay lenders or pay common and preferred dividends and repurchase equity.

[1]Cash from operating activities.
[2]Cash from investing activities.
[3]Cash from financing activities.

---

enterprise cash flow. The former reflects operating, investment, and financing activities, whereas the latter excludes cash flow from financing activities. Using actual data on Intel Corporation, Exhibit 7–4 reconciles the differences between conventional cash flow statements based on GAAP and valuation cash flow. Note that, in calculating enterprise cash flow, the analyst adds after-tax interest expense to net income to get cash available for both equity investors and lenders. While total interest expense is deducted from operating profits in calculating net income, the actual cash outlay is only the after-tax portion of interest expense, since interest expense is deductible for tax purposes. In contrast, in calculating equity cash flow or cash flow available for common shareholders, we must subtract after-tax interest expense from enterprise cash flow, since this is paid to lenders and therefore is not available to common shareholders.

Applying Income or Discounted Cash-Flow Methods

DCF methods provide estimates of the economic value of a company (i.e., the firm's ability to generate future cash flows), which do not need to be adjusted if the intent is to acquire a small portion of the company. However, if the intention is to obtain a controlling interest in the firm, a control premium must be added to the estimated economic value of the firm to determine the purchase price. A controlling interest generally is considered more valuable to an investor than a minority interest, because the investor has the right to final approval of important decisions affecting the business. Minority investment positions often are subject to discounts because of their lack of control. How control premiums and minority discounts are determined is discussed in detail in Chapter 10.

Exhibit 7–4 Reconciling GAAP-Based and Valuation Cash Flows

Standardized Intel Corporation GAAP Consolidated Statement of Cash Flows

	2007
Year ended December 31 ($millions)	
Cash and cash equivalents, beginning of year	$7,970
Cash Flows Provided by (used for) Operating Activities	
Net Income	3,117
Adjustments Reconciling Net Income to Net Cash from Operating Activities	
Nonoperating losses (gains) (e.g., net gain on sales of equity investments)	372
Depreciation and amortization expense	5,344
Long-term operating accruals (e.g., net gain on retirements of plant/equip.; deferred taxes)	681
Net change in operating working capital	(405)
Net cash provided by operating activities	9,109
Cash Flows Provided by (used for) Investing Activities	
Net (investment) liquidation in long-term operating assets (e.g., additions to plant/equip.)	(5,765)
Net cash used for investing activities	(5,765)
Cash Flows Provided by (used for) Financing Activities	
Net debt (repayments) or issuance	(64)
Net stock (repurchase) or issuance	(3,333)
Dividends paid on common stock	(533)
Net cash used for financing activities:	(3,930)
Net Increase (decrease) in cash and cash equivalents	($586)
Cash and cash equivalents, end of year	$7,384

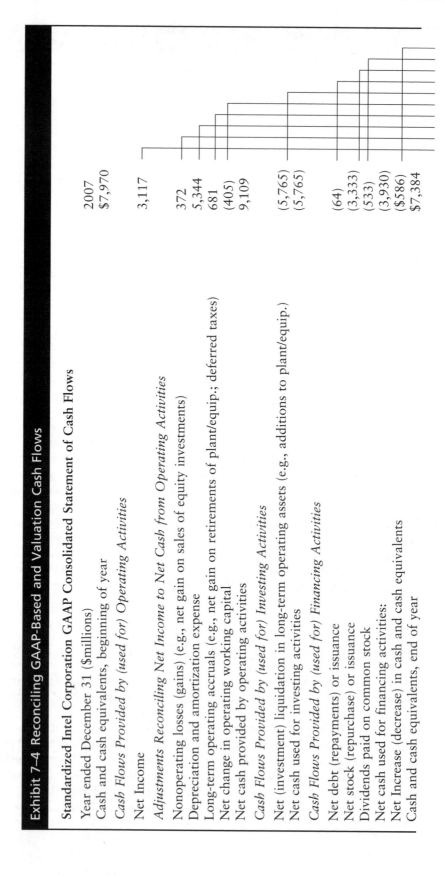

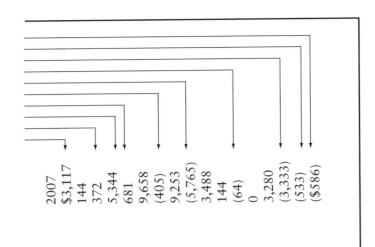

Intel Corporation Consolidated Valuation Cash Flows

Year ended December 31 ($millions)	2007
Net income	$3,117
After-tax net interest expense (income)	144
Nonoperating losses (gains)	372
Depreciation and amortization expense	5,344
Long-term operating accruals	681
Operating cash flow before operating working capital	9,658
Net change in operating working capital	(405)
Operating cash flow before investment in long-term operating assets	9,253
Net (investment in) or liquidation of operating long-term assets	(5,765)
Free cash flow to the firm (enterprise cash flow)	3,488
After-tax net interest expense (income)[1]	144
Net debt (repayment) or issuance	(64)
Dividends on preferred stock	0
Free cash flow available to equity (equity cash flow)	3,280
Net Stock (repurchase) or issuance	(3,333)
Dividends on common stock	(533)
Net increase (decrease) in cash and cash equivalents	($586)

[1]Subtracted from free cash flow to the firm in calculating free cash flow available to equity investors.

The various DCF models used to value acquisitions are special cases of the conventional capital budgeting process. Capital budgeting is the process for evaluating and comparing alternative investment opportunities to ensure the best long-term financial return for the firm. In the capital budgeting process, cash flows are projected over the expected life of the project and discounted to the present at the firm's cost of capital. M&As can be viewed as one of the alternative investment opportunities available to the firm.

Enterprise Discounted Cash-Flow Model (Enterprise or FCFF Method)

The enterprise valuation, or FCFF, approach discounts the after-tax free cash flow available to the firm from operations at the weighted average cost of capital to obtain the estimated enterprise value. The firm's estimated common equity value then is determined by subtracting the market value of the firm's debt and other investor claims on cash flow, such as preferred stock from the enterprise value. The estimate of equity derived in this manner equals the value of equity determined by discounting the cash flow available to the firm's shareholders at the cost of equity. This assumes that the discount rates used to calculate the present values of the firm's debt and other investor claims on cash flow reflect the risk associated with each cash-flow stream.

The enterprise approach is consistent with the capital budgeting process in that value is determined independently of how the business is financed. Moreover, it can be applied to individual business units or the parent firm in precisely the same manner. For example, for multiunit businesses, the value of equity using this method is equal to the sum of the value of each business unit owned by the parent firm plus excess cash balances less the present value of corporate overhead, debt, and preferred stock.

Equity Discounted Cash-Flow Model (Equity or FCFE Method)

The equity valuation, or FCFE approach, discounts the after-tax cash flows available to the firm's shareholders at the cost of equity. This approach is used primarily in special situations, such as for valuing highly leveraged transactions in which the capital structure is changing frequently and for financial services firms in which the cost of capital for various operations within the firm may be very difficult to estimate. For example, a retail commercial banking operation typically finances its operations using interest-free checking accounts. Determining the actual cost of acquiring such accounts is often quite arbitrary. By focusing on FCFE, the analyst needs to estimate only the financial services firm's cost of equity. The enterprise or FCFF method and the equity or FCFE method are illustrated in the following sections of this chapter using three cash-flow growth scenarios: zero growth, constant growth, and variable growth rates.

Zero-Growth Valuation Model

This model assumes that free cash flow is constant in perpetuity. The value of the firm at time zero (P_0) is the discounted or capitalized value of its annual cash flow. In this instance (Exhibit 7–5), the discount rate and the capitalization rate are the same (see Chapter 10 for a more detailed discussion of the difference between discount and capitalization rates). The present value of a constant payment in perpetuity is a diminishing series, because it represents the sum of the PVs for each future period. Each PV is smaller than the preceding one; therefore, the perpetuity is a diminishing series that converges to 1 divided by the discount rate. The subscript FCFF or FCFE refers to the definition of cash flow used in the valuation.

$$P_{0,FCFF} = FCFF_0/WACC \qquad (7-13)$$

where $FCFF_0$ is free cash flow to the firm at time 0 and WACC is the cost of capital.

$$P_{0,FCFF} = FCFF_0/k_e \qquad (7-14)$$

where $FCFE_0$ is free cash flow to common equity at time 0 and k_e is the cost of equity.

While simplistic, the zero-growth method has the advantage of being easily understood by all parties involved in a negotiation. Moreover, there is little evidence that more complex methods provide consistently better valuation estimates, due to their greater requirement for more inputs and assumptions. This method is commonly used to value commercial real estate transactions.

Exhibit 7–5 Zero-Growth Valuation Model

1. What is the enterprise value of a firm whose annual $FCFF_0$ of $1 million is expected to remain constant in perpetuity and whose cost of capital is 12 percent—see equation (7–13)?

$$P_{0,FCFF} = \$1/0.12 = \$8.3 \text{ million}$$

2. Calculate the weighted average cost of capital, see equation (7–4), and the enterprise value of a firm whose capital structure consists only of common equity and debt. The firm desires to limit its debt to 30 percent of total capital.[1] The firm's marginal tax rate is 0.4 and its beta is 1.5. The corporate bond rate is 8 percent and the 10-year U.S. Treasury bond rate is 5 percent. The expected annual return on stocks is 10 percent. Annual FCFF is expected to remain at $4 million indefinitely:

$$k_e = 0.05 + 1.5\,(0.10 - 0.05) = 0.125 = 12.5\%$$
$$WACC = 0.125 \times 0.7 + 0.08 \times (1 - 0.4) \times 0.3$$
$$= 0.088 + 0.014 = 0.102 = 10.2\%$$

$$P_{0,FCFF} = \$4/0.102 = \$39.2 \text{ million}$$

---

[1]If you know only a firm's debt-to-equity ratio (*D/E*), it is possible to calculate the firm's debt-to-total capital ratio [*D/(D + E)*] by dividing (*D/E*) by (1 + *D/E*), since *D/(D + E)* = (*D/E*)/(1 + *D/E*) = [(*D/E*)/(*D + E*)/*E*] = (*D/E*) × [*E/(D + E)*] = *D/(D + E)*.

Constant-Growth Valuation Model

The constant growth model (also known as the Gordon growth model) is applicable for firms in mature markets, characterized by a moderate and somewhat predictable rate of growth. Examples of such industries include beverages, cosmetics, personal care products, prepared foods, and cleaning products. To project growth rates, extrapolate the industry's growth rate over the past 5–10 years. The constant-growth model assumes that cash flow grows at a constant rate, g, which is less than the required return, k_e. The assumption that k_e is greater than g is a necessary mathematical condition for deriving the model (Gitman, 2008). In this model, next year's cash flow to the firm ($FCFF_1$), or the first year of the forecast period, is expected to grow at the constant rate of growth, g. Therefore, $FCFF_1 = FCFF_0\,(1 + g)$:

$$P_{0,FCFF} = FCFF_1/(WACC - g) \tag{7-15}$$

$$P_{0,FCFF} = FCFE_1/(k_e - g), \tag{7-16}$$

where $FCFE_1 = FCFE_0 (1 + g)$. Note that the zero growth model is a special case of the constant growth model for which g equals 0.

This simple valuation model also provides a means of estimating the risk premium component of the cost of equity as an alternative to relying on historical information, as is done in the capital asset pricing model. This model was developed originally to estimate the value of stocks in the current period (P_0) using the level of expected dividends (d_1) in the next period. This formulation provides an estimate of the present value of dividends growing at a constant rate forever. Assuming the stock market values stocks correctly and we know P_0, d_1, and g, we can estimate k_e. Therefore,

and

$$P_0 = d_1/(k_e - g)$$

$$k_e = (d_1/P_0) + g \tag{7-17}$$

This expression suggests that increases in a firm's share price relative to earnings (i.e., increases in the firm's P/E ratio) lowers the firm's required return on acquisitions financed by issuing stock. This explains why high levels of M&A activity frequently coincide with booming stock markets. For example, if d_1 is $1, g is 10 percent, and $P_0 = $10, k_e is 20 percent. However, if P_0 increases to $20 and g and d_1 remain the same, k_e declines to 15 percent. Note that an increase in P_0 without an increase in earnings growth, g, implies a higher P/E ratio for the firm. See Exhibit 7–6 for an illustration of how to apply the constant-growth model.

Variable-Growth Valuation Model

Many firms experience periods of high growth followed by a period of slower, more stable growth. Examples of such industries include cellular phones, personal computers, and cable TV. Firms within such industries routinely experience double-digit growth rates for periods of 5–10 years because of low penetration of these markets in the early years of the product's life cycle. As the market becomes saturated, growth inevitably slows to a

---

Exhibit 7–6 Constant-Growth Model

1. Determine the enterprise value of a firm whose projected free cash flow to the firm next year is $1 million, WACC is 12 percent, and expected annual cash-flow growth rate is 6 percent, see equation (7–15):

$$P_{0,FCFF} = \$1/(0.12 - 0.06) = \$16.7 \text{ million}$$

2. Estimate the equity value of a firm whose cost of equity is 15 percent and whose free cash flow to equity holders in the prior year is projected to grow 20 percent this year then at a constant 10 percent annual rate thereafter. The prior year's free cash flow to equity holders is $2 million, see equation (7–16):

$$P_{0,FFCE} = [(\$2.0 \times 1.2)(1.1)]/(0.15 - 0.10) = \$52.8 \text{ million}$$

rate more in line with the overall growth of the economy or the general population. The PV of such firms is equal to the sum of the PV of the discounted cash flows during the high-growth period plus the discounted value of the cash flows generated during the stable growth period. In capital budgeting terms, the discounted value of the cash flows generated during the stable growth period is called the *terminal, sustainable, horizon,* or *continuing growth value.*

The terminal value may be estimated using the constant-growth model. Free cash flow during the first year beyond the *n*th or final year of the forecast period, $FCFF_{n+1}$, is divided by the difference between the assumed cost of capital and the expected cash-flow growth rate beyond the *n*th year forecast period. The terminal value is the value in the *n*th year of all future cash flows beyond the *n*th year. Consequently, to convert the terminal value to its value in the current year, it is necessary to discount the terminal value, applying the discount rate used to convert the *n*th year value to a present value.

Although there are other ways to calculate the terminal value, the use of the constant growth model provides consistency in estimating the value of the firm created beyond the end of the forecast period. It enables the application of discounted cash-flow methodology in estimating value during both the variable and stable growth periods. However, the selection of the earnings growth rate and cost of capital must be done very carefully. Small changes in assumptions can result in dramatic swings in the terminal value and, therefore, in the valuation of the firm. Table 7–2 illustrates the sensitivity of a terminal value of $1 million to different spreads between the cost of capital and the stable growth rate. Note that, using the constant-growth model formula, the terminal value declines dramatically as the spread between the cost of capital and expected stable growth for cash flow increases by 1 percentage point.

Note that the expected stable growth rate in cash flow can be either positive or negative. The use of a positive growth rate suggests that the firm is expected to last forever. This assumption is not as bizarre as it may seem, because companies frequently are acquired or liquidated, thereby enabling the investors to earn a premium on their investment or recover at least some portion of their original investment. In contrast, the use of a negative growth rate implies that the firm's value will shrink each year until it eventually disappears. Therefore, we may use the constant-growth model to estimate the terminal value of a firm we do not expect to last forever.

Terminal values can be estimated in numerous other ways. The price-to-earnings, price-to-cash flow, or price-to-book techniques value the target as if it were sold at the end of a specific number of years. At the end of the forecast period, the terminal year's earnings, cash flow, or book value is projected and multiplied by a P/E, cash flow, or book value multiple believed to be appropriate for that year. The terminal value also may be estimated by assuming the firm's cash flow or earnings in the last year of the forecast period will continue in perpetuity. This is equivalent to the zero-growth valuation model discussed previously.

Table 7–2 Impact of Changes in Assumptions on a Terminal Value of $1 Million

Difference between Cost of Capital and Cash-Flow Growth Rate	Terminal Value ($ millions)
3%	33.3[1]
4%	25.0
5%	20.0
6%	16.7
7%	14.3

[1]$1.0/0.03.

Using the definition of free cash flow to the firm, $P_{0,\text{FCFF}}$ can be estimated using the variable growth model as follows:

$$P_{0,\text{FCFF}} = \sum_{t=1}^{n} \frac{\text{FCFF}_0 \times (1+g_t)^t}{1 + \text{WACC}} + \frac{P_n}{(1 + \text{WACC})^n} \qquad (7\text{--}18)$$

where

$$P_n = \frac{\text{FCFF}_n \times (1+g_m)}{\text{WACC}_m - g_m}$$

FCFF_0 = FCFF in year 0.
WACC = weighted average cost of capital through year n.
WACC_m = cost of capital assumed beyond year n (Note: $\text{WACC} > \text{WACC}_m$).
P_n = value of the firm at the end of year n (terminal value).
g_t = growth rate through year n.
g_m = stabilized or long-term growth rate beyond year n (Note: $g_t > g_m$).

Similarly, the value of the firm to equity investors can be estimated using equation (7–18). However, projected free cash flows to equity (FCFE) are discounted using the firm's cost of equity. See Exhibit 7–7 for an illustration of when and how to apply the variable growth model.

Supernormal "High-Flyer" Growth Valuation Model

Some companies display initial periods of what could be described as hypergrowth, followed by an extended period of rapid growth, before stabilizing at a more normal and sustainable growth rate. Initial public offerings and startup companies may follow this

---

Exhibit 7–7 Variable Growth Valuation Model

Estimate the enterprise value of a firm (P_0) whose free cash flow is projected to grow at a compound annual average rate of 35 percent for the next five years. Growth then is expected to slow to a more normal 5 percent annual growth rate. The current year's cash flow to the firm is $4 million. The firm's weighted average cost of capital during the high-growth period is 18 percent and 12 percent beyond the fifth year, as growth stabilizes. The firm's cash in excess of normal operating balances is assumed to be 0. Therefore, the present value of cash flows during the high-growth forecast period are as follows:

$$\text{PV}_{t-5} = \frac{4.00 \times 1.35}{1.18} + \frac{4.00 \times 1.35^2}{1.18^2} + \frac{4.00 \times 1.35^3}{1.18^3} + \frac{4.00 \times 1.35^4}{1.18^4} + \frac{4.00 \times 1.35^5}{1.18^5}$$

$$= 5.40/1.18 + 7.29/1.18^2 + 9.84/1.18^3 + 13.29/1.18^4 + 17.93/1.18^5$$

$$= 4.58 + 5.24 + 5.99 + 6.85 + 7.84 = 30.50$$

Calculation of the terminal value is as follows:

$$\text{PV}_5 = \frac{[(4.00 \times 1.35^5) \times 1.05]/(0.12 - 0.05)}{1.18^5} = \frac{18.83/0.07}{2.29} = 117.60$$

$$P_{0,\text{FCFF}} = \text{PV}_{t-5} + \text{PV}_5 = 30.50 + 117.60 = 148.10$$

model. This pattern reflects growth over their initially small revenue base, the introduction of a new product, or the sale of an existing product to a new or underserved customer group. Calculating the discounted cash flows is computationally more difficult for firms expected to grow for multiple periods, each of whose growth rates differ, before assuming a more normal long-term growth rate. Because each period's growth rate differs, the cost of capital in each period differs. Consequently, each year's cash flows must be discounted by the "cumulative cost of capital" from prior years. A more detailed discussion of this method is provided on the CD-ROM accompanying this book in the file folder entitled "Example of Supernormal Growth Model."

Determining Growth Rates

Projected growth rates for sales, profit, cash flow, or other financial variables can be readily calculated based on the historical experience of the firm or of the industry. See the document entitled "Primer on Cash Flow Forecasting" found on the CD-ROM accompanying this text for a discussion of how to apply regression analysis to projecting a firm's cash flow.

Duration of High-Growth Period

Intuition suggests that the length of the high-growth period should be longer when the current growth rate of a firm's cash flow is much higher than the stable growth rate. This is particularly true when the high-growth firm has a relatively small market share and there is little reason to believe that its growth rate will slow in the foreseeable future. For example, if the industry is expected to grow at 5 percent annually and the target firm, which has only a negligible market share, is growing at three times that rate, it may be appropriate to assume a high-growth period of 5–10 years. Moreover, if the terminal value constitutes a substantial percentage (e.g., three fourths) of total PV, the annual forecast period should be extended beyond the customary 5 years to at least 10 years. The extension of the time period reduces the impact of the terminal value in determining the market value of the firm.

According to Palepu, Healy, and Bernard (2004, pp. 10-2 and 10-3), historical evidence shows that sales and profitability tend to revert to normal levels within 5–10 years. Between 1979 and 1998, sales growth for the average U.S. firm reverted to an average of 7–9 percent within five years. Firms with initial growth rates in excess of 50 percent experience a decline to about 6 percent growth within three years; those with the lowest initial growth rate tend to increase to about 8 percent by year 5. This suggests that the conventional use of a 5–10-year annual forecast before calculating a terminal value makes sense.

More sophisticated forecasts of growth rates involve an analysis of the firm's customer base. Annual revenue projections are made for each customer or product and summed to provide an estimate of aggregate revenue. A product or service's life cycle (see Chapter 4) is a useful tool for making such projections. In some industries, a product's life cycle may be a matter of months (e.g., software) or years (e.g., an automobile). This information is readily available by examining the launch dates of new products and services in an industry in publications provided by the industry's trade associations. By determining where the firm's products are in their life cycle, the analyst can project annual unit volume by product.

Stable or Sustainable Growth Rate

The stable growth rate generally is going to be less than or equal to the overall growth rate of the industry in which the firm competes or the general economy. Stable growth rates in excess of these levels implicitly assume that the firm's cash flow eventually will exceed that of its industry or the general economy. Similarly, for multinational firms, the stable growth rate should not exceed the projected growth rate for the world economy or a particular region of the world.

High-growth rates usually are associated with increased levels of uncertainty. In applying discounted cash-flow methodology, the discount rate reflects risk. Consequently, the discount rate during the high-growth (i.e., less predictable) period or periods should generally be higher than during the stable growth period. For example, a high-growth firm may have a beta significantly above 1. However, when the growth rate becomes stable, it is reasonable to assume that the beta should approximate 1. A reasonable approximation of the discount rate to be used during the stable growth period is to adopt the industry average cost of equity or weighted average cost of capital.

Determining the Appropriate Discount Rate

The question of whether to use the acquirer's or the target's cost of capital to value the target's cash flows often arises in valuations. The appropriate discount rate is generally the target's cost of capital if the acquirer is merging with a higher-risk business, resulting in an increase in the cost of capital of the combined firms. However, either the acquirer's or the target's cost of capital may be used if the two firms are equally risky and based in the same country.

Valuing Firms under Special Situations

Firms with Temporary Problems

When cash flow is temporarily depressed due to strikes, litigation, warranty claims, employee severance, or other one-time events, it is generally safe to assume that cash flow will recover in the near term. One solution is to base projections on cash flow prior to the one-time event. Alternatively, actual cash flow could be adjusted for the one-time event by adding back the pretax reduction in operating profits of the one-time event and recalculating after-tax profits. If the cost of the one-time event is not displayed on the firm's financial statements, it is necessary to compare each expense item as a percent of sales in the current year with the prior year. Any expense items that look abnormally high should be "normalized" by applying an average ratio from prior years to the current year's sales. Alternatively, the analyst could use the prior year's operating margin to estimate the current year's operating income.

Firms with Longer-Term Problems

Deteriorating cash flow may be symptomatic of a longer-term deterioration in the firm's competitive position due to poor strategic decisions having been made by management. Under such circumstances, the analyst must decide whether the firm is likely to recover and how long it would take to restore the firm's former competitive position. The answer to such questions requires the identification of the cause of the firm's competitive problems. Firms with competitive problems often are less profitable than key competitors or the average firm in the industry. Therefore, the firm's recovery can be included in the forecast of cash flows by allowing its operating profit margin to increase gradually to the industry average or the level of the industry's most competitive firm. The speed of the adjustment depends on the firm's problems. For example, replacing outmoded equipment or back office processing systems may be done more quickly than workforce reductions when the labor force is unionized or if the firm's products are obsolete.

Cyclical Firms

The projected cash flows of firms in highly cyclical industries can be distorted, depending on where the firm is in its business cycle (i.e., the up and down movement of the economy). The most straightforward solution is to project cash flows based on an average historical growth rate during a prior full business cycle for the firm.

Valuing a Firm's Debt and Other Obligations

In the previous sections, we estimated the equity value of the firm by discounting the projected free cash flows to equity investors by the firm's cost of equity. Alternatively, the equity value may be estimated by subtracting the market or present value of the firm's debt and other obligations from the firm's estimated enterprise value. This section discusses how to value long-term debt, operating leases, and deferred tax liabilities to illustrate this alternative means of estimating the equity value of the firm.

Determining the Market Value of Long-Term Debt

In some instances, the analyst may not know the exact principal repayment schedule for the target firm's debt. To determine the market value of debt, treat the book value of all the firm's debt as a conventional coupon bond, in which interest is paid annually or semi-annually and the principal is repaid at maturity. The coupon is the interest on all of the firm's debt, and the principal at maturity is a weighted average of the maturity of all of the debt outstanding. The weighted average principal at maturity is the sum of the amount of debt outstanding for each maturity date multiplied by its share of total debt outstanding. The estimated current market value of the debt then is calculated as the sum of the annuity value of the interest expense per period plus the present value of the principal (see Exhibit 7–8). The only debt that must be valued is the debt outstanding on the valuation date. Future borrowing is irrelevant if we assume that cash inflows generated from investments financed with future borrowings are sufficient to satisfy interest and principal payments associated with these borrowings.

Exhibit 7–8 Estimating the Market Value of a Firm's Debt

According to its 10K report, Gromax, Inc. has two debt issues outstanding, with a total book value of $220 million. Annual interest expense on the two issues totals $20 million. The first issue, whose current book value is $120 million, matures at the end of 5 years; the second issue, whose book value is $100 million, matures in 10 years. The weighted average maturity of the two issues is 7.27 years, that is, $5 \times (120/220) + 10 \times (100/220)$. The current cost of debt maturing in 7–10 years is 8.5 percent. The firm's 10K also shows that the firm has annual operating lease expenses of $2.1, $2.2, $2.3, and $5.0 million in the fourth year and beyond (the 10K indicated the firm's cumulative value in the fourth year and beyond to be $5.0 million). For our purposes, we may assume that the $5.0 million is paid in the fourth year. What is the total market value of the firm's total long-term debt, including conventional debt and operating leases (dollars in millions)?

Continued

Exhibit 7–8 Estimating the Market Value of a Firm's Debt — Cont'd

$$PV_D \text{ (Long-term debt)}^1 = \$20 \times \frac{1 - [1/(1.085)^{7.27}]}{1.085} + \frac{\$220}{(1.085)^{7.27}}$$

$$= \$105.27 + \$121.55 = \$226.82$$

$$PV_{OL} \text{(Operating leases)} = \frac{\$2.1}{1.085} + \frac{\$2.2}{(1.085)^2} + \frac{\$2.3}{(1.085)^3} + \frac{\$5.0}{(1.085)^4}$$

$$= \$1.94 + \$1.87 + \$1.80 + \$3.61 = \$9.22$$

$$PV_{TD} \text{ (Total debt)} = \$226.82 + \$9.22 = \$236.04$$

[1]The present value of debt is calculated using the PV of an annuity formula for 7.27 years and an 8.5-percent interest rate plus the PV of the principal repayment at the end of 7.27 years. Alternatively, rather than using the actual formulas, a present value interest factor annuity table and a present value interest factor table could have been used to calculate the PV of debt.

Determining the Market Value of Operating Leases

Both capital and operating leases also should be counted as outstanding debt of the firm. When a lease is classified as a capital lease, the present value of the lease expenses is treated as debt. Interest is imputed on this amount that corresponds to debt of comparable risk and maturity. This imputed interest is shown on the income statement. Although operating lease expenses are treated as operating expenses on the income statement, they are not counted as part of debt on the balance sheet for financial reporting purposes. For valuation purposes, operating leases should be included in debt because failure to meet lease payments results in the loss of the leased asset, which contributes to the generation of operating cash flows. Future operating lease expenses are shown in financial statement footnotes. These future expenses should be discounted at an interest rate comparable to current bank lending rates for unsecured assets. The discount rate may be approximated using the firm's current pretax cost of debt. The pretax cost of debt is used to reflect the market rate of interest lessors would charge the firm. If future operating lease expenses are not available, the analyst can approximate the principal amount of the operating leases by discounting the current year's operating lease payment as a perpetuity using the firm's cost of debt (see Exhibit 7–8).

Capitalizing operating lease payments requires that the cost of capital incorporate the effects of this source of financing and operating income be adjusted to reflect lease expenses, as discussed earlier in this chapter. Finally, to calculate the value of the firm's equity, both debt and the capitalized value of operating leases must be subtracted from the estimated enterprise value of the firm (see Exhibit 7–9).

Determining the Cash Impact of Deferred Taxes

A firm that actually pays $40,000 in income taxes based on its tax accounting statements but would have paid $60,000 in taxes on the income reported on its financial statements must show $20,000 in deferred income tax liabilities on its balance sheet. Deferred tax liabilities measure income taxes saved in the current year. Such differences between when the tax provision is recorded and when taxes are actually paid represent temporary

Exhibit 7–9 Estimating Common Equity Value by Deducting the Market Value of Debt and Other Non-Equity Claims from the Enterprise Value

Operating income, depreciation, working capital, and capital spending are expected to grow 10 percent annually during the next five years and 5 percent thereafter. The book value of the firm's debt is $300 million, with annual interest expense of $25 million and term to maturity of four years. The debt is a conventional "interest only" note with a repayment of principal at maturity. The firm's annual preferred dividend expense is $20 million. The prevailing market yield on preferred stock issued by similar firms is 11 percent. The firm does not have any operating leases, and pension and healthcare obligations are fully funded. The firm's current cost of debt is 10 percent. The firm's weighted average cost of capital is 12 percent. Because of tax deferrals, the firm's current effective tax rate of 25 percent is expected to remain at that level for the next five years. The firm's current deferred tax liability is $300 million. The projected deferred tax liability at the end of the fifth year is expected to be paid off in ten equal amounts during the following decade. The firm's marginal tax rate is 40 percent and will be applied to the calculation of the terminal value. What is the value of the firm to common equity investors?

Financial Data

	Current Year	Year 1	Year 2	Year 3	Year 4	Year 5
EBIT	$200.0	$220.0	$242.0	$266.2	$292.8	$322.1
EBIT(1-t)	$150.0	$165.0	$181.5	$199.7	$219.6	$241.6
Depreciation (Straight line)	$8.0	$8.8	$9.7	$10.7	$11.7	$12.9
Δ Net Working Capital	$30.0	$33.0	$36.3	$39.9	$43.9	$48.3
Gross Capital Spending	$40.0	$44.0	$48.4	$53.2	$58.6	$64.4
Free Cash Flow to the Firm	$88.0	$96.8	$106.5	$117.3	$128.8	$141.8
Present Value		$86.40	$84.9	$83.5	$81.85	$80.46
Terminal Value[1]	$795.48					
Total Firm Value	$1,212.59					

Solution

$$PV_D \ (Debt)^2 = \$25 \times \frac{[1 - (1/(1.10)^4)]}{.10} + \frac{\$300}{1.10^4}$$

$$= \$25(3.17) + \$300(.683)$$
$$= \$79.25 + \$204.90$$
$$= \$284.15$$

PV_{PFD} (Preferred Stock)^3 = $20/.11 = $181.82

Deferred Tax Liability by end of Year 5 = $300 + ($220 + $242 + $266.2
                                                          +$292.8 + $322.1)(.40 − .25)
                                                = $501.47

Continued

Exhibit 7–9 Estimating Common Equity Value by Deducting the Market Value of Debt and Other Non-Equity Claims from the Enterprise Value — Cont'd

$$PV_{DEF} \text{ (Deferred Taxes)} = \left\{ (\$501.47/10) \times \frac{[(1 - (1/(1.12)^{10})]}{.12} \right\} /(1.12)^5$$

$$= \$(50.15 \times 5.65)/1.76$$

$$= \$160.99$$

$$P_{0,FCFE} = \$1,212.59 - \$284.15 - \$181.82 - \$160.99 = \$585.63$$

Notes:

[1]The terminal value reflects the recalculation of the fifth year after tax operating income using the marginal tax rate of 40% and applying the constant growth model.

[2]The present value of debt is calculated using the PV of an annuity for 4 years and a 10% interest rate plus the PV of the principal repayment at the end of 4 years. Alternatively, rather than using the actual formulas, a present value interest factor annuity table and a present value interest factor table could have been used to calculate the PV of debt. The firm's current cost of debt of 10% is higher than the implied interest rate of 8% ($25/$300) on the loan currently on the firm's books. This suggests that the market rate of interest has increased since the firm borrowed the $300 million "interest only" note.

[3]The market value of preferred stock (PV_{PFD}) is equal to the preferred dividend divided by the cost of preferred stock.

---

timing differences. The impact of timing differences can be incorporated into present value calculations by including the future impact of all factors affecting a firm's effective tax rate in projections of the individual components of cash flow (Copeland et al., 2005). Alternatively, the analyst could make assumptions about how the firm's effective tax rate will change and value current and future deferred tax liabilities separately from the calculation of the present value of the projected cash flows. As such, the impact on free cash flow of a change in deferred taxes can be approximated by the difference between a firm's marginal and effective tax rate multiplied by the firm's operating income before interest and taxes.

The author recommends calculating the impact of deferred taxes separately, since deferred tax liabilities can arise from many sources, such as uncollectible accounts receivable, warranties, options expensing, pensions, leases, net operating losses, depreciable assets, inventories, installment receivables, and intangible drilling and development costs (Stickney, Brown, and Wahlen, 2007). Which factors contribute the most to changes in deferred tax liabilities depends on the type of business. For example, the impact of timing differences due to depreciation is likely to be greater for manufacturing than for service or high-tech firms. Companies paying more in taxes than shown as an expense on their income statements show an asset item called a *deferred tax asset* on their balance sheets as a measure of the future tax savings the firm will realize.

The greatest challenge with deferred tax liabilities is determining when they are likely to come due. Such a liability is likely only when the firm's growth rate slows. The choice of tax rate in estimating future after-tax operating income has different implications under alternative scenarios. The first scenario assumes after-tax operating income is calculated using the firm's current effective tax rate indefinitely, implicitly assuming that the firm's deferred tax liabilities will never have to be repaid. In the second scenario, the analyst estimates after-tax operating income using the firm's marginal rate indefinitely, which implies that the firm cannot defer taxes beyond the current period. In the final scenario, the analyst assumes the effective tax rate is applicable for a specific number of years (for sake of discussion, assume five years) before reverting to the firm's marginal tax rate. The use of the effective tax rate for five years increases the deferred tax liability to the firm during that period, as long as the effective rate is below the marginal rate. The deferred tax liability at the end of the fifth year can be estimated by adding to the current cumulated deferred tax liability the incremental liability for each of the next five years. This incremental liability is the sum of projected EBIT times the difference between the marginal and effective tax rates. Assuming tax payments on the deferred tax liability at the end of the fifth year will be spread equally over the following 10 years, the present value of the tax payments during that 10-year period is then estimated and discounted back to the current period (see Exhibit 7–9).

Adjusting Firm Value for Nonequity Claims

Once we have estimated the market value of a firm's debt and other obligations, such as deferred tax liabilities, the firm's common equity value can be estimated by deducting the market value of the firm's non-common equity claims from the enterprise value of the firm (see Exhibit 7–9). Non-common equity claims could include the market value of the firm's debt and preferred stock, as well as the present value of expected liabilities from lawsuits, unfunded pension and health-care obligations, and deferred tax liabilities.

Valuing Nonoperating Assets

Other assets not directly used in operating the firm also may contribute to the value of the firm. Examples of such nonoperating assets include cash in excess of normal operating requirements, investments in other firms, and unused or underutilized assets. The value of such assets should be added to the value of the discounted cash flows from operating assets to determine the total value of the firm.

Cash and Marketable Securities

Cash and short-term marketable securities, held in excess of the target firm's minimum operating cash balance, represent value that should be added to the present value of net operating assets to determine the value of the firm. If a firm has large cash balances in excess of those required to satisfy operating requirements at the beginning of the forecast period, the valuation approach outlined in this chapter, which focuses on cash flow generated from net operating assets, assumes implicitly that it is treated as a one-time cash payout to the target firm's shareholders. Otherwise, the excess cash should be added to the present value of the firm's operating cash flows. On an ongoing basis, excess cash flows have already been taken into account in the valuation of cash flows from operating assets. Projected excess cash flows are assumed implicitly to be paid out to shareholders either as dividends or share repurchases. Note that the estimate of the firm's minimum cash balance should be used in calculating net working capital in determining free cash flow from operations.

What constitutes the minimum cash balance depends on the firm's cash conversion cycle. This cycle reflects the firm's tendency to build inventory, sell products on credit, and later collect accounts receivable. The delay between the investment of cash in the production of goods and the eventual receipt of cash inherent in this process reflects the amount of cash tied up in working capital. The length of time cash is committed to working capital can be estimated as the sum of the firm's inventory conversion period plus the receivables collection period less the payables deferral period.

The inventory conversion period is the average length of time in days required to produce and sell finished goods. The receivables collection period is the average length of time in days required to collect receivables. The payables deferral period is the average length of time in days between the purchase of and payment for materials and labor. To finance this investment in working capital, a firm must maintain a minimum cash balance equal to the average number of days its cash is tied up in working capital times the average dollar value of sales per day. The inventory conversion and receivables collection periods are calculated by dividing the dollar value of inventory and receivables by average sales per day. The payments deferral period is estimated by dividing the dollar value of payables by the firm's average cost of sales per day. See Exhibit 7–10 for an illustration of how to estimate minimum and excess cash balances.

Exhibit 7–10 Estimating Minimum and Excess Cash Balance

Prototype Incorporated's current inventory, accounts receivable, and accounts payable are valued at $14,000,000, $6,500,000, $6,000,000, respectively. Projected sales and cost of sales for the coming year total $100,000,000 and $75,000,000, respectively. Moreover, the value of the firm's current cash and short-term marketable securities is $21,433,000. What minimum cash balance should the firm maintain? What is the firm's current excess cash balance?

$$\frac{\$14,000,000}{\$100,000,000/365} + \frac{\$6,500,000}{\$100,000,000/365} - \frac{\$6,000,000}{75,000,000/365} =$$

$$51.1 \text{ days} \quad + \quad 23.7 \text{ days} \quad - \quad 29.2 \text{ days} \quad = 45.6 \text{ days}$$

Minimum Cash Balance = 45.6 days × $100,000,000/365 = $12,493,151
Excess Cash Balances = $21,433,000 − $12,493,151 = $8,939,849

While excess cash balances should be added to the present value of operating assets, any cash deficiency should be subtracted from the value of operating assets to determine the value of the firm. This reduction in the value reflects the need for the acquirer to invest additional working capital to make up any deficiency.

The method illustrated in Exhibit 7–10 may not work for firms that manage working capital aggressively, so that receivables and inventory are very low relative to payables. An alternative is to compare the firm's cash and marketable securities as a percent of revenue with the industry average. If the firm's cash balance exceeds the industry average, the firm has excess cash balances, assuming there are no excess cash balances for the average firm in the industry. For example, if the industry average cash holdings as a percent of annual revenue is 5 percent and the target firm has 8 percent, the target holds excess cash equal to 3 percent (8% − 5%) of its annual revenue.

Investments in Other Firms

Many target firms have investments in other firms. These investments generally have value and need to be included in any valuation of the target's nonoperating assets. Such investments, for financial reporting purposes, may be classified as minority passive investments, minority active investments, or majority investments. These investments

Table 7–3   Investments in Other Firms

% Ownership of Firm	Accounting Treatment	Valuation Methodology
Minority, passive investments (investment <20% of other firm)	Assets held to maturity are carried at book value with interest/dividends shown on income statement Investments available for sale are carried at market value with unrealized gains/losses included as equity and not as income Trading investments are shown at market value	For investments recorded on investing firm's balance sheet at book value 1. Value of firm in which investment is held 2. Multiply the firm's value by the proportionate share held by the investing firm to determine the investment's value 3. Add the investment's value to the value of the investing firm's nonoperating assets 4. For investments recorded at market value, add to the investing firm's nonoperating assets
Minority, active investments, equity method (investment is between 20% and 50% of the other firm's value)	Initial acquisition value is adjusted for proportional share of subsequent profits/losses Market value estimated on liquidation and gain/loss reported on income statement	1. Value the firms in which the investments are held 2. Estimate the investing firm's proportionate share 3. Add the resulting estimated value to the investing firm's nonoperating asset
Majority investments (investment >50% of other firm's value)	Requires consolidation of both firms' balance sheets[1] Shares held by other investors are shown as a minority interest on the liability side of the balance sheet	If the parent owns 100% of the subsidiary, value the two on a consolidated basis[2] If the parent owns less than 100%, value the parent and subsidiary on a consolidated basis and subtract the market value of minority interest shown as a liability on the parent's balance sheet[3]

[1]A firm may be required to consolidate both firms' balance sheets even if it owns less than 50%, if its ownership position gives it effective control of the other firm.

[2]If the subsidiary is in a different industry from the parent, a weighted average cost of capital reflecting the different costs of capital for the two businesses should be used to discount cash flows generated by the consolidated businesses.

[3]If a subsidiary is valued at $500 million and the parent owns 75 percent of the subsidiary, the value of the subsidiary to the parent is $375 million (i.e., $500 million − 0.25 × $500 million, to reflect the value owned by minority shareholders).

need to be valued individually and added to the present value of the firm's operating assets to determine the total value of the firm. Table 7–3 describes their accounting treatment and valuation methodology.

Unutilized and Undervalued Assets

Real estate on the books of the target firm at historical cost may have an actual market value substantially in excess of the value stated on the balance sheet. In other cases, a firm may have more assets on hand to satisfy future obligations than it currently might need. An illustration of such an asset would be an overfunded pension fund. Examples of intangible assets include patents, copyrights, licenses, and trade names. Intangible assets, so-called intellectual property, are becoming increasingly important for high-technology and service firms. Intangible assets may represent significant sources of value on a target firm's balance sheet. However, they tend to be difficult to value. A study by Chan, Lakonishok, and Sougiannis (1999) provides evidence that the value of intangible spending, such as R&D expenditures, is indeed factored into a firm's current share price. Despite this evidence, it is doubtful that intellectual property rights, such as patents, which a firm may hold but not currently use, contribute anything to the firm's current share price. In the absence of a predictable cash flow stream, their value may be estimated using the Black–Scholes model or the cost of developing comparable inventions or technologies. The Black–Scholes model is discussed in Chapter 8.

Patents

How patents are valued depends on whether they have current applications, are linked to existing products or services, or can be grouped and treated as a single patent portfolio.

Many firms have patents for which no current application within the firm has yet been identified. However, the patent may have value to an external party. Before closing, the buyer and seller may negotiate a value for a patent that has not yet been licensed to a third party based on the cash flows that can reasonably be expected to be generated over its future life. In cases where the patent has been licensed to third parties, the valuation is based on the expected future royalties to be received from licensing the patent over its remaining life.

When a patent is linked to a specific product, it is normally valued based on the "avoided cost" method. This method uses after-tax market-based royalty rates paid on comparable patents multiplied by the projected future stream of revenue from the products whose production depends on the patent discounted to its present value at the cost of capital.

Products and services often depend on a number of patents. This makes it exceedingly difficult to determine the amount of the cash flow generated by the sale of the products or services to be allocated to each patent. In this case, the patents are grouped together as a single portfolio and valued as a group using a single royalty rate applied to a declining percentage of the company's future revenue. The declining percentage of revenue reflects the likely diminishing value of the patents with the passage of time. This cash flow stream is then discounted to its present value.

Trademarks and Service Marks

A trademark is the right to use a name associated with a company, product, or concept. A service mark is the right to use an image associated with a company, product, or concept. Trademarks and service marks have recognition value. Examples include Bayer Aspirin and Kellogg's Corn Flakes. Name recognition reflects the firm's longevity, cumulative advertising expenditures, the overall effectiveness of its marketing programs, and the consistency of perceived product quality. The cost avoidance approach, the PV of projected license fees, or the use of recent transactions can be helpful in estimating a trademark's value.

The underlying assumption in applying the cost-avoidance approach to the valuation of trademarks and service marks is that cumulative advertising and promotion campaigns build brand recognition. The initial outlays for promotional campaigns are the largest and tend to decline as a percentage of sales over time as the brand becomes more recognizable. Consequently, the valuation of a trademark associated with a specific product or business involves multiplying projected revenues by a declining percentage to reflect the reduced level of spending, as a percentage of sales, required to maintain brand recognition. These projected expenditures then are adjusted for taxes (because marketing expenses are tax deductible) and discounted to the present at the acquiring firm's cost of capital.

Companies may license the right to use a trademark or service mark. The acquiring company may apply the license rate required to obtain the rights to comparable trademarks and service marks to a percentage of the cash flows that reasonably can be expected to be generated by selling the products or services under the licensed trademark or service mark. The resulting cash flows then are discounted to the present using the acquirer's cost of capital. Alternatively, a value may be determined by examining recent outright purchases of comparable trademarks or, in the case of the Internet, Web addresses or domain names. See Fernandez (2002) for an excellent discussion of alternative ways to value brands, service marks, and trade names.

Overfunded Pension Plans

Defined benefit pension plans require firms to accumulate an amount of financial assets to enable them to satisfy estimated future employee pension payments. During periods of rising stock markets, such as during the 1990s, firms with defined benefit pension plans routinely accumulated assets in excess of the amount required to meet expected obligations. As owners of the firm, shareholders have the legal right to these excess assets. In practice, if such funds are liquidated and paid out to shareholders, the firm has to pay taxes on the pretax value of these excess assets. Therefore, the after-tax value of such funds may be added to the present value of projected operating cash flows.

Adjusting the Target Firm's Equity Value for Nonoperating Assets, Debt, and Other Obligations

$$\mathrm{PV_{FCFE}} = \mathrm{PV_{FCFF}} \text{ (including terminal value)} - \mathrm{PV_D} + \mathrm{PV_{NOA}} - \mathrm{PV_{NOL}} \qquad (7\text{--}19)$$

where

$\mathrm{PV_{FCFE}}$ = PV of free cash flow to equity investors (i.e., equity value)

$\mathrm{PV_{FCFF}}$ = PV of free cash flow to the firm (i.e., enterprise value)

$\mathrm{PV_D}$ = PV of long-term debt

$\mathrm{PV_{NOA}}$ = PV of nonoperating assets

$\mathrm{PV_{NOL}}$ = PV of nonoperating liabilities

The value of the firm's equity may be understated or overstated if the estimated value provided by discounting operating cash flows is not adjusted for the existence of nonoperating assets and liabilities assumed by the acquirer. It is also important to include miscellaneous nonoperating cash outflows and inflows (if applicable) experienced on or about the closing date of the transaction in adjusting the firm's equity. These outflows include such items as investment banking, legal, and consulting fees. Cash inflows at closing could result from the sale of target assets to a third party negotiated prior to closing but not consummated until the closing date. Note that factors such as severance expenses and synergy-related items should already have been included in the valuation of operating cash flows. Exhibit 7–11 shows how firm value is adjusted for these factors to provide a more accurate estimate of the equity value of the firm.

Exhibit 7-11 Adjusting Firm Value

A target firm (which sells washing machines) initially is estimated to have a present value (PV) of annual cash flows for the next five years of $20 million and a terminal value of $34 million. The target firm has two million common shares outstanding, and the current market value of its long-term debt (LTD) and preferred stock are $12 million and $1 million, respectively. The present value of current and future deferred tax liabilities is $4 million. The acquirer is willing to assume these obligations. During due diligence, it is determined that the firm currently has excess operating cash balances of $2 million, unused patents that could be used by the acquiring firm with a present value of $3 million, and unused commercial property with an estimated market value of $3 million. Because the current commercial real estate market is depressed, it is expected to take 18–24 months to dispose of the property. Consequently, the PV of the surplus property is estimated to be $2.5 million.

It also is discovered that a product line consisting of several different models of washing machines was discontinued the year before due to quality problems. Potential warranty claims are estimated to have a PV of $2 million. Potential litigation with several customers could result in judgments against the target firm in the range of $5 to $10 million over the next four years. The PV of these judgments is $7 million. Note that the cash-flow impact of pending warranty claims and potential litigation expenses were not included in the projection of the target firm's future cash flows. Investment banking and other closing related cash outlays total $8 million. Calculate the adjusted equity value of the target firm as well as the equity value per share.

Table 7-4   Assets and Liabilities of Firm

Impact of Operating and Nonoperating Assets and Liabilities	($Millions)
PV of Cash Flow from Operations – Next 5 Years	20.0
PV of Terminal Value	34.0
Total PV (From Operating Cash Flows)	54.0
Plus Non-Operating Assets	
Excess Operating Cash & Short-Term Marketable Securities	2.0
PV of Surplus Commercial Property	2.5
PV of Unused Process Patents (Valued as a Call Option)	3.0
Total Non-Operating Assets	7.5
Less Miscellaneous Non-Operating Cash Outlays	8.0
Total Value of the Firm (Before Non-Operating Liabilities)	53.5
Less Non-Operating and Non-LTD Liabilities (not included in operating cash flows)	
PV of Warranty Claims	2.0
PV of Judgments	7.0
Total Non-Operating Liabilities	9.0
Less Long-Term Debt (including operating leases in present value terms)	12.0
Less: Preferred Stock	1.0
Less: PV of Deferred Tax Liabilities	4.0
Adjusted Equity Value	27.5
Adjusted Equity Value Per Share	$13.75

Things to Remember

The CAPM is used widely to estimate the cost of equity. The pretax cost of debt for non-rated firms can best be approximated by comparison with similar firms whose debt is rated by the major credit-rating agencies or by looking at interest rates on debt currently on the firm's books. Weights for the firm's cost of capital should be calculated using market rather than book values and reflecting the acquiring firm's target capital structure.

FCFF, free cash flow to the firm or enterprise cash flow, reflects cash from operating and investing activities. FCFE, free cash flow to equity investors or equity cash flow, includes cash from operating, investing, and financing activities. The present value of FCFF often is referred to as the *enterprise value* of the firm. Valuation based on FCFE commonly is called the *equity method* or *equity value*. Equity value also can be calculated by deducting the market value of the target firm's long-term debt (including operating leases expressed in present value terms) from the enterprise value.

Discounted cash-flow valuation is highly sensitive to the choice of the discount rate as well as the magnitude and timing of future cash flows. In the constant-growth model, free cash flow to the firm is expected to grow at a constant rate. In the variable-growth model, cash flow exhibits both high- and a stable-growth periods. The total PV in this case represents the sum of the discounted value of the cash flows over both periods.

The target firm's equity value should be adjusted for the value of nonoperating assets and liabilities not on the balance sheet. This value also is called the *adjusted equity value*. Thus, the equity value of the target firm is ultimately the sum of the firm's net operating cash flows, terminal value, and nonoperating assets less the current market value of long-term debt and nonoperating liabilities not fully reflected on the balance sheet.

Chapter Discussion Questions

7–1. What is the significance of the weighted average cost of capital? How is it calculated? Do the weights reflect the firm's actual or target debt-to-total-capital ratio? Explain your answer.

7–2. What does a firm's β measure? What is the difference between an unlevered and levered β? Why is this distinction significant?

7–3. Under what circumstances is it important to adjust the capital asset pricing model for firm size? Why?

7–4. What are the primary differences between FCFE and FCFF?

7–5. Explain the conditions under which it makes most sense to use the zero-growth and constant-growth DCF models. Be specific.

7–6. Which DCF valuation methods require the estimation of a terminal value? Why?

7–7. Do small changes in the assumptions pertaining to the estimation of the terminal value have a significant impact on the calculation of the total value of the target firm? If so, why?

7–8. How would you estimate the equity value of a firm if you knew its enterprise value and the present value of all nonoperating assets, nonoperating liabilities, and long-term debt?

7–9. Why is it important to distinguish between operating and nonoperating assets and liabilities when valuing a firm? Be specific.

7–10. Explain how you would value a patent under the following situations: a patent with no current application, a patent linked to an existing product, and a patent portfolio.

Answers to these Chapter Discussion Questions are available in the Online Instructor's Manual for instructors using this book.

Chapter Practice Problems and Answers

7–11. ABC Incorporated shares are currently trading for $32 per share. The firm has 1.13 billion shares outstanding. In addition, the market value of the firm's outstanding debt is $2 billion. The 10-year Treasury bond rate is 6.25 percent. ABC has an outstanding credit record and earned a AAA rating from the major credit rating agencies. The current interest rate on AAA corporate bonds is 6.45 percent. The historical risk premium over the risk-free rate of return is 5.5 percentage points. The firm's beta is estimated to be 1.1 and its marginal tax rate, including federal, state, and local taxes, is 40 percent.

a. What is the cost of equity?

b. What is the after-tax cost of debt?

c. What is the weighted average cost of capital?

Answers:

a. 12.3 percent.

b. 3.9 percent.

c. 11.9 percent.

7–12. HiFlyer Corporation does not currently have any debt. Its tax rate is 0.4 and its unlevered beta is estimated by examining comparable companies to be 2.0. The 10-year bond rate is 6.25 percent, and the historical risk premium over the risk-free rate is 5.5 percent. Next year, HiFlyer expects to borrow up to 75 percent of its equity value to fund future growth.

a. Calculate the firm's current cost of equity.

b. Estimate the firm's cost of equity after it increases its leverage to 75 percent of equity.

Answers:

a. 17.25 percent.

b. 22.2 percent.

7–13. Abbreviated financial statements are given for Fletcher Corporation in Table 7–5.
Yearend working capital in 2000 was $160 million and the firm's marginal tax rate was 40 percent in both 2001 and 2002. Estimate the following for 2001 and 2002:

a. Free cash flow to equity.

b. Free cash flow to the firm.

Answers:

a. $16.4 million in 2001 and –$26.8 million in 2002.

b. $44.4 million in 2001 and $1.2 million in 2002.

Table 7–5 Abbreviated Financial Statements for the Firm in Problem 7–13

	2001	2002
Revenues	$600.0	$690.0
Operating expenses	520.0	600.0
Depreciation	16.0	18.0
Earnings before interest and taxes	64.0	72.0
Less interest expense	5.0	5.0
Less taxes	23.6	26.8
Equals net income	35.4	40.2
Addendum:		
Yearend working capital	150	200
Principal repayment	25.0	25.0
Capital expenditures	20	10

7–14. In 2002, No Growth Incorporated had operating income before interest and taxes of $220 million. The firm was expected to generate this level of operating income indefinitely. The firm had depreciation expense of $10 million that year. Capital spending totaled $20 million during 2002. At the end of 2001 and 2002, working capital totaled $70 million and $80 million, respectively. The firm's combined marginal state, local, and federal tax rate was 40 percent, and its debt outstanding had a market value of $1.2 billion. The 10-year Treasury bond rate is 5 percent, and the borrowing rate for companies exhibiting levels of creditworthiness similar to No Growth is 7 percent. The historical risk premium for stocks over the risk-free rate of return is 5.5 percent. No Growth's beta was estimated to be 1.0. The firm had 2.5 million common shares outstanding at the end of 2002. No Growth's target debt-to-total-capital ratio is 30 percent.

a. Estimate free cash flow to the firm in 2002.

b. Estimate the firm's weighted average cost of capital.

c. Estimate the enterprise value of the firm (i.e., includes the value of equity and debt) at the end of 2002, assuming that it will generate the value of free cash flow estimated in (a) indefinitely.

d. Estimate the value of the equity of the firm at the end of 2002.

e. Estimate the value per share at the end of 2002.

Answers:

a. $112 million.

b. 8.61 percent.

c. $1,300.8 million.

d. $100.8 million.

e. $40.33.

7–15. Carlisle Enterprises, a specialty pharmaceutical manufacturer, has been losing market share for three years, since several key patents expired. Free cash flow to the firm is expected to decline rapidly as more competitive generic drugs enter the market. Projected cash flows for the next five years are $8.5 million, $7.0 million, $5.0 million, $2.0 million, and $.5 million. Cash flow after the fifth year is expected to be negligible. The firm's board has decided to sell the firm to a larger pharmaceutical company interested in using Carlisle's product offering to fill gaps in its own product offering until it can develop similar drugs. Carlisle's weighted average cost of capital is 15 percent. What purchase price must Carlisle obtain to earn its cost of capital?

Answer: $17.4 million.

7–16. Ergo Unlimited's current year's free cash flow to equity is $10 million. It is projected to grow at 20 percent per year for the next five years. It is expected to grow at a more modest 5 percent beyond the fifth year. The firm estimates that its cost of equity is 12 percent during the next 5 years then will drop to 10 percent beyond the fifth year, as the business matures. Estimate the firm's current market value.

Answer: $358.3 million.

7–17. In the year in which it intends to go public, a firm has revenues of $20 million and net income after taxes of $2 million. The firm has no debt, and revenue is expected to grow at 20 percent annually for the next five years and 5 percent annually thereafter. Net profit margins are expected to remain constant throughout. Annual capital expenditures equal depreciation, and the change in working capital requirements is minimal. The average beta of a publicly traded company in this industry is 1.50 and the average debt-to-equity ratio is 20 percent. The firm is managed conservatively and will not borrow through the foreseeable future. The Treasury bond rate is 6 percent, and the tax rate is 40 percent. The normal spread between the return on stocks and the risk-free rate of return is believed to be 5.5 percent. Reflecting the slower growth rate in the sixth year and beyond, the discount rate is expected to decline to the industry average cost of capital of 10.4 percent. Estimate the value of the firm's equity.

Answer: $63.41 million.

7–18. The information in Table 7–6 is available for two different common stocks: Company A and Company B.

Table 7–6 Information on the Stocks in Problem 7–18

	Company A	Company B
Free cash flow per share at the end of year 1	$1.00	$5.00
Growth rate in cash flow per share	8%	4%
Beta	1.3	.8
Risk-free return	7%	7%
Expected return on all stocks	13.5%	13.5%

a. Estimate the cost of equity for each firm.

b. Assume that the companies' growth rates will continue at the same rate indefinitely. Estimate the per share value of each company's common stock.

Answers:

a. Company A = 15.45 percent; Company B = 12.2 percent.

b. Company A = $13.42; Company B = $61.

7–19. You have been asked to estimate the beta of a high-technology firm that has three divisions with the characteristics shown in Table 7–7.

Table 7–7 Characteristics of the Firm in Problem 7–19

Division	Beta	Market Value ($ millions)
Personal computers	1.60	100
Software	2.00	150
Computer mainframes	1.20	250

    a. What is the beta of the equity of the firm?

    b. If the risk-free return is 5 percent and the spread between the return on all stocks is 5.5 percent, estimate the cost of equity for the software division.

    c. What is the cost of equity for the entire firm?

    d. Free cash flow to equity investors in the current year (FCFE) for the entire firm is $7.4 million and for the software division is $3.1 million. If the total firm and the software division are expected to grow at the same 8 percent rate into the foreseeable future, estimate the market value of the firm and of the software division.

Answer:

a. 1.52.

b. 16 percent.

c. 13.4 percent.

d. PV (total firm) = $147.96; PV (software division) = $41.88.

7–20. Financial Corporation wants to acquire Great Western Inc. Financial has estimated the enterprise value of Great Western at $104 million. The market value of Great Western's long-term debt is $15 million, and cash balances in excess of the firm's normal working capital requirements are $3 million. Financial estimates the present value of certain licenses that Great Western is not currently using to be $4 million. Great Western is the defendant in several outstanding lawsuits. Financial Corporation's legal department estimates the potential future cost of this litigation to be $3 million, with an estimated present value of $2.5 million. Great Western has 2 million common shares outstanding. What is the adjusted equity value of Great Western per common share?

Answer: $46.75/share.

Solutions to these Practice Problems are available in the Online Instructor's Manual for instructors using this book.

Chapter Business Cases

Case Study 7–1. Creating a Global Luxury Hotel Chain

Fairmont Hotels & Resorts Inc. ("Fairmont") announced on January 30, 2006, that it had agreed to be acquired by Kingdom Hotels ("Kingdom") and Colony Capital ("Colony") in an all-cash transaction valued at $45 per share. The transaction is valued at $3.9 billion, including assumed debt. The purchase price represents a 28 percent premium over Fairmont's closing price on November 4, 2005, the last day of trading when Kingdom and Colony expressed interest in Fairmont. The combination of Fairmont and Kingdom will create a luxury global hotel chain with 120 hotels in 24 countries. Discounted cash flow analyses, including estimated synergies and terminal value, value the firm at $43.10 per share. The net asset value of Fairmont's real estate is believed to be $46.70 per share.

Discussion Questions

1. Is it reasonable to assume that the acquirer could actually be getting the operation for "free," since the value of the real estate per share is worth more than the purchase price per share? Explain your answer.
2. Assume the acquirer divests all of Fairmont's hotels and real estate properties but continues to manage the hotels and properties under long-term management contracts. How would you estimate the net present value of the acquisition of Fairmont to the acquirer? Explain your answer.

Solutions to these questions are found in the Online Instructor's Manual available to instructors using this book.

Case Study 7–2. The Hunt for Elusive Synergy—@Home Acquires Excite

Background Information

Prior to @Home Network's merger with Excite for $6.7 billion, Excite's market value was about $3.5 billion. The new company combined the search engine capabilities of one of the best-known brands (at that time) on the Internet, Excite, with @Home's agreements with 21 cable companies worldwide. @Home gains access to the nearly 17 million households that are regular users of Excite. At the time, this transaction constituted the largest merger of Internet companies ever. As of July 1999, the combined firm, Excite @Home, displayed a P/E ratio in excess of 260 based on the consensus estimates for the year 2000 of $0.21 per share. The firm's market value was $18.8 billion, 270 times sales. Investors had great expectations for the future performance of the combined firms, despite their lackluster profit performance since their inception. Founded in 1995, @Home provided interactive services to home and business users over its proprietary network, telephone company circuits, and through the cable companies' infrastructure. Subscribers paid $39.95 per month for the service.

Assumptions

- Excite is properly valued immediately prior to announcement of the transaction.
- Annual customer service costs equal $50 per customer.
- Annual customer revenue in the form of @Home access charges and ancillary services equals $500 per customer. This assumes that declining access charges in this highly competitive environment will be offset by increases in revenue from the sale of ancillary services.
- None of the current Excite user households are current @Home customers.
- New @Home customers acquired through Excite remain @Home customers in perpetuity.
- @Home converts immediately 2 percent or 340,000 of the current 17 million Excite user households.

- @Home's cost of capital is 20 percent during the growth period and drops to 10 percent during the slower, sustainable growth period; its combined federal and state tax rate is 40 percent.
- Capital spending equals depreciation; current assets equal current liabilities.
- FCFF from synergy increases by 15 percent annually for the next 10 years and 5 percent thereafter. Its cost of capital after the high-growth period drops to 10 percent.
- The maximum purchase price @Home should pay for Excite equals Excite's current market price plus the synergy that results from the merger of the two businesses.

Discussion Questions

1. Use discounted cash flow (DCF) methods to determine if @Home overpaid for Excite.
2. What other assumptions might you consider in addition to those identified in the case study?
3. What are the limitations of the discounted cash flow method employed in this case?

Solutions to these questions are found in the Online Instructor's Manual available to instructors using this book.

8

Applying Relative, Asset-Oriented, and Real-Option Valuation Methods to Mergers and Acquisitions

You earn a living by what you get, but you build a life by what you give.
—Winston Churchill

Inside M&A: A Real Options' Perspective on Microsoft's Takeover Attempt of Yahoo

In a bold move to transform two relatively weak online search businesses into a competitor capable of challenging market leader Google, Microsoft proposed to buy Yahoo for $44.6 billion on February 2, 2008. At $31 per share in cash and stock, the offer represented a 62 percent premium over Yahoo's prior day closing price. Despite boosting its bid to $33 per share to offset a decline in the value of Microsoft's share price following the initial offer, Microsoft was rebuffed by Yahoo's board and management. In early May, Microsoft withdrew its bid to buy the entire firm and substituted an offer to acquire the search business only. Incensed at Yahoo's refusal to accept the Microsoft bid, activist shareholder Carl Icahn initiated an unsuccessful proxy fight to replace the Yahoo board. Throughout this entire melodrama, critics continued to ask how Microsoft could justify an offer valued at $44.6 billion when the market prior to the announcement had valued Yahoo at only $27.5 billion.

Microsoft could have continued to slug it out with Yahoo and Google, as it has been for the last five years, but this would have given Google more time to consolidate its leadership position. Despite having spent billions of dollars on Microsoft's online service (Microsoft Network or MSN) in recent years, the business remains a money loser (with losses exceeding one half billion dollars in 2007). Furthermore, MSN accounts for only 5 percent of the firm's total revenue.

Microsoft's Motives for Wanting Yahoo

Microsoft argued that its share of the online Internet search (i.e., ads appearing with search results) and display (i.e., website banner ads) advertising markets would be dramatically increased by combining Yahoo with MSN. Yahoo also is the leading consumer email service. Anticipated cost savings from combining the two businesses could reach $1 billion annually. Longer term, Microsoft could bundle search and advertising capabilities into the Windows operating system to increase the usage of the combined firms' online services by offering compatible new products and enhanced search capabilities.

The Challenges of Integration

The two firms have very different cultures. The iconic Silicon Valley–based Yahoo often is characterized as a company with a free-wheeling, fun-loving culture, potentially incompatible with Microsoft's more structured and disciplined environment. Melding or eliminating overlapping businesses represents a potentially mind-numbing effort given the diversity and complexity of the numerous sites available. To achieve the projected cost savings, Microsoft would have to choose which of the businesses and technologies would survive. Moreover, the software driving all of these sites and services is largely incompatible.

Microsoft's Decision-Making Flexibility

As an independent or stand-alone business, the market valued Yahoo at approximately $17 billion less than Microsoft's valuation. Microsoft was valuing Yahoo based on its intrinsic stand-alone value plus perceived synergy resulting from combining Yahoo and MSN. Standard discounted cash flow analysis assumes implicitly that, once Microsoft makes an investment decision, it cannot change its mind. In reality, once an investment decision is made, management often has a number of opportunities to make future decisions based on the outcome of things that are currently uncertain. These opportunities, or real options, include the decision to expand (i.e., accelerate investment at a later date), delay the initial investment, or abandon an investment. With respect to Microsoft's effort to acquire Yahoo, the major uncertainties dealt with the actual timing of an acquisition and whether the two businesses could be integrated successfully. In view of the current uncertainty, the so-called real options can be viewed as adjustments to the base case investment decision. For Microsoft's attempted takeover of Yahoo, such options could include the following:

- **Base case.** Buy 100 percent of Yahoo immediately.
- **Option to expand.** If Yahoo were to accept the bid, accelerate investment in new products and services contingent on the successful integration of Yahoo and MSN.
- **Option to delay.** (1) Temporarily walk away keeping open the possibility of returning for 100 percent of Yahoo if circumstances change or (2) offer to buy only the search business with the intent of purchasing the remainder of Yahoo at a later date.
- **Option to abandon.** If Yahoo were to accept the bid, spin off or divest combined Yahoo/MSN if integration is unsuccessful.

The decision tree in Figure 8–1 illustrates the range of real options (albeit an incomplete list) available to the Microsoft board. Each branch of the tree represents a specific option. The decision-tree framework is helpful in depicting the significant flexibility senior management often has in changing an existing investment decision at some point in the future.

Chapter Overview

Chapter 7 discussed in detail how DCF analysis is applied to M&A valuation. This chapter addresses alternative methods of valuation. These methods include relative-valuation (i.e., market-based) methods, asset-oriented methods, real-options analysis

FIGURE 8–1 Microsoft real options decision tree.

(i.e., contingent claims), and replacement cost. Relative-valuation methods include comparable company, comparable transactions, comparable industry techniques, and value-driver-based valuation. Asset-oriented methods include tangible book value and liquidation- or breakup-valuation techniques.

The chapter discusses in detail how to look at M&A valuation in the context of real options. This involves identifying preclosing and postclosing strategic and tactical alternatives and associated risks available to M&A participants. Real-options valuation is illustrated both in the context of a decision tree framework and as call and put options, when the assets underlying the option exhibit the characteristics of financial options. A weighted average valuation approach, which attempts to incorporate the analyst's relative confidence in the various valuation methods, also is discussed. The chapter concludes with a summary of the strengths and weaknesses of the alternative valuation methods (including discounted cash flow) and when it is appropriate to apply each methodology. The major segments of this chapter include the following:

• Applying Relative-Valuation (Market-Based) Methods
• Applying Asset-Oriented Methods

- Replacement-Cost Method
- Valuing the Firm Using the Weighted Average (Expected Value Method)
- Analyzing Mergers and Acquisitions in Terms of Real Options
- Determining When to Use Alternative Approaches to Valuation
- Things to Remember

A review of this chapter (including additional practice problems with solutions) is available in the file folder entitled Student Study Guide contained on the CD-ROM accompanying this book. The CD-ROM also contains a Learning Interactions Library, enabling students to test their knowledge of this chapter in a "real-time" environment.

Applying Relative-Valuation (Market-Based) Methods

Relative valuation involves valuing assets based on how similar assets are valued in the marketplace. Relative-valuation methods assume a firm's market value can be approximated by a value indicator for comparable companies, comparable transactions, or comparable industry averages. Value indicators could include the firm's earnings, operating cash flow, EBITDA (i.e., earnings before interest and taxes, depreciation, and amortization), sales, or book value. This approach often is described as market based, as it reflects the amounts investors are willing to pay for each dollar of earnings, cash flow, sales, or book value at a moment in time. As such, it reflects theoretically the collective wisdom of investors in the marketplace. Because of the requirement for positive current or near-term earnings or cash flow, this approach is meaningful only for companies with a positive, stable earnings or cash-flow stream.

If comparable companies are available, the market value of a target firm T (MV_T) can be estimated by solving the following equation:

$$MV_T = (MV_C/VI_C) \times VI_T \qquad (8-1)$$

where

MV_C = market value of the comparable company C.

VI_C = value indicator for comparable company C.

VI_T = value indicator for firm T.

(MV_C/VI_C) = market value multiple for the comparable company.

For example, if the P/E ratio for the comparable firm is equal to 10 (MV_C/VI_C) and the after-tax earnings of the target firm is $2 million ($VI_T$), the market value of the target firm is $20 million ($MV_T$). Relative-value methods are used widely for three reasons. First, such methods are relatively simple to calculate and require far fewer assumptions than discounted cash-flow techniques. Second, relative valuation is easier to explain than DCF methods. Finally, the use of market-based techniques is more likely to reflect current market demand and supply conditions. The relationship expressed in equation (8-1) can be used to estimate the value of the target firm in all the relative-valuation and asset-oriented methods discussed in this chapter.

The analyst must be careful to follow certain guidelines in applying relative valuation methods. First, when using multiples (i.e., MV_C/VI_C), it is critical to ensure that the multiple is defined in the same way for all comparable firms. For example, in using a price-to-earnings ratio, earnings may be defined as trailing (i.e., prior), current, or projected. Whichever way earnings are defined, the definition must be applied consistently to all firms in the sample. Also, the numerator and the denominator of the multiple must be defined in the same way. If the numerator in the price to earnings ratio is defined as price per share, the denominator also must be calculated as earnings per share. Second, the analyst must examine the distribution of the multiples of the firms being compared and eliminate outliers. Outliers are those whose values are substantially different from others in the sample. Failure to do so can distort the average or median of the sample. For a more detailed discussion of these issues, see Stowe et al. (2007).

Comparable Companies' Method

Applying the comparable companies' approach requires that the analyst identify companies that are substantially similar to the target firm. This approach is used widely in so-called fairness opinions, which investment bankers frequently are asked to give before a request for shareholder approval of an acquisition. Because it often is viewed as more objective than alternative approaches, the comparable companies' method enjoys widespread use in legal cases.

Generally speaking, a comparable firm is one whose profitability, potential growth rate in earnings or cash flows, and perceived risk is similar to the firm to be valued. By defining comparable companies so broadly, it is possible to utilize firms in other industries. As such, a computer hardware manufacturer can be compared to a telecommunications firm, as long as they are comparable in terms of profitability, growth, and risk. Consequently, if the firm to be valued has a 15 percent return on equity (i.e., profitability), expected earnings or cash-flow growth rates of 10 percent annually (i.e., growth), and a beta of 1.3 or debt to equity ratio of 1 (i.e., risk), the analyst must find a firm with similar characteristics in either the same industry or another industry. In practice, analysts often look for comparable firms in the same industry and that are similar in terms of such things as markets served, product offering, degree of leverage, and size.

To determine if the firms you have selected are truly comparable, estimate the correlation between the operating income or revenue of the firm to be valued and the comparable firms. If the correlation is positive and high, the firms are comparable. Similarly, if the firm has multiple product lines, collect comparable firms for each product line and estimate the degree of correlation.

Even when companies appear to be substantially similar, there are likely to be significant differences in these data at any one moment in time. These differences may result from investor overreaction to one-time events. For example, the announcement of a pending acquisition may boost the share prices of competitors as investors anticipate takeover bids for these firms. The impact of such events abates with the passage of time. Consequently, comparisons made at different times can provide distinctly different results. By taking an average of multiples over six months or one year, these differences may be minimized. Note that valuations derived using the comparable company method do not include a purchase price premium.

Exhibit 8–1 illustrates how to apply the comparable companies' method to value Repsol YPF, S.A. Headquartered in Buenos Aires, Argentina, Repsol is a geographically diversified integrated oil and gas firm engaged in all aspects of the petroleum business, including exploration, development and production of crude oil and natural gas, petroleum refining, petrochemical production, and marketing of petroleum products. Repsol

Exhibit 8–1 Valuing Repsol YPF Using Comparable Integrated Oil Companies					
	Target Valuation Based on Following Multiples (MV_C/VI_C)				
Comparable Company	Trailing P/E[1] Col. 1	Forward P/E[2] Col. 2	Price/ Sales Col. 3	Price/ Book Col. 4	Average Col. 1–4
Exxon Mobil Corp (XOM)	11.25	8.73	1.17	3.71	
British Petroleum (BP)	9.18	7.68	0.69	2.17	
Chevron Corp (CVX)	10.79	8.05	0.91	2.54	
Royal Dutch Shell (RDS)	7.36	8.35	0.61	1.86	
ConocoPhillips (COP)	11.92	6.89	0.77	1.59	
Total SA (TOT)	8.75	8.73	0.80	2.53	
Eni SpA (E)	3.17	7.91	0.36	0.81	
PetroChina Co. (PTR)	11.96	10.75	1.75	2.10	
Average multiple (MV_C/VI_C) times	9.30	8.39	0.88	2.16	
Repsol YPF projections (VI_T)[3]	$4.38	$3.27	$92.66	$26.49	
Equals estimated value of target	$40.72	$27.42	$81.77	$57.32	$51.81

[1]Trailing 52 week averages.
[2]Projected 52 week averages.
[3]Billions of dollars.

has economic and political risks and growth characteristics similar to other globally diversified integrated oil and gas companies. The estimated value of Repsol based on the comparable companies' method is $51.81 billion versus its actual June 25, 2008, market capitalization of $49.83 billion.

The analyst needs to be mindful of changes in fundamentals that can affect multiples. These fundamentals include a firm's ability to generate and grow earnings and cash flow through reinvestment in the firm's operations, as well as the risk associated with the firm's earnings and cash flows. Since multiples are affected by each of these variables, changes in them affect multiples. Firms with lower earnings and cash-flow generation potential, lower growth prospects, and higher risk should trade at multiples less than firms with higher earnings and cash-flow generation capability, higher growth prospects, and less risk. Consequently, the analyst needs to understand why one firm's multiple is less than a comparable firm's before concluding that it is under- or overvalued. For example, a firm with a P/E of 10 may not be more expensive than a comparable firm with a P/E of 8, if the former's growth prospects, profitability, and the rate at which profits are reinvested in the firm are higher than the latter firm's.

Table 8–1 summarizes the relationships between various multiples and their underlying determinants. The word *positive* or *negative* in parentheses next to the factors influencing the multiples indicates the direction of causality. For example, assuming nothing else is changing, price-to-earnings ratios should increase as expected earnings increase and decrease as dividend payout ratios rise, reflecting a lower rate of reinvestment of earnings in the firm

Table 8–1   Factors Influencing Valuation Multiples

Multiple	Factor[1]
Price-to-earnings ratio	Earnings growth rate (positive)
	Payout ratio (negative)[2]
Price-to-book ratio	Return on equity (positive)
	Payout ratio (negative)
	Earnings growth rate (positive)
Price-to-revenue ratio	Net profit margin (positive)
	Payout ratio (negative)
	Earnings growth rate (positive)
Enterprise-value multiples	Cash-flow growth rate (positive)

[1]For a derivation of the relationship between multiples and fundamentals, see Damodaran (2001), pp. 263–264.

[2]Payout ratios refer to dividends as a percent of earnings available for common equity, where (1 – the payout ratio) = the rate at which a firm is retaining earnings for reinvestment. Therefore, increasing payout ratios indicates a lower firm reinvestment rate.

Comparable Transactions Method

The comparable transactions approach is conceptually similar to the comparable companies approach. This valuation technique also is referred to as the *precedent* or *recent transactions method*. The multiples used to estimate the value of the target are based on purchase prices of comparable companies that recently were acquired. Price (i.e., market-value)-to-earnings, sales, cash-flow, EBITDA, and book-value ratios are calculated using the purchase price for the recent comparable transaction. Earnings, sales, cash flow, EBITDA, and book value for the target subsequently are multiplied by these ratios to obtain an estimate of the market value of the target company. The estimated value of the target firm obtained using recent comparable transactions already reflects a purchase price premium, unlike the comparable companies' approach to valuation. The obvious limitation to the comparable transactions method is the difficulty in finding truly comparable, recent transactions. Note that comparable recent transactions can be found in other industries, as long as they are similar to the target firm in terms of profitability, expected earnings, and cash flow, growth, and perceived risk. Exhibit 8–1 could be used to illustrate how the recent transaction valuation method may be applied simply by replacing the data in the column headed "Comparable Company" with data for "Recent Comparable Transactions."

Same or Comparable Industry Method

Using this approach, the target company's net income, revenue, cash flow, EBITDA, and book value are multiplied by the ratio of the market value of shareholders' equity to net income, revenue, cash flow, EBITDA, and book value for the average company in the target firm's industry or a comparable industry (see Exhibit 8–2). Such information can be obtained from Standard & Poor's, Value Line, Moody's, Dun & Bradstreet, and Wall Street analysts. The primary advantage of this technique is the ease of use. Disadvantages include the presumption that industry multiples are actually comparable. The use of the industry average may overlook the fact that companies, even in the same industry, can have drastically different expected growth rates, returns on invested capital, and debt-to-total capital ratios.

Exhibit 8–2 Valuing a Target Company Using the Same or Comparable Industries Method

As of June 25, 2008, Repsol YPB, an Argentine-based integrated oil and gas producer, had projected earnings per share for the coming year of $3.27 (see Exhibit 8–1). The industry average price-to-earnings ratio at that time for integrated oil and gas companies was 12.4. Estimate the firm's price per share, see equation (8–1):

$$MV_T = (MV_{IND}/VI_{IND}) \times VI_T$$
$$= 12.4 \times \$3.27$$
$$= \$40.54/\text{share} (6/25/08 \text{ actual price} = \$39.18)$$

where

MV_T = market value per share of the target company.

MV_{IND}/VI_{IND} = market value per share of the average firm in the industry divided by a value indicator for that average firm in the industry (e.g., industry average price-to-earnings ratio).

VI_T = value indicator for the target firm (e.g., projected earnings per share).

Valuations Based on Projections May be Superior to Those Based on Historical Data

An analyst using industry or comparable company multiples must decide whether to use multiples based on current or projected earnings or cash flows or some other measure of value. In using projections, the source of the information must be taken into account. For example, projections based on Wall Street analysts' forecasts may not be unbiased. Such concerns notwithstanding, empirical evidence suggests that forecasts of earnings and other value indicators are better predictors of firm value than value indicators based on historical data (Moonchul and Ritter, 1999; Liu, Nissim, and Thomas, 2002).

Earnings Show Stronger Short-Run Correlation with Stock Returns Than Cash Flow

Considerable attention has been paid to whether cash flow, earnings, or dividends are better predictors of firm value. In valuation, differences in earnings, cash flows and dividends are often attributable to timing differences (i.e., differences between when a cash outlay is recorded and when it is actually incurred). For example, when a firm buys a piece of equipment, it generally pays for the equipment in the period in which it is received. However, for financial reporting purposes, the purchase price of the equipment is amortized over its estimated useful life. Proponents of using earnings as a measure of value rather than cash flow argue that earnings reflect value changes regardless of when they occur. For example, a firm's contractual obligation to provide future health care or pension benefits when an employee retires is reflected in current compensation and earnings are reduced by an expense equal to the present value of that deferred compensation. In contrast, current cash flows are unaffected by this obligation. The bottom line is that, over the life of the firm, the present values of future earnings, cash flows, and dividends will be equal, if based on internally consistent assumptions (Liu et al., 2002).

Studies suggest that cash flows and earnings are highly positively correlated with stock returns over long periods, such as five-year intervals. However, for shorter time periods, earnings show a stronger correlation with stock returns than cash flows

(Cheng, Liu, Schaefer, 1996; Dechow, 1994; Sloan, 1996). As a practical matter, cash flow is more often used for valuation than earnings or dividends simply because firms often do not pay dividends or generate profits for a significant period.

For a sample of 25,843 firms in 10 countries from 1987 to 2004, Liu, Nissim, and Thomas (2007) argue that forecasted earnings may be better predictors of firm value than projected cash flows. The authors found that the use of industry multiples based on forecasted earnings are superior predictors of actual equity values of firms traded on public stock exchanges than industry multiples based forecasted cash flow. Forecasted earnings also were found to be superior as a measure of value than dividend-based valuations. In contrast to these findings, Kaplan and Ruback (1995) and Kim and Ritter (1999) argue that the choice of which multiple or method (relative valuation or DCF) to use is ambiguous. Furthermore, for a sample of 51 highly leveraged transactions between 1983 and 1989, Kaplan and Ruback question whether one forecasting method is superior to another by noting that both the DCF and the relative multiple methods exhibit similar levels of valuation accuracy.

Enterprise Value to EBITDA Method

In recent years, analysts have increasingly used the relationship between enterprise value to earnings before interest and taxes, depreciation, and amortization to value firms. Note that enterprise value can be defined either in terms of the asset or the liability side of the balance sheet (see Exhibit 8–3). Recall that, in Chapter 7, enterprise value was discussed from the perspective of the asset side or "left-hand side" of the balance sheet as the present value of free cash flow to the firm (i.e., cash flows generated from operating assets and liabilities available for lenders and common and preferred shareholders). Thus defined, enterprise value was adjusted for the value of nonoperating assets and liabilities to estimate the value of common equity, see equation (7–19). In this chapter, enterprise value is viewed from the perspective of the liability or "right-hand side" of the balance sheet.

The enterprise value to EBITDA multiple relates the total market value of the firm from the perspective of the liability side of the balance sheet (i.e., long-term debt plus preferred and common equity), excluding cash, to EBITDA. In practice, other long-term liabilities often are ignored and "excess cash" is assumed to be equal to cash and short-term marketable securities on the balance sheet. In constructing the enterprise value, the market value of the firm's common equity value (MV_{FCFE}) is added to the market value of the firm's long-term debt (MV_D) and the market value of preferred stock (MV_{PF}). Cash and short-term marketable securities are deducted from the enterprise value of the firm since interest income from such cash is not counted in the calculation of EBITDA. Consequently, the inclusion of cash would overstate the enterprise value to

---

Exhibit 8–3 Defining Enterprise Value from Either Side of the Balance Sheet

Excess cash (C)	Current liabilities (CL)
Current assets, excluding excess cash (CA)	Long-term debt (LTD)
Long-term assets (LTA)	Other long-term liabilities (OLTL)
	Shareholders equity, including common and preferred equity (SE)

Note: Enterprise value = C + CA − CL + LTA = SE + LTD + OLTL

EBITDA multiple, since the asset cash is included in the calculation of the enterprise value. The enterprise value (EV) to EBITDA method is commonly expressed as follows:

$$EV/EBITDA = [MV_{FCFE} + MV_{PF} + (MV_D - Cash)]/EBITDA \qquad (8\text{--}2)$$

where $(MV_D - Cash)$ is often referred to as net debt.

The enterprise value to EBITDA method is useful because more firms are likely to have negative earnings rather than negative EBITDA. Consequently, relative valuation methods are more often applicable when EBITDA is used as the value indicator. Furthermore, net or operating income can be significantly affected by the way the firm chooses to calculate depreciation (e.g., straight line versus accelerated). Such problems do not arise if the analyst uses a value indicator such as EBITDA that is estimated before deducting depreciation and amortization expense. Finally, the multiple can be compared more readily among firms exhibiting different levels of leverage than for other measures of earnings, since the numerator represents the total value of the firm irrespective of its distribution between debt and equity and the denominator measures earnings before interest. See Exhibit 8–4 for an illustration of how to apply the enterprise value to EBITDA method.

Exhibit 8–4 Valuing a Target Firm Using the Enterprise Value to EBITDA Method

Repsol and Eni are geographically diversified integrated oil and gas companies. As of December 31, 2006, the market value of Repsol's common equity was $40.36 billion and Eni's was $54.30 billion. Neither firm had preferred stock outstanding. Repsol's and Eni's outstanding debt primarily are interest only with a balloon payment at maturity. The average maturity date for Repsol's debt is 12 years and 10 years for Eni. Market rates of interest for firms like Repsol and Eni at that time for debt maturing within 10–12 years were 7.5 percent and 7 percent, respectively. Repsol's and Eni's current income, balance sheet, and cash flow statements as of December 31, 2006 are as shown in Table 8–2.

Which firm has the higher enterprise value to EBITDA ratio? Hint: Use equation (8–2).

Answer: Repsol

The market value of existing debt is calculated as follows:

$$PVD\,(\text{PV of Repsol long-term debt})^1 = \$0.7 \times \frac{1 - \left[1/(1.075)^{12}\right]}{0.075} + \frac{\$14.6}{(1.075)^{12}}$$

$$= \$0.7 \times 7.74 + \$6.13 = \$11.55\,\text{billion}$$

$$PVD\,(\text{PV of Eni long-term debt})^2 = \$0.3 \times \frac{1 - [1/(1.070)^{10}]}{0.07} + \frac{\$8.8}{(1.07)^{10}}$$

$$= \$0.3 \times 7.02 + \$4.47 = \$6.58\,\text{billion}$$

The enterprise to EBITDA ratio is

(Market value of equity + Market value of debt − Cash) / (EBIT + Depreciation)[3]

Repsol: ($40.36 + $11.55 − $3.8)/($8.0 + $4.1) = 3.98

Eni: ($54.30 + $6.58 − $6.2)/($27.60 + $8.1) = 1.53

Table 8–2   Financial Statements ($ billions)

	Repsol YPF ($ billions)	Eni SpA
Income Statement (12/31/06)		
Revenue	72.70	114.70
Cost of sales	48.60	75.90
Other expenses	16.10	11.20
Earnings before interest and taxes	8.00	27.60
Interest expense	0.70	0.30
Earnings before taxes	7.30	27.30
Taxes	3.10	14.10
Net income	4.20	13.20
Balance Sheet (12/31/06)		
Cash	3.80	6.20
Other current assets	14.60	29.80
Long-term assets	42.70	77.20
Total assets	61.10	113.20
Current liabilities	13.30	28.30
Long-term debt	14.60	8.80
Other long-term liabilities	8.80	26.40
Total liabilities	36.70	63.50
Shareholders' equity	24.40	49.70
Equity + Total liabilities	61.10	113.20
Cash Flow (12/31/06)		
Net income	4.20	13.20
Depreciation	4.10	8.10
Change in working capital	−0.40	1.10
Investments	−6.90	−9.30
Financing	−1.20	−9.40
Change in cash balances	−0.20	3.70

Source: Yahoo Finance.

---

[1]The present value of debt is calculated using the PV of an annuity formula for 12 years and a 7.5-percent interest rate plus the PV of the principal repayment of $14.6 billion at the end of 12 years. Alternatively, rather than using the actual formulas, a present value interest factor annuity table and a present value interest factor table could have been used to calculate the PV of debt. Note that only the annual interest expense of $0.7 million is used in the calculation of the PV of the annuity payment because the debt is treated as a balloon note.

[2]The present value of debt is calculated using the PV of an annuity formula for 10 years and a 7.0-percent interest rate plus the PV of the principal repayment of $8.8 billion at the end of 10 years.

[3]Note that a firm's financial statements frequently include depreciation expense in the cost of sales. Therefore, EBITDA may be calculated by adding EBIT from the income statement and depreciation expense shown on the cash-flow statement.

Adjusting Relative Valuation Methods for Firm Growth Rates

Assume Firm A and Firm B are direct competitors and have price-to-earnings ratios of 20 and 15, respectively. Which is the cheaper firm? It is not possible to answer this question without knowing how fast the earnings of the two firms are growing. The higher P/E ratio for Firm A may be justified if its earnings are expected to grow significantly faster than Firm B's future earnings.

For this reason, relative valuation methods may be adjusted for differences in growth rates among firms. The most common adjustment is the PEG ratio, commonly calculated by dividing the firm's price-to-earning ratio by the expected growth rate in earnings. This relative-valuation method is both simple to compute and provides a convenient mechanism for comparing firms with different growth rates. The comparison of a firm's P/E ratio to its projected earnings is helpful in identifying stocks of firms that are under- or overvalued. Conceptually, firms with P/E ratios less than their projected growth rates may be considered undervalued; while those with P/E ratios greater than their projected growth rates may be viewed as overvalued. It is critical for the analyst to remember that growth rates by themselves do not increase multiples, such as a firm's price-to-earnings ratio, unless coupled with improving financial returns. Investors are willing to pay more for each dollar of future earnings only if they expect to earn a higher future rate of return. Investors may be willing to pay considerably more for a stock whose PEG ratio is greater than 1 if they believe the increase in earnings will result in future financial returns that significantly exceed the firm's cost of equity.

Moreover, the PEG ratio can be helpful in evaluating the potential market values of a number of different firms in the same industry in selecting which may be the most attractive acquisition target. While the PEG ratio uses P/E ratios, other value indicators may be used. This method may be generalized as follows:

$$\frac{MV_T VI_T}{VI_{TGR}} = A$$

and

$$MV_T = A \times VI_{TGR} \times VI_T \qquad (8\text{--}3)$$

where

A = PEG ratio; that is, market-price-to-value-indicator ratio (MV_T/VI_T) relative to the growth rate of the value indicator (VI_{TGR}), which could include the growth in net income, cash flow, EBITDA, revenue, and the like.

VI_{TGR} = projected growth rate of the value indicator. Because this method uses an equity multiple (e.g., price per share/net income per share), consistency suggests that the growth rate in the value indicator should be expressed on a per-share basis. Therefore, if the value indicator is net income per share, the growth in the value indicator should be the growth rate for net income per share and not net income.

Equation (8–3) gives an estimate of the implied market value per share for a target firm based on its PEG ratio. As such, PEG ratios are useful for comparing firms whose expected future growth rates are positive and different to determine which is likely to have the higher firm value. For firms whose projected growth rates are 0 or negative, this method implies zero firm value for firms that are not growing and a negative value for those whose projected growth rates are negative. The practical implications for such firms is that those that are not growing are not likely to increase in market value, while those exhibiting negative growth are apt to experience declining firm values. Exhibit 8–5 illustrates how to apply the PEG ratio.

Exhibit 8–5 Applying the PEG Ratio

An analyst is asked to determine whether Basic Energy Service (BES) or Composite Production Services (CPS) is more attractive as an acquisition target. Both firms provide engineering, construction, and specialty services to the oil, gas, refinery, and petrochemical industries. BES and CPS have projected annual earnings per share growth rates of 15 percent and 9 percent, respectively. BES's and CPS's current earnings per share are $2.05 and $3.15, respectively. The current share prices as of June 25, 2008, for BES is $31.48 and for CPS is $26. The industry average price-to-earnings ratio and growth rate are 12.4 and 11 percent, respectively. Based on this information, which firm is a more attractive takeover target as of the point in time the firms are being compared? Hint: Use equation (8–3). The PEG ratio focuses on P/E ratios and earnings growth rates. What other factors, if known, might change your answer to the previous question?

Industry average PEG ratio: $12.4/0.11 = 112.73$[1]

BES: Implied share price $= 112.73 \times 0.15 \times \$2.05 = \$34.66$

CPX: Implied share price $= 112.73 \times 0.09 \times \$3.15 = \$31.96$

Answer: The difference between the implied and actual share prices for BES and CPS is $3.18 (i.e., $34.66 – $31.48) and $5.96 ($31.96 – $26.00), respectively. CPS is more undervalued than BES at that moment in time. However, BES could be a more attractive acquisition target than CPS if it can generate increasing future financial returns and its projected earnings stream is viewed as less risky. Therefore, BES could exhibit greater potential and less uncertain future profitability than CPS.

---

[1] Solving MVT = A × VITGR × VIT using an individual firm's PEG ratio provides the firm's current or share price in period T, since this formula is an identity. An industry average PEG ratio may be used to provide an estimate of the firm's intrinsic value. This implicitly assumes that both firms exhibit the same relationship between price-to-earnings ratios and earnings growth rates.

Data Source: Yahoo Finance.

Value-Driver-Based Valuation

In the absence of earnings, other factors that drive the creation of value for a firm may be used for valuation purposes. Such factors commonly are used to value startup companies and initial public offerings, which often have little or no earnings performance records. Measures of profitability and cash flow are simply manifestations of value indicators. These indicators are dependent on factors both external and internal to the firm. Value drivers exist for each major function within the firm including sales, marketing, and distribution; customer service; operations and manufacturing; and purchasing.

There are both micro value drivers and macro value drivers. *Micro value drivers* are those that directly influence specific functions within the firm. Micro value drivers for sales, marketing, and distribution could include product quality measures, such as part defects per 100,000 units sold, on-time delivery, the number of multiyear subscribers, and the ratio of product price to some measure of perceived quality. Customer service drivers could include average waiting time on the telephone, the number of billing errors as a percent of total invoices, and the time required to correct such errors. Operational value drivers include average collection period, inventory turnover, and the number of units produced per manufacturing employee hour. Purchasing value drivers include average payment period, on-time vendor delivery, and the quality of purchased materials and services. *Macro value drivers* are more encompassing than micro value drivers by affecting all aspects of the firm. Examples of macro value drivers include market share, overall customer satisfaction measured by survey results, total asset turns (i.e., sales to total assets), revenue per employee, and "same store sales" in retailing.

Using value drivers to value businesses is straightforward. First, the analyst needs to determine the key determinants of value (i.e., the value drivers for the target firm). Second, the market value for comparable companies is divided by the value driver selected for the target to calculate the dollars of market value per unit of value driver. Third, this figure is multiplied by the same indicator or value driver for the target company. For example, assume that the primary macro value driver or determinant of a firm's market value in a particular industry is market share. How investors value market share can be estimated by dividing the market leader's market value by its market share. If the market leader has a market value and market share of $300 million and 30 percent, respectively, the market is valuing each percentage point of market share at $10 million (i.e., $300 million/30). If the target company in the same industry has a 20 percent market share, an estimate of the market value of the target company is $200 million (20 points of market share times $10 million).

Similarly, the market value of comparable companies could be divided by other known value drivers. Examples include the number of visitors or page views per month for an Internet content provider, the number of subscribers to a magazine, cost per hotel room for a hotel chain, and the number of households with TVs in a specific geographic area for a cable TV company. Using this method, AT&T's acquisitions of the cable companies TCI and Media One in the late 1990s would appear to be a "bargain." AT&T spent an average of $5,000 per household (the price paid for each company divided by the number of customer households acquired) in purchasing these companies' customers. In contrast, Deutsche Telekom and Mannesmann spent $6,000 and $7,000 per customer, respectively, in buying mobile phone companies One 2 One and Orange PLC (*Business Week*, 2000a).

The major advantage of this approach is its simplicity. Its major disadvantage is the implied assumption that a single value driver or factor is representative of the total value of the business. The bankruptcy of many dotcom firms between 2000 and 2002 illustrates how this valuation technique can be misused. Many of these firms had never shown any earnings, yet they exhibited huge market valuations. Investors often justified these valuations by using page views and subscribers of supposedly comparable firms to value any firm associated with the Internet. These proved to be poor indicators of the firm's ability to generate future earnings or cash flow.

Despite the well-documented dangers of overpaying for firms, recent transactions involving Internet startups MySpace and YouTube suggest that what some might term "field of dreams" valuations pop up all too often. Amidst the euphoria of the moment, acquirers often overlook the risks associated with firms lacking meaningful revenues or profits and well-defined business models and base their valuations solely on the target firm's perceived potential.

Applying Asset-Oriented Methods

Tangible Book Value or Equity per Share Method

Book value is a much-maligned value indicator, because book asset values rarely reflect actual market values (Exhibit 8–6). They may over- or understate market value. For example, the value of land frequently is understated on the balance sheet, whereas inventory often is overstated if it is old or obsolete. The applicability of this approach varies by industry. Although book values generally do not mirror actual market values for manufacturing companies, they may be more accurate for distribution companies, whose assets are largely composed of inventory and that exhibit high inventory turnover rates. Examples of such companies include pharmaceutical distributor Bergen Brunswick and personal computer distributor Ingram Micro. Book value is also widely used for valuing financial services companies, where tangible book value is primarily cash or liquid assets. Tangible book value is book value less goodwill.

Exhibit 8–6 Valuing Companies Using Book Value

Ingram Micro Inc. and its subsidiaries distribute information technology products worldwide. The firm's market price per share on August 21, 2008 was $19.30. Ingram's projected five-year average annual net income growth rate is 9.5 percent, and its beta is 0.89. The firm's shareholders' equity is $3.4 billion and goodwill is $0.7 billion. Ingram has 172 million (0.172 billion) shares outstanding. Table 8–3 lists the firms that represent Ingram's primary competitors.

Based on the information provided, what is Ingram's tangible book value per share (VI_T)? What is the appropriate industry average market value to tangible book value ratio (MV_{IND}/VI_{IND})? Estimate the implied market value per share of Ingram (MV_T) using tangible book value as a value indicator. See equation (8–1). Based on this analysis, is Ingram under- or overvalued compared to its August 21, 2008, share price?

Ingram's tangible book value per share: (VI_T) = ($3.4 − $0.7)/0.172 = $15.70

Based on risk as measured by the firm's beta and the five-year projected earnings growth rate, Synnex is believed to exhibit significantly different risk and growth characteristics from Ingram and is excluded from the calculation of the industry average market-value-to-tangible-book-value ratio. Therefore, the appropriate industry average ratio (MV_{IND}/VI_{IND}) = 0.95; that is, (0.91 + 1.01 + 0.93)/3.

$$\text{Ingram's implied value per share} = MV_T = (MV_{IND}/VI_{IND}) \times VI_T$$
$$= 0.95 \times \$15.70 = \$14.92$$

Based on the implied value per share, Ingram was overvalued on August 21, 2008, when its share price was $19.30.

Table 8–3 Competitor Firms

	Market Value/Tangible Book Value	Beta	Projected 5-Year Net Income Growth Rate (%)
Tech Data	0.91	0.90	11.6
Synnex Corporation	0.70	0.40	6.9
Avnet	1.01	1.09	12.1
Arrow	0.93	0.97	13.2

Source: Yahoo Finance.

Liquidation or Breakup Value

The terms liquidation and breakup value often are used interchangeably. However, there are subtle distinctions. *Liquidation* or breakup value is the projected price of the firm's assets sold separately less its liabilities and expenses incurred in liquidating or breaking up the firm. Liquidation may be involuntary, as a result of bankruptcy, or voluntary, if a firm is viewed by its owners as worth more in liquidation than as a going concern. The *going concern value* of a company may be defined as the firm's value in excess of the sum of the value of its parts. The breakup value of the firm is synonymous with its voluntary liquidation value. Liquidation and breakup strategies are explored further in Chapter 15.

During the late 1970s and throughout most of the 1980s, highly diversified companies routinely were valued by investors in terms of their value if broken up and sold as discrete operations as well as their going concern value as a consolidated operation. Companies lacking real synergy among their operating units or sitting on highly appreciated assets often were viewed as more valuable when broken up or liquidated. In the mid-1980s, an investor group acquired the Ohio Mattress Company and promptly shut down its operations. The value of the firm's nonoperating assets, primarily some timberland, was valued far higher than the firm as a going concern. In early 2007, the Blackstone Group, a major private equity investor, acquired Equity Office Properties Trust (EOP) for $36 billion. While EOP had been slowly selling properties in less desirable markets, Blackstone intends to move much more aggressively to sell off the properties held by the real estate investment trust (see Case Study 11–1 for more details.).

In practice, the calculation of liquidation value, voluntary or as a consequence of bankruptcy, requires a concerted effort by appraisers who are intimately familiar with the operations to be liquidated. In some instances, the expenses incurred in terms of legal, appraisal, and consulting fees may constitute a large percentage of the dollar proceeds from the sale of the firm's assets. Guidelines exist for the probable liquidation value of various types of assets. However, they differ dramatically from one industry to another. They also depend on the condition of the economy and whether the assets must be liquidated in a hurry to satisfy creditors.

Analysts may estimate the liquidation value of a target company to determine the minimum value of the company in the worst-case scenario of business failure and eventual liquidation. It is particularly appropriate for financially distressed firms. Analysts often make a simplifying assumption that the assets can be sold in an orderly fashion, which is defined as a reasonable amount of time to solicit bids from qualified buyers. *Orderly fashion* often is defined as 9–12 months. Under these circumstances, high-quality receivables typically can be sold for 80–90 percent of their book value. Inventories might realize 80–90 percent of their book value, depending on the condition and the degree of obsolescence. The value of inventory may also vary depending on whether it consists of finished, intermediate, or raw materials. More rapid liquidation might reduce the value of inventories to 60–65 percent of their book value. The liquidation value of equipment varies widely depending on the age and condition.

Inventories need to be reviewed in terms of obsolescence, receivables in terms of the ease with which they may be collected, equipment in terms of age and effectiveness, and real estate in terms of current market value. Equipment such as lathes and computers with a zero book value may have a significant economic value (i.e., useful life). Land can be a hidden source of value, because it frequently is undervalued on GAAP balance sheets. Prepaid assets, such as insurance premiums, sometimes can be liquidated with a portion of the premium recovered. The liquidation value is reduced dramatically if the assets have to be liquidated in "fire sale" conditions, under which assets are sold to the first rather than the highest bidder (Exhibit 8–7).

Exhibit 8–7 Calculating Liquidation Value

Titanic Corporation has declared bankruptcy and the trustee has been asked by the firm's creditors to estimate its liquidation value assuming orderly sale conditions (Table 8–4). Note that this example does not take into account legal fees, taxes, management fees, and contractually required employee severance expenses. In certain cases, these expenses can constitute a substantial percentage of the proceeds from liquidation.

Table 8–4   Items for Liquidation

Balance Sheet Item	Book Value ($ millions)	Orderly Sale Value ($ millions)
Cash	100	100
Receivables	500	450
Inventory	800	720
Equipment (after depreciation)	200	60
Land	200	300
Total assets	1,800	1,630
Total liabilities	1,600	1,600
Shareholders' equity	200	30

Exhibit 8–8 illustrates a hypothetical estimation of the breakup value of a firm consisting of multiple operating units. The implicit assumption is that the interdependencies among the four operating units are limited such that they can be sold separately without a significant degradation of the value of any individual unit.

Exhibit 8–8 Calculating Breakup Value

Sea Bass Inc. consists of four operating units (Table 8–5). The value of operating synergies among the units is believed to be minimal. All but $10 million in debt can be allocated to each of the four units. Such debt is associated with financing the needs of the corporate overhead structure. Legal, consulting, and investment banking fees, as well as severance expenses associated with terminating corporate overhead personnel, amount to $10 million. What is the breakup value of Sea Bass Inc.?

Table 8–5   Value of Operating Units

Operating Unit	Estimated Equity Value ($ millions)
Unit 1	100
Unit 2	125
Unit 3	50
Unit 4	75
Total equity value	350
Less any unallocated liabilities held at the corporate level, corporate overhead expense, and costs associated with the breakup.	20
Total breakup value	330

Replacement-Cost Method

The replacement-cost approach estimates what it would cost to replace the target firm's assets at current market prices using professional appraisers less the present value of the firm's liabilities. The difference provides an estimate of the market value of equity. This approach does not take into account the going concern value of the company, which reflects how effectively the assets are being used in combination (i.e., synergies) to generate profits and cash flow. Valuing the assets separately in terms of what it would cost to replace them may seriously understate the firm's true going concern value. This approach may also be inappropriate if the firm has a significant amount of intangible assets on its books due to the difficulty in valuing such assets.

Valuing the Firm Using the Weighted-Average (Expected-Value) Method

Predicting future cash flows and determining the appropriate discount rate is often very difficult. Consequently, relative valuation multiples often are used in lieu of DCF valuation. However, no multiple is universally accepted as the best measure of a firm's value. Consequently, the weighted-average method of valuation represents a compromise position. This approach involves calculating the expected value (EXPV) or weighted average of a range of potential outcomes. Kaplan and Ruback (1995) and Liu et al. (2002) provide empirical support for using multiple methods of valuation to estimate the economic value of an asset.

Note that the weights reflect the analyst's relative confidence in the various methodologies employed to value a business. Note also that the value of the weights must sum to 1. Assuming an analyst is equally confident in the accuracy of both methods, the expected value of a target firm valued at \$12 million using discounted cash flow and \$15 million using the comparable companies' method can be written as follows:

$$EXPV = 0.5 \times \$12 + 0.5 \times \$15 = \$13.5 \, million$$

Neither valuation method in this example includes a purchase price premium. Consequently, a premium will have to be added to the expected value estimate to obtain a reasonable purchase estimate for the target firm.

Adjusting Valuation Estimates for Purchase Price Premiums

As explained in Chapter 1, the purchase premium reflects both the perceived value of obtaining a controlling interest in the target and the value of expected synergies (e.g., cost savings) resulting from combining the two firms. When using the weighted-average or expected-value valuation method, it is important to remember that, unless adjusted to reflect a premium, the individual valuation methods discussed in Chapters 7 and 8 do not reflect the amount over market value that must be paid to gain a controlling interest in the target firm. The exception is the recent transactions method, which already reflects a purchase price premium. The premium generally is determined as a result of the negotiation process and may reflect premiums paid on recent acquisitions of similar firms or the percentage of synergy provided by the target firm. If the investor is interested in purchasing less than 100 percent of the voting shares of the target, it is necessary to adjust the purchase price for control premiums or minority discounts. How these adjustments are made is explained in detail in Chapter 10.

Adjustments to estimated market values should be made with care. For example, the analyst should be careful not to mechanically add an acquisition premium to the target firm's estimated value based the comparable companies method if there is evidence that

Exhibit 8–9 Weighted-Average Valuation of Alternative Methodologies

An analyst has estimated the value of a company using multiple valuation methodologies. The discounted cash-flow value is $220 million, the comparable transactions value is $234 million, the P/E-based value is $224 million, and the firm's breakup value is $200 million (Table 8–6). The analyst has greater confidence in certain methodologies than others. The purchase price paid for the recent comparable transaction represented a 20 percent premium over the value of the firm at the time of the takeover announcement. Estimate the weighted average value of the firm using all valuation methodologies and the weights or relative importance the analyst assigns to each methodology.

Table 8–6   Valuation Methodologies

Estimated Value ($ millions) Col. 1	Estimated Value Incl. 20% Premium ($ millions) Col. 2	Relative Weight (as determined by analyst) Col. 3	Weighted Average ($ millions) Col. 2 × Col. 3
220	264.0	30	79.2
234	234.0[1]	40	93.6
224	268.8	20	53.8
200	240.0	10	24.0
		1.00	250.6

[1]Note that the comparable recent transactions estimate already contains a 20 percent purchase price premium.

the market values of "comparable firms" already reflect the effects of acquisition activity elsewhere in the industry. For example, rival firms' share prices will rise in response to the announced acquisition of a competitor, regardless of whether the proposed acquisition is ultimately successful or unsuccessful (Song and Walking, 2000). Akhigbe, Borde, and Whyte (2000) find that the increase in rivals' share prices may be even greater if the acquisition attempt is unsuccessful, because investors believe that the bidder will attempt to acquire other firms in the same industry. There is evidence the effects of merger activity in one country is also built into merger premiums in other countries in regions that are becoming more integrated, such as the European Union (Bley and Medura, 2003).

Exhibit 8–9 illustrates a practical way of calculating the expected value of the target firm, including a purchase premium, using estimates provided by multiple valuation methods. In the example, the purchase price premium associated with the estimate provided by the recent comparable transactions method is applied to estimates provided by the other valuation methodologies.

Analyzing Mergers and Acquisitions in Terms of Real Options

An option is the exclusive right, but not the obligation, to buy, sell, or use property for a specific period of time in exchange for a predetermined amount of money. Options traded on financial exchanges, such as puts and calls, are called *financial options*. Options that involve real assets, such as licenses, copyrights, trademarks, and patents, are called *real options*. Other examples of real options include the right to buy land, commercial property, and equipment. Such assets can be valued as call options if their current value exceeds the difference between the asset's current value and some predetermined level. For example, if a business has an option to lease office space at a predetermined price, the value of that option increases as lease rates for this type of office space increase. The asset can be valued as a put option if its value increases as the value of the underlying asset falls below a predetermined level. For example, if a business has an option to sell a commercial office building at a predetermined price, the value of that option increases as the value of the office building declines. In either instance, the option holder can choose to exercise (or not exercise) the option now or at some time in the future.

Real options refer to management's ability to adopt and later revise corporate investment decisions. They should not be confused with a firm's strategic options, such as adopting a cost leadership, differentiation, or a focus business strategy (see Chapter 4). Since management's ability to adopt and subsequently change investment decisions can greatly alter the value of a project, it should be considered in capital budgeting methodology. If we view a merger or acquisition as a single project, real options should be considered as an integral part of M&A valuation.

Traditional DCF techniques fail to account for management's ability to react to new information and make decisions that affect the outcome of a project. However, real options can be costly to obtain (e.g., the right to extend a lease or purchase property), complex to value, and dependent on highly problematic assumptions. They should not be considered unless they are clearly identifiable, management has the time and resources to exploit the option, and they would add significantly to the value of the underlying investment decision. For an intuitive discussion of real options, see Boer (2002) and Cromwell and Hodges (1998); for a more rigorous discussion of applying real options, see Damodaran (2002, pp. 772–815).

Identifying Real Options Embedded in M&A Decisions

Investment decisions, including M&As, often contain certain "embedded options," such as the ability to accelerate growth by adding to the initial investment (i.e., expand), delay the timing of the initial investment (i.e., delay), or walk away from the project (i.e., abandon). The case study at the beginning of this chapter illustrates the real options available to Microsoft in its attempt to takeover Yahoo. If Yahoo were to accept Microsoft's early 2008 bid, Microsoft could choose to accelerate investment contingent on the successful integration of Yahoo and MSN (i.e., option to expand) or spin off or divest the combined MSN/Yahoo business if the integration effort were unsuccessful (option to abandon). Absent a negotiated agreement with Yahoo, Microsoft could walk away, keeping open the possibility of returning for 100 percent of Yahoo at a later date if the Yahoo board became more receptive (option to delay).

In late 2008, Swiss mining company Xstrata PLC executed what could be characterized as an option to delay when it dropped its $10 billion bid for platinum producer Lonmin PLC, because of its inability to get financing due to turmoil in the credit markets. However, Xstrata signaled that it would resume efforts to acquire Lonmin at a later date by buying 24.9 percent of the firm's depressed shares in the open market. Already owning 10.7 percent of the target's shares, the additional purchase gave Xstrata a 35.6 percent stake in Lonmin at a low average cost, effectively blocking potential competing bids. Drug company Eli Lilly's purchase of ImClone Systems for $6.5 billion in late 2008 at a sizeable 51 percent premium may have reflected an embedded option to expand. A significant portion of ImClone's future value seems to depend on the commercial success of future drugs derived from the firm's colon cancer–fighting drug Erbitux.

Frequently, the existence of the real option increases the value of the expected NPV of an investment. For example, the NPV of an acquisition of a manufacturer operating at full capacity may have a lower value than if the NPV is adjusted for a decision made at a later date to expand capacity. If the additional capacity is fully utilized, the resulting higher level of future cash flows may increase the acquisition's NPV. In this instance, the value of the real option to expand is the difference between the NPV with and without expansion. An option to abandon an investment (i.e., divest or liquidate) often increases the NPV because of its effect on reducing risk. By exiting the business, the acquirer may be able to recover a portion of its original investment and truncate projected negative cash flows associated with the acquisition. Similarly, an acquirer may be able to increase the expected NPV by delaying the decision to acquire 100 percent of the target firm until the acquirer can be more certain about projected cash flows.

Pre-Closing Options and Associated Risks

Expand, delay, and abandon options exist in the period prior to closing an acquisition. An example of an option to delay closing occurs when a potential acquirer chooses to purchase a "toehold" position in the target firm to obtain leverage by acquiring voting shares in the target firm. The suitor is required to prenotify the target firm and publicly file its intentions with the SEC if its share of the target firm's outstanding stock reaches 5 percent. At this point the acquirer may choose to delay adding to its position or to move aggressively through a tender offer to achieve a controlling interest in the target firm. The latter option is an example of a option to expand its position. An opportunity cost is associated with each choice. If the suitor fails to expand its position, additional bidders made aware of its intentions may bid up the target firm's share price to a level considered prohibitive by the initial potential acquirer. Consequently, the initial acquirer may choose to abandon the entire effort. If the acquirer moves aggressively, it may lose the potential for reaching agreement with the target firm's board and management on friendly terms. The costs associated with a hostile takeover attempt include a potentially higher purchase price and the possible loss of key employees, customers, and suppliers during a more tumultuous integration of the target into the acquiring firm.

Other examples of delay options include an acquiring firm choosing to delay a merger until certain issues confronting the target are resolved, such as outstanding litigation or receiving regulatory approval (e.g., FDA approval for a new drug). The suitor may simply choose not to bid at that time and run the risk of losing the target firm to another acquirer or to negotiate an exclusive call option to buy the target at a predetermined price within a specified time period.

During the tumultuous credit markets of 2008 and 2009, bidders often were uncertain about lender commitments to finance the transaction and how the investors would view the proposed takeover immediately following the announcement of the transaction. Reverse termination fee structures became increasingly common among highly leveraged transactions such as Mars Corporation's takeover of Wrigley and InBev's buyout of Anheuser-Busch. Normally, a breakup or termination fee is paid by the seller to the buyer if the seller decides to sell to another bidder following the signing of agreement of purchase and sale with the initial bidder. In a reverse termination fee arrangement, the bidder pays the seller a fee to withdraw from the transaction, often due to "financial failure." Financial failure may reflect the inability to obtain bridge financing or permanent financing costs far exceeding the value of the reverse fee.

The reverse fee could be viewed as a real option held by the buyer to abandon the deal. In mid-2008, Excel Technologies' shares traded at a 7.5 percent discount to a tender offer that was scheduled to close in 30 days. The size of the discount reflected investor concern that the buyer, GSI Group, would exercise its $9 million reverse termination fee to withdraw from the contract since its stock had fallen by 35 percent since the deal's announcement, reflecting investor displeasure with the proposed takeover.

Postclosing Options and Associated Risks

Following closing, the acquirer also has the opportunity to expand, delay, or abandon new investment in the target firm. Acquiring firms generally have some degree of control over the timing of their investment decisions. For example, the acquiring firm's management may choose to make the level of investment in the target firm following closing contingent on the performance of actual cash flows compared to projected cash flows. If actual performance exceeds expectations, the acquirer may choose to accelerate its level of investment. In contrast, if performance is disappointing, the acquirer may opt to delay investment or even abandon the target firm either through divestiture or liquidation.

Valuing Real Options for Mergers and Acquisitions

Three ways to value real options are discussed in this book. The first is to use discounted cash flow, relative valuation, or asset-oriented methods and ignore alternative real options by assuming that their value is essentially zero. This suggests implicitly that management will not change the decision to invest once it has been made. The second is to value the real options in the context of a decision tree analysis. A decision tree is an expanded timeline that branches into alternative paths whenever an event can have multiple outcomes (see Lasher, 2005, pp. 428–433). The points at which the tree branches are called *nodes*. The decision tree is most useful whenever the investment decision is subject to a relatively small number of probable outcomes and the investment decision can be made in clearly defined stages. The third method involves the valuation of the real option as a put or call, assuming that the underlying asset has the characteristics of financial options. Valuing real options in this manner is often referred to as *contingent claim valuation*. A **contingent claim** is a claim that pays off only if certain events occur.

Several methods are employed for valuing financial options. The standard method for valuing a financial option is the Black–Scholes model, which is typically applied to European options. Such options can be exercised only at the expiration date of the option (i.e., a single, predefined date). This is an example of a "closed-form" model, in which the underlying assumptions do not vary over time. A more flexible, albeit often more complex, valuation method is a lattice-based option valuation technique, such as the binomial valuation model. Such models are sometimes used to value so-called American options, which may be exercised at any time before the expiration date. The binomial option-pricing model is based on the notion that the value of the underlying asset in any time period can change in one of two directions (i.e., either up or down), thereby creating a lattice of alternative asset pricing points. Because the lattice model, unlike the Black–Scholes model, values the asset (e.g., stock price) underlying the option at various points in time, such important economic assumptions as risk and the risk-free rate of return can be assumed to vary over time. While the binomial model allows for changing key assumptions over time, it often requires a large number of inputs, in terms of expected future prices at each node or pricing point. While the binomial options model offers greater flexibility in terms of allowing assumptions to vary over time, the Black–Scholes offers greater simplicity. For this reason, the valuation of real options expressed as call or put options are valued in this book using the Black–Scholes method. For a recent discussion of alternative real option valuation methods, see Hitchner (2006), Whaley (2006), and Shreve (2005).

Valuing Real Options Using a Decision Tree Framework

Exhibit 8–10 illustrates how the presence of real options may affect the NPV associated with an acquisition in which management has identified two cash flow scenarios (i.e., those associated with a successful acquisition and those with an unsuccessful one). Each

Exhibit 8-10 The Impact of Real Options on Valuing Mergers and Acquisitions

						Projected Target Firm Cash Flows				
	Year 0	Year 1	Year 2	Year 3	Year 4	Year 5	Year 6	Year 7	Year 8	Year 9
First Branch: Option for Immediate Investment/Acquisition										
Enterprise cash flows										
Successful case	−300	30	35	40	45	50	55	60	65	
Unsuccessful case	−300	−5	−5	−5	−5	−5	−5	−5	−5	
Weighted cash flows										
Successful case (60%)	0	18	21	24	27	30	33	36	39	
Unsuccessful case (40%)	0	−2	−2	−2	−2	−2	−2	−2	−2	
Expected enterprise cash flow	−300	16	19	22	25	28	31	34	37	
Expected NPV Yr 1–8 @ 15%										−166
Expected terminal value @ 13%; sustainable growth rate = 5%										159
Expected total NPV										−7
Second Branch: Option to Abandon (Divest or Liquidate)										
Enterprise cash flows										
Successful case	−300	30	35	40	45	50	55	60	65	
Unsuccessful case	−300	−5	−5	−5	−5	−5	−5	−5	−5	
Weighted cash flows										
Successful case (60%)	0	18	21	24	27	30	33	36	39	
Unsuccessful case (40%)	0	−2	−2	150	0	0	0	0	0	
Expected enterprise cash flow	−300	16	19	174	27	30	33	36	39	
Expected NPV Yr 1–6 @ 15%										−75
Expected terminal value @ 13%; sustainable growth rate = 5%										167
Expected total NPV										92

Continued

Exhibit 8–10 The Impact of Real Options on Valuing Mergers and Acquisitions — Cont'd

| | Projected Target Firm Cash Flows | | | | | | | | | |
	Year 0	Year 1	Year 2	Year 3	Year 4	Year 5	Year 6	Year 7	Year 8	Year 9
Third Branch: Option to Delay Investment or Acquisition										
Enterprise cash flows										
Successful case	0	−300	35	40	45	50	55	60	65	70
Unsuccessful case	0	−300	0	0	0	0	0	0	0	0
Weighted cash flows										
Successful case (60%)	0	0	21	24	27	30	33	36	39	42
Unsuccessful case (40%)	0	0	0	0	0	0	0	0	0	0
Expected enterprise cash flow	0	−300	21	24	27	30	33	36	39	42
Expected NPV @ 15%										−146
Expected terminal value @ 13%; sustainable growth rate = 5%										180
Expected total NPV										34

Note: The NPV for the delay option is discounted at the end of year 1, while the other options are discounted from year 0 (i.e., the present).

pair of cash flow scenarios is associated with what are believed to be the range of reasonable options associated with acquiring the target firm. These include the option to immediately acquire, delay, or to abandon the acquisition. Each outcome is shown as a "branch" on a tree. Each branch shows the cash flows and probabilities associated with each cash flow scenario displayed as a timeline. The probability of realizing the "successful" cash flow projections is assumed to be 60 percent and the "unsuccessful" one is 40 percent. The expected enterprise cash flow of the target firm is the sum of the projected cash flows of both the "successful" and "unsuccessful" scenarios multiplied by the estimated probability associated with each scenario. The target firm is assumed to have been acquired for $300 million, and the NPV is estimated using a 15 percent discount rate. The terminal value is calculated using the constant growth method with an assumed terminal-period growth rate of 5 percent. With an NPV of –$7 million, the immediate investment option suggests that the acquisition should not be undertaken. However, the analyst should evaluate alternative options to determine if they represent attractive investment strategies.

By recognizing that the target firm could be sold or liquidated, the expected NPV based on projected enterprise cash flows is $92 million, suggesting that the acquisition should be undertaken. This assumes that the target firm is sold or liquidated at the end of the third year following its acquisition for $152 million. Note that the cash flow in year 3 is $150 million, reflecting the difference between $152 million and the –$2 million in operating cash flow during the third year. The expected NPV with the option to delay is estimated at $34 million. Note that the investment is made after a one-year delay only if the potential acquirer feels confident that competitive market conditions will support the projected "successful" scenario cash flows. Consequently, the "unsuccessful" scenario's cash flows are zero.

Figure 8–2 summarizes the results provided in Exhibit 8–10 in a decision tree framework. Of the three options analyzed, valuing the target including the value of the cash flows associated with the option to abandon would appear to be the most attractive investment strategy based on NPV. The values of the abandon and delay options are estimated as the difference between each of their NPVs and the NPV for the "immediate investment or acquisition" case.

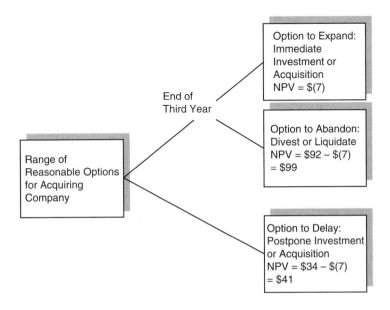

FIGURE 8–2 Real options' decision tree. *Note:* See Exhibit 8–10 for data.

Valuing Real Options Using the Black–Scholes Model

Options to assets whose cash flows have large variances and a long time before they expire are typically more valuable than those with smaller variances and less time remaining. The greater variance and time to expiration increases the chance that the factors affecting cash flows will change a project from one with a negative NPV to one with a positive NPV. If we know the values of five variables, we can use the Black–Scholes model to establish a theoretical price for an option. The limitations of the Black–Scholes model are the difficulty in estimating key assumptions (particularly risk), its assumptions that interest rates and risk are constant, that it can be exercised only on the expiration date, and that taxes and transactions costs are minimal. Modified versions of the Black–Scholes model are discussed in Arzac (2006). The basic Black–Scholes formula for valuing a call option is given as follows:

$$C = SN(d_1) - Ee^{-Rt}N(d_2) \tag{8–4}$$

where

C = theoretical call option value.

$$d_1 = \frac{\ln(S/E) + [R + (1/2)\sigma^2]t}{\sigma\sqrt{t}}$$

$d_2 = d_1 - \sigma\sqrt{t}$

S = stock price or underlying asset price.

E = exercise or strike price.

R = risk-free interest rate corresponding to the life of the option.

σ^2 = variance (a measure of risk) of the stock's or underlying asset's return.

t = time to expiration of the option.

$N(d_1)$ and $N(d_2)$ = cumulative normal probability values of d_1 and d_2.

The term Ee^{-Rt} is the present value of the exercise price when continuous discounting is used. The terms $N(d_1)$ and $N(d_2)$, which involve the cumulative probability function, are the terms that take risk into account. $N(d_1)$ and $N(d_2)$ measure the probability that the value of the call option will pay off and the probability that the option will be exercised, respectively. These two values are Z scores from the normal probability function, and they can be found in cumulative normal distribution function tables for the standard normal random variable in many statistics books.

The variance (i.e., risk) to be used in the Black–Scholes model can be estimated in number of ways. First, risk could be estimated as the variance in the stock prices of similar firms or the assets whose cash flows enable the valuation of the option. For example, the average variance in the share prices of U.S. oil services companies could be used as the variance in the valuation of a real option associated with the potential purchase of an oil services firm. In another example, assume a potential acquirer of an oil company recognizes that, in buying the target, it would have a call option (real option to expand) to develop the firm's oil reserves at a later date. The acquirer could choose to value the target firm as a stand-alone entity and the option to develop the firm's reserves at some time in the future separately. Assuming the volume of reserves is known with certainty, the variance in world oil prices may be used as a proxy for the risk associated with an option to develop the reserves. If there is uncertainty with respect to the volume of reserves and the price of oil, the uncertainties can be combined by recognizing that the value of the reserves represents the price of oil times the quantity of reserves and estimating the variance of the dollar value of the reserves.

Second, the variance of cash flows from similar prior investments can be used. For example, drugs often require more than 10 years and a cumulative expenditure of more than $1 billion before they become commercially viable. A pharmaceutical company may use the variance associated with the cash flows of previously developed comparable drugs in valuing an option to invest in a new drug.

A third method is to use the standard deviation (i.e., square root of the variance) calculated by using commonly available software to conduct so-called Monte Carlo simulation analyses. For each simulation, a range of outcomes are generated, based on the predefined probability distributions provided by the analyst for the inputs (e.g., sales growth, inflation) underlying the cash flows. The analyst selects one outcome from each simulation and calculates the present values of the cash flows based on the selected outcomes. The average of the range of present values calculated from running repeated simulations is the expected value of the project. By squaring the standard deviation associated with the range of present values, a variance can be calculated to be used in valuing the real option.

Assuming the necessary inputs (e.g., risk) can be estimated, a real option can be valued as a put or call option. The net present value (NPV) of an investment can be adjusted for the value of the real option as follows:

$$\text{Total NPV} = \text{Present value} - \text{Investment} + \text{Option value} \qquad (8\text{–}5)$$

Option to Expand   To value a firm with an option to expand, the analyst must define the potential value of the option. For example, suppose a firm has an opportunity to enter a new market. The analyst must project cash flows that accrue to the firm if it enters the market. The cost of entering the market becomes the option's exercise price and the present value of the expected cash flows resulting from entering the market becomes the value of the firm or underlying asset. The present value is likely to be less than the initial entry costs or the firm would already have entered the market. The variance of the firm's value can be estimated by using the variances of the market values of publicly traded firms that currently participate in that market. The option's life is the length of time during which the firm expects to achieve a competitive advantage by entering the market now. Exhibit 8–11 illustrates how to value an option to expand.

Exhibit 8–11 Valuing an Option to Expand Using the Black–Sholes Model

AJAX Inc. is negotiating to acquire Comet Inc. to broaden its product offering. Based on its projections of Comet's cash flows as a stand-alone business, AJAX cannot justify paying more than $150 million for Comet. However, Comet is insisting on a price of $160 million. Following additional due diligence, AJAX believes that, by applying its technology, Comet's product growth rate could be accelerated significantly. By buying Comet, AJAX is buying an option to expand in a market in which it is not participating currently by retooling Comet's manufacturing operations. The cost of retooling Comet's manufacturing operations to fully utilize AJAX's technology requires an initial investment of $100 million. The present value of the expected cash flows from making this investment today is $80 million. Consequently, based on this

Continued

Exhibit 8–11 Valuing an Option to Expand Using the Black–Sholes Model — Cont'd

information, paying the higher purchase cannot be justified by making the investment in retooling now.

However, if Comet (employing AJAX's new technology) could be first to market with the new product offering, it could achieve a dominant market share. While the new product would be expensive to produce in small quantities, the cost of production is expected to fall as larger volumes are sold, making Comet the low-cost manufacturer. Moreover, because of patent protection, AJAX believes that it is unlikely that competitors would be able to develop a superior technology for at least 10 years. An analysis of similar investments in the past suggests the variance of the projected cash flows is 20 percent. The option is expected to expire in 10 years, reflecting the time remaining on AJAX's patent. The current 10-year Treasury bond rate (corresponding to the expected term of the option) is 6 percent. Is the value of the option to expand, expressed as a call option, sufficient to justify paying Comet's asking price of $160 million? See equation (8–4).

Solution

Value of the asset (PV of cash flows from retooling Comet's operations)	= $80 million
Exercise price (PV of the cost of retooling Comet's operations)	= $100 million
Variance of the cash flows	= 0.20
Time to expiration	= 10 years
Risk-free interest rate	= 0.06

$$d_1 = \frac{\ln(\$80/\$100) + [.06 + (1/2)0.2]10}{\sqrt{.2} \times \sqrt{10}} = \frac{-.2231 + 1.600}{.4472 \times 3.1623} = \frac{1.3769}{1.4142} = .9736$$

$$d_2 = 0.9736 - 1.4142 = -0.4406$$

$$C = \$80(0.8340) - \$100(2.7183)^{-0.06 \times 10}(0.3300) = \$66.72 - \$18.11$$
$$= \$48.61 \text{ (value of the call option)}$$

The net present value of the investment in retooling Comet's operations including the value of the call option is $28.61 million (i.e., $80 – $100 + $48.61). Therefore, it does make sense for AJAX to exercise its option to retool Comet's operations, and AJAX can justify paying Comet its $160 million asking price.

Note: Z values for d_1 and d_2 were obtained from a cumulative standardized normal distribution, $N(d)$, table in Levine, Berenson, and Stephan, 1999, pp. E6–E7.

Option to Delay The underlying asset is the project to which the firm has exclusive rights. The current value is the present value of expected cash flows from undertaking the project now. The variance of cash flows from similar past projects or acquisitions can be used to estimate the variance for the project under consideration. A firm exercises an option to delay when it decides to postpone investing in a project. The option's exercise price is the cost of making the initial investment.

The option to delay expires whenever the exclusive rights to the project ends. Since the option eventually expires, excess profits associated with having the option disappear as other competitors emerge to exploit the opportunity. This opportunity cost associated with delaying implementation of an investment is similar to an adjustment made to the Black–Scholes model for stocks that pay dividends. The payment of a dividend is equivalent to reducing the value of the stock, since such funds are not reinvested in the firm to support future growth. Consequently, for a project whose expected cash flows are spread evenly throughout the option period, each year the project is delayed the firm will lose one year of profits that it could have earned. Therefore, the annual cost of delay is $1/n$, where n is the time period for which the option is valid. If cash flows are not spread evenly, the cost of delay may be estimated as the projected cash flow for the next period as a percent of the current present value (see Exhibit 8–12). Equation (8–4) may be modified to reflect these considerations.

$$C = SN(d_1)e^{-DYt} - Ee^{-Rt}N(d_2) \tag{8–6}$$

where

$$d_1 = \frac{\ln(S/E) + (R - DY + 1/2\sigma^2)t}{\sigma\sqrt{t}}$$

$$d_2 = d_1 - \sigma\sqrt{t}$$

DY = Dividend yield or opportunity cost.

Exhibit 8–12 Valuing an Option to Delay Using the Black–Scholes Model

Aztec Corp has an opportunity to acquire Pharmaceuticals Unlimited, which has a new cancer-fighting drug recently approved by the Federal Drug Administration. While current market studies indicate that the new drug's market acceptance will be slow, due to competing drugs, it is believed that the drug will have meteoric growth potential in the long-term as new applications are identified. The R&D and commercialization costs associated with exploiting new applications are expected to require an upfront investment of $60 million. However, Aztec can delay making this investment until it is more confident of the new drug's actual growth potential.

It is believed that Pharmaceuticals Unlimited's research and development efforts give it a five-year time period before competitors have similar drugs on the market to exploit these new applications. However, if the higher growth for the new drug and its related applications do not materialize, Aztec estimates that the NPV for Pharmaceuticals Unlimited to be $(30) million. That is, if the new cancer-fighting drug does not realize its potential, it makes no sense for Aztec to acquire Pharmaceuticals Unlimited. Cash flows from previous drug introductions have exhibited a variance equal to 50 percent of the present value of the cash flows. Simulating alternative growth scenarios for this new drug provides an expected value of $40 million. The five-year Treasury bond rate (corresponding to the expected term of the option) is 6 percent. Despite the negative NPV associated with the acquisition, does the existence of the option to delay, valued as a call option, justify Aztec acquiring Pharmaceuticals Unlimited? See equation (8–6).

Continued

Exhibit 8–12 Valuing an Option to Delay Using the Black–Scholes Model — Cont'd

Solution

Value of the asset (PV of projected cash flows for the new drug)	= $40 million
Exercise price (Investment required to fully develop the new drug)	= $60 million
Variance of the cash flows	= 0.5
Time to expiration (t)	= 5 years
Risk free interest rate	= 0.06
Dividend yield or opportunity cost (cost of delay = 1/5)	= 0.2

$$d_1 = \frac{\ln(\$40/\$60) + (0.06 - 0.2 + {}^1\!/_2 0.5)5}{\sqrt{0.5}\sqrt{5}}$$

$$= \frac{-0.4055 + 0.5500}{0.7071 \times 2.2361} = \frac{0.1445}{1.5811} = 0.0914$$

$$d_2 = .0914 - 1.5811 = -1.4897$$

$$C = \$40(0.5359)2.7183^{-0.2 \times 5} - \$60(0.0681)(2.7183)^{-0.06 \times 5}$$
$$= \$40 \times (0.5359) \times 0.3679 - \$60 \times (0.0681) \times 0.7408 = 7.89 - 3.03$$
$$= \$4.86 \text{ million (value of the call option)}$$

The modest $4.86 million value of the call option is insufficient to offset the negative NPV of $30 million associated with the acquisition. Consequently, Aztec should not acquire Pharmaceuticals Unlimited.

Note: Z values for d_1 and d_2 were obtained from a cumulative standardized normal distribution, $N(d)$, table in Levine, Berenson, and Stephan, 1999, pp. E6–E7.

Option to Abandon   For a project with a remaining life of n years, the value of continuing the project should be compared to its value in liquidation or sale (i.e., abandonment). The project should be continued if its value exceeds the liquidation value or sale value. Otherwise, the project should be abandoned. The option to abandon is equivalent to a put option (i.e., the right to sell an asset for a predetermined price at or before a stipulated time). The Black–Scholes formula for valuing a call option can (be rewritten to value a put option (P) as follows. See equation (8–4):

$$P = S[1 - N(d_2)]e^{-Rt} - E[1 - N(d_1)]e^{-DYt} \qquad (8\text{–}7)$$

where

P = Theoretical put option value

$$d_1 = \frac{\ln(S/E) + [R - DY + (1/2)\sigma^2]t}{\sigma\sqrt{t}}$$

$$d_2 = d_1 - \sigma\sqrt{t}$$

Exhibit 8–13 illustrates how the abandonment or put option can be applied.

Exhibit 8–13 Valuing an Option to Abandon Using the Black–Scholes Model

BETA Inc has agreed to acquire a 30 percent ownership stake in Bernard Mining for $225 million to help finance the development of new mining operations. The mines are expected to have an economically useful life of 35 years. BETA estimates that the present value of its share of the cash flows would be $210 million, resulting in a negative NPV of $15 million (i.e., $210 million – $225 million). To induce BETA to make the investment, Bernard Mining has given BETA a put option enabling it to sell its share (i.e., abandon its investment) to Bernard at any point during the next five years for $175 million. The put option limits the downside risk to BETA.

In evaluating the terms of the deal, BETA needs to value the put option, whose present value varies depending on when it is exercised. BETA estimates the average variance in the present values of future cash flows to be 20 percent based on the variance of the share prices of publicly traded similar mining companies. Since the value of the mines diminishes over time as the reserves are depleted, the present value of the investment will diminish over time because fewer years of cash flows will remain. The dividend yield or opportunity cost is estimated to be 1/number of years of profitable reserves remaining. The risk-free rate of return is 4 percent. Is the value of the put option sufficient to justify making the investment despite the negative net present value of the investment without the inclusion of the option value? See equation (8–7).

Solution

Present or expected value of BETA's 30 percent share of Bernard SA	= $210 million
Exercise price of put option	= $175 million
Time to expiration of put option	= 5 years
Variance	= 20 percent
Dividend yield (1/35)	= 0.029

$$d_1 = \frac{\ln(\$210/\$175) + (.04 - .029 + (1/2)0.2)5}{\sqrt{.2} \times \sqrt{5}}$$

$$= \frac{.1823 + .5550}{.4472 \times 2.2361} = \frac{.7373}{1.0} = .7373$$

$$d_2 = 0.7373 - 1.000 = -0.2627$$

$$P = \$210 \times (1 - 0.6026) \times 2.7183^{-0.04 \times 5} - \$175 \times (1 - 0.7673) \times 2.7183^{-0.029 \times 5}$$

$$= \$210 \times 0.3974 \times 0.8187 - \$175 \times 0.2327 \times 0.8650$$

$$= \$33.10$$

The value of the put option represents the additional value created by reducing the risk associated with the investment. This additional value justifies the investment, as the sum of the NPV of $(15) million and the put option of $33.10 million gives a total NPV of $18.10 million.

Note: Z scores for d_1 and d_2 were obtained from a cumulative standardized normal distribution, $N(d)$, table in Levine, Berenson, and Stephan, 1999, pp. E6–E7.

Determining When to Use the Different Approaches to Valuation

Table 8–7 summarizes the circumstances under which it would be most appropriate to use each valuation methodology. These methodologies include the discounted cash flow (DCF) approach discussed in detail in Chapter 7, as well as the relative, asset-oriented, replacement-cost, and contingent claims methods (i.e., real options) discussed in this chapter. If the intention is to obtain a controlling interest in the firm, a control premium must be added to the estimated economic value of the firm to determine the purchase price. The exception is the comparable recent transactions method, which already contains a premium.

Table 8–7   When to Use Various Valuation Methodologies

Methodology	Use Each Methodology When
Discounted cash flow	The firm is publicly traded or private with identifiable cash flows A startup has some history to facilitate cash flow forecasts An analyst has a long time horizon An analyst has confidence in forecasting the firm's cash flows Current or near-term earnings or cash flows are negative but are expected to turn positive in the future A firm's competitive advantage is expected to be sustainable The magnitude and timing of cash flows varies significantly
Comparable companies	Many firms exhibit similar growth, return, and risk characteristics An analyst has a short-term time horizon Prior, current, or near-term earnings or cash flows are positive An analyst has confidence that the markets are on average right Sufficient information to predict cash flows is lacking Firms are cyclical. For P/E ratios, use normalized earnings (i.e., earnings averaged throughout the business cycle) Growth rate differences among firms are large. Use the PEG ratio.
Comparable transactions	Many recent transactions of similar firms exist An analyst has a short-term time horizon An analyst has confidence the markets are on average right Sufficient information to predict cash flows is lacking
Same or comparable industry	Firms within an industry or comparable industry are substantially similar in terms of profitability, growth, and risk An analyst has confidence the markets are on average right Sufficient information to predict cash flows is lacking
Replacement cost approach	An analyst wants to know the current cost of replicating a firm's assets The firm's assets are easily identifiable, tangible, and separable The firm's earnings or cash flows are negative
Tangible book value	The firm's assets are highly liquid The firm is a financial services or product distribution business The firm's earnings and cash flows are negative
Breakup value	The sum of the value of the businesses or product lines constituting a firm are believed to exceed its value as a going concern
Liquidation value	An analyst wants to know asset values if they were liquidated today Assets are separable, tangible, and marketable Firms are bankrupt or subject to substantial financial distress An orderly liquidation is possible

Table 8–7 — Cont'd

Methodology	Use Each Methodology When
Real options (contingent claims)	Additional value can be created if management has a viable option to expand, delay, or abandon an investment
	Assets not currently generating cash flows have the potential to do so
	The markets have not valued the management decision-making flexibility associated with the option
	Assets have characteristics most resembling financial options
	The asset owner has some degree of exclusivity (e.g., a patent)

Things to Remember

Relative valuation and asset-oriented techniques offer a variety of alternatives to discounted cash-flow estimates. The comparable companies approach entails the multiplication of certain value indicators for the target, such as earnings by the appropriate valuation multiple for comparable companies. Similarly, the comparable transactions method involves the multiplication of the target's earnings by the same valuation multiple for recent, similar transactions. The comparable industry approach applies industry average multiples to earnings, cash flow, book value, or sales. Asset-oriented methods, such as tangible book value, are very useful for valuing financial services companies and distribution companies. Liquidation or breakup value is the projected price of the firm's assets sold separately less its liabilities and associated expenses. Of these methods, only the comparable recent transactions approach includes the value of the purchase price or control premium.

Since no single valuation approach ensures accuracy, analysts often choose to use a weighted average of several valuation methods to increase their level of confidence in the final estimate. This approach relies on an averaging process to achieve potentially more reliable estimates. It also allows the analyst to interject their own preferences for certain methods over others.

Real options refer to management's ability to revise corporate investment decisions after they have been made. Traditional DCF techniques do not recognize management's ability to react to new information. Since real options can be costly, complex, and dependent on questionable assumptions, they should not be considered unless they are clearly identifiable, realizable, and significantly add to the value of the underlying investment.

Chapter Discussion Questions

8–1. Does the application of the comparable companies valuation method require the addition of an acquisition premium? Why or why not?

8–2. Which is generally considered more accurate: the comparable companies or recent transactions method? Explain your answer.

8–3. What key assumptions are implicit in using the comparable companies valuation method? The recent comparable transactions method?

8–4. Explain the primary differences between the income (discounted cash flow), market-based, and asset-oriented valuation methods?

8–5. Under what circumstances might it be more appropriate to use relative valuation methods rather than the DCF approach? Be specific.

8–6. PEG ratios allow for the adjustment of relative valuation methods for the expected growth of the firm. How might this be helpful in selecting potential acquisition targets? Be specific.

8–7. How is the liquidation value of the firm calculated? Why is the assumption of orderly liquidation important?

8–8. What are real options and how are they applied in valuing acquisitions?

8–9. Give examples of pre- and postclosing real options. Be specific.

8–10. Conventional DCF analysis does not incorporate the effects of real options into the valuation of an asset. How might an analyst incorporate the potential impact of real options into conventional DCF valuation methods?

Answers to these Chapter Discussion Questions are available in the Online Instructor's Manual for instructors using this book.

Chapter Practice Problems and Answers

8–11. BigCo's chief financial officer is trying to determine a fair value for PrivCo, a non-publicly traded firm that BigCo is considering acquiring. Several of PrivCo's competitors, Ion International and Zenon, are publicly traded. Ion and Zenon have P/E ratios of 20 and 15, respectively. Moreover, Ion and Zenon's shares trade at a multiple of earnings before interest, taxes, depreciation, and amortization (EBITDA) of 10 and 8, respectively. BigCo estimates that next year PrivCo will achieve net income and EBITDA of $4 million and $8 million, respectively. To gain a controlling interest in the firm, BigCo expects to have to pay at least a 30 percent premium to the firm's market value. What should BigCo expect to pay for PrivCo?

a. Based on P/E ratios?

b. Based on EBITDA?

Answers:

a. $91 million.

b. $93.6 million.

8–12. LAFCO Industries believes that its two primary product lines, automotive and commercial aircraft valves, are becoming obsolete rapidly. Its free cash flow is diminishing quickly as it loses market share to new firms entering its industry. LAFCO has $200 million in debt outstanding. Senior management expects the automotive and commercial aircraft valve product lines to generate $25 million and $15 million, respectively, in earnings before interest, taxes, depreciation, and amortization next year. The operating liabilities associated with these two product lines are minimal. Senior management also believes that it will not be able to upgrade these product lines because of declining cash flow and excessive current leverage. A competitor to its automotive valve business last year sold for 10 times EBITDA. Moreover, a company similar to its commercial aircraft valve product line sold last month for 12 times EBITDA. Estimate LAFCO's breakup value before taxes.

Answer: $230 million.

8–13. Siebel Incorporated, a non-publicly traded company, has 2009 earnings before interest and taxes (EBIT) of $33.3 million, which is expected to grow at 5 percent annually into the foreseeable future. The firm's combined federal, state, and local tax rate is 40 percent; capital spending will equal the firm's rate of depreciation;

and the annual change in working capital is expected to be minimal. The firm's beta is estimated to be 2.0, the 10-year Treasury bond is 5 percent, and the historical risk premium of stocks over the risk-free rate is 5.5 percent. Rand Technology, a direct competitor of Siebel's, recently was sold at a purchase price of 11 times its 2009 EBIT, which included a 20 percent premium. Aware of the premium paid for the purchase of Rand, Siebel's equity owners would like to determine what it might be worth if they were to attempt to sell the firm in the near future. They chose to value the firm using the discounted cash flow and comparable recent transactions methods. They believe that either method provides an equally valid estimate of the firm's value.

a. What is the value of Siebel using the DCF method?

b. What is the value using the comparable recent transactions method?

c. What would be the value of the firm if we combine the results of both methods?

Answers:

a. $228.9 million.

b. $220 million.

c. $224.5 million.

8–14. Titanic Corporation reached an agreement with its creditors to voluntarily liquidate its assets and use the proceeds to pay off as much of its liabilities as possible. The firm anticipates that it will be able to sell off its assets in an orderly fashion, realizing as much as 70 percent of the book value of its receivables, 40 percent of its inventory, and 25 percent of its net fixed assets (excluding land). However, the firm believes that the land on which it is located can be sold for 120 percent of book value. The firm has legal and professional expenses associated with the liquidation process of $2.9 million. The firm has only common stock outstanding. Using Table 8–8, estimate the amount of cash that would remain for the firm's common shareholders once all assets have been liquidated.

Answer: $1.3 million.

8–15. Best's Foods is seeking to acquire the Heinz Baking Company, whose shareholders' equity and goodwill are $41 million and $7 million, respectively. A comparable bakery was recently acquired for $400 million, 30 percent more than its tangible book value (TBV). What was the tangible book value of the recently acquired bakery? How much should Best's Foods expect to have to pay for the Heinz Baking Company? Show your work.

Answer: The TBV of the recently acquired bakery = $307.7 million and the likely purchase price of Heinz = $44.2 million.

Table 8–8   Titanic's Assets in Problem 8–14

Balance Sheet Item	Book Value of Assets	Liquidation Value
Cash	$10	
Accounts receivable	$20	
Inventory	$15	
Net fixed assets excluding land	$8	
Land	$6	
Total assets	$59	
Total liabilities	$35	
Shareholders' equity	$24	

8–16. Delhi Automotive Inc. is the leading supplier of specialty fasteners for passenger cars in the U.S. market, with an estimated 25 percent share of this $5 billion market. Delhi's rapid growth in recent years has been fueled by high levels of reinvestment in the firm. While this has resulted in the firm having "state-of-the-art" plants, it also resulted in the firm showing limited profitability and positive cash flow. Delhi is privately owned and has announced that it is going to undertake an initial public offering in the near future. Investors know that economies of scale are important in this high-fixed-cost industry and understand that market share is an important determinant of future profitability. Thornton Auto Inc., a publicly traded firm and the leader in this market, has an estimated market share of 38 percent and an $800 million market value. How should investors value the Delhi IPO? Show your work.

Answer: $526.3 million.

8–17. Photon Inc. is considering acquiring one of its competitors. Photon's management wants to buy a firm it believes is most undervalued. The firm's three major competitors, AJAX, BABO, and COMET, have current market values of $375 million, $310 million, and $265 million, respectively. AJAX's FCFE is expected to grow at 10 percent annually, while BABO's and COMET's FCFE are projected to grow by 12 and 14 percent per year, respectively. AJAX, BABO, and COMET's current year FCFE are $24, $22, and $17 million, respectively. The industry average price-to-FCFE ratio and growth rate are 10 and 8 percent, respectively. Estimate the market value of each of the three potential acquisition targets based on the information provided. Which firm is the most undervalued? Which firm is most overvalued? Show your work.

Answer: AJAX is most overvalued and Comet is most undervalued.

8–18. Acquirer Incorporated's management believes that the most reliable way to value a potential target firm is by averaging multiple valuation methods, since all methods have their shortcomings. Consequently, Acquirer's chief financial officer estimates that the value of Target Inc. could range, before an acquisition premium is added, from a high of $650 million using discounted cash flow analysis to a low of $500 million using the comparable companies relative valuation method. A valuation based on a recent comparable transaction is $672 million. The CFO anticipates that Target Inc.'s management and shareholders would be willing to sell for a 20 percent acquisition premium, based on the premium paid for the recent comparable transaction. The CEO asks the CFO to provide a single estimate of the value of Target Inc. based on the three estimates. In calculating a weighted average of the three estimates, she gives a value of 0.5 to the recent transactions method, 3 to the DCF estimate, and 0.2 to the comparable companies estimate. What is the weighted average estimate she gives to the CEO? Show your work.

Answer: $690 million.

8–19. An investor group has the opportunity to purchase a firm whose primary asset is ownership of the exclusive rights to develop a parcel of undeveloped land sometime during the next five years. Without considering the value of the option to develop the property, the investor group believes the net present value of the firm is $(10) million. However, to convert the property to commercial use (i.e., exercise the option), the investors have to invest $60 million immediately in infrastructure improvements. The primary uncertainty associated with the property is how rapidly the surrounding area will grow. Based on their experience with similar properties, the investors estimate that the variance of the projected cash flows is 5 percent of NPV, which is $55 million. Assume the risk-free rate of return is 4 percent. What is the value of the call option the investor group would obtain by buying the firm? Is it sufficient to justify the acquisition of the firm? Show your work.

Answer: The value of the option is $13.47 million. The investor group should buy the firm since the value of the option more than offsets the $(10) million NPV of the firm if the call option were not exercised.

8–20. Acquirer Company's management believes that there is a 60 percent chance that Target Company's free cash flow to the firm will grow at 20 percent per year during the next five years from this year's level of $5 million. Sustainable growth beyond the fifth year is estimated at 4 percent per year. However, they also believe that there is a 40 percent chance that cash flow will grow at half that annual rate during the next five years, then at a 4 percent rate thereafter. The discount rate is estimated to be 15 percent during the high-growth period and 12 percent during the sustainable-growth period. What is the expected value of Target Company?

Answer: $94.93 million.

Solutions to these Practice Problems are available in the Online Instructor's Manual for instructors using this book.

Chapter Business Cases

Case Study 8–1. Google Buys YouTube—Brilliant or Misguided?

This case study illustrates how a value driver approach to valuation could have been used by Google to estimate the potential value of YouTube by collecting publicly available data for a comparable business. Note the importance of clearly identifying key assumptions underlying the valuation. The credibility of the valuation ultimately depends on the credibility of the assumptions.

How much would you pay for a business with no significant revenues, let alone profits? Ask Google. It purchased video-sharing website YouTube on October 9, 2006, for $1.65 billion in stock. At that time, the business had been in existence only for 14 months and consisted of 65 employees. However, what it lacked in size it made up in global recognition and a rapidly escalating number of site visitors. A little more than one year earlier, News Corp had paid $580 million for Intermix Media, the owner of MySpace, then the fifth most viewed Internet domain in the United States. MySpace.com users access the site for dating, making friends, professional networking, and sharing interests. With a larger percentage of advertising dollars moving from traditional outlets to the online venue, News Corp and Google, like most media firms, are attempting to further increase their Internet exposure.

Under pressure to continue to fuel its own meteoric 77 percent annual revenue growth rate, Google moved aggressively to acquire YouTube in an attempt to assume center stage in the rapidly growing online video market. With no debt, $9 billion in cash, and a net profit margin of about 25 percent, Google was in remarkable financial health for a firm growing so rapidly. The acquisition was by far the most expensive acquisition by Google in its relatively short eight-year history. In 2005, Google spent $130.5 million in acquiring 15 small firms. Google seems to be placing a big bet that YouTube will become a huge marketing hub as its increasing number of viewers attracts advertisers interested in moving from television to the Internet.

Started in February 2005 in the garage of one of the founders, YouTube displays more than 100 million videos daily and has an estimated 72 million visitors from around the world each month, of which 34 million are unique. Unique visitors are those whose IP addresses are counted only once no matter how many times they visit a website during a given period. As part of Google, YouTube would retain its name and current headquarters in San Bruno, California. In addition to receiving funding from Google, YouTube would be able to tap into Google's substantial technological and advertising expertise. Although YouTube does not currently run advertising within the videos shown on its sites, it has plans to do so to tap potentially lucrative advertising revenues.

While most videos on YouTube are homemade, the site also features material protected by copyright. This has spurred some observers to predict that the firm will be buried in an avalanche of copyright infringement lawsuits filed by media companies and artists in a manner similar to Napster, a music file sharing site. In an effort to ward off a similar fate, YouTube announced new partnerships with Universal Music Group, CBS Corp., Sony BMG Music Entertainment, Warner Music Group Inc., and other important content providers. To insulate itself from potential lawsuits and associated legal fees and possible penalties for copyright violations, Google withheld 12.5 percent of the purchase price (457,000 shares valued at $224 million as of November 14, 2006) for one year in an escrow account.

To determine if Google is likely to earn its cost of equity on its investment in YouTube, we have to establish a base-year free cash-flow estimate for YouTube. This may be done by examining the performance of a similar but more mature website, such as about.com. Acquired by *The New York Times* in February 2005 for $410 million, about.com is a website offering consumer information and advice and is believed to be one of the biggest and most profitable websites on the Internet, with estimated 2006 revenues of almost $100 million. With a monthly average number of unique visitors worldwide of 42.6 million, about.com's revenue per unique visitor is estimated to be about $0.15, based on monthly revenues of $6.4 million (Aboutmediakit, September 17, 2006, http://beanadvertiser.about.com/archive/news091606.html).

If we assume that these numbers can be duplicated by YouTube within the first full year of ownership by Google, YouTube could potentially achieve monthly revenue of $5.1 million (i.e., $0.15 per unique visitor × 34 million unique YouTube visitors) by the end of year. Assuming net profit margins comparable to Google's 25 percent, YouTube could generate about $1.28 million in after-tax profits on those sales. If that monthly level of sales and profits could be sustained for the full year, YouTube could achieve annual sales in the second year of $61.2 million (i.e., $5.1 × 12) and profit of $15.4 million ($1.28 × 12). Assuming optimistically that capital spending and depreciation grow at the same rate and that the annual change in working capital is minimal, YouTube's free cash flow would equal after-tax profits.

Recall that a firm earns its cost of equity on an investment whenever the net present value of the investment is zero. Assuming a risk-free rate of return of 5.5 percent, a beta of 0.82 (per Yahoo Finance), and an equity premium of 5.5 percent, Google's cost of equity would be 10 percent. For Google to earn its cost of equity on its investment in YouTube, YouTube would have to generate future cash flows whose present value would be at least $1.65 billion (i.e., equal to its purchase price). To achieve this result, YouTube's free cash flow to equity would have to grow at a compound annual average growth rate of 225 percent for the next 15 years, and then 5 percent per year thereafter. Note the present value of the cash flows during the initial 15-year period would be $605 million and the present value of the terminal period cash flows would be $1,005 million. Using a higher revenue per unique visitor assumption would result in a slower required annual growth rate in cash flows to earn the 10 percent cost of equity. However, a higher discount rate might be appropriate to reflect YouTube's higher investment risk. Using a higher discount rate would require revenue growth to be even faster to achieve an NPV equal to zero.

Google could easily have paid cash, assuming that the YouTube owners would prefer cash to Google stock. Perhaps Google saw its stock as overvalued and decided to use it now to minimize the number of new shares that it would have had to issue to acquire YouTube or perhaps YouTube shareholders simply viewed Google stock as more attractive than cash. Whatever the reason, Google appears to be placing a bet on the future that rests on highly optimistic valuation assumptions to justify the purchase price.

The events of early 2007 suggest that the valuation assumptions implicit in Google's initial valuation of YouTube may, indeed, turn out to be wildly optimistic. While YouTube continues to be a success in terms of the number of site visits, it appears to be a failure at this juncture in terms of advertising revenue, profit, and potential copyright infringements. In February 2007, Viacom filed a $1 billion lawsuit against YouTube for failure to pay "reasonable" licensing fees for the use of copyrighted material. In late March, NBC Universal and News Corp announced plans to create an online website, Hulu, to distribute professionally produced movies and TV content free to Internet users. The site would be funded by advertising. Early indications are that advertisers are getting a higher response rate to advertisements shown on Hulu than on YouTube. Although not broken out separately, Adegoke (2008) reported that YouTube's 2008 revenue reached about $200 million, about 1 percent of Google's $20 billion in annual revenue. It is unclear if the site is generating any profit.

Discussion Questions

1. What alternative valuation methods could Google have used to justify the purchase price it paid for YouTube? Discuss the advantages and disadvantages of each.

2. The purchase price paid for YouTube represented more than 1 percent of Google's then market value. If you were a Google shareholder at that time, how might you have evaluated the wisdom of the acquisition?

3. To what extent might the use of stock by Google have influenced the amount they were willing to pay for YouTube? How might the use of "overvalued" shares impact future appreciation of the stock?

4. What is the appropriate cost of equity for discounting future cash flows? Should it be Google's or YouTube's? Explain your answer.

5. What are the critical valuation assumptions implicit in the valuation method discussed in this case study? Be specific.

Solutions to these questions are provided in the Online Instructor's Guide accompanying this manual.

Case Study 8–2. Merrill Lynch and BlackRock Agree to Swap Assets

During the 1990s, many financial services companies began offering mutual funds to their current customers who were pouring money into the then booming stock market. Hoping to become financial supermarkets offering an array of financial services to their customers, these firms offered mutual funds under their own brand name. The proliferation of mutual funds made it more difficult to be noticed by potential customers and required the firms to boost substantially advertising expenditures at a time when increased competition was reducing mutual fund management fees. In addition, potential customers were concerned that brokers would promote their own firm's mutual funds to boost profits.

This trend reversed in recent years, as banks, brokerage houses, and insurance companies are exiting the mutual fund management business. Merrill Lynch agreed on February 15, 2006, to swap its mutual funds business for an approximate 49 percent stake in money-manager BlackRock Inc. The mutual fund or retail accounts represented a new customer group for BlackRock, founded in 1987, which had previously managed primarily institutional accounts.

At $453 billion in 2005, BlackRock's assets under management had grown four times faster than Merrill's $544 billion mutual fund assets. During 2005, BlackRock's net income increased to $270 million, or 63 percent over the prior year, as compared to Merrill's 27 percent growth in net income in its mutual fund business to $397 million. BlackRock and Merrill stock traded at 30 and 19 times estimated 2006 earnings.

Merrill assets and net income represented 55 percent and 60 percent of the combined BlackRock and Merrill assets and net income, respectively. Under the terms of the transaction, BlackRock would issue 65 million new common shares to Merrill. Based on BlackRock's February 14, 2005, closing price, the deal is valued at $9.8 billion. The common stock gave Merrill 49 percent of the outstanding BlackRock voting stock. PNC Financial and employees and public shareholders owned 34 percent and 17 percent, respectively. Merrill's ability to influence board decisions is limited since it has only 2 of 17 seats on the BlackRock board of directors. Certain "significant matters" require a 70 percent vote of all board members and 100 percent of the nine independent members, which include the two Merrill representatives. Merrill (along with PNC) must also vote its shares as recommended by the BlackRock board.

Discussion Questions

1. Merrill owns less than half of the combined firms, although it contributed more than one half of the combined firms' assets and net income. Discuss how you might use DCF and relative valuation methods to determine Merrill's proportionate ownership in the combined firms.
2. Why do you believe Merrill was willing to limit its influence in the combined firms?
3. What method of accounting would Merrill use to show its investment in BlackRock?

Solutions to these questions are found in the Online Instructor's Manual for instructors using this manual.

9

Applying Financial Modeling Techniques to Value, Structure, and Negotiate Mergers and Acquisitions

Great moments come from great opportunities.

—Herb Brooks

Inside M&A: HP Buys EDS—The Role of Financial Models in Decision Making

PC and printer behemoth, Hewlett-Packard (HP), had just announced its agreement to buy Electronic Data Systems (EDS) on May 9, 2008, for $13.9 billion (including assumed debt of $700 million) in an all-cash deal. The purchase price represented a 33 percent premium for EDS, a systems integration, consulting, and services firm. Expressing their dismay, investors drove HP's share price down by 11 percent in a single day following the announcement.

In a meeting arranged to respond to questions about the deal, HP's chief executive, Mark Hurd, found himself barraged by concerns about how the firm intended to recover the sizeable premium it had paid for EDS. The CEO has been a Wall Street darling since he assumed his position three years earlier. Under his direction, the firm's profits rose sharply as it successfully cut costs while growing revenue and integrating several acquisitions. Asked how HP expected to generate substantial synergies by combining two very different organizations, Mr. Hurd indicated that the firm and its advisors had done "double-digit thousands of hours" in due diligence and financial modeling and that they were satisfied that the cost synergies were there. In an effort to demonstrate how conservative they had been, the CEO indicated that potential revenue synergies had not even been included in their financial models. However, he was convinced that there were significant upside revenue opportunities (Richtel, 2008).

Chapter Overview

Financial modeling refers to the application of spreadsheet software to define simple arithmetic relationships among variables within the firm's income, balance sheet, and cash-flow statements and to define the interrelationships among the various financial statements. The primary objective in applying financial modeling techniques is to create a computer-based model, which facilitates the acquirer's understanding of the affect of changes in certain operating variables on the firm's overall performance and valuation (Benninga, 2000). Once in place, these models can be used to simulate alternative plausible valuation scenarios to determine which one enables the acquirer to achieve its financial objectives without violating identifiable constraints. Financial objectives could include earnings per share (EPS) for publicly traded firms, return on total capital for privately held firms, or return on equity for leveraged buyout firms. Typical constraints include Wall Street analysts' expectations for the firm's EPS, the acquirer's leverage compared with other firms in the same industry, and loan covenants limiting how the firm uses its available cash flow. Another important constraint is the risk tolerance of the acquiring company's management, which could be measured by the acquirer's target debt-to-equity ratio.

Financial models can be used to answer several sets of questions. The first set pertains to valuation. How much is the target company worth without the effects of synergy? What is the value of expected synergy? What maximum price should the acquiring company pay for the target? The second set of questions pertains to financing. Can the proposed purchase price be financed? What combination of potential sources of funds, both internally generated and external sources, provides the lowest cost of funds for the acquirer, subject to known constraints? The final set of questions pertains to deal structuring. What is the impact on the acquirer's financial performance if the deal is structured as a taxable rather than a nontaxable transaction? What is the impact on financial performance and valuation if the acquirer is willing to assume certain target company liabilities? Deal structuring considerations are discussed in more detail in Chapters 11 and 12.

The purpose of this chapter is to illustrate a process for building a financial model in the context of a merger or acquisition. The process allows the analyst to determine the minimum and maximum prices for a target firm and the initial offer price. The chapter contains numerous examples of how the effects of synergy can be included in a model. Simple formulas for calculating share-exchange ratios and assessing the impact on postmerger EPS are provided. The author also provides a simulation model for assessing the impact of various offer prices on postmerger EPS and discusses how this capability can be used in the negotiating process. Finally, the flexibility of these modeling techniques is illustrated by showing how they may be applied to special situations, such as when the acquirer or target is part of a parent firm or when the objective is to value, structure, and negotiate a joint venture or business alliance. The Microsoft Excel spreadsheets and formulas for the models described in this chapter are available in the file folder entitled Mergers and Acquisitions Valuation and Structuring Model on the CD-ROM accompanying this book.

Chapter Business Case Studies 9–1 and 9–2 illustrate the application of all the financial modeling concepts discussed in this chapter in the context of recent actual transactions. Case Study 9–1 uses the actual terms and conditions reported in the 2008 Cleveland Cliffs takeover attempt of Alpha Nutural Resources Incorporated to illustrate how a simple simulation model can be used to investigate the impact of alternative offer prices on postacquisition earnings per share. Case Study 9–2 shows how all of the concepts discussed in this chapter could be used to value, structure, and negotiate a transaction as exemplified by Alanco Technologies' takeover of StarTrak systems in 2006. Case Study 9–2 uses the M&A model available on the CD-ROM accompanying this textbook.

This highly sophisticated M&A model may be customized by readers to meet the requirements of their own situation. The model methodology developed in this chapter also may be applied to operating subsidiaries and product lines of larger organization as well as joint ventures and partnerships. The major segments of this chapter include the following:

- Limitations of Financial Data
- Model-Building Process
- Adjusting the Target's Offer Price for the Effects of Options and Convertible Securities
- Factors Affecting Postmerger Share Price
- Key Merger and Acquisition Model Formulas
- M&A Model Balance-Sheet Adjustment Mechanisms
- Applying Offer Price-Simulation Models in the Context of M&A Negotiations
- Alternative Applications of M&A Financial Models
- Things to Remember

A review of this chapter (including practice questions and answers) is available in the file folder entitled Student Study Guide included on the CD-ROM accompanying this book. The CD-ROM also contains a Learning Interactions Library, enabling students to test their knowledge of this chapter in a "real-time" environment as well as a document discussing how to interpret the financial ratios commonly generated by financial models. See the Appendix for more details on how to use the CD-ROM M&A model. For more advanced discussions on financial modeling, see Sengupta (2004) and Mun (2006).

Limitations of Financial Data

The output of models is only as good as the accuracy and timeliness of the numbers used to create them and the quality of the assumptions used in making projections. Consequently, analysts must understand on what basis numbers are collected and reported. Consistency and adherence to uniform standards become exceedingly important. However, imaginative accounting tricks threaten to undermine an analyst's ability to properly understand a firm's underlying dynamics. Recent examples of inordinate accounting abuses include WorldCom, Tyco, Enron, Sunbeam, Waste Management, and Cendant.

Generally Accepted Accounting Principles and International Accounting Standards

U.S. public companies prepare their financial statements in accordance with *generally accepted accounting practices* (GAAP). GAAP financial statements are those prepared in agreement with guidelines established by the Financial Accounting Standards Board (FASB). GAAP is a rules-based system, giving explicit instructions for every situation that the FASB has anticipated. In contrast, international accounting standards (IAS) is a principles-based system, with more generalized standards to follow. All European Union publicly traded companies had to adopt the IAS system in 2007. The more than 400 foreign firms also listed on U.S. stock exchanges have to continue to display their books in accordance with GAAP as well. GAAP and IAS currently exhibit significant differences. However, these differences are expected to narrow in the coming years.

Few would argue that GAAP ensures that all transactions are accurately recorded. Nonetheless, the scrupulous application of GAAP does ensure consistency in comparing one firm's financial performance to another. It is customary for definitive agreements of purchase and sale to require that a target company represent that its financial books are kept in accordance with GAAP. Consequently, the acquiring company at least understands how the financial numbers were assembled. During due diligence, the acquirer can look for discrepancies between the target's reported numbers and GAAP practices. Such discrepancies could indicate potential problems.

Pro Forma Accounting

In recent years, there has been a trend toward using *pro forma financial statements,* which present financial statements in a way that purports to more accurately describe a firm's current or projected performance. Because there are no accepted standards for pro forma accounting, pro forma statements may deviate substantially from standard GAAP statements. Pro forma statements frequently are used to show what an acquirer's and target's combined financial performance would look like if they were merged.

Although public companies still are required to file their financial statements with the Securities and Exchange Commission in accordance with GAAP, companies increasingly are using pro forma statements to portray their financial performance in what they argue is a more realistic (and usually more favorable) manner. Companies maintain that such statements provide investors with a better view of a company's core performance than GAAP reporting. Although pro forma statements provide useful insight into how a proposed combination of businesses might look, such liberal accounting techniques easily can be abused to hide a company's poor performance. Exhibit 9–1 suggests some ways in which an analyst can tell if a firm is engaging in inappropriate accounting practices. For a more detailed discussion of these issues, see Sherman and Young (2001).

Exhibit 9–1 Accounting Discrepancy Red Flags

1. The source of the revenue is questionable. Beware of revenue generated by selling to an affiliated party, selling something to a customer in exchange for something other than cash, or the receipt of investment income or cash received from a lender.
2. Income is inflated by nonrecurring gains. Gains on the sale of assets may be inflated by an artificially low book value of the assets sold.
3. Deferred revenue shows an unusually large increase. Deferred revenue increases as a firm collects money from customers in advance of delivering its products. It is reduced as the products are delivered. A jump in this balance sheet item could mean the firm is having trouble delivering its products.
4. Reserves for bad debt are declining as a percentage of revenue. This implies the firm may be boosting revenue by not reserving enough to cover probable losses from customer accounts that cannot be collected.
5. Growth in accounts receivable exceeds substantially the increase in revenue or inventory. This may mean that a firm is having difficulty in selling its products (i.e., inventories are accumulating) or collecting what it is owed.
6. The growth in net income is significantly different from the growth in cash from operations. Because it is more difficult to "manage" cash flow than net income (which is subject to distortion due to improper revenue recognition), this could indicate that net income is being deliberately misstated. Potential distortion may be particularly evident if the analyst adjusts end-of-period cash balances by deducting cash received from financing activities and adding back cash used for investment purposes. Consequently, changes in the adjusted cash balances should reflect changes in reported net income.

7. An increasing gap between a firm's income reported on its financial statements and its tax income. While it is legitimate for a firm to follow different accounting practices for financial reporting and tax purposes, the relationship between book and tax accounting is likely to remain constant over time, unless there are changes in tax rules or accounting standards.

8. Unexpected large asset write-offs. This may reflect management inertia in incorporating changing business circumstances into its accounting estimates.

9. Extensive use of related party transactions. Such transactions may not be subject to the same discipline and high standards of integrity as unrelated party transactions.

10. Changes in auditing firms that are not well justified. The firm may be seeking a firm that will accept its aggressive accounting positions.

Model-Building Process

The logic underlying the Excel-based M&A model found on the CD-ROM accompanying this book follows the process discussed in this chapter. This process involves four discrete steps. First, value the acquiring and target firms as stand-alone businesses. A *stand-alone business* is one whose financial statements reflect all the costs of running the business and all the revenues generated by the business. Second, value the consolidated acquirer and target firms including the effects of synergy. The appropriate discount rate for the combined firms is generally the target's cost of capital unless the two firms have similar risk profiles and are based in the same country. It is particularly important to use the target's cost of capital if the acquirer is merging with a higher-risk business, resulting in an increase in the acquirer's cost of capital. Third, determine the initial offer price for the target firm. Fourth, determine the acquirer's ability to finance the purchase using an appropriate financial structure (Table 9–1). The appropriate financial structure (debt-to-equity ratio) is that which satisfies certain predetermined criteria. The appropriate financial structure can be determined from a range of scenarios created by making small changes in selected value drivers. Value drivers are factors, such as product volume, selling price, and cost of sales, that have a significant impact on the value of the firm whenever they are altered (see Chapter 7).

Step 1. Value Acquirer (PV$_A$) and Target Firms (PV$_T$) as Stand-Alone Businesses

The following discussion applies to both the acquiring and target firms. The analyst should apply as many valuation methods as data availability and common sense allow. The estimates resulting from the various methods then can be averaged to arrive at a single valuation estimate using the weighted average valuation method (see Chapter 8).

Understand Specific Firm and Industry Competitive Dynamics

The accuracy of any valuation depends heavily on understanding the historical competitive dynamics of the industry, the historical performance of the company within the industry, and the reliability of the data used in the valuation. Competitive dynamics simply refer to the factors within the industry that determine industry profitability and cash flow. A careful examination of historical information can provide insights into key relationships among various operating variables. Examples of relevant historical relationships include seasonal or cyclical movements in the data, the relationship between

Table 9–1   The Mergers and Acquisition Model-Building Process

Step 1 Value Acquirer & and Target as Stand-Alone Firms	Step 2 Value Acquirer & and Target Firms, Including Synergy	Step 3 Determine Initial Offer Price for Target Firm	Step 4 Determine Combined Firms' Ability to Finance Transaction
1. Understand specific firm and industry competitive dynamics (see Chapter 4, Figure 4–2)	Estimate sources and destroyers of value and implementation costs incurred to realize synergy	Estimate minimum and maximum purchase price range	Estimate impact of alternative financing structures
2. Normalize 3–5 years of historical financial data (i.e., add or subtract nonrecurring losses and expenses or gains to smooth data)	Consolidate the acquirer and target stand-alone values including the effects of synergy	Determine amount of synergy acquirer is willing to share with target shareholders	Select financing structure that a. Meets acquirer's required financial returns b. Meets target's primary needs c. Does not raise cost of debt or violate loan covenants d. Minimizes EPS dilution and short-term reduction in financial returns
3. Project normalized cash flow based on expected market growth and industry dynamics; calculate stand-alone values of acquirer and target firms	Estimate value of net synergy (i.e., consolidated firms including synergy less stand-alone values of acquirer and target)	Determine appropriate composition of offer price (i.e., cash, stock, or some combination)	

Note: Key assumptions made for each step should be clearly stated.

fixed and variable expenses, and the impact on revenue of changes in product prices and unit sales. If these relationships can reasonably be expected to continue through the forecast period, they can be used to project valuation cash flows.

Normalizing Historical Data

To ensure that these historical relationships can be accurately defined, it is necessary to cleanse the data of anomalies, nonrecurring changes, and questionable accounting practices. For example, cash flow may be adjusted by adding back unusually large increases in reserves or deducting large decreases in reserves from free cash flow to the firm. Similar adjustments can be made for significant nonrecurring gains or losses on the sale of assets or nonrecurring expenses, such as those associated with the settlement of a lawsuit or warranty claim. Monthly revenue may be aggregated into quarterly or even annual data to minimize period-to-period distortions in earnings or cash flow resulting from inappropriate accounting practices. While public companies are required to provide financial data for only the current and two prior years, it is highly desirable to use data spanning at least one business cycle (i.e., about five to seven years).

Common-size financial statements are among the most frequently used tools to uncover data irregularities. These statements may be constructed by calculating the percentage each line item of the income statement, balance sheet, and cash flow statement is of annual sales for each quarter or year for which historical data are available. Common-size financial statements are useful for comparing businesses of different sizes in the same industry at a specific moment in time. Such analyses are called *cross-sectional comparisons*. By expressing the target's line-item data as a percentage of sales, it is possible to compare the target company with other companies' line-item data expressed in terms of sales to highlight significant differences. For example, a cross-sectional comparison may indicate that the ratio of capital spending to sales for the target firm is much less than for other firms in the industry. This discrepancy may simply reflect "catch-up" spending under way at the target's competitors, or it may suggest a more troubling development, in which the target is deferring necessary plant and equipment spending. To determine which is true, it is necessary to calculate common-size financial statements for the target firm and its primary competitors over a number of consecutive periods. This type of analysis is called a *multiperiod comparison*. Comparing companies in this manner helps confirm whether the target simply has completed a large portion of capital spending that others in the industry are undertaking currently or is woefully behind in making necessary expenditures.

Even if it is not possible to collect sufficient data to undertake cross-sectional and multiperiod comparisons of both the target firm and its direct competitors, constructing common-size statements for the target firm only provides useful insights. Abnormally large increases or decreases in these ratios from one period to the next highlight the need for further examination to explain why these fluctuations occurred. If it is determined that they are one-time events, these fluctuations may be eliminated by averaging the data immediately preceding and following the period in which these anomalies occurred. The anomalous data then are replaced by the data created through this averaging process. Alternatively, anomalous data can be completely excluded from the analysis. In general, nonrecurring events affecting more than 10 percent of the net income or cash flow for a specific period should be discarded from the data to allow for a clearer picture of trends and relationships in the firm's historical financial data.

Financial ratio analysis is the calculation of performance ratios from data in a company's financial statements to identify the firm's financial strengths and weaknesses. Such analysis helps in identifying potential problem areas that may require further examination during due diligence. Because ratios adjust for firm size, they enable the analyst to compare a firm's ratios with industry averages. A file entitled A Primer on Applying and Interpreting Financial Ratios on the CD-ROM accompanying this book lists commonly used formulas for financial ratios, how they are expressed, and how they should be interpreted. The analyst need not describe all the ratios listed; instead, only those that appear to have an impact on the firm's performance need be analyzed. These ratios should be compared with industry averages to discover if the company is out of line with others in the industry. A successful competitor's performance ratios may be used if industry average data is not available. Industry average data commonly is found in such publications as *The Almanac of Business and Industrial Financial Ratios* (Prentice Hall), *Annual Statement Studies* (Robert Morris Associates), *Dun's Review* (Dun and Bradstreet), *Industry Norms and Key Business Ratios* (Dun and Bradstreet), and *Value Line Investment Survey for Company and Industry Ratios* (Value Line).

Project Normalized Cash Flow

Normalized cash flows should be projected for at least five years and possibly more, until they turn positive or the growth rate slows to what is believed to be a sustainable pace. Projections should reflect the best available information about product demand growth, future pricing, technological changes, new competitors, new product and service offerings from current competitors, potential supply disruptions, raw material and labor cost increases, and possible new product or service substitutes. Projections also should include the revenue and costs associated with known new product introductions and capital expenditures, as well as additional expenses, required to maintain or expand operations by the acquiring and target firms during the forecast period.

A simple model to project cash flow involves the projection of revenue and the various components of cash flow as a percent of projected revenue. For example, cost of sales, depreciation, gross capital spending, and the change in working capital are projected as a percent of projected revenue. What percentage is applied to projected revenue for these components of free cash flow to the firm may be determined by calculating their historical ratio to revenue. In this simple model, revenue drives cash-flow growth. Therefore, special attention must be given to projecting revenue by forecasting unit growth and selling prices, the product of which provides estimated revenue. As suggested in Chapters 4 and 7, the product life cycle concept may be used to project unit growth and prices.

Revenue projections are commonly based on *trend extrapolation*, which entails extending present trends into the future using historical growth rates or multiple regression techniques. Another common forecasting method is to use *scenario analysis*. Cash flows under multiple scenarios are projected with each differing in terms of key variables (e.g., growth in gross domestic product, industry sales growth, fluctuations in exchange rates) or issues (e.g., competitive new product introductions, new technologies, and new regulations).

Step 2. Value Acquirer and Target Firms, Including Synergy

Synergy generally is considered to consist only of those factors or sources of value adding to the economic value (i.e., ability to generate future cash flows) of the combined firms. However, factors that destroy value also should be considered in the estimation of the economic value of the combined firms. **Net synergy** (NS) is the difference between estimated sources of value and destroyers of value. The present value of net synergy can be estimated in either of two ways. The common approach is to subtract the sum of the present values of the acquirer and target firms on a stand-alone basis from the present value of the consolidated acquirer and target firms including the estimated effects of synergy. Alternatively, the present value of net synergy can be estimated by calculating present value of the difference between the cash flows from sources and destroyers of value. The first approach is illustrated in detail in this chapter. This approach has the advantage of enabling the analyst to create an interactive model to simulate alternative scenarios including different financing and deal structuring assumptions.

Sources of Value

Look for quantifiable sources of value and destroyers of value while conducting due diligence. The most common include the potential for cost savings resulting from shared overhead, duplicate facilities, and overlapping distribution channels. Synergy related to cost savings that are generally more easily identified seems to have a much better chance of being realized than synergy due to other sources (Christofferson, McNish, and Sias, 2004).

Potential sources of value also include assets not recorded on the balance sheet at fair value and off-balance-sheet items. Common examples include land, "obsolete" inventory and equipment, patents, licenses, and copyrights. Underutilized borrowing capacity also can make an acquisition target more attractive. The addition of the acquired company's assets, low level of indebtedness, and strong cash flow from operations could enable the buyer to increase substantially the borrowing levels of the combined companies. The incremental borrowing capacity can be approximated by comparing the combined firms' current debt-to-total capital ratio with the industry average. For example, assume Firm A's acquisition of Firm B results in a reduction in the combined firms' debt-to-total capital ratio to 0.25 (e.g., debt represents $250 million of the new firm's total capital of $1 billion). If the same ratio for the industry is 0.5, the new firm may be able to increase its borrowing by $250 million to raise its debt-to-total capital ratio to the industry average. Such incremental borrowing often is used to finance a portion of the purchase price paid for the target firm. See Table 13–11 in Chapter 13 for a more rigorous discussion of how to estimate incremental borrowing capacity.

Other sources of value could include access to intellectual property (i.e., patents, trade names, and rights to royalty streams), new technologies and processes, and new customer groups. Gaining access to new customers is often given as a justification for mergers and acquisitions. Kmart Holding Corp's acquisition of Sears, Roebuck and Co. in 2004 was in part motivated by the opportunity to sell merchandise with strong brand equity, which had been sold exclusively at Kmart (e.g., Joe Boxer) to a whole new clientele in Sears stores.

Income tax loss carryforwards and carrybacks and tax credits also may represent an important source of value for an acquirer seeking to reduce its tax liability. Loss carryforwards and carrybacks represent a firm's losses that may be used to reduce future taxable income or recover some portion of previous taxes paid by the firm. Tax credits may be particularly valuable, since they can be deducted directly from a firm's current tax liability. See Chapter 12 for a more detailed discussion of tax-related issues.

Destroyers of Value

Factors that can destroy value include poor product quality, wage and benefit levels above comparable industry levels, poor productivity, and high employee turnover. A lack of customer contracts or poorly written contracts often result in customer disputes about terms and conditions and what amounts actually are owed. Verbal agreements made with customers by the seller's sales representatives also may become obligations for the buyer. These are particularly onerous, because commissioned sales forces frequently make agreements that are not profitable for their employer.

Environmental issues, product liabilities, unresolved lawsuits, and other current or pending liabilities are also major potential destroyers of value for the buyer. These also serve as ticking time bombs because the actual liability may not be apparent for years following the acquisition. Moreover, the magnitude of the liability actually may force a company into bankruptcy. In the 1980s, a major producer of asbestos, Johns Manville Corporation, was forced into bankruptcy because of the discovery that certain types of asbestos, which had been used for decades for insulating buildings, could be toxic. When China's Lenovo Group acquired IBM's PC business in 2005, it disclosed that high warranty costs attributable to a single problem component contributed significantly to the IBM PC business net losses in 2002 and 2003 of $171 million and $258 million, respectively.

Implementation Costs Often Overlooked

In calculating net synergy, it is important to include the costs associated with recruiting and training, realizing cost savings, achieving productivity improvements, and exploiting revenue opportunities. No matter how much care is taken to minimize employee attrition following closing, some employees will be lost. Often these are the most skilled. Once a merger or acquisition is announced, target company employees start to circulate their resumes. The best employees start to receive job solicitations from competitors or executive search firms. Consequently, the costs associated with replacing employees who leave following closing can escalate sharply. The firm will incur recruitment costs as well as the cost of training the new hires. Moreover, the new hires are not likely to reach the productivity levels of those they are replacing for some time.

Cost savings are likely to be greatest when firms with similar operations are consolidated and redundant or overlapping positions are eliminated. Many analysts take great pains to estimate savings in terms of wages, salaries, benefits, and associated overhead, such as support staff and travel expenses, without accurately accounting for severance expenses associated with layoffs. How a company treats its employees during layoffs has a significant impact on the morale of those that remain. Furthermore, if it is widely perceived that a firm treats laid off employees fairly, it will be able to recruit new employees more easily in the future. Consequently, severance packages should be as equitable as possible.

Realizing productivity improvements frequently requires additional spending in new structures and equipment, retraining employees that remain with the combined companies, or redesigning work flow. Similarly, exploiting revenue-raising opportunities may require training the sales force of the combined firms in selling each firm's products or services and additional advertising expenditures to inform current or potential customers of what has taken place.

Step 3. Determine Magnitude and Composition of Initial Offer Price for the Target Firm

Factors Affecting Offer Price and Composition

In practice, many factors affect the amount and form of payment of the purchase price. Which are most important depends largely on the circumstances surrounding the transaction. In some cases, these factors can be quantified (e.g., synergy), while others are largely subjective (e.g., the degree of acquirer shareholder and management risk aversion). Table 9–2 identifies many of the factors that affect the magnitude and composition of the purchase price. The remainder of this section of this chapter addresses how some of these factors can be incorporated into the model-building process.

Estimating Minimum and Maximum Offer Price Range (Stock and Asset Purchases)

For transactions in which there is potential synergy between the acquirer and target firms, the initial offer price for the target firm lies between the minimum and maximum offer prices. In a purchase of stock transaction, the minimum offer price may be defined as the target's stand-alone or present value (PV_T) or its current market value (MV_T) (i.e., the target's current stock price times its shares outstanding). The maximum price is the sum of the minimum price plus the present value of net synergy (PV_{NS}). Note that the maximum price may be overstated if the current market value of the target firm reflects investor expectations of an impending takeover. As such, the current market value may already reflect some portion of future synergies. Consequently, simply adding the present value of net synergy to the current market value of the target firm can result in double counting some portion of future synergy. The initial offer price (PV_{IOP}) is the sum of both the minimum purchase price and some percentage between 0 and 1 of the PV of net synergy (see Exhibit 9–2).

Table 9–2 Determinants of Magnitude and Composition of Initial Offer Price

Factors Affecting	Magnitude	Composition
Acquirer's Perspective	• Estimated net synergy • Willingness to share net synergy with target shareholders • Relative attractiveness of alternative investment opportunities • Number of potential bidders • Effectiveness of target's defenses • Public disclosure requirements (May result in preemptive bid) • Degree of management's risk aversion	• Current borrowing capacity • After-tax cost of debt versus cost of equity • Size and duration of potential EPS dilution (Reduces attractiveness of share exchange) • Size of transaction (May make borrowing impractical) • Desire for risk sharing (May result in contingent or deferred payments)
Target's Perspective	• Number of potential bidders • Perception of bidder as friendly or hostile • Effectiveness of defenses • Size of potential tax liability (May require increase in purchase price) • Standalone valuation • Availability of recent comparable transactions • Relative attractiveness of alternative investment opportunities	• Perceived attractiveness of acquirer stock • Shareholder preference for cash versus stock • Size of potential tax liability (May make share exchange most attractive option) • Perceived upside potential of target (May result in contingent payout)

Exhibit 9–2 Determining the Initial Offer Price (PV$_{IOP}$)—Purchase of Stock

PV_{MIN} = PV_T or MV_T, whichever is greater. MV_T is the target firm's current share price times the number of shares outstanding.

PV_{MAX} = $PV_{MIN} + PV_{NS}$, where PV_{NS} = PV (sources of value) – PV (destroyers of value).

PV_{IOP} = $PV_{MIN} + \alpha PV_{NS}$, where $0 \leq \alpha \leq 1$.

Offer price range for the target firm = $(PV_T$ or $MV_T) < PV_{IOP} < (PV_T$ or $MV_T) + PV_{NS}$.

The stand-alone value is applicable for privately held firms. In an efficient market in which both the buyer and seller have access to the same information, the stand-alone value would be the price the rational seller expects to receive. In practice, markets for small, privately owned businesses are often inefficient. Either the buyer or seller may not have access to all relevant information about the economic value of the target firm, perhaps due to the absence of recent comparable transactions. Consequently, the buyer may attempt to purchase the target firm at a discount from what it believes is the actual economic or fair market value.

In an asset purchase, the target's equity would have to be adjusted to reflect the fair market value of the target assets and liabilities that are to be excluded from the transaction. The adjustment would be similar to those made in Exhibit 7–11 entitled "Adjusting Firm Value" in Chapter 7. Exhibit 9–3 illustrates the target firm's balance sheet with the

---

Exhibit 9–3 Determining the Initial Offer Price (PV_{IOP})—Purchase of Assets

Included Assets (INA)	Included Liabilities (INL)
Excluded Assets (EXA)	Excluded Liabilities (EXL)
Total Assets (TA)	Total Liabilities (TL)
	Shareholders' Equity (SE)

$ADJEQ = (TA - EXA) - (TL - EXL) = INA - INL$ (included net assets)

PV_{MIN} = Liquidation value of adjusted equity.[1]

$PV_{MAX} = PV_{MIN} + PV_{NS}$, where $PV_{NS} = PV$ (sources of value) $- PV$ (destroyers of value).

$PV_{IOP} = PV_{MIN} + \alpha PV_{NS}$, where $0 \leq \alpha \leq 1$.

Offer price range for the target firm $= PV_{MIN} < PV_{IOP} < PV_{MIN} + PV_{NS}$.

---

[1] A rational seller would not sell assets at less than their liquidation value.

---

assets and liabilities categorized as those assets (INA) and liabilities (INL) included and those assets (EXA) and liabilities (EXL) excluded from the transaction. Included assets and liabilities are those to be purchased (assets) or assumed (liabilities) by the buyer and excluded assets and liabilities are those retained by the seller. Adjusted target firm equity equals the difference between total assets (TA) and excluded assets and total liabilities (TL) and excluded liabilities. As such, the present value of adjusted equity (PV_{ADJEQ}) is the PV of the cash flows generated by included net assets (i.e., INA – INL). As indicated in Exhibit 9–3, the initial offer price in an asset purchase equals the PV of adjusted target equity plus some portion of anticipated net synergy. The buyer is willing to pay the seller some portion of the strategic value to the buyer of the included net assets.

Determining Distribution of Synergy between Acquirer and Target

In determining the initial offer price, the acquiring company must decide how much of anticipated synergy it is willing to share with the target firm's shareholders. This is often determined by the portion of anticipated synergy contributed by the target firm. For example, if following due diligence, it is determined that the target would contribute 30 percent of the synergy resulting from combining the acquirer and target firms, the acquirer may choose to share up to 30 percent of estimated net synergy with the target firm's shareholders.

It is logical that the offer price should fall between the minimum and maximum prices for three reasons. First, it is unlikely that the target company can be purchased at the minimum price, because the acquiring company normally has to pay a premium over the current market value to induce target shareholders to transfer control to another firm. In an asset purchase, the rational seller would not sell at a price below the liquidation value of the net assets being acquired, as this represents what the seller could obtain by liquidating rather than selling the assets and using a portion of the proceeds to pay off liabilities that would have been assumed by the buyer. Second, at the maximum end of the range, the acquiring company would be ceding all of the net synergy value created by the combination of the two companies to the target company's shareholders. Third, it is prudent to pay significantly less than the maximum price, because the amount of synergy actually realized often tends to be less than the amount anticipated.

Adjusting Projections for Revenue- and Cost-Savings-Related Synergy

Broadly speaking, there are two general categories of synergy: revenue-related and cost-savings-related synergy. Revenue-related synergy arises from sales and marketing opportunities that can be realized as a result of combining the target and acquiring firms. Similarly, cost-savings-related synergy refers to the opportunities for the elimination of duplicate operations, processes, and personnel, as well as productivity improvements, resulting from combining firms.

- **Revenue-related synergy.** The customer base for the target and acquiring firms can be segmented into four categories: (1) those served only by the target, (2) those served only by the acquirer, (3) those served by both firms, and (4) those served by neither firm (Exhibit 9–4). The first two segments may represent revenue enhancement opportunities by enabling the target or the acquirer to sell its current products into the other's current customer base. The third segment could represent a net increase or decrease in revenue for the new firm. Incremental revenue may result from new products that could be offered only as a result of exploiting the capabilities of the target and acquiring firms in combination. However, revenue may be lost as some customers choose to have more than one source of supply. The last segment represents prospective customers who neither firm has been able to capture with its existing product offering but who may become customers for products that can be offered only as a result of combining the capabilities of the acquiring and target firms. The analysis is simplified by focusing on the largest customers, because it often is true that about 80 percent of a company's revenues come from about 20 percent of its customers.

- **Cost-savings-related synergies.** The cost of sales for the combined firms may be adjusted for cost savings resulting from such factors as the elimination of redundant jobs and bulk purchases of raw materials. Direct labor refers to those employees directly involved in the production of goods and services. Indirect labor refers to supervisory overhead. A distinction needs to be made because of likely differences in average compensation for direct and indirect labor. Sales, general, and administrative expenses (S, G, & A) may be reduced by the elimination of overlapping jobs and the closure of unneeded sales offices (see Table 9–3).

Table 9–4 illustrates how to adjust the combined firm's income statement for productivity improvements. Such improvements may result from the application of the "best practices" of either the acquirer or target firm to the combined firms. Note that the gross

---

Exhibit 9–4 Combined Firm Customer Base Segmentation Analysis

Segment: Customers Served By	Segment: Represents Potential
Target only	New customers for acquirer products
Acquirer only	New customers for target products

Both firms	Net gain or loss equal to
	    Gain from sale of new firm's products less
	    loss from existing customers seeking
	    to diversify suppliers

Neither firm	Prospective customers for new firm's combined product offering

Table 9–3 Adjusting Cost of Sales and S, G, & A Due to Head Count Reduction and Purchasing Economies

	Year 1 Head Count Reduction		Year 2 Head Count Reduction	
	Staff Reduction	**Dollar Savings**	**Staff Reduction**	**Dollar Savings**
Cost of sales				
Direct labor[1]	65	$4,057,143	129	$8,845,714
Indirect labor[2]	24	$2,228,571	59	$5,478,571
Total	89	$6,285,714	188	$14,324,285
Purchased materials[3]		$3,160,000		$3,360,000
S, G, & A				
Direct sales[4]	10	$1,071,421	25	$2,678,571
Sales administration[5]	5	$285,714	10	$571,429
Total	15	$1,357,135	30	$3,250,000
Lease buyouts		$765,000		$382,197

[1]Average direct annual salary of $48,000. Benefits equal 30 percent of annual salary.

[2]Averge indirect annual salary of $65,000. Benefits equal 30 percent of annual salary.

[3]Volume discount of 5 percent on total dollar value of purchased materials. Purchased materials equal to 40 percent of cost of sales. Therefore, the dollar value of purchased materials savings increases each year.

[4]Average direct sales annual salary of $75,000. Benefits equal 30 percent of annual salary.

[5]Average sales administration salary of $40,000. Benefits equal 30% of annual salary.

Table 9–4 Adjusting Cost of Sales for Productivity Improvements ($ millions)

	Year 1	Year 2	Year 3	Year 4	Year 5
Net revenue	1000.00	1040.00	1081.60	1124.86	1169.86
Cost of sales (COS)[1]	800.00	832.00	865.28	899.89	935.89
Training expense	25.00				
Cost savings		16.64	17.31	18.00	18.72
Adjusted cost of sales[2]	825.00	815.36	847.97	881.89	917.17
Gross profit	175.00	224.64	233.63	242.97	252.69
Gross profit margin (%)	17.5	21.6	21.6	21.6	21.6

Notes: Assumptions

Postmerger labor costs without productivity improvement:

One worker produces 10 widgets per hour.

Each worker is paid $20 per hour (including benefits).

Nonlabor costs (e.g., materials, depreciation) = $2 per widget.

Hourly labor cost per widget = $20/10 = $2.

Total COS per widget[1] = labor cost + nonlabor cost = $2 + $2 = $4.

Postmerger labor costs with productivity improvement:

Hourly productivity per worker increases by 20% due to improved worker training resulting in each worker producing 12 widgets per hour (10 × 1.2).

Training expense in the first year totals $25 million.

Three quarters of savings from productivity gain shared with labor to minimize turnover. (Actual amount shared depends on relative bargaining power of labor and management.)

Hourly labor cost per widget = $20/1.2 = $1.67.

Labor savings per widget due to productivity improvement = $2.00 − $1.67 = $0.33.

Portion of savings shared with labor = 0.75 × $0.33 = $0.25 (Hourly wage rate increases to $20.25 from $20.00.)

Total COS per widget[2] = labor + nonlabor costs = ($1.67 + $0.25) + $2 = $3.92.

Total COS per widget reduced by 2 percentage points (i.e., 1 − ($3.92/$4.00).

Cost savings = 0.02 × cost of sales in year 2, year 3, etc.

profit margin of the combined firms, as well as the wage rate, increases due to the improvement in productivity. Gross margin increases from 20 percent (i.e., what it would have been in Year 1 if the $25 million training expense had not been incurred) to 21.6 percent reflecting the productivity gain. Similarly, the average hourly wage rate increases from by 1.3 percent to $20.25 from $20.00.

To realize the savings shown in Tables 9–3 and 9–4, the combined firms experience certain one-time expenses, such as severance associated with layoffs, the cost of buying out leases for sales offices to be closed, and the cost of retraining the workforce to employ "best practices." Severance expenses are often equal to several months of salary, including benefits, for each employee whose job is terminated. Other one-time expenses could include the cost of facility, equipment, technology, and process upgrades. The COS and S, G, & A expenses including synergy then are used to calculate operating income (EBIT), which results in a higher free cash flow as a result of the effects of anticipated synergy (see Table 9–5). Note that operating earnings, including synergy, in Table 9–5, are calculated from the line items in bold type.

Table 9–5   Adjusting the Combined Acquirer and Target Company Projections for the Estimated Value of Synergy ($ millions)

	Forecast Period				
	Year 1	Year 2	Year 3	Year 4	Year 5
Revenue[1]	198	210	222	236	250
Revenue-Related Synergy					
Target customers	4	6	8	12	12
Acquirer customers	2	4	6	10	10
Both firms	(4)	0	3	4	8
Neither firm	0	0	2	2	6
Total	2	10	19	28	36
Revenue (including synergy)	**200**	**220**	**241**	**264**	**286**
Cost of sales	158	168	178	189	200
Cost of sales-related synergy	4	8	8	8	8
Direct labor	2	5	5	5	5
Indirect labor	3	3	4	4	4
Purchased materials					
Total	9	16	17	17	17
Cost of sales (including synergy)	**149**	**152**	**161**	**172**	**183**
S, G, & A expenses	20	21	22	24	25
S, G, & A-related synergy	2	3	3	3	3
S, G, & A expenses (including synergy)	**18**	**18**	**19**	**21**	**22**
Implementation expenses	**3**	**4**			
Operating earnings (EBIT) (including synergy and implementation expenses)	**30**	**46**	**61**	**71**	**81**
Addendum					
Cost of sales/revenue (%)	80	80	80	80	80
Cost of sales (including net synergy)/revenue (including synergy) (%)	75	69	67	65	64
S, G, & A/revenue (%)	10	10	10	10	10
S, G, & A (including synergy)/revenue (including synergy) (%)	9	8	7	8	8

[1]Revenue of the combined firms before the effects of synergy is projected to grow at an annual rate of 6 percent during the forecast period.

Determining the Appropriate Composition of the Offer Price

The purchase price offered to the target company could consist of the acquirer's stock, debt, cash, or some combination of all three. The actual composition of the purchase price depends on what is acceptable to the target and acquiring companies and what the financial structure of the combined companies can support. Consequently, the acquirer needs to determine the appropriate financing or capital structure of the combined companies, including debt, common equity, and preferred equity. In this chapter, the initial offer price is the market value or economic value (i.e., present value of the target firm defined as a stand-alone business) plus some portion of projected net synergy. In Chapter 5, the offer or purchase price was defined in a different context, as total consideration, total purchase price or enterprise value, and net purchase price. These definitions were provided with the implicit assumption that the acquiring company had determined the economic value of the firm on a stand-alone basis and the value of net synergy. Economic value is determined before any consideration is given to how the transaction will be financed.

Step 4. Determine Combined Firms' Ability to Finance the Transaction

Estimating Impact of Alternative Financing Structures

The consolidated target and acquiring firms' financial statements, adjusted to reflect the net effects of synergy, are run through a series of scenarios to determine the impact on such variables as earnings, leverage, covenants, and borrowing costs. For example, each scenario could represent different amounts of leverage as measured by the firm's debt-to-equity ratio.

Selecting an Appropriate Capital or Financing Structure

In theory, the optimal capital or financing structure is the one that maximizes the firm's share price. When borrowed funds are reinvested at a return above the firm's cost of capital, firm value is increased. However, higher debt levels also increase the firm's cost of earnings by raising its levered beta and, as such, work to lower the firm's share price. Since many factors affect share price, it is difficult to determine the exact capital structure that maximizes the firm's share price.

In practice, financial managers attempt to forecast how changes in debt will affect those ratios that have an impact a firm's creditworthiness. Such factors include the interest-coverage ratio, debt-to-equity ratio, times interest earned ratio, current ratio, and the like. They subsequently discuss their projected pro-forma financial statements with lenders and bond rating agencies, who may make adjustments to the firm's projected financial statements. The lenders and rating agencies then compare the firm's credit ratios with those of other firms in the same industry to assess the likelihood that the borrower will be able to repay the borrowed funds (with interest) on schedule. Ultimately, interaction among the borrower, lenders, and rating agencies is what determines the amount and composition of combined firms' (i.e., acquirer and target) capital structure.

For purposes of model-building, the appropriate financing structure can be estimated by selecting that structure which satisfies certain predetermined selection criteria. These selection criteria should be determined as part of the process of developing the acquisition plan (see Chapter 4). For a public company, the appropriate capital structure could be that scenario whose debt-to-equity ratio results in the highest net present value for cash flows generated by the combined businesses, the least near-term EPS dilution, no violation of loan covenants, and no significant increase in borrowing costs. Excluding EPS considerations, private companies could determine the appropriate capital structure in the same manner. In effect, the acquirer should select the financing structure that enables the following criteria to be satisfied:

1. The acquirer is able to achieve its financial return objectives for the combined companies.
2. The primary needs of the acquirer and target firm's shareholders are met.
3. There is no significant increase in the cost of debt or violation of loan covenants.
4. For public companies, EPS dilution, if any, is minimized and reductions in reported financial returns are temporary.

For publicly traded companies, financial return objectives often are couched in terms readily understood by investors, such as earnings per share. Acquiring companies must be able to convince investors that any EPS dilution is temporary and the long-term EPS growth of the combined companies will exceed what the acquirer could have achieved without the acquisition. Financial returns for both public and private companies also may be described as the firm's estimated cost of capital or in terms of the return on total capital, assets, or equity. Moreover, the combined companies' cash flow must be sufficient to meet any incremental interest and principal repayments resulting from borrowing undertaken to finance all or some portion of the purchase price without violating existing loan covenants or deviating from debt service ratios typical for the industry. If loan covenants are violated, lenders may require the combined companies to take immediate remedial action or be declared in technical default and forced to repay the outstanding loans promptly. Moreover, if the combined firms' interest coverage or debt-to-equity ratios deviate significantly from what is considered appropriate for similar firms in the same industry, borrowing costs may escalate sharply.

The Importance of Stating Assumptions

The credibility of any valuation ultimately depends on the validity of its underlying assumptions. Valuation-related assumptions tend to fall into five major categories: (1) market, (2) income statement, (3) balance sheet, (4) synergy, and (5) valuation. Note that implicit assumptions about cash flow already are included in assumptions made about the income statement and changes in the balance sheet, which together drive changes in cash flow. *Market assumptions* generally relate to the growth rate of unit volume and product price per unit. *Income statement assumptions* include the projected growth in revenue, the implied market share (i.e., the firm's projected revenue as a percent of projected industry revenue), and the growth in the major components of cost in relation to sales. *Balance sheet assumptions* may include the growth in the primary components of working capital and fixed assets in relation to the projected growth in sales. *Synergy assumptions* relate to the amount and timing associated with each type of anticipated synergy, including cost savings from workforce reductions, productivity improvements as a result of the introduction of new technologies or processes, and revenue growth as a result of increased market penetration or cross-selling opportunities. Finally, examples of important *valuation assumptions* include the acquiring firm's target debt-to-equity ratio used in calculating the cost of capital, the discount rates used during the forecast and stable growth periods, and the growth assumptions used in determining the terminal value.

Adjusting the Target's Offer Price for the Effects of Options and Convertible Securities

When the target firm has outstanding management stock options and convertible securities, it is necessary to adjust the offer price to reflect the extent to which options and convertible securities will be exchanged for new common shares. If the acquirer is intent on buying all the target's outstanding shares, these new shares also have to be purchased. Convertible securities commonly include preferred stock and debentures. Information on the number of options outstanding and their associated exercise prices, as well as convertible securities, generally are available in the footnotes to the financial statements of the target firm. Note that "out-of-the-money" options (i.e., those whose exercise or conversion price exceeds the firm's current shares price) often are exercisable if the firm faces a change of control. With respect to convertible securities, it is reasonable to assume that such securities will be converted to common equity if the conversion price is less than the current common share price. Such securities are said to be "in the money." Exhibit 9–5 illustrates how the offer price could be adjusted to reflect the conversion of outstanding options and convertible securities to new common equity.

Factors Affecting Postmerger Share Price

Determining the appropriate P/E ratio to apply to the combined firms' postmerger EPS is an important assumption in estimating the postmerger share price. Consequently, the analyst needs to anticipate how investors will react to the merger announcement.

Exhibit 9–5 Adjusting Offer Price for Options and Convertible Securities

Offer price = (Total shares outstanding × Offer price per share) – Option proceeds[1]
Key Assumptions:

1. Total shares outstanding = Issued shares + Shares from "in-the-money" options + Shares from "in-the-money" convertible securities.
2. Target's outstanding common stock (excluding "in-the-money" options and convertible securities) = 2 million.
3. In-the-money options outstanding = 150,000 at an exercise price equal to $15.
4. Convertible securities = $10 million (face value for each security = $1,000; conversion price = $20; implied conversion ratio = 50).
5. Offer price per share = $25.

$$\text{Therefore,}$$
$$\text{Total shares outstanding} = 2 \text{ million} + 150,000 + (\$10 \text{ million}/\$1000) \times 50$$
$$= 2 \text{ million} + 150,000 + 500,000$$
$$= 2,650,000$$
$$\text{Adjusted offer price} = 2,650,000 \times \$25 - 150,000 \times \$15$$
$$= \$66.25 \text{ million} - \$2.25 \text{ million}$$
$$= \$64 \text{ million}$$

---

[1]Cash proceeds received from option holders choosing to exercise their options. This is assumed to be 100 percent of "in-the-money" options.

Frequently, the price of both the acquirer's and the target's stock adjusts immediately following the announcement of a pending acquisition. The target's current stock price increases by somewhat less than the announced purchase price, as arbitrageurs buy the target's stock in anticipation of a completed transaction. The difference between what they pay and the announced purchase price is their potential profit. The current stock price of the acquiring company may decline, reflecting a potential dilution of its EPS or a growth in EPS of the combined companies that is somewhat slower than the growth rate investors had anticipated for the acquiring company without the acquisition. For these reasons, immediately following the acquisition announcement, investors may place a somewhat lower price-to-earnings ratio on the acquiring company's EPS and later on the combined companies' EPS than had prevailed for the acquiring company before the announcement of the acquisition.

Share-Exchange Ratios

For public companies, the exchange of the acquirer's shares for the target's shares requires the calculation of the appropriate exchange ratio. The share-exchange ratio (SER) can be negotiated as a fixed number of shares of the acquirer's stock to be exchanged for each share of the target's stock. Alternatively, SER can be defined in terms of the dollar value of the negotiated offer price per share of target stock (P_{TO}) to the dollar value of the acquirer's share price (P_A). The SER is calculated by the following equation:

$$SER = P_{TO}/P_A$$

The SER, defined in this manner, can be less than, equal to, or greater than 1, depending on the value of the acquirer's shares relative to the offer price on the date set during the negotiation for valuing the transaction. Exhibit 9–6 illustrates how the SER is calculated.

Estimating Postmerger Earnings per Share

The critical "go, no go" decision variable for senior management of many publicly traded acquiring companies often is the impact of the acquisition on EPS following closing. This measure is perhaps the simplest summary variable available of the economic impact of an acquisition or merger on the acquirer's share price. Moreover, as noted in Chapter 8, earnings per share are more closely correlated with share price than cash flow per share for periods of less than five years. As such, EPS is among the most widely followed indicators by market analysts and investors. Earnings dilution, although temporary, can cause a dramatic loss of market value for the acquiring company.

As illustrated in Exhibit 9–7, the calculation of postmerger EPS reflects the EPS of the combined companies, the price of the acquirer's stock, the price of the target's stock, and the number of shares of acquirer and target stock outstanding.

Exhibit 9–6 Calculating Share Exchange Ratios

The price offered and accepted by the target company is $40 per share, and the acquiring company's share price is $60. What is the SER?

$$SER = \$40/\$60 = 0.6667$$

Implication: To complete the merger, the acquiring company will give 0.6667 shares of its own stock for each share of the target company.

Exhibit 9–7 Calculating Postmerger Earnings per Share

The acquiring company's share price is $40 and the price offered to the target, including an appropriate premium, is $20. The combined earnings of the two companies, including estimated synergies, are $1 million. If the acquiring company has 200,000 shares outstanding and the target company has 100,000 shares outstanding, what is the postmerger EPS for the combined companies?

$$\text{Postmerger EPS} = \frac{\$1\,\text{million}}{200,000 + [100,000 \times (\$20/\$40)]}$$

$$= \frac{\$1\,\text{million}}{250,000} = \$4.00$$

$$\text{Postmerger EPS} = \frac{E_{T+A}}{N_A + [N_T \times (P_{TO}/P_A)]}$$

E_{T+A} = the sum of the current earnings of the target and acquiring companies plus any earnings increase because of synergy.
N_A = the acquiring company's outstanding shares.
P_{TO} = price offered for the target company.
N_T = number of target company's outstanding shares.
P_A = current price of the acquiring company's stock.

Estimating the Postmerger Share Price

The share price of the combined firms following an acquisition reflects both the anticipated EPS for the combined firms and the P/E ratio investors are willing to pay for the anticipated per-share earnings. Exhibit 9–8 provides an example of how this process works under three scenarios: a share-for-share exchange, an all-cash purchase, and a transaction whose purchase price includes a combination of stock and cash. The exhibit illustrates how the postmerger share price may be determined by multiplying the postmerger EPS by an appropriate P/E ratio. For simplicity, the prevailing postmerger P/E is assumed to be the acquiring firm's premerger P/E, and each scenario assumes no earnings gain in the current period due to synergy.

Exhibit 9–8 Calculating the Postmerger Share Price

Share-for-Share Exchange

The acquiring company is considering the acquisition of Target Company in a share-for-share transaction in which Target Company would receive $84.30 for each share of its common stock. Acquiring Company expects no change in its P/E multiple after the merger and chooses to value Target Company conservatively by assuming no earnings growth due to synergy. Data on the companies is in Table 9–6.

1. Exchange ratio = Price per share offered for Target Company/Market price per share for the Acquiring Company
   = $84.30/$56.25
   = 1.5 (i.e., Acquiring Company issues 1.5 shares of stock for each share of Target Company's stock)

Table 9–6   Data on Companies

	Acquiring Company	Target Company
Earnings available for common stock	$281,500	$62,500
Number of shares of common outstanding	112,000	18,750
Market price per share	$56.25	$62.50

2. New shares issued by Acquiring Company = 18,750 (shares of Target Company) × 1.5 (exchange ratio) = 28,125
3. Total shares outstanding of the combined companies = 112,000 + 28,125 = 140,125
4. Postmerger EPS of the combined companies = ($281,500 + $62,500)/140,125
   = $344,000/140,125
   = $2.46
5. Premerger EPS of Acquiring Company = $281,500/112,000 = $2.51
6. Premerger P/E = Premerger price per share/premerger earnings per share
   = $56.25/($281,500/112.000) = $56.25/$2.51
   = 22.4
7. Postmerger share price = Postmerger EPS × Premerger P/E
   = $2.46 × 22.4
   = $55.10 (compared with $56.25 premerger)
8. Postmerger equity ownership distribution:

Target Company = 28,125/140,125 = 20.1%

$$\text{Acquiring Company} = 100 - 20.1 = \frac{79.9}{100.0\%}$$

Implications: The acquisition results in a $1.15 reduction in the share price of Acquiring Company as a result of a $0.05 decline in the EPS of the combined companies. (Recall that Acquiring Company assumed no gains in earnings of the combined companies due to synergy.) Whether the acquisition is a poor decision depends on what happens to the earnings of the combined companies over time. If the combined companies' earnings grow more rapidly than Acquiring Company's earnings would have in the absence of the acquisition, the acquisition may contribute to the market value of Acquiring Company.

All-Cash Purchase

Instead of a share-for-share exchange, Target Company agrees to an all-cash purchase of 100 percent of its outstanding stock at $84.30 for each of its 18,750 shares of common stock outstanding. When the transaction is closed, the 18,750 shares of Target Company's stock are retired. The acquiring company believes that investors apply its premerger P/E to determine the postmerger share price. Moreover, Acquiring Company finances the purchase price by using cash balances on hand in excess of its normal cash requirements.

Continued

Exhibit 9–8 Calculating the Postmerger Share Price — Cont'd

1. Postmerger EPS of the combined companies = ($281,500 + $62,500)/112,000
   = $3.07
2. Postmerger share price = Postmerger EPS × Premerger P/E
   = $3.07 × 22.4
   = $68.77 (compared with $56.25 premerger)

Implications: The all-cash acquisition results in a $12.52 increase in the share price of the combined companies. This is a result of a $0.56 improvement in the EPS of the combined companies as compared with the $2.51 premerger EPS of Acquiring Company. In practice, the improvement in EPS would not have been as dramatic if the earnings of the combined companies had been reduced by accrued interest on the excess cash balances of the acquirer or by interest expense if the acquirer had chosen to finance the transaction using debt.

Combination Cash and Stock

If the offer price for the target firm consists of one share of acquirer stock valued at $56.25 (given in the problem) and $28.05 in cash ($84.30 offer price – $56.25), calculate the postmerger earnings per share and share price.

1. Postmerger EPS = ($281,500 + $62,500)/(112,000 + 18,750) = $2.63
2. Postmerger share price = 22.4 × $2.63 = $58.91

Implications: The combination cash and stock offer increases the share price of the combined firms by somewhat more than the all-stock offer, which actually destroys value, but far less than the increase in shareholder value provided by the all-cash offer. Moreover, as with the all-cash offer, the combined firms' EPS must be adjusted to reflect the loss of interest earnings on any excess cash balances used by the acquirer to buy the target firm or interest expense if the acquirer borrowed to pay the cash portion of the purchase price.

Key M&A Model Formulas

Each component of cash flow used to value the acquiring and target firms individually (Step 1) and the consolidated acquirer and target firms including the effects of synergy (Step 2) is estimated by projecting the appropriate line items of the firm's income statement and balance sheet. Often, many of the financial statement line items are forecast by calculating each item as a percentage of sales based on the last three to five years of historical information and applying these historical percentages to projections of sales. This method is intuitively appealing because sales are normally the principal determinant of changes in cash flow over long time periods. This method also is simple to apply. Of course, the implicit assumptions are that all financial statement line items projected in this manner grow at the same rate as sales over time and that the historical relationship between these line items and sales will continue to apply to the forecast period. All financial statement line items need not or conceptually should not be expressed as a function of sales. These include such line items as depreciation and amortization expense, interest income and expense, and borrowing. Exhibit 9–9 lists the key formulas used to create the M&A model outlined in Steps 1–4 and illustrated later in Case Study 9–1.

Exhibit 9–9 Key Financial Modeling Relationships

Projected financial data may be based on historical relationships observed in the normalized data.

1. Net sales equal net sales in the prior year $\times$ $(1 + g)$, where g is the expected sales growth rate.
2. The variable component of cost of sales and S, G, & A is determined as a percentage of sales.
3. Depreciation and amortization are determined as a percentage of gross fixed assets (GFA).
4. Gross profit equals net revenue less the variable component of cost of sales, depreciation and amortization, lease expense, and other expenses allocated to production activities.
5. Operating profit (EBIT) equals gross profit less S, G, & A.
6. Interest income equals the interest rate $\times$ cash and marketable securities.
7. Interest expense equals cost of borrowed funds $\times$ yearend debt outstanding.
8. Before-tax profit equals EBIT plus interest income less interest expense.
9. Tax liability equals before-tax profits $\times$ marginal tax rate (federal, state, and local = 0.4).
10. Net profits equal before-tax profits less tax liability.
11. Other current assets (e.g., receivables, inventories, and prepaid assets) are determined as a percentage of sales.
12. Cash and marketable securities equal cash needed for operations and short-term (nonoperating) investments.
13. Accumulated depreciation and amortization equal current depreciation and amortization plus accumulated depreciation and amortization in the prior year.
14. Net fixed assets (NFA) equal GFA less accumulated depreciation and amortization.
15. Total assets equal cash and marketable securities plus other current assets plus NFA.
16. Current liabilities are determined as a percentage of net sales.
17. Long-term debt (LTD) equals existing debt plus new debt.[1]
18. Retained earnings equal net income after taxes plus retained earnings in the prior year.
19. Shareholders' equity equals common stock (including earned surplus) plus retained earnings.
20. Total liabilities and shareholders' equity equal current liabilities plus LTD plus shareholders' equity.
21. Working capital equals current assets (excluding excess cash balances) less current liabilities. See Exhibit 7–10 in Chapter 7 for an illustration of how to estimate minimum and excess cash balances.[2]
22. Change in working capital equals working capital in the current year less working capital in the prior year.

Continued

Exhibit 9–9 Key Financial Modeling Relationships — Cont'd

23. Capital spending equals the actual change in gross fixed assets whenever the current year's sales growth exceeds some predetermined number; otherwise, it equals depreciation and amortization expense.[3]

24. Free cash flow (to the firm) equals EBIT times $(1 - t)$ plus depreciation and amortization less capital expenditures less the change in working capital.

---

[1]Existing debt on the firm's balance sheet consists of debt at the end of the year preceding the first annual forecast year. This debt declines throughout the annual forecast period by the amount of the yearly principal repayment. The terms (i.e., interest rate and maturity) of each type of loan and annual repayment schedule may be found in the footnotes associated with the firm's financial statements shown in the 10K. The annual interest expense associated with total debt outstanding is estimated by multiplying the weighted average interest on the outstanding debt times the amount of debt outstanding at the beginning of the year (i.e., beginning balance). The weights used to calculate the weighted average interest rate are determined by calculating each type of debt outstanding as a percent of total debt outstanding.

[2]Once determined, minimum cash balances may be projected by assuming they increase in direct proportion to the increase in sales.

[3]If sales grow at less than some predetermined rate, capital spending equals depreciation and amortization expenses, a proxy for the required level of maintenance spending. If sales growth exceeds that predetermined rate, the firm must add to its capacity. Therefore, capital spending equals the change in gross fixed assets, which reflects both spending for additional capacity and maintenance spending.

Note: In solving the model using Microsoft Excel, the analyst should make sure the iteration command is turned on. The use of Excel's iteration capability will accommodate the "circularity or circular references" inherent in many financial models. For example, the change in cash and marketable securities impacts interest income, which affects net income and in turn the change in cash and marketable securities. Iteration is the recalculation of the worksheet until certain conditions are reached. Excel will recalculate the model the maximum number of times specified or until the results between the calculations change by less than the amount specified in the maximum change box. To turn on the iteration command, on the menu bar click on Tools >>> Options >>> Calculation. Select iteration and specify the maximum number of iterations and amount of maximum change.

M&A Model Balance-Sheet Adjustment Mechanisms

Projecting each line item of the balance sheet as a percent of sales does not ensure that the projected balance sheet will balance. Financial analysts commonly "plug" into financial models an adjustment equal to the difference between assets and liabilities plus shareholders' equity. While this may make sense for one-year budget forecasting, it becomes very cumbersome in multiyear projections. Moreover, it becomes very time consuming to run multiple scenarios based on different sets of assumptions. By forcing the model to automatically balance, these problems can be eliminated. While practical, this automatic adjustment mechanism rests on the simplistic notion that a firm will borrow if cash flow is negative and add to cash balances if cash flow is positive. This assumption ignores other options available to the firm, such as using excess cash flow to reduce outstanding debt, repurchase stock, or pay dividends.

The balance-sheet adjustment methodology illustrated in Exhibit 9–10 requires that the analyst separate current assets into operating and nonoperating assets. Operating assets include minimum operating cash balances and other operating assets (e.g., receivables, inventories, and assets such as prepaid items). Current nonoperating assets are

Exhibit 9–10 Model Balance-Sheet Adjustment Mechanism

Assets	Liabilities
Current operating assets	Current liabilities (CL)
Cash needed for operations (C)	
Other current assets (OCA)	Other liabilities (OL)
Total current operating assets (TCOA)	
Short-term (nonoperating) investments (I)	Long-term debt (LTD)
	Existing debt (ED)
	New debt (ND)
Net fixed assets (NFA)	
Other assets (OA)	
Total assets (TA)	Total liabilities (TL)
	Shareholders' equity (SE)

Notes:
Cash outflows exceed cash inflows. If $(TA - I) > (TL - ND) + SE$, the firm must borrow.
Cash outflows are less than cash inflows. If $(TA - I) < (TL - ND) + SE$, the firm's nonoperating investments increase.
Cash outflows equal cash inflows. If $(TA - I) = (TL - ND) + SE$, there is no change in borrowing or non-operating investments.

investments (i.e., cash generated in excess of minimum operating balances invested in short-term marketable securities). The firm issues new debt whenever cash outflows exceed cash inflows. Investments increase whenever cash outflows are less than cash inflows. For example, if net fixed assets (NFA) were the only balance-sheet item that grew from one period to the next, new debt issued (ND) would increase by an amount equal to the increase in net fixed assets. In contrast, if current liabilities were the only balance-sheet entry to rise from one period to the next, nonoperating investments (I) would increase by an amount equal to the increase in current liabilities. In either example, the balance sheet will automatically balance.

Applying Offer Price-Simulation Models in the Context of M&A Negotiations

The acquirer's initial offer generally is at the lowest point in the range between the minimum and maximum prices consistent with the acquirer's perception of what constitutes an acceptable price to the target firm. If the target's financial performance is remarkable, the target firm will command a high premium and the final purchase price will be close to the maximum price. Moreover, the acquirer may make a bid close to the maximum price to preempt other potential acquirers from having sufficient time to submit competing offers. However, in practice, hubris on the part of the acquirer's management or an auction environment may push the final negotiated purchase price to or even above the maximum economic value of the firm. Under any circumstance, increasing the offer price involves trade-offs.

The value of the offer price simulation model is that it enables the acquirer to see trade-offs between changes in the offer price and postacquisition EPS. EPS is widely used by acquirers whose shares are publicly traded as a measure of the acceptability of an acquisition. Even a short-term reduction in EPS may dissuade some CEOs from pursuing a target firm. As noted in Chapter 8, studies suggest that cash flows and earnings are highly positively correlated with stock returns over long periods such as five-year intervals. However, for shorter time periods, earnings show a stronger correlation with stock returns than cash flows.

The acquiring firm may vary the offer price by changing the amount of net synergy shared with the target firm's shareholders. Increases in the offer price affect the postacquisition EPS for a given set of assumptions about the deal's terms and conditions and firm-specific data. Terms and conditions include the cash and stock portion of the purchase price. Firm-specific data include the preacquisition share prices, the number of common shares outstanding for the acquirer and target firms, and the present value of anticipated net synergy, as well as the postacquisition projected net income available for common equity of the combined firms. Note that alternative performance measures, such as cash flow per share, can be used in place of EPS.

Table 9–7 illustrates alternative scenarios for postacquisition EPS generated by varying the amount of synergy shared with the target firm's shareholders based on a 75 percent equity/25 percent cash offer price. The composition reflects what the acquirer believes will best meet both the target's and its own objectives. The table shows the trade-off between increasing the offer price for a given postacquisition projection of net income and EPS. The relatively small reduction in EPS in each year as the offer price increases reflects the relatively small number of new shares the acquirer has to issue to acquire the target's shares. The data in the table reflects the resulting minimum, maximum, and initial offer price, assuming that the acquirer is willing to give up 30 percent of projected synergy. At that level of synergy sharing, the equity of the new firm will be 95 percent owned by the acquirer's current shareholders, with the remainder owned by the target firm's shareholders. See Case Study 9–1, later, for an application of the offer price simulation model to Cleveland Cliffs' 2008 takeover attempt of Alpha Natural Resources Corporation. Readers are encouraged to examine the formulas underlying the Excel-Based Offer-Price Simulation Model available on the CD-ROM accompanying this book and to apply the model to an actual or potential transaction of their choosing. Note that the offer-price simulation model in Table 9–7 is embedded in Step 3 of the worksheets entitled Excel-Based Merger and Acquisition Valuation and Structuring Model on the CD-ROM accompanying this textbook.

Alternative Applications of M&A Financial Models

When the Acquirer or Target Is Part of a Larger Legal Entity

The acquirer or target may be a wholly owned subsidiary, operating division, business segment, or product line of a parent corporation. When this is the case, it should be treated as a stand-alone business (i.e., one whose financial statements reflect all the costs of running the business and all the revenues generated by the business). This is the methodology suggested for Step 1 in the modeling process outlined in this chapter (see Table 9–1).

Wholly owned subsidiaries differ from operating divisions, business segments, and product lines in that they are units whose stock is entirely owned by the parent firm. Operating divisions, business segments, or product lines may or may not have detailed income, balance-sheet, and cash-flow statements for financial reporting purposes. The parent's management may simply collect data it deems sufficient for tracking the unit's performance. For example, such operations may be viewed as "cost centers," responsible for controlling their own costs. Consequently, detailed costs may be reported, with little

Table 9-7   Offer Price Simulation Model

Deal terms and conditions

Cash portion of offer price (%)	0.25
Equity portion of offer price (%)	0.75
Anticipated synergy shared with target (%)	0.3

Specific firm data

Acquirer share price ($/share)	16.03
Target share price ($/share)	14.25
Target shares outstanding (millions)	19.10
Acquirer shares outstanding, preclosing (millions)	426.00
PV of anticipated net synergy ($ million)	368.00

Alternative Scenarios Based on Different Amounts of Synergy Shared with Target

Shared Synergy (%)	Offer Price ($ millions)	Offer Price per Share	Postacq. Total Shares	Postacquisition EPS				
				2008	2009	2010	2011	2012
0.1	309	16.18	445	1.09	1.29	1.43	1.60	1.61
0.2	346	18.10	448	1.08	1.28	1.42	1.59	1.61
0.3	383	20.03	450	1.08	1.27	1.41	1.58	1.60
0.4	419	21.96	452	1.07	1.27	1.40	1.57	1.59
0.5	456	23.88	454	1.07	1.26	1.40	1.57	1.58
0.6	493	25.81	457	1.06	1.25	1.39	1.56	1.58
0.7	530	27.74	459	1.06	1.25	1.38	1.55	1.57
0.8	567	29.66	461	1.05	1.24	1.38	1.54	1.56
0.9	603	31.59	464	1.05	1.24	1.37	1.54	1.55
1.0	640	33.52	466	1.04	1.23	1.36	1.53	1.54

Calculated data

Minimum offer price ($ millions)	272
Maximum offer price ($ millions)	640
Initial offer price ($ millions)	383
Initial offer price per share ($)	20.03
Purchase price premium per share (%)	0.41
Composition of purchase price per target share	
Acquirer equity per target share	15.02
Cash per target share ($)	5.01
Share exchange ratio	1.25
New shares issued by acquirer	23.87
Acquirer shares outstanding, postclosing (millions)	449.87
Ownership distribution in new firm	
Acquirer shareholders (%)	0.95
Target shareholders (%)	0.05

Consolidated Acquirer and Target Net Income

	2009	2010	2011	2012	2013
Postacquisition consolidated net income ($ millions)	485	573	635	712	719

Note: This model is available on the CD-ROM accompanying this book in a worksheet entitled Excel-Based Offer Price Simulation Model.

detail for assets and liabilities associated with the operation. This is especially true for product lines, which often share resources (e.g., manufacturing plants, shipping facilities, accounting and human resource departments) with other product lines and businesses. The solution is to allocate a portion of the cost associated with each resource shared by the business to the business's income statement and estimate the percentage of each asset and liability associated with the business to create a balance sheet.

Adjusting Revenue and Costs

As an operating unit within a larger company, administrative costs such as legal, tax, audit, benefits, and treasury may be heavily subsidized or even provided without charge to the subsidiary. Alternatively, these services may be charged to the subsidiary as part of an allocation equal to a specific percentage of the subsidiary's sales or cost of sales. If these expenses are accounted for as part of an allocation methodology, they may substantially overstate the actual cost of purchasing these services from outside parties. Such allocations are often ways for the parent to account for expenses incurred at the level of the corporate headquarters but have little to do with the actual operation of the subsidiary. Such activities may include the expense associated with maintaining the corporation's headquarters building and airplanes.

If the cost of administrative support services is provided for free or heavily subsidized by the parent, the subsidiary's reported profits should be reduced by the actual cost of providing these services. If the cost of such services is measured by using some largely arbitrary allocation methodology, the subsidiary's reported profits may be increased by the difference between the allocated expense and the actual cost of providing the services.

When the target is an operating unit of another firm, it is common for its reported revenue to reflect sales to other operating units of the parent firm. Unless the parent firm contractually commits as part of the divestiture process to continue to buy from the divested operation, such revenue may evaporate as the parent firm satisfies its requirements from other suppliers. Moreover, intercompany revenue may be overstated, because the prices paid for the target's output reflect artificially high internal transfer prices (i.e., the price products are sold by one business to another in the same corporation) rather than market prices. The parent firm may not be willing to continue to pay the inflated transfer prices following the divestiture.

If the unit, whose financials have been adjusted, is viewed by the parent firm as the acquirer, use its financials (not the parent's) as the acquirer in the computer model. Then proceed with Steps 1–4 of the model building process described earlier in this chapter. You may wish to eliminate the earnings per share lines in the model. Similar adjustments are made for targets that are part of larger organizations.

Joint Ventures and Business Alliances

For alliances and joint ventures, the process is very much the same. The businesses or assets contributed by the partners to a joint venture (JV) should be valued on a stand-alone basis. For consistency with the model presented in this chapter, one of the partners may be viewed as the acquirer and the other as the target. Their financials are adjusted so that they are viewed on a stand-alone basis. Steps 1 and 2 enable the determination of the combined value of the JV and Step 4 incorporates the financing requirements for the combined operations. Step 3 is superfluous, as actual ownership of the partnership or JV depends on the agreed-on (by the partners) relative value of the assets or businesses contributed by each partner and the extent to which these assets and businesses contribute to creating synergy.

Things to Remember

Financial modeling in the context of M&As facilitates the process of valuation, deal structuring, and selecting the appropriate financial structure. The methodology developed in this chapter also may be applied to operating subsidiaries and product lines of larger organizations as well as joint ventures and partnerships. The process outlined in this chapter entails a four-step procedure.

1. Value the acquirer and target firms as stand-alone businesses. All costs and revenues associated with each business should be included in the valuation. The analyst should understand industry and company competitive dynamics. This requires normalizing the components of historical valuation cash flow. Data aberrations should be omitted. Common-size financial statements applied at a point in time, over a number of periods, and compared with other companies in the same industry provide insights into how to properly value the target firm. Multiple valuation methods should be used and the results averaged to increase confidence in the accuracy of the estimated value.

2. Value the combined financial statements of the acquirer and target companies including the effects of anticipated synergy. Ensure that all costs likely to be incurred in realizing synergy are included in the calculation of net synergy. All key assumptions should be stated clearly to provide credibility for the valuation and to inject a high degree of discipline into the valuation process.

3. Determine the initial offer price for the target firm. For stock purchases, define the minimum and maximum offer price range where the potential for synergy exists as follows:

$$(PV_T \text{ or } MV_T) < P_{IOP} < (PV_T \text{ or } MV_T + PV_{NS})$$

where PV_T and MV_T are the economic value of the target as a stand-alone company and the market value of the target, respectively. PV_{NS} is the present value of net synergy, and P_{IOP} is the initial offer price for the target. For asset purchases, the minimum price is the liquidation value of acquired net assets (i.e., acquired assets – acquired/assumed liabilities).

4. Determine the combined companies' ability to finance the transaction. The appropriate capital structure of the combined businesses is that which enables the acquirer to meet or exceed its required financial returns, satisfies the seller's price expectations, does not significantly raise borrowing costs, and does not violate significant financial constraints. Examples of financial constraints include loan covenants and prevailing industry average debt service ratios.

Chapter Discussion Questions

9–1. Why are financial modeling techniques used in analyzing M&As?

9–2. Give examples of the limitations of financial data used in the valuation process.

9–3. Why is it important to analyze historical data on the target company as part of the valuation process?

9–4. Explain the process of normalizing historical data and why it should be done before the valuation process is undertaken.

9–5. What are common-size financial statements, and how are they used to analyze a target firm?

9–6. Why should a target company be valued as a stand-alone business? Give examples of the types of adjustments that might have to be made if the target is part of a larger company.

9–7. Define the minimum and maximum purchase price range for a target company.

9–8. What are the differences between the final negotiated price, total consideration, total purchase price, and net purchase price?

9–9. Can the offer price ever exceed the maximum purchase price? If yes, why? If no, why not?

9–10. Why is it important to clearly state assumptions underlying a valuation?

9–11. Assume two firms have little geographic overlap in terms of sales and facilities. If they were to merge, how might this affect the potential for synergy?

9–12. Dow Chemical, a leading manufacturer of chemicals, announced in 2008 that it had an agreement to acquire competitor Rhom and Haas. Dow expected to broaden its current product offering by offering the higher-margin Rohm and Haas products. What would you identify as possible synergies between these two businesses? In what ways could the combination of these two firms erode combined cash flows?

9–13. Dow Chemical's acquisition of Rhom and Haas included a 74 percent premium over the firm's preannouncement share price. What is the probable process Dow employed in determining the stunning magnitude of this premium?

9–14. For most transactions, the full impact of net synergy will not be realized for many months. Why? What factors could account for the delay?

9–15. How does the presence of management options and convertible securities affect the calculation of the offer price for the target firm?

Answers to these Chapter Discussion Questions are available in the Online Instructor's Manual for instructors using this book.

Chapter Practice Problems and Answers

9–16. Acquiring Company is considering the acquisition of Target Company in a share-for-share transaction in which Target Company would receive $50.00 for each share of its common stock. Acquiring Company does not expect any change in its P/E multiple after the merger.

Using the information provided on these two firms in Table 9–8 and showing your work, calculate the following:

a. Purchase price premium. (Answer: 25%.)

b. Share-exchange ratio. (Answer: 0.8333.)

c. New shares issued by Acquiring Company. (Answer: 16,666.)

d. Total shares outstanding of the combined companies. (Answer: 76,666.)

Table 9–8 Information of Firms in Problem 9–16

	Acquiring Co.	Target Co.
Earnings available for common stock	$150,000	$30,000
Shares of common stock outstanding	60,000	20,000
Market price per share	$60.00	$40.00

e. Postmerger EPS of the combined companies. (Answer: $2.35.)

f. Premerger EPS of Acquiring Company. (Answer: $2.50.)

g. Postmerger share price. (Answer: $56.40, compared with $60.00 premerger.)

9–17. Acquiring Company is considering buying Target Company. Target Company is a small biotechnology firm that develops products licensed to the major pharmaceutical firms. Development costs are expected to generate negative cash flows during the first two years of the forecast period of $(10) million and $(5) million, respectively. Licensing fees are expected to generate positive cash flows during years 3 through 5 of the forecast period of $5 million, $10 million, and $15 million, respectively. Because of the emergence of competitive products, cash flow is expected to grow at a modest 5 percent annually after the fifth year. The discount rate for the first five years is estimated to be 20 percent then to drop to 10 percent beyond the fifth year. Also, the present value of the estimated net synergy by combining Acquiring and Target companies is $30 million. Calculate the minimum and maximum purchase prices for Target Company. Show your work.

Answer: Minimum price: $128.5 million; Maximum price: $158.5 million.

9–18. Using the Excel-Based Offer Price Simulation Model (Table 9–7) found on the CD-ROM accompanying this book, what would the initial offer price be if the amount of synergy shared with the target firm's shareholders was 50 percent? What is the offer price and what would the ownership distribution be if the percentage of synergy shared increased to 80 percent and the composition of the purchase price were all acquirer stock?

Solutions to these Practice Problems are available in the Online Instructor's Manual for instructors using this book.

Chapter Business Cases

Case Study 9–1. Cleveland Cliffs Fails to Complete Takeover of Alpha Natural Resources in a Commodity Play

In an effort to exploit the long-term upward trend in commodity prices, Cleveland Cliffs (Cliffs), an iron ore mining company, failed in its attempt to acquire Alpha Natural Resources (Alpha), a metallurgical coal mining firm, in late 2008 for a combination of cash and stock. In a joint press release on November 19, 2008, the firms announced that their merger agreement had been terminated due to adverse "macroeconomic conditions" at that time. Nevertheless, the transaction illustrates how a simple simulation model can be used to investigate the impact of alternative offer prices on postacquisition earnings per share.

When first announced in mid-2008, the deal was valued at about $10 billion. Alpha shareholders would receive total consideration of $131.42 per share, an approximate 46 percent premium over the firm's preannouncement share price. The new firm would be renamed Cliffs Natural Resources and would become one of the largest U.S. diversified mining and natural resources firms. The additional scale of operations, purchasing economies, and eliminating redundant overhead were expected to generate about $290 million in cost savings annually. The cash and equity portions of the offer price were 17.4 percent and 82.6 percent, respectively (see Table 9–9). The present value of anticipated synergy discounted in perpetuity at Cliff's estimated cost of capital of 11 percent was about $2.65 billion. Posttransaction net income projections were derived from Wall Street estimates.

Table 9–9 Cleveland-Cliffs' Attempted Acquisition of Alpha Natural Resources: Offer Price Simulation Model

Deal terms and conditions

Cash portion of offer price (%)	0.174
Equity portion of offer price (%)	0.826
Anticipated synergy shared with target (%)	1.00

Specific firm data

Acquirer share price ($/share)	102.50
Target share price ($/share)	90.27
Target shares outstanding (millions)	64.40
Acquirer shares outstanding, preclosing (millions)	44.60
PV of anticipated net synergy ($ millions) (@11% WACC)	2650

Calculated data

Minimum offer price ($ millions)	5813
Maximum offer price ($ millions)	8463
Initial offer price ($ millions)	8463
Initial offer price per share ($)	131.42
Purchase price premium per share (%)	0.46
Composition of purchase price per target share	
Acquirer equity per target share	108.55
Cash per target share ($)	22.87
Share-exchange ratio	1.28
New shares issued by acquirer	82.57
Acquirer shares outstanding, postclosing (millions)	127.17
Ownership distribution in new firm	
Acquirer shareholders (%)	0.35
Target shareholders (%)	0.65

Alternative Scenarios Based on Different Amounts of Synergy Shared with Target

Shared Synergy (%)	Offer Price ($ millions)	Offer Price per Share	Postacq. Total Shares	Postacquisition EPS				
				2008	2009	2010	2011	2012
0.1	6078	94.38	104	3.72	4.09	4.42	4.73	4.96
0.2	6343	98.50	106	3.63	3.99	4.31	4.61	4.84
0.3	6608	102.61	109	3.55	3.90	4.21	4.50	4.72
0.4	6873	106.73	112	3.47	3.81	4.11	4.40	4.61
0.5	7138	110.84	114	3.39	3.72	4.02	4.30	4.51
0.6	7403	114.96	117	3.31	3.64	3.93	4.20	4.41
0.7	7668	119.07	119	3.24	3.56	3.84	4.11	4.31
0.8	7933	123.19	122	3.17	3.48	3.76	4.02	4.22
0.9	8198	127.30	125	3.11	3.41	3.68	3.94	4.13
1.0	8463	131.42	127	3.04	3.34	3.61	3.86	4.05

Consolidated Acquirer and Target Net Income

	2009	2010	2011	2012	2013
Postacquisition consolidated net income ($ millions)	387	425	459	491	515

Discussion Questions

1. Purchase price premiums contain a synergy premium and a control premium. The control premium represents the amount an acquirer is willing to pay for the right to direct the operations of the target firm. Assume that Cliffs would not have been justified in paying a control premium for acquiring Alpha. Consequently, the Cliffs' offer price should have reflected only a premium for synergy. According to Table 9–9, did Cliffs overpay for Alpha? Explain your answer.

2. Based on the information in Table 9–9 and the initial offer price of $10 billion, did this transaction implicitly include a control premium? How much? In what way could the implied control premium have simply reflected Cliffs potentially overpaying for the business? Explain your answer.

3. The difference in postacquisition EPS between an offer price in which Cliffs shared 100 percent of synergy and one in which it would share only 10 percent of synergy is about 22 percent (i.e., $3.72/$3.04 in 2008). To what do you attribute this substantial difference?

Answers to these questions are found in the Online Instructor's Manual available to instructors using this book.

Case Study 9–2. Determining the Initial Offer Price: Alanco Technologies Inc. Acquires StarTrak Systems

Background

In mid-2006, Alanco Technologies Inc. (Alanco) acquired all the outstanding stock of StarTrak Systems (StarTrak), a provider of global positioning satellite (GPS) tracking and wireless subscription data services to the transportation industry. StarTrak competes in the refrigerated segment of the transport industry and provides the dominant share of all wireless tracking, monitoring, and control services to this market segment. The firm's products increase efficiency and reduce logistical costs through the wireless monitoring and control of crucial data, including GPS location, cargo temperatures, and fuel levels. StarTrak has been growing rapidly and currently has a substantial order backlog. Management projects escalating cash flows during the next five years.

StarTrak's GPS tracking, wireless information services technology, and large commercial market opportunity complement Alanco's own TSI PRISM Radio Frequency identification tracking business. The acquisition would further establish Alanco's leadership role in developing new markets for wireless tracking and management of people and assets. Alanco had developed the TSI PRISM system to provide tracking services for the corrections industry. It tracks the location and movement of inmates and officers, resulting in prison operating cost reductions and enhanced officer and facility security.

Alanco's management understood that a successful acquisition would be one that would create more shareholder value at an acceptable level of risk than if the firm retained its current "go it alone" strategy. Consequently, Alanco valued its own business on a stand-alone basis, StarTrak's business as a stand-alone unit, and combined the two and included the effects of potential synergy. The difference between the combined valuation with synergy and the sum of the two businesses valued as stand-alone operations provided an estimate of the potential incremental value that could be created from the acquisition of StarTrak. Alanco's management also understood the importance of not paying too much for StarTrak, while offering enough to make the target's management take the bid seriously. Therefore, the challenge was to determine the initial StarTrak offer price.

Analysis

Tables 9–10 to 9–13 provide pro forma financial output from an M&A model used to determine the initial StarTrak offer price. Each table corresponds to one step in the four-step process outlined in this chapter. The total value created by combining Alanco and StarTrak is summarized in Table 9–14.

- Table 9–10. Based on management's best estimate of future competitive dynamics and the firm's internal resources, Alanco devised a business plan suggesting that, if Alanco continued its current strategy, it would be worth about $97 million. Reflecting limited data provided by StarTrak's management and publicly available information, Alanco normalized StarTrak's historical financial statements by eliminating nonrecurring gains, losses, and expenses. This provided Alanco with a better understanding of StarTrak's sustainable financial performance. Future performance was determined by adjusting the firm's past performance to reflect what Alanco's management thought was possible. Despite its significantly smaller size in terms of revenue, StarTrak's market value, determined by multiplying its share price by the number of shares outstanding, was about $103.5 million—about $6 million more than Alanco's stand-alone market value.

- Table 9–11. By consolidating the two firms and estimating potential synergy, Alanco believed that together they could achieve about $118 million in additional shareholder value. This incremental value was attributable to sustainable revenue increases of as much as $15 million annually as a result of improved product quality, a broader product offering, and cross-selling activities, as well as cost savings resulting from economies of scale and scope and the elimination of duplicate jobs.

- Table 9–12. After an extensive review of the data, Alanco's management proposed to StarTrak's CEO the acquisition of 100 percent of the firm's outstanding 3 million shares for $50.20 per share, a 46 percent premium over the current StarTrak share price. The initial offer consisted of 1.14 Alanco shares plus $12.55 in cash for each StarTrak share. If accepted, StarTrak shareholders would own about 77 percent of the stock of the combined firms.

- Table 9–13. It appeared that the combined firms would be able to finance the transaction without violating covenants on existing debt. Despite $40 million in additional borrowing to finance the transaction, the key credit ratios for the combined firms remained attractive relative to industry averages. This may enable the new firm to borrow additional funds to exploit selected future strategic opportunities as they arise. Finally, the after-tax return on total capital for the combined firms exceeded by 2010 what Alanco could have achieved on a stand-alone basis.

- Table 9–14. The estimated equity value for the combined firms is $251.7 million. This reflects the enterprise or total present value of the new firm, including synergy, adjusted for long-term debt and excess cash balances. The estimated posttransaction price per share is $56.95, $23.95 above Alanco's pretransaction share price.

Discussion Questions

1. Using the M&A model financial statements for the two firms in Tables 9–10 through 9–14, determine the differences between the market value and stand-alone value of StarTrak and Alanco. How would you explain these differences?

Table 9-10 Step 1. Acquiring Company—Alanco

Forecast Assumptions for 2006–2010	2006	2007	2008	2009	2010
Net sales growth rate	1.25	1.20	1.15	1.15	1.15
Cost of sales (variable)/sales (%)	0.65	0.65	0.65	0.65	0.65
Dep. and amort./gross fixed assets (%)	0.1	0.1	0.1	0.1	0.1
Selling expense/sales (%)	0.09	0.09	0.09	0.09	0.09
General and admin. expense/sales (%)	0.07	0.07	0.07	0.07	0.07
Interest on cash/marketable securities	0.04	04	0.04	0.04	0.04
Interest rate on debt (%)	0.1	0.1	0.1	0.1	0.1
Marginal tax rate	0.4	0.4	0.4	0.4	0.4
Other assets/sales (%)	0.3	0.3	0.3	0.3	0.3
Gross fixed assets/sales (%)	0.4	0.4	0.4	0.4	0.4
Minimum cash balances/sales (%)	0.12	0.12	0.12	0.12	0.12
Current liabilities/sales (%)	0.1	0.1	0.1	0.1	0.1
Common shares outstanding (millions)	1	1	1	1	1
Discount rate (2006–2010) (%)	0.15				
Discount rate (terminal period) (%)	0.10				
Sustainable cash-flow growth rate	1.06				
Sustainable cash-flow rate as %	0.06				
Market value of long-term debt ($ millions)[1]	23.8				

Alanco Stand-Alone Income, Balance Sheet, and Cash-Flow Statements

	Historical Financials						Projected Financials			
	2001	2002	2003	2004	2005	2006	2007	2008	2009	2010
Income statement ($ millions)										
Net sales	27.4	31.5	41.0	53.3	66.6	83.2	99.8	114.8	132.0	151.9
Less cost of sales										
Variable	17.8	20.5	26.6	34.6	43.3	54.1	64.9	74.6	85.8	98.7
Depreciation & amortization	1.1	1.3	1.6	2.1	2.7	3.3	4.0	4.6	5.3	6.1
Lease expense	0.4	0.4	0.6	0.7	0.8	1.0	1.2	1.2	1.3	1.3
Total cost of sales	19.3	22.1	28.9	37.4	46.7	58.4	70.1	80.4	92.4	106.1
Gross profit	8.1	9.4	12.1	15.8	19.8	24.8	29.8	34.4	39.6	45.8

Continued

Table 9–10 — Cont'd

	Historical Financials					Projected Financials				
	2001	2002	2003	2004	2005	2006	2007	2008	2009	2010
Less sales, general, and admin. expense										
Selling expense	2.5	2.8	3.7	4.8	6.0	7.5	9.0	10.3	11.9	13.7
General and admin. expense	1.9	2.2	2.9	3.7	4.7	5.8	7.0	8.0	9.2	10.6
Total S, G, & A	4.4	5.0	6.6	8.5	10.7	13.3	16.0	18.4	21.1	24.3
Operating profits (EBIT)	3.7	4.3	5.5	7.3	9.2	11.5	13.8	16.0	18.5	21.5
Plus interest income	0.2	0.2	0.2	0.3	0.4	0.4	0.5	0.6	0.6	0.7
Less interest expense	1.5	1.5	1.8	2.1	2.4	2.7	2.8	2.6	2.3	1.9
Net profits before taxes	2.4	3.0	4.0	5.5	7.2	9.2	11.4	14.0	16.9	20.3
Less taxes	0.9	1.2	1.6	2.2	2.9	3.7	4.6	5.6	6.7	8.1
Net profits after taxes	1.4	1.8	2.4	3.3	4.3	5.5	6.9	8.4	10.1	12.2
Earnings per share ($/share)	1.4	1.8	2.4	3.3	4.3	5.5	6.9	8.4	10.1	12.2
Balance sheet (12/31)										
Current assets										
Cash and marketable securities[2]	3.3	3.8	4.9	6.4	8.0	10.0	12.0	13.8	15.8	18.2
Other current assets	8.2	9.5	12.3	16.0	20.0	25.0	30.0	34.4	39.6	45.6
Total current assets	11.5	13.2	17.2	22.4	28.0	34.9	41.9	48.2	55.5	63.8
Gross fixed assets	11.0	12.6	16.4	21.3	26.6	33.3	39.9	45.9	52.8	60.7
Less accumulated deprec. and amortization.	0.6	1.9	3.5	5.6	8.3	11.6	15.6	20.2	25.5	31.6
Net fixed assets	10.4	10.7	12.9	15.7	18.3	21.7	24.3	25.7	27.3	29.2
Total assets	21.9	24.0	30.1	38.0	46.3	56.6	66.3	73.9	82.8	93.0
Current liabilities	2.7	3.2	4.1	5.3	6.7	8.3	10.0	11.5	13.2	15.2
Long-term debt[3]	15.1	15.0	17.8	21.2	23.8	26.9	28.1	25.9	22.9	18.9
Common stock[4]	2.0	2.0	2.0	2.0	2.0	2.0	2.0	2.0	2.0	2.0
Retained earnings	2.0	3.8	6.2	9.5	13.8	19.3	26.2	34.6	44.7	56.9
Shareholders' equity	4.0	5.8	8.2	11.5	15.8	21.3	28.2	36.6	46.7	58.9
Total liabilities + shareholders' equity	21.9	24.0	30.1	38.0	46.3	56.6	66.3	73.9	82.8	93.0
Free cash flow ($ millions)										
EBIT (1 – t)	2.2	2.6	3.3	4.4	5.5	6.9	8.3	9.6	11.1	12.9
Plus depreciation and amortization	1.1	1.3	1.6	2.1	2.7	3.3	4.0	4.6	5.3	6.1

	Historical Financials					Projected Financials				
	2001	2002	2003	2004	2005	2006	2007	2008	2009	2010
Less capital expenditures[5]	1.2	1.3	3.8	4.9	5.3	6.7	4.0	4.6	5.3	6.1
Less change in working capital	0.4	1.3	3.0	3.9	4.3	5.3	5.3	4.8	5.5	6.3
Equals free cash flow[6]	1.7	1.3	-1.8	-2.3	-1.4	-1.8	2.9	4.8	5.6	6.5
PV (2006–2010) @15%	10.3									
PV of terminal value @ 10%	86.3									
Total PV (market value of the firm)	96.6									

Alanco Stand-Alone Income, Balance-Sheet, and Cash-Flow Statements

	Historical Financials					Projected Financials				
Valuation Analysis	**2001**	**2002**	**2003**	**2004**	**2005**	**2006**	**2007**	**2008**	**2009**	**2010**
Plus excess cash balances	0.0									
Less mkt. value of long-term debt	23.8									
Equity value ($ millions)	72.8									
Equity value per share ($/share)	72.8									

Forecast Assumptions for 2006–2010 (Target Company: StarTrak)	**2006**	**2007**	**2008**	**2009**	**2010**
Net sales growth rate	1.4	1.35	1.3	1.3	1.2
Cost of sales (variable)/sales (%)	0.60	0.60	0.60	0.60	0.60
Dep. and amortization./gross fixed assets (%)	0.1	0.1	0.1	0.1	0.1
Selling expense/sales (%)	0.08	0.08	0.08	0.08	0.08
General and admin. expense/sales (%)	0.06	0.06	0.06	0.06	0.06
Interest on cash/marketable sec.	0.04	0.04	0.04	0.04	0.04
Interest rate on debt (%)	0.1	0.1	0.1	0.1	0.1
Marginal tax rate	0.4	0.4	0.4	0.4	0.4
Other assets/sales (%)	0.3	0.3	0.3	0.3	0.3
Gross fixed assets/sales (%)	0.35	0.35	0.35	0.35	0.35
Minimum cash balances/sales (%)	0.12	0.12	0.12	0.12	0.12
Current liabilities/sales (%)	0.1	0.1	0.1	0.1	0.1
Common shares outstanding (millions)	3	3	3	3	3
Discount rate (2006–2010) (%)	0.15				
Discount rate (terminal period) (%)	0.1				

Continued

Table 9–10 — Cont'd

Forecast Assumptions for 2006–2010 (Target Company: StarTrak)

	2006
Sustainable cash-flow growth rate	1.06
Sustainable cash-flow rate as %	0.06
Market value of long-term debt ($ millions)[1]	3.1

Valuation Analysis	Historical Financials					Projected Financials				
	2001	2002	2003	2004	2005	2006	2007	2008	2009	2010
Income statement ($ millions)										
Net sales	10.4	12.0	16.1	21.8	28.3	39.7	53.6	69.6	90.5	108.6
Less: cost of sales										
Variable	6.2	7.2	9.7	13.1	17.0	23.8	32.1	41.8	54.3	65.2
Depreciation and amortization	0.4	0.4	0.6	0.8	1.0	1.4	1.9	2.4	3.2	3.8
Lease expense	0.4	0.4	0.6	0.7	0.8	1.0	1.2	1.2	1.3	1.3
Total cost of sales	7.0	8.0	10.9	14.5	18.8	26.2	35.2	45.4	58.8	70.3
Gross profit	3.4	4.0	5.3	7.3	9.5	13.5	18.3	24.2	31.7	38.3
Less sales, general & administrative expenses										
Selling expense	0.8	1.0	1.3	1.7	2.3	3.2	4.3	5.6	7.2	8.7
General and admin. expense	0.6	0.7	1.0	1.3	1.7	2.4	3.2	4.2	5.4	6.5
Total S, G, & A	1.5	1.7	2.3	3.1	4.0	5.6	7.5	9.7	12.7	15.2
Operating profits (EBIT)	1.9	2.3	3.0	4.2	5.6	7.9	10.8	14.5	19.1	23.1
Plus interest income	0.1	0.1	0.1	0.1	0.2	0.2	0.3	0.3	0.4	0.6
Less interest expense	0.3	0.2	0.2	0.3	0.3	0.5	0.6	0.6	0.5	0.0
Net profits before taxes	1.7	2.2	2.9	4.0	5.4	7.6	10.5	14.2	19.0	23.7
Less taxes	0.7	0.9	1.2	1.6	2.2	3.1	4.2	5.7	7.6	9.5
Net profits after taxes	1.0	1.3	1.7	2.4	3.3	4.6	6.3	8.5	11.4	14.2
Earnings per share ($/share)	0.3	0.4	0.6	0.8	1.1	1.5	2.1	2.8	3.8	4.7
Balance sheet (12/31)										
Current assets										
Cash and marketable securities[2]	1.2	1.4	1.9	2.6	3.4	4.8	6.4	8.4	10.9	13.8
Other current assets	3.1	3.6	4.8	6.5	8.5	11.9	16.1	20.9	27.2	32.6
Total current assets	4.4	5.0	6.8	9.2	11.9	16.7	22.5	29.2	38.0	46.4
Gross fixed assets	3.6	4.2	5.7	7.6	9.9	13.9	18.7	24.4	31.7	38.0
Less accumulated depreciation and amortization	0.4	0.8	1.4	2.1	3.1	4.5	6.4	8.8	12.0	15.8

	Historical Financials					Projected Financials				
	2001	2002	2003	2004	2005	2006	2007	2008	2009	2010
Net fixed assets	3.2	3.4	4.3	5.5	6.8	9.4	12.3	15.5	19.7	22.2
Total assets	7.6	8.4	11.0	14.6	18.7	26.0	34.8	44.8	57.7	68.6
Current liabilities	1.0	1.2	1.6	2.2	2.8	4.0	5.4	7.0	9.1	10.9
Long-term debt[3]	2.6	1.9	2.4	3.0	3.1	4.7	5.9	5.7	5.1	0.0
Common stock[4]	2.0	2.0	2.0	2.0	2.0	2.0	2.0	2.0	2.0	2.0
Retained earnings	2.0	3.3	5.0	7.5	10.7	15.3	21.6	30.2	41.6	55.8
Shareholders' equity	4.0	5.3	7.0	9.5	12.7	17.3	23.6	32.2	43.6	57.8
Total liabilities + shareholders' equity	7.6	8.4	11.0	14.6	18.7	26.0	34.8	44.8	57.7	68.6
Free cash flow ($ millions)										
EBIT (1 − t)	1.2	1.4	1.8	2.5	3.3	4.8	6.5	8.7	11.4	13.9
Plus depreciation & amortization	0.4	0.4	0.6	0.8	1.0	1.4	1.9	2.4	3.2	3.8
Less capital expenditures[5]	1.2	0.4	1.5	2.0	1.0	4.0	4.9	2.4	3.2	3.8
Less change in working capital	0.4	0.5	1.3	1.8	2.1	3.6	4.4	5.1	6.7	6.6
Equals: free cash flow[6]	−0.1	0.9	−0.4	−0.5	1.3	−1.5	−0.9	3.5	4.8	7.3

	2005
PV (2006–2010) @ 15%	6.7
PV of terminal value @ 10%	96.0
Total PV (mkt. value of firm)	102.7
Plus excess cash balances	0.0
Less mkt. value of long-term debt	3.1
Equity value ($ millions)	99.6
Equity value per share ($/share)	33.2

[1]PV of Alanco's debt $= C \times PVIFA_{i,n} + P \times PVIF_{i,n}$, where C is the average coupon rate in dollars on Alanco's debt at an interest rate, i, for the average remaining maturity on the debt, n. P is the principal in dollars. PVIFA is the present value interest factor for an annuity and PVIF is the present value interest factor for a single value.

[2]Cash and marketable securities = long-term debt + current liabilities + shareholders' equity − other current assets − net fixed assets.

[3]See Exhibit 9-11.

[4]Common stock includes both stock issued at par plus additional paid in capital (i.e., premium paid to the firm over par or stated value of the stock).

[5]Capital spending is undertaken to maintain existing and provide additional capacity. Additions to capacity come at periodic intervals related to the level of utilization of existing production facilities. Consequently, capital spending equals the actual change in gross fixed assets (GFA) only if the current year's percentage change in sales exceeds 20 percent (a measure of facility utilization); otherwise, capital spending equals depreciation.

[6]Free cash flow equals after-tax EBIT + depreciation and amortization − capital expenditures − the change in working capital.

Table 9–11 Step 2. Acquirer and Target Consolidation

Forecast Assumptions for 2006–2010	2006	2007	2008	2009	2010
Sales-related synergy ($ millions)	2	10	15	15	15
Variable COS/sales (%)	0.63	0.63	0.63	0.63	0.63
Selling expense/sales (%)	0.085	0.08	0.08	0.08	0.08
General and admin./sales (%)	0.055	0.05	0.05	0.05	0.05
Integration expenses	−5	−3			
Discount rate (2006–2010)	0.15				
Discount rate (terminal period)	0.1				
Sustainable cash-flow growth rate	1.065				
Sustainable cash-flow rate as %	0.065				
Market value of long-term debt	26.9				

Consolidated Alanco and StarTrak Income, Balance-Sheet, and Cash-Flow Statements Including Synergy

	Historical Financials					Projected Financials				
Valuation analysis	2001	2002	2003	2004	2005	2006	2007	2008	2009	2010
Income statement ($ millions)										
Net sales	37.8	43.5	57.1	75.0	94.9	122.9	153.4	184.4	222.6	260.5
Sales-related synergy[1]						2.0	10.0	15.0	15.0	15.0
Total net sales	37.8	43.5	57.1	75.0	94.9	124.9	163.4	199.4	237.6	275.5
Less: cost of sales										
Variable[2]	24.1	27.7	36.3	47.7	60.3	78.7	102.9	125.7	149.7	173.5
Depreciation and amortization expense	1.5	1.7	2.2	2.9	3.7	4.7	5.9	7.0	8.4	9.9
Lease expense	0.8	0.8	1.2	1.4	1.6	2.0	2.4	2.4	2.6	2.6
Total cost of sales	26.3	30.1	39.7	52.0	65.5	85.4	111.2	135.1	160.7	186.0
Gross profit	11.5	13.3	17.4	23.1	29.4	39.5	52.2	64.4	76.8	89.4
Less sales, general, and admin. expense										
Selling expense	3.3	3.8	5.0	6.5	8.3	10.6	13.1	16.0	19.0	22.0
General and admin. expense	2.5	2.9	3.8	5.0	6.4	6.9	8.2	10.0	11.9	13.8
Total S, G, & A[3]	5.8	6.7	8.8	11.6	14.6	17.5	21.2	25.9	30.9	35.8
Integration expenses[4]						−5.0	−3.0	0.0	0.0	0.0
Operating profits (EBIT)	5.7	6.6	8.6	11.5	14.8	17.0	27.9	38.4	46.0	53.6
Plus interest income	0.2	0.3	0.3	0.5	0.6	0.6	0.7	0.9	1.1	1.3
Less interest expense	1.8	1.7	2.0	2.4	2.7	3.2	3.4	3.2	2.8	1.9
Net profits before taxes	4.1	5.2	6.9	9.5	12.6	14.4	25.3	36.2	44.2	53.0
Less taxes	1.6	2.1	2.8	3.8	5.1	5.8	10.1	14.5	17.7	21.2

Net profits after taxes[5]	2.5	3.1	4.1	5.7	7.6	8.7	15.2	21.7	26.5	31.8
Balance sheet (12/31)										
Current assets										
Cash and marketable securities	4.5	5.2	6.9	9.0	11.4	14.7	18.4	22.1	26.7	32.1
Other current assets	11.3	13.0	17.1	22.5	28.5	36.9	46.0	55.3	66.8	78.1
Total current assets	15.9	18.3	24.0	31.5	39.9	51.6	64.4	77.5	93.5	110.2
Gross fixed assets	14.6	16.8	22.0	28.9	36.5	47.2	58.7	70.3	84.5	98.8
Less accumulated depreciation	1.0	2.7	4.9	7.8	11.4	16.1	22.0	29.0	37.5	47.4
Net fixed assets	13.6	14.1	17.2	21.2	25.1	31.0	36.7	41.3	47.0	51.4
Total assets	29.5	32.4	41.1	52.7	65.0	82.6	101.1	118.7	140.5	161.6
Current liabilities	3.8	4.3	5.7	7.5	9.5	12.3	15.3	18.4	22.3	26.0
Long-term debt	17.7	16.9	20.2	24.2	26.9	31.7	33.9	31.5	28.0	18.9
Common stock	4.0	4.0	4.0	4.0	4.0	4.0	4.0	4.0	4.0	4.0
Retained earnings	4.0	7.1	11.3	17.0	24.5	34.6	47.8	64.8	86.3	112.7
Shareholders' equity	8.0	11.1	15.3	21.0	28.5	38.6	51.8	68.8	90.3	116.7
Total liabilities + shareholders' equity	29.5	32.4	41.1	52.7	65.0	82.6	101.1	118.7	140.5	161.6
Free cash flow ($ millions)										
EBIT (1 – t)	3.4	4.0	5.1	6.9	8.9	10.2	16.8	23.1	27.6	32.2
Plus depreciation & amortization	1.5	1.7	2.2	2.9	3.7	4.7	5.9	7.0	8.4	9.9
Less capital expenditures	2.4	1.7	5.2	6.9	6.3	10.6	8.9	7.0	8.4	9.9
Less change in working capital	0.8	1.8	4.4	5.7	6.4	9.0	9.8	9.9	12.2	12.9
Equals: free cash flow to the firm	1.7	2.2	–2.3	–2.8	–0.2	–0.7	4.0	13.1	15.4	19.2
PV (2006–2010) @ 15%					26.0					
PV of terminal value @ 10% (8)					291.2					
Total PV (market value of the firm)					317.2					
Plus excess cash balances					0.0					
Less mkt. value of long-term debt					26.9					
Equity value ($ millions)					290.2					
Equity value per share ($/share)					77.3					

[1] Revenue increases as a result of improved product quality, a broader product offering, and cross-selling to each firm's customers.

[2] Production cost-related savings are realized as a result of economies of scale (i.e., better utilization of existing facilities) and scope (i.e., existing operations are used to produce a broader product offering) and the elimination of duplicate jobs.

[3] Selling expenses and administrative overhead savings result from the elimination of duplicate jobs.

[4] Integration expenses include severance, training, marketing, and advertising expenses, as well as production, process, and technology upgrades.

[5] EPS is not shown because the consolidated valuation does not consider how the acquisition will be financed. The use of stock to finance a portion of the offer price would affect the estimation of the EPS of the combined companies by affecting the number of shares outstanding.

Table 9-12 Step 3. Offer Price Determination

Forecast assumptions

Acquirer (Alanco) share price[1]	$33.00
Target (StarTrak) share price[2]	$34.50
Synergy shared with target (%)[3]	0.4
Target firm shares outstanding (millions)	3
Acquirer shares outstanding (millions)	1
Cash portion of offer price (%)[4]	0.25

			Stand-Alone Value Consolidated Alanco and StarTrak		
Financing Metrics ($ millions)	**Alanco (1)**	**StarTrak (2)**	**Without Synergy (3) = (1) + (2)**	**With Synergy (4)**	**Value of Synergy (4) – (3) PV_{NS}**
Valuations (see PV in Tables 9–4 and 9–5)	72.8	99.6	172.4	290.2	117.9
Minimum offer price (PV_{MIN}) ($ millions)	103.5				
Maximum offer price (PV_{MAX}) ($ mil)	221.4				
Initial offer price ($ million)	150.6				
Initial offer price per share ($)	50.2				
Purchase price premium per share	0.46				
Cash per share ($)[5]	12.55				
Share-exchange ratio[6]	1.14				
New shares issued by Alanco	3.42				
Total shares outstanding (Alanco/StarTrak)	4.42				
Ownership distribution in new firm					
Alanco shareholders (%)	0.23				
StarTrak shareholders (%)	0.77				
Offer price composition	1.14 shares of Alanco stock + $12.55 for each share of StarTrak stock outstanding				
Offer price incl. assumed StarTrak debt[7]	153.8				

[1]Alanco share price at the close of business the day before the offer was presented to StarTrak management. Note that Alanco's market value estimated by Alanco management is substantially higher than that implied by its current share price, reflecting its greater optimism than investors.

[2]StarTrak share price at the close of business the day before the offer is received from StarTrak management.

[3]This fraction represents the share of net synergy Alanco's management is willing to share initially with StarTrak shareholders.

[4]Alanco management desired to limit the amount of borrowing associated with the transaction to 25 percent of the purchased price.

[5]Cash portion of the offer price equals 0.25 × $50.20.

[6]($50.20 – 0.25 × $50.20)/$33.00 = ($50.20 – $12.55)/$33.00 = 1.14 Alanco shares for each StarTrak share. Note that $12.55 is the cash portion of the purchase price Alanco management is willing to pay StarTrak shareholders.

[7]Alanco's management is willing to assume StarTrak's long-term debt outstanding of $3.1 million at the end of 2000.

Table 9–13   Step 4. Financing Feasibility Analysis

Forecast assumptions (2006–2010)

New transaction-related borrowing:

Principal ($ millions)[1]	40
Interest (%)	0.11
Loan covenants on existing debt	
Debt/total capital	<1.0
Fixed payment coverage ratio	>1.0
Current assets/current liabilities	>2.0
New Alanco shares issued (millions)	3.42

Consolidated Alanco and StarTrak Financial Statements Including Synergy and Financing Effects

	Projected Financials					Forecast Comments
Financial Reporting	**2006**	**2007**	**2008**	**2009**	**2010**	**Data from Tables 9–7 and 9–9 unless otherwise noted.**
Income statement ($ millions)						
Net sales	124.9	163.4	199.4	237.6	275.5	
Less cost of sales	85.4	111.2	135.1	160.7	186.0	
Gross profit	39.5	52.2	64.4	76.8	89.4	
Less sales, general, and admin. expense	17.5	21.2	25.9	30.9	35.8	
Integration expenses	–5.0	–3.0	0.0	0.0	0.0	
Operating profits (EBIT)	17.0	27.9	38.4	46.0	53.6	
Plus interest income	0.6	0.7	0.9	1.1	1.3	
Less interest expense	7.6	7.7	7.3	6.8	5.7	Includes interest on current and transaction-related debt.
Net profits before taxes	10.0	21.0	32.1	40.3	49.3	
Less taxes	4.0	8.4	12.8	16.1	19.7	
Net profits after taxes	6.0	12.6	19.2	24.2	29.6	
Earnings per share ($/share)	1.4	2.9	4.3	5.5	6.7	Includes 1 million existing and 3.42 million newly issued Alanco shares.
Balance sheet (12/31)						
Current assets						
Cash and marketable securities	53.5	55.9	58.1	61.0	64.6	
Other current assets	36.9	46.0	55.3	66.8	78.1	

Continued

Table 9-13 — Cont'd

Financial Reporting	Projected Financials					Forecast Comments
	2006	2007	2008	2009	2010	Data from Tables 9–7 and 9–9 unless otherwise noted.
Total current assets	90.4	101.9	113.4	127.8	142.7	
Gross fixed assets	47.2	58.7	70.3	84.5	98.8	
Less accumulated depreciation	16.1	22.0	29.0	37.5	47.4	
Net fixed assets	31.0	36.7	41.3	47.0	51.4	
Total assets	121.4	138.6	154.7	174.8	194.1	
Current liabilities	12.3	15.3	18.4	22.3	26.0	
Long-term debt	38.8	37.6	36.1	34.5	32.8	
Existing debt	31.7	33.9	31.5	28.0	18.9	
Transaction-related debt	38.8	37.5	36.0	34.3	32.5	$40 million, 15 year loan at 11% per annum
Total long-term debt	70.5	71.4	67.5	62.3	51.4	
Common stock	4.0	4.0	4.0	4.0	4.0	
Retained earnings	34.6	47.8	64.8	86.3	112.7	
Shareholders' equity	38.6	51.8	68.8	90.3	116.7	
Total liabilities + shareholders' equity	121.4	138.6	154.7	174.8	194.1	
Addendum						
Lease payments	2.0	2.4	2.4	2.6	2.6	
Principal repayments	5.6	5.6	5.6	5.6	5.6	¹$40 million, 15-year loan at 11% per annum
Financial scenario selection criteria						
After-tax return on capital, combined firms (%)	9.7	13.7	16.7	17.7	20.7	[Net income + (Interest and Lease expense) $\times$ (1–0.4)]/(Shareholders' equity + Long-term debt + PV of operating leases)
After-tax return on capital, Alanco (%)	12.6	14.4	15.1	15.6	16.2	Same
Key combined firm credit ratios and performance measures						
Debt to total capital	0.65	0.58	0.50	0.41	0.31	Total long-term debt/(Total long-term debt + equity)
Fixed-payment coverage ratio	1.01	1.56	2.15	2.60	3.20	(EBIT + Lease payments)/(Interest expense + Lease payment + Principal repayment $\times$ [1/(1 – 0.40)])

Current assets/current liabilities	7.36	6.64	6.15	5.74	5.48
Return on equity	15.5	24.3	27.9	26.8	25.4

Key industry average credit ratios
and performance measures

Debt to total capital	.72
Fixed-payment coverage ratio	.92
Current assets/current liabilities	3.15
Return on equity	16.4

[1]The $40 million in new debt borrowed to finance the cash portion of the purchase price is equal to $12.55 (i.e., the cash portion of the offer price per share) times 3 million StarTrak shares outstanding plus $2.35 million to cover anticipated acquisition-related investment banking, legal, and consulting fees.

[2]Level payment loan

Year	2006	2007	2008	2009	2010	2011	2012	2013	2014	2015	2016	2017	2018	2019	2020
Annual payment[3]	5.6	5.6	5.6	5.6	5.6	5.6	5.6	5.6	5.6	5.6	5.6	5.6	5.6	5.6	5.6
Interest[4]	4.4	4.3	4.1	4.0	3.8	3.6	3.4	3.1	2.8	2.5	2.5	1.8	1.4	.9	.4
Principal[5]	1.2	1.3	1.5	1.6	1.8	2.0	2.2	2.5	2.8	3.1	3.4	3.8	4.2	4.7	5.2
Ending balance[6]	38.8	37.5	36.0	34.3	32.5	30.5	28.2	25.7	23.0	19.9	16.5	12.7	8.5	3.8	-1.4

[3]Equal annual payments including principal and interest are calculated by solving PVA = PMT × PVIAF$_{11,15}$ (i.e., future value interest factor for 11 percent and 15 years) for PMT.

[4]Loan balance times annual interest rate.

[5]Annual payment less interest payment.

[6]Beginning loan balance less principal payment.

Table 9–14 Equity Value of the Combined Companies (Alanco and StarTrak)

	($ Millions)	Comments
Enterprise value of the combined companies	317.20	Total PV of free cash flow to the firm.
Less transaction-related debt	40.00	Alanco's incremental borrowing to finance the cash portion of the purchase price from Table 9–10.
Alanco's pretransaction debt	23.80	Alanco's long-term debt at closing from Table 9–10 at yearend 2005.
StarTrak's pretransaction debt	3.10	StarTrak's long-term debt at closing from Table 9–10 at yearend 2005.
Total debt of the combined companies	66.90	
Plus excess cash balances	1.40	Minimum desired operating cash balances for the combined companies are estimated to be 8% of 2005 net sales. This is less than the 12% held previously by each firm as a result of the presumed increase in operating efficiencies of the combined firms. Excess cash balances equal total cash and marketable securities of $11.4 million at the end of 2005 less 0.08 times net sales of $124.9 million in 2005.
Equals: equity value of the combined firms	251.70	
Estimated combined company price per share following acquisition ($/share)	56.95	$251.7/4.42 (total shares outstanding of the combined firms). Note that this share price compares quite favorably with the pretransaction share price of $33 for Alanco.

How would these differences affect the cost of the transaction to Alanco's pretransaction shareholders?

2. Alanco shareholders ceded only 40 percent of the synergy to StarTrak shareholders, yet StarTrak shareholders received 77 percent ownership of the combined firms. Why?

3. Alanco shareholders owned less than one fourth of the new firm. Was this a good deal for them? Explain your answer.

Answers to these questions are found in the Online Instructor's Manual available to instructors using this book.

Appendix: Utilizing the M&A Model on the CD-ROM Accompanying This Book

The spreadsheet model on the CD-ROM follows the four-step model building process discussed in this chapter. Each worksheet is identified by a self-explanatory title and an acronym or "short name" used in developing the worksheet linkages. Appendices A and B at the end of the Excel spreadsheets include the projected timeline, milestones, and individual(s) responsible for each activity required to complete the transaction. See Table 9–15 for a brief description of the purpose of each worksheet.

Table 9–15 Model Structure

Step	Worksheet Title	Objective (Tab Short Name)
1	Determine Acquirer and Target Standalone Valuation	Identify assumptions and estimate preacquisition value of stand-alone strategies
1	Acquirer 5-Year Forecast and Standalone Valuation	Provides stand-alone valuation (BP_App_B1)
1	Acquirer Historical Data and Financial Ratios	Provides consistency check between projected and historical data (BP_App_B2)
1	Acquirer Debt Repayment Schedules	Estimate firm's preacquisition debt (BP_App_B3)
1	Acquirer Cost of Equity and Capital Calculation	Displays assumptions (BP_App_B4)
1	Target 5-Year Forecast and Standalone Valuation	See above (AP_App_B1)
1	Target Historical Data and Financial Ratios	See above (AP_App_B2)
1	Target Debt Repayment Schedules	See above (AP_App_B3)
1	Target Cost of Equity & Capital Calculation	See above (AP_App_B4)
2	Value Combined Acquirer & Target Including Synergy	Identify assumptions and estimate postacquisition value
2	Combined Firm's 5-Year Forecast & Valuation	Provides valuation (AP_App_C)
2	Synergy Estimation	Displays assumptions underlying estimates (AP_App_D)
3	Determine Initial Offer Price for Target Firm	Estimate negotiating price range
3	Offer Price Determination	Estimate minimum and maximum offer prices (AP_App_E)
3	Alternative Valuation Summaries	Displays alternative valuation methodologies employed (AP_App_F)
4	Determine Combined Firm's Ability to Finance Transaction	Reality check (AP_App_G)
	Appendix A. Acquisition Timeline	Provides key activities schedule (AP_App_A1)
	Appendix B. Summary Milestones & Responsible Individuals	Benchmarks performance to timeline (AP_App_A2)

Each worksheet follows the same layout: the assumptions listed in the top panel, historical data in the lower left panel, and forecast period data in the lower right panel. In place of existing historical data, fill in the data for the firm you wish to analyze in cells not containing formulas. Do not delete existing formulas in the section marked "historical period" unless you wish to customize the model. Do not delete or change formulas in the "forecast period" cells unless you want to customize the model. To replace existing data in the forecast period panel, change the forecast assumptions at the top of the spreadsheet.

A number of the worksheets use Excel's "iteration" calculation option. This option may have to be turned on for the worksheets to operate correctly, particularly due to the inherent circularity in these models. For example, the change in cash and investments affects interest income, which in turn, affects net income and the change in cash and investments. If the program gives you a "circular reference" warning, please go to Tools, Options, and Calculation and turn on the iteration feature. One hundred iterations usually are enough to solve any "circular reference"; however, the number may vary with different versions of Excel.

Individual simulations may be made most efficiently by making relatively small incremental changes to a few key assumptions underlying the model. Key variables include sales growth rates, the cost of sales as a percent of sales, cash-flow growth rates during the terminal period, and the discount rate applied during the annual forecast period and the terminal period. Changes should be made to only one variable at a time.

10

Analysis and Valuation of Privately Held Companies

Maier's Law: If the facts do not conform to the theory, they must be disposed of.

Inside M&A: Cashing Out of a Privately Owned Enterprise[1]

In 2004, when he had reached his early sixties, Anthony Carnevale starting reducing the amount of time he spent managing Sentinel Benefits Group Inc., a firm he had founded. He planned to retire from the benefits and money management consulting firm in which he was a 26 percent owner. Mr. Carnevale, his two sons, and two nonfamily partners had built the firm to a company of more than 160 employees with $2.5 billion under management.

Selling the family business was not what the family expected to happen when Mr. Carnevale retired. He believed that his sons and partners were quite capable of continuing to manage the firm after he left. However, like many small businesses, Sentinel found itself with a succession planning challenges. If the sons and the company's two other nonfamily partners bought out Mr. Carnevale, the firm would have little cash left over for future growth. The firm was unable to get a loan, given the lack of assets for collateral and the somewhat unpredictable cash flow of the business. Even if a loan could have been obtained, the firm would have been burdened with interest and principal repayment for years to come.

Over the years, Mr. Carnevale had rejected buyout proposals from competitors as inadequate. However, he contacted a former suitor, Focus Financial Partners LLC (a partnership that buys small money management firms and lets them operate largely independently). In January 2007, Focus acquired 100 percent of Sentinel. Each of the five partners, Mr. Carnevale, his two sons, and two nonfamily partners, received an undisclosed amount of cash and Focus stock. A four-person Sentinel management team is now paid based on the company's revenue and growth.

The major challenges prior to the sale dealt with the many meetings held to resolve issues such as compensation, treatment of employees, how the firm would be managed subsequent to the sale, how client pricing would be determined, and who would make decisions about staff changes. Once the deal was complete, the Carnivales found it difficult to tell employees, particularly those who had been with the firm for years. Since most employees were not directly affected, only one left as a direct result of the sale.

---

[1]Adapted from Simona Covel, "Firm Sells Itself to Let Patriarch Cash Out," *Wall Street Journal*, November 1, 2007, p. B8.

Chapter Overview

If you own an interest in a privately held business, you cannot simply look in the *Wall Street Journal* or the local newspaper to see what your investment is worth. This is the situation with the vast majority of the nation's businesses. The absence of an easy and accurate method of valuing your investment can create significant financial burdens for both investors and business owners. Investors and business owners may need a valuation as part of a merger or acquisition, for settling an estate, or because employees wish to exercise their stock options. Employee stock ownership plans (ESOPs) also may require periodic valuations. In other instances, shareholder disputes, court cases, divorce, or the payment of gift or estate taxes may necessitate a valuation of the business.

In addition to the absence of a public market, there are other significant differences between publicly traded versus privately held companies. The availability and reliability of data for public companies tends to be much greater than for small private firms. Moreover, in large publicly traded corporations and large privately held companies, managers are often well versed in contemporary management practices, accounting, and financial valuation techniques. This is frequently not the case for small privately owned businesses. Finally, managers in large public companies are less likely to have the same level of emotional attachment to the business frequently found in family owned businesses.

A *private corporation* is a firm whose securities are not registered with state or federal authorities. Consequently, they are prohibited from being traded in the public securities markets. Buying a private firm is, in some ways, easier than buying a public firm, because there are generally fewer shareholders. However, the lack of publicly available information and the lack of public markets in which to value their securities constitute formidable challenges. Most acquisitions of private firms are friendly takeovers. However, in some instances, a takeover may occur despite opposition from certain shareholders. To circumvent such opposition, the acquirer seeks the cooperation of the majority shareholders, directors, and management, because only they have access to the information necessary to properly value the business.

The intent of this chapter is to discuss how the analyst deals with these problems. Issues concerning making initial contact and negotiating with the owners of privately held businesses were addressed in Chapter 5. Consequently, this chapter focuses on the challenges of valuing private or closely held businesses. Following a brief discussion of such businesses, this chapter discusses in detail the hazards of dealing with both limited and often unreliable data associated with privately held firms. The chapter then focuses on how to properly adjust questionable data as well as how to select the appropriate valuation methodology and discount or capitalization rate. Considerable time is spent discussing how to apply control premiums, minority discounts, and liquidity discounts in valuing businesses. The collapse of the credit markets for collateralized debt obligations in 2008 and 2009 underscores the importance of properly pricing assets to reflect potential market illiquidity. This chapter also includes a discussion of how corporate shells, created through reverse mergers, and leveraged ESOPs are used to acquire privately owned companies and how PIPE financing may be used to fund their ongoing operations. The major segments of this chapter include the following:

- Demographics of Privately Owned Businesses
- Challenges of Valuing Privately Owned Businesses
- Process for Valuing Privately Held Businesses
- Step 1. Adjusting the Income Statement
- Step 2. Applying Valuation Methodologies to Private Companies

- Step 3. Developing Discount (Capitalization) Rates
- Step 4. Applying Liquidity Discounts, Control Premiums, and Minority Discounts
- Reverse Mergers
- Using Leveraged Employee Stock Ownership Plans to Buy Private Companies
- Empirical Studies of Shareholder Returns
- Things to Remember

A review of this chapter (including practice questions) is available in the file folder entitled Student Study Guide contained on the CD-ROM accompanying this book. The CD-ROM also contains a Learning Interactions Library, enabling students to test their knowledge of this chapter in a "real-time" environment.

Demographics of Privately Owned Businesses

More than 99 percent of all businesses in the United States are small. They contribute about 75 percent of net new jobs added to the U.S. economy annually. Furthermore, such businesses employ about one half of the U.S. nongovernment-related workforce and account for about 41 percent of nongovernment sales (see U.S. Small Business Administration).

Privately owned businesses are often referred to as *closely held*, since they are usually characterized by a small group of shareholders controlling the operating and managerial policies of the firm. Most closely held firms are family-owned businesses. All closely held firms are not small, as families control the operating policies at many large, publicly traded companies. In many of these firms, family influence is exercised by family members holding senior management positions, seats on the board of directors, and through holding supervoting stock (i.e., stock with multiple voting rights). The last factor enables control, even though the family's shareholdings often are less than 50 percent. Examples of large, publicly traded family businesses include Wal-Mart, Ford Motor, American International Group, Motorola, Loew's, and Bechtel Group. Each of these firms has annual revenues of more than $16 billion.

Key Characteristics

The number of firms in the United States in 2004 (the last year for which detailed data are available) totaled 28.7 million, with about 7.4 million or one fourth having payrolls. The total number of firms and the number of firms with payrolls have grown at compound annual average growth rates of 2.6 percent and 1.3 percent, respectively, between 1990 and 2004. Of the firms without a payroll, most are self-employed persons operating unincorporated businesses, and they may or may not be the owner's primary source of income. Since such firms account for only 3 percent of the nation's private sector sales, they often are excluded from reported aggregate business statistics. However, since 1997, their numbers have been growing faster than firms with employees. Of the total number of firms in 2004, about 19, 9, and 72 percent were corporations, proprietorships, and partnerships, respectively (see Figure 10–1). These percentages have been relatively constant since the early 1990s. The M&A market for employer firms tends to be concentrated among smaller firms, as firms in the United States with 99 or fewer employees account for 98 percent of all firms with employees (see Tables 10–1 and 10–2).

Family-Owned Firms

Family-owned businesses account for about 89 percent of all businesses in the United States (Astrachan and Shanker, 2003). In such businesses, the family has effective control over the strategic direction of the business. Moreover, the business contributes

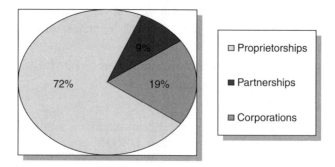

FIGURE 10–1 Percent distribution of U.S. firms filing income taxes in 2004.

significantly to the family's income, wealth, and identity. While confronted with the same business challenges as all firms, family-owned firms are beset by more severe internal issues than publicly traded firms. These issues include management succession, lack of corporate governance, informal management structure, less-skilled lower-level management, and a preference for ownership over growth.

Table 10–1   Number of U.S. Firms Filing Income Tax Returns

	Type of Firm (thousands)				Percent Distribution		
Year	Proprietorships	Partnerships	Corporations	Total	Proprietorships	Partnerships	Corporations
1990	14,783	1,554	3,717	20,054	73.72%	7.75%	18.53%
1991	15,181	1,515	3,803	20,499	74.06%	7.39%	18.55%
1992	15,495	1,485	3,869	20,849	74.32%	7.12%	18.56%
1993	15,848	1,468	3,965	21,281	74.47%	6.90%	18.63%
1994	16,154	1,494	4,342	21,990	73.46%	6.79%	19.75%
1995	16,424	1,581	4,474	22,479	73.06%	7.03%	19.90%
1996	16,955	1,654	4,631	23,240	72.96%	7.12%	19.93%
1997	17,176	1,759	4,710	23,645	72.64%	7.44%	19.92%
1998	17,409	1,855	4,849	24,113	72.20%	7.69%	20.11%
1999	17,576	1,937	4,936	24,449	71.89%	7.92%	20.19%
2000	17,905	2,058	5,045	25,008	71.60%	8.23%	20.17%
2001	18,338	2,132	5,136	25,606	71.62%	8.33%	20.06%
2002	18,926	2,242	5,267	26,435	71.59%	8.48%	19.92%
2003	19,710	2,375	5,401	27,486	71.71%	8.64%	19.65%
2004	20,591	2,547	5,558	28,696	71.76%	8.88%	19.37%

Source: Statistical Abstract of the United States, 2007, U.S. Bureau of the Census.

Table 10–2   Establishments with Payrolls (000)

	Number of Employees						Percent Distribution				
	Total	<20	20–99	100–499	500–999	>1,000	<20	20–99	100–499	500–999	>1,000
1990	6,176	5,354	684	122	10	6	86.69%	11.08%	1.98%	0.50%	0.10%
1995	6,613	5,733	730	135	10	6	86.69%	11.04%	2.04%	0.50%	0.09%
1999	7,008	6,036	802	152	12	7	86.13%	11.44%	2.17%	0.60%	0.10%
2000	7,070	6,069	826	157	12	7	85.84%	11.68%	2.22%	0.60%	0.10%
2001	7,095	6,083	836	157	12	7	85.74%	11.78%	2.21%	0.60%	0.10%
2002	7,201	6,199	835	149	11	7	86.09%	11.60%	2.07%	0.55%	0.10%
2003	7,255	6,240	845	151	11	7	86.01%	11.65%	2.08%	0.55%	0.10%
2004	7,388	6,359	856	154	12	7	86.07%	11.59%	2.08%	0.60%	0.09%

Source: Statistical Abstract of the United States, 2007, U.S. Bureau of Census, Table 735.

Firms that are family owned but not managed by family members are often well managed, as family shareholders with large equity stakes carefully monitor those charged with managing the business (Bennedsen et al., 2006; Perez-Gonzalez, 2006; and Villalonga and Amit, 2006). However, management by the children of the founders typically adversely affects firm value (Claessens et al., 2002; Morck and Yeung, 2000). This may result from the limited pool of family members available for taking control of the business.

Succession is one of the most difficult challenges to resolve, with family-owned firms viewing succession as the transfer of ownership more than as a transfer of management. Problems arise from inadequate preparation of the younger generation of family members and the limited pool of potential successors who might not even have the talent or the interest to take over. For many such firms, the founder always made key decisions and other family members often did not have the opportunity to develop business acumen. In such firms, mid-level management expertise often resides among non-family members, who often leave due to perceived inequity in pay scales with family members and limited promotion opportunities. While some firms display an ability to overcome the challenges of succession, others look to sell the business (see Case Study 10–1). Unlike the case study at the beginning of the chapter, the owner lacked confidence that his existing management team had the level of sophistication to continue to grow the firm. Consequently, he looked to sell the firm, not only as a means of "cashing out" but also as a way of sustaining growth in the firm he had founded.

Case Study 10–1 Deb Ltd. Seeks an Exit Strategy

In late 2004, Barclay's Private Equity acquired slightly more than one half the equity in Deb Ltd. (Deb), valued at about $250 million. The private equity arm of Britain's Barclay's bank outbid other suitors in an auction to acquire a controlling interest in the firm. PriceWaterhouseCooper had been hired by the Williamson family, the primary stockholder in the firm, to find a buyer.

The sale solved a dilemma for Nick Williamson, the firm's CEO and son of the founder, who had invented the firm's flagship product, Swarfega. The company had been founded some 60 years earlier based on a single product, a car cleaning agent. Since then, the Swarfega brand name had grown into a widely known brand associated with a broad array of cleaning products.

In 1990, the elder Williamson wanted to retire and his son Nick, along with business partner Roy Tillead, bought the business from his father. Since then, the business has continued to grow, and product development has accelerated. The company developed special Swarfega-dispensing cartridges that have applications in hospitals, clinics, and other medical faculties.

After 13 years of sustained growth, Williamson realized that some difficult decisions had to be made. He knew he did not have a natural successor to take over the company. He no longer believed the firm could be managed successfully by the same management team. It was now time to think seriously about succession planning. So in early 2004, he began to seek a buyer for the business. He preferably wanted somebody who could bring in new talents, ideas, and up-to-date management techniques to continue the firm's growth.

The terms of the agreement called for Williamson and Tillead to work with a new senior management team until Barclays decided to take the firm public. This was expected some time during the five-to-seven year period following the sale. At that point, Williamson would sell the remainder of his family's stock in the business (Goodman, 2005).

Continued

Case Study 10–1 Deb Ltd. Seeks an Exit Strategy — Cont'd

Discussion Questions

1. Succession planning issues are often a reason for family-owned businesses to sell. Why do you believe it may have been easier for Nick than his father to sell the business to a non-family member?
2. What other alternatives could Nick have pursued? Discuss the advantages and disadvantages of each.
3. What do you believe might be some of the unique challenges in valuing a family-owned business? Be specific.

Governance Issues in Privately Held and Family-Owned Firms

The approach taken to promote good governance in the Sarbanes–Oxley Act of 2002 (see Chapter 2) and under the market model of corporate governance (see Chapter 3) is to identify and apply "best practices." The focus on "best practices" has led to the development of generalized laundry lists, rather than specific actions leading to measurable results (Robinson 2002b). Moreover, what works for publicly traded companies may not be readily applicable to privately held or family-owed firms.

The market model relies on a large dispersed class of investors in which ownership and corporate control are largely separate. Moreover, the market model overlooks the fact that family owned firms often have different interests, time horizons, and strategies from investors in publicly owned firms. In many countries, family owned firms have been successful because of their shared interests and because investors place a higher value on the long-term health of the business rather than on short-term performance (Habersham and Williams, 1999; de Visscher, Aronoff, and Ward, 1995). Consequently, the control model of corporate governance discussed in Chapter 3 may be more applicable where ownership tends to be concentrated and the right to control the business is not fully separate from ownership.

Astrachan and Shanker (2003) conclude that the control model (or some variation) is more applicable to family-owned firms than the market model. The authors argue that director independence is less important for family-owned firms, since outside directors often can be swayed by various forms of compensation. A board consisting of owners focused on the long-term growth of the business for future generations of the family may be far more committed to the firm than outsiders. While the owners are ultimately responsible for strategic direction, the board must ensure that strategy formulated by management is consistent with the owners' desires.

Nevertheless, there is evidence that many private businesses are adopting many of the Sarbanes–Oxley procedures as part of their own internal governance practices. A 2004 survey conducted by Foley and Lardner found that more than 40 percent of the private firms surveyed voluntarily adopted the following SOX provisions: (1) executive certification of financial statements, (2) whistleblower initiatives, (3) board approval of nonaudit services provided by external auditors, and (4) adoption of corporate governance policy guidelines (Foley and Lardner, 2007).

Challenges of Valuing Privately Held Companies

The anonymity of many privately held firms, the potential for manipulation of information, problems specific to small firms, and the tendency of owners of private firms to manage in a way to minimize tax liabilities creates a number of significant valuation issues. The challenges of valuation are compounded by the emotional attachments private business owners often have to their businesses. These issues are addressed in the next sections of this chapter.

Lack of Externally Generated Information

There is generally a lack of analyses of private firms generated by sources outside of the company. Private firms provide little incentive for outside analysts to cover them because of the absence of a public market for their securities. Consequently, there are few forecasts of their performance other than those provided by the firm's management. Press coverage is usually quite limited, and what is available is again often based on information provided by the firm's management. Even highly regarded companies (e.g., Dun & Bradstreet) purporting to offer demographic and financial information on small privately held firms use largely superficial and infrequent telephone interviews with the management of such firms as their primary source of such information.

Lack of Internal Controls and Inadequate Reporting Systems

Private companies are generally not subject to the same level of rigorous controls and reporting systems as public firms. Public companies are required to prepare audited financial statements for their annual reports. The SEC enforces the accuracy of these statements under the authority provided by the Securities and Exchange Act of 1934. The use of audits is much more rigorous and thorough than other types of reports, known as accounting reviews and compilations. Although accounting reviews are acceptable for quarterly 10Q reports, compilation reports are not acceptable for either 10Ks or 10Qs. The *audit* consists of a professional examination and verification of a company's accounting documents and supporting data for the purpose of rendering an opinion as to their fairness, consistency, and conformity with generally accepted accounting principles.

Although reporting systems in small firms are generally poor or nonexistent, the lack of formal controls, such as systems to monitor how money is spent and an approval process to ensure that funds are spent appropriately, invites fraud and misuse of company resources. Documentation is another formidable problem. Intellectual property is a substantial portion of the value of many private firms. Examples of such property include system software, chemical formulas, and recipes. Often only one or two individuals within the firm know how to reproduce these valuable intangible assets. The lack of documentation can destroy a firm if such an individual leaves or dies. Moreover, customer lists and the terms and conditions associated with key customer relationships also may be largely undocumented, creating the basis for customer disputes when a change in ownership occurs. Furthermore, as is explained in the next section of this chapter, both revenue and costs may be manipulated to minimize the firm's tax liabilities or make the business more attractive for sale.

Firm-Specific Problems

Also, a number of factors may be unique to the private firm that make valuation difficult. The company may lack product, industry, and geographic diversification. There may be insufficient management talent to allow the firm to develop new products for its current markets or expand into new markets. The company may be highly sensitive to fluctuations in demand because of significant fixed expenses. Its small size may limit its influence with regulators and unions. The company's size also may limit its ability to gain access to efficient distribution channels and leverage with suppliers and customers. Finally, the company may have an excellent product but very little brand recognition. Such considerations normally tend to reduce the stand-alone value of the business because of the uncertainty associated with efforts to forecast future cash flows.

Common Forms of Manipulating Reported Income

Misstating Revenue

Revenue may be over- or understated, depending on the owner's objectives. If the intent is tax minimization, businesses operating on a cash basis may opt to report less revenue because of the difficulty outside parties have in tracking transactions. Private business owners intending to sell a business may be inclined to inflate revenue if the firm is to be sold. Common examples include manufacturers, which rely on others to distribute their products. These manufacturers can inflate revenue in the current accounting period by booking as revenue products shipped to resellers without adequately adjusting for probable returns. Membership or subscription businesses, such as health clubs and magazine publishers, may inflate revenue by booking the full value of multiyear contracts in the current period rather than prorating the payment received at the beginning of the contract period over the life of the contract. Such booking activity results in a significant boost to current profitability, because not all the costs associated with multiyear contracts, such as customer service, are incurred in the period in which the full amount of revenue is booked.

Manipulation of Operating Expenses

Owners of private businesses attempting to minimize taxes may overstate their contribution to the firm by giving themselves or family members unusually high salaries, bonuses, and benefits. Because the vast majority of all businesses are family owned, this is a widespread practice. The most common distortion of costs comes in the form of higher than normal salary and benefits provided to family members and key employees. Other examples of cost manipulation include extraordinary expenses that are really other forms of compensation for the owner, his or her family, and key employees, which may include the rent on the owner's summer home or hunting lodge and salaries for the pilot and captain for the owner's airplane and yacht. Current or potential customers sometimes are allowed to use these assets. Owners frequently argue that these expenses are necessary to maintain customer relationships or close large contracts and are therefore legitimate business expenses. One way to determine if these are appropriate business expenses is to ascertain how often these assets are used for the purpose for which the owner claims they were intended. Other areas commonly abused include travel and entertainment, personal insurance, and excessive payments to vendors supplying services to the firm. Due diligence frequently uncovers situations in which the owner or a family member is either an investor in or an owner of the vendor supplying the products or services.

Alternatively, if the business owner's objective is to maximize the selling price of the business, salaries, benefits, and other operating costs may be understated significantly. An examination of the historical trend in the firm's reported profitability may reveal that the firm's profits are being manipulated. For example, a sudden improvement in operating profits in the year in which the business is being offered for sale may suggest that expenses had been overstated, revenues understated, or both during the historical period. The onus of explaining this spike in profitability should be put on the business owner.

Process for Valuing Privately Held Businesses

To address the challenges presented by privately owned firms, an analyst should adopt a four-step procedure. Step 1 requires adjustment of the target firm's financial data to reflect true profitability and cash flow in the current period. Determining what the business is actually capable of doing in terms of operating profit and cash flow in the current period is critical to the valuation, since all projections are biased if the estimate of current performance is skewed. Step 2 entails determining the appropriate valuation methodology (e.g., discounted cash flow, relative valuation). Step 3 requires the determination of the appropriate discount or capitalization rate. Finally, the fourth step involves adjusting the estimated value of the private firm for a control premium (if appropriate), a liquidity discount, and a minority discount (if an investor takes a less than controlling ownership position in a firm).

Step 1. Adjusting the Income Statement

The purpose of adjusting the income statement is to provide an accurate estimate of the current year's net or pretax income, earnings before interest and taxes (EBIT), or earnings before interest, taxes, depreciation, and amortization (EBITDA). The various measures of income should reflect accurately all costs actually incurred in generating the level of revenue, adjusted for doubtful accounts the firm booked in the current period. They also should reflect other expenditures (e.g., training and advertising) that must be incurred in the current period to sustain the anticipated growth in revenue.

The importance of establishing accurate current or base-year data is evident when we consider how businesses—particularly small, closely held businesses—are often valued. If the current year's profit data are incorrect, future projections of the dollar value would be inaccurate, even if the projected growth rate is accurate. Furthermore, valuations based on relative valuation methods such as price-to-current year earnings ratios would be biased to the extent estimates of the target's current income are inaccurate.

EBITDA has become an increasingly popular measure of value for privately held firms. The use of this measure facilitates the comparison of firms, because it eliminates the potential distortion in earnings performance due to differences in depreciation methods and financial leverage among firms. Furthermore, this indicator is often more readily applicable in relative valuation methods than other measures of profitability since firms are more likely to display positive EBITDA than EBIT or net income figures. Despite its convenience, the analyst needs to be mindful that EBITDA is only one component of cash flow and ignores the impact on cash flow of changes in net working capital, investing, and financing activities. See Chapter 8 for a more detailed discussion of the use of EBITDA in relative valuation methods.

Making Informed Adjustments

While finding reliable current information on privately held firms is generally challenging, some information is available, albeit often fragmentary and inconsistent. The first step for the analyst is to search the Internet for references to the target firm. This search should unearth a number of sources of information on the target firm. Table 10–3 provides a partial list of websites containing information on private firms.

Owner's and Officer's Salaries

Before drawing any conclusions, the analyst should determine the actual work performed by all key employees and the compensation generally received for performing the same or a similar job in the same industry. Comparative salary information can be obtained by employing the services of a compensation consultant familiar with the industry or simply by scanning "employee wanted" advertisements in the industry trade press and magazines and the "help wanted" pages of the local newspaper. Such an effort should be part of any comprehensive due diligence activity. Case Study 10–2 illustrates how the failure to complete this type of analysis can lead to a substantial disruption to the business following a change in ownership.

Table 10–3   Information Sources on Private Firms

Source/Web Address	Content
Research Firms	
Washington Researchers/ www.washingtonresearchers.com Fuld & Company/www.fuld.com	Listing of sources such as local government officials, local chambers of commerce, state government regulatory bodies, credit reporting agencies, and local citizen groups.
Databases	
Dun & Bradstreet/smallbusiness.dnb.com	Information on firms' payment histories and limited financial data.
Hoover/www.hoovers.com	Data on 40,000 international and domestic firms, IPOs, not-for profits, trade associations, and small businesses and limited data on 18 million other companies
Integra/www.integrainfo.com	Industry benchmarking data
Standard & Poor's Net Advantage/ www.netadvantage.standardpoor.com	Financial data and management and directors' bibliographies on 125,000 firms
InfoUSA/www.infousa.com	Industry benchmarking and company specific data
Forbes/www.forbes.com/list	List of top privately held firms annually
Inc/www.inc.com/inc500	List of 500 of fastest growing firms annually

---

Case Study 10–2 Loss of Key Employee Causes Carpet Padding Manufacturer's Profits to Go Flat

A manufacturer of carpet padding in southern California had devised a unique chemical process for converting such materials as discarded bedding and rags to high-quality commercial carpet padding. Over a period of 10 years, the firm established itself as the regional leader in this niche market. With annual sales in excess of $10 million, the firm consistently earned pretax profits of 18–20 percent of sales.

The owner and founder of the company had been trained as a chemist and developed the formula for decomposing the necessary raw materials purchased from local junkyards into a mixture to produce the foam padding. In addition, the owner routinely calibrated all of the company's manufacturing equipment to ensure that the machines ran at peak efficiency, with no deterioration in product quality. Over the years, the owner also had developed relationships with a network of local junk dealers to acquire the necessary raw materials. The owner's reputation for honesty and the firm's ability to produce consistently high-quality products ensured very little customer turnover. The owner was also solely responsible for acquiring several large accounts, which consistently contributed about 30 percent of annual revenue.

When the firm was sold, the owner's salary and benefits of $300,000 per year were believed to be excessive by the buyer. Efforts to reduce his total compensation caused him to retire. The new owner soon was forced to hire several people to replace the former owner, who had been performing the role of chemist, maintenance engineer, and purchasing agent. These were functions that did not appear on any organization chart when the buyer performed due diligence. Consequently, the buyer did not increase the budget for salaries and benefits to provide personnel to perform these crucial functions. This tended to overstate profits and inflated the purchase price paid by the buyer, since the price paid represented a multiple of the firm's current earnings.

Ultimately, replacing the owner required hiring a chemist, a machinist, a purchasing agent, and a salesperson at an annual cost in salary and benefits of more than $450,000. Despite the additional personnel, the new owner also found it necessary to hire the former owner under a consulting contract valued at $35,000 per year.

To add insult to injury, because of the change in ownership the firm lost several large customers who had had a long-standing relationship with the former owner. These customers accounted for more than $2 million in annual sales.

Discussion Questions

1. Explain how the buyer's inadequate due diligence contributed to its postclosing problems.
2. How could the buyer have retained the firm's president? Give several examples.

Benefits

Depending on the industry, benefits can range from 14–50 percent of an employee's base salary. Certain employee benefits, such as Social Security and Medicare taxes, are mandated by law and, therefore, an uncontrollable cost of doing business. Other types of benefits may be more controllable. These include items such as pension contributions and life insurance coverage, which are calculated as a percentage of base salary. Consequently, efforts by the buyer to trim salaries, which appear to be excessive, also reduce these types of benefits. Efforts to reduce such benefits may contribute to higher overall operating costs in the short run. Operating costs may increase as a result of higher employee turnover and the need to retrain replacements, as well as the potential negative impact on the productivity of those that remain.

Travel and Entertainment

Travel and entertainment (T&E) expenditures tend to be one of the first cost categories cut when a potential buyer attempts to value a target company. The initial reaction is almost always that actual spending in this area is far in excess of what it needs to be. However, what may look excessive to one relatively unfamiliar with the industry may in fact be necessary for retaining current customers and acquiring new customers. Establishing, building, and maintaining relationships is particularly important for personal and business services companies, such as consulting and law firms. Account management may require consultative selling at the customer's site. A complex product like software may require on-site training. Indiscriminant reduction in the T&E budget could lead to a loss of customers following a change in ownership.

Auto Expenses and Personal Life Insurance

Before assuming auto expenses and life insurance are excessive, ask if they represent a key component of the overall compensation required to attract and retain key employees. This can be determined by comparing total compensation paid to employees of the target firm with compensation packages offered to employees in similar positions in the same industry in the same region. A similar review should be undertaken with respect to the composition of benefits packages. Depending on the demographics and special needs of the target firm's workforce, an acquirer may choose to alter the composition of the benefits package by substituting other types of benefits for those eliminated or reduced. By carefully substituting benefits that meet the specific needs of the workforce, such as on-site day-care services, the acquirer may be able to provide an overall benefits package that better satisfies the needs of the employees.

Family Members

Similar questions need to be asked about family members on the payroll. Frequently, they perform real services and tend to be highly motivated because of their close affinity with the business. If the business has been in existence for many years, the loss of key family members who built relationships with customers over the years may result in a subsequent loss of key accounts. Moreover, family members may be those who possess proprietary knowledge necessary for the ongoing operation of the business.

Rent or Lease Payments in Excess of Fair Market Value

Check who owns the buildings housing the business or equipment used by the business. This is a frequent method used by the owner to transfer company funds to the owner in excess of their stated salary and benefits. However, rents may not be too high if the building is a "special-purpose" structure retrofitted to serve the specific needs of the tenant.

Professional Services Fees

Professional services could include legal, accounting, personnel, and actuarial services. This area is frequently subject to abuse. Once again, check for any nonbusiness relationship between the business owner and the firm providing the service. Always consider any special circumstances that may justify unusually high fees. An industry that is subject to continuing regulation and review may incur what appear to be abnormally high legal and accounting expenses when compared with firms in other industries.

Depreciation Expense

Accelerated depreciation methodologies may make sense for tax purposes, but they may seriously understate current earnings. For financial reporting purposes, it may be appropriate to convert depreciation schedules from accelerated to straight-line depreciation, if this results in a better matching of when expenses actually are incurred and revenue actually is received.

Reserves

Current reserves may be inadequate to reflect future events. An increase in reserves lowers taxable income, whereas a decrease in reserves raises taxable income. Collection problems may be uncovered following an analysis of accounts receivable. It may be necessary to add to reserves for doubtful accounts. Similarly, the target firm may not have adequately reserved for future obligations to employees under existing pension and health-care plans. Reserves also may have to be increased to reflect known environmental and litigation exposures.

Accounting for Inventory

During periods of inflation, businesses frequently use the last-in, first-out (LIFO) method to account for inventories. This approach results in an increase in the cost of sales that reflects the most recent and presumably highest-cost inventory; therefore, it reduces gross profit and taxable income. During periods of inflation, the use of LIFO also tends to lower the value of inventory on the balance sheet, because the items in inventory are valued at the lower cost of production associated with earlier time periods. In contrast, the use of first-in, first-out (FIFO) accounting for inventory assumes that inventory is sold in the chronological order in which it was purchased. During periods of inflation, the FIFO method produces a higher ending inventory, a lower cost of goods sold, and higher gross profit. Although it may make sense for tax purposes to use LIFO, the buyer's objective for valuation purposes should be to obtain as realistic an estimate of actual earnings as possible in the current period. FIFO accounting appears to be most logical for products that are perishable or subject to rapid obsolescence and, therefore, are most likely to be sold in chronological order. In an environment in which inflation is expected to remain high for an extended time period, LIFO accounting may make more sense.

Areas Commonly Understated

Projected increases in sales normally require more aggressive marketing efforts, more effective customer service support, and enhanced employee training. Nonetheless, it is common to see the ratio of annual advertising and training expenses to annual sales decline during the period of highest projected growth in forecasts developed by either the buyer or the seller. The seller has an incentive to hold costs down during the forecast period to provide the most sanguine outlook possible. The buyer simply may be overly optimistic about how much more effectively the business can be managed as a result of a change in ownership. The buyer may also be excessively optimistic in an effort to induce lenders to finance the transaction. Other areas that are commonly understated in projections but that can never really be escaped include the expense associated with environmental cleanup, employee safety, and pending litigation. Even in an asset purchase, the buyer still may be liable for certain types of risks, such as environmental problems, pension obligations, and back taxes. From a legal standpoint, both the buyer and the seller often are held responsible for these types of obligations.

Areas Commonly Overlooked

Understandably, buyers find the valuation of tangible assets easier than intangible assets. Unfortunately, in many cases, the value in the business is more in its intangible than tangible assets. The best examples include the high valuations placed on many Internet-related and biotechnology companies. The target's intangible assets may include customer lists, patents, licenses, distributorship agreements, leases, regulatory approvals (e.g., U.S. Food and Drug Administration approval of a new drug), noncompete agreements, and employment contracts. Note that, for these items to represent sources of incremental value, they must represent sources of revenue or cost reduction not already reflected in the target's cash flows.

Table 10–4 illustrates how historical and projected financial statements received from the target as part of the due diligence process could be restated to reflect what the buyer believes to be a more accurate characterization of revenue and costs. Adjusting the historical financials provides insight into what the firm could have done had it been managed differently. Similarly, adjusting the projected financials enables the analyst to use what he or she considers to be more realistic assumptions. Note that the cost of sales is divided into direct and indirect expenses. Direct cost of sales relates to costs incurred directly in the production process. Indirect costs are those incurred as a result of the various functions (e.g., senior management, human resources, sales, accounting) required to support the production process. The actual historical costs are displayed above the "Explanation of adjustments" line. Some adjustments represent "add backs" to profit while others reduce profit. The adjusted EBITDA numbers at the bottom of the table represent what the buyer believes to be the most realistic estimate of the profitability of the business. Finally, by displaying the data historically, the buyer can see trends that may be useful in projecting the firm's profitability.

Specific adjustments require further explanation. The buyer believes that, because of the nature of the business, inventories are more accurately valued on a FIFO rather

Table 10–4   Adjusting the Target Firm's Financial Statements ($ thousands)

	Year 1	Year 2	Year 3	Year 4	Year 5
Revenue	8000.0	8400.0	8820.0	9261.0	9724.1
Less direct cost of sales (COS), excluding depreciation and amortization	5440.0	5712.0	5997.6	6297.5	6612.4
Equals gross profit	2560.0	2688.0	2822.4	2963.5	3111.7
Less indirect cost of sales					
Salaries and benefits	1200.0	1260.0	1323.0	1389.2	1458.6
Rent	320.0	336.0	352.8	370.4	389.0
Insurance	160.0	168.0	176.4	185.2	194.5
Advertising	80.0	84.0	88.2	92.6	97.2
Travel and entertainment	240.0	252.0	264.6	277.8	291.7
Director fees	50.0	50.0	50.0	50.0	50.0
Training	10.0	10.0	10.0	10.0	10.0
All other indirect expenses	240.0	252.0	264.6	277.8	291.7
Equals EBITDA	260.0	276.0	292.8	310.4	329.0
Explanation of Adjustments: Add Backs/(Deductions)					
LIFO direct COS is higher than FIFO cost; adjustment converts to FIFO costs	200.0	210.0	220.5	231.5	243.1
Eliminate part-time family members' salaries and benefits	150.0	157.5	165.4	173.6	182.3
Eliminate owner's salary, benefits, and director fees	125.0	131.3	137.8	144.7	151.9
Increase targeted advertising to sustain regional brand recognition	(50.0)	(52.5)	(55.1)	(57.9)	(60.8)
Increase T&E expense to support out-of-state customer accounts	(75.0)	(78.8)	(82.7)	(86.8)	(91.2)
Reduce office space (rent) by closing regional sales offices	120.0	126.0	132.3	138.9	145.9
Increase training budget	(25.0)	(26.3)	(27.6)	(28.9)	(30.4)
Adjusted EBITDA	705.0	743.3	783.4	825.6	869.9

Note: The reader may simulate alternative assumptions by accessing the file entitled Excel-Based Spreadsheet of How to Adjust Target Firm's Financial Statements, available on the CD-ROM accompanying this book.

than LIFO basis. This change in inventory cost accounting results in a sizeable boost to the firm's profitability. Furthermore, due diligence revealed that the firm was overstaffed and it could be operated adequately by eliminating the full-time position held by the former owner (including fees received as a member of the firm's board of directors) and a number of part-time positions held by the owner's family members. Note that, although some cost items are reduced, others are increased. The implications for other categories of cost reductions in one area must be determined. For example, office space is reduced, thereby lowering rental expense as a result of the elimination of out-of-state sales offices. However, the sales- and marketing-related portion of the travel and entertainment budget is increased to accommodate the increased travel necessary to service out-of-state customer accounts due to the closure of the regional offices. Furthermore, it is likely that advertising expense will have to be increased to promote the firm's products in those regions. The new buyer also believes that the firm's historical training budget has been woefully inadequate to sustain the growth of the business and more than doubles spending in this category. The reader may simulate alternative assumptions by accessing the file entitled Excel-Based Spreadsheet of How to Adjust Target Firm's Financial Statements, available on the CD-ROM accompanying this book.

Step 2. Applying Valuation Methodologies to Private Companies

Defining Value

The most common generic definition of value used by valuation professionals is fair market value. Hypothetically, *fair market value* is the cash or cash-equivalent price that a willing buyer would propose and a willing seller would accept for a business if both parties have access to all relevant information. Furthermore, fair market value assumes that neither the seller nor the buyer is under any obligation to buy or sell.

It is easier to obtain the fair market value for a public company because of the existence of public markets in which stock in the company is actively traded. The concept may be applied to privately held firms if similar publicly traded companies exist. However, because finding substantially similar companies is difficult, valuation professionals have developed a related concept called *fair value. Fair value* is applied when no strong market exists for a business or it is not possible to identify the value of substantially similar firms. Fair value is, by necessity, more subjective, because it represents the dollar value of a business based on an appraisal of the tangible and intangible assets of the business.

Unfortunately, the standard for fair value is ambiguous, since it is interpreted differently in the context of state statutes and financial reporting purposes. In most states, fair value is the statutory standard of value applicable in cases of dissenting stockholders' appraisal rights. Following a merger or corporate dissolution, shareholders in these states have the right to have their shares appraised and receive fair value in cash. In states adopting the Uniform Business Corporation Act, fair value means the value of the shares immediately before the corporate decision to which the shareholder objects, excluding any appreciation or depreciation in anticipation of the corporate decision. Fair value tends to be interpreted by judicial precedents or prior court rulings in each state. In contrast, according to the Financial Accounting Standards Board Statement 157 effective November 15, 2007, fair value is the price determined in an orderly transaction between market participants (Pratt and Niculita, 2008).

Selecting the Appropriate Valuation Methodology

As noted in Chapters 7 and 8, appraisers, brokers, and investment bankers generally classify valuation methodologies into four distinct approaches: income (discounted cash flow), relative or market based, replacement cost, and asset oriented.

Income or Discounted Cash-Flow Approach

The validity of this method depends heavily on the particular definition of income or cash flow, the timing of those cash flows, and the selection of an appropriate discount or capitalization rate. The terms *discount rate* and *capitalization rate* often are used interchangeably. Whenever the growth rate of a firm's cash flows is projected to vary over time, *discount rate* generally refers to the factor used to convert the projected cash flows to present values. In contrast, if the cash flows of the firm are not expected to grow or are expected to grow at a constant rate indefinitely, the discount rate used by practitioners often is referred to as the *capitalization rate.*

The conversion of a future income stream into a present value also is referred to as the *capitalization process.* It often applies when future income or cash flows are not expected to grow or are expected to grow at a constant rate. When no growth in future income or cash flows is expected, the capitalization rate is defined as the perpetuity growth model. When future cash flow or income is expected to grow at a constant rate, the capitalization rate commonly is defined as the difference between the discount rate and the expected growth rate (i.e., the constant growth model). Present values calculated in this manner are sometimes referred to as *capitalized values*. See Chapter 7.

Capitalization rates are commonly converted to multiples by dividing 1 by the discount rate or the discount rate less the anticipated constant growth rate in cash flows. These *capitalization multiples* can be multiplied by the current period's cash flow (i.e., if applying the perpetuity model) or the subsequent period's anticipated cash flow (i.e., if applying the constant growth model) to estimate the market value of a firm. For example, if the discount rate is assumed to be 8 percent and the current level of a firm's cash flow is $1.5 million, which is expected to remain at that level in perpetuity, the implied valuation is $18.75 million, that is, $(1/0.08) \times \$1.5$. Alternatively, if the current level of cash flow is expected to grow at 4 percent annually in perpetuity, the implied valuation is $39.0 million, that is, $[(1.04)/(0.08 - 0.04)] \times \$1.5$. The capitalization multiples in the perpetuity and constant growth cases are $1/0.08$ and $1.04/(0.08 - 0.04)$, respectively.

Several alternative definitions of income or cash flow can be used in either the discounting or capitalization process. These include free cash flow to equity holders or the firm; earnings before interest and taxes; earnings before interest, taxes, and depreciation; earnings before taxes (EBT); and earnings after taxes (EAT or NI). The discount rate must be adjusted to reflect these definitions before applying the discounting process. Capitalized values and capitalization rates often are used in valuing small businesses because of their inherent simplicity. Many small business owners lack sophistication in financial matters. Consequently, a valuation concept, which is easy to calculate, understand, and communicate to the parties involved, may significantly facilitate completion of the transaction. Finally, there is little empirical evidence that more complex valuation methods necessarily result in more accurate valuation estimates.

Relative-Value or Market-Based Approach

This approach is used widely in valuing private firms by business brokers or appraisers to establish a purchase price. The Internal Revenue Service (IRS) and the U.S. tax courts have encouraged the use of market-based valuation techniques. Therefore, in valuing private companies, it is always important to keep in mind what factors the IRS thinks are relevant to the process, because the IRS may contest any sale requiring the payment of estate, capital gains, or unearned income taxes. The IRS's positions on specific tax issues can be determined by reviewing revenue rulings. A *revenue ruling* is an official interpretation by the IRS of the Internal Revenue Code, related statutes, tax treaties, and regulations. These rulings represent the IRS's position on how the law is applied to a specific set of circumstances and are published in the *Internal Revenue Bulletin* to assist taxpayers, IRS personnel, and other concerned parties in interpreting the Internal Revenue Code.

Issued in 1959, Revenue Ruling 59–60 describes the general factors that the IRS and tax courts consider relevant in valuing private businesses. These factors include general economic conditions, the specific conditions in the industry, the type of business, historical trends in the industry, the firm's performance, and the firm's book value. In addition, the IRS and tax courts consider the ability of the company to generate earnings and pay dividends, the amount of intangibles such as goodwill, recent sales of stock, and the stock prices of companies engaged in the "same or similar" line of business.

Replacement-Cost Approach

This approach states that the assets of a business are worth what it would cost to replace them. The approach is most applicable to businesses that have substantial amounts of tangible assets for which the actual cost to replace them can be determined easily. In the case of a business whose primary assets consist of intellectual property, it may be difficult to determine the actual cost of replacing the firm's intangible assets using this method. The accuracy of this approach depends heavily on the skill and specific industry knowledge of the appraisers employed to conduct the analyses. Moreover, the replacement-cost approach ignores the value created in excess of the cost of replacing each asset by operating the assets as a going concern. For example, an assembly line may consist of a number of different machines, each performing a specific task in the production of certain products. The value of the total production coming off the assembly line over the useful lives of the individual machines is likely to far exceed the sum of the costs to replace each machine. Consequently, the business should be valued as a going concern rather than the sum of the costs to replace its individual assets.

The replacement-cost approach sometimes is used to value intangible assets by examining the amount of historical investment associated with the asset. For example, the cumulative historical advertising spending targeted at developing a particular product brand or image may be a reasonable proxy for the intangible value of the brand name or image. However, because consumer tastes tend to change over time, applying historical experience to the future may be highly misleading.

Asset-Oriented Approach

Like the replacement-cost approach, the accuracy of asset-oriented approaches depends on the overall proficiency of the appraiser hired to establish value and the availability of adequate information. Book value is an accounting concept and generally not considered a good measure of market value, because book values usually reflect historical rather than current market values. However, as noted in Chapter 8, tangible book value (i.e., book value less intangible assets) may be a good proxy for the current market value for both financial services and product distribution companies. Breakup value is an estimate of what the value of a business would be if each of its primary assets were sold independently. This approach may not be practical if there are few public markets for the firm's assets. Liquidation value is a reflection of the firm under duress. A firm in liquidation normally must sell its assets within a specific time period. Consequently, the cash value of the assets realized is likely to be much less than their actual replacement value or value if the firm were to continue as a viable operation. Liquidation value is a reasonable proxy for the minimum value of the firm. For a listing of when to use the various valuation methodologies, see Table 8–7 in Chapter 8.

Step 3. Developing Discount (Capitalization) Rates

While the discount or capitalization rate can be derived using a variety of methods, the focus in this chapter is on the weighted-average cost of capital or the cost of equity in the absence of debt. As noted in Chapter 7, the capitalization process of converting future cash flows to a current value requires an estimate of a firm's cost of equity and, if debt is involved, the cost of debt. The capital asset pricing model (CAPM) provides an estimate of the acquiring firm's cost of equity, which may be used as the discount or capitalization rate when no debt is involved in the transaction.

Estimating a Private Firm's Beta

Like public firms, private firms are subject to nondiversifiable risk, such as changes in interest rates, inflation, war, and terrorism. However, to estimate the firm's beta, it is necessary to have sufficient historical data. Private firms and divisions of companies are not publicly traded and, therefore, have no past stock price information. The common solution is to estimate the firm's beta based on comparable publicly listed firms.

Assuming the private firm is leveraged, the process commonly employed for constructing the private firm's leveraged beta is to assume that it can be estimated based on the unlevered beta for comparable firms adjusted for the private firm's target debt-to-equity ratio. The process involves the following steps. First, calculate the average beta for publicly traded comparable firms. If the comparable firms are leveraged, the resulting average is a leveraged beta for the comparable firms. Second, estimate the average debt-to-equity ratio in terms of the market values of the comparable firms. Third, estimate the average unlevered beta for the comparable firms based on information determined in the first two steps. Fourth, compute the levered beta for the private firm based on the firm's target debt-to-equity ratio set by management. Alternatively, the industry average leveraged beta could be used by assuming the private firm's current debt-to-equity ratio will eventually match the industry average.

Once estimated using the CAPM, the cost of equity may have to be adjusted to reflect risk specific to the target when it is applied to valuing a private company. The CAPM may understate significantly the specific business risk associated with acquiring the firm, because it may not adequately reflect the risk associated with such firms. As noted earlier, private firms are often subject to risks not normally found in public firms. Consequently, it is appropriate to adjust the CAPM for the additional risks associated with private or closely held firms.

Recall from Chapter 7 that risk premiums for public companies often are determined by examining the historical premiums earned by stocks over some measure of risk-free returns, such as 10-year Treasury bonds. This same logic may be applied to calculating specific business risk premiums for small private firms. The specific business risk premium can be measured by the difference between the junk bond and risk-free rate or the return on comparable small stocks and the risk-free rate. Note that comparable small companies are more likely to be found on the NASDAQ, OTC, or regional stock exchanges than on the New York Stock Exchange. Other adjustments for the risks associated with firm size are given by Ibbotson Associates in Table 7–1 found in Chapter 7.

For example, consider an acquiring firm attempting to value a small, privately owned software company. If the risk-free return is 6 percent, the historical return on all stocks minus the risk-free return is 5.5 percent, the firm's financial returns are highly correlated with the overall stock market (i.e., the firm's β is approximately 1), and the historical return on OTC software stocks minus the risk-free return is 9 percent, the cost of equity (k_e) can be calculated as follows:

$$k_e = \text{Risk-free return} + \beta \times \text{Market risk or equity premium}$$
$$+ \text{Specific business risk premium}$$
$$= 6\% + 1.0 \times 5.5\% + 9\% = 20.5\%$$

Note that the rationale for this adjustment for specific business risk is similar to that discussed in Chapter 7 in adjusting the CAPM for firm size (i.e., small firms generally are less liquid and subject to higher default risk than larger firms).

Estimating the Cost of Private Firm Debt

Private firms seldom can access public debt markets and are therefore usually not rated by the credit rating agencies. Most debt is bank debt, and the interest expense on loans on the firm's books that are more than a year old may not reflect what it actually would cost the firm to borrow currently. There are a number of possible solutions. The common solution is to assume that private firms can borrow at the same rate as comparable publicly listed firms or estimate an appropriate bond rating for the company based on financial ratios and use the interest rate that public firms with similar ratings would pay.

For example, an analyst can easily identify publicly traded company bond ratings by going to any of the various Internet bond screening services (e.g., finance.yahoo.com/bonds) and searching for bonds using various credit ratings. Royal Caribbean Cruise Lines LTD had a BBB rating and a 2.7 interest coverage ratio (i.e., EBIT/interest expense) in 2008 and would have to pay 7.0 to 7.5 percent for bonds maturing in 7–10 years. Consequently, firms with similar interest coverage ratios could have similar credit ratings. If the private firm to be valued had a similar interest coverage ratio and wanted to borrow for a similar time period, it is likely that it would have had to pay a comparable rate of interest. Other sources of information about the interest rates firms of a certain credit rating pay often is available in major financial newspapers such as the *Wall Street Journal, Investors' Business Daily*, and *Barron's*. Unlike the estimation of the cost of equity for small, privately held firms, it is unnecessary to adjust the cost of debt for specific business risk, since such risk should already be reflected in the interest rate charged to firms of similar risk.

Estimating the Cost of Capital

In the presence of debt, the cost of capital method should be used to estimate the discount or capitalization rate. This method involves the calculation of a weighted average of the cost of equity and the after-tax cost of debt. The weights should reflect market values rather than book values. Private firms represent a greater challenge than public firms in that the market value of their equity, and debt is not readily available in public markets. Calculating the cost of capital requires the use of the market rather than the book value of debt-to-total-capital ratios. Private firms provide such ratios only in book terms. A common solution is to use what the firm's management has set as its target debt-to-equity ratio in determining the weights to be used or assume that the private firms will eventually adopt the industry average debt-to-equity ratio.

Note the importance of keeping assumptions used for the management's target debt-to-equity ratio (D/E) in computing the firm's cost of equity consistent with the weights used in calculating the weighted-average cost of capital. For example, the firm's target D/E should be consistent with the debt-to-total-capital and equity-to-total-capital weights used in the weighted-average cost of capital. This consistency can be achieved simply by dividing the target D/E (or the industry D/E if that is what is used) by (1 + D/E) to estimate the implied debt-to-total-capital ratio. Subtracting this ratio from 1 provides the implied equity-to-total-capital ratio.

When the growth period for the firm's cash flow is expected to vary, the cost of capital estimated for the high-growth period can be expected to decline when the firm begins to grow at a more sustainable rate. This rate often is the industry average rate of growth. At that point, the firm presumably begins to take on the risk and growth characteristics of the typical firm in the industry. Thus, the discount rate may be assumed to be the industry average cost of capital during the sustainable or terminal growth period. Exhibit 10–1 illustrates how to calculate a private firm's beta, cost of equity, and cost of capital.

Exhibit 10–1 Valuing Private Firms

Acuity Lighting, a regional manufacturer and distributor of custom lighting fixtures, has revenues of $10 million and an EBIT of $2 million in the current year (i.e., year 0). The book value of the firm's debt is $5 million. The firm's debt matures at the end of five years and has annual interest expense of $400,000. The firm's marginal tax rate is 40 percent, the same as the industry average. Capital spending equals depreciation in year 0, and both are expected to grow at the same rate. As a result of excellent working capital management, the future change in working capital is expected to be essentially zero. The firm's revenue is expected to grow 15 percent annually for the next five years and 5 percent per year thereafter. The firm's current operating profit margin is expected to remain constant throughout the forecast period. As a result of the deceleration of its growth rate to a more sustainable rate, Acuity Lighting is expected to assume the risk and growth characteristics of the average firm in the industry during the terminal growth period. Consequently, its discount rate during this period is expected to decline to the industry average cost of capital of 11 percent.

The industry average beta and debt-to-equity ratio are 2.00 and, .4, respectively. The 10-year U.S. Treasury bond rate is 4.5 percent, and the historical average equity premium on all stocks is 5.5 percent. The specific business risk premium as measured by the difference between the junk bond and risk-free rate or the return on comparable small stocks and the risk-free rate is estimated to be 9 percent.

Acuity Lighting's interest coverage ratio is 2.89, which is equivalent to a BBB rating by the major credit rating agencies. BBB-rated firms are currently paying a pretax cost of debt of 7.5 percent. Acuity Lighting's management has established the firm's target debt-to-equity ratio at .5 based on the firm's profitability and growth characteristics. Estimate the equity value of the firm.

Calculate Acuity's cost of equity and weighted average cost of capital:

1. Unlevered beta for publicly traded firms in the same industry = $2.00 / (1 + .6 \times .4)$ = 1.61, where 2.00 is the industry's average levered beta, .6 is (1-tax rate), and .4 is the average debt-to-equity ratio for firms in this industry. See Chapter 7 for more detail on estimating levered and unlevered betas.
2. Acuity's levered beta = $1.61 \times (1 + .6 \times .50)$ = 2.09, where .5 is the target debt-to-equity ratio established by Acuity's management.
3. Acuity's cost of equity = $4.5 + 2.09 \times 5.5 + 9.0$ = 25.0, where 4.5 is the risk free rate and 9.0 is the firm size or firm specific business risk premium.
4. Acuity's after-tax cost of debt = $7.5 \times (1 - .4)$ = 4.5, where 7.5 is the pre-tax cost of debt.
5. Acuity's WACC = $25.0 \times .67 + 4.5 \times .33$ = 18.24, where the firm's debt-to-total capital ratio (D/TC) is determined by dividing Acuity's debt-to-equity target (D/E) by 1+D/E. Therefore, D/TC = $.5/(1 + .5)$ = .33 and equity to total capital is 1 − .33 or 67.

Value Acuity using the FCFF model using the data provided in Table 10–5.

Table 10–5   FCFF Model

Year	1	2	3	4	5	6
EBIT[1]	$2,300,000	$2,645,000	$3,041,750	$3,498,012	$4,022,714	$4,223,850
EBIT (1-Tax Rate)[2]	$1,380,000	$1,587,000	$1,825,050	$2,098,807	$2,413,628	$2,534,310

[1]EBIT grows at 15 percent annually for the first five years and 5 percent thereafter.

[2]Capital spending equals depreciation in year 0 and both are expected to grow at the same rate. Moreover, the change in working capital is zero. Therefore, free cash flow equals after-tax EBIT.

Exhibit 10–1 Valuing Private Firms — Cont'd

$$\text{Present Value of FCFF} = \frac{\$1,380,000}{1.1824} + \frac{\$1,587,000}{1.1824^2} + \frac{\$1,825,050}{1.1824^3}$$

$$+ \frac{\$2,098,807}{1.1824^4} + \frac{\$2,413,628}{1.1824^5}$$

$$= \$1,167,118 + \$1,135,136 + \$1,104,032$$
$$+ \$1,073,779 + \$1,044,355$$
$$= \$5,524,420$$

PV of Terminal value $= [\$2,534,310 / (.11 - .05)]/1.1824^5 = \$18,276,220$
Total Present Value $= \$5,524,420 + \$18,276,220 = \$23,800,640$

$$\text{Market value of the Acuity's debt} = \$400,000 \times \frac{1 - [1/(1.075)^5]}{.075}$$

$$+ \frac{\$5,000,000}{(1.075)^5}$$

$$= \$1,618,354 + \$3,482,793$$
$$= \$5,101,147$$

Value of Equity $= \$23,800,640 - \$5,101,147 = \$18,699,493$

Step 4. Applying Liquidity Discounts, Control Premiums, and Minority Discounts

In Exhibit 9–2 in Chapter 9, the maximum purchase price of a target firm (PV_{MAX}) is defined as its current market or stand-alone value (i.e., the minimum price or PV_{MIN}) plus the value of anticipated net synergies (i.e., PV_{NS}):

$$PV_{MAX} = PV_{MIN} + PV_{NS} \tag{10-1}$$

This is a reasonable representation of the maximum offer price for firms whose shares are traded in liquid markets and where no single shareholder (i.e., block shareholder) can direct the activities of the business. Examples of such firms could include Microsoft, IBM, and General Electric. However, when markets are illiquid and there are block shareholders with the ability to influence strategic decisions made by the firm, the maximum offer price for the firm needs to be adjusted for liquidity risk and the value of control.

Liquidity Discounts

Liquidity is the ease with which investors can sell their stock without a serious loss in the value of their investment. An investor in a private company may find it difficult to quickly sell his or her shares because of limited interest in the company. As such, the investor may find it necessary to sell at a significant discount from what was paid for the shares. Liquidity or marketability risk may be expressed as a *liquidity* or *marketability discount* or the reduction in the offer price for the target firm by an amount equal to the potential loss of value when sold due to the lack of liquidity in the market.

Empirical Studies of the Liquidity Discount

Liquidity discounts have been estimated using a variety of methodologies. The most popular involves so-called restricted stocks. Other studies have involved analyzing conditions prior to initial public offerings (IPOs), the cost of IPOs, option pricing models, and the value of subsidiaries of parent firms.

Restricted Stock (Letter Stock) Studies   Issued by public companies, such shares are identical to the firm's equities that are freely traded except for the restriction that they not be sold for a specific period of time. Letter stock gets its name from the practice of requiring investors to provide an "investment letter" stipulating that the purchase is for investment and not for resale. The restriction on trading results in a lack of marketability of the security. Registration (with the SEC) exemptions on restricted stocks are granted under Rule 144 of Section 4(2) of the 1933 Securities Act. Restricted stock may be sold in limited amounts through private placements to investors, usually at a significant discount. However, it cannot be sold to the public, except under provisions of the SEC's Rule 144. Prior to 1990, a holder of restricted stock had to register the securities with the SEC or qualify for exemption under Rule 144 to sell stock in the public markets. This made trading letter stock a time-consuming, costly process, as buyers had to perform appropriate due diligence. In 1990, the SEC adopted Rule 144A, allowing institutional investors to trade unregistered securities among themselves without filing registration statements. This change created a limited market for letter stocks and reduced discounts. In 1997, this rule was again amended to reduce the holding period for letter stocks from two years to one.

Empirical studies of restricted equities examine the difference in the price at which the restricted shares trade versus the price at which the same unrestricted equities trade in the public markets on the same date. Table 10–6 provides the results of 17 restricted stock studies. A comprehensive study undertaken by the SEC in 1971 examined restricted stock for 398 publicly traded companies and found that the median discount involving the restricted stock sales was about 26 percent (Institutional Investor, 1971). Size effects appeared to be important with firms having the highest sales volumes exhibiting the lowest discounts and the smallest firms, the largest discounts. An analysis completed by Gelman (1972) on a smaller sample of 146 publicly traded firms found that restricted shares traded at a discount of 33 percent. Other studies by Maher (1976) and Trout (1977) estimated the discount to be in the 33–35 percent range. Silber (1991) estimated a median discount of 33.50 percent, with outliers as high as 84 percent. Silber also found that the size of the liquidity discounts tended to decrease for firms with larger revenues and profitability and for smaller block sales of stock. The magnitude of these estimates from the pre-1990 studies is problematic in view of the types of investors in unregistered equities. These include insurance companies and pension funds, which typically have long-term investment horizons and well-diversified portfolios. Such investors are unlikely to be deterred by a one or two year restriction on selling their investments.

The Management Planning Study cited in Mercer (1997) reported a median 28.9 percent discount and found five factors to be reliable indicators of liquidity discounts: revenues, earnings, market price per share, price stability, and earnings stability. Hall and Polacek (1994) found that firms that were the most profitable showed 11 percent discounts, while Johnson (1999) showed discounts of 13 percent for firms with the highest sales volume. Firms showing the greatest stability had a median discount of 16.4 percent. As the lowest among pre-1990 studies, Wruck (1989) estimated a median discount of 13 percent

More recent studies of restricted stock sales since 1990 indicate a median discount of about 20 percent (Johnson, 1999; Aschwald, 2000; Finnerty, 2002; Loughran and

Table 10–6   Empirical Studies of Liquidity Discounts

Study	Time Period (Sample Size)	Median Discount (%)
Restricted Stock Studies		
Institutional Investor Study Report (1971)	1966–1969 (398)	25.8
Gelman (1972)	1968–1970 (89)	33.0
Trout (1972)	1968–1972 (NA)	33.5
Morony (1973)	1969–1972 (146)	35.6
Maher (1976)	1969–1973 (NA)	35.4
Standard Research Consultants (1983)	1978–1982 (NA)	45.0
Wruck (1989)	1979–1985 (99)	13.5
Hertzel and Smith (1993)	1980–1987 (106)	20.1
Oliver and Meyers (2000)	1980–1996 (53)	27.0
Willamette Management Associates Inc., cited in Pratt (2001)	1981–1984 (NA)	31.2
Silber (1991)	1981–1988 (69)	33.8
Management Planning, Inc., cited in Pratt (2005)	1980–1995 (NA)	28.9
Hall and Polacek (1994)	1979–1992 (NA)	23.0
Johnson (1999)	1991–1995 (72)	20.0
Aschwald (2000)	1996–1997 (23)	21.0
Aschwald (2000)	1997–1998 (15)	13.0
Finnerty (2002)	1991–1997 (101)	20.1
Pre-IPO Studies		
Willamette Management Associates Inc., cited in Pratt (2001)	1981–1984 (NA)	45.0
Emory (2001)	1981–2000 (631)	45.9
IPO Cost Studies		
Loughran and Ritter (2002)[1]	1990–2000 (NA)	22.0
Option Studies		
Longstaff (1995)	NA	25–35
Parent Subsidiaries		
Studies Officer (2007)	1997–2004 (122)	15–30

NA = Not available.

[1]Measures maximum discount.

Ritter, 2002). Aschwald (2000) showed a decline in the median discount to 13 percent following the holding period change under Rule 144 from two years to one after 1997.

Pre-IPO Studies   An alternative to estimating liquidity discounts is to compare the value of a firm's stock sold before an IPO, usually through private placements, with the actual IPO offering price. Firms undertaking IPOs are required to disclose all transactions in their stocks for a period of three years before the IPO. Because the liquidity available is substantially less before the IPO, this difference is believed to be an estimate of the liquidity discount. In 10 separate studies of 631 firms between 1980 and 2000, Emory (2001) found a median discount of 45.9 percent between the pre-IPO transaction prices and the actual post-IPO prices. The magnitude of the estimate remained relatively unchanged in each study. Reporting on a study by Willamette Management Associates, Pratt (2001) noted a median discount of 45 percent. Such studies are subject to selection bias as only IPOs that were completed are studied. IPOs that were withdrawn because of unattractive market conditions may have received valuations more in line with pre-IPO private placements and therefore exhibited smaller discounts. Furthermore, changes in a firm's financial structure and product offering between the pre- and post-IPO periods suggest that projected cash flows on which investors base their valuations differ between the two periods.

IPO Cost Studies The total cost of an IPO includes both direct costs of flotation and indirect underpricing costs. The direct costs entail management fees, underwriting fees, and selling concession (i.e., difference between gross and net proceeds of the issue) as a percentage of the amount of the issue. Indirect costs are measured by the frequent underpricing of the securities by underwriters interested in selling the entire issue quickly. Direct costs run about 7 percent and indirect costs about 15 percent, implying that firms seeking to achieve liquidity incur an average cost of 22 percent (Chaplinsky and Ramchand, 2000; Loughran and Ritter, 2002).

Option Pricing Studies Option pricing studies suggest that uncertainty and time are important determinants of liquidity discounts. With respect to uncertainty, the greater the volatility of the shares, the greater the magnitude of the discount. The longer the length of time the shareholder is restricted from selling the shares, the greater the discount. If a shareholder holds restricted stock and purchases a put option to sell the stock at the market price, the investor has effectively secured access to liquidity. The liquidity discount is the cost of the put option with an exercise price equal to the share price at the date of issue as a percent of the exercise price (Alli and Thompson, 1991). Longstaff (1995) found maximum liquidity discounts in the 25–35 percent range for two-year holding periods and 15–25 percent for one-year holding periods.

Studies of Parent Subsidiaries Officer (2007) found that sales of subsidiaries of other firms and privately owned firms sell at discounts of 15–30 percent below acquisition multiples for comparable publicly traded firms. He argues that this discount is the price paid by such firms for the liquidity provided by the acquiring firm. Discounts tend to be greater when debt is relatively expensive to obtain and when the parent's stock returns tend to underperform the market in the 12 months prior to the sale. This is consistent with the findings of several restricted stock studies, which identify profitability as a reliable indicator of the size of a firm's liquidity discount.

In summary, empirical studies of liquidity discounts demonstrate that they exist, but there is substantial disagreement over their magnitude. Most empirical studies conducted prior to 1992 indicated that liquidity discounts ranged from 33 to 50 percent when compared to publicly traded securities of the same company (Gelman, 1972; Moroney, 1973; Maher, 1976; Silber, 1991). More recent studies indicate that such securities trade at more modest discounts, ranging from 13 to 35 percent (Hertzel and Smith, 1993; Hall and Polacek, 1994; Longstaff, 1995; Oliver and Meyers, 2000; Aschwald, 2000; Koeplin, Sarin, and Shapiro, 2000; Finnerty, 2002; Officer, 2007). This range excludes the results of the pre-IPO studies that, for reasons discussed previously, are believed to be outliers. Four recent studies show a clustering of the discount around 20 percent. The decline in the liquidity discount since 1990 reflects a reduction in the required holding period for Rule 144 security issues and improved overall market liquidity during the periods covered by these studies. The latter is due to enhanced business governance practices, lower transaction costs, and greater accessibility to information via the Internet and other sources about private firms and the industries in which they compete. Note that the 2008–2009 capital market meltdowns are likely an aberration and, as such, should not affect the magnitude of the liquidity discount in the long term.

Purchase Price Premiums, Control Premiums, and Minority Discounts

For many transactions, the purchase price premium, which represents the amount a buyer pays the seller in excess of the seller's current share price, includes both a premium for anticipated synergy and a premium for control. The value of control is distinctly different from the value of synergy. The value of synergy represents revenue increases and cost savings that result from combining two firms, usually in the same line of business. In contrast, the value of control provides the right to direct the activities of the target firm on an ongoing basis.

Control can include the ability to select management, determine compensation, set policy and change the course of the business, acquire and liquidate assets, award contracts, make acquisitions, sell or recapitalize the company, and register the company's stock for a public offering. Control also involves the ability to declare and pay dividends, change the articles of incorporation or bylaws, or block any of the aforementioned actions. Owners of controlling blocks of voting stock may use this influence to extract special privileges or benefits not available to other shareholders, such as directing the firm to sell to companies owned by the controlling shareholder at a discount to the market price and to buy from suppliers owned by the controlling shareholder at premium prices. Furthermore, controlling shareholders may agree to pay unusually high salaries to selected senior managers, who may be family members. For these reasons, the more control a block investor has, the less influence a minority investor has and the less valuable is that person's stock. Therefore, a **control premium** is the amount an investor is willing to pay to direct the activities of the firm. Conversely, a **minority discount** is the reduction in the value of the investment because the minority owners have little influence on the firm's operations.

Purchase price premiums may reflect only control premiums, when a buyer acquires a target firm and manages it as a largely independent operating subsidiary. The **pure control premium** is the value the acquirer believes can be created by replacing incompetent management, changing the strategic direction of the firm, gaining a foothold in a market not currently served, or achieving unrelated diversification. Other examples of pure control premiums include premiums paid for firms going private through a leveraged buyout, in that the target firm generally is merged into a shell corporation with no synergy being created and managed for cash after having been recapitalized. Recapitalization refers to the change in the composition of the target's pre-LBO capital (i.e., equity and debt) structure to one consisting of substantially more debt. While the firm's management team may remain intact, the board of directors usually consists of representatives of the financial sponsor (i.e., equity or block investor).

Empirical Studies of the Pure Control Premium

While many empirical studies estimate the magnitude of the liquidity risk discount, the empirical evidence available to measure the control premium is limited. As is true of the liquidity discount, empirical studies confirmed the existence of a pure control premium. However, considerable disagreement continues over their size. Empirical studies to date focused on block transaction premiums, dual-class ownership, and M&A transactions.

Evidence from Block Transaction Premiums   Barclay and Holderness (1989) argue that an estimate of the magnitude of the pure control premium can be obtained by examining the difference between prices paid for privately negotiated sales of blocks of voting stock (defined as greater than 10,000 shares) constituting more than 5 percent of a firm's equity with the posttransaction share price. Analyzing 63 block trades between 1980 and 1982, the authors found the median premium paid for these private blocks of voting stock compared to the publicly traded price to be about 20 percent.

In a cross-country comparison, Dyck and Zingales (2004) studied 412 block transactions in 39 countries from 1990 to 2000. Although the median was about 14 percent, estimates of the control premium ranged from –4 percent to 65 percent. Negative results occur whenever the price paid for the block is less than the market price. This could occur whenever a firm is facing bankruptcy, management is widely viewed as incompetent, or the firm's products are obsolete. For example, Morgan Stanley's offer price for 40 percent of financially insolvent Bear Stearns voting shares in 2008 at $10 per share was $2 less than the market price on the day of the announcement.

In the Dyck and Zingales study, countries such as the United States, United Kingdom, and the Netherlands exhibited median premiums of 2 percent compared to premiums in Brazil and the Czech Republic of 65 and 58 percent, respectively. The authors argue that the value of control tends to be less in countries with better accounting standards, better legal protection for minority shareholders, more active competition in product markets, an independent press, and high tax compliance. Massari, Monge, and Zanetti (2006) found that block transaction (tender) premiums equal about 12 to 14 percent, depending on the size of the block of shares to be acquired. The authors found that the value of special privileges accruing to controlling shareholders is less than in prior studies. The findings are based on 27 control transactions in Italy between 1993 and 2003. Weifeng, Zhaoguo, and Shasa (2008) estimate median control premiums in China of 18.5 percent. The wide variation in results across countries may reflect the small samples used in evaluating transactions in each country as well as significantly different circumstances in each country.

Evidence from Dual-Class Ownership   Dual-class ownership structures involve classes of stock that differ in voting rights. Those shares having more voting rights than other shares typically trade at much higher prices. Zingales (1995) found that control premiums for most countries studied fell within a range of 10–20 percent of the firm's current share price. The United States, Sweden, and the United Kingdom displayed premiums of 5.4, 6.5, and 12.8 percent, respectively, compared to Israel and Italy, at 45.5 and 82 percent, respectively. In a more recent study, Nenova (2003), in an 18 country study in 1997, estimated a median control premium of 13 percent. However, the results varied widely across countries, with the United States and Sweden at 2 percent and Italy and Mexico at 29.4 and 36.4 percent, respectively. The author found that two thirds of the cross-country variance could be explained by a nation's legal environment, law enforcement, investor protection, and corporate charter provisions that tend to concentrate power (e.g., supermajority voting).

Evidence from Mergers and Acquisition Transactions   The premium paid to target company shareholders in part reflects what must be paid to get the firm's shareholders to relinquish control. Hanouna, Sarin, and Shapiro (2001) analyzed two samples: one in which buyers acquired a minority position and a second where the buyers acquired a controlling position. The study examined 9,566 transactions between 1990 and 2000 in the United States, Japan, Germany, France, Italy, the United Kingdom, and Canada. The authors found that a controlling position commanded a premium 20–30 percent higher than the price paid for minority positions in United States transactions. Similar premiums were found in other market-oriented nations, such as the United Kingdom and Canada. However, premiums were much smaller in those nations (i.e., Japan, Germany, France, and Italy) in which banks routinely make equity investments in publicly traded firms.

In summary, country comparison studies indicate a huge variation in median control premiums from as little as 2–5 percent in countries where corporate ownership often is widely dispersed and investor protections are relatively effective (e.g., United States and United Kingdom) to as much as 60–65 percent in countries where ownership tends to be concentrated and governance practices relatively poor (e.g., Brazil and the Czech Republic). Median estimates across countries are 10–12 percent.

The Relationship between Liquidity Discounts and Control Premiums

Control premiums and liquidity discounts are related by the degree of ownership concentration in a firm. Increasing control premiums reflect greater ownership concentration as investors able to buy large blocks of stock see increasing value in control and the amount they are willing to pay for such control rises. The resulting increased concentration of ownership reduces liquidity for a firm's stock, since controlling shareholders are more intent on managing the direction of the firm or extracting benefits that accrue to those in control than in trading their shares. This reduces market liquidity, since minority shareholders lack the influence to force the sale of the firm to liquidate their shareholdings. Nor can they sell to the block holders who are less inclined to buy more shares because the incremental benefit to them is relatively small. Consequently, increasing control premiums often are associated with increasing liquidity discounts, reflecting the illiquidity of shares held by minority investors.

In contrast, decreasing control premiums, reflecting the lower value investors place on control, often are associated with decreasing liquidity discounts. When markets are liquid, investors place a lower value on control. If investors are dissatisfied with the way a firm is being run, they can sell their shares easily and drive down the value of the controlling stockholder's shares. Hence, factors that contribute to improving liquidity reduce the value of control. For example, improving corporate governance mandated for public companies by Sarbanes–Oxley and the exchanges on which they trade contribute to greater investor understanding of firms' financial statements. This increased "transparency" limits the ability of controlling shareholders to take actions inimical to the interests of minority shareholders.

While it would seem that controlling blocks of stock placed on the market at the same time could only be sold at a significant discount, the ease with which they can be sold depends ultimately on what investors believe they can do with a controlling position in the firm. A study by Koeplin et al. (2000) suggests that the liquidity discounts in control situations should not exceed 30 percent. The authors analyze only transactions in which a controlling interest was acquired and create a matched pair (i.e., for each private transaction, a public acquisition of a firm in the same industry, country, and year is identified). By comparing multiples based on earnings before taxes and EBITDA for each matched pair, the authors find liquidity discounts of 20 and 28 percent, respectively.

Equation (10–1) can be rewritten to reflect the interdependent relationship between the control premium (CP) and the liquidity discount (LD) as follows:

$$\mathrm{PV_{MAX}} = (\mathrm{PV_{MIN}} + \mathrm{PV_{NS}})(1 + \mathrm{CP\%})(1 - \mathrm{LD\%})$$

and

$$\mathrm{PV_{MAX}} = (\mathrm{PV_{MIN}} + \mathrm{PV_{NS}})(1 - \mathrm{LD\%} + \mathrm{CP\%} - \mathrm{LD\%x\ CP\%}) \qquad (10\text{–}2)$$

where

CP% = control premium expressed as a percentage of the maximum purchase price.

LD% = liquidity discount expressed as a percentage of the maximum purchase price.

The multiplicative form of equation (10–2) results in a term (i.e., LD% × CP%) that serves as an estimate of the interaction between the control premium and the liquidity discount. Note that, while CP% can be positive if it is a premium or negative if it is a minority discount, the value of LD% always is negative.

Estimating Liquidity Discounts, Control Premiums, and Minority Discounts

Given the wide variability of estimates, it should be evident that premiums and discounts must be applied to the value of the target firm with great care. The implication is that there is no such thing as a standard liquidity discount or control premium. In general, the size of the discount or premium should reflect factors specific to the firm.

Factors Affecting the Liquidity Discount

The median discount for empirical studies since 1992 is about 20 percent, with about 90 percent of the individual studies' estimated median discounts falling within a range of 13–35 percent.

Table 10–7 suggests a subjective methodology for adjusting a private firm for liquidity risk, in which the analyst starts with the median liquidity discount of 20 percent and adjusts for factors specific to the firm to be valued. Such factors include firm size, liquid assets as a percent of total assets, financial returns, and cash-flow growth and leverage compared to the industry. While this is not intended to be an exhaustive list, these factors were selected based on the findings of empirical studies of restricted stocks.

The logic underlying the adjustments to the median liquidity discount is explained next. Firms whose cash, receivables, and inventory levels constitute a relatively larger percentage of their total assets are likely to be more liquid than firms whose liquid assets constitute a relatively smaller percentage. As such, the liquidity discount should be smaller for more highly liquid firms, since liquid assets generally can be converted quickly to cash with minimal loss of value. Furthermore, firms whose financial returns exceed significantly the industry average have an easier time attracting investors and should be subject to a smaller liquidity discount than firms underperforming the industry. Likewise, firms with relatively low leverage and high cash-flow growth should be subject to a smaller liquidity discount than more leveraged firms with slower cash-flow growth, because they have a lower breakeven point and are less likely to default or become insolvent.

Table 10–7   Estimating the Size of the Liquidity Discount

Factor	Guideline	Adjust 20% Median Discount as Follows[1]
Firm size	Large	Reduce discount
	Small	Increase discount
Liquid assets as % of total assets	>50%	Reduce discount
	<50%	Increase discount
Financial returns	2 × industry median[1]	Reduce discount
	½ × industry median	Increase discount
Cash flow growth rate	2 × industry median	Reduce discount
	½ × industry median	Increase discount
Leverage	½ × industry median	Reduce discount
	2 × industry median	Increase discount
Estimated firm-specific liquidity discount		???

[1]Industry median financial information often is available from industry trade associations, conference presentations, Wall Street analyst's reports, Yahoo! Finance, *Barron's, Investors Business Daily,* the *Wall Street Journal,* and similar publications and websites.

Factors Affecting the Control Premium

Factors affecting the size of the control premium include the perceived competence of the target's current management, the extent to which operating expenses are discretionary, the value of nonoperating assets, and the perceived net present value of currently unexploited business opportunities. The value in replacing incompetent management is difficult to quantify since it reflects the potential for better future decision making. The value of nonoperating assets and discretionary expenses are quantified by estimating the after-tax sale value of redundant assets and the pretax profit improvement from eliminating noncritical operating activities or individual positions. While relatively easy to measure, such decisions may be impossible to implement without having control of the business. This is true because they could involve eliminating the positions of members of the family owning the business or selling an asset owned by the business but used primarily by the family owning the business.

State statutes also affect the rights of controlling and minority shareholders. In more than one half of the states, major corporate actions, such as a merger, sale, liquidation, or recapitalization of a firm, may be approved by a simple majority vote of the firm's shareholders. In contrast, other states require at least a two thirds majority to approve such decisions. In these states, a minority of slightly more than one third can block such actions. Furthermore, a majority of the states have dissolution statutes enabling minority shareholders to force dissolution of a corporation if they can show there is a deadlock in their negotiations with the controlling shareholders or that their rights are being violated. If the suit is successful and the controlling shareholders do not want to dissolve the firm, the solution is to pay minority shareholders fair value for their shares.

If the target business is to be run by the acquirer as it is currently, no control premium should be added to the purchase price. However, if the acquirer intends to take actions that are possible only if the acquirer owns enough of the voting stock to achieve control, the purchase price should include a control premium large enough to obtain a controlling interest. Table 10–8 provides a subjective methodology for adjusting a control premium to be applied to a specific business. Note that the 10 percent premium used in the table is for illustrative purposes only and is intended to provide a starting point. The actual premium selected should reflect the analyst's perception of what is appropriate given the country's legal system and propensity to enforce laws and the extent to which firm ownership tends to be concentrated or widely dispersed. The percentages applied to the discretionary expenses' share of total expenses, nonoperating assets as a percent of total assets, and the NPV of alternative strategies are intended to reflect risks inherent in cutting costs, selling assets, and pursuing alternative investment opportunities. These risks include a decline in morale and productivity following layoffs, the management time involved in selling assets and the possible disruption of the business, and the potential for overestimating the NPV of alternative investments. In other words, the perceived benefits of these decisions should be large enough to offset the associated risks.

As a practical matter, business appraisers frequently rely on the *Control Premium Study,* published annually by Mergerstat. Another source is Duff and Phelps. Mergerstat estimates median control premiums and control premiums by industry by comparing the per-share total consideration paid to the target to the "unaffected" price. The "unaffected" price is determined by examining the target price and volume statistics for the year preceding the takeover announcement. The use of these data is problematic, since the control premium estimates provided by Mergerstat include the estimated value of synergy as well as the amount being paid to replace current management or change the firm's strategy. Damodaran (2002) suggests that the way to estimate a control premium is to view it as equal to the difference between the present value of a firm if it were being operating optimally and

Table 10–8   Estimating the Size of the Control Premium to Reflect the Value of Changing the Target's Business Strategy and Operating Practices

Factor	Guideline	Adjust 10% Median Control Premium as Follows[1]
Target management	Retain	No change in premium
	Replace	Increase premium
Discretionary expenses	Cut if potential savings >5% of total expenses	Increase premium
	Do not cut if potential savings <5% of total expenses	No change in premium
Nonoperating assets	Sell if potential after-tax gain >10% of purchase price[2] of net acquired target assets	Increase premium
	Defer decision if potential after-tax gain <10% of purchase price	No change in premium
Alternative business opportunities	Pursue if NPV > 20% of target's stand-alone value	Increase premium
	Do not pursue if NPV < 20% of target's stand-alone value	No change in premium
Estimated firm-specific control premium		???

[1]The 10 percent premium represents the median estimate from the Nenova (2003) and Dyck and Zingales (2004) studies for countries perceived to have relatively stronger investor protection and law enforcement.

[2]The purchase price refers to the price paid for the controlling interest in the target.

its present value the way it is currently being managed. This approach presumes that the analyst is able to determine accurately the value-optimizing strategy for the target firm.

Factors Affecting the Minority Discount

Minority discounts reflect the loss of influence due to the power of a controlling block investor. Intuitively, the magnitude of the discount should relate to the size of the control premium. The larger the control premium, the greater the perceived value of being able to direct the activities of the business and the value of special privileges that come at the expense of the minority investor. Reflecting the relationship between control premium and minority discounts, Mergerstat estimates minority discounts by using the following formula:

$$\text{Implied median minority discount} = 1 - [1/(1 + \text{Median premium paid})] \qquad (10\text{–}3)$$

Equation (10–3) implies that an investor would pay a higher price for control of a company and a lesser amount for a minority stake (i.e., larger control premiums are associated with larger minority discounts). While equation (10–3) is routinely used by practitioners to estimate minority discounts, there is little empirical support for this largely intuitive relationship.

Exhibit 10–2 illustrates what an investor should be willing to pay for a controlling interest and for a minority interest. Note that the example assumes that 50.1 percent ownership is required for a controlling interest. In practice, control may be achieved with less than a majority ownership position if there are numerous other minority investors. The reader should note how the 20 percent median liquidity discount rate (based on recent empirical studies) is adjusted for the specific risk and return characteristics of the target firm. Furthermore, note that the control premium is equal to what the acquirer believes is the minimum increase in value created by achieving a controlling interest. Also, observe how the direct relationship between control premiums and minority discounts is used to estimate the size of the minority discount. Finally, see how median estimates of liquidity discounts and control premiums can serve as guidelines in valuation analyses.

Lighting Group Incorporated (LGI), a holding company, wants to acquire a controlling interest in Acuity Lighting, whose estimated stand-alone equity value equals $18,699,493 (see Exhibit 10–1). LGI believes that the present value of synergies is $2,250,000 ($PV_{SYN}$) due to the potential for bulk purchase discounts and cost savings related to eliminating duplicate overhead and combining warehousing operations. LGI believes that the value of Acuity, including synergy, can be increased by at least 10 percent by applying professional management methods (and implicitly by making better management decisions) and reducing the cost of borrowing by financing the operations through the holding company. To achieve these efficiencies, LGI must gain control of Acuity. LGI is willing to pay a control premium of as much as 10 percent. The minority discount is derived from equation (10–3). The factors used to adjust the 20 percent median liquidity discount are taken from Table 10–7. The magnitudes of the adjustments are the opinion of LGI analysts. LGI's analysts have used Yahoo! Finance to obtain the industry data for the home furniture and fixtures industry shown in Table 10–9.

What is the maximum purchase price LGI should pay for a 50.1 percent controlling interest in the business? For a minority 20 percent interest in the business?

To adjust for presumed liquidity risk of the target firm due to lack of a liquid market, LGI discounts the amount it is willing to offer to purchase 50.1 percent of the firm's equity by 16 percent.

$$
\begin{aligned}
\text{Using equation } (10\text{–}2), PV_{MAX} &= (PV_{MIN} + PV_{NS})(1 - LD\%)(1 + CP\%) \\
&= [(\$18,699,493 + \$2,250,000)(1 - 0.16)(1 + 0.10)] \\
&\quad \times 0.501 \\
&= \$20,949,493 \times 0.924 \times 0.501 \\
&= \$9,698,023 \text{ (Maximum purchase price for 50.1\%)}
\end{aligned}
$$

If LGI were to acquire only a 20 percent stake in Acuity, it is unlikely that there would be any synergy, because LGL would lack the authority to implement potential cost saving measures without the approval of the controlling shareholders. Because it is a minority investment, there is no control premium, but a minority discount for lack of control should be estimated. The minority discount is estimated using equation (10–3); that is, $1 - [1/(1 + 0.10)] = 9.1$:

$$
\begin{aligned}
PV_{MAX} &= [\$18,699,493 \times (1 - 0.16)(1 - 0.091)] \times 0.2 \\
&= \$2,855,637 \text{ (Maximum purchase price for 20\%)}
\end{aligned}
$$

Table 10–9 Industry Data

Factor	Acuity Lighting	Home Furniture and Fixtures Industry	Adjustments to 20% Median Liquidity Discount
Median liquidity discount[1]	NA	NA	20.0%
Firm size	Small	NA	+2.0
Liquid assets as % of total assets	>50%	NA	−2.0
Return on equity	19.7%	9.7%	−2.0
Cash flow growth rate	15%	12.6%	0.0
Leverage (debt to equity)	0.27[2]	1.02	−2.0
Estimated Liquidity Discount for Acuity Lighting			16.0%

[1]Median estimate of the liquidity discount of empirical studies (excluding pre-IPO studies) since 1992.

[2]From Exhibit 10–1: the market value of Acuity's debt to the market value of its equity = $5,101,147/$18,699,493 = 0.27

NA = Not available or not applicable.

Case Study 10–3 is a highly summarized version of how a business valuation firm evaluated the liquidity risk associated with Taylor Devices' unregistered common stock, registered common shares, and a minority investment in a business that it was planning to sell following its merger with Tayco Development. The estimated liquidity discounts were used in a joint proxy statement submitted to the SEC by the two firms to justify the value of the offer the boards of Taylor Devices and Tayco Development had negotiated.

Case Study 10–3 Determining Liquidity Discounts: The Taylor Devices and Tayco Development Merger

Taylor Devices (Taylor) and Tayco Development (Tayco) agreed to merge in early 2008. Tayco would be merged into Taylor, with Taylor as the surviving entity. The merger would enable Tayco's patents and intellectual property to be fully integrated into Taylor's manufacturing operations, as intellectual property rights transfer with the Tayco stock. Each share of Tayco common would be converted into one share of Taylor common stock, according to the terms of the deal. Taylor's common stock is traded on the NASDAQ Small Cap Market under the symbol TAYD and, on January 8, 2008 (the last trading day before the date of the filing of the joint proxy statement with the SEC), the stock closed at $6.29 per share. Tayco common stock is traded over the counter on "Pink Sheets" (i.e., an informal trading network) under the trading symbol TYCO.PK, and it closed on January 8, 2008, at $5.11 per share.

A business appraisal firm was hired to value Taylor's unregistered (with the SEC) shares. The appraisal firm treated the shares as if they were restricted shares, because there was no established market for trading in these shares. The appraiser reasoned that the risk of Taylor's unregistered shares is greater than for letter stock, which have a stipulated period during which the shares cannot be sold, because the Taylor shares lacked a date indicating when they could be sold. Using this line of reasoning, the appraisal firm estimated a liquidity discount of 20 percent, which it believed approximated the potential loss that holders of these shares might incur in attempting to sell their shares.

The block of registered Taylor common stock differs from the unregistered shares, in that they are not subject to Rule 144. Based on the trading volume of Taylor common over the preceding 12 months, the appraiser believed that it was likely that it would take less than one year to convert the block of registered stock into cash and estimated the discount at 13 percent, consistent with the Aschwald (2000) studies.

The appraisal firm also was asked to estimate the liquidity discount for the sale of Taylor's minority investment in a real estate development business. Due to the increase in liquidity of restricted stocks since 1990, the business appraiser argued that restricted stock studies conducted before that date might provide a better proxy for liquidity discounts for this type of investment. Interests in closely held firms are more like letter stock transactions occurring before the changes in SEC Rule 144 beginning in 1990, when the holding period was reduced from three to two years and later to one after 1997. Such firms have little ability to raise capital in public markets due to their small size and face high transaction costs.

Based on the SEC and other prior 1990 studies, the liquidity discount for this investment was expected to be between 30 and 35 percent. Pre-IPO studies could push it higher, to a range of 40–45 percent. Consequently, the appraisal firm argued that the discount for most minority interest investments tended to fall in the range of 30–45 percent. Because the real estate development business is smaller than nearly all the firms in the restricted stocks studies, the liquidity discount is believed by the appraisal firm to be at the higher end of the range.

Discussion Questions

1. Describe how the various historical restricted stock studies were used by the appraiser to estimate the liquidity discount.
2. What other factors could the appraiser have used to estimate the liquidity discount on the unregistered stock?
3. In view of your answer to question 2, how might these factors have changed the appraiser's conclusions? Be specific.
4. Based on the 13 percent liquidity discount estimated by the business appraiser, what was the actual purchase price premium paid to Tayco shareholders for each of their common shares?

Solutions to these questions are available on the Online Instructor's Manual for instructors using this textbook.

Source: SEC Form S4 filing of a joint proxy statement for Taylor Devices and Tayco Development dated January 15, 2008.

Reverse Mergers

Many small businesses fail each year. In a number of cases, all that remains is a business with no significant assets or operations. Such companies are referred to as *shell corporations.* Shell corporations can be used as part of a deliberate business strategy in which a corporate legal structure is formed in anticipation of future financing, a merger, joint venture, spin-off, or some other infusion of operating assets. This may be accomplished in a transaction called a *reverse merger* in which the acquirer (a private firm) merges with a publicly traded target (often a corporate shell) in a statutory merger in which the public firm survives. The target is the surviving entity, which must hold the assets and liabilities of both the target and shell subsidiary. See Chapter 11 for more on reverse mergers.

The Value of Corporate Shells

Is there any value in shells resulting from corporate failure or bankruptcy? The answer may seem surprising, but it is a resounding yes. Merging with an existing corporate shell of a publicly traded company may be a reasonable alternative for a firm wanting to go public that is unable to provide the two years of audited financial statements required by the SEC or unwilling to incur the costs of going public. Thus, merging with a shell corporation may represent an effective alternative to an IPO for a small firm.

After the private company acquires a majority of the public shell corporation's stock and completes the merger, it appoints new management and elects a new board of directors. The owners of the private firm receive most of the shares of the shell corporation (i.e., more than 50 percent) and control the shell's board of directors. The new firm must have a minimum of 300 shareholders to be listed on the NASDAQ Small Cap Market.

Shell corporations usually are of two types. The first is a failed public company whose shareholders want to sell what remains to recover some of their losses. The second type is a shell that has been created for the sole purpose of being sold as a shell in a reverse merger. The latter type typically carries less risk of having unknown liabilities.

Are Reverse Mergers Cheaper than IPOs?

As noted previously, direct and indirect costs of an IPO can be as much as 22 percent of gross proceeds, or about $1.1 million for a $5 million IPO. Reverse mergers typically cost between $50,000 and $100,000, about one quarter of the expense of an IPO, and can be completed in about 60 days or one third of the time to complete a typical IPO (Sweeney, 2005).

Despite these advantages, reverse takeovers may take as long as IPOs and are sometimes more complex. The acquiring company must still perform due diligence on the target and communicate information on the shell corporation to the exchange on which its stock will be traded and prepare a prospectus. It can often take months to settle outstanding claims against the shell corporation. Public exchanges often require the same level of information for companies going through reverse mergers as those undertaking IPOs. The principal concern is that the shell company may contain unseen liabilities, such as unpaid bills or pending litigation, which in some instances can make the reverse merger far more costly than an IPO.

Arellano-Ostoa and Brusco (2002) found that 32.6 percent of their sample of 121 reverse mergers between 1990 and 2000 were delisted within three years. The authors argue that reverse mergers may represent a means by which a private firm can achieve listing on a public stock exchange when it may not be fully able to satisfy the initial listing requirements if it were to undertake an IPO. However, this claim is disputed in a larger and more recent study. In a sample of 286 reverse mergers and 2,860 IPOs between 1990 and 2002, Cyree and Walker (2008) found that private firms using the reverse merger technique to go public rather than the IPO method tend to be smaller, younger, and exhibit poorer financial performance than those that choose to go public using an IPO. Of those private firms listed on public exchanges either through a reverse merger or an IPO, 42 percent using reverse mergers are delisted within three years versus 27 percent of firms using IPOs. However, the authors found that only 1.4 percent of their sample of reverse mergers were unable to satisfy the initial listing requirements of public exchanges. See Case Study 10–4 for an example of a company taken public via a reverse merger.

Financing Reverse Mergers

Private investment in public equities (PIPEs) is a commonly used method of financing reverse mergers. In a PIPE offering, a firm with publicly traded shares sells, usually at a discount, newly issued but unregistered securities, typically stock or debt convertible into stock, directly to investors in a private transaction. Hedge funds are common buyers of such issues. The issuing firm is required to file a shelf registration statement on Form S-3 with the SEC as quickly as possible (usually between 10 and 45 days after issuance) and to use its "best efforts" to complete registration within 30 days after filing. Registration enables investors to resell the shares in the public market well before the Rule 144 required holding period expires.

PIPEs often are used in conjunction with a reverse merger to provide companies with not just an alternative way to go public but also financing once they are listed on the public exchange. For example, assume a private company is merged into a publicly traded firm through a reverse merger. As the surviving entity, the public company raises funds through a privately placed equity issue (i.e., PIPE financing). The private firm is now a publicly traded company with the funds to finance future working capital requirements and capital investments.

To issuers, PIPEs offer the advantage of being able to be completed more quickly, cheaply, and confidentially than a public stock offering, which requires registration up front and a more elaborate investor "road show" to sell the securities to public investors. To investors, PIPEs provide an opportunity to identify stocks that overoptimistic public investors have overvalued. Such shares can be purchased as a private placement at a discount to compensate investors for the stocks underperformance following the issue (Hertzel et al., 2002). Once registered, such shares can be resold in the public markets often before the extent of the overvaluation is recognized by public investors. As private placements, PIPEs are most suitable for raising small amounts of financing, typically in the $5–10 million range. Firms seeking hundreds of millions of dollars are more likely to be successful in going directly to the public financial markets in a public stock offering.

Using Leveraged Employee Stock Ownership Plans to Buy Private Companies

An ESOP is a means whereby a corporation can make tax-deductible contributions of cash or stock into a trust. The assets are allocated to employees and are not taxed until withdrawn by employees. ESOPs generally must invest at least 50 percent of their assets in employer stock. Three types of ESOPs are recognized by the 1974 Employee Retirement Income Security Act: (1) leveraged, the ESOP borrows to purchase qualified employer securities; (2) leverageable, the ESOP is authorized but not required to borrow; and (3) nonleveraged, the ESOP may not borrow funds. As noted in Chapter 1, ESOPs offer substantial tax advantages to sponsoring firms, lenders, and participating employees.

Employees commonly use leveraged ESOPs to buy out owners of private companies who have most of their net worth in the firm. The firm establishes an ESOP. The owner sells at least 30 percent of his or her stock to the ESOP, which pays for the stock with borrowed funds. The owner may invest the proceeds and defer taxes if the investment is made within 12 months of the sale of the stock to the ESOP, the ESOP owns at least 30 percent of the firm, and neither the owner nor his or her family participates in the ESOP. The firm makes tax-deductible contributions to the ESOP in an amount sufficient to repay interest and principal. Shares held by the ESOP are distributed to employees as the loan is repaid. As the outstanding loan balance is reduced, the shares are allocated to employees, who eventually own the firm.

Empirical Studies of Shareholder Returns

As noted in Chapter 1, target shareholders of both public and private firms routinely experience abnormal positive returns when a bid is announced for the firm. In contrast, acquirer shareholders often experience abnormal negative returns on the announcement date, particularly when using stock to purchase publicly traded firms. However, substantial empirical evidence shows that public acquirers using their stock to buy privately held firms experience significant abnormal positive returns around the transaction announcement date. Other studies suggest that acquirers of private firms often experience abnormal positive returns regardless of the form of payment. These studies are discussed next.

Chang (1998), in a study of the returns to public company shareholders when they acquire privately held firms, found an average positive 2.6 percent abnormal return for shareholders of bidding firms for stock offers but not cash transactions. The finding of positive abnormal returns earned by buyers using stock to acquire private companies is in sharp contrast with the negative abnormal returns earned by U.S. bidders using stock to acquire publicly traded companies. Chang (1998) notes that ownership of privately held companies tends to be highly concentrated, so that an exchange of stock tends to create a few very large stockholders (often called blockholders). Close monitoring of management and the acquired firm's performance may contribute to abnormal positive returns experienced by companies bidding for private firms. Draper and Padyal (2006), in an exhaustive study of 8,756 firms from 1981 to 2001, also found that acquirers of private firms in the United Kingdom paying with stock achieved the largest positive abnormal returns due to increased monitoring of the target firm's performance. These findings are consistent with the positive abnormal announcement returns of more than 2 percent for acquirers of private firms in Canadian and European studies, where owner-ship is often highly concentrated than the highly dispersed ownership of publicly traded firms in the United States (Ben-Amar and Andre, 2006; Bigelli and Mengoli, 2004; Boehmer, 2000; Dumontier and Pecherot, 2001). This conclusion is consistent with stud-ies of returns to companies that issue stock and convertible debt in private placements (Fields and Mais, 1991; Hertzel and Smith, 1993; Wruck, 1989). It generally is argued that, in private placements, large shareholders are effective monitors of managerial per-formance, thereby enhancing the prospects of the acquired firm (Demsetz and Lehn, 1996).

Ang and Kohers (2001) found positive excess returns to the shareholders of firms acquiring private firms regardless of the form of payment. Fuller, Netter, and Stegemoller (2002) also found that acquirers earn excess returns of as much as 2.1 percent when buying private firms or 2.6 percent for subsidiaries of public companies. They attribute the abnormal returns to the tendency of acquirers to pay less for non-publicly traded companies, due to the relative difficulty in buying private firms or subsidiaries of public companies. In both cases, shares are not publicly traded and access to information is limited. Moreover, there may be fewer bidders for non-publicly traded companies. Consequently, these targets may be acquired at a discount from their actual economic value. As a consequence of this discount, bidder shareholders are able to realize a larger share of the anticipated synergies.

Other factors that may contribute to these positive abnormal returns for acquirers of private companies include the introduction of more professional management into the privately held firms and tax considerations. Public companies may introduce more professional management systems into the target firms thereby enhancing the target's value. The acquirer's use of stock rather than cash may also induce the seller to accept a lower price since it allows sellers to defer taxes on any gains until they decide to sell their shares (see Chapter 11). Poulsen and Stegemoller (2002) found that the favorable tax consequences of a share-for-share exchange were an important factor in privately held firms selling to public companies for more than one third of sellers surveyed.

Things to Remember

Private businesses often are characterized by a lack of professional managers and a small group of shareholders controlling the firm's decision making. Valuing private companies is more challenging than valuing public companies, due to the absence of published share price data. Private firms often face problems that may be unique to their size. Owners considering the sale of their firms may overstate revenue and understate cost. However, during the normal course of business, private firms are more likely to overstate costs and understate revenues to minimize tax liabilities. Although many small businesses have few hard assets, they may have substantial intangible value in terms of customer lists, intellectual property, and the like. As such, it is crucial to restate the firm's financial state-ments to determine the current period's true profitability.

Calculating the weighted average cost of capital also represents a challenge. Because private firms lack a share price history, betas often are estimated based on those of comparable publicly traded firms; CAPM often needs to be adjusted for risks specific to the private firm. The cost of borrowing frequently is estimated based on what similar public firms are paying. Weights used in estimating the cost of capital may be either management's target debt-to-equity ratio or the industry average ratio.

When markets are illiquid and block shareholders exert substantial control over the firm's operations, the maximum offer price for the target must be adjusted for liquidity risk and the value of control. Given the wide variability of estimates, it should be evident that premiums and discounts must be applied to the value of the target firm with great care. In general, the size of the premium or discount should reflect factors specific to the firm. The median liquidity discount from empirical studies since 1992 is about 20 percent, with some evidence that discounts exceeding 30 percent cannot be justified (especially in control situations). While varying widely, recent studies indicate that median pure control premiums across countries are about 12–14 percent. However, such premiums in the United States fall in the 2–5 percent range. Increasing control premiums are associated with increasing minority discounts. Published data on control premiums and minority discounts are much higher, but they often include synergy as well as control considerations. These data are provided for the sole purpose of serving as guidelines. The author suggests that factors specific to each circumstance need to be analyzed and used to adjust these medians to the realities of the situation.

In contrast to studies involving acquisitions of U.S. public firms, buyers of private firms in the United States often realize significant abnormal positive returns, particularly in share-for-share transactions. This result reflects the concentration of ownership in private firms and the resulting aggressive monitoring of management. This is in contrast to publicly traded firms, where the impact of incompetent management is spread over many shareholders rather than shouldered by a few. This finding is also supported by many studies of mergers in other countries, where ownership tends to be more heavily concentrated than in the United States. A tendency of buyers to acquire private firms at a discount from their economic value and tax considerations also are factors in positive abnormal returns experienced by these acquirers.

Chapter Discussion Questions

10–1. Why is it more difficult to value privately held companies than publicly traded firms?

10–2. What factors should be considered in adjusting target company data?

10–3. What is the capitalization rate, and how does it relate to the discount rate?

10–4. What are the common ways of estimating the capitalization rate?

10–5. What is the liquidity discount, and what are common ways of estimating this discount?

10–6. Give examples of private company costs that might be understated, and explain why.

10–7. How can an analyst determine if the target firm's costs and revenues are understated or overstated?

10–8. What is the difference between the concepts of fair market value and fair value?

10–9. What is the importance of IRS Revenue Ruling 59–60?

10–10. Why might shell corporations have value?

10–11. Why might succession planning be more challenging for a family firm?

10–12. How are governance issues between public and private firms the same and how are they different?

10–13. What are some of the reasons a family-owned or privately owned business may want to go public? What are some of the reasons that discourage such firms from going public?

10–14. Why are family-owned firms often attractive to private equity investors?

10–15. Rank from the highest to lowest the liquidity discount you would apply if you, as a business appraiser, had been asked to value the following businesses: (a) a local, profitable hardware store; (b) a money-losing laundry; (c) a large privately owned firm with significant excess cash balances and other liquid short-term investments; and (d) a pool cleaning service whose primary tangible assets consist of a two-year-old truck and miscellaneous equipment. Explain your ranking.

Answers to these Chapter Discussion Questions are available in the Online Instructor's Manual for instructors using this book.

Chapter Practice Problems and Answers

10–16. It is usually appropriate to adjust the financials received from the target firm to reflect any changes that you, as the new owner, would make to create an adjusted EBITDA. Using the Excel-Based Spreadsheet on How to Adjust Target Firm's Financial Statements on the CD-ROM accompanying this book, make at least three adjustments to the target's hypothetical financials to determine the impact on the adjusted EBITDA. (Note: The adjustments should be made in the section on the spreadsheet entitled "Adjustments to Target Firm's Financials.") Explain your rationale for each adjustment.

10–17. Based on its growth prospects, a private investor values a local bakery at $750,000. While wanting to own the operation, she intends to keep the current owner to manage the business. To do so, she wishes to purchase 50.1 percent ownership, with the current owner retaining the remaining equity. Furthermore, she has no plans to change the way in which the business is managed or combine the business with any other operations. Based on recent empirical studies, she believes the appropriate liquidity discount is 20 percent. What is the most she should be willing to pay for a 50.1 percent stake in the bakery?

Answer: $300,600.

10–18. You have been asked by an investor to value a local restaurant. In the most recent year, the restaurant earned pretax operating income of $300,000. Income has grown an average of 4 percent annually during the last five years, and it is expected to continue growing at that rate into the foreseeable future. By introducing modern management methods, you believe the pretax operating income growth rate can be increased to 6 percent beyond the second year and sustained at that rate through the foreseeable future. The investor is willing to pay a 10 percent premium to reflect the value of control. The beta and debt-to-equity ratio for publicly traded firms in the restaurant industry are 2.0 and 1.5, respectively. The business's target debt-to-equity ratio is 1.0 and its pretax cost of borrowing, based on its recent borrowing activities, is 7 percent. The business-specific risk for firms of this size is estimated to be 6 percent. The investor concludes that the specific risk of this business is less than other firms in this industry due to its sustained profit growth, low leverage, and high return on assets compared to similar restaurants in this geographic area. Moreover, per capita income in this region is expected to grow more rapidly than elsewhere in the country, adding to the growth prospects of the restaurant business. At an estimated 15 percent, the liquidity risk premium is believed to be relatively low due to the excellent reputation of the restaurant. Since the current chef and the staff are expected to remain if the business is sold, the quality of the restaurant is expected to be maintained. The 10-year Treasury bond rate is 5 percent, the equity risk premium is 5.5 percent, and the federal, state, and local tax rate is 40 percent. The annual change in working capital is $20,000, capital spending for maintenance exceeded depreciation in the prior year by $15,000. Both working capital and the excess of capital spending over depreciation are projected to grow at the same rate as operating income. What is the business worth?

Answer: $2,110,007.

Solutions to these practice exercises and problems are available in the Online Instructor's Manual for instructors using this book.

Chapter Business Cases

Case Study 10–4. Panda Ethanol Goes Public in a Shell Corporation

In early 2006, Panda Ethanol (Panda), owner of ethanol plants in west Texas, decided to explore the possibility of taking its ethanol production business public to take advantage of the high valuations placed on ethanol-related companies in the public market at that time. The firm was confronted with the choice of taking the company public through an initial public offering or by combining with a publicly traded shell corporation through a reverse merger.

After enlisting the services of a local investment banker, Grove Street Investors, Panda chose to "go public" through a reverse merger. This process entailed finding a shell corporation with relatively few shareholders, who were interested in selling their stock. The investment banker identified Cirracor Inc., a publicly traded firm headquartered in Oceanside, California, as a potential merger partner. Cirracor was formed on October 12, 2001, to provide website development services and was traded on the over-the-counter bulletin board market (i.e., a market for very low priced stocks). The website business was not profitable, and the company had only 10 shareholders. As of June 30, 2006, Cirracor listed $4,856 in assets and a negative shareholders' equity of $(259,976). The continued financial viability of the firm was clearly problematic. Given the poor financial condition of Cirracor, the firm's shareholders were interested in either selling their shares for cash or owning even a relatively small portion of a financially viable company to recover their initial investments in Cirracor. Acting on behalf of Panda, Grove Street formed a limited liability company, called Grove Panda, and purchased 2.73 million Cirracor common shares, or 78 percent of the company, for about $475,000.

The merger proposal provided for one share of Cirracor common to be exchanged for each share of Panda Ethanol common outstanding and for Cirracor shareholders to own 4 percent of the newly issued and outstanding common stock of the surviving company. Panda Ethanol shareholders would own the remaining 96 percent. At the end of 2005, Panda had 13.8 million shares outstanding. On June 7, 2006, the merger

Table 10–10 Effects of Reverse Stock Split

	Before Reverse Split		After Reverse Split	
	Shares Outstanding (millions)	Ownership Distribution (%)	Shares Outstanding (millions)	Ownership Distribution (%)
Panda Ethanol	28.8	89.2	28.8	96
Cirracor Inc.	3.5	10.8	1.2	4

agreement was amended to permit Panda Ethanol to issue 15 million new shares through a private placement to raise $90 million. This brought the total Panda shares outstanding to 28.8 million. Cirracor common shares outstanding at that time totaled 3.5 million. However, to achieve the agreed-on ownership distribution, the number of Cirracor shares outstanding had to be reduced. This would be accomplished by an approximate three-for-one reverse stock split immediately prior to the completion of the reverse merger (i.e., each Cirracor common share would be converted into 0.340885 shares of Cirracor common stock). As a consequence of the merger, the previous shareholders of Panda Ethanol were issued 28.8 million new shares of Cirracor common stock. The combined firm now has 30 million shares outstanding, with the Cirracor shareholders owning 1.2 million shares. Table 10–10 illustrates the effect of the reverse stock split.

A special Cirracor shareholders' meeting was required by Nevada law (i.e., the state in which Cirracor was incorporated) in view of the substantial number of new shares that were to be issued as a result of the merger. The proxy statement filed with the Securities and Exchange Commission and distributed to Cirracor shareholders indicated that Grove Panda, a 78 percent owner of Cirracor common, had already indicated that it would vote its shares for the merger and the reverse stock split. Since Cirracor's articles of incorporation required only a simple majority to approve such matters, it was evident to all that approval was imminent.

On November 7, 2006, Panda completed its merger with Cirracor Inc. As a result of the merger, all shares of Panda Ethanol common stock (other than Panda Ethanol shareholders who had executed their dissenters' rights under Delaware law) would cease to have any rights as a shareholder, except the right to receive one share of Cirracor common per share of Panda Ethanol common. Panda Ethanol shareholders choosing to exercise their right to dissent would receive a cash payment for the fair value of their stock on the day immediately before closing Cirracor shareholders had similar dissenting rights under Nevada law. While Cirracor is the surviving corporation, Panda is viewed for accounting purposes as the acquirer. Accordingly, the financial statements shown for the surviving corporation are those of Panda Ethanol.

Discussion Questions

1. Who were Panda Ethanol, Grove Street Investors, Grove Panda, and Cirracor? What were their roles in the case study? Be specific.
2. Discuss the pros and cons of a reverse merger versus an initial public offering for taking a company public. Be specific.
3. Why did Panda Ethanol undertake a private equity placement totaling $90 million shortly before implementing the reverse merger?
4. Why did Panda not directly approach Cirracor with an offer? How were the Panda Grove investment holdings used to influence the outcome of the proposed merger?

Solutions to this case are provided in the Online Instructor's Manual available for instructors using this book.

Case Study 10–5. Cantel Medical Acquires Crosstex International

On August 3, 2005, Cantel Medical Corporation (Cantel), as part of its strategic plan to expand its infection prevention and control business, announced that it had completed the acquisition of Crosstex International Incorporated (Crosstex). Cantel is a leading provider of infection prevention and control products. Crosstex is a privately owned manufacturer and reseller of single-use infection control products used primarily in the dental market.

As a consequence of the transaction, Crosstex became a wholly owned subsidiary of Cantel, a publicly traded firm. For the fiscal year ended April 30, 2005, Crosstex reported revenues of approximately $47.4 million and pretax income of $6.3 million. The purchase price, which is subject to adjustment for the net asset value at July 31, 2005, was $74.2 million, comprising $67.4 million in cash and 384,821 shares of Cantel stock (valued at $6.8 million). Furthermore, Crosstex shareholders could earn another $12 million payable over three years based on future operating income. Each of the three principal executives of Crosstex entered into a three-year employment agreement.

James P. Reilly, president and CEO of Cantel, stated, "We continue to pursue our strategy of acquiring branded niche leaders and expanding in the burgeoning area of infection prevention and control. Crosstex has a reputation for quality branded products and seasoned management." Richard Allen Orofino, Crosstex's president, noted, "We have built Crosstex over the past 50 years as a family business and we continue growing with our proven formula for success. However, with so many opportunities in our sights, we believe Cantel is the perfect partner to aid us in accelerating our growth plans."

Discussion Questions

1. What were the primary reasons Cantel wanted to buy Crosstex? Be specific.
2. What do you believe could have been the primary factors causing Crosstex to accept Cantel's offer? Be specific.
3. What factors might cause Crosstex's net asset value (i.e., the difference between acquired assets and liabilities) to change between signing and closing the agreement of purchase and sale?
4. Speculate why Cantel may have chosen to operate Crosstex as a wholly owned subsidiary following closing. Be specific
5. The purchase price consisted of cash, stock, and an earn-out. What are some factors that might have determined the purchase price from the seller's perspective? From the buyer's perspective? Be specific.

Solutions to this case are provided in the Online Instructor's Manual for instructors using this book.

Deal Structuring and Financing Strategies

11

Structuring the Deal

Payment and Legal Considerations

If you can't convince them, confuse them.

—Harry S. Truman

Inside M&A: News Corp's Power Play in Satellite Broadcasting Seems to Confuse Investors

The share prices of Rupert Murdoch's News Corp, Fox Entertainment Group Inc., and Hughes Electronics Corp (a subsidary of General Motors Corporation) tumbled immediately following the announcement that News Corp had reached an agreement to take a controlling interest in Hughes on April 10, 2003. Investors may have been reacting unfavorably to the complex financial structure of News Corp's proposed deal, the potential earnings dilution, and perhaps to parallels that could be drawn to the ill-fated AOL–Time Warner merger in 2000.

Hughes Electronics is a world leader in providing digital television entertainment, broadband satellite networks and services (DirecTV), and global video and data broadcasting. News Corp is a diversified international media and entertainment company. News Corp's chairman, Rupert Murdoch, had pursued control of Hughes, the parent company of DirecTV, for several years. News Corp's bid, valued at about $6.6 billion, to acquire control of Hughes Electronics Corp and its DirecTV unit gives News Corp a U.S. presence to augment its satellite TV operations in Britain and Asia. By transferring News Corp's stake in Hughes to Fox, in which it owns an 81 percent interest, Fox gained control over 11 million subscribers. It gives Fox more leverage for its cable networks when negotiating rights fees with cable operators that compete with DirecTV. General Motors was motivated to sell its investment in Hughes because of its need for cash.

News Corp financed its purchase of a 34.1 percent stake in Hughes (i.e., GM's 20 percent ownership and 14.1 percent from public shareholders) by paying $3.1 billion in cash to GM, plus 34.3 million in nonvoting American depository receipts (ADRs) in News Corp shares. Hughes's public shareholders were paid with 122.2 million nonvoting ADRs in News Corp, an Australian corporation. (ADRs are shares of foreign companies trading on U.S. exchanges.) Immediately following closing, News Corp's ownership interest was transferred to Fox in exchange for a $4.5 billion promissory note from Fox and 74 million new Fox shares. This transfer saddled Fox with $4.5 billion in debt.

In early 2005, News Corp announced plans to buy all shares of Fox that it did not currently own in a stock swap worth roughly $6 billion. The deal was undertaken to simplify News Corp's capital structure. By owning 100 percent of Fox's shares, control would be centralized in News Corp, enabling the firm to more easily make major business decisions. A simplified deal structure may have been the best strategy for News Corp all along.

Chapter Overview

Once management has determined that an acquisition is the best way to implement the firm's business strategy, a target has been selected, the target's fit with the strategy is well understood, and the preliminary financial analysis is satisfactory, it is time to consider how to properly structure the transaction. In this chapter, the deal-structuring process is described in terms of seven interdependent components. These include the acquisition vehicle, the postclosing organization, the form of payment, the legal form of the selling entity, the form of acquisition, and accounting and tax considerations.

This chapter briefly addresses the form of the acquisition vehicle, postclosing organization, and the legal form of the selling entity because these are discussed in some detail elsewhere in this book. The chapter also discusses the interrelatedness of payment, legal, and tax forms by illustrating how decisions made in one area affect other aspects of the overall deal structure. The focus in this chapter is on the form of payment, form of acquisition, and alternative forms of legal structures in which ownership is conveyed. The implications of alternative tax structures for the deal structuring process, how transactions are recorded for financial reporting purposes, and how they might affect the deal structuring process are discussed in detail in Chapter 12. The major segments of this chapter include the following:

- The Deal Structuring Process
- Form of Acquisition Vehicle
- Postclosing Organization
- Legal Form of the Selling Entity
- Form of Payment or Total Consideration
- Managing Risk and Closing the Gap on Price
- Using Collar Arrangements (Fixed and Variable) to Preserve Shareholder Value
- Form of Acquisition
- Things to Remember

A review of this chapter (including practice questions and answers) is available in the file folder entitled Student Study Guide contained on the CD-ROM accompanying this book. The CD-ROM also contains a Learning Interactions Library, enabling students to test their knowledge of this chapter in a "real-time" environment.

The Deal-Structuring Process

The *deal-structuring process* is fundamentally about satisfying as many of the primary objectives (or needs) of the parties involved and determining how risk will be shared. Common examples of high-priority buyer objectives include paying a "reasonable" purchase price, using stock in lieu of cash (if the acquirer's stock is believed to be overvalued), and having the seller finance a portion of the purchase price by carrying a seller's note. Buyers may also want to put a portion of the purchase price in an escrow account, defer a portion of the price, or make a certain percentage of the purchase price contingent on realizing some future event to minimize risk. Common closing conditions desired by buyers include obtaining employee retention and noncompete agreements. Sellers, who also are publicly traded companies, commonly are driven to maximize purchase price. However, their desire to maximize price may be tempered by other considerations, such as the perceived ease of doing the deal or a desire to obtain a tax-free transaction. Private or family-owned firms may be less motivated by price than by other factors, such as protecting the firm's future reputation and current employees, as well as obtaining rights to license patents or utilize other valuable assets.

Risk sharing refers to the extent to which the acquirer assumes all, some, or none of the liabilities, disclosed or otherwise, of the target. The appropriate deal structure is that which satisfies, subject to an acceptable level of risk, as many of the primary objectives of the parties involved as necessary to reach overall agreement. The process may be highly complex in large transactions involving multiple parties, approvals, forms of payment, and sources of financing. Decisions made in one area inevitably affect other areas of the overall deal structure. Containing risk associated with a complex deal is analogous to catching a water balloon. Squeezing one end of the balloon simply forces the contents to shift elsewhere.

Key Components of the Deal-Structuring Process

Figure 11–1 summarizes the deal-structuring process. The process begins with addressing a set of key questions, whose answers greatly influence the primary components of the entire structuring process. Answers to these questions help define initial negotiating positions, potential risks, options for managing risk, levels of tolerance for risk, and conditions under which the buyer or seller will "walk away" from the negotiations.

The *acquisition vehicle* refers to the legal structure created to acquire the target company. The *postclosing organization*, or structure, is the organizational and legal framework used to manage the combined businesses following the consummation of the transaction. Commonly used structures for both the acquisition vehicle and postclosing organization include the corporate or division, holding company, joint venture (JV), partnership, limited liability company (LLC), and employee stock ownership plan (ESOP) structures.

For transactions in which the target shares are purchased using the acquirer's stock or cash, the acquirer often creates a wholly owned acquisition subsidiary to transfer ownership. The transfer of ownership is commonly accomplished through a forward triangular three-party merger or a reverse triangular three-party merger. The *forward triangular merger* involves the acquisition subsidiary being merged with the target and the acquiring subsidiary surviving. The *reverse triangular merger* entails the merger of the target with the acquiring subsidiary, with the target surviving. Because the surviving entity is owned entirely by the parent, the parent now indirectly owns the target's assets and liabilities. The advantages and disadvantages of the forward and reverse triangular mergers, along with other mechanisms for conveying ownership, are discussed in more detail later in this chapter.

Although the two structures are often the same before and after completion of the transaction, the postclosing organization may differ from the acquisition vehicle depending on the acquirer's strategic objectives for the combined firms. An acquirer may choose a corporate or division structure to purchase the target firm and rapidly integrate the acquired business to realize synergies. Alternatively, the acquirer may opt to undertake the transaction using a JV or partnership vehicle to share risk. Once the operation of

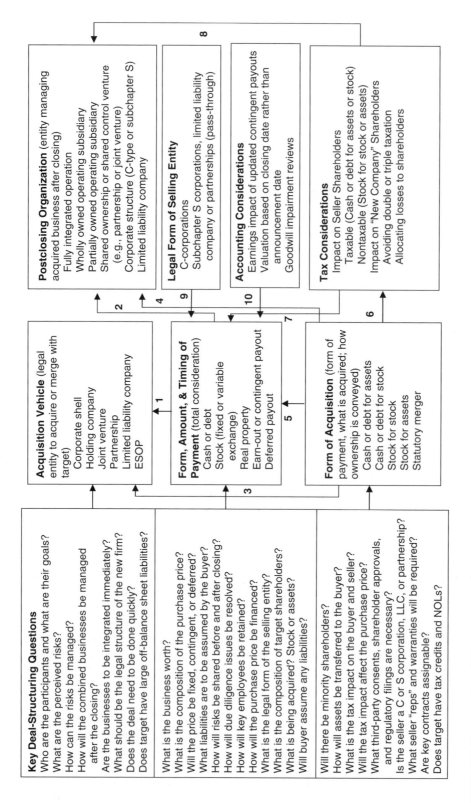

FIGURE 11–1 Mergers and acquisitions deal structuring process.

the acquired entity is better understood, the acquirer may choose to buy out its partners and operate within a corporate or division structure. Similarly, the acquirer may complete the transaction using a holding company legal structure. The acquirer may operate the acquired firm as a wholly owned subsidiary to preserve the attractive characteristics of its culture for an extended time period and later move to a more traditional corporate or division framework.

The *form of payment*, or total consideration, may consist of cash, common stock, debt, or a combination of all three types. The payment may be fixed at a moment in time, contingent on the future performance of the acquired unit, or payable over time. The form of payment influences the selection of the appropriate form of acquisition and postclosing organization. The *form of acquisition* reflects what is being acquired (stock or assets) and, as such, tax considerations. *Accounting considerations* refer to the potential impact of financial reporting requirements on the earnings volatility of business combinations due to the need to periodically revalue acquired assets to their fair market value as new information becomes available. *Tax considerations* entail tax structures and strategies that determine whether a transaction is taxable or nontaxable to the seller's shareholders and influence the choice of postclosing organization, which affects the potential for double taxation and the allocation of losses to owners. The form of acquisition also defines how the ownership of assets will be conveyed from the seller to the buyer, either by rule of law, as in a merger, or through transfer and assignment, as in a purchase of assets. The *legal form of the selling entity* (i.e., whether it is a C or S chapter corporation, LLC, or partnership) also has tax implications. These considerations are explored in greater detail later in this chapter.

Common Linkages

For simplicity, many of the linkages or interactions that reflect how decisions made in one area affect other aspects of the deal are not shown in Figure 11–1. Common linkages or interactions among various components of the deal structure are illustrated through examples, described next.

Form of Payment Influences Choice of Acquisition Vehicle and Postclosing Organization (Figure 11–1, Arrows 1 and 2)

If the buyer and seller agree on a price, the buyer may offer a purchase price that is contingent on the future performance of the target. The buyer may choose to acquire and operate the acquired company as a wholly owned subsidiary within a holding company during the term of the "earn-out." This facilitates monitoring the operation's performance during the earn-out period and minimizes the potential for postearn-out litigation initiated by earn-out participants.

Form of Acquisition (Figure 11–1, Arrows 3–6) Effects

- **Choice of acquisition vehicle and postclosing organization.** If the form of acquisition is a statutory merger, all known and unknown or contingent liabilities are transferred to the buyer. Under these circumstances, the buyer may choose to change the type of acquisition vehicle to one better able to protect the buyer from the liabilities of the target, such as a holding company arrangement. Acquisition vehicles and postclosing organizations that facilitate a sharing of potential risk or the purchase price include JV or partnership arrangements.

- **Form, timing, and amount of payment.** The assumption of all seller liabilities through a merger also may induce the buyer to change the form of payment by deferring some portion of the purchase price to decrease the present value of the cost of the transaction. The buyer also may attempt to negotiate a lower overall purchase price.
- **Tax considerations.** The transaction may be tax free to the seller if the acquirer uses its stock to acquire substantially all of the seller's assets or stock in a stock-for-stock or stock-for-assets purchase. See Chapter 12 for M&A-related tax issues.

Tax Considerations (Figure 11–1, Arrows 7 and 8) Effects

- **Amount, timing, and composition of the purchase price.** If the transaction is taxable to the target's shareholders, it is likely that the purchase price will be increased to compensate the target's shareholders for their tax liability. The increase in the purchase price may affect the form of payment. The acquirer may maintain the present value of the total cost of the acquisition by deferring some portion of the purchase price by altering the terms to include more debt or installment payments.
- **Selection of the postclosing organization.** The decision as to what constitutes the appropriate organizational structure of the combined businesses is affected by several tax-related factors: the desire to minimize taxes and pass through losses to the owners. The S corporation, LLC, and the partnership eliminate double-taxation problems. Moreover, current operating losses, loss carryforwards or carrybacks, or tax credits generated by the combined businesses can be passed through to the owners if the postclosing organization is a partnership or a LLC.

Legal Form of Selling Entity Affects the Form of Payment (Figure 11–1, Arrow 9)

Because of the potential for deferring shareholder tax liabilities, target firms that qualify as C corporations often prefer to exchange their stock or assets for acquirer shares. In contrast, owners of S corporations, LLCs, and partnerships are largely indifferent as to whether the transaction is taxable or nontaxable, because 100 percent of the proceeds of the sale are taxed at the shareholders ordinary tax rate. Table 11–1 provides a summary of these common linkages.

Table 11–1   Summary of Common Linkages within the Deal-Structuring Process

Component of Deal-Structuring Process	Influences Choice Of
Form, amount, and timing of payment	Acquisition vehicle Postclosing organization Accounting considerations
Form of acquisition	Acquisition vehicle Postclosing organization Tax structure (taxable or nontaxable) Form, amount, and timing of payment
Tax considerations	Form, amount, and timing of payment Postclosing organization
Legal form of selling entity	Tax structure (taxable or nontaxable)

Accounting Considerations Affect the Form, Amount, and Timing of Payment (Figure 11–1, Arrow 10)

Earn-outs and other forms of contingent considerations are recorded at fair value on the acquisition date under recent changes in financial reporting guidelines (i.e., SFAS 141R and SFAS 157) effective December 15, 2009, and subsequently adjusted to fair value as new information comes available. Such changes can increase or decrease reported earnings. Since earn-outs must be recorded at fair value on the acquisition date and subsequently adjusted, the potential for increased earnings volatility may make performance-related payouts less attractive as a form of payment. Furthermore, the use of equity securities to pay for target firms may be less attractive due to recent changes in financial reporting requirements. The value of the transaction is not known until the closing, since the value of the transaction is measured at the close of the deal rather than at the announcement date. If the length of time between announcement and closing is substantial due to the need to obtain regulatory approval, the value of the deal may change significantly. Finally, the requirement to review periodically the book or carrying value of such assets as goodwill for impairment (e.g., fair market value is less than book value) may discourage acquirers from overpaying for a target firm due to the potential for future asset write-downs. These financial reporting requirements are discussed in more detail in Chapter 12.

Form of Acquisition Vehicle

The acquisition vehicle is the legal entity used to acquire the target and generally to continue to own and operate the acquired company after closing. Which form of legal entity is used has markedly different risk and tax implications for the acquirer. The various forms of potential acquisition vehicles and their specific advantages and disadvantages are discussed in considerable detail in Chapter 14. They include the corporate or division structure, limited liability companies, JV corporations, holding companies, general and limited liability partnerships (LLPs), and ESOPs.

The corporate structure or some variation is the most commonly used acquisition vehicle. In such an arrangement, the acquired company generally is integrated into an existing operating division or product line within the corporation. Used as an acquisition vehicle, the JV corporation or partnership offers a lower level of risk than a direct acquisition of the target firm by one of the JV corporate owners or individual partners. By acquiring the target firm through the JV, the corporate investor limits the potential liability to the extent of its investment in the JV corporation. For small, privately owned firms, an ESOP structure may be a convenient vehicle for transferring the owner's interest in the business to the employees (see Chapter 10). Non-U.S. buyers intending to make additional acquisitions may prefer a holding company structure. The advantages of this structure over a corporate merger for both foreign and domestic firms are the ability to control other companies by owning only a small portion of the company's voting stock and to gain this control without getting shareholder approval.

Postclosing Organization

What form the postclosing structure takes depends largely on the objectives of the acquiring company. These objectives could include the following: (1) facilitating postclosing integration, (2) minimizing risk to owners from the target's known and unknown liabilities, (3) minimizing taxes, and (4) passing through losses to shelter the owners' tax liabilities.

If the acquirer is interested in integrating the target business immediately following closing, the corporate or division structure may be most desirable, because the acquirer is most likely to be able to gain the greatest control using this structure. In other structures, such as JVs and partnerships, decision making may be slower or more contentious as a result of dispersed ownership. Decision making is more likely to depend on close cooperation and consensus building, which may slow efforts to rapidly integrate the acquired company (see Chapter 6).

In contrast, a holding company structure in which the acquired company is managed as a wholly owned subsidiary may be preferable when an earn-out is involved, the target is a foreign firm, or the acquirer is a financial investor. In an earn-out agreement, the acquired firm must be operated largely independently from other operations of the acquiring firm to minimize the potential for lawsuits. If the acquired firm fails to achieve the goals required to receive the earn-out payment, the acquirer may be sued for allegedly taking actions that prevented the acquired firm from reaching the necessary goals. When the target is a foreign firm, it is often appropriate to operate it separately from the rest of the acquirer's operations because of the potential disruption from significant cultural differences. Prevailing laws in the foreign country may also affect the form of the organization. Finally, a financial buyer may use a holding company structure because it has no interest in operating the target firm for any length of time.

A partnership or JV structure may be appropriate if the risk associated with the target firm is believed to be high. Consequently, partners or JV owners can limit their financial exposure to the amount they invested in the partnership or JV. The acquired firm also may benefit from being owned by a partnership or JV because of the expertise that may be provided by the different partners or owners. The availability of such expertise actually may reduce the overall risk of managing the business.

Finally, a partnership or LLC may be most appropriate for eliminating double taxation and passing through current operating losses, tax credits, and loss carryforwards and carrybacks to the owners. Cerberus Capital Management's conversion of its purchase of General Motors Acceptance Corporation (GMAC) from General Motors in 2006 from a C corporation to a limited liability company at closing reflects the desire to eliminate the double-taxation of income while continuing to limit shareholder liability. Similarly, legendary investor Sam Zell masterminded a leveraged buyout of media company Tribune Corporation in 2007 in which an ESOP was used as the acquisition vehicle and a subchapter-S corporation as the postclosing organization. The change in legal structure enabled the firm to save an estimated $348 million in taxes. S corporation profits are not taxed if distributed to shareholders, which in this case included a tax-exempt ESOP as the primary shareholder. However, the deal's complexity and extensive leverage rendered it unable to withstand the meltdown of the credit markets in 2008. See Case Study 12–3 for more details.

Legal Form of the Selling Entity

Whether the seller will care about the form of the transaction (i.e., whether stock or assets are sold) may depend on whether the seller is an S, limited liability company, partnership, or C corporation (i.e., corporations for which an election to be subject to subchapter S of the Internal Revenue Code has not been made). As noted previously, C corporations are subject to double taxation, whereas owners of S corporations, partnerships and LLCs are not (see Exhibit 11–1).

Exhibit 11–1 How the Legal Form of the Seller Affects the Form of Payment

Assume a business owner starting with an initial investment of $100,000 sells her business for $1 million. Different legal structures have different tax impacts.

1. After-tax proceeds of a stock sale are ($1,000,000 – $100,000) × (1 – 0.15) = $765,000. The S corporation shareholder or limited liability company member holding shares for more than one year pays a maximum capital gains tax equal to 15 percent of the gain on the sale.[1]

2. After-tax proceeds from an asset sale are ($1,000,000 – $100,000) × (1 – 0.4) × (1 – 0.15) = $900,000 × 0.51 = $459,000. A C corporation typically pays tax equal to 40 percent (i.e., 35 percent federal and 5 percent state and local) and the shareholder pays a maximum capital gains tax equal to 15 percent, resulting in double taxation of the gain on sale.

Implications

1. C corporation shareholders generally prefer acquirer stock for their stock or assets to avoid double taxation.

2. S corporation and LLC owners often are indifferent to an asset sale or stock sale because 100 percent of the corporation's income passes through the corporation untaxed to the owners, who are subject to their own personal tax rates. The S corporation shareholders or LLC members still may prefer a share-for-share exchange if they are interested in deferring their tax liability or are attracted by the long-term growth potential of the acquirer's stock.

---

[1]This is the current capital gains tax as of the publication date of this text.

Form of Payment or Total Consideration

Determining the proper form of payment can be a complicated exercise. Each form of payment can have significantly different implications for the parties involved in the transaction. Of the total transactions between 1980 and 2006, on average, cash accounted for 45 percent, stock for 30 percent, and cash–stock combinations for 25 percent of the transactions (*Mergerstat Review*, 2007).

Cash

The use of cash is the simplest and most commonly used means of payment for acquiring shares or assets. Although cash payments generally result in an immediate tax liability for the target company's shareholders, there is no ambiguity about the value of the transaction, as long as no portion of the payment is deferred. Whether cash is the predominant form of payment depends on a variety of factors. These include the acquirer's current leverage, potential near-term earnings per share dilution, the seller's preference for cash or acquirer stock, and the extent to which the acquirer wishes to maintain control.

A highly leveraged acquirer may be unable to raise sufficient funds at an affordable rate of interest to make a cash purchase practical. Issuing new shares may result in significant erosion of the combined firm's earnings per share immediately following closing, which may prove to be unacceptable to investors. The sellers' preference for stock or cash reflects their potential capital gains and the attractiveness of the acquirer's shares. Finally, a bidder may choose to use cash rather than issue voting shares if the voting control of its dominant shareholder is threatened as a result of the issuance of voting stock to acquire the target firm (Faccio and Marsulis, 2005). The preference for using cash appears to be much higher in western European countries, where ownership tends to be more heavily concentrated in publicly traded firms than in the United States. In Europe, 63 percent of publicly traded firms have a single shareholder who directly or indirectly controls 20 percent or more of the voting shares; in the United States, the figure is 28 percent (Faccio and Lang, 2002).

Noncash Forms of Payment

The use of common equity may involve certain tax advantages for the parties involved. This is especially true for the selling company shareholders. However, the use of shares is much more complicated than cash, because it requires compliance with the prevailing security laws (see Chapter 2). Moreover, the acquirer's share price may suffer if investors believe that the newly issued shares will result in a long-term dilution in earnings per share (EPS, a reduction in an individual shareholder's claim on future earnings and the assets that produce those earnings). The use of convertible preferred stock or debt can be attractive to both buyers and sellers. Convertible preferred stock provides some downside protection to sellers in the form of continuing dividends, while providing upside potential if the acquirer's common stock price increases above the conversion point. Acquirers often find convertible debt attractive because of the tax deductibility of interest payments. The major disadvantage in using securities of any type is that the seller may find them unattractive. Debt instruments may be unacceptable because of the perceived high risk of default associated with the issuer. When offered common equity, shareholders of the selling company may feel the growth prospects of the acquirer's stock may be limited or the historical volatility of the stock makes it unacceptably risky. Finally, debt or equity securities may be illiquid because of the small size of the resale market.

Other forms of payment include real property, rights to intellectual property, royalties, earn-outs, and contingent payments. Real property consists of such things as a parcel of real estate. So-called like-kind exchanges or swaps may have favorable tax consequences (see Chapter 12). Real property exchanges are most common in commercial real estate transactions. Granting the seller access to valuable licenses or franchises limits the use of cash or securities at the time of closing; however, it does raise the possibility that the seller could become a future competitor. The use of debt or other types of deferred payments reduces the overall present value of the purchase price to the buyer by shifting some portion of the purchase price into the future.

Using a Combination of Cash and Stock

Bidders may use a combination of cash and noncash forms of payment as part of their bidding strategies to broaden the appeal to target shareholders. Payment options may include all cash, all stock, and a combination of cash and stock. The cash option appeals to those shareholders who either place a high value on liquidity or do not view acquirer stock as attractive. The all-stock option is attractive to target shareholders who may be interested in deferring their tax liabilities in a share-for-share exchange or who find the acquirer shares attractive. Finally, the combination of cash and stock should appeal to those who value cash but also want to participate in any appreciation in the acquirer's stock.

The bidding strategy of offering target firm shareholders multiple-payment options increase the likelihood that more target firm shareholders will participate in a tender offer. Such bidding strategies are common in "auction" environments or when the bidder is unable to borrow the amount necessary to support an all-cash offer or unwilling to absorb the potential earnings per share dilution in an all-stock offer. However, the multiple-option bidding strategy introduces a certain level of uncertainty in determining the amount of cash the acquirer ultimately has to pay out to target firm shareholders, since the number choosing the all-cash or cash-and-stock option is not known prior to the completion of the tender offer. Acquirers resolve this issue by including a "proration clause" in tender offers and merger agreements, which allows them to fix the total amount of cash they ultimately have to pay out at the time the tender offer is initiated. How this is done is illustrated later in Case Study 11–6.

Case Study 11–1 illustrates how the form of payment can be used as a key component of a takeover strategy. Note how Equity Office Properties' board carefully weighed the greater certainty of Blackstone's all-cash offer against the greater value of the combination of cash and stock offered by Vornado in making its decision of to whom to sell.

Case Study 11–1 Blackstone Outmaneuvers Vornado to Buy Equity Office Properties

Reflecting the wave of capital flooding into commercial real estate and the growing power of private equity investors, the Blackstone Group (Blackstone) succeeded in acquiring Equity Office Properties (EOP) following a bidding war with Vornado Realty Trust (Vornado). On February 8, 2007, Blackstone Group closed the purchase of EOP for $39 billion, consisting of about $23 billion in cash and $16 billion in assumed debt.

EOP was established in 1976 by Sam Zell, a veteran property investor known for his ability to acquire distressed properties. Blackstone, one of the nation's largest private equity buyout firms, entered the commercial real estate market for the first time in 2005. In contrast, Vornado, a publicly traded real estate investment trust, had a long-standing reputation for savvy investing in the commercial real estate market. EOP's management had been under fire from investors for failing to sell properties fast enough and distribute the proceeds to shareholders.

EOP signed a definitive agreement to be acquired by Blackstone for $48.50 per share in cash in November 2006, subject to approval by EOP's shareholders. Reflecting the view that EOP's breakup value exceeded $48.50 per share, Vornado bid $52 per share, 60 percent in cash and the remainder in Vornado stock. Blackstone countered with a bid of $54 per share, if EOP would raise the breakup fee to $500 million from $200 million. Ostensibly designed to compensate Blackstone for expenses incurred in its takeover attempt, the breakup fee also raised the cost of acquiring EOP by another bidder, which as the new owner would actually pay the fee. Within a week, Vornado responded with a bid valued at $56 per share. While higher, EOP continued to favor Blackstone's offer since the value was more

Continued

> ### Case Study 11–1 Blackstone Outmaneuvers Vornado to Buy Equity Office Properties — Cont'd
>
> certain than Vornado's bid. It could take as long as three to four months for Vornado to get shareholder approval. The risks were that the value of Vornado's stock could decline and shareholders could nix the deal. Reluctant to raise its offer price, Vornado agreed to increase the cash portion of the purchase price and pay shareholders the cash more quickly than had been envisioned in its initial offer. However, Vornado did not offer to pay EOP shareholders a fee if Vornado's shareholders did not approve the deal. The next day, Blackstone increased its bid to $55.25 and eventually to $55.50 at Zell's behest in exchange for an increase in the breakup fee to $720 million. Vornado's failure to counter gave Blackstone the win. On the news that Blackstone had won, Vornado 's stock jumped by 5.8 percent and EOP's fell by 1 percent to just below Blackstone's final offer price.
>
> *Discussion Questions*
>
> 1. Describe Blackstone's negotiating strategy with EOP to counter Vornado's bids.
> 2. What could Vornado have done to assuage EOP's concerns about the certainty of the value of the stock portion of its offer? Be specific.
> 3. Explain the reaction of EOP's and Vornado's share prices to the news that Blackstone was the wining bidder. What does the movement in Vornado's share price tell you about the likelihood that the firm's shareholders would have approved the takeover of EOP?
>
> *A solution to this case is provided in the Online Instructor's Manual for instructors using this book.*

Managing Risk and Closing the Gap on Price

In an all-cash transaction, the risks accrue entirely to the buyer. Despite exhaustive due diligence, there is no assurance that the buyer will have uncovered all the risks associated with the target. During the negotiation phase, the buyer and seller maneuver to share the perceived risk and apportion the potential returns. In doing so, substantial differences arise between what the buyer is willing to pay and what the seller believes the business is worth.

Postclosing balance-sheet adjustments and escrow accounts, earn-outs and other contingent payments, contingent value rights, staging investment, rights to intellectual property, licensing fees, and consulting agreements commonly are used to consummate the deal, when buyers and sellers cannot reach agreement on purchase price.

Postclosing Price Adjustments

Postclosing adjustment price mechanisms include escrow or holdback accounts and adjustments to the target's balance sheet. Both mechanisms rely on an audit of the target firm to determine its "true" value. Generally, the cost of the audit is shared by the buyer and seller. Such mechanisms generally are applicable only when what is being acquired is clearly identifiable, such as in a purchase of tangible assets. Moreover, such mechanisms most often are used in cash rather than stock-for-stock purchases, particularly when the number of target shareholders is large. Attempting to recover a portion of the shares paid to target shareholders may trigger litigation. Also, retaining a portion of the shares paid to target shareholders may communicate suspected problems with the target and trigger a sale by target shareholders of the shares. Google's share-for-share purchase of YouTube involved a holdback of a portion of the purchase price because of the potential for copyright infringement litigation.

With *escrow accounts*, the buyer retains a portion of the purchase price until a post-closing audit has been completed. Balance-sheet adjustments most often are used in purchases of assets when the elapsed time between the agreement on price and the actual closing date is lengthy. This may be a result of the need to obtain regulatory or shareholder approvals or a result of ongoing due diligence. During this period, balance-sheet items, particularly those related to working capital, may change significantly.

As indicated in Table 11–2, to protect the buyer or seller, the buyer reduces the total purchase price by an amount equal to the decrease in net working capital or shareholders' equity of the target and increases the purchase price by any increase in these measures during this period. Buyers and sellers generally view purchase price adjustments as a form of insurance against any erosion or accretion in asset values, such as receivables or inventories. Such adjustments protect the buyer from receiving a lower dollar value of assets than originally anticipated or the seller from transferring to the buyer more assets than expected. The actual payments are made between the buyer and seller after a comprehensive audit of the target's balance sheet by an independent auditor is completed some time after closing.

Earn-Outs and Other Contingent Payments

Earn-outs and warrants frequently are used whenever the buyer and seller cannot agree on the probable performance of the seller's business over some future period or when the parties involved wish to participate in the upside potential of the business. Earn-out agreements may also be used to retain and motivate key target firm managers. An *earn-out agreement* is a financial contract in which a portion of the purchase price of a company is to be paid in the future, contingent on the realization of a previously agreed-on future earnings level or some other performance measure. The terms of the earn-out are stipulated in the agreement of purchase and sale. Subscription warrants, more commonly known as *warrants*, represent a type of security often issued with a bond or preferred stock. The warrant entitles the holder to purchase an amount of common stock at a stipulated price. The exercise price is usually higher than the price at the time the warrant is issued. Warrants may be converted over a period of many months to many years. In contrast, a rights offering to buy common shares normally has an exercise price below the current market value of the stock and a life of four to eight weeks.

The earn-out normally requires that the acquired business be operated as a wholly owned subsidiary of the acquiring company under the management of the former owners or key executives of the business. Both the buyer and seller are well advised to keep the calculation of such goals and resulting payments as simple as possible, because disputes frequently arise as a result of the difficulty in measuring actual performance to the goals.

Table 11–2 Balance-Sheet Adjustments ($ millions)

| | Purchase Price | | Purchase Price Reduction | Purchase Price Increase |
	At Time of Negotiation	At Closing		
If working capital equals	110	100	10	
If working capital equals	110	125		15

Earn-outs may take many forms. Some earn-outs are payable only if a certain performance threshold is achieved; others depend on average performance over a number of periods. Still other arrangements may involve periodic payments depending on the achievement of interim performance measures rather than a single, lump-sum payment at the end of the earn-out period. Moreover, the value of the earn-out is often capped. In some cases, the seller may have the option to repurchase the company at some predetermined percentage of the original purchase price in case the buyer is unable to pay the earn-out at maturity.

Exhibit 11–2 illustrates how an earn-out formula could be constructed, reflecting the considerations outlined in the preceding paragraph. The purchase price consists of two components. At closing, the seller receives a lump-sum payment of $100 million. The seller and the buyer agree to a baseline projection for a three-year period and that the seller would receive a fixed multiple of the average annual performance of the acquired business in excess of the baseline projection. Thus, the earn-out provides an incentive for the seller to operate the business as effectively as possible. Normally, the baseline projection is what the buyer used to value the seller's business. Shareholder value for the buyer is created whenever the acquired business's actual performance exceeds the baseline projection and the multiple applied by investors at the end of the three-year period exceeds the multiple used to calculate the earn-out payment. This assumes that the baseline projection accurately values the business and the buyer does not overpay. By multiplying the anticipated multiple investors will pay for operating cash flow at the end of the three-year period by projected cash flow, it is possible to estimate the potential increase in shareholder value.

Exhibit 11–2 Hypothetical Earn-Out as Part of the Purchase Price

Purchase Price

1. **Lump sum payment at closing.** The seller receives $100 million.
2. **Earn-out payment.** The seller receives four times the excess of the actual average annual net operating cash flow over the baseline projection at the end of three years not to exceed $35 million. This is calculated in Table 11–3.

Table 11–3 Calculations for Earn-Out Payment

	Year 1	Year 2	Year 3
Baseline projection (net cash flow)	$10	$12	$15
Actual performance (net cash flow)	$15	$20	$25

Note: The first full year of ownership is the base year, on which calculations are based.

Earn-out at the end of three years:[1]

$$\frac{(\$15 - \$10) + (\$20 - \$12) + (\$25 - \$15)}{3} \times 4 = \$30.67$$

Potential increase in shareholder value:[2]

$$\left[\frac{(\$15 - \$10) + (\$20 - \$12) + (\$25 - \$15)}{3} \times 10\right] - \$30.67 = \$46$$

---

[1]The cash flow multiple of 4 applied to the earn-out is a result of negotiation before closing.

[2]The cash flow multiple of 10 applied to the potential increase in shareholder value for the buyer is the multiple the buyer anticipates that investors would apply to a three-year average of actual operating cash flow at the end of the three-year period.

Earn-outs tend to shift risk from the acquirer to the seller, in that a higher price is paid only when the seller has met or exceeded certain performance criteria. However, earn-outs also may create some perverse results during implementation. Management motivation may be lost if the acquired firm does not perform well enough to achieve any payout under the earn-out formula or if the acquired firm substantially exceeds the performance targets, effectively guaranteeing the maximum payout under the plan. Moreover, the management of the acquired firm may have an incentive to take actions not in the best interests of the acquirer. For example, management may cut back on certain expenses such as advertising and training to improve the operation's current cash-flow performance. In addition, management may make only those investments that improve short-term profits at the expense of investments that may generate immediate losses but favorably affect profits in the long term. As the end of the earn-out period approaches, management may postpone all investments to maximize their bonus under the earn-out plan. To avoid various pitfalls associated with earn-outs, it may be appropriate to establish more than one target. For example, it may be appropriate to include a revenue, income, and investment target, although this adds to the complexity.

Earn-outs, also known as *contingent payouts*, accounted for roughly 2.5 percent of total transactions in the 1990s. Kohers and Ang (2000) and Datar, Frankel, and Wolfson (2001) found that earn-outs are more commonly used when the targets are small, private firms or subsidiaries of larger firms rather than for large, publicly traded firms. Such contracts are more easily written and enforced when there are relatively few shareholders. Earn-outs tend to be most common in high-tech and service industries, when the acquirer and target firms are in different industries, when the target firm has a significant number of assets not recorded on the balance sheet or access to information not known to the buyer, and when little integration will be attempted.

The Kohers and Ang study also showed that earn-outs on average account for 45 percent of the total purchase price paid for private firms and 33 percent for subsidiary acquisitions. Moreover, target firm shareholders tend to realize about 62 percent of the potential earn-out amount. In transactions involving earn-outs, acquirers earn abnormal returns of 5.39 percent around the announcement date, in contrast to transactions not involving contingent payments, in which abnormal returns to acquirers tend to be zero or negative. The authors argue that the positive abnormal returns to acquiring company shareholders are a result of investor perception that, with an earn-out, the buyer is less likely to overpay and more likely to retain key target firm talent.

Earn-outs may also be based on share of equity ownership when the business is sold. For example, assume an entrepreneur believes the business is worth $20 million without additional investment and the private equity investor estimates the business to be worth only $15 million without additional investment. The entrepreneur who wants $5 million in equity investment perceives the market value including the equity infusion to be $25 million (i.e., $20 million stand alone plus $5 million in equity). The implied ownership distribution is 80/20, with the entrepreneur receiving 80 percent (i.e., $20/$25) and the equity investor receiving 20 percent (i.e., $5/$25).

However, the equity investor sees the value of the business including the equity investment to be only $20 million (i.e., $15 million stand alone plus $5 million equity investment). The implied ownership is 75/25, with the entrepreneur receiving only 75 percent ownership (i.e., $15/$20) and the equity investor 25 percent ownership (i.e., $5/$20). The ownership gap of 5 percentage points can be closed by the entrepreneur and equity investor agreeing to the 80/20 distribution if certain cash flow or profit targets can be reached prior to exiting the business sufficient to justify the $25 million net present value (see Exhibit 11–3).

Exhibit 11–3 Earn-Outs Based on Ownership Distribution

Distribution of ownership equity if average annual free cash flow is less than $5 million in years 3–5:[1]

Entrepreneur	75%
Private investor	25%
Total	100%

Distribution of ownership equity if average annual free cash flow is greater than $5 million in years 3–5:

Entrepreneur	80%
Private Investor	20%
Total	100%

---

[1]A three-year average cash flow figure is used to measure performance to ensure that the actual performance is sustainable as opposed to an aberration.

Effective January 1, 2009, revisions to accounting standards (Statement of Financial Accounting Standards 141R) that apply to business combinations may make earn-outs less attractive than in the past. The fair value of earn-outs and other contingent payouts must be estimated and recorded on the acquisition closing date. Changes in fair value resulting from changes in the likelihood or amount of the contingent payout must be recorded as charges to the income statement at that time. Under earlier accounting standards, contingent payments were charged against income only when they were actually paid. For more detail on SFAS 141R, see Chapter 12.

Contingent Value Rights

In M&A transactions, *contingent value rights* (CVRs) are commitments by the issuing company (i.e., the acquirer) to pay additional cash or securities to the holder of the CVR (i.e., the seller) if the share price of the issuing company falls below a specified level at some date in the future. CVRs provide a guarantee of future value as of a point in time of one of various forms of payment made to the seller, such as cash, stock, or debt. While relatively rare, such rights are sometimes granted in deals in which there are large differences between the buyer and seller with respect to the purchase price. Such rights may also be used when the target firm wants protection for any remaining minority shareholders fearful of being treated unfairly by the buyer. In Tembec, Inc.'s 1999 acquisition of Crestbrook Forest Products, Ltd., each Crestbrook shareholder received a contingent value right, enabling the shareholder to receive a one-time payment, on March 31, 2000, of up to a maximum of $1.50 per share. The size of the payout depended on the amount by which the average price of wood pulp for 1999 exceeded $549/ton. MacAndrews & Forbes provided each shareholder of Abex Inc., in a 1995 transaction, a contingent value right per common share equal to $10 to ensure that Abex shareholders would receive at least that amount per share. In 2008, French utility EDF was able to overcome resistance from certain British Energy shareholders by offering a combination of cash and a contingent value right enabling investors to share in future profits whenever electrical output and energy prices rise. The amount of future payouts to shareholders would depend on the amount of the increase in profits.

Chatterjee and Yan (2008) argue that CVRs are issued most often when the acquiring firm issues stock to the target firm's shareholders, because it believes its shares are undervalued. Such a situation often is referred to as *information asymmetry*, in which one party has access to more information than others. The CVR represents a declaration by the acquirer that its current share price represents a floor and it is confident the price will rise in the future. Firms offering CVRs in their acquisitions tend to believe their shares are more undervalued than those acquirers using cash or stock without CVRs as a form of payment. The authors found that most CVRs are issued in conjunction with either common or preferred stock. Acquirers offering CVRs experience announcement period abnormal returns of 5.3 percent. Targets receiving CVRs earn abnormal announcement period returns of 18.4 percent. The size of the abnormal announcement period return is greater than for firms not offering CVRs. The authors argue that investors view acquirers who offer CVRs as having knowledge of the postmerger performance of the acquired business not available to the broader market. Hence, the issuance of the CVR expresses buyer confidence in the future success of the transaction.

Earn-outs are different from CVRs. Earn-outs represent call options for the target representing claims on future upside performance and are employed when there is substantial disagreement between the buyer and seller on price. In contrast, CVRs are put options limiting downside loss on the form of payment received by sellers.

Distributed or Staged Payouts

The purchase price payments can be contingent on the target satisfying an agreed-on milestone. Such milestones could include achieving a profit or cash-flow target, the successful launch of a new product, obtaining regulatory or patent approval, and the like. By distributing the payout over time, the risk to the acquirer is managed, in that it reduces some of the uncertainty about future cash flows. An acquirer could also avoid having to finance the entire cash purchase price in a large transaction at one time. In 2008, Novartis, a Swiss pharmaceuticals firm, acquired Nestle's controlling interest in Alcon, an eye care company, for $39 billion. Novartis would pay $11 billion for 25 percent of Alcon at closing and $28 billion in 2010 or 2011 for Nestle's remaining 52 percent stake. In doing so, Novartis was able to defer financing the bulk of the transaction amid the 2008 credit crisis.

Rights, Royalties, and Fees

Other forms of payment that can be used to close the gap between what the buyer is willing to offer and what the seller expects include such things as the rights to intellectual property, royalties from licenses, and fee-based consulting or employment agreements. Having the right to use a proprietary process or technology for free or below the prevailing market rate may be of interest to the former owners who are considering pursuing business opportunities in which the process or technology would be useful. Note that such an arrangement, if priced at below market rates or free to the seller, represent taxable income to the seller. Obviously, such arrangements should be coupled with reasonable agreements not to compete in the same industry as their former firm. Contracts may be extended to both the former owners and their family members. By spreading the payment of consulting fees or salary over a number of years, the seller may be able to reduce the income tax liability that might have resulted from receiving a larger lump-sum purchase price.

Table 11–4 summarizes the various forms of payment in terms of their advantages and disadvantages. Note the wide range of options available to satisfy the various needs of the parties to the transaction.

Using Collar Arrangements (Fixed and Variable) to Preserve Shareholder Value

A *share-exchange ratio* is the number of shares of acquirer stock offered for each share of target stock (see Chapter 9). A *fixed or constant share-exchange agreement* is one in which the number of acquirer shares exchanged for each target share is unchanged

Table 11–4   Form of Payment Risk Evaluation

Form of Payment	Advantages	Disadvantages
Cash (including highly marketable securities)	*Buyer*: Simplicity.	*Buyer*: Must rely solely on protections afforded in contract to recover claims.
	Seller: Ensures payment if acquirer's creditworthiness is questionable.	*Seller*: Creates immediate tax liability.

Stock
  Common
  Preferred
  Convertible preferred
	Buyer: High P/E relative to seller's P/E may increase value of combined firms	*Buyer*: Adds complexity; potential EPS dilution.

	Seller: Defers taxes and provides potential price increase. Retains interest in the business.	*Seller*: Potential decrease in purchase price if the value of equity received declines. May delay closing because of registration requirements.

Debt
  Secured
  Unsecured
  Convertible
	Buyer: Interest expense tax is deductible.
	Seller: Defers tax liability on principal.
		Buyer: Adds complexity and increases leverage.
		Seller: Risk of default.

Performance-related earn-outs	*Buyer*: Shifts some portion of risk to seller.	*Buyer*: May limit integration of businesses.
	Seller: Potential for higher purchase price.	*Seller*: Increases uncertainty of sales price.
Purchase price adjustments	*Buyer*: Protection from eroding values of working capital before closing.	*Buyer*: Audit expense.
	Seller: Protection from increasing values of working capital before closing.	*Seller*: Audit expense. (Note that buyers and sellers often split the audit expense.)

Real property
  Real estate
  Plant and equipment
  Business or product line
	Buyer: Minimizes use of cash.
	
	Seller: May minimize tax liability.
		Buyer: Opportunity cost.
		
		Seller: Real property may be illiquid.

Table 11–4 — Cont'd

Form of Payment	Advantages	Disadvantages

Rights to intellectual property
  License
  Franchise
	Buyer: Minimizes cash use.
	
	Seller: Gains access to valuable rights and spreads taxable income over time.
		Buyer: Potential for setting up new competitor.
		Seller: Illiquid; income taxed at ordinary rates.

Royalties from
  Licenses
  Franchises
	Buyer: Minimizes cash use.
	Seller: Spreads taxable income over time.
		Buyer: Opportunity cost.
		Seller: Income taxed at ordinary rates.

Fee based
  Consulting contract
  Employment agreement
	Buyer: Uses seller's expertise and removes seller as potential competitor for a limited time.
	Seller: Augments purchase price and allows seller to stay with the business.
		Buyer: May involve demotivated employees.
		
		Seller: Limits ability to compete in same line of business. Income taxed at ordinary rates.

Contingent value rights	*Buyer*: Minimizes upfront payment. *Seller*: Provides for minimum payout guarantee.	*Buyer*: Commits buyer to minimum payout. *Seller*: Buyer may ask for purchase price reduction.
Staged or distributed payouts	*Buyer*: Reduces amount of upfront investment. *Seller*: Reduces buyer angst about certain future events.	*Buyer*: May result in underfunding of needed investments. *Seller*: Lower present value of purchase price.

between the signing of the agreement of purchase and sale and closing. However, the value of the buyer's share price is allowed to fluctuate. While the buyer knows exactly how many shares have to be issued to consummate the transaction, both the acquirer and the target are subject to significant uncertainty about what the final purchase price will be. The acquirer may find that the transaction is much more expensive than anticipated if the value of its shares rises; in contrast, the seller may be greatly disappointed if the acquirer's share price declines.

In a *fixed value agreement*, the value of the price per share is fixed by allowing the number of acquirer shares issued to vary to offset fluctuations in the buyer's share price. For example, an increase in the value of the acquirer's share price results in the issuance of fewer acquirer shares to keep the value of the deal unchanged; a decrease in the acquirer's share price requires more new shares to be issued. Because of potential dilution to acquirer shareholders if more new shares than originally anticipated had to be issued, the buyer would usually want to ask for a reduction in the purchase price in exchange for a collar arrangement.

Most stock mergers have a fixed share exchange ratio. To compensate for the uncertain value of the deal, some transactions allow the share-exchange ratio to fluctuate within limits or boundaries. Such limits are referred to as a *collar*. Collar arrangements have become more common in recent years, with about 20 percent of stock mergers employing some form of collar as part of the bid structure. **Collar agreements** provide for certain changes in the exchange ratio contingent on the level of the acquirer's share price around the effective date of the merger. This date is often defined as the average acquirer share price during a 10–20-day period preceding the closing date. The two primary types of collar arrangements are the floating and fixed collar agreement.

A *floating collar agreement* may involve a fixed exchange ratio as long as the acquirer's share price remains within a narrow range, calculated as of the effective date of merger. For example, the acquirer and target may agree that the target would receive 0.5 shares of acquirer stock for each share of target stock, as long as the acquirer's share price remains between $20 and $24 per share during a 10-day period just prior to closing. This implies a collar around the bid price of $10 (i.e., 0.5 × $20) to $12 (i.e., 0.5 × $24) per target share. The collar arrangement may further stipulate that, if the acquirer price falls below $20 per share, the target shareholder would receive $10 per share; if the acquirer share price exceeds $24 per share, the target shareholder would receive $12 per share. Therefore, the acquirer and target shareholders can be assured that the actual bid or offer price will be between $10 and $12 per target share.

A *fixed-payment*, or value, *collar agreement* guarantees that the target firm shareholder receives a certain dollar value in terms of acquirer stock, as long as the acquirer's stock remains within a narrow range, and a fixed exchange ratio, if the acquirer's average stock price is outside the bounds around the effective date of the merger. For example, the acquirer and target may agree that target shareholders would receive $40 per share, as long as the acquirer's share price remains within a range of $30 to $34 per share. This would be achieved by adjusting the number of acquirer shares exchanged for each target share (i.e., the number of acquirer shares exchanged for each target share increases if the acquirer share price declines toward the lower end of the range and decreases if the acquirer share price increases). If the acquirer share price increases above $34 per share, target shareholders would receive 1.1765 shares of acquirer stock (i.e., $40/$34); if the acquirer share price drops below $30 per share, target shareholders would receive 1.333 shares of acquirer stock (i.e., $40/$30) for each target share they own. Table 11–5 identifies the advantages and disadvantages of various types of collar arrangements.

Both the acquirer and target boards of directors have a fiduciary responsibility to demand that the merger terms be renegotiated if the value of the offer made by the bidder changes materially relative to the value of the target's stock or if there has been any other material change in the target's operations. Merger contracts routinely contain "material adverse effects clauses," which provide a basis for buyers to withdraw from or renegotiate the contract. For example, in 2006, Johnson and Johnson (J&J) demanded that Guidant Corporation, a leading heart pacemaker manufacturer, accept a lower purchase price than that agreed to in their merger agreement. J&J was reacting to news of government recalls of Guidant pacemakers and federal investigations that could materially damage the value of the firm.

Renegotiation can be expensive for either party due to the commitment of management time and the cost of legal and investment banking advice. Collar agreements protect the acquiring firm from "overpaying" in the event that its share price is higher or the target firm's share price is lower on the effective date of the merger than it was on the day agreement was reached on merger terms. Similarly, the target shareholders are protected from receiving less than the originally agreed-to purchase price if the acquirer's stock declines in value by the effective date of the merger. If the acquirer's share price has historically been highly volatile, the target may demand a collar to preserve the agreed-on share price. Similarly, the acquirer may demand a collar if the target's share price has shown great variation in the past to minimize the potential for overpaying if the target's share price declines significantly relative to the acquirer's share price. Officer (2004) concludes, in an evaluation of 1,127 stock mergers between 1991 and 1999, of which approximately one fifth had collar arrangements, that collars are more likely to be used

Table 11–5 Advantages and Disadvantages of Alternative Collar Agreements

Agreement Type	Advantages	Disadvantages
Fixed share-exchange agreement	*Buyer:* Number of acquirer shares to be issued is known with certainty; minimizes potential for overpaying. *Seller:* Share exchange ratio is known with certainty.	*Buyer:* Actual value of transaction is uncertain until closing; may necessitate renegotiation. *Seller:* Same.
Fixed-value agreement	*Buyer:* Transaction value is known; protects acquirer from overpaying. *Seller:* Transaction value is known; prevents significant reduction in purchase price due to acquirer share price variation.	*Buyer:* Number of acquirer shares to be issued is uncertain. *Seller:* May have to reduce purchase price to get acquirer to fix value.
Floating collar agreement	*Buyer:* Number of acquirer shares to be issued is known within a narrow range. *Seller:* Greater certainty about share exchange ratio.	*Buyer:* Actual value of transaction subject to some uncertainty. *Seller:* May have to reduce purchase price to get acquire to float exchange ratio.
Fixed-payment collar agreement	*Buyer:* Reduces uncertainty about transaction value and potential for renegotiation. *Seller:* Same.	*Buyer:* May still result in some overpayment. *Seller:* May still result in some underpayment.

if the volatility of the acquirer share price is greater than the target share price. He further concludes that the use of collars reduces substantially the likelihood that merger terms would have to be renegotiated. How collars may be used to reduce risk to both the acquirer's and the target's shareholders is illustrated in Northrop Grumman's bid for TRW (Case Study 11–2).

Case Study 11–2 Northrop Grumman Makes a Bid for TRW: How Collar Arrangements Affect Shareholder Value

On March 5, 2002, Northrop Grumman initiated a tender offer for 100 percent of TRW's common shares by offering to exchange $47.00 in market value of Northrop Grumman common stock for each share of TRW common stock. The tender offer would expire at the end of the month. Northrop implicitly was offering to exchange 0.4352 (i.e., $47/$108) of its own common shares (based on its March 5 share price of $108.00) for each share of TRW stock. However, the actual share-exchange ratio would be based on the average Northrop share price during the last five business days of the month. The $47 offer price is assured within a narrow range to TRW shareholders by placing a collar of +5 percent ($113.40) or –5 percent ($102.60) around the $108 Northrop share price on the tender offer announcement date. The range of share-exchange ratios implied by this collar is as follows:

$$0.4581(\text{i.e.,} \$47/\$102.60) < 0.4352(\text{i.e.,} \$47/\$108) < 0.4145(\$47/\$113.40)$$

The 0.4581 and 0.4145 share-exchange ratios represent the maximum and minimum fraction of a share of Northrop stock that would be offered for each TRW share

Continued

Case Study 11–2 Northrop Grumman Makes a Bid for TRW: How Collar Arrangements Affect Shareholder Value — Cont'd

during this tender offer period. The collar gave TRW shareholders some comfort that they would receive $47 per share and enabled Northrop to determine the number of new shares it would have to issue within a narrow range to acquire TRW and the resulting impact on EPS of the combined firms.

An increase in Northrop's share price to $117.40 on April 10, 2002, enabled Northrop to increase its offer price to $53 per share of TRW stock outstanding on April 15, 2002, without issuing more than the maximum number of shares they were willing to issue in their March 5 offer. This could be accomplished because the maximum share-exchange ratio of 0.4581 would not be exceeded as long as the share price of Northrop stock remained above $115.75 per share (i.e., $0.4581 \times \$115.75 = \$53$).

In an effort to boost its share price, TRW repeatedly rejected Northrop's offers as too low and countered with its own restructuring plan. This plan would split the firm into separate defense and automotive parts companies while selling off the aeronautical systems operation. TRW also moved aggressively to solicit bids from other potential suitors. TRW contended that its own restructuring plan was worth as much as $60 per share to its shareholders. In June, TRW reached agreement with Goodrich Corporation to sell the aeronautical systems unit for $1.5 billion.

Northrop Grumman and TRW finally reached an agreement on July 1, 2002. Under the terms of the agreement, Northrop would acquire all of TRW's outstanding common stock for $60 per share in a deal valued at approximately $7.8 billion. Northrop also agreed to assume approximately $4 billion of TRW's debt. Moreover, Northrop withdrew its original tender offer. The actual share exchange ratio would be determined by dividing the $60 offer price by the average of the reported prices per share of Northrop common stock on the five consecutive trading days prior to the closing date. Under a revised collar arrangement, the exchange ratio would not be less than 0.4348 or more than 0.5357 of Northrop's shares.

Discussion Questions

1. What type of collar arrangement did Northrop use (i.e., fixed exchange rate or fixed payment)? Explain your answer.
2. What would have been the implications for TRW shareholders had a fixed exchange ratio without a collar been used? Explain your answer.
3. How did the collar arrangement facilitate the completion of the transaction? Explain your answer.

Form of Acquisition

The form of acquisition describes the mechanism for conveying or transferring ownership of assets or stock and associated liabilities from the target to the acquiring firm. The most commonly used methods include the following: asset purchases for cash or acquirer stock, stock purchases for cash or acquirer stock, and statutory mergers using cash or acquirer stock as the form of payment. For excellent discussions of commonly used methods of conveying ownership, see Bainbridge (2003), Hunt (2003), Lajoux and Nesvold (2004), Oesterlie (2005), Sherman (2006), Aspatore (2006), and Ginsburg and Levin (2006).

Asset purchases involve the sale of all or a portion of the assets of the target to the buyer or its subsidiary in exchange for buyer stock, cash, or debt. The buyer may assume all, some, or none of the target's liabilities. *Stock purchases* involve the sale of the outstanding stock of the target to the buyer or its subsidiary by the target's shareholders. The target's shareholders may receive acquirer stock, cash, or debt for their shares. The biggest difference between a stock and an asset purchase is that, in a stock purchase, the purchase price is paid to the target firm's shareholders and not directly to the target firm, as in an asset purchase. A *statutory merger* involves the combination of the target with the buyer or a subsidiary formed to complete the merger. The corporation surviving the merger (i.e., the surviving corporation) can be the buyer, target, or the buyer's subsidiary. The assets and liabilities of the corporation, which ceases to exist, are merged into the surviving firm as a "matter of law." The statutes of the state in which the combined businesses will be incorporated govern such transactions. State statutes typically address considerations such as the percentage of the total voting stock required for approval of the transaction, who is entitled to vote, how the votes are counted, and the rights of the dissenting voters. In a statutory merger, dissenting or minority shareholders are required to sell their shares, although they may have the right to be paid the appraised value of their shares under some state statutes. Minority shareholders are forced out to avoid a hold-out problem, in which a minority of shareholders can delay the completion of a transaction unless they receive compensation in excess of the acquisition purchase price. Stock-for-stock or stock-for-assets transactions represent alternatives to a merger.

An important advantage of an asset purchase over a purchase of stock is that no minority shareholders remain. Without a merger, shareholders cannot be forced to sell their shares. The acquirer may choose to operate the target firm as a subsidiary, in which some target shareholders, albeit a minority, could remain. Consequently, the buyer's subsidiary must submit annual reports to these shareholders, hold shareholder meetings, elect a board of directors by allowing shareholder votes, while being exposed to potentially dissident shareholders. Moreover, a new owner may void a previously existing labor contract if less than 50 percent of the newly created firm belongs to the union. However, if the collective bargaining agreement covering the workforce in the target firm contains a "successor clause" that has been negotiated by the employer and the union, the terms of the agreement may still apply to the workforce of the new business. Table 11–6 highlights the primary advantages and disadvantages of these alternative forms of acquisition. Each alternative form of acquisition is discussed in more detail during the remainder of this chapter.

Purchase of Assets

In an asset purchase, a buyer acquires all rights a seller has to an asset for cash, stock, or some combination. Many state statutes require shareholder approval of a sale of "substantially all" of the target's assets. In many cases, when the acquirer is interested in only a product line or division of the parent firm with multiple product lines or divisions that are not organized as separate legal subsidiaries, an asset purchase is the most practical way to complete the transaction.

In a *cash-for-assets* acquisition, the acquirer pays cash for the seller's assets and may choose to accept some or all of the seller's liabilities. Seller shareholders must vote to approve the transaction, whenever the seller's board votes to sell all or "substantially all" of the firm's assets. What constitutes "substantially all" does not necessarily mean that most of the firm's assets have been sold; rather, it could mean that the assets sold,

Table 11–6 Advantages and Disadvantages of Alternative Forms of Acquisition

Alternative Forms	Advantages	Disadvantages
Cash purchase of assets	*Buyer*: Allows targeted purchase of assets	*Buyer*: Lose NOLs[1] and tax credits
	Asset write-up	Lose rights to intellectual property
	May renegotiate union and benefits agreements	May require consents to assignment of contracts
	May avoid need for shareholder approval	Exposed to liabilities transferring with assets (e.g., warranty claims)
	No minority shareholders	Subject to taxes on any gains resulting in asset write-up
		Subject to lengthy documentation of assets in contract
	Seller: Maintains corporate existence and ownership of assets not acquired	*Seller*: Potential double taxation if shell is liquidated
	Retains NOLs and tax credits	Subject to state transfer taxes
		Necessity of disposing of unwanted residual assets
Cash purchase of stock	*Buyer*: Assets and liabilities transfer automatically	*Buyer*: Responsible for known and unknown liabilities
	May avoid need to get consents to assignment for contracts	No asset write-up unless 338 election taken by buyer[2]
	Less documentation	Union and employee benefit agreements do not terminate
	NOLs and tax credits pass on to buyer	Potential for minority shareholders[3]
	No state transfer taxes	
	May be insulated from target liabilities if kept as subsidiary	
	No shareholder approval if funded by cash or debt	
	Enables circumvention of target's board in hostile tender offer	
	Seller: Liabilities generally pass on to the buyer	*Seller*: Loss of NOLs and tax credits
	May receive favorable tax treatment if acquirer stock received in payment	Favorable tax treatment lost if buyer adopts 338 election
Statutory merger	*Buyer*: Flexible form of payment (stock, cash, or debt)	*Buyer*: May have to pay dissenting shareholders appraised value of stock
	Assets and liabilities transfer automatically, without lengthy documentation	May be time consuming because of the need for target shareholders and board approvals, which may delay closing
	No state transfer taxes	
	No minority shareholders as shareholders are required to tender shares (minority freeze-out)	
	May avoid shareholder approval	
	Seller: Favorable tax treatment if purchase price primarily in acquirer stock	*Seller*: May be time consuming
	Allows for continuing interest in combined companies	Target firm often does not survive
	Flexible form of payment	May not qualify for favorable tax status

Table 11–6 — Cont'd

Alternative Forms	Advantages	Disadvantages
Stock-for-stock transaction	*Buyer*: May operate target company as a subsidiary	*Buyer*: May postpone realization of synergies
	See purchase of stock above	See purchase of stock above
	Seller: See purchase of stock	*Seller*: See purchase of stock
Stock-for-assets transaction	*Buyer*: See purchase of assets	*Buyer*: May dilute buyer's ownership position
		See purchase of assets
	Seller: See purchase of assets	*Seller*: See purchase of assets
Staged transactions	Provides greater strategic flexibility	May postpone realization of synergies

[1]Net operating loss carryforwards or carrybacks.

[2]In Section 338 of the U.S. tax code, the acquirer in a purchase of 80 percent or more of the stock of the target may elect to treat the acquisition as if it were an acquisition of the target's assets.

[3]Minority shareholders in a subsidiary may be eliminated by a so-called backend merger following the initial purchase of target stock. As a result of the merger, minority shareholders are required to abide by the majority vote of all shareholders and sell their shares to the acquirer. If the acquirer owns more than 90 percent of the target's shares, it may be able to use a short-form merger, which does not require any shareholder vote.

while comprising a relatively small percentage of the firm's total assets, are critical to the ongoing operation of the business. Hence, any sale of assets that does not leave the firm with "significant continuing business activity" may force the firm to liquidate. Significant business activity remains following the sale of assets if the selling firm retains at least 25 percent of total pretransaction operating assets and 25 percent of pretransaction income or revenue. Unless required by the firm's bylaws, the buyer's shareholders do not vote to approve the transaction.

After receiving the cash from the buyer, the selling firm may reinvest all the cash in its operations, reinvest some and pay a dividend to shareholders with the remaining cash, or pay it out in a single liquidating distribution. The selling firm's shares are extinguished if shareholders approve the liquidation of the firm. After paying for any liabilities not assumed by the buyer, the assets remaining with the seller and the cash received from the acquiring firm are transferred to the seller's shareholders in a liquidating distribution.

Valero Oil and Gas purchased substantially all of the assets of bankrupt ethanol manufacturer VeraSun for $280 million in cash in early 2009. Valero would buy five refineries as well as a refinery under construction. While this purchase would constitute only six of VeraSun's 14 refineries, it would constitute a purchase of about three quarters of the firm's production capacity and therefore required VeraSun shareholder approval.

In a stock-for-assets transaction, once approved by the seller's board and shareholders, the seller's shareholders receive buyer stock in exchange for the seller's assets and liabilities. In a second stage, the seller dissolves the corporation, following shareholder ratification of such a move, leaving its shareholders with buyer stock. Consequently, the shareholders of the two firms have effectively pooled their ownership interests in the buyer's corporation, which holds the combined assets and liabilities of both firms. Many states and public stock exchanges give acquiring firm shareholders the right to vote to approve a stock for assets transaction if the new shares issued by the buyer exceed more than 20 percent of the firm's total shares outstanding before the transaction.

Advantages: Buyer's Perspective

Buyers can be selective as to which assets of the target will be purchased. The buyer is generally not responsible for the seller's liabilities, unless specifically assumed under the contract. However, the buyer can be held responsible for certain liabilities, such as environmental claims, property taxes, and in some states, substantial pension liabilities and product liability claims. To protect against such risks, buyers usually insist on seller **indemnification** (i.e., the seller is held responsible for payment of damages resulting from such claims). Of course, such indemnification is worthwhile only as long as the seller remains solvent. (Note that, in most agreements of purchase and sale, buyers and sellers agree to indemnify each other from claims for which they are directly responsible. Liability under such arrangements usually is subject to specific dollar limits and is in force only for a specific time period.)

Acquired assets may be revalued to market value on the closing date under the purchase method of accounting. (Purchase accounting is a form of financial reporting of business combinations discussed in detail in Chapter 12.) This increase or *step-up* in the tax basis of the acquired assets to fair market value provides for higher depreciation and amortization expense deductions for tax purposes. Such deductions are said to shelter pretax income from taxation. Buyers are generally free of any undisclosed or contingent liabilities. In the absence of successor clauses in the contract, the asset purchase results in the termination of union agreements, thereby providing an opportunity to renegotiate agreements viewed as too restrictive. Benefit plans may be maintained or terminated at the discretion of the acquirer. While termination of certain contracts and benefit plans is possible in a purchase of assets, buyers may be reluctant to do so because of the potential undermining of employee morale and productivity.

Advantages: Seller's Perspective

Sellers are able to maintain their corporate existence and hence ownership of tangible assets not acquired by the buyer and intangible assets, such as licenses, franchises, and patents. The seller retains the right to use the corporate identity in subsequent marketing programs, unless ceded to the buyer as part of the transaction. The seller also retains the right to use all tax credits and accumulated net operating losses, which can be used to shelter future income from taxes. Such tax considerations remain with the holders of the target firm's stock.

Disadvantages: Buyer's Perspective

The buyer loses the seller's net operating losses and tax credits. Rights to assets such as licenses, franchises, and patents cannot be transferred to buyers. Such rights are viewed as belonging to the owners of the business (i.e., target stockholders). These rights sometimes can be difficult to transfer because of the need to obtain consent from the agency (e.g., U.S. Patent Office) issuing the rights. The buyer must seek the consent of customers and vendors to transfer existing contracts to the buyer. The transaction is more complex and costly, because acquired assets must be listed on appendixes to the definitive agreement and the sale of and titles to each asset transferred must be recorded and state title *transfer taxes* must be paid. Moreover, a lender's consent may be required if the assets to be sold are being used as collateral for loans.

Disadvantages: Seller's Perspective

Taxes also may be a problem, because the seller may be subject to double taxation. If the tax basis in the assets or stock is low, the seller may experience a sizable gain on the sale. In addition, if the corporation subsequently is liquidated, the seller may be responsible for the recapture of taxes deferred as a result of the use of accelerated rather than straight-line depreciation. If the number of assets transferred is large, the amount of state transfer taxes may become onerous. Whether the seller or the buyer actually pays the transfer taxes or they are shared is negotiable.

In late 2007, the largest banking deal in history was consummated through a purchase of the assets of one of Europe's largest financial services firms (see Case Study 11–3). The deal was made possible by a buyer group banding together to buy the firm after reaching agreement as to which of the target's assets would be owned by the each member of the consortium.

Case Study 11–3 Buyer Consortium Wins Control of ABN Amro

The biggest banking deal on record was announced on October 9, 2007, resulting in the dismemberment of one of Europe's largest and oldest financial services firms, ABN Amro (ABN). A buyer consortium consisting of The Royal Bank of Scotland (RBS), Spain's Banco Santander (Santander), and Belgium's Fortis Bank (Fortis) won control of ABN, the largest bank in the Netherlands, in a buyout valued at $101 billion.

European banks are under pressure to grow through acquisitions and compete with larger American rivals to avoid becoming takeover targets themselves. ABN had been viewed for years as a target because of its relatively low share price. However, rival banks were deterred by its diverse mixture of businesses, which was unattractive to any single buyer. Under pressure from shareholders, ABN announced that it had agreed, on April 23, 2007, to be acquired by Barclay's Bank of London for $85 billion in stock. The RBS-led group countered with a $99 billion bid consisting mostly of cash. In response, Barclay's upped its bid by 6 percent with the help of state-backed investors from China and Singapore. ABN's management favored the Barclay bid because Barclay had pledged to keep ABN intact and its headquarters in the Netherlands. However, a declining stock market soon made Barclay's mostly stock offer unattractive.

While the size of the transaction was noteworthy, the deal is especially remarkable in that the consortium had agreed prior to the purchase to split up ABN among the three participants. The mechanism used for acquiring the bank represents an unusual means of completing big transactions amidst the subprime-mortgage-induced turmoil in the global credit markets at the time. The members of the consortium were able to select the ABN assets they found most attractive. The consortium agreed in advance of the acquisition that Santander would receive ABN's Brazilian and Italian units; Fortis would obtain the Dutch bank's consumer lending business, asset management, and private banking operations; and RBS would own the Asian and investment banking units. Merrill Lynch served as the sole investment advisor for the group's participants. Caught up in the global capital market meltdown, Fortis was forced to sell the ABN Amro assets it had acquired to its Dutch competitor ING in October 2008.

Continued

Case Study 11–3 Buyer Consortium Wins Control of ABN Amro — Cont'd

Discussion Questions

1. In your judgment, what are likely to be some of the major challenges in assembling a buyer consortium to acquire and subsequently dismember a target firm such as ABN Amro? In what ways do you think the use of a single investment advisor might have addressed some of these issues?
2. The ABN Amro transaction was completed at a time when the availability of credit was limited due to the subprime-mortgage-loan problem originating in the United States. How might the use of a group rather than a single buyer have facilitated the purchase of ABN Amro?
3. The same outcome could have been achieved if a single buyer had reached agreement with other banks to acquire selected pieces of ABN before completing the transaction. The pieces could then have been sold at the closing. Why might the use of the consortium been a superior alternative?

Solutions to these questions are given in the Online Instructors' Guide for instructors using this textbook.

Purchase of Stock

In cash-for-stock or stock-for-stock transactions, the buyer purchases the seller's stock directly from the seller's shareholders. If the target is a private firm, the purchase is completed by a stock purchase agreement signed by the acquirer and the target's shareholders, if they are few in number. For a public company, the acquiring firm making a tender offer to the target firm's shareholders would consummate the purchase. A tender offer is employed because public company shareholders are likely to be too numerous to deal with separately. The tender offer would be considered friendly if supported by the board and management of the target firm; otherwise, it would be considered a hostile tender offer.

This is in marked contrast to a statutory merger, in which the boards of directors of the firms involved must first ratify the proposal before submitting it to their shareholders for approval. Consequently, a purchase of stock is the approach most often taken in hostile takeovers. If the buyer is unable to convince all the seller's shareholders to tender their shares, then a minority of seller shareholders remains outstanding. The target firm would then be viewed not as wholly owned but rather as a partially owned subsidiary of the buyer or acquiring company. No seller shareholder approval is required in such transactions as the seller's shareholders are expressing approval by tendering their shares. As required by most major stock exchanges, acquiring company shareholders have the right to approve a stock-for-stock transaction if the amount of new acquirer shares issued exceeds 20 percent of the firm's total outstanding shares before the transaction takes place.

Advantages: Buyer's Perspective

All assets are transferred with the target's stock, resulting in less need for documentation to complete the transaction. State asset transfer taxes may be avoided with a purchase of shares. Net operating losses and tax credits pass on to the buyer with the purchase of stock. The right of the buyer to use the target's name, licenses, franchises, patents, and permits also is preserved. Furthermore, the purchase of the seller's stock provides for the continuity of contracts and corporate identity. This obviates the need to renegotiate contracts and enables the acquirer to utilize the brand recognition that may be associated with the name of the target firm. However, some customer and vendor contracts, as well as permits, may stipulate that the buyer must obtain their consent before the contract is transferred. While the acquirer's board normally approves any major acquisition, approval by shareholders is not required if the purchase is financed primarily with cash or debt. If stock that has not yet been authorized is used, shareholder approval is likely to be required. Neither the target's board nor shareholders need to approve a sale of stock; however, shareholders may simply refuse to sell their stock.

Advantages: Seller's Perspective

The seller is able to defer paying taxes. If stock is received from the acquiring company, taxes are paid by the target's shareholders only when the stock is sold. All obligations, disclosed or otherwise, transfer to the buyer. This advantage for the seller usually is attenuated by the insistence by the buyer that the seller indemnify the buyer from damages resulting from any undisclosed liability. However, as previously noted, indemnification clauses in contracts generally are in force for only a limited time period. Finally, the seller is not left with the problem of disposing of assets that the seller does not wish to retain but that were not purchased by the acquiring company.

Disadvantages: Buyer's Perspective

The buyer is liable for all unknown, undisclosed, or contingent liabilities. The seller's tax basis is carried over to the buyer at historical cost, unless the seller consents to take certain tax code elections. These elections could create a tax liability for the seller. Therefore, they are used infrequently. Consequently, there is no step-up in the cost basis of assets and no tax shelter is created. Dissenting shareholders have the right to have their shares appraised, with the option of being paid the appraised value of their shares or remaining as minority shareholders. The purchase of stock does not terminate existing union agreements or employee benefit plans.

The existence of minority shareholders creates significant administrative costs and practical concerns. Significant additional expenses are incurred as the parent must submit annual reports, hold annual shareholder meetings, and allow such shareholders to elect a board through a formal election process. Furthermore, implementing strategic business moves may be inhibited. In an effort to sell its MTU Friedrichshafen diesel engine assembly operations, DaimlerChrysler announced the purchase of minority shareholders' interests whose holdings constituted less than 10 percent of firm's outstanding stock. Prior to the buyout, DaimlerChrysler had been unable to reach agreement with enough shareholders to enable it to sell the business.

Disadvantages: Seller's Perspective

The seller cannot pick and choose the assets to be retained. Furthermore, the seller loses all net operating losses and tax credits.

Mergers

Unlike purchases of target stock, mergers require approval of the acquirer's board and the target's board of directors and the subsequent submission of the proposal to the shareholders of both firms. Unless otherwise required by a firm's bylaws, a simple majority of all the outstanding voting shares must ratify the proposal. The merger agreement must then be filed with the state (usually the Secretary of State) in which the merger is to be consummated. Under several exceptions, no vote is required by the acquirer's (i.e., surviving firm) shareholders. The first exception involves a transaction that is not considered material, in that the acquirer issues new shares to the target's shareholders in an amount which constitutes less than 20 percent of the acquirer's voting shares outstanding before the transaction. The second exception under which a vote is not required in a statutory merger occurs when a subsidiary is being merged into the parent and the parent owns a substantial majority (over 90 percent in some states) of the subsidiary's stock before the transaction.

The purchase price in a merger can consist of cash, stock, or debt, giving the acquiring company more latitude in how it will pay for the purchase of the target's stock. If the seller receives acquirer shares in exchange for its shares (with the seller's shares subsequently canceled), the merger is a *stock-for-stock*, or stock swap, *statutory merger*. If the shareholders of the selling firm receive cash or some form of nonvoting investment (e.g., debt or nonvoting preferred or common stock) for their shares, the merger is referred to as a *cash-out*, or cash, *statutory merger*. Mergers are generally not suitable for hostile transactions, because they require the approval of the target's board.

An alternative to a traditional merger that accomplishes the same objective is the two-step acquisition. First, through a stock purchase, the acquirer buys the majority of the target's outstanding stock from the target's shareholders in a tender offer and follows up with a "squeeze-out" or backend merger approved by the acquirer as majority shareholder. Minority shareholders are required to take the acquisition consideration in the backend merger because of the state statutory provisions designed to prevent a minority from delaying completion of a merger until they receive better terms. Two-step acquisitions sometimes are used to make it more difficult for another firm to make a bid, because the merger can be completed quickly. In summary, whether through a one-step or two-step merger involving a stock purchase followed by a backend merger, all the stock held by each target shareholder gets converted into the merger consideration, regardless of whether the shareholder voted for the merger.

In March 2009, Merck Pharmaceuticals acquired a much smaller rival Schering-Plough through a two-step merger in order to quickly close the deal and to prevent a potential bidding war with Johnson & Johnson and the loss of the profits from a joint venture Schering had with Johnson & Johnson. The deal was constructed as a reverse triangular merger in which a wholly owned shell subsidiary (i.e., a merger subsidiary) of Schering would be merged into Merck, with Merck surviving as a wholly owned Schering subsidiary. Thus, Schering is viewed as the acquiring firm even though the combined firms will be renamed Merck, the Merck CEO will become the CEO of the merged firms, and Merck is putting up all the money to finance the transaction. Merck would be merged into Schering subsequent to closing. By positioning Schering as the acquirer, Merck was attempting to avoid triggering a change of control provision in a long-standing drug distribution agreement between Johnson & Johnson and Schering under which Johnson & Johnson would be able to cancel the agreement and to take full ownership of the drugs covered by the agreement.

In contrast, Roche, the Swiss Pharmaceutical giant, reached agreement on March 12, 2009, to acquire the remaining 44 percent of Genentech they did not already own. Roche was unable to squeeze out the minority Genentech shareholders through a backend merger even though they held a majority of the shares, because they were bound by an affiliation agreement between the two firms which governed their prior joint business relationships. The affiliation agreement required that in the event of a merger with Genentech that Roche must either receive a favorable vote from the majority of the remaining Genentech shares not already owned by Roche or offer the remaining Genentech shareholders a price equal to or greater than the average of fair values of such shares as determined by two investment banks appointed by the Genentech board of directors.

Most mergers are structured as subsidiary mergers, in which the acquiring firm creates a new corporate subsidiary that merges with the target. By using this reverse triangular merger, the acquirer may be able to avoid seeking approval from its shareholders. While merger statutes require approval by the shareholders of the target and acquiring firms, the parent of the acquisition subsidiary is the shareholder. Just as in a stock purchase, an assignment of contracts is generally not necessary as the target survives. In contrast, an assignment is required in a forward triangular merger, since the target is merged into the subsidiary with the subsidiary surviving.

Advantages

The primary advantage of a merger is that the transfer of assets and the exchange of stock between the acquirer and the target happen automatically by "rule of law." (*Rule of law* refers to the accumulation of applicable federal and state laws and legal precedents resulting from numerous court cases establishing when and how ownership is transferred.) When a majority (i.e., 50.1 percent) of target shareholders has approved the merger, all shareholders are required to sell their shares, even if they did not support the transaction. Such shareholders are said to have been "frozen out" of their position. Transfer taxes are not paid because there are no asset transfer documents. Contracts, licenses, patents, and permits automatically transfer, unless they require "consent to assignment." This means that the buyer convinces all parties to the contracts to agree to consign them to the new owner. This transfer can be accomplished by merging a subsidiary set up by the buyer with the target. The subsidiary can be merged with the parent immediately following closing.

Disadvantages

Mergers of public corporations can be costly and time consuming because of the need to obtain shareholder approval and comply with proxy regulations (see Chapter 2). The resulting delay can open the door to other bidders, create an auction environment, and boost the purchase price.

Staged Transactions

An acquiring firm may choose to complete a takeover of another firm in stages spread over an extended period of time. Staged transactions may be used to structure an earn-out, enable the target to complete the development of a technology or process, await regulatory approval, eliminate the need to obtain shareholder approval, and minimize cultural conflicts with the target.

As part of an earn-out agreement, the acquirer may agree to allow the target to operate as a wholly owned but largely autonomous unit until the earn-out period expires. This suggests that little attempt will be made to integrate facilities, overhead operations, and distribution systems during the earn-out period.

The value of the target may be greatly dependent on the target developing a key technology or production process, receiving approval from a regulatory authority such as the Federal Communications Commission (FCC), or signing a multiyear customer or vendor contract. The target's ability to realize these objectives may be enhanced if it is aligned with a larger company or receives a cash infusion to fund the required research. A potential acquirer may assume a minority investment in the target with an option to acquire the company at a later date.

If the long-term value of the acquirer's stock offered to the target is dependent on the acquirer receiving approval from a regulatory agency, developing a new technology, or landing a key contract, the target may be well advised to wait. The two parties may enter into a letter of intent, with the option to exit the agreement without any liability to either party if certain key events are not realized within a stipulated time.

Case Study 11–4 illustrates a staged transaction in which Phelps Dodge attempted to acquire two other metals companies by acquiring all of the outstanding stock of Inco. The strategy was, in one grand gesture, to make Phelps Dodge the world's second largest metals mining company, behind Australia's BHP Billiton. This three-way transaction is reminiscent of U.S.-based Andarko's acquisition of Western Gas Resources and Kerr-McGee for $21 billion in early 2006 (see the Inside M&A case study in Chapter 4 for more detail).

Case Study 11–4 Phelps Dodge Attempts to Buy Two at the Same Time

Buoyed by high metals prices, many major mining companies were experiencing huge increases in their cash reserves. Expectations of continued high prices sparked an M&A boom among Canadian mining companies late in 2005. These companies were seeking to rapidly increase revenue and improve profitability through savings generated by consolidating the industry.

In October 2005, Inco made a bid to buy Falconbridge. However, in early May 2006, another Canadian mining company, Teck Cominco, offered to buy Inco. By mid-May, Swiss mining company Xstrata initiated a bidding war with Inco for Falconbridge. Finally, Phelps Dodge (Phelps) entered the fray with a complex plan involving three companies.

In what was heralded by some as a bold strategic move, Phelps proposed to acquire Canadian mining companies Inco Ltd. and Falconbridge Ltd. in a three-way transaction valued at $47.9 billion. The new company would be named Phelps Dodge Inco Company and would be the world's largest producer of nickel and the second largest producer of copper and molybdenum, a mineral used to strengthen steel.

The transaction was to be completed in two stages. The first stage called for Inco to complete its acquisition of Falconbridge by offering a combination of Inco shares and cash. Regulators in North America had already approved the deal. In the second stage, Inco shareholders would receive a combination of cash and Phelps's stock for their shares, once Falconbridge shares were converted to Inco shares. Inco shareholders were to receive a healthy premium for their shares. Phelps was betting that the premium could be easily recovered by realizing huge cost savings in combining the operations of the three businesses. Phelps's bid for Inco was not contingent on Inco successfully acquiring Falconbridge. When the deal was completed, Phelps anticipated buying back $5 billion worth of its shares. Financing the transaction (including the share buyback) would require that Phelps borrow more than $27 billion. The complex three-way deal is illustrated in Figure 11–2, with the dollar figures in parentheses indicating the market value of each company.

As many deals do, this one looked good on paper but was very difficult to execute. In late July, Inco lost to Xstrata in its effort to acquire Falconbridge. Phelps's share price continued to drop as investors recognized that the loss of Falconbridge significantly reduced the value of anticipated cost savings that would have been realized by combining the three firms. Without Falconbridge, expected annual cost savings fell from $900 million to $350 million.

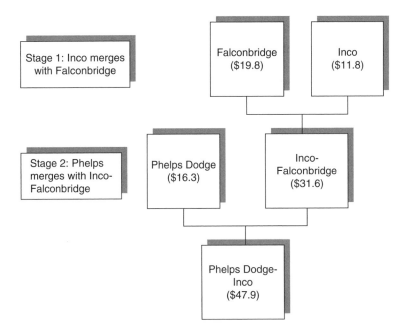

FIGURE 11–2 Three-way deal.

The skies darkened further for Phelps Dodge in mid-August, when Inco's board entered into talks with Brazil's Companhia Vale do Rio Doce (CVRD), which offered to buy Inco for $17.6 billion in cash. Simultaneously, Inco's board urged shareholders to support the earlier agreement it had made with Phelps Dodge to avoid triggering penalties in the agreement and recommended the rejection of a third competing bid from Teck Cominco Ltd.

Amid concerns among its own shareholders about dilution and lack of support among Inco shareholders for its offer, Phelps Dodge withdrew its bid to buy Inco in early September 2006. Phelps Dodge stated publicly that they would focus on increasing its own copper production from the firm's current mines. The firm's share price rose as the firm's shareholders celebrated the demise of the deal. The firm's institutional shareholders had long been critical of what they believed was an excessive offer price that would dilute owners' equity and saddle Phelps Dodge with too much debt. Phelps was entitled to receive a breakup fee from Inco of $125 million and potentially another $350 if Inco was acquired anytime during the following year.

Within a little more than two months of Phelps's aborted takeover attempt, the hunter was itself acquired. In late November of 2006, Freeport-McMoran Copper & Gold Inc. announced that it had reached agreement to acquire Phelps for $25.9 billion.

Discussion Questions

1. Given the complexity of the three-way transaction, what factors may have motivated Phelps Dodge's management to adopt this strategy? Be specific.
2. What are the primary risks associated with a three-way transaction? Be specific.
3. With the loss of the potential cost savings from integrating Falconbridge, why do you believe Phelps continued to pursue Inco?
4. How might Phelps's effort to execute this complex three-way transaction contributed to its eventually being acquired?

Things to Remember

The deal-structuring process addresses satisfying as many of the primary objectives of the parties involved and determines how risk will be shared. The process begins with addressing a set of key questions, whose answers help define initial negotiating positions, potential risks, options for managing risk, levels of tolerance for risk, and conditions under which the buyer or seller will "walk away" from the negotiations. The deal-structuring process can be defined in terms of seven major components: the form of the acquisition vehicle, the postclosing organization, the form of payment, the form of acquisition, the legal form of the selling entity, and accounting and tax considerations.

The form of the acquisition vehicle refers to the legal structure used to acquire the target. The postclosing organization is the legal framework used to manage the combined businesses following the consummation of the transaction. The postclosing organization may differ from the acquisition vehicle, depending on the acquirer's strategic objectives for the combined firms. The form of payment or total consideration may consist of cash, common stock, debt, or some combination of all three. The form of acquisition refers to what is being acquired: stock or assets. The form of acquisition affects the form of payment, tax considerations, as well as the choice of acquisition vehicle and postclosing organization. Tax considerations also are affected by the legal structure of the selling entity. Financial reporting requirements may affect the form, amount, and timing of payment.

Chapter Discussion Questions

11–1. Describe the deal-structuring process. Be specific.

11–2. Provide two examples of how decisions made in one area of the deal-structuring process are likely to affect other areas.

11–3. For what reasons may acquirers choose a particular form of acquisition vehicle?

11–4. Describe techniques used to "close the gap" when buyers and sellers cannot agree on price.

11–5. Why do bidders sometimes offer target firm shareholders multiple payments options (e.g., cash and stock)?

11–6. What are the advantages and disadvantages of a purchase of assets from the perspective of the buyer and seller?

11–7. What are the advantages and disadvantages of a purchase of stock from the perspective of the buyer and seller?

11–8. What are the advantages and disadvantages of a statutory merger?

11–9. What are the reasons some acquirers choose to undertake a staged or multistep takeover?

11–10. What forms of acquisition represent common alternatives to a merger? Under what circumstances might these alternative structures be employed?

11–11. Comment of the following statement. A premium offered by a bidder over a target's share price is not necessarily a fair price; a fair price is not necessarily an adequate price.

11–12. In early 2008, a year marked by turmoil in the global credit markets, Mars Corporation was able to negotiate a reverse breakup fee structure in its acquisition of Wrigley Corporation. This structure allowed Mars to walk away from the transaction at any time by paying a $1 billion fee to Wrigley.

Speculate as to the motivation behind Mars and Wrigley negotiating such a fee structure.

11–13. Despite disturbing discoveries during due diligence, Mattel acquired The Learning Company (TLC), a leading developer of software for toys, in a stock-for-stock transaction valued at $3.5 billion on May 13, 1999. Mattel had determined that TLC's receivables were overstated because product returns from distributors were not deducted from receivables and its allowance for bad debt was inadequate. A $50 million licensing deal also had been prematurely put on the balance sheet. Finally, TLC's brands were becoming outdated. TLC had substantially exaggerated the amount of money put into research and development for new software products. Nevertheless, driven by the appeal of rapidly becoming a big player in the children's software market, Mattel closed on the transaction, aware that TLC's cash flows were overstated. Despite being aware of extensive problems, Mattel proceeded to acquire The Learning Company. Why? What could Mattel have done to better protect its interests? Be specific.

11–14. Describe the conditions under which an earn-out may be most appropriate.

11–15. In late 2008, Deutsche Bank announced that it would buy the commercial banking assets (including a number of branches) of the Netherlands' ABN Amro for $1.13 billion. What liabilities, if any, would Deutsche Bank have to (or want to) assume? Explain your answer.

Solutions to these Chapter Discussion Questions are found in the Online Instructor's Manual for instructors using this book.

Chapter Business Cases

Case Study 11–5. Vivendi Universal and GE Combine Entertainment Assets to Form NBC Universal

Ending a four-month-long auction process, Vivendi Universal SA agreed on October 5, 2003, to sell its Vivendi Universal Entertainment (VUE) businesses, consisting of film and television assets, to General Electric Corporation's wholly owned NBC subsidiary. Vivendi received a combination of GE stock and stock in the combined company valued at approximately $14 billion. Vivendi would combine the Universal Pictures movie studio, its television production group, three cable networks, and the Universal theme parks with NBC. The new company would have annual revenues of $13 billion based on 2003 pro forma statements.

This transaction was among many made by Vivendi in its effort to restore the firm's financial viability. Having started as a highly profitable distributor of bottled water, the French company undertook a diversification spree in the 1990s, which pushed the firm into many unrelated enterprises and left it highly in debt. With its stock plummeting, Vivendi had been under considerable pressure to reduce its leverage and refocus its investments.

Applying a multiple of 14 times estimated 2003 EBITDA of $3 billion, the combined company had an estimated value of approximately $42 billion. This multiple is well within the range of comparable transactions and is consistent with the share price multiples of television media companies at that time. Of the $3 billion in 2003 EBITDA, GE would provide $2 billion and Vivendi $1 billion. This values GE's assets at $28 billion and Vivendi's at $14 billion. This implies that GE assets contribute two thirds and Vivendi's one third of the total market value of the combined company.

NBC Universal's total assets of $42 billion consist of VUE's assets valued at $14 billion and NBC's at $28 billion. Vivendi chose to receive an infusion of liquidity at closing consisting of $4.0 billion in cash by selling its right to receive $4 billion in GE stock and the transfer of $1.6 billion in debt carried by VUE's businesses to NBC Universal.

Vivendi would retain an ongoing approximate 20 percent ownership in the new company valued at $8.4 billion after having received $5.6 billion in liquidity at closing. GE would have 80 percent ownership in the new company in exchange for providing $5.6 billion in liquidity (i.e., $4 billion in cash and assuming $1.6 billion in debt). Vivendi had the option to sell its 20 percent ownership interest in the future, beginning in 2006, at fair market value. GE would have the first right (i.e., the first right of refusal) to acquire the Vivendi position. GE anticipated that its 80 percent ownership position in the combined company would be accretive for GE shareholders beginning in the second full year of operation.

Discussion Questions

1. From a legal standpoint, identify the acquirer and the target firms.
2. What is the form of acquisition? Why might this form have been agreed to by the parties involved in the transaction?
3. What is the form of acquisition vehicle and the postclosing organization? Why do you think the legal entities you have identified were selected?
4. What is the form of payment or total consideration? Why do you believe the parties to this transaction agreed to this form of payment?
5. Based on a total valuation of $42 billion, Vivendi's assets contributed one third and GE's two thirds of the total value of NBC Universal. However, after the closing, Vivendi would own only a 20 percent equity position in the combined business. Why?

Solutions to these questions are provided in the Online Instructor's Manual for instructors using this book.

Case Study 11–6. Using Form of Payment as a Takeover Strategy: Chevron's Acquisition of Unocal

Background

Unocal ceased to exist as an independent company on August 11, 2005, and its shares were delisted from the New York Stock Exchange. The new firm is known as Chevron. In a highly politicized transaction, Chevron battled Chinese oil producer CNOOC for almost four months for ownership of Unocal. A cash and stock bid by Chevron, the nation's second largest oil producer, made in April and valued at $61 per share, was accepted by the Unocal board when it appeared that CNOOC would not counterbid. However, CNOOC soon followed with an all-cash bid of $67 per share. Chevron amended the merger agreement with a new cash and stock bid valued at $63 per share in late July. Despite the significant difference in the value of the two bids, the Unocal board recommended to its shareholders that they accept the amended Chevron bid in view of the growing doubt that U.S. regulatory authorities would approve a takeover by CNOOC.

Winning Approval by Appealing to the Varied Interests of Target Shareholders

In its strategy to win Unocal shareholder approval, Chevron offered Unocal shareholders three options for each of their shares: (1) $69 in cash, (2) 1.03 Chevron shares, or (3) 0.618 Chevron shares plus $27.60 in cash. Unocal shareholders not electing any specific option would receive the third option. Moreover, the all-cash and all-stock offers were subject to proration to preserve an overall per share mix of 0.618 of a share of Chevron common stock and $27.60 in cash for all of the 272 million outstanding shares of Unocal common stock. This mix of cash and stock provided a "blended" value of about $63 per share of Unocal common stock on the day that Unocal and Chevron entered into the amendment to the merger agreement on July 22, 2005. The "blended" rate was calculated by multiplying 0.618 by the value of Chevron stock on July 22 of $57.28 plus $27.60 in cash. This resulted in a targeted purchase price that was about 56 percent Chevron stock and 44 percent cash.

This mix of cash and stock implied that Chevron would pay approximately $7.5 billion (i.e., $27.60 × 272 million Unocal shares outstanding) in cash and issue approximately 168 million shares of Chevron common stock (i.e., 0.618 × 272 million of Unocal shares) valued at $57.28 per share as of July 22, 2005. The implied value of the merger on that date was $17.1 billion (i.e., $27.60 × 272 million Unocal common shares outstanding plus $57.28 × 168 million Chevron common shares). An increase in Chevron's share price to $63.15 on August 10, 2005, the day of the Unocal shareholders' meeting, boosted the value of the deal to $18.1 billion.

Option 1 was intended to appeal to those Unocal shareholders who were attracted to CNOOC's all-cash offer of $67 per share. Option 2 was designed for those shareholders interested in a tax-free exchange. Finally, it was anticipated that option 3 would attract those Unocal shareholders who were interested in cash but also wished to enjoy any appreciation in the stock of the combined companies.

Adjusting Unocal Investor Elections

The agreement of purchase and sale between Chevron and Unocal contained a "proration clause." This clause enabled Chevron to limit the amount of total cash it would pay out under those options involving cash that it had offered to Unocal shareholders and to maintain the "blended" rate of $63 it would pay for each share of Unocal stock. Approximately 242 million Unocal shareholders elected to receive all cash for their shares, 22.1 million opted for the all-stock alternative, and 10.1 million elected the cash and stock combination. No election was made for approximately .3 million shares. Based on these results, the amount of cash needed to satisfy the number shareholders electing the all-cash option far exceeded the amount that Chevron was willing to pay. Consequently, as permitted in the merger agreement, the all-cash offer was prorated resulting in the Unocal shareholders who had elected the all-cash option receiving a combination of cash and stock rather than $69 per share. The mix of cash and stock was calculated as shown in Table 11–7.

If too many Unocal shareholders had elected to receive Chevron stock, those making the all-stock election would not have received 1.03 shares of Chevron stock for each share of Unocal stock. Rather, they would have received a mix of stock and cash to help preserve the approximate 56 percent stock and 44 percent cash composition of the purchase price desired by Chevron. For illustration only, assume the number of Unocal shares to be exchanged for the all-cash and all-stock options are 22.1 and 242 million, respectively. This is the reverse of what actually happened. The mix of stock and cash would have been prorated as shown in Table 11–8.

Conclusions

It is typical of large transactions in which the target has a large, diverse shareholder base that acquiring firms offer target shareholders a "menu" of alternative forms of payment. The objective is to enhance the likelihood of success by appealing to a broader group of

Table 11–7 Prorating All-Cash Elections

1. **Determine the available cash election amount** (ACEA). Aggregate cash amount minus the amount of cash to be paid to Unocal shareholders selecting the combination of cash and stock (i.e., option 3):
ACEA = $27.60 × 272 million (Unocal shares outstanding) − 10.1 million (shares electing cash and stock option) × $27.60
= $7.5 − $0.3
= $7.2 billion
2. **Determine the elected cash amount** (ECA). Amount equal to $69 multiplied by the number of shares of Unocal common stock electing the all-cash option:
ECA = $69 × 242 million = $16.7 billion
3. **Determine the cash proration factor** (CPF). ACEA/ECA:
CPF = $7.2/$16.7 = 0.4311
4. **Determine the prorated cash merger consideration** (PCMC). An amount in cash equal to $69 multiplied by the cash proration factor:
PCMC = $69 × 0.4311 = $29.74
5. **Determine the prorated stock merger consideration** (PSMC). 1.03 multiplied by 1 − CPF:
PSMC = 1.03 × (1 − 0.4311) = 0.5860
6. **Determine the stock and cash mix** (SCM). Sum of the prorated cash (PCMC) and stock (PSMC) merger considerations exchanged for each share of Unocal common stock:
SCM = $29.74 + 0.5860 of a Chevron share

Table 11–8 Prorating All-Stock Elections

1. **Determine the available cash election amount** (ACEA). Same as step 1 in Table 11–7:
ACEA = $7.2 billion
2. **Determine the elected cash amount** (ECA). Amount equal to $69 multiplied by the number of shares of Unocal common stock electing the all-cash option:
ECA = $69 × 22.1 million = $1.5 billion
3. **Determine the excess cash amount** (EXCA). Difference between ACEA and ECA:
EXCA = $7.2 − $1.5 = $5.7
4. **Determine the prorated cash merger consideration** (PCMC). EXCA divided by number of Unocal shares elected the all-stock option:
PCMC = $5.7/242 million = $23.55
5. **Determine the stock proration factor** (SPF). $69 minus the prorated cash merger consideration divided by $69:
SPF = ($69 − $23.55)/$69 = $45.45 / $69 = 0.6587
6. **Determine the prorated stock price consideration** (PSPC). The number of shares of Chevron stock equal to 1.03 multiplied by the stock proration factor:
PSPC = 1.03 × 0.6587 = 0.6785
7. **Determine the stock and cash mix** (SCM). Each Unocal share to be exchanged in an all-stock election is converted into the right to receive the prorated cash merger consideration and the prorated stock merger consideration:
SCM = $23.55 + 0.6785 of a Chevron share for each Unocal share

shareholders. To the unsophisticated target shareholder, the array of options may prove appealing. However, it is likely that those electing all-cash or all-stock purchases are likely to be disappointed due to probable proration clauses in merger contracts. Such clauses enable the acquirer to maintain an overall mix of cash and stock in completing the transaction. This enables the acquirer to limit the amount of cash it must borrow or the number of new shares it must issue to levels it finds acceptable.

Discussion Questions

1. What was the form of payment employed by both bidders for Unocal? In your judgment, why were they different? Be specific.
2. How did Chevron use the form of payment as a potential takeover strategy?
3. Is the "proration clause" found in most merger agreements in which target shareholders are given several ways in which they can choose to be paid for their shares in the best interests of the target shareholders? In the best interests of the acquirer? Explain your answer.

Solutions to these case study discussion questions are available in the Online Instructor's Manual for instructors using this book.

12

Structuring the Deal

Tax and Accounting Considerations

One person of integrity can make a difference, a difference of life and death.
—Elie Wiesel

Inside M&A: Teva Pharmaceuticals Acquires Ivax Corp

Teva Pharmaceutical Industries (Teva), a leading manufacturer and distributor of generic drugs in the United States, announced on July 25, 2005, that it would acquire Ivax Corp (Ivax) for about $7.4 billion to become the world's largest manufacturer of generic drugs. For Teva, based in Israel, and Ivax, headquartered in Miami, the merger eliminated a large competitor and created a distribution chain that spans 50 countries. The two firms would have combined annual revenues of more than $7 billion.

Under the terms of the merger agreement, Ivax shareholders could elect to receive for each of their shares either of the following: (1) 0.8471 of American depository receipts representing Teva shares or (2) $26 in cash. ADRs represent the receipt given to U.S. investors for the shares of a foreign-based corporation held in the vault of a U.S. bank. Holders of ADRs are entitled to all dividends paid and capital gains associated with the stock. Ivax shareholders have the opportunity to receive a significant portion of the total consideration (i.e., purchase price) in cash, thereby receiving immediate liquidity and the remainder in Teva ADRs. By receiving Teva ADRs, Ivax shareholders would be able to participate in any future appreciation of Teva stock.

As a result of the merger, each previously outstanding share of Ivax common stock was canceled. Each canceled share represented the right to receive, at the election of the Ivax shareholders made at least two business days prior to the closing of the merger, either of these two payments options. The merger agreement also provided for the acquisition of Ivax by Teva through a merger of Merger Sub, a newly formed and wholly owned subsidiary of Teva, into Ivax. As the surviving corporation, Ivax would be a wholly owned subsidiary of Teva. The merger involving the exchange of Teva ADRs for Ivax shares would be considered as tax-free under U.S. law.

Chapter Overview

In Chapter 11, the deal-structuring process was described in terms of the acquisition vehicle, the postclosing organization, the form of payment, the legal form of the selling entity, the form of acquisition, and accounting and tax considerations. The author stressed how changes made in one area of the process could affect other areas of the overall deal structure significantly.

While Chapter 11 discusses in detail the first five components of the process, this chapter focuses on the implications of tax and accounting considerations for the deal-structuring process. As noted previously, tax considerations can affect the amount, timing, and composition of the purchase price. If a transaction is taxable, target shareholders typically demand a higher purchase price to offset the anticipated tax liability. The increase in the purchase price may cause the acquirer to defer some portion of the purchase price by altering the terms to include more debt or installment payments to maintain the same purchase price in present value terms. Moreover, the decision as to the appropriate organizational structure of the combined businesses is affected by such factors as the desire to minimize taxes and pass through losses to owners. The S corporation, LLC, and the partnership eliminate double-taxation problems. Current operating losses, loss carryforwards or carrybacks, or tax credits generated by the combined businesses can be passed through to the owners if the postclosing organization is a partnership or an LLC.

With the elimination of pooling of interests as an alternative to purchase accounting in 2001 and further changes in financial reporting standards that took effect in late 2008, acquirers are likely to be more circumspect in making acquisitions. Overpayment for target firms and the use of contingent payout mechanisms can result in significant increases in future earnings volatility for acquiring firms. Furthermore, equity may become less attractive as a form of payment due to the requirement to record business combinations on the closing rather than the announcement date, although these concerns may be mitigated by the use of collar arrangements. The ever-present threat of these factors may exert some discipline into the negotiating process, affecting both the amount and timing of offer prices and the length and intensity of M&A due diligence. The major segments of this chapter include the following:

- General Tax Considerations
- Taxable Transactions
- Tax-Free Transactions
- Other Tax Considerations Affecting Corporate Restructuring Activities
- Financial Reporting of Business Combinations
- Impact of Purchase Accounting on Financial Statements
- International Accounting Standards
- Recapitalization Accounting
- Things to Remember

A review of this chapter (including practice questions and answers) is available in the file folder entitled Student Study Guide contained on the CD-ROM accompanying this book. The CD-ROM also contains a Learning Interactions Library, enabling students to test their knowledge of this chapter in a "real-time" environment. See Stickney, Brown, and Wahlen (2007) and Gale and Morris (2006) for an excellent discussion of financial reporting and statements analysis. See Carrington (2007) for an in-depth discussion of tax accounting for mergers and acquisitions.

General Tax Considerations

Taxes are an important consideration in almost any transaction. However, taxes are seldom the primary motivation for an acquisition. The fundamental economics of the transaction always should be the deciding factor. Tax benefits accruing to the buyer

Table 12–1 Alternative Taxable and Nontaxable Structures

Taxable Transactions: Immediately Taxable to Target Shareholders	Nontaxable Transactions: Tax Deferred to Target Shareholders
Purchase of assets with cash	Type A reorganization (statutory stock merger or consolidation)
Purchase of stock with cash	Type B reorganization (stock for stock)
Statutory cash merger or consolidation	Type C reorganization (stock for assets)
Triangular statutory cash mergers	Triangular statutory stock mergers
Forward	Forward
Reverse	Reverse

should simply reinforce a purchase decision. From the viewpoint of the seller or target company shareholder, transactions may be tax free or entirely or partially taxable. The sale of stock, rather than assets, is generally preferable to the target firm shareholders to avoid double taxation, if the target firm is structured as a C corporation. Various taxable and tax-free structures, including both statutory mergers (two-party transactions) and triangular mergers (three-party transactions), are summarized in Table 12–1. The structure of transactions that create an immediate tax liability for the target's shareholders is discussed next, followed by those structures that enable such taxes to be deferred to a later date. For a detailed discussion of the application of the tax code to M&As, see PricewaterhouseCoopers (2006); CCH Tax Law Editors (2005); Hurter, Petersen, and Thompson: (2005); Ginsburg and Levin (2004); and Tillinghast (1998).

Taxable Transactions

A transaction generally is considered taxable to the target firm's shareholders if it involves the purchase of the target's stock or assets for substantially all cash, notes, or some other nonequity consideration. In this type of transaction, the term *cash* often is synonymous with the use of notes or other nonequity consideration as part of or as the entire purchase price. Using the term *cash* to represent all forms of non-equity payment, such transactions may take the form of a cash purchase of target assets, a cash purchase of target stock, a statutory cash merger or consolidation, or a triangular statutory cash merger. In a triangular cash merger, the target firm may either be merged into an acquirer's operating or a shell acquisition subsidiary, with the subsidiary surviving (i.e., a forward triangular cash merger) or the acquirer's subsidiary merged into the target firm with the target surviving (i.e., a reverse triangular cash merger).

The major advantages of using a triangular structure are limitations of the voting rights of acquiring shareholders and gaining the acquirer control of the target through a subsidiary without being directly responsible for the target's known and unknown liabilities. Recall that the acquiring firm is not required to get shareholder approval if the stock used to purchase the target represents less than 20 percent of the firm's total shares outstanding. However, this advantage may be nullified if the stock is newly issued and the firm's bylaws require such approval.

Taxable Purchase of Target Assets with Cash

If a transaction involves a cash purchase of target assets, the target company's tax cost or basis in the acquired stock or assets is increased or "stepped up" to their fair market value (FMV), which is equal to the purchase price paid by the acquirer. The resulting additional depreciation and amortization in future years reduces the present value of the tax liability of the combined companies. The target firm realizes an immediate gain or loss on assets sold equal to the difference between the FMV of the asset and the asset's adjusted tax basis (i.e., book value less accumulated depreciation).

The target's shareholders could be taxed twice, once when the firm pays taxes on any gains and a second time when the proceeds from the sale are paid to the shareholders either as a dividend or distribution following liquidation of the corporation. A liquidation of the target firm may occur if a buyer acquires enough of the assets of the target to cause it to cease operations. To compensate the target company shareholders for any tax liability they may incur, the buyer usually has to increase the purchase price (Ayers, Lefanowicz, and Robinson, 2003). Buyers are willing to do this only if the present value of the tax savings resulting from the step-up of the target's assets is greater than the increase in the purchase price required to compensate the target's shareholders for the increase in their tax liability.

There is little empirical evidence that the tax shelter resulting from the ability of the acquiring firm to increase the value of acquired assets to their FMV is a highly important motivating factor for a takeover (Auerbach and Reishus, 1988). However, taxable trans-actions have become somewhat more attractive to acquiring firms since 1993, when a change in legislation allowed acquirers to amortize intangible assets qualifying under Section 197 of the Internal Revenue Service Code. Such assets include goodwill, going concern value, books and records, customer lists, licenses, permits, franchises, and trade-marks. A "197" intangible must be amortized over 15 years for tax purposes. Moreover, the current tax code allows operating losses (including those resulting from the write down of impaired goodwill) to be used to recover taxes paid in the preceding 2 years and reduce future tax liabilities up to 20 years. The treatment of net operating loss carrybacks and carryforwards is discussed in more detail later in this chapter in a section entitled "Net Operating Losses."

Taxable Purchase of Target Stock with Cash

Taxable transactions often involve the purchase of the target's voting stock, because the purchase of assets automatically trigger a taxable gain for the target if the FMV of the acquired assets exceeds the target firm's tax basis in the assets. All stockholders are affected equally in a taxable purchase of assets, because the target firm is paying the taxes. In contrast, in a taxable stock purchase, double taxation does not occur, as the transaction takes place between the acquirer and the target firm's shareholders. Therefore, the target firm pays no taxes on the transaction.

The target firm does not restate (i.e., revalue) its assets and liabilities for tax pur-poses to reflect the amount that the acquirer paid for the shares of common stock. Rather, the tax basis (i.e., their value on the target's financial statements) of assets and liabilities of the target before the acquisition carries over to the acquirer after the acqui-sition. This represents a potential problem for the buyer in a purchase of stock, since the buyer loses the additional tax savings that would result from acquiring assets and writing them up to fair market value. Consequently, the buyer may want to reduce what it is willing to pay to the seller.

Section 338 Election

The acquirer and target firms can jointly elect Section 338 of the Internal Revenue Code and thereby record assets and liabilities at their fair market value for tax purposes. According to Section 338 of the U.S. tax code, a purchaser of 80 percent or more of the stock of the target may elect to treat the acquisition as if it were an acquisition of the target's assets for tax purposes. This enables the acquiring corporation to avoid having to transfer assets and obtain consents to assignment of all contracts (as would be required in a direct purchase of assets), while still benefiting from the write-up of assets. By not being viewed as a transfer of assets, asset transfer, sales, and use taxes may be avoided. However, the 338 election generates an immediate tax liability for the target firm, which is viewed by the IRS as an "old" corporation selling its assets to a "new" corporation. Consequently, the target must recognize and pay taxes on any gains of the sale of assets. To compensate for the immediate tax liability, the target firm may demand a higher selling price.

Triangular Cash-Out Mergers

The IRS generally views forward triangular cash mergers as a purchase of target assets followed by a liquidation of the target, for which target shareholders recognize a taxable gain or loss, as if they had sold their shares. Having in effect sold its operating assets, the target firm is frequently liquidated. Because the target firm ceases to exist, its tax attributes in the form of any tax loss carryforwards or carrybacks or investment tax credits do not carry over to the acquirer. However, its assets and liabilities do transfer, as it is a merger. Taxes are paid by the target firm on any gain on the sale of its assets and again by target shareholders who receive a liquidating dividend. With the merger, no minority shareholders remain, as all shareholders are required to accept the terms of the merger, although dissident shareholders may have appraisal rights for the stock they are required to sell. See Figure 12–1.

In contrast, the IRS treats the reverse triangular cash merger as a purchase of target shares, with the target firm, including its assets, liabilities, and tax attributes, surviving. Consequently, the cash is taxed only once when the target firm shareholders pay taxes on any gain on the sale of their stock. However, if the acquirer and target agree to invoke a 338 election (i.e., treating a stock purchase as a purchase of assets), the target will have had to pay taxes on any gains on assets written up to their fair market value. As a result of the 338 election, the IRS treats the purchase of target shares as a taxable purchase of assets, which can be stepped up to fair market value. See Figure 12–2. Table 12–2 summarizes the key characteristics of taxable transaction structures.

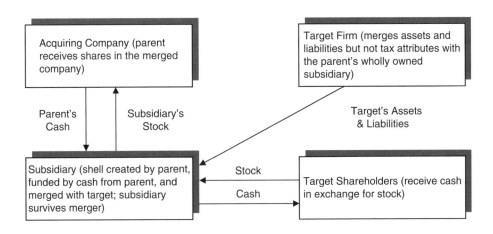

FIGURE 12–1 Forward triangular cash merger.

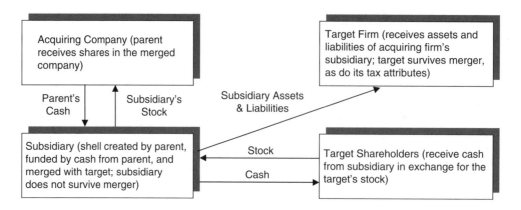

FIGURE 12–2 Reverse triangular cash merger.

Tax-Free Transactions

As a general rule, a transaction is tax free if the form of payment is primarily acquirer's stock. Transactions may be partially taxable if the target shareholders receive some non-equity consideration, such as cash or debt, in addition to the acquirer's stock. This non-equity consideration, or **boot**, is taxable if paid as a dividend to all shareholders, and it is taxed as ordinary income.

Acquirers and targets planning to enter into a tax-free transaction frequently seek to get an *advance ruling* from the IRS to determine its tax-free status. This is a binding formal ruling from the IRS. However, the certainty of the formal letter may diminish if any of the key assumptions underlying the transaction change prior to closing. Moreover, the process of requesting and receiving a letter may take five or six months. Alternatively, acquirers may rely on the opinion of trusted legal counsel.

If the transaction is tax free, the acquiring company is able to transfer or carry over the target's tax basis to its own financial statements. In the tax-free transaction, there is no increase or step-up in assets to FMV. A tax-free reorganization envisions the acquisition of all or substantially all of a target company's assets or shares. Consequently, the tax-free structure is generally not suitable for the acquisition of a division within a corporation.

Continuity of Interests and Continuity of Business Enterprise Requirements

Under the law, tax-free transactions contemplate substantial continuing involvement of the target company's shareholders. To demonstrate continuity of interests, target share-holders must continue to own a substantial part of the value of the combined target and acquiring firms. To demonstrate the continuity of a business enterprise, the acquiring corporation must either continue the acquired firm's "historic business enterprise" or use a significant portion of the target's "historic business assets" in a business. This continued involvement is intended to demonstrate a long-term or strategic commitment on the part of the acquiring company to the target. Nontaxable or tax-free transactions usually involve mergers, with the acquirer's stock exchanged for the target's stock or assets. Nontaxable transactions also are called *tax-free reorganizations*. The purpose of the continuity of interests' requirement is to prevent transactions that more closely resemble a sale from qualifying as a tax-free reorganization.

Table 12-2 Key Characteristics of Alternative Taxable (to Target Shareholders) Transaction Structures

Transaction Structure	Form of Payment	Acquirer Retains Target's Tax Attributes	Target Survives?	Parent Exposure to Target Liabilities	Shareholder Vote Required? Acquirer	Shareholder Vote Required? Target	Minority Freeze Out?	Automatic Transfer of Contracts?[2]
Purchase of stock	Mostly cash, debt, or other nonequity payment	Yes, but no asset step-up without 338 election[1]	Yes	High	No[4]	No, but shareholder may not sell shares	No	Yes
Purchase of assets	Mostly cash, debt, other nonequity payment	No, but can step up assets	Perhaps[3]	Low, except for assumed liabilities	No[4]	Yes, if sale of assets is substantial	No minority created	No
Statutory merger or consolidation	Mostly cash, debt, or other nonequity payment	Yes	No	High	No[4]	Yes	Yes[5]	Yes
Forward triangular cash merger (treated as an asset purchase by IRS as target generally liquidated)	Mostly cash, debt, or other nonequity payment	No	No	Low—limited by subsidiary	No[4]	Yes	Yes	No
Reverse triangular cash merger (treated as a stock purchase by IRS)	Mostly cash, debt, or other nonequity payment	Yes	Yes	Low—limited by subsidiary	No[4]	Yes	Yes	Yes

[1]An acquirer may treat a stock purchase as an asset purchase if it and the target agree to invoke a Section 338 (of the Tax Code) election.

[2]Contracts, leases, licenses, and rights to intellectual property automatically transfer unless contracts stipulate consent to assignment required.

[3]The target may choose to liquidate if the sale of assets is substantial, to distribute the proceeds to its shareholders, or to continue as a shell.

[4]May be required by public stock exchanges or by legal counsel if deemed material to the acquiring firm or if the parent needs to authorize new stock. In practice, most big mergers require shareholders' approval.

[5]Target shareholders must accept terms due to merger, although in some states dissident shareholders have appraisal rights for their shares.

Alternative Tax-Free Reorganizations

The eight principal forms of tax-free reorganizations are described in Section 368 of the Internal Revenue Code. Three are excluded from our discussion. These include Type D, transfers between related corporations; Type E, the restructuring of a firm's capital structure; and Type F, a reorganization in which the firm's name or location is changed. What follows is a discussion of the Type A reorganization, involving statutory mergers and consolidations; the Type B reorganization, involving a stock-for-stock purchase; the Type C reorganization, entailing a stock-for-assets purchase; and the forward and reverse triangular subsidiary mergers, in which the acquiring company creates a shell subsidiary as an intermediary to complete the transaction.

Types A and B are the most common tax-free reorganizations for mergers in which a combination of stock, cash, or debt is used to acquire the target's stock or assets. Forward and reverse triangular mergers are used primarily when the acquirer stock is the predominate form of payment used to purchase the target's stock or assets. Since the IRS requires that target shareholders continue to hold a substantial equity interest in the acquiring company, the tax code defines what constitutes a substantial equity interest. The definition varies with the type of tax-free reorganization used. Reorganizations under the tax code may be wholly (all stock) or partially (stock and other nonequity consideration) tax free. Triangular mergers are commonly used for tax-free transactions.

Type A reorganizations are statutory mergers or consolidations governed by state law. To qualify for a Type A reorganization, the transaction must be either a merger or a consolidation. There are no limitations on the type of consideration involved. Target company shareholders may receive cash, voting or nonvoting common or preferred stock, notes, or real property. Target shareholders need not be treated equally, in that some may receive all stock, others all cash, and still other a combination of the two. At least 40 percent of the purchase price must be acquiring company stock to ensure that the IRS's continuity of interests' requirement is satisfied.

The acquirer may choose not to purchase all the target's assets. Unlike a direct statutory merger, in which all known and unknown target assets and liabilities transfer to the buyer by rule of law, a subsidiary merger often results in the buyer, acquiring only a majority interest in the target, carries the target as a subsidiary of the parent. The target may later be merged into the parent in a backend merger (see Chapter 3). To ensure the target does not resemble an actual sale (therefore, making the transaction taxable), the acquirer must purchase a significant percentage of the target's net assets to satisfy the continuity of business enterprise principle. For forward and reverse triangular stock mergers, the acquirer must purchase at least 80 percent of the fair market value of the target's net assets.

Type A reorganizations are used widely as a result their great flexibility. Because there is no requirement to utilize voting stock, acquiring firms enjoy more options. By issuing nonvoting stock, the acquiring corporation may acquire control over the target without diluting control over the combined or newly created company. Moreover, there is no stipulation as to the amount of target net assets that must be acquired. Finally, there is no maximum amount of cash that may be used in the purchase price, and the limitations articulated by both the IRS and the courts allow significantly more cash than Types B or C reorganizations. Flexibility with respect to the amount of cash being used may be the most important consideration, because it enables the acquirer to better satisfy the disparate requirements of the target's shareholders. Some will want cash, and some will want stock.

In a *Type B stock-for-stock reorganization*, the acquirer, using its voting common stock, must purchase an amount of voting stock that constitutes at least 80 percent of the voting power of all voting stock outstanding (recall that some voting shares may have multiple voting rights). In addition, the acquirer must purchase at least 80 percent of each class of nonvoting shares. Any cash or debt disqualifies the transaction as a Type B reorganization. However, cash may be used to purchase fractional shares. Type B reorganizations are used as an alternative to a merger or consolidation. The target's stock may be purchased over 12 months or less as part of a formal acquisition plan. Type B reorganizations may be appropriate if the acquiring company wishes to conserve cash or its borrowing capacity. Since shares are being acquired directly from shareholders, there is no need for a target shareholder vote. Finally, contracts, licenses, and the like transfer with the stock, thereby obviating the need to receive consent to assignment, unless specified in the contract.

A *Type C stock-for-assets reorganization* requires that at least 80 percent of the FMV of the target's assets, as well as the assumption of certain specified liabilities, are acquired solely in exchange for acquirer voting stock. Since the cash portion of the purchase price must be reduced by assumed liabilities (which are viewed by the IRS as equivalent to cash), cash may be used to purchase the remainder of the stock only if the assumed liabilities amount to less than 20 percent of the FMV of the acquired assets. Since assumed liabilities frequently exceed 20 percent of the FMV of the acquired assets, the form of payment as a practical matter is generally 100 percent stock.

As part of the plan of reorganization, the target subsequent to closing dissolves and distributes the acquirer's stock to the target's shareholders for the now-canceled target stock. The Type C reorganization is used when it is essential for the acquirer not to assume any undisclosed liabilities. The requirement to use only voting stock is a major deterrent to the use of this type of reorganization. While a purchase of assets allows the acquirer to step up the basis of the acquired assets, asset purchases result in the target recognizing a taxable gain if the purchase price exceeds the firm's tax basis in the assets. If the target is liquidated to enable the firm to pay the sale proceeds to its shareholders, target shareholders then have to pay taxes on such payouts. The potential for double taxation generally makes the purchase of stock more attractive than an asset purchase. In contrast to a stock-for-stock reorganization, in which the target remains a wholly owned subsidiary of the buyer, the stock-for-assets reorganization result in the assessment of sales, use, and other transfer taxes.

A *forward triangular merger* is the most commonly used form of reorganization for tax-free asset acquisitions in which the form of payment is acquirer stock. It involves three parties: the acquiring firm, the target firm, and a shell subsidiary of the acquiring firm (Figure 12–3). As with the forward triangular cash merger described earlier, the

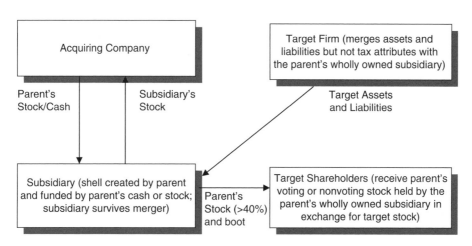

FIGURE 12–3 Forward triangular stock merger.

parent funds the shell corporation by buying stock issued by the shell with its own stock. All the target's stock is acquired by the subsidiary with the stock of the parent, and the target's stock is canceled, with the acquirer subsidiary surviving. The target company's assets and liabilities are merged into the acquirer's subsidiary in a statutory merger. The parent's stock may be voting or nonvoting, and the acquirer must purchase substantially all of the target's assets and liabilities. *Substantially all* is defined as 80 percent of the fair market value of the target's net assets (i.e., assets minus liabilities). According to new rules announced by the IRS in 2006, the substantially all requirement may not apply if a so-called disregarded unit, such as a limited liability company, is used as the acquiring subsidiary and the target firm (structured as a C corporation) ceases to exist. As such, no limitations would be placed on the amount of target net assets that have to be acquired to qualify as a tax-free reorganization. This is explained in more detail later in this chapter.

Asset sales by the target firm just prior to the transaction may threaten the tax-free status of the deal. Moreover, tax-free deals are disallowed within two years of a spin-off. The IRS imposes these limitations to preclude sellers from engaging in restructuring activities that make them more attractive to potential acquirers, which might be willing to consummate a tax-free deal if the size of the target firm were smaller. At least 40 percent of the purchase price must consist of acquirer stock, with the remainder consisting of boot, tailored to meet the needs of the target's shareholders. The transaction qualifies as a Type A tax-free reorganization. The parent indirectly owns all of the target's assets and liabilities, because it owns all the subsidiary's voting stock.

The advantages of the forward triangular merger may include the avoidance of approval by the parent firm's shareholders. However, public exchanges on which the parent firm's stock trades still may require parent shareholder approval if the amount of the parent stock used to acquire the target exceeds some predetermined percentage of parent voting shares outstanding. Other advantages include the possible insulation of the parent from the target's liabilities, which remain in the subsidiary, and the avoidance of asset recording fees and transfer taxes, because the target's assets go directly to the parent's wholly owned subsidiary.

The *reverse triangular merger* most commonly is used to effect tax-free stock acquisitions in which the form of payment is predominately the acquirer's voting stock (Figure 12–4). The acquirer forms a new shell subsidiary, which is merged into the target

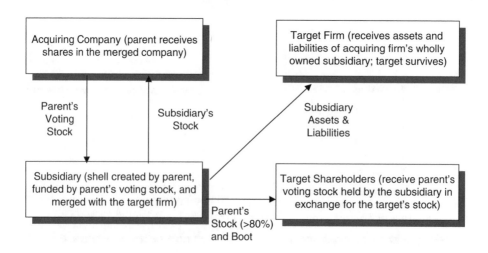

FIGURE 12–4 Reverse triangular stock merger.

in a statutory merger. The target is the surviving entity and must hold substantially all the assets and liabilities of both the target and shell subsidiary. *Substantially all* is generally defined as at least 80 percent of the FMV of net assets. The target firm's shares are canceled. The target shareholders receive the acquirer's or parent's shares. The parent corporation, which owned all of the subsidiary stock, now owns all the new target stock and, indirectly, all of the target's assets and liabilities. To qualify as a tax-free transaction, at least 80 percent of the total consideration paid to the target must be in the form of the acquirer's parent voting stock. This stock may be common or preferred equity. Like the forward triangular merger, a reverse triangular merger precludes asset sales or spin-offs just prior to the completion of the transaction. This transaction qualifies as a Type A tax-free reorganization. Note that, unlike a forward triangular merger, the substantially all requirement cannot be circumvented by merging a LLC created by a parent corporation with a target C Corporation and exchanging parent stock for target stock.

Although the reverse triangular merger is similar to a Type A reorganization, in which the acquiring company purchases the target's stock in exchange for its stock, it permits the acquirer to use up to 20 percent cash. The reverse merger also may avoid the need for parent company shareholder approval. Because the target firm remains in existence, the target can retain any nonassignable franchise, lease, or other valuable contract rights. Also, the target's liabilities are isolated in a subsidiary of the acquirer. Moreover, by avoiding the dissolution of the target firm, the acquirer avoids the possible acceleration of loans outstanding. Finally, insurance, banking, and public utility regulators may require the target to remain in existence in exchange for their granting regulatory approval. See Table 12–3 for a summary of the key characteristics of alternative tax-free deal structures.

Expanding the Role of Mergers in Tax-Free Reorganizations

In late 2006, the IRS finalized regulations under Treasury Regulation Section 1.368–2 defining the term *statutory merger* or *consolidation* for purposes of using tax-free reorganizations. The new regulations offer more flexibility to businesses in using the statutory merger or consolidation with respect to transactions involving so-called disregarded entities. Such entities include separate limited liability companies, a corporation that is a qualified real estate investment trust subsidiary, and a corporation that is a qualified subchapter S subsidiary, as well as transactions completed under the laws of foreign jurisdictions. The new rules apply to transactions taking place on or after January 22, 2006.

Under the new regulations, only the continuity of interests and the continuity of business enterprise tests, and not the more restrictive substantially all requirement, must be satisfied. Previously, two-party statutory Type A mergers offered greater flexibility than three-party transactions, since they placed no restriction on the amount of target net assets that could be acquired and allowed the use of nonvoting stock. In contrast, Type A triangular mergers generally require the use of voting stock and require the purchase of at least 80 percent of the fair market value of the net assets of the target firm.

It is now possible for a merger of a corporation into a single-member (i.e., parent firm) limited liability company established by the parent corporation in a triangular merger to qualify as a two-party Type A merger. However, the target firm must be a C corporation that ceases to exist after the transaction is completed. As a two-party Type A statutory merger, there is no limitation on the amount of target net assets the buyer must acquire. Because three parties are involved in the forward triangular merger, the target firm can be operated as a subsidiary, thereby insulating the parent from its liabilities. Furthermore, no vote of parent firm shareholders is required because the parent firm is

Table 12-3 Key Characteristics of Alternative Tax-Free (to Target Shareholders) Transaction Structures[1]

Transaction Structure (Type of Reorganization)	Form of Payment	Limitation[2]	Acquirer Retains Target Tax Attributes	Target Survives?	Parent Exposure to Target Liabilities	Shareholder Vote Required?		Minority Freeze Out?	Automatic Transfer of Contracts?[3]
						Acquirer	Target		
Statutory merger or consolidation (Type A reorganization)	At least 40% parent voting or nonvoting stock	No limitations on target net assets purchased	Yes, but no asset step up	No	High, unless merged into subsidiary[4]	No[6,7]	Yes	Yes	Yes
Forward triangular stock merger (Type A reorganization)	At least 40% parent voting or nonvoting stock	Must purchase at least 80% of FMV of net assets unless LLC acquiring sub	Yes, but no asset step up	No	Low, limited by subsidiary	No[6,7]	Yes	Yes	No
Reverse triangular stock merger (Type A reorganization)	At least 80% parent voting stock (common or preferred)	Must purchase at least 80% of FMV of net assets	Yes, but no asset step up	Yes	Low, limited by subsidiary	No[6,7]	Yes	Yes	Target retains non-assignable contracts, etc.
Purchase of stock without a merger (Type B reorganization)	100% parent voting stock (common or preferred)	Must purchase at least 80% of voting and nonvoting shares	Yes, but no asset step up	Yes	Low, limited by subsidiary	No[6]	No, as shares bought directly from shareholders	No	Yes
Purchase of assets (Type C reorganization)	100% voting stock[8]	Must purchase at least 80% FMV of net assets	No and no asset step up	No	Low,[5] except for assumed liabilities	No[6]	Yes, if sale of assets substantial	No minority created	No

[1] Target shareholders are taxed at ordinary rates on any "boot" received (i.e., anything other than acquiring stock).

[2] Asset sales or spin-offs two years prior (may reflect effort to reduce size of purchase) or subsequent to (violates continuity requirement) closing may invalidate tax-free status. Forward triangular mergers do not require any limitations on purchase of target net assets if a so-called "disregarded unit" such as an LLC is used as the acquiring entity and the target is a C corporation which ceases to exist as a result of the transaction.

[3] Contracts, leases, licenses, and rights to intellectual property automatically transfer with the stock unless contracts stipulate consent to assignment required. Moreover, target retains any non-assignable franchise, lease or other contract right, as long as target is the surviving entity as in a reverse triangular merger.

[4] Acquirer may be insulated from a target's liabilities as long as it is held in a subsidiary, except for liabilities such as unpaid taxes, unfunded pension obligations, and environmental liabilities.

[5] The parent is responsible for those liabilities conveying with the assets, such as warranty claims.

[6] May be required by public stock exchanges or legal counsel if deemed material to the acquiring firm or if the parent needs to authorize new stock.

[7] Mergers are generally ill-suited for hostile transactions, because they require approval of both the target's board and shareholders.

[8] While cash may be used to pay for up to 20% of the FMV of net assets, it must be offset by assumed liabilities, making the purchase price usually 100% stock.

the sole owner of the subsidiary unless the increase in shares issued to complete the transaction exceeds 20 percent of total parent shares outstanding. All of this can be accomplished without endangering the tax-free status of the transaction.

For years, the IRS had contended that a foreign corporation could not participate in a Type A tax-free reorganization, because the term *statutory merger* referred only to a merger completed under the laws of the United States, a state, or the District of Columbia. With the advent of the new regulations, the merger of a foreign corporation into another foreign corporation (or the creation of a new corporation in a consolidation) in accordance with the host country's laws qualifies as a Type A reorganization. As such, the exchange would be tax free for any U.S. shareholders in the target firm receiving acquirer shares or shares in the new company formed as a result of the consolidation. The new regulations make it easier to qualify foreign acquisitions, both unrelated party transactions and internal restructurings and reorganizations, as Type A tax-free reorganizations. Therefore, if a U.S. firm buys a foreign firm having U.S. shareholders, the transaction can be structured so that the purchase is free of U.S. taxes to the U.S. shareholders.

Tax-Free Transactions Arising from 1031 "Like-Kind" Exchanges

The prospect of being able to defer taxable gains indefinitely is often associated with 1031 exchanges of real estate property. The potential benefits are significant, with capital gains taxes (as of the publication of this book) of 15 percent at the federal level and between 10 percent and 15 percent at the state level. Furthermore, depreciation recapture taxes (i.e., applied to the difference between accelerated and straight-line depreciation) also may be postponed with applicable federal income tax rates as high as 35 percent (as of the printing of this book) and some state income tax rates approaching 10 percent.

The concept involves selling one property and buying another subject to certain restrictions and time limitations. The 1031 exchanges are relevant to M&As in that they represent a means of using "like-kind" assets to finance all or a portion of the purchase price of the target firm, while deferring the payment of taxes. A section of the U.S. tax code, known as 1031, allows investors to make a "like-kind" exchange of investment properties. A wide variety of investment properties can be swapped for others, such as an apartment complex for land or an oil and gas property for a commercial strip mall. Investors can continue exchanging existing properties for new properties of equal or greater value, while deferring any tax consequences.

By postponing the tax payments, investors have more money to reinvest in new properties. For example, assume a property was purchased 10 years ago for $5 million and it is now worth $15 million. If the property is sold with no subsequent purchase of a substantially similar property within the required time period, the federal capital gains tax bill would be $1.5 million (i.e., ($15 − $5) × 0.15). This ignores the potential for state taxes or depreciation recapture taxes, which could be owed if the owner took deductions for depreciation. However, by entering into a 1031 exchange, the owner could use the entire $15 million from the sale of the property as a down payment on a more expensive property. If the investor acquires a property of a lesser value, taxes are owed on the difference.

To qualify for a 1031 exchange, the property must be an investment property or one that is used in a trade or business (e.g., a warehouse, store, or commercial office building). Delayed exchanges are the most common means of implementing this type of a tax strategy. When a property is sold, a replacement property must be identified within 45 days of the closing. The deal for the replacement property must be closed within 180 days. An independent party, known as a *qualified intermediary*, must hold the proceeds of the sale until the next property is purchased. The intermediary cannot be a party directly involved in the transaction, such as your real estate broker, lawyer, or accountant. Moreover, if the taxpayer were to take control of the proceeds of the sale, it would invalidate the "like-kind" exchange. Qualified intermediaries can be found by contacting the Federation of Exchange Accommodators (www.1031.org).

In a tax-free asset swap, News Corp reached agreement in early 2007 to buy Liberty Media's 19 percent or $11 billion stake in the media giant in exchange for News Corp's 38.6 percent stake in the satellite TV firm DirecTV Group, $550 million in cash, and three sports TV channels. While the two investments were approximately equal in value, Liberty's management believed that DirecTV's stock was inflated by speculation about the impending deal. The cash and media assets were added to ensure that Liberty Media is exchanging its stake in News Corp for "like-kind" assets of an equivalent or higher value to qualify as a tax-free exchange. By structuring the deal in this manner, the transaction is viewed as an asset swap rather than a sale of assets, resulting in Liberty Media being able to save billions of dollars in taxes that would have been owed due to its low basis in its investment in News Corp. If the assets had been divested, the two companies would have had to pay an estimated $4.5 billion in taxes due to likely gains on the sale of these assets (Angwin and Drucker, 2006). Similarly, Berkshire Hathaway Inc. traded its 16.3 percent stake in White Mountains Insurance Group for two of the firm's subsidiaries and $751 million in cash. The terms of the deal value Berkshire's White Mountains stock at $836 million. Because the deal is structured as an asset swap, neither firm expects to record a taxable gain on the transaction.

Other Tax Considerations Affecting Corporate Restructuring Activities

Many areas of the tax code affect corporate restructuring activities. Treatment of net operating losses, corporate capital gains taxes, the alternative corporate minimum tax, the treatment of greenmail for tax purposes, Morris Trust transactions, and leveraged partnerships are discussed in this section of this chapter.

Net Operating Losses

Net operating loss (NOL) carrybacks and carryforwards are provisions in the tax laws allowing firms to use NOLs generated in the past to carry those losses back two years (to obtain a tax refund if those years were profitable) and forward 20 years to offset future taxable income. The Tax Reform Act of 1986 introduced an annual limit on the use of net operating loss carryforwards. The limit takes effect if there is a greater than 50 percent change in ownership in a corporation generating cumulative losses during the three years preceding the change in ownership. Such corporations are referred to as *loss corporations*. The maximum amount of the NOL that can be used annually to offset earnings is limited to the value of the "loss corporation" on the date of the acquisition multiplied by the long-term tax-exempt bond rate. Furthermore, "loss corporations" cannot use a net operating loss carryforward unless they remain viable and in essentially the same business for at least two years following the closing of the acquisition.

Despite the limitations imposed by the tax code, NOLs may still represent a potentially significant source of value to acquirers that should be considered during the process of valuing an acquisition target. Lucent Technologies had accumulated numerous losses since the bursting of the Internet bubble in 2000. By acquiring Lucent in 2006, Alcatel obtained $3.5 billion in net operating losses that could be used to shelter future income for many years (Drucker and Silver, 2006). Exhibit 12–1 illustrates how the analyst might value NOLs on the books of a target corporation.

Exhibit 12–1 Valuing Net Operating Losses

Acquiring Company is contemplating buying Target Company, which has a tax loss carryforward of $8 million. Acquiring Company has a 40-percent tax rate. Assume the tax-loss carryforward is within the limits of the Tax Reform Act of 1986 and the firm's cost of capital is 15 percent. Information on the two firms is given in Table 12–4.

Table 12–4   Information on the Firms

Years Remaining in Loss Carryforward	Amount ($000)	Years after Acquisiton	Earnings before Tax ($000)
1	2,000	1	1,800
2	2,000	2	2,000
3	800	3	1,000
4	1,200	4	1,000
5	800	5	2,000
Total	6,800	Total	7,800

Calculate Acquiring Company's tax payments without the acquisition.

Years	Tax Benefit
1	720
2	800
3	400
4	400
5	800

Calculate Acquiring Company's tax payment for each year with the proposed acquisition.

Years	Earnings before Taxes ($000)	Tax Loss ($000)	Amount Carried Forward ($000)	Use of Tax Loss ($000)	Taxable Income ($000)	Tax Payment ($000)
1	1,800	2,000		1,800	0	0
2	2,000	2,000	200	2,000	0	0
3	1,000	800	0	1,000	0	0
4	1,000	1,200	200	1,000	0	0
5	2,000	800	0	1,000	1,000	400

What is the most the Acquiring Company should pay for the Target Company if its only value is its tax loss?

Answer

The Acquiring Company should not pay more than the present value of the net tax benefit: $720,000, $800,000, $400,000, $400,000, and $400,000. The present value of the cumulative tax benefits discounted at a 15 percent cost of capital is $1,921,580.

Notes

1. Tax benefits are equal to earnings before tax times the 40 percent marginal tax rate of the Acquiring Company. Therefore, the tax benefit in year 1 is $1.8 million $\times$ 0.4 = $720,000.

2. The net tax benefit in the fifth year is equal to the $800,000 tax benefit less the $400,000 in tax payments required in the fifth year.

Although NOLs represent a potential source of value, their use must be monitored carefully to realize the full value resulting from the potential for deferring income taxes. An acquirer must be highly confident that the expected future pretax income stream will be realized. Without the future income, the NOLs expire worthless. Because the acquirer can never be certain that future income will be sufficient to fully realize the value of the NOLs, loss carryforwards alone rarely justify an acquisition. Studies show that it is easy to overstate the value of loss carryforwards because of the potential for them to expire before they can be fully used. Empirical analyses indicate that the actual tax savings realized from loss carryforwards tend to be about one half of their expected value (Auerbach and Poterba, 1987).

In late 2007, General Motors Corporation announced a $39 billion noncash charge on its income statement (and the addition of an equivalent reserve to its balance sheet) to write down deferred-tax assets. The deferred-tax assets had resulted from cumulative losses and could be used to offset taxes on current or future profits for a number of years. However, the write-down suggests that the firm, currently experiencing huge operating losses, does not expect to return to profitability any time soon. Consequently, some portion of the tax deferrals is likely to expire before they can be used to offset future taxable income. If the corporation were to return to profitability, the firm could reverse (i.e., remove) the valuation reserve and utilize some portion of the unexpired deferred tax credits to reduce its tax liability.

Corporate Capital Gains Taxes

Since both short-term and long-term corporate capital gains are taxed as ordinary income and subject to a maximum federal corporate tax rate of 34 percent, acquirers often adopt alternative legal structures having more favorable tax attributes in making acquisitions. These include master limited partnerships (MLPs), subchapter S corporations, and limited liability companies (LLCs). Profits distributed directly to MLP partners, subchapter S corporation shareholders, and LLC members are taxed at their personal tax rates. See Chapter 14 for a more detailed discussion of taxation concerning these types of so-called pass-through organizations.

Alternative Corporate Minimum Tax

Under certain circumstances in which corporate taxes have been significantly reduced, corporations may be subject to an alternative minimum tax with a flat rate of 20 percent. The introduction of the alternative minimum tax has proven to be particularly burdensome for leveraged buyouts. LBOs are by intent highly leveraged and have little if any taxable income because of their high annual interest expense. Consequently, the imposition of the alternative minimum tax reduced the potential returns to equity investors that could be achieved as a result of highly leveraged transactions. See Chapter 13 for a more detailed discussion of LBOs.

Greenmail Payments

Greenmail refers to payments made to "corporate raiders" to buy back positions they had taken in target companies (see Chapter 3). Greenmail was made more expensive by changes in the tax code, which sharply reduced the amount of such payments that could be deducted from before tax profits.

Morris Trust Transactions

So-called Morris Trust transaction tax code rules restrict how certain types of corporate deals can be structured to avoid taxes. Assume Firm A sells an operating unit to Firm B and makes a profit on the transaction on which it would owe taxes. To avoid the payment of taxes, Firm A spins off the operating unit as a dividend to its shareholders. The operating unit, still owned by Firm A's shareholders, is subsequently merged with Firm B. This causes shareholders in Firm A to become shareholders in Firm B. By spinning off the operating unit, Firm A was able to avoid the payment of corporate taxes on taxable gains, and Firm A's shareholders were able to defer the payment of personal taxes on any gains until they sold their stock in Firm B.

To make such transactions less attractive, the tax code was amended in 1997 to require that taxes would not have to be paid only if no cash changed hands and Firm A's shareholders end up as majority owners in Firm B. Without the maintenance of "continuity of ownership" in the operating unit, the IRS views this type of transaction as a sale having taken place. The practical effect of the requirement that Firm A maintain majority ownership is that merger partners such as Firm B in these types of transactions must be significantly smaller than Firm A. This reduces significantly the number of potential deal candidates.

The tax code was changed in 1997 in response to deals that were done on a tax-free basis that appeared to be sales in disguise. In some instances, parent companies would borrow money through a subsidiary and keep the money, while leaving responsibility for repaying the debt with the subsidiary. The subsidiary was then spun off to its shareholders. Later, the former subsidiary would be merged with another company. The cash was effectively transferred from the merger partner to the former parent company tax free, even if the parent would have earned a profit on the transaction if it had sold the business outright. (Note that, if a corporation borrows funds, retains the funds, but later transfers responsibility for repayment to another entity, the funds are viewed as taxable income to the original borrower by the IRS.)

The change in the law has had a material impact on the way M&A business is conducted. For example, in 2005, Alltel announced it was getting rid of its local telephone business. Although Alltel had been in talks with phone companies, their size made the prospects of tax-free transaction more complicated. In the end, Alltel sold the business to a far smaller firm, Valor Communications Group Inc., to meet the requirements of the tax code.

Leveraged Partnerships

Leveraged partnerships may permit a C corporation to sell appreciated assets for cash without incurring an immediate tax liability. Assume Firm A wants to sell appreciated assets to Firm B but also wishes to defer the payment of taxes on the resulting profit on the sale. Firm A may be able to avoid recognizing the gain immediately by forming a partnership with B. This could be accomplished in the following manner.

The two firms form a partnership called AB. A contributes the appreciated assets to AB and retains a minimal ownership position in AB. In turn, B contributes a substantial amount of assets to AB in exchange for the remaining ownership equity. AB subsequently borrows an amount equal to the value of the assets contributed by A from a third-party lender, with A guaranteeing the debt. The proceeds of the debt are distributed to A. As guarantor, A has effectively borrowed the funds. Therefore, the transaction is not viewed as a sale and no gain must be recorded for tax purposes. The debt is structured as consisting of annual interest payments and a single payment of principal at maturity paid by the partnership. Immediately before the debt is retired, B also acquires A's interest in AB for a small amount of money and A is released from the loan guarantee. B, as the sole owner of AB, owns the assets initially contributed by A.

This appears to have been the structure employed by Cablevision and the Tribune Company on May 12, 2008, when they announced a new partnership through which Cablevision would acquire 97 percent of Newsday (see Case Study 12–1).

Case Study 12–1 Cablevision Acquires Majority of Newsday Media Group

Cablevision Systems Corporation (CVC) prevailed in early 2008 in the bidding for Newsday Media Group (Newsday) after News Corporation withdrew from the running. Under the terms of the transaction, CVC would have about 97 percent and the Tribune Company (Tribune) 3 percent equity ownership in the partnership. Tribune would contribute the Newsday assets, and CVC would contribute newly issued parent company bonds with a fair market value of $650 million of senior debt maturing in 10 years. The CVC debt is equivalent to contributing a deferred cash payment, with the cash actually paid to the partnership when the bonds mature. The partnership would borrow $650 million for 10 years from the Bank of America, guaranteed by Tribune Company. The proceeds would be distributed to Tribune.

Tribune would not have to pay capital gains taxes on the $650 million, despite having earned a profit on the "deferred sale" of Newsday. In 2007, turnaround specialist Sam Zell, after taking the Tribune Company private, converted the firm from a C corporation to an S corporation to take advantage of favorable tax treatment. C corporation profits are taxed twice (once when earned and a second time when distributed to shareholders). In contrast, S corporations must distribute all profits, which are taxed at their shareholders ordinary tax rates. Asset sales within 10 years of the conversion from a C to an S corporation are subject to capital gains taxes.

By structuring the transaction as a leveraged partnership, the Tribune Corporation need not recognize the contribution of Newsday to the partnership as a sale, on which it would have to pay capital gains taxes, since CVC does not own Newsday outright until the debt matures in 10 years. At that time, the 10-year holding period following the conversion of Tribune from a C to an S corporation would have expired, and Tribune would not be required to recognize the gain on the sale of Newsday as taxable event.

Discussion Questions

1. Assume that this transaction could not have been structured as nontaxable to the Tribune Company. Speculate under what circumstances it might still have taken place. Be specific.
2. To what extent do tax laws affect the efficiency of free markets for M&As? (Note: Efficiency refers to the cost of doing business.) Be specific.

Financial Reporting of Business Combinations

Since 2001, all M&As must be accounted for using the purchase method (also called the *acquisition method*) as required by the Financial Accounting Standards Board (FASB), an independent organization funded entirely by the private sector. A company maintaining its financial statements under international financial reporting standards (IFRS) or generally accepted accounting principles (GAAP) needs to account for its business combinations according IFRS 3 and SFAS (statements of financial accounting standards) 141, respectively.

According to **purchase accounting**, the purchase price or acquisition cost is determined and, using a cost allocation approach, assigned first to tangible then intangible net assets, at their value on the date of the signing of the agreement of purchase and sale and recorded on the books of the acquiring company. *Net assets* refer to acquired assets less assumed liabilities. Any excess of the purchase price over the fair value of the acquired net assets is recorded as goodwill. Goodwill is an asset representing future economic benefits arising from acquired assets that were not identified individually. However, effective for transactions whose acquisition date occurs on or after December 15, 2008, revised accounting rules, SFAS 141R, changed the standards covering business combinations to require the acquiring entity to recognize, separately from goodwill, identifiable assets and assumed liabilities at their acquisition date (closing date) fair values and account for future changes in fair value. The introduction of SFAS 141R was intended to achieve greater conformity with international accounting standards as applied to business combinations.

In addition to SFAS 141R, another recent accounting standard change that could have a significant impact on the way mergers and acquisition are done is SFAS 157, which introduces a new definition of *fair value*. Previously, the definition of *fair value* was ambiguous and it often was used inconsistently. The implications of SFAS 141R and SFAS 157 for M&As are discussed next.

Differences between SFAS 141 and SFAS 141R

The revised standards require an acquirer to recognize the assets acquired, the liabilities assumed, and any noncontrolling interest in the acquirer to be measured at their fair value as of the acquisition or closing date. This directive replaces Statement 141's cost-allocation process, which required the cost of an acquisition to be allocated to the individual assets acquired and liabilities assumed based on their estimated fair values on the announcement date. The announcement date often coincides with the signing of the agreement of purchase of sale by the acquirer and target firms. Guidance given in SFAS 141 resulted in not recognizing items, such as acquisition-related expenses, on the date of the acquisition. The revised standards retain the fundamental requirements of SFAS 141 that the applicable acquisition method of accounting for all business combinations be the purchase method of accounting and for an acquirer to be identified for each business combination. The revised standard defines the *acquirer* as the entity that obtains control of one or more businesses in the business combination and establishes the acquisition date as the date the acquirer achieves control. The acquisition date generally corresponds to the closing date rather than the announcement or signing date, as was true previously. SFAS 141R is more inclusive than the earlier standards.

Under the new standard, a *business* is defined as an integrated set of activities and assets utilized in such a way as to provide a stream of benefits, such as dividends, increasing share price, or lower costs. As such, a business need not actually generate outputs. Consequently, what had been classified previously as asset purchases, such as pipeline purchases, or assets still in their development stage, such as reserves of natural resources, must now be treated as business combinations. Other major differences between SFAS 141 and SFAS 141R are discussed next.

Recognizing Acquired Net Assets and Goodwill at Fair Value

To increase the ability to compare different transactions, Statement 141R requires the acquirer to recognize goodwill as of the acquisition date, measured as the excess of the purchase price plus the fair value of any noncontrolling (i.e., minority) interest in the target at the acquisition date over the fair value of the acquired net assets. Previously, guidelines as to how to treat noncontrolling interests were ambiguous.

Statement 141R requires recognizing 100 percent of the assets acquired and liabilities assumed, even if less than 100 percent of the target's ownership interests are acquired by the buyer. In other words, this results in the recognition of the target's business in its entirety regardless of whether 51 percent or 100 percent (or any amount in between) of the target is acquired. Consequently, the portion of the target that was not acquired (i.e., the noncontrolling or minority interest) is also recognized, causing the buyer to account for both the goodwill attributable to it and to the noncontrolling interest. Minority interest is reported in the consolidated balance sheet within the equity account, separately from the parent's equity. Moreover, the revenues, expenses, gains, losses, net income or loss, and other income associated with the noncontrolling interest should be reported on the consolidated income statement.

A *bargain purchase* is defined as a business combination in which the total acquisition date fair value of the acquired net assets exceeds the fair value of the purchase price plus the fair value of any noncontrolling interest in the target. Such a purchase may arise due to forced liquidation or distressed sales. Statement 141R requires the acquirer to recognize that excess on the consolidated income statement as a gain attributable to the acquirer. Previously, Statement 141 required the "negative goodwill" to be allocated on a pro-rata basis to particular assets acquired.

Recognizing and Measuring Net Acquired Assets in Step or Stage Transactions

The revised standards require an acquirer in a business combination undertaken in stages (i.e., a stage or step transaction) to recognize the acquired net assets as well as the noncontrolling interest in the target firm, at the full amounts of their fair values. Previously, under Statement 141, an entity that acquired another entity in a series of purchases identified the cost of each investment, the fair value of the acquired net assets, and the goodwill at each step. Consequently, business combinations consummated under a step transaction resulted in a blend of historical costs and fair values. Under the revised standard, net acquired assets at each step must be revalued to the current fair market value. The acquirer is obligated to disclose gains or losses that arise due to the reestimation of the formerly noncontrolling interests on the income statement. Furthermore, if prior gains or losses on the noncontrolling interests were reported under "other comprehensive income," the acquirer is required to reclassify such gains or losses and report their impact on earnings.

Recognizing Contingent Considerations

Revised standards pertaining to contingencies and contingent considerations also may affect how deals are done. Contingencies are uncertainties that may result in future assets or liabilities. Examples include potential legal, environmental, and warranty claims about which the future may not be fully known at the time a transaction is consummated. The new standards require the acquirer to report an asset or liability arising from a contingency to be recognized at its acquisition date fair value, absent new information about the possible outcome. However, as new information becomes available, the acquirer must revalue the asset or liability to its current fair value, reflecting the new information, and record the impact of changes in the fair values of these assets or liabilities on earnings. In the past, uncertain liabilities, such as contingent obligations, need not be recorded until their dollar amount was known. The revised standards are likely to encourage more rigorously defined limits on liability (i.e., indemnification) in acquisitions. Rather than a general indemnification clause, indemnification clauses likely will cover specific issues.

Contingent consideration or payments are an important component of many transactions and include the transfer of additional equity or cash to the previous owners of the target firm (e.g., earn-outs). Payment of contingent consideration depends on the achievement of certain prespecified performance benchmarks by the acquired business over a period of time. Statement 141R treats contingent consideration as part of the total consideration paid (i.e., purchase price) for the acquired business, which is measured at the acquisition date fair value. The revised standard also requires the reporting entity to reestimate the fair value of the contingent consideration at each reporting date until the amount of the payout (if any) is determined, with changes in fair value during the period reported as a gain or loss on the income statement. The potential for increased earnings volatility due to changes in the value of contingent liabilities may reduce the attractiveness of earn-outs as a form of consideration.

In-Process Research and Development Assets

Prior to Statement 141R, R&D assets acquired in a business combination that had no alternative future use were to be measured at their acquisition date fair values then immediately expensed. If the R&D assets were later found to have commercial value, the firm could recognize its value on the balance sheet and record a gain on the firm's income statement. Under the new standards, the acquirer must recognize separately from goodwill the acquisition date fair values of R&D assets acquired in the business combination. Such assets would remain on the books as an asset with an indefinite life until the project's outcome is known. If the specific project is deemed a success, the firm would begin to amortize the asset over the estimated useful life of the technology; if the research project is abandoned, the R&D asset booked at the date of the acquisition would be considered impaired and expensed.

Expensing Deal Costs

Under Statement 141, acquisition expenses, such as legal, accounting, and investment banking fees, were capitalized and allocated to the acquired assets and assumed liabilities. Consequently, their cost was amortized over time, even though they were incurred on the closing date. Under the new standard, such transaction-related costs are recorded as an expense on the closing date and charged against current earnings. As such, firms may need to explain the nature of the costs incurred in closing a deal and the impact of such costs on the earnings of the combined firms. This could result in downward pressure on such fees, as acquirers become more aggressive in negotiating the cost of legal and advisory services. Financing costs, such as expenses incurred as a result of new debt and equity issues, will continue to be capitalized and amortized over time.

SFAS 157: The New Fair Value Framework

The effective date for SFAS 157 for financial assets and liabilities on financial statements was November 15, 2007, and November 15, 2008 for nonfinancial assets and liabilities. The new definition of fair value under this standard is the price that would be received to sell an asset or paid to transfer a liability in an orderly transaction (i.e., not a forced liquidation or distress sale) between market participants on the date on which the asset or liability is to be estimated. The new definition of fair value introduces the notion that fair value is an "exit" price that a market participant would pay the seller for a company, asset, or investment. An asset's "entry" price would always be the price that was paid. However, the asset's exit price could fluctuate dramatically, reflecting changing market, industry, or regulatory conditions. The purpose of SFAS 157 was to establish a single definition of fair value and a consistent framework for measuring fair value under GAAP that would result in increased consistency and comparability in fair value estimates.

SFAS 157 allows acquirers to use the market approach (i.e., valuation based on prices paid for comparable assets or in recent transactions), the income approach (i.e., discounted cash flow), or the replacement cost approach (i.e., estimating what it would cost to physically replace an asset). Once a valuation approach is selected, SFAS 157 requires sufficient disclosure to enable users of financial statements to understand how an asset was valued. So-called Level 1 assets are those whose valuation is based on quoted prices for identical assets or liabilities in an active or liquid market. Level 2 assets and liabilities are valued based on either a quote for an identical item in an inactive or illiquid market or a quote for similar items in active or liquid market. Finally, Level 3 assets and liabilities are valued using the firm's own data and valuation models. Whenever possible, firms are required to use actual market information.

Some have argued that the requirement for banks to continuously "mark to market" the value of distressed financial assets contributed to the extreme financial instability of the global credit markets during 2008 and 2009. Succumbing to U.S. Congressional pressure, the U.S. Financial Accounting Standards Board on April 3, 2009 relaxed the fair value accounting standards allowing banks more freedom to use their own valuation models rather than current market prices to value assets whose markets had become illiquid. In contrast, the International Accounting Standards Board, which sets rules for more than 100 countries including the European Union, indicated that, rather than weaken current rules, it would accelerate efforts to review how it accounts for financial assets.

Impact of Purchase Accounting on Financial Statements

A long-term asset is an *impaired asset* if its fair value falls below its book or carrying value. If this is the case, the firm is required to report a loss equal to the difference between the asset's fair value and its carrying value. Impairment could occur due to loss of customers, loss of contracts, loss of key personnel, obsolescence of technology, litigation, patent expiration, failure to achieve anticipated cost savings, overall market slowdown, and so forth. The write-down of assets associated with an acquisition constitutes a public admission by the firm's management of having substantially overpaid for the acquired assets. In an effort to minimize goodwill, auditors often require that factors underlying goodwill be tied to specific intangible assets for which fair value can be estimated, such as customer lists and brand names. These intangible assets must be capitalized and shown on the balance sheet. Consequently, if the anticipated cash flows associated with an intangible asset, such as a customer list, have not materialized, the carrying value of the customer list must be written down to reflect its current value.

Balance Sheet Considerations

For financial reporting purposes, the purchase price (PP) paid (including the fair value of any noncontrolling interest in the target at the acquisition date) for the target company consists of the fair market value of total identifiable acquired tangible and intangible assets (FMV_{TA}) less total assumed liabilities (FMV_{TL}) plus goodwill (FMV_{GW}). The difference between FMV_{TA} and FMV_{TL} is called *net asset value*.

These relationships can be summarized as follows:

$$\text{Purchase price (total consideration): } PP = FMV_{TA} - FMV_{TL} + FMV_{GW} \qquad (12\text{--}1)$$

$$\begin{aligned} \text{Calculation of goodwill: } FMV_{GW} &= PP - FMV_{TA} + FMV_{TL} \\ &= PP - (FMV_{TA} - FMV_{TL}) \end{aligned} \qquad (12\text{--}2)$$

From equation (12–2), it should be noted that, as net asset value increases, FMV_{GW} decreases. Also note that, from equation (12–2), the calculation of goodwill can result in either a positive (i.e., PP > net asset value) or negative (i.e., PP < net asset value) value. Negative goodwill arises if the acquired assets are purchased at a discount to their FMV, referred under Statement 141R as a *bargain purchase*. Exhibit 12–2 illustrates the calculation of goodwill in a transaction in which the acquirer purchases less than 100 percent of the target's outstanding shares. Valuation guidelines for each major balance-sheet category are listed in Exhibit 12–3.

Exhibit 12–2 Estimating Goodwill

On January 1, 2009, Acquirer Inc. purchased 80 percent of Target Inc.'s 1 million shares outstanding at $50 per share for a total value of $40 million (i.e., 0.8 × 1 million shares outstanding × $50/share). On that date, the fair value of total Target net assets was estimated to be $42 million. Acquirer paid a 20 percent control premium, which was already included in the $50 per share purchase price. The implied minority discount of the minority shares is 16.7 percent, that is, $1 - (1/1 + 0.2)$.[1] What is the value of the goodwill shown on Acquirer's consolidated balance sheet? What portion of that goodwill is attributable to the minority interest retained by Target's shareholders? What is the fair value of the 20 percent minority interest measured on a fair value per share basis?

Goodwill Shown on Acquirer's Balance Sheet

From equation (12–2), goodwill (FMV_{GW}) can be estimated as follows:

$$FMV_{GW} = PP - (FMV_{TA} - FMV_{TL}) = \$50 \text{ million } - \$42 \text{ million } = \$8 \text{ million}$$

where $50 million = $50/share × 1 million shares outstanding

Goodwill Attributable to the Minority Interest

Note that 20 percent of the total shares outstanding equals 200,000 shares with a market value of $10 million ($50/share × 200,000). Therefore, the amount of goodwill attributable to the minority interest is calculated as follows:

Fair value of minority interest:	$10,000,000
Less 20% fair value of total net assets (0.2 × $42,000,000):	$ 8,400,000
Equals goodwill attributable to minority interest:	$ 1,600,000

Fair Value of the Minority Interest per Share

Since the fair value of Acquirer's interest in Target and Target's retained interest are proportional to their respective ownership interests, the value of the ownership distribution of the majority and minority owners is as follows:

Acquirer interest (0.8 × 1 million × $50/share)	$40 million
Target minority interest (0.2 × 1 million × $50/share)	$10 million
Total market value	$50 million

The fair market value per share of the minority interest is $41.6, that is, ($10 million/200,000) × (1 – 0.167). The minority share value is less than the share price of the controlling shareholders (i.e., $50/share), because it must be discounted for the relative lack of influence on the firm's decision-making process of minority shareholders.

---

[1]See Chapter 10 for a discussion of how to calculate control premiums and minority discounts.

Exhibit 12–3 Guidelines for Valuing Acquired Assets and Liabilities

1. Cash and accounts receivable, reduced for bad debt and returns, are valued at their values on the books of the target on the acquisition date.
2. Marketable securities are valued at their realizable value after any transaction costs.
3. Inventories are broken down into finished goods and raw materials. Finished goods are valued at their liquidation value; raw material inventories are valued at their current replacement cost. Last-in, first-out inventory reserves maintained by the target before the acquisition are eliminated.
4. Property, plant, and equipment are valued at fair market value on the acquisition date.
5. Accounts payable and accrued expenses are valued at the levels stated on the target's books on the acquisition date.
6. Notes payable and long-term debt are valued at their net present value of the future cash payments discounted at the current market rate of interest for similar securities.
7. Pension fund obligations are booked at the excess or deficiency of the present value of the projected benefit obligations over the present value of pension fund assets. This may result in an asset or liability being recorded by the consolidated firms.
8. All other liabilities are recorded at their net present value of future cash payments.
9. Intangible assets are booked at their appraised values on the acquisition date.
10. Goodwill is the difference between the purchase price less the fair market value of the target's net asset value. Positive goodwill is recorded as an asset, whereas negative goodwill (i.e., a bargain purchase) is shown as a gain on the acquirer's consolidated income statement.

Many assets, such as intangibles, are not specifically identified on the firm's balance sheet. In the United States, companies expense the cost of investing in intangibles in the year in which the investment is made. The rationale for immediately expensing such assets is the difficulty in determining whether a particular expenditure results in a future benefit (i.e., an asset) or not (i.e., an expense). For example, the value of the Coca-Cola brand name clearly has value extending over many years, but there is no estimate of this value on the firm's balance sheet.

Firms capitalize (i.e., value and display as assets on the balance sheet) the costs of acquiring identifiable intangible assets. The value of such assets can be ascertained from similar transactions made elsewhere. The acquirer must consider the future benefits of the intangible asset to be at least equal to the price paid. Specifically, identifiable assets must have a finite life. Intangible assets are listed as identifiable if the asset can be separated from the firm and sold, leased, licensed, or rented. Examples of separable intangible assets include patents and customer lists. Intangible assets also are viewed as identifiable if they are contractually or legally binding. An example of a contractually binding intangible asset would the purchase of a firm that has a leased manufacturing facility whose cost is less than the current cost of a comparable lease. The difference would be listed as an intangible asset on the consolidated balance sheet of the acquiring firm.

Firms must amortize the value of the asset over this estimated life span. Firms must periodically test the value of intangible assets that are amortized for impairment following a procedure similar to that used for goodwill. The test compares the "carrying value" (i.e., value as shown on the firm's financial statements) to the fair value of the intangible asset and requires recognition of an impairment loss whenever the carrying value exceeds the fair value.

The test for intangibles not requiring amortization (e.g., goodwill) is different from that of tangibles. The test for assets requiring amortization (i.e., tangibles) necessitates the comparison of the undiscounted future cash flows of the asset to the asset's carrying (i.e., book) value. The dollar value of any write down is equal to the difference between the undiscounted value of future cash flows and the book or carrying value of the asset. Impaired asset values are subsequently written down in direct proportion to their share of the purchase price of net acquired assets. Intangibles not requiring amortization have an indefinite life and thus no defined period over which to project cash flows. Therefore, determining the fair value of goodwill is often difficult. It entails estimating the fair value of the reporting unit that resulted from a previously acquired firm in which the purchase price exceeded the fair value of net acquired assets, resulting in the creation of goodwill. Generally, the reporting unit has no shares trading on a public exchange. Firms often employ comparable company valuation methods to value the reporting unit (see Chapter 8).

Intangible assets can be classified into three categories: operational intangibles, production or product intangibles, and marketing intangibles (Table 12–5). Those intangible assets marked with an asterisk in Table 12–5 are generally not viewed as identifiable assets and would be subsumed under goodwill. The other intangible assets often are viewed as identifiable and are capitalized on the acquirer's balance sheet. *Operational intangibles* have been defined as the ability of a business to continue to function and generate income without interruption because of a change in ownership. Production or **product intangibles** are values placed on the accumulated intellectual capital resulting from the production and product design experience of the combined entity. *Marketing intangibles* are those factors that help a firm to sell a product or service. For tax and financial reporting purposes, goodwill is a residual item equal to the

Table 12–5   Intangible Asset Categories

Intangible Asset Categories	Examples
Operating intangibles	Assembled and trained workforce*
	Operating and administrative systems*
	Corporate culture*
Production or product intangibles	Patents
	Technological know-how
	Production standards
	Copyrights
	Software
	Favorable leases and licenses
Marketing intangibles	Customer lists and relationships
	Price lists and pricing strategies*
	Marketing strategies, studies, and concepts*
	Advertising and promotional materials*
	Trademarks and service marks
	Trade names
	Covenants not to compete
	Franchises

*Intangible assets are often included as part of goodwill since they are not easily separable from other assets or contractually/ legally binding.

difference between the purchase price for the target company and fair market value of net assets, including identifiable operational, production, and marketing intangible assets. In most cases, intangible assets, like tangible assets, have separately determinable values with limited useful lives. In certain cases, the useful lives are defined by the legal protection afforded by the agency issuing the protection, such as the U.S. Patent Office. In contrast, the useful life of such intangible assets as customer lists is more difficult to define. The concepts and methodologies discussed in Chapters 7 and 8 may be applied to value different types of intangible assets.

Exhibit 12–4 illustrates the balance-sheet impacts of purchase accounting on the acquirer's balance sheet and the effects of impairment subsequent to closing. Assume that Acquirer Inc. purchases Target Inc. on December 31, 2009 (the acquisition date) for $500 million. Identifiable acquired assets and assumed liabilities are shown at their fair value on the acquisition date. The excess of the purchase price over the fair value of net acquired assets is shown as goodwill. The fair value of the "reporting unit" (i.e., Target Inc.) is determined annually to ensure that its fair value exceeds its carrying value. As of December 31, 2010, it is determined that the fair value of Target Inc. has fallen below its carrying value due largely to the loss of a number of key customers.

Exhibit 12–4 Balance Sheet Impacts of Purchase Accounting

Target Inc. 12/31/2009, purchase price (total consideration)		$500 million
Fair values of Target Inc.'s net assets @ 12/31/2009		
Current assets	$40 million	
Plant and equipment	200 million	
Customer list	180 million	
Copyrights	120 million	
Current liabilities	(35 million)	
Long-term debt	(100 million)	
Value assigned to identifiable net assets		$405 million
Value assigned to goodwill		95 million
Carrying value as of 12/31/2009		$500 million
Fair value of Target Inc.'s net assets @ 12/31/2010		$400 million[1]
Current assets	$ 30 million	
Plant and equipment	175 million	
Customer list	100 million	
Copyrights	120 million	
Current liabilities	(25 million)	
Long-term debt	(90 million)	
Fair value of identifiable net assets		$310 million
Value of goodwill		90 million
Carrying value after impairment @12/31/2010		$400 million
Impairment loss (difference between 12/31/2010 and 12/31/2009 carrying values)		$100 million

[1]Note that the 12/31/2010 carrying value is estimated based on the fair market value of the net acquired assets on that date. The fair value is composed of the sum of the fair value of identifiable net assets plus goodwill.

Income Statement and Cash-Flow Considerations

For financial reporting purposes, an upward valuation of tangible and intangible assets, other than goodwill, raises depreciation and amortization expenses, which lowers operating and net income. For tax purposes, goodwill created after July 1993 may be amortized up to 15 years and is tax deductible. Goodwill booked before July 1993 is not tax deductible. Cash-flow benefits from the tax deductibility of additional depreciation and amortization expenses are written off over the useful lives of the assets. This assumes that the acquirer paid more than the target's net asset value. If the purchase price paid is less than the target's net asset value, the acquirer records a one-time gain equal to the difference on its income statement. If the carrying value of the net asset value subsequently falls below its fair market value, the acquirer records a one-time loss equal to the difference.

International Accounting Standards

Ideally, financial reporting would be the same across the globe but that has not yet occurred. The discussion of financial reporting for business combinations is focused on the application of generally accepted accounting principles of the Financial Accounting Standards Board in the United States. Many of the same challenges are addressed in the application of international financial reporting standards of the International Accounting Standards Board (IASB). When comparing financial information for companies operating in multiple countries, it is important to achieve comparability of the reporting methods and accounting principles employed by the acquisition and merger targets.

The overarching objective of the IASB is the convergence of accounting standards worldwide and the establishment of global standards, sometimes referred to as *global GAAP*. The IASB issues international financial reporting standards, and as of 2005, firms across the European Union have to conform to IFRS directives. FASB and IASB have pledged that they will work diligently to ensure that GAAP and IFRS will be compatible as soon as practicable.

Non-U.S. firms that have debt or equity securities trading in the United States must either file a form 10K using GAAP or file a Form 20-F report with the U.S. Securities and Exchange Commission. The Form 20-F report must include a reconciliation of shareholders' equity and net income as reported in the firm's local country with GAAP in the United States. Such information enables the translation of the financial statements of a non-U.S. firm to achieve comparable accounting principles in the United States.

Recapitalization Accounting

An acquisition resulting in a change in control (i.e., a change in majority voting power) must use purchase accounting for recording the net assets of the acquired business on the acquirer's financial statements. However, under certain circumstances, control may change without changing the basis of the acquired assets and liabilities. Such circumstances arise with a leveraged buyout. In an LBO, some of the target's shareholders continue to own stock in the postacquisition firm. For example, assume the buyer makes an equity investment in the firm by acquiring new shares issued directly by the target. The target uses this equity infusion to borrow money to repurchase some, but not all, of the target's outstanding shares. Consequently, some old target shareholders continue to own a significant part of the firm.

Recapitalization accounting applies under the following conditions. First, there is no change in control of the target firm, since the target's old investors continue to own a substantial portion of the target's equity after the acquisition. Second, there is change of control of the target but the target survives as an entity (e.g., a reverse triangular merger) and the target's shareholders own more than 20 percent of the resulting business.

The advantage of recapitalization accounting is that acquired net assets need not be restated for book purposes. If value of the acquired assets is revised upward, net income would be reduced as a result of an increase in depreciation expense. Furthermore, since the acquired net assets are not restated to their fair market value, no goodwill is created. The absence of goodwill eliminates concern about future goodwill write-offs due to impairment and the potential violation of loan covenants requiring a certain minimum level of debt to total assets. Therefore, when the target is to be taken public or sold to a strategic buyer, its financials will be more favorable, since recapitalization rather than purchase accounting was applied to the target's financial statements when the firm was taken private.

Things to Remember

Taxes are an important, but rarely an overarching, consideration in most M&A transactions. The deciding factor in any transaction should be whether it makes good business sense. Transactions may be either partly or entirely taxable to the target firm's shareholders or tax free. A transaction generally is considered taxable to the seller if the buyer uses mostly cash, notes, or some nonequity consideration to purchase the target's stock or assets. Conversely, the transaction is generally considered tax free, if mostly acquirer stock is used to purchase the stock or assets of the target firm. Tax considerations and strategies are likely to have an important impact on how a deal is structured by affecting the amount, timing, and composition of the price offered to a target firm. Moreover, tax factors are likely to affect how the combined firms are organized following closing, as the tax ramifications of a corporate structure are quite different from those of a limited liability company or partnership.

For financial reporting purposes, all M&As (except those qualifying for recapitalization accounting) must be recorded using the purchase method of accounting. The excess of the purchase price, including the fair value of any noncontrolling (i.e., minority) interest in the target at the acquisition date, over the fair market value of acquired net assets is treated as goodwill on the combined firm's balance sheet. If the fair value of the target's net assets later falls below its carrying value, the acquirer must record a loss equal to the difference. The threat of this possibility may introduce additional discipline for acquirers when negotiating with target company boards and management, since such an event would be a public admission that management had overpaid for past acquisitions. Furthermore, recent changes in accounting standards requiring business combinations to be valued on the closing date may make equity financed transactions less attractive due to the potential for significant changes in value between signing and closing. However, this concern may be mitigated somewhat by the use of collar arrangements. The requirement to value contingent liabilities at closing and update them over time could contribute to earnings instability and make earn-outs a less attractive form of payment.

Chapter Discussion Questions

12–1. When does the IRS consider a transaction to be nontaxable to the target firm's shareholders? What is the justification for the IRS' position?

12–2. What are the advantages and disadvantages of a tax-free transaction for the buyer? Be specific.

12–3. Under what circumstances can the assets of the acquired firm be increased to fair market value when the transaction is deemed a taxable purchase of stock?

12–4. When does it make sense for a buyer to use a Type A tax-free reorganization?

12–5. When does it make sense for a buyer to use a Type B tax-free reorganization?

12–6. What are net operating loss carryforwards and carrybacks? Why might they add value to an acquisition?

12–7. Explain how tax considerations affect the deal structuring process.

12–8. How does the purchase method of accounting affect the income statement, balance sheet, and cash-flow statements of the combined companies?

12–9. What is goodwill and how is it created?

12–10. Under what circumstances might an asset become impaired? How might this event affect the way in which acquirers bid for target firms?

12–11. Why do boards of directors of both acquiring and target companies often obtain so-called fairness opinions from outside investment advisors or accounting firms? What valuation methodologies might be employed in constructing these opinions? Should stockholders have confidence in such opinions? Why or why not?

12–12. Archer Daniel Midland (ADM) wants to acquire AgriCorp to augment its ethanol manufacturing capability. AgriCorp wants the transaction to be tax free for its shareholders. ADM wants to preserve AgriCorp's significant investment tax credits and tax loss carryforwards so that they transfer in the transaction. Also, ADM plans on selling certain unwanted AgriCorp assets to help finance the transaction. How would you structure the deal so that both parties' objectives could be achieved?

12–13. Tangible assets are often increased to fair market value following a transaction and depreciated faster than their economic lives. What is the potential impact on posttransaction EPS, cash flow, and balance sheet?

12–14. Discuss how the form of acquisition (i.e., asset purchase or stock deal) could affect the net present value or internal rate of return of the deal calculated postclosing.

12–15. What are some of the important tax-related issues the boards of the acquirer and target companies may need to address prior to entering negotiations? How might the resolution of these issues affect the form of payment and form of acquisition?

Solutions to these Chapter Discussion Questions are found in the Online Instructor's Manual for instructors using this book.

Chapter Practice Problems and Answers

12–16. Target Company has incurred $5 million in losses during the past three years. Acquiring Company anticipates pretax earnings of $3 million in each of the next three years. What is the difference between the taxes that Acquiring Company would have paid before the merger as compared to actual taxes paid after the merger? Show your work.

Answer: $2 million.

12–17. Acquiring Company buys Target Company for $5 million in cash. As an analyst, you are given the premerger balance sheets for the two companies (Table 12–6). Assuming plant and equipment are revalued upward by

Table 12–6   Premerger Balance Sheets for Companies in Problem 12–17 (in dollars)

	Acquiring Company	Target Company
Current assets	600,000	800,000
Plant and equipment	1,200,000	1,500,000
Total assets	1,800,000	2,300,000
Long-term debt	500,000	300,000
Shareholders' equity	1,300,000	2,000,000
Shareholders' equity + total liabilities	1,800,000	2,300,000

$500,000, what will be the combined companies' shareholders' equity plus total liabilities? What is the difference between Acquiring Company's shareholders' equity and the shareholders' equity of the combined companies? Show your work.

Answer: The combined companies' shareholders' equity plus total liabilities is $7.1 million and the change between the combined companies' and Acquiring Company's shareholders' equity is $5 million. Note that the change in the acquirer's equity equals the purchase price.

Solutions to these problems are found in the Online Instructor's Manual available to instructors using this text.

Chapter Business Cases

Case Study 12–2. Boston Scientific Overcomes Johnson & Johnson to Acquire Guidant—A Lesson in Bidding Strategy

Background

Johnson and Johnson (J&J), the behemoth American pharmaceutical company, announced an agreement in December 2004 to acquire Guidant for $76 per share for a combination of cash and stock. Guidant is a leading manufacturer of implantable heart defibrillators and other products used in angioplasty procedures. The market for such defibrillators has been growing at 20 percent annually. J&J desired to reenergize its slowing growth rate by diversifying into the more rapidly growing medical stent market. Soon after the agreement was signed, Guidant's defibrillators became embroiled in a regulatory scandal over failure to inform doctors about rare malfunctions. Guidant suffered a serious erosion of market share when it recalled five models of its defibrillators. Part of the risk in completing the takeover of Guidant is the potential jeopardy the company faces from federal investigations and civil lawsuits.

The apparent erosion in the value of Guidant prompted J&J to renegotiate the deal under a material adverse change clause common in most M&A agreements. Such clauses are predicated on a continuation of the target business without any significant changes that degrade value between the signing of the agreement and the actual closing. J&J was able to get Guidant to accept a lower price of $63 a share in mid-November. However, this new agreement was not without risk.

An Auction Emerges

The renegotiated agreement gave Boston Scientific an opportunity to intervene with a more attractive informal offer on December 5, 2005, of $72 per share. The offer price consisted of 50 percent stock and 50 percent cash. Boston Scientific, a leading supplier of heart stents, saw the proposed acquisition as a vital step in the company's strategy of diversifying into the high-growth implantable defibrillator market. Heart stents prop open arteries leading to the heart, potentially preventing heart attacks; implantable defibrillators regulate heart beats through a series of electrical impulses. The bid pitted Boston Scientific against its major competitor in the drug-coated stent market. The two firms had been embroiled in litigation over stent technology.

Despite the more favorable offer, Guidant board's decided to reject Boston Scientific's offer in favor of an upwardly revised offer of $71 per share made by J&J on January 11, 2005. The board continued to support J&J's lower bid, despite the furor it caused among big Guidant shareholders. With a market capitalization nine times the size of Boston Scientific, the Guidant board continued to be enamored with J&J's size and industry position relative to Boston Scientific. The board argued that a J&J combination would result in much more rapid growth than merging with the much smaller Boston Scientific.

Boston Scientific's Bidding Strategy

Boston Scientific realized that it would be able to acquire Guidant only if it made an offer that Guidant could not refuse without risking major shareholder lawsuits. Boston Scientific reasoned that, if J&J hoped to match an improved bid, it would have to be at least $77, slightly higher than the $76 J&J had offered in its initial agreement with Guidant in December 2004. With its greater borrowing capacity, Boston Scientific knew that J&J also had the option of converting its combination stock and cash bid to an all-cash offer. Such an offer could be made a few dollars lower than Boston Scientific's bid, since Guidant investors might view such an offer more favorably than one consisting of both stock and cash, whose value could fluctuate between the signing of the agreement and the actual closing. This was indeed a possibility, since the J&J offer did not include a collar arrangement.

Boston Scientific decided to boost the new bid to $80 per share, which it believed would deter any further bidding from J&J. J&J had been saying publicly that Guidant was already "fully valued." Boston Scientific reasoned that J&J had created a public relations nightmare for itself. If J&J raised its bid, it would upset J&J shareholders and make it look like an undisciplined buyer. According to the agreement it had with Guidant, J&J had five days to respond to the sweetened Boston Scientific bid. J&J refused to up its offer saying that such an action would not be in the best interests of its shareholders. Table 12–7 summarizes the key events timeline.

Abbott Labs Helps Seal the Deal

A side deal with Abbott Labs made the lofty Boston Scientific offer possible. The firm entered into an agreement with Abbott Laboratories in which Boston Scientific would divest Guidant's stent business, while retaining the rights to Guidant's stent technology.

Table 12–7 Boston Scientific and Johnson & Johnson Bidding Chronology

Date	Comments
December 15, 2004	J&J reaches agreement to buy Guidant for $25.4 billion in stock and cash
November 15, 2005	Value of J&J deal is revised downward to $21.5 billion
December 5, 2005	Boston Scientific offers $25 billion
January 11, 2006	Guidant accepts a J&J counteroffer valued at $23.2 billion
January 17, 2006	Boston Scientific submits a new bid valued at $27 billion.
January 25, 2006	Guidant accepts the Boston Scientific bid when J&J fails to improve its offer.

In return, Boston Scientific received $6.4 billion in cash on the closing date, consisting of $4.1 billion for the divested assets, a loan of $900 million, and Abbott's purchase of $1.4 billion of Boston Scientific stock. The additional cash helped fund the purchase price. This deal also helped Boston Scientific gain regulatory approval by enabling Abbott Labs to become a competitor in the stent business. Merrill Lynch and Bank of America each would lend $7 billion to fund a portion of the purchase price and provide the combined firms with additional working capital.

Boston Scientific's Investors Express Nervousness

To complete the transaction, Boston Scientific paid $27 billion, consisting of cash and stock, to Guidant shareholders and another $800 million as a breakup fee to J&J. In addition, the firm is burdened with $14.9 billion in new debt. Within days of Boston Scientific's winning bid, the firm received a warning from the U.S. Food and Drug Administration to delay the introduction of new products until the firm's safety procedures improve. Longer term, whether the deal would earn Boston Scientific shareholders an appropriate return on their investments depends largely on the continued rapid growth in the defibrillator market and the outcome of civil suits surrounding the recall of Guidant products.

Between December 2004, the date of Guidant's original agreement with J&J, and January 25, 2006, the date of its agreement with Boston Scientific, Guidant's stock rose by 16 percent reflecting the bidding process. During the same period, J&J's dropped by a modest 3 percent, while Boston Scientific's shares plummeted by 32 percent, as investors fretted over the earnings outlook for the firm.

Epilogue

As a result of product recalls and safety warnings on more than 50,000 Guidant cardiac devices, the firm's sales and profits plummeted. Between the announcement date of its purchase of Guidant in December 2005 and yearend 2006, Boston Scientific lost more than $18 billion in shareholder value. The operations acquired in the Guidant transactions are not profitable and no recovery is anticipated until product quality problems are resolved. By yearend 2006, Boston Scientific's shares dropped to the high teens, reflecting the enormous dilution of the firm's earnings per share. In acquiring Guidant, Boston Scientific increased its total shares outstanding by more than 80 percent and assumed responsibility for $6.5 billion in debt, with no proportionate increase in earnings. To add insult to injury, in late September 2006, Johnson & Johnson sued Boston Scientific, Guidant, and Abbott for $5.5 billion, arguing that they had violated terms of J&J's deal with Guidant.

Discussion Questions

1. What might J&J have done differently to avoid igniting a bidding war?
2. What evidence is given that J&J may not have taken Boston Scientific as a serious bidder?
3. Explain how differing assumptions about market growth, potential synergies, and the size of the potential liability related to product recalls affected the bidding?

Solutions to these questions are provided in the Online Instructor's Manual for instructors using this book.

Case Study 12–3. "Grave Dancer" Takes Tribune Corporation Private in an Ill-Fated Transaction

At the closing in late December 2007, well-known real estate investor Sam Zell described the takeover of the Tribune Company as "the transaction from hell." His comments were prescient, in that what had appeared to be a cleverly crafted, albeit highly leveraged deal from a tax standpoint was unable to withstand the credit malaise of 2008. The end came swiftly when the 161-year-old Tribune filed for bankruptcy on December 8, 2008.

Background

On April 2, 2007, the Tribune Corporation (Tribune) announced that the firm's publicly traded shares would be acquired in a multistage transaction valued at $8.2 billion. Tribune owns nine newspapers, 23 television stations, a 25 percent stake in Comcast's SportsNet Chicago, and the Chicago Cubs baseball team. Publishing accounts for 75 percent of the firm's total $5.5 billion annual revenue, with the remainder coming from broadcasting and entertainment. Advertising and circulation revenue had fallen by 9 percent at the firm's three largest newspapers (the *Los Angeles Times*, *Chicago Tribune*, and *Newsday* in New York) between 2004 and 2006. Despite aggressive efforts to cut costs, Tribune's stock had fallen more than 30 percent since 2005.

The deal involved famed turnaround specialist Sam Zell, fresh from earning as much as $900 million in the sale of Equity Office Properties to the Blackstone Group for $39 billion (including debt) in March 2007. Mr. Zell often refers to himself as the "grave dancer" for his skill in resurrecting failing businesses. This represented Zell's second investment in the media industry. In 1992, he acquired a failing radio station operator, Jacor Broadcasting, for $79 million and sold it seven years later for $4.4 billion. Mr. Zell became the Tribune's CEO.

Deal Structure

The transaction was implemented in a two-stage transaction (Figure 12–5), in which Zell acquired a controlling 51 percent interest in the first stage followed by a backend merger in the second stage in which the remaining outstanding Tribune shares were acquired. In the first stage, Tribune initiated a cash tender offer for 126 million shares (51 percent of total shares) for $34 per share, totaling $4.2 billion. The tender was financed using

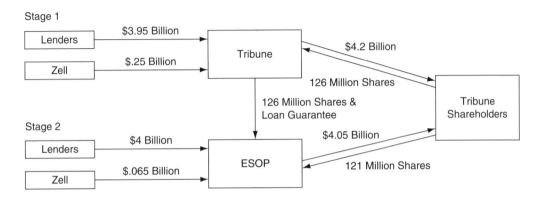

FIGURE 12–5 Tribune deal structure.

$250 million of the $315 million provided by Sam Zell in the form of subordinated debt, plus additional borrowing to cover the balance. Stage 2 was triggered when the deal received regulatory approval. During this stage, an employee stock ownership plan (ESOP) bought the rest of the shares at $34 a share (totaling about $4 billion), with Zell providing the remaining $65 million of his pledge. Most of the ESOP's 121 million shares purchased were financed by debt guaranteed by the firm on behalf of the ESOP. At that point, the ESOP held all of the remaining stock outstanding valued at about $4 billion. In exchange for his commitment of funds, Mr. Zell received a 15-year warrant to acquire 40 percent of the common stock (newly issued) at a price set at $500 million.

Following closing in December 2007, all company contributions to employee pension plans were funneled into the ESOP in the form of Tribune stock. Over time, the ESOP would hold all the stock. Furthermore, Tribune was converted from a C corporation to a subchapter S corporation, allowing the firm to avoid corporate income taxes. However, it would have to pay taxes on gains resulting from the sale of assets held less than 10 years after the conversion from a C to an S corporation.

Financing the Transaction

The purchase of Tribune's stock was financed almost entirely with debt, with Zell's equity contribution amounting to less than 4 percent of the purchase price. The transaction resulted in the Tribune being burdened with $13 billion in debt (including the approximate $5 billion currently owed by Tribune). At this level, the firm's debt was 10 times EBITDA, more than 2.5 times that of the average media company. Annual interest and principal repayments reached $800 million (almost three times their preacquisition level), about 62 percent of the firm's previous EBITDA cash flow of $1.3 billion. While the ESOP owned the company, it was not be liable for the debt guaranteed by Tribune.

The conversion of the Tribune into a subchapter S corporation eliminated the firm's current annual tax liability of $348 million. Such entities pay no corporate income tax but must pay all profit directly to shareholders, who then pay taxes on these distributions. Since the ESOP was the sole shareholder, the restructured Tribune was expected to be largely tax exempt, since ESOPs are not taxed.

In an effort to reduce the firm's debt burden, the Tribune Company announced in early 2008 the formation of a partnership in which Cablevision Systems Corporation would own 97 percent of Newsday for $650 million, with Tribune owning the remaining 3 percent (see Case Study 12–1 for more detail). However, the Tribune was unable to sell the Chicago Cubs (which had been expected to fetch as much as $1 billion) and the minority interest in SportsNet Chicago to help reduce the debt amid the 2008 credit crisis. The worsening of the recession, accelerated the decline in newspaper and TV advertising revenue, as well as newspaper circulation, thereby eroded the firm's ability to meet its debt obligations.

Sifting through the Carnage

By filing for Chapter 11 bankruptcy protection, the Tribune Company, unable to meet pending quarterly interest and principal repayments, sought a reprieve from its creditors while it attempted to restructure its business. Although the extent of the losses to employees, creditors, and other stakeholders is difficult to determine at this time, some things are clear. Any pension funds set aside prior to the closing remain with the employees, but it is likely that equity contributions made to the ESOP on behalf of the employees since the closing would be lost. The employees would become general creditors of the Tribune.

As a holder of subordinated debt, Mr. Zell had priority over the employees if the firm was liquidated and the proceeds distributed to the creditors.

Those benefiting from the deal included the Tribune's public shareholders, including the Chandler family, which owed 12 percent of the Tribune as a result of its prior sale of the Times Mirror to Tribune, and Dennis FitzSimons, the firm's former CEO, who received $17.7 million in severance and $23.8 million for his holdings of Tribune shares. Citigroup and Merrill Lynch walked away with $35.8 million and $37 million, respectively, in advisory fees. Morgan Stanley received $7.5 million for writing a fairness opinion letter. Finally, Valuation Research Corporation received $1 million for providing a solvency opinion indicating that Tribune could satisfy its loan covenants.

What appeared to be one of the most complex deals of 2007, designed to reap huge tax advantages, soon became a victim of the downward spiraling economy, the credit crunch, and its own leverage. A lawsuit filed in late 2008 on behalf of the Tribune employees contended that the transaction was flawed from the outset and intended to benefit Sam Zell and his advisors and the Tribune board. Even if the employees win, they will simply have to stand in line with other Tribune creditors awaiting the resolution of the bankruptcy court proceedings.

Discussion Questions

1. What is the acquisition vehicle, postclosing organization, form of payment, form of acquisition, and tax strategy described in this case study?
2. Describe the firm's strategy to finance the transaction.
3. Is this transaction best characterized as a merger, acquisition, leveraged buyout, or spin-off? Explain your answer.
4. Is this transaction taxable or nontaxable to Tribune's public shareholders? To its posttransaction shareholders? Explain your answer.
5. Comment on the fairness of this transaction to the various stakeholders involved. How would you apportion the responsibility for the eventual bankruptcy of Tribune among Sam Zell and his advisors, the Tribune board, and the largely unforeseen collapse of the credit markets in late 2008? Be specific.

Solutions to these case study discussion questions are available in the Online Instructor's Manual for instructors using this book.

13

Financing Transactions

Private Equity, Hedge Funds, and Leveraged Buyout Structures and Valuation

A billion dollars isn't what it used to be.

—Nelson Bunker Hunt

Inside M&A: HCA's LBO Represents a High-Risk Bet on Growth

While most LBOs are predicated on improving operating performance through a combination of aggressive cost cutting and revenue growth, HCA laid out an unconventional approach in its effort to take the firm private. On July 24, 2006, management again announced that it would "go private" in a deal valued at $33 billion including the assumption of $11.7 billion in existing debt.

The approximate $21.3 billion purchase price for HCA's stock was financed by a combination of $12.8 billion in senior secured term loans of varying maturities and an estimated $8.5 billion in cash provided by Bain Capital, Merrill Lynch Global Private Equity, and Kohlberg Kravis Roberts & Company. HCA also would take out a $4 billion revolving credit line to satisfy immediate working capital requirements. The firm publicly announced a strategy of improving performance through growth rather than through cost cutting. HCA's network of 182 hospitals and 94 surgery centers is expected to benefit from an aging U.S. population and the resulting increase in health-care spending. The deal also seems to be partly contingent on the government assuming a larger share of health-care costs in the future. Finally, with many nonprofit hospitals faltering financially, HCA may be able to acquire them inexpensively.

While the longer-term trends in the health-care industry are unmistakable, shorter-term developments appear troublesome, including sluggish hospital admissions, more uninsured patients, and higher bad debt expenses. Moreover, with Medicare and Medicaid financially insolvent, it is unclear if future increases in government health-care spending would be sufficient to enable HCA investors to achieve their expected financial returns. With the highest operating profit margins in the industry, it is uncertain if

HCA's cash flows could be significantly improved by cost cutting, if the revenue growth assumptions fail to materialize. HCA's management and equity investors have put themselves in a position in which they seem to have relatively little influence over the factors that directly affect the firm's future cash flows.

Chapter Overview

The purpose of this chapter is to discuss how transactions are financed, with an emphasis on the financing, structuring, and valuation of highly leveraged transactions. Such transactions saw a surge in the 1980s, culminating in the $31.5 billion (including assumed debt) buyout in 1988 of RJR Nabisco by Kohlberg Kravis Roberts & Company. This boom period dissipated, due to the 1991 recession and political backlash to such transactions. Following the tech boom in the late 1990s, the terrorist attacks of 9/11, and the 2001 recession, highly leveraged transactions once again surged upward, peaking in early 2007. The boom was fueled largely by a strong economy, low interest rates, and easy credit conditions. While private equity investors and hedge funds played an important role as *financial sponsors* (i.e., equity investors) in highly leveraged transactions throughout the three merger waves since the early 1980s, their role was largely a secondary one during the tech boom of the 1990s. The buyout binge came to a grinding halt when LBO financing dried up in late 2007 and throughout 2008, forcing private equity and hedge funds to retrench. As a sign of the times, there were 91 defaults globally, totaling $295 billion by private equity backed companies during 2008 according to the credit-rating agency Standard and Poor's.

In a *leveraged buyout* (LBO), borrowed funds are used to pay for most of the purchase price, with the remainder provided by a financial sponsor, such as a private equity investor group or hedge fund. LBOs can be of an entire company or divisions of a company. LBO targets can be private or public firms. Typically, the tangible assets of the firm to be acquired are used as collateral for the loans. The most highly liquid assets often are used as collateral for obtaining bank financing. Such assets commonly include receivables and inventory. The firm's fixed assets commonly are used to secure a portion of long-term senior financing. Subordinated debt, either unrated or low-rated debt, is used to raise the balance of the purchase price. This debt often is referred to as *junk bond financing*. When a public company is subject to an LBO, it is said to be *going private* in a public-to-private transaction, because the equity of the firm has been purchased by a small group of investors and is no longer publicly traded. Buyers of the firm targeted to become a leveraged buyout often consist of managers from the firm that is being acquired. The LBO that is initiated by the target firm's incumbent management is called a *management buyout* (MBO).

In recent years, private equity and hedge funds have exhibited increasing similarities. Both raise money from institutions, such as pension funds and insurance companies, and wealthy individuals. Both use borrowed funds aggressively in their investment strategies. Private equity funds tend to make longer-term investments, often waiting years before realizing significant financial returns. Hedge funds tend to engage in more short-term trading. However, as noted in Chapter 1, more and more their investment strategies are converging. Some private equity and hedge funds raise funds in public markets. Hedge funds are increasingly willing to provide longer-term loans in financing leveraged buyouts. On February 10, 2007, Fortress Investment Group LLC, which manages $30 billion, became the first private equity and hedge fund manager to sell shares on the U.S. equity market (Zuckerman, Sender, and Patterson, 2007).

Academic research generally suggests that recent private equity sponsored LBOs have had a positive impact on the financial performance of the acquired firms. However, it is difficult to determine whether this association resulted from actions taken by the private equity firms or other factors (United States General Accountability Office, 2008). Moreover, only time will tell how well the highly leveraged transactions of recent years will perform during the turbulence of the global slowdown that began in 2008.

This chapter begins with a discussion of the changing face of LBOs. Subsequent sections discuss how such transactions often are financed, alternative LBO structures, the risks associated with poorly constructed deals, how to take a company private, how to develop viable exit strategies, and how to estimate a firm's financing capacity. The terms *buyout firm* and *financial sponsor* are used interchangeably, as they are in the literature on the subject, throughout the chapter to include the variety of investor groups, such as private equity investors and hedge funds, that commonly engage in LBO transactions. Empirical studies of pre- and postbuyout returns to shareholders also are reviewed. The chapter concludes with a discussion of how to analyze and value highly leveraged transactions and to construct LBO models. The major segments of this chapter include the following:

- Characterizing Leveraged Buyouts
- When Do Firms Go Private?
- Financing Transactions
- Common Forms of Leveraged Buyout Deal Structures
- What Factors Are Critical to Successful LBOs?
- Prebuyout and Postbuyout Shareholder Returns
- Valuing Leveraged Buyouts
- Building an LBO Model
- Things to Remember

A detailed Microsoft Excel-Based Leveraged Buyout Valuation and Structuring Model is available on the CD-ROM that accompanies this book. The model reflects the sophistication used by professionals who engage in such transactions and may be customized by the reader to meet the unique characteristics of the situation. How the model may be applied is illustrated in Case Study 13–5 at the end of this chapter. A review of this chapter (including practice questions and answers) is available in the file folder entitled Student Study Guide contained on the CD-ROM accompanying this book. The CD-ROM also contains a Learning Interactions Library, enabling students to test their knowledge of this chapter in a "real-time" environment.

Characterizing Leveraged Buyouts

An LBO investor is frequently called a *financial buyer*. Such investors are inclined to use a large amount of debt to finance as much of the target's purchase price as possible. Financial buyers tend to concentrate on actions that enhance the target firm's ability to generate cash to satisfy their substantial debt service requirements. Leverage makes the potential returns to equity much more attractive than less-leveraged transactions (see Table 13–1).

Historically, empirical studies of LBOs have been subject to a series of limitations. First, such studies often were conducted on small samples due to the limited availability of data. Second, the studies were subject to "survival bias" in that failed firms were excluded from the performance studies because they no longer existed. Third, these

Table 13–1   Impact of Leverage on Return to Shareholders

	All-Cash Purchase	50% Cash/50% Debt	20% Cash/80% Debt
Purchase price	$100	$100	$100
Equity (cash investment)	$100	$50	$20
Borrowings	0	$50	$80
Earnings before interest and taxes	$20	$20	$20
Interest at 10%	0	$5	$8
Income before taxes	$20	$15	$12
Less income taxes at 40%	$8	$6	$4.8
Net income	$12	$9	$7.2
After-tax return on equity	12%	18%	36%

Note: Unless otherwise noted, all numbers are in millions of dollars.

studies focused on transactions involving the conversion of public companies to private entities (largely ignoring private firms acquired in LBO-type transactions) due to the availability of data.

Recent studies based on larger samples make some of the conclusions of earlier studies problematic. The data for the large sample studies comes from Standard & Poor's Capital IQ and the U.S. Census Bureau databases. The studies compare a sample of LBO target firms with a "control sample." Selected for comparative purposes, firms in control samples are known to be similar to the private equity transaction sample in all respects except for not having undergone an LBO. While not conclusive, these studies shed more light on how LBOs have changed in recent years. These more recent studies are discussed next.

The Changing Nature of LBOs since 1970

In an exhaustive study of 21,397 private equity transactions that could be identified between 1970 and 2007, Stromberg (2008) confirmed that private equity transactions accelerated sharply in recent years from their longer-term trend. Such transactions accounted for more than 40 percent of the M&A transactions that occurred between 2001 and 2007. In 2007, more than 14,000 LBOs operated globally as compared to about 5,000 in the year 2000 and only 2,000 in the mid-1990s.

The Private Equity Market Is a Global Phenomenon

While private equity investors have been more active in the United States for a longer time period, the number of non-U.S. private equity transactions has grown to be larger than that of the United States. The ability to conduct public-to-private LBO transactions in different countries is influenced by the ability to squeeze out minority shareholders. The United States, United Kingdom, and Ireland tend to be at the less-restrictive end of the spectrum while Italy, Denmark, Finland, and Spain tend to be far more restrictive (Wright et al., 2008). While the U.S. market started to develop in the middle to late 1970s, the market in western Europe was slow to expand. Only the United Kingdom and the Netherlands showed any significant activity by the mid-1980s. While remaining relatively flat throughout the 1990s in both the United States and western Europe following the recession early in the decade, LBO growth exploded between 2001 and 2007, particularly outside the United States (see Table 13–2).

Table 13-2   LBO Transactions by Region (% distribution)

	Number of Deals		Dollar Value[1]	
	1970–2000	2001–2007	1970–2000	2001–2007
United States	55.1	34.8	64.5	42.8
Canada	1.5	3.5	1.5	2.4
Continental Europe	15.6	17.6	13.2	26.1
Scandinavia	3.1	3.6	2.3	4.5
United Kingdom	20.1	28.7	15.0	15.5
Africa and Middle East	.7	2.8	.3	1.3
Asia	1.5	2.8	1.8	4.0
Australia	.5	2.5	.3	1.3
Eastern Europe	1.1	2.5	.2	1.0
Latin America	.8	1.2	.9	1.1
	100.0	100.0	100.0	100.0

[1]Millions of 2007 dollars.

Source: Adapted from Stromberg (2008).

Pure Management Buyouts Rare

Only one in five LBOs deals between 1970 and 2007 involved pure management buy-outs, in which individual investors (typically the target firm's management) acquired the firm in a leveraged transaction. The majority were undertaken by a traditional private equity sponsor or LBO fund providing most of the equity financing.

LBO Transactions Widespread

While Stromberg (2008) confirms that private equity transactions take place in a wide variety of industries, including chemicals, machinery, and retailing, buyout activity increasingly shifted to the high- growth, "high-tech" market segments. The shift in the type of target may reflect a change in the composition of U.S. industry or simply a short-age of targets deemed appropriate by private equity investors in the more traditional industries

Sales to Strategic Buyers Represent Primary Exit Strategy

LBO sponsors and management are able to realize their expected financial returns on exiting or "cashing out" of the business. Constituting about 13 percent of total transac-tions since the 1970s, initial public offerings (i.e., IPOs) declined in importance as an exit strategy. At 39 percent of all exits, the most common ways of exiting buyouts is through a sale to a strategic buyer; the second most common method, at 24 percent, is a sale to another buyout firm. See Table 13–3 for a breakdown of alternative methods of exiting LBOs.

Selling to a strategic buyer usually results in the best price, as the buyer may be able to generate significant synergies by combining the firm with its existing business. If the original buyout firm's investment fund is coming to an end, the firm may be able to sell the LBO to another buyout firm that is looking for new investment opportunities. This option is best used when the LBO's management is still enthusiastic about growing the firm rather than cashing out. Consequently, the LBO may be attractive to another buyout

Table 13–3 Method of Exiting LBO Transaction (% of total exits)

All Deals	1970–84	1985–89	1990–94	1995–99	2000–02	2003–05	2006–07	Total
Bankruptcy	7	6	5	8	6	4	3	6
IPO	28	25	22	11	8	10	1	13
Sold to strategic buyer	32	34	38	39	39	41	38	39
Sold to buyout firm	6	13	17	24	30	30	22	24
Sold to LBO-backed firm[1]	2	3	3	5	5	6	14	5
Sold to mangement[2]	1	1	1	2	2	1	1	2
Other/unknown	24	18	14	11	10	8	21	11
	100	100	100	100	100	100	100	100

[1]Firms having undergone LBOs frequently grow by making acquisitions.

[2]While MBOs represent about one fifth of all leveraged buyouts, they represent a very small percentage of exit strategies.

Source: Adapted from Stromberg (2008).

firm. An IPO is often less attractive, due to the massive amount of public disclosure required, the substantial commitment of management time, the difficulty in timing the market, and the potential for incorrectly valuing the IPO. The original investors also can cash out while management remains in charge of the business through a leveraged recapitalization. This strategy entails borrowing additional monies to repurchase stock from other shareholders, leaving the firm with a more conventional capital structure. This strategy may be employed once the firm has paid down its original debt level.

LBOs Not Prone to "Quick Flips"

"Quick flips," those LBO exited in less than two years of the initial investment, accounted for only 8 percent of the total deals and declined in recent years. LBOs tend to remain in place for long periods, with almost 40 percent continuing to operate 10 years after the initial LBO announcement. Smaller firms tend to stay in the LBO ownership form longer than larger firms. The median firm remains under LBO ownership for nine years. These findings are in stark contrast to earlier studies of public to private transactions, which found the median LBO target remained private for 6.8 years (Kaplan 1991).

Most LBOs Involve Acquisitions of Private Firms

Most highly leveraged transactions consist of acquisitions of private rather public firms. While receiving most of the research in prior studies, public-to-private (going private) transactions accounted for 6.7 percent of all transactions between 1970 and 2007, although they did make up about 28 percent of the dollar value of such transactions, since public companies tend to be larger than private firms. Acquisitions of private firms constituted 47 percent of all transactions between 1970 and 2007. During the same period, buyouts of divisions of companies accounted for 31 percent of the transactions and 31 percent of the total value of transactions. Table 13–4 illustrates the dramatic shift in the types of deals between the 1970–2000 and 2001–2007 time periods, with more than two thirds of all deals and the dollar value of such deals consummated between 2001 and 2007.

Pricing Multiples Reached Record Levels in 2006–2007

In the United States, purchase price multiples paid for target firms generally rose in recent years. Using Standard & Poor's data on transaction values (measured by enterprise value)

Table 13–4   LBO Transactions by Type of Deal (% distribution)

	Number of Deals		Dollar Value	
	1970–2000	**2001–2007**	**1970–2000**	**2001–2007**
Public to private	6.0	6.8	26.9	28.8
Private to private	63.8	36.9	37.2	14.7
Divisional buyout	22.8	36.3	25.9	31.6
Buyout firm	6.2	16.8	9.4	23.5
Distressed (buyout from bankruptcy)	1.2	3.2	.6	1.4
	100.0	100.0	100.0	100.0
Percent of total sample (1970–2007)	37	63	32	68

Note: Total LBO transactions 1970 to 2007 in sample = 21,397.

Source: Adapted from Stromberg (2008).

as a multiple of EBITDA, U.S. buyouts over $250 million have risen from 6 in 1995 to 7.5 by the end of 2007. For buyouts between $250 and $500 million, multiples declined from a peak, in 1998 of 8.7 to 6.5 in 2001 before rising to 8.5 by the end of 2007. Similarly, LBO values above $500 million peaked in 1998 at about 9 before falling to 6.7 in 2001 and subsequently rising to 12.7 in 2007.

The Effects of LBOs on Innovation

The rate of innovation has long been recognized as an important factor in economic growth. Early studies found a correlation between more debt and lower R&D spending (Hall, 1992; Himmelberg and Petersen, 1994). In contrast, Hao and Jaffe (1993) conclude that more debt can be shown to reduce R&D only for the smallest firms. Lichtenberg and Siegel (1990) found that LBOs increase R&D spending on an absolute basis and relative to their peers.

While there is no perfect measurement of the rate of innovation, the number of patents and the number of times they are cited in the literature are widely recognized as an appropriate measure (Jaffe and Trajtenberg, 2002). Sorensen, Stromberg, and Lerner (2008) examined the impact of private equity investment on the rate of innovation for a sample of 495 firms with at least one successful patent application filed from three years prior to five years following a private equity investment. The authors found that the rate of innovation, as measured by the quantity and generality of patents, does not change following private equity investments. However, such firms tend to concentrate their innovation efforts in areas in which the firm has historically focused. In fact, the patents of private equity backed firms applied for in the years following the investment by the private equity firm are more frequently cited, suggesting some improvement in the rate of innovation.

The Effects of LBOs on Employment Growth

In a study of 5,000 LBOs between 1980 and 2005 (the largest such study to date), Davis et al. (2008) found that companies owned by buyout firms maintained employment levels on par with competitors in the first year after the buyout. The sample included 300,000 sites operated by buyout firms at the time of the transactions. However, their employment levels dropped relative to the control sample in the second and third years following the buyout. By the end of five years, cumulative job growth was in the aggregate about 2 percentage points less than firms in the control sample. In manufacturing, employment levels at firms subject to buyout were very similar to those at competitor firms; while in retailing, services, and financial services, employment tended to be significantly lower. Job creation as a result of investment in new ventures (i.e., greenfield operations) tends to be higher at firms experiencing buyouts than at competitor firms.

The authors note that their findings are consistent with the notion that private equity groups act as catalysts to shrink inefficient segments of underperforming firms. Furthermore, greenfield operations undertaken by firms having undergone buyouts accelerate the expansion of such firms in new, potentially more productive directions. The job creation rate in these new ventures tends to be substantially higher than those in current businesses, creating the potential for higher long-term employment gains than at firms not having undergone buyouts. Firms having undergone buyouts also tend to engage in more acquisitions and divestitures than their competitors.

Corporate Governance Structures in LBOs

Jensen (1989) argues that the LBO would become the dominant form of corporate governance structure in view of its emphasis on concentrated ownership by active owners, substantial managerial incentives, and leveraged capital structure. However, LBO activity slowed considerably during the early 1990s. Kaplan (1997) argues that this slowdown in part reflected the elimination of many incompetent managers in the 1980s and therefore lessened the need for an LBO-imposed governance system. In contrast to Jensen, LBOs were viewed by others largely as a temporary form of corporate governance structure aimed at public companies that were inefficiently using excess cash flows (Baker and Wruck, 1989). Rappaport (1990) views LBOs as a short-term phenomenon of the 1980s, in which highly inefficient firms with poor corporate governance were taken private to restore profitability and the proper corporate governance and that they would be returned to public ownership a few years later.

These views no longer accurately characterize today's private equity market. LBO investors are no longer primarily motivated by correcting governance problems in publicly traded firms (i.e., removing incompetent managers, restoring profitability, and returning the target to the public markets). Public-to-private transactions accounted for about 15 percent of the number of transactions and about one half of the value during the 1980s. As noted previously, current LBO transactions target both public and private companies in a wide variety of industries (Stromberg, 2008). Between 2001 and 2007, public-to-private transactions accounted for less than 7 percent and 29 percent of the number of and value of LBO transactions. Moreover, increasingly LBOs are exited by selling to another LBO buyout firm rather than to strategic buyers with more conventional governance structures.

The role of the board of directors is crucial in private equity. Having private equity partners can be very helpful in restructuring the target firm. For a sample of 142 public-to-private transactions (of which 88 were sponsored by a private equity investor) in the United Kingdom between 1998 and 2002, Cornelli and Karakas (2008) found that the board size and the number of outside directors was substantially reduced. Outside directors were replaced by employees of the private equity firm. In the case of MBOs, outside directors disappeared and only management remained. Private equity investors are most active in challenging complex transactions. Directors appointed by financial sponsors tend to remain actively engaged for years after the initial investment.

In the largest management buyout in U.S. history at that time, Kinder Morgan Inc.'s management proposed to take the oil and gas pipeline firm private in 2006 in a transaction that valued the firm's outstanding equity at $13.5 billion. Under the proposal, chief executive Richard Kinder and other senior executives would contribute shares valued at $2.8 billion to the newly private company. An additional $4.5 billion would come from private equity investors, including Goldman Sachs Capital partners, American International Group Inc., and the Carlyle Group. Including assumed debt, the transaction was valued at about $22 billion. The transaction also was notable for the governance and ethical issues it raised (see Case Study 13–1).

Case Study 13–1 Kinder Morgan Buyout Raises Ethical Questions

The top management of Kinder Morgan Inc. waited more than two months before informing the firm's board of its desire to take the company private. It is customary for boards governing firms whose managements were interested in buying out public shareholders to create a committee within the board consisting of independent board members (i.e., nonmanagement) to solicit other bids. While the Kinder Morgan board did eventually create such a committee, the board's lack of awareness of the pending management proposal gave management an important lead over potential bidders in structuring a proposal. By being involved early on in the process, a board has more time to negotiate terms more favorable to shareholders. The transaction also raises questions about the potential conflicts of interest of investment bankers hired to advise management and the board on the "fairness" of the offer price but who also are potential investors in the buyout.

Kinder Morgan's management hired Goldman Sachs, in February 2006, to explore "strategic" options for the firm to enhance shareholder value. The leveraged buyout option was proposed by Goldman Sachs on March 7, followed by their proposal to become the primary investor in the LBO on April 5. Subsequently, the management buyout group hired a number of law firms and other investment banks as advisors and discussed the proposed buyout with credit-rating firms to assess how much debt the firm could support without experiencing a significant downgrade in its credit rating.

On May 13, 2006, the full board was finally made aware of the proposal. The board immediately demanded that a standstill agreement that had been signed by Richard Kinder, CEO and leader of the buyout group, not to talk to any alternative bidders for a period of 90 days be terminated. While investment banks and buyout groups often propose such an agreement to ensure that they can perform adequate due diligence, this extended period is not necessarily in the interests of the firm's shareholders, because it puts alternative suitors coming in later at a distinct disadvantage. Later bidders simply lack sufficient time to make as adequate assessment of the true value of the target and structure their own proposals. In this way, the standstill agreement could discourage alternative bids for the business.

The special committee of the board set up to negotiate with the management buyout group was ultimately able to secure a $107.50 per share price for the firm, significantly higher than the initial offer. The discussions were rumored to have been very contentious due to the board's annoyance with the delay in informing them (Berman and Sender, 2006). The deal between the management group and the board was hammered out in about two weeks.

In contrast to the Kinder Morgan deal, a management group within HCA, a large U.S. hospital operator, took less than one month to inform its board of their interest in an LBO. The special committee of the board took three months to negotiate a deal with the firm's buyout group.

Continued

Case Study 13–1 Kinder Morgan Buyout Raises Ethical Questions — Cont'd

Discussion Questions

1. What potential conflicts of interest could arise in a management buyout in which the investment bank is also likely to be an investor? Be specific.
2. Do you believe standstill agreements, in which the potential LBO firm agrees not to shop for alternative bidders for a specific period of time, are reasonable? Explain your answer.

Competition in the LBO Market

To finance the increased average size of targets taken private in 2006, buyout firms started to bid for target firms as groups of investors. The increased tendency of buyout firms to invest as a group is often referred to as *clubbing*. The HCA, SunGard, and Kinder Morgan transactions all involved at least four private equity investor funds. While mitigating risk, banding together to buy large LBO targets also made buyout firms vulnerable to accusations of colluding in an effort to limit the prices offered for target firms. The empirical evidence concerning whether club deals actually benefit target firm shareholders by enabling the payment of higher purchase prices is mixed. Meuleman and Wright (2007) and Guo et al. (2008) found some evidence that "clubbing" is associated with higher target transaction prices. However, Officer, Ozbas, and Berk (2008) argue that club deals are likely to be detrimental to public company shareholders by undermining the auction process that might result from having multiple suitors. In analyzing 325 public-to-private LBO transactions between 1998 and 2007, the United States General Accountability Office (2008) could find no correlation between club deals and prices paid for target firms.

When Do Firms Go Private?

In general, public firms are inclined to go private if the board and management believe that the firm's current share price is undervalued when compared to what they perceive to be future cash flows. In addition, Boot, Gopalan, and Thankor (2009) argue that other factors affecting the timing of the decision of when to go private include the firm's need for liquidity, the potential for loss of control to activist investors (i.e., those who intervene in board and management decision making through proxy contests), and the cost of governance (e.g., SEC reporting requirements, Sarbanes–Oxley). Access to liquid public capital markets enables a firm to lower its cost of capital. However, participating in public markets creates the potential for greater instability of the firm's shareholder base as investors can easily buy and sell the firm's outstanding shares. This instability creates uncertainty between management and shareholder expectations, as the composition of the base potentially changes from one that is largely passive to one more inclined to intervene in management decisions.

There is evidence that the Sarbanes–Oxley Act of 2002 contributed to the cost of governance for firms as a result of the onerous reporting requirements of the bill. This has been a particular burden to smaller firms. Some studies estimate that the cost of being a public firm was more than $14 million in 2004, almost twice the cost incurred in the prior year (Engel, Hayes, and Xang, 2004; Hartman, 2005; and Kamar, Karaca-Mandic, and Talley, 2006). Leuz, Triantis, and Wang (2008) document a spike in delistings of public firms attributable to the passage of the Sarbanes–Oxley Act of 2002.

In summary, the incentive to go private is greatest when management and the board believe the firm is undervalued. Moreover, public firms are more likely to go private if the cost of governance is high, the need for liquidity is low, and the potential loss of control is high.

Financing Transactions

Once a prospective target has been identified, the buyer has a number of financing options. For the risk-adverse acquirer, the ideal mechanism might be to finance the transaction out of cash held by the target in excess of normal working capital requirements. Such situations are usually very difficult to find. Venture capital, or so-called angel, investors also may be available to fund the transaction. However, this may represent very expensive financing, because the buyer may have to give up majority ownership of the acquired company. Use of the buyer's stock may be an appropriate way to minimize the initial cash outlay, but such an option is rarely available in an MBO or a buyout by privately held companies. The seller may be willing to accept debt issued by the buyer if an upfront cash payment is not important. The use of a public issue of long-term debt to finance the transaction may minimize the initial cash outlay, but it is also subject to restrictions placed on how the business may be operated by the investors buying the issue. Moreover, public issues are expensive in terms of administrative, marketing, and regulatory reporting costs. For these reasons, asset-based lending has emerged as an attractive alternative to the use of cash, stock, or public debt issues if the target has sufficient tangible assets to serve as collateral.

Asset-Based or Secured Lending

Under asset-based lending, the borrower pledges certain assets as collateral. Asset-based lenders look at the borrower's assets as their primary protection against the borrower's failure to repay. Such loans are often short term (i.e., less than 1 year in maturity) and secured by assets that can be liquidated easily, such as accounts receivable and inventory. Borrowers often seek *revolving credit lines* that they draw upon on a daily basis to run their business. Under a revolving credit arrangement, the bank agrees to make loans up to a specified maximum for a specified period, usually a year or more. As the borrower repays a portion of the loan, an amount equal to the repayment can be borrowed again under the terms of the agreement. In addition to interest on the notes, the bank charges a fee for the commitment to hold the funds available. For a fee, the borrower may choose to convert the revolving credit line into a term loan. A *term loan* usually has a maturity of 2 to 10 years and is secured by the asset that is being financed, such as new capital equipment.

Acquiring firms generally prefer to borrow funds on an unsecured basis because the added administrative costs involved in pledging assets as security significantly raise the total cost of borrowing. Secured borrowing also can be onerous because the security agreements can severely limit a company's future borrowing. However, in many instances, borrowers may have little choice but to obtain secured lending for at least a portion of the purchase price. Asset-based lenders generally require personal guarantees from the buyer, in which the buyer pledges such personal assets as his or her principal residence.

Loan Documentation

The lending process entails the negotiation of a loan agreement, security agreement, and promissory note. The *loan agreement* stipulates the terms and conditions under which the lender would loan the firm funds. The *security agreement* specifies which of the borrower's assets are pledged to secure the loan. The *promissory note* commits the borrower to repay the loan, even if the assets, when liquidated, do not fully cover the unpaid balance. These agreements contain certain security provisions and protective covenants limiting what the borrower may do as long as the loan is outstanding. The security agreement is filed at a state regulatory office in the state where the collateral is located. Future lenders can check with this office to see which assets a firm has pledged and which are free to be used as future collateral. The filing of this security agreement legally establishes the lender's security interest in the collateral. If the borrower defaults on the loan or otherwise fails to honor the terms of the agreement, the lender can seize and sell the collateral to recover the value of the loan. The process of determining which of a firm's assets are free from liens is made easier today by commercial credit reporting repositories such as Dun & Bradstreet, Experian, Equifax, and Transunion.

Pledging Receivables and Inventory

Depending on the extent to which they are collectable, lenders may lend up to 80–90 percent of the book value of the receivables (Kretlow, McGuigan, and Moyer, 1998). Asset-based lenders generally are willing to lend against only those receivables due within 90 days. Those that are more than 90 days past due are likely to be difficult to collect. Lenders are not willing to lend up to 100 percent of the value of the more current receivables, because they are aware that some portion of those receivables will not be collectable.

Inventories also are commonly used to provide collateral for LBO transactions. As is true of receivables, inventories are often highly liquid. Inventory consists of raw material, work in process, and finished goods. Lenders generally consider only raw material and finished goods inventories as suitable collateral. The amount a lender will advance against the book value of inventory depends on its ease of identification and its liquidity. Normally, lenders loan between 50 and 80 percent of the value of inventory. Lenders tend to loan less if the inventory is viewed as perishable, subject to rapid obsolescence, or having relatively few potential buyers.

Pledging Equipment and Real Estate to Support Term Loans

Borrowers often prefer term loans because they need not be concerned that the loan will have to be renewed. A term loan can be structured in such a way that the period of the loan corresponds with the economic life of the item being financed. Durable equipment and real estate often are used to secure loans. Lenders are frequently willing to lend up to 80 percent of the appraised value of equipment and 50 percent of the value of land, if such land can be converted to cash quickly. The cash flows generated by the assets will be used to pay off the loan. Term loans sometimes are used in LBO transactions to reduce the overall cost of borrowing. Because term loans are negotiated privately between the borrower and the lender, they often are much less expensive than the cost of floating a public debt or stock issue.

Security Provisions and Protective Covenants

Security provisions and protective covenants in loan documents are intended to ensure that the interest and principal of outstanding loans will be repaid in a timely fashion. Typical security features include the assignment of payments due under a specific contract to the lender, an assignment of a portion of the receivables or inventories, and a pledge of marketable securities held by the borrower. Other features could include a mortgage on property, plant, and equipment held by the borrower and the assignment of the cash surrender value of a life insurance policy held by the borrower on key executives.

An *affirmative covenant* is a portion of a loan agreement that specifies the actions the borrowing firm agrees to take during the term of the loan. These typically include furnishing periodic financial statements to the lender, carrying sufficient insurance to cover insurable business risks, maintaining a minimum amount of net working capital, and retaining key management personnel acceptable to the lending institution. A *negative covenant* restricts the actions of the borrower. It could include limiting the amount of dividends that can be paid, the level of salaries and bonuses that may be given to the borrower's employees, the total amount of indebtedness that can be assumed by the borrower, investments in plant and equipment and acquisitions, and the sale of certain assets. All loan agreements have default provisions permitting the lender to collect the loan immediately under certain conditions. These conditions might include the borrower failing to pay interest, principal, or both according to the terms of the loan agreement; the borrower materially misrepresenting information on the firm's financial statements; and the borrower failing to observe any of the affirmative or negative covenants. Loan agreements also commonly have *cross-default provisions*, allowing a lender to collect its loan immediately if the borrower is in default on a loan to another lender.

Cash-Flow or Unsecured Lenders

Cash-flow lenders view the borrower's future cash-flow generation capability as the primary means of recovering a loan and the borrower's assets as a secondary source of funds in the event of default by the borrower. Cash-flow-based lending for LBOs became more commonplace during the middle to late 1980s. Many LBOs' capital structures assumed increasing amounts of unsecured debt. To compensate for additional risk, the unsecured lenders would receive both a higher interest rate and warrants that were convertible into equity at some future date.

Unsecured debt often is referred to as *mezzanine financing.* Such debt lies between senior debt and the equity layers. It includes senior subordinated debt, subordinated debt, bridge financing, and LBO partnership financing. It frequently consists of high-yield junk bonds, which may also include zero coupon deferred interest debentures (i.e., bonds whose interest is not paid until maturity) used to increase the postacquisition cash flow of the acquired entity. In liquidation, it lies between the secured or asset-based debt and preferred and common equity. Unsecured financing often consists of several layers of debt, each subordinate in liquidation to the next more senior issue. Those with the lowest level of security normally offer the highest yields to compensate for their higher level of risk in the event of default. *Bridge financing* consists of unsecured loans often provided by investment banks or hedge funds to supply short-term financing pending the placement of subordinated debt (i.e., long-term or "permanent" financing). Bridge financing is usually expected to be replaced six to nine months after the closing date of the LBO transaction.

On March 17, 2009, Pfizer Pharmaceuticals announced that it had successfully sold $13.5 billion in senior, unsecured long-term debt in maturities of three, six, 10 and 20 years to replace short-term bridge financing that had been issued to complete its acquisition of Wyeth Pharmaceuticals. Accounting for about one third of the $68 billion purchase price, the bridge financing, consisting of $22.5 billion, had to be repaid by December 31, 2009. The five banks that originally had provided the bridge loans had syndicated (sold) portions of the loans to a total of 29 other banks such that no single bank financed more than $1.5 billion of the total $22.5 billion.

Types of Long-Term Financing

Long-term debt generally is classified according to whether it is secured or not. *Secured debt* issues usually are called *mortgage bonds* or *equipment trust certificates.* Issues not secured by specific assets are called *debentures.* Because debentures are unsecured, their quality depends on the general creditworthiness of the issuing company. The attractiveness of long-term debt is its relatively low after-tax cost as a result of the tax deductibility of interest.

Senior and Junior Debt

Long-term debt issues also are classified by whether they are senior or junior in liquidation. Senior debt has a higher-priority claim to a firm's earnings and assets than junior debt. Unsecured debt also may be classified according to whether it is subordinated to other types of debt. In general, subordinated debentures are junior to other types of debt, including bank loans, and even may be junior to all of a firm's other debt. The extent to which a debt issue is junior to other debt depends on the restrictions placed on the company by the purchasers of the issue in an agreement called an *indenture*.

Indentures

An **indenture** is a contract between the firm that issues the long-term debt securities and the lenders. The indenture details the nature of the issue, specifies the way in which the principal must be repaid, and specifies affirmative and negative covenants applicable to the long-term debt issue. Typical covenants include maintaining a minimum interest coverage ratio, a minimum level of working capital, a maximum amount of dividends that the firm can pay, and restrictions on equipment leasing and issuing additional debt.

Seller Financing

A sometimes overlooked source of financing is to have the seller agree to carry a promissory note for some portion of the purchase price. This may be especially important when the buyer is unable to finance the bulk of the purchase price and is unwilling or unable to put in more equity capital. Such financing generally is unsecured. If the business being purchased is part of a larger parent company, the borrower may be able to obtain certain concessions from the parent. For example, the parent may be willing to continue to provide certain products and services to the business at cost to increase the likelihood that the business is successful and its note will be repaid in a timely fashion.

Bond Ratings

Debt issues are rated by various rating agencies according to their relative degree of risk. These agencies include Moody's Investors Services and Standard and Poor's (S&P) Corporation. Factors considered by these agencies when assessing risk include a firm's earnings stability, interest coverage ratios, the relative amount of debt in the firm's capital structure, the degree of subordination of the issue being rated, and the firm's past performance in meeting its debt service requirements. Each rating agency has a scale for identifying the risk of an issue. For Moody's, the ratings are Aaa, Aa, A, Baa, Ba, B, Caa, Ca, and C, with Aaa the lowest- and C the highest-risk category. AAA denotes the lowest-risk category for S&P. This rating is followed by AA, A, BBB, BB, B, CCC, CC, C, and D.

Junk Bonds

Junk bonds are high-yield bonds either rated by the credit-rating agencies as below investment grade or not rated at all. Noninvestment grade bonds usually are rated Ba or lower by Moody's or BB or lower by S&P. When originally issued, junk bonds frequently yield more than 4 percentage points above the yields on U.S. Treasury debt of comparable maturity. Junk bond financing exploded in the 1980s. Although junk bonds were a popular source of financing for takeovers, about three fourths of the total proceeds of junk bonds issued between 1980 and 1986 were used to finance the capital requirements of high-growth corporations (Yago, 1991). The remainder was used to finance corporate takeovers. This source of LBO financing dried up as a result of a series of defaults of overleveraged firms in the late 1980s, coupled with alleged insider trading and fraud at such companies as Drexel Burnham, the primary market maker for junk bonds at that time.

The rapid growth of the junk bond market coincided with a growing deterioration in the quality of such issues. Wigmore (1994) found that the quality of the junk bonds issued during the 1980s deteriorated in terms of such measures as interest coverage ratios (i.e., earnings before interest and taxes/interest expense), debt/net tangible book value, and cash flow as a percentage of debt. Cumulative default rates for junk bonds issued in the late 1970s reached as high as 34 percent by 1986 (Asquith, Mullins, and Wolff, 1989). Despite these high default rates, some portion of the face value of the junk bond issues often was recovered because firms formerly in default emerged from bankruptcy. Altman and Kishore (1996) found that recovery rates for senior secured debt averaged about 58 percent of the original principal. Taking recovery rates into consideration, they found the actual realized spread between junk bonds and 10-year U.S. Treasury securities was actually about 2 percentage points between 1978 and 1994 rather than more than 4 percentage points when they were issued originally.

Leveraged Bank Loans

Leveraged loans often are defined as unrated or noninvestment grade bank loans whose interest rates are equal to or greater than the London Interbank Rate (LIBOR) plus 150 basis points (1.5 percentage points). Leveraged loans also include second mortgages, which typically have a floating rate and give lenders a lower level of security than first mortgages. Some analysts include other forms of debt instruments in this market, such as mezzanine or senior unsecured debt, discussed earlier in this chapter, and *payment-in-kind notes,* for which interest is paid in the form of more debt. In the United States, the volume of such loans substantially exceeds the volume of junk bond issues. This represents a resurgence in bank loan financing as an alternative to financing transactions by using junk bonds. Leveraged loans are often less costly than junk bonds for borrowers, because they often provide a higher level of security than unsecured junk bonds.

Globally, the syndicated loan market (which includes leveraged loans, senior unsecured debt, and payment-in-kind notes) is growing more rapidly than public markets for debt and equity. Syndicated loans are those typically issued through a consortium of institutions, including hedge funds, pension funds, and insurance companies, to individual borrowers. Since such lending usually avoids the public debt markets, it often is referred to as the *private debt market.* With the drying up of credit in 2008 and 2009, reflecting a loss of confidence due to the proliferation of imprudent lending practices, this market is likely to be subject to considerably more regulation in the future.

Other Sources of Funds

Common stockholders participate in the firm's future earnings, because they may receive a larger dividend if earnings increase. Like common stock, preferred stock is part of shareholders' equity. Although preferred stockholders receive dividends instead of interest payments, it is considered a fixed-income security. Dividends on preferred stock are generally constant over time, like interest payments on debt, but the firm is generally not obligated to pay them at a specific point in time. Unpaid dividends may cumulate for eventual payment by the issuer if the preferred stock is a special cumulative issue. In liquidation, bondholders are paid first, then preferred stockholders; common stockholders are paid last. Preferred stock often is issued in LBO transactions, because it provides investors a fixed-income security, which has a claim that is senior to common stock in the event of liquidation. To conserve cash, LBOs frequently issue payment-in-kind (PIK) preferred stock, where the dividend obligation can be satisfied by issuing additional par amounts of the preferred security. Table 13–5 summarizes the key characteristics of an LBO's capital structure.

How Solid Are Loan Commitments?

Like buyers, lenders also invoke material adverse-change clauses to back out of lending commitments. Concerned that they will have to discount such loans when they are resold, Morgan Stanley and UBS balked at commitments to fund the purchase of Reddy Ice Holdings and Genesco in late 2007. Similarly, Lehman and J.P. Morgan were part of a group of banks that helped force Home Depot to take $1.8 billion less for its construction supply business. Although only the 10th largest transaction of 2007 in terms of price, the Home Depot Supply deal became one of the 2007's most important by mid-year. It represented one of the first large, highly leveraged transactions to be renegotiated following the collapse of the subprime mortgage market in late summer (see Case Study 13–2).

Table 13–5 Leveraged Buyout Capital Structure

Type of Security		Debt	
	Backed By	Lenders Loan Up To	Lending Source
Secured debt			
Short-term (<1 year) debt	Liens generally receivables and inventories	50–80% depending on quality	Banks and finance companies
Intermediate term (1–10 years) debt	Liens on land and equipment	Up to 80% of appraised value of equipment and 50% of real estate	Life insurance companies, private equity investors, pension, and hedge funds

Unsecured or mezzanine debt (subordinated and junior subordinated debt, including seller financing)
  First layer
  Second layer
  Etc.
Bridge financing
Payment in kind
	Cash generating capabilities of the borrower	Face value of securities	Life insurance companies, pension funds, private equity, and hedge funds

		Equity	
Preferred stock Payment in kind	Cash-generating capabilities of the borrower		Life insurance companies, pension funds, hedge funds, private equity, and angel investors
Common stock	Cash generating capabilities of the borrower		Life insurance, pension, private equity, hedge, and venture capital funds and angel investors

Case Study 13–2 Financing Challenges in the Home Depot Supply Transaction

Buyout firms Bain Capital, Carlyle Group, and Clayton, Dubilier & Rice (CD&R) bid $10.3 billion in June 2007 to buy Home Depot Inc.'s HD Supply business. HD Supply represented a collection of small suppliers of construction products. Home Depot had announced earlier in the year that it planned to use the proceeds of the sale to pay for a portion of a $22.5 billion stock buyback.

Three banks, Lehman Brothers, J.P. Morgan Chase, and Merrill Lynch agreed to provide the firms with a $4 billion loan. The repayment of the loans was predicated on the ability of the buyout firms to improve significantly HD Supply's current cash flow. Such loans are normally made with the presumption that they can be sold to investors, with the banks collecting fees from both the borrower and investor groups. However, by July, concern about the credit quality of subprime mortgages spread to the broader debt market and raised questions about the potential for default of loans made to finance highly leveraged transactions. The concern was particularly great for so-called covenant-lite loans, for which the repayment terms were very lenient.

Fearing they would not be able to resell such loans to investors, the three banks involved in financing the HD Supply transaction wanted more financial protection. Additional protection, they reasoned, would make such loans more marketable to investors. They used the upheaval in the credit markets as a pretext for reopening negotiations on their previous financing commitments. Home Depot was willing to lower the selling price, thereby reducing the amount of financing required by the buyout firms, and to guarantee payment in the event of default by the buyout firms. While Bain, Carlyle, and CD&R were willing to increase their cash investment and pay higher fees to the banks, they were unwilling to alter the original terms of the loans. Eventually the banks agreed to provide financing consisting of a $1 billion "covenant-lite" loan and a $1.3 billion "payment-in-kind" loan. Home Depot agreed to assume the loan payments on the $1 billion loan if the investor firms were to default and lower the selling price to $8.5 billion for 87.5 percent of HD Supply, with Home Depot retaining the remaining 12.5 percent.

By the end of August, Home Depot had succeeded in raising the cash needed to help pay for its share repurchase, and the banks had reduced their original commitment of $4 billion in loans to $2.3 billion. While they had agreed to put more money into the transaction, the buyout firms had been successful in limiting the number of new restrictive covenants.

Discussion Questions

1. Based on the information given it the case, determine the amount of the price reduction Home Depot accepted for HD Supply and the amount of cash the three buyout firms put into the transaction.
2. Why did banks lower their lending standards in financing LBOs in 2006 and early 2007? How did the lax standards contribute to their inability to sell the loans to investors? How did the inability to sell the loans once made curtail their future lending?

A solution to this case study is provided in the Online Instructor's Manual for instructors using this book.

Common Forms of Leveraged Buyout Deal Structures

As a result of the epidemic of bankruptcies of overleveraged cash-flow-based LBOs in the late 1980s, the most common form of LBO today is the asset-based LBO. This type of LBO can be accomplished in two ways: (1) the sale of assets by the target to the acquiring company or (2) a merger of the target into the acquiring company (direct merger) or a wholly owned subsidiary of the acquiring company (subsidiary merger) (see Chapter 11). For small companies, a reverse stock split may be used to take the firm private. An important objective of "going private" transactions is to reduce the number of shareholders to below 300 to enable the public firm to delist from many public stock exchanges.

Lender Commitment Letters

The acquirer often is asked by the seller for a *commitment letter* from a lender, which commits the lender to providing financing for the transaction. Closing is conditioned on the acquirer's ability to obtain financing. The commitment letter allows the lender access to the target company's records for credit evaluation and to conduct asset appraisals. It outlines the maximum loan amounts, interest charges, repayment schedule, and ratio of advances to assets pledged (i.e., collateral). The commitment letter is conditioned on the lender having performed adequate due diligence and the execution of an agreement of purchase and sale between the buyer and seller.

Direct Merger

In a direct or cash merger, the company to be taken private merges with a company controlled by the majority stockholder or a stockholder group. If the LBO is structured as a direct merger, in which the seller receives cash for stock, the lender will make the loan to the buyer once the appropriate security agreements are in place and the target's stock has been pledged against the loan. The target then is merged into the acquiring company, which is the surviving corporation. Payment of the loan proceeds usually is made directly to the seller in accordance with a "letter of direction" drafted by the buyer.

Subsidiary Merger

LBOs may be consummated by establishing a new subsidiary that merges with the target. The subsidiary, or affiliated entity, then makes a tender offer for the outstanding public shares. This may be done to avoid any negative impact that the new company might have on existing customer or creditor relationships. If some portion of the parent's assets are to be used as collateral to support the ability of its operating subsidiary to fund the transaction, both the parent and the subsidiary may be viewed as having a security interest in the debt. As such, they may be held jointly and severally liable for the debt. To avoid this situation, the parent may make a capital contribution to the subsidiary rather than provide collateral or a loan guarantee.

Reverse Stock Splits

A reverse stock split is a process whereby a corporation reduces the number of shares outstanding. The total number of shares will have the same market value immediately after the reverse split as before, but each share will be worth more. Reverse splits may be used to take a firm private where a firm is short of cash. Therefore, the majority shareholders retain their stock after the split while the minority shareholders receive a cash payment. On January 9, 2008, MagStar Technologies, a Minnesota-based manufacturer of conveyor systems, announced a 1 for 2,000 reverse split of the firm's common stock intended to take it private. Under the terms of the split, each 2,000 shares of the firm's common stock would be converted into 1 share of common stock and holders of fewer than 2,000 shares of common stock on the record date would receive cash of $0.425 per presplit share. The anticipated split would reduce the number of shareholders to less than 300, the minimum required to list on many public exchanges. The company immediately stopped filing reports with the SEC. Under Minnesota law, the board of directors of a company may amend the firm's articles of incorporation to conduct the reverse split without shareholder approval.

Legal Pitfalls of Improperly Structured LBOs

Fraudulent conveyance laws are applicable whenever a company goes into bankruptcy following events such as a highly leveraged transaction. Under the law, the new company created by the LBO must be strong enough financially to meet its obligations to current and future creditors. If the new company is found by the court to have been inadequately capitalized, the lender could be stripped of its secured position in the company's assets or its claims on the assets could be made subordinate to those of the general or unsecured creditors. Consequently, lenders, sellers, directors, or their agents, including auditors and investment bankers, may be required to compensate the general creditors. Fraudulent conveyance laws are intended to preclude shareholders, secured creditors, and others from benefiting at the expense of unsecured creditors.

Lender Due Diligence

The lender can be expected to make a careful evaluation of the quality of the assets to be used as collateral. Receivables are analyzed to determine the proportion beyond normal collection terms. An assessment of the likelihood that the receivables realistically could be converted to cash also is made. A physical inspection of the inventory is made to establish both the quantitative and qualitative values of the inventory. Fixed assets are appraised at their realistic "quick-sale" values by professional appraisers. Values also should be placed on off-balance-sheet assets, such as patents, trademarks, licenses, franchises, copyrights, and blueprints.

Leveraged Buyout Capital Structures

LBOs tend to have complicated capital structures consisting of bank debt, high-yield debt, mezzanine debt (intervening unsecured debt between senior debt and equity), and private equity provided primarily by the LBO sponsor. As secured debt, the bank debt generally is the most senior in the capital structure in the event of liquidation. Usually maturing within five to seven years, interest rates on such loans often vary at a fixed spread or difference over the London interbank offering rate. Bank loans usually must be paid off before other types of debt. Bank debt often consists of term loans in tranches or slices, denoted as A, B, C, and D, with A the most senior and D the least of all bank financing. While bank debt in the A tranche usually must be amortized or paid off before other forms of debt can be paid, the remaining tranches generally involve little or no amortization. While lenders in the A tranche often sell such loans to other commercial banks, loans in the B, C, and D tranches often are sold to hedge funds and mutual funds. In recent years, bank debt would make up about 40 percent of the total capital structure.

The remainder of the LBO capital structure consists of unsecured subordinated debt, also referred to as *junk bonds*. Interest is fixed and represents a constant percentage or spread over the U.S. Treasury bond rate. The amount of the spread depends on the credit quality of the debt. Often callable at a premium, this debt usually has a 10-year maturity date when the debt is paid off in a single payment. Such loans often are referred to as *bullet loans*, to reflect their repayment at a single point in time.

As an alternative to high-yield publicly traded junk bonds, second mortgage or lien loans became popular between 2003 and mid-2007. Such loans are privately placed with hedge funds and collateralized loan obligation (CLO) investors. They are secured by the firm's assets but are subordinated to the bank debt in liquidation. By pooling large numbers of first and second mortgage loans (so-called leverage loans) and subdividing the pool into tranches, CLO investors sell the tranches to institutional investors such as pension funds and insurance companies.

Case Study 13–3 provides an example of a nontraditional LBO target (SunGard Corporation). Note how the sponsors of the LBO banded together to defray risk and how the torrid pace of capital flowing into buyout funds and their need to achieve higher financial returns spurred their willingness to assume greater risk and to pay ever-increasing prices. Also note the merger structure and complex capital structure required to support the size of the transaction.

Case Study 13–3 Financing LBOs—The SunGard Transaction

With their cash hoards accumulating at an unprecedented rate, there was little that buyout firms could do but to invest in larger firms. Consequently, the average size of LBO transactions grew significantly during 2005. In a move reminiscent of the blockbuster buyouts of the late 1980s, seven private investment firms acquired 100 percent of the outstanding stock of SunGard Data Systems Inc. (SunGard) in late 2005. SunGard is a financial software firm known for providing application and transaction software services and creating backup data systems in the event of disaster. The company's software manages 70 percent of the transactions made on the NASDAQ stock exchange, but its biggest business is creating backup data systems in case a client's main systems are disabled by a natural disaster, blackout, or terrorist attack. Its large client base for disaster recovery and backup systems provides a substantial and predictable cash flow.

SunGard's new owners include Silver Lake Partners, Bain Capital LLC, The Blackstone Group L.P., Goldman Sachs Capital Partners, Kohlberg Kravis Roberts & Co., Providence Equity Partners Inc., and Texas Pacific Group. Buyout firms in 2005 tended to band together to spread the risk of a deal this size and reduce the likelihood of a bidding war. Indeed, with SunGard, there was only one bidder, the investor group consisting of these seven firms.

The software side of SunGard is believed to have significant growth potential, while the disaster-recovery side provides a large stable cash flow. Unlike many LBOs, the deal was announced as being all about growth of the financial services software side of the business. The deal is structured as a merger, since SunGard would be merged into a shell corporation created by the investor group for acquiring SunGard. Going private allows SunGard to invest heavily in software without being punished by investors, since such investments are expensed and reduce reported earnings per share. Going private also allows the firm to eliminate the burdensome reporting requirements of being a public company.

The buyout represented potentially a significant source of fee income for the investor group. In addition to the 2 percent management fees buyout firms collect from investors in the funds they manage, they receive substantial fee income from each investment they make on behalf of their funds. For example, the buyout firms receive a 1 percent deal completion fee, which was more than $100 million in the Sun-Gard transaction. Buyout firms also receive fees paid for by the target firm that is "going private" for arranging financing, as well as fees for conducting due diligence and monitoring the ongoing performance of the firm taken private. Finally, when the buyout firms exit their investments in the target firm via a sale to a strategic buyer or a secondary IPO, they receive 20 percent (i.e., so-called carry fee) of any profits.

Under the terms of the agreement, SunGard shareholders received $36 per share, a 14 percent premium over the SunGard closing price as of the announcement date of March 28, 2005, and 40 percent more than when the news first leaked about the deal a week earlier. From the SunGard shareholders' perspective, the deal is valued at $11.4 billion dollars consisting of $10.9 billion for outstanding shares and "in-the-money" options (i.e., options whose exercise price is less than the firm's market price per share) plus $500 million in debt on the balance sheet.

The seven equity investors provided $3.5 billion in capital with the remainder of the purchase price financed by commitments from a lending consortium consisting of Citigroup, J.P. Morgan Chase & Co., and Deutsche Bank. The purpose of the loans is to finance the merger, repay or refinance SunGard's existing debt, provide ongoing working capital, and pay fees and expenses incurred in connection with the merger. The total funds necessary to complete the merger and related fees and expenses is approximately $11.3 billion, consisting of approximately $10.9 billion to pay SunGard's stockholders and about $400.7 million to pay fees and expenses related to the merger and the financing arrangements. Note that the fees to be financed constitute almost 4 percent of the purchase price. Ongoing working capital needs and capital expenditures required obtaining commitments from lenders well in excess of $11.3 billion.

The merger financing consists of several tiers of debt and "credit facilities." Credit facilities are arrangements for extending credit. The senior secured debt and senior subordinated debt are intended to provide "permanent" or long-term financing. Senior debt covenants include restrictions on new borrowing, investments, sales of assets, mergers and consolidations, prepayments of subordinated indebtedness, capital expenditures, liens and dividends and other distributions, as well as a minimum interest coverage ratio and a maximum total leverage ratio.

If the offering of notes is not completed on or prior to the closing, the banks providing the financing have committed to provide up to $3 billion in loans under a senior subordinated bridge credit facility. The bridge loans are intended as a form of temporary financing to satisfy immediate cash requirements until permanent financing can be arranged. A special-purpose SunGard subsidiary will purchase receivables from SunGard, with the purchases financed through the sale of the receivables to the lending consortium. The lenders would subsequently finance the purchase of the receivables by issuing commercial paper, which is to be repaid as the receivables are collected. The special-purpose subsidiary is not shown on the SunGard balance sheet. Based on the value of receivables at closing, the subsidiary could provide up to $500 million. The obligation of the lending consortium to buy the receivables would expire on the sixth anniversary of the closing of the merger.

Table 13–6 provides SunGard's postmerger pro forma capital structure. Note that the pro forma capital structure is portrayed as if SunGard uses 100 percent of bank lending commitments. Also, note that individual LBO investors may invest monies from more than one fund they manage. This may be due to the perceived attractiveness of the opportunity or the limited availability of money in any single fund. Of the $9 billion in debt financing, bank loans constitute 56 percent and subordinated or mezzanine debt represents 44 percent.

Continued

Case Study 13–3 Financing LBOs—The SunGard Transaction — Cont'd

Table 13–6   SunGard Pro Forma Capital Structure ($ millions)

Premerger Existing SunGard Debt Outstanding	
Senior notes (3.75% due in 2009)	250,000,000
Senior notes (4.785% due in 2014)	250,000,000
Total existing debt outstanding	500,000,000
Debt Portion of Merger Financing	
Senior secured notes (≤$5 billion)	5,000,000,000
$1 billion revolving credit facility with 6-year term	
$4 billion term loan maturing in 7½ years	
Senior subordinated notes (≤$3 billion)	3,000,000,000
Payment-in-kind senior notes (≤$0.5 billion)	500,000,000
Receivables credit facility (≤$0.5 billion)	500,000,000
Total merger financing (as if fully utilized)	9,000,000,000

Equity Portion of Merger Financing	
Equity investor	**Commitment**
Silver Lake Partners II, LP[1]	540,000,000
Bain Capital Fund VIII, LP	540,000,000
Blackstone Capital Partners IV, L.P.	270,000,000
Blackstone Communications Partners I, L.P.	270,000,000
GS Capital Partners 2000, L.P.	250,000,000
GS Capital Partners 2000 V, L.P.	250,000,000
KKR Millennium Fund, L.P.	540,000,000
Providence Equity Partners V, L.P.	300,000,000
TPG Partners IV, L.P.	540,000,000
Total equity portion of merger financing	3,500,000,000
Total debt and equity	13,000,000,000

[1]The roman numeral II refers to the fund providing the equity capital managed by the partnership.

Discussion Questions

1. In what ways is this transaction similar to and different from those that were common in the 1980s? Be specific.
2. Why are payment-in-kind securities (debt or preferred stock) particularly well suited for financing LBOs? Under what circumstances might they be most attractive to lenders or investors?
3. Explain how the way in which an LBO is financed affects the way in which it is operated and the timing of when equity investors or sponsors choose to exit the business.

A solution to this case study is provided in the Online Instructor's Manual for instructors using this book.

What Factors Are Critical to Successful LBOs?

While many factors contribute to the success of leveraged buyouts, studies suggest that selecting suitable targets, not overpaying, and improving operating performance are among the most important.

Knowing What to Buy

Traditionally, firms that represent good candidates for an LBO are those that have substantial tangible assets, unused borrowing capacity, predictable positive operating cash flow, and assets that are not critical to the continuing operation of the business (Carow and Roden, 1998). Competent and highly motivated management is always crucial to the eventual success of the LBO. Finally, firms in certain types of industries or that are part of larger firms often represent attractive opportunities.

Unused Borrowing Capacity, Tax Shelter, and Redundant Assets

A number of factors enhance borrowing capacity. These include cash balances on the books of the target company in excess of working capital requirements, a low debt-to-total capital ratio (as compared with the industry average), and a demonstrated ability to generate consistent earnings and cash-flow growth. Firms with undervalued assets may use such assets as collateral for loans from asset-based lenders. Such assets also provide a significant tax shelter, because they may be revalued and depreciated or amortized over their allowable tax lives. In addition, operating assets, such as subsidiaries that are not germane to the target's core business and that can be sold quickly for cash, can be divested to accelerate the payoff of either the highest cost debt or the debt with the most restrictive covenants.

Management Competence and Motivation

Although the quality of management is always an important factor in the eventual success of a merger or acquisition, it tends to be critical to LBOs. Even though management competence is a necessary condition for success, it does not ensure that the firm's performance will meet investor expectations. Management must be highly motivated by the prospect of abnormally large returns in a relatively short time. Consequently, management of the firm to be taken private is normally given an opportunity to own a significant portion of the equity of the firm.

Attractive Industries

Typical targets are in mature industries, such as manufacturing, retailing, textiles, food processing, apparel, and soft drinks. Such industries usually are characterized by large tangible book values, modest growth prospects, relatively stable cash flow, and limited research and development, new product, or technology requirements. Such industries are generally not dependent on technologies and production processes that are subject to rapid change. Empirical studies have shown that industries that have high free cash flows and limited growth opportunities are good candidates for LBOs (Opler and Titman, 1993; Phan, 1995). However, reflecting the need to deploy large unused monies held by their funds and attract future money by striving for ever-higher financial returns, buyout firms have expanded their range of investments to include high-tech firms in recent years.

Large-Company Operating Divisions

The best candidates for management buyouts often are underperforming divisions of larger companies, in which the division is no longer considered critical to the parent firm's overarching strategy. Frequently, such divisions are saddled with excessive administrative overhead, often required by the parent, and expenses are allocated to the division by the parent for services, such as legal, auditing, and treasury functions, that could be purchased less expensively from sources outside the parent firm.

Firms without Change of Control Covenants

Change of control covenants in bond indentures are clauses either limiting the amount of debt a firm can add or requiring the company to buy back outstanding debt, sometimes at a premium, whenever a change of control occurs. Billett, Jiang, and Lie (2008) report that firms with bonds lacking such covenants are twice as likely to be the target of an LBO.

Not Overpaying

Although overpaying for any acquisition, highly leveraged or otherwise, almost always impairs the ability of the acquiring firm to achieve expected financial returns, it can be disastrous for LBOs. Failure to meet debt service obligations in a timely fashion often requires that the LBO firm renegotiate the terms of the loan agreements with the lenders. If the parties to the transaction cannot reach a compromise, the firm may be forced to file for bankruptcy, often wiping out the value of the initial investors' investment. Highly leveraged firms also are subject to aggressive tactics from major competitors. Such competitors understand that taking on large amounts of debt raises the breakeven point for the firm. If the amount borrowed is made even more excessive as a result of having paid more than the economic value of the target firm, competitors may opt to gain market share by cutting product prices. The ability of the LBO firm to match such price cuts is limited because of the need to meet required interest and principal repayments.

Improving Operating Performance

Tactics employed to improve performance include negotiating employee wage and benefit concessions in exchange for a profit-sharing or stock ownership plan and outsourcing services once provided by the parent. Other options include moving the corporate headquarters to a less-expensive location, pruning unprofitable customer accounts, and eliminating such perks as corporate aircraft. As board members, buyout specialists, such as LBO funds, tend to take a much more active role in monitoring management performance.

Prebuyout and Postbuyout Shareholder Returns

The following sections summarize the key factors affecting financial returns to shareholders before and after a leveraged buyout transaction.

Prebuyout Returns to Target Shareholders

The studies cited in Table 13–7 show that the premium paid by LBOs and MBOs to target company shareholders often exceeds 40 percent in nondivisional buyouts. These empirical studies also include so-called *reverse LBOs* (RLBOs). These are public companies that are taken private and later are taken public again through an IPO. The second effort to take the firm public is called a *secondary public offering.*

Divisional buyouts represent opportunities for improved operating efficiency, as the division is removed from the bureaucracy of the parent. Although this may be a source of gain for the acquirer, it does not seem to be true for the shareholders of the parent firm divesting the division. The parent firm's shareholders receive only miniscule returns. The size of these returns often may reflect the division's relatively small share of the parent corporation's total market value. Alternatively, the parent's management may forego the auction process in favor of the division's management. The fact that parent

Table 13–7 Empirical Studies of Returns to Shareholders (Prebuyout Returns)

Nondivisional Buyouts	Premium Paid to Target Shareholders[1]
DeAngelo, DeAngelo, and Rice (1984)	56% (1973–1983)
(Sample size = 72 U.S. MBOs)	76% (when there are three or more bids)
Lowenstein (1985) (Sample size = 28 U.S. MBOs)	48% (1979–1984)
Lehn and Poulsen (1988) (Sample size = 92 U.S. LBOs)	41% (1980–1984)
Kaplan (1989a) (Sample size = 76 U.S. LBOs)	42% (1980–1986)
Renneboog, Simons, and Wright (2007) (Sample size = 97 U.K. LBOs)	40% (1997–2003)
Divisional Buyouts	**Return to Parent Corporation Shareholders**
Hite and Vetsuypens (1989) (Sample size = 151 MBOs)	0.55% (1983–1987)
Muscarella and Vetsuypens (1990) (Sample size = 45 MBOs)	1.98% (1983–1988)

Note: MBO, management buyout; LBO, leveraged buyout.

[1]The years in parentheses represent the time period in which the study took place.

shareholders experience any gain at all may suggest that the parent's resources are redeployed to higher return investments.

Factors Determining Prebuyout Target Shareholder Returns

Table 13–4 summarizes a portion of the extensive empirical research, which attempts to identify the factors that explain the sizable gains in share price that accrue to prebuyout target shareholders. Although a number of factors are at work, the sizeable returns to prebuyout shareholders as noted in Table 13–8 seem to reflect buyout firms' anticipated improvements in operating performance (i.e., cost reduction, productivity improvement, and revenue enhancement) due to management incentives as well as large tax benefits. The anticipated improved operating performance is consistent with arguments made by Renneboog et al. (2007) and Weir, Liang, and Wright (2005) that large abnormal returns to LBO target shareholders reflect investor undervaluation of the target prior to the announcement of an LBO.

Anticipated Improvement in Operating Performance and Tax Benefits

The most often cited sources of these returns are from tax benefits and expected post-LBO improvements in operating performance as a result of management incentives and the discipline imposed by the need to repay debt, which motivate aggressive cost cutting. Jensen (1986) argues that debt imposes a discipline that forces managers to stay focused on maximizing operating cash flows. Tax benefits are largely predictable and built into the premium offered for the public shares of the target firm as a result of the negotiation process (Kaplan, 1989b; Newbould, Chatfield, and Anderson, 1992). Successful MBOs are associated with improved operating performance, including increased efficiency and more aggressive marketing plans, while firms undertaking MBOs that were not completed showed no subsequent improvement in operating performance (Ofek, 1994).

Table 13–8 Factors Contributing to Pre-LBO Buyout Returns to Target Shareholders

Factor	Theory	Evidence
Management Incentives		
Equity ownership Kaplan (1991) (Sample size = 76 MBOs)	Management will improve performance when its ownership stake increases.	Management ownership increased for MBOs between 1980 and 1986 from 8.3% before the buyout to 29% after the buyout.
Incentive (profit-sharing) plans Muscarella and Vetsuypens (1990) (Sample size = 72 reverse LBOs)	Stock-option and share-appreciation plans motivate management to take cost-cutting actions that might otherwise have been unacceptable.	96% of LBOs had at least one and 75% had two incentive plans in place during the 1983–1988 period. Moreover, the change in shareholder gain is positively correlated with the fraction of shares owned by LBO's officers.
Improved operating performance Holthausen and Larker (1996) (Sample size = 90 reverse LBOs)	Equity ownership and incentive plans motivate management to initiate aggressive cost-reduction plans and to change marketing strategies.	For the 1983–1988 period, sales were up by 9.4% in real terms and operating profits were up by 45.4% between the LBO announcement date and the secondary initial public offering. Firm performance also was highly correlated with the amount of ownership by officers and directors
Kaplan (1989b)		Operating income in LBO firms increased more than in other firms in the same industry during 2 years following the LBO.
Tax Shelter Benefits		
Kaplan (1989a)	An LBO can be tax free for as long as 5–7 years.	Median value of tax shelter contributed 30% of the premium.
Lehn and Poulsen (1988)		Premium paid to pre-LBO shareholders positively correlated with pre-LBO tax liability or equity.
Undervaluation		
Renneboog et al. (2007) Weir et al. (2005)	Investors undervalue the target firm prior to LBO.	Report of large abnormal returns in recent LBO wave consistent with those recorded in the 1980s.
Wealth Transfer Effects		
Lehn and Poulsen (1988)	Premiums represent a transfer of wealth from bondholders to common stockholders.	Found no evidence that bondholders and preferred stockholders lose value when an LBO is announced.
Travlos and Cornett (1993)		Found small losses associated with the LBO announcement.
Billet, King, and Mauer (2004) Sample size = 3073 LBOs		Found no evidence of wealth transfer between bondholders and stockholders
Investor Group Has Better Information than Public Shareholders on MBO Target		
Kaplan (1988) and Smith (1990)	Investor group believes target worth more than shareholders believe it is.	Found no evidence to support this theory.
Improved Efficiency in Decision Making		
Travlos and Cornett (1993)	Private firms are less bureaucratic and do not incur reporting and servicing costs associated with public shareholders.	Shareholder-related expenses are not an important factor; difficult to substantiate more efficient decision making.

Note: MBO, management buyout; LBO, leveraged buyout.

Wealth Transfer Effects

The evidence supporting wealth transfer effects is mixed for most LBO transactions. The exception may be for very large LBOs, such as RJR Nabisco, where largely anecdotal evidence seems to suggest that a significant transfer of wealth may have taken place between the firm's pre-LBO debt holders and shareholders.

Superior Knowledge

There is little evidence to support that LBO investors have knowledge of a business that is superior to that held by the firm's public shareholders. Such knowledge is sometimes referred to as *asymmetric information*, in that it is not equally available to both investors and public shareholders. Therefore, the LBO investors are motivated to pay such high premiums because they understand better how to achieve cost savings and productivity improvements.

More Efficient Decision Making

There is also little empirical evidence to support the notion that decision making is more efficient. Nonetheless, the intuitive appeal of the simplified decision-making process of a private company is compelling when contrasted with a public company with multiple constituents directly or indirectly affecting decision making. Examples of such constituents include a board of directors with outside directors, public shareholders, public company regulatory agencies, and Wall Street analysts.

Postbuyout Returns to LBO Shareholders

Table 13–9 summarizes a cross-section of the studies of returns to shareholders following a leveraged buyout. A number of empirical studies suggest that investors in LBOs earned abnormal profits on their initial investments.

Factors Determining Postbuyout Returns

The presumption in postbuyout empirical studies seems to be that the full effect of increased operating efficiency following a leveraged buyout is not fully reflected in the pre-LBO premium. These studies may be subject to selection or survivor bias, in that only LBOs that are successful in significantly improving their operating performance are able to undertake a secondary public offering. Mian and Rosenfeld (1993) note that, in many instances, the abnormal returns earned by postbuyout shareholders were the result of the LBO being acquired by another firm in the three years immediately following the LBO announcement.

Using a larger sample and longer time period than earlier studies, Cao and Lerner (2006) found that reverse LBOs showed a much larger three-year cumulative return (except for those "flipped" within one year of acquisition) than earlier studies. The authors suggest that new owners choosing to retain their investment longer have more time to put the proper controls and reporting–monitoring systems in place for firms to survive the rigor of being a public company. In contrast, unless in place when acquired, firms resold within a year simply lack the time to adequately prepare for participating in public markets. Consistent with these findings, Katz (2008) reports that private equity sponsored firms display superior long-term share price performance after they go public, reflecting professional ownership, tighter monitoring, and often the reputations of the private equity firm owners. Gurung and Lerner (2008) find that private equity groups have a greater capacity to squeeze more productivity out of companies they buy during times of financial stress than other types of acquirers. The authors attribute this success to the willingness of private equity sponsors to make the difficult choices of restructuring

Table 13–9   Postbuyout Returns to LBO Shareholders

Empirical Study	Impact on Postbuyout Performance
Muscarella and Vetsuypens (1990) (Sample size = 45 MBOs, 1983–1987)	Of 41 firms going public, median annual return was 36.6% in 3 years following buyout.
Kaplan (1991) (Sample size = 21 MBOs, 1979–1986)	Median annualized return was 26% higher than the gain on the S&P 500 during the 3-year postbuyout period.
Mian and Rosenfeld (1993) (Sample size = 85 reverse LBOs, 1983–1989)	Of the 33 LBOs acquired by another firm during the 3 years following the LBO, cumulative abnormal returns exceeded 21%; of those not acquired, cumulative abnormal returns were zero.
Holthausen and Larker (1996) (Sample size = 90 reverse LBOs, 1983–1988)	Firms outperformed their industries over the 4 years following the secondary IPO.
Cao and Lerner (2006) (Sample size = 496 reverse LBOs, 1980–2002)	Reverse LBOs outperformed other IPOs and the overall stock market, exhibiting a cumulative 3 year return of 43.8%. In contrast, "quick flips" (i.e., buyout firm sells its investment within a year of acquisition) underperformed the S&P 500 by a cumulative 5 percentage points during the following 3-year period.
Groh and Gottschaig (2006) (Sample size = 152 LBOs, 1981–2004)	Risk-adjusted performance of U.S. LBOs was significantly superior to S&P 500 stock index.
Renneboog et al. (2006) (Sample size = 97 LBOs, 1997–2004)	Share prices higher in aftermath of LBO.
Guo et al. (2008) (Sample size = 192 LBOs, 1990–2006)	Median pre- and post-buyout returns are 78 and 36 percent, respectively. Gains tended to be larger for more leveraged firms and when the CEO was replaced at the time of the buyout.

Note: MBO, managed buyout; LBO, leveraged buyout.

and shutting down poorly performing operations in times of economic downturns. The authors also find that private equity-owned firms are particularly strong at adopting "lean manufacturing" practices.

Valuing Leveraged Buyouts

An LBO can be evaluated from the perspective of common equity investors only or all those who supply funds, including common and preferred investors and lenders. Conventional capital budgeting procedures may be used to evaluate the LBO. The transaction makes sense from the viewpoint of all investors in the transaction if the present value (PV) of the cash flows to the firm (PV_{FCFF}) or enterprise value, discounted at the weighted-average cost of capital, equals or exceeds the total investment consisting of debt, common equity, and preferred equity ($I_{D+E+PFD}$) required to buy the outstanding shares of the target company:

$$PV_{FCFF} - I_{D+E+PFD} \geq 0 \qquad (13–1)$$

If this is true, the target firm can earn its cost of capital and return sufficient cash flow to all parties to the transaction, enabling them to meet or exceed their minimum required returns.

However, it is possible for a leveraged buyout to make sense to common equity investors but not to other investors such as pre-LBO debt holders and preferred stockholders. The market value of the debt and preferred stock on the books of the target firm before the announcement of the LBO reflects two factors. First, the firm must be able to repay, in a timely fashion, both principal and interest. Second, the firm must be able to continue to make required dividend payments on preferred equity. The future ability to meet these obligations often is measured by comparing such ratios for the target firm as debt to equity and interest coverage with those of comparable firms. Once the LBO has been consummated, the firm's perceived ability to meet these obligations often deteriorates, because the firm takes on a substantial amount of new debt. The firm's pre-LBO debt and preferred stock may be revalued in the open market by investors to reflect this higher perceived risk, resulting in a significant reduction in the market value of both debt and preferred equity owned by pre-LBO investors. Although there is little empirical evidence to show that this is typical of LBOs, this revaluation may characterize large LBOs, such as RJR Nabisco in 1989, HCA in 2006, and TXU Corp in 2007.

What follows is a discussion of two methods for valuing leveraged buyouts. The cost of capital method attempts to adjust future cash flows for changes in the cost of capital as the firm reduces its outstanding debt. The second method, adjusted present value, sums the value of the firm without debt plus the value of future tax savings resulting from the tax-deductibility of interest.

Valuing LBOs: The Cost of Capital Method

As long as the debt-to-equity ratio is expected to be constant, applying conventional capital budgeting techniques that discount future cash flows with a constant weighted average cost of capital (CC) is appropriate. However, the extremely high leverage associated with leveraged buyouts significantly increases the riskiness of the cash flows available to equity investors, as a result of the increase in fixed interest and principal repayments that must be made to lenders. Consequently, the cost of equity should be adjusted for the increased leverage of the firm. However, since the debt is to be paid off over time, the cost of equity decreases over time. Therefore, in valuing a leveraged buyout, the analyst must project free cash flows; but instead of discounting the cash flows at a constant discount rate, the discount rate must decline with the firm's declining debt-to-equity ratio. To determine if the deal makes sense, the analyst compares the estimated value of the firm with the purchase price of the firm.

What follows is a five-step procedure (sometimes referred to the *cost of capital method*) that allows for the discount rate to vary with changes in leverage to determine if a leveraged buyout opportunity makes sense.

Project Annual Cash Flows (Step 1)

Step 1 involves projecting free cash flow to equity (FCFE). FCFE measures the cash flow available for common equity investors after all other financing obligations have been satisfied. These cash flows should be projected annually until the LBO has achieved its target debt-to-equity ratio. Because LBO investors wish to recover their investment and required return by either selling to a strategic buyer or engaging in a secondary public offering, they must determine the appropriate debt-to-equity ratio. The appropriate ratio is that level of outstanding debt relative to equity at which the firm resumes paying taxes and appears to be acceptable to strategic buyers or investors in a secondary public offering.

Project Debt-to-Equity Ratios (Step 2)

The decline in debt-to-equity ratios depends on known debt repayment schedules and the projected growth in the market value of shareholders' equity. The market value of common equity can be assumed to grow in line with the projected growth in net income available to common shareholders.

Calculate Terminal Value (Step 3)

Calculate the terminal value of equity (TVE) and of the firm in year t:

$$\text{Terminal value of equity (TVE)} = \text{FCFE}_{t+1}/(k_e - g) \qquad (13\text{--}2)$$

The cost of equity, k_e, and g represent the cost of equity and the cash flow growth rate that can be sustained during the stable-growth or terminal period. TVE represents the present value of equity of the dollar proceeds available to the firm at time t. These proceeds are commonly generated by selling equity to the public or to a strategic buyer.

Adjust the Discount Rate to Reflect Changing Risk (Step 4)

The high leverage associated with a leveraged buyout increases the risk of the cash flows available for equity investors by increasing debt service requirements. As the LBO's extremely high initial debt level is reduced, the firm's cost of equity needs to be adjusted to reflect the decline in risk, as measured by the firm's levered beta (β_{FL}). This adjustment may be estimated starting with the firm's levered beta in period 1 (β_{FL1}) as follows:

$$\beta_{FL1} = \beta_{IUL1}\left[1 + (D/E)_{F1}(1 - t_F)\right] \qquad (13\text{--}3)$$

where β_{IUL1} is the industry unlevered β in period 1; $(D/E)_{F1}$ and t_F are the firm's debt-to-equity ratio and marginal tax rate, respectively; and $\beta_{IUL1} = \beta_{IL1}/[1 + (D/E)_{I1}(1 - t_I)]$, where β_{IL1}, $(D/E)_{I1}$, and t_I are the industry's levered β, debt-to-equity ratio, and tax rate, respectively. The firm's β in each successive period should be recalculated, using the firm's projected debt-to-equity ratio for that period. The firm's cost of equity (k_{eF}) must be recalculated each period using that period's estimated β determined by equation (13–3).

Because the firm's cost of equity changes over time, the firm's cumulative cost of equity is used to discount projected cash flows. Recall that the future value of $1 ($\text{FV}_{\$1}$) in two years invested at a 5 percent return in the first year and 8-percent in the second year is $1 \times [(1 + 0.05)(1 + 0.08)] = \$1.13$; the present value of $1 received in two years earning the same rates of return ($\text{PV}_{\$1}$) is $\$1/[(1 + 0.05)(1 + 0.08)] = \$0.88$. This reflects the fact that each period's cash flows generate a different rate of return. The cumulative cost of equity is represented as follows:

$$PV_1 = \text{FCFE}_1/(1 + \text{COE}_1)$$
$$PV_2 = \text{FCFE}_2/[(1 + \text{COE}_1)(1 + \text{COE}_2)]$$
$$\bullet$$
$$\bullet \qquad (13\text{--}4)$$
$$\bullet$$
$$PV_n = \text{FCFE}_n/[(1 + \text{COE}_1)(1 + \text{COE}_2)\ldots(1 + \text{COE}_{n-1})(1 + \text{COE}_n)]$$

Determine If Deal Makes Sense (Step 5)

Making sense of the deal requires calculating the PV of FCFE discounted by the cumulative cost of equity generalized by equation (13–4) in Step 4, including the terminal value estimated by equation (13–2) in Step 3. Compare this result to the value of the equity invested in the firm, including transaction-related fees. The deal makes sense to common equity investors if the PV of FCFE exceeds the value of the equity investment in the deal. The deal makes sense to lenders and non-common equity investors if the PV of FCFF exceeds the total cost of the deal, see equation (13–1). See Exhibit 13–1 for an illustration of how to calculate the value of an LBO using the cost of capital method. Exhibit 13–1 uses data from the financial statements shown in Case Study 13–5, at the end of the chapter.

Exhibit 13–1 Present Value of California Kool's Adjusted Equity Cash Flow Using the Cost of Capital Method

Assumptions:	2003	2004	2005	2006	2007	2008	2009	2010
Market value of preferred equity ($ millions)	22	24.6	27.6	30.9	34.6	38.8	43.4	48.6
Market value of common equity ($ millions)	3	2.3	3.3	4.0	5.0	5.4	5.7	6.0
Equity[1] ($ millions)	25	27.0	30.9	34.9	39.6	44.2	49.1	54.6
Debt ($ millions)	47	39.5	31.5	23.8	19.2	14.3	8.8	2.7
Comparable firm:								
Price/earnings ratio	6							
Levered beta (β)	2.4							
Debt/equity ratio	0.3							
Unlevered beta[2]	2.0							
Marginal tax rate	0.4							
10-yr. Treasury bond rate	0.05							
Risk premium on stocks (%)	0.055							
Terminal period growth rate (%)	0.045							
Terminal period cost of equity (%)	0.10							

Year	Debt/ Equity	Leveraged Beta[3]	Cost of Equity	Cumulative Discount Factor[4]	Adjusted Equity Cash Flow[5]	PV of Adjusted Equity Cash Flow[6]
2004	1.5	3.8	0.260	1/(1.26) = 0.7937	0.3	0.3
2005	1.0	3.3	0.230	1/[(1.26)(1.23)] = 0.6452	0.2	0.1
2006	0.7	2.9	0.208	1/[(1.26)(1.23)(1.208)] = 0.5341	1.8	1.0
2007	0.5	2.6	0.194	1/[(1.26)(1.23)(1.208)(1.194)] = 0.4474	7.4	3.3
2008	0.3	2.4	0.184	1/[(1.26)(1.23)(1.208)(1.194)(1.184)] = 0.3778	7.7	2.9

Continued

Exhibit 13–1 Present Value of California Kool's Adjusted Equity Cash Flow Using the Cost of Capital Method — Cont'd

Year	Debt/Equity	Leveraged Beta[3]	Cost of Equity	Cumulative Discount Factor[4]	Adjusted Equity Cash Flow[5]	PV of Adjusted Equity Cash Flow[6]
2009	0.2	2.3	0.174	$1/[(1.26)(1.23)(1.208)(1.194)(1.184)(1.174)] = 0.3218$	8.1	2.6
2010	0.0	2.1	0.165	$1/[(1.26)(1.23)(1.208)(1.194)(1.184)(1.174)(1.165)] = 0.2762$	8.5	2.4
PV(2004–2010) ($M)						12.5
Terminal value ($M)						44.7
Total PV ($M)						57.2

[1]Market value of common equity is assumed to grow by the rate of growth in income available to common equity; preferred equity is assumed to equal to its book value; and debt outstanding reflects the projected repayment schedule. See Table 13–15 in Case Study 13–5.

[2]Comparable firm unlevered $\beta_u = \beta/[1 + (D/E)(1 - t)]$.

[3]Firm's levered beta $\beta_l = \beta_u[1 + (D/E)(1 - t)]$.

[4]Because of the changing D/E ratio, the discount factor is expressed in multiplicative form to reflect the differing cash-flow streams generated by investments made at each level of the D/E ratio.

[5]Adjusted equity cash flows come from Table 13–13 in Case Study 13–5.

[6]PV of adjusted equity cash flow equals the cumulative discount factor times the adjusted equity cash flow.

Valuing LBOs: Adjusted Present Value Method

Some analysts suggest that the problem of a variable discount rate can be avoided by separating the value of a firm's operations into two components: (1) the firm's value as if it were debt free and (2) the value of interest tax savings. The total value of the firm is the present value of the firm's free cash flows to equity investors plus the present value of future tax savings discounted at the firm's unlevered cost of equity. This is the basis of the adjusted present value (APV) method. Brigham and Ehrhardt (2005, p. 597) argue that the unlevered cost of equity is the appropriate discount rate rather than the cost of debt or a risk-free rate, because tax savings are subject to risk since the firm may default on its debt or be unable to utilize the tax savings due to continuing operating losses.

The justification for the APV method reflects the theoretical notion that the value of a firm should not be affected by the way in which it is financed (Brealey and Myers, 1996). This concept assumes investors have access to perfect information, the firm is not growing and no new borrowing is required, and there are no taxes and transaction costs and implicitly that the firm is free of default risk. Under these assumptions, the earning power and risk associated with the firm's assets determine the value of the firm.

In the presence of taxes, Graham (2000) argues that firms are often less leveraged than they should be, given the potentially large tax benefits associated with debt. According to Graham, firms can increase market value by increasing leverage to the point at which the additional contribution of the tax shield to the firm's market value begins to decline. In contrast, Molina (2006) contends that management's decision to increase leverage affects and, in turn, is affected by the firm's credit rating. Consequently, the tax benefits of higher leverage may be partially or entirely offset by the higher probability of default associated with an increase in leverage.

For the APV method to be applicable in highly leveraged transactions, the analyst needs to introduce the costs of financial distress, as suggested by Molina's findings. Financial distress is most evident whenever a firm is unable to pay interest and principal on its debt on a timely basis for an extended period. The direct cost of financial distress includes the costs associated with reorganization in bankruptcy and ultimately liquidation (see Chapter 16). However, financial distress can have a material cost even on firms that are able to avoid bankruptcy or liquidation. These indirect costs include the loss of customers (and revenue), employee turnover, less favorable terms from suppliers, and higher borrowing costs.

Consequently, in applying the APV method, the present value of a highly leveraged transaction (PV_{HL}) would reflect the present value of the firm without leverage (PV_{UL}) plus the present value of tax savings (i.e., interest expense, i, times the firm's marginal tax rate, t, or tax shield PV_{ti} resulting from leverage) less the present value of expected financial distress PV_{FD}).

$$PV_{HL} = PV_{UL} + PV_{ti} - PV_{FD} \qquad (13-5)$$

where $PV_{FD} = \mu FD$.

FD is the expected cost of financial distress and μ is the probability of financial distress. Unfortunately, FD and μ cannot be easily or reliably estimated and are often ignored by analysts using the APV method. Failure to include an estimate of the cost and probability of financial distress is likely to result in an overestimate of the value of the firm using the APV method. The importance of estimating the likelihood of financial distress was made evident during the meltdown of the financial markets in 2008. Despite these concerns, many analysts continue to apply the APV method because of its relative simplicity, as illustrated in the following five-step process.

Project Annual Cash Flows and Interest Tax Savings (Step 1)

For the period during which the debt-to-total capital ratio (i.e., the firm's capital structure) is changing, the analyst should project free cash flows to equity and the interest-related tax savings. During the firm's terminal period, the debt-to-total capital structure is assumed to be stable and the free cash flows are projected to grow at a constant rate.

Value Target Excluding Tax Savings (Step 2)

Estimate the unlevered cost of equity (COE) for discounting cash flows during the period in which the capital structure is changing and the weighted-average cost of capital (WACC) for discounting during the terminal period. The WACC is estimated using the COE and after-tax cost of debt and the proportions of debt and equity that make up the firm's capital structure in the final year of the period during which the capital structure is changing.

Estimate Present Value of Tax Savings (Step 3)

Project the annual tax savings resulting from the tax deductibility of interest. Discount projected tax savings at the firm's unlevered cost of equity, since it reflects a higher level of risk than either the WACC or after-tax cost of debt. Tax savings are subject to risk comparable to the firm's cash flows, in that a highly leveraged firm may default and the tax savings go unused.

Calculate Total Value of Firm (Step 4)

To determine the total value of the firm, add the present value of the firm's cash flows to equity, interest tax savings, and terminal value discounted at the firm's unlevered cost of equity and subtract the present value of the expected cost of financial distress, see equation (13–5). Note that the terminal value is calculated using WACC but that it is discounted to the present using the unlevered COE. This is done because it represents the present value of cash flows in the final year of the period in which the firm's capital structure is changing and beyond.

Determine If the Deal Makes Sense (Step 5)

This requires that the present value of equation (13–5) less the value of equity invested in the transaction (i.e., NPV) be greater than or equal to 0. Exhibit 13–2 illustrates how to calculate the value of an LBO using the APV method. The data used in this exhibit comes from Table 13–13 in Case Study 13–5. According to Andrade and Kaplan (1998), the magnitude of the indirect cost of financial distress can range from 10 to 25 percent of a firm's market value. The probability of financial distress can be estimated by analyzing bond ratings. Altman and Kishore (2001) estimated the cumulative probabilities of default for bonds in different ratings classes over 5 and 10 year periods. The cumulative probability of default for each rating over five years is given in parentheses: AAA (.03), AA (0.18), A (0.20), BBB (2.50), BB (9.27), B (24.04), and CCC (39.15). Over 10 years, the cumulative probability of default for each rating is as follows: AAA (0.03), Aa (0.25), A (0.56), BBB (4.27), BB (16.89), B (32.75), and CCC (51.38). Assuming California Kool (see Case Study 13–5) is a B rated firm, the present value of the expected cost of

Exhibit 13–2 Present Value of California Kool Adjusted Equity Cash Flows Using the Adjusted Present Value Method

Assumptions	2004	2005	2006	2007	2008	2009	2010
Marginal tax rate	0.4						
Comparable company unlevered beta	2						
10-year Treasury bond rate	0.05						
Firm's credit rating	B						
Expected cost of bankruptcy as % of firm market value (per Andrade and Kaplan, 1998)	.2500						
Cumulative probability of default for a B rated firm over 10 years (per Altman and Kishore, 2001)	.3275						
Risk premium on stocks	0.0550						
Terminal period growth rate	0.0450						
2004–2010 unlevered cost of equity[1]	0.1700						
Terminal period WACC[2]	0.1200						
Adjusted equity cash flow[3]	0.3	0.2	1.8	7.4	7.7	8.1	8.5
Plus tax shield[4]	1.8	1.6	1.3	1.0	0.8	0.6	0.4
Plus terminal value[5]							123.8
Equals total cash flow	2.2	1.8	3.2	8.4	8.5	8.7	132.7
PV of 2004–2010 cash flows ($M)							$61.07
Less PV expected cost of bankruptcy ($M)[6]							5.00
PV of cash flows adjusted for expected cost of bankruptcy ($M)							$56.07

---

[1]COE = 0.06 + 2.0(.055).

[2]WACC = COE × W1 + Pref × W2 + i × (1 − 0.t) × W3, where COE = unlevered cost of equity; Pref = yield on preferred stock; i = interest rate on outstanding debt; W1 = common equity's share of total terminal year capital; W2 = preferred stock's share of total terminal year capital; W3 = debt's share of total terminal year capital; and t = marginal tax rate.

[3]Adjusted equity cash flows come from Table 13–13 in Case Study 13–5.

[4]Tax shield is the product of total interest expense times the marginal tax rate.

[5]The terminal value is calculated using the constant growth method estimated based on total 2010 cash flow, terminal period WACC, and terminal period sustainable period cash-flow growth rate.

[6]Equals cumulative probability of default over 10 years for a B rated company (i.e., 0.3275) × expected cost of bankruptcy (0.25 × $61.07).

bankruptcy in Exhibit 13–2 is $5 million and is calculated as the cumulative probability of default over 10 years for a B rated company (i.e., 0.3275) times the expected cost of bankruptcy: 0.25 (per Andrade and Kaplan, 1998) × $61.07 million. Note that the estimate provided by the APV method is $61.07 million before the adjustment for financial distress. This is an about 7 percent more than the estimate provided using the CC method, shown in Exhibit 13–1. After adjusting for financial distress, the estimate declines to $56.07 million versus $57.2 million estimated using the CC method in Exhibit 13–1, a difference of approximately 2 percent.

Comparing Cost of Capital and Adjusted Present Value Methods

Although the proposition that the value of the firm should be independent of the way in which it is financed may make sense for a firm whose debt-to-capital ratio is relatively stable and similar to the industry's, it is highly problematic when it is applied to highly leveraged transactions. In these situations, the LBO's leverage may be three or four times the industry's average, thereby dramatically increasing the potential for financial distress. Intuitively, the APV method is likely to overestimate the value of the firm unless the resulting estimated value is adjusted for both the likelihood of and costs associated with financial distress, see equation (13–5). Without such an adjustment, the APV method implies that the value of the firm could be increased by continuously taking on more debt. Therefore, the primary drawback to the APV method is the implication that the firm should optimally use 100 percent debt financing to take maximum advantage of the tax shield created by the tax deductibility of interest (Booth, 2002).

The primary advantage of the APV method is its relative computational simplicity. Although somewhat more complex, the cost of capital method attempts to adjust for the changing level of risk over time, as the LBO reduces its leverage over time. Thus, the CC method takes into account what is actually happening in practice. For an excellent discussion of alternative valuation methods for highly leveraged firms, see Ruback (2002). Table 13–10 summarizes the process steps as well as the strengths and weaknesses of the cost of capital and adjusted present value methods.

Building an LBO Model

The following sections discuss a typical approach to developing a leveraged buyout model and how to estimate a firm's borrowing capacity in order to finance transactions. The underlying Excel-based spreadsheets, found on the CD-ROM accompanying this book, are entitled Excel-Based LBO Valuation and Structuring Model and Excel-Based Model to Estimate Borrowing Capacity. The reader is encouraged to examine the formulas underlying these spreadsheets.

Typical LBO Model Formats

The process of valuing highly leveraged transactions using an LBO valuation and structuring model is illustrated in Case Study 13–5. Once constructed, the model enables the evaluation of alternative scenarios reflecting different levels of leverage and their implications for credit ratios monitored by lenders and investors. Table 13–13 of the case study displays a sources and uses of funds table which shows how the transaction is to be financed. Representing total funds required, the uses section includes payments to the

Table 13–10   Comparative LBO Valuation Methodologies

	Cost of Capital Method	Adjusted Present Value Method
Process Steps		
Step 1	Project annual cash flows, including all financing considerations and tax savings until anticipate exiting the business	Project annual cash flows to equity investors and interest tax savings
Step 2	Project annual debt-to-equity ratios	Value target without tax savings, including terminal value
Step 3	Calculate terminal value	Estimate PV of tax savings
Step 4	Adjust discount rate to reflect declining cost of equity as debt is repaid	Add PV of firm without debt including terminal period and PV of tax savings
Step 5	Determine if NPV of projected cash flows ≥ 0	Determine if NPV of projected cash flows ≥ 0
Advantages	Adjusts discount rate to reflect diminishing risk	Simplicity
Disadvantages	Calculations more tedious than alternative methods	Ignores effects of leverage on discount rate as debt repaid To incorporate effects of leverage, requires estimation of cost of and probability of financial distress for highly leveraged firms Unclear whether true discount rate is cost of debt, unlevered COE, or somewhere between the two

target firm's owners, including cash, any equity retained by the seller, any seller's notes, and any excess cash retained by the sellers. The uses section also contains the refinancing of any existing debt on the balance sheet of the target firm and any transaction fees. The sources section describes various sources of financing including new debt, any existing cash that is being used to finance the transaction, and the common and preferred equity being contributed by the financial sponsor. The equity contribution represents the difference between uses and all other sources of financing.

Table 13–14 and 13–15 of the case study contain the pro forma income statement and balance sheet for the target firm. The pro forma balance sheet reflects changes to the existing balance sheet of the target firm altered to reflect the new capital structure of the firm. The new balance sheet also typically reflects the creation of goodwill resulting from the excess of the purchase price over the fair market value of the net acquired assets and any interest expense that can be capitalized under current accounting rules (see Chapter 12). Table 13–16 contains the pro forma cash flow statement. All financial statements are projected annually until the financial sponsor expects to exit the firm. The balance sheet projections are based on the pro forma balance sheet, with the debt outstanding and interest expense reflecting the repayment schedules associated with each type of debt. The model also reflects a projected sale value on the assumed exit date. The internal rates of return represent the average annual compounded rate at which the financial sponsor's equity investment grows, assuming no dividend payments or additional equity contributions.

Estimating Borrowing Capacity

Borrowing capacity is defined as the amount of debt a firm can borrow without materially increasing its cost of borrowing or violating loan covenants on existing debt. By using a net debt (D) to enterprise cash-flow (FCFF) ratio to measure the firm's borrowing capacity, we link borrowing capacity to the purchase price multiple and the financial sponsor's equity contribution, see equation (13–6). Recall that net debt equals total debt less cash and marketable securities. Note that the purchase price is financed either from debt or equity contributed by the buyout firm. For example, assume that a buyout firm determines that it can borrow an amount equal to six times the target firm's FCFF by analyzing recent comparable transactions and the buyout firm is willing to contribute an amount of equity (E) equal to one times FCFF. Therefore, the maximum purchase price (PP) for the firm should not exceed seven times FCFF:

$$D/FCFF + E/FCFF = PP/FCFF \qquad (13\text{–}6)$$

Analysts differ as to which measure of cash flow should be used for this purpose. Some analysts use EBITDA as a proxy for cash flow. By not deducting interest, taxes, depreciation, and amortization, EBITDA supporters argue that it represents a convenient proxy for the cash available to meet the cost (i.e., interest, depreciation, and amortization) of long-term assets. In essence, EBITDA provides a simple way of determining how long the firm can continue to service its debt without additional financing. Furthermore, EBITDA is not affected by the method the firm employs in depreciating its assets.

Critics of the use of EBITDA as a measure of cash flow argue that it can be dangerously misleading since it ignores changes in working capital. It implicitly assumes that capital expenditures needed to maintain the business are equal to depreciation. However, from the dotcom debacle in 2000, we know that a firm could have an attractive EBITDA to interest expense ratio but still have insufficient cash to finance interest expense, working capital, and needed capital outlays that exceed the long-term growth trend. Such critics argue that free cash flow to the firm (i.e., enterprise cash flow) is a better measure of how much cash a company is generating, since it includes changes in working capital and capital expenditures.

Table 13–11 illustrates a simple model to estimate a firm's borrowing capacity. The model is contained on the CD-ROM accompanying this text in the file folder entitled Excel-Based Model to Estimate Borrowing Capacity. The estimate of borrowing capacity is expressed as a multiple of EBITDA. Even though the author prefers to use enterprise cash flow, it is important to recognize that EBITDA is commonly used for this purpose. The model is divided into three panels: assumptions, estimating cash available for debt reduction, and estimating total debt to EBITDA and interest coverage ratios. Key assumptions are that all cash available for paying off debt will be used to repay senior bank debt, such debt will be amortized over eight years, and subordinated debt matures sometime after the eighth year.

Assume that, based on similar transactions, the analyst believes that a buyout firm will be able to borrow about 5.5 times first year EBITDA of $200 million (i.e., about $1.1 billion) and the buyout firm has a target debt mix consisting of 75 percent senior and 25 percent subordinated debt. Further assume that investors in the buyout firm wish to exit the business within eight years after having repaid all the senior debt. To accomplish this objective, the investors intend to use 100 percent of cash available for debt reduction to pay off senior debt, and the subordinated debt is payable as a balloon note beyond year 8. Using a trial-and-error method, insert a starting value for senior debt of $800 million in year 0. This $800 million starting number is in line with the firm's assumed target debt mix (i.e., 0.75 × total potential borrowing of $1.1 billion is

Table 13–11 Determining a Firm's Borrowing Capacity

	Year 0	Year 1	Year 2	Year 3	Year 4	Year 5	Year 6	Year 7	Year 8
Assumptions									
Sales growth (%)	0	1.05	1.05	1.05	1.05	1.05	1.05	1.05	1.05
Cost of sales (COS) as % of sales	0.5	0.5	0.5	0.5	0.5	0.5	0.5	0.5	0.5
Sales, general, and administrative expense as % of sales	0.1	0.1	0.1	0.1	0.1	0.1	0.1	0.1	0.1
Depreciation as % of sales	0.03	0.03	0.03	0.03	0.03	0.03	0.03	0.03	0.03
Amortization as % of sales	0.01	0.01	0.01	0.01	0.01	0.01	0.01	0.01	0.01
Interest on cash and marketable securities (%)	0.03	0.03	0.03	0.03	0.03	0.03	0.03	0.03	0.03
Interest on senior debt (%)	0.07	0.07	0.07	0.07	0.07	0.07	0.07	0.07	0.07
Interest on subordinated debt (%)	0.09	0.09	0.09	0.09	0.09	0.09	0.09	0.09	0.09
Tax rate	0.4	0.4	0.4	0.4	0.4	0.4	0.4	0.4	0.4
Cash and marketable securities as % sales	0.01	0.01	0.01	0.01	0.01	0.01	0.01	0.01	0.01
Change in working capital as % of sales	0.02	0.02	0.02	0.02	0.02	0.02	0.02	0.02	0.02
Capital expenditures as % of sales	0.03	0.03	0.03	0.03	0.03	0.03	0.03	0.03	0.03
Estimating Cash Available for Debt Reduction ($ millions)									
Sales	500.0	525.0	551.3	578.8	607.8	638.1	670.0	703.6	738.7
Less cost of sales	250.0	262.5	275.6	289.4	303.9	319.1	335.0	351.8	369.4
Less sales, general & administrative expense	50.0	52.5	55.1	57.9	60.8	63.8	67.0	70.4	73.9
Equals EBITDA	200.0	210.0	220.5	231.5	243.1	255.3	268.0	281.4	295.5
Less depreciation	15.0	15.8	16.5	17.4	18.2	19.1	20.1	21.1	22.2
Less amortization	5.0	5.3	5.5	5.8	6.1	6.4	6.7	7.0	7.4
Plus interest Income	0.2	0.2	0.2	0.2	0.2	0.2	0.2	0.2	0.2

Continued

Table 13–11 — Cont'd

	Year 0	Year 1	Year 2	Year 3	Year 4	Year 5	Year 6	Year 7	Year 8
Less interest expense									
Senior debt		52.2	47.9	43.1	37.7	31.7	24.9	17.4	9.1
Subordinated debt		27.0	27.0	27.0	27.0	27.0	27.0	27.0	27.0
Total interest expense		79.2	74.9	70.1	64.7	58.7	51.9	44.4	36.1
Equals income before tax		110.0	123.7	138.4	154.3	171.3	189.5	209.1	230.0
Less taxes paid		44.0	49.5	55.4	61.7	68.5	75.8	83.6	92.0
Equals net income after tax		66.0	74.2	83.1	92.6	102.8	113.7	125.4	138.0
Plus depreciation and amortization expense		21.0	22.1	23.2	24.3	25.5	26.8	28.1	29.5
Less change in working capital		10.5	11.0	11.6	12.2	12.8	13.4	14.1	14.8
Less capital expenditures		15.8	16.5	17.4	18.2	19.1	20.1	21.1	22.2
Equals cash available for debt reduction		60.7	68.7	77.3	86.5	96.4	107.0	118.4	130.6
Estimating Total Debt to EBITDA and EBITDA to Interest Coverage Ratios									
Cash balance	5.0	5.3	5.5	5.8	6.1	6.4	6.7	7.0	7.4
Senior debt outstanding at yearend[1]	745.6	684.8	616.1	538.9	452.4	356.0	249.0	130.6	0.0
Subordinated debt Outstanding at yearend[2]	300.0	300.0	300.0	300.0	300.0	300.0	300.0	300.0	300.0
Total debt	1045.6	984.8	916.1	838.9	752.4	656.0	549.0	430.6	300.0
Total debt to EBITDA ratio	5.2	4.7	4.2	3.6	3.1	2.6	2.0	1.5	1.0
Interest coverage (EBITDA/Net interest expense)	2.5	2.8	3.2	3.6	4.2	4.9	6.1	7.8	8.2

[1] Assumes 100% of cash available for debt reduction is used to pay off senior debt.

[2] Subordinated debt payable as a balloon note beyond year 8.

approximately equal to $800 million). The amount of senior debt outstanding at the end of the eighth year is $75.7 million. If we now try $700 million in senior debt in year 0, the amount of senior debt outstanding at the end of the eighth year is $(63.3). Using the midpoint between $700 and $800 million, we insert $750 million for senior debt in year 0, resulting in $6.2 million in remaining debt at the end of the eighth year. Further fine-tuning results in a zero balance at the end of year 8, if we use a starting value of $745.6 million for senior debt.

Things to Remember

Success in structuring a leveraged buyout is a result of knowing what to buy, not over-paying, and being able to substantially improve operating performance. Good LBO candidates are those that have substantial tangible assets, unused borrowing capacity, predictable positive operating cash flow, and assets that are not critical to the continuing operation of the business. Although overpaying for any acquisition, highly leveraged or otherwise, almost always impairs the ability of the acquiring firm to achieve expected financial returns, it can be disastrous for highly leveraged transactions.

Successful LBOs rely heavily on management incentives to improve operating performance and the discipline imposed by the demands of satisfying interest and principal repayments. The premium paid to target company shareholders by LBO and MBO investors may exceed 40 percent, often as a result of expected improvements in operating performance and tax benefits. Tax benefits are largely predictable; and as such, they are often built into the premium offered for the public shares of the target firm as a result of the negotiation process. Post-LBO financial returns often exceed the broader stock market averages during the three years following the announcement of the LBO. The primary reasons for these gains seem to be improvements in operating performance, whose value was not captured fully in the premium paid to pre-LBO stockholders and the potential for the firm having undergone the LBO to be acquired by another firm.

The high leverage associated with the LBO increases the risk of the cash flows available for equity investors by increasing debt service requirements. As the LBO's extremely high initial debt level is reduced, the firm's cost of equity needs to be adjusted to reflect the decline in risk. This implies a changing cost of equity over time. Excessive leverage and the resultant higher level of fixed expenses makes LBOs vulnerable to business cycle fluctuations and aggressive competitor actions, which LBOs often cannot counteract.

Chapter Discussion Questions

13–1. What potential conflicts arise between management and shareholders in an MBO? How can these conflicts be minimized?

13–2. In what ways have private equity and hedge funds exhibited increasing similarities in recent years?

13–3. What are the primary ways in which an LBO is financed?

13–4. How do loan and security covenants affect the way in which an LBO is managed? Note the differences between positive and negative covenants.

13–5. What are the primary factors that explain the magnitude of the premium paid to pre-LBO shareholders?

13–6. What are the primary uses of junk bond financing?

13–7. Describe common strategies LBO firms use to exit their investment. Discuss the circumstances under which some methods of "cashing out" are preferred to others.

13–8. Describe some of the legal problems that can arise from an improperly structured LBO.

13–9. Is it possible for an LBO to make sense to equity investors but not to other investors in the deal? If so, why? If not, why not?

13–10. How does the risk of an LBO change over time? How can the impact of changing risk be incorporated into the valuation of the LBO?

13–11. In an effort to take the firm private, Cox Enterprises announced on August 3, 2004, a proposal to buy the remaining 38 percent of Cox Communications's shares that it did not already own. Cox Enterprises stated that the increasingly competitive cable industry environment makes investment in the cable industry best done through a private company structure. Why would the firm believe that increasing future levels of investment would be best done as a private company?

13–12. Following Cox Enterprises' announcement on August 3, 2004, of its intent to buy the remaining 38 percent of Cox Communications's shares that it did not already own, the Cox Communications board of directors formed a special committee of independent directors to consider the proposal. Why?

13–13. Qwest Communications agreed to sell its slow but steadily growing yellow pages business, QwestDex, to a consortium led by the Carlyle Group and Welsh, Carson, Anderson and Stowe for $7.1 billion in late 2002. Why do you believe the private equity groups found the yellow pages business attractive? Explain the following statement: "A business with high growth potential may not be a good candidate for an LBO."

13–14. Describe the potential benefits and costs of LBOs to stakeholders including shareholders, employers, lenders, customers, and communities in which the firm undergoing the buyout may have operations. Do you believe that on average LBOs provide a net benefit or cost to society? Explain your answer.

13–15. Sony's long-term vision has been to create synergy between its consumer electronics products business and its music, movies, and games. On September 14, 2004, a consortium, consisting of Sony Corp of America, Providence Equity Partners, Texas Pacific Group, and DLJ Merchant Banking Partners, agreed to acquire MGM for $4.8 billion. In what way do you believe that Sony's objectives might differ from those of the private equity investors making up the remainder of the consortium? How might such differences affect the management of MGM? Identify possible short-term and long-term effects.

Answers to these Chapter Discussion Questions are available in the Online Instructor's Manual for instructors using this book.

Chapter Practice Problems

13–16. Assume that, based on similar transactions, an analyst believes that a buyout firm will be able to borrow about 5.5 times first year EBITDA of $200 million (i.e., about $1.1 billion) and that the buyout firm has a target senior to subordinated debt split of 75 to 25 percent. Further assume that investors in the buyout firm wish to exit the business within eight years after having repaid all of the senior debt. To accomplish this objective, the investors intend to use 100 percent of cash available for debt reduction to pay off senior debt, and the subordinated debt is payable as a balloon note beyond year 8. Using the scenario in the template Excel-Based Model to Estimate Firm Borrowing Capacity on the CD-ROM accompanying this textbook as the base case, answer the following questions:

a. Will the buyout firm be able to exit its investment by the eighth year if sales grow at 3 percent rather than 5 percent assumed in the base case and still satisfy the assumptions in the base case scenario? After rerunning the model using the lower sales growth rate, what does this tell you about the model's sensitivity to relatively small changes in assumptions?

b. How does this slower sales growth scenario affect the amount the buyout firm could borrow initially if the investors still want to exit the business by the eighth year after paying off 100 percent of the senior debt and maintain the same senior to subordinated debt split?

13–17. By some estimates, as many as one fourth of the LBOs between 1987 and 1990 (the first mega LBO boom) went bankrupt. The data in Table 13–12 illustrate the extent of the leverage associated with the largest completed LBOs of 2006 and 2007 (the most recent mega-LBO boom). Equity Office Properties and Alltel have been sold. Use the data given in the table to calculate the equity contribution made by the buyout firms as a percent of enterprise value and the dollar value of their equity contribution. What other factors would you want to know in evaluating the likelihood that these LBOs will end up in bankruptcy?

Table 13–12   Top Ten Completed Buyouts of 2006 and 2007 Ranked by Deal Enterprise Value

Target	Bidder(s)	Enterprise Value (EV) ($ billions)	Net Debt % of EV	Equity % of EV	Value of Equity ($ billions)	Interest Coverage Ratio
TXU	KKR, TPG, Goldman Sachs	43.8	89.5	?	?	1.0
Equity Office Properties	Blackstone	38.9	Sold	NA	NA	Sold
HCA	Bain, KKR, Merrill Lynch	32.7	82.4	?	?	1.6
Alltel	TPG, Goldman Sachs	27.9	Sold	NA	NA	Sold
First Data	KKR	27.7	79.2	?	?	1.0
Harrah's Entertainment	TPG, Appollo	27.4	83.7	?	?	0.8
Hilton Hotels	Blackstone	25.8	75.9	?	?	1.1
Alliance Boots	KKR	20.8	83.5	?	?	1.1
Freescale Semiconductor	Blackstone, Permira, Carlyle, TPG	17.6	49.6	?	?	1.6
Intelsat	BC Partners	16.4	88.9	?	?	1.0
Average		27.9	81	?	?	1.0

[1]EBITDA less capital expenditures divided by estimated interest expense.

Source: The Economist (July 2008), p. 85.

A solution to this problem is available in the Online Instructor's Manual for instructors using this book.

Chapter Business Cases

Case Study 13–4. Cerberus Capital Management Acquires Chrysler Corporation

According to the terms of the transaction, Cerberus would own 80.1 percent of Chrysler's auto manufacturing and financial services businesses in exchange for $7.4 billion in cash. Daimler would continue to own 19.9 percent of the new business, Chrysler Holdings LLC. Of the $7.4 billion, Daimler would receive $1.35 billion while the remaining $6.05 billion would be invested in Chrysler (i.e., $5.0 billion is to be invested in the auto manufacturing operation and $1.05 billion in the finance unit). Daimler also agreed to pay to Cerberus $1.6 billion to cover Chrysler's long-term debt and cumulative operating losses during the four months between the signing of the merger agreement and the actual closing. In acquiring Chrysler, Cerberus assumed responsibility for an estimated $18 billion in unfunded retiree pension and medical benefits. Daimler also agreed to loan Chrysler Holdings LLC $405 million.

The transaction is atypical of those involving private equity investors, which usually take public firms private, expecting to later sell them for a profit. The private equity firm pays for the acquisition by borrowing against the firm's assets or cash flow. However, the estimated size of Chrysler's retiree health-care liabilities and the uncertainty of future cash flows make borrowing impractical. Therefore, Cerberus agreed to invest its own funds in the business to keep it running while it restructured the business.

By going private, Cerberus would be able to focus on the long-term without the disruption of meeting quarterly earnings reports. Cerberus was counting on paring retiree health-care liabilities through aggressive negotiations with the United Auto Workers (UAW). Cerberus sought a deal similar to what the UAW accepted from Goodyear Tire and Rubber Company in late 2006. Under this agreement, the management of $1.2 billion in health-care liabilities was transferred to a fund managed by the UAW, with Goodyear contributing $1 billion in cash and Goodyear stock. By transferring responsibility for these liabilities to the UAW, Chrysler believed that it would be able to cut in half the $30 dollar per hour labor cost advantage enjoyed by Toyota. Cerberus also expected to benefit from melding Chrysler's financial unit with Cerberus's 51 percent ownership stake in GMAC, GM's former auto financing business. By consolidating the two businesses, Cerberus hoped to slash cost by eliminating duplicate jobs, combining overlapping operations such as data centers and field offices, and increasing the number of loans generated by combining back-office operations.

However, the 2008 credit market meltdown, severe recession, and subsequent free fall in auto sales threatened the financial viability of Chrysler, despite an infusion of U.S. government capital, and its leasing operations as well as GMAC. GMAC applied for commercial banking status to be able to borrow directly from the U.S. Federal Reserve. In late 2008, the U.S. Treasury purchased $6 billion in GMAC preferred stock to provide additional capital to the financially ailing firm. To avoid being classified as a bank holding company under direct government supervision, Cerberus reduced its ownership in 2009 to 14.9 percent of voting stock and 33 percent of total equity by distributing equity stakes to its coinvestors in GMAC. By surrendering its controlling interest in GMAC, it is less likely that Cerberus would be able to realize anticipated cost savings by combining the GMAC and Chrysler Financial operations. In early 2009, Chrysler entered into negotiations with Italian auto maker Fiat to gain access to the firm's technology in exchange for a 20 percent stake in Chrysler.

Discussion Questions

1. What were the motivations for this deal from Cerberus's perspective? From Daimler's perspective?
2. What are the risks to this deal's eventual success? Be specific.
3. Cite examples of potential economies of scale and scope.
4. Cerberus and Daimler would own 80.1 percent and 19.9 percent of Chrysler Holdings LLC, respectively. Why do you think the two parties agreed to this distribution of ownership?
5. Which of the leading explanations of why deals often fail to meet expectations (i.e., tendency to overpay, slow integration, and bad business plan) best explains why the combination of Daimler and Chrysler failed? Explain your answer.
6. The new company, Chrysler Holdings, is a limited liability company. Why do you think Cerberus chose this legal structure over a more conventional corporate structure?

A solution to this case study is provided in the Online Instructor's Manual for instructors using this book.

Case Study 13–5. Pacific Investors Acquires California Kool in a Leveraged Buyout

Pacific Investors (PI) is a small private equity limited partnership with $3 billion under management. The objective of the fund is to give investors at least a 30-percent annual average return on their investment by judiciously investing these funds in highly leveraged transactions. PI has been able to realize such returns over the last decade because of its focus on investing in industries that have slow but predictable growth in cash flow, modest capital investment requirements, and relatively low levels of research and development spending. In the past, PI made several lucrative investments in the contract packaging industry, which provides packaging for beverage companies that produce various types of noncarbonated and carbonated beverages. Because of its commitments to its investors, PI likes to liquidate its investments within four to six years of the initial investment through a secondary public offering or sale to a strategic investor.

Following its past success in the industry, PI currently is negotiating with California Kool (CK), a privately owned contract beverage packaging company with the technology required to package many types of noncarbonated drinks. CK's 2003 revenue and net income are $190.4 million and $5.9 million, respectively. With a reputation for effective management, CK is a medium-sized contract packaging company that owns its own plant and equipment and has a history of continually increasing cash flow. The company also has significant unused excess capacity, suggesting that production levels can be increased without substantial new capital spending.

The owners of CK are demanding a purchase price of $70 million. This is denoted on the balance sheet (see Table 13–15 at the end of the case) as a negative entry in additional paid-in capital. This price represents a multiple of 11.8 times 2003's net income, almost twice the multiple for comparable publicly traded companies. Despite the "rich" multiple, PI believes that it can finance the transaction through an equity investment of $25 million and $47 million in debt. The equity investment consists of $3 million in common stock, with PI's investors and CK's management each contributing $1.5 million. Debt consists of a $12 million revolving loan to meet immediate working capital requirements, $20 million in senior bank debt secured by CK's fixed assets, and $15 million in a subordinated loan from a pension fund. The total cost of acquiring CK is $72 million, $70 million paid to the owners of CK and $2 million in legal and accounting fees.

As indicated in Table 13–15, the change in total liabilities plus shareholders' equity (i.e., total sources of funds or cash inflows) must equal the change in total assets (i.e., total uses of funds or cash outflows). Therefore, as shown in the adjustments column, total liabilities increase by $47 million in total borrowings and shareholders' equity declines by $45 million (i.e., $25 million in preferred and common equity provided by investors less $70 million paid to CK owners). The excess of sources over uses of $2 million is used to finance legal and accounting fees incurred in closing the transaction. Consequently, total assets increase by $2 million and total liabilities plus shareholders' equity increase by $2 million between the pre- and postclosing balance sheets as shown in the adjustments column.[1]

Revenue for CK is projected to grow at 4.5 percent annually through the foreseeable future. Operating expenses and sales, general, and administrative expenses as a percent of sales are expected to decline during the first three years of operation due to aggressive cost cutting and the introduction of new management and engineering processes. Similarly, improved working capital management results in significant declines in working capital as a percent of sales during the first year of operation. Gross fixed assets as percent of sales is held constant at its 2003 level during the forecast period, reflecting reinvestment requirements to support the projected increase in net revenue. Equity cash flow adjusted to include cash generated in excess of normal operating requirements (i.e., denoted by the change in investments available for sale) is expected to reach $8.5 million annually by 2010. Using the cost of capital method, the cost of equity declines in line with the reduction in the firm's beta as the debt is repaid from 26 percent in 2004 to 16.5 percent in 2010. In contrast, the adjusted present value method employs a constant unlevered COE of 17 percent.

The deal would appear to make sense from the standpoint of PI, since the projected average annual internal rates of return (IRRs) for investors exceed PI's minimum desired 30 percent rate of return in all scenarios considered between 2007 and 2009 (see Table 13–13). This is the period during which investors would like to "cash out." The rates of return scenarios are calculated assuming the business can be sold at different multiples of adjusted equity cash flow in the year in which the business is assumed to be sold. Consequently, IRRs are calculated using the cash outflow (initial equity investment in the business) in the first year offset by any positive equity cash flow from operations generated in the first year, equity cash flows for each subsequent year, and the sum of equity cash flow in the year in which the business is sold or taken public plus the estimated sale value (e.g., eight times equity cash flow) in that year. Adjusted equity cash flow includes free cash flow generated from operations and the increase in "investments available for sale." Such investments represent cash generated in excess of normal operating requirements; and as such, this cash is available to LBO investors.

The actual point at which CK would either be taken public, sold to a strategic investor, or sold to another LBO fund depends on stock market conditions, CK's leverage relative to similar firms in the industry, and cash flow performance as compared to the plan. Discounted cash flow analysis also suggests that PI should do the deal, since the total present value of adjusted equity cash flow of $57.2 million using the CC method is more than twice the magnitude of the initial equity investment. At $56 million, the APV method results in a slightly lower estimate of total present value. See Tables 13–14, 13–15, and 13–16 for the income, balance-sheet, and cash-flow statements, respectively,

---

[1]ΔTotal assets = ΔTotal liabilities + ΔShareholders' equity: $2 million = $47 million − $45 million = $2 million.

associated with this transaction. Exhibits 13–1 and 13–2 illustrate the calculation of present value of the transaction based on the cost of capital and the adjusted present value methods, respectively. Note the actual Excel spreadsheets and formulas used to create these financial tables are available on the CD-ROM accompanying this book in a worksheet, Excel-Based Leveraged Buyout Valuation and Structuring Model.

Discussion Questions

1. What criteria did Pacific Investors (PI) use to select California Kool (CK) as target for an LBO? Why were these criteria employed?
2. Describe how PI financed the purchase price. Speculate as why each source of financing was selected. How did CK pay for fees incurred in closing the transaction?
3. What are the advantages and disadvantages of using enterprise cash flow in valuing CK? In what way might EBITDA have been a superior (inferior) measure of cash flow for valuing CK?
4. Compare and contrast the cost of capital method and the adjusted present value method of valuation.

A solution to this case study is provided in the Online Instructor's Manual for instructors using this book.

Table 13-13 California Kool Model Output Summary

Sources (Cash Inflows) and Uses (Cash Outflows) of Funds						Pro Forma Capital Structure		
Sources of Funds	Amount ($)	Interest Rate (%)	Uses of Funds	Amount ($)		Form of Debt and Equity	Market Value	% of Total Capital
Cash from balance sheet	$0.0	0.0%	Cash to owners	$70.0		Revolving loan	$12.0	16.7%
New revolving loan	$12.0	9.0%	Seller's equity	$0.0		Senior debt	$20.0	27.8%
New senior debt	$20.0	9.0%	Seller's note	$0.0		Subordinated debt	$15.0	20.8%
New subordinated debt	$15.0	12.0%	Excess cash	$0.0		Total debt	$47.0	65.3%
New preferred stock (PIK)	$22.0	12.0%	Paid to owners	$70.0		Preferred equity	$22.0	30.6%
New common stock	$3.0	0.0%	Debt repayment	$0.0		Common equity	$3.0	4.2%
			Buyer expenses	$2.0		Total equity	$25.0	34.7%
Total sources	$72.0		Total uses	$72.0		Total capital	$72.0	

Equity Investment	Ownership Distribution ($)			% Distribution		Fully Diluted Ownership Distribution				
	Common	Preferred	Total	Common	Preferred	Common	Warrants	Preoption Ownership	Perform. Options	Fully Dil. Ownership
Equity investor	1.5	22.0	23.5	50.0%	100.0%	50.0%	0.0%	50.0%	0.0%	50.0%
Management	1.5	0.0	1.5	50.0%	0.0%	50.0%	0.0%	50.0%	0.0%	50.0%
Total equity investment	$3.0	$22.0	$25.0	100.0%	100.0%	100.0%	0.0%	100.0%	0.0%	100.0%

Internal Rates of Return	Total Investor Return (%)			Equity Investor Investment Gain ($)			Management Investment Gain ($)		
	2007	2008	2009	2007	2008	2009	2007	2008	2009
Multiple of adjusted equity cash flow[1]									
8 × Terminal year CF	0.42	0.35	0.33	$66.6	$78.9	$96.0	$4.3	$5.0	$6.1
9 × Terminal year CF	0.46	0.39	0.35	$73.8	$86.6	$104.5	$4.7	$5.5	$6.7
10 × Terminal year CF	0.51	0.42	0.37	$81.0	$94.2	$113.0	$5.2	$6.0	$7.2

Net sales	$177.6	$183.5	$190.4	$197.1	$205.0	$214.2	$223.8	$233.9	$244.4	$255.4
Annual growth rate	4.2%	3.3%	3.8%	3.5%	4.0%	4.5%	4.5%	4.5%	4.5%	4.5%
EBIT as % of net revenue	5.5%	1.3%	5.1%	8.5%	9.5%	10.2%	11.2%	11.4%	11.4%	11.4%
Adjusted enterprise cash flow[2]	$4.2	$0.2	$0.1	$9.5	$9.6	$10.8	$13.0	$13.4	$14.2	$14.9
Adjusted equity cash flow	$4.2	$0.2	$0.1	$0.3	$0.2	$1.8	$7.4	$7.7	$8.1	$8.5
Total debt outstanding	0	0	$47.0	$39.5	$31.5	$23.8	$19.2	$14.3	$8.8	$2.7
Total debt/Adjusted enterprise cash flow	0.0	0.0	NA	4.1	3.3	2.2	1.5	1.1	0.6	0.2
EBIT/Interest expense	0	0	0	3.6	4.9	6.6	10.1	13.3	18.6	30.9
PV of adjusted equity cash flow at 26%	$57.2									
PV of 2004–2010 adj. equity CF/Terminal value	28.1%									

[1] Net income + Depreciation and amortization – Gross capital spending – Change in working capital – Principal repayments – Change in investments available for sale (i.e., increases in such investments are a negative cash flow entry but represent cash in excess of normal operating needs).

[2] EBIT(1 – t) + Depreciation and amortization – Gross capital spending – Change in working capital – Change in investments available for sale.

Table 13–14   California Kool Income Statement and Forecast Assumptions

	Historical Period				Projections: Twelve Months Ending December 31					
	2001	2002	2003	2004	2005	2006	2007	2008	2009	2010
Income Statement Assumptions										
Net sales growth (%)	0.042	0.033	0.038	0.035	0.040	0.045	0.045	0.045	0.045	0.045
Cost of sales as % of sales	0.805	0.814	0.780	0.765	0.758	0.755	0.750	0.750	0.750	0.750
SG&A as % of sales	0.133	0.144	0.142	0.135	0.130	0.125	0.120	0.120	0.120	0.120
Effective tax rate (%)	0.400	0.400	0.400	0.400	0.400	0.400	0.400	0.400	0.400	0.400
Income Statement										
Net sales	$177.6	$183.5	$190.4	$197.1	$205.0	$214.2	$223.8	$233.9	$244.4	$255.4
Cost of sales	143.0	149.3	148.5	150.8	155.4	161.7	167.9	175.4	183.3	191.6
Gross profit	34.6	34.1	41.9	46.3	49.6	52.5	56.0	58.5	61.1	63.9
Depreciation	1.3	5.4	5.1	2.4	2.9	3.4	3.5	3.7	3.8	4.0
Amortization of financing fees				0.5	0.5	0.5	0.5			
Total depreciation and amortization	1.3	5.4	5.1	2.9	3.4	3.9	4.0	3.7	3.8	4.0
SG&A	23.6	26.4	27.0	26.6	26.6	26.8	26.9	28.1	29.3	30.7
Management fee			0.1	0.1	0.1	0.1	0.1	0.1	0.1	0.1
Operating income (EBIT)	9.7	2.3	9.7	16.7	19.5	21.7	25.0	26.6	27.8	29.1
(Interest income)	0.1	0.1	0.1	0.0	0.1	0.1	0.1	0.1	0.1	0.1
New revolver interest expense				1.0	0.7	0.4	0.0	0.0	0.0	0.0
New senior debt interest expense				1.8	1.6	1.4	1.2	0.9	0.6	0.3
Subordinated debt interest expense				1.8	1.7	1.5	1.3	1.1	0.9	0.6
Total interest expense	0	0	0	4.6	4.0	3.3	2.5	2.0	1.5	0.9
Earnings before taxes	9.8	2.4	9.8	12.1	15.6	18.5	22.6	24.7	26.4	28.3
Taxes at 40%	3.9	0.9	3.9	4.8	6.2	7.4	9.0	9.9	10.6	11.3
Net income	$5.9	$1.4	$5.9	$7.3	$9.4	$11.1	$13.6	$14.8	$15.9	$17.0
PIK preferred dividend				2.6	3.0	3.3	3.7	4.2	4.7	5.2
Net income to common	$5.9	$1.4	$5.9	$4.6	$6.4	$7.8	$9.9	$10.7	$11.2	$11.7

Table 13–15 California Kool Balance Sheet and Forecast Assumptions

	Historical Period			Closing			Projections: Twelve Months Ended December					
	2001	2002	2003	Adjust.	2003	2004	2005	2006	2007	2008	2009	2010
Balance Sheet Assumptions												
Cash and marketable securities (% sales)	0.02	0.02	0.02	0.0	0.02	0.02	0.02	0.02	0.02	0.02	0.02	0.02
Accounts receivable (%sales)	0.161	0.158	0.167	0.0	0.167	0.155	0.155	0.155	0.155	0.155	0.155	0.155
Other current assets (% sales)	0.054	0.057	0.063	0.0	0.063	0.055	0.055	0.055	0.055	0.055	0.055	0.055
Gross prop., plant, and equip. (% sales)	0.473	0.5	0.52	0.0	0.52	0.52	0.52	0.52	0.52	0.52	0.52	0.52
Accumulated depreciation (% GP&E)	0.7	0.7	0.7	0.0	0.7	0.7	0.7	0.7	0.7	0.7	0.7	0.7
Accounts payable (% sales)	0.08	0.083	0.084	0.0	0.084	0.078	0.078	0.078	0.078	0.078	0.078	0.078
Other current liabilities (% sales)	0.074	0.079	0.076	0.0	0.076	0.07	0.07	0.07	0.07	0.07	0.07	0.07
Assets ($ millions)												
Current assets												
Cash and marketable securities	3.6	3.7	3.8	0.0	3.8	4.1	4.3	4.5	4.7	4.9	5.1	5.1
Accounts receivable	28.6	29.0	31.8	0.0	31.8	30.6	31.8	33.2	34.7	36.3	37.9	39.6
Other current assets	9.6	10.5	12.0	0.0	12.0	10.8	11.3	11.8	12.3	12.9	13.4	14.0
Total current assets	41.7	43.1	47.6	0.0	47.6	45.5	47.3	49.5	51.7	54.0	56.4	58.8
Investments available for sale	0.0		0.0		0.0	0.0	0.0	0.0	8.9	16.3	24.2	32.7
Gross property, plant, and equipment	84.0	91.7	99.0	0.0	99.0	102.5	106.6	111.4	116.4	121.6	127.1	132.8
Less: accumulated depreciation	58.8	64.2	69.3	0.0	69.3	71.7	74.6	78.0	81.5	85.1	89.0	93.0
Net property, plant & equipment	25.2	27.5	29.7	0.0	29.7	30.7	32.0	33.4	34.9	36.5	38.1	39.8
Transaction fees and expenses	0.0	0.0	0.0	2.0	2.0	1.5	1.0	0.5	0.0	0.0	0.0	0.0
Purchase price in excess of book value					0.0	0.0	0.0	0.0	0.0	0.0	0.0	0.0
Total assets	66.9	70.6	77.3	2.0	79.3	77.7	80.3	83.4	95.5	106.8	118.8	131.3
Liabilities and Shareholders' Equity ($ millions)												
Current liabilities												
Accounts payable	14.2	15.2	16.0	0.0	16.0	15.4	16.0	16.7	17.5	18.2	19.1	19.9
Other current liabilities	13.1	14.5	14.5	0.0	14.5	13.8	14.3	15.0	15.7	16.4	17.1	17.9
Total current liabilities	27.4	29.7	30.5	0.0	30.5	29.2	30.3	31.7	33.1	34.6	36.2	37.8

Continued

Table 13-15 — Cont'd

	Historical Period			Adjust.	Closing		Projections: Twelve Months Ended December						
	2001	2002	2003		2003	2004	2005	2006	2007	2008	2009	2010
Long-term debt												
Revolving loan				12.0	12.0	7.9	3.7	0.0	0.0	0.0	0.0	0.0
Senior debt				20.0	20.0	17.8	15.5	12.9	10.1	7.0	3.7	0.0
Subordinated debt				15.0	15.0	13.8	12.4	10.9	9.2	7.2	5.1	2.7
Total long-term debt	0.0	0.0	0.0		47.0	39.5	31.5	23.8	19.2	14.3	8.8	2.7
Shareholders' equity												
Preferred stock (PIK)				22.0	22.0	24.6	27.6	30.9	34.6	38.8	43.4	48.6
Common stock				3.0	3.0	3.0	3.0	3.0	3.0	3.0	3.0	3.0
Additional paid-in capital				(70.0)	(70.0)	(70.0)	(70.0)	(70.0)	(70.0)	(70.0)	(70.0)	(70.0)
Retained earnings	39.5	40.9	46.8	0.0	46.8	51.4	57.8	65.7	75.5	86.2	97.4	109.1
Total shareholders' equity	39.5	40.9	46.8		1.8	9.1	18.4	29.6	43.1	58.0	73.8	90.8
Total liabilities and shareholders' equity	66.9	70.6	77.3	2.0	79.3	77.7	80.3	85.0	95.5	106.8	118.8	131.3

Table 13–16 California Kool Cash Flow Statement and Analysis

GAAP Cash Flow ($ millions)	Historical Data				Projections: Twelve Months Ended December 31,					
	2001	2002	2003	2004	2005	2006	2007	2008	2009	2010
Cash flow from operating activities										
Net income available to common equity	5.9	1.4	5.9	4.6	6.4	7.8	9.9	10.7	11.2	11.7
Adjustments to reconcile net income to net cash flow										
Depreciation	1.3	5.4	5.1	2.4	2.9	3.4	3.5	3.7	3.8	4.0
Amortization of financing fees	0.0	0.0	0.0	0.5	0.5	0.5	0.5	0.0	0.0	0.0
PIK preferred dividends	0.0	0.0	0.0	2.6	3.0	3.3	3.7	4.2	4.7	5.2
Net change in working capital	0.0	1.1	(3.6)	1.1	(0.5)	(0.6)	(0.6)	(0.6)	(0.7)	(0.7)
Net cash flow from operations	7.2	5.7	14.6	11.3	12.2	14.4	17.0	17.9	19.0	20.3
Cash flow from investing activities										
(Increase) decrease in investments available for sale				0.0	0.0	0.0	(8.9)	(7.4)	(7.9)	(8.5)
(Increase) decrease in gross property, plant, and equipment				(3.5)	(4.1)	(4.8)	(5.0)	(5.2)	(5.5)	(5.7)
Net cash used in investments	0.0	0.0	0.0	(3.5)	(4.1)	(4.8)	(13.9)	(12.7)	(13.3)	(14.2)
Cash flows from financing activities										
Net debt (repayment) or issuance	0.0	0.0	0.0	(7.5)	(8.0)	(7.8)	(4.5)	(5.0)	(5.5)	(6.1)
Net cash (used in) provided by financing activities	0.0	0.0	0.0	(7.5)	(8.0)	(7.8)	(4.5)	(5.0)	(5.5)	(6.1)
Net increase (decrease) in cash and marketable securities				0.3	0.2	1.8	(1.5)	0.2	0.2	0.0
Beginning balances—cash and marketable securities				3.8	4.1	4.3	6.1	4.7	4.9	5.1
Ending balances—cash and marketable securities				4.1	4.3	6.1	4.7	4.9	5.1	5.1

Continued

Table 13–16 — Cont'd

	Historical Data				Projections: Twelve Months Ended December 31,					
	2001	2002	2003	2004	2005	2006	2007	2008	2009	2010
Valuation Cash Flow ($ millions)										
Net income to available to common equity	5.9	1.4	5.9	4.6	6.4	7.8	9.9	10.7	11.2	11.7
After-tax net interest expense (income)	0	0	0	1.7	1.4	1.2	1.0	0.8	0.6	0.4
Depreciation	1.3	5.4	5.1	2.4	2.9	3.4	3.5	3.7	3.8	4.0
Amortization of financing fees	0	0	0	0.5	0.5	0.5	0.5	0	0	0
PIK preferred dividend	0	0	0	2.6	3.0	3.3	3.7	4.2	4.7	5.2
Net cash flow before working capital	7.2	6.8	11.0	11.9	14.2	16.1	18.6	19.3	20.3	21.3
Net change in working capital	0.0	1.1	(3.6)	1.1	(0.5)	(0.6)	(0.6)	(0.6)	(0.7)	(0.7)
Net cash flow before gross property, plant & equip. spending	7.2	7.9	7.4	13.0	13.7	15.6	18.0	18.7	19.6	20.7
(Increase) decrease in invest available for sale				0.0	0.0	0.0	(8.9)	(7.4)	(7.9)	(8.5)
(Increase) decrease in gross property, plant & equipment	(3.0)	(7.7)	(7.3)	(3.5)	(4.1)	(4.8)	(5.0)	(5.2)	(5.5)	(5.7)
Enterprise cash flow	4.2	0.2	0.1	9.5	9.6	10.8	4.1	6.0	6.3	6.5
After-tax net interest expense (income)	0.0	0.0	0.0	1.7	1.4	1.2	1.0	0.8	0.6	0.4
Net debt (repayments) or issuance	0.0	0.0	0.0	(7.5)	(8.0)	(7.8)	(4.5)	(5.0)	(5.5)	(6.0)
Equity cash flow	4.2	0.2	0.1	0.3	0.2	1.8	(1.5)	0.2	0.2	0.0
Dividends on common stock	0.0	0.0	0.0	0.0	0.0	0.0	0.0	0.0	0.0	0.0
Net stock (repurchase) or issuance	0.0	0.0	0.0	0.0	0.0	0.0	0.0	0.0	0.0	0.0
Net increase (decrease) in cash balance	4.2	0.2	0.1	0.3	0.2	1.8	(1.5)	0.2	0.2	0.0
Beginning balances—cash and marketable securities		3.6	3.8	3.9	4.2	4.4	6.2	4.8	5.0	5.2
Ending balances—cash and marketable securities	3.6	3.8	3.9	4.2	4.4	6.2	4.8	5.0	5.2	5.2
Adjusted equity cash flow	4.2	0.2	0.1	0.3	0.2	1.8	7.4	7.7	8.1	8.5

Alternative Business and Restructuring Strategies

14

Joint Ventures, Partnerships, Strategic Alliances, and Licensing

Humility is not thinking less of yourself. It is thinking less about yourself.
—Rick Warren

Inside M&A: Garmin Utilizes Supply Agreement as Alternative to Acquiring Tele Atlas

Following an aggressive bidding process, Garmin Ltd., the largest U.S. maker of car-navigation devices, withdrew its bid for the Netherlands-based Tele Atlas NV on November 16, 2007. Tele Atlas provides maps of 12 million miles of roads in 200 countries. The move cleared the way for TomTom NV to buy the mapmaker for $4.25 billion. Both Garmin and TomTom are leading manufacturers of global positioning systems (GPSs), which enable users to navigate more easily through unfamiliar territory. The most critical component of such navigation systems is the map.

In lieu of acquiring Tele Atlas, Garmin entered into a six-year deal with an option to extend for an additional four years to obtain maps from Tele Atlas's competitor Navteq Corp. In doing so, Garmin avoided the EPS-dilutive effects of owning money-losing Tele Atlas. Garmin can focus on building traffic information and business listings into its products without having to own the underlying maps. An acquisition would have diluted Garmin's profit until 2010. Building maps comparable to those owned by Tele Atlas could take up to 10 years and cost $1 billion.

By owning the maps, TomTom is seeking to become more of a service provider than simply a manufacturer of GPS devices. Such devices are widely used in the automotive industry, as well as aviation and boating. The biggest growth opportunity is the increased use of GPS tracking capabilities in the market for mobile phones. This application is expected to dwarf the transportation and sports markets for GPS devices.

Because it will own the underlying maps, TomTom may be able to more easily combine the data with navigation devices and add traffic, gas station, and restaurant information. In contrast, Garmin will have to obtain proprietary data from others. Garmin may also have to pay more for maps or even lose access after the contract (including the option to extend) expires.

Chapter Overview

For many years, joint ventures (JVs) and alliances have been commonplace in high-technology industries; many segments of manufacturing; the oil exploration, mining, and chemical industries; media and entertainment; financial services; pharmaceutical and biotechnology firms; and real estate. They have taken the form of licensing, distribution, comarketing, research and development agreements, and equity investments. The term *business alliance* is used throughout this chapter to include joint ventures, partnerships, strategic alliances, equity partnerships, licensing agreements, and franchise alliances. What all of these arrangements have in common is that they generally involve sharing the risk, reward, and control among all participants.

The primary theme of this chapter is that well-constructed business alliances often represent viable alternatives to mergers and acquisitions (M&As), and they always should be considered one of the many options for achieving strategic business objectives. The principal differences in the various types of business alliances were discussed in some detail in Chapter 1; as such, they only are summarized in Table 14–1. This chapter

Table 14–1 Key Differences among Business Alliances

Type	Key Characteristics
Joint ventures (JV)	Independent entity involving two or more parties May be organized as a corporation, partnership, or other legal or business organization selected by the parties Ownership, responsibilities, risks, and rewards allocated to parties Each party retains corporate identity and autonomy Created by parties contributing assets for a specific purpose and for a limited duration
Strategic alliances (e.g., technology transfer, R&D sharing, and cross-marketing)	Do not involve the formation of separate legal entities May be precursor to JV, partnership, or acquisition Generally not passive but involve cross-training, coordinated product development, and long-term contracts based on performance metrics such as product quality rather than price
Equity partnerships	Have all the characteristics of an alliance Involve making minority investment in other party (e.g., 5–10 percent) Minority investor may have an option to buy a larger stake in other party

Licensing
  Product
  Process
  Merchandise and
  Trademark
	Patent, trademark, or copyright licensed in exchange for royalty or fee
	Generally no sharing of risk or reward
	Generally stipulates what is being sold, how and where it can be used, and for how long
	Payments usually consist of an initial fee and royalties based on a percentage of future license sales

Franchising alliances	Network of alliances in which partners are linked by licensing agreements (e.g., fast food chains, hardware stores) Often grant exclusive rights to sell or distribute goods or services in specific geographic areas or markets Licensees may be required to purchase goods and services from other firms in the alliance
Network alliances	Interconnecting alliances among companies crossing international and industrial boundaries May involve companies collaborating in one market while competing in others (e.g., computers, airlines, cellular telephones) Most often formed to access skills from different but converging industries
Exclusive agreements	Usually involve rights for manufacturing or marketing specific products or services Each party benefits from the specific skills or assets the other party brings to the relationship

discusses the wide variety of motives for business alliances and the factors common to most successful alliances. Also addressed are the advantages and disadvantages of alternative legal structures, important deal-structuring issues, and empirical studies that purport to measure the contribution of business alliances to creating shareholder wealth. The major segments of this chapter include the following:

- Motivations for Business Alliances
- Critical Success Factors for Business Alliances
- Alternative Legal Forms of Business Alliances
- Strategic and Operational Plans
- Resolving Business Alliance Deal-Structuring Issues
- Empirical Findings
- Things to Remember

A review of this chapter (including practice questions and answers) is available in the file folder entitled Student Study Guide contained on the CD-ROM accompanying this book. The CD-ROM also contains a Learning Interactions Library, enabling students to test their knowledge of this chapter in a "real-time" environment.

Motivations for Business Alliances

Money alone rarely provides the basis for a successful long-term business alliance. A partner often can obtain funding from a variety of sources but may be able to obtain access to a set of skills or nonfinancial resources only from a specific source. The motivation for an alliance can include risk sharing, gaining access to new markets, globalization, cost reduction, a desire to acquire (or exit) a business, or the favorable regulatory treatment often received compared with M&As.

Risk Sharing

Risk is the potential for losing, or at least not gaining, value. Risk often is perceived to be greater the more money, management time, or other resources a company has committed to an endeavor and the less certain the outcome. To mitigate perceived risk, companies often enter into alliances to gain access to know-how and scarce resources or reduce the amount of resources they would have to commit if they were to do it on their own. For example, in late 2004, General Motors and DaimlerChrysler, the world's largest and fifth largest auto manufacturers, agreed to jointly develop hybrid gasoline–electric engines for cars and light trucks. Neither corporation felt comfortable in assuming the full cost and risk associated with developing this new automotive technology. Moreover, each company would be willing to contribute the results of its own internal R&D efforts to the joint development of a technology to be shared by the two companies. In early 2009, Disney Studio entered into a long-term film distribution agreement with Dream-Works Studios, giving DreamWorks's productions access to the substantial Disney film distribution network.

Sharing Proprietary Knowledge

Developing new technologies can be extremely expensive. Given the pace at which technology changes, the risk is high that a competitor will be able to develop a superior technology before a firm can bring its own new technology to market. Consequently, high-technology companies with expertise in a specific technology segment often combine their efforts with another company or companies with complementary know-how to reduce the risk of failing to develop the "right" technology. Moreover, by having multiple contacts throughout an industry, it is unlikely that a firm will overlook new innovations or best practices. For example, TiVo, a small manufacturer of set-top boxes that provide interactive TV service, raised $32 million in 1999 through a series of private debt placements with CBS, NBC, Disney/ABC, Hughes's Direct TV satellite service, and Comcast (a leading cable TV service). By lending to TiVo, these companies would be able to obtain access to the latest technologies that may someday be necessary to remain competitive in their respective markets.

In 1983, Rockwell, Sperry, Boeing, Control Data, Honeywell, Digital Equipment, Kodak, Harris, Lockheed, 3M, Martin Marietta, Motorola, NCR, National Semiconductor, and RCA formed Micro-Electronics Computer Corporation (MCC). MCC was formed to share the cost of developing semiconductor, computer, and software technology that could not otherwise be developed cost effectively by these companies. In 1988, Sematech was founded as a research alliance consisting of IBM, National Semiconductor, Advanced Micro Devices, and other major companies. In the late 1980s, Union Carbide and AlliedSignal combined their skills to launch UOP, a joint venture that develops process technology for the oil-refining and petrochemical industries. Since its inception, it has become the world's largest process-licensing organization, with annual revenues exceeding $800 million. The Microsoft and Intel relationship is one of the better known technology partnerships in which the two cooperate to enhance the "Wintel" world, which combines Windows operating systems with Intel microchips.

Sharing Management Skills and Resources

Firms often lack the management skills and resources to solve complex tasks and projects. These deficiencies can be remedied by aligning with other firms that possess the requisite skills and proprietary knowledge. Building contractors and real estate developers have collaborated for years by pooling their resources to construct, market, and manage large, complex commercial projects. Similarly, the contribution of Dow Chemical management personnel to a JV with Cordis, a small pacemaker manufacturer, enabled the JV to keep pace with accelerating production.

The huge research and development (R&D) requirements, the relatively low success rate, near-term patent expiration of profitable drugs, and the high cost of marketing new drugs have resulted in a dramatic escalation of the use of partnerships in the pharmaceutical industry. Reflecting the bureaucratic inertia often found in mega-corporations, large pharmaceutical firms also actively seek partnerships with smaller, more nimble and innovative firms as a way of revitalizing their new drug pipelines. Such relationships are also commonplace among biotechnology firms. Lerner, Shane, and Tsai (2003) found that small biotechnology firms are in fact likely to fund their R&D through JVs with large corporations, with the larger partner receiving the controlling interest.

In mid-2006, Nokia, a Finnish firm specializing in wireless communications, and Siemens, a German company with a strong position in fixed-line telecommunications, agreed to pool their networking equipment divisions in a joint venture. The new firm, called Nokia Siemens Networks, based in Finland, is the third largest telecom equipment maker in the world. By pooling their technical and manufacturing resources, the partners believe they can develop integrated products for the major telecommunications companies competing to sell a combination of fixed-line, broadband Internet, wireless, and television. In early 2009, Walt Disney Studios announced that it had entered a long-term distribution agreement with DreamWorks Studios to utilize its vaunted marketing capabilities to distribute six DreamWorks' films annually.

In mid-2009, Italy's Fiat acquired a 35 percent stake in U.S. car maker Chrysler in exchange for sharing products and platforms for small cars with Chrysler. The deal was designed to help Fiat boost its sales volumes to compete in the global auto market and to enable Chrysler to enter more foreign markets, gain access to fuel-efficient technology, and to expand its small car product offering.

Sharing Substantial Capital Outlays

As the U.S. cellular phone market became saturated, wireless carriers fought tenaciously to increase market share in a maturing market. Increased price competition and the exorbitant costs of creating and supporting national networks contributed to consolidation in the industry. Regional and foreign carriers were encouraged to join forces to achieve the scale necessary to support these burdensome costs. Vodafone and Verizon Communications joined forces in 1999 to form Verizon Wireless. SBC and Bell Atlantic formed the Cingular Wireless partnership, which acquired AT&T Wireless in early 2004.

Securing Sources of Supply

The chemical industry is highly vulnerable to swings in energy costs and other raw materials. Chemical companies such as Dow, Hercules, and Olin, have used JVs to build new plants throughout the world. When shortages of raw materials threaten future production, these firms commonly form JVs to secure future sources of supply. Similarly, CNOOC, the large Chinese oil concern, has been busily trying to invest in oil and natural gas assets in highly diverse geographic areas to obtain reliable sources of supply. CNOOC's efforts have ranged from outright acquisition (e.g., the attempted takeover of Unocal in the United States), to long-term contracts (e.g., Canadian tar sands), to joint ventures in various locations in Africa (e.g., Sudan and Kenya).

Cost Reduction

In the 1980s and 1990s, retailers and financial services firms outsourced such back-office activities as information and application processing to such firms as IBM and EDS. Others outsourced payroll processing and benefits management to such firms as ADP. More recently, firms entered so-called logistics alliances. Such alliances cover both transportation and warehousing services and utilize a single provider for these services. In January 2001, the U.S. Postal Service (USPS) and Federal Express (FedEx) announced an agreement in which FedEx would haul the USPS's Express Mail and Priority Mail as well as some first class mail. FedEx would provide guaranteed space at a cost of $6.3 billion over seven years. Moreover, FedEx would pay the USPS at least $126 million to place its collection boxes at post offices. The USPS is expected to save more than $1 billion by phasing out its Indianapolis hub and by allowing a number of leases to expire. In turn, FedEx is guaranteed a specific volume of mail and would have access to a large number of package drop-off points at USPS offices (Schmid, 2001).

Companies also may choose to combine their manufacturing operations in a single facility with the capacity to meet the production requirements of all parties involved. By building a large facility, the firms jointly can benefit from lower production costs resulting from spreading fixed costs over larger volumes of production. This type of arrangement is commonplace within the newspaper industry in major cities in which several newspapers are engaged in "head-to-head" competition. Similar cost benefits may be realized if one party closes its production facility and satisfies its production requirements by buying at preferred prices from another party with substantial unused capacity. Other examples of competitors combining operating units to achieve economies of scale include Sony and Ericsson combining their mobile-handset units to compete with Nokia and Motorola in the late 1990s, as well as Hitachi and Mitsubishi forming an $8 billion a year semiconductor joint venture in 2000. In 2005, Canon and Toshiba created a new manufacturing operation to satisfy their requirements for SED displays for TVs by investing a combined $1.8 billion in a JV.

Gaining Access to New Markets

Gaining access to new customers is often a highly expensive proposition involving substantial initial marketing costs, such as advertising, promotion, warehousing, and distribution expenses. The cost may be prohibitive unless alternative distribution channels providing access to the targeted markets can be found. For example, despite concerns about the viability of many Chinese banks awash in bad loans, Bank of America paid $2.5 billion in 2005 for a 9 percent stake in China Construction Bank to gain access to what could be potentially a large and lucrative market. Despite competing in various markets, Google was able to inexpensively gain access to eBay's non-U.S. customers. In an alliance with eBay in late 2006, eBay granted Google the exclusive right to display text advertisements on eBay's auction websites outside the United States, with eBay sharing in the revenue generated by the advertisements. Earlier that same year, Yahoo signed a similar agreement with eBay for sites within the United States.

A company may enter into an alliance to sell its products through another firm's direct sales force, telemarketing operation, retail outlets, or Internet site. The alliance may involve the payment of a percentage of revenue generated in this manner to the firm whose distribution channel is being used. Alternatively, firms may enter into a "cross-marketing" relationship in which they agree to sell the other firm's products through their own distribution channels. The profitability of these additional sales can be significant, because neither firm has to add to its significant overhead expense or to its investment in building or expanding its distribution channels.

In October 2008, Morgan Stanley and Goldman Sachs, the then largest independent investment banks, converted to bank holding companies and joined the U.S. Federal Reserve System. While the move will subject the firms to Fed regulation, it also provides the ability to borrow from the central bank to satisfy short-term liquidity needs. While Morgan Stanley owned a small commercial banking operation, its total deposit base was miniscule compared to competitors. Consequently, the firm sought an international alliance in which it could obtain a capital infusion, as well as access to a larger deposit base and new customer markets. See Case Study 14–1.

Case Study 14–1 Morgan Stanley Sells Mitsubishi 21 Percent Ownership Stake

Japan's largest bank, Mitsubishi UFJ Financial Group (MFUG), announced on October 13, 2008, that it had invested $9 billion in Morgan Stanley (Morgan). MFUG agreed to purchase 9.9 percent of Morgan's common stock at $25.75 per share for $3 billion and acquire $6 billion in perpetual convertible preferred stock yielding a 10 percent dividend. The preferred shares can be converted into common stock at $31.25 per share. After one year, one half of the preferred stock would convert into common shares if Morgan's common stock trades above the conversion price for a predetermined time period.

Despite its $1 trillion in assets, Morgan was seen as being highly leveraged with assets 24 times tangible shareholders' equity. This compares to 14 times tangible shareholders' equity for most major commercial banks. Reflecting its perceived precarious financial position, the cost of insuring its debt increased from 2 to 10 percentage points. While the immediate benefit to Morgan would be to bolster the firm's capital base, the deal allows Morgan to accelerate its transition from a pure independent investment bank to large bank holding company. The deal envisions cooperation between Morgan and MFUG in global corporate lending and security underwriting, retail banking, asset management, and investment banking.

Discussion Questions

1. Speculate as to why Mitsubishi was willing to invest in Morgan Stanley, despite its perceived investment risk.
2. How would Morgan Stanley benefit from the automatic conversion feature embedded in the preferred stock? What would be the impact on current Morgan Stanley shareholders of the conversion feature?

Globalization

The dizzying pace of international competition increased the demand for alliances and JVs to enable companies to enter markets in which they lack production or distribution channels or in which laws prohibit 100 percent foreign ownership of a business. Moreover, a major foreign competitor might turn out to be an excellent partner in fighting domestic competition. Alternatively, a domestic competitor could become a partner in combating a foreign competitor.

The automotive industry uses alliances to provide additional production capacity, distribution outlets, technology development, and parts supply. Many companies, such as General Motors and Ford, take minority equity positions in other companies within the industry to gain access to foreign markets. By aligning with Lenovo Group as a strategic partner, IBM has an opportunity to enlarge dramatically its market share in China (Case Study 14–2).

Case Study 14–2 IBM Partners with China's Lenovo Group

IBM was able to satisfy two objectives in selling its ailing PC business to China's Lenovo Group for $1.75 billion in cash, stock, and assumed liabilities in late 2004. First, the firm is able to eliminate the business's ongoing operating losses from its financial statements. Second, IBM could sharply enhance its position in information technology in China, which is rapidly emerging as one of the world's largest information technology markets.

Under the terms of the transaction, Lenovo would relocate its world headquarters from Beijing to Armonk, New York, near IBM's headquarters. Lenovo would be managed by senior IBM executives. IBM owns an 18.9-percent stake in the new company, which would sell PCs under the IBM brand name. IBM gets to continue selling PCs, which help it sell other products and services to corporations as packages. IBM hopes to exploit Lenovo's influence in China to sell additional information technology products. As China's number 1 PC maker, Lenovo has a 27 percent overall market share and strong positions in both the government and education markets. The firm's presence in these markets is expected to strengthen, because the Chinese government owns 46 percent of the new company. Lenovo hopes to benefit by obtaining a global PC operation, which places it third in market share behind number one Dell and

Continued

Case Study 14–2 IBM Partners with China's Lenovo Group — Cont'd

number two Hewlett Packard, and expand its sales under the widely recognized and respected IBM brand.

Discussion Questions

1. Which party (i.e., IBM or Lenovo) to this transaction do you think will benefit more? Explain your answer.
2. What other challenges to making this relationship work would you anticipate? Be specific.
3. What challenges might arise for IBM due to the Chinese government's ownership of such a large part of Lenovo? Be specific.

A Prelude to Acquisition or Exit

Rather than acquire a company, a firm may choose to make a minority investment in another company. In exchange for the investment, the investing firm may receive board representation, preferred access to specific proprietary technology, and an option to purchase a controlling interest in the company. The investing firm is able to assess the quality of management, cultural compatibility, and the viability of the other firm's technology without having to acquire a controlling interest in the firm.

Favorable Regulatory Treatment

As noted in Chapter 2, the Department of Justice has looked on JVs far more favorably than mergers or acquisitions. Mergers result in a reduction in the number of firms. In contrast, JVs increase the number of firms because the parents continue to operate while another firm is created. Project-oriented JVs often are viewed favorably by regulators. Regulatory authorities tend to encourage collaborative research, particularly when the research is shared among all the parties to the JV.

Critical Success Factors for Business Alliances

Research suggests that the success of a JV or alliance depends on a specific set of identifiable factors (Kantor, 2002; Child and Faulkner, 1998; Lynch, 1990, 1993). These factors most often include the following: synergy; cooperation; clarity of purpose, roles, and responsibilities; accountability; a "win–win" situation; compatible time frames and financial expectations for the partners; and support from top management.

Synergy

Successful alliances are usually characterized by partners that have attributes that either complement existing strengths or offset significant weaknesses. Examples include economies of scale and scope, access to new products, distribution channels, and proprietary know-how. As with any merger or acquisition, the perceived synergy should be measurable to the extent possible. Interestingly, successful alliances are often those in which the partners contribute a skill or resource in addition to or other than money. Such alliances often make good economic sense and, as such, are able to get financing.

Cooperation

All parties involved must be willing to cooperate at all times. A lack of cooperation contributes to poor communication and reduces the likelihood that the objectives of the JV or alliance will be realized. Not surprisingly, companies with similar philosophies, goals, rewards, operating practices, and ethics are more likely to cooperate over the long run.

Clarity of Purpose, Roles, and Responsibilities

The purpose of the business alliance must be evident to all involved. A purpose that is widely understood drives timetables, division of responsibility, commitments to milestones, and measurable results. Internal conflict and lethargic decision making inevitably result from poorly defined roles and responsibilities of those participating in the alliance.

Accountability

Successful alliances hold managers accountable for their actions. Once roles and responsibilities have been clearly defined and communicated, measurable goals to be achieved in identifiable timeframes should be established for all managers. Such goals should be directly tied to the key objectives for the alliance. Incentives should be in place to reward good performance with respect to goals and those failing to perform should be held accountable.

Win–Win Situation

All parties to an alliance must believe they are benefiting from the activity for it to be successful. Johnson & Johnson's (J&J) alliance with Merck & Company in the marketing of Pepcid AC is a classic win–win situation. Merck contributed its prescription drug Pepcid AC to the alliance so that J&J could market it as an over-the-counter drug. With Merck as the developer of the upset stomach remedy and J&J as marketer, the product became the market share leader in this drug category. In contrast, the attempt by DaimlerChrysler, Ford, and GM to form an online auction network for parts, named Covisint, in early 2000 failed in part because the partners did not feel they were benefiting equally. Cooperation disintegrated when the automakers and suppliers believed that they would lose competitive information.

Compatible Time Frames and Financial Expectations

The length of time an alliance agreement remains in force depends on the partners' objectives, the availability of resources needed to achieve these objectives, and the accuracy of the assumptions on which the alliance's business plans are based. Incompatible time frames are a recipe for disaster. The management of a small Internet business may want to "cash out" within the next 18–24 months, whereas a larger firm may wish to gain market share over a number of years.

Support from the Top

Top management of the parents of a business alliance must involve themselves aggressively and publicly. Such support should be unambiguous and consistent. Tepid support or, worse, indifference filters down to lower-level managers and proves to be highly demotivating. Middle-level managers tend to focus their time and effort on those activities that tend to maximize their compensation and likelihood of promotion. These activities may divert time and attention from the business alliance.

Alternative Legal Forms of Business Alliances

As is true of M&As, determining the legal form of a business alliance should follow the creation of a coherent business strategy. The choice of legal structure should be made only when the parties to the business alliance are comfortable with the venture's objectives, potential synergy, and preliminary financial analysis of projected returns and risk. Business alliances may assume a variety of legal structures. These include the following: corporate, partnership, franchise, equity partnership, or written contract. Technically, a "handshake" agreement is also an option. However, given the inordinate risk associated with the lack of a written agreement, those seeking to create a business alliance are encouraged to avoid this type of arrangement. However, in some cultures, this type of informal agreement may be most appropriate. Efforts to insist on a detailed written agreement or contractual relationship may be viewed as offensive. The five basic legal structures, excluding the handshake agreement, are discussed in detail in this section. Each has its own implications with respect to taxation, control by the owners, ability to trade ownership positions, limitations on liability, duration, and ease of raising capital. The relative merits of each legal form are summarized in Table 14–2.

Corporate Structures

A corporation is a legal entity created under state law in the United States with an unending life and limited financial liability for its owners. Corporate legal structures include a generalized corporate form (also called C-type corporation) and the subchapter S (S-type) corporation. The S-type corporation contains certain tax advantages intended to facilitate the formation of small businesses, which are perceived to be major contributors to job growth. For an excellent discussion of the corporation, see Truitt (2006).

C-Type Corporations

A JV corporation normally involves a stand-alone business. The corporation's income is taxed at the prevailing corporate tax rates. Corporations, other than S-type corporations, are subject to "double" taxation. Taxes are paid by the corporation when profits are earned and again by the shareholders when the corporation issues dividends. Moreover, setting up a corporate legal structure may be more time consuming and costly than other legal forms because of legal expenses incurred in drafting a corporate charter and bylaws. Although the corporate legal structure has adverse tax consequences and may be more costly to establish, it does offer a number of important advantages over other legal forms. The four primary characteristics of a C-type corporate structure include managerial autonomy, continuity of ownership or life, ease of transferring ownership and raising money, and limited liability. These characteristics are discussed next.

Managerial autonomy most often is used when the JV is large or complex enough to require a separate or centralized professional management organization. The corporate structure works best when the JV requires a certain amount of operational autonomy to be effective. The parent companies would continue to set strategy, but the JV's management would manage the day-to-day operations.

Unlike other legal forms, the corporate structure has an indefinite life, as it does not have to be dissolved as a result of the death of the owners or if one of the owners wishes

Table 14–2 Alternative Legal Forms Applicable to Business Alliances

Legal Form	Advantages	Disadvantages
Corporate Structures		
C Corporation	Continuity of ownership Limited liability Provides operational autonomy Provides for flexible financing Facilitates tax-free merger	Double taxation Inability to pass losses on to shareholders Relatively high setup costs including charter and bylaws
Subchapter S	Avoids double taxation Limited liability	Maximum of 100 shareholders Excludes corporate shareholders Must distribute all earnings Allows only one class of stock Lacks continuity of C corporate structure Difficult to raise large sums of money
Limited liability company (LLC)	Limited liability Owners can be managers without losing limited liability Avoids double taxation Allows an unlimited number of members or owners Allows corporate shareholders Can own more than 80 percent of another company Allows flexibility in allocating investment, profits, losses, and operational responsibilities among members Life set by owners Can sell shares to "members" without SEC registration Allows foreign corporations as investors	Owners also must be active participants in the firm Lacks continuity of a corporate structure State laws governing LLC formation differ, making it difficult for LLCs doing business in multiple states Member shares often are illiquid because consent of members required to transfer ownership
Partnership structures		
General partnerships	Avoids double taxation Allows flexibility in allocating Investment, profits, losses, and operational responsibilities Life set by general partner	Partners have unlimited liability Lacks continuity of corporate structure Partnership interests illiquid Partners jointly and severally liable Each partner has authority to bind the partnership to contracts
Limited liability partnerships	Limits partner liability (except for general partner) Avoids double taxation State laws consistent (covered under the Uniform Limited Partnership Act)	Partnership interests illiquid Partnership dissolved if a partner leaves Private partnerships limited to 35 partners
Franchise alliances	Allows repeated application of a successful business model Minimizes startup expenses Facilitates communication of common brand and marketing strategy	Success depends on quality of franchise sponsor support Royalty payments (3–7 percent of revenue)
Equity partnerships	Facilitates close working relationship Potential prelude to merger May preempt competition	Limited tactical and strategic control
Written contracts	Easy startup Potential prelude to merger	Limited control Lacks close coordination Potential for limited commitment

to liquidate his or her ownership position. A corporate legal structure may be warranted if the JV's goals are long term and the parties choose to contribute cash directly to the JV. In return for the cash contribution, the JV partners receive stock in the new company. If the initial strategic reasons for the JV change and the JV no longer benefits one of the partners, the stock in the JV can be sold. Alternatively, the partner–shareholder can withdraw from active participation in the JV corporation but remain a passive shareholder in anticipation of potential future appreciation of the stock. In addition, the corporate structure facilitates a tax-free merger in which the stock of the acquiring firm can be exchanged for the stock or assets of another firm. In practice, the transferability of ownership interests is strictly limited by the stipulations of a shareholder agreement created when the corporation is formed.

Under a corporate structure ownership can be easily transferred, which facilitates raising money. A corporate structure also may be justified if the JV is expected to have substantial future financing requirements. A corporate structure provides a broader array of financing options than other legal forms. These include the ability to sell interests in the form of shares and the issuance of corporate debentures and mortgage bonds. The ability to sell new shares enables the corporation to raise funds to expand while still retaining control if less than 50.1 percent of the corporation's shares are sold.

Under the corporate structure, the parent's liability is limited to the extent of its investment in the corporation. Consequently, an individual stockholder cannot be held responsible for the debts of the corporation or of other shareholders. Creditors cannot take the personal assets of the owners. However, an owner of a corporation can be held personally liable if he or she directly injures someone or personally guarantees a bank loan or a business debt on which the corporation defaults. Other exceptions to personal liability include the failure to deposit taxes withheld from employees' wages or the commission of intentional fraud that causes harm to the corporation or someone else. Finally, an owner may be liable who treats the corporation as an extension of his or her personal affairs by failing to adequately capitalize the corporation, hold regular directors and shareholders meetings, or keeps business records and transactions separate from the other owners.

Subchapter S Corporations

Effective December 31, 2004, a firm having 100 or fewer shareholders may qualify as an S-type corporation and elect to be taxed as if it were a partnership, and thus avoid double taxation. The maximum number of shareholders was increased from 76 to 100 under the 2004 American Jobs Creation Act. This act allows the members of a single family to be considered as a single shareholder. For example, a husband and wife (and their estates) would be treated as a single shareholder. Members of a family refer to individuals with a common ancestor, lineal descendants of the common ancestor, and the spouses (or former spouses) of such lineal descendants or common ancestor. Moreover, an ESOP maintained by an S corporation is not in violation of the maximum number of shareholders' requirement because the S corporation contributes stock to the ESOP.

The major disadvantages to an S-type corporation are the exclusion of any corporate shareholders, the requirement to issue only one class of stock, the necessity of distributing all earnings to the shareholders each year, and that no more than 25 percent of the corporation's gross income may be derived from passive income. To be treated as an S-type corporation, all shareholders must simply sign and file IRS Form 2553.

C corporations may convert to subchapter S corporations to eliminate double taxation on dividends. Asset sales within 10 years of the conversion from a C to an S corporation are subject to capital gains taxes. However, after 10 years such gains are tax free to the S corporation but are taxable when distributed to shareholders at their personal tax rates. In 2007, turnaround specialist Sam Zell, after taking The Tribune Corporation private, converted the firm to an S corporation to take advantage of the favorable tax treatment (see Case Study 12–3). Sales of assets acquired by an S corporation or after a 10-year period following conversion from one form of legal entity to an S corporation are taxed at the more favorable capital gains tax rate. The 10-year "built-in-gains" period is designed by the IRS to discourage C corporations from converting to subchapter S corporations to take advantage of the more favorable capital gains tax rates on gains realized by selling corporate assets. Gains on the sale of assets by C corporations are taxed at the prevailing corporate tax rate rather than a more favorable capital gains tax rate.

As discussed next, the limited liability company offers its owners the significant advantage of greater flexibility in allocating profits and losses and is not subject to the many restrictions of the S corporation. Consequently, the overall popularity of the S corporation has declined.

Limited Liability Company

Like a corporation, the limited liability corporation (LLC) limits the liability of its owners (called *members*) to the extent of their investment. Like a limited partnership, the LLC passes through all of the profits and losses of the entity to its owners without itself being taxed. To obtain this favorable tax status, the IRS generally requires that the LLC adopt an organization agreement that eliminates the characteristics of a C corporation: management autonomy, continuity of ownership or life, and free transferability of shares. Management autonomy is limited by expressly placing decisions about major issues pertaining to the management of the LLC (e.g., mergers or asset sales) in the hands of all its members. LLC organization agreements require that they be dissolved in case of the death or retirement or resignation of any member, thereby eliminating continuity of ownership or life. Free transferability is limited by making a transfer of ownership subject to the approval of all members.

Unlike S-type corporations, LLCs can own more than 80 percent of another corporation and have an unlimited number of members. Also, corporations as well as non-U.S. residents can own LLC shares. Equity capital is obtained through offerings to owners or members. Capital is sometimes referred to as *interests* rather than *shares*, since the latter denotes something that may be freely traded. The LLC can sell shares or interests to members without completing the costly and time-consuming process of registering them with the Securities and Exchange Commission (SEC), which is required for corporations that sell their securities to the public. However, LLC shares are not traded on public exchanges. This arrangement works well for corporate JVs or projects developed through a subsidiary or affiliate. The parent corporation can separate a JV's risk from its other businesses while getting favorable tax treatment and greater flexibility in the allocation of revenues and losses among owners. Finally, LLCs can incorporate before an initial public offering tax free. This is necessary, as they must register such issues with the SEC. The life of the LLC is determined by the owners and is generally set for a fixed number of years in contrast to the typical unlimited life for a corporation.

While a limited liability company must have members or owners, its management structure may be determined in whatever manner the members desire. Members may manage the LLC directly or provide for the election of a manager, officer, or board to conduct LLC's activities. Members hold final authority in the LLC, having the right to approve extraordinary actions such as mergers or asset sales. Member approval may be granted through meetings, written consents, and conference calls. Managers may represent the LLC in dealings with third parties.

The LLC's drawbacks are evident if one owner decides to leave. All other owners must formally agree to continue the firm. Also, all the LLC's owners must take active roles in managing the firm. LLC interests are often illiquid, as transfer of ownership is subject to the approval of other members. LLCs must be set for a limited time, typically 30 years. Each state has different laws about LLC formation and governance, so an LLC that does business in several states might not meet the requirements in every state. LLCs are formed when two or more "persons" (i.e., individuals, LLPs, corporations, etc.) agree to file articles of organization with the secretary of state's office. The most common types of firms to form LLCs are family-owned businesses, professional services firms such as lawyers, and companies with foreign investors.

Partnership Structures

Partnership structures frequently are used as an alternative to a corporation. Partnership structures include general partnerships and limited partnerships. While the owners of a partnership are not legally required to have a partnership agreement, it usually makes sense to have one. The partnership agreement spells out how business decisions are to be made and how profits and losses will be shared.

General Partnerships

Under the general partnership legal structure, investment, profits, losses, and operational responsibilities are allocated to the partners. The arrangement has no effect on the autonomy of the partners. Because profits and losses are allocated to the partners, the partnership is not subject to tax. The partnership structure also offers substantial flexibility in how the profits and losses are allocated to the partners. Typically, a corporate partner forms a special-purpose subsidiary to hold its interest. This not only limits liability but also may facilitate disposition of the JV interest in the future. The partnership structure is preferable to the other options when the business alliance is expected to have short (three to five years) duration and if high levels of commitment and management interaction are necessary for short time periods.

The primary disadvantage of the general partnership is that all the partners have unlimited liability and may have to cover the debts of less financially sound partners. Each partner is said to be jointly and severally liable for the partnership's debts. For example, if one of the partners negotiates a contract resulting in a substantial loss, each partner must pay for a portion of the loss, based on a previously determined agreement on the distribution of profits and losses. Because each partner has unlimited liability for all the debts of the firm, creditors of the partnership may claim assets from one or more of the partners if the remaining partners are unable to cover their share of the loss. Another disadvantage includes the ability of any partner to bind the entire business to a contract or other business deal. Consequently, if one partner purchases inventory at a price that the partnership cannot afford, the partnership is still obligated to pay.

Partnerships also lack continuity in that they must be dissolved if a partner dies or withdraws, unless a new partnership agreement can be drafted. To avoid this possibility, a partnership agreement should include a buy–sell condition or right of first refusal allowing the partners to buy out a departing partner's interest so the business can continue. Finally, partnership interests may also be difficult to sell because of the lack of a public market, thus making the partnership difficult to liquidate or to transfer partnership interests.

Forming a partnership generally requires applying for a local business license or tax registration certificate. If the business name does not contain all of the partners' last names, the partnership must register a fictitious or assumed business name in the county in which it is established. The body of law governing partnerships is the Uniform Partnership Act (UPA).

Limited Partnerships

A limited liability partnership is one in which one or more of the partners can be designated as having limited liability as long as at least one partner has unlimited liability. It is governed by state law and, unless the partnership strictly conforms to state restrictions, is regarded as a general partnership. Limited partners usually cannot lose more than their capital contribution. Those who are responsible for the day-to-day operations of the partnership's activities, whose individual acts are binding on the other partners, and who are personally liable for the partnership's total liabilities are called *general partners*. Those who contribute only money and are not involved in management decisions are called *limited partners*. Usually limited partners receive income, capital gains, and tax benefits, whereas the general partner collects fees and a percentage of the capital gain and income.

Typical limited partnerships are in real estate, oil and gas, and equipment leasing, but they also are used to finance movies, R&D, and other projects. Public limited partnerships are sold through brokerage firms, financial planners, and other registered securities representatives. Public partnerships may have an unlimited number of investors and their partnership plans must be filed with the SEC. Private limited partnerships are constructed with fewer than 35 limited partners, who each invest more than $20,000. Their plans do not have to be filed with the SEC.

The sources of equity capital for limited partnerships are the funds supplied by the general and limited partners. The total amount of equity funds needed by the limited partnerships is typically committed when the partnership is formed. Therefore, ventures that are expected to grow are not usually set up as limited partnerships. LLPs are very popular for accountants, physicians, attorneys, and consultants. With the exception of Louisiana, every state has adopted either the Uniform Limited Partnership Act or the Revised Uniform Limited Partnership Act.

Franchise Alliance

Franchises typically involve a franchisee making an initial investment to purchase a license, plus additional capital investment for real estate, machinery, and working capital. For this initial investment, the franchisor provides training, site-selection assistance, and discounts resulting from bulk purchasing. Royalty payments for the license typically run 3–7 percent of annual franchisee revenue. Franchise success rates exceed 80 percent over a five-year period as compared with some types of startups, which have success rates of less than 10 percent after 5 years (Lynch, 1990). The franchise alliance is preferred when a given business format can be replicated many times. Moreover, franchise alliances are also appropriate when there needs to be a common, recognizable identity presented to customers of each of the alliance partners and close operational coordination is required. In addition, a franchise alliance may be desirable when a common marketing program needs to be coordinated and implemented by a single partner. Multistate franchises must be careful to be in full compliance with the franchise laws of the states in which they have franchisees.

The franchisor and franchisee operate as separate entities, usually as corporations or LLCs. The four basic types of franchises are distributor (auto dealerships), processing (bottling plants), chain (restaurants), and area franchises (a geographic region is licensed to new franchisee to subfranchise to others). Franchisors are required to comply with the Federal Trade Commission's Franchise Rule, which requires franchisors to make presale disclosure nationwide to prospective franchisees. Registration of franchises falls under state law modeled on the Uniform Franchise Offering Circular, which requires franchisors to make specific presale disclosures to prospective franchisees, including their balance sheets, income statements for preceding three years, terms and conditions of the franchise agreement, territory restrictions, and the like.

Equity Partnership

An equity partnership involves a company's purchase of stock (resulting in a less than controlling interest) in another company or a two-way exchange of stock by the two companies. It often is referred to as a *partnership* because of the equity ownership exchanged. Equity partnerships commonly are used in purchaser–supplier relationships, technology development, marketing alliances, and in situations in which a larger firm makes an investment in a smaller firm to ensure its continued financial viability. In exchange for an equity investment, a firm normally receives a seat on the board of directors and possibly an option to buy a controlling interest in the company. The equity partnership may be preferred when there is a need to have a long-term or close strategic relationship, to preempt a competitor from making an alliance or acquisition, or as a prelude to an acquisition or merger.

Written Contract

The written contract is the simplest form of legal structure. This form is used most often with strategic alliances, because it maintains an "arms-length" or independent relationship between the parties to the contract. The contract normally stipulates such things as how the revenue is divided, the responsibilities of each party, the duration of the alliance, and confidentiality requirements. No separate business entity is established for legal or tax purposes. The written contract most often is used when the business alliance is expected to last less than three years, frequent close coordination is not required, capital investments are made independently by each party to the agreement, and the parties have had little previous contact.

Strategic and Operational Plans

Planning should precede deal-structuring activities. Too often, the parties to a proposed alliance get bogged down early in the process in such details as legal structure, control, ownership, and other deal-structuring issues. They spend insufficient energy in determining if the proposal makes good strategic and operational sense in terms of the participants' financial and nonfinancial objectives. Before any deal-structuring issues are addressed, the prospective parties must agree on the basic strategic direction and purpose of the alliance as defined in the alliance's strategic plan, as well as the financial and nonfinancial goals established in the operation's plan.

The strategic plan identifies the primary purpose or mission of the business alliance; communicates specific quantifiable targets, such as financial returns or market share and milestones; and analyzes the business alliance's strengths and weaknesses and opportunities and threats relative to the competition. The purpose of a business alliance could take various forms, as diverse as R&D, cross-selling the partners' products, or jointly developing an oil field. The roles and responsibilities of each partner in conducting the day-to-day operations of the business alliance are stipulated in an operations plan. Teams representing all parties to the alliance should be involved from the outset of the discussions in developing both a strategic and operations plan for the venture. The operations plan (i.e., annual budget) should reflect the specific needs of the proposed business alliance. The operations plan should be written by those responsible for implementing the plan. The operations plan is typically a one-year plan that outlines for managers what is to be accomplished, when it is to be accomplished, and what resources are required.

Resolving Business Alliance Deal-Structuring Issues

Generally speaking, the purpose of deal structuring in a business alliance is to allocate fairly risks, rewards, resource requirements, and responsibilities among participants. The formation of a successful alliance requires that a series of issues be resolved before signing an alliance agreement. Table 14–3 summarizes the key issues and related

Table 14–3 Business Alliance Deal-Structuring Issues

Issue	Key Questions
Scope	What products are included and what are excluded? Who receives rights to distribute, manufacture, acquire, or license technology or purchase future products or technology?
Duration	How long is the alliance expected to exist?
Legal form	What is the appropriate legal structure: stand-alone entity or contractual?
Governance	How are the interests of the parents to be protected? Who is responsible for specific accomplishments?
Control	How are strategic decisions to be addressed? How are day-to-day operational decisions to be handled?
Resource contributions and ownership determination	Who contributes what and in what form? Cash? Assets? Guarantees or loans? Technology, including patents, trademarks, copyrights, and proprietary knowledge? How are contributions to be valued? How is ownership determined?
Financing ongoing capital requirements	What happens if additional cash is needed?
Distribution	How are profits and losses allocated? How are dividends determined?
Performance criteria	How is performance to the plan measured and monitored?
Dispute resolution	How are disagreements resolved?
Revision	How will the agreement be modified?
Termination	What are the guidelines for termination? Who owns the assets on termination? What are the rights of the parties to continue the alliance activities after termination?
Transfer of interests	How are ownership interests to be transferred? What restrictions are placed on the transfer of interests? How will new alliance participants be handled? Will there be rights of first refusal, drag-along, tag-along, or put provisions?
Tax	Who receives tax benefits?
Management or organization	How is the alliance to be managed?
Confidential information	How is confidential information handled? How are employees and customers of the parent firms protected?
Regulatory Restrictions and notifications	What licenses are required? What regulations need to be satisfied? What agencies need to be notified?

questions that need to be addressed as part of the business alliance deal-structuring process. This section discusses how these issues most often are resolved. For an excellent discussion of deal structuring in this context, see Ebin (1998), Freeman and Stephens (1994), Fusaro (1995), and Lorange and Roos (1992).

Scope

A basic question in setting up a business alliance involves which products specifically are included and excluded from the business alliance. This question deals with defining the scope of the business alliance. Scope outlines how broadly the alliance will be applied in pursuing its purpose. For example, an alliance whose purpose is to commercialize products developed by the partners could be broadly or narrowly defined in specifying what products or services are to be offered, to whom, in what geographic areas, and for what time period. Failure to define scope adequately can lead to situations in which the alliance may be competing with the products or services offered by the parent firms. Products developed for one purpose may prove to have other applications in the future. With respect to both current and future products, the alliance agreement should identify who receives the rights to market or distribute products, manufacture products, acquire or license technology, or purchase products from the venture.

In certain types of alliances, intellectual property may play a very important role. It is common for a share in the intangible benefits of the alliance, such as rights to new developments of intellectual property, to be more important to an alliance participant than its share of the alliance's profits. What started out as a symbiotic marketing relationship between two pharmaceutical powerhouses, Johnson & Johnson and Amgen, deteriorated into a highly contentious feud. The failure to properly define which parties would have the right to sell certain drugs for certain applications and future drugs that may have been developed as a result of the alliance laid the groundwork for a lengthy legal battle between these two corporations.

Duration

The participants need to agree on how long the business alliance is to remain in force. Participant expectations must be compatible. The expected longevity of the alliance is also an important determinant in the choice of a legal form. For example, the corporate structure more readily provides for a continuous life than a partnership structure because of its greater ease of transferring ownership interests. There is conflicting evidence on how long most business alliances actually last. Mercer Management Consulting, in ongoing research, concludes that most JVs last only about three years (Lajoux, 1998), whereas Booz-Allen and Hamilton (1993) reported an average life span of seven years. The critical point is that most business alliances have a finite life, corresponding to the time required to achieve their original strategic objectives.

Legal Form

Businesses that are growth oriented or intend to eventually go public through an IPO generally become a C corporation due to its financing flexibility, unlimited life, continuity of ownership, and ability to combine on a tax-free basis with other firms. With certain exceptions concerning frequency, firms may convert from one legal structure to a C corporation before going public. The nature of the business greatly influences the legal form chosen. See Table 14–4.

Table 14–4   Key Factors Affecting Choice of Legal Entity

Determining Factors: Businesses With	Should Select
High liability risks	C corporation, LLP, or LLC
Large capital or financing requirements	C corporation
Desire for continuity of existence	C corporation
Desire for managerial autonomy	C corporation
Desire for growth through M&A	C corporation
Owners who are also active participants	LLCs
Foreign corporate investors	LLCs
Desire for allocation of investments, profits, losses, and operating responsibilities among owners	LLCs and LLPs
Project focus or expected limited existence	LLPs
Owners who want to remain inactive	LLPs and C corporations
Large marketing expenses	Franchise
Strategies that are easily replicated	Franchise
Close coordination among participants not required	Written "arms length" agreement
Low risk and low capital requirements	Sole proprietorship or partnership

Governance

In the context of a business alliance, *governance* may be defined broadly as an oversight function providing for efficient, informed communication between two or more parent companies. The primary responsibilities of this oversight function are to protect the interests of the corporate parents, approve changes to strategy and annual operating plans, allocate resources needed to make the alliance succeed, and arbitrate conflicts among lower levels of management. Historically, governance of business alliances has followed either a quasi-corporate or quasi-project approach. For example, the oil industry traditionally has managed alliances by establishing a board of directors to provide oversight of managers and protect the interests of nonoperating owners. In contrast, in the pharmaceutical and automotive industries, where nonequity alliances are common, firms treat governance like project management by creating a steering committee that allows all participants to comment on issues confronting the alliance. For highly complex alliances, governance may have to be implemented through multiple boards of directors, steering committees, operating committees, alliance managers, and project committees.

Resource Contributions and Ownership Determination

As part of the negotiation process, the participants must agree on a fair value for all tangible and intangible assets contributed to the business alliance. The valuation of partner contributions is important, in that it often provides the basis for determining ownership shares in the business alliance. The shares of the corporation or the interests in the partnership are distributed among the owners in accordance with the value contributed by each participant. The partner with the largest risk, the largest contributor of cash, or the person who contributes critical tangible or intangible assets generally is given the greatest equity share in a JV.

It is relatively easy to value tangible or "hard" contributions such as cash, promissory cash commitments, contingent commitments, stock of existing corporations, and assets and liabilities associated with an ongoing business in terms of actual dollars or their present values. A party contributing "hard" assets, such as a production facility, may want the contribution valued in terms of the value of increased production rather than its replacement cost or lease value. The contribution of a fully operational, modern facility to a venture interested in being first to market with a particular product may provide far greater value than if the venture attempted to build a new facility because of the delay inherent in making the facility fully operational.

In contrast, intangible or "soft" or "in-kind" contributions such as skills, knowledge, services, patents, licenses, brand names, and technology are often much more difficult to value. Partners providing such services may be compensated by having the business alliance pay a market-based royalty or fee for such services. If the royalties or fees paid by the alliance are below standard market prices for comparable services, the difference between the market price and what the alliance actually is paying may become taxable income to the alliance. Alternatively, contributors of intellectual property may be compensated by receiving rights to future patents or technologies developed by the alliance. Participants in the business alliance contributing brand identities, which facilitate the alliance's entry into a particular market, may require assurances that they can purchase a certain amount of the product or service, at a guaranteed price, for a specific time period. See Exhibit 14–1 for an illustration of how the distribution of ownership between General Electric and Vivendi Universal Entertainment may have been determined in the formation of NBC Universal.

Exhibit 14–1 Determining Ownership Distribution in a Joint Venture

In 2003, Vivendi Universal Entertainment (VUE) contributed film and television assets valued at $14 billion to create NBC Universal, a joint venture with NBC, General Electric's (GE) wholly owned TV subsidiary. NBC Universal was valued at $42 billion at closing. NBC Universal's EBITDA was estimated to be $3 billion, of which GE contributed two thirds and VUE accounted for the remaining one third. EBITDA multiples for recent transactions involving TV media firms averaged 14 times EBITDA at that time. GE provided VUE an option to buy $4.0 billion in GE stock, assumed $1.6 in VUE debt, and paid the remainder of the $14 billion purchase price in the form of NBC Universal stock. At closing, VUE converted the option to buy GE stock into $4 billion in cash. GE owned 80 percent of NBC Universal and VUE 20 percent. How might this distribution have been determined?

Solution

Step 1. Estimate the total value of the joint venture.

$$\$3 \text{ billion} \times 14 = \$42 \text{ billion}$$

Step 2. Estimate the value of assets contributed by each partner. Reflecting the relative contribution of each partner to EBITDA (⅔ from GE, ⅓ from VUE), GE's contributed assets were valued at $28 billion (i.e., ⅔ of $42 billion) and VUE's at $14 billion (i.e., ⅓ of $42 billion).

Step 3. Determine the form of payment.

$ 4.0 billion (GE stock)

$ 1.6 billion (assumed Vivendi debt)

$ 8.4 billion (value of VUE's equity position in NBC Universal = $14 − $4.0 − $1.6)

$14.0 billion (purchase price paid by GE to Vivendi for VUE assets)

Step 4. Determine ownership distribution. At closing, Vivendi chose to receive a cash infusion of $5.6 billion (i.e., $4 billion in cash in lieu of GE stock + $1.6 billion in assumed VUE debt). Therefore,

$$\text{VUE's ownership of NBC Universal} = \frac{\$14 \text{ billion} - \$5.6 \text{ billion}}{\$42 \text{ billion}}$$

$$= \frac{\$8.4 \text{ billion}}{\$43 \text{ billion}}$$

$$= 0.2$$

$$\text{GE's ownership of NBC Universal} = 1 - 0.2 = 0.8$$

Financing Ongoing Capital Requirements

The business alliance may finance future capital requirements that cannot be financed out of operating cash flow by calling on the participants to make a capital contribution, issuing additional equity or partnership interests, or borrowing. Cingular's 2004 purchase of AT&T Wireless in an all-cash offer totaling $41 billion (the largest all-cash purchase on record) resulted in SBC and Bell Atlantic (coowners of the Cingular JV) contributing 60 percent and 40 percent of the purchase price, respectively, to the joint venture to fund the acquisition. Their percentage equity contributions reflected their ownership shares of the joint venture.

If it is decided that the alliance should be able to borrow, the participants must agree on an appropriate financial structure for the enterprise. *Financial structure* refers to the amount of equity that will be contributed to the business alliance and how much debt it will carry. Alliances established through a written contract obviate the need for such a financing decision, because each party to the contract finances its own financial commitments to the alliance. Because of their more predictable cash flows, project-based JVs, particularly those that create a separate corporation, sometimes sell equity directly to the public or though a private placement.

Owner or Partner Financing

The equity owners or partners may agree to make contributions of capital in addition to their initial investments in the enterprise. The contributions usually are made in direct proportion to their equity or partnership interests. If one party chooses not to make a capital contribution, the ownership interests of all the parties are adjusted to reflect the changes in their cumulative capital contributions. This adjustment results in an increase in the ownership interests of those making the contribution and a reduction in the interests of those not making contributions.

Equity and Debt Financing

JVs formed as a corporation may issue different classes of either common or preferred stock. JVs established as partnerships raise capital through the issuance of limited partnership units to investors, with the sponsoring firms becoming general partners. An LLC structure may be necessary when one of the owners is a foreign investor. When a larger company aligns with a smaller company, it may make a small equity investment in the smaller firm to ensure it remains solvent or to benefit from potential equity appreciation. Such investments often include an option to purchase the remainder of the shares, or at least a controlling interest, at a predetermined price if the smaller firm or the JV satisfies certain financial targets. Non-project-related alliances or alliances without financial track records often find it very difficult to borrow. Banks and insurance companies generally require loan guarantees from the participating owners. Such guarantees give lenders recourse to the participating owners in the event the alliance fails to repay its debt.

Control

Control is distinguishable from ownership by the use of agreements among investors or voting rights or by issuing different classes of shares. The most successful JVs are those in which one party is responsible for most routine management decisions, with the other parties participating in decision making only when the issue is fundamental to the success of the business alliance. The business alliance agreement must define what issues are to be considered fundamental to the alliance and address how they are to be resolved, either by majority votes or by veto rights given to one or more of the parties. Whichever owner is responsible for the results of the alliance will want operational control. Operational control should be placed with the owner best able to manage the JV. In some cases, the partner with operational control could be a minority owner.

The owner who has the largest equity share but not operational control as well is likely to insist on being involved in the operation of the business alliance by having a seat on the board of directors or steering committee. The owner also may insist on having veto rights over issues it views as fundamental to the success of the alliance. These issues often include changes in the alliance's purpose and scope, overall strategy, capital expenditures over a certain amount of money, key management promotions, salary increases applying to the general employee population, the amount and timing of dividend payments, buyout conditions, and acquisitions or divestitures.

Distribution Issues

Distribution issues relate to dividend policies and how profits and losses are allocated among the owners. The dividend policy determines the cash return each partner should receive. How the cash flows of the venture will be divided generally depends on the initial equity contribution of each partner, ongoing equity contributions, and noncash contributions in the form of technical and managerial resources. Allocation of profits and losses normally follow directly from the allocation of shares or partnership interests. When the profits flow from intellectual property rights contributed by one of the parties, royalties or payments for expertise may be used to compensate the party contributing the property rights. When profits are attributable to distribution or marketing efforts of a partner, fees and commission can be used to compensate the partners. Similarly, rental payments can be used to allocate profits attributable to specific equipment or facilities contributed by a partner.

Performance Criteria

The lack of adequate performance measurement criteria can result in significant disputes among the partners and eventually contribute to the termination of the venture. In early 2000, the Carlyle Group took a 20-percent stake in French paper products manufacturer Otor for $54 million. The shareholder agreement included provisions for Carlyle to assume majority control of the business should Otor fail to meet certain profitability targets. Two years later, incumbent management, which remained with the firm after the investment, resisted Carlyle's efforts to take control after claiming that the targets had not been met. After more than three years in the French court system, Carlyle finally received ownership of 80 percent of the firm.

Performance criteria should be both measurable and simple enough to be understood and used by the partners and managers at all levels. Performance criteria should be spelled out clearly in the business alliance agreement. Nonfinancial performance measures should be linked to financial return drivers. For example, factors such as market share, consistent product quality, and customer service may be critical to success in the marketplace. In licensing arrangements, the licensor should require that the licensee provide a forecast of unit sales and the value contributed by the license in such sales to provide a basis for auditing the licensee royalty payments.

The balanced scorecard technique may be applied to measuring alliance performance by having the partners agree on a small number (i.e., 5–10) of relevant indicators. The indicators should include financial and nonfinancial, short- and long-term, and internal and customer-focused measures. Examples of performance indicators include return on investment, operating cash flow, profit margins, asset turnover, market share, on-time delivery, and customer satisfaction survey results. Managers will ignore performance indicators if their compensation is not linked to their actual performance against these measures. The top alliance managers should be evaluated against the full list of balanced scorecard performance measures. The performance of lower-level managers should be evaluated only against those measures over which they have some degree of control.

Dispute Resolution

No matter how well the participants draft the venture agreement, disputes between parties to the agreement will arise. There are several ways to resolve such disputes. One is a ***choice of law provision*** in the alliance agreement, indicating which state's or country's laws have jurisdiction in settling disputes. This provision should be drafted with an understanding of the likely outcome of litigation in any of the participants' home countries or states and the attitude of these countries' or states' courts in enforcing choice of law provisions in the JV agreements.

In international JVs, the choice of common law or civil law countries for settling disputes can have profoundly different outcomes. Common law countries, found typically in North America and western Europe, rely on case law (i.e., resolutions of prior disputes) for guidance in resolving current disputes. In contrast, civil law countries, located primarily in Asia, do not rely on case law but allow magistrates to apply their interpretation of existing statutes to resolve current disputes. Consequently, the outcome of certain types of disputes may be less predictable in civil rather than common law countries, which rely heavily on historical precedents.

Another important clause is the definition of what constitutes a deadlock or impasse when a disagreement arises. This clause should include a statement of what events trigger dispute-resolution procedures. Care should be taken not to define the events triggering dispute-resolution procedures so narrowly that minor disagreements are subject to the dispute mechanism. Finally, an ***arbitration clause*** usually is used to address major disagreements. Such a clause should define the type of dispute subject to arbitration and how the arbitrator will be selected.

Revision

No matter how well conceived the business alliance was at the time of formation, changing circumstances and partner objectives may prompt a need to revise the objectives of the business alliance. If one of the parties to the agreement wishes to withdraw, the participants should have agreed in advance how the withdrawing party's ownership interest would be divided among the remaining parties. Moreover, a product or technology may be developed that was not foreseen when the alliance first was conceived. The alliance agreement should indicate that the rights to manufacture and distribute the product or technology might be purchased by a specific alliance participant. If agreement cannot be reached on revising the original agreement, it may be necessary to terminate the enterprise. The events triggering dissolution usually are spelled out in the *deadlock clause.*

Termination

A business alliance may be terminated as a result of the completion of a project, successful operations resulting in merger of the partners, diverging strategic objectives of the partners, and failure of the alliance to achieve stated objectives. Termination provisions in the alliance agreement should include buyout clauses enabling one party to purchase another's ownership interests, prices of the buyout, and how assets and liabilities are to be divided if the venture fails or the partners elect to dissolve the operation. In some instances, a JV may convert to a simple licensing arrangement. Consequently, the partner may disengage from the JV without losing all benefits by purchasing rights to the product or technology.

Transfer of Interests

JV and alliance agreements often limit how and to whom parties to the agreements can transfer their interests. This is justified by noting that each party entered the agreement with the understanding of who its partners would be. In agreements that permit transfers under certain conditions, the partners or the JV itself may have *right of first refusal* (i.e., the party wishing to leave the JV first must offer its interests to other participants in the JV). Parties to the agreement may have the right to "put" or sell their interests to the venture, and the venture may have a call option or right to purchase such interests. There also may be "tag-along" and "drag-along" provisions, which have the effect of a third-party purchaser acquiring not only the interest of the JV party whose interest it seeks to acquire but also the interests of other parties as well. A *drag-along* provision *requires* a party not otherwise interested in selling its ownership interest to the third party to do so. A *tag-along* provision gives a party to the alliance, who was not originally targeted by the third party, the *option* to join the targeted party in conveying its interest to the third party.

Buyout clauses in alliances that give one party an option to sell its share of the partnership to the other at a fixed price can backfire. Examples abound. AOL Time Warner had to pay a German media firm $6.75 billion for its half of AOL Europe, four times its estimated value at the time. The best alliance agreements avoid clauses such as fixed or minimum buyout prices, short payment periods, and strict payment options, such as cash only, to avoid giving substantial leverage to one party over the other. In early 2005, General Motors and Fiat agreed to dissolve their five-year partnership after GM agreed to pay Fiat $2 billion in cash to avoid having to exercise a put option to buy the financially weak Fiat Auto.

Taxes

Although tax considerations should never drive the transaction, failure to explore their different implications can have painful financial consequences for all parties involved. As is true for a merger, the primary tax concerns of the JV partners are to avoid the recognition of taxable gains on the formation of the venture and minimize taxes on the distribution of its earnings. In addition to the double taxation of dividends discussed earlier, the corporate structure may have other adverse tax consequences. If the partner owns less than 80 percent of the alliance, its share of the alliance's results cannot be included in its consolidated income tax return. This has two effects. First, when earnings are distributed, they are subject to an intercorporate dividend tax, which can be 7 percent if the partner's ownership interest in the venture is 20 percent or more. Second, losses of the business alliance cannot be used to offset other income earned by the participant (Tillinghast, 1998). For tax purposes, the preferred alternative to a corporate legal structure is to use a pass-through legal structure, such as a limited liability company or partnership.

A partnership can be structured in such a way that some partners receive a larger share of the profits, whereas others receive a larger share of the losses. This flexibility in tax planning is an important factor stimulating the use of partnerships and LLCs. These entities can allocate to each JV partner a portion of a particular class of revenue, income, gain, loss, or expense. These special allocations can be made in the documents governing the creation of the partnership or LLC. Thus, partners or LLC members need not share the results of the venture on a pro-rata basis. When one of the partners contributes technology, patent rights, or other property to the JV, the contribution may be structured so that the partner receives equity in exchange for the contribution. Otherwise, it will be viewed by the IRS as an attempt to avoid making cash contributions and treated as taxable income to the JV.

Services provided to the JV, such as accounting, auditing, legal, human resource, and treasury services, are not viewed by the IRS as being "at risk" if the JV fails. The JV should pay prevailing market fees for such services. Services provided to the JV in return for equity may be seen as taxable to the JV by the IRS if such services are not truly "at risk."

Management and Organizational Issues

Before a business alliance agreement is signed, the partners must decide what type of organizational structure provides the most effective management and leadership.

Steering or Joint Management Committee

Control of business alliances most often is accomplished through a steering committee. The steering committee is the ultimate authority for ensuring that the venture stays focused on the strategic objectives agreed to by the partners. To maintain good communication, coordination, and teamwork, the committee should meet at least monthly. The committee should provide operations managers with sufficient autonomy so they can take responsibility for their actions and be rewarded for their initiative.

Methods of Dividing Ownership and Control

A common method of control is the *majority–minority* framework, which relies on identifying a clearly dominant partner, usually the one having at least a 50.1 percent ownership stake. In this scenario, the equity, control, and distribution of rewards reflect the majority–minority relationship. This type of structure tends to promote the ability to make rapid midcourse corrections and clearly defines who is in charge. This framework is most appropriate for high-risk ventures where quick decisions often are required. The major disadvantage of this approach is that the minority partner may feel powerless and become passive or alienated.

Another method of control is the *equal division of power* framework, which usually means that equity is split equally. This assumes that the initial contribution, distribution, decision making, and control are split equally. This approach helps keep the partners actively engaged in the management of the venture. It is best suited for partners sharing a strong common vision for the venture and possessing similar corporate cultures. However, the approach can lead to deadlocks and the eventual dissolution of the alliance.

Under the *majority rules* framework, the equity distribution may involve three partners. Two of the partners have large equal shares, whereas the third partner may have less than 10 percent. The minority partner is used to break deadlocks. This approach enables the primary partners to remain actively engaged in the enterprise without stalemating the decision-making process.

In the *multiple party* framework, no partner has control. Instead, control resides with the management of the venture. Consequently, decision making can be nimble and made by those that best understand the issues. This framework is well suited for international ventures, where a country's laws may prohibit a foreign firm from having a controlling interest in a domestic firm. In this instance, it is commonplace for a domestic company to own the majority of the equity but for the operational control of the venture to reside with the foreign partner. In addition to a proportional split of the dividends paid, the foreign company may receive additional payments in the form of management fees and bonuses (Armstrong and Hagel, 1997).

Regulatory Restrictions and Notifications

From an antitrust perspective, the Department of Justice historically looked on business alliances far more favorably than mergers or acquisitions. Nonetheless, JVs may be subject to Hart–Scott–Rodino filing requirements, because the parties to the JV are viewed as acquirers and the JV itself is viewed as a target. For JVs between competitors to be acceptable to regulators, competitors should be able to do something together that they could not do alone.

In general, competitors can be relatively confident that a partnership will be acceptable to regulators if, in combination, they control no more than 20 percent of the market. Project-oriented ventures are looked at most favorably. Collaborative research is encouraged, particularly when the research is shared among all the parties to the alliance. Alliances among competitors are likely to spark a review by the regulators, because they have the potential to result in price fixing and dividing up the market. See Chapter 2 for a more detailed discussion of regulations covering business combinations. Case Study 14–3 illustrates many of the previously discussed deal-structuring issues.

Case Study 14–3 Pixar and Disney Part Company

The announcement on February 5, 2004, of the end of the wildly successful partnership between Walt Disney Company ("Disney") and Pixar Animation Studios ("Pixar") rocked the investment and entertainment world. While the partnership continued until the end of 2005, the split-up underscores the nature of the rifts that can develop in business alliances of all types. The dissolution of the partnership ends a relationship in existence since 1995 in which Disney produced and distributed the highly popular films created by Pixar. Under the terms of the original partnership agreement, the two firms cofinanced each film and split the profits evenly. Moreover, Disney received 12.5 percent of film revenues for distributing the films. Negotiations to renew the partnership after 2005 foundered on Pixar's desire to get a greater share of the partnership's profits. Disney CEO Michael Eisner refused to accept a significant reduction in distribution fees and film royalties; while Steve Jobs, Pixar's CEO, criticized Disney's creative capabilities and noted that marketing alone does not make a poor film successful.

After 10 months of talks between Disney and Pixar, Disney rejected a deal that would have required it to earn substantially less from future Pixar releases. Disney also would have had to relinquish potentially lucrative copyrights to existing films such as *Toy Story* and *Finding Nemo*. Disney shares immediately fell by almost 2 percent on the news of the announcement, while Pixar's shares skyrocketed almost 4 percent by the end of the day. Pixar contributed more than 50 percent of Disney Studio's operating profits, and Disney Studios accounted for about one fourth of Disney's total operating profits. While Disney now faces Pixar as a competitor, it retains the rights to make video and theatrical sequels and TV shows to the movies covered by the current partnership agreement. However, while Disney does retain the right to make sequels to Pixar films, it does not own the underlying technology and must recreate the millions of lines of computer code for each character.

The key challenge for Disney will be to fill the creative vacuum left by the loss of Pixar writers and animators. Disney is particularly vulnerable in that it has severely cut back its own feature animation department and stumbled in recent years with a variety of box office duds (e.g., *Treasure Planet*). Reflecting concern that Disney would not be able to compete with Pixar, bond-rating service, Fitch Ratings suggested a possible downgrade of Disney debt. Pixar announced that it was seeking another production studio. Immediately following this announcement, Sony and others approached Pixar with proposals to collaborate in making animated films.

Epilogue

In early 2006, Pixar agreed to be acquired by Disney. See Case Study 4–2 in Chapter 4 for a detailed discussion of this transaction.

Discussion Questions

1. In your opinion, what were the motivations for forming the Disney-Pixar partnership in 1995? Which partner do you believe had the greatest leverage in these negotiations? Explain your answer.
2. What happened since 1995 that might have contributed to the breakup? (Hint: Consider partner objectives, personalities of Steve Jobs and Michael Eisner, perceived relative contribution, and Disney's in-house capabilities.)
3. How does the dissolution of the partnership leave Disney vulnerable? What could Disney have done to protect itself from these vulnerabilities in the original negotiations? (Hint: Consider scope of the agreement, management and control, dispute resolution mechanisms, valuation of tangible and intangible assets, ownership of partnership assets following dissolution, and performance criteria.)
4. What does the reaction of the stock market and credit rating agencies tell you about how investors value the contribution of the two partners to the partnership? Do you think investors may have overreacted? Explain your answer.

Solutions to these questions are found in the Online Instructor's Manual for this book.

Empirical Findings

Abnormal Returns

There is empirical evidence that JVs and strategic alliances create value for their participants (see Table 14–5). Abnormal returns (i.e., those in excess of what would have been predicted by the capital asset pricing model) average about 1.5 percent around the announcement date. Participants in horizontal relationships (i.e., those involving partners in the same industry) tend to share equally in the wealth creation. However, for vertical JVs, suppliers experienced a greater portion of the wealth created (Johnson and Houston, 2000). Moreover, the increase in wealth was much greater for horizontal alliances involving the transfer of technical knowledge than for nontechnical alliances (Chan, Kensinger, Keown, and Martin, 1997; Das, Sen, and Sengupta, 1998). Firms with greater alliance experience enjoy a greater likelihood of success and greater wealth creation than those with little experience (Kale, Dyer, and Singh, 2002). Finally, Marciukaityte, Roskelley, and Wang (2009) found, in a study of financial services firms spanning from 1986 to 2003, that strategic alliances most often represent the final form of cooperation between partners rather than representing a prelude to a more formal arrangement, such as a joint venture corporation or a merger. However, the authors did find that investors react more favorably around the announcement date if they believe the partners will eventually merge.

Chang (2008) investigated the impact of alliances on customers, suppliers, and rivals. He found evidence that strategic alliances can have a salutary effect on the share prices of their suppliers and customers and a negative impact on the share prices of competitors. This is particularly true of alliances created to share technologies or develop new technical capabilities, where suppliers benefit from increased sales to the alliance and customers benefit from using the enhanced technology developed by the alliance in their products. Lost sales by competitors result in reduced future earnings and a deteriorating share price.

The Growing Role of Business Alliances

The average large company, which may have had no alliances in 1990, now has more than 30 (Kalmbach and Roussel, 1999). Robinson (2002a) reported that the number of merger transactions per year between 1985 through 1989 averaged almost four times the number of alliances. Between 1990 and 1995, the average annual rate at which

Table 14–5   Abnormal Returns to Allaince Participants around Announcement Dates

Empirical Study	Abnormal (Excess) Return
McConnell and Nantell (1985): 136 JVs, 1972–1979	2.15%
Woolridge and Snow (1990): 767 JVs, 1972–1987	2.45%
Koh and Venkatraman (1991): 239 technology firms in JVs, 1972–1986	0.87%
Chan et al. (1997): 345 strategic alliances, 1983–1992	0.64% for both horizontal and nonhorizontal alliances 3.54% for horizontal alliances involving technical knowledge transfer
Das et al. (1998): 119 strategic alliances, 1987–1991	1% for technology transfer alliances
Johnson and Houston (2000): 191 JVs, 1991–1995	1.67%
Kale et al. (2002): 1,572 strategic allliances, 1988–1997	1.35% for firms with significant alliance experience; otherwise .18%

alliances were formed accelerated to almost twice the rate of M&A transactions. The sharp acceleration in alliance formation in part reflected a loosening of antitrust regulatory policies that extended the encouragement of alliances for R&D activities to joint production operations.

Despite rapid growth, there is evidence that most companies have yet to develop the skill to implement alliances successfully. The Kalmbach and Roussel study indicates that 61 percent of the alliances are viewed as either disappointments or outright failures. This figure substantiates earlier findings by Robert Spekman of the Darden Graduate School of Business Administration that 60 percent of all ventures fail to meet expectations (Ellis, 1996). Klein (2004) reports that 55 percent of alliances fall apart within three years of their formation. These studies make no allowance for different levels of experience in forming and managing alliances among the firms in their samples. Cumulative experience seems to be an important factor in increasing the likelihood that an alliance will meet expectations. According to a Booz-Allen survey of 700 alliances (Booz-Allen and Hamilton, 1993), financial returns on investment are directly related to a company's experience in forming and managing business alliances. Companies with one or two alliances in place tended to earn a 10 percent average return on investment as compared with 15 percent for those with three to five, 17 percent for those with six to eight, and 20 percent for those with nine or more.

Things to Remember

Business alliances may represent attractive alternatives to M&As. The motivations for business alliances can include risk sharing, gaining access to new markets, accelerating the introduction of new products, technology sharing, globalization, a desire to acquire (or exit) a business, and the perception that they are often more acceptable to regulators than acquisitions or mergers.

Business alliances may assume a variety of legal structures: corporate, limited liability company, partnership, franchise, equity partnership, or written contract. Corporate legal structures include a C-type and an S-type structure. Although the C corporate structure is subject to double taxation, it does provide for centralized management, continuity of ownership, ease of raising capital, and limited liability. Limited liability companies and partnerships frequently are used as an alternative to the corporate structure because of their greater flexibility in allocating gains and losses and their more favorable tax treatment. The written contract is the simplest legal structure and most often is used in strategic alliances.

Deal structuring in the context of a business alliance concerns the fair allocation of risks, rewards, resource requirements, and responsibilities among participants. Key issues that must be resolved include the alliance's scope, duration, legal form, governance, and control mechanism. The valuation of resource contributions ultimately determines ownership interests. How profits and losses will be distributed and how performance will be measured also must be determined. Alliance agreements also must be flexible enough to be revised when necessary and contain mechanisms for breaking deadlocks, transferring ownership interests, and dealing with the potential for termination.

Empirical studies suggest that business alliances contribute to shareholder value and are likely to become increasingly popular in the future. Studies suggest that alliances formed by partners in the same industry are more likely to create value than those that are not. Partners in such horizontal alliances are more likely to share equally in the benefits than parties to vertical alliances between a customer and a supplier. In such arrangements, studies suggest that suppliers tend to experience a disproportionate amount of the benefit. Finally, the greatest value creation seems to occur for horizontal alliances that result in a technology or knowledge transfer among the parties to the alliance. Nonetheless, the success rate of business alliances in terms of meeting participants' expectations does not seem to be materially different from that of M&As.

Chapter Discussion Questions

14–1. Under what circumstances does a business alliance represent an attractive alternative to a merger or acquisition?

14–2. Compare and contrast a corporate and partnership legal structure.

14–3. What are the primary motives for creating a business alliance? How do they differ from the motives for a merger or acquisition?

14–4. What factors are critical to the success of a business alliance?

14–5. Why is a handshake agreement a potentially dangerous form of business alliance? Are there any circumstances under which such an agreement may be appropriate?

14–6. What is a limited liability company? What are its advantages and disadvantages?

14–7. Why is defining the scope of a business alliance important?

14–8. Discuss ways of valuing tangible and intangible contributions to a JV.

14–9. What are the advantages and disadvantages of the various organizational structures that could be used to manage a business alliance?

14–10. What are the common reasons for the termination of a business alliance?

14–11. In 2005, Google invested $1 billion for a 5 percent stake in Time Warner's America Online unit as part of a partnership that expands the firm's existing search engine deal to include collaboration on advertising, instant messaging, and video. Under the deal, Google would have the usual customary rights afforded a minority investor. What rights or terms do you believe Google would have negotiated in this transaction? What rights do you believe Time Warner might want? Be specific.

14–12. In late 2004, Conoco Phillips (Conoco) announced the purchase of 7.6 percent of Lukoil's (a largely government-owned Russian oil and gas company) stock for $2.36 billion during a government auction of Lukoil's stock. Conoco would have one seat on Lukoil's board. As a minority investor, how could Conoco protect its interests?

14–13. In 1999, Johnson & Johnson (J&J) sued Amgen over their 14-year alliance to sell a blood-enhancing treatment called erythropoietin. The relationship had begun in the mid-1980s with J&J helping commercialize Amgen's blood-enhancing treatment, but the partners ended up squabbling over sales rights and a spin-off drug. The companies could not agree on future products for the JV. Amgen won the right in arbitration to sell a chemically similar medicine that can be taken weekly rather than daily. Arbitrators ruled that the new formulation was different enough to fall outside the licensing pact between Amgen and J&J. What could these companies have done before forming the alliance to have mitigated the problems that arose after the alliance was formed? Why do you believe they may have avoided addressing these issues at the outset?

14-14. In late 1999, General Motors (GM), the world's largest auto manufacturer, agreed to purchase 20 percent of Japan's Fuji Heavy Industries, Ltd., the manufacturer of Subaru vehicles, for $1.4 billion. Why do you believe that initially General Motors may have wanted to limit its investment to 20 percent?

14-15. Through its alliance with Best Buy, Microsoft is selling its products—including Microsoft Network (MSN) Internet access services and hand-held devices such as digital telephones, hand-held organizers, and WebTV that connect to the Web—through kiosks in Best Buy's 354 stores nationwide. In exchange, Microsoft has invested $200 million in Best Buy. What were the motivations for this strategic alliance?

Answers to these Chapter Discussion Questions are available in the Online Instructor's Manual for instructors using this book.

Chapter Business Cases

Case Study 14–4. SABMiller in Joint Venture with Molson Coors

On October 10, 2007, SABMiller (SAB) and Molson Coors (Coors) agreed to combine their U.S. brewing operations into a joint venture corporation. The stated objective was to create a rival capable of competing with Anheuser-Busch, the maker of Budweiser beer. SAB and Coors, the second and third largest breweries, respectively, in the United States in terms of market share, would have equal voting rights in the newly formed entity. Each firm would have five representatives on the board. In terms of ownership, SAB, the larger of the two in terms of sales and profits, would have a 58-percent stake and Coors a 42-percent position. The combined operations, named MillerCoors, would have about a 30 percent market share versus Anheuser's 48 percent. MillerCoors would have a full-year revenue of $6.6 billion and EBITDA of $842 million. Leo Kiely, chief executive at Coors, would be the chief executive officer of MillerCoors and Tom Long, head of the SAB business in the United States, would be president and chief commercial officer. Peter Coors, vice chairman of Coors, would be the chairman and Graham Mackey, SAB's chief executive officer, would be vice chairman of MillerCoors. Both Coors and SAB would continue to operate separate global businesses.

From its roots in South Africa, the former SAB PLC grew rapidly over the previous decade by expanding into fast growing economies such as China, Eastern Europe, and Latin America. SAB acquired Miller Brewing Company in 2002, but the U.S. business failed to gain significant market share in competing with Anheuser-Busch's pervasive brand awareness and distribution strength. Molson Coors was formed by the 2005 merger of Colorado's Adolph Coors Co. and Canada's Molson Inc., both family-controlled companies. The families were unwilling to sell their entire companies to another firm. The JV allows them to keep some control. Molson Coors, with dual headquarters in Montreal and Denver, has major operations in Canada and Britain that would remain independent of SABMiller. Reflecting its larger market share, brand recognition, and negotiating clout with distributors, Anheuser-Busch has operating profit margins of 23 percent, double SAB's or Coors's margins. SAB is larger in terms of both revenue and profit than Coors.

The major U.S. breweries have been experiencing growing competition from wine, specialty beers, spirits, and imported beers. Spirits companies have raised the pressure on beer giants to merge by rolling out sweet cocktails and other drinks to lure younger consumers. Premixed bottled drinks such as Smirnoff Ice have seen sales triple in the last decade. The U.S. beer market is largely mature, with consumption growing at an annual rate of about 1.5 percent.

MillerCoors expects annual cost savings to reach $500 million by the third year of operation and be accretive for both parent firms by the second full year of combined operations. The cost savings result from streamlining production, reducing shipping distances between plants and distribution sites, and cutting corporate staff. Shipping costs represent a significant cost, given the nature of the product. By producing both firms' products in the eight plants geographically distributed across the midwestern and western United States, MillerCoors should realize significant savings in meeting customer demand for both products in the immediate proximity of each plant.

SAB and Coors hope to become one-stop shops for distributors, allowing them to save time and money by dealing with one company instead of two. About 60 percent of Miller's volume is distributed by wholesalers also selling Molson Coors brands. U.S. federal law dating back to the repeal of prohibition requires beer to be sold in many states through wholesalers. The resulting savings to distributors could increase Miller-Coors overall market share.

By combining their U.S. advertising budgets, MillerCoors expects to have more clout at the bargaining table with U.S. media outlets, enabling the combined firm to get lower prices and better sports marketing deals. Such deals are viewed as critical to marketing beer in the United States. MillerCoors will find it easier to negotiate for better placement for its ads and compete more effectively for ad rights to major sporting events. The two firms are also geographically complementary. Miller is strong in the Midwest, while Coors has large market share in the West.

Immediately following the joint venture announcement, Anheuser-Busch's CEO August A. Busch IV said in a message to employees that the brewer must capitalize on the significant transition confusion he predicted would occur when Miller and Molson Coors blend their U.S. operations. Such confusion, he predicted, would create great concern within the SABMiller/Coors field sales and wholesale organizations, as people attempt to determine if they will have a role in this new structure.

Discussion Questions

1. What tactics do you think Anheuser-Busch might employ to exploit the predicted confusion during the integration of the SABMiller and Coors operations?
2. How did the combination of the U.S. operations of SABMiller and MolsonCoors meet the needs of the two parties? Why was a JV viewed as preferable to a merger of the two firm's global operations?
3. How do you believe the ownership distribution for MillersCoors was determined?
4. Why do you believe that SAB and Coors agreed to equal board representation and voting rights in the new JV? What types of governance issues might arise in view of the governance structure of MillersCoors? What mechanisms might have been put in place by the partners prior to closing to resolve possible governance issues?

Solutions to these case study questions are found in the Online Instructor's Manual for instructors using this book.

Case Study 14–5. Coca-Cola and Procter & Gamble's Aborted Effort to Create a Global Joint Venture Company

Coca-Cola (Coke), arguably the world's best-known brand, manufactures and distributes Coca-Cola as well as 230 other products in 200 countries through the world's largest distribution system. Procter & Gamble (P&G) sells 300 brands to nearly 5 billion consumers in 140 countries and holds more food patents than the three largest U.S. food companies combined. Moreover, P&G has a substantial number of new food and beverage products under development. Both firms have been competing in the health and wellness segment of the food market for years. P&G spends about 5 percent of its annual sales, about $1.9 billion, on R&D and holds more than 27,000 patents. The firm employs about 6,000 scientists, including about 1,200 people with PhDs.

Both firms have extensive distribution systems. P&G uses a centralized selling and warehouse distribution system for servicing high-volume outlets, such as grocery store chains. With a warehouse distribution system, the retailer is responsible for in-store presentations of the brands, including shelving, display, and merchandising. The primary disadvantage of this type of distribution system is that it does not reach many smaller outlets cost effectively, resulting in many lost opportunities. In contrast, Coke uses three distinct systems. Direct store delivery consists of a network of independently operated bottlers, which bottle and deliver the product directly to the outlet. The bottler also is responsible for in-store merchandising. Coke's warehouse distribution is similar to P&G's and is used primarily to distribute Minute Maid products. Coke also sells beverage concentrates to distributors and food service outlets.

On February 21, 2001, Coca-Cola and Procter & Gamble announced, amid great fanfare, plans to create a stand-alone joint venture corporation focused on developing and marketing new juice and juice-based beverages as well as snacks on a global basis. The new company expected to benefit from Coca-Cola's worldwide distribution, merchandising, and customer marketing skills and P&G's R&D capabilities and wide range of popular brands. The new company would focus on the health and wellness segment of the food market. Less than nine months later, Coke and P&G released a one-sentence joint statement on September 21, 2001, that they could achieve better returns for their respective shareholders if they pursued this opportunity independently. Although it is unclear what may have derailed what initially had seemed to the potential partners like such a good idea, it is instructive to examine the initial rationale for the proposed joint effort.

Each parent would own 50 percent of the new company. Because of the businesses each partner was to contribute to the JV, the firm would have annual sales of $4 billion. The new firm would be an LLC, having its own board of directors consisting of two directors each from Coke and P&G. Moreover, the new firm would have its own management and dedicated staff providing administrative and R&D services. Coke was contributing a number of well-known brands including Minute Maid, Hi-C, Five Alive, Cappy, Kapo, Sonfil, and Qoo; P&G contributed Pringles, Sunny Delight, and Punica beverages. The new company would have had 15 manufacturing facilities and about 6,000 employees.

Although the new firm was to have access to all distribution systems of the parents, it would have been free to choose the best route to market for each product. Although Minute Maid was to continue to use Coke's distribution channels, it also was to take advantage of existing refrigerated distribution systems built for Sunny Delight. Pringles was to use a variety of distribution systems, including the existing warehouse system. The Pringles brand was expected to take full advantage of Coke's global distribution and merchandising capabilities. Minute Maid was to gain access to new outlets through Coke's fountain and direct store distribution system.

The new company's sales were expected to grow from $4 billion during the first 12 months of operation to more than $5 billion within two years. The combination of increasing revenue and cost savings was expected to contribute about $200 million in pretax earnings annually by 2005. Specifically, Pringles's revenue growth as a result of enhanced distribution was expected to contribute about $120 million of this projected improvement in pretax earnings. The importance of improved distribution is illustrated by noting that Coke has access to 16 million outlets globally. In the United States alone, that represents a 10-fold increase for Pringles, from its current 150,000 points of outlet. Similarly, improved merchandising and distribution of Sunny Delight was expected to contribute an additional $30 million in pretax income. The remaining $50 million in pretax earnings was to come from lower manufacturing, distribution, and administrative expenses and through discounts received on bulk purchases of foodstuffs and ingredients. P&G and Coke were hoping to stimulate innovation by combining global brands and distribution with talent from both firms in what was hoped would be a highly entrepreneurial corporate culture. The parents also hoped that the stand-alone firm would be able to achieve focus and economies of scale that could not have been achieved by either firm separately.

The results of the LLC were not to be consolidated with those of the parents but rather shown using the equity method of accounting. Under this method of accounting, each parent's proportionate share of earnings (or losses) is shown on its income statement, and its equity interest in the LLC is displayed on its balance sheets. The new company was expected to be nondilutive of the earnings of the parents during its first full year of operations and contribute to earnings per share in subsequent years. The incremental earnings were expected to improve the market value of the parents by at least $1.5–2.0 billion (Bachman, 2001).

Some observers suggested that P&G would stand to benefit the most from the JV. It would have gained substantially by obtaining access to the growing vending machine market. Historically, P&G's penetration in this market had been miniscule. This perceived disproportionate benefit accruing to P&G may have contributed to the eventual demise of the joint venture effort. Coke may have sought additional benefits from the JV that P&G was simply not willing to cede. Once again, we see that, no matter how attractive the concept may seem to be on the surface, the devil is indeed in the details when comes to making it happen.

Discussion Questions

1. In your opinion, what were the motivating factors for the Coke and P&G business alliance?
2. Why do you think the parents selected a limited liability corporate structure for the new company? What are the advantages and disadvantages of this structure over alternative legal structures?
3. The parents estimated that the new company would add at least $1.5–2.0 billion to their market values. How do you think this estimated incremental value was determined?
4. Why do you think the parents opted to form a 50–50 distribution of ownership? What are some possible challenges of operating the new company with this type of an ownership arrangement? What can the parents do to overcome these challenges?
5. Do you think it is likely that the new company would be highly entrepreneurial and innovative? Why or why not? What could the parents do to stimulate the development of this type of an environment within the new company?
6. What factors may have contributed to the decision to discontinue efforts to implement the joint venture? Consider control, scope, financial, and resource contribution issues.

Solutions to these case study questions are provided in the Online Instructor's Manual for instructors using this book.

15

Alternative Exit and Restructuring Strategies

Divestitures, Spin-Offs, Carve-Outs, Split-Ups, and Split-Offs

Experience is the name everyone gives to their mistakes.

—Oscar Wilde

Inside M&A. Financial Services Firms Streamline their Operations

During 2005 and 2006, a wave of big financial services firms announced their intentions to spin-off operations that did not seem to fit strategically with their core business. In addition to realigning their strategies, the parent firms noted the favorable tax consequences of a spin-off, the potential improvement in the parent's financial returns, the elimination of conflicts with customers, and the removal of what, for some, had become a management distraction.

American Express announced plans in early 2005 to jettison its financial advisory business through a tax-free spin-off to its shareholders. The firm also noted that it would incur significant restructuring-related expenses just before the spin-off. Such one-time write-offs by the parent are sometimes necessary to "clean up" the balance sheet of the unit to be spun off and unburden the newly formed company's earnings performance. American Express anticipated substantial improvement in future financial returns on assets as it will be eliminating more than $410 billion in assets from its balance sheet that had been generating relatively meager earnings.

Investment bank Morgan Stanley announced in mid-2005 its intent to spin off its Discover Credit Card operation. While Discover Card generated about one fifth of the firm's pretax profits, Morgan Stanley had been unable to realize significant synergies with its other operations. The move represented an attempt by senior Morgan Stanley management to mute shareholder criticism of the company's lackluster stock performance due to what many viewed had been the firm's excessive diversification.

Similarly, J.P. Morgan Chase announced plans in 2006 to spin off its $13 billion private equity fund, J.P. Morgan Partners. The bank would invest up to $1 billion in a new fund J.P. Morgan Partners plans to open as a successor to the current Global Fund.

Because the bank's ownership position would be less than 25 percent, it would be classified as a passive partner. The expectation is that, by jettisoning this operation, the bank would be able to reduce earnings volatility and decrease competition between the bank and large customers when making investments.

Chapter Overview

Many corporations, particularly large, highly diversified organizations, are reviewing constantly ways in which they can enhance shareholder value by changing the composition of their assets, liabilities, equity, and operations. These activities generally are referred to as restructuring strategies. In early 2009, ailing mega-bank, Citigroup, spun off its Smith Barney brokerage operations in a joint venture with Morgan Stanley. The bank also announced plans to jettison as much as one third of the its operations over the next several years bringing to a close the bank's rapid diversification initiated in the late 1990s.

Restructuring may embody both growth and exit strategies. Growth strategies have been discussed elsewhere in this book. The focus in this chapter is on those strategic options that allow the firm to maximize shareholder value by redeploying assets through downsizing the parent corporation. The intent of this chapter is to discuss the myriad motives for exiting businesses, the various restructuring strategies for doing so, why firms select one strategy over other options, and selected empirical studies of restructuring strategies. In this context, equity carve-outs, spin-offs, divestitures, and split-offs are discussed separately rather than discussed as a specialized form of a carve-out. In some accounting texts, divestitures (referred to as *sell-offs*), spin-offs, and split-offs are all viewed as different forms of equity carve-outs and discussed in terms of how they affect the parent firm's shareholders' equity for financial reporting purposes. The chapter concludes with a discussion of what empirical studies say are the primary determinants of financial returns to shareholders resulting from undertaking the various restructuring strategies. The major segments of this chapter include the following:

- Commonly Stated Motives for Exiting Businesses
- Divestitures
- Spin-Offs and Split-Ups
- Equity Carve-Outs
- Split-Offs
- Voluntary Liquidations (Bust-Ups)
- Tracking, Targeted, and Letter Stocks
- Comparing Alternative Exit and Restructuring Strategies
- Choosing among Divestiture, Carve-Out, and Spin-Off Restructuring Strategies
- Determinants of Returns to Shareholders from Restructuring Strategies
- Things to Remember

Voluntary and involuntary restructuring and reorganization (both inside and outside the protection of bankruptcy court) also represent exit strategies for firms. Chapter 16 includes a detailed discussion of these restructuring strategies. A review of Chapter 15 (including practice questions with answers) is available in the file folder entitled Student Study Guide contained on the CD-ROM accompanying this book. The CD-ROM also contains a Learning Interactions Library, enabling students to test their knowledge of this chapter in a "real-time" environment.

Commonly Stated Motives for Exiting Businesses

There are numerous theories as to why corporations choose to exit certain businesses. They include increasing corporate focus, a desire to exit underperforming businesses, a lack of fit, regulatory concerns, and tax considerations. Other motives include a need to raise funds, reduce risk, discard unwanted businesses from prior acquisitions, avoid conflicts with customers, and increase financial transparency.

Increasing Corporate Focus

Managing highly diverse and complex portfolios of businesses is both time consuming and distracting and may result in funding those businesses with relatively unattractive investment opportunities with cash flows generated by units offering more favorable opportunities. This is particularly true when the businesses are in largely unrelated industries and senior managers lack sufficient understanding of such businesses to make appropriate investment decisions. Consequently, firms often choose to simplify their business portfolio by focusing on those units with the highest growth potential by exiting those businesses that are not germane to the firm's core business strategy.

In 1999, Allegheny Teledyne spun off its software and engineering systems, communication and electronics, and aircraft engine businesses to concentrate on its specialty metals businesses. In 2005, Agilent announced that it had reached agreement to sell its semiconductor unit and its stake in a lighting technology company for $3.6 billion to emphasize its core measurement products business. Similarly, Sara Lee announced in early 2006 that it would divest or spin off businesses accounting for as much as 40 percent of its current revenue to concentrate its resources on its food and beverage business.

Underperforming Businesses

Parent firms often exit businesses that consistently fail to meet or exceed the parent's hurdle rate requirements. These hurdle rates frequently consist of the parent's cost of capital adjusted for any special risks associated with the business or the industry in which it competes. Baxter International Inc. announced in late 1999 its intention to spin off its underperforming cardiovascular business, creating a new company specializing in treatments for heart disease. In 2004, IBM announced the sale of its ailing PC business to China's Lenovo Group. In May 2007, General Electric announced the sale of its plastics operations for $11.6 billion to Saudi Basic Industries Corporation as part of the firm's strategy to sell lower financial return businesses and move into faster growing and potentially higher return businesses such as health care and water processing. In late 2007, Daimler announced it was divesting its Chrysler operations to private equity investor firm, Cerberus, in exchange for Cerberus's willingness to pay off $18 billion in future retirement and health-care liabilities. Daimler had acquired Chrysler in 1998 for $36 billion.

Regulatory Concerns

A firm with substantial market share purchasing a direct competitor may create concerns about violations of antitrust laws. Regulatory agencies still may approve the merger if the acquiring firm is willing to divest certain operations that, in combination with similar units in the acquiring company, are deemed to be anticompetitive. As a result of an antitrust suit filed by the Department of Justice, the government and AT&T reached an agreement effective January 1, 1984, to breakup AT&T's 22 operating companies into 7 regional Bell operating companies (RBOCs). The RBOCs became responsible for local telephone service, and AT&T kept responsibility for long-distance service and certain telecommunications equipment manufacturing operations. See Case Study 2–1 (Chapter 2) for a more detailed discussion of how the Justice Department required AlliedSignal and Honeywell to divest overlapping businesses before approving their merger in 1999.

Lack of Fit

Individual businesses may be undervalued because investors believe that insufficient bene-fits accrue from synergy to offset the overhead expenses associated with being part of a holding company. This may have been a factor in AT&T's choice to implement a split-up of its business in the mid-1990s into three separate entities, each with its own stock traded on the public exchanges. In late 1999, a failed attempt to redirect the business into more lucrative telecommunications industry segments, such as broadband and wireless, caused AT&T to again undertake a strategy to spin off or divest some portions of the firm. See Case Study 15–5 at the end of the chapter.

Companies may divest units after they have had time to learn more about the busi-ness. Raytheon sold its D.C. Heath textbook publishing company to Houghton Mifflin Company in 1995. Although large on a stand-alone basis, D.C. Heath did not fit with the other three larger core Raytheon businesses, which included defense electronics, engi-neering, and avionics. Similarly, TRW's decision to sell its commercial and consumer information services businesses in 1997 came after years of trying to find a significant fit with its space and defense businesses.

Tax Considerations

Restructuring actions may provide tax benefits that cannot be realized without undertak-ing a restructuring of the business. Marriott Corporation contributed its hotel real estate operations to a Real Estate Investment Trust (REIT) in 1989 through a spin-off. Because REITs do not pay taxes on income that is distributed to shareholders, Marriott was able to enhance shareholder value by eliminating the double taxation of income. The income from these properties had been taxed as rental income to the parent and again when distributed to shareholders.

Raising Funds or Worth More to Others

Parent firms may choose to fund new initiatives or acquisitions or reduce leverage through the sale or partial sale of units no longer considered strategic or underperforming corporate expectations. Sales may also result from a financially failing firm's need to raise capital. Examples include Andarko's announcement in late 2006 to sell its Canadian gas properties to Canadian Natural Resources for $4.1 billion to help finance its purchase of two smaller competitors earlier in the year and Chrysler's sale of its highly profitable tank division to avoid bankruptcy in the early 1980s. Similarly, Navistar, formerly Interna-tional Harvester, sold its profitable Solar Turbines operation to Caterpillar Tractor to reduce its indebtedness. Others may view a firm's operating units as much more valuable than the parent and be willing to pay a "premium" price for such businesses.

Risk Reduction

A firm may reduce its perceived risk associated with a particular unit by selling a portion of the business to the public. For example, American Express viewed Shearson Lehman as much riskier than its credit card business. Although the firm believed that there were opportunities to sell its credit cards to Shearson Lehman customers, it decided to reduce its exposure to the cyclical securities business by selling a portion of the unit in 1987. In addition, major tobacco companies have been under pressure for years to divest or spin off their food businesses because of the litigation risk associated with their tobacco subsidiaries. RJR Nabisco bowed to such pressure in 1998 with the spin-off of Nabisco Foods. For similar reasons, Altria spun off its Kraft food operations in 2007. Parent firms may attempt to dump debt or other liabilities by assigning them to a subsidiary and later exiting those businesses. In early 2002, Citigroup sold 21 percent of its Travelers Property Casualty unit in a $3.9 billion initial public offering (IPO), announcing that the remainder would be sold off later. The parent's motivation for this exit strategy could have been to distance itself from the potential costs of asbestos-related claims by Travelers' policyholders. Similarly, Goodrich passed on its asbestos liabilities to EnPro Industries, its diversified industrial products subsidiary, which it spun off in mid-2002.

Discarding Unwanted Businesses from Prior Acquisitions

Acquiring companies often find themselves with certain assets and operations of the acquired company that do not fit their primary strategy. These redundant assets may be divested to raise funds to help pay for the acquisition and enable management to focus on integrating the remaining businesses into the parent without the distraction of having to manage nonstrategic assets. In 2002, Northrop Grumman Corporation announced that it would acquire TRW. Northrop stated that it would retain TRW's space and defense businesses and divest its automotive operations, which were not germane to Northrop's core defense business. Nestle acquired Adams, Pfizer's chewing gum and confectionery business, in early 2003 for $4.6 billion. Pfizer viewed Adams as a noncore business it had acquired as part of its $84 billion acquisition of Warner-Lambert in 2000.

Avoiding Conflicts with Customers

For years, many of the RBOCs spun off by AT&T in 1984 have been interested in competing in the long-distance market, which would put them in direct competition with their former parent. Similarly, AT&T sought to penetrate the regional telephone markets by gaining access to millions of households by acquiring cable TV companies. In preparation for the implementation of these plans, AT&T announced in 1995 that it would split up the company into three publicly traded global companies. The three companies included Communications Services (long-distance services), Communications Systems (later renamed Lucent Technologies, a provider of network switches and transmission equipment), and Global Information Solutions (later renamed NCR, a provider of systems integration services). The primary reason for the split-up was to avoid conflicts between AT&T's former equipment manufacturer and its main customers, the RBOCs.

Increasing Transparency

Firms may be largely opaque to investors due to their complexity. Complexity may take the form of the extreme diversity and number of the businesses the firm operates. General Electric is an example of such a corporation, operating dozens of separate businesses in many countries. Even with access to financial and competitive information on each business, it is challenging for any analyst or investor to value properly such a diversified business. Furthermore, certain parties (i.e., insiders) have access to certain types of information not available to others. Such situations sometimes are called *information asymmetries* (i.e., relevant information is not available to everyone). By reducing the complexity of its operations and making information more readily available, a firm may increase the likelihood that investors value the corporation accurately.

Divestitures

A *divestiture* is the sale of a portion of a firm's assets to an outside party, generally resulting in a cash infusion to the parent. Such assets may include a product line, subsidiary, or division. Between 1970 and 2008, divestitures averaged about 33 percent of total M&A transactions (*Mergerstat Review*). The number of divestitures as a percentage of M&A volume surged in the early to mid-1970s (reaching a peak of 54 percent in 1975), in the early 1990s (reaching a high of 42 percent in 1992), and again in the early 2000s (hitting 40 percent in 2002). These peak activity levels followed the merger boom periods of the late 1960s, the 1980s, and the second half of the 1990s.

Motives for Divestitures

Divestitures often represent a way of raising cash. A firm may choose to sell an undervalued or underperforming operation that it determined to be nonstrategic or unrelated to the core business and use the proceeds of the sale to fund investments in potentially higher return opportunities, including paying off debt. Alternatively, the firm may choose to divest the undervalued business and return the cash to shareholders through either a liquidating dividend or share repurchase. A liquidating dividend is a payment made to shareholders exceeding the firm's net income. It is a liquidating dividend because the firm must sell assets to make the payment. Moreover, an operating unit may simply be worth more if sold than if retained by the parent. While investment bankers or business brokers representing a buyer interested in acquiring an operating unit frequently approach firms, some firms choose to be proactive by periodically conducting portfolio reviews.

Corporate Portfolio Reviews

Many corporations review their business portfolio periodically to determine which operations continue to fit their core strategies. As part of this review, the parent conducts a financial analysis to determine if the business is worth more to shareholders if it is sold and the proceeds either returned to the shareholders or reinvested in opportunities offering higher returns. Weighing the future of certain current businesses with other perceived opportunities, General Electric announced in late 2006 that it was selling its silicone and quartz business for $3.4 billion to private equity firm Apollo Management. GE's portfolio of companies has been undergoing change since the current CEO, Jeffrey Immelt, took control in September 2001. Since then, GE has completed transactions valued at more than $100 billion in buying and selling various operating units.

To Sell or Not to Sell

An analysis undertaken to determine if a business should be sold involves a multistep process. These steps include determining the after-tax cash flows generated by the unit, an appropriate discount rate reflecting the risk of the business, the after-tax market value of the business, and the after-tax value of the business to the parent. The decision to sell or retain the business depends on a comparison of the after-tax value of the business to the parent with the after-tax proceeds from the sale of the business. These steps are outlined next.

Step 1. Calculating After-Tax Cash Flows

To decide if a business is worth more to the shareholder if sold, the parent must first estimate the after-tax cash flows of the business viewed on a stand-alone basis (i.e., as if it were operated as an independent operating unit). This requires adjusting the cash flows for intercompany sales and the cost of services (e.g., legal, treasury, and audit) provided by the parent. *Intercompany sales* refer to operating unit revenue generated by selling products or services to another unit owned by the same parent. For example, in a vertically integrated business, such as a steel manufacturer that obtains both iron ore and coal from its operating subsidiaries, the majority of the revenue generated by the iron ore and coal operations often comes from sales to the parent company's steelmaking operations. The parent may value this revenue for financial reporting purposes using product transfer prices, which may reflect current market prices or some formula, such as a predetermined markup over the cost of production. If the transfer prices do not reflect actual market prices, intercompany revenue may be artificially high or low, depending on whether the transfer prices are higher or lower than actual market prices. Intercompany revenues associated with the operating unit should be restated to reflect actual market prices. Moreover, services provided by the parent to the business may be subsidized (i.e., provided at below actual cost) or at a markup over actual cost. To reflect these factors, operating profits should be reduced by the amount of any subsidies and increased by any markup over what the business would have to pay if it purchased comparable services from sources outside of the parent firm.

Step 2. Estimating the Discount Rate

Once the after-tax stand-alone cash flows have been determined, a discount rate should be estimated that reflects the risk characteristics of the industry in which the business competes. The cost of capital of other firms in the same industry (or firms in other industries exhibiting similar profitability, growth, and risk characteristics) is often a good proxy for the discount rate of the business being analyzed.

Step 3. Estimating the After-Tax Market Value of the Business

The discount rate then is used to estimate the present or market value of the projected after-tax cash flows of the business, as if it were a stand-alone business. The valuation is based on cash flows adjusted for intercompany revenues not on the books at market prices and services provided the operating unit by the parent firm at something other than actual cost.

Step 4. Estimating the Value of the Business to the Parent

The after-tax equity value (EV) of the business as part of the parent is estimated by subtracting the market value of the business's liabilities (L) from its after-tax market value (MV) as a stand-alone operation. This relationship can be expressed as follows:

$$EV = MV - L$$

EV is a measure of the after-tax market value of shareholder equity of the business, where the shareholder is the parent firm.

Step 5. Deciding to Sell

The decision to sell or retain the business is made by comparing the EV with the after-tax sale value (SV) of the business. Assuming other considerations do not outweigh any after-tax gain on the sale of the business, the decision to sell or retain can be summarized as follows:

If SV > EV, divest.

If SV < EV, retain.

Although the sale value may exceed the equity value of the business, the parent may choose to retain the business for strategic reasons. For example, the parent may believe that the business's products (e.g., ties) may facilitate the sale of other products the firm offers (e.g., custom shirts). The firm may lose money on the sale of ties but make enough money on the sale of custom shirts to earn a profit on the combined sales of the two products. In another instance, one subsidiary of a diversified parent may provide highly complex components critical to the assembly of finished products produced by other subsidiaries of the parent firm. Under these circumstances, the parent may choose to incur a small loss on the production of components to ensure the continued high quality of its highly profitable finished products.

Timing of the Sale

Obviously, the best time to sell a business is when the owner does not need to sell or the demand for the business to be divested is greatest. The decision to sell also should reflect the broader financial environment. Selling when business confidence is high, stock prices are rising, and interest rates are low is likely to fetch a higher price for the unit. If the business to be sold is highly cyclical, the sale should be timed to coincide with the firm's peak year earnings. Businesses also can be timed to sell when they are considered most popular. In 1980, the oil exploration business was booming; by 1983, it was in the doldrums. It recovered again by the mid-1990s. What's hot today can fizzle tomorrow. A similar story could be told about many of the high-flying Internet-related companies of the late 1990s.

The Selling Process

The selling process may be reactive or proactive (see Figure 15–1). *Reactive sales* occur when the parent is unexpectedly approached by a buyer, either for the entire firm or for a portion of the firm, such as a product line or subsidiary. If the bid is sufficiently attractive, the parent firm may choose to reach a negotiated settlement with the bidder without investigating other options. This may occur if the parent is concerned about potential degradation of its business, or that of a subsidiary, if its interest in selling becomes public knowledge.

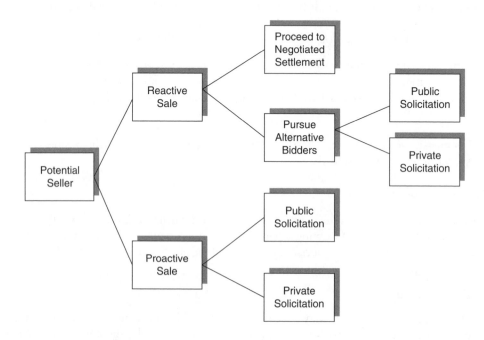

FIGURE 15–1 The selling process.

In contrast, *proactive sales* may be characterized as public or private solicitations. In a **public solicitation**, a firm can announce publicly that it is putting itself, a subsidiary, or a product line up for sale. In this instance, potential buyers contact the seller. This is a way to identify relatively easily interested parties. Unfortunately, this approach can also attract unqualified bidders (i.e., those lacking the financial resources necessary to complete the deal). In a **private solicitation**, the parent firm may hire an investment banker or undertake on its own to identify potential buyers to be contacted. Once a list of what are believed to be qualified buyers has been compiled, contact is made. (See the discussion of the screening and contacting process in Chapter 5 for more detail.)

In either a public or private solicitation, interested parties are asked to sign confidentiality agreements before they are given access to proprietary information. In a private solicitation, they may also be asked to sign a standstill agreement requiring them not to make an unsolicited bid. Parties willing to sign these agreements are then asked to submit preliminary, nonbinding "indications of interest" (i.e., a single number or a bid expressed as a range).

Those parties submitting preliminary bids are then ranked by the selling company in terms of the size of the bid, form of payment (i.e., composition), the ability of the bidder to finance the transaction, form of acquisition (i.e., whether the bidder proposes to buy stock or assets), and ease of doing the deal. The last factor involves an assessment of the difficulty in obtaining regulatory approval, if required, and the integrity of the bidder. A small number of those submitting preliminary bids are then asked to submit a best and final offer. Such offers must be binding on the bidder. At this point, the seller may choose to initiate an auction among the most attractive bids or go directly into negotiating a purchase agreement with a single party.

Tax and Accounting Considerations for Divestitures

The divesting firm is required to recognize a gain or loss for financial reporting purposes equal to the difference between the fair value of the consideration received for the divested operation and its book value. However, if the transaction is an exchange of similar assets or an equivalent interest in similar productive assets, the company should not recognize a gain or loss other than a loss resulting from the impairment of value. If the divested division or subsidiary is a discontinued segment, the parent firm must estimate the gain or loss from the divestiture on the date that management approves a formal plan to dispose of the division or subsidiary. For tax purposes, the gain or loss is the difference between the proceeds and the parent's tax (i.e., cost) basis in the stock or assets. Net gains (i.e., capital gains in excess of losses) are taxed at the same rate as other business income.

Spin-Offs and Split-Ups

A *spin-off* is a transaction in which a parent creates a new legal subsidiary and distributes shares it owns in the subsidiary to its current shareholders as a stock dividend. Such distributions are made in direct proportion to the shareholders' current holdings of the parent's stock. Consequently, the proportional ownership of shares in the new legal subsidiary is the same as the stockholders' proportional ownership of shares in the parent firm. The new entity has its own management and operates independently from the parent company. Unlike the divestiture or equity carve-out (explained later in this chapter), the spin-off does not result in an infusion of cash to the parent company. The average size of spin-offs is about 25 percent of the parent's original market value. According to Thomson Reuters, the dollar value and number of U.S. spin-offs peaked in 1999 at $146 billion and 92, respectively. Although U.S. spin-off activity waned following the bursting of the

Internet bubble, spin-off activity recovered in 2007, with 88 spin-offs valued at $79 billion. Some of the more notable spin-offs include the spin-off of Medco by Merck, Allstate by Sears, Payless by May Department Stores, Dean Witter/Discover by Sears, CBS by Westinghouse, and Pizza Hut, KFC, and Taco Bell by PepsiCo. A *split-up* involves creating a new class of stock for each of the parent's operating subsidiaries, paying current shareholders a dividend of each new class of stock, and then dissolving the remaining corporate shell. See Case Study 15–1 for an example of a split-up.

Case Study 15–1 Motorola Splits in Two

Motorola announced on March 26, 2008, its intention to create two independent, publicly traded companies in 2009. The decision by the Motorola board followed an extensive evaluation of the growth prospects and cash-flow-generating potential of all the firm's units. The two new companies would consist of the firm's former Mobile Devices and Broadband & Mobility Solutions businesses. The Mobile Devices business designs, manufactures, and sells mobile handsets and accessories globally. The Broadband & Mobility Solutions business manufactures, designs, integrates, and services voice and data communication solutions and wireless broadband networks for business enterprises and government agencies. By splitting the company in this manner, Motorola is able to separate its loss-generating handset division from its other businesses. Although the third largest handset manufacturer globally, the handset business had been losing market share to Nokia and Samsung Electronics for years. The split-up would take the form of a tax-free distribution to Motorola's shareholders, with shareholders holding shares of two independent and publicly traded firms.

Once independent, the handset operation could become more attractive to Asian handset manufacturers eager to improve their U.S. market share. Such a split-up could be a prelude to a joint venture with a Chinese or Japanese firm that finds it easier to negotiate with an independent firm. A stand-alone firm is unencumbered by intracompany relationships including such things as administrative support or parts and services supplied by other areas of Motorola. Moreover, all liabilities and assets associated with the handset business already would have been determined making it easier for a potential partner to value the business. Motorola had been seeking a buyer for the business for months, but none had emerged.

Under pressure from an intensifying proxy battle against activist investor Carl Icahn (who owned a 6.3 percent stake in Motorola), the firm felt compelled to make a dramatic move before the May 2008 shareholders' meeting. Icahn had submitted a slate of four directors to replace those up for reelection. Shares of Motorola, which had a market value of $22 billion, had fallen more than 60 percent since October 2006, making the Motorola board vulnerable in the proxy contest.

Discussion Questions

1. In your judgment, did the breakup of Motorola make sense? Explain your answer.
2. What other restructuring alternatives could Motorola have pursued to increase shareholder value? Why do you believe it pursued this split-up strategy rather than some other alternative? Explain your answer.

Motives for Spin-Offs

In addition to the motives for exiting businesses discussed earlier, spin-offs provide a means of rewarding shareholders with a nontaxable dividend (if properly structured). Parent firms with a low tax basis in a business may choose to spin off the unit as a tax-free distribution to shareholders rather than sell the business and incur a substantial tax liability. In addition, the unit, now independent of the parent, has its own stock to use for possible acquisitions. Finally, the managers of the business that is to be spun off have a greater incentive to improve the unit's performance if they own stock in the unit.

Tax and Accounting Considerations for Spin-Offs

If properly structured, spin-offs or split-ups are generally not taxable to shareholders. According to the Internal Revenue Service Code Section 355, a spin-off must satisfy five conditions for it to be considered tax free to the parent firm's shareholders:

1. **Control.** The parent firm must have a controlling interest in the subsidiary before it is spun off. Control is defined as the parent owning at least 80 percent of the voting stock in the subsidiary and 80 percent of each class of nonvoting stock.
2. **Active business.** After the spin-off, both the parent and the subsidiary must remain in the same line of business in which each was involved for at least five years before the spin-off.
3. **Prohibition against tax avoidance.** The spin-off cannot have been used as a means of avoiding dividend taxation by converting ordinary income into capital gains.
4. **Continuity of interest.** The parent's shareholders must maintain significant ownership in both the parent and the subsidiary following the transactions.
5. **Business purpose.** The transaction must have a significant business purpose separate from tax savings.

For financial reporting purposes, the parent firm should account for the spin-off of a subsidiary's stock to its shareholders at book value with no gain or loss recognized, other than any reduction in value due to impairment. The reason for this treatment is that the ownership interests are essentially the same before and after the spin-off. See Case Study 15–2 for a description of how a spin-off may be structured.

Case Study 15–2 Anatomy of a Spin-Off

On October 18, 2006, Verizon Communication's board of directors declared a dividend to the firm's shareholders consisting of shares in a company comprising the firm's domestic print and Internet yellow pages directories publishing operations (Idearc Inc.). The dividend consisted of one share of Idearc stock for every 20 shares of Verizon common stock. Idearc shares were valued at $34.47 per share. On the dividend payment date, Verizon shares were valued at $36.42 per share. The 1-to-20 ratio constituted a 4.73 percent yield—that is, $34.47/($36.42 \times 20)$—approximately equal to Verizon's then-current cash dividend yield.

Because of the spin-off, Verizon would contribute to Idearc all its ownership interest in Idearc Information Services and other assets, liabilities, businesses, and

Continued

Case Study 15–2 Anatomy of a Spin-Off — Cont'd

employees currently employed in these operations. In exchange for the contribution, Idearc would issue to Verizon shares of Idearc common stock to be distributed to Verizon shareholders. In addition, Idearc would issue senior unsecured notes to Verizon in an amount approximately equal to the debt Verizon incurred in financing Idearc's operations historically. Idearc would also transfer $2.5 billion in excess cash to Verizon. Verizon believed it owned such cash balances, since they were generated while Idearc was part of the parent.

Verizon announced that the spin-off would enable the parent and Idearc to focus on their core businesses, which may facilitate expansion and growth of each firm. The spin-off would also allow each company to determine its own capital structure, enable Idearc to pursue an acquisition strategy using its own stock, and permit Idearc to enhance the effectiveness of equity-based compensation programs offered to its employees. Because of the spin-off, Idearc would become an independent public company, although Idearc would continue to have a number of significant commercial arrangements with Verizon. Moreover, no vote of Verizon shareholders was required to approve the spin-off, since it constitutes the payment of a dividend permissible by the board of directors according to the bylaws of the firm. Finally, Verizon shareholders have no appraisal rights in connection with the spin-off.

Discussion Questions

1. How do you believe the Idearc shares were valued for purposes of the spin-off? Be specific.
2. Do you believe that it is fair for Idearc to repay a portion of the debt incurred by Verizon relating to Idearc's operations even though Verizon included Idearc's earnings in its consolidated income statement? Is the transfer of excess cash to the parent fair? Explain your answer.
3. Do you believe shareholders should have the right to approve a spin-off? Explain your answer.

Equity Carve-Outs

Equity carve-outs exhibit characteristics similar to spin-offs. Both result in the subsidiary's stock being traded separately from the parent's stock. They also are similar to divestitures and IPOs in that they provide cash to the parent. However, unlike the spin-off or divestiture, the parent generally retains control of the subsidiary in a carve-out transaction. Retention of at least 80 percent of the unit enables consolidation for tax purposes and retention of more than 50 percent enables consolidation for financial reporting purposes. Allen and McConnell (1998) found a median retention of subsidiary shares of 69 percent, while Vijh (2002) found a median ownership stake of 72 percent. A potentially significant drawback to the carve-out is the creation of minority shareholders. General Motors 2006's sale of a 51 percent stake in its then-profitable GMAC finance unit to private investor group Cerberus for $14 billion is a recent example of an equity carve-out. In this transaction, GM retained the right (i.e., a call option) to buy back GMAC during the 10-year period following the close of the transaction.

Motives for Equity Carve-Outs

As is true of a divestiture, equity carve-outs provide an opportunity to raise funds for reinvestment in the subsidiary, paying off debt, or paying a dividend to the parent firm. Moreover, a carve-out frequently is a prelude to a divestiture since it provides an opportunity to value the business by selling stock in a public stock exchange. The stock created for purposes of the carve-out often is used in incentive programs for the unit's management and as an acquisition currency (i.e., form of payment) if the parent later decides to grow the subsidiary. The two basic forms of an equity carve-out are the initial public offering and the subsidiary equity carve-out. These are discussed in the following section.

Initial Public Offerings

An *initial public offering* is the first offering to the public of common stock of a formerly privately held firm. The sale of the stock provides an infusion of cash to the parent. The cash may be retained by the parent or returned to shareholders. United Parcel Service's IPO of a small share of its stock in 1999 is an example of an IPO.

Subsidiary Equity Carve-Outs

The *subsidiary carve-out* is a transaction in which the parent creates a wholly owned independent legal subsidiary, with stock and a management team that is different from the parent's, and issues a portion of the subsidiary's stock to the public. Alternatively, a portion of the stock of an existing subsidiary could be sold to the public for the first time. Usually, only a minority share of the parent's ownership in the subsidiary is issued to the public. Although the parent retains control, the shareholder base of the subsidiary may be different than that of the parent as a result of the public sale of equity. The cash raised may be retained in the subsidiary or transferred to the parent as a dividend, a stock repurchase, or an intercompany loan. An example of a subsidiary carve-out is the sale to the public by Phillip Morris in 2001 of 15 percent of its wholly owned Kraft subsidiary. While the firm was able to raise $8.68 billion, Phillip Morris's voting power over Kraft was reduced only to 97.7 percent because Kraft had a dual-class share structure (i.e., different classes of stock had different numbers of votes) in which only low-voting shares were issued in the public stock offering.

Equity Carve-Outs as Staged Transactions

Equity may be sold to the public in several stages. A partial sale of equity either in a wholly owned subsidiary (a subsidiary equity carve-out) or in the consolidated business (an IPO) may be designed to raise capital and establish a market price for the stock. Later, once a market has been established for the stock, the remainder of the subsidiary's stock may be issued to the public. Alternatively, the parent may choose to spin off its remaining shares in the subsidiary to the parent's shareholders as a dividend. Few carve-outs remain under the parent's control in the long term. In a study of more than

200 carve-outs, only 8 percent of the firms held more than 50 percent of the equity of their carve-outs after five years, 31 percent of the parents held less than 25 percent of the equity, and 39 percent of the carve-outs had been acquired or merged with third parties (Annema, Fallon, and Goedhart, 2002). Hewlett-Packard's staged spin-off of its Agilent Technologies subsidiary is an example of a staged transaction. It began with an equity carve-out of a minority position in its wholly owned Agilent subsidiary in late 1999. The remainder of the unit's stock was sold in 2000.

Split-Offs

A *split-off* is similar to a spin-off in that a firm's subsidiary becomes an independent firm and the parent firm does not generate any new cash. However, unlike a spin-off, the split-off involves an offer to exchange parent stock for stock in the parent firm's subsidiary. For example, in 2001, AT&T spun off its 86-percent-owned wireless operations to investors holding tracking shares in the subsidiary. Shareholders owning tracking shares (i.e., shares whose dividends fluctuate with the unit's profitability) exchanged their shares for common shares in the wireless unit. In 2004, Viacom spun off its movie rental chain by exchanging shares in its 81-percent-owned Blockbuster Inc. subsidiary for Viacom common shares. In late 2003, GM split off Hughes by distributing its 19.9-percent stake in Hughes Corporation common stock to the holders of GM Class H common stock (a tracking stock) in exchange for the shares they owned. Consequently, Hughes became a separate, independent company.

Split-offs normally are non-pro-rata stock distributions in contrast to spin-offs, which generally are pro-rata or proportional distributions of shares. In a pro-rata distribution, a shareholder owning 10 percent of the outstanding parent company stock would receive 10 percent of the subsidiary whose shares were distributed. A non-pro-rata distribution takes the form of a tender offer in which shareholders can accept or reject the distribution. The tax treatment of split-offs is identical to that previously described for a spin-off.

Motives for Split-Offs

Divestiture may not be an option for disposing of a business in which the parent owns less than 100 percent of the stock, because potential buyers often want to acquire all of a firm's outstanding stock. By acquiring less than 100 percent, a buyer inherits minority shareholders who may disagree with the new owner's future business decisions. Consequently, split-offs are best suited for disposing of a less than 100 percent investment stake in a subsidiary. Moreover, the split-off also reduces the pressure on the spun-off firm's share price, because shareholders who exchange their stock are less likely to sell the new stock. Presumably, those shareholders willing to make the exchange believe the stock in the subsidiary has greater appreciation potential than the parent's stock. The exchange also increases the earnings per share of the parent firm by reducing the number of its shares outstanding, as long as the impact of the reduction in the number of shares outstanding exceeds the loss of the subsidiary's earnings.

Split-offs and spin-offs undertaken as part of a merger must be structured to satisfy Morris Trust tax code rules if they are to be tax free. Such rules require that the shareholders of the parent undertaking the split-off or spin-off end up as majority shareholders in the merged firm (see Case Study 15–3). See Chapter 12 for a detailed discussion of Morris Trust rules.

Case Study 15–3 Kraft Foods Undertakes Split-Off of Post Cereals in Merger-Related Transaction

In late August 2008, Kraft Foods (Kraft) announced an exchange offer related to the split-off of its Post Cereals unit and the closing of the merger of its Post Cereals business (Post) into a wholly owned subsidiary of Ralcorp Holdings (Ralcorp). Kraft is a major manufacturer and distributor of foods and beverages, whose brands include Kraft cheeses, Oscar Mayer meats, Philadelphia cream cheese, Maxwell House coffee, Nabisco cookies, and Oreo cookies. Post is a leading manufacturer of breakfast cereals. Ralcorp manufactures, distributes, and markets brand-name products in grocery, mass merchandise, and other food service channels.

Prior to the transaction, Kraft borrowed $300 million from outside lenders and established Kraft Sub, a shell corporation wholly owned by Kraft. Kraft subsequently transferred the Post assets and associated liabilities, along with the liability Kraft incurred in raising $300 million, to Kraft Sub in exchange for all of Kraft Sub's stock and $660 million in debt issued by Kraft Sub to be paid to Kraft at the end of 10 years.

In the related split-off transaction, Kraft shareholders had the option to exchange their shares of Kraft common stock for shares of Kraft Sub, which owned the assets and liabilities of Post. With the completion of the merger of Kraft Sub with Ralcorp Sub (a Ralcorp wholly owned subsidiary), the common shares of Kraft Sub were exchanged for shares of Ralcorp stock on a one-for-one basis. Consequently, Kraft shareholders that had tendered their Kraft shares as part of the exchange offer owned 0.6606 of Ralcorp stock for each Kraft share exchanged as part of the split-off. Concurrent with the exchange offer, Kraft closed the merger of Post with Ralcorp. Kraft shareholders received 30,466,805 shares of Ralcorp stock valued at $1.6 billion, resulting in their owning 54 percent of the merged firm. By satisfying the Morris Trust tax code regulations, the transaction was tax free to Kraft shareholders.

The purchase price for Post equaled $2.560 billion. This price consisted of $1.6 billion in Ralcorp stock received by Kraft shareholders and $960 million in cash equivalents received by Kraft. The $960 million included the assumption of the $300 million liability by Kraft Sub and the $660 million in debt securities received from Kraft Sub.[1] The steps involved in the transaction are described next.

Step 1. Kraft creates a shell subsidiary (Kraft Sub) and transfers Post assets and liabilities and $300 million in Kraft debt into the shell in exchange for Kraft Sub stock plus $660 million in Kraft Sub debt securities (Figure 15–2).

Step 2. Kraft implements an exchange offer in which Kraft shareholders could exchange their Kraft shares for shares in Kraft Sub (Figure 15–3). The resulting split-off makes Kraft Sub an independent company.

Step 3. Kraft Sub, as an independent company, is merged with a sub of Ralcorp (Ralcorp Sub) (Figure 15–4).

---

[1]The $600 million represents the book value of the debt on the merger closing date. The more correct representation in calculating the purchase price would be to estimate its market value.

Continued

Case Study 15–3 Kraft Foods Undertakes Split-Off of Post Cereals in Merger-Related Transaction — Cont'd

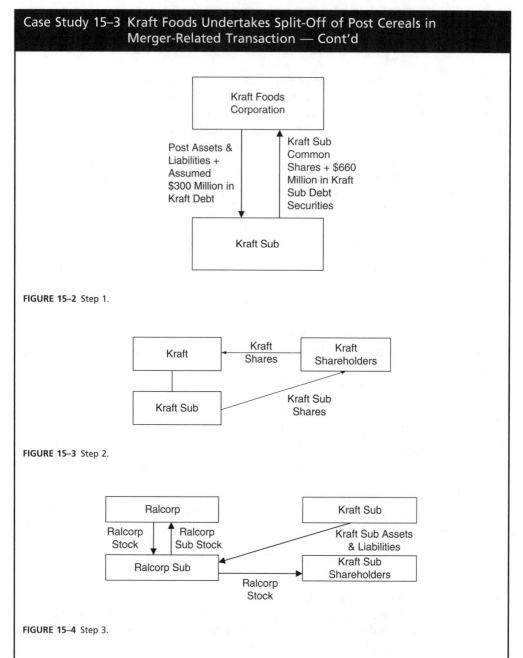

FIGURE 15–2 Step 1.

FIGURE 15–3 Step 2.

FIGURE 15–4 Step 3.

Discussion Questions

1. The merger of Post with Ralcorp could have been achieved through a spin-off. Explain the details of how this might happen.
2. Speculate as to why Kraft chose to split off rather than spin off Post as part of its plan to merge Post with Ralcorp. Be specific.

Solutions to this case study are found in the Online Instructor's Manual for instructors using this book.

Voluntary Liquidations (Bust-Ups)

Chapter 16 includes a detailed discussion of involuntary, bankruptcy-related liquidations. Such transactions occur when creditors and the bankruptcy court concur that they will realize more value through liquidation than by reorganizing the firm. *Voluntary liquidations* reflect the judgment that the sale of individual parts of the firm could realize greater value than the value created by a continuation of the combined corporation. This may occur when management views the firm's growth prospects as limited. This option generally is pursued only after other restructure actions have failed to improve the firm's overall market value.

In 2005, Cendant, a leisure and real estate conglomerate, announced it would split into four separate businesses in an attempt to revive its stock. The new entities included real estate, travel, hospitality (hotels), and car rental. Each unit became a separate publicly traded company. Cendant shareholders received shares in each and continued to receive dividends. Cendant's decision came six months after Viacom announced plans to separate CBS and its cable television operations into two companies. In 2006, conglomerate Tyco International announced the separation of the company into three independent units as the best approach to achieve their full potential. Tyco shareholders received shares in Tyco Healthcare, Tyco Electronics, and Tyco Fire and Security. Tyco International distributed the firm's debt among the three entities.

In general, a merger has the advantage over the voluntary bust-up of deferring the recognition of a gain by the stockholders of the selling company until they eventually sell the stock. In liquidation, the selling shareholders must recognize the gain immediately. Unused tax credits and losses belonging to either of the merged firms carry over in a nontaxable merger but are lost in liquidation.

Tracking, Targeted, and Letter Stocks

Tracking, *targeted*, or *letter stocks* are separate classes of common stock of the parent corporation. The parent firm divides its operations into two or more operating units and assigns a common stock to each operation. Tracking stock is a class of common stock that links the shareholders' return to the operating performance of a particular business segment or unit (i.e., the targeted business unit). Dividends paid on the tracking stock rise or fall with the performance of the business segment. Tracking stock represents an ownership interest in the company as a whole, rather than a direct ownership interest in the targeted business segment. For voting purposes, holders of tracking stock with voting rights may vote their shares on issues related to the parent and not the subsidiary. The parent's board of directors and top management retain control of the subsidiary for which a tracking stock has been issued, since the subsidiary is still legally a part of the parent. Tracking stocks may be issued to current parent company shareholders as a dividend, used as payment for an acquisition, or more commonly, issued in a public offering. Once the tracking stock is listed on a public exchange, the subsidiary must file separate financial statements with the Securities and Exchange Commission.

Thirty-two U.S. firms had issued 50 tracking stocks as of the end of 2008. The concept was introduced in 1984 when General Motors issued a class of stock identified as E stock, often referred to as *letter stock* at that time, to buy Electronic Data Systems (EDS). In 1985, GM issued another class of stock called H stock when it acquired Hughes Corporation. In 1991, U.S. Steel Company created a USX-Marathon stock for its oil business and a USX stock for its steel operations. The next year, USX created a third tracking stock when it sold shares of the USX-Delhi group in an IPO. Few tracking stocks have been issued in recent years, perhaps due to inherent governance issues and their poor long-term performance. Relatively recent issues include AT&T Wireless, Alcatel, and Disney in 2000, as well as Sony, Sprint PCS, and CarMax in 2001.

Motives for Tracking Stocks

The purpose in creating tracking stock is to enable the financial markets to value the different operations within a corporation based on their own performance. Such stocks represent *pure plays* to the extent that they give investors an opportunity to invest in a single operating unit of a diversified parent firm. Moreover, the operating unit files financial statements with the SEC separate from those of the parent's, even though its financial performance is included in the parent's consolidated financial statements. However, there is little empirical evidence that issuing a tracking stock for a subsidiary creates pure-play investment opportunities, as the tracking stock tends to be correlated more with the parent's other outstanding stocks than with the stocks in the industry in which the subsidiary competes (D'Souza and Jacob, 2000). Tracking or targeted stocks provide the parent company with an alternative means of raising capital for a specific operation by selling a portion of the stock to the public and an alternative "currency" for making acquisitions. In addition, stock-based incentive programs to attract and retain key managers can be implemented for each operation with its own tracking stock. Although tracking stocks may not be created initially for the purpose of exiting a business, they make such a move easier for the parent at a later date. Tracking stocks also give the parent and the subsidiary the opportunity to share overhead expenses such as data processing centers, tax preparation, risk management, and the like.

Tax and Accounting Considerations for Tracking Stocks

For financial reporting purposes, a distribution of tracking stock splits the parent firm's equity structure into separate classes of stock without a legal split-up of the firm. Tracking stocks may be issued as dividends to the parent's current shareholders. Unlike the case with spin-offs, the IRS currently does not require the business for which the tracking stock is created to be at least five years old and that the parent retain a controlling interest in the business for the stock to be exempt from capital gains taxes. Unlike a spin-off or carve-out, the parent retains complete ownership of the business. In general, a proportionate distribution by a company to its shareholders in the company's stock is tax free to shareholders.

Problems with Tracking Stocks

Tracking stocks may create internal operating conflicts among the parent's business units. Such conflicts arise in determining how the parent's overhead expenses are allocated to the business units and what price one business unit is paid for selling products to other business units. In addition to creating internal problems, tracking stocks can stimulate shareholder lawsuits. Although the unit for which a tracking stock has been created may be largely autonomous, the potential for conflict of interest is substantial because the parent's board and the target stock's board are the same. The parent's board approves overall operating unit and capital budgets. Decisions made in support of one operating unit may appear to be unfair to those holding a tracking stock in another unit. Thus, tracking stocks can pit classes of shareholders against one another and lead to lawsuits. When GM sold part of its Hughes unit and all of EDS, holders of H shares sued the GM board of directors, complaining that they were underpaid.

Tracking stocks may be penalized if the parent's management continues to operate them conservatively. With a spin-off, the firm has a separate board of directors that can introduce a more aggressive management style than the parent may have been willing to tolerate. In addition, tracking stocks may not have voting rights. Finally, the chances of a hostile takeover of a firm with a tracking stock are virtually zero, because the firm is controlled by the parent. Hence, there is no takeover premium built into the stock price. Reflecting investor disenchantment with the longer-term performance of tracking stocks, Billet and Vijh (2004) found average excess returns to shareholders of 13.9 percent around the date of the announcement that target stock structures would be removed in 11 instances between 1984 and 1999.

Comparing Alternative Exit and Restructuring Strategies

Table 15–1 summarizes the primary characteristics of each of the restructuring strategies discussed thus far in this chapter. Note that divestitures and carve-outs provide cash to the parent, whereas spin-offs, split-ups, and bust-ups do not. Equity ownership does not change in spin-offs, but it may change in split-ups or split-offs, as parent company shareholders may exchange their shares or shares in one or more of the spin-offs. The parent remains in existence in all restructuring strategies except split-ups and bust-ups. A new legal entity generally is created with each restructuring strategy, except for voluntary liquidations. With the exception of the carve-out, the parent generally loses control of the division involved in the restructuring strategy. Only spin-offs, split-ups, and split-offs are generally not taxable to shareholders.

Table 15–1   Key Characteristics of Alternative Exit and Restructuring Strategies

Characteristics	Divestitures	Equity Carve-outs and IPOs	Spin-Offs	Split-Ups	Split-Offs	Voluntary Liquidation (Bust-Ups)	Tracking Stocks
			Alternative Strategies				
Cash infusion to parent	Yes	Yes	No	No	No	No	Yes
Change in equity ownership	Yes	Yes	No	Sometimes[1]	Yes	Yes	Sometimes
Parent ceases to exist	No	No	No	Yes	No	Yes	No
New legal entity created	Sometimes	Yes[2]	Yes	Yes	No	No	No
New shares issued	Sometimes	Yes	Yes	Yes	No	No	Yes
Parent remains in control	No	Generally	No	No	No	No	Yes
Taxable to shareholders	Yes[3]	Yes[3]	No[4]	No[4]	No[4]	Yes	No[5]

[1]Parent firm shareholders may exchange their shares for one or more of the spin-off's shares or immediately sell their shares resulting in a different distribution of ownership.

[2]Applies to subsidiary carve-outs only.

[3]The proceeds are taxable if returned to shareholders as a dividend or tax deferred if used to repurchase the parent's stock.

[4]The transaction is generally not taxable if properly structured.

[5]Only dividend payments and shareholder gains on the sale of stock are taxable.

Choosing among Divestiture, Carve-Out, and Spin-Off Restructuring Strategies

The reasons for selecting a divestiture, carve-out, or spin-off strategy are inherently different. Parent firms that engage in divestitures often are highly diversified in largely unrelated businesses and have a desire to achieve greater focus or raise cash (Bergh, Johnson, and Dewitt, 2007). Parent firms that use carve-out strategies usually operate businesses in somewhat related industries exhibiting some degree of synergy and desire to raise cash. Consequently, the parent firm may pursue a carve-out rather than a divestiture or spin-off strategy to retain perceived synergy (Powers, 2001). There is empirical evidence that the timing of the carve-out is influenced by when management sees its subsidiary's assets as overvalued (Powers, 2003; Chen and Guo, 2005). Firms engaging in spin-offs often are highly diversified but less so than those that are prone to pursue divestiture strategies and have little need to raise cash (John and Ofek, 1995; Kaplan and Weisbach, 1992). Table 15–2 identifies characteristics of parent firm operating units that often are subject to certain types of restructuring activities.

The decision to exit a business is essentially a two-stage process. The first stage involves the firm deciding to exit a line of business or product line for one or more of the reasons described earlier in this chapter. The second stage entails selecting the appropriate exit strategy. Divestitures, carve-outs, and spin-offs are the most commonly used restructuring strategy when a parent corporation is considering partially or entirely exiting a business. The decision as to which of these three strategies to use is often heavily influenced by the parent firm's need for cash, the degree of synergy between the business to be divested or spun off and the parent's other operating units, and the potential selling price of the division (Powers, 2001). However, these factors are not independent. Parent firms needing cash are more likely to divest or engage in an equity carve-out for operations exhibiting high selling prices relative to their synergy value. Parent firms not needing cash are more likely to spin off units exhibiting low selling prices and synergy with the parent. Parent firms with moderate cash needs are likely to engage in equity carve-outs when the unit's selling price is low relative to perceived synergy. Table 15–3 illustrates this two-stage procedure.

Table 15–2   Characteristics of Parent Company Operating Units That Undergo Divestiture, Carve-Out, or Spin-Off

Exit or Restructuring Strategy	Characteristics
Divestitures	Usually unrelated to other businesses owned by parent
	Operating performance generally worse than the parent's consolidated performance
	Slightly underperform their peers in year before announcement date
	Generally sell at a lower price than carve-outs measured by market value to book assets
Carve-outs	Generally more profitable and faster growing than spun-off or divested businesses
	Operating performance often exceeds parent's
	Usually operate in industries characterized by high market to book values
	Generally outperform peers in year before announcement date
Spin-offs	Generally faster growing and more profitable than divested businesses
	Most often operate in industries related to other industries in which the parent operates
	Operating performance worse than parent's
	Slightly underperform peers in year before announcement date

Sources: Ravenscroft and Scherer (1991), Cho and Cohen (1997), Hand and Skantz (1997), Kang and Shivdasani (1997), Powers (2001, 2003), Chen and Guo (2005), and Bergh et al. (2007).

Table 15–3   Divestitures, Carve-Outs, and Spin-Offs: Selecting the Appropriate Restructuring Strategy

Stage 1 Considerations (Primary Motive for Restructuring)	Stage 2 Considerations — Need for Cash	Stage 2 Considerations — Value of Business/Degree of Synergy	Appropriate Restructuring Strategy	Restructuring Strategy More Likely If Parent
Change strategy/increase focus	Needs cash	High price/high synergy	Carve-out	Can retain synergy
	Needs cash	Low price/high synergy	Carve-out	Can retain synergy
	Needs cash	High price/low synergy	Divestiture	Can shield taxable gains[1]
	Needs cash	Low price/low synergy	Divestiture	Can retain synergy
	Little need for cash	High price/high synergy	Carve-out	Can retain synergy
	Little need for cash	Low price/high synergy	Carve-out	Cannot shield potential gains
	Little need for cash	High price/low synergy	Spin-off	Can shield taxable gains
	Little need for cash	Low price/low synergy	Spin-off	Cannot shield potential gains
Underperforming businesses	Needs cash		Divestiture	Carve-out not an option
	Little need for cash		Spin-off	Can shield taxable gains
Regulatory concerns			Divestiture/spin-off	Cannot shield potential gains
Lack of fit	Needs cash		Divestiture	Cannot shield potential gains
	Little need for cash		Spin-off	Can shield taxable gains
Tax considerations			Spin-off	Can shield taxable gains
Raising funds/worth more to others			Divestiture	Can shield taxable gains
Risk reduction			Carve-out	Can shield taxable gains
Moving away from core business			Divestiture/carve-out	Can shield taxable gains
Discarding unwanted businesses from prior acquisitions			Divestiture	
Avoiding customer conflicts	Need cash		Divestiture	
	Little need for cash		Spin-off	Cannot shield taxable gains

[1]Parent can shield any taxable gains on the sale by offsetting such gains with losses incurred elsewhere in the consolidated firm.

It may seem that a divestiture or carve-out generally would be preferable to a spin-off if the after-tax proceeds from the sale of all or a portion of the operating unit exceeds its after-tax equity value to the firm. Unlike a spin-off, a divestiture or carve-out generates a cash infusion to the firm. However, a spin-off may create greater shareholder wealth for several reasons. First, a spin-off is tax free to the shareholders if it is properly structured. In contrast, the cash proceeds from an outright sale may be taxable to the parent to the extent a gain is realized. Moreover, management must be able to reinvest the after-tax proceeds in a project that has a reasonable likelihood of returning the firm's cost of capital. If management chooses to return the cash proceeds to shareholders as a dividend or through a stock repurchase, the shareholders also must pay taxes on the dividend at their ordinary tax rate or on any gain realized through the share repurchase at the generally lower capital gains tax rate. Second, a spin-off enables the shareholders to decide when to sell their shares. Third, a spin-off may be less traumatic than a divestiture for an operating unit. The divestiture process can degrade value if it is lengthy. Employees leave, worker productivity generally suffers, and customers may not renew contracts until the new owner is known.

Determinants of Returns to Shareholders Resulting from Restructuring Strategies

Preannouncement Abnormal Returns

Empirical studies indicate that the alternative restructure and exit strategies discussed in this chapter generally provide positive abnormal returns to the shareholders of the company implementing the strategy. This should not be surprising since such actions often are undertaken to correct many of the problems associated with highly diversified firms, such as having invested in underperforming businesses, having failed to link executive compensation to the performance of the operations directly under their control, and being too difficult for investors and analysts to evaluate. Alternatively, restructuring strategies involving a divisional or asset sale may create value simply because the asset is worth more to another investor. See Table 15–4 for a summary of the results of selected empirical studies of restructuring activities.

Divestitures

The empirical evidence suggests that divestitures generally create value by increasing the diversified firm's focus and reducing the conglomerate discount (see Chapter 1), transferring assets to those that can use them more effectively, resolving agency conflicts, and mitigating financial distress. Abnormal returns around the announcement date of the restructure strategy average 1.6 percent for sellers. Buyers average abnormal returns of about 0.5 percent (Hanson and Song, 2000; John and Ofek, 1995; Sicherman and Pettway, 1992). While both sellers and buyers gain from a divestiture, most of the gain appears to accrue on average to the seller. However, how the total gain is divided ultimately depends on the relative bargaining strength of the seller and the buyer.

Increasing Focus A substantial body of evidence indicates that reducing a firm's complexity (i.e., increasing its focus) can improve financial returns to shareholders. The difficulty in managing diverse portfolios of businesses in many industries and the difficulty in accurately valuing these portfolios contributed to the breakup of conglomerates in the 1970s and 1980s. Of the acquisitions made between 1970 and 1982 by companies in industries unrelated to the acquirer's primary industry focus, 60 percent were divested by 1989 (Petty, Keown, Scott, and Martin, 1993). John and Ofek (1995) found that abnormal returns earned by the shareholders of a firm divesting a business result largely from improved management of the assets that remain after the divestiture is completed. They

Table 15–4   Returns to Shareholders of Firms Undertaking Restructuring Actions

Restructuring Action	Average Preannouncement Abnormal Returns
Divestitures	1.6%
Spin-offs	3.7%
Tracking stocks	3.0%
Equity carve-outs	4.5%
Voluntary bust-ups	17.3%

Study	Preannouncement Abnormal Returns by Study[1]
Divestitures	
Alexander, Benson, and Kampmeyer (1984): 53, 1964–1973	0.17%
Linn and Rozeff (1984): 77, 1977–1982	1.45%
Jain (1985): 1,107, 1976–1978	0.70%
Klein (1986): 202, 1970–1979	1.12%
	When percentage of equity sold is
	<10%, none
	>10<50%, 2.53%
	>50%, 8.09%
Lang, Poulsen, and Stulz (1995): 93, 1984–1989	2.0% for firms distributing proceeds to shareholders; (0.5)% for those reinvesting proceeds
Allen (2000): 48, 1982–1991	0.8%
Mulherin and Boone (2000): 139, 1990–1998	2.6%
Clubb and Stouraitis (2002): 187, 1984–1994	1.1%
Dittmar and Shivdasani (2002): 188, 1983–1994	2.6%
Bates (2005): 372, 1990–1998	1.2% for firms using proceeds to reduce debt .7% for firms using proceeds to repurchase stock or pay dividends
Slovin, Sushka, and Polonchek (2005): 327, 1983–2000	1.9% for seller receiving cash 3.2% for seller receiving equity
Spin-Offs	
Hite and Owers (1983): 56, 1963–1979	3.8%
Miles and Rosenfeld (1983): 62, 1963–1981	2.33%
Michaely and Shaw (1995): 91 master limited partnerships, 1981–1989	4.5%
Loh, Bezjak, and Toms (1995): 59, 1982–1987	1.5%
J.P. Morgan (1995): 77 since beginning of 1995	5% 6% if spin-off >10% of parent's equity 4% if spin-off <10% of parent's equity
Vroom and van Frederikslust (1999): 210 worldwide spin-offs, 1990–1998	2.6%
Mulherin and Boone (2000): 106, 1990–1998	4.51%
Davis and Leblond (2002): 93, 1980–1999	2.92%
Veld and Veld-Merkoulova (2002): 200, 1987–2000	2.66%
Maxwell and Rao (2003): 80, 1976–1997	3.60%
McNeil and Moore (2005): 153, 1980–1996	3.5%
Harris and Glegg (2007): 58 cross-border spin-offs, 1990–2006	2.23%
Tracking Stocks:	
Logue, Seward, and Walsh (1996): 9, 1991–1995	2.9%
D'Souza and Jacob (2000)	3.6%

Continued

Table 15–4 — Cont'd

Study	Preannouncement Abnormal Returns by Study[1]
Elder and Westra (2000): 35, 1984–1999	3.1%
Haushalter and Mikkelson (2001): 31, 1994–1996	3.0%
Chemmanur and Paeglis (2000): 19, 1984–1998	3.1%
Billet and Vijh (2004): 29, 1984–1999	2.2%
Equity Carve-Outs and IPOs	
Schipper and Smith (1986): 81, 1965–1983	1.7%
Michaely and Shaw (1995): 91 limited partnerships, 1981–1989	4%
Allen and McConnell (1998): 188, 1978–1993	6.63% when proceeds used to pay off debt; zero otherwise
Vijh (1999): 628, 1981–1995	6.2%
Mulherin and Boone (2000): 125, 1990–1998	2.3%
Prezas, Tarimcilar, and Vasduevan (2000): 237, 1985–1996	5.8%
Hulburt, Miles, and Wollridge (2002): 245, 1981–1994	2.1%
Hogan and Olson (2004): 458, 1990–1998	8.8%
Wagner (2004): 71, 1984 to 2002	1.7%
Voluntary Liquidations	
Skantz and Marchesini (1987): 37, 1970–1978	21.4%[2]
Hite, Owers, and Rogers (1987): 49, 1966–1975	13.6%[2]
Kim and Schatzberg (1987): 73, 1963–1981	14%
Erwin and McConnell (1997): 61, 1970–1991	20%

[1]Abnormal mean returns measured from one to three days before and including announcement date of restructure action.

[2]Abnormal mean returns measured during the month of the announced restructure action.

attribute these returns to increased focus and the ability of management to understand fewer lines of business. As evidence of the challenges of understanding businesses in diverse industries, they also found that 75 percent of divested units were unrelated to the selling company. Dittmar and Shivdasani (2003) show that divesting firms tend to improve their investment decisions in their remaining businesses following divestitures by achieving levels of investment in core businesses comparable to their more focused peers.

Maksimovic and Phillips (2001) and Kaplan and Weisback (1992) found that firms tend to sell noncore operations; while Moeller, Schlingemann, and Stulz (2004) demonstrated that divested units tend to represent a relatively small portion of the parent's operations. Kaplan and Weisback (1992) argue that firms tend to sell previously acquired units more because of the improvement in their profitability or because they no longer support the parent's strategy than for having failed to achieve expectations.

Colak and Whited (2007) argue that restructure decisions, such as divestitures, and investment decisions are interdependent. A parent may divest a unit to raise cash to finance what ultimately turns out to be a successful investment decision. While the divestiture was related to the successful investment, it does not follow that the decision to divest resulted in better investment decision making. Therefore, Colak and Whited argue that other factors unrelated to the divestiture decision, such as the firm's competitive position in high-growth markets, often explain the success of the firm's investment decisions.

Transferring Assets to Those Who Can Use Them More Efficiently   Maksimovic and Phillips (2001) document that divestitures result in productivity gains by redeploying assets from less productive sellers to more productive buyers, who believe they can generate a higher financial return than the seller. Using Tobin q ratios (i.e., the ratio of the market value of a firm to the cost of replacing the firm's assets) as a proxy for better managed firms, Datta, Iskandar-Datta, and Raman (2003) found that announcement period returns are highest for transactions in which the buyer's q ratio is higher than the seller's. This implies that the assets are being transferred to a better managed firm.

Resolving Differences between Management and Shareholders (Agency Conflicts) A firm's senior managers serve as agents of the shareholders in conducting the firm's operations. Conflicts arise when management and shareholders disagree about major corporate decisions. What to do with the proceeds of the sale of assets can result in such a conflict, since they can be used in a variety of ways. The proceeds can be reinvested in the seller's remaining operations, paid to shareholders, or used to reduce the firm's outstanding debt. Abnormal returns on divestiture announcement dates tend to be positive when the proceeds are used to pay off debt (Lang et al. 1995; Kaiser and Stouraitis, 2001) or distributed to the shareholders (Slovin et al., 1995). Such results are consistent with a lack of shareholder confidence in the ability of management to invest funds at or above the firm's cost of capital.

Slovin et al. (2005) investigated the extent to which the form of payment affects excess returns. The authors found that abnormal returns to sellers are much smaller when the seller receives cash rather than buyer equity. Asset for buyer equity sales generate abnormal or excess returns of about 10 percent for buyers and 3 percent for sellers on or about the announcement date of the divestiture. The higher returns for buyers may reflect information communicated to the seller not generally known by the investing public about the synergy between the divested asset and the buyer's operations and the overall future earnings potential of the buyer's business. In contrast, excess returns to sellers receiving cash average about 3 percent for sellers and about zero for buyers.

Mitigating Financial Distress   Not surprisingly, empirical studies indicate that firms sell assets when they need cash. The period before a firm announces asset sales often is characterized by deteriorating operating performance (Lang et al., 1995; Schlingemann et al., 2002). Firms that divest assets often have lower cash balances, cash flow, and bond credit ratings than firms exhibiting similar growth, risk, and profitability characteristics (Officer, 2007). Firms experiencing financial distress are more likely to utilize divestitures as part of their restructuring programs than other options because they generate cash (Nixon, Roenfeldt, and Sicherman, 2000; Ofek, 1993).

Spin-Offs

At 3.7 percent, the average abnormal return to parent firm shareholders associated with spin-off announcements is more than twice the 1.6 percent average return on divestitures. However, the differences in announcement date returns between spin-offs and divestitures is smaller than it appears if we note that some portion of the total gain in wealth created by divestitures is shared with the buying firm's shareholders. In contrast, the jump in the parent firm's share price following the announcement of a spin-off reflects the total gain due to the spin-off. Including the abnormal return to the buyer's shareholders of 0.5 percent, the total gain from a divestiture is 2.1 percent. Much of the remaining gap between abnormal returns to shareholders from spin-offs versus divestitures may be attributable to tax considerations. Spin-offs generally are tax free, while any gains on divested assets can be subject to double taxation. With spin-offs, shareholder value is created by increasing the focus of the parent by spinning off unrelated units, providing greater transparency, and transferring wealth from bondholders to shareholders.

Increasing Focus   Daley, Mehrotra, and Sivakumar (1997) show significant positive announcement date returns for spin-offs that increase the focus of the parent but not for those parents for which the spin-off is in the same industry and therefore does little to enhance corporate focus. Desai and Jain (1997) demonstrate that spin-offs that increase focus are associated with significantly higher positive abnormal announcement date returns and improvements in operating performance than spin-offs that do not increase focus. Burch and Nanda (2001) found a reduction in the diversification discount when a spin-off increases corporate focus but not for those do not.

Like divestitures, spin-offs eliminate the tendency to use the cash flows of efficient business to finance investment in less efficient business units. Gertner, Powers, and Scharfstein (2002) find that firms are more likely to invest in their attractive businesses, as measured by the magnitude of the business's q ratio, after a spin-off. Seoungpil and Denis (2004) demonstrate that spin-offs reduce the magnitude of the discount for firms trading at a conglomerate discount prior to the spin-off. Such firms are also more inclined to invest in their remaining high-growth segments.

Greater Transparency (Eliminating Information Asymmetries)   Divestitures and spin-offs that tend to reduce a firm's complexity help to improve investors' ability to evaluate the firm's operating performance. The coverage of publicly traded firms by financial analysts provides an important source of information for investors. By reducing complexity, financial analysts are better able to forecast earnings accurately. Gilson et al. (2001) note a substantial increase in analyst coverage and earnings forecast accuracy in the three years following a spin-off or equity carve-out. Huson and MacKinnon (2003) found that analysts revise upward their earnings forecasts in response to a spin-off. These findings are consistent with the observation that reduced information asymmetries tend to increase shareholder value.

Wealth Transfers   There is evidence that spin-offs transfer wealth from bondholders to stockholders for several reasons. First, spin-offs reduce the assets available for liquidation in the event of business failure. Therefore, investors may view the firm's existing debt as more risky. (Note that assets actually pledged as collateral to current debt may not be spun off without violating loan covenants.) Second, the loss of the cash flow generated by the spin-off may result in less total parent cash flow to cover interest and principal repayments on the parent's current debt. Maxwell and Rao (2003), in a sample of 80 spin-offs between 1976 and 1997, note that bondholders on average suffer a negative abnormal return of 0.8 percent in the month of the spin-off announcement. Stockholders experience an increase of about 3.6 percent during the same period.

Equity Carve-Outs

Announcement date abnormal returns average 4.5 percent. These returns tend to increase with the size of the carve-out (Allen and McConnell, 1998; Vijh, 2002). Value is created by increased parent focus, providing a source of financing, and resolving differences between the parent firm's management and shareholders (i.e., agency issues).

Increasing Focus   Vijh (2002) demonstrates that parents and subsidiaries involved in carve-outs are frequently in different industries. He found that positive announcement date returns often are higher for carve-outs of unrelated subsidiaries. This is consistent with the common observation that carve-outs are undertaken for businesses that do not fit with the parent's business strategy. It is unclear if operating performance improves following equity carve-outs. Hulbert et al. (2002) found evidence that both parents and carved-out subsidiaries improve their operating performance relative to their industry peers in the year following the carve-out. However, Powers et al. (2003) and Boone, Haushalter, and Mikkelson (2003) found evidence that operating performance declines following a carve-out.

Providing a Source of Financing   Equity carve-outs can help to finance the needs of the parent or the subsidiary involved in the carve-out. Schipper and Smith (1986) suggest that firms use carve-outs to finance their high-growth subsidiaries. Chen and Guo (2005) find that corporations tend to choose equity carve-outs and divestitures over spin-offs when market to book value and revenue growth of the carved-out unit are high to maximize the cash proceeds of the sale of equity or asset sales.

Resolving Agency Issues   Arguing that some managers are less likely to sell assets because their compensation is based on the size of the firm, Allen and McConnell (1998) suggest equity carve-outs may be used instead of divestitures to allow the managers to retain control over the assets involved in the carve-out. The authors also found that investor reaction to the announcement of a carve-out is determined by how the proceeds are used. Firms announcing that the proceeds will be used to repay debt or pay dividends earn a 7 percent abnormal return compared to minimal returns for those announcing that the proceeds will be reinvested in the firm. Powers (2003) argues that managers use their inside information about the subsidiary's growth prospects to decide how much of the subsidiary to issue to the public. They are more inclined to retain a larger percentage of the business if they feel the unit's growth prospects are favorable. Atanasov, Boone, and Haushalter (2005) demonstrate that carve-outs show poorer operating performance than their peers when their parents keep less than 50 percent of the subsidiary's equity. The authors argue that either the parent chooses not to consolidate the carved-out unit due to its expected poor performance or it intends to transfer cash from minority-owned businesses through intercompany loans or dividends.

Tracking Stocks

As indicated on Table 15–4, a number of studies show that tracking stocks experience significant positive abnormal returns around their announcement date. Studies addressing the issue of whether the existence of publicly listed tracking shares increase the demand for other stock issued by the parent give mixed results. Clayton and Qian (2004) found evidence that parent shares rise following the issuance of publicly listed tracking stocks. However, Elder et al. (2000) find no evidence that tracking shares lead to greater interest in the parent's and other subsidiary shares.

Voluntary Liquidations and Bust-Ups

The exceptional average 17.3 abnormal returns for voluntary bust-ups may reflect investors' concurrence with management that continued operation of the firm is likely to erode shareholder value. Busting up the firm enables shareholders to redeploy the proceeds of the liquidation to potentially more attractive alternative investments. Consistent with a perceived lack of investment options, Fleming and Moon (1995) found that firms that voluntarily liquidate have low market-to-book ratios, cash balances well in excess of their operating needs, and low debt-to-equity levels. Such firms also tend to have high equity ownership by senior managers who tend to gain significantly by liquidating the firm.

Postspin-Off Returns to Shareholders

Carve-outs and spin-offs are more likely to outperform the broader stock market indices because their share prices reflect speculation that they will be acquired rather than any improvement in the operating performance of the units once they have been spun off from the parent. One third of spin-offs are acquired within three years after the unit is spun off by the parent. Once those spin-offs that have been acquired are removed from the sample, the remaining spin-offs perform no better than their peers (Cusatis, Miles, and Woolridge, 1993). McConnell, Ozbilgin, and Wahal (2001) conclude that many historical studies showing superior postspin-off returns are indeed heavily biased by the inclusion of one or two firms in the sample whose excess returns are the result of having been acquired. Spin-offs simply may create value by providing an efficient method of transferring corporate assets to acquiring companies. Hulbert et al. (2002) found that the probability of acquisition is higher for units subject to a carve-out than for similar firms in the same industry. Harris and Glegg (2008) found significant positive abnormal returns involving cross-border spin-off announcements, in which the parent and the subsidiary are in different countries. The magnitude of the wealth gain accruing to holders of stock in the unit spun-off by the parent is higher in countries where takeover activity is high. This reflects the increased likelihood that the spun-off units will become takeover targets.

In a study of 232 spin-offs and equity carve-outs during the 1990s, Booz Allen Hamilton found that only 26 percent of the units outperformed the broader stock market indices during the two years following their separation from the parent (Scherreik, 2002). Smaller spin-offs (i.e., those with a market cap of less than $200 million) tend to outperform larger ones (i.e., those with a market cap greater than $200 million) (J.P. Morgan, 1999). This may be a result of a tendency of investors relatively unfamiliar with the business that is spun off by the parent to undervalue the spin-off. Carve-outs that are largely independent of the parent (i.e., in which the parent tended to own less than 50 percent of the equity) tended to significantly outperform the S&P 500 (Annema et al., 2002).

The evidence for the long-term performance of tracking stocks is mixed. Chemmanur and Paeglis (2000) found that the stock of parent firms tends to underperform the major stock indices, while the average tracking stock outperforms its industry stock index. However, Billett and Vijh (2004) found negative financial returns following the issue date for tracking stocks and positive, but statistically insignificant, returns for parents.

Things to Remember

Divestitures, spin-offs, equity carve-outs, split-ups, split-offs, and voluntary bust-ups are commonly used restructuring and exit strategies to redeploy assets by returning cash or noncash assets through a special dividend to shareholders or to use cash proceeds to pay off debt. On average, these restructuring strategies create positive abnormal financial returns for shareholders around the announcement date, because they tend to correct problems facing the parent. However, the longer-term performance of spin-offs, carve-outs, and tracking stocks is problematic. The extent to which such stocks outperform their industry stock indices reflects more the likelihood that they will be acquired than improved operating performance. The motives for firms undertaking these strategies include a changing corporate strategy or a desire to exit underperforming businesses. Tax and regulatory considerations, a desire to reduce risk, abandoning the core business, discarding unwanted businesses from prior acquisitions, increasing corporate transparency, and avoiding conflicts with customers are also factors causing firms to restructure.

A divestiture is the sale of a portion of the firm to an outside party, generally resulting in a cash infusion to the parent. Equity carve-outs tend to fall into two categories. The first type, the IPO, involves a transaction in which a privately held firm offers a portion of the stock of the consolidated entity to the general public. The second category, the subsidiary equity carve-out, involves a parent selling a portion of the stock in a newly created, wholly owned subsidiary to the public. As is true with subsidiary equity carve-outs, spin-offs entail the creation of a new legal entity. However, there is no cash infusion to the parent, as these new shares are distributed, as a stock dividend, to the parent's current shareholders.

In a split-up, the entire company is broken up into a series of spin-offs, with the parent ceasing to exist. Tracking stock transactions are those in which a parent divides its operations into two or more operating units and assigns a common stock to each operation. The tracking stock is owned by the parent and not by the subsidiary. Voluntary liquidations or bust-ups reflect the judgment that the sale of individual parts of the firm could realize greater value than by continuing the combined corporation. A split-off is a variation of a spin-off, in which some parent company shareholders receive shares in a subsidiary in return for exchanging their parent company shares.

Chapter Discussion Questions

15-1. How do tax and regulatory considerations influence the decision to exit a business?

15-2. How would you decide when to sell a business?

15-3. What are the major differences between a spin-off and an equity carve-out?

15-4. Under what conditions is a spin-off tax free to shareholders?

15-5. Why would a firm decide to voluntarily split up?

15-6. What are the advantages and disadvantages of tracking stocks to investors and the firm?

15-7. What factors contribute to the high positive abnormal returns to shareholders before the announcement of a voluntary bust-up?

15-8. What factors influence a parent firm's decision to undertake a spin-off rather than a divestiture or equity carve-out?

15-9. How might the form of payment affect the abnormal return to sellers and buyers?

15-10. How might spin-offs result in a wealth transfer from bondholders to shareholders?

15-11. Explain how executing successfully a large-scale divestiture can be highly complex. This is especially true when the divested unit is integrated with the parent's functional departments and other units operated by the parent. Consider the challenges of timing, interdependencies, regulatory requirements, and customer and employee perceptions.

15-12. On April 25, 2001, in an effort to increase shareholder value, USX announced its intention to split U.S. Steel and Marathon Oil into two separately traded companies. The breakup gives holders of Marathon Oil stock an opportunity to participate in the ongoing consolidation within the global oil and gas industry. Holders of USX–U.S. Steel Group common stock (target stock) would become holders of newly formed Pittsburgh-based United States Steel Corporation. What other alternatives could USX have pursued to increase shareholder value? Why do you believe they pursued the breakup strategy rather than some of the alternatives?

15-13. Hewlett-Packard (HP) announced in early 1999 the spin-off of its Agilent Technologies unit to focus on its main business of computers and printers. HP retained a controlling interest until mid-2000, when it spun off the rest of its shares in Agilent to HP shareholders as a tax-free transaction. Discuss the reasons why HP may have chosen a staged transaction rather than an outright divestiture or spin-off of the business.

15–14. After months of trying to sell its 81-percent stake in Blockbuster Inc., Viacom undertook a spin-off in mid-2004. Why would Viacom choose to spin off rather than divest its Blockbuster unit? Explain your answer.

15–15. Since 2001, GE, the world's largest conglomerate, had been underperforming the S&P 500 stock index. In late 2008, the firm announced that it was considering spinning off its consumer and industrial unit. What do you believe are GE's motives for their proposed restructuring? Why do you believe it chose a spin-off rather than an alternative restructuring strategy?

Answers to these Chapter Discussion Questions are found in the Online Instructor's Manual for instructors using this book.

Chapter Business Cases

Case Study 15–4. Hughes Corporation's Dramatic Transformation

In one of the most dramatic redirections of corporate strategy in U.S. history, Hughes Corporation transformed itself from a defense industry behemoth into the world's largest digital information and communications company. Once California's largest manufacturing employer, Hughes Corporation built spacecraft, the world's first working laser, communications satellites, radar systems, and military weapons systems. However, by the late 1990s, the firm had undergone substantial gut-wrenching change to reposition the firm in what was viewed as a more attractive growth opportunity. This transformation culminated in the firm being acquired in 2004 by News Corp, a global media empire.

To accomplish this transformation, Hughes divested its communications satellite businesses and its auto electronics operation. The corporate overhaul created a firm focused on direct-to-home satellite broadcasting with its DirecTV service offering. DirecTV's introduction to nearly 12 million U.S. homes was a technology made possible by U.S. military spending during the early 1980s. Although military spending had fueled much of Hughes's growth during the decade of the 1980s, it was becoming increasingly clear by 1988 that the level of defense spending of the Reagan years was coming to a close with the winding down of the cold war.

For the next several years, Hughes attempted to find profitable niches in the rapidly consolidating U.S. defense contracting industry. Hughes acquired General Dynamics's missile business and made about 15 smaller defense-related acquisitions. Eventually, Hughes's parent firm, General Motors, lost enthusiasm for additional investment in defense-related businesses. The decision was made that, if Hughes could not participate in the shrinking defense industry, there was no reason to retain any interests in the industry at all. In November 1995, Hughes initiated discussions with Raytheon, and two years later, it sold its aerospace and defense business to Raytheon for $9.8 billion. The firm also merged its Delco product line with GM's Delphi automotive systems. What remained was the firm's telecommunications division. Hughes had transformed itself from a $16 billion defense contractor to a svelte $4 billion telecommunications business.

Hughes's telecommunications unit was its smallest operation but, with DirecTV, its fastest growing. The transformation was to exact a huge cultural toll on Hughes's employees, most of whom had spent their careers dealing with the U.S. Department of Defense. Hughes moved to hire people aggressively from the cable and broadcast businesses. By the late 1990s, former Hughes's employees constituted only 15–20 percent of DirecTV's total employees.

Restructuring continued through the end of the 1990s. In 2000, Hughes sold its satellite manufacturing operations to Boeing for $3.75 billion. This eliminated the last component of the old Hughes and cut its workforce in half. In December 2000, Hughes paid about $180 million for Telocity, a firm that provides digital subscriber line service through phone lines. This acquisition allowed Hughes to provide high-speed Internet connections through its existing satellite service, mainly in more remote rural areas, as well as phone lines targeted at city dwellers. Hughes now could market the same combination of high-speed Internet services and video offered by cable providers, Hughes's primary competitor.

In need of cash, GM put Hughes up for sale in late 2000, expressing confidence that there would be a flood of lucrative offers. However, the faltering economy and stock market resulted in GM receiving only one serious bid, from media tycoon Rupert Murdoch of News Corp in February 2001. But, internal discord within Hughes and GM over the possible buyer of Hughes Electronics caused GM to backpedal and seek alternative bidders. In late October 2001, GM agreed to sell its Hughes Electronics subsidiary and its DirecTV home satellite network to EchoStar Communication for $25.8 billion. However, regulators concerned about the antitrust implications of the deal disallowed this transaction. In early 2004, News Corp, General Motors, and Hughes reached a definitive agreement in which News Corp acquired GM's 19.9 percent stake in Hughes and an additional 14.1 percent of Hughes from public shareholders and GM's pension and other benefit plans. News Corp paid about $14 per share, making the deal worth about $6.6 billion for 34.1 percent of Hughes. The implied value of 100 percent of Hughes was, at that time, $19.4 billion, about three fourths of EchoStar's valuation three years earlier.

Discussion Questions

1. How did changes in Hughes's external environment contribute to its dramatic 20-year restructuring effort? Cite specific influences in answering this question. (Hint: Consider the motivations discussed in this chapter for engaging in restructuring activities.) Cite examples of how Hughes took advantage of its core competencies in pursuing other alternatives.
2. Why did Hughes's board and management seem to rely heavily on divestitures rather than other restructuring strategies discussed in this chapter to achieve the radical transformation of the firm? Be specific.
3. What risks did Hughes face in moving completely away from its core defense business and into a high-technology commercial business? In your judgment, did Hughes move too quickly or too slowly? Explain your answer.
4. Why did Hughes move so aggressively to hire employees from the cable TV and broadcast industry?
5. Speculate as to why News Corp, a major entertainment industry content provider, might have been interested in acquiring Hughes. Be specific.

Solutions to these questions are found in the Online Instructor's Manual available for instructors using this book.

Case Study 15–5. AT&T (1984–2005)—A Poster Child for Restructuring Gone Awry

Between 1984 and 2000, AT&T underwent four major restructuring programs. These included the government-mandated breakup in 1984, the 1996 effort to eliminate customer conflicts, the 1998 plan to become a broadband powerhouse, and the most recent restructuring program announced in 2000 to correct past mistakes. It is difficult to identify another major corporation that has undergone as much sustained trauma as AT&T. Ironically, a former AT&T operating unit acquired its former parent in 2005.

The 1984 Restructure: Changed the Organization but Not the Culture

The genesis of Ma Bell's problems may have begun with the consent decree signed with the Department of Justice in 1984, which resulted in the spin-off of its local telephone operations to its shareholders. AT&T retained its long-distance and telecommunications equipment manufacturing operations. Although the breadth of the firm's product offering changed dramatically, little else seems to have changed. The firm remained highly bureaucratic, risk averse, and inward looking. However, a substantial market share in the lucrative long-distance market continued to generate huge cash flow for the company, thereby enabling the company to be slow to react to the changing competitive dynamics of the marketplace.

The 1996 Restructure: Lack of a Coherent Strategy

Cash accumulated from the long-distance business was spent on a variety of ill-conceived strategies, such as the firm's foray into the personal computer business. After years of unsuccessfully attempting to redefine the company's strategy, AT&T once again resorted to a major restructure of the firm. In 1996, AT&T spun off Lucent Technologies (its telecommunications equipment business) and NCR (a computer services business) to shareholders to facilitate Lucent equipment sales to former AT&T operations and eliminate the noncore NCR computer business. However, this had little impact on the AT&T share price.

The 1998 Restructure: Vision Exceeds Ability to Execute

In its third major restructure since 1984, in June 1998, AT&T CEO Michael Armstrong passionately unveiled a daring strategy to transform AT&T from a struggling long-distance telephone company into a broadband Internet access and local phone services company. To accomplish this end, he outlined his intentions to acquire cable companies MediaOne Group and Telecommunications Inc. for $58 billion and $48 billion, respectively. The plan was to use cable-TV networks to deliver the first fully integrated package of broadband Internet access and local phone service via the cable-TV network.

AT&T Could Not Handle Its Early Success

During the next several years, Armstrong seemed to be up to the task, cutting sales, general, and administrative expenses' share of revenue from 28 percent to 20 percent, giving AT&T a cost structure comparable to its competitors. He attempted to change the bureaucratic culture to one able to compete effectively in the deregulated environment of the post-1996 Telecommunications Act by issuing stock options to all employees, tying compensation to performance, and reducing layers of managers. He used AT&T's stock, as well as cash, to buy the cable companies before the decline in AT&T's long-distance business pushed the stock into a free fall. He also transformed AT&T Wireless from a collection of local businesses into a national business.

Notwithstanding these achievements, AT&T experienced major missteps. Employee turnover became a big problem, especially among senior managers. Armstrong also bought Telecommunications and MediaOne when valuations for cable-television assets were near their peak. He paid about $106 billion in 2000, when they were worth about $80 billion. His failure to cut enough deals with other cable operators (e.g., Time Warner) to sell AT&T's local phone service meant that AT&T could market its services only in regional markets rather than on a national basis. In addition, AT&T moved large corporate customers to its Concert joint venture with British Telecom, alienating many AT&T salespeople, who subsequently quit. As a result, customer service deteriorated rapidly and major customers defected. Finally, Armstrong seriously underestimated the pace of erosion in AT&T's long-distance revenue base.

AT&T May Have Become Overwhelmed by the Rate of Change

What happened? Perhaps AT&T fell victim to the same problems as many other acquisitive companies. AT&T is capable of exceptional vision but incapable of effective execution. Effective execution involves buying or building assets at a reasonable cost. Its substantial overpayment for its cable acquisitions meant that it would be unable to earn the returns required by investors in what they would consider a reasonable period. Moreover, Armstrong's efforts to shift from the firm's historical business by buying into the cable-TV business through acquisition had saddled the firm with $62 billion in debt.

AT&T tried to do too much too quickly. New initiatives, such as high-speed Internet access and local telephone services over cable-television network, were too small to pick up the slack. Much time and energy seems to have gone into planning and acquiring what were viewed as key building blocks to the strategy. However, there appears to have been insufficient focus and realism in terms of the time and resources required to make all the pieces of the strategy fit together. Some parts of the overall strategy were at odds with other parts. For example, AT&T undercut its core long-distance wired telephone business by offers of free long-distance wireless to attract new subscribers. Despite aggressive efforts to change the culture, AT&T continued to suffer from a culture that evolved in the years before 1996, during which the industry was heavily regulated. That atmosphere bred a culture based on consensus building, ponderously slow decision making, and a low tolerance for risk. Consequently, the AT&T culture was unprepared for the fiercely competitive deregulated environment of the late 1990s (Truitt, 2001).

Furthermore, AT&T created individual tracking stocks for AT&T Wireless and Liberty Media. The intention of the tracking stocks was to link the unit's stock to its individual performance, create a currency for the unit to make acquisitions, and provide a new means of motivating the unit's management by giving them stock in their own operation. Unlike a spin-off, AT&T's board continued to exert direct control over these units. In an IPO in April 2000, AT&T sold 14 percent of AT&T's Wireless tracking stock to the public to raise funds and to focus investor attention on the true value of the Wireless operations.

Investors Lose Patience

Although all these actions created a sense that grandiose change was imminent, investor patience was wearing thin. Profitability foundered. The market share loss in its long-distance business accelerated. Although cash flow remained strong, it was clear that a cash machine so dependent on the deteriorating long-distance telephone business soon could grind to a halt. Investors' loss of faith was manifested in the sharp decline in AT&T stock that occurred in 2000.

The 2000 Restructure: Correcting the Mistakes of the Past

Pushed by investor impatience and a growing realization that achieving AT&T's vision would be more time and resource consuming than originally believed, Armstrong announced on October 25, 2000, the breakup of the business for the fourth time. The plan involved the creation of four new independent companies: AT&T Wireless, AT&T Consumer, AT&T Broadband, and Liberty Media.

By breaking the company into specific segments, AT&T believed that individual units could operate more efficiently and aggressively. AT&T's consumer long-distance business would be able to enter the digital subscriber line (DSL) market. DSL is a broadband technology based on the telephone wires that connect individual homes with the telephone network. AT&T's cable operations could continue to sell their own fast Internet connections and compete directly against AT&T's long-distance telephone business. Moreover, the four individual businesses would create "pure-play" investor opportunities. Specifically, AT&T proposed splitting off AT&T Wireless in early 2001 and issuing tracking stocks to the public in late 2001 for AT&T's Consumer operations, including long-distance and Worldnet Internet service, and AT&T's Broadband (cable) operations. The tracking shares would later be converted to regular AT&T common shares as if issued by AT&T Broadband, making it an independent entity. AT&T would retain AT&T Business Services (i.e., AT&T Lab and Telecommunications Network) with the surviving AT&T entity. Investor reaction was swift and negative. Not swayed by the proposal, investors caused the stock to drop 13 percent in a single day. Moreover, it ended 2000 at 17½, down 66 percent from the beginning of the year.

The More Things Change the More They Stay the Same

On July 10, 2001, AT&T Wireless Services became an independent company, in accordance with plans announced during the 2000 restructure program. AT&T Wireless became a separate company when AT&T converted the tracking shares of the mobile-phone business into common stock and split off the unit from the parent. AT&T encouraged shareholders to exchange their AT&T common shares for Wireless common shares by offering AT&T shareholders 1.176 Wireless shares for each share of AT&T common. The exchange ratio represented a 6.5 percent premium over AT&T's current common share price. AT&T Wireless shares have fallen 44 percent since AT&T first sold the tracking stock in April 2000. On August 10, 2001, AT&T spun off Liberty Media.

After extended discussions, AT&T agreed, on December 21, 2001, to merge its broadband unit with Comcast to create the largest cable television and high-speed Internet service company in the United States. Without the future growth engine offered by Broadband and Wireless, AT&T's remaining long-distance businesses and business services operations had limited growth prospects. After a decade of tumultuous change, AT&T was back where it was at the beginning of the 1990s. At about $15 billion in late 2004, AT&T's market capitalization was about one sixth of that of such major competitors as Verizon and SBC. SBC Communications (a former local AT&T operating company) acquired AT&T on November 18, 2005, in a $16 billion deal and promptly renamed the combined firms AT&T.

Discussion Questions

1. What were the primary factors contributing to AT&T's numerous restructuring efforts since 1984? How did they differ? How were they similar?
2. Why do you believe that AT&T chose to split off its wireless operations rather than divest the unit? What might you have done differently?
3. Was AT&T proactive or reactive in initiating its 2000 restructuring program? Explain your answer.
4. AT&T overpaid for many of its largest acquisitions made during the 1990s. How might this have contributed to its subsequent restructuring efforts?

5. To what extent were AT&T's ineffectual restructuring efforts a function of factors beyond management's control and to what extent were they due to poor implementation? Be specific.
6. What challenges did AT&T face in trying to split up the company in 2000? What might you have done differently to overcome these obstacles?

Solutions to these case study questions are found in the Online Instructor's Manual for instructors using this book.

16

Alternative Exit and Restructuring Strategies

Reorganization and Liquidation

What is important is not adding more years to life but more life to your years.
—Doug Fields

Inside M&A: Calpine Emerges from the Protection of Bankruptcy Court

Following approval of its sixth Plan of Reorganization by the U.S. Bankruptcy Court for the Southern District of New York, Calpine Corporation was able to emerge from Chapter 11 bankruptcy on January 31, 2008. Burdened by excessive debt and court battles with creditors on how to use its cash, the electric utility had sought Chapter 11 protection by filing a petition with the bankruptcy court in December 2005. After settlements with certain stakeholders, all classes of creditors voted to approve the Plan of Reorganization, which provided for the discharge of claims through the issuance of reorganized Calpine Corporation common stock, cash, or a combination of cash and stock to its creditors.

Shortly after exiting bankruptcy, Calpine canceled all its then outstanding common stock and authorized the issuance of 485 million shares of reorganized Calpine Corporation common stock for distribution to holders of unsecured claims. In addition, the firm issued warrants (i.e., securities) to purchase 48.5 million shares of reorganized Calpine Corporation common stock to the holders of the canceled (i.e., previously outstanding) common stock. The warrants were issued pro rata (i.e., on a proportionate basis) reflecting the number of shares of "old common stock" held at the time of cancellation. These warrants carried an exercise price of $23.88 per share and expired on August 25, 2008. Relisted on the New York Stock Exchange, the reorganized Calpine Corporation common stock began trading under the symbol CPN on February 7, 2008, at about $18 per share.

The firm had improved its capital structure while in bankruptcy. On entering bankruptcy, Calpine carried $17.4 billion of debt with an average interest rate of 10.3 percent. By retiring unsecured debt with reorganized Calpine Corporation common stock and selling certain assets, Calpine was able to repay or refinance certain project debt, thereby reducing the prebankruptcy petition debt by approximately $7.0 billion. On exiting bankruptcy, Calpine negotiated approximately $7.3 billion of secured "exit facilities" (i.e., credit lines) from Goldman Sachs, Credit Suisse, Deutsche Bank, and Morgan Stanley. About $6.4 billion of these funds were used to satisfy cash payment obligations under the Plan of Reorganization. These obligations included the repayment of a portion of unsecured creditor claims and administrative claims, such as legal and consulting fees, as well as expenses incurred in connection with the "exit facilities" and immediate working capital requirements. On emerging from Chapter 11, the firm carried $10.4 billion of debt with an average interest rate of 8.1 percent.

Chapter Overview

In countries where court enforcement of creditor rights is inconsistent, reforms in creditor rights have relatively little impact on the availability and cost of commercial bank lending. However, reforms in creditor rights tend to increase the availability and reduce the cost of credit in countries where court enforcement is quick and fair (Safavian and Sharma, 2007). Haselmann, Pistor, and Vig (2006) show that, in their sample of bank loans in 12 emerging countries, the availability of credit increased and the cost of credit declined in response to bankruptcy laws enforcing creditor rights to the collateral underlying loans. Hence, the quick and fair enforcement of creditor rights to the collateral underlying loans tends to lower borrowing costs and increase access to credit. The effective enforcement of bankruptcy laws is integral to the success of this process.

This chapter focuses on bankruptcy and liquidation as alternative restructuring or exit strategies for failing firms. Bankruptcy enables a failing firm to reorganize, while protected from its creditors, or to cease operation by selling its assets to satisfy all or a portion of the firm's outstanding debt. This chapter addresses how reorganization and liquidation take place both inside and outside the protection of the bankruptcy court. The chapter also discusses common strategic options for failing firms, the current state of bankruptcy prediction models, and empirical studies of the performance of firms experiencing financial distress. The major segments of this chapter include the following:

- Business Failure
- Voluntary Settlements with Creditors outside of Bankruptcy
- Reorganization and Liquidation in Bankruptcy
- Analyzing Strategic Options for Failing Firms
- Predicting Corporate Default and Bankruptcy
- Empirical Studies of Financial Distress
- Things to Remember

A review of this chapter (including practice questions with answers) is available in the file folder entitled Student Study Guide contained on the CD-ROM accompanying this book. The CD-ROM also contains a Learning Interactions Library, enabling students to test their knowledge of this chapter in a "real-time" environment.

Business Failure

Failing firms may be subject to financial distress as measured by declining asset values, liquidity, and cash flow. The term *financial distress* does not have a strict technical or legal definition. The term could apply to a firm unable to meet its obligations or a specific security on which the issuer has defaulted. Firms whose debt yields more than 10 percentage points above the risk-free rate often are considered financially distressed. Moody's credit rating agency defines *default* as any missed or delayed disbursement of interest or principal, bankruptcy, receivership, or an exchange diminishing the value of what is owed to bondholders. For example, the issuer might offer bondholders a new security or package of securities (such as preferred or common stock or debt with a lower coupon or par value) that are worth less than what they are owed (Keenan, Shotgrin, and Sobehart, 1999).

Technical insolvency arises when a firm is unable to pay its liabilities as they come due. *Legal insolvency* occurs when a firm's liabilities exceed the fair market value of its assets. Creditors' claims cannot be satisfied unless the firm's assets can be liquidated for more than the book value of the firm's liabilities. U.S. courts treat both technical insolvency and legal insolvency as a financial failure of the firm. *Bankruptcy* is a federal legal proceeding designed to protect the technically or legally insolvent firm from lawsuits by its creditors until a decision can be made to shut down or continue to operate the firm. A firm is not bankrupt or in bankruptcy until it files, or its creditors file, a petition for reorganization or liquidation with the federal bankruptcy courts.

The terms *liquidity* and *solvency* often are used inappropriately. Liquidity is the ability of a business to have sufficient cash on hand (as opposed to tied up in receivables and inventory) to meet its immediate obligations without having to incur significant losses in selling assets. Insolvency means that a firm simply cannot pay its bills under any circumstances. A liquid business is more likely to be solvent (i.e., able to pay its bills); however, not all businesses that are liquid are solvent and not all solvent businesses have adequate liquidity.

Initially, some observers diagnosed giant U.S. investment bank Lehman Brothers' problems as insufficient liquidity to meet its obligations if many creditors demanded immediate payment. Loan agreements often have so called cross-default clauses enabling a lender to demand immediate payment if a borrower is in default on any loan. Depending on loan covenants, default could be triggered by the borrower's share price declining below some predetermined level. Short selling pushed the firm's share price down precipitously triggering such clauses. It soon became clear that Lehman would not be able to pay its debt even if its entire asset portfolio were sold. What may have started as a liquidity problem soon became an insolvency issue. For detail on the Lehman Bankruptcy, see Case Study 16–2 later in the chapter.

Receivership can be an alternative to bankruptcy in which a court- or government-appointed individual (i.e., a receiver) takes control of the assets and affairs of a business to administer them according to the court's or government's directives. The purpose of a receiver may be to serve as a custodian while disputes between officers, directors, or stockholders are settled or to liquidate the firm's assets. Under no circumstance can the firm's debt be discharged without the approval of the bankruptcy court. In most states, receivership cannot take effect unless a lawsuit is underway and the court has determined that receivership is appropriate. *Conservatorship* represents a less restrictive alternative to receivership. While the receiver is expected to terminate the rights of shareholders and managers, a conservator is expected to merely assume these rights temporarily.

For example, in July 2008, the failing IndyMac Bank was taken into administrative receivership by the Federal Deposit Insurance Corporation, and the bank's assets and secured liabilities were transferred into a "bridge bank" called *IndyMac Federal Bank*, until the assets could be liquidated. Also in September 2008, the CEO and the boards of the Federal National Mortgage Association and the Federal Home Loan Mortgage Corporation were dismissed and the firms were put under the conservatorship of the Federal Housing Finance Agency while the their asset portfolios were reduced.

The conservatorship status leaves open the possibility that smaller versions of these firms will emerge as privately owned companies in the future, but without any implicit or explicit government backing.

A debtor firm and its creditors may choose to reach a negotiated settlement outside of bankruptcy, within the protection of the court, or through a prepackaged bankruptcy. The last represents a blend of the first two scenarios. The following pages discuss each of these scenarios.

Voluntary Settlements with Creditors outside of Bankruptcy

An insolvent firm may reach an agreement with its creditors to restructure its obligations out of court to avoid the costs of bankruptcy proceedings. The debtor firm usually initiates the voluntary settlement process, because it generally offers the best chance for the current owners to recover a portion of their investments either by continuing to operate the firm or through a planned liquidation of the firm. This process normally involves the debtor firm requesting a meeting with its creditors. At this meeting, a committee of creditors is selected to analyze the debtor firm's financial position and recommend an appropriate course of action. The committee can recommend that the firm either continue to operate or be liquidated.

Increasingly, distressed companies are choosing to restructure outside of bankruptcy court (Lovely, 2007). Smaller firms are inclined to use out-of-court settlements because of the excessive expenses associated with reorganizing in bankruptcy courts. Small business bankruptcy filings cost $50,000 to $100,000 in legal expenses and court filing fees. Legal and fee expenses well in excess of $100,000 are common (Buljevich, 2005). More mid-sized companies moving into international markets also contribute to the growth in out-of-court restructurings. Such firms may not be able to restructure through U.S. bankruptcy courts if the ruling is not recognized overseas. Large companies often have a difficult time achieving out-of-court settlements because they usually have hundreds of creditors.

Voluntary Settlement Resulting in Continued Operation

Plans to restructure the debtor firm developed cooperatively with creditors commonly are called *workouts*. A **workout** is an arrangement outside of bankruptcy by a debtor and its creditors for payment or rescheduling of payment of the debtor's obligations. Because of the firm's weak financial position, the creditors must be willing to restructure the insolvent firm's debts to enable it to sustain its operations. **Debt restructuring** involves concessions by creditors that lower an insolvent firm's payments so that it may remain in business. Restructuring normally is accomplished in three ways: an extension, a composition, or a debt-for-equity swap.

An **extension** occurs when creditors agree to lengthen the period during which the debtor firm can repay its debt. Creditors often agree to temporarily suspend both interest and principal repayments. A **composition** is an agreement in which creditors agree to settle for less than the full amount they are owed. A **debt-for-equity swap** occurs when creditors surrender a portion of their claims on the firm in exchange for an ownership position in the firm. If the reduced debt service payments enable the firm to prosper, the value of the stock in the long run may far exceed the amount of debt the creditors were willing to forgive. In 2004, Revlon reached agreement with Fidelity

Management & Research Company and MacAndrews & Forbes to exchange $155 million and $775 million, respectively, in debt for common stock.

Exhibit 16-1 depicts a debt restructure of a bankrupt company that would enable the firm to continue operation by converting debt to equity. Although the firm, Survivor Incorporated, has positive earnings before interest and taxes, it is not enough to meet its interest payments. When principal payments are considered, cash flow becomes significantly negative. Therefore, it is technically insolvent. As a result of the restructuring of the firm's debt, Survivor Incorporated is able to continue to operate. However, the firm's lenders now have a controlling interest in the firm. Note the same type of restructuring could take place either voluntarily outside the courts or as a result of reorganizing under the protection of the bankruptcy court. The latter scenario is discussed later in this chapter.

Exhibit 16–1 Survivor Inc. Restructures Its Debt

Survivor Inc. currently has 400,000 shares of common equity outstanding at a par value of $10 per share. The current rate of interest on its debt is 8 percent and the debt is amortized over 20 years. The combined federal, state, and local tax rate is 40 percent. The firm's cash flow and capital position are shown in Table 16–1.

Assume bondholders are willing to convert $5 million of debt to equity at the current par value of $10 per share. This necessitates that Survivor Inc. issue 500,000 new shares. These actions result in positive cash flow, a substantial reduction in the firm's debt-to-total capital ratio, and a transfer of control to the bondholders. The former stockholders now own only 44.4 percent (4 million/9 million) of the company. The revised cash flow and capital position are shown in Table 16–2.

Table 16–1   Cash Flow and Capital Position

Income and Cash Flow		Total Capital	
Earnings before interest and taxes	$500,000	Debt	$10 million
Interest	$800,000	Equity	$4 million
Earnings before taxes	$(300,000)	Total	$14 million
Taxes	$120,000		
Earnings after taxes	$(180,000)	Debt/Total capital	71.4%
Depreciation	$400,000		
Principal repayment	$(500,000)		
Cash flow	$(280,000)		

Table 16–2   Revised Cash Flow and Capital Position

Income and Cash Flow		Total Capital	
Earnings before interest and taxes	$500,000	Debt	$5 million
Interest	$400,000	Equity	$9 million
Earnings before taxes	$100,000	Total	$14 million
Taxes	$40,000		
Earnings after taxes	$60,000	Debt/Total capital	35.7%
Depreciation	$400,000		
Principal repayment	$(250,000)		
Cash flow	$210,000		

Voluntary Settlement Resulting in Liquidation

If the creditors conclude that the insolvent firm's situation cannot be resolved, liquidation may be the only acceptable course of action. Liquidation can be conducted outside the court in a private liquidation or through the U.S. bankruptcy court. If the insolvent firm is willing to accept liquidation and all creditors agree, legal proceedings are not necessary. Creditors normally prefer private liquidations to avoid lengthy and costly litigation. Through a process called an assignment, a committee representing creditors grants the power to liquidate the firm's assets to a third party, called an *assignee or trustee*. The responsibility of the assignee is to sell the assets as quickly as possible while obtaining the best possible price. The assignee distributes the proceeds of the asset sales to the creditors and the firm's owners if any monies remain.

Case Study 16–1 describes how CompUSA voluntarily reached agreement with its creditors without seeking protection from the U.S. bankruptcy court. Note that the decision to liquidate the firm came only after completing an exhaustive attempt to sell the business.

Case Study 16–1 CompUSA Liquidates outside of Bankruptcy Court

Succumbing to pressure from rivals like Best Buy and Wal-Mart, CompUSA, the computer retailer announced, in early December 2007, that it had been sold to an investment firm, Gordon Brothers Group. Gordon Brothers, a firm specializing in restructuring and liquidating retail assets, intended to liquidate the business. Gordon Brothers announced that active discussions were underway to sell its technical services business, CompUSA TechPro, its online sales operation CompUSA.com, and certain stores in key geographic markets.

The firm reached agreement with its creditors that an orderly liquidation was the preferred way to maximize the value of the business. In early 2007, CompUSA had closed more than half its U.S. retail stores in a bid to streamline operations and bolster margins in top-performing stores. The firm shifted its strategy to catch the big-screen HDTV wave and focus on the small business segment. At the end of 2007, CompUSA had about 103 stores operating in 68 markets.

In 2006, its Mexican parent company, Grupo Carso SZ (controlled by billionaire Carlos Slim Helu) hired Credit Suisse to explore alternatives. Credit Suisse had unsuccessfully tried to sell the business for more than a year. CompUSA would be run on an interim basis by Bill Weinstein, a principal at Gordon Brothers, and by Stephen Gray, a managing partner at restructuring firm CRG Partners, who would serve as chief restructuring officer. Current CompUSA CEO Roman Ross would stay on in an executive advisory capacity during the transition.

Discussion Questions

1. Describe the options available to Grupo Carso, CompUSA's parent, for maximizing the value of the firm. Be specific.
2. Why did CompUSA's creditors agree to liquidation outside of bankruptcy court?

Solutions to these questions are found in the Online Instructor's Manual for instructors using this book.

Reorganization and Liquidation in Bankruptcy

In the absence of a voluntary settlement out of court, the debtor firm may seek protection from its creditors by initiating bankruptcy or may be forced into bankruptcy by its creditors. When the debtor firm files the petition with the bankruptcy court, the bankruptcy is said to be *voluntary bankruptcy*. When creditors do the filing, the action is said to be *involuntary bankruptcy*. Once either a voluntary or involuntary petition is filed, the debtor firm is protected from any further legal action related to its debts until the bankruptcy proceedings are completed. The filing of a petition triggers an *automatic stay* once the court accepts the request, which provides a period suspending all judgments, collection activities, foreclosures, and repossessions of property by the creditors on any debt or claim that arose before the filing of the bankruptcy petition.

The Evolution of U.S. Bankruptcy Laws and Practices

U.S. bankruptcy laws and practices focus on rehabilitating and reorganizing debtors in distress. Except for Chapter 12, all the chapters of the present bankruptcy code are odd numbered and enumerated with Arabic numerals. (Roman numerals were used to number the chapters, prior to the Reform Act of 1978.) Chapters 1, 3, and 5 cover matters of general application, while Chapters 7, 9, 11, 12, and 13 concern liquidation (business or nonbusiness), municipality bankruptcy, business reorganization, family farm debt adjustment, and wage-earner or personal (i.e., nonbusiness) reorganization, respectively. Chapter 15 applies to international cases.

The Bankruptcy Reform Act of 1978

The Bankruptcy Reform Act of 1978 substantially changed the bankruptcy laws by adding a strong business reorganization mechanism, referred to as Chapter 11 of the U.S. bankruptcy code. Chapter 11 replaced the old Chapters 10 through 12 of the U.S. bankruptcy code. Similarly, a more powerful personal bankruptcy, Chapter 13, replaced the old laws. In general, the Reform Act of 1978 made it easier for both businesses and individuals to file a bankruptcy and reorganize.

The 1978 Bankruptcy Reform Act also broadened the conditions under which companies could file, so that a firm could declare bankruptcy without having to wait until it was virtually insolvent. The intent of making the bankruptcy code less rigid was to increase the likelihood that creditors and owners would reach agreement on plans to reorganize rather than liquidate insolvent firms. Reorganization rather than liquidation offered the prospect of saving jobs and government tax revenues, while enabling creditors to recover a larger portion of their claims. Moreover, debtor firm shareholders also potentially could recover some or all of their original investment in instances where they received warrants to purchase the newly reorganized company's shares.

The Bankruptcy Reform Act of 1994

During the 1980s and early 1990s the number of bankruptcy filings reached record levels. Such notable companies as R. H. Macy, LTV, Continental Airlines, Pan Am, Texaco, Eastern Airlines, Allied Stores, Federated Department Stores, and Greyhound filed for bankruptcy. Most of the filings were for Chapter 11 reorganization. With operations in different countries, Chapter 11 filings for Maxwell Communication and Olympia & York involved insolvency laws in different legal jurisdictions. As the frequency and complexity of cases grew, concerns about the level of professional fees and the perceived loss of value of assets in a number of bankruptcy cases increased the demand for new legislation. In response, the U.S. Congress passed the Bankruptcy Reform Act of 1994, which represented the most comprehensive piece of bankruptcy legislation since the 1978 act. The 1994 act contains provisions to expedite bankruptcy proceedings and encourage individual debtors to use Chapter 13 to reschedule their debts rather than use Chapter 7 to liquidate.

The Bankruptcy Abuse Prevention and Consumer Protection Act of 2005

On April 19, 2005, the Bankruptcy Abuse Prevention and Consumer Protection Act (BAPCPA) became law. The new legislation primarily affects consumer filings, making it more difficult for a person or estate to file for Chapter 7 bankruptcy. The BAPCPA affects business filers as well, with the heaviest influence on smaller (i.e., those with less than $2 million in debt) businesses.

This act represents the most comprehensive bankruptcy reform since 1978. Prior to BAPCPA, commercial enterprises used Chapter 11 reorganization to continue operating a business and repay creditors through a court-approved plan of reorganization. The debtor had the exclusive right to file a plan of reorganization for the first 120 days after it filed the case. The debtor also had to provide creditors with a disclosure statement containing information sufficient to enable them to evaluate the plan. The court ultimately approved or disapproved the plan of reorganization. If approved, the plan enabled the debtor to reduce its debts by repaying a portion of its obligations and discharging other obligations. The debtor could also terminate onerous contracts and leases, recover assets, and restructure its operations to restore profitability.

BPCPA changed this process as follows: (1) reducing the maximum length of time debtors' have the exclusive right to submit a plan; (2) shortening debtors' time to accept or reject leases; and (3) limiting compensation under key employee retention programs. Prior to BAPCPA, a debtor corporation had the opportunity to request a bankruptcy judge to extend the period for submission of the plan of reorganization as long as it could justify its request. Once the judge ruled that the debtor has been given sufficient time, any creditor could submit a reorganization plan. The new law caps the exclusivity period at 18 months from the day of the bankruptcy filing. The debtor then has an additional two months to win the creditors' acceptance of the plan thereby providing a debtor-in-position a maximum of 20 months before creditors can submit their reorganization plans.

In addition to increased privileges for creditors via the amended bankruptcy laws, lessors (i.e., owners of the leased asset) also benefit from BAPCPA amendments. "Good-cause" extensions are restricted to 90 days without written consent of the lessor. Under prior legislation, leases could be extended indefinitely, as long as the debtor-in-position continued making payments due under the commercial lease. Under the new legislation, the trustee or debtor-in-possession no longer would be able to get endless extensions, even if the debtor is paying the rent according to the terms of the lease agreement.

BAPCPA also limits pay for key employees. Payments to management employees cannot be more than 10 times the amount paid to nonmanagement employees. Absent the retention of nonmanagement employees subsequent to filing for bankruptcy, payment cannot exceed 25 percent of any other payment made to a management employee during the prior year.

Before BAPCPA, Chapter 11 litigation often took several years before the reorganized firm emerged from bankruptcy. United Airlines (UAL) exited from bankruptcy in February 2006 after 38 months in Chapter 11, the longest period under court protection in U.S. bankruptcy history. UAL used the time to radically restructure the company and trim $7 billion in annual costs, including two rounds of employee pay cuts and the elimination of 25,000 jobs. The firm also transferred successfully its defined benefit pension plans to the U.S Pension Benefit Guaranty Corporation and further reduced its cost structure by shedding more than 100 planes from its fleet, cutting some U.S. flights and expanding internationally.

Finally, Chapter 15 was added to the U.S. Bankruptcy Code by BAPCPA of 2005 to reflect the adoption of the Model Law on Cross-Border Insolvency passed by the United Nations Commission on International Trade Law (UNCITRAL) in 1997. Chapter 15 replaces section 304 of the U.S. Bankruptcy Code. The purpose of UNCITRAL is to provide for better coordination among legal systems for cross-border bankruptcy cases. The application of Chapter 15 is discussed in more detail later in this chapter.

Figure 16–1 provides annual historical data on U.S. business bankruptcy filings. Such filings follow closely trends in the economy. The peaks in 1993, 2002, and 2008 mirrored the effects of a recession in the early 1990s, 2001, and 2008. Despite a robust economy, business bankruptcy filings remained at relatively high levels through 2005 as firms rushed to avoid the more stringent new requirements of the Bankruptcy Abuse Prevention and Consumer Protection Act of 2005, which did not become effective until October 17 of that year.

Filing for Chapter 11 Reorganization

Chapter 11 reorganization may involve a corporation, sole proprietorship, or partnership. Since a corporation is viewed as separate from its owners (i.e., the shareholders), the Chapter 11 bankruptcy of a corporation (i.e., the corporation as debtor) does not put the personal assets of the stockholders at risk, other than the value of their investment in the firm's stock. In contrast, sole proprietorships (i.e., the owner as debtor) and owners are not separate. Therefore, a bankruptcy case involving a sole proprietorship includes both the business and personal assets of the owner–debtor. Like a corporation, a partnership exists as a separate entity apart from its partners. In a partnership bankruptcy case (i.e., the partnership as debtor), the partners may be sued such that their personal assets are used to pay creditors. Consequently, the partners, themselves, may file for bankruptcy protection.

Figure 16–2 summarizes the process for filing for reorganization under Chapter 11. The process begins by filing in a federal bankruptcy court. In the case of an involuntary petition, a hearing must be held to determine whether the firm is insolvent. If the firm is

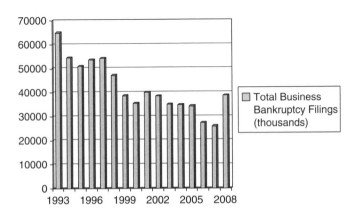

FIGURE 16–1 U.S. total business bankruptcy filings by fiscal year including Chapters 7, 11, 12, (farm), and 13 (single proprietorships). *Source:* Administrative Office of the United States Courts.

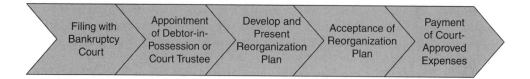

FIGURE 16–2 Procedures for reorganizing in bankruptcy.

found to be insolvent, the court enters an ***order for relief,*** which initiates the bankruptcy proceedings. On the filing of a reorganization petition, the filing firm becomes the ***debtor-in-possession*** of all the assets. As previously noted, under current BAPCPA legislation, the debtor has a maximum of 20 months to convince creditors to accept its plan of reorganization, after which the creditors can submit their own proposal. In the case of fraud, creditors may request that the court appoint a trustee instead of the debtor to manage the firm during the reorganization period.

The debtor-in-position and creditors have considerable flexibility in working together during Chapter 11 reorganization. This enables them to negotiate debt repayment schedules, the restructuring of debt, and the granting of loans by the creditors to the debtor. Without a workable plan, the firm is liquidated in accordance with the procedures outlined in Chapter 7 of the U.S. bankruptcy code.

The U.S. Trustee, the bankruptcy department of the U.S. Justice Department, appoints one or more committees to represent the interests of creditors and shareholders. The purpose of these committees is to work with the debtor-in-possession to develop a reorganization plan for exiting Chapter 11. Creditors and shareholders are grouped according to the similarity of claims. In the case of creditors, the plan must be approved by holders of at least two thirds of the dollar value of the claims as well as a simple majority of the creditors in each group. In the case of shareholders, two thirds of those in each group (e.g., common and preferred shareholders) must approve the plan. Following acceptance by creditors, bondholders, and stockholders, the bankruptcy court also must approve the reorganization plan. Even if creditors or shareholders vote to reject the plan, the court is empowered to ignore the vote and approve the plan if it finds the plan to be fair to creditors and shareholders as well as feasible. Finally, the debtor-in-position is responsible for paying the expenses approved by the court of all parties whose services contributed to the approval or disapproval of the plan.

Although intended to give firms time to restructure, whether a business is likely to be successful in Chapter 11 in part depends on the type of business and the circumstances under which it seeks the protection of the bankruptcy court. The credit crisis of 2008, which saw global banks write down more than $300 billion in assets and caused the hurried sales of Bear Stearns, Merrill Lynch, Wachovia, and Washington Mutual, also forced investment-banking behemoth Lehman Brothers to seek protection from its creditors. Case Study 16–2 illustrates the race against time to salvage as much of the firm's franchise as possible and how circumstances overcame Lehman's plans to restructure the business. Lehman Brothers had a plan in place to restructure operations, reduce the overall cost structure, and improve performance. Top executives intended to sell a majority of the firm's investment management business, which included money manager Neuberger Berman, and spin off its troubled real estate loans into a publicly traded unit. The firm also had explored the sale of its broker–dealer operations (i.e., a broker network and securities trading business). However, plans take time to implement and, with the loss of confidence in the capital markets in general and Lehman in particular, the firm simply ran out of time and options.

Case Study 16–2 Lehman Brothers Files for Chapter 11 in the Biggest Bankruptcy in U.S. History

A casualty of the 2008 credit crisis that shook Wall Street to its core, Lehman Brothers Holdings, Inc. (LBHI), a holding company, on September 15, 2008, announced that it had filed a petition under Chapter 11 of the U.S. bankruptcy code. Lehman's board of directors decided to opt for court protection after attempts to find a buyer for the entire firm collapsed. With assets of $639 billion and liabilities of $613 billion, Lehman is the largest bankruptcy in history in terms of assets. The next biggest bankruptcies were WorldCom and Enron with $126 billion and $81 billion in assets, respectively.

None of the holding company's subsidiaries was included in the filing, enabling customers of Lehman's brokerage, Neuberger Berman Holdings, to continue to use their accounts to trade. Furthermore, by excluding its units from the bankruptcy filing, customers of its broker–dealer operations would not be subject to claims by LBHI's more than 100,000 creditors in the bankruptcy case.

When a financial services firm goes bankrupt, counterparties have a right to cancel contracts. Lehman would normally hedge or protect its investments by taking opposite positions to minimize potential losses in its derivatives portfolios. Derivatives are financial instruments whose value changes in response to the value of the underlying assets over a specific period. For example, if the firm purchased a contract to buy oil at a specific price at some point in the future, it would also sell a contract at a somewhat lower price to another party (called a *counterparty*) to minimize losses if the price of oil dropped. Thus, filing for Chapter 11 reorganization left Lehman's investment positions unprotected.

On September 20, 2008, Barclays PLC., a major U.K. bank, acquired Lehman's broker–dealer operations for $250 million and paid an additional $1.5 billion for the firm's New York headquarters building and two New Jersey–based data centers. Coming just five days after Lehman filed for bankruptcy, the deal reflected the urgency to find buyers for those businesses whose value consisted primarily of their employees. Barclays did not buy any of Lehman's commercial real estate assets or private equity and hedge fund investments. However, Barclays did agree to take $47.4 billion in securities and assume $45.5 billion in trading liabilities. On September 24, 2008, Japanese brokerage Nomura Securities acquired Lehman's Japanese and Australian operation for $250 million. Lehman's investment management group, Neuberger Berman, was sold in late December 2008 to a Neuberger management group for $922 million. Under the deal, Neuberger's management would own 51 percent of the firm and Lehman's creditors would control the remainder. Other Lehman assets, consisting primarily of complex derivatives ranging from oil price futures to insuring corporate debt (i.e., credit default swaps) to options on stock indices, with more than 8,000 counterparties, were expected to take years to identify, value, and liquidate. The firm also could expect to face numerous lawsuits.

The October 18, 2008, auction of $400 billion of Lehman's debt issues was valued at 8.5 cents on the dollar. Because such debt was backed by only the firm's creditworthiness, the buyers of the Lehman debt had purchased insurance from other financial institutions to mitigate the risk of a Lehman default. The existence of these credit default swap arrangements meant that the insurers were required to pay Lehman bondholders $366 billion (i.e., .915 times $400 billion). Purchasers of this debt at the auction were betting that, following Lehman's eventual liquidation, holders

Continued

Case Study 16–2 Lehman Brothers Files for Chapter 11 in the Biggest Bankruptcy in U.S. History — Cont'd

of this debt would receive more than 8.5 cents on the dollar and the insurers would be able to satisfy their obligations.

Hedge funds also were affected significantly by the Lehman bankruptcy. Hedge funds borrowed heavily from Lehman (a so-called prime broker), putting up certain assets as collateral for the loans. While legal, Lehman was using this collateral to borrow from other firms. By using its customers' collateral as its own collateral, Lehman and other firms could borrow more money, using the proceeds to make additional investments. When Lehman filed for bankruptcy, the court took control of such assets until who was entitled to the assets could be determined. Moreover, while derivative agreements are designed to terminate whenever a party declares bankruptcy and be settled outside of court, Lehman's general creditors may lay claim to any collateral whose value exceeds the value of the derivative agreements.

Discussion Questions

1. Why did Lehman choose not to seek Chapter 11 protection for its subsidiaries?
2. How does Chapter 11 bankruptcy protect Lehman's creditors? How does it potentially hurt them? Explain your answers.
3. Do you believe the U.S. bankruptcy process was appropriate in this instance? Explain your answer.
4. Do you believe the U.S. government's failure to bail out Lehman, thereby forcing the firm to file for bankruptcy, exacerbated the global credit meltdown in October 2008? Explain your answer.

Case Study 16–3 illustrates how an automotive parts manufacturer used Chapter 11 bankruptcy to achieve substantial cost savings from employees and suppliers, price increases from customers, and concessions from its creditors. These actions enabled the firm to avoid liquidation, which may have resulted in a much larger loss of jobs and tax revenue in the communities in which the firm had operations, while enabling creditors to recover a larger portion of their claims.

Case Study 16–3 A Reorganized Dana Corporation Emerges from Bankruptcy Court

Dana Corporation announced on February 1, 2008, that it had emerged from bankruptcy court with an exit financing facility of $2 billion. The firm had entered Chapter 11 reorganization on March 3, 2006. During the ensuing 21 months, the firm and its constituents identified, agreed on, and won court approval for approximately $440 million to $475 million in annual cost savings and the elimination of unprofitable products. These annual savings resulted primarily from achieving better plant utilization due to changes in union work rules, wage and benefit reductions, the reduction of ongoing obligations for retiree health and welfare costs, and streamlining administrative expenses.

Dana is a leading supplier of axles and drive shafts, as well as structural, sealing, and thermal management products. The company's customer base includes virtually every major vehicle and engine manufacturer in the global automotive, commercial vehicle, and off-highway markets, which collectively produce more than 70 million vehicles annually. The company employed about 35,000 people in 26 countries and had annual sales of $8.5 billion in 2006 (in the year in which it entered Chapter 11 bankruptcy), with more than half coming from outside the United States.

The plan of reorganization accepted by the court, creditors, and investors included a $750 million equity investment provided by Centerbridge Capital Partners to fund a portion of the firm's health-care and pension obligations. Under the plan, shareholders received no payout. Bondholders of some $1.62 billion in various maturities and holders of $1.63 billion in unsecured claims recovered about 60–90 percent of their claims. Centerbridge would acquire $250 million of convertible preferred stock in the reorganized Dana operation, and creditors, who had agreed to support the reorganization plan, could acquire up to $500 million of the convertible preferred shares. The preferred shares were issued as an inducement to get creditors to support the plan of reorganization. Under the reorganization plan, Dana sold some businesses, cut plants in the United States and Canada, reduced its hourly and salaried workforce, and sought price increases on parts from customers.

Dana also agreed to retain sponsorship of its retirement plans. During the bankruptcy proceedings, the company continued to make legally required contributions and consolidated 32 defined-benefit plans into seven pension funds. These changes reduced Dana's minimum funding contributions by $60 million through the year 2012. These moves would significantly improve the financial health of Dana's remaining seven plans that cover more than 53,000 participants, of which almost 15,000 are active employees. By reducing the number of plans, Dana made its pension obligations more affordable and lessened the possibility that the plans would have to be assumed by the U.S. Pension Benefit Guaranty Corporation (PBGC) in the future. The PBGC is a federal corporation created under the Employee Retirement Income Security Act of 1974.

Discussion Questions

1. Does the process outlined in this business case seem equitable for all parties to the bankruptcy proceedings? Why? Why not? Be specific.
2. Why did Centerbridge receive convertible preferred rather than common stock?
3. What was the motivation for Dana to agree to continue to sponsor its retirement plans rather than simply suspend payments and discharge these obligations to the PBGC? Be specific.

Implementing Chapter 7 Liquidation

If the bankruptcy court determines that reorganization is infeasible, the failing firm may be forced to liquidate. A trustee is appointed by the court to handle the administrative aspects of the liquidation. The trustee is given the responsibility to liquidate the firm's assets, keep records, examine creditors' claims, disburse the proceeds, and submit a final report on the liquidation. The priority in which the claims are paid is stipulated in Chapter 7 of the Bankruptcy Reform Act, which must be followed by the trustee when the firm is liquidated. All secured creditors are paid when the firm's assets that were pledged as collateral are liquidated. If the proceeds of the sale of these assets are inadequate to satisfy all of the secured creditors' claims, they become unsecured or general creditors for the amount that was not recovered. If the proceeds of the sale of pledged assets exceed secured creditors' claims, the excess proceeds are used to pay general creditors.

Chapter 7 distributes the liquidation proceeds according to the following priorities: (1) administrative claims (e.g., lawyers' fees, court costs, accountants' fees, trustees' fees, and other costs necessary to liquidate the firm's assets), (2) statutory claims (e.g., tax obligations, rent, consumer deposits, and unpaid wages and benefits owed before the filing up to some threshold), (3) secured creditors' claims, (4) unsecured creditors' claims, and (5) equity claims. Liquidation under Chapter 7 does not mean that all employees lose their jobs. When a large firm enters Chapter 7 bankruptcy, an entire division of the company may be sold intact to other companies during the liquidation. For example, the sale of several Lehman Brothers operating units in 2008, while the firm was in bankruptcy, preserved the jobs of as many as 10,000 of the firm's 25,000 employees in place before the bankruptcy.

Fully secured creditors, such as bondholders or mortgage lenders, have a legally enforceable right to the collateral securing their loans or the equivalent value. A creditor is fully secured if the value of the collateral for its loan to the debtor equals or exceeds the amount of the debt. For this reason, fully secured creditors are not entitled to participate in any distribution of liquidated assets that the bankruptcy trustee might make.

Exhibit 16–2 describes how a legally bankrupt company could be liquidated. In this illustration, the bankruptcy court, owners, and creditors could not agree on an appropriate reorganization plan for DOA Inc. Consequently, the court ordered that the firm be liquidated in accordance with Chapter 7. Note that this illustration would differ from a private or voluntary out-of-court liquidation in two important respects. First, the expenses associated with conducting the liquidation would be lower, because the liquidation would not involve extended legal proceedings. Second, the distribution of proceeds could reflect the priority of claims negotiated between the creditors and the owners that differs from that set forth in Chapter 7 of the Bankruptcy Reform Act.

Exhibit 16–2 Liquidation of DOA Inc. under Chapter 7

DOA has the balance sheet in Table 16–3. The only liability not shown on the balance sheet is the cost of the bankruptcy proceedings, which are treated as expenses and are not capitalized.

The sale of DOA's assets generates $5.4 million in cash. The distribution of the proceeds results in the following situation as displayed in Table 16–4. Note that the proceeds are distributed in accordance with the priorities stipulated in the current commercial bankruptcy law and that the cost of administering the bankruptcy totals 18 percent (i.e., $972,000/$5,400,000) of the proceeds from liquidation.

Once all prior claims have been satisfied, the remaining proceeds are distributed to the unsecured creditors. The pro rata or proportional settlement percentage of 27.64 percent is calculated by dividing funds available for unsecured creditors by the amount of unsecured creditor claims (i.e., $1368/$4950). The shareholders receive nothing because not all unsecured creditor claims have been satisfied. See Table 16–5.

Table 16–3   DOA Balance Sheet

Assets		Liabilities	
Cash	$35,000	Accounts payable	$750,000
Accounts receivable	2,300,000	Bank notes payable	3,000,000
Inventories	2,100,000	Accrued salaries	720,000
Total current assets	$4,435,000	Unpaid benefits	140,000
Land	1,500,000	Unsecured customer deposits	300,000
Net plant and equipment	2,000,000	Taxes payable	400,000
Total fixed assets	$3,500,000	Total current liabilities	$5,310,000
Total assets	$7,935,000	First mortgage	2,500,000
		Unsecured debt	200,000
		Total long term debt	$2,700,000
		Preferred stock	50,000
		Common stock	100,000
		Paid in surplus	500,000
		Retained earnings	(725,000)
		Total stockholders' equity	$(75,000)
		Total shareholders' equity and total liabilities	$7,935,000

Table 16–4   Distribution of Liquidation Proceeds

Distribution of Liquidation Proceeds	
Proceeds from Liquidation	$5,400,000
Expenses of Administering Bankruptcy	972,000
Salaries Owed Employees	720,000
Unpaid Employee Benefits	140,000
Unsecured Customer Deposits	300,000
Taxes	400,000
Funds Available for Creditors	$2,868,000
First Mortgage (From sale of fixed assets)	1,500,000
Funds Available for Unsecured Creditors	$1,368,000

Table 16–5   Distribution of Funds among Unsecured Creditors

Unsecured Creditor Claims	Amount	Settlement at 27.64%
Unpaid Balance from First Mortgage	$1,000,000	$276,400
Accounts Payable	750,000	207,300
Notes Payable	3,000,000	829,200
Unsecured Debt	200,000	55,280
Total	$4,950,000	$1,368,000

Case Study 16–4 describes how NetBank had to liquidate because of its inability to provide an acceptable reorganization plan to its creditors, shareholders, and the bankruptcy court. Note how ING bank acquired NetBank's assets and deposits while it was in bankruptcy.

Case Study 16–4 NetBank Liquidates in Bankruptcy

As the largest commercial bank to fail in 14 years, NetBank announced in late 2007 that it had filed for bankruptcy protection and expected to liquidate its assets. The Chapter 11 reorganization plan it filed described how such liquidation would take place. Shareholders would receive no distribution from the proceeds of the liquidation. NetBank was the nation's oldest Internet bank, serving retail and business customers in all 50 states. NetBank filed for voluntary petition for relief from its creditors on September 28, 2007, under Chapter 11 of the U.S. Bankruptcy Code with the bankruptcy court in Jacksonville, Florida. Factors contributing to the filing included mounting losses from mortgage defaults, weak underwriting standards, poor documentation, a lack of controls, and what the U.S. Office of Thrift Supervision labeled as failed business strategies.

The Federal Deposit Insurance Corporation closed NetBank's operations, and ING Groep NV's banking unit took over much of the firm's deposits. NetBank had $2.5 billion in assets and $2.3 billion in deposits as of June 30, 2007. ING Direct, a unit of ING Groep NV and nation's fourth largest thrift, acquired $1.4 billion in deposits and 104,000 NetBank customers for $14 million. NetBank shares traded on the day of the announcement at one cent. At that time, the Federal Deposit Insurance Corporation insured deposit accounts up to $100,000. Customers whose accounts contained less than that amount continued to have full access to their money. However, customers whose accounts were in excess of $100,000 became creditors of the receivership for their uninsured funds.[1] How much these 1,500 accounts would recover depended on the liquidation of the firm's assets.

Discussion Questions

1. Speculate as to why NetBank sought the protection of the bankruptcy court rather than to try to reach some accommodation with creditors prior to going to court.
2. In what way does the existence of FDIC insurance impede the efficient reallocation of bank assets? Explain your answer.

---

[1]Effective October 28, 2008, FDIC-insured deposit limits were raised to $250,000 per deposit owner through December 31, 2009.

Chapter 15. Dealing with Cross-Border Bankruptcy

As noted previously in this chapter, the purpose of Chapter 15 of the U.S. Bankruptcy Code is to provide effective mechanisms for resolving insolvency cases involving assets, lenders, and other parties in various countries. In general, a Chapter 15 case is ancillary or secondary to the primary proceeding brought in another country, which is typically the debtor's home country. As an alternative to Chapter 15, the debtor may proceed with a Chapter 7 or Chapter 11 case in the United States, if warranted by the complexity of the assets. As part of a Chapter 15 proceeding, the U.S. bankruptcy court may authorize a trustee to act in a foreign country on behalf of the U.S. Bankruptcy Court.

Under Chapter 15, an ancillary case is initiated by a "foreign representative" filing a petition for recognition of a "foreign proceeding." As such, Chapter 15 gives the foreign representative the right to access the U.S. court system for resolving insolvency issues. The petition must include documentation showing the existence of the foreign proceeding and the appointment of the foreign representative. Once processed by the U.S. court, the petition gives the court the authority to issue an order recognizing the foreign proceeding as either a "foreign main proceeding" or a "foreign nonmain proceeding." A foreign main proceeding is a proceeding in a country where the debtor's main interests are located. A foreign nonmain proceeding is a proceeding in a country where the debtor has an establishment not representing its main holdings. If recognized as a foreign main proceeding, the court imposes an automatic stay on assets in dispute in the United States and authorizes the foreign representative to operate the debtor's business. Chapter 15 also gives foreign creditors the right to participate in U.S. bankruptcy cases and prohibits discrimination against foreign creditors. The Chapter 15 proceeding attempts to promote collaboration between U.S and foreign courts, as the participants in the proceeding must cooperate fully.

In late 2008, judges in Canada and the United States approved key elements of an agreement enabling Hollinger Inc., a Canadian-based newspaper holding company, to emerge from the protection of bankruptcy court. Bondholders sent Hollinger into insolvency protection in Canada and Chapter 15 in the United States. A key component of the agreement with Davidson Kempner, holder of about 40 percent of the more than $100 million owed by Hollinger, involved the elimination of the super-voting control shares held by a major stockholder. The shareholder agreed to convert super-voting shares in Hollinger's largest investment (i.e., Sun-Times Media Group) for one-vote, one-share common stock. Hollinger's creditors would receive the new shares as part of an agreement to dispense with the debt they are owed. In early 2009, Icelandic bank Glitnir banki hf sought Chapter 15 bankruptcy protection from U.S. creditors in the U.S. Bankruptcy Court for the Southern District of New York. Court documents indicated that the purpose of the filing was to have the firm's court proceedings in Iceland recognized in the United States.

Motivations for Filing for Bankruptcy

Although most companies that file for bankruptcy do so because of their deteriorating financial position, companies increasingly are seeking bankruptcy protection to avoid litigation and hostile takeovers. In the mid-1980s, Johns Manville Corporation used bankruptcy to negotiate a reduction in huge liability awards granted in the wake of asbestos-related lawsuits. Similarly, Texaco used the threat of bankruptcy in the early 1990s as a negotiating ploy to reduce the amount of court-ordered payments to Occidental Petroleum resulting from the court's determination that Texaco had improperly intervened in a pending merger transaction. Saddled with crushing pension and other retiree benefit obligations, 33 steel companies in the United States have sought the protection of the bankruptcy court to either reorganize or liquidate their businesses. In 2001, LTV sold its plants while in bankruptcy to W.L. Ross and Company, which restarted the plants in 2002 in a new company named the International Steel Group (ISI). By simply buying assets, ISI has no obligation to pay pension, health-care, or insurance liabilities, which remained with LTV.

More recently, a bankruptcy judge in late 2004 approved a settlement enabling two subsidiaries of the energy giant, Halliburton, to emerge from bankruptcy. Under the settlement, Halliburton agreed to establish a $4.2 billion trust fund to pay potential future asbestos claims. Delphi, the ailing auto parts manufacturer, used its bankrupt status to threaten to abrogate union contracts to gain substantial wage and benefit concessions from its employees in 2007. In September 2008, the Federal Deposit Insurance Corporation (FDIC), as receiver, took control of Washington Mutual (WaMu) and simultaneously sold selected bank assets and liabilities out of receivership in a precedent-setting move (see Case Study 16–5).

Case Study 16–5 U.S. Government Seizes Washington Mutual to Minimize Impact on U.S. Taxpayer

On September 26, 2008, J.P. Morgan Chase acquired Washington Mutual's (WaMu) insured and uninsured deposits and operations, including branches and data centers for $1.9 billion, after the FDIC (a regulator and deposit insurance agency) seized the bank's operations in the largest bank failure in U.S. history. The purchase of the uninsured deposits eliminated the need for the already financially strapped FDIC to cover any losses. J.P. Morgan did not assume any of WaMu's unsecured debt or the assets or liabilities of the holding company. The $1.9 billion paid for WaMu's operations went into a fund overseen by the FDIC to pay a portion of WaMu's $7 billion senior unsecured debt at a rate of 27 cents (i.e., $1.9/$7.0) on the dollar. The WaMu financial collapse wiped out common shareholders, $4 billion in preferred equity, and more than 90 percent of its $22.6 billion in unsecured debt.

Historically, banks considered too big to fail were auctioned off to the highest bidder, with the FDIC covering any losses on qualifying deposits. In this instance, WaMu was placed in receivership before a sale had been arranged. With the withdrawal of billions of dollars in WaMu deposits in recent weeks, it became apparent that there was no time to allow bidders to perform due diligence. Through a secret auction process, four banks submitted bids on the due date of September 24, 2008, and J.P. Morgan was notified, later the same day, that it had won. A secret auction was used to avoid exacerbating the run on deposits already underway. By waiting until WaMu was in receivership, J.P. Morgan Chase was able to pay "fire-sale" prices for only those assets and liabilities it wanted. While saving the U.S. taxpayer money in this instance, the precedent-setting transaction may make it more expensive for banks to raise capital in the future.

Discussion Questions

1. Discuss the fairness of this government-brokered takeover to unsecured creditors.
2. What alternatives to this type of takeover could the FDIC have pursued?
3. Investors speculated that WaMu would sell itself to J.P. Morgan Chase, Citigroup, Wells Fargo, or some European bank by buying the firm's common stock despite its dramatic decline. How did the speculators affect market liquidity?
4. How might the way in which the FDIC intervened affect the ability of banks to raise capital in the future? Explain your answer.

Effectiveness of Chapter 11 Reorganization versus Chapter 7 Liquidation

Bris, Welch, and Zhu (2006) argue that Chapter 7 liquidations appear to be as costly in terms of legal expenses and related fees, as well as the time required to complete the proceedings, as Chapter 11 reorganization. However, Chapter 11 reorganization allows creditors to recover relatively more of their claims than under liquidation. In liquidation, bankruptcy professionals, including attorneys, accountants, and trustees, often end up with the majority of the proceeds generated by selling the assets of the failing firm.

Professional Fees Associated with the Bankruptcy Process

Lopucki and Doherty (2007) found that company size (measured by assets), case duration (measured in days), and the number of parties involved in the proceedings (measured in terms of the numbers of professional firms working) explain 87 percent of the case-to-case variation in professional fees. The study reviewed 74 large public company bankruptcies between 1998 and 2003. Fees and expenses increased about 9 percent annually during that period. The authors argue that these factors measure not only the need for professional services but also the opportunity for professionals to bill. The authors came to the same conclusion after adjusting for differences in case complexity by including such variables in their analysis as the number of employees, docket length, and the number of parties to the reorganization plan.

These costs prompted a greater use of auctions and other market-based techniques to privatize bankruptcy. These techniques include "prepackaged bankruptcies" with a reorganization plan in place at the time of the bankruptcy filing, acquisition of distressed debt by "vulture" investors willing to support the proposed plan of reorganization, and voluntary auction-based sales in Chapter 11.

Prepackaged Bankruptcies

Under a *prepackaged bankruptcy*, the debtor negotiates with creditors well in advance of filing for a Chapter 11 bankruptcy. Because there is general approval of the plan before the filing, the formal Chapter 11 reorganization that follows generally averages only a few months and results in substantially lower legal and administrative expenses (Altman, 1993; Betker, 1995; Tashjian, Lease, and McConnell, 1996). More than one fifth of major bankruptcy cases between 2001 and 2005 were prepackaged deals (Lovely, 2007). Prepackaged bankruptcies are often a result of major creditors anticipating a potential liquidation in bankruptcy as occurring at "fire-sale" prices (Eckbo and Thorburn, 2008).

In a true prepackaged bankruptcy, creditors circulate and approve a plan of reorganization before filing the petition of bankruptcy. The bankruptcy court then approves the plan and the company emerges from bankruptcy quickly. Minority creditors are often required by the court to accept a plan of reorganization. The confirmation of a plan of reorganization over the objections of one or more classes of creditors sometimes is referred as a *cram down*.

Prepackaged bankruptcy provides tax benefits not found in workouts. If a firm enters into a workout in which a voluntary negotiated agreement with debtors is achieved, the firm may lose its right to claim net operating losses in its tax filing. This could occur if the original creditors exchange their debt for equity and the original equity holders own less than 50 percent of the company. As such, the Internal Revenue Service would view this as a loss of control by the original shareholders and a violation of the "continuity of interests" principle discussed in Chapter 12. In bankruptcy, the firm may claim the right to NOLs, if the court rules the firm insolvent (i.e., negative net worth). In addition, if a debtor company reaches a voluntary agreement whereby creditors agree to cancel a certain percentage of debt, the amount is treated as income for tax purposes. A similar debt restructuring in bankruptcy does not create such a tax liability.

In a so-called prearranged bankruptcy, U.S. cable giant, Charter Communications, reached agreement with several major lenders in mid-2009 to reduce its crushing debt load from $21.7 billion to about $12 billion before seeking Chapter 11 protection. Most of the debt reduction was accomplished through a debt for equity swap. Unlike a prepackaged bankruptcy in which the debtor deals with all classes of creditors prior to seeking Chapter 11, the debtor may reach agreement with only certain lenders before filing for bankruptcy in a prearranged bankruptcy strategy. Similarly, in what appeared to be a largely U.S. government sponsored prearranged bankruptcy, Chrysler LLC sought Chapter 11 protection in May 2009 against the protestations of several secured lenders with the intent of introducing a reorganization plan involving its sale to Italian automaker, Fiat.

Debtor-in-Possession Financing

Lenders provide so-called debtor-in-possession (DIP) loans to firms in Chapter 11 reorganization to finance their operating expenses and pay their bankruptcy advisors. Such loans either are considered by the bankruptcy court to have a "superpriority" claim, such that the lender is paid from the firm's operating cash flows or financing arranged when the firm emerges from the protection of the bankruptcy court. Historically, such loans were issued at the London Inter Bank Offered Rate (LIBOR) plus 250 basis points (i.e., 2½ percentage points). Due to the 2008–2009 credit crunch, interest rates on DIP loans rose to more than 600 basis points above the LIBOR. In the past, such loans had terms of 12 to 18 months; however, during 2008 and 2009, maturities ranged from 2 to 6 months, as lenders became increasingly concerned debtor firms would be unable to reorganize successfully and that the proceeds of liquidation would be insufficient to repay DIP loans.

Trading in Bankrupt Company Securities

Once in Chapter 11, a firm's securities may continue to trade, as no federal law prohibits trading in bankrupt securities. While bankrupt firms generally are unable to meet the listing requirements of the major stock exchanges, their shares may trade in the over-the-counter market. In this market, securities' transactions are conducted through a telephone and computer network connecting dealers or market makers in stocks and bonds rather than on the floor of an exchange. So-called pink-sheet bid and ask prices for stocks and yellow sheets for bonds are available to subscribers of Pink Sheets LLC (www.pinksheets.com).

Investing in such securities is very risky. When firms emerge from bankruptcy, creditors are generally the new owners. The bankrupt firm's reorganization plan often requires the cancellation of the existing equity. In some instances, following emergence from Chapter 11, two types of common stock (with different ticker symbols) may be trading for the same firm. One is the old common stock identified with a five-letter ticker symbol ending in Q, and the other is the newly issued equity, whose ticker symbol does not end in Q.

Analyzing Strategic Options for Failing Firms

A failing firm's strategic options are to merge with another firm, reach an out-of-court voluntary settlement with creditors, or file for Chapter 11 bankruptcy. Note the prepackaged bankruptcy discussed earlier in this chapter constitutes a blend of the second and third options. The firm may voluntarily liquidate as part of an out-of-court settlement or be forced to liquidate under Chapter 7 of the bankruptcy code. Table 16–6 summarizes the implications of each option. The choice of which option to pursue is critically dependent on which provides the greatest present value for creditors and shareholders. To evaluate these options, the firm's management needs to estimate the going concern, selling price, and liquidation values of the firm.

Merging with Another Firm

If the failing firm's management estimates that the sale price of the firm is greater than the going concern or liquidation value, management should seek to be acquired by or to merge with another firm. If there is a strategic buyer, management must convince the firm's creditors that they will be more likely to receive what they are owed and shareholders are more likely to preserve share value if the firm is acquired rather than liquidated or allowed to remain independent. In some instances, buyers are willing to

Table 16–6   Alternative Strategies for Failing Firms

Assumptions	Options: Failing Firm	Outcome: Failing Firm
Selling price > Going concern or liquidation value	Is acquired by or merges with another firm	Continues as subsidiary of acquirer Merged into acquirer and ceases to exist
Going concern value > Sale or liquidation value	Reaches out-of-court settlement with creditors Seeks bankruptcy protection under Chapter 11 Seeks prepackaged settlement with primary creditors before entering Chapter 11	Continues with debt-for-equity swap, extension, and composition Continues in reorganization
Liquidation value > Sale or going concern value	Reaches out-of-court settlement with creditors Liquidates under Chapter 7	Ceases to exist; assignee liquidates assets and distributes proceeds, reflecting terms of negotiated settlement with creditors Ceases to exist; trustee supervises liquidation and distributes proceeds according to statutory priorities

acquire failing firms only if their liabilities are reduced through the bankruptcy process. Hence, it may make sense to force the firm into bankruptcy to have some portion of its liabilities discharged during the process of Chapter 11 reorganization. To protect it from litigation, Washington Construction Group required Morrison Knudsen Corporation to file for bankruptcy as a closing condition in the agreement of purchase and sale in 2000. Alternatively, the potential buyer could reach agreement in advance or bankruptcy reorganization with the primary creditors (i.e., a prepackaged bankruptcy) and employ the bankruptcy process to achieve compliance from the minority creditors.

Sales within the protection of Chapter 11 reorganization may be accomplished either by a negotiated private sale to a particular purchaser or through a public auction. The latter is often favored by the court since the purchase price is more likely to reflect the true market value of the assets. Generally, a public auction can withstand any court challenge by creditors questioning whether the purchaser has paid fair market value for the failing firm's assets. International Steel Group's acquisition of LTV Steel's assets in 2002 and bankrupt Bethlehem Steel in early 2003, along with U.S. Steel's purchase of bankrupt National Steel shortly thereafter, are examples of such transactions. In 2005, Time Warner Inc. and Comcast Corp reached an agreement to buy bankrupt cable operator Adelphia Communications Corp while in Chapter 11 for nearly $18 billion. Time Warner and Comcast paid Adelphia bondholders and other creditors in cash and warrants for stock in a new company formed by combining Time Warner's cable business and Adelphia.

In a study of 38 takeovers of distressed firms from 1981 to 1988, Clark and Ofek (1994) found that bidders tend to overpay for these types of firms. Although this strategy may benefit the failing firm's shareholders, such takeovers do not seem to benefit the acquirer's shareholders. Clark and Ofek also found that, in most cases, the acquiring firms fail to restructure successfully the target firms.

Case Study 16–6 illustrates how complex and contentious buying a firm in Chapter 11 can become. In this instance, Asarco, a U.S.-based mining firm, claimed that its parent company, Grupo Mexico, fraudulently moved assets beyond the reach of creditors before taking the firm into bankruptcy. In an effort to regain control of its subsidiary, Grupo Mexico submitted a reorganization plan, which it claimed would pay off a larger percentage of Asarco's creditors than Sterlite Industries's proposal to acquire Asarco.

Case Study 16–6 Grupo Mexico and Sterlite Industries Compete to Acquire Asarco from Chapter 11

Accused of illegally stripping U.S.-based copper mining company Asarco of its most valuable assets before putting the firm into bankruptcy to avoid paying environmental liabilities, Grupo Mexico asserted that, as the parent, it never wanted to put the subsidiary into bankruptcy. However, it was compelled to do so because of Asarco's deteriorating cash position and open-ended environmental liabilities. At stake was $11.3 billion in assets that Asarco wanted returned.

Asarco's Position

Asarco argued, in its lawsuit against Grupo Mexico filed in early 2007, that it was interested in only Asarco's 54.2 percent interest in the Southern Peru Copper Company (SPCC) when Grupo Mexico acquired Asarco for $817 million in 1999. Asarco also alleged that the subsequent transfer of its investment in SPCC to American Mining Company (AMC), another Grupo Mexico subsidiary, on March 31, 2003, was made at less than fair value and left the firm insolvent. Dividends from this investment had been a major contributor to Asarco's cash flow. Furthermore, the removal of this investment seriously reduced the firm's balance-sheet assets. Asarco also claimed that Grupo Mexico managed Asarco for cash by forcing it to sell its land at below market prices, failing to make necessary maintenance investments, and selling its highest grade ore at bargain prices. Allegedly, this was done to enable Asarco to avoid insolvency long enough to exceed the statutes of limitation on fraudulent asset transfers. Asarco has asked a federal court for a 30 percent stake in SPCC shares, currently valued at $9.6 billion and $1.7 billion in dividends Asarco would have received if it had retained the investment in SPCC.

Grupo Mexico's Position

Grupo Mexico has argued that the sale of Asarco's majority stake in SPCC to Grupo Mexico's AMC subsidiary allowed Asarco to eliminate all its existing short-term debt obligations through 2013. According to Asarco's lawsuit, AMC made an undisclosed deal with its lender, Banco Inbursa, to obtain financing for the transfer of the stake in SPCC in which it agreed to pay principal and interest on $100 million in Asarco unsecured debt. Asarco also alleged that the lender and its primary shareholder, Carlos Slim Helu (Mexico's richest citizen), had jointly purchased at deep discounts as much as 90 percent of the outstanding debt. If true, the clandestine purchase of the bonds guaranteed the lender and Mr. Helu a huge profit on their investment.

In contrast, Grupo Mexico notes that the transfer of the SPCC investment enabled Asarco to reduce substantially its current and future financing costs, improve its credit ratings, and reach a standstill agreement with the Justice Department to help resolve its environmental problems. Grupo Mexico also argued that, in addition to Asarco's cash shortage, another reason for putting its subsidiary into bankruptcy on August 9, 2005, was to reach consensus on the extent of its environmental liabilities. Having achieved consensus with all claimants in the reorganization process, a final determination could be made of the Asarco's total current and future obligations. Up to this point, the firm was unsure about the total dollar value of the environmental liabilities. During two and one half years in Chapter 11,95,000 asbestos-related claims were submitted to the court totaling $2.7 billion.

Competing Reorganization Plans

Asarco argued that the best means of satisfying claimants was through a sale of the firm. Several potential buyers submitted bids. In early 2008, Asarco accepted a $2.6 billion cash offer from India-based Vedanta Resources' U.S. subsidiary Sterlite Industries as the winning bid for its assets. This sale represented the cornerstone of Asarco's reorganization plan. The plan required approval by the judge and a majority of creditors and shareholders. In response, Grupo Mexico introduced its own reorganization plan. The plan entailed the firm providing as much as $4.1 billion to pay off claims against Asarco and take Asarco out of Chapter 11. In doing so, Grupo Mexico would resume control of Asarco, its U.S. subsidiary.

In September 2008, the U.S. District Court ruled that Grupo Mexico had fraudulently transferred shares in SPCC to its own subsidiary, AMC, leaving Asarco without sufficient operating cash to survive. Although creditors voted to support the Sterlite Industries's proposal in mid-October, albeit at a lower price due to the then crisis in the credit markets and declining copper prices, Asarco announced on October 22, 2008, that it had terminated the sales agreement it had with Sterlite because it was unwilling to accept a lower purchase price. Nonetheless, in view of the continued global weakness in commodity prices, Sterlite overcame Asarco's resistance announcing it had reached an agreement to buy Asarco in March 2009 for $1.7 billion, $900 million less than its earlier offer. Grupo Mexico now had to turn its attention to resolving the outstanding $11.3 billion fraudulent conveyance lawsuit.

Discussion Questions

1. What was the primary reason Asarco claimed that its stake in SPCC was fraudulently conveyed to AMC? As the parent firm, should Grupo Mexico have the right to restructure (including transferring assets) the assets as it believes is appropriate? Explain your answer.
2. Why do you believe Grupo Mexico was interested in once again obtaining control over Asarco? Be specific.
3. Why would Grupo Mexico be willing to bid as much as $4.1 billion for Asarco when Sterlite's bid was only $2.6 billion? Explain your answer.

Reaching an Out-of-Court Voluntary Settlement with Creditors

Alternatively, the going concern value of the firm may exceed the sale or liquidation value. Management must be able to demonstrate to creditors that a restructured or downsized firm would be able to repay its debts if creditors were willing to accept less, extend the maturity of the debt, or exchange debt for equity. If management cannot reach agreement with the firm's creditors, it may seek protection under Chapter 11.

A voluntary settlement may be difficult to achieve because the debtor often needs the approval of all its creditors. Known as the ***holdout problem***, smaller creditors have an incentive to attempt to hold up the agreement unless they receive special treatment. Consensus may be accomplished by paying all small creditors 100 percent of what they are owed and the larger creditors an agreed-on percentage. Other factors limiting voluntary settlements, such as a debt-for-equity swap, include a preference by some creditors for debt rather than equity and the lack of the necessary information to enable proper valuation of the equity offered to the creditors. Because of these factors, there is some evidence that firms attempting to restructure outside of Chapter 11 bankruptcy have more difficulty in reducing their indebtedness than those that negotiate with creditors while under the protection of Chapter 11 (Gilson, 1997).

Voluntary and Involuntary Liquidations

The failing firm's management, shareholders, and creditors may agree that the firm is worth more in liquidation than in sale or as a continuing operation. If management cannot reach agreement with its creditors on a private liquidation, the firm may seek Chapter 7 liquidation. The proceeds of a private liquidation are distributed in accordance with the agreement negotiated with creditors, while the order in which claimants are paid under Chapter 7 is set by statute.

Predicting Corporate Default and Bankruptcy

Alternative Models

The research undertaken to develop models to predict the incidence of default and bankruptcy is varied and extensive. Bellovary, Giacomino, and Akers (2007) reviewed 165 bankruptcy prediction studies published from 1930 to 2006. Examining modeling trends by decade, the authors note that discriminant analysis was the primary method used to develop models in the 1960s and 1970s. However, the primary modeling methods shifted by the 1980s to logit analysis and neural networks. While the number of factors used in building the models varied by decade, the average model used about 10 variables. In analyzing model accuracy, the authors conclude that multivariate discriminant analysis and neural networks are the most promising and increasing the number of variables in the model does not guarantee greater accuracy. Two-factor models are often as accurate as models with as many as 21 factors.

In an international study, Aziz and Dar (2006) analyzed the empirical findings and methodologies employed in 46 studies applied in 10 countries from 1968 to 2003. Observing that bankruptcy prediction models typically use financial ratios to forecast business failure, about 60 percent of the studies reviewed used only financial ratios. The remaining studies use both financial ratios and other information. The financial ratios typically include measures of liquidity, solvency, leverage, profitability, asset composition, firm size, and growth rate. Other variables include macroeconomic, industry-specific, location, and firm-specific variables. The authors concluded that the predictive accuracy of the various types of models investigated is very similar, correctly identifying failing firms about 80 percent of the time for firms in the sample employed in estimating the models. However, the accuracy drops substantially for out-of-sample predictions. Unlike Bellovary et al. (2007), the authors argue that there still seems to be a lack of consensus as to which methodology is the most reliable.

Grice and Dugan (2001) document potential problems with bankruptcy prediction models. They note that model results often vary by industry and time period. They also found that model accuracy declined when applied to periods different from those employed to develop the models (i.e., in sample versus out-of-sample predictions). Moreover, applying models to industries other than those used to develop the models often results in greatly diminished accuracy.

In view of the extensive literature on the subject, the following subsections discuss categories of models that differ by methodology and choice of variables used to predict bankruptcy. The intent of these subsections is to provide a cursory overview of the state of such models. For a more rigorous discussion of bankruptcy prediction models, see Jones and Hensher (2008).

Models That Differ by Methodology
Credit-Scoring Models

Using discriminant analysis to distinguish between bankrupt and nonbankrupt firms, Altman (1968) developed one of the first quantitative models for predicting bankruptcy. Discriminant analysis uses a combination of independent variables to assign a score (i.e., a Z score) to a particular firm. This score then is used to discriminate between bankrupt and nonbankrupt firms by using a cutoff point. The Z-score model formalized the more qualitative analysis of default risk offered by credit rating agencies such as Moody's Investors Services. Using five key financial ratios, Altman determined a firm's Z score. The likelihood of default for firms with low Z scores is less than for firms with high Z scores. The most significant financial ratios for predicting default are earnings before income and taxes as a percent of total assets and the ratio of sales to total assets. The major shortcoming of this approach is that it is a snapshot of a firm's financial health at a moment in time, and it does not reflect changes in a company's financial ratios over time. Grice and Ingram (2001) retested the Altman (1968) model on a more recent sample and found that its ability to classify bankrupt companies fell from 83.5 percent to 57.8 percent.

To compensate for the shortcomings of the discriminant model, Shumway (2001) developed a model to predict the probability of a firm defaulting over some future period. The model postulated that the default rate depended not only on the firm's current financial ratios but also on such forward-looking market variables as market capitalization, abnormal financial returns, and the volatility of such financial returns. He found that the only financial ratios with significant predictive power are earnings before interest and taxes to total liabilities and the market value of equity to total liabilities.

Structural Models

While credit scoring models do not estimate the probability of default, structural models attempt to do so. Often employing probit analysis, structural models are debt-pricing models that link the probability of default to the structure of a firm's assets and liabilities. Structural models of credit risk assume that firms default when they violate a debt covenant, their cash flow falls short of required debt payments, their assets become more valuable in competitors' hands, or their shareholders decide that servicing the debt is no longer in their best interests. Structural models can be very difficult to develop for firms with complex debt structures.

Ohlson (1980) and Zavgren (1985) used logistic (logit) or probit regression models, which provide a conditional probability of an observation belonging to a particular category. Logit and probit models do not require assumptions as restrictive as discriminant analysis. Supporters of this approach argue that logit regression fits the characteristics of the default prediction problem. The dependent variable is binary (default/nondefault). The logit model yields a score between 0 and 1, which gives the probability of the firm defaulting. A partial list of structural credit risk models include the following: Kim, Ramaswamy, and Sundaresan, 1993; Leland, 1994; Longstaff and Schwartz, 1995; and Hsu, Saa-Requejo, and Santa-Clara, 2002.

Reduced Form Models

In contrast to structural models, reduced form models use market prices of the distressed firm's debt as the only source of information about the firm's risk profile. Such prices are a proxy for the variables used in the structural models. Although easier to estimate, such models lack a specific link between credit risk and the firm's assets and liabilities and assume that the timing of default is random, in that investors with incomplete information do not know how far the firm is from default. Default is triggered by some measure of distress crossing a threshold level or default boundary. See Jarrow and Turnbull (1995) and Singleton (1999) for examples of reduced form models.

Other Modeling Methods

While statistical discriminant analysis and probit or logit methods dominate the literature, they are not the only techniques used in bankruptcy prediction (Aziz and Dar, 2006). Neural networks are a type of artificial intelligence that attempts to mimic the way a human brain works. Neural networks are particularly effective when the networks have a large database of prior examples (Platt et al., 1999). The cumulative sums (CUSUM) methods represent a class of models that account for serial correlation (i.e., interdependencies) in the data and incorporate information from more than one period (Kahya and Theodossiou, 1999). The options-based approach to bankruptcy prediction builds on option-pricing theory to explain business bankruptcy relying on such variables as firm volatility to predict default (Charitou and Trigeorgis, 2000).

Models Differing in Choice of Variables Used to Predict Bankruptcy

Blume, Lim, and MacKinlay (1998); Molina (2006); and Avamov et al. (2006, 2007) use accounting data to predict credit ratings, which serve as proxies for the probability of default. Duffie, Saita, and Wang (2007) argue that the probability of failure depends on the length of the time horizon considered. Altman et al. (2003) demonstrate a correlation between default rates and loss in the event of default and the business cycle. Hennessy and Whited (2007); Anderson and Carverhill (2007); and Asvanunt, Broadie, and Sundaresan (2007) demonstrate that "shocks," such as recession and credit crunches, contribute to default by negatively affecting firm assets or cash flow. Other studies use net worth as a key factor that affects a firm's ability to raise financing in a liquidity crisis (White, 1989). Gilson, John, and Lang (1990) and Asquith, Gertner, and Scharfstein (1994) use equity returns and debt service ratios as measures of distress.

Empirical Studies of Financial Distress

Attractive Returns to Firms Emerging from Bankruptcy Often Temporary

When firms emerge from bankruptcy, they often cancel the old stock and issue new common stock. Empirical studies show that such firms often show very attractive financial returns to holders of the new stock immediately following the announcement that the firm is emerging from bankruptcy (Alderson and Betker, 1996; Eberhart, Altman, and Aggarwal, 1999). However, long-term performance often deteriorates. Hotchkiss (1995) found that 40 percent of the firms studied experienced operating losses in the three years after emerging from Chapter 11. Almost one third subsequently filed for bankruptcy or had to restructure its debt. After five years, about one quarter of all firms that reorganized were liquidated, merged, or refiled for bankruptcy (France, 2002).

Returns to Financially Distressed Stocks Unexpectedly Low

Campbell, Hilscher, and Szilagyi (2009) note that, as a class, distressed stocks (i.e., firms often characterized by deteriorating asset values and liquidity) offer low financial rates of return despite their high risk of business failure. In theory, one would expect such risky assets to offer financial returns commensurate with risk. The low financial return for distressed stocks tends to be worse for stocks with low analyst coverage, institutional ownership, and price per share. Factors potentially contributing to these low rates of return could include unexpected events, valuation errors by uninformed investors, and the characteristics of distressed stocks. Unexpected events could include the economy being worse than expected. Valuation errors include investors not understanding the relationship between variables used to predict failure and the risk of failure and therefore may not have fully discounted the value of stocks to offset this risk. The characteristics of failing firms are such that some investors may have an incentive to hold such stocks, despite their low financial returns. For example, majority owners of distressed stocks can benefit by buying the firm's output or assets at bargain prices. Consequently, the benefits from having control could exceed the low returns associated with financially distressed stocks.

IPOs More Likely to Experience Bankruptcy than Established Firms

Firms that have recently undergone IPOs tend to experience a much higher incidence of financial distress and bankruptcy than more established firms. Beneda (2007) examines the post-IPO returns and incidence of bankruptcies and distress of firms that had initial public offerings between 1995 and 2002. These findings are consistent with other studies showing that owning a portfolio of IPOs for up to five years after the firms go public performs well below the return on the S&P 500 stock index (Aggarwal and Rivoli, 1990; Ritter, 1991; and Loughran, Ritter, and Rydqvist, 1994). Greenblatt and Titman (2002) attribute this underperformance to the limited amount of information available on these firms.

Things to Remember

Bankruptcy is a federal legal proceeding designed to protect the technically or legally insolvent firm from lawsuits by its creditors until a decision is made to liquidate or reorganize the firm. An insolvent firm may reach an agreement with its creditors to restructure its obligations out of court to avoid the costs of bankruptcy proceedings. Whether the debtor firm reorganizes inside or outside the protection of bankruptcy, concessions by creditors are necessary to lower an insolvent firm's payments so that it may remain in business. Common forms of debt restructuring include an extension of payment terms, a composition or reduction in the amount owed, or a debt-for-equity swap.

In the absence of a voluntary settlement out of court, the debtor firm may voluntarily seek protection from its creditors by initiating bankruptcy or be forced involuntarily into bankruptcy by its creditors. Once a petition is filed, the debtor firm is protected from any further legal action related to its debts until the bankruptcy proceedings are completed Under a prepackaged bankruptcy, the debtor negotiates with creditors well in advance of filing for a Chapter 11 bankruptcy. Because there is general approval of the plan before the filing, the formal Chapter 11 reorganization that follows generally averages only a few months and results in substantially lower legal and administrative expenses.

Bankruptcy prediction models typically use financial ratios to predict firm failure. The financial ratios normally include measures of liquidity, solvency, leverage, profitability, asset composition, firm size, and growth rate. Other informational variables include macroeconomic, industry-specific, location, and firm-specific factors. Model accuracy declines when applied to periods and industries not used to develop the model. There is evidence that multivariate discriminant analysis and neural networks offer the greatest promise for improving accuracy.

Chapter Discussion Questions

16–1. Why are strong creditor rights important to an efficiently operating capital market? What is the purpose of bankruptcy in promoting capital market efficiency?

16–2. Of all possible stakeholders to the bankruptcy process, which are likely to benefit the most? Which are likely to benefit the least? Explain your answer.

16–3. What are the advantages to the lender and the debtor firm's shareholders of reaching a negotiated settlement outside of bankruptcy court? What are the primary disadvantages?

16–4. How does the Bankruptcy Abuse Prevention and Consumer Protection Act of 2005 differ from the Bankruptcy Reform Act of 1978? It what ways do you feel that it represents an improvement? In what ways could the more recent legislation discourage reorganization in Chapter 11? Be specific.

16–5. What are prepackaged bankruptcies? In what ways do they represent streamlining of the credit recovery process?

16–6. Why would creditors make concessions to a debtor firm? Give examples of common types of concessions. Describe how these concessions affect the debtor firm.

16–7. Although most companies that file for bankruptcy do so because of their deteriorating financial position, companies increasingly are seeking bankruptcy protection to avoid litigation. Give examples of how bankruptcy can be used to avoid litigation.

16–8. What are the primary options available to a failing firm? What criteria might the firm use to select a particular option? Be specific.

16–9. Describe the probable trend in financial returns to shareholders of firms that emerge from bankruptcy. To what do you attribute these trends? Explain your answer.

16–10. Identify at least two financial or nonfinancial variables that have been shown to affect firm defaults and bankruptcies. Explain how each might affect the likelihood the firm will default or seek Chapter 11 protection.

16–11. On June 25, 2008, JHT Holdings, Inc., a Kenosha, Wisconsin–based package delivery service, filed for bankruptcy. The firm had annual revenues of $500 million. What would the firm have to demonstrate for its petition to be accepted by the bankruptcy court?

16–12. Dura Automotive emerged from Chapter 11 protection in mid-2008. The firm obtained exit financing consisting of a $110 million revolving credit facility, a $50 million European first-lien term loan, and an $84 million U.S. second-lien loan. The reorganization plan specified how a portion of the proceeds of these loans would be used. What do you believe might be typical stipulations in reorganization plans for using such funds? Be specific.

16–13. What are the primary factors contributing to business failure? Be specific.

16–14. In recent years, hedge funds engaged in so-called loan-to-own prebankruptcy investments, in which they acquired debt from distressed firms at a fraction of face value. Subsequently, they moved the company into Chapter 11, intent on converting the acquired debt to equity in a firm with sharply reduced liabilities. The hedge fund also provided financing to secure its interest in the business. The emergence from Chapter 11 was typically accomplished under section 363(k) of the bankruptcy code, which gives debtors the right to bid on the firm in a public auction sale. During the auction, the firm's debt was valued at face rather than market value, discouraging other bidders other than the hedge fund, which acquired the debt prior to bankruptcy at distressed levels. Without competitive bidding, there was little chance of generating additional cash for the general creditors. Is this an abuse of the Chapter 11 bankruptcy process? Explain your answer.

16–15. American Home Mortgage Investments filed for Chapter 11 bankruptcy in late 2008. The company indicated that it chose this course of action because it represented the best means of preserving the firm's assets. W.L. Ross and Company agreed to provide the firm $50 million in debtor-in-possession financing to meet its anticipated cash needs while in Chapter 11. Comment on the statement that bankruptcy provides the best means of asset preservation. Why would W.L. Ross and Company lend money to a firm that had just filed for bankruptcy?

Answers to these Chapter Discussion Questions are found in the Online Instructor's Manual for instructors using this book.

Chapter Business Cases

Case Study 16–7. The Enron Shuffle—A Scandal to Remember

What started in the mid-1980s as essentially a staid "old-economy" business became the poster child in the late 1990s for companies wanting to remake themselves into "new-economy" powerhouses. Unfortunately, what may have started with the best of intentions emerged as one of the biggest business scandals in U.S. history. Enron was created in 1985 as a result of a merger between Houston Natural Gas and Internorth Natural Gas. In 1989, Enron started trading natural gas commodities and eventually became the world's largest buyer and seller of natural gas. In the early 1990s, Enron became the nation's premier electricity marketer and pioneered the development of trading in such commodities as weather derivatives, bandwidth, pulp, paper, and plastics. Enron invested billions in its broadband unit and water and wastewater system management unit and in hard assets overseas. In 2000, Enron reported $101 billion in revenue and a market capitalization of $63 billion.

The Virtual Company

Enron was essentially a company whose trading and risk management business strategy was built on assets largely owned by others. The complex financial maneuvering and off-balance-sheet partnerships that former CEO Jeffrey K. Skilling and chief financial officer Andrew S. Fastow implemented were intended to remove everything from telecommunications fiber to water companies from the firm's balance sheet and into partnerships. What distinguished Enron's partnerships from those commonly used to share risks were their lack of independence from Enron and the use of Enron's stock as collateral to leverage the partnerships. If Enron's stock fell in value, the firm was obligated to issue more shares to the partnership to restore the value of the collateral underlying the debt or immediately repay the debt. Lenders in effect had direct recourse to Enron stock if at any time the partnerships could not repay their loans in full. Rather than limiting risk, Enron was assuming total risk by guaranteeing the loans with its stock.

Enron also engaged in transactions that inflated its earnings, such as selling time on its broadband system to a partnership at inflated prices at a time when the demand for broadband was plummeting. Enron then recorded a substantial profit on such transactions. The partnerships agreed to such transactions because Enron management seems to have exerted disproportionate influence in some instances over partnership decisions, although its ownership interests were very small, often less than 3 percent. Curiously, Enron's outside auditor, Arthur Andersen, had a dual role in these partnerships, collecting fees for helping to set them up and auditing them.

Time to Pay the Piper

At the time the firm filed for bankruptcy on December 2, 2001, it had $13.1 billion in debt on the books of the parent company and another $18.1 billion on the balance sheets of affiliated companies and partnerships. In addition to the partnerships created by Enron, a number of bad investments both in the United States and abroad contributed to the firm's malaise. Meanwhile, Enron's core energy distribution business was deteriorating. Enron was attempting to gain share in a maturing market by paring selling prices. Margins also suffered from poor cost containment.

Dynegy Corp. agreed to buy Enron for $10 billion on November 2, 2001. On November 8, Enron announced that its net income would have to be restated back to 1997, resulting in a $586 million reduction in reported profits. On November 15, chairman Kenneth Lay admitted that the firm had made billions of dollars in bad investments. Four days later, Enron said it would have to repay a $690 million note by mid-December and it might have to take an additional $700 million pretax charge. At the end of the month, Dynegy withdrew its offer and Enron's credit rating was reduced to junk bond status. Enron was responsible for another $3.9 billion owed by its partnerships. Enron had less than $2 billion in cash on hand.

The end came quickly as investors and customers completely lost faith in the energy behemoth as a result of its secrecy and complex financial maneuvers, forcing the firm into bankruptcy in early December. Enron's stock, which had reached a high of $90 per share on August 17, 2001, was trading at less than $1 by December 5, 2001.

In addition to its angry creditors, Enron faced class-action lawsuits by shareholders and employees, whose pensions were invested heavily in Enron stock. Enron also faced intense scrutiny from congressional committees and the U.S. Department of Justice. By the end of 2001, shareholders had lost more than $63 billion from its previous 52-week high, bondholders lost $2.6 billion in the face value of their debt, and banks appeared to be at risk on at least $15 billion of credit they had extended to Enron. In addition, potential losses on uncollateralized derivative contracts totaled $4 billion. Such contracts involved Enron commitments to buy various types of commodities at some point in the future.

Questions remain as to why Wall Street analysts, Arthur Andersen, federal or state regulatory authorities, the credit rating agencies, and the firm's board of directors did not sound the alarm sooner. It is surprising that the audit committee of the Enron board seems to have somehow been unaware of the firm's highly questionable financial maneuvers. Inquiries following the bankruptcy declaration seem to suggest that the audit committee followed all the rules stipulated by federal regulators and stock exchanges regarding director pay, independence, disclosure, and financial expertise. Enron seems to have collapsed in part because such rules did not do what they were supposed to do. For example, paying directors with stock may have aligned their interests with shareholders, but it also is possible to have been a disincentive to question aggressively senior management about their financial dealings.

The Lessons of Enron

Enron may be the best recent example of a complete breakdown in corporate governance, a system intended to protect shareholders. Inside Enron, the board of directors, management, and the audit function failed to do the job. Similarly, the firm's outside auditors, regulators, credit rating agencies, and Wall Street analysts also failed to alert investors. What seems to be apparent is that if the auditors fail to identify incompetence or fraud, the system of safeguards is likely to break down. The cost of failure to those charged with protecting the shareholders, including outside auditors, analysts, credit-rating agencies, and regulators, was simply not high enough to ensure adequate scrutiny.

What may have transpired is that company managers simply undertook aggressive interpretations of accounting principles then challenged auditors to demonstrate that such practices were not in accordance with GAAP accounting rules (Weil, 2002). This type of practice has been going on since the early 1980s and may account for the proliferation of specific accounting rules applicable only to certain transactions to insulate both the firm engaging in the transaction and the auditor reviewing the transaction from subsequent litigation. In one sense, the Enron debacle represents a failure of the free market system and its current shareholder protection mechanisms, in that it took so long for the dramatic Enron shell game to be revealed to the public. However, this incident highlights the remarkable resilience of the free market system. The free market system worked quite effectively in its rapid imposition of discipline in bringing down the Enron house of cards, without any noticeable disruption in energy distribution nationwide.

Epilogue

Due to the complexity of dealing with so many types of creditors, Enron filed its plan with the federal bankruptcy court to reorganize one and a half years after seeking bankruptcy protection on December 2, 2001. The resulting reorganization has been one of the most costly and complex on record, with total legal and consulting fees exceeding $500 million by the end of 2003. More than 350 classes of creditors, including banks, bondholders, and other energy companies that traded with Enron said they were owed about $67 billion.

Under the reorganization plan, unsecured creditors received an estimated 14 cents for each dollar of claims against Enron Corp., while those with claims against Enron North America received an estimated 18.3 cents on the dollar. The money came in cash payments and stock in two holding companies, CrossCountry containing the firm's North American pipeline assets and Prisma Energy International containing the firm's South American operations.

After losing its auditing license in 2004, Arthur Andersen, formerly among the largest auditing firms in the world, ceased operation. In 2006, Andrew Fastow, former Enron chief financial officer, and Lea Fastow plead guilty to several charges of conspiracy to commit fraud. Andrew Fastow received a sentence of 10 years in prison without the possibility of parole. His wife received a much shorter sentence. Also in 2006, Enron chairman Kenneth Lay died while awaiting sentencing, and Enron president Jeffery Skilling received a sentence of 24 years in prison.

Citigroup agreed in early 2008 to pay $1.66 billion to Enron creditors who lost money following the collapse of the firm. Citigroup was the last remaining defendant in what was known as the Mega Claims lawsuit, a bankruptcy lawsuit filed in 2003 against 11 banks and brokerages. The suit alleged that, with the help of banks, Enron kept creditors in the dark about the firm's financial problems through misleading accounting practices. Because of the Mega Claims suit, creditors recovered a total of $5 billion or about 37.4 cents on each dollar owed to them. This lawsuit followed the settlement of a $40 billion class action lawsuit by shareholders, which Citicorp settled in June 2005 for $2 billion.

Discussion Questions

1. In your judgment, what were the major factors contributing to the demise of Enron? Of these factors, which were the most important? Explain your answer.
2. In what way was the Enron debacle a breakdown in corporate governance (oversight)? Explain your answer.
3. How were the Enron partnerships used to hide debt and inflate the firm's earnings? Should partnership structures be limited in the future? If so, how?
4. What should (or can) be done to reduce the likelihood of this type of situation arising in the future? Assess the impact of your proposals on the willingness of corporate managers to take risks. Be specific.

Solutions to these Case Study questions are found in the Online Instructor's Manual available for instructors using this book.

Case Study 16–8. Delta Airlines Rises from the Ashes

On April 30, 2007, Delta Airlines (Delta) emerged from bankruptcy leaner but still an independent carrier after a 19-month reorganization, during which it successfully fought off a $10 billion hostile takeover attempt by US Airways. The challenge facing Delta's management was to convince creditors that it would become more valuable as an independent carrier than it would be as part of US Airways.

An Industry Pushed to the Brink

Ravaged by escalating jet fuel prices and intensified competition from low-fare, low-cost carriers, Delta had lost $6.1 billion since the September 11, 2001, terrorist attack on the World Trade Center. The final crisis occurred in early August 2005, when the bank that was processing the airline's Visa and MasterCard ticket purchases started holding back money until passengers had completed their trips as protection in case of a bankruptcy filing. The bank was concerned that it would have to refund the passengers' ticket prices if the airline curtailed flights and the bank had to be reimbursed by the airline. This move by the bank cost the airline $650 million, further straining the carrier's already limited cash reserves. Delta's creditors were becoming increasingly concerned about the airline's ability to meet its financial obligations. Running out of cash and unable to borrow to satisfy current working capital requirements, the airline felt compelled to seek the protection of the bankruptcy court in late August 2005.

Delta's decision to declare bankruptcy occurred about the same time as a similar decision by Northwest Airlines. United Airlines and US Airways were already in bankruptcy. United had been in bankruptcy almost three years at the time Delta entered Chapter 11, and US Airways had been in bankruptcy court twice since the 9/11 terrorist attacks shook the airline industry. At the time Delta declared bankruptcy, about one half of the domestic carrier capacity was operating under bankruptcy court oversight.

Consequences of Bankruptcy Reorganization

Delta underwent substantial restructuring of its operations. An important component of the restructuring effort involved turning over its underfunded pilot's pension plans to the Pension Benefit Guaranty Corporation (PBGC), a federal pension agency, while winning concessions on wages and work rules from its pilots. The agreement with the pilot's union would save the airline $280 million annually and the pilots would be paid 14 percent less than they were before the airline declared bankruptcy. To achieve an agreement with its pilots to transfer control of their pension plan to the PBGC, Delta agreed to give the union a $650 million interest-bearing note on terminating and transferring the pension plans to the PBGC. The union would then use the airline's payments on the note to provide supplemental payments to members who would lose retirement benefits due to the PBGC limits on the amount of Delta's pension obligations it would be willing to pay. The pact covers more than 6,000 pilots.

The overhaul of Delta, the nation's third largest airline, left it a much smaller carrier than the one that sought protection of the bankruptcy court. Delta shed about one jet in six used by its mainline operations at the time of the bankruptcy filing, and it cut more than 20 percent of the 60,000 employees it had just prior to entering Chapter 11. Delta's domestic carrying capacity fell by about 10 percent since it petitioned for Chapter 11 reorganization, allowing it to fill about 84 percent of its seats on U.S. routes. This compared to only 72 percent when it filed for bankruptcy. The much higher utilization of its planes boosted revenue per mile flown by 15 percent since it entered bankruptcy, enabling the airline to better cover its fixed expenses. Delta also sold one of its "feeder" airlines, Atlantic Southeast Airlines, for $425 million.

Delta Obtains Financing to Exit Chapter 11

Delta would have $2.5 billion in exit financing to fund operations and a cost structure of about $3 billion a year less than when it went into bankruptcy. The purpose of the exit financing facility is to repay the company's $2.1 billion debtor-in-possession credit facilities provided by GE Capital and American Express, make other payments required on exiting bankruptcy, and increase its liquidity position. With 10 financial institutions providing the loans, the exit facility consists of a $1.6 billion first-lien revolving credit line, secured by virtually all the airline's unencumbered assets, and a $900 million second-lien term loan.

Final Approval of the Reorganization Plan

The bankruptcy court judge gave final approval to Delta's reorganization after rejecting four last minute objections filed by bondholders and shareholders, who complained that they were not being treated fairly. As required by the Plan of Reorganization approved by the Bankruptcy Court, Delta canceled its preplan common stock on April 30, 2007. Holders of preplan common stock did not receive a distribution of any kind under the Plan of Reorganization. The company issued new shares of Delta common stock as payment of bankruptcy claims and as part of a postemergence compensation program for Delta employees. Issued in May 2007, the new shares were listed on the New York Stock Exchange.

Discussion Questions

1. To what extent do you believe the factors contributing to the airline's bankruptcy were beyond the control of management? To what extent do you believe past airline mismanagement may have contributed to the bankruptcy?
2. Comment on the fairness of the bankruptcy process to shareholders, lenders, employees, communities, government, and so forth. Be specific.

3. Why would lenders be willing to lend to a firm emerging from Chapter 11? How did the lenders attempt to manage their risks? Be specific.

4. In view of the substantial loss of jobs, as well as wage and benefit reductions, do you believe that firms should be allowed to reorganize in bankruptcy? Explain your answer.

5. How does Chapter 11 potentially affect adversely competitors of those firms emerging from bankruptcy? Explain your answer.

Solutions to these case study questions are found in the Online Instructor's Manual for instructors using this book.

17

Cross-Border Mergers and Acquisitions

Analysis and Valuation

Courage is not the absence of fear. It is doing the thing you fear the most.
— Rick Warren

Inside M&A: Arcelor Outbids ThyssenKrupp for Canada's Dofasco Steelmaking Operations

Arcelor Steel of Luxembourg, the world's second largest steel maker, was eager to make an acquisition. Having been outbid by Mittal, the world's leading steel firm, in its efforts to buy Turkey's state-owned Erdemir and Ukraine's Kryvorizhstal, Guy Dolle, Arcelor's CEO, seemed determined not to let that happen again. Arcelor and Dofasco had been in talks for more than four months before Arcelor decided to initiate a tender offer on November 23, 2005, valued at $3.8 billion in cash. Dofasco, Canada's largest steel manufacturer, owned vast coal and iron ore reserves, possessed a nonunion workforce, and sold much of its steel to Honda assembly plants in the United States. The merger would enable Arcelor, whose revenues were concentrated primarily in Europe, to diversify into the United States. Contrary to their European operations, Arcelor found the flexibility offered by Dofasco's nonunion labor force highly attractive. Moreover, by increasing its share of global steel production, Arcelor's management reasoned that it would be able to exert additional pricing leverage with both customers and suppliers.

Serving the role of "white knight," Germany's ThyssenKrupp, the sixth largest steel firm in the world, offered to acquire Dofasco one week later for $4.1 billion in cash. Dofasco's board accepted the bid, which included a $187 million breakup fee should another firm acquire Dofasco. Investors soundly criticized Dofasco's board for not opening up the bidding to an auction. In its defense, the board expressed concern about stretching out the process in an auction over several weeks. In late December, Arcelor topped the ThyssenKrupp bid by offering $4.2 billion. Not to be outdone, ThyssenKrupp matched the Arcelor offer on January 4, 2006. The Dofasco board reaffirmed its preference for the ThyssenKrupp bid, due to the breakup fee and ThyssenKrupp's willingness (unlike Arcelor) to allow Dofasco to continue to operate under its own name and management.

In a bold attempt to put Dofasco out of reach of the already highly leveraged ThyssenKrupp, Arcelor raised its bid to $4.8 billion on January 16, 2006. This bid represented an approximate 80 percent premium over Dofasco's closing share price on the day Arcelor announced its original tender offer. The Arcelor bid was contingent on Dofasco withdrawing its support for the ThyssenKrupp bid. On January 24, 2006, ThyssenKrupp said it would not raise its bid. Events in the dynamically changing global steel market were not to end here. The Arcelor board and management barely had time to savor their successful takeover of Dofasco before Mittal initiated a hostile takeover of Arcelor. Ironically, Mittal succeeded in acquiring its archrival, Arcelor, just six months later in a bid to achieve further industry consolidation. See Chapter 3 (Case Study 3–1) for a discussion of the Mittal–Arcelor transaction.

Chapter Overview

There are as many motives as there are strategies for international expansion. This chapter addresses common motives for international expansion as well as the advantages and disadvantages of a variety of international market entry strategies. However, the focus in this chapter is on M&A as a market entry or expansion mode, because cross-border M&As comprise on average one fourth of total global transactions and more than one half of direct foreign investment annually (Hopkins, 2008; Kang and Johansson, 2000–2001; Letto-Gillies, Meschi, and Simonetti, 2001; and Chen and Findlay, 2002). Moreover, foreign direct investment (i.e., M&As and greenfield investment) has replaced international trade (i.e., exports and imports) as the driving force behind global integration of product markets. Given its focus on M&As, this chapter also addresses the challenges of M&A deal structures, financing, valuation, and execution in both developed and emerging countries. Finally, the chapter summarizes empirical studies investigating the actual benefits to both target and acquiring company shareholders of international diversification. Major chapter segments include the following:

- Distinguishing between Developed and Emerging Economies
- Globally Integrated versus Segmented Capital Markets
- Motives for International Expansion
- Common International Market Entry Strategies
- Structuring Cross-Border Transactions
- Financing Cross-Border Transactions
- Planning and Implementing Cross-Border Transactions in Emerging Countries
- Valuing Cross-Border Transactions
- Empirical Studies of Financial Returns to International Diversification
- Things to Remember

A review of this chapter (including practice questions with answers) is available in the file folder entitled Student Study Guide contained on the CD-ROM accompanying this book. The CD-ROM also contains a Learning Interactions Library, enabling students to test their knowledge of this chapter in a "real-time" environment.

Distinguishing between Developed and Emerging Economies

Throughout the chapter, the term *local country* refers to the target's country of residence, while *home country* refers to the acquirer's country of residence. *Developed countries* are those having significant and sustainable per capita economic growth, globally integrated capital markets, a well-defined legal system, transparent financial statements, currency convertibility, and a stable government. According to the World Bank, *emerging countries* have a growth rate in per capita gross domestic product significantly below that of developed countries. Note that, while many emerging countries show annual gross domestic product (GDP) growth well in excess of that of developed countries, their per capita GDP growth rate, generally considered a better measure of economic well-being, is usually much lower. Moreover, emerging countries frequently lack many of the other characteristics normally associated with developed nations.

Table 17–1 provides examples of developed and emerging economies as defined by Morgan Stanley Capital International. Other organizations, such as the Organization for Economic Cooperation and Development and the United Nations, include a somewhat different mix of countries. Despite definitional differences, Brazil, Russia, India, and China make everyone's list of emerging nations. These four countries (often grouped together under the acronym BRIC) constitute about four fifths of the total GDP of emerging countries (see *Economist*, 2006b).

Globally Integrated versus Segmented Capital Markets

While both developed and emerging country economies have become increasingly interdependent in recent years, there also is substantial evidence that regional and individual country capital markets have become increasingly integrated. Reflecting the emergence of a global capital market, correlation among individual countries' capital markets, on average, has increased (Bekaert and Harvey, 2002). For example, in 2005, foreigners held 12 percent of U.S. stocks, 25 percent of U.S. corporate bonds, and 44 percent of U.S. Treasury securities, as compared to 4, 1, and 20 percent, respectively, in 1975 (Farrell, Key, and Shavers, 2006). Reflecting this increasing integration among country capital markets, correlation between the performance of U.S. and European stocks has increased from less than 30 percent in the 1970s to 90 percent in recent years (Blackman, 2006).

Globally integrated capital markets provide foreigners with unfettered access to local capital markets and local residents to foreign capital markets. Factors contributing to the integration of global capital markets include the reduction in trade barriers, removal of capital controls, the harmonization of tax laws (which reduce the impact of

Table 17–1 Examples of Developed and Emerging Economies

Developed Economies		Emerging Economies	
Australia	Japan	Argentina	Mexico
Austria	Netherlands	Brazil	Morocco
Belgium	New Zealand	China	Pakistan
Canada	Norway	Colombia	Peru
Denmark	Portugal	Czech Republic	Philippines
Finland	Singapore	Egypt	Poland
France	Spain	Hungary	Russia
Germany	Sweden	India	South Africa
Greece	Switzerland	Indonesia	Sri Lanka
Hong Kong	United Kingdom	Israel	Taiwan
Ireland	United States	Jordan	Thailand
Italy		Korea	Turkey
		Malaysia	Venezuela

Source: Morgan Stanley Capital International (www.msci.com).

different tax rates on trade and investment), floating exchange rates, and the free convertibility of currencies. Improving accounting standards and shareholder protections (i.e., corporate governance) also encourage cross-border capital flows. Transaction costs associated with foreign investment portfolios have also fallen because of advances in information technology and competition. Consequently, multinational corporations can more easily raise funds in both domestic and foreign capital markets. This increase in competition among lenders and investors has resulted in a reduction in the cost of capital for such firms.

Unlike globally integrated capital markets, **segmented capital markets** exhibit different bond and equity prices in different geographic areas for identical assets in terms of risk and maturity. Arbitrage should drive the prices in different markets to be the same, as investors sell those assets that are overvalued to buy those that are undervalued. Segmentation arises when investors are unable to move capital from one market to another due to capital controls or simply because they prefer to invest in their local markets. Segmentation or local bias may arise because of investors having better information about local rather than more remote firms (Kang, 2008).

Investors in segmented markets bear a higher level of risk by holding a disproportionately large share of their investments in their local market as opposed to the level of risk if they invested in a globally diversified portfolio. Reflecting this higher level of risk, investors and lenders in such markets require a higher rate of return to local market investments than if investing in a globally diversified portfolio of stocks. Therefore, the cost of capital for firms in segmented markets without easy access to global markets often is higher than the global cost of capital.

Despite the increasing correlation of cash flows and share prices among firms in developed countries, there is evidence that capital markets in these countries may be segmented to the extent that local factors are more important in determining the cash flows, access to capital, and share prices of small firms than of large firms (Eun, Huang, and Lai, 2007). Consequently, the share price of a major French retailer like Carrefour may trade very much like the giant U.S. retailer Wal-Mart. However, the stock of a small French retail discount chain, affected more by factors in its local market segment, may trade differently from either Carrefour or Wal-Mart and exhibit a much higher cost of capital.

Motives for International Expansion

The reasons firms expand internationally include the desire to achieve geographic diversification, accelerate growth, consolidate industries, utilize natural resources and lower labor costs elsewhere, and leverage intangible assets. Other motives include minimizing tax liabilities, avoiding entry barriers, fluctuating exchange rates, and following customers into foreign markets.

Geographic and Industrial Diversification

Firms may diversify by investing in different industries in the same country, the same industries in different countries, or different industries in different countries. Firms investing in industries or countries whose economic cycles are not highly correlated may lower the overall volatility in their consolidated earnings and cash flows. By increasing earnings and cash flow predictability, such firms may reduce their cost of capital. Numerous studies show that diversified international firms often exhibit a lower cost of capital than firms whose investments are not well-diversified (Chan, Karolyi, and Stulz, 1992; Stulz 1995a, 1995b; Stulz and Wasserfallen, 1995; Expinosa, 1996; Seth, Song, and Petit, 2002).

Accelerating Growth

Foreign markets represent an opportunity for domestic firms to grow. Graham, Martey, and Yawson (2008) found that large firms experiencing slower growth in their domestic markets have a greater likelihood of making foreign acquisitions, particularly in rapidly growing emerging markets. U.S. firms have historically invested in potentially higher-growth foreign markets. Similarly, the United States represents a large, growing, and politically stable market. Consequently, foreign firms have increased their exports to and direct investment (including M&As) in the United States. Facing increasingly saturated home markets, many European telecommunications companies, such as Vodafone and Spain's Telefonica, set their sights on emerging markets to fuel future expansion. The number of cell phone subscribers in Europe has been increasing at a tepid 6–8 percent pace as compared to 34 percent in the Middle East and 55 percent per annum in Africa (Bryan-Low, 2005).

Industry Consolidation

Excess capacity in many industries often drives M&A activity, as firms strive to achieve greater economies of scale and scope, as well as pricing power with customers and suppliers. The highly active consolidation in recent years in the metals industries (e.g., steel, nickel, and copper) represents an excellent example of this global trend. Global consolidation has also been common in such industries as financial services, media, oil and gas, telecommunications, and pharmaceuticals.

Once industries become more concentrated, smaller competitors often are compelled to merge, thereby accelerating the pace of consolidation. In late 2006, midsize European drug maker Merck KFaA agreed to buy Swiss biotechnology company Serono SA for $11 billion, and Germany's Alana AF said it would sell its comparatively low-market-share pharmaceutical business to Danish drug manufacturer Nycomed for $5 billion. Smaller drug companies found it difficult to compete with behemoths Pfizer Inc. and GlaxoSmithKline PLC, which have much larger research budgets and sales forces. Midsize firms also are more likely to be reliant on a few drugs for the bulk of their revenue, which makes them highly vulnerable to generic copies of their drugs.

Utilization of Lower Raw Material and Labor Costs

Emerging markets may be particularly attractive since they often represent low labor costs, access to inexpensive raw materials, and low levels of regulation (Dunning, 1988). Thus, shifting production overseas represents an opportunity to reduce significantly operating expenses and become more competitive in global markets. The salutary impact of lower labor costs often is overstated because worker productivity in emerging countries tends to be significantly lower than in more developed countries. Consequently, while emerging country workers are paid less they also produce far less than their counterparts in developed nations do.

Leveraging Intangible Assets

Firms with significant expertise, brands, patents, copyrights, and proprietary technologies seek to grow by exploiting these advantages in emerging markets. Foreign buyers may seek to acquire firms with intellectual property, so that they can employ such assets in their own domestic markets (Eun, Kolodny, and Scherage, 1996; Morck and Yeung, 1991). Caves (1982) demonstrates that firms with a reputation for superior products in their home markets might find that they can successfully apply this reputation in foreign markets (e.g., Coke, Pepsi, and McDonald's). Ferreira and Tallman (2005) argue that firms seeking to leverage their capabilities are likely to acquire controlling interests in foreign firms. However, as Wal-Mart discovered, sometimes even a widely recognized brand name is insufficient to overcome the challenges of foreign markets (see Case Study 17–1).

Case Study 17–1 Wal-Mart Stumbles in Its Global Expansion Strategy

The year 2006 marked the most significant retrenchment for Wal-Mart since it undertook its international expansion in the early 1990s, in an effort to rejuvenate sales growth. Wal-Mart, the world's largest retailer, admitted defeat in its long-standing effort to penetrate successfully the German retail market. On July 30, 2006, the behemoth announced that it was selling its operations in Germany to German retailer Metro AG. Wal-Mart had been trying to make its German stores profitable for eight years. Wal-Mart announced a pretax loss on the sale of $1 billion. Wal-Mart had previously announced in May that it would sell its 16 stores in South Korea.

Wal-Mart apparently underestimated the ferocity of German competitors, the frugality of German shoppers, and the extent to which regulations, cultural differences, and labor unions would impede its ability to apply in Germany what had worked so well for it in the United States. German discount retailers offer very low prices, and German shoppers have shown they can be very demanding. Germany's shoppers are accustomed to buying based primarily on price. They are willing to split their shopping activities among various retailers, which blunt the effectiveness of the "superstores" offering one location for all the shoppers needs. Employees filed a lawsuit against the retailer's policy against romantic relationships between employees and supervisors. Accustomed to putting their own groceries in shopping bags, German shoppers were alienated by clerks who bagged groceries. Moreover, German regulations limited Wal-Mart's ability to offer extended and weekend hours, as well to sell merchandise below cost in an effort to lure consumers with so-called loss leaders. Strong unions also limited the firm's ability to contain operating costs.

Wal-Mart also experienced a loss of seasoned executives when it acquired several German retailers. The two retailers were headquartered in different cities. Following the mergers, Wal-Mart consolidated the two headquarters in one city, prompting many executives to leave rather than relocate. Perhaps reflecting this "brain drain," Wal-Mart's German operations had four presidents in eight years. Wal-Mart has not been alone in finding the German discount market challenging. Nestle SA and Unilever are among the large multinational retailers that had to change the way they do business in Germany. France's Carrefour SA, Wal-Mart's largest competitor worldwide, diligently avoided Germany.

With the withdrawal from the German and South Korean markets, Wal-Mart is currently operating in 11 countries. This compares to Carrefour of France (29 countries), and Metro of Germany (30 countries), the second and third largest global retailers, respectively. Wal-Mart's international ambitions are now centered in Asia and Latin America, with India and China the firm's most promising growth markets. However, Wal-Mart can expect to experience similar growth challenges in these countries. For example, India does not permit foreign firms to establish stores unless they sell only one brand. In late 2006, Wal-Mart agreed with China's state-run union to set up unions at its 60 stores in that country. Moreover, China is limiting the size of large-scale retail outlets, which is likely to limit Wal-Mart's plans to introduce the superstore concept.

Discussion Questions

1. Wal-Mart's missteps in Germany may represent an example of the limitations of introducing what works in one market (i.e., so-called best practices) in another. To what extent do you believe that Wal-Mart's failure represented a strategic error? To what extent did the firm's lack of success represent an implementation error?
2. Based on this experience, do you believe Wal-Mart should limit its international expansion? Explain your answer.
3. In your judgment, what criteria should Wal-Mart employ in selecting other foreign markets to enter? Be specific.

Minimizing Tax Liabilities

Firms in high-tax countries may shift production and reported profits by building or acquiring operations in countries with more favorable tax laws. Evidence supporting the notion that such strategies are common is mixed. Servaes and Zenner (1994) found a positive correlation between cross-border mergers and differences in tax laws. However, Manzon, Sharp, and Travlos (1994) and Dewenter (1995) found little correlation.

Avoiding Entry Barriers

Quotas and tariffs on imports imposed by governments to protect domestic industries often encourage foreign direct investment. Foreign firms may acquire existing facilities or start new operations in the country imposing the quotas and tariffs to circumvent such measures.

Fluctuating Exchange Rates

Changes in currency values can have a significant impact on where and when foreign direct investments are made. Appreciating foreign currencies relative to the dollar reduce the overall cost of investing in the United States. The impact of exchange rates on cross-border transactions has been substantiated in a number of studies: Georgopoulos (2008); Feliciano and Lipsey (2002); Vasconcellos and Kish (1998); Harris and Ravenscraft (1991); and Vaconcellos, Madura, and Kish (1990).

Following Customers

Often suppliers are encouraged to invest abroad to better satisfy the immediate needs of their customers. For example, auto parts suppliers worldwide have set up operations next to large auto manufacturing companies in China. By doing so, parts suppliers were able to reduce costs and make parts available as needed by the auto companies.

Common International Market Entry Strategies

The method of market entry chosen by a firm reflects the firm's risk tolerance, perceived risk, competitive conditions, and the firm's overall resources. Common entry strategies include greenfield or solo ventures, mergers and acquisitions, joint ventures, export, and licensing. The literature discussing the reasons why a firm chooses one strategy over another is extensive. Figure 17–1 summarizes the factors influencing the choice of entry strategy.

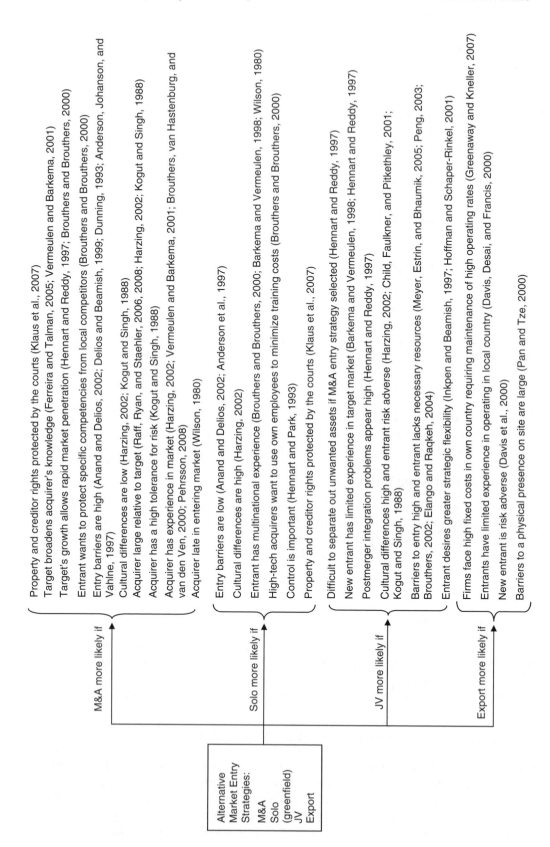

FIGURE 17–1 Alternative market entry strategies.

M&As can provide quick access to a new market; however, they are subject to many of the same problems associated with domestic M&As. They often are very expensive, complex to negotiate, subject to myriad regulatory requirements, and sometimes beset by intractable cultural issues. *The Economist* (1999) estimated that only one fifth of cross-border bids result in a completed transaction, as compared to a success rate of more than 40 percent for domestic transactions. The challenges of implementing cross-border transactions are compounded by substantial cultural differences and frequently by local country political and regulatory considerations.

In a greenfield or solo venture, a foreign firm starts a new business in the local country, enabling the firm to control technology, production, marketing, and product distribution. Studies show that firms with significant intangible assets (e.g., proprietary know-how) are frequently able to earn above average returns, which can be leveraged in a greenfield or startup venture (Brouthers and Brouthers, 2000). However, the firm's total investment is at risk, and the need to hire local residents ensures that the firm faces the challenges associated with managing a culturally diverse employee base.

Joint ventures allow firms to share the risks and costs of international expansion, develop new capabilities, and gain access to important resources (Zahra and Elhagrasey, 1994). Most strategic alliances are with a local firm that understands the competitive conditions, legal and social norms, and cultural standards of the country. Local firms may be interested in alliances to gain access to the technology, brand recognition, and innovative products of the foreign firm. Despite these benefits, many alliances fail, due to conflict between partners (see Chapter 14). Alliances are also difficult to manage. Pan, Li, and Tse (1999) show that alliances tend to produce higher financial returns if the partners have an equity interest. In contrast to earlier studies showing increasing use of alliances and joint ventures in entering foreign markets, Desai, Foley, and Hines (2002) show a decline between 1982 and 1997 in the frequency of such activity. Factors contributing to this decline include lower coordination costs between domestic and foreign operations, due to easier communication, reduced transportation costs, and integration of global financial markets. During the sample period, minority-owned foreign affiliates declined from 17.9 percent to 10.6 percent, while wholly owned affiliates increased from 72.3 percent to 80.4 percent. Alliances are often a precursor to acquisition. Wal-Mart's successful entry into Mexico started with a joint venture in 1991 with Grupo Cifra, Mexico's largest retail chain, culminating in the acquisition of the Mexican retailer in 1997. Grupo Cifra brought name recognition, while Wal-Mart contributed expertise in merchandising, distribution, warehousing, logistics, and data management.

Exporting does not require the expense of establishing local operations. However, exporters must establish some means of marketing and distributing their products at the local level. The disadvantages of exporting include high transportation costs, exchange rate fluctuations, and possible tariffs placed on imports into the local country. Moreover, the exporter has limited control over the marketing and distribution of its products in the local market. Raff, Ryan, and Staehler (2008) found that firms exhibiting relatively low productivity (a proxy for cash flow) are more likely to enter foreign markets by exporting than via acquisition or investing in greenfield operation.

Licensing allows a firm to purchase the right to manufacture and sell another firm's products within a specific country or set of countries. The licensor is normally paid a royalty on each unit sold. The licensee takes the risks and makes the investments in facilities for manufacturing, marketing and distribution of goods and services. Consequently, licensing is possibly the least costly form of international expansion. Therefore, licensing is an increasingly popular entry mode for smaller firms with insufficient capital and limited brand recognition (Hitt and Ireland, 2000). Disadvantages include the lack of control over the manufacture and marketing of the firm's products in other countries.

The risk may be high if the firm's brand or trademark is put in jeopardy. Furthermore, licensing often is the least profitable entry strategy, because the profits must be shared between the licensor and licensee. Finally, the licensee may learn the technology and sell a similar competitive product after the license expires.

Structuring Cross-Border Transactions

Acquisition vehicles, forms of payment and acquisition, and tax strategies are discussed in detail elsewhere in this book. This section discusses only those aspects of deal structuring pertinent to cross-border transactions.

Acquisition Vehicle

Non-U.S. firms seeking to acquire U.S. companies often use C corporations, limited liability companies, or partnerships to acquire the shares or assets of U.S. targets. C corporations are relatively easy to organize quickly, since all states permit such structures and no prior government approval is required. There is no limitation on non-U.S. persons or entities acting as shareholders in U.S. corporations, except for certain regulated industries. A limited liability company is attractive for joint ventures in which the target would be owned by two or more unrelated parties, corporations, or nonresident investors. While not traded on public stock exchanges, LLC shares can be sold freely to members. This facilitates the parent firm operating the acquired firm as a subsidiary or JV. A partnership may have advantages for investors from certain countries (e.g., Germany), where income earned from a U.S. partnership is not subject to taxation. Holding company structures enable a foreign parent to offset gains from one subsidiary with losses generated by another, serve as a platform for future acquisitions, and provide the parent with additional legal protection in the event of lawsuits.

U.S. companies acquiring businesses outside the United States encounter obstacles atypical of domestic acquisitions. These include investment and exchange control approvals, tax clearances, clearances under local competition (i.e., antitrust) laws, and unusual due diligence problems. Other problems involve the necessity of agreeing on an allocation of the purchase price among assets located in various jurisdictions and compliance with local law relating to the documentation necessary to complete the transaction. Much of what follows also applies to non-U.S. firms acquiring foreign firms.

The laws governing foreign firms have an important impact on the choice of acquisition vehicle, since the buyer must organize a local company to hold acquired shares or assets in a way consistent with local country law. In common-law countries (e.g., the United Kingdom, Canada, Australia, India, Pakistan, Hong Kong, Singapore, and other former British colonies), the acquisition vehicle will be a corporationlike structure. Corporations in the United Kingdom and other commonwealth countries are similar to those in the United States. In civil-law countries (which include western Europe, South America, Japan, and Korea), the acquisition will generally be in the form of a share company or limited liability company. *Civil law* is synonymous with *codified law, continental law*, or the *Napoleonic Code*. Practiced in some Middle Eastern Muslim and in some countries in Southeast Asia (e.g., Indonesia and Malaysia), Islamic law is based on the Koran and is sometimes referred to as *Muslim law*.

In the European Union, there is no overarching law or EU directive requiring a specific corporate form. Rather, corporate law is the responsibility of each member nation. In many civil-law countries, smaller enterprises often use a limited liability company, while larger enterprises, particularly those with public shareholders, are referred to as *share companies*. The rules applicable to limited liability companies tend to be flexible and are particularly useful for wholly owned subsidiaries. In contrast, share companies are subject to numerous restrictions and applicable securities laws. However, their shares trade freely on public exchanges.

Share companies tend to be more heavily regulated than U.S. corporations. Share companies must register with the commercial registrar in the location of its principal place of business. Bureaucratic delays from several weeks to several months between the filing of the appropriate documents and the organization of the company may occur. Most civil-law countries require that there be more than one shareholder. Usually there is no limitation on foreigners acting as shareholders. The directors in many share companies function as both officers and directors, as they do in a U.S. corporation.

Limited liability companies outside the United States are generally subject to fewer restrictions than share companies. LLCs have interests or quotas rather than shares, since a share denotes something traded freely on an exchange. A limited liability company typically is required to have more than one quota holder. In general, either domestic or foreign corporations or individuals may be quota holders in the LLC. For an excellent discussion of alternative corporate structures in common and civil law countries, see Truitt (2006).

Form of Payment

U.S. target shareholders most often receive cash rather than shares in cross-border transactions (Ceneboyan, Papaiaoannou, and Travlos, 1991). Shares and other securities require registration with the Securities and Exchange Commission and compliance with all local securities (including state) laws if they are resold in the United States. Target shareholders are interested in receiving acquirer shares only if there is a significant public market for the shares. Payment in transactions involving non-U.S. firms also are most likely to be cash. Acquirer shares often are less attractive to potential targets because of the absence of a liquid market for resale or the acquirer is not widely recognized by the target firm's shareholders.

Form of Acquisition

While a foreign buyer may acquire shares or assets directly, share acquisitions are generally the simplest form of acquisition. Share acquisitions result in all assets and liabilities of the target firm, on or off the balance sheet, transferred to the acquirer by "rule of law." In certain cases, the seller may choose to retain selected assets or liabilities. Asset purchases result in the transference of all or some of the assets of the target firm to the acquirer (see Chapter 11).

For acquisitions outside the United States, share acquisitions are often the simplest mechanism for conveying ownership. All assets and liabilities remain with the target; as such, they transfer to the buyer when the target's shares are purchased. Since assets remain with the target, few transfer documents are required and transfer taxes may be limited or avoided. This is particularly important in countries where transfer taxes (i.e., those paid whenever asset ownership transfers) are onerous. In share acquisitions, licenses, permits, franchises, contracts, and leases generally transfer to the buyer, without the need to get approval from licensors, permit holders, and the like, unless otherwise stipulated in the contract. The major disadvantage of a share purchase is that all the target's known and unknown liabilities transfer to the buyer. When the target is in a foreign country, full disclosure of liabilities is often limited and some target assets transfer encumbered by tax liens or other associated liabilities.

While asset sales generally make sense in acquiring a single line of business, they often are more complicated in foreign countries when the local law requires that the target firm's employees automatically become the acquirer's employees with the sale of the assets. Mergers are not legal in all countries, often due to the requirement that minority shareholders must assent to the will of the majority vote.

Tax Strategies

There are three basic deal-structuring strategies for determining whether the transaction is tax free or taxable to shareholders of U.S. firms acquired by foreign companies. The first strategy is the *tax-free reorganization*, or merger, in which target shareholders receive acquirer stock in exchange for substantially all of the target's assets or shares. The target firm merges with a U.S. subsidiary of the foreign acquirer in a statutory merger under state laws. To qualify as a U.S. corporation for tax purposes, the foreign firm must own at least 80 percent of the stock of the domestic subsidiary. As such, the transaction can qualify as a Type-A tax-free reorganization (see Chapter 12). Shareholders of the target company receive stock of the foreign acquirer in exchange for their stock in the target firm. The stock of the foreign acquirer may be voting or nonvoting. The U.S. subsidiary must acquire substantially all the assets of the target company. The most commonly used forms of tax-free *share* acquisitions is the *reverse triangular merger*. The foreign acquirer forms a new shell U.S. subsidiary, which merges with the target in a statutory merger, with the target surviving.

The second form of deal structure is the taxable purchase, which involves the acquisition by one company of the shares or assets of another, usually in exchange for cash or debt. Such a transaction is called *taxable* because the target firm's shareholders recognize a taxable gain or loss on the exchange. The *forward triangular merger* in cash is the most common form of *taxable transaction*. The target company merges with a U.S. subsidiary of the foreign acquirer, with shareholders of the target firm receiving acquirer shares as well as cash, although cash is the predominate form of payment. This structure is useful when the foreign acquirer is willing to issue some shares and some target company shareholders want shares, while others want cash.

Hybrid transactions represent a third form of transaction used in cross-border transactions. This type of structure affords the U.S. target corporation and its shareholders tax-free treatment, while avoiding the issuance of shares of the foreign acquirer. In general, a hybrid transaction may be taxable to some target shareholders and tax free to others. To structure hybrid transactions, some target company shareholders may exchange their common shares for a nonvoting preferred stock, while the foreign acquirer or its U.S. subsidiary buys the remaining common stock for cash. This transaction is tax free to target company shareholders taking preferred stock and taxable to those selling their shares for cash. For an excellent discussion of the different tax laws in various countries, see PriceWaterhouseCoopers (2006). Case Study 17–2 illustrates the complexity of international transactions.

Case Study 17-2 Cadbury Buys Adams in a Sweet Deal

Cadbury Schweppes PLC is a confectionary and beverage company headquartered in London, England. Cadbury Schweppes (Cadbury) acquired Adams Inc., a chewing gum manufacturer, from Pfizer Corporation in 2003 for $4.2 billion. The acquisition enables Cadbury to gain access to new markets, especially in Latin America. The purchase also catapulted Cadbury to the top spot in the global confectionary market. Adams's major brands are in the fastest growing segments of the global market and complement Cadbury's existing chocolate business.

Cadbury bought 100 percent of the business of the Adams Division of Pfizer. The decision whether to transfer assets or stock depended on which gave Cadbury and Pfizer optimum tax advantages. Furthermore, many employees had positions with both the parent and the operating unit. In addition, the parent supplied numerous support services for its subsidiary. While normal in the purchase of a unit of a larger company, this purchase was complicated by Adams operating in 40 countries representing 40 legal jurisdictions.

Cadbury and Pfizer representatives agreed on a single asset and stock sale and purchase agreement (i.e., the master agreement), which transferred the relevant U.S. assets and stock in Adams's subsidiaries to Cadbury. The master agreement contained certain overarching terms, including closing conditions, representations and warranties, covenants, and indemnification clauses that applied to all legal jurisdictions. However, the master agreement required Pfizer or Adams to enter into separate local "implementation" agreements. This was done to complete the transfer of either Adams's assets in non-U.S. jurisdictions or shares in non-U.S. Adams's subsidiaries to local Cadbury subsidiaries depending on which provided the most favorable tax advantages and where necessary to accommodate differences in local legal conditions. The parties entered into more than 20 such agreements to transfer asset and stock ownership. All the agreements used the master agreement as a template. Written in English, the various contracts were governed by New York law, the state in which Pfizer is headquartered, except where there was a requirement that the law governing the contract be that of the local country.

A team of 5 Cadbury in-house lawyers and 40 outside attorneys conducted the legal review. Cadbury staff members carried out separate environmental due diligence exercises, because Adams had long-standing assets in the form of plant and machinery in each of 22 factories in 18 countries. Cadbury filed with antitrust regulators in a number of European and non-European countries, including Germany, the Czech Republic, Turkey, Greece, Italy, Portugal, Spain, the United Kingdom, South Africa, and Brazil. The requirements varied in each jurisdiction. It was necessary to obtain regulatory clearance before closing in countries where prenotification was required. The master agreement was conditional on antitrust regulatory approval in the United States, Canada, and Mexico, Adams's largest geographic markets.

Cadbury wanted all 12,900 Adams employees across 40 countries to transfer to it with the business. However, because not all of them were fully dedicated Adams employees (i.e., some had both Adams and Pfizer functions), it was necessary to determine on a site-by-site basis which employees should remain with Pfizer and which should transfer to Cadbury. Partly due to the global complexity of the deal, the preclosing and closing meetings lasted three full days and nights. The closing checklist was 129 pages long (Birkett, 2003).

Discussion Questions

1. Discuss how cross-border transactions complicate the negotiation of the agreement of purchase and sale as well as due diligence. Be specific.
2. How does the complexity described in your answer to the first question add to the potential risk of the transaction? Be specific.
3. What conditions would you, as a buyer, suggest be included in the agreement of purchase and sale that might minimize the potential risk mentioned in your answer to the second question? Be specific.

Financing Cross-Border Transactions

Debt is most often used to finance cross-border transactions. The proceeds of the debt financing may be used either to purchase the target's outstanding shares for cash or repurchase acquirer shares issued to target shareholders to minimize potential earnings dilution. Sources of financing exist in capital markets in the acquirer's home, the target's local country, or in some third country. Domestic capital sources available to cross-border acquirers include banks willing to provide bridge financing and lines of credit, bond markets, and equity markets.

Debt Markets

Eurobonds represent a common form of financing for cross-border transactions. Eurobonds are debt instruments expressed in terms of U.S. dollars or other currencies and sold to investors outside the country in whose currency they are denominated. A typical Eurobond transaction could be a dollar-denominated bond issued by a French firm through an underwriting group. The underwriting group could comprise the overseas affiliate of a New York commercial bank, a German commercial bank, and a consortium of London banks. Bonds issued by foreign firms and governments in local markets have existed for many years. Such bonds are issued in another country's domestic bond market, denominated in its currency, and subject to that country's regulations. Bonds of a non-U.S. issuer registered with the SEC for sale in the U.S. public bond markets are called *yankee bonds*. Similarly, a U.S. company issuing a bond in Japan would be issuing a "samurai" bond.

Equity Markets

The American depository receipt (ADR) market evolved as a means of enabling foreign firms to raise funds in the U.S. equity markets. ADRs represent the receipt for the shares of a foreign-based corporation held in a U.S. bank. The ADR entitles the holder to all dividends and capital gains. American depositary shares (ADS) are shares issued under a deposit agreement representing the underlying common share, which trades in the issuer's market. The acronyms ADS and ADR often are used interchangeably. Euroequity markets are equivalent to the Eurobond market. The Euroequity market reflects equity issues by a foreign firm tapping a larger investor base than the firm's home equity market. The foreign firm may also be trying to avoid its domestic market regulations and expenses.

Often the target's shareholders are reluctant to accept an acquirer's shares if the buyer is not well known in the target's home market. Target shareholders may be able to sell the shares only at a discount in their home market. In this instance, the buyer may have to issue shares in its home market or possibly to the international equities market and use the proceeds to acquire the target for cash. Alternatively, the acquirer may issue shares in the target's market, if by doing so, it creates a resale market for target shareholders. The buyer could also offer target shareholders the opportunity to sell the shares in the buyer's home market through an investment banker.

Sovereign Funds

Sovereign wealth funds (SWFs) are government-backed or -sponsored investment funds whose primary function is to invest profitably accumulated reserves of foreign currencies. For years, such funds, in countries that had accumulated huge quantities of dollars, would reinvest these funds in U.S. Treasury securities. However, in recent years, such funds have become more sophisticated, increasingly taking equity positions in foreign firms.

Table 17–2   Sovereign Wealth Funds Ranked by Size

Country of Origin	Fund Name	Assets (Estimated)	Year Founded
Abu Dhabi	Abu Dhabi Investment Authority	$900 billion	1976
Norway	Government Pension Fund of Norway	$380 billion	1990
Singapore	Government of Singapore Investment Corporation	$340 billion	1981
Kuwait	Kuwait Investment Authority	$225 billion	1953
China	China Investment Corporation	$210 billion	2007
Singapore	Temasek Holdings	$115 billion	1974
Libya		$45 billion	2007
Russia	National Wealth Fund	$35 billion	2008
Korea	Korea Investment Corporation	$20 billion	2005
Dubai	Istithmar	Unknown	2003
Abu Dhabi	Mubabdala	Unknown	2002
Total funds held by all SWFS		$3.7 trillion (estimated)	

Source: Deutsche Bank, Standard Charter, and various news reports.

While the growth of such funds is relatively new, the funds themselves have been around for years. The oldest SWF, Kuwait Investment Authority, started in 1953. AbuDhabi Investment Authority and Temasek Holdings of Singapore have been around for more than 30 years. Collectively, the sovereign funds control almost $4 trillion in assets. The biggest shift in recent years has been the funds' willingness to make high-profile investments in public companies. For the most part, the sovereign funds appear to be long-term, sophisticated investors. Having invested more than $40 billion in UBS, Morgan Stanley, Merrill Lynch, and Citigroup during 2008, the funds often are attracted by marquee brands. Moreover, thus far they have not demonstrated a desire to seek controlling interests. Table 17–2 ranks the world's largest sovereign wealth funds by estimated assets as of the end of 2008.

Planning and Implementing Cross-Border Transactions in Emerging Countries

Entering emerging economies poses a host of new challenges not generally encountered in developed countries. These challenges may include a range of political and economic risks.

Political and Economic Risks

It is difficult to differentiate between political and economic risks, since they are often highly interrelated. Examples of political and economic risk include excessive local government regulation, confiscatory tax policies, restrictions on cash remittances, currency inconvertibility, restrictive employment policies, outright expropriation of assets of foreign firms, civil war or local insurgencies, and corruption. Another, sometimes overlooked, challenge is the failure of the legal system in an emerging country to honor contracts (Khanna, Palepu, and Sinha, 2005).

Many of these risks result in gyrating exchange rates, which heighten the level of risk associated with foreign direct investment in an emerging country. Unanticipated changes in exchange rates can influence substantially the competitiveness of products produced in the local market for export to the global marketplace. Furthermore, changes in exchange rates alter the value of assets invested in the local country and earnings repatriated from the local operations to the parent corporation in the home country. Not surprisingly, the degree of economic and political freedom correlates positively with foreign direct investment. When they believe that their property rights are going to respected and relatively few restrictions are placed on managing investments and repatriating earnings, foreigners are more inclined to invest directly in the local country. Bengoa and Sanchez-Robles (2003) and Berggren and Jordahl (2005) demonstrate a strong positive relationship between foreign direct investment and the Heritage Foundation's Freedom Index. This index contains about 50 variables divided into 10 categories, measuring various aspects of economic and political freedoms.

Sources of Information for Assessing Political and Economic Risk

Information sources include consultants in the local country, joint venture partners, a local legal counsel, or appropriate government agency such as the U.S. Department of State. Other sources of information include the major credit-rating agencies such as Standard and Poor's, Moody's, and Fitch IBCA. Trade magazines, such as *Euromoney* and *Institutional Investor*, provide overall country risk ratings updated semiannually. The Economic Intelligence Unit also provides numerical risk scores for individual countries. The *International Country Risk Guide*, published by the Political Risk Services Group, offers overall numerical risk scores for individual countries as well as separate scores for political, financial, and economic risks. While such publications provide a means of ranking countries in terms of risk, they provide little insight in measuring the magnitude of the risk.

Using Insurance to Manage Risk

The decision to buy political risk insurance depends on the size of the investment and the perceived level of political and economic risk. Parties have a variety of sources from which to choose. For instance, the export credit agency in a variety of countries such as Export Import Bank (United States), SACE (Italy), Hermes (Germany), and so forth may offer coverage for companies based within their jurisdictions. The Overseas Private Investment Corporation is available to firms based in the United States while the World Bank's Multilateral Investment Guarantee Agency is available to all firms. These government and quasi-governmental insurers are the only substantial providers of war and political violence coverage.

Using Options and Contract Language to Manage Risk

In theory, a thorough due diligence of the target firm should uncover the majority of significant risks for the acquirer. However, in emerging countries, where financial statements may be haphazard and gaining access to the information necessary to adequately assess risk is limited, it may be impossible to perform an adequate due diligence. Under these circumstances, acquirers may protect themselves by including a put option in the agreement of purchase and sale. Such an option enables the buyer to require the seller to repurchase shares from the buyer at a predetermined price under certain circumstances. Alternatively, the agreement could include a clause requiring a purchase price adjustment. For example, in late 2005, the Royal Bank of Scotland purchased shares in the Bank of China. If subsequent to closing, there were material restatements to the Bank of China's financial statements, the purchase price would be adjusted in the Royal Bank's favor.

Valuing Cross-Border Transactions

The methodology for valuing cross-border transactions using discounted cash flow analysis is similar to that employed when both the acquiring and target firms are within the same country. The basic differences between within-country and cross-border valuation methods is that the latter involves converting cash flows from one currency to another and adjusting the discount rate for risks not generally found when the acquirer and target firms are within the same country.

Converting Foreign Target Cash Flows to Acquirer Domestic Cash Flows

Cash flows of the target firm can be expressed in its own currency including expected inflation (i.e., in nominal terms), its own currency without inflation (i.e., real terms), or the acquirer's currency. Real cash-flow valuation adjusts all cash flows for inflation and uses real discount rates. Normally, M&A practitioners utilize nominal cash flows except when inflation rates are high. Under these circumstances, real cash flows are preferable. Real cash flows are determined by dividing the nominal cash flows by the country's gross domestic product deflator or some other broad measure of inflation. Future real cash flows are estimated by dividing future nominal cash flows by the current GDP deflator, increased by the expected rate of inflation. Real discount rates are determined by subtracting the expected rate of inflation from nominal discount rates. Nominal or real cash flows should give the same net present values if the expected rate of inflation used to convert future cash flows to real terms is the same inflation rate used to estimate the real discount rate.

Inflation in the target country may affect the various components of the target firm's cash flows differently. For example, how the inventory component of working capital is affected by inflation reflects in part how sensitive certain raw materials and the like are to inflation and how such inventory is recorded (i.e., LIFO or FIFO basis). Moreover, straight-line depreciation may not adequately account for the true replacement cost of equipment in an inflationary environment. Since conversion of the various components of cash flow from local to home country currency may result in unnecessary distortions, it is advisable to project the target's cash flows in terms in its own currency then convert the cash flows into the acquirer's currency. This requires estimating future exchange rates between the target (local) and acquirer's (home) currency.

Interest rates and expected inflation in one country compared to another country affect exchange rates between the two countries. The current rate at which one currency can be exchanged for another is called the *spot exchange rate*. Consequently, the translation to the acquirer's currency can be achieved by using future spot exchange rates estimated either from relative interest rates (the interest rate parity theory) in each country or by the relative rates of expected inflation (the purchasing power parity theory). For a detailed discussion of the interest rate parity and purchasing power parity theories, see Shapiro (2005).

When Target Firms Are in Developed (Globally Integrated) Capital Market Countries

For developed countries, such as those in western Europe, the interest rate parity theory provides a useful framework for estimating forward currency exchange rates (i.e., future spot exchange rates). To illustrate this process, consider a U.S. acquirer's valuation of a firm in the European Union (EU), with projected cash flows expressed in terms of euros. The target's cash flows can be converted into dollars by using a forecast of future dollar-to-euro spot rates. The *interest rate parity theory* relates forward or future spot exchange rates to differences in interest rates between two countries adjusted by the spot rate. Therefore, dollar/euro exchange rate $(\$/€)_n$ (i.e., the future or forward exchange rate), n periods into the future, is expected to appreciate (depreciate) according to the following relationship:

$$(\$/€)_n = [(1 + R_{\$n})^n/(1 + R_{€n})^n] \times (\$/€)_0 \qquad (17\text{--}1)$$

Similarly, the euro-to-dollar exchange rate $(€/\$)_n$, n periods into the future, would be expected to appreciate (depreciate) according to the following relationship:

$$(€/\$)_n = [(1 + R_{€n})^n/(1 + R_{\$n})^n] \times (€/\$)_0 \qquad (17\text{--}2)$$

Note that $(\$/€)_0$ and $(€/\$)_0$ represent the spot rate for the dollar to euro and euro to dollar exchange rates, respectively; $R_{\$n}$ and $R_{€n}$ represent the interest rate in the United States and the European Union, respectively. Equations (17–1) and (17–2) imply that if U.S. interest rates rise relative to those in the European Union, investors will buy dollars with euros at the current spot rate and sell dollars for euros in the forward or futures market to offset the risk of exchange rate changes n periods into the future. By doing so, investors avoid the potential loss of the value of their investment expressed in terms of dollars when they wish to convert their dollar holdings back into euros. In this way, the equality in these two equations is maintained. Exhibit 17–1 illustrates how to convert a target company's nominal free cash flows to the firm (FCFF) expressed in euros (i.e., the local country or target's currency) to those expressed in dollars (i.e., home country or acquirer's currency).

When Target Firms Are in Emerging (Segmented) Capital Market Countries

Cash flows are converted as before using the interest rate parity theory or the purchasing power parity theory. The latter is used if there is insufficient information about interest rates in the emerging market. The *purchasing power parity theory* states that one currency appreciates (depreciates) with respect to another currency according to the

---

Exhibit 17–1 Converting Euro-Denominated into Dollar-Denominated Free Cash Flows Using the Interest Rate Parity Theory

	2008	2009	2010
Target's euro-denominated FCFF cash flows (millions)	€124.5	€130.7	€136.0
Target country's interest rate (%)	4.50	4.70	5.30
U.S. interest rate (%)	4.25	4.35	4.55
Current spot rate ($/€) = 1.2044			
Projected spot rate ($/€)	1.2015	1.1964	1.1788
Target's dollar-denominated FCFF cash flows (millions)	$149.59	$156.37	$160.32

Note: Calculating the projected spot rate using equation (17–1):

$(\$/€)_{2008} = [(1.0425)/(1.0450)] \times 1.2044 = 1.2015$

$(\$/€)_{2009} = [(1.0435)^2/(1.0470)^2] \times 1.2044 = 1.1964$

$(\$/€)_{2010} = [(1.0455)^3/(1.0530)^3] \times 1.2044 = 1.1788$

expected relative rates of inflation between the two countries. To illustrate, the dollar/Mexican peso exchange rate, ($/Peso)$_n$, and the Mexican peso/dollar exchange rate, (Peso/$)$_n$, n periods from now (i.e., future exchange rates) is expected to change according to the following relationships:

$$(\$/Peso)_n = [(1 + P_{us})^n/(1 + P_{mex})^n] \times (\$/Peso)_0 \qquad (17\text{--}3)$$

and

$$(Peso/\$)_n = [(1 + P_{mex})^n/(1 + P_{us})^n] \times (Peso/\$)_0 \qquad (17\text{--}4)$$

where P_{us} and P_{mex} are the expected inflation rates in the United States and Mexico, respectively, and ($/Peso)$_0$ and (Peso/$)$_0$ are the dollar-to-peso and peso-to-dollar spot exchange rates, respectively. If future U.S. inflation is expected to rise faster than the Mexican inflation rate, the forward dollar to peso exchange rate, that is, future spot rates shown by equation (17–3), would depreciate, as U.S. citizens sell dollars for pesos to buy relatively cheaper Mexican products. See Exhibit 17–2 for an illustration of how this might work in practice.

Selecting the Correct Marginal Tax Rate

In general, the correct marginal tax rate should be that prevailing in the country in which the cash flows are generated. If the acquirer's country makes foreign income exempt from further taxation once taxed in the foreign country, the correct tax rate would be the marginal tax rate in the foreign country because that is where taxes are paid. Consequently, taxes paid on earnings in the foreign country would satisfy the acquirer's total taxes owed on income earned from this investment. Otherwise, the correct tax rate should be the acquirer's country rate, if it is higher than the target's country rate and taxes paid in a foreign country are deductible from the taxes owed by the acquirer in its home country. The acquirer must still pay taxes owed in the country in which it resides in excess of any credits received for foreign taxes paid.

Exhibit 17–2 Converting Peso-Denominated into Dollar-Denominated Free Cash Flows to the Firm Using the Purchasing Power Parity Theory

	2008	2009	2010
Target's peso-denominated FCFF cash flows (millions of pesos)	P1,050.5	P1,124.7	P1,202.7
Current Mexican expected inflation rate = 6%			
Current U.S. expected inflation rate = 4%			
Current spot rate ($/Peso) = .0877			
Projected spot rate ($/Peso)	.0860	.0844	.0828
Target's dollar-denominated FCFF cash flows (millions of dollars)	$90.34	$94.92	$99.58

Note: Calculating the projected spot rate using equation (17–3):

$(\$/Peso)_{2008} = [(1.04)/(1.06)] \times 0.0877 = 0.0860$

$(\$/Peso)_{2009} = [(1.04)^2/(1.06)^2] \times 0.0877 = 0.0844$

$(\$/Peso)_{2010} = [(1.04)^3/(1.06)^3] \times 0.0877 = 0.0828$

Estimating the Cost of Capital in Cross-Border Transactions

While almost three fourths of U.S. corporate chief financial officers surveyed use the capital asset pricing model to calculate the cost of equity, there is considerable disagreement in how to calculate the cost of equity in cross-border transactions (Graham and Harvey, 2001). To the extent a consensus exists, the basic capital asset pricing model or a multi-factor model (e.g., CAPM plus a factor to adjust for the size of the firm, etc.) should be used in developed countries with liquid capital markets. For emerging countries, the estimation of the cost of equity is more complex. Harvey (2005) documents 12 approaches to estimating the international cost of equity. Each method endeavors to incorporate adjustments to the discount rate to account for potential capital market segmentation and specific country risks. Still other approaches attempt to incorporate the risk of investing in emerging countries not by adjusting the discount rate but by adjusting projected cash flows. In either case, the adjustments often appear arbitrary.

Developed economies seem to exhibit little differences in the cost of equity, due to the relatively high integration of their capital markets with the global capital market. Thus, adjusting the cost of equity for specific country risk does not seem to make any significant difference (Koedijk and Van Dijk, 2000; Koedijk et al., 2002; Mishra and O'Brien, 2001; Bodnar, Dumas, and Marston, 2003). However, for emerging market countries, the existence of segmented capital markets, political instability, limited liquidity, currency fluctuations, and currency inconvertibility seem to make adjusting the target firm's cost of equity for these factors (to the extent practical) desirable. Bodnar et al. (2003) argue that, in addition to the risk-free rate of return, the firm's cost of equity (k_e) should be adjusted for such factors as the risk arising from variation in returns on a global stock market, country-specific stock market risk, and industry-specific risk. Other factors include exchange rate, political, and liquidity risk. Unfortunately, the substantial amount of information needed to estimate the adjustments required in such extensive multifactor models usually makes this approach impractical.

The following discussion incorporates the basic elements of valuing cross-border transactions, distinguishing between the different adjustments made when investing in developed and emerging countries. Nonetheless, the reader must keep in mind that that considerable debate continues in this area. See Harvey (2005) for an excellent discussion of the issues.

Estimating the Cost of Equity in Developed (Globally Integrated) Countries

What follows is a discussion of how to adjust the basic CAPM formulation for valuing cross-border transactions where the target is located in a developed country. The discussion is very similar to the capital asset pricing model formulation (CAPM) outlined in Chapter 7, except for the use of either national or globally diversified stock market indices in estimating beta and calculating the equity market risk premium.

Estimating the Risk-Free Rate of Return (Developed Countries)   For developed countries, the risk-free rate is the local country's government bond rate, whenever the projected cash flows for the target firm are expressed in local currency. Conversely, the risk-free rate is the U.S. Treasury bond rate if projected cash flows are in terms of dollars.

Adjusting CAPM for Risk (Developed Countries)   The equity premium, reflecting the difference between the return on a well-diversified portfolio and the risk-free return, is the incremental return required to induce investors to buy stock. The use of a well-diversified portfolio eliminates risk specific to a business or so-called diversifiable risk.

The firm's β is a measure of nondiversifiable risk. In a world in which capital markets are fully integrated, equity investors hold globally diversified portfolios. When measured in the same currency, the equity premium is the same for all investors, because each security's β is estimated by regressing its historical financial returns, or that of a comparable firm, against the historical returns on a globally diversified equity index.

Alternatively, an analyst could use a well-diversified country index that is highly correlated with the global index. In the United States, an example of a well-diversified portfolio is the Standard and Poor's 500 stock index (S&P 500); in the global capital markets, the Morgan Stanley Capital International World Index (MSCI) is commonly used as a proxy for a well-diversified global equity portfolio. Thus, the equity premium may be estimated on a well-diversified portfolio of U.S. equities, another developed country's equity portfolio, or on a global equity portfolio.

Adjusting CAPM for Firm Size   As noted in Chapter 7, studies show that the capital asset pricing model should be adjusted for the size of the firm. The size factor serves as a proxy for factors such as smaller firms being subject to higher default risk and generally being less liquid than large capitalization firms (Berk, 1995). See Chapter 7 (Table 7–1) for estimates of the amount of the adjustment to the cost of equity to correct for firm size, as measured by market value.

Global CAPM Formulation (Developed Countries)   In globally integrated markets, non-diversifiable or systematic market risk is defined relative to the rest of the world. Therefore, an asset has systematic risk only to the extent that the performance of the asset correlates with the overall world economy. When using a global equity index, the resulting CAPM often is called the *global* or *international capital asset pricing model*. If the risk associated with the target firm is similar to that faced by the acquirer, the acquirer's cost of equity may be used to discount the target's cash flows.

The global capital asset pricing model for the target firm may be expressed as follows:

$$k_{e,\text{dev}} = R_f + \beta_{\text{devfirm,global}}(R_m - R_f) + \text{FSP} \qquad (17\text{–}5)$$

where

$k_{e,\text{dev}}$ = required return on equity for a firm operating in a developed country.

R_f = local country's risk-free financial rate of return if cash flows are measured in the local country's currency or U.S. Treasury bond rate if in dollars.

$(R_m - R_f)$ = difference between the expected return on the global market portfolio (i.e., MSCI), U.S. equity index (S&P 500), or a broadly defined index in the target's local country and R_f. This difference is the equity premium, which should be approximately the same when expressed in the same currency for countries with globally integrated capital markets.

$\beta_{\text{devfirm,global}}$ = measure of nondiversifiable risk with respect to a globally diversified equity portfolio or a well-diversified country portfolio highly correlated with the global index. Alternatively, $\beta_{\text{devfirm,global}}$ may be estimated indirectly as illustrated in equation (17–7).

FSP = firm size premium reflecting the additional return smaller firms must earn relative to larger firms to attract investors.

Note the similarity of the global capital asset pricing model, equation (17–5), with the capital asset pricing model adjusted for firm size discussed in Chapter 7, equation (7–2).

An analyst may wish to value the target's future cash flows in both the local and home currencies. The Fisher effect allows the analyst to convert a nominal cost of equity from one currency to another. Assuming the expected inflation rates in the two countries are accurate, the real cost of equity should be the same in either country.

Applying the Fisher Effect   The so-called Fisher effect states that nominal interest rates can be expressed as the sum of the real interest rate (i.e., interest rates excluding inflation) and the anticipated rate of inflation. The Fisher effect can be shown for the United States and Mexico as follows:

$$(1 + i_{us}) = (1 + r_{us})(1 + P_{us})$$

and

$$(1 + r_{us}) = (1 + i_{us})/(1 + P_{us})$$
$$(1 + i_{mex}) = (1 + r_{mex})(1 + P_{mex})$$

and

$$(1 + r_{mex}) = (1 + i_{mex})/(1 + P_{mex})$$

If real interest rates are constant among all countries, nominal interest rates between countries vary by only the difference in the anticipated inflation rates. Therefore,

where
$$(1 + i_{us})/(1 + P_{us}) = (1 + i_{mex})/(1 + P_{mex}) \qquad (17\text{--}6)$$

i_{us} and i_{mex} = nominal interest rates in the United States and Mexico, respectively.

r_{us} and r_{mex} = real interest rates in the United States and Mexico, respectively.

P_{us} and P_{mex} = anticipated inflation rates in the United States and Mexico, respectively.

If the analyst knows the Mexican interest rate and the anticipated inflation rates in Mexico and the United States, solving equation (17–6) provides an estimate of the U.S. interest rate; that is, $i_{us} = (1 + i_{mex}) \times [(1 + P_{us})/(1 + P_{mex})] - 1$. Exhibit 17–3 illustrates how the cost of equity estimated in one currency is converted easily to another using equation (17–6). Although the historical equity premium in the United States is used in calculating the cost of equity, the historical U.K. or MSCI premium also could have been employed.

Exhibit 17–3 Calculating the Target Firm's Cost of Equity in Both Home and Local Currency

Acquirer, a U.S. multinational firm, is interested in purchasing Target, a small U.K.-based competitor, with a market value of £550 million or about $1 billion. The current risk-free rate of return for U.K. 10-year government bonds is 4.2 percent. The anticipated inflation rates in the United States and the United Kingdom are 3 and 4 percent, respectively. The estimated size premium for a small capitalization firm is 1.2 percent (see Chapter 7, Table 7–1). The historical equity risk premium in the United States is 5.5%.[1] Acquirer estimates Target's β to be 0.8, by regressing Target's historical financial returns against the S&P 500. What cost of equity ($k_{e,uk}$) should be used to discount Target's projected cash flows when they are expressed in terms of British pounds (i.e., local currency)? What cost of equity ($k_{e,us}$) should be used to discount Target's projected cash flows when they are expressed in terms of U.S. dollars (i.e., home currency)?[2]

$k_{e,\text{uk}}$, see equation (17–5), $= 0.042 + 0.8 \times (0.055) + 0.012 = 0.098 = 9.80\%$

$k_{e,\text{us}}$, see equation (17–6), $= (1 + 0.098) \times [(1 + 0.03)/(1 + 0.04)] - 1$
$$= 0.0875 = 8.75\%$$

[1]The U.S. equity premium or U.K. equity premium could have been used since equity markets in both countries are highly correlated.

[2]The real rate of return is the same in the United Kingdom (r_{uk}) and the United States (r_{us}): $r_{\text{uk}} = 9.8\% - 4.0\% = 5.8\%$ and $r_{\text{us}} = 8.8\% - 3.0\% = 5.8\%$.

Estimating the Cost of Equity in Emerging (Segmented) Capital Market Countries

If the individual country's capital markets are segmented, the global capital asset pricing model must be adjusted to reflect the tendency of investors in individual countries to hold local country rather than globally diversified equity portfolios. Consequently, equity premiums differ among countries reflecting the nondiversifiable risk associated with each country's equity market index. What follows is a discussion of how to adjust the basic CAPM formulation for valuing cross-border transactions where the target is located in an emerging country.

Estimating the Risk-Free Rate of Return (Emerging Countries)   For emerging economies, data limitations often preclude using the local country's government bond rate as the risk-free rate. If the target firm's cash flows are in terms of local currency, the U.S. Treasury bond rate often is used to estimate the risk-free rate. To create a local nominal interest rate, the Treasury bond rate should be adjusted (using the Fisher effect) for the difference in the anticipated inflation rates in the two countries. See equation (17–6) to determine how to make this adjustment.

Adjusting CAPM for Risk (Emerging Countries)   An analyst can determine if a country's equity market is likely to be segmented from the global equity market if the β derived by regressing returns in the foreign market with returns on the global equity market is significantly different from 1. This implies that the local country's equity premium differs from the global equity premium, reflecting the local country's nondiversifiable risk.

Nondiversifiable risk for a firm operating primarily in its emerging country's home market, whose capital market is segmented, is measured mainly with respect to the country's equity market index ($\beta_{\text{emfirm,country}}$) and to a lesser extent with respect a globally diversified equity portfolio ($\beta_{\text{country,global}}$). The emerging country firm's global beta ($\beta_{\text{emfirm,global}}$) can be adjusted to reflect the relationship with the global capital market as follows:

$$\beta_{\text{emfirm,global}} = \beta_{\text{emfirm,country}} \times \beta_{\text{country,global}} \qquad (17-7)$$

The value of $\beta_{\text{emfirm,country}}$ is estimated by regressing historical returns for the local firm against returns for the country's equity index. In the absence of sufficient historical information, $\beta_{\text{emfirm,country}}$ may be estimated by using the beta for a similar local firm or a similar foreign firm. The value of $\beta_{\text{country,global}}$ can be estimated by regressing the financial returns for the local country index (or for the index in a similar country) against the historical financial returns for a global index. Alternatively, a more direct approach is to regress the local firm's historical returns against the financial returns for a globally diversified portfolio of stocks to estimate $\beta_{emfirm,global}$. Furthermore, the β between a similar local or foreign firm and the global index could be used for this purpose. However, the regression of the local firm's historical financial returns against the global index may not work for many local firms whose business is not dependent on exports and is not highly correlated with the global economy.

Due to absence of historical data in many emerging economies, the equity risk premium often is estimated using the "prospective method" implied in the constant growth valuation model. As noted in Chapter 7, equation (7–17), this formulation provides an estimate of the present value of dividends growing at a constant rate in perpetuity. Recall that this method requires that the dividends paid in the current period (d_0) are grown at a constant rate of growth (g) such that d_1 equals $d_0(1 + g)$.

Assuming the stock market values stocks correctly and we know the present value of a broadly defined index in the target firm's country ($P_{country}$) or in a similar country, dividends paid annually on this index in the next period (d_1), and the expected dividend growth (g), we can estimate the expected return ($R_{country}$) on the stock index as follows:

$$P_{country} = d_1/(R_{country} - g)$$

and

$$R_{country} = (d_1/P_{country}) + g \qquad (17\text{–}8)$$

From equation (17–8), the equity risk premium for the local country's equity market is $R_{country} - R_f$, where R_f is the local country's risk-free rate of return. Exhibit 17–4 illustrates how to calculate the cost of equity for a firm in an emerging country in the absence of perceived significant country or political risk not captured in the beta or equity risk premium. Note that the local country's risk-free rate of return is estimated using the U.S. Treasury bond rate adjusted for the expected inflation in the local country relative to the United States. This converts the U.S. Treasury bond rate into a local country nominal interest rate.

Exhibit 17–4 Calculating the Target Firm's Cost of Equity for Firms in Emerging Countries

Assume next year's dividend yield on an emerging country's stock market is 5 percent and earnings for the companies in the stock market index are expected to grow by 6 percent annually in the foreseeable future. The country's global beta ($\beta_{country,global}$) is 1.1. The U.S. Treasury bond rate is 4 percent, and the expected inflation rate in the emerging country is 4 percent compared to 3 percent in the United States. Estimate the country's risk free rate (R_f), the return on a diversified portfolio of equities in the emerging country ($R_{country}$), and the country's equity risk premium ($R_{country} - R_f$). What is the cost of equity for a local firm ($k_{e,em}$), whose country beta ($\beta_{emfirm,country}$) is 1.3, in the local currency?

Solution

$$R_f = (1 + 0.04)[(1 + 0.04)/(1 + 0.03)] - 1 = 0.0501 = 5.01\%$$

$$R_{country}, \text{ see equation (17–8)}, = 5.00 + 6.00 = 11.00\%$$

$$(R_{\text{country}} - R_f) = 11.00 - 5.01 = 5.99\%$$

$$\beta_{\text{emfirm,global}}, \text{see equation}(17\text{–}7), = 1.3 \times 1.1 = 1.43$$

$$k_{e,em} = 5.01 + 1.43\,(5.99) = 13.58\%$$

Adjusting the CAPM for Country or Political Risk   Recall that a country's equity premium reflects systematic risk (i.e., factors affecting all firms). However, the country's equity premium may not capture all the events that could jeopardize a firm's ability to operate. For example, political instability could result in a government that assumes an antiforeign business stance, resulting in potential nationalization, limits on repatriation of earnings, capital controls, the levying of confiscatory or discriminatory taxes, and the like. Such factors could increase significantly the firm's likelihood of default. Unless the analyst includes the risk of default by the firm in projecting a local firm's cash flows, the expected cash flow stream would be overstated to the extent that it does not reflect the costs of financial distress (e.g., higher borrowing costs). If the U.S. Treasury bond rate is used as the risk-free rate in calculating the CAPM, adding a country risk premium to the basic CAPM estimate is appropriate. The country risk premium (CRP) often is measured as the difference between the yield on the country's sovereign or government bonds and the U.S. Treasury bond rate of the same maturity. The difference or "spread" is the additional risk premium that investors demand for holding the emerging country's debt rather than U.S. Treasury bonds.

Note a country risk premium should not be added to the cost of equity if the risk-free rate is the country's sovereign or government bond rate, since the effects of specific country or political risk would be reflected already. Consequently, adding a country risk premium would double count the effects of country or political risk. Standard and Poor's (www.standardardandpoors.com), Moody's Investors Service (www.moodys.com), and Fitch IBCA (www.fitchibca.com) provide sovereign bond spreads. In practice, the sovereign bond spread is computed from a bond with the same maturity as the U.S. benchmark Treasury bond used to compute the risk-free rate for the calculation of the cost of equity. The U.S. benchmark rate usually is the 10-year Treasury bond rate.

Global CAPM Formulation (Emerging Countries)   To estimate the cost of equity for a firm in an emerging economy ($k_{e,em}$), equation (17–5) can be modified for specific country risk as follows:

$$k_{e,em} = R_f + \beta_{\text{emfirm,global}}(R_{\text{country}} - R_f) + \text{FSP} + \text{CRP} \qquad (17\text{–}9)$$

where

R_f = local risk-free rate or the U.S. Treasury bond rate converted to a local nominal rate if cash flows are in the local currency, see equation (17–6); if cash flows are in dollars, the U.S. Treasury bond rate.

$(R_{\text{country}} - R_f)$ = difference between expected return on a well-diversified equity index in the local country or a similar country and the risk-free rate.

$\beta_{\text{emfirm,global}}$ = emerging country firm's global beta, see equation (17–7).

FSP = firm size premium reflecting the additional return smaller firms must earn relative to larger firms to attract investors.

CRP = specific country risk premium, expressed as difference between the local country's (or a similar country's) government bond rate and the U.S. Treasury bond rate of the same maturity. Add to the CAPM estimate only if the U.S. Treasury bond rate is employed as a proxy for the local country's risk-free rate.

Estimating the Local Firm's Cost of Debt in Emerging Markets

The cost of debt for an emerging market firm (i_{emfirm}) should be adjusted for default risk due to events related to the country and those specific to the firm. When a local corporate bond rate is not available, the cost of debt for a specific local firm may be estimated by using an interest rate in the home country (i_{home}) that reflects a level of creditworthiness comparable to the firm in the emerging country. The country risk premium is added to the appropriate home country interest rate to reflect the impact of such factors as political instability on i_{emfirm}. Therefore, the cost of debt can be expressed as follows:

$$i_{emfirm} = i_{home} + \text{CRP} \tag{17–10}$$

Most firms in emerging markets are not rated. Therefore, to determine which home country interest rate to select, it is necessary to assign a credit rating to the local firm. This "synthetic" credit rating may be obtained by comparing financial ratios for the target firm to those used by U.S. rating agencies. The estimate of the unrated firm's credit rating may be obtained by comparing interest coverage ratios used by Standard and Poor's to the firm's interest coverage ratio to determine how S&P would rate the firm. See Exhibit 17-5 for an illustration of how to calculate the cost of emerging market debt.

Exhibit 17–6 illustrates the calculation of WACC in cross-border transactions. Note the adjustments made to the estimate of the cost of equity for firm size and country risk. Note also the adjustment made to the local borrowing cost for country risk. The risk-free rate of return is the U.S. Treasury bond rate converted to a local nominal rate of interest.

Exhibit 17–5 Estimating the Cost of Debt in Emerging Market Countries

Assume a firm in an emerging market has annual operating income before interest and taxes of $550 million and annual interest expense of $18 million. This implies an interest coverage ratio of 30.6 (i.e., $550/$18). For Standard and Poors, this corresponds to an AAA rating. According to S&P, default spreads for AAA firms are 0.85 currently. The current interest rate on U.S. triple A rated bonds is 6.0 percent. Assume further that the country's government bond rate is 10.3 percent and that the U.S. Treasury bond rate is 5 percent. Assume the firm's marginal tax rate is 0.4. What is the firm's cost of debt before and after tax?

Solution

Cost of debt before taxes, see equation (17–10), $= 6.0 + (10.3 - 5.0) = 11.3\%$

After-tax cost of debt $= 11.3 \times (1 - 0.4) = 6.78\%$

Exhibit 17–6 Estimating the Weighted-Average Cost of Capital in Cross-Border Transactions

Acquirer Inc., a U.S.-based corporation, wants to purchase Target Inc. Acquirer's management believes that the country in which Target is located is segmented from global capital markets, because the beta estimated by regressing the financial returns on the country's stock market with those of a global index is significantly different from one.

Assumptions

The current U.S. Treasury bond rate (R_{us}) is 5 percent. The expected inflation rate in the target's country is 6 percent annually compared to 3 percent in the United States. The country's risk premium provided by Standard and Poor's is estimated to be 2.0 percent. Based on Target's interest coverage ratio, its credit rating is estimated to be AA. The current interest rate on AA rated U.S. corporate bonds is 6.25 percent. Acquirer Inc. receives a tax credit for taxes paid in a foreign country. Since its marginal tax rate is higher than the target's, Acquirer's marginal tax rate of 0.4 is used in calculating the weighted-average cost of capital (WACC). Acquirer's pretax cost of debt is 6 percent. The firm's total capitalization consists only of common equity and debt. Acquirer's projected debt to total capital ratio is 0.3.

Target's beta and the country beta are estimated to be 1.3 and 0.7, respectively. The equity premium is estimated to be 6 percent, based on the spread between the prospective return on the country's equity index and the estimated risk free rate of return. In view of its relatively small $1 billion market capitalization, Target's size premium is estimated at 1.2 percent (see Chapter 7, Table 7–1). What weighted-average cost of capital should Acquirer use to discount appropriately Target's projected annual cash flows expressed in its own local currency?

Solution

$$k_{e,em}, \text{see equation (17–9),} = \{(1 + 0.05) \times [(1 + 0.06)/(1 + 0.03)] - 1\}$$
$$\times 100 + 1.3 \times 0.7(6.0) + 1.2 + 2.0 = 16.72\%$$

$$i_{local}, \text{see equation (17–10),} = 6.25 + 2.0 = 8.25\%$$

$$\text{WACC}_{em}, \text{see equation (7–4),} = 16.72 \times (1 - 0.3) + 8.25 \times (1 - 0.4) \times 0.3 = 13.19\%$$

---

[1]Note that the expression $\{(1 + 0.05) \times [(1 + 0.06)/(1 + 0.03)] - 1\} \times 100$ represents the conversion of the U.S. Treasury bond rate to a local nominal rate of interest using equation (17–6). Also, note that 1.3×0.7 results in the estimation of the target's global beta, as indicated in equation (17–7).

Table 17–3 summarizes methods commonly used for valuing cross-border transactions involving firms in developed and emerging countries. The WACC calculation assumes the firm uses only common equity and debt financing. Note that the country risk premium is added to both the cost of equity and the after-tax cost of debt in calculating the WACC for a target firm in an emerging country, if the U.S. Treasury bond rate is used as the risk-free rate of return. The analyst should avoid adding the country risk premium to the cost of equity if the risk-free rate used to estimate the cost of equity is the local country's government bond rate. References to home and local countries in Table 17–3 refer to the acquirer's and the target's countries, respectively.

Table 17–3 Common Methodologies for Valuing Cross-Border Transactions

Developed Countries (Integrated Capital Markets)	Emerging Countries (Segmented Capital Markets)
Step 1. Project and Convert Cash Flows	
Project target's cash flows in local currency. Convert local cash flows into acquirer's home currency employing forward exchange rates projected using the interest rate parity theory.	Project target's cash flows in local currency. Convert local cash flows into acquirer's home currency using forward exchange rates. Project exchange rates using the purchasing power parity theory, if little reliable data on interest rates is available.
Step 2. Adjust Discount Rates	
$k_{e,dev} = R_f + \beta_{devfirm,gloabal}{}^1 (R_m - R_f) + \text{FSP}$ $i = \text{cost of debt}^3$ $\text{WACC} = k_e W_e + i(1-t) \times W_d$	$k_{e,em} = R_f + \beta_{emfirm,global}{}^1 (R_{country} - R_f)^2 + \text{FSP} + \text{CRP}$ $i_{local} = i_{home} + \text{CRP}$ $\text{WACC} = k_e W_e + i_{local}(1-t) \times W_d$
R_f is the long-term government bond rate in the home country	R_f is long-term government bond rate in the local country or the U.S. Treasury bond rate converted to a local nominal rate if cash flows in local currency; if cash flows in dollars, the U.S. Treasury bond rate. Note: If local risk-free rate used, do not add CRP.
$\beta_{devfirm,global}$ is nondiversifiable risk associated with a well-diversified global, U.S., or local country equity index.	$\beta_{emfirm,global}$ is nondiversifiable risk associated with target's local country β and local country's global β.
R_m is the return on a well-diversified U.S., local, or global equity index	$R_{country}$ is the return on a diversified local equity index or a similar country's index
FSP is the firm size premium	CRP is the country risk premium
t is the appropriate marginal tax rate	i_{home} is the home country cost of debt
W_e is the acquirer's target equity to total capital ratio and W_d is $1 - W_e$	i_{local} is the local country cost of debt

[1]β may be estimated directly for firms, whose business is heavily dependent on exports or operating in either developing or emerging countries, by directly regressing the firm's historical financial returns against returns on a well-diversified global equity index. For firms operating primarily in their home markets, β may be estimated indirectly using equation (17–7).

[2]$(R_{country} - R_f)$ also could be the equity premium for well-diversified U.S. or global equity indices if the degree of local segmentation is believed to be small.

[3]For developed countries, either the home or local country cost of debt may be used. There is no need to add a country risk premium, as would be the case in estimating a local emerging country's cost of debt.

Evaluating Risk Using Scenario Planning

Many emerging countries have few publicly traded firms and even fewer M&A transactions to serve as guides in valuing companies. Furthermore, with countries like China and India growing at or near double-digit rates, the future may be too dynamic to rely on discounted cash flows. Projecting cash flows beyond three years may be pure guesswork.

As an alternative to making seemingly arbitrary adjustments to the target firm's cost of capital, the acquirer may incorporate risk into the valuation by considering alternative economic scenarios for the emerging country. The variables that define these alternative scenarios could include GDP growth, inflation rates, interest rates, and foreign exchange rates. Each of these variables can be used to project cash flows using regression analysis (see the file entitled Primer on Cash Flow Forecasting on the CD-ROM accompanying this book). The scenarios may also be built on alternative industry or political conditions. For example, a best-case scenario can be based on projected cash flows assuming the emerging market's economy grows at a moderate real growth rate of 2 percent per annum for the next five years. Alternative scenarios could assume a one- to two-year recession. A third scenario could assume a dramatic devaluation of the country's currency. The NPVs are weighted by subjectively determined probabilities. The actual valuation of the target firm reflects the expected value of the three scenarios. Note that, if a scenario approach is used to incorporate risk in the valuation, there is no need to modify the discount rate for perceived political and economic risk in the local country. See Chapter 8, Exhibit 8–10, for a more detailed discussion and illustration of scenario planning in the context of a decision tree framework.

While building risk into the projected cash flows is equivalent to adjusting the discount rate in applying the discounted cash flow method, it also appears to be subject to making arbitrary or highly subjective adjustments. What are the appropriate scenarios to be simulated? How many such scenarios are needed to incorporate adequately risk into the projections? What is the likelihood of each scenario occurring? The primary advantage of adopting a scenario approach is that it forces the analyst to evaluate a wider range of possible outcomes. The major disadvantage is the substantial additional effort required.

Empirical Studies of Financial Returns to International Diversification

International Diversification May Contribute to Higher Financial Returns

Empirical studies suggest that international diversification may increase financial returns by reducing risk, if economies are relatively uncorrelated (Delios and Beamish, 1999; Tang and Tikoo, 1999; Madura and Whyte, 1990). Higher financial returns from international diversification may also be attributable to potential economies of scale and scope, geographic location advantages associated with being nearer customers, increasing the size of the firm's served market, and learning new technologies (Zahra, Ireland, and Hitt, 2000; Caves, 1982). Controversy continues as to whether returns are higher for multinational companies that diversify across countries or across industries, spanning political boundaries. In either case, the importance of selecting an appropriate country remains very important. Diermeier and Solnik (2001) provide evidence that supports diversifying across industries; Isakov and Sonney (2002) found evidence of the importance of country choice. Francis, Hasan, and Sun (2008) provide evidence that buyers of targets in segmented markets realize larger abnormal returns than if they were to buy firms in globally integrated countries. The authors argue that targets in segmented markets benefit from the acquirer's lower cost of capital.

Foreign Buyers of U.S. Firms Tend to Pay Higher Premiums than U.S. Buyers

Foreign bidders have historically paid higher premiums to acquire U.S. firms than domestic acquirers of U.S. firms. Harris and Ravenscraft (1991) show that, between 1970 and 1987, foreign acquirers paid an average of 10 percentage points in higher premiums than U.S. acquirers. The higher premiums often resulted from more favorable foreign currency exchange rates, contributing to lower overall purchase prices when expressed in terms of foreign currency. Between 1990 and 2007, the premium paid by foreign buyers of U.S. firms over those paid by U.S. acquirers narrowed to about 4 percentage points on average. The continued higher premiums paid by foreign buyers may reflect their efforts to preempt U.S. buyers, U.S. target firm shareholders lack of familiarity with foreign acquirers, and concern that the transaction would not be consummated due to political (e.g., Unocal and CNNOC) and economic considerations (i.e., lack of financial resources).

Returns for Cross-Border Transactions Consistent with Domestic Results

Shareholders of target firms in cross-border transactions receive substantial abnormal returns. Such returns for shareholders of U.S. targets of foreign buyers range from about 23 percent (Kuipers, Miller, and Patel, 2003) to about 40 percent (Seth, Song, and Pettit, 2000; Eun, Kolodny, Scheraga, 1996; Servaes and Zenner, 1994; Harris and Ravenscraft, 1991). Abnormal returns to shareholders of U.S. and non-U.S. buyers of foreign firms are about zero to slightly negative (Kuipers et al., 2003; Seth et al., 2000; Eckbo and Thorburn, 2000; Markides and Oyon, 1998; Cakici and Tandon, 1996). Moeller and Schlingemann (2002), in a sample of 4,430 transactions between 1985 and 1995, compared returns in cross-border transactions to domestic deals and found that U.S. acquirers realized stock returns for cross-border transactions as much as 1 percent lower than for U.S. deals. The authors argue that increasing global integration, while providing new investment opportunities for multinational businesses, is increasing the level of competition for attractive foreign targets and reducing the gains from diversification into formerly segmented markets. Chatterjee and Aw (2004) for U.K. and Eckbo and Thorburn (2000) for Canadian targets acquired by U.S. firms also found that bidders buying foreign targets underperform those acquiring domestic firms. In contrast, Chari, Ouimet, and Tesar (2004) found that acquirer returns increase on average by 1.65–3.1 percent when the targets are in emerging markets. This improvement is attributable to the achievement of control (e.g., enabling the protection of intellectual property), the elimination of minority shareholders, and the encouragement of investment in the target by the parent.

Good Corporate Governance Supports Cross-Border M&A Activity

Higher firm valuations are often found in countries with better shareholder protections (La Porta, Lopez-De-Silanes, and Shliefer, 2002; Lemmons and Lins, 2003; Peng, Lee, and Lang, 2005). This is especially true in emerging countries, where firms typically have a single dominant investor (Young et al., 2008). Leuz, Lins, and Warnock (2004) found that inflows of foreign investment are highest in countries that enforce laws requiring firms to disclose information and provide good shareholder protections. This finding underscores the importance of countries' having legal systems that actively enforce contracts and prevailing securities laws. Rossi and Volpin (2004) also found that M&A activity is substantially larger in countries with better accounting standards and shareholder safeguards. Moreover, the authors found that targets in cross-border deals are typically from countries with poorer investor protection than the acquirer's country. The transference of corporate governance practices through cross-border mergers may improve shareholder safeguards and, in turn, financial returns to target firm shareholders (Bris and Cabolis, 2004). Target firms in weaker corporate governance countries relative to the acquirer often adopt the better practices because of a change in the country of incorporation of the firm. Martynova and Renneboog (2008b) note that, when the bidder is from a country with stronger governance practices and gains full control of a target firm in a country with weaker governance practices, part of the total synergy value of the takeover may result from imposing the stricter practices of the bidder on the target firm.

Aggarwal et al. (2007) found that foreign firms that invest less in corporate governance than a comparable U.S. firm have a lower market value than the U.S. firm. They attribute the level of investment to the characteristics of the country (e.g., legal system, extent of enforcement of exiting laws). The underinvestment is greatest in countries in which it is in the best interests of the controlling shareholders, who often can obtain benefits at the expense of minority shareholders. Consequently, efforts to increase minority shareholder protection can increase the attractiveness of the firm's shares to a broader array of investors.

Things to Remember

The motives for international corporate expansion include a desire to accelerate growth, achieve geographic diversification, consolidate industries, and take advantage of natural resources and lower labor costs available elsewhere. Other motives include applying a firm's widely recognized brand name or unique intellectual property in new markets, minimizing tax liabilities, following customers into foreign markets, as well as avoiding such entry barriers as tariffs and import barriers. Alternative strategies for entering foreign markets include exporting, licensing, alliances or joint ventures, solo ventures or greenfield operations (i.e., establishing new wholly owned subsidiaries), and mergers and acquisitions.

The methodology for valuing cross-border transactions is quite similar to that employed when both the acquiring and target firms are within the same country. The methodology involves projecting the target firm's cash flows and converting these future cash flows to current or present values using an appropriate discount rate. The basic differences between within-country and cross-border valuation methods is that the latter involves converting cash flows from one currency to another and adjusting the discount rate for risks not generally found when the acquirer and target firms are within the same country. An important issue in calculating the cost of equity for cross-border transactions is the degree of integration of global capital markets. If markets are integrated, a global beta and a global equity premium are appropriate. However, in segmented markets, a local beta and a local equity premium should be used.

Chapter Discussion Questions

17–1. Find a recent example of a cross-border merger or acquisition in the business section of a newspaper. Discuss the motives for the transaction. What challenges would the acquirer experience in managing and integrating the target firm? Be specific.

17–2. Classify the countries of the acquirer and target in a recent cross-border merger or acquisition as developed or emerging. Identify the criteria you use to classify the countries. How might your classification of the target firm's country affect the way you analyze the target firm?

17–3. Describe the circumstances under which a firm may find a merger or acquisition a more favorable market entry strategy than a joint venture with a firm in the local country.

17–4. Discuss some of the options commonly used to finance international transactions. If you were the chief financial officer of the acquiring firm, what factors would you consider in determining how to finance a transaction?

17–5. Compare and contrast laws that might affect acquisitions by a foreign firm in the United States. In the European Union.

17–6. Discuss the circumstances under which a non-U.S. buyer may choose a U.S. corporate structure as its acquisition vehicle. A limited liability company? A partnership?

17–7. What factors influence the selection of which tax rate to use (i.e., the target's or the acquirer's) in calculating the weighted-average cost of capital in cross-border transactions?

17–8. Discuss adjustments commonly made in estimating the cost of debt in emerging countries.

17–9. Find an example of a recent cross-border transaction in the business section of a newspaper. Discuss the challenges an analyst might face in valuing the target firm.

17–10. Discuss the various types of adjustments for risk that might be made to the global CAPM before valuing a target firm in an emerging country. Be specific.

17–11. Do you see the growth in sovereign wealth funds as important sources of capital to the M&A market or as a threat to the sovereignty of the countries in which they invest? Explain your answer.

17–12. What primary factors contribute to the increasing integration of the global capital markets? Be specific.

17–13. Give examples of economic and political risk that you could reasonably expect to encounter in acquiring a firm in an emerging economy. Be specific.

17–14. During the 1980s and 1990s, changes in the S&P 500 (a broadly diversified index of U.S. stocks) were about 50 percent correlated with the MSCI EAFE Index (a broadly diversified index of European and other major industrialized countries' stock markets). In recent years, the correlation has increased to more than 80 percent. Why? If an analyst wishes to calculate the cost of equity, which index should they use in estimating the equity risk premium?

17–15. Comment on the following statement: "The conditions for foreign buyers interested in U.S. targets could not be more auspicious. The dollar is weak, M&A financing is harder to come by for financial sponsors (private equity firms), and many strategic buyers in the United States are hard-pressed to make acquisitions at a time when earnings targets are being missed."

Answers to these Chapter Discussion Questions are found in the Online Instructor's Manual for instructors using this book.

Chapter Business Cases

Case Study 17–3. Political Risk of Cross-Border Transactions—CNOOC's Aborted Attempt to Acquire Unocal

Background

In what may be the most politicized takeover battle in U.S. history, Unocal announced on August 11, 2005, that its shareholders approved overwhelmingly the proposed buyout by Chevron. The combined companies would produce the equivalent of 2.8 million barrels of oil per day and the acquisition would increase Chevron's reserves by about 15 percent. With both companies owning assets in similar regions, it was easier to cut duplicate costs. The deal also made Chevron the top international oil company in the fast growing southeast Asia market. Unocal is much smaller than Chevron. As a pure exploration and production company, Unocal had operations in nine countries. Chevron operated gas stations, drilling rigs, and refineries in 180 countries.

The Transaction Timeline

Sensing an opportunity, Chevron moved ahead with merger talks and made an all-stock $16 billion offer for Unocal in late February 2005. Unocal rebuffed the offer as inadequate and sought bids from China's CNOOC and Italy's ENI SPA. While CNOOC offered

$17 billion in cash, ENI was willing to offer only $16 billion. Chevron subsequently raised its all-stock offer to $16.5 billion, in line with the board's maximum authorization. Hours before final bids were due, CNOOC informed Unocal it was not going to make any further bids. Believing that the bidding process was over, Unocal and Chevron signed a merger agreement on April 4, 2005. The merger agreement was endorsed by Unocal's board and cleared all regulatory hurdles. Despite its earlier reluctance, CNOOC boosted its original bid to $18.5 billion in late June to counter the Chevron offer. About three fourths of CNOOC's all-cash offer was financed through below-market-rate loans provided by its primary shareholder, the Chinese government. On July 22, 2005, Chevron upped its offer to $17.7 billion, of which about 60 percent was in stock and 40 percent in cash. By the time Unocal shareholders actually approved the deal, the appreciation in Chevron's stock boosted the value of the deal to more than $18.1 billion.

The Political Firestorm

CNOOC's all-cash offer of $67 per share in June sparked instant opposition from members of Congress, who demanded a lengthy review by President George W. Bush and introduced legislation to place even more hurdles in CNOOC's way. Hoping to allay fears, CNOOC offered to sell Unocal's U.S. assets and promised to retain all of Unocal's workers, something Chevron was not prone to do. CNOOC also argued that its bid was purely commercial and not connected in any way with the Chinese government. U.S. lawmakers expressed concern that Unocal's oil drilling might have military applications and CNOOC's ownership structure (i.e., 70 percent owned by the Chinese government) would enable the firm to secure low-cost financing that was unavailable to Chevron. The final blow to CNOOC's bid was an amendment to an energy bill passed in July requiring the Departments of Energy, Defense, and Homeland Security to spend four months studying the proposed takeover before granting federal approval.

China's Reaction

Perhaps somewhat naively, the Chinese government viewed the low-cost loans as a way to "recycle" a portion of the huge accumulation of dollars it was experiencing. While the Chinese remained largely silent through the political maelstrom, CNOOC's management appeared to be greatly surprised and embarrassed by the public criticism in the United States about the proposed takeover of a major U.S. company. Up to that point, the only other major U.S. firm acquired by a Chinese firm was the 2004 acquisition of IBM's personal computer business by Lenovo, the largest PC manufacturer in China. While the short-term effects of the controversy appear benign, the long-term implications are less clear. It remains to be seen how well international business and politics can coexist between the world's major economic and military superpower and China, an emerging economic and military superpower in its own right.

Conclusions

Cross-border transactions often require considerable political risk. In emerging countries, this is viewed as the potential for expropriation of property or disruption of commerce due to a breakdown in civil order. However, as CNOOC's aborted effort to takeover Unocal illustrates, foreign firms have to be highly sensitive to political and cultural issues in any host country, developed or otherwise.

Discussion Questions

1. Should CNNOC have been permitted to buy Unocal? Why or why not?
2. How might the Chinese have been able to persuade U.S. regulatory authorities to approve the transaction?
3. The U.S. and European firms are making substantial investments (including M&As) in China. How should the Chinese government react to this rebuff?

Solutions to these questions are found in the Online Instructor's Manual available for instructors using this book.

Case Study 17–4. Vodafone AirTouch Acquires Mannesmann in a Record-Setting Deal

On February 4, 2000, Vodafone AirTouch PLC, the world's largest wireless communications company, agreed to buy Mannesmann AG in a $180.0 billion stock swap. At that time, the deal was the largest transaction in M&A history. The value of this transaction exceeded the value of the AOL Time Warner merger at closing by an astonishing $74 billion. Including $17.8 billion in assumed debt, the total value of the transaction soared to $198 billion. After a protracted and heated contest with Mannesmann's management as well as German labor unions and politicians, the deal finally closed on March 30, 2000. In this battle of titans, Klaus Esser, CEO of Mannesmann, the German cellular phone giant, managed to squeeze nearly twice as much money as first proposed out of Vodafone, the British cellular phone powerhouse. This transaction illustrates the intricacies of international transactions in countries in which hostile takeovers are viewed negatively and antitakeover laws generally favor target companies. (See Chapter 3 for a more detailed discussion of antitakeover laws.)

Vodafone AirTouch Corporate Profile

Vodafone AirTouch, itself the product of a $60 billion acquisition of U.S.-based AirTouch Communications in early 1999, is focused on becoming the global leader in wireless communication. Although it believes the growth opportunities are much greater in wireless than in wired communication systems, Vodafone AirTouch has pursued a strategy in which customers in certain market segments are offered a package of integrated wireless and wired services. Vodafone AirTouch is widely recognized for its technological innovation and pioneering creative new products and services. Vodafone has been a global leader in terms of geographic coverage since 1986 in terms of the number of customers, with more than 12 million at the end of 2000. Vodafone AirTouch's operations cover the vast majority of the European continent, as well as potentially high-growth areas such as Eastern Europe, Africa, and the Middle East. Vodafone AirTouch's geographic coverage received an enormous boost in the United States by entering into the joint venture with Bell Atlantic. Vodafone AirTouch has a 45 percent interest in the joint venture. The JV has 23 million customers (including 3.5 million paging customers). Covering about 80 percent of the U.S. population, the joint venture offers cellular service in 49 of the top 50 U.S. markets and is the largest wireless operator in the United States.

Mannesmann's Corporate Profile

Mannesmann is an international corporation headquartered in Germany and focused on the telecommunications, engineering, and automotive markets. Mannesmann transformed itself during the 1990s from a manufacturer of steel pipes, auto components, and materials-handling equipment into Europe's biggest mobile-phone operator. Rapid growth in its telecom activities accounted for much of the growth in the value of the company in recent years.

Strategic Rationale for the Merger

With Mannesmann, Vodafone AirTouch intended to consolidate its position in Europe and undertake a global brand strategy. In Europe, Vodafone and Mannesmann would have controlling stakes in 10 European markets, giving the new company the most extensive European coverage of any wireless carrier. Vodafone AirTouch would benefit from the additional coverage provided by Mannesmann in Europe, whereas Mannesmann's operations would benefit from Vodafone AirTouch's excellent U.S. geographic coverage. The merger would create a superior platform for the development of mobile data and Internet services.

Mannesmann's "Just-Say-No" Strategy

What supposedly started on friendly terms soon turned into a bitter battle, involving a personal duel between Chris Gent, Vodafone's CEO, and Klaus Esser, Mannesmann's CEO. In November 1999, Vodafone AirTouch announced for the first time its intention to make a takeover bid for Mannesmann. Mannesmann's board rebuked the overture as inadequate, noting its more favorable strategic position. After the Mannesmann management had refused a second, more attractive bid, Vodafone AirTouch went directly to the Mannesmann shareholders with a tender offer. A central theme in Vodafone AirTouch's appeal to Mannesmann shareholders was what it described as the extravagant cost of Mannesmann's independent strategy. Relations between Chris Gent and Klaus Esser turned highly contentious. The decision to undertake a hostile takeover was highly risky. Numerous obstacles stood in the way of foreign acquirers of German companies.

Culture Clash

Hostile takeovers of German firms by foreign firms are rare. It is even rarer when it turns out to be one of the nation's largest corporations. Vodafone AirTouch's initial offer immediately was decried as a job killer. The German tabloids painted a picture of a pending bloodbath for Mannesmann and its 130,000 employees if the merger took place. Vodafone AirTouch had said that it was interested in only Mannesmann's successful telecommunications operations and it was intending to sell off the company's engineering and automotive businesses, which employ about 80 percent of Mannesmann's total workforce. The prospect of what was perceived to be a less caring foreign firm doing the same thing led to appeals from numerous political factions for government protection against the takeover.

German law at the time also stood as a barrier to an unfriendly takeover. German corporate law required that 75 percent of outstanding shares be tendered before control is transferred. In addition, the law allows individual shareholders to block deals with court challenges that can drag on for years. In a country where hostile takeovers are rare, public opinion was squarely behind management.

To defuse the opposition from German labor unions and the German government, Chris Gent said that the deal would not result in any job cuts and the rights of the employees and trade unions would be fully preserved. Moreover, Vodafone would accept fully the Mannesmann corporate culture including the principle of codetermination through employee representation on the Mannesmann supervisory board. Because of these reassurances, the unions decided to support the merger.

The Offer Mannesmann Couldn't Refuse

When it became clear that Vodafone's attempt at a hostile takeover might succeed, the Mannesmann management changed its strategy and agreed to negotiate the terms for a friendly takeover. The final agreement was based on an improved offer for Mannesmann shareholders to exchange their shares in the ratio of 58.96 Vodafone AirTouch shares for 1 Mannesmann share, an improvement over the previous offer of 53.7 to 1. Furthermore, the agreement defined terms for the integration of the two companies. For example, Dusseldorf was retained as one of two European headquarters with responsibility for Mannesmann's existing continental European mobile and fixed-line telephone business. Moreover, with the exception of Esser, all Mannesmann's top managers would remain in place.

Epilogue

Throughout the hostile takeover battle, Vodafone AirTouch said that it was reluctant to offer Mannesmann shareholders more than 50 percent of the new company; in sharp contrast, Mannesmann said all along that it would not accept a takeover that gives its shareholders a minority interest in the new company. Esser managed to get Mannesmann shareholders almost 50 percent ownership in the new firm, despite Mannesmann contributing only about 35 percent of the operating earnings of the new company.

Vodafone, currently the world's largest (by revenue) cell phone service provider, has experienced continuing share price erosion amidst intensifying price erosion from competition in western European markets and new technologies, such as Internet calling, that are slowing revenue growth and shrinking profit margins. Shares in Vodafone have underperformed the UK market by 40 percent since the firm acquired Mannesmann. In 2006, the company recorded an impairment charge of $49 billion. This charge reflected the lower current value of the Mannesmann assets acquired by Vodafone in 2000, effectively making it official that the firm substantially overpaid for Mannesmann.

While hostile bids were relatively rare at the time of the Vodafone–Mannesmann transaction, they have become increasingly more common in recent years. Since 2002, Europe has seen more hostile or unsolicited deals than in the United States. In part, Europe is simply catching up to the United States after many years in which there were virtually no hostile bids. For years, national governments and regulators in Europe had been able to deter easily cross-border deals that they felt could threaten national interests, even though European Union rules are supposed to allow a free and fair market within its jurisdiction. However, the rise of big global rivals, as well as a rising tide of activist investors, is making companies more assertive.

Discussion Questions

1. Who do you think negotiated the best deal for their shareholders, Chris Gent or Klaus Esser? Explain your answer in terms of short- and long-term impacts.
2. Both firms were pursuing a similar strategy of expanding their geographic reach. Does this strategy make sense? Why or why not? What risks are associated with this strategy?
3. Do you think the use of all stock, rather than cash or a combination of cash and stock, to acquire Mannesmann helped or hurt Vodafone AirTouch's shareholders?

4. Do you think that Vodafone AirTouch conceded too much to the labor unions and Mannesmann's management to get the deal done? Explain your answer.

5. What problems do you think Vodafone AirTouch might experience if they attempt to introduce what they view as "best operating practices" to the Mannesmann culture? How might these challenges be overcome? Be specific.

Solutions to these questions are found in the Online Instructor's Manual available to instructors using this book.

References

A

Aboutmediakit, 2006. http://beanadvertiser.about.com/archive/news091606.html

Abrams, J. B., 2001. Quantitative Business Valuation: A Mathematical Approach for Today's Professionals. McGraw-Hill, New York.

Acharya, V. V., Franks, J., Servaes, H., 2007. Private Equity: Boom or Bust? Journal of Applied Corporate Finance 19 (Fall), 44–53.

ACNielsen, Retailer Support is Essential for New Product Success. Bases www.bases.com/news/news112002.html

Adams, R., Ferreira, D., 2007. A Theory of Friendly Boards. Journal of Finance 62, 217–250.

Adegoke, Y., 2008. YouTube Rolls out Sponsored Videos in Revenue Drive. Reuters.

Adolph, G., 2006. Mergers: Back to Happily Ever After. In: Strategy and Business. Booz Allen Hamilton, New York.

Aggarwal, R., Rivoli, P., 1990. Fads in the Initial Public Offering Market. Financial Management 19, 45–57.

Aggarwal, R., Erel, I., Stulz, R., Williamson, R., 2007. Differences in Governance Practices between U.S. and Foreign Firms: Measurement, Causes, and Consequences. NBER Working Paper 13288, August.

Aggdata.com, 2008. www.aggdata.com/business/fortune_500

Agrawal, A., Jaffe, J. F., 1999. The Post-Merger Performance Puzzle. Working Paper Series, Social Science Research Network, December.

Agrawal, A., Jaffe, J. F., Mandelker, G. N., 1992. The Post-Merger Performance of Acquiring Firms: A Reexamination of an Anomaly. Journal of Finance 47, 1605–1621.

Akhigbe, A., Borde, S. F., Whyte, A. M., 2000. The Source of Gains to Targets and Their Industry Rivals: Evidence Based on Terminated Merger Proposals. Financial Management 29 (Winter), 101–118.

Alderson, M. J., Betker, B. L., 1996. Assessing Post-Bankruptcy Performance: An Analysis of Reorganized Firms' Cash Flows. Working Paper, Saint Louis University.

Alexander, G. J., Benson, G., Kampmeyer, J. M., 1984. Investigating the Valuation Effects Announcements on Valuing Corporate Sell-Offs. Journal of Finance 39, 503–517.

Alexander, M., Campbell, A., Gould, M., 1995. Parenting Advantage. In: Prism. Arthur D. Little, Inc. 2nd Quarter, pp. 23–33.

Allen, J., McConnell, J. J., 1998. Equity Carve Outs and Managerial Discretion. Journal of Finance 53, 163–186.

Allen, J., 2001. Private Information and Spin-off Performance. Journal of Business 74, 281–306.

Allen, P., 2000. Corporate Equity Ownership, Strategic Alliances, and Product Market Relationships. Journal of Finance 55, 2791–2816.

Alli, K. L., Thompson, D. J., 1991. The Value of the Resale Limitation on Restricted Stock: An Option Theory Approach. Valuation 36, 22–34.

Altman, E. I., 1968. Financial Ratios, Discriminant Analysis and the Prediction of Corporate Bankruptcy. Journal of Finance 23, 509–609.

Altman, E. I., 1993. Corporate Financial Distress and Bankruptcy, second ed. John Wiley & Sons, New York.

Altman, E. I., 2000. Predicting Financial Distress of Companies: Revisiting the Z-Score and ZETA Models. Working Paper, New York University.

Altman, E. I., Brady, B., Resti, A., Sironi, A., 2003. The Link between Default and Recovery Rates: Theory, Empirical Evidence and Implications. Journal of Business.

Altman, E. I., Kishore, V. M., 1996. Almost Everything You Wanted to Know about Recoveries on Defaulted Bonds. Financial Analysts Journal November/December, 57–64.

Altman, E. I., Kishore, V., 2001. The Default Experience of U.S. Bonds. Working Paper, Salomon Center, New York.

American Bar Association, 2006. Mergers and Acquisitions: Understanding Antitrust Issues, second ed.

Anand, J., Delios, A., 2002. Absolute and Relative Resources as Determinants of International Acquisitions. Journal of Strategic Management 23, 119–134.

Anderson, R. W., Coverhill, A., 2007. Liquidity and Capital Structure. Center for Economic Policy Research, Working Paper No. 6044.

Anderson, U., Johanson, J., Vahlne, J. E., 1997. Organic Acquisitions in the International Process of the Business Firm. Management International Review 37, 67.

Andrade, G., Kaplan, S., 1998. How Costly Is Financial (Not Economic) Distress? Evidence from Highly Leveraged Transactions That Become Distressed. Journal of Finance 53, 1443–1493.

Andrade, G., Mitchell, M. L., Stafford, E., 2006. New Evidence and Perspectives on Mergers. J. Econ. Perspect. 15, 103–120.

Ang, J. S., Cheng, Y., 2006. Direct Evidence on the Market-Driven Acquisition Theory. Journal of Financial Research 29, 199–216.

Ang, J., Kohers, N., 2001. The Takeover Market for Privately Held Companies: The U.S. Experience. Cambridge Journal of Economics 25, 723–748.

Angwin, J., Drucker, J., 2006. How News Corp. and Liberty Media Can Save $4.5 Billion. Wall St. J. p. A3.

Annema, A., Fallon, W. C., Goedhart, M. H., 2002. When Carve-outs Make Sense. McKinsey Quarterly 2.

Annema, A., Goedhart, M. H., 2006. Betas: Back to Normal. McKinsey Quarterly.

Arellano-Ostoa, A., Brusco, S., 2002. Understanding Reverse Mergers: A First Approach. University of Madrid Working Paper, Business Economics Series 11.

Armstrong, A., Hagel, J., 1997. Net Gain: Expanding Markets through Virtual Communities, Harvard Business School Press, Boston.

Arzac, E. R., 2006. Valuation for Mergers, Buyouts, and Restructuring. John Wiley & Sons, New York.

Aschwald, K. F., 2000. Restricted Stock Discounts Decline as Result of One-Year Holding Period. Shannon Pratt's Business Valuation Update May, 1–5.

Ascioglu, N. A., McInish, T. H., Wook, R. A., 2002. Merger Announcements and Trading. Journal of Financial Research 25 (2), Summer, 263–278.

Aspatore Staff, 2006. M&A Negotiations: Leading Lawyers on Negotiating Deals: Structuring Contracts and Resolving Merger and Acquisition Disputes, Aspatore Books, Boston.

Asquith, P., 1983. Merger Bids and Stock Returns. Journal of Financial Economics 11, 51–83.

Asquith, P., Gerther, R., Scharfstein, D., 1994. Anatomy of Financial Distress: An Examination of Junk Bond Issuers. Quarterly Journal of Economics 109, 625–658.

Asquith, P., Kim, E. H., 1982. The Impact of Merger Bids on the Participating Firms' Security Holders. Journal of Finance 37, 1209–1228.

Asquith, P., Mullins, D., Wolff, E., 1989. Original Issue High Yield Bonds: Aging Analysis of Defaults, Exchanges and Calls. Journal of Finance 44, 923–952.

Astrachan, J., Keys, A., Lane, S., McMillan, K., 2003. Loyola Guidelines for Family Business Boards of Directors. Loyola University of Chicago, Family Business Center.

Astrachan, J. H., Shanker, M. C., 2003. Family Businesses Contributions to the U.S. Economy: A Closer Look. Family Business Review 15, 211–219.

Attakrit, A., Broadie, M., Sundaresan, S., 2007. Managing Corporate Liquidity: Welfare and Pricing Implications. Working Paper, Columbia University.

Atanasov, V., Boone, A., Haushalter, D., 2005. Minority Shareholder Expropriation in U.S. Publicly Traded Subsidiaries. Babson College Working Paper.

Atkinson, A., Salterio, S., 2002. Shaping Good Conduct. Management 49, 18–34.

Auerbach, A. J., Poterba, J., 1987. Tax Loss Carry Forwards and Corporate Tax Incentives. In: Martin, F. (Ed.), The Effect of Taxation on Capital Accumulation. University of Chicago Press, Chicago.

Auerbach, A. J., Reishus, D., 1988. Taxes and the Merger Decision. In: Coffee Jr., J. C., Lowenstein, L., Ackerman, S. R. (Eds.), Knights, Raiders, and Targets. Oxford University Press, New York, pp. 69–88.

Avramov, D., Chordia, T., Jostova, G., Philipov, A., 2006. Credit Ratings and the Cross-Section of Stock Returns. Working Paper, University of Maryland, Emory University, George Washington University, and American University.

Ayers, B. C., Lefanowicz, C. E., Robinson, J. R., 2003. Shareholder Taxes in Acquisition Premiums: The Effect of Capital Gains Taxation. Journal of Finance 58, 2783–2801.

Aziz, M. A., Dar, H. A., 2006. Predicting Corporate Bankruptcy: Where We Stand? Corporate Governance 6 (1), 18–33.

B

Bachman, J., 2001. Coke, P&G Try to Juice Snack Sales. Associated Press, Orange County Register, Business Section, p. 2.

Bainbridge, S. M., 2003. Mergers and Acquisitions. Foundation Press, New York.

Baker, G., Smith, G., 1998. The New Financial Capitalists. Cambridge University Press, Cambridge, England.

Baker, G., Wruck, K., 1989. Organizational Changes and Value Creation in Leveraged Buyouts: The Case of O. M. Scott and Sons Company. Journal of Financial Economics 25, 163–190.

Ball, M., 1997. How a Spin-off Could Lift Your Share Value. Corporate Finance May, 23–29.

Bao, J., Edmans, A., 2008. How Should Acquirers Select Advisors? Persistence in Investment Bank Performance. Social Science Research Network.

Barber, B. M., Lyon, J. D., 1997. Detecting Long-Run Abnormal Stock Returns: The Empirical Power and Specification of Test Statistics. Journal of Financial Economics 43, 341–372.

Barclay, M. J., Holderness, C. G., 1989. Private Benefits from Control of Public Companies. Journal of Financial Economics 25, 371–395.

Barkema, H. G., Schijven, M., 2008. Towards Unlocking the Full Potential of Acquisitions: The Role of Organizational Restructuring. Acad. Manage. J. 34, 594–611.

Barkema, H. G., Vermeulen, F., 1998. International Expansion through Start-up or Acquisition: A Learning Perspective. Journal of the Academy of Management 7–26.

Barnett, T. R., 2008. Message from the AAG, U.S. Department of Justice. Antitrust Division Update Spring.

Bates, T. W., 2005. Asset Sales, Investment Opportunities, and the Use of Proceeds. Journal of Finance.

Bebchuk, L., Coates, J., Subramaniam, G., 2002. The Powerful Anti-Takeover Force of Staggered Boards: Theory, Evidence, and Policy. Stanford Law Rev. 54, 887–951.

Bebchuk, L. J., Coates IV, J. C., Subramanian, G., 2003. The Powerful Antitkeover Force of Staggered Boards. Working Paper, Harvard Law School and NBER.

Bebchuk, L., Cohen, A., Ferrell, A., 2005. What Matters in Corporate Governance. Harvard University Law School Discussion Paper, No. 49.

Bekaert, G., Harvey, C. R., 2002. Research in Emerging Markets Finance: Looking to the Future. Presentation to the Conference on Valuation in Emerging Markets at the University of Virginia, May 28–30, p. 3.

Bekier, M. M., Bogardus, A. J., Oldham, T., 2001. Why Mergers Fail. McKinsey Quarterly 4, 3.

Bellovary, J. L., Giacomino, D. E., Akers, M. D., 2007. A Review of Bankruptcy Prediction Studies: 1930 to the Present. Journal of Financial Education Winter, 262–298.

Ben-Amar, W., Andre, P., 2006. Separation of Ownership from Control and Acquiring Firm Performance: The Case of Family Ownership in Canada. Journal of Business Finance and Accounting 33, 517–543.

Beneda, N., 2007. Performance and Distress Indicators of New Public Companies. Journal of Asset Management 8, 24–33.

Benerjee, A., Woodrow Eckard, E., 1998. Are Mega-Mergers Anti-Competitive? Evidence from the First Great Merger Wave. Rand J. Econ. 29 (Winter), 803–827.

Bengoa, M., Sanchez-Robles, B., 2003. Foreign Direct Investment, Economic Freedom and Growth. European Journal of Political Economy 19, 529–545.

Bennedsen, M., Nielsen, K., Perez-Gonzalez, F., Wolfenson, D., 2006. Inside the Family Firm: The Role of Families in Succession Decisions and Performance. Working Paper, New York University.

Benninga, S., 2000. Financial Modeling. MIT Press, Cambridge, MA.

Berenson, M. L., Levine, D. M., Stephan, D., 1999. Statistics for Managers, second ed. Prentice-Hall, Upper Saddle River, NJ.

Berger, P. G., Ofek, E., 1995. Diversification's Effect on Firm Value. Journal of Financial Economics 37, 39–65.

Berger, P. G., Ofek, E., 1996. Bustup Takeovers of Value Destroying Diversified Firms. Journal of Finance 51, 1175–1200.

Berggren, N., Jordahl, H., 2005. Does Free Trade Reduce Growth? Further Testing Using the Economic Freedom Index. Public Choice 22, 99–114.

Bergh, D., Johnson, R., Dewitt, R. L., 2007. Restructuring through Spin-off or Sell-Off: Transforming Information Asymmetries into Financial Gain. Strategic Management Journal 29, 133–148.

Berk, J. B., 1995. A Critique of Size Related Anomalies. The Review of Financial Studies 8, 275–286.

Berman, D. K., Sender, H., 2006. Back-Story of Kinder LBO Underscores Web of Ethical Issues Such Deals Face. Wall St. J. p. A6.

Bernard, V., Healy, P., Palepu, K. G., 2000. Business Analysis and Valuation, second ed. Southwestern College Publishing Company, Georgetown, TX.

Best, R., Hodges, C. W., 2004. Does Information Asymmetry Explain the Diversification Discount? Journal of Financial Research 27 (Summer), 235–249.

Betker, B., 1995. An Empirical Examination of Prepackaged Bankruptcy. Financial Management (Spring), 3–18.

Bhagat, S., Dong, M., Hirshleifer, D., Noah, R., 2005. Do Tender Offers Create Value? New Methods and Evidence. Journal of Financial Economics 76, 3–60.

Bhagat, S., Hirshleifer, D., 1996. Do Takeovers Create Value?: An Intervention Approach. University of Michigan Business School, Working Paper 9505-03-R, http://eres.bus.umich.edu/docs/workpap/wp9505-03-R.pdf, December, p. 35.

Bhagat, S., Jefferis, R. H., 1994. The Cause and Consequence of Takeover Defense: Evidence from Greenmail. Journal of Corporate Finance 1.

Bigelli, M., Mengoli, S., 2004. Sub-Optimal Acquisition Decision under a Majority Shareholder System. J. Manage. Governance 8, 373–403.

Billett, M. T., Jiang, Z., Lie, E., 2008. The Role of Bondholder Wealth Expropriation in LBO Transactions. SSRN, http://ssrn.comabstract=1107448

Billett, M. T., King, T.-H. D., Mauer, D. C., 2004. Bondholder Wealth Effects n Mergers and Acquisitions: New Evidence from the 1980s and 1990s. Journal of Finance 107–135.

Billett, M. T., Mauer, D. C., 2000. Diversification and the Value of Internal Capital Markets: The Case of Tracking Stock. Journal of Banking and Finance 24, 1457–1490.

Billett, M. T., Qian, Y., 2006. Are Overconfident Managers Born or Made? Evidence of Self-Attribution Bias from Frequent Acquirers. AFA. Boston Meetings Paper, http://ssrn.com/abstract=687534

Billett, M. T., Vijh, A. M., 2004. The Wealth Effects of Tracking Stock Restructurings. Journal of Financial Research 27 (Winter), 559–583.

Billett, M. T., Xue, H., 2007. The Takeover Deterrent Effect of Open Market Share Repurchases. Journal of Finance 62, 1827–1851.

Birkett, K., 2003. Sweets to the Sweet: Cadbury Schweppes Buys Adams. Shearman & Sterling, crossborder. practicallaw.com/3-102-3481?jurisFilter=&tab=5

Black, B. S., 1998. Shareholder Activism and Corporate Governance in the United States. In: Peter, N. (Ed.), The New Palgrave Dictionary of Economics and the Law. Palgrave Macmillan, New York.

Black, E. L., Carnes, T. A., Jandik, T., 2000. The Long-Term Success of Cross-Border Mergers and Acquisitions. Social Science Research Network Electronic Paper Collection, December http://papers.ssrn.com/5013/delivery.cfn/ssrn_id272782_010705100.pdf

Blackman, A., 2006. Your U.S. Fund May Be Scurrying Abroad. Wall St. J. p. C2.

Bley, J., Madura, J., 2003. Intra-Industry and Inter-Country Effects of European Mergers. Journal of Economics and Finance 27 (3), Fall, 373–392.

Bloomberg.com, 2000. Glaxo, SmithKline Agree to Merge. January 18.

Blume, M. E., Lim, F., MacKinlay, A. C., 1998. The Declining Credit Quality of U.S. Corporate Debt: Myth or Reality? Journal of Finance 53, 1389–1413.

Bodnar, G., Dumas, B., Marston, R., 2003. Cross-Border Valuations: The International Cost of Capital. INSEAD Working Paper, Fontainebleau, France.

Boehmer, E., 2000. Business Groups, Bank Control, and Large Shareholders: An Analysis of German Takeovers. Journal of Financial Intermediation 9, 117–148.

Boer, P. E., 2002. The Real Options Solution: Finding Total Value in a High Risk World. John Wiley & Sons, New York.

Bogler, D., 1996. Post-Takeover Stress Disorder, Summary of a PA Consulting Study. Financial Times p. 11.

Boone, A. L., Casares Field, L., Karpoff, J. M., 2007. The Determinants of Corporate Board Sizes and Composition: An Empirical Analysis. Journal of Financial Economics 85, 66–101.

Boone, A., Haushalter, D., Mikkelson, W., 2003. An Investigation of the Gains from Specialized Equity Claims. Financial Management 32, 67–83.

Boone, A. L., Mulherin, J. H., 2006. How Are Firms Sold?. Journal of Finance.

Boot, A. W. A., Gopalan, R., Thakor, A. V., 2008. Market Liquidity, Investor Participation, and Managerial Autonomy: Why Do Firms Go Private. Journal of Finance 2013–2059.

Booth, L., 2002. Finding Value Where None Exists: Pitfalls in Using Adjusted Present Value. Journal of Applied Corporate Finance 15 (Spring), 1–15.

Booz-Allen & Hamilton, 1993. A Practical Guide to Alliances: Leapfrogging the Learning Curve, Booz-Allen & Hamilton, Los Angeles.

Borden, A. M., 1987. Going Private. Law Journal Seminar Press, New York.

Boston Consulting Group, 1985. The Strategy Development Process. The Boston Consulting Group, Boston.

Boston Consulting Group, 2003. Weak Economy is Ideal Time for Mergers and Acquisitions. July 10, www.srimedia.com/artman/ppublish/printer_657.shtml

Boyle, G. W., Carer, R. B., Stover, R. D., 1998. Extraordinary Anti-Takeover Provisions and Insider Ownership Structure: The Case of Converting Savings and Loans. Journal of Financial and Quantitative Analysis 33, 291–304.

Boyson, N., 2008. Hedge Fund Performance Persistence: A New Approach Financial Analysts Journal 64.

Bradley, M., Desai, A., Kim, E. H., 1988. Synergistic Gains from Corporate Acquisitions and Their Division between the Stockholders of Target and Acquiring Firms. Journal of Financial Economics 21, 3.

Bradley, M., Jarrell, G., 1988. Comment on Mergers and Acquisitions. In: Coffee Jr., J., Lowenstein, L., Rose-Ackerman, S. (Eds.), Knights, Raiders, and Targets. Oxford University Press, Oxford, England, pp. 253–259.

Brav, A., Jiang, W., Partnoy, F., Thomas, R., 2006. Hedge Fund Activism, Corporate Governance, and Firm Performance. ECGI-Finance Working Paper 13912006, Duke University.

Brealey, R. A., Myers, S. C., 1996. Principles of Corporate Finance, fifth ed. McGraw-Hill, New York.

Brealey, R. A., Myers, S. C., 2003. Principles of Corporate Finance, seventh ed. McGraw-Hill, New York.

Brickley, J. A., Coles, J. L., Jarrell, G., 1997. Leadership Structure: Separating the CEO and Chairman of the Board. Journal of Corporate Finance 3, 89220.

Brigham, E. F., Ehrhardt, M. C., 2005. Financial Management: Theory and Practice. Thomson-Southwestern Publishing, Mason, OH.

Bris, A., Cabolis, C., 2004. Adopting Better Corporate Governance: Evidence from Cross-Border Mergers. Yale Working Paper, January.

Bris, A., Welch, I., Zhu, N., 2006. Chapter 7 Liquidation Versus Chapter 11 Reorganization. Journal of Finance (June), 1253–1303.

Brookings Institute, 2000. Antitrust Goes Global. November.

Brouthers, K. D., 2002. Institutional, Cultural, and Transaction Cost Influences on Entry Mode Choice and Performance. Journal of International Business Studies 33, 203–221.

Brouthers, K. D., Brouthers, L. E., 2000. Acquisition, Greenfield Start-Up: Institutional, Cultural, and Transaction Cost Influences. Strategic Management Journal 21, 89–97.

Brouthers, K. D., van Hastenburg, P., van den Ven, J., 2000. If Most Mergers Fail Why Are They So Popular? Long Range Plann. 31, 347–353.

Bryan-Low, C., 2005. European Telecoms Vie for Emerging Markets. Wall St. J. p. B2.

Buljevich, E. C., 2005. Cross Border Debt Restructuring: Innovative Approaches for Creditors, Corporate and Sovereigns. Euromoney Institutional Investor, London.

Bumgardner, L., 2005. Antitrust Law in the European Union: The Law is Changing—But to What Effect? Journal of Relevant Business Information and Analysis 8.

Burch, T. R., 2001. Locking out Rival Bidders: The Use of Lockup Options in Corporate Mergers. Journal of Financial Economics 60, 103–141.

Burch, T. R., Nanda, V., 2001. Divisional Diversity and the Conglomerate Discount: Evidence from Spin-Offs. Journal of Financial Economics 70, 233–257.

Burkhart, M., Gromb, D., Panunzi, F., 1997. Larger Shareholders, Monitoring and the Value of the Firm. Quarterly Journal of Economics 693–728.

Burrus, A., McNamee, M., 2002. Evaluating the Rating Agencies. Bus. Week 8, pp. 39–40.

Bus. Week, 1995. The Case against Mergers. pp. 122–125.

Bus. Week, 2000a. Burying the Hatchet Buys a Lot of Drug Research. p. 43.

Bus. Week, 2000b. Jack's Risky Last Act. pp. 40–45.

Bus. Week, 2001. A Merger's Bitter Harvest. p. 112.

Bus. Week, 2008. Easygoing Trustbusters. p. 8.

Byers, S. S., Scott Lee, D., Opler, T. C., 1996. Equity Carve-outs and Management Change. Idaho State University Working Paper.

Bygrave, W. D., Timmons, J. A., 1992. Venture Capital at the Crossroads. Harvard Business School Press, Boston.

Byrd, J., Hickman, K., 1992. Do Outside Directors Monitor Managers? Evidence from Tender Offer Bids. Journal of Financial Economics 32, 195–207.

C

Cakici, N. G., Tandon, K., 1996. Foreign Acquisitions in the U.S.: Effects on Shareholder Wealth of Foreign Acquiring Firms. Journal of Banking and Finance 20, 307–329.

Campa, J., Simi, K., 2002. Explaining the Diversification Discount. Journal of Finance 57, 135–160.

Campbell, J. Y., Hilscher, J., Szilagyi, J., 2008. In Search of Distress Risk. Journal of Finance 63, 2899–2939.

Campbell, A., Sadler, D., Koch, R., 1997. Breakup! When Companies Are Worth More Dead than Alive. Capstone, Oxford, England.

Cao, J. X., 2008. An Empirical Study of LBOs and Takeover Premium. Available at SSRN, http://ssrn.com/abstrat=1100059, February 10.

Cao, J., Lerner, J., 2006. The Success of Reverse Leveraged Buyouts. In: Working Knowledge for Business Leaders. Harvard Business School, October 11.

Capron, L., Shen, J. C., 2007. Acquisitions of Private versus Public Firms: Private Information, Target Selection, and Acquirer Returns. Strategic Management Journal 28, 891–911.

Carey, D. C., Ogden, D., 2004. The Human Side of M&A. Oxford University Press, Oxford, England.

Carleton, J. R., Lineberry, C. S., 2004. Achieving Post-Merger Success. John Wiley & Sons, New York.

Carline, N., Linn, S., Yadav, P., 2002. The Impact of Firm-Specific and Deal-Specific Factors on the Real Gains in Corporate Mergers and Acquisitions. University of Oklahoma Working Paper.

Carlton, D., Perloff, J., 1999. Modern Industrial Organization, third ed., AddisonWesley Longman, New York.

Carow, K. A., Roden, D. M., 1998. Determinants of the Stock Price Reaction to Leveraged Buyouts. Journal of Economics and Finance 22 (Spring), 37–47.

Carrington, G. R., 2007. Tax Accounting in Mergers and Acquisitions. CCH Inc., New York.

Caves, R. E., 1982. Multinational Enterprise and Economic Analysis. Cambridge University Press, Cambridge, MA.

CCH Tax Law Editors, 2005. U.S. Master Tax Code. Commerce Clearinghouse, New York.

Ceneboyan, A. S., Papaioannou, G. J., Travlos, N., 1991. Foreign Takeover Activity in the U.S. and Wealth Effects for Target Firm Shareholders. Financial Management 31, 58–68.

Chaffee, D. B., 1993. Option Pricing as a Proxy for Discount for Lack of Marketability in Private Company Valuation. Business Valuation Review, 182–188.

Chakrabarti, A., 1990. Organizational Factors in Post-Acquisition Performance. IEEE Transactions in Engineering Management EM-37 135, 259–266.

Chakrabarti, R., Jayaraman, N., Mukherjee, S., 2005. Mars-Venus Marriages: Culture and Cross-Border M&A. Working Paper, Georgia Institute of Technology, March.

Chambers, D. R., Lacey, N. J., 2008. Modern Corporate Finance: Theory and Practice, fifth ed. Hayden-McNeil, Plymouth, MI.

Chan, K. C., Karolyi, G. A., Stulz, R. M., 1992. Global Financial Markets and the Risk Premium of U.S. Equity. Journal of Financial Economics 32, 137–167.

Chan, S. H., Kensinger, J. W., Keown, A. J., Martin, J. D., 1997. Do Strategic Alliances Create Value? Journal of Financial Economics 46, 199–221.

Chan, L. K. C., Lakonishok, J., Sougiannis, T., 1999. Investing in High R&D Stocks. Bus. Week, 28.

Chang, S., 1998. Takeovers of Privately Held Targets, Methods of Payment, and Bidder Returns. Journal of Finance 53.

Chang, S.-C., 2008. How Do Strategic Alliances Affect Suppliers, Customers, and Rivals. Social Science Research Network, *Working Paper Series*, February 1.

Chaochharia, V., Grinstein, Y., 2007. Corporate Governance and Firm Value: The Impact of the 2002 Governance Rules. Journal of Finance 62, 1789–1825.

Chapman, T. L., Dempsey, J. J., Ramsdell, G., Bell, T. E., 1998. Purchasing's Big Moment—After a Merger. McKinsey Quarterly 1, 56–65.

Chaplinsky, S., Ramchand, L., 2000. The Impact of Global Equity Offers. Journal of Finance 2767–2789.

Chari, A., Ouiment, P., Tesar, L., 2004. Cross-Border Mergers and Acquisitions in Emerging Markets: The Stock Market Valuation of Corporate Control. University of Michigan Working Paper, March.

Charitou, A., Trigeorgis, L., 2000. Option-Based Bankruptcy Prediction. University of Cyprus Working Paper.

Chatterjee, R. A., Aw, M. S. B., 2004. The Performance of UK: Fiirms Acquiring Large Cross-Border and Domestic Takeover Targets. Applied Financial Economics 14, 337–349.

Chatterjee, S., Yan, A., 2008. Using Innovative Securities Under Asymmetric Information: Why Do Some Firms Pay with Contingent Value Rights? Journal of Financial and Quantitative Analysis.

Chemmanur, T., Paeglis, I., 2000. Why Issue Tracking Stock? Working Paper, available by email from chemmanu@bc.edu

Chen, C., Findlay, C., 2002. A Review of Cross-Border Mergers and Acquisitions in APEC. Australian National University, Canberra.

Chen, H. L., Guo, R. J., 2005. On Corporate Divestitures, Rev. Quant. Finan. Acc. 25, 399–421.

Cheng, C. S., Liu, C. S., Schaefer, T. F., 1996. Earnings Permanence and the Incremental Information Content of Cash Flow from Operations. Journal of Accounting Research (Spring), 173–181.

Child, J., Faulkner, D., 1998. Strategies of Cooperation: Managerial Alliances, Networks, and Joint Ventures. Oxford University Press, Oxford, England.

Child, J., Faulkner, D., Pitkethley, R., 2001. The Management of International Acquisitions. Oxford University Press, Oxford, UK.

Cho, M. H., Cohen, M. A., 1997. The Economic Causes and Consequences of Corporate Divestiture. Managerial and Decision Economics 18, 367–374.

Christofferson, S. A., McNish, R. S., Sias, D. L., 2004. Where Mergers Go Wrong. McKinsey Quarterly.

Claessens, S., Djankov, S., Fan, J., Lang, H. P. I., 2002. Disentangling the Incentive and Entrenchment Effects of Large Shareholders. Journal of Finance 57, 2741–2771.

Clark, K., Ofek, E., 1994. Mergers as a Means of Restructuring Distressed Firms: An Empirical Investigation. Journal of Financial and Quantitative Analysis 29, 541–565.

Claus, J., Thomas, J., 2001. Equity Premia as Low as Three Percent? Empirical Evidence from Analysts' Earnings Forecasts for Domestic and International Stock Markets. Journal of Finance 56, 1629–1666.

Clifford, C., 2007. Value Creation or Destruction: Hedge Funds as Shareholder Activists. Working Paper, Arizona State University.

Clubb, C., Stouraitis, A., 2000. The Significance of Sell-off Profitability in Explaining the Market Reaction to Divestiture Announcements. Journal of Banking and Finance 26, 671–688.

Coates, J. C., 2000. Takeover Defenses in the Shadow of the Pill: A Critique of the Scientific Evidence. Texas Law Review 79, 271–382.

Coates, J. C., 2001. Explaining Variation in Takeover Defenses: Blame the Lawyers. California Law Review 89, 1376.

Coates, J. C., 2007. The Goals and Promise of the Sarbanes-Oxley Act. J. Econ. Perspect. 21 (Winter), 91–116.

Coffee, J., Seligman, J., Sale, H., 2008. Federal Securities Laws: Selected Statutes, Rules, and Forms. Foundation Press, New York.

Colak, G., Whited, T., 2007. Spin-Offs, Divestitures, and Conglomerate Investment. The Review of Financial Studies 20, 557–595.

Coles, J. L., Daniel, N. D., Naveen, L., 2008. Boards: Does One Size Fit All? Journal of Financial Economics 87, 329–356.

Comment, R., Jarrell, G., 1993. Corporate Focus and Stock Returns, Journal of Financial Economics 37, 67–87.

Comment, R., William Schwert, G., 1995. Poison or Placebo: Evidence on the Deterrence and Wealth Effects of Modern Anti-Takeover Measures. Journal of Financial Economics 39, 3–43.

Conn, R. L., Cost, A., Guest, P. M., Hugues, A., 2005. Why Must All Good Things Come to an End? The Performance of Multiple Acquirers. Working Paper, University of Cambridge http://ssrn.com/abstract=499310

Cooper, S. & Lybrand, 1996. Most Acquisitions Fail, C&L Study Says. Mergers & Acquisitions Report 7, 47, p. 2.

Copeland, T., Koller, T., Murrin, J., 2005. Valuation: Measuring, and Managing the Value of Companies, fourth ed. John Wiley & Sons, New York.

Cornelli, F., Karakas, O., Private Equity and Corporate Governance: Do LBOs Have More Effective Boards? Globalization of Alternative Investments. In: Working Papers, Vol. 1, The Global Economic Impact of Private Equity Report, OECD, 2008.

Cossey, B., 1991. Systems Assessment in Acquired Subsidiaries. Accountancy, 98–99.

Cotter, J. F., Peck, S. W., 2001. The Structure of Debt and Active Equity Investors: The Case of the Buyout Specialist. Journal of Finance 59.

Cotter, J. F., Shivdasani, A., Zenner, M., 1997. Do Independent Directors Enhance Target Shareholder Wealth during Tender Offers? Journal of Financial Economics 43, 237–266.

Cremers, M., Nair, V., 2005. Governance Mechanisms and Equity Prices. Journal of Finance 60, 2859–2894.

Cremers, M. K. J., Nair, V. B., Wei, C., 2004. The Impact of Shareholder Control on Bondholders. Working Paper, Yale University and New York University.

Creswell, J., 2001. Would You Give This Man Your Company? Fortune 127–129.

Croci, E., 2005. Why Do Managers Make Serial Acquirers? An Investigation of Performance Predictability in Serial Acquirers. Available SSRN: http:ssrn.com/abstract=727503

Cromwell, N. O., Hodges, C. W., 1998. Teaching Real Options in Corporate Finance Classes. Journal of Financial Education 24 (Spring), 33–48.

Cusatis, P. J., Miles, J. A., Randall Woolridge, J., 1993. Restructuring through Spin-Offs. Journal of Financial Economics 33, 293–311.

Cyree, K. B., Walker, M. M., 2008. The Determinants and Survival of Reverse Mergers Versus IPOs. Journal of Economics and Finance 32, 176–194.

D

Dahya, J., McConnell, J. J., 2001. Outside Directors and Corporate Board Decisions: A Natural Experiment. Working Paper Purdue University.

Dai, N., 2007. Do Venture Capitalists Add Value to Public Firms? Evidence from Venture Capital-Led PIPEs. Journal of Corporate Finance.

Daley, L., Mehrotra, V., Sivakumar, R., 1997. Corporate Focus and Value Creation, Evidence from Spin-Offs. Journal of Financial Economics 45, 257–281.

Dalton, D. R., Dalton, C. M., 2007. Sarbanes-Oxley and the Guideline of the Listing Exchanges: What Have We Wrought? Bus. Horiz. 50, 93–100.

Dalton, D. R., 2006. CEO Tenure, Boards of Directors, and Acquisition Performance. Journal of Business Research 60, 331–338.

Damadoran, A., 1997. Corporate Finance: Theory and Practice. John Wiley & Sons, New York.

Damodaran, A., 2001. The Dark Side of Valuation: Valuing Old Tech, New Tech, and New Economy Companies. Upper Saddle River, NJ, Prentice-Hall, New York.

Damodaran, A., 2002. Investment Valuation: Tools and Techniques for Determining the Value of Any Asset, second ed. John Wiley & Sons, New York.

Daniel, K. D., Hirshleifer, D., Subrahmanyam, A., Investor Psychology and Security Market Under- and Over-Reactions. Journal of Finance 53, 1839–1886.

Das, S., Sen, P. K., Sengupta, S., 1998. Impact of Strategic Alliances on Firm Valuation, Academy of Management Journal 41, 27–41.

Datta, S., Iskandar-Datta, M., Raman, K., 2003. Value Creation in Corporate Asset Sales: The Role of Managerial Performance and Lender Monitoring. Journal of Banking and Finance 27, 351–375.

Davis, P. S., Desai, A. B. Francis, J. D., 2000. Mode of International Entry: An Isomorphian Perspective. Journal of International Business Studies 31, 239–258.

Davis, S. J., Haltiwanger, J., Jarmin, R., Lerner, J., Miranda, J., 2008. Private Equity and Employment. U.S. Census Bureau, Center for Economic Studies, Paper No. CES-WP-08-07.

Davis, G., Kim, H., 2007. Business Ties and Proxy Voting by Mutual Funds. Journal of Financial Economics 85, 552–570.

Davis, A., Leblond, M., 2002. A Spin-off Analysis: Evidence from New and Old Economies. Working Paper, Queen's University, available by email from adavis@business.queensu.ca

DeAngelo, H., DeAngelo, L., 1989. Proxy Contests and the Governance of Publicly Held Corporations. Journal of Financial Economics 23, 29–60.

DeAngelo, H., DeAngelo, L., Rice, E., 1984. Going Private: Minority Freezeouts and Stockholder Wealth. Journal of Law and Economics 27, 367–401.

DeAngelo, H., Rice, E., 1983. Anti-Takeover Charter Amendments and Stockholder Wealth. Journal of Financial Economics 11, 329–360.

Dechow, P. M., 1994. Accounting Earnings and Cash Flows as Measures of Firm Performance: The Role of Accounting Accruals. Journal of Accounting and Economics, 3–42.

Delios, A., Beamish, P. W., 1999. Ownership Strategy of Japanese Firms: Transactional and Institutional Influence. Strategic Management Journal 20, 915–933.

DeLong, G., 2003. Does Long-Term Performance of Mergers Match Market Expectations? Financial Management (Summer), 5–25.

Delos, A., Beamish, P. S., 1999. Geographic Scope, Product Diversification, and the Corporate Performance of Japanese Firms. Strategic Management Journal 20, 711–727.

Demsetz, H., Lehn, K., 1996. The Structure of Corporate Ownership: Causes and Consequences. Journal of Political Economy 93, 1155–1177.

Deogun, N., Lipin, S., 2000. Big Mergers in '90s Prove Disappointing to Shareholders. Salomon Smith Barney study, quoted in Wall St. J. p. C12.

De Pamphilis, D. M., 2001. Managing Growth Through Acquisition: Time Tested Techniques for the Entrepreneur. International Journal of Entrepreneurship and Innovation 2 (3), 195–205.

DePamphilis, D. M., 2010a. M&A Basics: All You Need to Know. Elsevier, Boston.

DePamphilis, D. M., 2010b. M&A Negotiations and Deal Structuring: All You Need to Know. Elsevier, Boston.

Desai, M., Frity Foley, C., Hines, J. R., 2002. The Costs of Shared Ownership: Evidence from International Joint Ventures. Harvard Business School Working Paper, No. 03-017, July.

Desai, H., Jain, P., 1997. Firm Performance and Focus: Long-Run Stock Market Performance Following Spin-Offs. Journal of Financial Economics 54, 75–101.

Deusen, C., Williamson, S., Babson, H. C., 2007. Business Policy and Strategy: The Art of Competition, seventh ed. Auerbach, New York.

De Visscher, F. M., Arnoff, C. E., Ward, J. L., 1995. Financing Transitions: Managing Capital and Liquidity in the Family Business. Business Owner Resources, Marietta, GA.

Dewenter, K. L., 1995. Does the Market React Differently to Domestic and Foreign Takeover Announcements? Evidence from the U.S. Chemical and Retail Industries. Journal of Financial Economics 37, 421–441.

Dichev, I., 1998. Is the Risk of Bankruptcy a Systematic Risk? Journal of Finance 53, 1141–1148.

Diermeier, J. Solnik, B., 2001. Global Pricing of Equity. Financial Analysts Journal 57, 17–47.

Dimson, E., March, P., Staunton, M., 2002. Triumph of the Optimists. Princeton University Press, Princeton NJ.

Dimson, E., Marsh, P., Staunton, M., 2003. Global Evidence on the Equity Risk Premium. Journal of Applied Corporate Finance 15 (Fall), 27–38.

Dittmar, A., Shivdasani, A., 2002. Divestitures and Divisional Investment Policies, Journal of Finance 58, 2711–2744.

Dodd, P., Warner, J., 1983. On Corporate Government: A Study of Proxy Contests, Journal of Financial Economics 11, 401–438.

Dong, M., Hirshleifer, D., Richardson, S., Teoh, S. H., 2006. Does Investor Misvaluation Drive the Takeover Market? Journal of Finance 61, 725–762.

Donn, L. E., 2006. The Best and Worst of the Bankruptcy Abuse Prevention and Consumer Protection Act of 2005: Its Effect on Bankruptcy Courts, Reorganizing Business, and the American People. Rutgers Law General 38, 574–597.

Doukas, J., Travlos, N. G., 1988. The Effect of Corporate Multinationalism on Shareholders' Wealth: Evidence from International Acquisitions. Journal of Finance 43, 1161–1175.

Down, J. W., 1995. The M&A Game Is Often Won or Lost after the Deal, Management Review Executive Forum p. 10.

Draper, P., Paudyal, K., 2006. Acquisitions: Private versus Public. European Financial Management 12, 57–80.

Drucker, J., Silver, S., 2006. Alcatel Stands to Reap Tax Benefits on Merger. Wall St. J. p. C3.

D'Souza, J., Jacob, J., 2000. Why Firms Issue Targeted Stock. Journal of Financial Economics 56, 459–483.

Duffie, D., Saita, L., Wang, K., 2007. Multi-Period Corporate Default Prediction with Stochastic Covariates. Journal of Financial Economics 83, 635–665.

Duffie, D., Singleton, K. J., 1999. Modeling Term Structures of Defaultable Bonds. Review of Financial Studies 12, 687–720.

Dukes, W., Frohlich, C., Ma, C., 1992. Risk Arbitrage in Tender Offers: Handsome Rewards—And Not for Insiders Only. Journal of Portfolio Management 18, 47–55.

Dumontier, P., Pecherot, B., 2001. Determinants of Returns to Acquiring Firms around Tender Offer Announcement Dates: The French Evidence,. ESA Universite de Grenoble, Working Paper.

Dunning, J. H., 1988. The Eclectic Paradigm of International Production: A Restatement and Some Possible Extensions. Journal of International Business Studies 1–31.

Dunning, J., 1993. Multinational Enterprises and the Global Economy. Addison-Wesley Publishing, Reading, MA.

Dutta, S., Iskandar-Dutta, M., Raman, K., 2001. Executive Compensation and Corporate Acquisition Decisions. Journal of Finance 56, 2299–2396.

Dyck, A., Zingales, L., 2004. Control Premiums and the Effectiveness of Corporate Governance Systems. Journal of Applied Finance 16 (Spring–Summer), 51–72.

E

Easton, P., Taylor, G., Shroff, P., Sougiannis, T., June 2001. Using Forecasts of Earnings to Simultaneously Estimate Growth and the Rate of Return on Equity Investment. Journal of Accounting Research 40, 657–676.

Eberhart, A. C., Altman, E. I., Aggarwal, R., 1999. The Equity Performance of Firms Emerging from Bankruptcy. Journal of Finance 54.

Ebin, R. F., 1998. Legal Aspects of International Joint Ventures and Strategic Alliances. In: BenDaniel, D. J., Rosenbloom, A. H. (Eds.), International M&A, Joint Ventures and Beyond: Doing the Deal. John Wiley & Sons, New York, pp. 315–360.

Eckbo, E., Thorburn, K. S., March 2000. Gains to Bidder Firms Revisited: Domestic and Foreign Acquisitions in Canada. Journal of Financial and Quantitative Analysis 35, 1–25.

Eckbo, B., 2008. Espen, and Karin S. Thorburn, Automatic Bankruptcy Auctions and Fire-Sales. Journal of Financial Economics 89, 404–422.

Economic Report to the President, 2003. U.S. Government Printing Office, Washington DC. February.

Economist, 2006a. Battling for Corporate America. pp. 69–71.

Economist, 2006b. A Survey of the World Economy. p. 12.

Elango, B., Rakeh, B., 2004. The Influence of Industry Structure on the Entry Mode Choice of Overseas Entrants in Manufacturing Industries. Journal of International Management 107–124.

Elder, J., Westra, P., 2000. The Reaction of Security Prices to Tracking Stock Announcements. Journal of Economics and Finance 24, 36–55.

Ellis, C., 1996. Briefings from the Editors. Harv. Bus. Rev. 74, p. 8.

Ellison, S., 2006. Clash of Cultures Exacerbates Woes for Tribune Co. Wall St. J. p. 1.

Emery, D. R., Finnerty, J. D., 1992. A Review of Recent Research Concerning Corporate Debt Provisions. Financial Markets, Institutions, and Instruments 1, 23–39.

Emory, J. D., 2001. The Value of Marketability as Illustrated in Initial Public Offerings of Common Stock. Business Valuation Review 20, 21–24.

Engel, E., Hayes, R., Xang, X., 2004. The Sarbanes–Oxley Act and Firms' Going Private Decisions. Working Paper, University of Chicago.

Ertimur, Y., Ferri, F., Stubben, S., 2008. Board of Directors Responsiveness to Shareholders: Evidence from Shareholder Proposals. Harvard Business School Working Paper, February.

Erwin, G. R., McConnell, J. J., 1997. To Live or Die? An Empirical Analysis of Piecemeal Voluntary Liquidations, Journal of Corporate Finance 3, 325–354.

Escherich, R., 1998. Selected Results from Our Survey of U.S. Valuation Techniques. In: Global Mergers & Acquisition Review. J.P. Morgan, New York and London, p. 31. January.

Eun, C. S., Kolodny, R., Scherage, C., 1996. Cross-Border Acquisition and Shareholder Wealth: Tests of the Synergy and Internationalization Hypotheses. Journal of Banking and Finance 20, 1559–1582.

Eun, C. S., Huang, W., Lai, S., 2007. International Diversification with Large and Small Cap Stocks. Journal of Financial and Quantitative Analysis.

F

Faccio, M., Lang, L. H. P., 2002. The Ultimate Ownership of Western European Corporations. Journal of Financial Economics 65, 365–395.

Faccio, M., Masulis, R., 2005. The Choice of Payment Method in European Mergers and Acquisitions. Journal of Finance 60, 1345–1388.

Faccio, M., McConnell, J., Stolin, D., 2006. Returns to Acquirers of Listed and Unlisted Companies. Journal of Financial and Quantitative Analysis 47, 197–220.

Faleye, O., 2004. Cash and Corporate Control. Journal of Finance.

Fama, E. F., French, K. R., 1992. The Cross-Section of Expected Stock Returns. Journal of Finance 47, 427–465.

Fama, E. F., 1998. Market Efficiency, Long-Term Returns, and Behavioral Finance. Journal of Financial Economics 47, 427–465.

Fama, E. F., French, K. R., 1993. Common Risk Factors in the Returns on Stocks and Bonds. Journal of Financial Economics 33, 3–56.

Fama, E. F., French, K. R., 2006. The Value Premium and the CAPM, Journal of Finance.

Fama, E. F., Jensen, M. C., 1983. Separation of Ownership and Control. Journal of Law and Economics 26, 301–325.

Fan, J. P. H., Goyal, V. K. 2006. On the Pattern and Wealth Effects of Vertical Mergers. Journal of Business 79, 877–902.

Farrell, D., Key, A. M., Shavers, T., 2006. Mapping the Global Capital Markets. McKinsey Quarterly.

Farzad, R., 2006. Fidelity's Divided Loyalties. Bus. Week, p. 12.

Fauver, L., Houston, J., Narango, A., 2003. Capital Market Development, International Integration, and the Value of Corporate Diversification: A Cross-Country Analysis. Journal of Financial and Quantitative Analysis 38, 138–155.

Federal Reserve Bulletin, 2003. Board of Governors, U.S. Federal Reserve System, December p. 33.

Federal Trade Commission, 1999a. Merger Guidelines www.ftc.com.

Federal Trade Commission, Bureau of Competition, 1999b. A Study of the Commission's Divestiture Process.

Fee, C., 2004. Edward, and Shawn Thomas, Sources of Gains in Horizontal Mergers: Evidence from Customer, Supplier, and Rival Firms. Journal of Financial Economics 74, 423–460.

Feliciano, Z., Lipsey, R. E., 2002. Foreign Entry Into U.S. Manufacturing by Takeovers and the Creation of New Firms. Working Paper 9122, National Bureau of Economic Research, Cambridge, MA.

Ferenczy, I., 2005. Employee Benefits in Mergers and Acquisitions. Aspen Publishers, New York.

Fernandez, P., 2002. Valuation Methods and Shareholder Value Creation. Academic Press, New York.

Ferreira, M. P., Tallman, S. B., 2005. Building and Leveraging Knowledge Capabilities through Cross-Border Acquisitions. Presentation to the Academy of Management Meeting.

Field, L. C., Karpoff, J. M., 2002. Takeover Defenses of IPO Firms. Journal of Finance 57, 1629–1666.

Fields, L. P., Mais, E. L., 1991. The Valuation Effects of Private Placements of Convertible Debt. Journal of Finance 46, 1925–1932.

Financial Times, 1996. Bugged by Failures. p. 8.

Finnerty, J. D., 2002. The Impact of Transfer Restrictions on Stock Prices. Working Paper, Analysis Group/Economics, Cambridge MA.

Fisher, D., 2006. A Dangerous Game. Forbes Magazine, 40–43.

Flanagan, D. J., O'Shaughnessy, K. C., 1998. Determinants of Layoff Announcements following Mergers and Acquisitions: An Empirical Investigation. Strategic Management Journal 19, 989–999.

Fleming, M. J., Moon, J. J., 1995. Preserving Firm Value through Exit: The Case of Voluntary Liquidations. Federal Reserve Bank of New York, Staff Reports 8.

Foley, Lardner, L. L. P., 2007. What Private Companies and Non-Profits Need to Know About SOX. Report presented at Foley and Lardner's 2004 National Directors Institute Meeting, Chicago.

Foster, R., Kaplan, S., 2001. Why Companies That Are Built to Last Under-Perform—and How to Successfully Transform Them. Prentice-Hall, Upper Saddle River, NJ.

France, M., 2002. Bankruptcy Reform Won't Help Telecom. Bus. Week, p. 40.

Francis, B., Hasan, I., Sun, X., 2008. Financial Market Integration and the Value of Global Diversification: Evidence for U.S. Acquirers in Cross-Border Mergers and Acquisitions. Journal of Banking and Finance 32, 1522–1540.

Frank, R., Sidel, R., 2002. Firms That Lived by the Deal in the 1990s Now Sink by the Dozens. Wall St. J. p. A1.

Franks, J. R., Harris, R. S., Titman, S., 1991. The Post-Merger Share-Price Performance of Acquiring Firms. Journal of Financial Economics 29, 81–96.

Franks, J., Mayer, C., 1996. Hostile Takeovers and the Correction of Managerial Failure. Journal of Financial Economics 40, 163–181.

Freeman, L. S., Stephens, T. M., 1994. Advantages, Key Issues, and Tax Strategies in the Use of Partnerships by Corporate Joint Ventures. In: Tax Strategies for Corporate Acquisitions, Dispositions, Spin-Offs, Joint Ventures and Other Strategic Alliances, Financings, Reorganizations, and Restructurings, Practicing Law Institute, New York.

Frick, K. A., Torres, A., 2002. Learning from High Tech Deals. McKinsey Quarterly 1, p. 2.

Fubini, D. G., Price, C., Zollo, M., 2006. Successful Mergers Start at the Top. McKinsey Quarterly.

Fuller, K., Netter, J., Stegemoller, M. A., 2002. What Do Returns to Acquiring Firms Tell Us? Evidence from Firms That Make Many Acquisitions. Journal of Finance 57, 1763–1793.

Fusaro, R. F. X., 1995. Issues to Consider in Drafting Joint Venture Agreements. In: Drafting Corporate Agreements, Practicing Law Institute, New York.

G

Gale, W. J., Morris, J. M., 2006. Mergers and Acquisition: Business Strategy for Accountants, second ed. Cumulative Supplement, Wiley & Sons, New York.

Galpin, T., Herndon, M., 2007. The Complete Guide to Mergers and Acquisitions: Process Tools to Support Integration at Every Level, second ed. Jossey-Bass, San Francisco.

Garten, J. E., 2000. As Business Goes Global, Antitrust Should Too. Bus. Week, p. 38.

Gaspara, J. M., Massa, P., 2005. Shareholder Investment Horizons and the Market for Corporate Control. Journal of Financial Economics 76, 135–165.

Gell, J., Kengelbach, J., Roos, A., 2008. The Return of the Strategist: Creating Value with M&A in Downturns. Boston Consulting Group, Boston.

Gelman, M., 1972. An Economist-Financial Analyst's Approach to Valuing Stock of a Closely Held Company. Journal of Taxation, 46–53.

Georgopoulos, G., 2008. Cross-Border Mergers and Acquisitions: Do Exchange Rates Matter? Some Evidence for Canada. Canadian Journal of Economics 41, 450–474.

Gertner, R., Powers, E., Scharfstein, D., 2002. Learning about Internal Capital Markets from Corporate Spin-Offs. Journal of Finance 57, 2479–2506.

Ghosh, A., Lee, C. W. J., 2000. Abnormal Returns and Expected Managerial Performance of Target Firms. Financial Management 29 (Spring), 40–52.

Ghosh, A., 2001. Does Operating Performance Really Improve Following Corporate Acquisitions? Journal of Corporate Finance 7, 151–178.

Ghosh, A., 2004. Increasing Market Share as a Rationale for Corporate Acquisitions, Journal of Business, Finance, and Accounting 31, 78–91.

Gillan, S., Starks, L., 2007. The Evolution of Shareholder Activism in the United States, Journal of Applied Corporate Finance 19, 55–73.

Gilson, R. J., Black, B. S., 1995. The Law and Finance of Corporate Acquisitions, second ed. The Foundation Press, Inc., Westbury, NY.

Gilson, S., March 1997. Transactions Costs and Capital Structure Choice: Evidence from Financially Distressed Firms. Journal of Finance 52, 161–196.

Gilson, S. C., Healy, P. M., Noe, C. F., Palepu, L. G., 2001. Analyst Specialization and Conglomerate Stock Breakups. Journal of Accounting Research 39, 565–582.

Gilson, S., John, K., Lang, L. H., 1990. Troubled Debt Restructuring: An Empirical Study of Private Reorganization of Firms in Default. Journal of Financial Economics 27, 315–353.

Ginsburg, M. D., Levin, J. S., 2004. Mergers, Acquisitions and Buyouts: A Transactional Analysis of Governing Tax, Legal, and Accounting Considerations. Aspen Publishers, New York.

Ginsburg, M. D., Levin, J. S., 2006. Mergers, Acquisitions, and Buyouts. Aspen Publishers, New York.

Gitman, L. J., 2008. Principles of Managerial Finance, twelfth ed. Addison-Wesley, New York.

Goldblatt, H., 1999. Merging at Internet Speed. Fortune, 164–165.

Gompers, P. A., Ishii, J., Metrick, A., 2009. Extreme Governance: An Analysis of U.S. Dual Class Companies in the United States. Review of Financial Studies forthcoming.

Goodman, M., 2005. The Role of Private Equity Firms. SME Magazine http://sme.atalink.co.uk/articles/150

Gorton, G., Kahl, M., Rosen, R. J., 2009. Eat or Be Eaten: A Theory of Mergers and Firm Size. Journal of Finance Forthcoming.

Goyal, V. K., Park, C. W., 2002. Board Leadership Structure and CEO Turnover. Journal of Corporate Finance 8, 49–66.

Graham, J. R., 2000. How Big Are the Tax Benefits of Debt? Journal of Finance 55, 1901–1941.

Graham, J. R., Harvey, C. R., 2001. The Theory and Practice of Corporate Finance: Evidence from the Field. Journal of Financial Economics 60, 187–243.

Graham, J., Lemmon, M., Wolf, J., 2002. Does Diversification Destroy Firm Value? Journal of Finance 57, 695–720.

Graham, M., Martey, E., Yawson, A., 2008. Acquisitions from UK Firms into Emerging Markets. Global Finance Journal 19, 56–71.

Grant, J., 2007. SEC Hopes Sarbox Fix Will Revive Foreign Listings in U.S. Financial Times, p. 2.

Greenaway, D., Kneller, R., 2007. Firm Heterogeneity, Exporting, and Foreign Direct Investment. Economic Journal, Deposition/Interrogatory Review 117, 134–161.

Greenwald, J., 1988. Where's the Limit? Time, 66–70.

Greenwood, R., Schor, M., 2007. Hedge Fund Investor Activism and Takeovers. Harvard Business School Working Paper, Working Knowledge.

Grice, S., Dugan, M., 2001. The Limitations of Bankruptcy Prediction Models: Some Cautions for the Researcher. Rev. Quant. Finan. Acc. 17.

Grice, S., Ingram, R., 2001. Tests of the Generalizability of Altman's Bankruptcy Prediction Model. Journal of Business Research 54, 53–61.

Grinblatt, M., Titman, S., 2002. Financial Markets and Corporate Strategy, second ed. McGraw-Hill, New York.

Groh, A. Gottschaig, O., 2006. The Risk-Adjusted Performance of U.S. Buyouts. Working Paper, HEC, Paris.

Gugler, K., Mueller, D. C., Yurtoglu, B. B., Zulehner, C., May 2003. The Effects of Mergers: An International Comparison. International Journal of Industrial Organization 21 (5), 625–653.

Guo, S., Hotchkiss, E. S., Song, W., 2008. Do Buyouts (Still) Create Value? Available at SSRN, http://ssrn.com/abstract=1009281

Guo, R. J., Kruse, T. A., Nohel, T., 2008. Undoing the Powerful Anti-Takeover Force of Staggered Boards, Journal of Corporate Finance 14, 274–288.

Gurung, A., Lerner, J., 2008. The Global Economic Impact of Private Equity. World Economic Forum and Harvard Business School.

H

Habbershon, T. G., Williams, M. L., 1999. A Resource-Based Framework for Assessing the Strategic Advantages of Family Firms. Family Business Review 12, 1–26.

Hackbarth, D., Morellec, E., 2008. Stock Returns in Mergers and Acquisitions, Journal of Finance 63, 1213–1252.

Hall, B., 1992. Investment and Research and Development at the Firm Level: Does the Source of Financing Matter? National Bureau of Economic Research, Working Paper No. 4096.

Hall, L. S., Polacek, T. C., 1994. Strategies for Obtaining the Largest Valuation Discounts. Estate Planning, 38–44.

Hamel, G. C., Prahalad, C. K., 1994. Competing for the Future. Harvard Business School Press, Cambridge, MA.

Hand, J. R., Skantz, T. R., 1997. Market Timing Through Equity Carve-Outs. University of North Carolina Working Paper.

Hanke, J. E., Wichern, D. W., 2005. Business Forecasting, eighth ed. Prentice Hall, Upper Saddle River NJ.

Hanouna, P., Sarin, A., Shapiro, A., 2001. The Value of Corporate Control: Some International Evidence. Working Paper, Marshall School of Business, University of Southern California, Los Angeles.

Hansen, R., 1986. Evaluating the Costs of a New Equity Issue. Midland Corporate Finance Journal (Spring), 42–55.

Hanson, R. C., Song, M. H., 2000. Managerial Ownership, Board Structure, and the Division of Gains. Journal of Corporate Finance 6.

Hao, K. Y., Jaffe, A. B., 1993. The Impact of Corporate Restructuring on Industrial Research and Development. Brookings Papers on Economic Activity 1, 275–282.

Harding, D., Rovit, S., 2004. Mastering the Merger: Four Critical Decisions That Make or Break the Deal. Harvard Business School Press.

Harford, J., 1999. Corporate Cash Reserves and Acquisitions. Journal of Finance 54, 1969–1997

Harford, J., 2005. What Drives Merger Waves? Journal of Financial Economics 77, 529–560.

Harper, N. W., Schneider, A., 2004. Where Mergers Go Wrong. McKinsey Quarterly, Number 2.

Harris, O., Glegg, C., 2007. The Wealth Effects of Cross-Border Spin-Offs. Journal of Multinational Financial Management.

Harris, R. S., Ravenscraft, D., 1991. The Role of Acquisitions in Foreign Direct Investment: Evidence from the U.S. Stock Market. Journal of Finance 46, 825–844.

Harrison, J. S., Oler, D., Allen, M. R., 2005. Event Studies and the Importance of Longer-Term Measures in Assessing the Performance of Outcomes of Complex Events. Working Paper, Indiana University.

Hartman, T. E., 2005. The Costs of Being Public in the Era of Sarbanes-Oxley. Foley & Lardner LLP Annual Survey.

Harvey, C. R., 2005. Twelve Ways to Calculate the International Cost of Capital. Duke University and National Bureau of Economic Research Working Paper, October 14.

Harvey, C. R., Lins, K. V., Roper, A. H., 2004. The Effect of Capital Structure When Expected Agency Costs Are Extreme. Journal of Financial Economics 74, 3–30.

Harzing, A. W., 2002. Acquisitions versus Greenfield Investments: International Strategy and Management of Entry Modes. Strategic Management Journal 23, 211–227.

Haselmann, R., Pistor, K., Vig, V., 2006. How Law Affects Lending. Working Paper No. 285, Columbia Law School.

Haushalter, D., Mikkelson, W., 2001. An Investigation of the Gains from Specialized Equity: Tracking Stocks and Minority Carve-Outs. Working Paper, University of Oregon.

Hayes, R. H., 1979. The Human Side of Acquisitions. Manage. Rev. 41.

Hayward, M. L., 2002. When Do Firms Learn from Their Acquisition Experience? Evidence from 1990–1995. Strategic Management Journal 23, 21–39.

Healy, P. M., Palepu, K. G., Ruback, R. S., 1992. Does Corporate Performance Improve after Mergers? Journal of Financial Economics 31, 135–175.

Hennart, J. F., Park, Y. R., 1993. Location, Governance, and Strategic Determinants of Japanese Manufacturing Investment in the United States. Journal of Strategic Management 15, 419–436.

Hennart, J. F., Reddy, S., 1997. The Choice between Mergers, Acquisitions, and Joint Ventures: The Case of Japanese Investors in the United States. Strategic Management Journal 18, 1–12.

Hennessy, C. A., Whited, T. M., 2007. How Costly Is External Financing? Evidence from a Structural Estimation. Journal of Finance 62, 1705–1745.

Henry, D., 2001. The Numbers Game. Bus. Week, 100–103.

Henry, D., 2002. Mergers: Why Most Big Deals Don't Pay Off. Bus. Week, 60–64.

Henry, D., 2003. A Fair Deal—But for Whom. Bus. Week, 108–109.

Heron, R., Lie, E., 2002. Operating Performance and the Method of Payment in Takeovers. Journal of Financial and Quantitative Analysis 137–155.

Hermalin, B. E., 2006. Trends in Corporate Governance. Journal of Finance 60, 2351–2384.

Hertzel, M., Smith, R. L., 1993. Market Discounts and Shareholder Gains for Placing Equity Privately, Journal of Finance 48, 459–485.

Hertzel, M., Lemmon, M., Linck, J. S., Rees, L., 2002. Long-Run Performance Following Private Placements of Equity, Journal of Finance 47, 2595–2641.

Hill, C. W. L., Jones, G. R., 2001. Strategic Management: An Integrated Approach, fifth ed. Houghton-Mifflin, Boston.

Himmelberg, C. P., Petersen, B. C., 1994. R&D and Internal Finance: A Panel Study of Small Firms in High Tech Industries. Review of Economics and Statistics 76, 38–51.

Hillyer, C., Smolowitz, I., 1996. Why Do Mergers Fail to Achieve Synergy? Director's Monthly, p. 13.

Hirschey, M., 2003. Tech Stock Valuation. Academic Press, New York.

Hitchner, J. R., 2006. Financial Valuation: Applications and Models. second ed. Wiley & Sons, New York.

Hite, G., Owers, J. E., 1983. Security Price Reactions around Corporate Spin-off Announcements. Journal of Financial Economics 12, 409–436.

Hite, G., Owers, J., Rogers, R., 1987. The Market for Inter-Firm Asset Sales: Partial Sell-offs and Total Liquidations. Journal of Financial Economics 18, 229–252.

Hite, G. L., Vetsuypens, M. R., 1989. Management Buyouts of Divisions and Shareholder Wealth. Journal of Finance 44, 953–970.

Hitt, M. A., Hoskisson, R. E., Kim, H., 1999. International Diversification: Effects on Innovation and Firm Performance in Product Diversified Firms. Academy of Management Journal 40, 767–798.

Hitt, M. A., Ireland, R. D., 2000. The Intersection of Entrepreneurship and Strategic Management Research. In: Sexton, D., Landstrom, H. (Eds.), The Blackwell Handbook of Entrepreneurship. Blackwell Publishers, Ltd., Oxford, UK.

Hoffman, W. H., Schaper-Rinkel, W., 2001. Acquire or Ally?—A Strategic Framework for Deciding between Acquisition and Cooperation. Management International Review 41, 131–159.

Hogan, K. M., Olson, G. T., 2004. The Pricing of Equity Carve-outs during the 1990s. Journal of Financial Research 27 (Winter), 521–537.

Holthausen, R. W., Larker, D. F., 1996. The Financial Performance of Reverse Leveraged Buyouts. Journal of Financial Economics 42, 293–332.

Holmstrom, B. R., Kaplan, S. N., 2001. Corporate Governance and Merger Activity in the U.S.: Making Sense of the 1980s and 1990s. MIT Department of Economics Working Paper, No. 01-11.

Hopkins, H. D., 2008. International Acquisitions: Strategic Considerations. International Research Journal of Finance and Economics 15, 261–270.

Hotchkiss, E. S., 1995. The Post-Emergence Performance of Firms Emerging from Chapter 11. Journal of Finance 50, 3–21.

Hotchkiss, E., Qian, J., Song, W., 2005. Holdup, Renegotiation, and Deal Protection in Mergers. Working Paper, Boston College.

Houston, J., James, C., Ryngaert, M., 2001. Where Do Merger Gains Come From? Journal of Financial Economics, 285–331.

Hsu, J. C., Saa-Requejo, J., Santa-Clara, P., 2002. Bond Pricing and Default Risk. Working Paper, UCLA.

Hulburt, H. M., Miles, J. A., Wollridge, J. R., 2002. Value Creation from Equity Carve-Outs. Financial Management 31 (Spring), 83–100.

Hunger, D., Wheeler, T. L., 2007. Concepts: Strategic Management and Business Policy, eleventh ed. Prentice Hall, Upper Saddle River, NJ.

Hunt, P., 2003. Structuring Mergers and Acquisitions: A Guide to Creating Shareholder Value. Aspen Publishers, New York.

Hurter, W. H., Petersen, J. R., Thompson, K. E., 2005. Merger, Acquisitions, and 1031 Tax Exchanges. Lorman Education Services, New York.

Huson, M. R., MacKinnon, G., 2003. Corporate Spin-offs and Information Asymmetry between Investors. Journal of Economics and Management Strategy 9, 481–501.

Huson, M. R., Parrino, R., Starks, L. T., 2001. Internal Monitoring Mechanism and CEO Turnover: A Long-Term Perspective, Journal of Finance 55, 2265–2297.

Hyland, D., 2001. Why Firms Diversify: An Empirical Examination. Working Paper, University of Texas, Arlington.

I

Ibbotson Associates, 2002. Stock, Bonds, Bills, and Inflation, Valuation Edition Yearbook. Ibbotson Associates Inc., Chicago IL.

Inkpen, A. C., Beamish, P. W., 1997. Knowledge, Bargaining Power, and the Instability of International Joint Ventures. Academy of Management Review 22, 177–202.

Institutional Investor Study Report, 1971. Securities and Exchange Commission, US Government Printing Office, Washington, DC, Document No. 93-64, March 10.

Isakov, D., Sonney, F., 2002. Are Parishioners Right? On the Relative Importance of Industrial Factors in International Stock Returns. Working Paper, HEC-University of Geneva.

Ismail, A., 2005. Will Multiple Acquirers Ever Learn? The U.S. Evidence from Single versus Multiple Acquirers. http://ssrn.com/abstract=765245

J

Jackson, H., Roe, M., 2008. Private and Public Enforcement of Securities Laws: Resource-Based Evidence. Available on SSRN: http://ssrn.com/abstract=1003177

Jaffe, A. B., Trajtenberg, M., 2002. Patents, Citations, and Innovations: A Window on the Knowledge Economy. MIT Press, Cambridge, MA.

Jain, P. C., 1985. The Effects of Voluntary Sell-off Announcements on Shareholder Wealth. Journal of Finance 40, 209–224.

Jarrell, G., 1985. Wealth Effects of Litigating by Targets: Do Interests Diverge in a Merger? Journal of Law and Economics 28, 151–177.

Jarrell, G. A., Brickley, J. A., Netter, J. M., 1988. The Market for Corporate Control: The Empirical Evidence Since 1980. J. Econ. Perspec. 2, 49–68.

Jarrell, G., Poulsen, A. B., 1987. Shark Repellents and Stock Prices: The Effects of Antitakeover Amendments since 1980. Journal of Financial Economics 19, 127–168.

Jarrell, G., Poulsen, A., 1989. The Returns to Acquiring Firms in Tender Offers: Evidence from Three Decades. Financial Management 18, 12–19.

Jarrow, R. A., Protter, P., 2004. Structural versus Reduced Form Models: A New Information Based Perspective. Journal of Investment Management 2, 1–10.

Jarrow, R., Turnbull, S., 1995. Pricing Derivative on Financial Securities Subject to Credit Risk. Journal of Finance 50, 1449–1470.

Jensen, M. C., 1993. The Modern Industrial Revolution: Exit and the Failure of Internal Control Systems. Journal of Finance 48, 831–880.

Jensen, M. C., 1986. Agency Costs of Free Cash Flow, Corporate Finance, and Takeovers. American Economic Association Papers and Proceedings (May), 323–329.

Jensen, M. C., 1989. The Eclipse of the Public Corporation. Harv. Bus. Rev. 67, 61–74.

Jensen, M. C., 2005. Agency Costs of Overvalued Equity. Financial Management 34 (Spring), 5–19.

Jensen, M. C., Ruback, R. S., 1983. The Market for Corporate Control: The Scientific Evidence. Journal of Financial Economics 11, 5–53.

Jindra, J., Walkling, R., 1999. Arbitrage Spreads and the Market Pricing of Proposed Acquisitions. Working Paper, Ohio State University.

John, K., Ofek, E., 1995. Asset Sales and Increase in Focus. Journal of Financial Economics 37, 105–126.

Johnson, B., 1999. Quantitative Support for Discounts for Lack of Marketability. Business Valuation Review, 132.

Johnson, S. A., Houston, M. B., 2000. A Re-examination of the Motives and Gains in Joint Ventures. Journal of Financial and Quantitative Analysis 35.

Jones, S., Hensher, D., 2008. Advances in Credit Risk Modeling and Corporate Bankruptcy Prediction. Cambridge University Press, Cambridge, England.

Morgan, J. P., 1995. Monitoring spin-off performance. Morgan Markets, New York.

Morgan, J. P., 1999. Monitoring spin-off performances. Morgan Markets, New York.

Kahya, E., Theodosiou, P., 1999. Predicting corporate financial distress: a time-series cusum methodology. Review of Quantitative Finance and Accounting 13, 323–345.

Kaiser, K. M. J., Stouraitis, A., 2001. Revering Corporate Diversification and the Use of the Proceeds from Asset Sales: The Case of Thorn Emi. Financial Management 30, 63–101.

Kale, P., Dyer, J. H., Singh, H., August 2002. Alliance Capability, Stock Market Response, and Long-Term Alliance Success: The Role of the Alliance Function. Strategic Management Journal 23, 747–767.

Kalmbach Jr., C., Roussel, C. 1999. Dispelling the Myths of Alliances. Andersen Consulting. Available at www.accenture.com/xd/xd.asp?it=enWeb&xd=ideas/outlook/special99/over_special_intro.xml

Kamar, E., Karaca-Mandic, P., Talley, E., 2006. Going-Private Decisions and the Sarbanes-Oxley Act of 2002: A Cross-Country Analysis,. University of Southern California Law School, Working Paper.

Kang, J. K., 2008. The Geography of Block Acquisitions. SSRN, http://ssrn.com/abstract=891110

Kang, J. K., Shivdasani, A., 1997. Corporate Restructuring during Performance Declines in Japan. Journal of Financial Economics 46, 29–65.

Kang, N. H., Johansson, S., 2001. Cross-Border Mergers and Acquisitions: Their Role in Industrial Globalization. STI Working Papers 2000/1, OECD, Paris.

Kantor, R. M., 2002. Collaborative Advantage: The Art of Alliances. In: Harvard Business Review on Strategic Alliances. Harvard Business School Press.

Kaplan, S., 1988. Management Buyouts: Efficiency Gains or Value Transfers. University of Chicago Working Paper 244.

Kaplan, S., 1991. The Staying Power of Leveraged Buyouts. Journal of Financial Economics 29, 287–314.

Kaplan, S., 1989. The Effects of Management Buyouts on Operating Performance and Value. Journal of Financial Economics 24, 217–254.

Kaplan, S., 1989b. Management Buyouts: Efficiency Gains or Value Transfers. Journal of Finance 3, 611–632.

Kaplan, S. N., 1991. The Staying Power of Leveraged Buyouts. Journal of Financial Economics 29, 287–313.

Kaplan, S. N., 1997. The Evolution of U.S. Corporate Governance: We Are All Henry Kravis Now. Journal of Private Equity (Fall), 7–14.

Kaplan, S. N., Ruback, R. S., 1995. The Valuation of Cash Flow Forecasts. Journal of Finance 50, 1059–1094.

Kaplan, S. N., Schoar, A. 2005. Returns, Persistence and Capital Flows. Journal of Finance 60, 1791–1823.

Kaplan, S. N., Weisbach, M. S. 1992. The Success of Acquisitions: Evidence from Divestitures. Journal of Finance 47, 107–138.

Karolyi, G. A., Shannon, J., 1998. Where's the Risk in Risk Arbitrage? Working Paper, Richard Ivey School of Business, University of Western Ontario.

Karpoff, J. M., 2001. The Impact of Shareholder Activism on Target Companies: A Survey of Empirical Findings. Working Paper, University of Washington.

Karpoff, J. M., Malatesta, P. H., 1989. The Wealth Effects of Second Generation State Takeover Legislation. Journal of Financial Economics 25, 291–322.

Karpoff, J. M., Walkling, R. A., 1996. Corporate Governance and Shareholder Initiatives: Empirical Evidence. Journal of Financial Economics 42, 365–395.

Katz, S., 2008. Earnings Quality and Ownership Structure: The Role of Private Equity Sponsors. NBER Working Paper No. W14085.

Kennan, S. C., Shotgrin, I., Sobehart, J., 1999. Historical Default Rates of Corporate Bond Issuers: 1920–1988. Moody's Investors Services, Working Paper.

Kennedy, K., Moore, M., 2003. Going the Distance: Why Some Companies Dominate and Others Fail. Prentice Hall, Upper Saddle River, NJ.

Khanna, T., Palepu, K., Sinha, J., 2005. Strategies that fit emerging markets. Harv. Bus. Rev. 83.

Kim, E. H., McConnell, J. J., 1977. Corporate Mergers and the Co-Insurance of Corporate Debt. Journal of Finance 32, 349–365.

Kim, I. J., Ramaswamy, K., Sundaresan, S., 1993. Does Default Risk in Coupons Affect the Valuation of Corporate Bonds? A Contingent Claims Model. Financial Management 22, 117–131.

Kim, M., Ritter, J. R., 1999. Valuing ipos. Journal of Financial Economics 53, 409–437.

Kim, E. H., Schatzberg, H., 1987. Voluntary corporate liquidations. Journal of Financial Economics 19 (2), 311–328.

Kini, I., Kracaw, W., Mian, S., 2004. The Nature of Discipline by Corporate Takeovers. Journal of Finance.

Kirkland, R., 2007. Private money. Fortune.

Kirkpatrick, D., 2006. Dell in the Penalty Box. Fortune, 69–77.

Klaus, G., Mueller, D. C., Burein Yurtoglu, B., Zulehner, C., 2003. The Effects of Mergers: An International Comparison. International Journal of Industrial Organization 21 (5), 625–653.

Klaus, M., Estrin, S., Bhaumik, S., Peng, M., 2007. Institutions, Resources, and Entry Strategies in Emerging Countries. University of Bath, U.K., Working Paper.

Klein, A., 1986. The Timing and Substance of Divestiture Announcements: Individual, Simultaneous and Cumulative Effects. Journal of Finance 41, 685–697.

Klein, K. E., 2004. Urge to Merge? Take Care to Beware. Bus. Week July 1, p. 68.

Klein, A., Zur, E., 2009. Entrepreneurial Shareholder Activism: Hedge Funds and Other Private Investors. Journal of Finance.

Koedijk, K., Van Dijk, M., 2000. The Cost of Capital of Cross-Listed Firms, Rotterdam. Erasmus University, Working Paper.

Koedijk, K., Kool, C., Schotman, P., Van Kijk, M., 2002. The Cost of Capital in International Markets: Local or Global. Centre for Economic Policy Research, Working Paper.

Koeplin, J., Sarin, A., Shapiro, A. C., 2000. The private equity discount. Journal of Applied Corporate Finance 12, 94–101.

Kogut, B., Singh, H., 1988. The Effect of National Culture on the Choice of Entry Mode. Journal of International Business Studies 19, 411–432.

Koh, J., Venkatraman, N., 1991. Joint Venture Formations and Stock Market Reactions: An Assessment in the Information Technology Sector. Academy of Management Journal 34, 869–892.

Kohers, N., Ang, J., 2000. Earnouts in Mergers: Agreeing to Disagree and Agreeing to Stay. Journal of Finance 73, 445–476.

Koons, C., 2007. Junk bond holders losing their status. Wall St. J. p. B4.

KPMG, 2006. When Hedge Funds Start to Look Like Private Equity Firms. Global M&A Spotlight (Spring).

KPMG, 2006. Mergers and Acquisitions, 2006 M&A Outlook Survey.

Kranhold, K., 2006. GE's Water Unit Remains Stagnant as It Struggles to Integrate Acquisitions. Wall St. J. p. C2.

Kretlow, J. R., McGuigan, J. R., Charles Moyer, R., 1998. Contemporary Financial Management, seventh ed. Southwestern College Publishing, Georgetown, TX.

Krishnaswami, S., Subramaniam, V., 1999. Information Asymmetry, Valuation and the Corporate Spin-off Decision. Journal of Financial Economics 53, 73–112.

Kuipers, D., Miller, D., Patel, A., 2003. The Legal Environment and Corporate Valuation: Evidence from Cross-Border Mergers. Texas Tech Working Paper.

L

Lajoux, A. R., 1998. The Art of M&A Integration. McGraw-Hill, New York.

Lajoux, A. R., Peter Nesvold, H., 2004. The Art of M&A Structuring: Techniques for Mitigating Financial, Tax, and Legal Risk. McGraw-Hill, New York.

Lamont, O., Polk, C., 1997. The Diversification Discount: Cash Flows versus Returns. Journal of Finance 56, 1693–1721.

Lang, L., Poulsen, A., Stulz, R., 1995. Asset Sales, Firm Performance, and the Agency Costs of Managerial Discretion. Journal of Financial Economics 37, 3–37.

Lang, L., Stulz, R. M., Walkling, R. A., 1989. Managerial Performance, Tobin's Q, and the Gains from Successful Tender Offers. Journal of Financial Economics 24, 137–154.

Langford, R., Brown, C., 2004. Making M&A Pay: Lessons from the World's Most Successful Acquirers. Strategy and Leadership 32, 5–14.

La Porta, R., Lopez-de-Silanes, F., Shleifer, A., 2002. Investor Protection and Corporate Valuation. Journal of Finance 57, 147–170.

La Porta, R. F., Shleifer, A., Vishny, R., 1997. Legal Determinants of External Finance. Journal of Finance 52, 1131–1150.

La Porta, R. F., Shleifer, A., 1999. Corporate Ownership around the Word. Journal of Finance 54, 471–518.

Larsen, P. T., Hughes, C., 2008. Sovereign Wealth Funds: The New Kids on the Block. FT.com, January 23.

Lasher, W. R., 2005. Practical Financial Management, fourth ed. Southwestern College Publishing, Mason, OH.

Leeth, J. D., Rody Borg, J., 2000. The Impact of Takeovers on Shareholders' Wealth during the 1920's Merger Wave. Journal of Financial and Quantitative Analysis 35, 29–38.

Lehn, K., Poulsen, A., 1988. Leveraged Buyouts: Wealth Created or Wealth Redistributed? In: Weidenbaum, M., Chilton, K. (Eds.), Public Policy towards Corporate Takeovers. Transaction Publishers, New Brunswick, NJ.

Lehn, K. M., Zhao, M., 2006. CEO Turnover after Acquisitions: Are Bad Bidders Fired? Journal of Finance 61, 1383–1412.

Leland, H. E., 1994. Corporate Debt Value, Bond Covenants, and Optimal Capital Structure. Journal of Finance 49, 1213–1252.

Lemmons, M. L., Lins, K. V., 2003. Ownership Structure, Corporate Governance, and Firm Value: Evidence from the East Asian Financial Crisis. Journal of Finance 58, 1147–1170.

Lerner, J., Shane, H., Tsai, A., 2003. Do equity financing cycles matter? Journal of Financial Economics 67, 411–446.

Letto-Gilles, G., Meschi, M., Simonetti, R., 2001. Cross-Border Mergers and Acquisitions: Patterns in the EU and Effects. South Bank University, London.

Levine, D. M., Berenson, M. L., Stephan, D., 1999. Statistics for Managers, second ed. Prentice Hall, New York.

Leuz, C., Lins, K. V., Warnock, F. E., 2004. Do Foreigners Invest Less in Poorly Governed Firms. University of Virginia, ECGI-Finance Working Paper No. 43.

Leuz, C., Triantis, A., Wang, T. Y., 2008. Why Do Firms Go Dark? Causes and Economic Consequences of Voluntary SEC Deregistrations. Journal of Accounting and Economics 45, 181–208.

Levy, G., 2004. Computational Finance: Numerical Methods for Pricing Financial Instruments. Elsevier, Butterworth–Heinemann, New York.

Lichtenberg, F. R., Siegel, D., 1990. The Effects of lbos on Productivity and Related Aspects of Firm Behavior. Journal of Financial Economics 27, 165–194.

Linck, J. S., Netter, J. M., Yang, T., 2008. The Determinants of Board Structure. Journal of Financial Economics 87, 308–328.

Lindell, C. K., 2006. More Merger Reviews, Fewer Hurdles. Law and Regulation.

Lindsay, D., Campbell, A., 1996. A Chaos Approach to Bankruptcy Prediction. Journal of Applied Business Research 12, 1–9.

Linn, S. C., McConnell, J. J., 1983. An Empirical Investigation of the Impact of Anti-Takeover Amendments on Common Stock Prices. Journal of Financial Economics 11, 361–399.

Linn, S. C., Rozeff, M. S., 1984. The Corporate Sell-off. Midland Corporate Finance Journal 2, Summer, 17–26.

Linn, S. C., Switzer, J. A., 2001. Are Cash Acquisitions Associated with Better Post Combination Operating Performance Than Stock Acquisitions. Journal of Banking and Finance 25, 1113–1138.

Lins, K. V., 2004. Equity Ownership and Firm Value in Emerging Markets. Journal of Financial and Quantitative Analysis 38, 159–184.

Lins, K., Servaes, H., 1999. International Evidence on the Value of Corporate Diversification. Journal of Finance 54, 2215–2239.

Liu, J., Nissim, D., Thomas, J. K., 2002. Equity valuation using multiples. Journal of Accounting Research 40 (1), 135–172.

Liu, J., Nissim, D., Thomas, J., 2007. Is Cash Flow King in Valuations? Financial Analysts Journal 63, 56–65.

Logue, D. E., Seward, J. K., Walsh, J. W., 1996. Rearranging Residual Claims: A Case for Targeted Stock. Financial Management 25, Spring, 43–61.

Loh, C., Bezjak, J. R., Toms, H., 1995. Voluntary Corporate Divestitures as an Anti-Takeover Mechanism. Financial Review 30, 21–24.

Longstaff, F. A., 1995. How Can Marketability Affect Security Values. Journal of Finance 50, 1767–1774.

Longstaff, F. A., Schwartz, E. S., 1995. A Simple Approach to Valuing Risky Fixed and Floating Rate Debt. Journal of Finance 50, 789–819.

Loomis, C. J., 2001. Sandy Weill's Monster. Fortune, 107–110.

Lopucki, L. M., Doherty, J. W., 2007. The Determinants of Professional Fees in Large Bankruptcy Reorganization Cases Revisited. UCLA School of Law, Law-Econ Research Paper No. 06-16, Second Annual Conference on Empirical Legal Studies Paper, July 1.

Lorange, P., Roos, J., 1992. Strategic Alliances: Formation, Implementation, and Evolution. Blackwell, Oxford, UK.

Lord, M. D., Ranft, A. L., 2000. Acquiring New Knowledge: The Role of Retaining Human Capital in Acquisitions of High Tech Firms. Journal of High Technology Management Research 11, Autumn, 295–320.

Loss, L., Seligman, J., 1995. Fundamentals of Securities Regulation, third ed. Little, Brown, Boston.

Loughran, T., Ritter, J., 2002. Why Don't Issuers Get Upset about Leaving Money on the Table in IPOs? Review of Financial Studies 15, 413–443.

Loughran, T., Ritter, J., Rydqvist, K., 1994. Initial Public Offerings: International Insights. Pacific Basin Finance Journal 2, 165–199.

Loughran, T., Anand, M., Vijh, 1997. Do Long-Term Shareholders Benefit from Corporate Acquisitions? Journal of Finance 22, 321–340.

Lovley, E., 2007. How Troubled Firms Skip Bankruptcy Court. Wall St. J. p. C2.

Lowenstein, L., 1985. Management Buyouts. Columbia Law Review 85, 730–784.

Lowenstein, L., 1987. What's Wrong with Wall Street? Addison-Wesley, Reading, MA.

Lyon, J. D., Barber, B. M., Tsai, C. L., 1999. Improved Methods for Tests of Long-Run Abnormal Stock Returns, Journal of Finance 54, 165–201.

Lynch, R. P., 1990. The Practical Guide to Joint Ventures and Corporate Alliances. John Wiley & Sons, New York.

Lynch, R. P., 1993. Business Alliance Guide: The Hidden Competitive Weapon. John Wiley & Sons, New York.

M

Madura, J., Whyte, A., 1990. Diversification Benefits of Direct Foreign Investment. Management International Review 30, 73–85.

Maguire, S., Phillips, N., 2008. Citibankers at Citigroup: A Study of the Loss on Institutional Trust after a Merger. Journal of Management Studies 45, 372–401.

Maher, J., 1976. Michael, Discounts for Lack of Marketability for Closely Held Business Interests. Taxes 54, 562–571.

Maier, A., Atzler, E., 2006. Hedge Funds Seek Private Equity. Financial Times Deutschland.

Maksimovic, V., Phillips, G. M., 2001. The Market for Corporate Assets: Who Engages in Mergers and Asset Sales and Are There Efficiency Gains. Journal of Finance, 332–355.

Malatesta, P. H., Walkling, R. A., 1988. Poison Pills Securities: Stockholder Wealth, Profitability and Ownership Structure. Journal of Financial Economics 20, 347–376.

Malekzadeh, A. R., Nahavandi, A., 1990. Making Mergers Work by Managing Cultures. Journal of Business Strategy 11, 55–57.

Malekzadeh, A. R., McWilliams, V. B., Sen, N., 1998. Implications of CEO Structural and Ownership Power, Ownership, and Board Composition on the Market's Reaction to antitakeover Charter Amendments. Journal of Applied Business Research 14, 53–62.

Mallea, J., 2008. A Review of Mergers of Equals. FactSetmergermetrics.com.

Mangenheim, E. B., Mueller, D. C., 1988. Are Acquiring Firm Shareholders Better off after an Acquisition. In: Coffee Jr., J., Lowenstein, L., Rose-Ackerman, S. (Eds.), Knight, Raiders, and Targets. Oxford University Press, Oxford, England, pp. 171–193.

Manzon, K. G. K., Sharp, D. J., Travlos, N., 1994. An Empirical Study of the Consequences of U.S. Tax Rules for International Acquisitions by U.S. Firms. Journal of Finance 49, 1893–1904.

Maquierira, C. P., Megginson, W. L., Nail, L. A., 1998. Wealth Creation versus Wealth Redistributions in Pure Stock-for-Stock Mergers. Journal of Financial Economics 48, 3–33.

Marciukaityte, D., Roskelley, K., Wang, H., 2009. Strategic Alliances by Financial Services Firms. Journal of Business Research.

Markides, C., Oyon, D., 1998. International Acquisitions: Do They Create Value for Shareholders? European Management Journal 16, 125–135.

Marks, M. L., 1996. From Turmoil to Triumph: New Life after Mergers, Acquisitions, and Downsizing. Lexington Books, Lanham, MD.

Marks, S. G., Samuelson, W. F., 2003. Managerial Economics, fourth ed. John Wiley & Sons, New York.

Martynova, M., Renneboog, L., 2008a. A Century of Corporate Takeovers: What Have We Learned and Where Do We Stand? Journal of Banking and Finance.

Martynova, M., Renneboog, L., 2008b. Spillover of Corporate Governance Standards in Cross-Border Mergers and Acquisitions. ECGI-Finance Working Paper No. 197/2008, SSRN http://ssrn.com/abstract=1094661

Massari, M., Monge, V., Zanetti, L., 2006. Control Premium in the Presence of Rules Imposing Mandatory Tender Offers: Can It Be Measured. Journal of Management and Governance 101–110.

Masulis, R. W., Wang, C., Xie, F., 2007. Corporate Governance and Acquirer Returns. Journal of Finance 62, 1851–1890.

Masulis, R. W., Wang, C., Xie, F., 2009. Agency Problems at Dual-Class Companies. Journal of Finance Forthcoming.

Maxwell, W. F., Rao, R. P., 2003. Do Spin-offs Expropriate Wealth from Bondholders, Journal of Finance 58 (5), 2087–2108.

McCarthy, P., 1998. Legal Aspects of Acquiring U.S. Enterprises. In: BenDaniel, D. J., A. H. Rosenbloom (Eds.), International M&A, Joint Ventures & Beyond: Doing the Deal. Wiley & Sons, New York, pp. 27–57.

McCartney, S., 2001. Flying lessons. Wall Street J. p. 1.

McConnell, J. J., Nantell, T. J., June 1985. Corporate Combinations and Common Stock Returns: The Case of Joint Ventures. Journal of Finance 40, 519–536.

McConnell, J. J., Ozbilgin, M., Wahal, S., 2001. Spin-Offs: Ex Ante. Journal of Business 74, 245–280.

McKinsey & Company, 1990. Creating Shareholder Value through Merger and/or Acquisition: A McKinsey & Company Perspective. An internal 1987 memorandum cited in Copeland T., Koller, T., Murrin, J. (Eds.), Valuation: Measuring and Managing the Value of Companies. John Wiley & Sons, New York, p. 321.

McKinsey & Co., 1999. Spin-offs May Overshadow Other Investments. Bus. Week, 196–197.

McKinsey & Co., 2008. Making the Board More Strategic: A McKinsey Global Survey. McKinsey Quarterly.

McNamara, G., Dykes, B. J. Haleblian, J., 2008. The Performance Implications of Participating in an Acquisition Wave. Acad Manage J.

McNatt, R., 2000. Chrysler Not Quite So Equal. Bus. Week.

McNeil, C. R., Moore, W. T., 2005. Dismantling Internal Capital Markets via Spin-Off: Effects on Capital Allocation Efficiency and Firm Valuation. Journal of Corporate Finance 11, 253–275.

McWilliams, V. B., 1993. Tobin's Q and the Stock Price Effects of Anti-Takeover Amendment Proposals. Financial Management 22, 16–18.

Megginson, W. L., Morgan, A., Nail, L., 2003. The Determinants of Positive Long-term Performance in Strategic Mergers: Corporate Focus and Cash. Journal of Banking and Finance.

Mehran, H., Peristiani, S., 2006. Financial Visibility and the Decision to Go Private. Working Paper, April. Federal Reserve Bank of New York, April.

Melicher, R. W., Norton, E. A., 1999. Finance: Introduction to Institutions, Investments, and Management. Southwestern College Publishing, Mason, OH.

Mercer, C., 1997. The Management Panning Study, Quantifying Marketability Discounts. Peabody Publishing, New York.

Mercer Management Consulting, 1998. 1995 and 1997 Surveys. Cited in Lajoux, A. R. (Eds.), The Art of M&A Integration. McGraw-Hill, New York.

Mergerstat, L. P., 2002. Dealmakers Hope for Better Days Ahead in 2002. Press release, www.mergerstat.com

Mergerstat, G. M., Information, A., 2005. Mergerstat Review. Santa Monica, CA.

Mergerstat Review, 1988. p. 85.

Mergerstat Review, 2001. p. 38.

Mergerstat Review, 2007. p. 22.

Metrick, A., Yasuda, A., 2007. The Economics of Private Equity Funds. University of Pennsylvania Wharton School of Finance Working Paper.

Meuleman, M., Wright, M., 2007. Industry Concentration, Syndication Networks and Competition in the UK Private Equity Market. CMBOR Working Paper.

Meyer, K. E., Estrin, S., Bhaumik, S., 2005. Institutions and Business Strategies in Emerging Economies: A Study of Entry Mode Choice. Working Paper, London Business School.

Mian, S., Rosenfeld, J., 1993. Takeover Activity and the Long-Run Performance of Reverse Leveraged Buyouts. Financial Management 22, Winter, 46–57.

Michaely, R., Shaw, W. H., 1995. The Choice of Going Public: Spin-offs vs. Carve-Outs. Financial Management 24, Autumn, 15–21.

Miles, J., Rosenfeld, J., 1983. An Empirical Analysis of the Effects of Spin-off Announcements on Shareholder Wealth. Journal of Finance 38, 15–28.

Mishra, D., O'Brien, T., 2001. A Comparison of Cost of Equity Estimates of Local and Global capms. Financial Review 36, 27–48.

Mitchell, D., 1998. Survey conducted by Economist Intelligence Unit, cited in Lajoux, A. R. (Eds.), The Art of M&A Integration. McGraw-Hill, New York, p. 19.

Mitchell, M. L., Mulherin, J. H., 1996. The Impact of Industry Shocks on Takeover and Restructuring Activity. Journal of Financial Economics 41, 193–229.

Mitchell, M. L., Pulvino, T. C., 2001. Characteristics of Risk and Return in Arbitrage. Journal of Finance 56, 2135–2175.

Mitchell, M., Pulvino, T., Stafford, E., 2004. Price Pressure around Mergers. Journal of Finance 31–63.

Moeller, S. B., Schlingemann, F. P., 2002. Are Cross-Border Acquisitions Different from Domestic Acquisitions? Evidence on Stock and Operating Performance for U.S. Acquirers. University of Pittsburgh Working Paper.

Moeller, S. B., Schlingemann, F. P., Stulz, R. M., 2004. Firm Size and the Gains from Acquisitions. Journal of Financial Economics 73, 201–228.

Moeller, S. B., Schlingemann, F. P., Stulz, R. M., 2005. Wealth Destruction on a Massive Scale? A Study of the Acquiring Firm Returns in the Recent Merger Wave. Journal of Finance 60, 757–782.

Moeller, S. B., Schlingemann, F. P., Stulz, R. M., 2007. How Do Diversity of Opinion and Information Asymmetry Affect Acquirer Returns. Review of Financial Studies 20, 2047–2078.

Molina, C. A., 2006. Are Firms Unleveraged? An Examination of the Effect of Leverage on Default Probabilities. Journal of Finance 60, 1427–1459.

Moonchul, K., Ritter, J. R., 1999. Valuing IPOs. Journal of Financial Economics 53, 409–437.

Morck, R., Shleifer, A., Vishny, R. W., 1988. Characteristics of Targets of Hostile and Friendly Takeovers. In: Auerbach, A. J. (Ed.), Corporate Takeovers: Causes and Consequences. University of Chicago Press, Chicago.

Morck, R., Shleifer, A., Vishny, R. W., 1990. Do Managerial Objectives Drive Bad Acquisitions? Journal of Finance 45, 31–48.

Morck, R., Yeung, B., 1991. Why Investors Value Multinationality. Journal of Business 64, 165–188.

Morck, R., Yeung, B., 2000. Inherited Wealth, Corporate Control, and Economic Growth: The Canadian Experience. In: Morck, R. (Ed.), Concentrated Corporate Ownership. National Bureau of Economic Research, Cambridge, MA, pp. 319–369.

Morellec, E., Zhdanov, A., 2008. Financing and Takeovers. Journal of Financial Economics 87, 556–581.

Moroney, R. E., 1973. Most Courts Overvalue Closely Held Stocks. Taxes 144–154.

Morosoni, P., Shane, S., Singh, H., 1998. National Cultural Distance and Cross-Border Acquisition Performance. Journal of International Business Studies 29, 137–156.

Morrow, D. J., 1988. Why the IRS Might Love Those lbos. Fortune 145–146.

Moyer, C. R., McGuigan, J. R., Kretlow, W. J., 1998. Contemporary Financial Management. SouthWestern College Publishing, Mason, OH.

Mueller, D., 1985. Mergers and Market Share. Review of Economics and Statistics 47, 259–267.

Mulherin, J. H., Boone, A. L., 2000. Comparing Acquisitions and Divestitures. Social Science Research Network Working Paper Series, p. 38.

Mulherin, J. H., Poulsen, A. B., 1998. Proxy Contests and Corporate Change: Implications for Shareholder Wealth. Journal of Financial Economics 47, 279–313.

Mun, J., 2006. Modeling Risk: Applying Monte Carlo Simulation, Real Option Analysis, Forecasting, and Optimization. Wiley & Sons, New York.

Murray, M., 2001. GE's Honeywell Deal Is More Than the Sum of Airplane Parts. Wall St. J. p. B6.

Muscarella, C. J., Vetsuypens, M. R., 1990. Efficiency and Organizational Structure: A Study of Reverse lbos. Journal of Finance 45, 1389–1413.

Myer, S., Majluf, N., 1984. Corporate Financing and Investment Decisions when Firms Have Information Investors Do Not Have. Journal of Financial Economics 13, 187–211.

N

Navarro, E., 2005. Merger Control in the EU: Law, Economics, and Practice, second ed. Oxford University Press, Oxford, England.

New York Times, 2001. The Spread of Antitrust Authorities. Section 3, p. 4.

Nelson, B., 2004. The lbo Method. Forbes 173 (13), 187–190.

Nenova, T., The Value of Corporate Voting Rights and Control: A Cross-Country Analysis. Journal of Financial Economics 68, 325–351.

Newbould, G. D., Chatfield, R. E., Anderson, R. F., 1992. Leveraged Buyouts and Tax Incentives, Financial Management 21, 1621–1637.

Nixon, T. D., Roenfeldt, R. L., Sicherman, N. W., 2000. The Choice between Spin-offs and Sell-Offs. Review of Quantitative Finance and Accounting 14, 277–288.

O

Oesterle, D. A., 2006. Mergers and Acquisitions in a Nutshell, third edition. West Publishing, St. Paul, MN.

Ofek, E., 1993. Capital Structure and Firm Response to Poor Performance: An Empirical Analysis. Journal of Financial Economics 34, 3–30.

Ofek, E., 1994. Efficiency Gains in Unsuccessful Management Buyouts. Journal of Finance 49, 627–654.

Offenberg, D., 2008. Firm Size and The Effectiveness of the Market for Corporate Control. Journal of Corporate Finance.

Officer, M. S., 2003. Termination Fees in Mergers and Acquisitions. Journal of Financial Economics 69, 431–467.

Officer, M. S., 2004. Collars and Renegotiation in Mergers and Acquisitions. Journal of Finance 59, 2719–2743.

Officer, M. S., 2007. The Price of Corporate Liquidity: Acquisition Discounts for Unlisted Targets. Journal of Financial Economics.

Officer, M. S., Ozbas, O., Sensoy, B. A., 2008. Club Deals in Leveraged Buyouts. Available at SSRN, http://ssrn.com/abstract=1128404

Officer, M. S., Poulsen, A. B., Stegemoller, M., 2009. Information Asymmetry and Acquirer Returns. Review of Finance forthcoming.

Ohlson, J. A., 1980. Financial Ratios and the Probabilistic Prediction of Bankruptcy. Journal of Accounting Research 109–131.

Oliver, R. P. I., Meyers, R. H., 2000. Discounts Seen in Private Placements of Restricted Stock. Chapter 5. In: Reilly, R.F., Schweihs, R. P. (Eds.), Handbook of Advanced Business Valuation, McGraw-Hill, New York.

Opler, T., Titman, S., 1993. The Determinants of Leveraged Buyout Activity: Free Cash Flow vs. Financial Distress Costs. Journal of Finance 48, 1985–2000.

Oppenheimer & Company, 1981. The Sum of the Parts. Oppenheimer & Company, New York.

P

Page, M., 2006. Beth, Done Deal, Your Guide to Mergers and Acquisitions Due Diligence. Authenticity Press, Chicago.

Palepu, K. G., Healy, P. M., Bernard, V. L., 2004. Business Analysis and Valuation, third ed. Thomson, Skokie, IL.

Palter, R. N., Srinivasan, D., 2006. Habits of the Busiest Acquirers. McKinsey Quarterly.

Pan, Y., Chi, P. S. K., 1999. Financial Performance and Survival of Multinational Corporations in China. Strategic Management Journal 20, 359–374.

Pan, Y., Tse, D. K., 2000. The Hierarchical Model of Market Entry Modes. Journal of International Business Studies 31, 535–554.

Pan, Y., Li, S., Tse, D., 1999. The Impact of Order and Mode of Entry on Profitability and Market Share. Journal of International Business Studies 30, 81–104.

Park, S. H., Ungson, G. R., 1997. The Effect of National Culture, Organizational Complementarity, and Economic Motivation on Joint Venture Dissolution. Academy of Management Journal 40, 279–307.

Pastor, L., Stambaugh, R. F., 2001. The Equity Premium and Structural Breaks. Journal of Finance 56, 1207–1239.

Pay, Y., Li, S., Tse, K. K., 1999. The Impact of Order and Mode of Market Entry on Profitability and Market Share. Journal of International Business Studies 30, 81–104.

Pehrsson, A., 2008. Strategy Antecedents of Mode of Entry into Foreign Markets. Journal of Business Research 61, 132–140.

Peng, M. W., 2003. Institutional Transitions and Strategic Choices. Acad. Manage. Rev. 28, 275–296.

Peng, M. W., Lee, S. H., Lang, D. Y. L., 2005. What Determines the Scope of the Firm over Time? A Focus on Institutional Relatedness. Acad. Manage. Rev. 30, 622–633.

Perez-Gonzalez, F., 2006. Inherited Control and Firm Performance. American Economic Review.

Pergola, T. M., 2005. Management Entrenchment: Can It Negate the Effectiveness of Recently Legislated Governance Reforms? Journal of American Academy of Business 6, 177–185.

Petty, J. W., Keown, A. J., Scott, D. F., Jr., Martin, J. D., 1993. Basic Financial Management, sixth ed. Prentice-Hall, Englewood Cliffs, NJ, 798.

Phan, P. H., 1995. Organizational Restructuring and Economic Performance in Leveraged Buyouts: An Ex Post Study. Acad. Manage. J. 38, 704–739.

Pinkowitz, L., 2002. The Market for Corporate Control and Corporate Cash Holdings. Working Paper, Georgetown University.

Platt, D., Platt, B., Yang, Z., 1999. Probabilistic Neural Networks in Bankruptcy Prediction. Journal of Business Research 44, 67–74.

Porter, M. E., 1985. Competitive Advantage. The Free Press, New York.

Porter, R., Wood, C. N., 1998. Post-merger Integration. In: BenDaniel, D. J., Rosenbloom, A. H., (Eds.), International M&A, Joint Ventures & Beyond: Doing the Deal. Wiley & Sons, New York, pp. 459–477.

Poulsen, A., Stegemoller, M., 2002. Transitions from Private to Public Ownership,. Working Paper, University of Georgia.

Poulsen, A., Stegemoller, M., 2007. Moving from Private to Public Ownership: Selling out to Public Firms versus Initial Public Offerings. Financial Management.

Powers, E. A., 2001. Spinoffs, Selloffs, and Equity Carveouts: An Analysis of Divestiture Method Choice, Social Science Research Network. Working Paper Series, pp. 2–4.

Powers, E. A., 2003. Deciphering the Motives for Equity Carve-Outs. Journal of Financial Research 26 (1), Spring, 31–50.

Pratt, S., 1998. Cost of Capital: Estimation and Applications. John Wiley & Sons, New York.

Pratt, S. Niculita, A., 2008. Valuing a Business: The Analysis and Appraisal of Closely Held Businesses. McGraw-Hill, New York.

Pratt, S. P., Reilly, R. F., Scheweihs, R. P., 1995. Valuing a Business: The Analysis and Appraisal of Closely Held Companies, third ed. Irwin Professional Publishers, Toronto.

Prezas, A., Tarmicilar, M., Vasudevan, G., 2000. The Pricing of Equity Carve-Outs. Financial Review 35, 123–138.

PriceWaterhouseCoopers, Mergers and Acquisitions, 2006. A Global Tax Guide. Wiley & Sons, New York.

Pursche, W. A., 1996. Pharmaceuticals—The Consolidation Isn't Over. McKinsey Quarterly 2, 110–119.

R

Raff, H., Ryan, M., Staehler, F., 2006. Asset Ownership and Foreign-Market Entry. CESifo Working Paper No. 1676, Category 7: Trade Policy, February.

Raff, H., Ryan, M., Staehler, F., 2008. Firm Productivity and Foreign Market Entry Decision. Christian-Albrechts-Universitat Kiel, New Zealand. Economics Working Paper, No. 2008-02.

Rajan, R., Servaes, H., Zingales, L., 2000. The Cost of Diversity: The Diversification Discount and Inefficient Investment. Journal of Finance 55, 35–38.

Rappaport, A., 1990. The Staying Power of the Public Corporation. Harv. Bus. Rev. 76-1-4.

Rau, P. R., Vermaelen, T., 1998. Glamour, Value, and the Post-Acquisition Performance of Acquiring Firms. Journal of Financial Economics 49, 223–253.

Ravenscraft, D., Scherer, F., 1987. Life after Takeovers. Journal of Industrial Economics 36, 147–156.

Ravenscraft, D., Scherer, F., 1988. Mergers and Managerial Performance. In: Coffee, J., Lowenstein, L., Ackerman, S. R. (Eds.), Knights and Targets. Oxford University Press, New York, pp. 194–210.

Ravenscroft, D. J., Scherer, F. M., 1991. Divisional Sell-Off: A Hazard Function Analysis. Managerial and Decision Economics 12, 429–438.

Renneboog, L., Simons, T., Wright, M., 2007. Why Do Public Firms Go Private in the U.K.? Journal of Corporate Finance 13, 591–628.

Renneboog, L., Szilagyi, P., 2006. How Do Mergers and Acquisitions Affect Bondholders in Europe? Evidence on the Impact and Spillover of Governance and Legal Standards. ECGI Finance Working Paper 125.

Renneboog, L., Szilagyi, P., 2007. Corporate Restructuring and Bondholder Wealth. European Financial Management 14, 792–819.

Rezaee, Z., 2009. Corporate Governance and Ethics. Wiley and Sons, New York.

Rhodes-Kropf, M., Viswanathan, S., 2004. Market Valuation and Merger Waves. Journal of Finance 59.

Richtel, M., 2008. Hewlett-Packard Is Facing Skepticism on E. D. S. Deal. New York Times nytimes.com

Rickertsen, R., 2001. Buyout: The Insider's Guide to Buying Your Own Company. AMACOM, New York.

Ritter, J., 1991. The Long-Run Performance of Initial Public Offerings. Journal of Finance 46, 3–27.

Robinson, A., 2002a. Is Corporate Governance the Solution or the Problem? Corporate Board 23, 12–16.

Robinson, D. T., 2002b. Strategic Alliances and the Boundaries of the Firm. Working Paper. Columbia University.

Roll, R., 1986. The Hubris Hypothesis of Corporate Takeovers. Journal of Business 59, 197–216.

Romano, R., 1993. Competition for Corporate Charters and the Lesson of Takeover Statutes. Fordham Law Rev. 61, 843–864.

Romano, R., 2001. Less Is More: Making Institutional Investor Activism a Valuable Mechanism of Corporate Governance. Yale Journal of Regulation 18, 174–251.

Rosenbloom, A. H. (Ed.), 2002. Due Diligence for Global Deal Making: The Definitive Guide to Cross-Border Mergers and Acquisitions, Joint Ventures, Financings, and Strategic Alliances. Bloomberg Press, Princeton, NJ.

Rossi, S., Volpin, P. F., 2004. Cross-Country Determinants of Mergers and Acquisitions. ECGI- Finance Working Paper No. 25/2003, AFA 2004 San Diego Meetings, September.

Ruback, R. S., 2002. Capital Cash Flows: A Simple Approach to Valuing Risky Cash Flows. Financial Management Summer, 85–103.

Ryngaert, M., 1988. The Effects of Poison Pill Securities on Stockholder Wealth. Journal of Financial Economics 20, 377–417.

S

Safavian, M., Sharma, S., 2007. When Do Creditor Rights Matter? Journal of Comparative Economics 35, 484–508.

Salter, M. S., Weinhold, W. A., 1979. Diversification through Acquisition: Strategies for Creating Economic Value. The Free Press, New York.

Sanderson, S., Uzumeri, M., 1997. The Innovative Imperative: Strategies for Managing Products, Models, and Families. Irwin Professional, Publishing, Burr Ridge, IL.

Savor, P. G., Lu, Q., 2009. Do Stock Mergers Create Value for Acquirers? Journal of Finance forthcoming.

Scannell, K., Ng, S., MacDonald, A., 2006. Can Anyone Police Swaps. Wall St. J. pp. C1–C2.

Scharfstein, D., Stein, J., 2000. The Dark Side of Internal Capital Markets: Divisional Rent-Seeking and Inefficient Investment. Journal of Finance 55, 2537–2564.

Schenker, J. L., 2008. Nokia makes its power play. Bus. Week pp. 30–31.

Scherer, P. M., Scannell, K., 2000. Deals and Deal Makers. Wall St. J. pp. 17.

Scherreik, S., 2002. Gems among the Trash, Bus. Week pp. 112–113.

Schipper, K., Smith, A., 1983. Effects of Re-Contracting on Shareholder Wealth, Journal of Financial Economics 12, 437–467.

Schipper, K., Smith, A., 1986. A Comparison of Equity Carve-outs and Equity Offerings: Share Price Effects and Corporate Restructuring. Journal of Financial Economics 15, 153–186.

Schmid, R. E., 2001. Post Office, FedEx Become Partners. Orange County Register, Business Section, p. 2.

Schor, M., Greenwood, R., 2007. Investor Activism and Takeovers. http://ssrn.com/abstracts=1003792

Schweiger, D. M., 2002. M&A Integration: Framework for Executives and Managers. McGraw-Hill, New York.

Schwert, W., 1996. Markup Pricing in Mergers and Acquisitions. Journal of Financial Economics 41, 153–192.

Schwert, G., 2000. William, Hostility in Takeovers: In the Eyes of the Bidder? Journal of Finance 55, 2599–2640.

Selim, G., 2003. Mergers, Acquisitions and Divestitures: Control and Audit Best Practices. Institute of Internal Auditing Research Foundation, New York.

Sender, H., 2006. High Risk Debt Still Has Allure for Buyout Deals. Wall St. J. p. C2.

Sengupta, C., 2004. Financial Modeling Using Excel and VBA. Wiley & Sons, New York.

Seoungpil, A., Denis, D. J., 2004. Internal Capital Market and Investment Policy: Evidence of Corporate Spin-Offs. Journal of Financial Economics 71, 489–516.

Servaes, H., Zenner, M., 1994. Taxes and the Returns to Foreign Acquisitions in the U.S. Financial Management 23, 42–56.

Seth, A., Song, K. P., Petit, R., 2000. Synergy, Managerialism or Hubris: An Empirical Examination of Motives for Foreign Acquisitions of U.S. Firms. Journal of International Business Studies 31, 387–405.

Seth, A., Song, K. P., Petit, R., 2002. Value Creation and Destruction in Cross-Border Acquisitions: An Empirical Analysis of Foreign Acquisitions of U.S. Firms. Strategic Management 23, 921–940.

Shahrur, H., 2005. Industry Structure and Horizontal Takeovers: Analysis of Wealth Effects on Rivals, Suppliers, and Corporate Customers. Journal of Financial Economics 76, 61–98.

Shapiro, A. C., 2005. Foundations of Multinational Financial Management, fifth ed. John Wiley & Sons, New York.

Sherman, D. H., David Young, S., 2001. Tread Lightly Through These Accounting Minefields. Harv. Bus. Rev. 129–137.

Sherman, A., 2006. Mergers and Acquisitions from A to Z: Strategic and Practical Guidance for Small- and Middle-Market Buyers and Sellers, second ed. AMACOM, New York.

Shin, H. H., Stulz, R., 1998. Are Internal Capital Markets Efficient? Quarterly Journal of Economics 113, 531–552.

Shivdasani, A., 1993. Board Composition, Ownership Structure, and Hostile Takeovers. Journal of Accounting and Economics 16, 167–198.

Shleifer, A., Vishny, R., 1997. A Survey of Corporate Governance. The Journal of Finance 52, 737–784.

Shleifer, A., Vishny, R. W., 2003. Stock Market Driven Acquisitions. Journal of Financial Economics 70, 295–311.

Shreve, S., 2005. Stochastic Calculus for Finance: The Binomial Asset Pricing Model. Springer Publishing, New York.

Shumway, T., 2001. Forecasting Bankruptcy More Accurately: A Simple Hazard Model. Journal of Business 74, 101–124.

Shuttleworth, R., 2004. Twelve Keys to Venture Capital. Tech Coast Angels, http://techcoastangels.com

Sicherman, N. W., Pettway, R. H., 1992. Wealth Effects for Buyers and Sellers for the Same Divested Assets. Financial Management 21, 119–128.

Silber, W. L., 1991. Discounts on Restricted Stocks: The Impact of Illiquidity on Stock Prices. Financial Analysts Journal 47, 60–64.

Siliconix Inc., 2001. Shareholders Litigation, Delaware Court, C.A., No. 18700, July 19.

Singh, H., Montgomery, C., 2008. Corporate Acquisition Strategies and Economic Performance. Strategic Management Journal 8, 377–386.

Sirower, M., 1997. The Synergy Trap. The Free Press, New York.

Skantz, T., Marchesini, R., 1987. The Effect of Voluntary Corporate Liquidation on Shareholder Wealth. Journal of Financial Research 10, Spring, 65–75.

Sloan, R. G., 1996. Do Stock Prices Fully Reflect Information in Accruals and Cash Flows about Future Earnings. Accounting Review 289–315.

Slovin, M. B., Sushka, M. E., Polonchek, J. A., 2005. Methods of Payment in Asset Sales: Contracting with Equity versus Cash. Journal of Finance 60, 2385–2407.

Smith, A., 1990. Corporate Ownership Structure and Performance: The Case of Management Buy-Outs. Journal of Financial Economics 27, 143–164.

Smith, C. W., 1993. A Perspective on Accounting Based Debt Covenant Violations. Accounting Review 68, 289–303.

Solomon, D., 2001. AT&T Prepares Its Cable-Access Program. Wall St. J. p. C1.

Song, H. H., Walking, R. A., 2000. Abnormal Returns to Rivals of Acquisitions Targets: A Test of the Acquisition Probability Hypothesis. Journal of Financial Economics 55, 439–457.

Sorensen, M., Stromberg, P., Lerner, J., 2008. Private Equity and Long-Run Investment: The Case of Innovation. http://ssrn.com/abstract=1088543

Srikant, D., Frankel, R., Wolfson, M., 2001. Earnouts: The Effects of Adverse Selection and Agency Costs on Acquisition Techniques. Journal of Law, Economics, and Organization 17, 201–238.

Standard Research Consultants, 1983. Revenue Ruling 77-287 Revisited. SRC Quarterly Reports 1-3, Spring.

Stefanini, F., 2006. Investment Strategies of Hedge Funds. John Wiley & Sons, New York.

Stickney, C. P., Brown, P. R., Wahlen, J. M., 2007. Financial Reporting, Financial Statement Analysis, and Valuation, sixth ed. Thomson SouthWestern, Mason, OH.

Stout, L. A., 2002. Do Antitakeover Defenses Decrease Shareholder Wealth? The Ex Post/Ex Ante Valuation Problem. Stanford Law Rev. 845–861.

Stowe, J. D., Robinson, T. R., Pinto, J. E., McLeavey, D. W., 2007. Equity Asset Valuation. John Wiley & Sons, Hoboken, NJ.

Stromberg, P., 2008. The New Demography of Private Equity. In: Globalization of Alternative Investments, Working Paper, Vol. 1, The Global Economic Impact of Private Equity Report, World Economic Forum, pp. 3–26.

Stromfeld v. Great Atlantic & Pacific Tea Company, 484F. Supplement, 1264 (S.D.N.Y. 1980), aff'd 6464 F.2d 563 (2nd Circuit 1980).

Stryker, S. C., 1986. Plan to Succeed: A Guide to Strategic Planning. Petrocelli Books, Princeton, NJ.

Stulz, R. M., 1995a. Globalization of the Capital Markets and the Cost of Capital: The Case of Nestle. Journal of Applied Corporate Finance 8, 30–38.

Stulz, R. M., 1995b. The Cost of Capital in Internationally Integrated Markets: The Case of Nestle. European Financial Management 1, 11–22.

Stulz, R. M., Wasserfallen, W., 1995. Foreign Equity Invest Restrictions, Capital Flight, and Shareholder Wealth Maximization: Theory and Evidence. Review of Financial Studies 8, Winter, 1019–1057.

Sullivan, M. J., Jensen, M. R. H., Hudson, C. D., 1994. The Role of Medium of Exchange in Merger Offers: Examination of Terminated Merger Proposals. Financial Management 23, 51–62.

Sweeney, P., 1999. Who Says It's a Fair Deal? Journal of Accountancy 188, 6.

Sweeney, P., 2005. Gap. Financial Executives Magazine 33–40.

T

Tam, P. W., 2003. An Elaborate Plan Forces HHP Union to Stay on Target. Wall St. J. p. 1.

Tang, C. Y., Tikoo, S., 1999. Operational Flexibility and Market Valuation of Earnings. Strategic Management Journal 20, 749–761.

Tashjian, E., Lease, R., McConnell, J. J., 1996. Prepacks: An Empirical Analysis of Prepackaged Bankruptcies. Journal of Financial Economics 40, 135–162.

The Deal, 2006. February 6–10.

Thompson, S. C., 2007. Business Planning for Mergers and Acquisitions. Carolina Academic Press, Durham, NC.

Thompson Financial Securities Data Corporation, 2000. The World's Urge to Merge. Press release, January 5.

Tierney, C., 2000. Can Schremp Stop the Careening at Chrysler? Bus. Week p. 40.

Tillinghast, D. R., 1998. Tax Aspects of Inbound Merger and Acquisitions and Joint Venture Transactions. In: BenDaniel, D. J., Rosenbloom, A. H. (Eds.), International M&A, Joint Ventures and Beyond: Doing the Deal. John Wiley & Sons, New York, pp. 151–180.

Travlos, N. G., Cornett, M. N., 1993. Going Private Buyouts and Determinants of Shareholders' Returns. Journal of Accounting, Auditing and Finance 8, 1–25.

Trout, R. R., 1977. Estimation of the Discount Associated with the Transfer of Restricted Securities, Taxes 55, 381–385.

Truitt, W. B., 2001. Business Planning: A Comprehensive Framework and Process. Greenwood Publishing, Westport CT.

Truitt, W. B., 2006. The Corporation. Greenwood Press, Westport, CT.

U

Uhlaner, R. T., West, A. S., 2008. Running a Winning M&A Shop. McKinsey Quarterly.

United States V. Primestar, L. P., 58 Fed Register, 33944, June 22, 1993 (Proposed Final Judgment and Competitive Impact Study).

United States Attorney General, 2000. Global Antitrust Regulation: Issues and Solutions. Final Report of the International Competition Policy Advisory Committee.

United States Department of Justice, 1999. Antitrust Division. www.usdoj.gov

United States General Accountability Office, 2008. Private Equity: Recent Growth in Leveraged Buyouts Exposes Risk. GAO-08-885.

United States Small Business Administration, 1999. Financial Difficulties of Small Businesses and Reasons for Their Failure. Office of Advocacy, RS 188.

United States Small Business Administration, 2003. State small business profile. Office of Advocacy.

Unocal v. Mesa, 493 A.2d 949, (Del. 1985).

Uysal, V., 2006. Deviation from the Target Capital Structure and Acquisition Choices. University of Oklahoma, Working Paper.

V

Vachon, M., 1993. Venture capital reborn. Venture Capital Journal, p. 32.

Vasconcellos, G. M., Kish, R. J., 1998. Cross-border Mergers and Acquisitions: The European-U.S. Experience. Journal of Multinational Financial Management 8, p. 173–189.

Vasconcellos, G. M., Madura, J., Kish, R. J., 1990. An Empirical investigation of Factors Affecting Cross-Border Acquisitions: U.S. versus Non-U.S. Experience. Global Finance Journal 1, 173–189.

Veld, C., Veld-Merkoulova, Y., 2004. Do Spin-offs Really Create Value? Journal of Banking and Finance 28, 1111–1135.

Vermeulen, F., Barkema, H. G., 2001. Learning through Acquisitions. Journal of the Academy of Management 44, 457–476.

Vijh, A. M., 1999. Long-Term Returns from Equity Carveouts. Journal of Financial Economics 51, 273–308.

Vijh, A. M., 2002. The Positive Announcement Period Returns of Equity Carve-Outs: Asymmetric Information or Divestiture Gains. Journal of Business 75, 153–190.

Villalonga, B., 2004. Diversification Discount or Premium? New Evidence from the Business Information Tracking Series. Journal of Finance 59, 479–506.

Villalonga, B., Amit, R., 2006. How Do Family Ownership, Control, and Management Affect Firm Value. Journal of Financial Economics 80, 385–417.

Vodafone AirTouch, 1999. Listing Particulars Relating to the Issue of Ordinary Shares in Vodafone Airtouch PLC in Connection with the Offer for Mannesmann AG. Filing with the Registrar of Companies in England and Wales, pp. 363–369.

Vroom, H. J. de, Frederikslust, R. van, 1999. Shareholder Wealth Effects of Corporate Spinoffs: The Worldwide Experience 1990–1998,. SSRN Working Paper Series, August 9.

W

Wagner, H. F., 2004. The Equity Carve Out Decision. University of Munich Working Paper.

Walker, M., 2000. Corporate Takeovers, Strategic Objectives, and Acquiring Firm Shareholder Wealth. Financial Management 29, 53–66.

Wall St. J., 1996a. Together but Equal. p. R-20.

Wall St. J., 1996b. When Things Go Wrong. p. R-25.

Wall St. J., 1996c. Disability Claims Mirror Rising Job Cuts. p. A-2.

Walsh, J. P., 1989. Doing a Deal: Merger and Acquisition Negotiations and Their Impact upon Target Company Top Management Turnover. Strategic Management Journal 10, 307–322.

Walsh, J. P., Ellwood, J. W., 1991. Mergers, Acquisitions, and the Pruning of Managerial Deadwood. Strategic Management Journal 12, 201–217.

Wasserstein, B., 1998. Big Deal: The Battle for Control of America's Leading Corporations. Warner Books, New York.

Weifeng, W., Zhaoguo, Z., Shasa, Z., 2008. Ownership Structure and the Private Benefits of Control: An Analysis of Chinese Firms. Corporate Governance 8, 286–298.

Weil, R. L., 2002. Fundamental Causes of the Accounting Debacle at Enron: Show Me Where It Says I Can't, Testimony before the U.S. House of Representatives Committee on Energy and Commerce.

Weir, C., Laing, D., Wright, M., 2005. Incentive Effects, Monitoring Mechanisms and the Threat from the Market for Corporate Control: An Analysis of the Factors Affecting Public to Private Transactions in the U.K. Journal of Business Finance and Accounting 32, 909–944.

Welch, I., 2001. The Equity Premium Consensus Forecast Revisited. Working Paper, University School of Management, Yale.

Whaley, R. E., 2006. Derivatives, Markets, Valuation, and Risk Management. Wiley & Sons, New York.

White, M., 1989. The Corporate Bankruptcy Decision. J. Econ. Perspect. 3, 129–152.

White, E., Joann, S., 2007. Lublin, Companies Trim Executive Perks to Avoid Glare. Wall St. J. 13, p. A1.

Whitehouse, K., 2007. Your Vote Can Count in Company Elections. Wall St. J. p. 5.

Wigmore, B., 1994. The Decline in Credit Quality of Junk Bond Issues, 1980–1988. In: Gaughan, P. A. (Ed.), Readings in Mergers and Acquisitions. Basil Blackwell, Cambridge, UK, pp. 171–184.

Wilson, B. D., 1980. The Propensity of Multinational Companies to Expand through Acquisitions. Journal of International Business Studies 11, 59–64.

Wiltbank, R., Boeker, W., 2007. Returns to Angel Investors in Groups,. SSRN, http://ssrn.com/abstracts-1028592

Woolridge, J. R., Snow, C. C., 1990. Stock Decisions. Strategic Management Journal 11, 353–363.

Wright, M., Renneboog, L., Simons, T., Scholes, L., 2006. Leveraged Buyouts in the U.K. and Continental Europe: Retrospect and Prospect. Journal of Applied Corporate Finance 18, 38–55.

Wright, M. N. W., Robbie, K., 1996. The Longer Term Effects of Management-Led Buyouts. Journal of Entrepreneurial and Small Business Finance 5, 213–234.

Wright, M., Burros, A., Ball, R., Scholes, L., Meuleman, M., Amess, K., 2008. The Implications of Alternative Investment Vehicles for Corporate Governance: A Survey of Empirical Research,. Organization for Economic Cooperation and Development, www.oecd,org/daf/corporate-affairs

Wruck, K. H., 1989. Equity Ownership Concentration and Firm Value: Evidence from Private Equity Financing. Journal of Financial Economics 23, 3–28.

Wulf, J., 2004. Do CEOs in Mergers Trade Power for Premium? Evidence from Mergers of Equals. Journal of Law and Organization 20, 60.

Wulf, J., Rajan, R., 2003. The Flattening Firm: Evidence from Panel Data on the Changing Nature of Corporate Hierarchies. Working Paper, University of Chicago.

Y

Yago, G., Bonds, J., 1991. How High Yield Securities Restructured Corporate America. Oxford University Press, New York.

You, V., Caves, R., Smith, M., Henry, J., 1986. Mergers and Bidders' Wealth: Managerial and Strategic Factors. In: Thomas III, L. G. (Ed.), The Economics of Strategic Planning, third ed. Lexington Books, Lexington, MA, pp. 201–220.

Young, M., Peng, M., Ahlston, D., Brinton, G., Jiang, Y., 2008. Corporate Governance in Emerging Economies. Journal of Management Studies.

Z

Zahra, S., Elhagrasey, G., 1994. Strategic Management of International Joint Ventures. European Management Journal 12, 83–93.

Zahra, S. A., Ireland, R. D., Hitt, M. A., 2000. International Expansion by New Venture Firms: International, Mode of Market Entry, Technological Learning and Performance. Academy of Management Journal pp. 244–257.

Zavgren, C. V., 1985. Assessing the Vulnerability of Failure of American Industrial Firms: A Logistic Analysis. Journal of Business Finance and Accounting 12, 19–45.

Zellner, W., 2005. This Big Oil Deal Shouldn't Hurt a Bit. Bus. Week p. 42.

Zingales, L., 1995. What Determines the Value of Corporate Control. The Quarterly Journal of Economics, 110, 1047–1073.

Zola, M., Meier, D., 2008. What is M&A Performance? Academy of Management Perspectives 22, 55–77.

Zuckerman, G., Sender, H., Patterson, S., 2007. Henny Sender, and Scott Patterson, Hedge Fund Crowd Sees More Green as Fortress Hits Jackpot with IPO. Wall St. J. p. A1.

Glossary

Abnormal return   The return to shareholders due to nonrecurring events that differs from what would have been predicted by the market. It is the return due to an event such as a merger or acquisition.

Accounting considerations   The potential impact of financial reporting requirements on the earnings volatility of business combinations due to the need to periodically revalue acquired assets to their fair market value as new information becomes available.

Acquisition   The purchase by one company of a controlling ownership interest in another firm, a legal subsidiary of another firm, or selected assets of another firm.

Acquirer   A firm that attempts to acquire a controlling interest in another company.

Acquisition vehicle   The legal structure used to acquire another company.

Advance notice provision   The requirement for announcement of shareholder proposals well in advance of the actual vote.

Advance ruling   An IRS ruling sought by acquirers and targets planning to enter into a tax-free transaction. A favorable ruling is often a condition of closing.

Affirmative covenant   A portion of a loan agreement that specifies the actions the borrowing firm agrees to take during the term of the loan.

Agency problems   The conflict of interest between a firm's incumbent managers and shareholders.

Antigreenmail provisions   Amendments to corporate charters restricting the firm's ability to repurchase shares from specific shareholders at a premium.

Antitakeover amendments   Amendments to corporate charters designed to slow or make more expensive efforts to take control of the firm.

Antitrust laws   Federal laws prohibiting individual corporations from assuming too much market power.

Appraisal rights   Rights to seek "fair value" for their shares in court given to target company shareholders who choose not to tender shares in the first or second tier of a tender offer.

Arbitrageurs ("arbs")   In the context of M&As, arbs are speculators who attempt to profit from the difference between the bid price and the target firm's current share price.

Arbitration clause   Wording in a contract defining the type of dispute subject to arbitration and how the arbitrator will be selected.

Articles of incorporation   A document filed with a state government by the founders of a corporation.

Asset-based lending   A type of lending in which the decision to grant a loan is based largely on the quality of the assets collateralizing the loan.

Asset impairment   An asset is said to be impaired according to FASB Statement 142 if its fair value falls below its book or carrying value.

Asset purchases   Transactions in which the acquirer buys all or a portion of the target company's assets and assumes all, some, or none of the target's liabilities.

Assignment   The process through which a committee representing creditors grants the power to liquidate a firm's assets to a third party, called an *assignee* or *trustee*.

Asymmetric information   Information about a firm that is not equally available to both managers and shareholders.

Auction   Multiple bidders competing for the same target firm.

Audit   The professional examination and verification of a company's accounting documents and supporting data to render an opinion as to their fairness, consistency, and conformity with generally accepted accounting principles.

Automatic stay   The requirement for a period of time following the submission of a petition for bankruptcy in which all judgments, collection activities, foreclosures, and repossessions of property are suspended and may not be pursued by the creditors on any debt or claim that arose before the filing of the bankruptcy petition.

Back end merger   The merger following either a single- or two-tier tender offer consisting of either a long-form or short-form merger, with the latter not requiring a target firm shareholder vote.

Backend value   The amount paid in the second stage to those shareholders not participating in the first stage of a two-tier tender offer.

Balance sheet assumptions   Anticipated growth in major balance-sheet components.

Bankruptcy   A federal legal proceeding designed to protect the technically or legally insolvent firm from lawsuits by its creditors until a decision can be made to shut down or continue to operate the firm.

Bear hug   A takeover tactic involving the mailing of a letter containing an acquisition proposal to the board of directors of a target company without prior warning and demanding a rapid decision.

Beta   A measure of nondiversifiable risk or the extent to which a firm's (or asset's) return changes because of a change in the market's return.

Blank check preferred stock   Preferred stock that has been authorized but not yet issued.

Bidder   See *acquirer.*

Boot   The nonequity portion of the purchase price.

Breakup fee   A fee that would be paid to the potential acquirer if the target firm decides to accept an alternative bid. Also called a *termination fee.*

Bridge financing   Temporary unsecured short-term loans provided by investment banks to pay all or a portion of the purchase price and meet immediate working capital requirements until permanent or long-term financing is found.

Buildup method   A method of adjusting a firm's discount rate to reflect risks associated with such businesses.

Business alliance   A generic term referring to all forms of business combinations other than mergers and acquisitions.

Business combination provisions   State laws forbidding the sale of a target firm's assets for a specific period of time following closing in an attempt to discourage highly leveraged transactions.

Business judgment rule. A code of conduct for directors requiring them to act in a manner that could reasonably be seen as being in the best interests of the shareholders. It is a presumption with which the courts will not interfere or second guess, business decisions made by directors.

Business-level strategies Strategies pertaining to a specific operating unit or product line within a firm.

Business-market attractiveness matrix A way of comparing the attractiveness of markets with a firm's capabilities.

Business plan A comprehensive analysis of all aspects of a business resulting in a vision for the firm and a strategy for achieving that vision.

Business strategy That portion of a business plan detailing the way the firm intends to achieve its vision.

Buyback See *share repurchase plans.*

Buyout Change in controlling interest in a corporation.

Capital asset pricing model A framework for measuring the relationship between expected risk and return.

Capital budgeting process A process of allocating available investment funds by giving projects priority based on projected rates of return.

Capitalization multiple The multiple estimated by dividing 1 by the estimated discount or capitalization rate that can be used to estimate the value of a business by multiplying it by an indicator of value such as free cash flow.

Capitalization rate The discount rate used by practitioners if the cash flows of the firm are not expected to grow or are expected to grow at a constant rate indefinitely.

Cash-for-assets An acquisition in which the acquirer pays cash for the seller's assets and may choose to accept some or all of the seller's liabilities.

Cash cows Businesses generating cash in excess of their reinvestment requirements.

Cash-out provisions State statutes that require a bidder whose purchases of stock exceed a stipulated amount to buy the remainder of the target stock on the same terms granted to those shareholders whose stock was purchased at an earlier date.

Cash-out statutory merger A merger in which the shareholders of the selling firm receive cash or some form on nonvoting investment (e.g., debt, or nonvoting preferred or common stock) for their shares.

Casual pass An informal communication with a board member or executive of the target firm to assess the potential interest in a takeover.

Certificate of incorporation A document received from the state once the articles of incorporation have been approved.

Chapter 7 The portion of the U.S. Bankruptcy Code dealing with liquidation of a firm that cannot be reorganized while under the protection of the bankruptcy court.

Chapter 11 That portion of the U.S. Bankruptcy Code dealing with reorganization, which provides for the debtor to remain in possession, unless the court rules otherwise, of the business and in control of its operations.

Chewable poison pill A poison pill that becomes void in the face of a fully financed offer at a substantial premium to the target firm's current share price.

Choice of law provision   A contract provision in an M&A or alliance agreement indicating which state's or country's laws have jurisdiction in settling disputes.

Classified board election   An antitakeover defense involving the separation of a firm's board into several classes, only one of which is up for election at any one point in time. Also called a *staggered board.*

Closing   The phase of the acquisition process in which ownership is transferred from the target to the acquiring firm in exchange for some agreed-on consideration following the receipt of all necessary shareholder, regulatory, and third-party approvals.

Closing conditions   Stipulations that must be satisfied before closing can take place.

Coinsurance   The combination of firms whose cash flows are relatively uncorrelated.

Collar agreement   An arrangement providing for certain changes in the share exchange ratio contingent on the level of the acquirer's share price around the effective date of the merger.

Collateralized loan obligations   Loans packaged into pools from which different securities are created to sell to investors.

Commitment letter   A document obligating a lender to provide financing.

Common-size financial statements   Valuation calculated by taking each line item as a percentage of revenue.

Composition   An agreement in which creditors consent to settling for less than the full amount they are owed.

Concentration   The percentage of an industry's total sales accounted for by a specific number of firms.

Confidentiality agreement   A mutually binding accord defining how information exchanged among the parties may be used and the circumstances under which the discussions may be made public. Also known as a *nondisclosure agreement.*

Conglomerate discount   The share prices of conglomerates often trade at a discount from focused firms or their value if they were broken up and sold in pieces.

Conglomerate mergers   Transactions in which the acquiring company purchases firms in largely unrelated industries.

Consent decree   Requires the merging parties to divest overlapping businesses or restrict anticompetitive practices.

Consent solicitation.   A process enabling dissident shareholders in certain states to obtain shareholder support for their proposals by simply obtaining their written consent.

Conservatorship   Represents the temporary assumption of shareholder and manager rights in contrast to a receiver who terminates such rights in taking over responsibility for a business or organization.

Consolidation   A business combination involving two or more companies joining to form a new company, in which none of the combining firms survive.

Constant growth model   A valuation method that assumes that cash flow will grow at a constant rate.

Contingency plans   Actions that are undertaken if the firm's current business strategy appears not to be working.

Contingent claims   A claim that pays off only under certain contingencies.

Contingent payments   Payments to the seller that depend on the achievement of certain revenue, profit, or cash flow targets.

Contingent value rights   (CVR) Commitments by the issuing company to pay additional cash or securities to the holder of the CVR if the share price of the issuing company falls below a specified level at some future date.

Control premium   The excess over the target's current share price the acquirer is willing to pay to gain a controlling interest. A pure control premium is one in which the anticipated synergies are small and the perceived value of the purchase is in gaining control to direct the activities of the target firm.

Core competencies   Bundles of skills that can be applied to extend a firm's product offering in new areas.

Corporate bylaws   Rules governing the internal management of the corporation, which are determined by the corporation's founders.

Corporate charters   A state license defining the powers of the firm and the rights and responsibilities of its shareholders, board of directors, and managers. The charter consists of articles of incorporation and a certificate of incorporation.

Corporate culture   The common set of values, traditions, and beliefs that influence behavior of a firm's employees.

Corporate governance   The systems and controls in place to protect the rights of corporate stakeholders.

Corporate-level strategies   Strategies cutting across business unit organizational lines, which entail such decisions as financing the growth of certain businesses, operating others to generate cash, divesting some units, or pursuing diversification.

Corporate restructuring   Actions taken to expand or contract a firm's basic operations or fundamentally change its asset or financial structure.

Corporate vision   A statement intended to describe the corporation's purpose for existing and where the corporation hopes to go.

Cost leadership   A strategy designed to make a firm the cost leader in its market by constructing efficient production facilities, tightly controlling overhead expense, and eliminating marginally profitable customer accounts.

Covenants   Promises made by the borrower that certain acts will be performed and others will be avoided.

Cram down   A legal reorganization occurring whenever one or more classes of creditors or shareholders approve, even though others may not.

Creeping takeover   Takeovers in which bidders acquire target voting shares in relatively small amounts until they achieve effective control of the target.

Cross-default provisions   Clauses in loan agreements allowing a lender to collect its loan immediately if the borrower is in default on a loan to another lender.

Crown jewels lockup   An arrangement in which the initial bidder obtains an option to buy important strategic assets of the target, if the target chooses to sell to another party.

Cumulative voting rights   In an election for a board of directors, each shareholder is entitled to as many votes as equal the number of shares the shareholder owns multiplied by the number of directors to be elected. Furthermore, the shareholder may cast all of these votes for a single candidate or any two or more of them.

Data room   The seller limits the acquirer's due diligence team to management presentations and selected data made available in a single room or via the Internet.

Dead hand poison pill   A poison pill security containing special features, which prevent the board of directors from taking action to redeem or rescind the pill unless the directors were the same directors who adopted the pill.

Deadlock clause   The portion of a contract that specifies the events triggering a dissolution of the joint venture or partnership.

Deal breakers   Issues that a party to the negotiation cannot concede without making the deal unacceptable.

Deal-structuring process   The process focused on satisfying as many of the primary objectives of the parties involved and determining how risk will be shared.

Debentures   Debt issued that is secured primarily by the cash flow of the issuer.

Debt-for-equity swap   Creditors surrender a portion of their claims on the firm in exchange for an ownership position in the firm.

Debtor-in-possession   On the filing of a reorganization petition, the firm's current management remains in place to conduct the ongoing affairs of the firm.

Debt restructuring   Involves concessions by creditors that lower an insolvent firm's payments so that it may remain in business.

Defensive acquisition   One made to reduce a firm's cash position or borrowing capacity.

Deferred purchase price payments   The placement of some portion of the purchase price in escrow until certain contractual conditions have been realized.

Definitive agreement of purchase and sale   The legal document indicating all of the rights and obligations of the parties both before and after closing.

Destroyers of value   Factors that can reduce the future cash flow of the combined companies.

Developed country   That having significant and sustainable per capita economic growth, globally integrated capital markets, a well-defined legal system, transparent financial statements, currency convertibility; and a stable government.

Differentiation   A strategy in which the product or service offered is perceived to be slightly different by customers from other product or service offerings in the marketplace.

Discounted cash flow   The conversion of future to current cash flows by applying an appropriate discount rate.

Discount rate   The opportunity cost associated with investment in the firm used to convert the projected cash flows to present values.

Discretionary assets   Undervalued or redundant assets not required to run the acquired business.

Dissident shareholders   Those that disagree with a firm's incumbent management and attempt to change policies by initiating proxy contests to gain representation on the board of directors.

Diversifiable risk   The risk specific to an individual firm, such as strikes and lawsuits.

Diversification   A strategy of buying firms outside of the company's primary line of business.

Divestiture   The sale of all or substantially all of a company or product line to another party for cash or securities.

Divisional organization   An organizational structure in which groups of products are combined into independent divisions or "strategic business units."

Dogs   Businesses with low growth and market share.

Drag-along   A contract provision common to joint venture or partnership agreements specifically requiring a party not otherwise interested in selling its ownership interest to a third party to do so.

Dual class recapitalization   A takeover defense in which a firm issues multiple classes of stock in which one class has voting rights that are 10 to 100 times those of another class. Such stock is also called *supervoting stock*.

Due diligence   The process by which the acquirer seeks to determine the accuracy of the target's financial statements, evaluate the firm's operations, validate valuation assumptions, determine fatal flaws, and identify sources and destroyers of value.

Earn-out agreement   A financial contract in which a portion of the purchase price of a company is to be paid in the future.

Earn-outs   Payments to the seller based on the acquired business achieving certain profit or revenue targets.

Economic value   The present value of a firm's projected cash flows.

Economies of scale   The spreading of fixed costs over increasing production levels.

Economies of scope   The use of a specific set of skills or an asset currently used to produce a specific product to produce related products.

Effective control   Control achieved when one firm has purchased another firm's voting stock, it is not likely to be temporary, there are no legal restrictions on control such as from a bankruptcy court, and there are no powerful minority shareholders.

Emerging country   A country whose sustainable growth rate in per capita gross domestic product is below that realized by developed countries. Such countries generally lack many of the characteristics of developed countries.

Employee stock ownership plan   (ESOP) A trust fund or plan that invests in the securities of the firm sponsoring the plan on behalf of the firm's employees. Such plans are generally defined contribution employee-retirement plans.

Enterprise cash flow   Cash available to shareholders and lenders after all operating obligations of the firm have been satisfied.

Enterprise value   Viewed from the liability side of the balance sheet, it is the sum of the market or present value of a firm's common equity plus preferred stock and long-term debt. For simplicity, other long-term liabilities are often excluded from the calculation. From the perspective of the asset side of the balance sheet, it is equal to cash plus the market value of current operating and nonoperating assets less current liabilities plus long-term assets.

Equity beta   A measure of the risk of a stock's financial returns, as compared with the risk of the financial returns to the general stock market, which in turn is affected by the overall economy.

Equity carve-out   A transaction in which the parent firm issues a portion of its stock or that of a subsidiary to the public.

Equity cash flow   Cash available to common shareholders after all operating obligations of the firm have been satisfied.

Equity premium   The rate of return in excess of the risk-free rate investors require to invest in equities.

Escape clause   A feature, common to poison pills, enabling the board of the issuing company to redeem the pill through a nominal payment to the shareholders.

Excess returns   See *abnormal returns*.

Exchange offer   A tender offer involving a share-for-share exchange.

Exit strategy   A strategy enabling investors to realize their required returns by undertaking an initial public offering or selling to a strategic buyer.

Expense investments   Expenditures made that are not capitalized on the balance sheet, such as application software development, database construction, research and development, training, and advertising to build brand recognition.

Experience curve   The theory that postulates that, as the cumulative historical volume of a firm's output increases, cost per unit of output decreases.

Extension   Creditor agreement to lengthen the period during which the debtor firm can repay its debt and, in some cases, to temporarily suspend both interest and principal repayments.

External analysis   The development of an in-depth understanding of the business's customers and their needs, underlying market dynamics or factors determining profitability, and emerging trends that affect customer needs and market dynamics.

Fair market value   The cash or cash-equivalent price a willing buyer would propose and a willing seller would accept for a business if both parties have access to all relevant information.

Fairness opinion letter   A written and signed third-party assertion certifying the appropriateness of the price of a proposed deal involving a tender offer, merger, asset sale, or leveraged buyout.

Fair price provisions   A takeover defense requiring that all target shareholders of a successful tender offer receive the same price as those tendering their shares.

Fair value   An estimate of the value of an asset when no strong market exists for a business or it is not possible to identify the value of substantially similar firms.

Financial buyer   Acquirers that focus on relatively short to intermediate financial returns.

Financial ratio analysis   Calculation of performance ratios from data in a company's financial statements.

Financial restructuring   Actions by the firm to change its total debt and equity structure.

Financial risk   The buyer's willingness and ability to leverage a transaction as well as the willingness of shareholders to accept near-term earnings per share dilution.

Financial sponsor   An investor group providing equity financing in leveraged buyout transactions.

Financial synergy   The reduction in the cost of capital as a result of more stable cash flows, financial economies of scale, or a better matching of investment opportunities with available funds.

First-generation poison pill   Issuance of preferred stock, which had to be registered with the SEC, in the form of a dividend to shareholders convertible into the common stock but only after the takeover is completed.

Fixed or constant share-exchange agreement   An exchange agreement in which the number of acquirer shares exchanged for each target share is unchanged between the signing of the agreement of purchase and sale and closing.

Fixed-payment collar agreement   A guarantee that the target firm's shareholders receive a certain dollar value in terms of acquirer stock as long as the acquirer's stock remains within a narrow range.

Fixed value agreement   The value of the price per share is fixed by allowing the number of acquirer shares issued to vary to offset fluctuations in the buyer's share price.

Flip-in poison pill   A shareholders' rights plan in which the shareholders of the target firm can acquire stock in the target firm at a substantial discount.

Flip-over poison pill   A shareholders' rights plan in which target firm shareholders may convert such rights to acquire stock of the surviving company at a substantial discount.

Float   The amount of stock that can be purchased most easily by the acquirer.

Floating collar agreement   May involve a fixed exchange ratio as long as the acquirer's share price remains within a narrow range.

Focus strategy   A strategy in which firms tend to concentrate their efforts by selling a few products or services to a single market and compete primarily on the basis of understanding their customers' needs better than the competition.

For-cause provisions   These specify the conditions for removing a member of the board of directors.

Form of acquisition   The determination of what is being acquired (i.e., stock or assets).

Form of payment   of the means of payment: cash, common stock, debt, or some combination. Some portion of the payment may be deferred or dependent on the future performance of the acquired entity.

Forward triangular merger   The acquisition subsidiary being merged with the target and the acquiring subsidiary surviving.

Franchise   A privilege given to a dealer by a manufacturer or franchise service organization to sell the franchisor's product or service in a given area.

Fraudulent conveyance   Laws governing the rights of shareholders if the new company created following an acquisition or LBO is inadequately capitalized to remain viable. In bankruptcy, the lender could be stripped of its secured position in the assets of the company or its claims on the assets could be made subordinate to those of the unsecured creditors.

Free cash flow   The difference between cash inflows and cash outflows, which may be positive, negative, or zero.

Freeze-out   A situation in which the remaining shareholders are dependent on the decisions made by the majority shareholders, if the acquirer does not decide to acquire 100 percent of the target's stock.

Friendly takeover   Acquisition when the target's board and management are receptive to the idea and recommend shareholder approval.

Functional organization   Employees are assigned to specific groups or departments, such as accounting, engineering, marketing, sales, distribution, customer service, manufacturing, or maintenance.

Functional strategies   Description in detail of how each major function (e.g., manufacturing, marketing, and human resources) within the firm will support the business strategy.

Generally accepted accounting principles   (GAAP) Accounting guidelines established by the Financial Accounting Standards Board.

General partner   An individual responsible for the daily operations of a limited partnership.

Global capital asset pricing model   A version of the capital asset pricing model in which a global equity index is used in calculating the equity risk premium.

Globally integrated capital markets Capital markets providing foreigners with unfettered access to local capital markets and local residents to foreign capital markets.

Going concern value The value of a company defined as the firm's value in excess of the sum of the value of its parts.

Going private The purchase of the publicly traded shares of a firm by a group of investors.

Golden parachutes Employee severance arrangements that are triggered whenever a change in control takes place.

Goodwill The excess of the purchase price over the fair value of the acquired net assets on the acquisition date. Goodwill is an asset representing future economic benefits arising from net acquired assets that were not identified individually.

Go-shop provision A provision allowing a seller to continue to solicit other bidders for a specific time period after an agreement has been signed but before closing. However, the seller that accepts another bid must pay a breakup fee to the bidder with which it had a signed agreement.

Greenmail The practice of a firm buying back its shares at a premium from an investor threatening a takeover.

Growth strategy A business strategy that concentrates on growing a firm's revenues, profit, and cash flow.

Hedge fund Private investment limited partnerships (for U.S. investors) or off-shore investment corporations (for non-U.S. or tax exempt investors) in which the general partner has made a substantial personal investment. Hedge fund bylaws generally allow the fund to engage in a wide variety of investing activities.

Herfindahl–Hirschman Index The measure of industry concentration used by the Federal Trade Commission as one criterion in determining when to approve mergers and acquisitions.

High yield debt See *junk bond financing*.

Highly leveraged transactions Those involving a substantial amount of debt relative to the amount of equity invested.

Holding company A legal entity often having a controlling interest in one or more companies.

Holdout problem Tendency for smaller creditors to hold up the agreement among creditors during reorganization unless they receive special treatment.

Home country The acquirer's country of residence.

Horizontal merger A combination of two firms within the same industry.

Hostile takeover Acquisition when the initial bid was unsolicited, the target was not seeking a merger at the time of the approach, the approach was contested by the target's management, and control changed hands.

Hostile tender offer A tender offer that is unwanted by the target's board.

Hubris An explanation for takeovers that attributes a tendency to overpay to excessive optimism about the value of a deal's potential synergy or excessive confidence in management's ability to manage the acquisition.

Hybrid transaction Affords the U.S. target corporation and its shareholders tax-free treatment while avoiding the issuance of shares of the foreign acquirer.

Impaired asset As defined by FASB, a long-term asset whose fair value falls below its book or carrying value.

Implementation strategy   The way in which the firm chooses to execute the business strategy.

Income statement assumptions   Projected growth in revenue, the implicit market share, and the major components of cost.

Incentive systems   Bonus, profit sharing, or other performance-based payments made to motivate both acquirer and target company employees to work to implement the business strategy for the combined firms.

Indemnification   A common contractual clause requiring the seller to indemnify or absolve the buyer of liability in the event of misrepresentations or breaches of warranties or covenants. Similarly, the buyer usually agrees to indemnify the seller. In effect, it is the reimbursement to the other party for a loss for which it was not responsible.

Indenture   A contract between the firm that issues the long-term debt securities and the lenders.

Industry   A collection of markets.

Internal analysis   The determination of the firm's strengths and weaknesses as compared to its competitors.

Initial offer price   A price that lies between the estimated minimum and maximum offer prices for a target firm.

Initial public offering   (IPO) The first offering to the public of common stock of a formerly privately held firm.

In play   A firm believed by investors to be vulnerable to or willing to undergo a takeover due to a bid or rumors of a bid.

Insider trading   Individuals buying or selling securities based on knowledge not available to the general public.

Interest rate parity theory   A theory that relates forward or future spot exchange rates to differences in interest rates between two countries adjusted by the spot rate.

Investment bankers   Advisors who offer strategic and tactical advice and acquisition opportunities, screen potential buyers and sellers, make initial contact with a seller or buyer, and provide negotiation support, valuation, and deal structuring advice.

Involuntary bankruptcy   A situation in which creditors force a debtor firm into bankruptcy.

Joint venture   A cooperative business relationship formed by two or more separate entities to achieve common strategic objectives.

Junk bond financing   Subordinated debt, either unrated or noninvestment grade. Also called *high-yield debt*.

Junk bonds   High-yield bonds either rated by the credit-rating agencies as below investment grade or not rated at all.

Legal form of the selling entity   Whether the seller is a C or subchapter S corporation, a limited liability company, or a partnership.

Legal insolvency   When a firm's liabilities exceed the fair market value of its assets.

Letter of intent   Preliminary agreement between two companies intending to merge that stipulates major areas of agreement between the parties.

Leveraged buyout   Purchase of a company financed primarily by debt.

Leveraged loans   Unrated or noninvestment grade bank loans whose interest rates are equal to or greater than the London Inter Bank Rate plus 150 basis points.

Limited partner   Partners who contribute only money and are not involved in management decisions.

Liquidating dividend   Proceeds left to shareholders after company is liquidated and outstanding obligations to creditors are paid off.

Liquidation   The value of a firm's assets sold separately less its liabilities and expenses incurred in breaking up the firm.

Liquidity discount   The discount or reduction in the offer price for the target firm made by discounting the value of the target firm estimated by examining the market values of comparable publicly traded firms to reflect the potential loss in value when sold due to the illiquidity of the market for similar types of investments. The liquidity discount also is referred to as a *marketability discount*.

Liquidity risk   See *marketability risk*.

Loan agreement   Contract that stipulates the terms and conditions under which the lender will loan the firm funds.

Local country   The target firm's country of residence.

Long-form merger   Mergers requiring shareholder approval.

Management buyout   A leveraged buyout in which managers of the firm to be taken private are also equity investors in the transaction.

Management entrenchment theory   A theory that managers use a variety of takeover defenses to ensure their longevity with the firm.

Management integration team   Senior managers from the two merged organizations charged with delivering on sales and operating synergies identified during the preclosing due diligence.

Management preferences   The boundaries or limits that senior managers of the acquiring firm place on the acquisition process.

Managerialism theory   A theory espousing that managers acquire companies to increase the acquirer's size and their own remuneration.

Market   Collection of customers, whether individual consumers or other firms, exhibiting common characteristics and needs.

Marketability discount   See *liquidity discount*.

Marketability risk   The risk associated with an illiquid market for the specific stock. Also called *liquidity risk*.

Market assumptions   Anticipated growth rate of unit volume and product price per unit.

Market-based valuation methods   Techniques that assume a firm's market value can be approximated by an indicator of value for comparable companies, comparable transactions, or comparable industry averages. Also referred to as *relative valuation methods*.

Market power   A situation in which the merger of two firms enables the resulting combination to profitably maintain prices above competitive levels for a significant period.

Market power hypothesis   A theory that firms merge to gain greater control over pricing.

Market segmentation   A process involving identifying customers with common characteristics and needs.

Maximum offer price   The sum of the minimum price plus the present value of net synergy.

Merger   A combination of two or more firms in which all but one legally cease to exist.

Merger–acquisition plan A specific type of implementation strategy that describes in detail the motivation for the acquisition and how and when it will be achieved.

Merger arbitrage An investment strategy that attempts to profit from the spread between a target firm's current share price and a pending takeover bid.

Merger of equals A merger framework usually applied whenever the merger participants are comparable in size, competitive position, profitability, and market capitalization.

Mezzanine financing Capital that in liquidation has a repayment priority between senior debt and common stock.

Minimum offer price The target's stand-alone or present value or its current market value.

Minority discount The reduction in the value of their investment in a firm since the minority investors cannot direct the activities of the firm.

Minority investment A less than controlling interest in another firm.

Monitoring systems Implemented to track the actual performance of the combined firms against the business plan.

Negative covenant Restriction found in loan agreements on the actions of the borrower.

Negotiating price range The difference between the minimum and maximum offer prices.

Net asset value The difference between the fair market value of total identifiable acquired assets and the value of acquired liabilities.

Net debt The market value of debt assumed by the acquirer less cash and marketable securities on the books of the target firm.

Net operating loss carryforward and carrybacks Provisions in the tax laws allowing firms to use accumulated net tax losses to offset income earned over a specified number of future years or recover taxes paid during a limited number of prior years.

Net purchase price The total purchase price plus other assumed liabilities less the proceeds from the sale of discretionary or redundant target assets.

Net synergy The difference between estimated sources of value and destroyers of value.

Nondiversifiable risk Risk generated by factors that affect all firms, such as inflation and war.

Nonrecourse financing Loans granted to a venture without partner guarantees.

Normal financial returns The rate of return that would have been expected by assessing normal risk and return factors in the absence of any specific events, such as an M&A.

No-shop agreement That which prohibits the takeover target from seeking other bids or making public information not currently readily available while in discussions with a potential acquirer.

One-tiered offer A bidder announces the same offer to all target shareholders.

Open market share repurchase The act of a corporation buying its shares in the open market at the prevailing price as any other investor, as opposed to a tender offer for shares or a repurchase resulting from negotiation such as with an unwanted investor.

Operating risk The ability of the buyer to manage the acquired company.

Operating synergy of the combination of economies of both scale and scope.

Operational restructuring The outright or partial sale of companies or product lines or downsizing by closing unprofitable or nonstrategic facilities.

Opportunity cost   The foregone opportunity precluded by an action.

Option   The exclusive right, but not the obligation, to buy, sell, or utilize property for a specific period of time in exchange for an agreed-on sum of money.

Order for relief   A court order initiating bankruptcy proceedings if it is determined that a firm is insolvent.

Overpayment risk   The dilution of EPS or a reduction in the earnings growth rate resulting from paying significantly more than the economic value of the acquired company.

Pac-Man defense   A rarely used defense in which the target makes a hostile tender offer for the bidder.

Payment-in-kind (PIK) notes   Equity or debt that pays dividends or interest in the form of additional equity or debt.

Permanent financing   Financing usually consisting of long-term unsecured debt.

Poison pills   A new class of securities issued as a dividend by a company to its shareholders, giving shareholders rights to acquire more shares at a discount. These securities have no value unless an investor acquires a specific percentage of the target firm's voting stock.

Poison puts   A takeover defense in which the target issues bonds containing put options exercisable into cash or more debt if and only if an unfriendly takeover occurs.

Portfolio companies   Companies in which the hedge or private equity fund has made investments.

Postclosing organization   The organizational and legal framework used to manage the combined businesses following the completion of the transaction.

Prepackaged bankruptcies   A situation in which the failing firm starts negotiating with its creditors well in advance of filing for a Chapter 11 bankruptcy in order to reach agreement on major issues before formally filing for bankruptcy.

Private corporation   A firm whose securities are not registered with state or federal authorities.

Private equity fund   Limited partnerships in which the general partner has made a substantial personal investment.

Private placements   The sale of securities to institutional investors, such as pension funds and insurance companies, for investment rather than for resale. Such securities do not have to be registered with the SEC.

Private solicitation   A firm hires an investment banker or undertakes on its own to identify potential buyers to be contacted as potential buyers for the entire firm or a portion of the firm.

Product or service organization   Organizations in which functional specialists are grouped by product line or service offering.

Product intangible   Values placed on the accumulated intellectual capital resulting from the production and product design experience of the combined acquiring and target firms.

Product life cycle   Characterizes a product's evolution in four stages: embryonic, growth, maturity, and decline.

Pro forma financial statements   A form of accounting that presents financial statements in a way that purports to more accurately describe a firm's current or projected performance.

Promissory note   A legal document committing the borrower to repay a loan, even if the assets when liquidated do not fully cover the unpaid balance.

Proxy contest An attempt by dissident shareholders to obtain representation on the board of directors or to change a firm's bylaws.

Public solicitation Public announcement by a firm that it is putting itself, a subsidiary or a product line up for sale.

Purchase accounting A form of accounting for financial reporting purposes in which the acquired assets and assumed liabilities are revalued to their fair market value on the date of acquisition and recorded on the books of the acquiring company.

Purchasing power parity theory The theory stating that one currency will appreciate (depreciate) with respect to another currency according to the expected relative rates of inflation between the two countries.

Purchase premium The excess of the offer price over the target's current share price, which reflects both the value of expected synergies and the amount necessary to obtain control.

Pure control premium The value the acquirer believes can be created by replacing incompetent management or changing the strategic direction of the firm,

Pure play A firm whose products or services focus on a single industry or market.

q-ratio The ratio of the market value of a firm to the cost of replacing its assets.

Real options Management's ability to adopt and later revise corporate investment decisions.

Receivership Court appointment of an individual to administer the assets and affairs of a business in accordance with its directives.

Reincorporation The act of a firm changing its state of incorporation to one in which the laws are more favorable for implementing takeover defenses.

Retention bonuses Incentives granted key employees of the target firm if they remain with the combined companies for a specific period following completion of the transaction.

Revenue ruling An official interpretation by the IRS of the Internal Revenue Code, related statutes, tax treaties, and regulations.

Reverse breakup fee Fees paid to a target firm in the event the bidder wants to withdraw from a signed contract.

Reverse LBOs Public companies that are taken private and later are taken public again. The second effort to take the firm public is called a *secondary public offering*.

Reverse merger Process by which a private firm goes public by merging with a public firm with the public firm surviving.

Reverse triangular merger The merger of the target with a subsidiary of the acquiring firm, with the target surviving.

Revolving credit line A credit line allowing borrowers to borrow on a daily basis to run their business. Under a revolving credit arrangement, the bank agrees to make loans up to a specified maximum for a specified period, usually a year or more.

Right of first refusal A contract clause requiring that a party wishing to leave a joint venture or partnership to first offer its interests to other participants in the JV or partnership.

Risk The degree of uncertainty associated with the outcome of an investment.

Risk-free rate of return The return on a security with an exceedingly low probability of default, such as U.S. Treasury securities, and minimal reinvestment risk.

Risk premium The additional rate of return in excess of the risk-free rate that investors require to purchase a firm's equity. Also called the *equity premium*.

Road show   On-site visits to lenders to arrange both bridge and permanent financing in which the buyer often develops elaborate presentations to convince potential lenders and investors of its attractiveness as a borrower or investment.

Secondary public offering   A stock offering by a private company that had previously been a public company.

Second generation poison pill   Also known as a *flip-over pill*, it includes a rights plan that can be exercised if 100 percent of the firm's stock has been acquired.

Secured debt   Debt backed by the borrower's assets.

Security agreement   A legal document stipulating which of the borrower's assets are pledged to secure the loan.

Segmented capital markets   Capital markets exhibiting different bond and equity prices in different geographic areas for identical assets in terms of risk and maturity.

Self-tender offer   A tender offer used when a firm seeks to repurchase its stock from its shareholders.

Share control provisions   State statutes requiring that a bidder obtain prior approval from stockholders holding large blocks of target stock once the bidder's purchases of stock exceed some threshold level.

Share-exchange ratio   The number of shares of the acquirer's stock to be exchanged for each share of the target's stock.

Shareholders' interest theory   The presumption that management resistance to proposed takeovers is a good bargaining strategy to increase the purchase price for the benefit of the target firm shareholders.

Share repurchase plans   Stock purchases undertaken by a firm to reduce the number of shares that could be purchased by the potential acquirer or by those, such as arbitrageurs, that will sell to the highest bidder. Also called a *stock buyback*.

Shark repellants   Specific types of takeover defenses that can be adopted by amending either a corporate charter or its bylaws.

Shell corporation   One that is incorporated but has no significant assets or operations.

Short form merger   A merger not requiring the approval of the parent's shareholders if the parent's ownership in the acquiring subsidiary exceeds the minimum threshold set by the state in which the firm is incorporated.

Sources of value   Factors increasing the cash flow of the combined companies.

Sovereign wealth funds   Government-backed or -sponsored investment funds whose primary function is to invest profitably accumulated reserves of foreign currencies.

Spin-off   A transaction in which a parent creates a new legal subsidiary and distributes shares it owns in the subsidiary to its current shareholders as a stock dividend.

Split-off   A variation of a spin-off in which some parent company shareholders receive shares in a subsidiary in return for relinquishing their parent company shares.

Split-up   A transaction creating a new class of stock for each of the parent's operating subsidiaries, paying current shareholders a dividend of each new class of stock, then dissolving the remaining corporate shell.

Staggered board election   A takeover defense involving the division of the firm's directors into a number of different classes, with no two classes up for reelection at the same time. Also called a *classified board*.

Stakeholders Groups having interests in a firm, such as customers, shareholders, employees, suppliers, regulators, and communities.

Stand-alone business One whose financial statements reflect all the costs of running the business and all the revenues generated by the business.

Standstill agreement A contractual arrangement in which the acquirer agrees not to make any further investments in the target's stock for a stipulated period.

State blue sky laws Statutes intended to protect individuals from investing in fraudulent security offerings by requiring significant disclosure of information.

Statutory consolidation Involves two or more companies joining to form a new company.

Statutory merger The combination of the acquiring and target firms, in which one firm ceases to exist, in accordance with the statutes of the state in which the combined businesses will be incorporated.

Stock-for-stock statutory merger A merger in which the seller receives acquirer shares in exchange for its shares (with the seller shares subsequently canceled); also called a *stock swap merger*.

Stock lockup An option granted the bidder to buy the target firm's stock at the first bidder's initial offer, triggered whenever a competing bid (usually higher) is accepted by the target firm.

Stock purchases The exchange of the target's stock for either cash, debt, or the stock of the acquiring company.

Strategic alliance An informal cooperative arrangement, such as an agreement to codevelop a technology, product, or process.

Strategic buyer An acquirer primarily interested in increasing shareholder value by realizing long-term synergies.

Strategic realignment A theory suggesting that firms use takeovers as a means of rapidly adjusting to changes in their external environment, such as deregulation and technological innovation.

Subsidiary carve-out A transaction in which the parent creates a wholly owned independent legal subsidiary, with stock and a management team different from the parent's, and issues a portion of the subsidiary's stock to the public.

Subsidiary merger A transaction in which the target becomes a subsidiary of the parent.

Success factors Those strengths or competencies necessary to compete successfully in the firm's chosen market.

Supermajority rules A takeover defense requiring a higher level of approval for amending the charter or for certain types of transactions, such as a merger or acquisition.

Super voting stock A class of voting stock having voting rights many times those of other classes of stock.

SWOT analysis The external and internal analyses undertaken to determine a business's strengths, weaknesses, opportunities, and threats.

Syndicate An arrangement in which a group of investment banks agrees to purchase a new issue of securities from the acquiring company for sale to the investing public.

Synergy The notion that the value of the combined enterprises will exceed the sum of their individual values.

Synergy assumptions Anticipated amount and timing of expected synergy.

Tag-along A provision in a partnership agreement that enables a partner to sell to a third party that had been interested in buying only another partner's ownership interest.

Takeover Generic term referring to a change in the controlling ownership interest of a corporation.

Takeover defenses Protective devices put in place by a firm to frustrate, slow down, or raise the cost of a takeover.

Target company The firm that is being solicited by the acquiring company.

Taxable transaction Transactions in which the form of payment is primarily something other than acquiring company stock.

Tax considerations Structures and strategies determining whether a transaction is taxable or nontaxable to the seller's shareholders.

Tax-free reorganization Nontaxable transactions usually involving mergers, with the form of payment primarily acquirer stock exchanged for the target's stock or assets.

Tax-free transactions Transactions in which the form of payment is primarily acquiring company stock. Also called *tax-free reorganizations*.

Tax shield The reduction in the firm's tax liability due to the tax deductibility of interest.

Technical insolvency A situation in which a firm is unable to pay its liabilities as they come due.

Tender offer The offer to buy shares in another firm, usually for cash, securities, or both.

Tender offer statement Schedule on which acquirer must disclose its intentions and business plans with respect to the target.

Terminal growth value The discounted value of the cash flows generated during the stable growth period. Also called the *sustainable*, *horizon*, or *continuing growth value*.

Term loan A loan usually having a maturity of 2 to 10 years and secured by the asset being financed, such as new capital equipment.

Term sheet A document outlining the primary areas of agreement between the buyer and the seller, which is often used as the basis for a more detailed letter of intent.

Third generation poison pill Also known as the *flip-in pill*, the rights can be exercised with a less than 100 percent change in ownership.

Toehold strategy A variation of the two-tier tender offer in which the buyer purchases a minority position in the target firm on the open-market and subsequently initiates a tender offer to gain a controlling interest. After control has been achieved, the buyer offers a lower purchase price for any remaining shares.

Total capitalization The sum of a firm's debt and all forms of equity.

Total consideration A commonly used term in legal documents to reflect the different types of remuneration received by target company shareholders.

Total purchase price The total consideration plus the market value of the target firm's debt assumed by the acquiring company. Also referred to as *enterprise value*.

Tracking stocks Separate classes of common stock of the parent corporation whose dividend payouts depend on the financial performance of a specific subsidiary. Also called *target* or *letter stocks*.

Transfer taxes State taxes paid whenever titles to assets are transferred, as in an asset purchase.

Trigger points Milestones or events causing a firm to pursue an alternative course of action.

Two-tiered offer A tender offer in which target shareholders receive an offer for a specific number of shares. Immediately following this offer, the bidder announces its intentions to purchase the remaining shares at a lower price or using something other than cash.

Type A reorganization A tax-free merger or consolidation in which target shareholders receive cash, voting or nonvoting common or preferred stock, or debt for their shares. At least 40 percent of the purchase price must be in acquirer stock.

Type B stock-for-stock reorganization A tax-free transaction in which the acquirer uses its voting common stock to purchase at least 80 percent of the voting power of the target's outstanding voting stock and at least 80 percent of each class of nonvoting shares. Used as an alternative to a merger.

Type C stock-for-assets reorganization A tax-free transaction in which acquirer voting stock is used to purchase at least 80 percent of the fair market value of the target's net assets.

Underwriter spread The difference between the price the underwriter receives for selling a firm's securities to the public and the amount it pays to the firm.

Valuation assumptions Anticipated acquirer's target debt-to-equity ratio, discount rates, and growth assumptions.

Valuation cash flows Restated GAAP cash flows used for valuing a firm or a firm's assets.

Variable growth valuation model A valuation method that assumes that a firm's cash flows will experience periods of high growth followed by a period of slower, more sustainable growth.

Vertical merger One in which companies that do not own operations in each major segment of the value chain choose to backward integrate by acquiring a supplier or to forward integrate by acquiring a distributor.

Vision What a business hopes to achieve. Also called a mission statement.

Voluntary bankruptcy A situation in which the debtor firm files for bankruptcy.

Voluntary liquidation Sale by management, which concludes that the sale of the firm in parts could realize greater value than the value created by a continuation of the combined corporation.

Weighted-average cost of capital A broader measure than the cost of equity that represents the return that a firm must earn to induce investors to buy its stock and bonds.

White knight A potential acquirer that is viewed more favorably by a target firm's management and board than the initial bidder.

White squires Firms that agree to purchase a large block of the target's stock in an effort to support incumbent management in its efforts to prevent a hostile takeover.

Winner's curse The tendency of the auction winners to show remorse, believing that they may have paid too much.

Workouts Plans to restructure the debtor firm developed cooperatively with creditors.

Zero-growth valuation model A valuation model that assumes that free cash flow is constant in perpetuity.

Index

Page numbers followed by "*f*" indicate figures, "*t*" indicate tables, and "*b*" indicate boxes.